Bali & Lombok

written and researched by

Lesley Reader and Lucy Ridout

ROUGH
GUIDES

www.roughguides.com

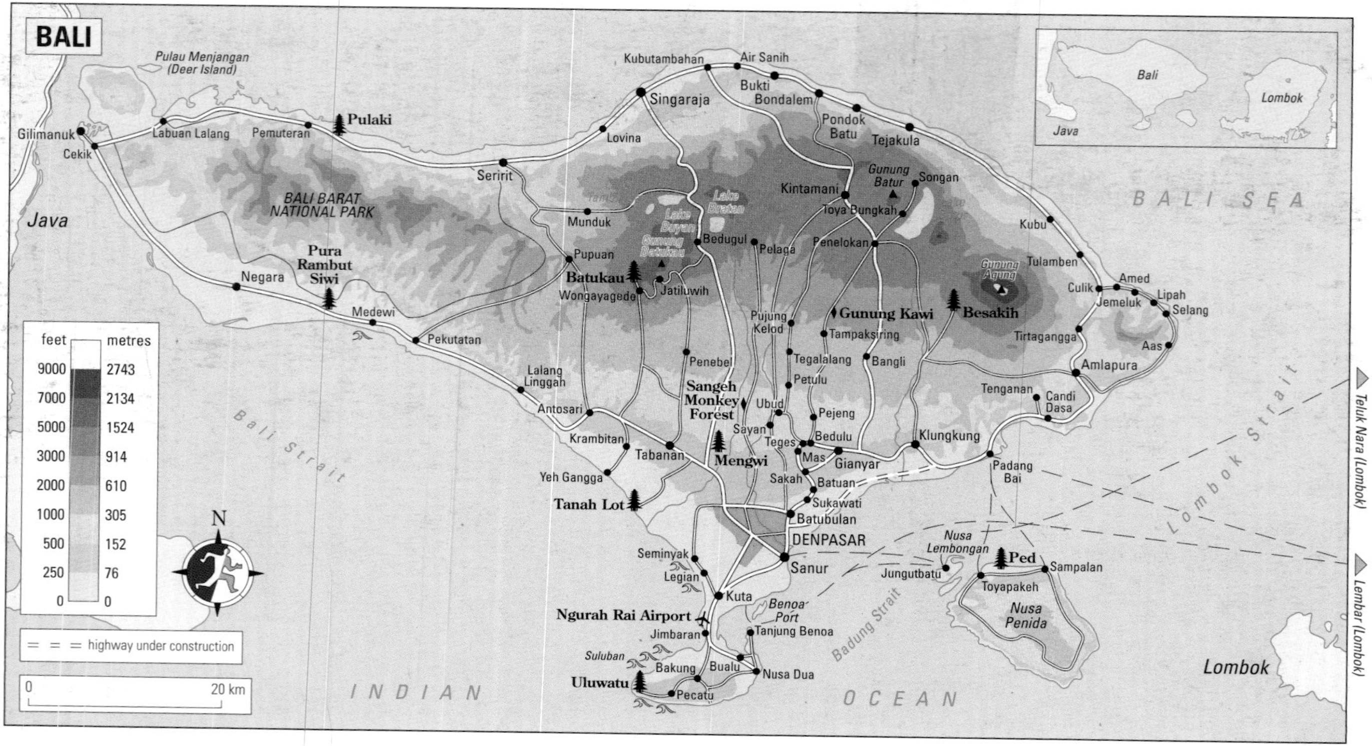

BALI

△ Teluk Nara (Lombok) △ Lembar (Lombok)

BALI SEA

LOMBOK STRAIT

Lombok

Java

Bali

Lombok

Gilimanuk
Cekik
Labuan Lalang
Pulau Menjangan
(Deer Island)
Pemuteran
Pulaki
Negara
Medewi
Pura Rambut Siwi
BALI BARAT NATIONAL PARK
Pekutatan
Cekik
Seririt
Pupuan
Munduk
Lovina
Singaraja
Kubutambahan
Air Sanih
Bukti
Bondalem
Pondok Batu
Tejakula
Songan
Tirtagangga
Candi Dasa
Tenganan
Padang Bai
Klungkung
Bangli
Tampaksiring
Pejeng
Bedulu
Mas
Gianyar
Batuan
Sukawati
Batubulan
DENPASAR
Sanur
Benoa Port
Tanjung Benoa
Nusa Dua
Kuta
Jimbaran
Ngurah Rai Airport
Bakung
Suluban
Pecatu
Uluwatu
Bualu
Seminyak
Legian
Tabanan
Krambitan
Yeh Gangga
Tanah Lot
Mengwi
Sangeh Monkey Forest
Penebel
Jatiluwih
Antosari
Lalang Linggah
Batukau
Wongayagede
Bedugul
Pelaga
Penelokan
Kintamani
Toya Bungkah
Gunung Batur
Gunung Kawi
Penelokan
Pupuan
Pujung Kelod
Ubud
Sayan
Teges
Tegalalang
Pelaga
Petulu
Besakih
Gunung Agung
Kubu
Tulamben
Culik
Amed
Jemeluk
Lipah
Selang
Aas
Amlapura
Ped
Nusa Penida
Sampalan
Toyapakeh
Nusa Lembongan
Jungutbatu
Badung Strait
Bali Strait
Bali Strait

INDIAN OCEAN

N

20 km

= = highway under construction

feet	metres
9000	2743
7000	2134
5000	1524
3000	914
2000	610
1000	305
500	152
250	76
0	0

0

Java

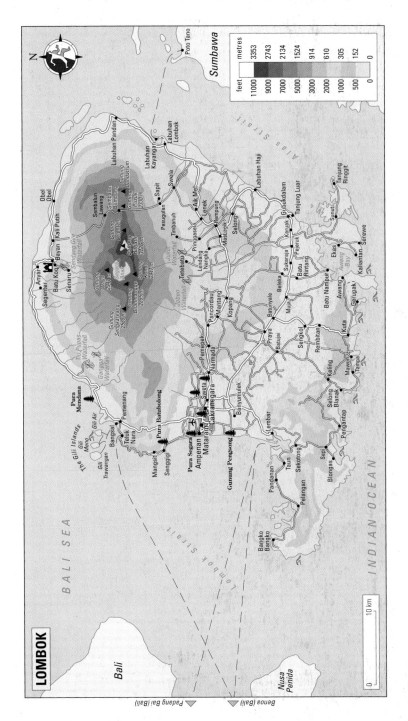

LOMBOK

N

Bali

BALI SEA

Nusa Penida

INDIAN OCEAN

Lombok Strait

Alas Strait

Sumbawa

Poto Tano

Places (clockwise / labels)

Obel Obel
Labuhan Pandan
Labuhan Lombok
Labuhan Kayangan
Sapit
Svela
Ak Mel
Labuhan Haji
Tanjung Ringgit
Gubukdalam
Tanjung Luar
Sanur
Serewe
Kaliantan
Tampa
Ekas
Awang Bay
Gerupak
Kuta
Mawan
Tampa
Tiampa
Batu Nampur
Remitan
Sengkol
Batujai
Praya
Keling
Selong Blanak
Pengantap
Sepi
Blongas
Bangko Bangko
Pelangan
Pandanan
Sekotong
Taun
Lembar
Banyumulek
Gunung Pengsong
Cakranegara
Mataram
Ampenan
Sveta
Narmada
Pemepek
Pura Segara
Pura Batubolong
Senggigi
Mangsit
Pura Meru
Pura Mendana
Pemenang
Tebuh Nara
Bangsal
The Gill Islands
Gili Meno
Gili Air
Gili Trawangan
Segenter
Anyar
Batu Koq
Senaru
Bayan Kali Putih
Sembalun Lawang
Sembalun Bumbung
Pesugulan
Timbanuh
Lenek
Aikmel
Pringasela
Lendang Nangka
Rempung
Masbagik
Salong
Sukaraja
Keruak
Prejerak
Batu Rintang
Muja
Beleke
Baturiyale
Kopang
Mantang
Pancordaul
Tetebatu
Joben Waterfall
Lendur Waterfall

Mountains
Gunung Rinjani 3726m
Gunung Kondo 2907m
Gunung Buahnanga 2895m
Gunung Senkareang 2580m
Gunung Baru 2330m
Gunung Joyo 2340m
Gunung Nangi 2330m
Gunung Nangi 2330m
Gunung Sundatum
Gunung Bumbun
Segara Anak

Sindang Gili Waterfall
Tiu Pupas Waterfall
Gangsal Waterfall

Padang Bai (Bali)
Benoa (Bali)

Elevation legend

feet	metres
11000	3353
9000	2743
7000	2134
5000	1524
3000	914
2000	610
1000	305
500	152
0	0

0 ___ 10 km

Introduction to

Bali
& Lombok

The islands of Bali and Lombok are part of the Indonesian archipelago, a 5200-kilometre-long string of over thirteen thousand islands, stretching between Malaysia in the west and Australia in the east. Sandy beaches punctuate the dramatically rugged coastlines and world-class surf pounds both shorelines.

Located just east of the island of Java, Bali has long been the primary focus of Indonesia's tourist industry; its eastern neighbour, Lombok, has also recently grown in popularity. Both islands are small (Bali extends less than 150km at its longest point, Lombok a mere 80km), volcanic and graced with swathes of extremely fertile land, much of it – particularly on Bali – sculpted into terraced **rice-paddies**. Culturally, however, Bali and Lombok could hardly be more different. Bali remains the only **Hindu** society in Southeast Asia, and exuberant religious observance permeates every aspect of contemporary Balinese life; the Sasak people of Lombok, on the other hand, are **Muslim**, like the vast majority of other Indonesians.

The tiny island of **Bali** (population three million) draws in more than one and a half million foreign visitors every year, plus around a million domestic tourists. As a result, it has become very much a mainstream destination, offering all the comforts and facilities expected by better-off tourists, and suffering the predictable problems of congestion, commercialization and breakneck Westernization. However, its original charm is still very much in evidence, its stunning temples and spectacular festivals

v

Fact file

- Bali and Lombok are part of the Republic of Indonesia, an ethnically diverse democracy of 228 million people. Everyone over the age of 17 is eligible to vote in the national elections, held at least every five years for the five hundred members of the House of Representatives (DPR), who subsequently elect a president.

- As one of 27 self-contained provinces (*propinsi*) of Indonesia, Bali is overseen by a governor; the current incumbent, Drs. I Dewa Made Beratha, was appointed in 1998. The province is divided into eight districts or *kabupaten* (reflecting the borders of the old regencies) and one municipality, Denpasar.

- Lombok and its eastern neighbour, Sumbawa, together form the province of Nusa Tenggara Barat, which has been governed by Harun Al Rasyid since 1998 from Lombok's capital, Mataram.

- Both islands are volcanic and subject to earthquakes. The last major eruption was in 1963, when 100,000 Balinese homes were destroyed (see box on p.268). But volcanic ash is also a life-enhancer – both an exceptionally rich medium for growing crops and an excellent fertilizer when carried down the hillsides by rivers. The highest peak in Bali's spine of volcanoes is Gunung Agung (3142m). Lombok's highest point, amidst a cluster of volcanoes topping 2300m, is the summit of Gunung Rinjani (3726m). Separating the two islands is the Lombok Strait – just 35km wide, but 1300m deep in places.

set off by the gorgeously lush landscape of the interior. Meanwhile, **Lombok** (population 2.3 million) plays host to only 250,000 foreign visitors annually (and about the same number of domestic tourists), and boasts only a handful of burgeoning tourist resorts, retaining its reputation as a more adventurous destination than its neighbour. While there are established resorts on the coast and in the hill villages, Lombok still has extensive areas that have yet to be fully explored by visitors.

Until the nineteenth century, both Bali and Lombok were divided into small **kingdoms**, each domain ruled by a succession of rajas whose territories fluctuated so much that, at times, parts of eastern Bali and western Lombok

were joined under a single ruler. More recently, both islands endured years of colonial rule under the Dutch East Indies government, which only ended with hard-won **independence** for Indonesia in 1949. Since then, the Jakarta-based government of Indonesia has tried hard to foster a sense of national identity among its extraordinarily diverse islands, both by implementing a unifying five-point political philosophy, the Pancasila, and through the mandatory introduction of Bahasa Indonesia, now the lingua franca for the whole archipelago. Politically, Bali is administered as a province in its own right, while Lombok is the most westerly island of Nusa Tenggara province, which stretches east as far as Timor.

Where to go

Bali's best-known resort is **Kuta** beach, an eight-kilometre sweep of golden sand whose international reputation as a hangout for week-ending Australian surfers is enhanced by its numerous restaurants, bars, clubs and shops. Travellers seeking more relaxed alternatives generally head across the southern peninsula to **Sanur** or, increasingly, to peaceful **Candi Dasa** further east, or the black volcanic sands of **Lovina** on the north coast. Quieter, but more upmarket, seaside options can be found at **Jimbaran** in the south and **Pemuteran** in the northwest. On Lombok, the **Senggigi** coastline offers the widest range of accommodation, while the nearby and rapidly developing **Gili**

Stunning temples and spectacular festivals are set off by gorgeously lush landscape

Islands have long been a favourite with backpackers. All these resorts make comfortable bases for **divers** and **snorkellers**, within easy reach of the islands' fine reefs; Bali also boasts an unusually accessible wreck dive. **Surfers** on Bali head for the famed south-coast swells (particularly around Uluwatu) and the offshore island breaks of Nusa Lembongan, though less experienced wave-riders find Kuta and Medewi more manageable. There's also plenty of surfing potential off Lombok's south coast.

Despite the obvious attractions of the beach resorts, most visitors also venture inland to experience more traditional island life. On Bali, the once-tiny village of **Ubud** has become a hugely popular cultural centre, still charming but undeniably commercialized, where traditional dances are staged every night of the week and the streets are full of arts and crafts galleries. **Tetebatu** on Lombok occupies a similarly cool position in the foothills, although, like the island as a whole, it lacks the artistic heritage of Bali. In general, the villages on both islands are far more appealing than the towns, but Bali's capital **Denpasar**, its former capital **Singaraja**, and Lombok's **Ampenan-Mataram-Cakranegara-Sweta** conurbation are all worth a day-trip for their museums, markets and temples.

Garden bathrooms

Perhaps inspired by the traditional use of the outdoors for ablutions (some villagers still bathe in the river every evening), some losmen and many hotels design their bathrooms with garden features. You may simply find a couple of shrubs and an artistically mossed-over stonecarving in your smallest room, or you may be greeted with elegant creations of riverbed pebbles, bamboo shower spouts, miniature ponds and waterfalls and perhaps even a sunken bathtub (with jacuzzi in the poshest places). Many garden bathrooms have a partially open roof – never compromising your privacy of course, but ideal for star-gazing or even a private shower in the rain.

Bali's other big draw is its proliferation of elegant Hindu **temples**, particularly the spectacular island temple of Tanah Lot and the extensive Besakih complex on the slopes of Gunung Agung. Temple **festivals** are also well worth attending: held throughout the island and at frequent intervals during the year, most are open to tourists.

Both islands hold a number of hiking possibilities, many of them up **volcanoes**. The best is undoubtedly the climb to the crater lake of Lombok's **Gunung Rinjani** – one of the highest peaks in Indonesia – though the ascent to the summit of Bali's **Gunung Batur** is less arduous and therefore

Despite the attractions of the beach resorts, most visitors also venture inland to experience more traditional island life

Rice-farming

Emerald-green rice terraces, or *sawah*, are one of the most memorable sights on Bali and Lombok, and you'll see them almost everywhere – ranged in steps up hillsides, tumbling down steep-sided river valleys, and encircling villages. The fertile volcanic soil, plentiful sunshine and regular downpours create ideal growing conditions that sustain at least two crops a year, and an ancient system of *subak* irrigation co-operatives (see p.545) ensures that neighbours help each other where possible. For rice-farming is unrelenting, back-breaking work, nearly all of it done by hand, from the painstaking planting of the seedlings to the harvesting and threshing of the paddy. Spiritual help is also enlisted from the rice goddess Dewi Sri, who is courted with numerous rituals and worshipped at tiny shrines in every expanse of *sawah*.

more popular. Bali's sole **national park**, Bali Barat, has relatively few interesting trails, but is a rewarding place for **bird-watching**, as is the area around Lake Bratan in the centre of the island. Even if you don't want to go hiking, it's worth considering a trip to the northern hills for the change of scenery and refreshing temperatures; the little village of **Munduk** makes a satisfying focus.

When to go

L ocated firmly in the **tropical** zone, just eight degrees south of the equator, Bali and Lombok enjoy fairly constant year-round temperatures, averaging 27°C in the shade in the coastal areas and the hills around Ubud, and 22°C in the central

Surfing

Bob Koke, co-founder of one of Kuta's first hotels, claims to have started Bali's surfing craze in 1936: he'd learnt to surf in Hawaii and, once established in Kuta, began to make his own boards and to teach his staff and guests the rudiments. Since then, Bali's surf breaks have become a major draw for enthusiasts from Australia, Japan and beyond – and local people have taken up the sport with equal zeal, perfecting a distinctive Bali style which even 6-year-olds execute with finesse. Bali's most awesome, and challenging, breaks are at Uluwatu and Padang Padang, though experts rate Lombok's Desert Point even higher. For more on surfing in Bali and Lombok, see p.60.

volcanoes around Kintamani. Both islands are hit by an annual **monsoon** which brings rain, wind and a sometimes unbearable 97 percent humidity from October through to March.

The **best time to visit** is outside the monsoon season, from May to September, though monsoons are, like many other events in Indonesia, notoriously unpunctual, and you should be prepared to get rained on in Ubud at any time of year. However, the prospect of a daily rainstorm shouldn't put you off: you're far more likely to get an hour-long downpour than day-long drizzle. In addition, the landscape is at its most verdant during this time, and the rivers and waterfalls at their most dramatic; mountain-climbing, though, is both unrewarding and dangerous at this time of year. You should also be aware of the peak **tourist seasons**: resorts on both islands get packed out

between mid-June and mid-September and again over the Christmas–New Year period, when prices rocket and rooms can be fully booked for days or weeks in advance.

For a two-day **weather forecast** for the different regions of Bali, and to request a customized forecast for weather-sensitive activities such as diving, sailing or hiking, visit Ⓦwww.baliweather.net.

Average monthly temperatures and rainfall

	Jan	Feb	Mar	Apr	May	Jun	Jul	Aug	Sep	Oct	Nov	Dec
Kintamani												
°C	22	22	22	22	22	21	21	21	22	22	22	22
mm	444	405	248	174	72	43	30	21	35	50	166	257
Kuta												
°C	28	28	28	28	27	27	26	26	27	27	28	28
mm	394	311	208	115	79	67	57	31	43	95	176	268
Mataram												
°C	27	27	26	26	26	25	25	25	26	27	27	27
mm	253	254	209	155	84	67	38	21	36	168	250	209
Singaraja												
°C	27	27	27	27	28	28	27	27	28	29	28	28
mm	318	318	201	123	57	36	31	7	21	54	115	180
Ubud												
°C	27	27	27	27	27	26	26	26	26	27	27	27
mm	412	489	274	224	101	172	128	132	142	350	374	398

30
things not to miss

It's not possible to see everything that Bali and Lombok have to offer in one trip – and we don't suggest you try. What follows is a selective and subjective taste of the islands' highlights: great places to stay, outstanding beaches, spectacular hikes and exquisite crafts. They're arranged in five colour-coded categories, so you can browse through to find the very best things to see, do, buy and experience. All highlights have a page reference to take you straight into the guide, where you can find out more.

01 **South Lombok beaches** Page **473** • Some of the most glorious coastline on the islands features sweeping bays and pristine coves between dramatic headlands.

02 **Pura Luhur Batukau** Page **385** • Secluded high in the foothills of a sacred mountain, this is one of Bali's most beautiful and atmospheric temples.

03 **Sunrise from Gunung Batur** Page **319** • Pre-dawn climbers are rewarded by a fabulous sunrise silhouetting Abang, Agung and Rinjani to the east.

04 **Temple festivals** Page **510** • Every one of Bali's 20,000 Hindu temples holds at least one annual festival to entertain the gods with processions, offerings and music.

05 **Kuta nightlife** Page **130** • Quaffing jugfuls of Bali Hai beer and dancing till dawn are the most popular pastimes in Bali's liveliest resort.

06 **Nusa Penida's south coast** Page **278** • Stunning limestone cliffs rise sheer from the ocean crashing hundreds of metres below.

07 **Gunung Agung** Page **269** • A perfectly conical summit, impressively visible from much of central and eastern Bali.

08 **Tenganan** Page **291** • An ancient Balinese village that is a centre for crafts, including weaving and calligraphy.

09 **Pemuteran** Page **404** • Traditional fishing boats are a common sight at this inviting little beach haven on the northwest coast.

10 **Kerta Gosa paintings, Klungkung** Page **257** • Intricate and superbly crafted examples of classical Balinese paintings.

11 Rice-paddies of Iseh and Sidemen Page **304** • Among the most beautiful of the many sweeping, soaring terraces carved from the hillsides that adorn the foothills of both islands.

12 Seafood barbecues, Jimbaran Page **138** • Fresh fish grilled to order on the beach.

13 Bali Museum, Denpasar Page **96** • A good ethnological introduction to traditional life on the island.

14 **Tirtagangga Water Palace** Page **301** • Soothing pools amidst pretty gardens, surrounded by rice-fields and impressive mountains.

15 Street food Page **47** • Chicken sate, noodle soup and spicy fruit salad are just a few of the local specialities sold from handcarts and food stalls on nearly every street corner.

16 Ubud Page **186** • With fine countryside nearby, myriad craft shops and exceptionally pleasant accommodation, Ubud is Bali's top inland destination.

17 Spas Page **67** • Pamper yourself with some of the local beauty treatments, including the famous *mandi lulur* turmeric scrub.

18 Gili Islands Page **441** • Pure white sand, crystal-clear turquoise waters and a laid-back atmosphere make these perennial favourites well worth a visit.

19 Gamelan music Page **515** • The frenetic syncopations of the Balinese xylophone provide the island's national soundtrack.

20 Diving and snorkelling Page **63** • Teeming shallow reefs, submerged canyons and resident oceanic sunfish are just a few of the underwater attractions.

21 Sanur Page **156** • Sumptuous hotel gardens and a distinct village atmosphere make this one of south Bali's nicest resorts.

22 Shopping Page **70** • A tantalizing range of goodies to browse and buy, including fashions in Kuta, arts and crafts in Ubud and pottery on Lombok.

23 Tanah Lot Page **374** • Bali's most photographed temple sits serenely atop its own tiny island off the southwest coast.

24 **Barong-Rangda dance** Page **521** • This theatrical enactment of the battle between good and evil makes for a gripping show.

25 **Lombok crafts** Page **429** • Textiles, pottery, basketware, carving, furniture... great-value crafts for even the most avid shopper.

26 **Kecak dance** Page **523** • Unforgettable torchlit performance narrated by an *a cappella* chorus of fifty men.

27 **Neka Art Museum, Ubud** Page **206** • An unrivalled selection of the finest art in Bali, from seventeenth-century narratives to 1960s expressionism and contemporary abstracts.

28 **Learning to paint, cook or dance** Page **225** • Ubud is the best place to take short, tourist-oriented courses in Balinese arts and crafts.

29 **Pura Meduwe Karang** Page **348** • A wonderful example of Bali's highly ornate northern temple architecture.

30 **Climbing Rinjani** Page **458** • The most challenging and rewarding climb on the islands takes in forest, rocky peaks and a dramatic crater lake.

contents

Using the Rough Guide

We've tried to make this Rough Guide a good read and easy to use. The book is divided into six main sections, and you should be able to find whatever you want in one of them.

colour section

The front colour section offers a quick tour of Bali and Lombok. The **introduction** aims to give you a feel for the islands, with suggestions on where to go. We also tell you what the weather is like and include a basic fact file. Next, our authors round up their favourite aspects of Bali and Lombok in the **things not to miss** section – whether it's great food, amazing sights or a special hotel. Right after this comes a full **contents** list.

basics

The Basics section covers all the **pre-departure** nitty-gritty to help you plan your trip. This is where to find out which airlines fly to your destination, what paperwork you'll need, what to do about money and insurance, about internet access, food, security, public transport, car rental – in fact just about every piece of **general practical information** you might need.

guide

This is the heart of the Rough Guide, divided into user-friendly chapters, each of which covers a specific region. Every chapter starts with a list of **highlights** and an **introduction** that helps you to decide where to go, depending on your time and budget. Likewise, introductions to the various towns and smaller regions within each chapter should help you plan your itinerary. We start most town accounts with information on arrival and accommodation, followed by a tour of the sights, and finally reviews of places to eat and drink, and details of nightlife. Longer accounts also have a directory of practical listings. Each chapter concludes with **public transport details** for that region.

contexts

Read Contexts to get a deeper understanding of what makes Bali and Lombok tick. We include a brief **history**, articles about **religion**, **arts**, **music** and **dance**, and a detailed further reading section that reviews dozens of **books**.

language

The **language** section gives useful guidance for speaking Bahasa Indonesia and pulls together all the vocabulary you might need on your trip, including a comprehensive **menu reader** and some words of Bahasa Bali and Sasak. Here you'll also find a **glossary** of terms peculiar to the islands.

index + small print

Apart from a **full index**, which includes maps as well as places, this section covers publishing information, credits and acknowledgements, and also has our contact details in case you want to send in updates and corrections to the book – or suggestions as to how we might improve it.

Chapter list and map

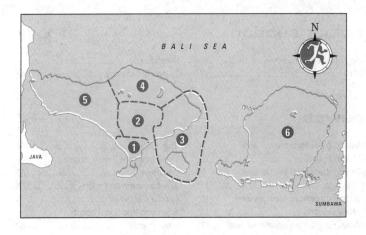

contents

colour section

basics

guide

contexts

485–560

language

561–571

index + small print

573–586

map symbols

maps are listed in the full index using coloured text

▪▪▪▪▪	International boundary	★	Bemo stop
▪▪▪▪	Chapter division boundary	⊠	Gate
═══	Main road	⊙	Statue
══	Minor road	◉	Accommodation
◄═══	One-way street	◼	Restaurant/bar
▬▬▬	Pedestrianized street	ⓘ	Information office
▪▪▪▪▪▪	Path	ℂ	Telephone
▪ ▪ ▪	Ferry route	@	Internet access
✈	Airport	⊠	Post office
✦	Point of interest	⊞	Hospital
♠	Temple	⊞	Clinic
♙	Mosque	▮	Fuel station
⚘	Waterfall	⛳	Golf course
⚶	Spring	▮	Building
▲	Mountain peak	▭	Hotel compound
◖	Cave	▦	Park
⌇	Surfing beach	▨	Mangrove swamp
⌇	Snorkelling area		

basics

basics

Getting there

There's no shortage of international and domestic flights to Bali's only airport, Ngurah Rai Airport – sometimes referred to as being in Denpasar, though it's actually 3km south of Kuta and 11km south of Denpasar (see box on pp.110–111 for full details). Lombok's Selaparang Airport, 2km north of Mataram, is much less busy, served mainly by domestic Indonesian carriers, but also by the Singapore Airlines subsidiary Silk Air.

The most expensive times to fly to Bali and Lombok are during **high season**, which on most airlines runs from the beginning of July through to the middle or end of August and also includes most of December and the first half of January. Flights get booked solid during these peak periods and should be reserved several weeks in advance. Prices drop considerably at other times of the year.

You can often cut costs by going through a specialist **flight agent** – either a consolidator, who buys up blocks of tickets from the airlines and sells them at a discount, or a discount agent, who may offer other travel-related services such as insurance and tours, or even a few nights' free accommodation. Periodic **special offers** (direct from airlines, through flight agents, or on the web) are invariably good deals, although they may come with restrictions. Otherwise, you'll be looking at a **restricted economy** fare such as Apex or SuperApex, often requiring booking – and paying – at least 21 days before departure, with minimum and maximum stays and penalties for date-changes. Many airlines and discount travel **websites** offer you the opportunity to book your tickets online, cutting out the costs of agents and middlemen. Good deals can often be found through discount or auction sites, as well as through the airlines' own websites. The *Rough Guide to Travel Online* has more. A few airlines offer **youth** or **student** fares, while some have very good-value **flight-plus-accommodation deals**, usually at mid-range hotels in the resorts of south-coast Bali.

If flying long-haul from Europe or North America, it's worth considering **stopping off** for a few days en route – an option offered free of charge by a number of Asian airlines, such as Malaysia Airlines for stops in Kuala Lumpur, or Thai for a break in Bangkok. Alternatively, if your time is not too limited, buying a ticket to a Southeast Asian hub such as Bangkok, and then buying an onward flight to Bali or Lombok from there, can often work out cheaper than flying direct: you can pick up a return flight to Bangkok from London for about £400, from Los Angeles for $800, and many Bangkok travel agents can sell you a return ticket to Bali for around £200/$290.

If Bali or Lombok is only one stop on a longer journey, you might want to consider buying a Circle Pacific, Circle Asia or **Round-the-World** (RTW) ticket. Some travel agents can sell you an "off-the-shelf" ticket that will have you touching down in about six cities (Denpasar is on many itineraries); others will have to assemble one for you, which can be tailored to your needs but is apt to be more expensive. The only way to include Lombok on such a ticket is to go via Bali.

Organized tours and packages

Options with **tour operators** are pretty varied, from resort-based trips to overland excursions or cruises. inevitably, package tours are more expensive and less spontaneous than you could manage if you travelled independently but can be useful if you have limited time or want everything organized with as few hassles as possible. You may be able to add a bit of private travel onto your organized trip, so it's worth checking whether you can stay on independently and fly back at a later date.

Tying the knot

Plenty of companies worldwide offer packages catering for those intending to get **married** in Bali; these generally involve certain formalities ahead of the wedding day at your consulate in Bali. There are some restrictions on age and religion, and things are complicated if you're divorced or widowed; the tour company can advise. On top of the standard holiday, you should reckon on an extra £400/US$600/A$1100 as a minimum: there are plenty of optional extras and it's important to check exactly what is and isn't included. Several wedding companies in Bali will organize the wedding for you; Bali Weddings International (ⓦwww.baliweddingsinternational .com) and Romantic Weddings (ⓦwww.romantic-weddings.com) get good reports. Some top-class hotels, including the *Bali Intercontinental Resort* at Jimbaran Bay, will also plan the entire event for you. Bali International Diving Professionals (ⓦwww.bidp-balidiving.com) arranges **underwater weddings**. *The Good Honeymoon Guide* (published by Trailblazer) includes details on planning weddings abroad.

A large chunk of the package price goes on the flight: you need to be vigilant when reading brochures. If you're planning a **hotel-based holiday**, the range of accommodation on offer will be from the mid to the top end of the market; the majority of hotels used by tour operators are in the Sanur, Legian and Nusa Dua areas on Bali, with some available in Ubud, and in Senggigi, the *Oberoi* or *Coralia Lombok Novotel*. There's an enormous spread of quality and price available if you use tour operators – from extremely good-value, no-frills places up to some of the plushest hotels on the islands. There are also plenty of specialist tailor-made companies that will assemble a trip to your specifications and make all the arrangements for you.

For a more varied and energetic experience, several companies offer **overland trips** from Java to Bali, calling in at the main central and eastern Java sights on the way; some offer extensions of basic Bali holidays with a **cruise** eastwards, usually as far as Flores, taking in Komodo on the way (it's always worth checking how long you have ashore at each stop).

Walking and hiking tours, activity trips and tours based on art, crafts and culture have become especially popular in Bali, and there's a wide range of **surf** or **dive** packages at every level of ability, experience and budget.

From the UK and Ireland

There are no nonstop flights **from the UK or Ireland** to Bali. Singapore Airlines and

Qantas offer the fastest, most comfortable, and generally most expensive London–Denpasar flights; both require a (short) transfer in Singapore, and usually get you to Bali in around 16 hours. Garuda also offers a fast, less expensive, though less luxurious, service, with a change of plane in Jakarta; seats can get booked up very far ahead. Several other cheaper airlines fly to Denpasar, with the drawback being longer transit times at airports en route, which push some journey times up to around 22 hours. All fares quoted below include tax.

From London, sample **low-season fares** for flights booked through a discount agent (always cheaper than those booked direct with an airline) are around £550 with Garuda (via Jakarta), Malaysia (via Kuala Lumpur) or Royal Brunei (via Bandar Seri Begawan), around £675 with Qantas (via Singapore) or Singapore (via Singapore). In **high season**, add £70–120 to all these. Flying from elsewhere in the UK or from Ireland, you'll need to add on the return fare to London.

If continuing **to Australia**, you'll find it much cheaper to buy a through-ticket on Qantas to Perth (£725–810 depending on the season) or Sydney (£810–950), with a stopover in Denpasar; Austravel and Quest have especially good deals on these routes. If you've managed to get a really cheap return fare to Bali, it might be worth contacting travel agents in Bali for quotes on return Bali–Sydney flights (from £360); see the listings sections of Denpasar (p.104), Kuta (p.137) or Ubud (p.228), or surf the Bali chapter of PATA (Pacific Asia Travel

Association) at ⓦwww.patabali.com/members. A typical one-year open **RTW ticket** from London taking in Delhi, Denpasar, Sydney, Auckland and Los Angeles can cost as little as £850.

To Lombok

The most convenient way of getting **to Lombok** is to fly nonstop London–Singapore with Singapore Airlines and then change onto their subsidiary carrier, Silk Air, for the nonstop flight to Mataram (4–6 weekly; 3hr). The complete return journey from London costs around £690 in low season (add £100 at peak times). You can buy the return Singapore–Mataram flight direct from the Silk Air website for £180/200. A cheaper alternative is to go with Garuda via Jakarta, though this may entail having to spend one night in Jakarta at your own expense; this varies between low/high-season fares of about £550/670. It's also possible to take the cheapest flight you can find to Kuala Lumpur, then change onto the Indonesian carrier Merpati, which flies from there to Mataram via Surabaya (3 weekly).

Depending on the time of year and your travel plans, you could save a lot by taking the cheapest available flight to Bali; from there, a flight to Mataram costs about £30 return (see p.41), a bus from £7 return (see p.417), or a ferry from £2 return (see p.416). For full details on getting from Bali to Lombok, see pp.416–417.

Airlines in the UK and Ireland

British Airways UK ☎0845/773 3377, Republic of Ireland ☎1800/626 747, ⓦwww.ba.com. No direct flights to Bali or Lombok, but daily partnership flights with Singapore Airlines from London via Singapore.
Garuda Indonesia UK ☎020/7467 8600, ⓦwww.garuda-indonesia.com. Four flights a week via Jakarta.
Malaysia Airlines (MAS) UK ☎0870/607 9090, Republic of Ireland ☎01/676 1561, ⓦwww.mas.com.my. Daily flights via Kuala Lumpur.
Merpati ⓦwww.merpati.co.id. Three flights a week from Kuala Lumpur to Mataram via Surabaya; six flights daily from Denpasar to Mataram.

Qantas UK ☎0845/774 7767, ⓦwww.qantas.com.au. Three flights weekly via Singapore.
Royal Brunei Airlines UK ☎020/7584 6660, ⓦwww.bruneiair.com. Two flights a week, via Bandar Seri Begawan, one of which requires an overnight stopover.
Silk Air Contact via Singapore Airlines ⓦwww.silkair.com.sg. Four to six flights a week from Singapore to Mataram.
Singapore Airlines UK ☎0870/608 8886, Republic of Ireland ☎01/671 0722, ⓦwww.singaporeair.com. Three times daily from London via Singapore to Bali and four to six weekly via Singapore to Lombok (using Silk Air).

Flight agents in the UK and Ireland

UK

Austravel ☎0870/166 2020, ⓦwww.austravel.com. Very good deals on flights to Australia and New Zealand via Indonesia, also on RTW tickets. Branches in Birmingham, Bristol, Edinburgh, Leeds, London and Manchester.
Bridge the World ☎020/7911 0900, ⓦwww.bridgetheworld.com. Specialists in RTW tickets, with good deals aimed at the backpacker market.
Co-op Travel Care ☎028/9047 1717. Budget fares agent, based in Belfast.
Flightbookers ☎0870/010 7000, ⓦwww.ebookers.com. Low fares on an extensive selection of scheduled flights.
North South Travel ☎01245/608291, ⓦwww.northsouthtravel.co.uk. Travel agency whose profits are used to support projects in the developing world, especially sustainable tourism.
Premier Travel ☎028/7126 3333, ⓦwww.premiertravel.uk.com. Discount flight specialists, based in Derry.
Quest Worldwide ☎020/8547 3322, ⓦwww.questtravel.com. Specialists in RTW and Australasian discount fares.
Rosetta Travel ☎028/9064 4996, ⓦwww.rosettatravel.com. Belfast flight and holiday agent.
STA Travel ☎0870/160 0599, ⓦwww.statravel.co.uk. Worldwide specialists in low-cost flights and tours for students and under-26s, though other customers welcome. Over 40 branches.
Top Deck ☎020/7370 4555, ⓦwww.topdecktravel.co.uk. Long-established agent dealing in discount flights.

Trailfinders ℡020/7938 3366, ⓦwww.trailfinders
.com. One of the best-informed and most efficient
agents for independent travellers, with ten branches.
Travel Bag ℡0870/900 1350,
ⓦwww.travelbag.co.uk. Discount flights to
Australia and the Far East; official Qantas agent.
The Travel Bug ℡0870/444 0045,
ⓦwww.flynow.com. Large range of discounted
tickets.
Travel Cuts ℡020/7255 2082, ⓦwww.travelcuts
.co.uk. Specializes in budget, student and youth
travel and RTW tickets.

Republic of Ireland

Apex Travel ℡01/241 8000, ⓦwww.apextravel.ie.
Specialists in flights to Australia and the Far East.
Aran Travel International ℡091/562595,
ⓦhomepages.iol.ie/~arantvl/aranmain.htm. Good-
value flights.
CIE Tours International ℡01/703 1888,
ⓦwww.cietours.ie. General flight and tour agent.
Joe Walsh Tours ℡01/676 0991 or ℡021/427
7959, ⓦwww.joewalshtours.ie. General budget
fares agent.
Lee Travel ℡021/427 7111, ⓦwww.leetravel.ie.
Flights and holidays worldwide.
McCarthy's Travel ℡021/427 0127, ⓦwww
.mccarthystravel.ie. General flight agent.
Trailfinders ℡01/677 7888, ⓦwww.trailfinders
.ie. Good service and range of flights.

Online

ⓦwww.cheapflights.com Very user-friendly site
that lists the cheapest fares from about thirty
travel agents.
ⓦwww.expedia.co.uk Discount airfares, all-
airline search engine and daily deals.
ⓦwww.lastminute.com Last-minute holiday
package and flight-only deals.
ⓦwww.priceline.com Name-your-own-price
website that has deals at around forty percent off
standard fares.

UK tour operators

Arc Journeys ℡020/7681 3175,
ⓦwww.travelarc.com. Tailor-made specialists with
a large and enticing portfolio of trips to Indonesia,
including special-interest tours such as art and
architecture, music, dance and drama, textiles and
climbing volcanoes, which can be combined with
Torajaland in Sulawesi, orangutans in Kalimantan,
sultanates of Java or the islands east of Bali.
Asiaworld ℡0870/079 9788, ⓦwww.asiaworld
.co.uk. Plenty of Bali and Lombok beach-based

holidays with possible add-on tours such as
exploring the islands or Yogyakarta on Java. Plenty
of combinations with stays in other parts of Asia
including Sabah. They are tailor-made specialists,
so can put together pretty much anything on
request.
Audley ℡01869/276200,
ⓦwww.audleytravel.com. Tailor-made specialists,
with lots of information and itinerary ideas which
feature Bali and Lombok, ideas on exploring Java
en route or extending with a cruise east to
Komodo.
British Airways Holidays ℡0870/442 3815,
ⓦwww.baholidays.co.uk. Luxury hotel-based
holidays in Bali and Lombok which can also be
combined with stays in Bangkok, Hong Kong or
Singapore. A 17-day "Overland to Bali" trip is also
available from Jakarta (this can also finish in
Lombok). Wedding specialists.
Exodus ℡020/8675 5550, ⓦwww.exodus.co.uk.
A well-respected, long-standing overland
expedition company. They sell trips from Peregrine
in Australia (see p.17), including the nine-day
"Secrets of Bali" taking in Ubud, many of the
central volcanoes and the west; and an eight-day
tour of Lombok, including the Gili Islands, Sapit
and Tetebatu. These two can be combined.
Explore ℡01252/760000,
ⓦwww.exploreworldwide.com. An established
adventure holiday company. "Exotic Java and Bali"
is a 16-day overland trip through Java and Bali
visiting all the highlights. The 15-day "Rinjani
Challenge" takes in the Bali highlights, the climb
up Rinjani and relaxation on the Gili Islands. Their
15-day "East Indies Seatrek" starts and ends in
Bali and is a traditional Buginese schooner cruise
via Sumbawa to Komodo and Rinca.
Footprint Adventures ℡01522/804929,
ⓦwww.footprint-adventures.com. This trekking,
wildlife and birding specialist offers the ten-day
"Mount Rinjani Adventure", including the climb to
the summit, and trips of varying length to Komodo,
the longer ones including Lombok and Sumbawa.
Handmade Holidays ℡01285/642555,
ⓦwww.handmade-holidays.co.uk. Tailor-made
specialists offering holidays in some of the
loveliest hotels in Bali and Lombok which can be
combined with individual cultural and adventure
tours around Indonesia.
Hayes and Jarvis ℡0870/898 9890,
ⓦwww.hayes-jarvis.com. A range of beach-based
Bali holidays, mostly in the resorts in the south
and multi-centre trips in various locations around
the island.
Holidays 4 Less ℡020/7400 7054,
ⓦwww.holidays4less.co.uk. A good range of south

Bali beach-based holidays, with often extremely good deals to be had at four- and five-star hotels.

Imaginative Traveller ☎020/8742 8612, ⓦwww.imaginative-traveller.com. A range of imaginative trips: their 13-day "Bali and Lombok Explored" includes all the highlights plus a trek to the crater rim on Rinjani, optional diving and snorkelling and jungle and beach walking.

Kuoni Travel ☎01306/742888, weddings 747007, ⓦwww.kuoni.co.uk. Hotel-based holidays in Bali and Lombok with a big selection of hotels. These can be combined with stays in other parts of Asia or Australia or with a Bali Explorer Tour or a cruise east on the MSY *Perintis* to Flores taking in Sumbawa and Komodo. Wedding arrangements are a speciality.

Magic of the Orient ☎01293/537700, ⓦwww.magic-of-the-orient.com. Holidays based in fine hotels throughout Bali and Lombok that can be combined with private tours or a five-day cruise east to Komodo and on to Sumba. Weddings arranged.

Silk Steps ☎01454/888850, ⓦwww.silksteps.co.uk. Suggested tailor-made itineraries include "The Garuda Way", six nights from Jakarta covering Yogyakarta and Bali; "Bali Puri", eight nights in Ubud, Munduk, Pemuteran, Pupuan and Kuta; "Island Hopper", visiting Java, Kalimantan, Sulawesi and Bali in thirteen nights; and "Dragon Discovery" covering Lombok, Sumbawa and Komodo. Also many other itineraries.

Symbiosis Expedition Planning ☎020/7924 5906, ⓦwww.symbiosis-travel.com. Mostly tailor-made holidays which can include diving (including liveaboards), trekking, whitewater rafting, mountain-biking or anything to do with the arts. They send clients a questionnaire to assess their interests and make suggestions accordingly. They also operate occasional small-group specialist trips such as "Bali, Madura and the Volcanoes of East Java by Bike", "Java Bali Birdwatching Expedition" and "Batik Painting and the Creative Arts in Bali and Java".

Travelbag Adventures ☎01420/541007, ⓦwww.travelbag-adventures.co.uk. Offers a small-group, fifteen-day trip "Island Volcanoes", taking in much of central Bali and Lombok, and a family adventure called "Monkeys and Volcanoes" to Ubud, Lovina, Tirtagangga and Batur which includes a stay with a Balinese family.

From the US and Canada

At the time of writing, all flights **from the US and Canada** to Indonesia on the national airline Garuda have been suspended, though it's hoped that the service will resume. Despite this, there's still a choice of flights to Bali on other carriers, although none goes direct. Note that flying on **weekends** can add $70–100.

Flights leaving from the **west coast** cross the Pacific to Asian and Australasian hubs such as Taipei, Seoul, Tokyo, Hong Kong, Sydney or Melbourne, from where there are plenty of flights on to Bali. The best journey times (often on Air Canada, Cathay Pacific or China Airlines) are around 24 hours, although considerably more than this is not unusual; the slower journeys invariably put down midway, perhaps in Honolulu and/or Guam, while Japan Airlines' schedules, for instance, force you to overnight in Tokyo. The cheapest low-season round-trip **fare** from LA is $820, with different deals running as high as $3000. In the shoulder season, reckon on $880 upwards, high season $1200.

From the **east coast**, it makes sense to check out routes via one of the major European gateways – most typically London, Frankfurt or Amsterdam. These also work out, at best, around 24 hours, although you'll need to make specific research enquiries: airline alliances mean that any North American carrier with links to an Asian partner would automatically send you west across the Pacific instead, pushing up the journey time. Similarly, consolidators and discount flight agents tend to quote the lowest prices – which are also often on Asian carriers flying west. **Fares** are around $2000 minimum in the low and shoulder seasons, $2700 in the high season.

RTW tickets starting from New York or Los Angeles can include combinations of Sydney, Denpasar, Jakarta, Singapore, Bangkok, Rome, Milan, London or Paris; **Circle Pacific** tickets starting from NY, San Francisco or LA can take in stops at Hong Kong, Bangkok, Kuala Lumpur and/or Bangkok in addition to Denpasar. Sample prices for either are around $2100. Yet another possibility, which could also work out cheaper, is Cathay Pacific's **"Asia Pass"**, which you purchase before you arrive at their hub in Hong Kong, and allows you up to six sectors of travel on the network at advantageous prices. Prices depend on the season and your destinations; contact the airline for details.

If Lombok is your destination, you can either fly from Denpasar on a local airline, or to Singapore with Singapore Airlines and then take the three-hour flight to Mataram on their subsidiary Silk Air.

Airlines in the US and Canada

Air Canada ☏1-888/247-2262, ⓦwww.aircanada.ca.
Cathay Pacific ☏1-800/233-2742, ⓦwww.cathay-usa.com.
China Airlines ☏1-800/227-5118, ⓦwww.china-airlines.com.
Continental Airlines ☏1-800/231-0856, ⓦwww.continental.com.
EVA Airways ☏1-800/695-1188, ⓦwww.evaair.com.
Garuda Indonesia ☏1-800/342-7832, ⓦwww.garuda-indonesia.com.
Japan Airlines ☏1-800/525-3663, ⓦwww.japanair.com.
Northwest/KLM ☏1-800/447-4747, ⓦwww.nwa.com.
Qantas Airways ☏1-800/227-4500, ⓦwww.qantas.com.
Singapore Airlines ☏1-800/742-3333, ⓦwww.singaporeair.com.

Flight agents in the US and Canada

Air Brokers International ☏1-800/883-3273 or 415/397-1383, ⓦwww.airbrokers.com. Consolidator and specialist in RTW and Circle Pacific tickets.
Educational Travel Center ☏1-800/747-5551 or 608/256-5551, ⓦwww.edtrav.com. Student/youth discount agent with plenty of fares available for older and non-student travellers.
High Adventure Travel ☏1-800/350-0612 or 415/912-5600, ⓦwww.airtreks.com. RTW, Circle Asia and Circle Pacific tickets. The website features an interactive database that lets you build and price your own RTW itinerary.
STA Travel ☏1-800/777-0112 or 1-800/781-4040, ⓦwww.sta-travel.com. Worldwide specialists in independent travel.
TFI Tours International ☏1-800/745-8000 or 212/736-1140, ⓦwww.lowestairprice.com. Consolidator.
Travac ☏1-800/872-8800, ⓦwww.thetravelsite.com. Consolidator and charter broker.
Travelers Advantage ☏1-877/259-2691, ⓦwww.travelersadvantage.com. Discount travel club; annual membership fee required (currently $1 for 3 months' trial).
Travel Avenue ☏1-800/333-3335, ⓦwww.travelavenue.com. Full-service travel agent that offers discounts (typically 7%) in the form of rebates.
Travel Cuts US ☏1-866/246-9762, Canada ☏1-800/667-2887, ⓦwww.travelcuts.com. Student and budget-travel organization.
Worldtek Travel ☏1-800/243-1723, ⓦwww.worldtek.com. Discount agency.

Online

ⓦ**www.expedia.com** Discount airfares, all-airline search engine and daily deals.
ⓦ**www.hotwire.com** Bookings from the US only. Last-minute savings of up to forty percent on regular published fares.
ⓦ**www.priceline.com** Name-your-own-price website that has deals at around forty percent off standard fares.
ⓦ**www.skyauction.com** Bookings from the US only. Auctions tickets and travel packages using a "second bid" scheme.
ⓦ**www.travelocity.com** Destination guides, hot web fares and best deals for car rental, accommodation and lodging as well as fares.

Tour operators in the US and Canada

Absolute Asia ☏1-800/736-8187 or 212/627-1950, ⓦwww.absoluteasia.com. Small-group plus custom-designed trips. They can put together themed, country-specific or multi-country trips to suit. The 13-day "Bali and Lombok Naturally" journey focuses on the countryside, including hiking, horseriding, mountain-biking and snorkelling. The 14-day "Nusa Tenggara Explorer" takes in Bali, Lombok, Sumbawa, Komodo and Flores, while "Textiles of Eastern Indonesia" covers Bali, Lombok, Flores and west Sumba in 13 days.
Adventure Center ☏1-800/228-8747 or 510/654-1879, ⓦwww.adventure-center.com. Hiking and "soft adventure" specialists. In addition to beach-based holidays and their own active trips, they are also agents for Explore (UK) and Intrepid (Australia).
Asian Pacific Adventures ☏1-800/825-1680 or 818/886-5190, ⓦwww.asianpacificadventures.com. Special small-group tours along with an à la carte menu of small units that customers can combine into a longer journey. "Bali: Through an Artist's Eye" is a fifteen-day trip based in Ubud concentrating on art and crafts, visiting workshops and galleries and including temples and performances. "Fire, Water, Earth and Tribal Life: an Indonesian Cultural

Odyssey" covers Bali, Sulawesi, Flores and Sumba in 22 days.

Backroads ☎1-800/462-2848 or 510/527-1555, ⓦwww.backroads.com. Cycling, hiking and multi-sport tours. "Biking Bali" is six days of pedalling from Ubud to Candi Dasa via Lovina and Tulamben; the nine-day "Bali Multisport" includes cycling, hiking and snorkelling.

Goway Travel ☎1-800/387-8850, ⓦwww.goway.com Canada-based operator with plenty of ideas for Bali trips and good-value all-in packages.

Himalayan Travel ☎1-800/225-2380 or 203/743-2349, ⓦwww.himalayantravelinc.com. Customized tours plus set packages. Their 15-day "Indonesian Experience" concentrates on wildlife and trekking while travelling overland through Java to Bali. They also offer shorter trips and a six-day "Rinjani Trek" that aims to reach the summit.

Maupintour ☎1-800/255-4266, ⓦwww.maupintour.com. Luxury escorted tours that pack a huge amount into a small time; their "Allure of the Orient" covers Hong Kong, Bangkok, Chiang Mai, Singapore and Bali in fourteen days.

Nature Expeditions International ☎1-800/869-0639, ⓦwww.naturexp.com. Experts in educational adventure trips that include a large element of activity and culture. "Treasures of Bali and Java" lasts 12 days and includes whitewater rafting, cycling in the Batur area and learning gamelan and a *topeng* dance. Lectures on relevant topics are included in trips and extensions are possible to Borneo, Java, Komodo and Sumatra.

Pacific Delight Tours ☎1-800/221-7179, ⓦwww.pacificdelighttours.com. Specialists in deluxe tours to the Orient and Southeast Asia. Their "Asian Vistas" trips combine Bali with destinations such as Hong Kong, Singapore and Bangkok.

Real Bali ☎1-800/699-1995. A good selection of all-in package trips to Bali with plenty of options in quieter spots, away from the main tourist centres.

Vacationland ☎1-800/245-0050, ⓦwww.vacation-land.com. An Asian specialist offering some Bali hotel-based packages that are generally good deals when compared to the cost of flights alone.

From Australia and New Zealand

From Australia, both Qantas and Garuda have direct flights to Denpasar (5hr 30min from Sydney, 4hr from Perth, 2hr from Darwin). Low-season fares from Sydney, Melbourne, Brisbane, Cairns or Adelaide are about A$1075 (plus tax) on Garuda, A$1300

on Qantas; in high season, reckon on A$1330/A$1650. All other airlines require a transit in an Asian capital, which will literally double your journey time and rarely saves much money. From Perth, expect to pay A$870 for Garuda or A$1100 for Qantas in low season, about A$200 more in high season. (The cheapest Perth flight takes you via Bandar Seri Begawan on Royal Brunei for just A$770 in high season, but journey time on the single day with a decent connection is almost nine hours.) Being such a popular short-break destination, Bali is a less obvious stopover on a **round-the-world** trip, but you can get good return flights to London featuring a stay in Bali from A$1449, while a **Circle Asia** ticket with stops in Denpasar, Singapore, Mumbai, Kathmandu and Bangkok costs from A$1129.

From New Zealand, Garuda has one direct Auckland–Denpasar flight a week (10hr), and two weekly flights via Brisbane. Fares for either are NZ$1300 in low season, NZ$1600 high. You'll usually need to add NZ$200–300 return if flying from Christchurch or Wellington – which makes Qantas' fares from Auckland, Christchurch or Wellington via Melbourne or Sydney competitive, at NZ$1500 low, NZ$1800 high.

It's always worth checking for **flight-plus-accommodation deals** offered by travel agents and tour operators, which can sometimes work out cheaper than flight-only offers. In Australia, Travelshop has especially good deals, such as seven nights in low season in a Kuta three-star plus return flights from major east-coast cities for A$1372, from Perth for A$1114; four-night packages from Perth can even drop as low as A$679 in quiet periods. In New Zealand, STA Travel offers deals as low as NZ$1100 on Garuda from Auckland plus six nights in a three-star hotel, or NZ$1229 from Auckland, Wellington or Christchurch for a Qantas flight (with optional Australia stopover) plus six nights in a three-star hotel.

There are no direct flights to Lombok from either country, so you'll either need to change in Bali onto a half-hour domestic Denpasar–Mataram flight (cheapest if booked through a travel agent in Kuta, Denpasar or Sanur) or take one of the cheaper ferry routes, as described on p.416.

Airlines in Australia and New Zealand

Air New Zealand Australia ☎13 24 76, New Zealand ☎0800/737 000, ⓦwww.airnz.com. Daily flights from Auckland with an overnight stop in Singapore.

Garuda Australia ☎02/9334 9970, New Zealand ☎09/366 1862, ⓦwww.garuda-indonesia.com. Direct to Denpasar several times a week from Adelaide, Brisbane, Cairns, Sydney, Melbourne, Perth and Darwin. One direct flight a week from Auckland, and twice weekly from Auckland via Brisbane.

Merpati ⓦwww.merpati.co.id. Six flights a day from Denpasar to Mataram.

Qantas Australia ☎13 13 13, New Zealand ☎09/357 8900, ⓦwww.qantas.com.au. Several direct flights a week to Denpasar from Darwin, Melbourne, Sydney and Perth, with flights from other cities via Sydney, Melbourne and Darwin. Several flights a week from Auckland, Christchurch and Wellington via either Melbourne or Sydney. Also good flight-plus-accommodation deals.

Royal Brunei Airlines Australia ☎07/3017 5000, ⓦwww.bruneiair.com. Two or three flights a week from Perth, Brisbane and Darwin via Bandar Seri Begawan. Most flights from Perth entail an overnight stop.

Singapore Airlines Australia ☎13 10 11, New Zealand ☎09/303 2129 or ☎0800/808 909, ⓦwww.singaporeair.com. Several flights a week to Denpasar or Mataram from Australasian capital cities via either a transfer or an overnight stopover in Singapore.

Flight agents in Australia and New Zealand

Australia

Flight Centre ☎13 16 00, ⓦwww.flightcentre
.com.au. Some of the cheapest fares to Bali, plus a comprehensive range of tours, cruises and accommodation packages.

Harvey World Travel ☎13 27 57, ⓦwww.harveyworld.com.au. Good RTW deals.

STA Travel ☎1300/360 960, ⓦwww.statravel.com.au. Specialists in student and discount travel.

Trailfinders ☎02/9247 7666, ⓦwww.trailfinders .com.au. Specializes in low-cost airfares.

Travel.com ☎02/9249 5232 or 1300/130 482, ⓦwww.travel.com.au. Independent travel specialists with online discounts.

Travelshop ☎1800/108 108, ⓦwww.travelshop.com.au. Exceptional deals on

Qantas and Garuda flights to Bali from all major departure points, with free accommodation.

New Zealand

Budget Travel ☎09/366 0061 or 0800/808 040, ⓦwww.budgettravel.co.nz. Flights and packages.

Destinations Unlimited ☎09/373 4033, ⓦwww.travel-nz.com. Good deals on airfares and holidays.

Flight Centre ☎0800/243 544, ⓦwww.flightcentre.co.nz. Some of the cheapest fares to Bali, plus a comprehensive range of tours, cruises and accommodation packages.

STA Travel ☎0508/782 872, ⓦwww.statravel.co.nz. Specialists in student and discount travel, plus good flight-plus-accommodation package deals.

Thomas Cook ☎09/379 3920. Airfares and holidays.

Travel.com ☎09/359 3860, ⓦwww.travel.co.nz. Independent travel specialists with online discounts.

Tour operators in Australia and New Zealand

Adventure World Australia ☎02/9956 7766 or 1300/363 055, ⓦwww.adventureworld.com.au, New Zealand ☎09/524 5118, ⓦwww.adventureworld.co.nz. Agents for a vast array of international adventure travel companies.

Allways Padi Travel Australia ☎03/9885 8863, ⓦwww.allwaysdive.com.au. Tailored dive and accommodation packages to some of the best sites in Bali and Lombok including dive safaris taking in diving and sightseeing and all-inclusive liveaboard trips with unlimited diving from Bali east to Komodo.

Asian Explorer Holidays Australia ☎03/9245 0777, ⓦwww.asianexplorer.com.au. All-in flight and room deals available in many locations across Bali and Lombok. These can be supplemented with day tours around the islands, an extended trip to Mount Bromo on Java or day cruises to Nusa Penida or Nusa Lembongan. There are regular special deals which are extremely good value.

Bali Travel Service Australia ☎02/9264 5895. Huge range of ever-changing accommodation package deals.

Flight Centre Australia ☎02/9235 3522, New Zealand ☎09/358 4310, ⓦwww.flightcentre.com.au. Although they mostly deal in flights, it is worth a look here for their "Holiday Specials" which are extremely good-value all-in deals.

Golden Bali Travel Australia ☎08/8227 1522, ⓦwww.goldenbali.com. All aspects of travel, including accommodation, tours and transport.

Intrepid Adventure Travel Australia ☎1300/360 667, ⓦwww.intrepidtravel.com.au. Several types of holiday that include Bali and Lombok; some small group trips, some private itineraries and more adventurous exploratory adventures. Many include walking, cycling, snorkelling and trekking. Trips on offer range from beach breaks in Kuta, stays in the Sacred Mountain Sanctuary in Sidemen and active explorations of Bali and Lombok. They also offer the 15-day "East Indies Explorer" overland trip eastwards or westwards between Jakarta and Bali taking in most of the highlights on Java and Lovina, Tirtagangga and Ubud on Bali.

Peregrine Adventures Australia ☎03/9662 2700 or 02/9290 2770, ⓦwww.peregrine.net.au. Well-established adventure company. They offer a ten-day "Bali–Lombok" trip, and a 15-day "Indonesia Experience" taking in Jakarta, Bogor, Bandung, Yogyakarta, Gunung Bromo and Bali.

Plan It Holidays Australia ☎03/9245 0747, ⓦwww.planit.com.au. Very good-value discounted airfares and accommodation packages to the main resorts in Bali.

Pro-Dive Travel Australia ☎02/9281 5066 or ☎1800/820 820, ⓦwww.prodive.com.au. Dive packages to Bali and Lombok including airfares, accommodation, dive gear and transport to dive sites. Dive safaris also available.

San Michele Travel Australia ☎1800/222 244, ⓦwww.asiatravel.com.au. Long-running Asia specialists with an emphasis on Indonesia. They can arrange all-inclusive holidays for all budgets in locations across Bali and Lombok. Their Bali Bus is used for day-trips and to transfer clients between hotels. They also offer a six-day "Bali Bus Extravaganza" multi-centre trip. "Sacred Retreats" is six nights of yoga, meditation and spa treatments. It's possible to add on a trip east to Komodo on the MSY *Perintis*, an old-style sailing schooner.

Surf Travel Company Australia ☎1800/687 873, New Zealand ☎09/473 8388, ⓦwww.surftravel .com.au. Detailed information on surfing throughout Indonesia (and beyond). They offer flights, accommodation packages, transport, all-in surfing deals and yacht charters depending on individual requirements and levels of experience.

Travelshop Australia ☎1800/108 108, ⓦwww.travelshop.com.au. Information about Bali and plenty of good-value all-in "Hot Bali" deals. These can be supplemented with day, culinary or cultural tours and day or evening cruises.

Travel from Southeast Asia

It's relatively easy to fly to Bangkok and then continue your journey to Bali or Lombok overland via Malaysia and Singapore.

There's a choice of **train** routes from Bangkok to Singapore, via Penang or Kuala Lumpur, detailed on the Malaysian Railways website (ⓦwww.ktmb.com.my). One Malaysia-bound **train** leaves Bangkok's Hualamphong station every day (book at least one day in advance at the station ticket office or designated agencies), arriving at Butterworth (for Penang) 23 hours later; second-class sleeper tickets cost about £20/US$35. If continuing to Singapore you'll need to change trains here for the remaining fifteen-hour journey (a through ticket costs about £40/$70 for a second-class sleeper).

Alternatively, you could take one of the four daily trains from Bangkok to Thailand's main southern terminal at Hat Yai (16hr) and change onto the once-daily train from Hat Yai to Kuala Lumpur (14hr); second-class sleeper through-fares to Kuala Lumpur are around £30/$55. **Buses** and share-taxis from Hat Yai to Penang run throughout the day (about £9/$13 per person; 6hr). There are also long-distance buses and minibuses from the tourist centres of Krabi, Phuket and Surat Thani to Penang, KL and Singapore.

From Malaysia and Singapore you have a choice of **ferry** routes into Indonesia. A variety

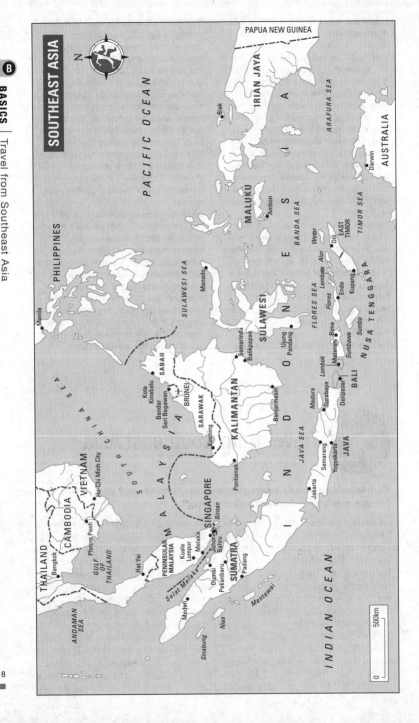

SOUTHEAST ASIA

N

PACIFIC OCEAN

PAPUA NEW GUINEA

IRIAN JAYA

Biak

ARAFURA SEA

AUSTRALIA

Darwin

TIMOR SEA

MALUKU

Ambon

BANDA SEA

EAST TIMOR

Dili

Wetar

Alor

Lembata

Kupang

PHILIPPINES

Manila

SULAWESI SEA

Manado

SULAWESI

Samarinda

Balikpapan

Ujung Pandang

FLORES SEA

Flores

Ende

Bima

NUSA TENGGARA

Sumba

Sumbawa

Lombok

Mataram

SABAH

Kota Kinabalu

Bandar Seri Begawan

BRUNEI

SARAWAK

KALIMANTAN

Banjarmasin

I N D O N E S I A

SOUTH CHINA SEA

VIETNAM

Ho Chi Minh City

THAILAND

Bangkok

CAMBODIA

Phnom Penh

GULF OF THAILAND

Hat Yai

ANDAMAN SEA

M A L A Y S I A

PENINSULAR MALAYSIA

Kuala Lumpur

Melaka

Johor Bahru

SINGAPORE

Bintan

Kuching

Pontianak

JAVA SEA

Jakarta

Semarang

JAVA

Yogyakarta

Surabaya

Madura

Denpasar

BALI

Dumai

Pekanbaru

SUMATRA

Padang

Medan

Nias

Mentawai

Sinabung

Selat Melaka

INDIAN OCEAN

500km

0

Official immigration gateways into Indonesia

When planning an overland trip through Indonesia, check that your proposed ports of entry and exit are officially recognized **immigration gateways**; if not, you'll need to buy an Indonesian visa before you arrive in the country. See below for a current list of gateways, and p.22 for full visa requirements, though it's always worth checking with your nearest Indonesian embassy for any recent or temporary alterations.

Airports

Bali Denpasar (Ngurah Rai).
Irian Jaya Biak (Frans Kaisiepo).
Java Bandung (Husein Sastranegara); Jakarta (Sukarno Hatta); Solo (Adi Sumarmo); Surabaya (Adi Juanda).
Kalimantan Balikpapan (Sepinggan); Pontianak (Soepadio).
Lombok Mataram (Selaparang).
Maluku Ambon (Pattimura).
Riau Batam Island (Hang Nadim).
Sulawesi Manado (Sam Ratulangi); Makassar (Hasanuddin).
Sumatra Medan (Polonia); Pekanbaru (Simpang Tiga); Padang (Tabing).
Timor Kupang (El Tari).

Seaports

Bali Sanur (Benoa); Padang Bai.

Java Jakarta (Tanjung Priok); Surabaya (Tanjung Perak); Semarang (Tanjung Mas).
Lombok Mataram (Lembar).
Maluku Ambon.
Riau Batam Island (Batu Ampar, Nongsa Terminal Bahari, Sekupang & Teluk Senimba); Bintan Island (Sri Bay Intan, Selat Kijang & Tanjung Pinang); Karimum (Tanjung Balai).
Sulawesi Manado (Bitung).
Sumatra Medan (Belawan); Dumai; Lhok Seumawe; Aceh (Malahayati & Sultan Iskandar Muda).
Timor Kupang (Tebau).

Land borders

Kalimantan Etikong.

---

of slow ferries and high-speed boats depart Penang daily for Medan in northern Sumatra (4–14hr), and daily services also run between Melaka and Dumai, south of Medan (2hr 30min). You can reach the islands of Batam, Bintan and Karimun, in Indonesia's Riau archipelago, from Johor Bahru in southern Malaysia or from Singapore.

Singapore Airlines **flies** Singapore–Denpasar several times a day, and Silk Air, a subsidiary, operates three or four flights a week from Singapore to Lombok.

From around Indonesia

With a sixty-day visa in your pocket it's quite feasible to make a leisurely journey **through Indonesia** to Bali or Lombok, taking in several other islands en route. You can do this in a variety of ways – by road, rail, inter-island ferry and by plane. Details on **ferry** crossings from Java to Bali are given on p.394, from Bali to Lombok on p.416, and from Sumbawa to Lombok on p.417. Other routes are sketched out below. To qualify for a full sixty-day visa, you need to enter and exit Indonesia via an **official immigration gateway** (see box).

When booking flights or working out bus and ferry connections, remember that the Indonesian archipelago spans three **time zones**: Sumatra, Java, West Kalimantan and Central Kalimantan are on Western Indonesian Time (GMT+7); Bali, Lombok, the Nusa Tenggara islands, Sulawesi, South Kalimantan and East Kalimantan are on Central Indonesian Time (GMT+8); and Irian Jaya and Maluku are on Eastern Indonesian Time (GMT+9).

"Overland"

Travelling **"overland" from Java,** the easiest and cheapest option is to buy a through-ticket on a public bus all the way to Denpasar. More expensive tourist services will take you to Ubud or Kuta.

Through-tickets to Denpasar (Bali) or Bertais (also known as Mandalika terminal at Sweta on Lombok) generally start from **Jakarta**, **Yogyakarta** or **Surabaya**, and passengers stay on the same bus right the way through, including on the ferry crossing. From Jakarta, reckon on paying around Rp200,000 for air-con and reclining seats to Denpasar (24hr) or Lombok (32hr); from Yogyakarta Rp165,000 (15hr/22hr); from Medan on Sumatra Rp500,000 (72hr/84hr). On Bali, most Java buses terminate at Denpasar's Ubung terminal (see box on p.372). There are also some direct Surabaya–Singaraja buses which pass through Lovina in north Bali, or you can buy a ticket to the west Balinese port of Gilimanuk, from where connections run to Singaraja or Lovina (see p.393). On Lombok, inter-island buses end at Bertais, also known as Mandalika terminal, on the eastern edge of the Mataram-Ampenan-Cakranegara-Sweta conurbation (see p.420).

Tourist travel services will bus you direct from your location in Java right through to one of the tourist centres in Bali. Perama Travel, for example, has departures from Jakarta, Yogyakarta, Surabaya and Malang to Kuta, Sanur and Ubud on Bali.

Travelling **from Australia** and then **overland from eastern Indonesia**, the most popular route begins in Timor (at Kupang or Dili), from where you can island-hop all the way to Lombok and Bali or get a direct Pelni ferry (see

box below). There are direct buses from Flores, Ruteng (36hr) and Labuhanbajo (24hr), and Sumbawa, Sape (14hr), Bima (12hr), Domphu (10hr), Sumbawa Besar (6hr) and Taliwang (5hr), to Lombok where you can then connect to Bali. Perama have offices or agents in Sumbawa Besar (☎0371/21555), Domphu (☎0373/623031), Bima (☎0374/427792), Labuhanbajo (☎0385/41009) and Maumere (☎0382/21321).

By sea

With over 13,000 islands tempting you to stop off and explore, it's hardly surprising that an increasing number of travellers are choosing to travel **by sea** through the Indonesian archipelago.

The national shipping company is **Pelni** (W www.pelni.co.id – beware that the website isn't always properly updated), which runs about twenty sizeable passenger ships, each one doing a fortnightly circuit of different inter-island routes. On the whole, this means that the boats dock at each port once every two weeks, but timetables can be confusing (and are reissued about every three months), so before you travel you should definitely contact one of the Pelni offices (see below). On Bali, the Pelni port

Pelni sea routes

KM Awu Waingapu, Lembar, Benoa, Waingapu, Ende, Kupang, Kalabahi, Maumere, Makassar, Parepare, Berau, Tarakan, Nunukan; and return.

KM Dobonsolo Tanjung Priok (Jakarta), Surabaya, Benoa, Kupang, Ambon, Sorong, Manokwari, Biak, Jayapura; and return.

KM Dorolonda Bitung, Kwandang, Pantoloan, Balikpapan, Surabaya, Benoa, Kupang, Ambon, Sorong, Fak Fak; and return.

KM Kelimutu Surabaya, Lembar, Labuhanbajo, Larantuka, Kupang, Saumlaki, Dobo, Timika, Merauke; and return.

KM Tatamailou Merauke, Agats, Timika, Kaimana, Fak Fak, Amahai, Ambon, Bau Bau, Makassar, Badas, Benoa, Banyuwangi, Bima,

Labuhanbajo, Larantuka, Saumlaki, Tual, Timika, Dobo; and return.

KM Tilongkabila Kumai, Surabaya, Benoa, Lembar, Bima, Labuhanbajo, Makassar, Bau Bau, Raha, Kendari, Kolonedale, Luwuk, Gorontalo, Bitung, Liruna, Lirung, Tahuna; and return.

Pelni offices

Jakarta Jl Gajah Mada 14 ☎021/384 3307, ℱ384 4342 or 385 4130; the ticket office is at Jl Angkasa 18 ☎021/421 1921.

Bali On Jalan Pelabuhan in Benoa Harbour ☎0361/723689 (Mon–Fri 8am–4pm, Sat 8am–12.30pm); also at Jl Raya Tuban 299 in Kuta, about 250m south of Supernova ☎0361/763963.

Lombok Jl Majapahit 2, Ampenan ☎0370/637212, ℱ631604 (Mon–Fri 8.30am–3.30pm, Sat 8.30am–1pm).

is at **Benoa Harbour** (Pelabuhan Benoa; see p.171) southwest of Sanur; on Lombok, it's at **Lembar** (see p.430). Life on board is relatively comfortable, with central air-conditioning and reasonable restaurants and bars. Each ship has four cabin classes and one deck class (actually a large air-conditioned lounge), and all rates include meals. **Fares** in the most luxurious class cost considerably more than airfares, while the cheapest are about 25 percent of this. Children pay two-thirds of the adult fare. Booking ahead is vital. Fares between Lembar and Bali (6hr) are Rp20,500–61,500, from Lembar to Surabaya (24hr) Rp85,000–284,500.

Pelni is no longer the only ocean-going option for getting around Indonesia. **Barito express boats** (tickets through travel agents in Kuta) operate to Benoa Harbour from Surabaya on Java (1 weekly; 7hr; Rp170,000), Bima on Sumbawa (1–2 weekly; 7hr; Rp200,000), Maumere on Flores (1 weekly; 12hr; Rp200,000), Waingapu on Sumba (1 weekly; 13hr; Rp300,000) and Kupang on Timor (1 weekly; 20hr; Rp425,000).

By air

There are several **domestic airlines** serving the Indonesian archipelago: Garuda, Merpati, Pelita, Awair and Air Mark all offer direct connections between Bali and/or Lombok and major provincial capitals. **Fares** tend to be pretty competitive, but it's always worth shopping around; sample fares to Denpasar include Rp235,000 from Lombok, Rp430,000 from Yogyakarta, Rp810,000 from Jakarta.

If you're planning to island-hop, you could consider a **domestic air pass**. For several years Garuda offered a Visit Indonesia Pass, which allowed visitors arriving from overseas on Garuda to make three advance bookings anywhere on their network (but not on other domestic carriers) for advantageous rates. A far better deal was the Asean Air Pass,

allowing travel between and within Brunei, Indonesia, Malaysia, Philippines, Singapore, Thailand and Vietnam for around US$95 for each sector. At the time of writing, amidst general airline uncertainty, both had been suspended.

For domestic flights, the **departure tax** from Ngurah Rai Airport (Bali) is Rp20,000, from Selaparang Airport (Lombok) Rp8000.

Domestic airlines

Air Mark Bali: at Ngurah Rai Airport ☎0361/759769. Lombok: at Selaparang Airport ☎0370/643564, and Jl Pejanggik 40–44 ☎0370/633235. Six times daily between Denpasar and Lombok, and daily between Lombok and Bima and Labuhanbajo.

Awair ⓦ www.awairlines.com. Bali: Denpasar ☎0361/768403. Java: Jakarta ☎021/520 1688. Daily flights between Denpasar and Jakarta.

Garuda ⓦ www.garuda-indonesia.com. Bali: *Sanur Beach Hotel* ☎0361/270535 and *Natour Kuta Beach Hotel* ☎0361/751179. Lombok: *Lombok Raya Hotel*, Jl Panca Usaha 11, Mataram ☎0370/637951; Selaparang Airport ☎0370/622987 ext 246. Java: Jl Merdeka Selatan 13, Jakarta ☎021/231 1817. Several flights daily from their hub, Jakarta, to Denpasar, as well as daily flights from Makassar to Denpasar.

Merpati ⓦ www.merpati.co.id. Bali: Jl Melati 51, Denpasar ☎0361/235358. Lombok: Jl Pejanggik 69, Cakranegara ☎0370/636745; Selaparang Airport ☎0370/633691. Java: Jl Angkasa 7, Blok B-15 Kav 2 & 3, Jakarta ☎021/654 8888; plus 24-hour check-in office at Gambir Station. Twice daily flights between Bali and Lombok, with less frequent direct connections to Bali and Lombok from Ambon, Bandung, Biak, Bima, Dili, Kupang, Labuhanbajo, Maumere, Sorong, Sumbawa, Surabaya, Tambulaka, Timika and Waingapu.

Pelita ⓦ www.pelita-airventure.com. Bali and Lombok: book through travel agents. Java: Jl Abdul Muis 52–56, Jakarta ☎021/231 2222, toll-free ☎800-1-778899. Twice-daily flights (Fri–Sun only) between Surabaya and Denpasar; also daily flights from Bandung to Surabaya, Denpasar and Kupang that return the same day. The company is in alliance with Mandala, and also flies Yogyakarta–Surabaya–Denpasar.

Visas and red tape

At the time of writing, citizens of Britain, Ireland, most European states, Australia, New Zealand, Canada and the US, do not need a visa for Bali or Lombok if intending to stay for less than sixty days, and if entering and exiting Indonesia via one of the designated gateway ports. There are 42 of these ports (see box on p.19), at which you can get a free, non-extendable sixty-day tourist visa on arrival. Your passport must be valid for at least six months and you must be able to show proof of onward travel (a return or onward ticket).

In 2002, the government proposed significant **changes to the visa regulations**, reducing the length of stay to thirty days and charging all tourists a fee on arrival. It may still be possible to obtain a sixty-day visa, but at a higher cost. Contact your nearest Indonesian embassy for up-to-date information.

Some international airlines may ask for proof of onward travel before letting you board a flight to Indonesia, and they may request to see relevant documents such as visas for your destinations beyond Indonesia; if you don't have the right documents you'll probably have to sign a form which waives the airline's responsibility. In theory you're also supposed to be in possession of **sufficient funds** for your stay (the sum of US$1000 is quoted, but very rarely enforced).

If you want to stay more than sixty days, or are entering via a non-designated gateway, you'll need to obtain a **tourist or business visa** before entering Indonesia. Non-extendable tourist visas are valid for four weeks only, and cost UK£10, US$35, C$50, A$125 or NZ$110. Business visas are valid for five weeks, cost the same (except in the UK, at £30), and can be extended for up to six months at immigration offices in Indonesia, if you can convince the authorities that your need is legitimate.

All tourist visas are absolutely **non-extendable**, but it's quite simple, if expensive, to get yourself a **new visa** by leaving the country for a few hours and then coming straight back in through a designated port of entry: most people choose to fly to Singapore (about £200/US$300 return; 2hr 30min). Immigration officials at Bali's Ngurah

Rai Airport don't seem to worry about this procedure, and numerous unofficial expat "residents" do the Singapore hop on a regular basis.

Penalties for **overstaying your visa** are quite severe: on departure, you'll be fined up to $10 for each day that you've exceeded the sixty-day limit. If you've stayed more than fourteen days over the limit, you'll probably get blacklisted from Bali for several years.

The Denpasar government **immigration office** (*kantor immigrasi*) is in Renon, at the corner of Jalan Panjaitan and Jalan Raya Puputan (Mon–Thurs 8am–3pm, Fri 8–11am, Sat 8am–2pm; ☎0361/227828). The Lombok *kantor immigrasi* is at Jl Udayana 2, Mataram (same hours; ☎0370/622520).

Indonesian embassies and consulates abroad

Australia 8 Darwin Ave, Yarralumla, Canberra, ACT 2600 ☎02/6250 8600, ⊛www.welcome.to/kbri-canberra.org.au; Level 2, 45 King William St, Adelaide, SA 5000 ☎08/8217 8282; Level 20, Riverside Centre, 123 Eagle St, Brisbane, QLD 4000 ☎07/3309 0888; 20 Harry Chan Ave, Darwin, NT 0801 ☎08/8941 0048; 72 Queen Rd, Melbourne, VIC 3004 ☎03/9525 2755; 134 Adelaide Terrace, East Perth, WA 6004 ☎08/9221 5858; 236–238 Maroubra Rd, Maroubra, Sydney, NSW 2035 ☎02/9344 9933, ⊛www.indosyd.org.au.
Canada 55 Parkdale Ave, Ottawa, ON K1Y 1E5 ☎613/724-1100, ⊛www.indonesia-ottawa.org; 129 Jarvis St, Toronto, ON M5C 2H6 ☎416/360-4020; 1630 Alberni St, Vancouver, BC V6G 1A6 ☎604/682-8855.

Malaysia 233 Jl Tun Razak, 50400 Kuala Lumpur ☏03/245 2011; 723 Jl Anyer Molek, 80000 Johor Bahru ☏07/221 2000; 467 Jl Burma, 10350 Penang ☏04/227412.

New Zealand 70 Glen Rd, Kelburn, PO Box 3543, Wellington ☏04/475 8697; 2nd floor, Beca Carter Hollings Femer Ltd, 132 Vincent St, Auckland ☏09/300 9000.

Singapore 7 Chatsworth Rd, Singapore 1024 ☏737 7422.

Thailand 600–602 Petchaburi Rd, Bangkok 10400 ☏02/252 3135; 19 Sadao Rd, Songkhla 90000 ☏074/311-544.

UK and Ireland 38 Grosvenor Sq, London W1X 9AD (personal callers: 38 Adams Row, W1) ☏020/7499 7661, ⓦwww.indonesianembassy.org.uk. Recorded visa information ☏0906/550 8962.

USA 2020 Massachusetts Ave NW, Washington, DC 20036 ☏202/775-5200, ⓦwww.embassyofindonesia.org; 72 E Randolph St, Chicago, IL 60601 ☏312/345-9300; 10900 Richmond Ave, Houston, TX 77057 ☏713/785-1691; 3457 Wilshire Blvd, Los Angeles, CA 90010 ☏213/383-5126, ⓦwww.kjri-la.com; 5 E 68th St, New York, NY 10021 ☏212/879-0600, ⓦwww.indony.org; 1111 Columbus Ave, San Francisco, CA 94133 ☏415/474-9571.

Worldwide listing at ⓦwww.dfa-deplu.go.id/ diplomatic/diplmission.htm.

Foreign embassies and consulates

Most countries maintain an **embassy** in the Indonesian capital, Jakarta, and some also have **consulates** in Bali. Your first point of contact should always be the Bali consulate; they may then refer you on to the embassy if necessary.

Australia Consulate in Bali: Jl Mochammad Yamin 4, Renon, Denpasar ☏0361/235092, ⓔausconbali@denpasar.wasantara.net.id. Embassy: Jl H.R. Rasuna Said Kav C15-16, Kuningan, Jakarta ☏021/2550 5555, ⓦwww.austembjak.or.id.

Canada Contact the Australian consulate in Denpasar first. Embassy: World Trade Centre, 6th floor, Jl Jen Sudirman, Kav 29, Jakarta ☏021/525 0709, ⓦwww.dfait-maeci.gc.ca/jakarta.

Ireland Contact the UK consul in Sanur first. Consulate: c/o Jakarta International School, Jl Terogong Raya 33, Jakarta ☏021/769 5142.

Netherlands Consulate in Bali: c/o KCB Tour and Travel, Jl Raya Kuta 99, Kuta ☏0361/751517, ⓔpurwa@denpasar.wasantara.net.id. Embassy: Jl H.R. Rasuna Said Kav S-3, Kuningan, Jakarta ☏021/525 1515, ⓦwww.netherlandsembassy.or.id.

New Zealand Contact the Australian consulate in Denpasar first. Embassy: Gedung BRII, 23rd floor, Jl Jen Sudirman, Kav 44, Jakarta ☏021/570 9460, ⓔnzembjak@cbn.net.id.

UK Honorary consul in Bali: Jl Mertasari 2, Sanur ☏0361/270601, ⓔtamarind@dps.centrin.net.id. Embassy: Jl M.H. Thamrin 75, Jakarta ☏021/315 6264, ⓦwww.britain-in-indonesia.or.id.

USA Consulate in Bali: Jl Hayam Wuruk 188, Renon, Denpasar ☏0361/233605, ⓔamcobali@indo.net.id. Embassy: Jl Merdeka Selatan 4–5, Jakarta ☏021/3435 9000, ⓦwww.usembassyjakarta.org.

Customs regulations

Indonesia's **customs regulations** allow foreign nationals to import one litre of alcohol, 200 cigarettes or 50 cigars or 100g of tobacco, and a reasonable amount of perfume. Cars, typewriters, TV sets and video cameras are supposed to be declared on entry and re-exported on departure. Import restrictions cover the usual banned items, including narcotics, weapons and pornographic material, and foreigners are also forbidden to bring in any printed matter written in Chinese characters, Chinese medicines and amounts of Rp5,000,000 or more in Indonesian currency. Indonesia is a signatory to the Convention on International Trade in Endangered Species (CITES), and so forbids import or export of products which are banned under this treaty, which include anything made from turtle flesh or turtle shells (including tortoiseshell jewellery and ornaments), as well as anything made from ivory. Indonesian law also prohibits the export of antiquities and cultural relics, unless properly sanctioned by the customs department.

Information, websites and maps

Since the economic crisis of the late 1990s, all overseas government tourist promotion offices have been closed down, so for information before you go, you should contact your nearest Indonesian embassy or consulate (listed on pp.22–23). Their resources are limited, but you'll probably get a glossy brochure or two. You'll find much more information about Bali and Lombok on the internet.

In Australia, it's also worth contacting DWI Tour Australia in Sydney (℡02/9211 3383), as they send out tourist literature on Indonesia.

Tourist offices

On Bali and Lombok, you'll find **government tourist offices** in the major tourist destinations – sometimes several in one town (Mon–Thurs 7am–2pm, Fri 7–11am, Sat 7am–12.30pm; those in the main tourist centres keep longer hours). Kanwil Depparpostel offices are run by the Jakarta-based directorate-general of tourism and give Indonesia-wide information; Diparda offices are run by each of the provinces of Indonesia; and there are smaller concerns operated by the individual districts. The amount and quality of information available in the offices varies widely: they'll usually have some brochures, but rarely any maps. There will generally be someone in each office who speaks English, but while staff are extremely willing, they may be hampered by a lack of hard information.

Wherever you go, you'll see signs offering tourist information – but these are usually private operators selling their own tours or renting out transport.

Websites

Only general tourist-oriented **websites** are listed below: online accommodation-booking services are listed in the box on p.44, and other, specialist sites are mentioned in their relevant sections in Basics.

Umbrella sites

Access Bali Online ⓦ www.baliwww.com/bali. One of the best umbrella sites for Bali, offering heaps of different tourist-oriented links and services, including a room-finder, tour planner, web directory with links, the latest tourism news, plus a travellers' forum.

Bali Paradise Online ⓦ www.bali-paradise.com. Another excellent wide-ranging umbrella site, with dozens of categories ranging from architecture, airline information, banks and car rental to the lowdown on nightlife, real estate and weather. Also has a travellers' forum.

Best of Bali ⓦ www.bali.com. Useful selection of links, from hotel finders to sights, weather forecasts to property issues, plus a handy section on local ISPs and phone charges.

Lombok Island ⓦ www.lombok.com. Small site featuring a general introduction to tourist spots plus links to Lombok hotels.

Travellers' forums

Bali and Lombok Travel Forum ⓦ www.travelforum.org/bali. Very good forum with lots of regular contributors who make frequent trips to Bali; especially useful for getting first-hand recommendations on drivers, tailors and particular room numbers. Also has a hotel reservation site.

Bali Travel Forum ⓦ www.balitravelforum.com. Another very helpful forum offering masses of advice and recommendations from recent travellers to Bali. It gets a lot of traffic, nearly all of it good-humoured, and also includes polls on the best and worst of Bali.

Lonely Planet Thorn Tree ⓦ thorntree.lonelyplanet.com. Very popular travellers' bulletin boards. Ideal for exchanging information with other travellers and for starting a debate, though it does attract an annoying number of regular posters just itching for an argument.

Rough Guides Travel Talk ⓦ roughguides.atinfopop.com. Forum section of the site for independent travellers, which also has travel tips and spotlight destination articles, plus the travel guides online.

Online publications

Inside Indonesia ⓦ www.insideindonesia.org. Web version of the hard-hitting bimonthly

magazine, full of articles about political, social and environmental issues across the archipelago.
Jakarta Post Ⓦ www.thejakartapost.com. Domestic Indonesian news hot off the press.
Tempo Interactive
Ⓦ www.tempointeractive.com. Online version of Indonesia's respected weekly news magazine (English-language edition), with the day's headline stories.

Government websites

Australian Dept of Foreign Affairs
Ⓦ www.dfat.gov.au. Advice and reports on unstable countries and regions.
Canadian Foreign Affairs Dept Ⓦ www.dfait-maeci.gc.ca. Country-by-country travel advisories.
UK Foreign and Commonwealth Office
Ⓦ www.fco.gov.uk. Constantly updated advice for travellers on circumstances affecting safety in over 130 countries.
US State Dept Ⓦ travel.state.gov. Details the dangers of travelling in most countries of the world.

Maps

There are plenty of **maps** of Bali available abroad, but it's harder to find specific maps of Lombok. If you are intending to rent your own transport, a detailed road map is vital.

For **Bali**, the best options are Periplus Travel Maps (1:250,000) and Berndtson and Berndtson (1:200,000). Both include some city plans and area maps but both suffer from inaccuracies. Although they're available in some bookshops on Bali, it's safest buying them before you leave. Recommended regional maps that are only available in Bali are mentioned in the relevant guide accounts; one attractive souvenir map of the whole island is by Studio Satumata (1:74,000), which shows the mountainous contours with exceptional clarity and may also be a useful driving map. It's sold at Ganesha Bookstore in Ubud.

For **Lombok**, go for the Periplus Travel Maps sheet covering Lombok and Sumbawa (1:200,000); if you wait until you get to Mataram, the free maps given out by the Diparda office are almost as good. There's also the prettier, but less practical, Travel Treasure Indonesia III series, distributed by Periplus, which has annotated sketches of tourist sights.

Map outlets

UK and Ireland

Blackwell's Map and Travel Shop 50 Broad St, Oxford OX1 3BQ ☎ 01865/793550, Ⓦ maps.blackwell.co.uk.
Easons 40 O'Connell St, Dublin 1 ☎ 01/873 3811, Ⓦ www.eason.ie.
Heffers Map and Travel 20 Trinity St, Cambridge CB2 1TJ ☎ 01223/568568, Ⓦ www.heffers.co.uk.
Hodges Figgis 56–58 Dawson St, Dublin 2 ☎ 01/677 4754, Ⓦ www.hodgesfiggis.com.
James Thin 53–59 South Bridge, Edinburgh EH1 1YS ☎ 0131/622 8222, Ⓦ www.jthin.co.uk.
John Smith & Son 100 Cathedral St, Glasgow G4 0RD ☎ 0141/552 3377, Ⓦ www.johnsmith.co.uk.
Map Shop 30a Belvoir St, Leicester LE1 6QH ☎ 0116/247 1400, Ⓦ www.mapshopleicester.co.uk.
National Map Centre 22–24 Caxton St, London SW1H 0QU ☎ 020/7222 2466, Ⓦ www.mapsnmc.co.uk.
Newcastle Map Centre 55 Grey St, Newcastle NE1 6EF ☎ 0191/261 5622.
Stanfords 12–14 Long Acre, London WC2E 9LP ☎ 020/7836 1321, and 29 Corn St, Bristol BS1 1HT ☎ 0117/929 9966, Ⓦ www.stanfords.co.uk.
Travel Bookshop 13–15 Blenheim Crescent, London W11 2EE ☎ 020/7229 5260, Ⓦ www.thetravelbookshop.co.uk.

US and Canada

Adventurous Traveler 102 Lake St, Burlington, VT 05401 ☎ 1-800/282-3963, Ⓦ www.adventuroustraveler.com.
Book Passage 51 Tamal Vista Blvd, Corte Madera, CA 94925 ☎ 1-800/999-7909, Ⓦ www.bookpassage.com.
Distant Lands 56 S Raymond Ave, Pasadena, CA 91105 ☎ 1-800/310-3220, Ⓦ www.distantlands.com.
Elliot Bay Book Company 101 S Main St, Seattle, WA 98104 ☎ 1-800/962-5311, Ⓦ www.elliotbaybook.com.
Forsyth Travel Library 226 Westchester Ave, White Plains, NY 10604 ☎ 1-800/367-7984, Ⓦ www.forsyth.com.
Globe Corner 28 Church St, Cambridge, MA 02138 ☎ 1-800/358-6013, Ⓦ www.globecorner.com.
GORP Books & Maps ☎ 1-877/440-4677, Ⓦ www.gorp.com.
Map Link 30 S La Patera Lane #5, Santa Barbara, CA 93117 ☎ 805/692-6777, Ⓦ www.maplink.com.

Rand McNally Stores across the US ☎1-800/333-0136, ⊛www.randmcnally.com.
Travel Books and Language Center 4437 Wisconsin Ave NW, Washington, DC 20016 ☎1-800/220-2665, ⊛www.bookweb.org/bookstore/travelbks.
Travel Bug 2667 W Broadway, Vancouver V6K 2G2 ☎604/737-1122, ⊛www.swifty.com/tbug.
World of Maps 1235 Wellington St, Ottawa, ON K1Y 3A3 ☎1-800/214-8524, ⊛www.worldofmaps.com.

Australia and New Zealand

Map Shop 6–10 Peel St, Adelaide, SA 5000 ☎08/8231 2033, ⊛www.mapshop.net.au.
Mapland 372 Little Bourke St, Melbourne, VIC 3000 ☎03/9670 4383, ⊛www.mapland.com.au.
MapWorld 173 Gloucester St, Christchurch ☎0800/627 967, ⊛www.mapworld.co.nz.
Perth Map Centre 1/884 Hay St, Perth, WA 6000 ☎08/9322 5733, ⊛www.perthmap.com.au.
Specialty Maps 46 Albert St, Auckland 1001 ☎09/307 2217, ⊛www.ubdonline.co.nz/maps.

Insurance

Before travelling to Bali or Lombok it is important to take out travel insurance. A typical policy usually provides cover for medical expenses due to illness or injury, the loss of baggage, tickets and – up to a certain limit – cash or cheques, plus cancellation or curtailment of your journey. Most exclude so-called dangerous sports unless an extra premium is paid: in Bali and Lombok this can mean scuba-diving, kayaking and whitewater rafting.

Before buying a policy, check that you're not already covered. Your **home insurance policy** may cover your possessions against loss or theft even when overseas, or you can extend cover through your household contents insurer. Many **charge cards** include some form of travel cover, and insurance is also sometimes thrown in if you pay for your trip with a **credit card** (though this usually only gives very limited medical or accident cover). Many **private medical schemes** include cover when abroad. In Canada, provincial health plans usually provide partial cover for medical mishaps overseas, while holders of official student/teacher/youth cards in Canada and the US are entitled to meagre accident coverage and hospital in-patient benefits. Students will often find that their student health coverage extends during the vacations and for one term beyond the date of last enrolment.

After exhausting the possibilities above, you might want to contact a **specialist travel insurance company**, or consider the travel insurance deal we offer (see box opposite). Many policies can be chopped and changed to exclude coverage you don't need – for example, sickness and accident benefits can often be excluded or included at will. If you do take medical coverage, ascertain whether benefits will be paid as treatment proceeds or only after return home, and whether there is a 24-hour medical emergency number (which you should carry with you at all times while you are away, along with the policy number). Always make a note of the policy details and leave them with someone at home in case you lose the original. When securing baggage cover, make sure that the per-article limit – typically under £500 – will cover your most valuable possession.

It can very often be more economical for couples and families travelling together to arrange joint insurance. Some insurance companies refuse to cover travellers over 65, or stop at 69 or 74 years of age; older travellers or anyone with health problems is advised to start researching insurance well in advance of their trip.

If you need to make a **claim**, you should keep receipts for medicines and treatment, and, if possible, contact the insurance company before making any major payment (for example on additional convalescence expenses). In the event you have anything stolen, you must obtain an official report from the police.

Health

Travelling in Bali and Lombok, most people end up with nothing more serious than a bout of traveller's diarrhoea ("Bali belly").

However, there are an increasing number of road accidents involving tourists on motorbikes, and surfers also suffer their share of mishaps. In the event of serious illness or accident, you'll need to be evacuated to Singapore or back home, so it is vital that you arrange adequate **health insurance** before you travel.

It's advisable to discuss your trip with your **doctor** as early as possible before you travel to allow time to complete any courses of inoculations you need. If you have any long-standing medical conditions or are travelling with children, you'll need to be particularly careful to get appropriate advice. If you need regular medication, take a certificate from

your doctor detailing your condition – it can be handy if you encounter over-zealous customs officials. It's also wise to get a dental check-up before you leave home.

No **inoculations** are legally required for entry into Indonesia, unless you've come directly from a country that is infected with yellow fever, in which case you'll need to make sure you've been immunized and have a certificate. It's recommended that you have inoculations against hepatitis A, polio, tetanus and typhoid fever, and it's also worth asking about inoculations against rabies, Japanese encephalitis, hepatitis B, tuberculosis and diphtheria. The *Rough Guide to Travel Health* has full details.

A traveller's first-aid kit

Items you might want to carry with you include:

- Antiseptic cream
- Insect repellent
- Plasters/bandaids
- Water sterilization tablets or water purifier
- Lint and sealed bandages
- Knee supports
- A course of Flagyl antibiotics
- Rehydration sachets

- Emergency diarrhoea treatment
- Paracetamol/aspirin/tylenol
- Multivitamin and mineral tablets
- Hypodermic needles and sterilized skin wipes (more for the security of knowing you have them, than any fear that a local hospital would fail to observe basic sanitary precautions)

Treatment in Bali and Lombok

There's a network of pharmacies and doctors across the islands offering Western medical services. **Pharmacies** (apotik) in towns and cities sell a wide range of medicines, many of which you would need a prescription to buy back home. Only in the main tourist areas will assistants speak English. In the **village health posts**, staff are generally well-meaning, but ill-equipped to cope with serious illness. Most Balinese use these in conjunction with traditional healers (balian) as they believe that physical symptoms are a sign of spiritual illness (see p.547 for more on this).

If you need an English-speaking **doctor**, seek advice at your hotel (some of the luxury ones have in-house doctors) or at the local tourist office. For more serious problems, you'll find a public **hospital** in each district capital and in some towns such as Singaraja; these are supplemented by private hospitals, many of which operate an accident and emergency department. There are two chains of **tourist-friendly clinics** in Bali – the Legian Clinics, and the SOS Clinics, with branches in Denpasar, Jimbaran, Kuta-Legian, Nusa Dua, Sanur and Ubud – plus several other independent clinics and doctors in the main resorts. Most function 24 hours a day, are staffed by English-speaking doctors and nurses and offer consultations (Rp100,000), emergency call-out (Rp250,000–400,000), ambulances, minor surgery and dental services. The widest range of facilities is in Denpasar, which is also the location of the only **decompression chamber** on the island. For full details, see the Listings sections of each city account. A couple of places on the outskirts of Kuta also have good reputations for dealing with expat emergencies: Bali International Medical Centre (BIMC), Jl Bypass Ngurah Rai 100x, ☏0361/761263, ⓦwww.bimcbali.com; and International SOS, Jl Bypass Ngurah Rai 24x ☏0361/755768, ⓦwww.sos-bali.com.

There are plenty of **dentists** (doktor gigi) in Bali and Lombok, but it is probably best to get a recommendation from a local tourist office if you need treatment.

Major diseases

There are several types of **hepatitis**, but the symptoms of all of them are a yellow colouring of the skin and eyes, extreme exhaustion, fever and diarrhoea. It's one of the most common illnesses that afflicts travellers to Asia and can last for several months. Treatment involves rest and complete abstinence from alcohol. The most common types are hepatitis A and hepatitis B, both caused by viruses; vaccines can offer some protection against them. Hepatitis A is transmitted via contaminated food and water or saliva. The initial vaccine can be boosted with another jab six to twelve months later which confers ten years' protection. Hepatitis B is more serious and is transmitted via sexual contact or by contaminated blood, needles or syringes, which means that medical treatment itself can pose something of a risk if sterilization procedures are not up to scratch. There are two types of immunization available against Hepatitis B and also **combined vaccines** available against Hepatitis A and Hepatitis B and against Hepatitis A and typhoid.

Many Western travellers will have had routine inoculations against **polio**, **diphtheria** and **tuberculosis**. These illnesses are far more common throughout Asia than in the West these days, and travellers should check that they are still covered against them. **Typhoid** is passed through contaminated food or water and can be lethal. It produces an extremely high fever accompanied by abdominal pains, headaches, diarrhoea and red spots on the body. Immunization is via injection or orally. **Cholera** is an extremely dangerous illness transmitted through contaminated food and water, with symptoms of severe watery diarrhoea, cramps, weakness and vomiting. Dehydration is the danger here, so take rehydration salts and get medical help urgently. The vaccine is considered to be so ineffectual and short-lived that it is not recommended. **Tetanus** (or lockjaw) is potentially fatal and is picked up through contaminated open wounds: if you cut or puncture yourself on something dirty, you will be at risk. You should make sure your jabs are up to date before leaving home. **Japanese encephalitis** is a serious viral illness causing inflammation of the brain. It is endemic across Asia and is transmitted from infected birds and animals via mosquitoes. Those planning extended periods of travel in rural areas are most at risk and inoculation is a course of three injections.

Avoid contact with all animals, no matter how cute. **Rabies** is spread via the saliva of infected animals, most commonly cats, dogs or monkeys, and is endemic throughout Asia. If you get bitten, wash the wound immediately with antiseptic and get medical help. Treatment involves a course of injections, but you won't need all of them if you have had a course of pre-departure jabs.

Malaria

Both Bali and Lombok are within **malarial zones**, although current advice seems to be that there's little risk of the disease in the most popular tourist resorts on Bali. If you're visiting Lombok you should take full precautions. However, information regarding the prevalence, prevention and treatment of malaria is being constantly updated so you must check the advice of your doctor at least a couple of weeks before you travel. Be sure to let them know if you're visiting other parts of Indonesia or Asia, even in transit. The latest information shows an increase in infections of the most serious form of malaria across Asia and there are reports of resistance to certain drug treatments by some strains. Pregnant women and children need particular advice on dosage and the different drugs available.

Malaria is caused by a parasite in the saliva of the anopheles **mosquito** which is passed into humans when they're bitten by the mosquito. There are various prophylactic drug regimes available, depending on your destination, all of which must be taken according to a strict timetable beginning before you go and continuing after leaving the area – the timetable depends on the exact drug regime. If you don't follow instructions precisely, you're in danger of developing the illness once you have returned home. The symptoms are fever, headache and shivering, similar to a severe dose of flu and often coming in cycles, but a lot of people have additional symptoms. Don't delay in seeking help fast: malaria can be fatal. If you develop flu-like symptoms any time up to a year after returning home, you should inform a doctor of the areas you have been travelling in and ask for a blood test.

Many of the **drugs** used in prevention have proved fairly effective, with a reasonably low incidence of side-effects, over many years of use. None is one hundred percent effective and it is equally important in prevention to stop the mosquitoes biting you: sleep under a **mosquito net** – preferably one impregnated with an insecticide especially suited to the task – burn mosquito coils, and use **repellent** on exposed skin when the mosquitoes are around, mostly after dark. One drug, mefloquine (sold as **Larium**), has received some very critical media coverage: in some people it appears to produce disorientation, depression and sleep disturbance – although it suits other people very well. If you're intending to use Larium you should begin to take it two weeks before you depart to see whether it will agree with your metabolism. If it doesn't, there are other drugs that can be used instead. If you're intending to scuba-dive, you should discuss the use of Larium very carefully with your medical adviser, as there has been some indication of an increased risk of the "bends".

Dengue fever

Another important reason to avoid getting bitten is **dengue fever**, caused by a virus carried by a different species of mosquito, which bites during the day. There is no vaccine or tablet available to prevent the illness – which causes fever, headache and joint and muscle pains among the least serious symptoms, and internal bleeding and circulatory system failure among the most serious – and no specific drug to cure it. Reports indicate that the disease is on the increase across Indonesia, part of a steady increase across the tropics and sub-tropics in recent years. It is vital to get an early medical diagnosis and obtain treatment to relieve symptoms.

AIDS

The Indonesian government admits to there being 343 cases of **AIDS** in the archipelago. The true figure is undoubtedly many times that, and the World Health Organization estimates 50,000 Indonesians may be HIV positive. Unofficial estimates of the infection rate are higher still; Java, Irian Jaya and Bali are the three most affected places in the country, although there are no separate figures for Bali alone. Many people with HIV are also infected with hepatitis. **Condoms** can be bought on both islands, but it's as well to bring your own.

General precautions

It's worth taking some sensible **precautions** while you are travelling to reduce your chances of getting ill. Be scrupulous about **personal hygiene** and treat even small cuts or scrapes with antiseptic. Wear flip-flops or thongs in the bathroom rather than walk around barefoot.

Avoid **food** that has sat around in the heat of the sun and always opt for freshly cooked meals rather than food that has been reheated; bear in mind too that food prepared in the fancy tourist places is just as likely to be suspect as that from simple streetside stalls. **Ice** is supposedly prepared under carefully regulated conditions in Indonesia, but it's impossible to be sure how it has been transported or stored once leaving the factory. If you're being really careful, avoid ice in your drinks – a lot easier said than done in the tropical heat.

Water hygiene

Although **water** may look clean, it can contain a huge population of disease-causing micro-organisms responsible for diseases such as diarrhoea, gastroenteritis, dysentery, giardia, typhoid, cholera and hepatitis A. While you'll need to increase water intake in the heat to avoid dehydration, you should avoid drinking untreated tap water on Bali and Lombok. **Bottled water** is available just about everywhere and there are several methods of treating either tap water or natural ground water to make it safe for drinking (and this also avoids creating mountains of waste with your empty plastic water bottles). The most traditional method is **boiling**, although the water needs to be kept at a boil for at least five minutes to ensure all the micro-organisms are dead, which isn't particularly convenient when you're travelling. A more convenient method is **chemical sterilization** using chlorine or iodine tablets or tincture of iodine. The disadvantage of this method is that it leaves a rather chemical taste in the water, isn't effective against everything and doesn't remove dirt or other matter from the water. **Filters** will remove visible impurities and the larger pathogenic organisms (most bacteria and cysts) according to the rated size of the filter. But, however fine the filter, it will not remove viruses, dissolved chemicals, pesticides and herbicides. A variety of filters is available from travel clinics, specialist outdoor equipment retailers and some pharmacies.

A more complete treatment, **purification**, involves two stages, filtration and then sterilization, destroying the viruses left behind by the filter. They come in all capacities and are available from travel clinics (see pp.32–33) and specialist outdoor equipment retailers.

Heat and skin problems

Travellers who are unused to tropical climates regularly suffer from **sunburn** and **dehydration**. Limit your exposure to the sun in the hours around midday, use high-factor sunscreen and wear dark glasses and a sun hat. You'll be sweating a great deal in the heat, so the important thing is to make sure that you drink enough. If you're urinating very little or your urine turns dark (this can also indicate hepatitis), increase your fluid intake. When you sweat you lose salt, so make sure your intake covers this: add some extra to your food or take oral **rehydration salts**. The home-made form of these is eight teaspoons of sugar and half a teaspoon of salt dissolved in a litre of clean water; this tastes no saltier than tears and gives you roughly the correct mineral balance.

A more serious result of the heat is **heatstroke**, indicated by high temperature, dry skin and a fast erratic pulse. As an emergency measure, try to cool the patient off by covering them in sheets or sarongs soaked in cold water and turn the fan on them; they may need to go to hospital though. Heat rashes, prickly heat and **fungal infections** are also common; wear loose cotton clothing, dry yourself carefully after bathing and use medicated talcum powder or anti-fungal powder if you fall victim.

Some travellers get persistent, long-lasting, itchy red rashes from sitting bare-legged on cane or bamboo chairs. Apparently this is caused by cane mites, and can be alleviated by Silver Clove cream, available in local pharmacies, markets and supermarkets.

Intestinal trouble

The number one priority if you have an **upset stomach** is not to get dehydrated. Start drinking rehydration salts as soon as the attack starts, even if you're vomiting as well, and worry about a diagnosis later. Rehydration salts are widely available in pharmacies but it makes sense to carry some with you. They come under several brand names in Bali and Lombok – Oralit and Pharolit are two common examples.

The problem with stomach upsets is that they can either be a straightforward reaction to a change of diet, or can signal something more serious. You should seek medical advice if the attack is particularly severe, lasts more than a couple of days or is accompanied by constant, severe abdominal pain or fever. Any blood or mucus in your diarrhoea is a sign you may have bacillic or amoebic **dysentery** and you should see a doctor at once. **Giardia** is another intestinal illness that produces, among other things, smelly farts and burps; it requires medical treatment.

In general, drugs such as Lomotil and Imodium should only be used if you get taken ill on a journey or must travel while ill; they are not a cure, and simply paralyse your gut, temporarily plugging you up.

Cuts, bites and stings

If you're contemplating **diving**, you should familiarize yourself with the potential dangers and what first-aid measures are required, although you're probably more at risk from the cold and scrapes from coral than from tangling with hazards like sharks, barracuda, sea snakes, stingrays, scorpionfish, jellyfish, stinging hydroids and sea urchins. All cuts should be cleansed thoroughly to remove any bits of coral, disinfected immediately, covered and kept dry until healed.

On the land, **snakes** are shy and are only likely to attack if you step on them. Take extra care when in jungle areas: wear long thick socks to protect your legs when trekking and walk noisily. If you're bitten, try to remember what the snake looked like (kill and keep it if possible), move as little as you can and send someone for medical help. Under no circumstances should you try doing anything heroic with a Swiss army knife. There are also a few poisonous **spiders** and if you're bitten by one you should also immobilize the limb and get medical help. If you get **leeches** attached to you while trekking in the jungle in the rainy season, use a dab of salt, suntan oil, or a cigarette to persuade them to let go, rather than just pulling them off.

Medical resources for travellers

Online

ⓦ **www.cdc.gov** Run by the US Centers for Disease Control and Prevention. An enormous amount of information, including an excellent section debunking the latest health myths and rumours.

Ⓦ**health.yahoo.com** Information on specific diseases and conditions, drugs and herbal remedies, as well as advice from health experts.

Ⓦ**www.tmvc.com.au** A list of all Travellers' Medical and Vaccination Centres throughout Australia, New Zealand and in Singapore, plus general information on travel health.

Ⓦ**www.istm.org** The International Society for Travel Medicine, with a full list of clinics specializing in international travel health.

Ⓦ**www.tripprep.com** Comprehensive database of information about diseases and necessary vaccinations for most countries, as well as destination and medical service provider information.

Ⓦ**www.fitfortravel.scot.nhs.uk** UK website carrying information about travel-related diseases and how to avoid them.

UK and Ireland

British Airways Travel Clinics Clinics throughout the UK; call ☎01276/685040 for the nearest, or consult Ⓦwww.ba.com. All offer vaccinations, tailored advice from an online database and a complete range of travel healthcare products.

Dun Laoghaire Medical Centre 5 Northumberland Ave, Dun Laoghaire, Co. Dublin ☎01/280 4996. Advice on medical matters abroad.

Hospital for Tropical Diseases Travel Clinic 2nd floor, Mortimer Market Centre, off Capper St, London WC1 (by appointment only; ☎020/7388 9600; £15 consultation fee is waived if you have your injections here). Their Health Line ☎0906/133 7733 gives hints on hygiene and illness prevention as well as listing appropriate immunizations.

Liverpool School of Tropical Medicine Pembroke Place, Liverpool L3 ☎0151/708 9393. Walk-in clinic Mon–Fri 1–4pm; appointment required only for yellow fever jab.

Malaria Helpline 24-hour recorded message ☎0900/160 0350.

MASTA (Medical Advisory Service for Travellers Abroad) Clinics throughout the UK; call ☎01276/685040 for the nearest, or consult Ⓦwww.masta.org. Recorded Travellers' Health Line ☎0906/822 4100 (Republic of Ireland ☎01560/147000) gives written information tailored to your journey by return of post.

Nomad Pharmacy 40 Bernard St, London, WC1 ☎020/7833 4114; 3–4 Wellington Terrace, London

N8 ☎020/8889 7014; 43 Queen's Rd, Clifton, Bristol ☎0117/922 6567. Free advice in person, or on ☎0906/863 3414. Ⓦwww.nomadtravel.co.uk.

Trailfinders Clinic at 194 Kensington High St, London W8 ☎020/7938 3999.

Travel Health Centre Department of International Health and Tropical Medicine, Royal College of Surgeons in Ireland, Mercers Medical Centre, Stephen's St Lower, Dublin ☎01/402 2337. Expert pre-trip advice and inoculations.

Travel Medicine Services 16 College St, Belfast ☎028/9031 5220. Medical advice before a trip and help afterwards in the event of a tropical disease.

Tropical Medical Bureau Grafton Buildings, 34 Grafton St, Dublin 2 ☎01/671 9200; 5 Northumberland Ave, Dun Laoghaire ☎01/280 4996. Ⓦtmb.exodus.ie.

US and Canada

Canadian Society for International Health 1 Nicholas St #1105, Ottawa, ON, K1N 7B7 ☎613/241-5785, Ⓦwww.csih.org. Distributes a free pamphlet, "Health Information for Canadian Travellers", containing an extensive list of travel health centres in Canada.

Centers for Disease Control 1600 Clifton Rd NE, Atlanta, GA 30333 ☎1-800/311-3435 or 404/639-3534, Ⓦwww.cdc.gov. Publishes outbreak warnings, suggested inoculations, precautions and other background information for travellers, including a vast amount of information about specific diseases. International Travelers Hotline on ☎1-877/394-8747.

International Association for Medical Assistance to Travellers (IAMAT) 417 Center St, Lewiston, NY 14092 ☎716/754-4883, and 40 Regal Rd, Guelph, ON, N1K 1B5 ☎519/836-0102, Ⓦwww.sentex.net/~iamat. A non-profit organization supported by donations. Membership is free and members can access a list of English-speaking doctors overseas, climate charts and leaflets on various diseases and inoculations.

International SOS Assistance Eight Neshaminy Interplex #207, Trevose, PA 19053-6956 ☎1-800/523-8930, Ⓦwww.intsos.com. Members receive pre-trip medical referral info, as well as overseas emergency services designed to complement travel insurance coverage.

Travel Medicine ☎1-800/872-8633, Ⓦwww.travmed.com. Sells first-aid kits, mosquito netting, water filters, reference books and other health-related travel products and also provides vaccine information and details of travel clinics in North America.

Australia and New Zealand

Travellers' Medical and Vaccination Centres Ⓦwww.tmvc.com.au. Travel clinics throughout Australia and New Zealand, including: 27–29 Gilbert Place, Adelaide, SA 5000 ℡08/8212 7522; 5th floor, 247 Adelaide St, Brisbane, QLD 4000 ℡07/3221 9066; Level 5, 8–10 Hobart Place, Canberra, ACT 2600 ℡02/6257 7156; 270 Sandy Bay Rd, Sandy Bay, Hobart, TAS 7005 ℡03/6223 7577; Level 2, 393 Little Bourke St, Melbourne, VIC 3000 ℡03/9602 5788; 45 Stirling Highway, Nedlands, WA 6009 ℡08/9386 4511, plus branch in Fremantle; Level 7, 428 George St, Sydney, NSW 2000 ℡02/9221 7133, plus branches in Chatswood and Parramatta. New Zealand: 1/170 Queen St, Auckland ℡09/373 3531; Moorhouse Medical Centre, 9 Washington Way, Christchurch ℡03/379 4000; 16 Beale St, Hamilton ℡07/839 1232; Avenue 7 Health, 56 7th Ave, Tauranga ℡07/578 9059; Shop 15, Grand Arcade, 14–16 Willis St, Wellington ℡04/473 0991.

Costs, money and banks

Foreign tourists visiting Bali and Lombok, wherever they come from, invariably find that hotel rooms at all levels of comfort, goods and services are relatively inexpensive when compared with their home countries.

Standards of living in all parts of Indonesia plummeted drastically as a result of the economic crisis in 1997–98, and have still not recovered. Prices of daily necessities such as rice and fuel have soared, with more price rises scheduled for the near future, while wages have remained almost static, creating great hardship for Indonesians. The Balinese are considered to enjoy a relatively high standard of living when compared with other Indonesians (including Lombok residents), but many of them are feeling the pinch, especially since the drop in tourist numbers in late 2001, when a lot of work on the island dried up overnight.

Many tourist businesses quote for their goods and services in **US dollars**. This includes hotels, dive operators, tour agents and car rental outlets, particularly in the larger resorts such as Kuta, Sanur, Nusa Dua, Ubud and Senggigi. Even where prices are displayed in US dollars, you're usually given the option of paying with cash, travellers' cheques, credit card or rupiah; it's worth checking the dollar exchange rate as it can be very advantageous.

Currency

The Indonesian currency is the **rupiah** (abbreviated to "Rp"). **Notes** come in denominations of Rp100 (red), Rp500 (green), Rp1000 (blue), Rp5000 (green and brown), Rp10,000 (browny-purple), Rp20,000 (green and black, or plain green), Rp50,000 (grey, blue and green) and small, plasticy, non-tearable Rp100,000 (pastel shades). They are all clearly inscribed with English numbers and letters. Be warned that most people won't accept ripped or badly worn banknotes, so you shouldn't either. There are also a few notes still around carrying a picture of ex-president Suharto, mostly the pink-purple Rp10,000 one. These are not legal tender, so don't accept them.

Coins are mainly used for public telephones and bemo rides. They come in five denominations: Rp25 (silver), Rp50 (silver-coloured plastic), Rp100 (silver-coloured plastic), Rp500 (larger, round, bronze), Rp1000 (large, round, bronze with silver rim). Some **old-style coins** are still in circulation: the old Rp50 are small, round and silver or small, round and bronze, and the old Rp100 are large, round and silver or octagonal bronze.

Despite the glossy tourist veneer, Bali is part of a poor country with limited resources to provide good-quality education and healthcare to its citizens, whose opportunities, quality of life and very survival are compromised as a result. Below are some suggestions for **charities** that would welcome help in some way from visitors.

• The US-Balinese-run Pondok Anak-Anak **Children's Library and Learning Centre** in Ubud (see p.227) offers a free library service to the children of Ubud and runs children's activities such as multi-language singing, dancing, and drawing. The library is open to all and is contained within its long-established parent project, the adult-oriented Pondok Pekak Library and Resource Centre, which has an excellent collection of English-language books on Bali as well as novels and travelogues. Visitors can support the Children's Library by using the adult library, by donating children's and adults' books (in English or Indonesian), or by donating funds. For more information, contact Pondok Pekak Library and Resource Centre, Jl Dewi Sinta, Ubud ☎0361/976194, ⓔpondok@denpasar .wasantara.net.id.

• In the grounds of *Balian Beach Bungalows* in Lalang Linggah, west Bali (see p.388) there's a small **workshop** where former drug and alcohol addicts produce soaps, candles, citronella and massage oils as part of the Yakeba rehabilitation programme. The project was set up by the owner of *Balian Beach* and has its main centre in the hills to the north, but visitors can buy the products from reception at *Balian Beach*. For more information, contact *Balian Beach Bungalows* ☎0361/814997, ⓔbobbali@denpasar.wasantara.net.id.

• In Klungkung (see p.256), the Panti Asuhan Kristen (**Christian Orphanage**), Jl Jempiring 20 ☎0366/21367, has been helping orphans from all over Indonesia since 1972. Children range from the age of two years old upwards, staying until the time when they find employment and can support themselves. Visitors wishing to see the work of the orphanage should come after 4pm when the children are home from school and donations of clothes, toys, books and money are all needed. To reach the orphanage, head south from the town centre along Jalan Puputan. After about 500m there's a large junction marked by a family statue on the corner; Jalan Jempiring is the road to the right.

• The **East Bali Poverty Project** ☎0361/410071, ⓦwww.eastbalipovertyproject .org, helps isolated mountain villages on the arid slopes of Gunung Agung and Gunung Abang in a number of ways, including setting up projects in sustainable and organic agriculture, establishing schools and health centres, and running awareness programmes on nutrition and sanitation. Visit *Cafe Bunga* in Ubud (see p.182), whose profits help the project directly, for more information about the work of the project.

• The **Crisis Care Centre** in Lovina (mobile ☎081/755 1158, ⓔgloriacrisiscare@ hotmail.com) is open to the local people for free healthcare (Mon–Fri 8am–noon) and is run totally on charitable donations, which are always needed. They also do outreach work to patients who cannot visit the clinic, and you're welcome to visit at any time. The clinic is in the hamlet of Lebah; take a side road away from the sea in Kaliasem, marked by a red-bordered sign with a blue cross, and the clinic is a couple of kilometres up on the left. The driving force is an Englishwoman, Gloria, and if the clinic is closed, visitors are welcome to visit her at home nearby; local people will give directions. You can also drop donations off at the *Legian Garden Restaurant* on Jl. Melasti in Kuta-Legian. There's more information and a Wish List at ⓦwww.wonderfulbali.com/ringo/picturealbum/ccc001.html.

In mid-2002 the official **exchange rate** was US\$1 to Rp10,300, and £1 to Rp14,500. Many of the websites listed on p.24 have links to Indonesian banks giving the daily exchange rate for Indonesian rupiah; one of the most reliable is the Bank Internasional Indonesia at ⓦbii.intnet.mu/ forex_calculator.htm. Alternatively, check out the useful "Currency CheatSheets" at ⓦwww.oanda.com.

Costs

If you're happy to eat where the locals do, use the public transport system and stay in simple accommodation, then you could scrape by on a **daily budget** of £8/US\$12 per person (less if you share a room). Food and lodgings are a little more costly in the larger resorts like Kuta (Bali) and Senggigi, and there's more to spend your money on in these places too. For around £20/\$30 a day (less if you share a room), you'll get quite a few extra comforts, like the use of a swimming pool and possibly hot water and air-conditioning as well, three good meals and a few beers. Staying in luxury hotels and eating at the flashiest restaurants, you're likely to spend a minimum of £100/\$140 per day. The sky's the limit at this end of the market, with \$1000-a-night accommodation, helicopter, yacht or sea-plane charters, dive or surf safaris, and fabulous gourmet meals all on offer.

Most government-run **museums** and **archeological sites** charge a standard Rp3100 per person (Rp1600 for under 14s), but elsewhere youth and student discounts are very rarely offered in Bali and Lombok. Few temples have fixed entry prices, but all visitors to any temple, whatever the size or status, are expected to give a small donation (about Rp5000) and, if necessary, to rent a sarong and sash as well.

Bargaining

Bargaining is one of the most obvious ways of keeping your costs down. The first price given is rarely the real one, and most stallholders and shopkeepers expect to engage in some financial banter before finalizing the sale; on average, buyers will start their counterbid at about 30 to 40 percent of the vendor's opening price and the bartering continues from there. Pretty much everything, from newspapers and cigarettes to woodcarvings and car rental is negotiable, and even accommodation rates can often be knocked down, from the humblest losmen through to the top-end places where the published price is only rarely what guests are expected to pay. Places that are oriented towards the upmarket tourist trade usually don't like to bargain, and many such shops display "fixed price" notices prominently, although even here it's worth asking about low-season discounts.

Bargaining is definitely an art, and requires not only a sense of humour but also a fair amount of tact – it's easy to forget that you're quibbling over just a few cents or pennies, and that such an amount is likely to mean a lot more to an Indonesian than to you. We've quoted prices in the book to give you a guide, but do remember that they will go up.

Cash and travellers' cheques

Before you leave home, banks, building societies and American Express travel offices should all be able to get some **cash** rupiah for you with enough warning: order at least a week ahead of your departure, as there is always a shortage of rupiah stocks outside Indonesia. The current import limit is Rp5,000,000 per person. On arrival, there are exchange counters at Bali's Ngurah Rai Airport, Lombok's Selaparang Airport and inside Jakarta's Sukarno Hatta Airport (domestic and international terminals), which all open for arriving passengers.

Most people carry at least some of their money as **travellers' cheques**, which are widely accepted at banks and exchange counters across Bali and in the tourist centres of west Lombok, the Gili Islands and the four cities area of Mataram-Ampenan-Cakranegara-Sweta. Outside these areas on Lombok, facilities are much rarer, so be sure to carry enough cash. The best cheques to take are those issued by the most familiar names, particularly American Express and Visa, ideally in US dollars or pounds sterling, though numerous other currencies are accepted in the largest resorts. Hold onto the **receipt** (or proof of purchase)

Money-changing scams

It's becoming increasingly common for unscrupulous staff at exchange counters to rip you off, and there are several well-known **money-changing scams** practised in the bigger resorts, in particular in Kuta on Bali.

Some common rip-offs

• Confusing you with the number of **zeros**. With over Rp10,000 to every pound or dollar, that's a lot of zeros every time you change money: it's quite easy for staff to give you Rp100,000 instead of Rp1,000,000.

• Giving you all your money in tiny Rp10,000 **denominations**, so that you lose track of the amount you're supposed to be getting.

• Tampering with the **calculator**, so that it shows a low sum even if you borrow the calculator and use it yourself.

• **Folding notes** over to make it look as if you're getting twice as much as you actually are.

• Turning the lights out or otherwise **distracting** you while the pile of money is on the counter.

• **Stealing** some notes as they "check" it for the last time.

• Once you've rumbled them and complained, telling you that the discrepancy in the figures is due to "**commission**".

Some advice

• **Avoid** any place that offers a ridiculously good rate. Better still, stick to banks, hotel counters or exchange desks attached to the losmen where you're staying.

• Always try to work out the **total amount** you're expecting beforehand, and write it down.

• Always ask whether there is **commission**.

• Before signing your cheque, ask for notes in **reasonable denominations** (Rp10,000 is unreasonable, Rp50,000 is acceptable), and ask to see them first.

• Always **count your money** carefully, and never hand back your pile of money to the exchange staff as this is when they whip away some notes without you noticing. You should be the last person to count the money before you put it away.

• So long as you haven't already **signed** a travellers' cheque, you can walk away at any point. If you have signed the cheque, stay calm, don't get distracted and count everything slowly and methodically.

that you get when you buy your travellers' cheques, as banks and exchange booths in smaller places may ask to see it before they agree to cash your cheques. It's important to realize that if you lose your passport your travellers' cheques will be useless as you can't encash them, so a **back-up** access to funds (a credit or debit card) in case of emergency is useful.

If you're staying in a developed tourist centre, you'll probably find that the money **exchange counters** and offices are the most convenient places to cash your cheques. Most of these open daily from around 8am to 8pm (slightly shorter hours on Lombok) and rates generally compare favourably with those offered by the banks. However, be wary of **money-changing** scams (see box above), particularly in Kuta.

Normal **banking hours** are Mon–Fri 8am–noon and, in some branches, Sat 8–11am, but these do vary. Also, in many banks the foreign exchange counter only opens for a limited period. You may find that banks in the smaller towns won't accept travellers' cheques. Most villages don't have a bank.

Plastic

Major **credit cards,** most commonly Visa and MasterCard, are accepted by most top hotels and by a growing number of tourist shops and businesses in the resort areas. However, outlets often add to your bill the entire fee that is charged to them (currently four percent), bumping costs up.

Lost or stolen credit cards

American Express *Grand Bali Beach Hotel*, north Sanur ☎0361/288449.
MasterCard Bank Central Asia (BCA), Jl Hasanudin 58, Denpasar ☎0361/431012.
Visa Bank Duta, Jl Hayam Wuruk 165, Denpasar ☎0361/226578.

In Bali and Lombok's biggest tourist centres (Kuta, Sanur, Nusa Dua, Ubud and Senggigi) and cities (Denpasar, Gianyar, Klungkung and Mataram), there are a useful number of **ATMs** that accept international cards, both **Visa** and **MasterCard** as well as debit cards on the Cirrus and Visa Delta network. Remember that all cash advances on credit cards are treated as loans, with interest accruing daily from the date of withdrawal and, possibly, a transaction fee on top. Debit card withdrawals are not liable to interest payments, and the flat transaction fee is usually quite small – your bank will be able to advise on this. Make sure you have a personal identification number (PIN) that's designed to work overseas. See the relevant sections of resort and city accounts for ATM locations; for an up-to-the-minute list, check ⓦwww.mastercard.com and ⓦwww.visa.com.

Visa TravelMoney (see ⓦwww.visa.com/pd) combines the security of travellers' cheques with the convenience of plastic. It's a disposable, prepaid debit card which you purchase before you leave home, and which gives access to your money from any Visa ATM. You can buy up to nine cards to access the same funds (useful for families or couples) and when all the money is gone you just throw the card away.

Wiring money

Wiring money through a specialist agent is a fast but expensive way to receive money abroad and should be considered a last resort. Money should be available for collection, usually in local currency, from the company's local agent within twenty minutes of being sent via Western Union or Moneygram; both charge on a sliding scale, so sending larger amounts of cash is better value.
Western Union has around a dozen agents in Bali and Lombok. Bali's main branch is located at Jl Udayana 1, Denpasar; the Bank Internasional Indonesia (BII) branches in Kuta, Nusa Dua, Singaraja, and Mataram also offer the service, as do main post offices in Denpasar, Gianyar, Singaraja and Mataram. See the relevant town accounts for locations; check opening hours on the website. Cash sent by **Moneygram** can be picked up in just four locations; at Bali's American Express office in Sanur (see p.169) and at Lippo Bank in Denpasar and at the Kuta Centre in Tuban (see p.135) and Bali International Convention Centre in Nusa Dua. Check the website for locations and opening hours.

It's also possible to have money wired **directly** from a bank in your home country to a bank in Indonesia, although this is somewhat less reliable because it involves two separate institutions. It's a good idea to check with your bank before travelling to see which branch of which bank they have reciprocal arrangements with, and precisely which details they'll need in order to complete the transaction.

Agents

Moneygram North America ☎1-800/MONEYGRAM (666-3947), all other countries toll-free ☎+800/6663-9472, ⓦwww.moneygram.com.
Western Union UK ☎0800/833833, Ireland ☎1800/395395, US ☎1-800/325-6000, Canada ☎1-800/235-0000, Australia ☎1800/649565, New Zealand ☎09/270 0050, ⓦwww.westernunion.com.

Getting around

Bali and Lombok are both small enough to traverse in a couple of hours by road (there's no rail transport on either island), although the lack of road or route numbers can make things confusing. On busy routes, the roads are good, wide enough for two-way traffic and fairly well maintained, although they see a lot of large trucks. On slightly less frequented routes, the roads are narrow and more likely to be potholed while, off the beaten track (on the southeast peninsula of Lombok for example), they may be no more than rough tracks.

The state of the road is also a reasonable indication of the frequency of **public transport**, which is generally cheap, but offers little in the way of space or comfort. In addition to the public transport system, **tourist shuttle buses** operate between major destinations on both Bali and Lombok, and although these are considerably more expensive, they are convenient on certain routes where public transport involves several changes or is especially time-consuming. If you prefer to drive yourself, bicycles, motorbikes, cars and jeeps are available to **rent** throughout the islands, or you can rent cars or motorbikes with a driver.

Getting **between the islands** is easy enough, with a choice of plane, catamaran or ferry. For details of services, see p.416.

Bemos and buses

On both Bali and Lombok, public transport predominantly consists of buses and bemos. **Bemos** are minibuses of varying sizes: tiny ones, with space for about ten people (although they often take many more), scurry around the local routes, while larger versions travel further and offer a reasonably comfortable ride. **Buses** operate long-distance routes such as Denpasar to Singaraja, Denpasar to Amlapura, and Bertais (also known as Mandalika terminal) in Sweta, Lombok to Labuhan Lombok. As there isn't quite so much stopping and starting, journey times by bus are a bit faster than by bemo.

You can pick up a ride from the bus or bemo station (terminal) or flag down a vehicle on the road. All fares are paid to the driver or their conductor, if there is one. You can't buy

tickets in advance – except for inter-island trips, such as from Bali to Java or Lombok.

No local person would dream of negotiating the **fare**. At the point they want to get off they yell "stoppa", hop out and pay the fixed local fare. The extent to which this system is accessible to tourists depends largely on where you are and your own approach to things. Some bemo drivers won't let you get in without agreeing the price beforehand; tourists are usually charged several times the local fare. At some of the biggest bus and bemo stations in Denpasar there are fare charts of prices to major destinations around the island, but as it can be hard to find them, we've tried to give a guide to prices for some routes. Bear in mind, though, that these rise every time that petrol prices go up: there's no substitute for asking a few local people what the fare should be. It's useful to carry coins and small notes with you to pay the exact fare; more unscrupulous drivers have been known to drive off without giving tourists their change. If you sit with your luggage on your knees, you should not be charged extra for it.

Tourist shuttle buses

The longest-established firm of **tourist shuttle buses**, with the widest choice of routes, is **Perama**. They have offices in most major tourist destinations and produce a useful leaflet outlining all their routes. **Fares** are roughly four or five times that of public transport, but their service is a lot more convenient and luggage isn't a problem; there's also plenty of room for wheelchairs, baby buggies and surfboards. Sample prices are Rp15,000 from Kuta to Ubud (7 daily);

Rp25,000 Candi Dasa to Kuta (3 daily); Rp40,000 Ubud to Lovina (2 daily); and Rp70,000 Lovina to Senggigi (daily). As above, fares rise when petrol prices go up but are displayed prominently in the Perama brochure; **discounts** are available if you've travelled with Perama previously and present your old ticket. You generally need to **book** the day before, but from popular destinations you can sometimes get a seat the same day. Phone bookings are usually acceptable and you can sometimes arrange a pick-up from your hotel as well. The company is constantly adding new routes to its services: Yeh Sanih, Tulamben and Tirtagangga on Bali have recently been added to the options as has Tetebatu on Lombok. The section "Travel Details", at the end of every guide chapter, lists frequencies and journey times of all routes. Perama also book tickets to further-flung destinations such as Malang, Surabaya, Yogyakarta and Jakarta on Java and Bima and Sape on Sumbawa; these routes are sometimes on Perama buses and sometimes on public transport – check at the time of booking.

There are several **rival companies** to Perama operating on both Bali and Lombok, including Wannen Wisata and Lombok Mandiri. They advertise throughout the tourist areas and offer a similar service, but are not as pervasive, frequent or high-profile as Perama. These are worth checking out if, for example, the Perama office is inconveniently far from the town centre (as in Lovina and Ubud): a rival company may well drop you more centrally. They can also make for a far calmer arrival: every hotel tout in every town knows precisely when and where the Perama bus arrives and will be waiting to entice passengers to their lodging. While this has advantages when beds are limited, it can be an unpleasant way to arrive when a crowd of thirty touts gathers to accost new arrivals. Other, smaller companies attract far less notice. Some, in fact, just book you onto public buses but take you to the bus station themselves; it's worth checking this out before you make a reservation.

Taxis

Metered **taxis** – with a "Taxi" sign on the roof – cruise for business in Denpasar, Nusa Dua, Jimbaran and Kuta on Bali, and Ampenan-Mataram-Cakranegara-Sweta, Lembar and Senggigi on Lombok. They're not expensive and are a straightforward alternative to bemos. It's usual to round the fare up to the nearest Rp1000 when paying.

On Bali there are several companies, the most common being the light-blue Blue Bird Taxis (☏0361/701111) and the white Ngurah Rai Airport Taxis (☏0361/724724). They charge Rp4000 flagfall and then Rp2000 per kilometre, day and night. Always double-check that the meter is turned on when you get in. As an example of fares, to get from Jalan Bagus Taruna in northern Legian to Waterbom Park in Tuban should cost around Rp16,000.

On Lombok, the light-blue Lombok Taxis (☏0370/627000) have roughly similar charges: to get from Mataram to Senggigi will cost around Rp15,000–20,000.

As an alternative, you can simply flag down an empty bemo and charter it like a taxi, although you'll have to bargain hard before you get in.

Dokar/cidomo

The traditional form of transport on the islands is quaint **horse and cart**. The horses wear heavy leather harnesses adorned with silver bells that jingle as they move, so you'll hear them coming long before they trot into view. Called **dokar** on Bali and **cidomo** on Lombok, where the carts have pneumatic tyres, they tend to ply the less popular routes, often transporting heavy loads. They're also used for city transport in Denpasar and as tourist vehicles in Kuta and Senggigi. Negotiate a price before you get in; as a tourist, you won't get far for less than Rp3000.

Rental vehicles

There are multinational **car rental agencies** on Bali, but not on Lombok – although with prices starting at around US$400 per week, it's far more economical to rent a car from local outlets after you arrive. However, you need to think about what you're planning to do before you decide on a vehicle. If you're heading into the mountains, you'll appreciate getting something as powerful as possible to cope with the slopes; if you're heading into rougher terrain make sure the vehicle is up to the job. Wherever you get the vehicle from, take a telephone contact number to get in touch in case of breakdown.

On both islands you'll need to produce an **international drivers' licence** or **tourist driving licence** before you rent. Be warned that on major holidays (like Galungan and Nyepi) vehicles are snapped up quickly by Balinese going home for the festivities. Rental vehicles need to have both Balinese and Lombok registration to travel on both islands, so you must tell the rental agency if you intend to take the vehicle between the islands, and check with them exactly what paperwork is required.

The more expensive operations, such as JBA in Sanur (see p.159), charge around $25 a day for a 800cc Suzuki Jimney, which can fit two people in the front and up to four on bench seats in the back, and $35 per day for a more comfortable jeep-like 1600cc Toyota Kijang. With a driver, add $12 per day; insurance adds $15 daily. Prices in less upmarket but still reputable places are Rp70,000–85,000 for a Suzuki Jimney, Rp100,000–120,000 for a Toyota Kijang, and Rp50,000 per day for a driver. Insurance deals vary. All prices exclude fuel, and note that a "one day" rental normally means twelve hours. On Lombok expect to pay towards the top end of the price ranges given. The rates drop quite considerably if you rent for a week or more.

Some outfits offer partial **insurance** as part of the fee; typically the maximum you'll end up paying in the event of any accident will be $150–500. The conditions of the insurance policies vary considerably and it's worth making certain you know what you're signing. Bear in mind that under this system, if there is more minor damage – for example if you smash a wing or a light – you'll probably end up paying the whole cost of it. Before you take a vehicle, check it thoroughly and get something in writing about any damage that has already been done, or you may end up being blamed for it. Most vehicle rental agencies keep your passport as security, so you don't have a lot of bargaining power in the case of any dispute.

Tourist driving licences

If you don't have an international driving licence it is possible to obtain a **tourist driving licence**, which allows you to drive. You can get one at Jalan Cok. Agung Tresna 14, in Renon in Denpasar. Go to the Pelayanan Samsat Building, BPKB Section, and you'll find a service window for foreigners (Mon–Thurs & Sat 8.30am–2.30pm, Fri 8.30am–1pm; ☎0361/243939). You'll need a photocopy of the pages of the passport showing your identity, your photo and your entry stamp to Indonesia, and a photocopy of your valid driving licence from home. Once you've completed the application form, paid the fee (Rp75,000 for a car or motorcycle licence) and got your photo taken, the licence will be ready immediately.

On the road

Traffic in Indonesia drives **on the left**. There's a maximum **speed limit** of 70kph. Fuel costs Rp1600 a litre, but is due to rise again during 2002 to at least Rp2175.

If you're driving a vehicle, you must carry an **international driving licence** or **tourist driving licence** and the registration documents of the vehicle at all times, or you're liable to a fine. Some vehicles are fitted with seatbelts but there are no regulations requiring them to be used. All motorcyclists, both drivers and passengers, must wear a **helmet**; these will be provided by the rental outlet, but most aren't up to much. The police carry out regular spot checks and you'll be fined for any infringements.

In south Bali in particular, there are certain roads that change during the day from two-way to one-way. This isn't publicized in any way that is comprehensible to foreigners, but if you're caught you'll be fined quite steeply. In recent years there have been regular reports of police stopping tourists who are driving for supposed infringements and "fining" them on the spot – accepting only foreign currency – in what is essentially an extortion racket. Official clean-up campaigns have followed, with police offenders sacked; if it happens to you the best advice is probably to keep calm and have a small amount of notes easily accessible well away from your main stash of cash that you can hand over if you have to.

It's worth driving extremely defensively. Accidents are always unpleasant, especially if people are hurt – more so in a foreign country where you may not speak the language. Disagreements over payment for repairs can be lengthy, frustrating and costly if the insurance situation is unclear and many local people have a straightforward attitude to accidents involving tourists – the visitor must be to blame. It really isn't a good idea to do any **driving at night** unless you absolutely have to, largely because pedestrians, cyclists, food carts and horse carts all use the roadway without any lights. There are also plenty of roadside ditches.

Car rental agencies abroad

Avis UK ☎0870/606 0100, Ireland ☎01/605 7500, US ☎1-800/331-1084, Canada ☎1-800/272-5871, Australia ☎13 63 33, New Zealand ☎0800/655111, ⓦwww.avis.com.
Hertz UK ☎0870/844 8844, Ireland ☎01/813 3416, US ☎1-800/654-3001, Canada ☎1-800/263-0600, Australia ☎13 30 39, New Zealand ☎0800/654321, ⓦwww.hertz.com.

Chartered transport

Hundreds of drivers patrol the tourist areas offering **chartered transport** – this means you rent their vehicle with them as the driver. Most have cars or jeeps but you can usually find somebody with a motorbike. You're expected to pay for the driver's meals and accommodation if the trip takes more than a day, and you must be very clear about who is paying for fuel, where you want to go and stop, and how many people will be travelling. With somebody driving who knows the roads, you've got plenty of time to look around and fewer potential problems to worry about, but it's very difficult to guarantee the quality of the driving. Expect to pay Rp50,000 per day for the driver in addition to the cost of the vehicle rental; you'll need to bargain. For first-hand recommendations of good drivers, check the Bali and Lombok Travel Forum ⓦwww.travelforum.org/bali.

Motorbike and bicycle rental

Motorbikes available for rent vary from small 100cc Yamahas to more robust trail bikes. Prices start at Rp30,000 per day without insurance, with discounts for longer rentals. You'll need to show an international motorcycle licence or a tourist driving licence. Conditions on Bali and Lombok are not really suitable for inexperienced drivers, with heavy traffic on major routes, steep hills and difficult driving once you get off the beaten track. There are increasing numbers of accidents involving tourists, so don't take risks.

In most tourist areas, it's possible to rent a **bicycle** for around Rp10,000 a day; check the condition of it before you set off and carry plenty of water as it's hot and thirsty work. If you are planning to tour the island by bike, bear in mind that, should you get tired or stranded somewhere, bemos will be extremely reluctant to pick you and your bike up.

Planes

Bali's domestic terminal is adjacent to the international one at Ngurah Rai Airport, 3km south of Kuta; **Lombok**'s shares the Selaparang Airport runway in Mataram with the handful of international flights. All domestic airlines have ticket sales counters in the domestic terminal at Bali's Ngurah Rai Airport; the other main offices in Bali, Lombok and Jakarta are listed on p.21. Including statutory taxes, the local **fare** between the two islands is a fixed-price Rp235,000. If you're planning to travel further afield in Indonesia by plane, you might want to consider an air pass (see p.21 for details and also for information on connections to the rest of Indonesia).

Chartered air transport

For special occasions or fantasy journeys – or if you're not counting the rupiah – it's possible to get around the islands by chartered plane or helicopter. Benoa Harbour is the main departure point for the **sea planes** run by Island Sea Planes (☎0361/728967, ⓦwww.islandseaplanes.org). These can be chartered for fixed-route sightseeing flights (from $55 per person for a half-hour round-trip), or used to get to and from Nusa

Lembongan on a day-trip, with the option of returning by sailing boat ($125 day return). They can also be rented as private air-taxis, for example to get to Pemuteran on the northwest coast ($225 per person; takes 30min). All prices are per person, with a minimum of two people.

For **helicopters**, Air Bali (☎0361/763151, ⓦwww.airbali.com) offers sightseeing trips of the south or centre of the island. Their helicopters can be chartered for $1000 per hour for either sightseeing or transport to one of the dozen or so helipads that are now dotted around the island.

Accommodation

Whatever your budget, the overall standard of accommodation in Bali and Lombok is high. Even the smallest and most inexpensive lodgings are enticing, nearly always set in a tropical garden and with some kind of outdoor seating area – a covered communal verandah or a shaded terrace with easy chairs and a garden view. Interiors can be a bit sparse, but the terraces encourage you to do as local people do, and spend most of your leisure time in the open air.

The majority of cheap places to stay are classed as **losmen**, a term which literally means homestay, but is most commonly used to describe any fairly small-scale and inexpensive accommodation, be it in the grounds of the family home or not. Nearly everything else comes into the **hotels** category, most of which offer air-conditioning and a swimming pool. **Villas** are private holiday homes, usually pretty luxurious, catering for couples, small groups and families. **Check-out time** in losmen and hotels is usually noon.

Most losmen and all hotel rooms have en-suite **bathrooms** (*kamar mandi*), though in a few of the older homestays you might have to share a communal one. Except in the most basic places, **toilets** (*wc*, pronounced *wey sey*) are usually Western-style, but flushing is sometimes done manually, with water scooped from the pail that stands alongside. The same pail and scoop is used by the Balinese to wash themselves after defecating (using the left hand, never the right which is for eating), so if you need toilet paper you may have to provide it yourself.

Many Balinese still **bathe** in the rivers and public bathing pools, but indoor bathing is traditionally done by means of the scoop and slosh method, or **mandi**. This entails dipping a scoop into a huge basin of water (which is often built into the bathroom wall) and then sloshing the water over yourself. The basin functions as a water supply only and not a bath, so never get in it; all washing is done outside it and the basin should not be contaminated by soap or shampoo. Many losmen and all hotels in the bigger resort areas provide showers as well as mandi, and some of the more upmarket places offer Western-style bathtubs as well. Hot water (*air panas*) rarely features in any room under category ❷.

In the more stylish establishments, bathrooms can be delightful, particularly if they are designed with open roofs and decked out with plants and flowers. These "**garden bathrooms**" often have showers and mandi fed by water piped through sculpted flues and floors covered in a carpet of smooth, rounded pebbles.

Prices

On the whole, both losmen and hotels are inexpensive. For the simplest double room, **prices** start at around Rp30,000 in the least visited areas, and Rp50,000 in the smaller resorts such as Lovina, Candi Dasa and

Accommodation price codes

All the accommodation listed in this book has been given one of the following price codes, corresponding to the **cheapest double room** in high season excluding tax – though, as with most commodities, a spot of skilful bargaining can work wonders. During the low season you can often get discounts of up to fifty percent if you negotiate; you can also save money by reserving your room online where possible. Nearly all losmen and hotels quote their rates exclusive of the obligatory ten percent government **tax**; many of the more expensive hotels add an extra eleven percent **service charge** (in hotel-speak, these supplements are usually referred to as "plus-plus"). Outside peak periods, a proprietor will often agree to do away with them.

In general, losmen in the ❶–❹ categories post their prices in **rupiah**. The most upmarket hotels quote their rates in **US dollars**, and usually accept cash, travellers' cheques or credit cards, but will also convert to rupiah on the spot if you want. Credit-card transactions are always in rupiah so you should check the in-house exchange rate. Unless otherwise indicated, hotels in the ❾ category charge $150–250 for their standard rooms; however, certain super deluxe establishments have nothing available under $300, and these details are given in the review.

Where we've given a significant **spread of prices** in an establishment's price codes (such as ❸–❺), the text of the review will explain what extra facilities you get for more money (usually air-conditioning, hot water and maybe a TV or fridge or both).

❶ under Rp45,000
❷ Rp45,000–85,000
❸ Rp85,000–135,000
❹ Rp135,000–195,000

❺ Rp195,000–305,000;
   US$19–30
❻ Rp305,000–505,000;
   US$30–50

❼ US$50–80
❽ US$80–150
❾ over US$150

Padang Bai. In Kuta, Ubud and Senggigi, you will find a handful of places charging Rp40,000, but these fill up very fast, so you should be prepared to pay a minimum of Rp70,000. In the more developed resorts, the choice of accommodation is phenomenal, with rows and rows of losmen and hotels competing for your custom.

During **off-season** (Feb–June and Sept–Nov) you can do some serious bargaining, saving up to fifty percent of the published rate in some of the moderate and expensive hotels, or at the very least getting the service tax deducted or an extra night thrown in for nothing.

Things are rather different in **peak season** (July, Aug, Dec & Jan), when rates can be hiked at whim and rooms are at a premium. Off-season weekends can also get pretty busy, particularly in Kuta, with planeloads of Australian surfers pitching up on Friday afternoons and sticking around until Monday morning. With this in mind, it's worth trying to reserve a room in advance (lots of mid-range places and some cheaper options can be booked over the internet) and, if you're arriving straight from Bali's Ngurah Rai Airport, asking to be picked up from the airport – many hotels offer this service free of charge. Losmen, unfortunately, rarely take advance bookings, but to find the best bargains in high season it's often worth listening to the touts who hang around the transport terminals in the main resort areas. They'll guarantee to find you a room, albeit at a rate that's slightly inflated to cover their commission.

Losmen

While most **losmen** provide far more sophisticated facilities than the "homestay" tag implies, many are still family-run operations with an emphasis on friendly service and simple, inexpensive accommodation. Rooms tend to be in single-storey detached or semi-detached "cottages" (sometimes known as "bungalows"), which can be anything from whitewashed concrete cubes to artful rattan and bamboo structures built to resemble traditional rice barns. Some are even embellished with woodcarvings and set

Booking accommodation online

Wherever possible, we've included in our reviews **website** and/or **email addresses**. Not all hotels in Bali and Lombok have their own websites: many have only a web page hosted by one or more of the main online accommodation services (listed below), where you can see photos and usually get a discounted rate.

Most of the following online accommodation finders offer **discounts** of up to fifty percent on the published rates (US$40 and upwards) of standard and upmarket hotels; they don't deal in genuine budget hotels and losmen. It's always worth doing a web-wide search on your selected hotel as discounted rates can vary.

Access Bali ⓦwww.villas-bali.com. Hotel rooms and a few private villas for rent by the day or week in both Bali and Lombok, with nightly rates from $40 to $3000.

Asia Travel ⓦwww.asiatravel.com/bali .html. Online booking service for a fair number of mid-range and upmarket hotels, most with substantial discounts.

Bali Hotel Bargain Finder ⓦwww .balivillas.com/hotels.html. Discounts of at least fifty percent on a few three-, four- and five-star hotels in the major resort areas of Bali.

Bali Hotels ⓦwww.balihotels.com. Forty percent discounts on a wide-ranging portfolio of hotels, most with online booking facilities. From $25.

Bali Hotels and Accommodations Company ⓦwww.travelideas.net/bali .hotels. Useful hotel booking service which includes extensive hotel reviews and information about facilities, and claims to take no agent's fee. Some direct booking with individual hotels. Rates from $11.

Bali Online Hotels ⓦwww.indo.com/ hotels. Online reservations for a selection of hotels in major resorts on

Bali. A few are under $15, but most start over $30. Discounts of up to fifty percent on published rates.

Bali Paradise ⓦwww.bali-paradise .com/properties. Good starting point for long-term rentals and properties for sale. Links to estate agents' websites, plus some individual rentals and accommodation classifieds.

Last Minute Bargains ⓦwww .last-minute-bargains.com/bali.hotels. As it says, with a few bargains at 25 percent off usual internet rates.

Lombok Hotels ⓦwww.lombokhotels .com. A handful of hotels in Lombok's main resorts that can be booked online. From $35.

Private Vacation Villas in Bali ⓦwww .balivillas.com. Luxurious, fully serviced hideaways for up to ten people, to rent by the day or by the week, complete with tropical gardens, swimming pools, cook, driver and housekeeper. Prices from $280 to $2000 a day.

Roomfinder ⓦwww.baliwww.com/bali/ roomfinder. Standard and upmarket accommodation in Bali, with savings offered on nearly all. Double rooms from $30.

in their own walled gardens. Furnishings tend to be fairly stark: hard beds and even harder bolsters are the norm, and you may or may not be provided with a light blanket. Most losmen rooms come with fans and net-ted windows (sticky tape comes in handy for repairing holes), and nearly all have attached cold-water bathrooms. Certain losmen offer a range of rooms, charging more for hot water, air-conditioning and a prime location, and possibly even a swimming pool as well.

Aside from the inevitable garden setting, what makes the best losmen especially delightful is the complimentary flask of tea left

on your garden table every morning and, better still, the **breakfasts** (*makan pagi*), which are occasionally included in the price of the room. If you're lucky this might run to fruit salad and banana pancakes, or may simply include toast and coffee. Following the economic crises of recent years, however, a decreasing number of losmen now offer these extras.

Very few losmen offer **single rooms** (*kamar untuk satu orang*), so lone travellers will normally get put in a double room at about 75 percent of the full price, which rarely works out at less than Rp30,000.

Hotels

The least attractive type of lodgings on Bali and Lombok are the **cheap urban hotels** (❶–❺) such as those in Denpasar and Singaraja, which cater for short-stay Indonesian businesspeople rather than tourists, and can feel rather soulless and lonely. Nonetheless, they are usually clean enough and tend to be located near transport terminals, so can suffice for overnight stops en route to more pleasant environs.

Moderately priced hotels (❹–❻) are larger and more formal operations than losmen. Accommodation is often in "cottages" or "bungalows" which may or may not be air-conditioned, but will almost certainly have hot-water showers and possibly bathtubs as well. Fridges, phones and TVs feature in the more costly ones. Breakfast is sometimes included in the smaller mid-priced hotels and there are nearly always swimming pools (*kolam renang*) on the premises.

Balinese gardens

Blessed with rich volcanic soil, abundant rivers, lots of sunshine and plenty of hearty downpours, Bali blooms year-round with stunning displays of tropical flora. Roadsides are planted with a rainbow of decorative and shade-giving trees, including scarlet **flame trees** (*flamboyan*), fiery orange **African tulip trees** (*kacret-kacretan*), banyans, and red, pink and white **oleanders** (*kenyeri*), as well as hedges of **croton**, **cordyline** and **coleus shrubs** in variegations that run from burgundy and scarlet through amber and lime. The clustered heads of the red **Javanese ixora** (*soka*) and the pink and orange **lantana** (*kerasi*) are common sights, as are purple and white **bougainvillea** (*kertas*), and the trumpet blossoms of the white **datura** (*kecubung bali*) and the yellow **allamanda**. The two woody **frangipani** shrubs (*jepun jawa* and *jepun bali*) are a staple feature of temple courtyards as their scented white, pink and yellow blossoms are, like the scarlet blooms of the ubiquitous **hibiscus** (*pucuk*), used in offerings and for decorating religious statues. Many households also cultivate fruit trees such as **papayas**, **bananas**, **guavas**, **mangoes** and **coconuts**. Even the exotic-looking flame-tipped **heliconias** are not uncommon sights in public and private gardens around the island, and the myriad foliage plants can be equally stunning, not least the large, white-veined, heart-shaped leaves of the **crystal anthurium**.

You'll find all this and more in Bali's **hotel gardens**, whose designers have taken inspiration from the horticultural principles of the traditional courtyard garden, which strives to create a balance of "abundance" and "stillness", and embellished the concept to often breathtaking effect. Perhaps the most famous Balinese hotel garden is the thirty-six acres at the *Bali Hyatt* in Sanur (see p.161), designed by the prolific expat architect and landscape gardener Made Wijaya to evoke a tropical park, complete with coconut groves, contemplative vistas and the all-important series of pools and ponds, interlaced with shrine-like lanterns and artfully sited mossy-green statues. **Water** is an essential feature of any Balinese garden, and even the smallest losmen courtyard is likely to harbour a few pink **lotus flowers** (*tunjung*) or a couple of white **water lilies** (also known as *tunjung*) in an earthenware water jar. At the most refined end of the spectrum, the bungalows at the *Watergarden* hotel in Candi Dasa (see p.284) are an exquisite example of harmony in an aquatic garden. Other outstanding hotel gardens in Bali and Lombok include the stepped terraces at *Hotel Tjampuhan* in Ubud (see p.200); the innovative integration of an elegant pond and a small, working rice-field into the hotel landscape at *Ananda Cottages*, also in Ubud (see p.199); the compact labyrinthine exuberance at *Gazebo* in Sanur (see p.161); and the lush extravaganza that falls just this side of wilderness at the *Sheraton* in Senggigi (see p.436). There are many fine small-scale hotel gardens too, often the product of a single gardener's enthusiasm, as at *Flamboyant* losmen in Candi Dasa (see p.285) and *Sri Ratu* in Legian (see p.119). For a selection of inspirational and educational **books** on Balinese gardens and tropical plants, see p.558.

Of all the **expensive hotels** (❼–❾) on Bali and Lombok, only one is high-rise – the nine-storey *Grand Bali Beach* in Sanur. This caused such consternation when built that a local law was subsequently passed forbidding any other hotel to be taller than a coconut palm. As a result, even the massive international hotels such as Kuta's *Holiday Inn*, Sanur's *Bali Hyatt* and Senggigi's *Sheraton* are low-rise structures, many of them designed to evoke traditional Balinese palaces (*puri*) and temples (*pura*). This *puri-pura* style, dubbed **Bali baroque** or Baliesque because of its excessive use of ornamentation, works better in some buildings than others, but certainly adds a distinct character to the upmarket resorts. Their grounds are designed in similarly grand style, with waterfalls, arbours, endless lawns and borders of tropical shrubs, and many include a series of free-form swimming pools as well. Facilities are top class, with most top-end places offering tennis courts and a gym, as well as several restaurants and a stage for nightly culture shows. The rooms themselves, though luxuriously equipped, can lack local colour or flair; throughout the guide we've tried to highlight those places which do make an effort to incorporate Balinese designs.

If you're looking for smaller-scale hotels with more character that are not prohibitively expensive, opt for those that classify themselves as **boutique hotels**. Some comprise as few as half a dozen rooms, and they're generally stylish and luxurious. Outstanding examples include *The Watergarden* and *Kubu Bali* in Candi Dasa, *Damai Lovina Villas* in Lovina, *Cabé Bali* in Tirtagangga, *Waka Gangga* in Yeh Gangga, *Alam Jiwa* and *Waka di Ume* in Ubud, and *Cempaka Belimbing* in Belimbing.

If you can afford to stay in **super-luxury hotels** (US$250–700), you'll almost certainly be treated to supremely indulgent and tasteful accommodation, often designed in chic modern-Asian style and perhaps inspired by the traditional homes of the Balinese rajas, with your own private garden-compound and possibly a personal plunge-pool as well. We've detailed some of these places, most notably the *Four Seasons* in Jimbaran, the *Tugu* in Canggu, the *Amandari* in Ubud, Nusa Dua's *Amanusa*, Candi Dasa's *The Serai*, and the *Oberoi* near Tanjung in Lombok.

Villas

If you want posh accommodation for a family or small group, or extremely private accommodation for a couple, it's worth considering a **villa**. Sometimes the home of an expat that is rented out for most of the year, or sometimes purpose-built for holiday rentals, villas are generally very smart and well maintained and are usually designed in appealing Balinese style and equipped with a private pool and kitchen. They can be rented, often at quite reasonable rates, by the day or the week, and prices often include the services of a housekeeper and cook. Be aware, though, that some hotels advertise their bungalows as "villas" even though they don't have kitchens and lack the privacy of genuine holiday homes. For weekly and monthly rental opportunities, see Long-Term Accommodation below.

Youth hostels and camping

There is just one registered **youth hostel** in Bali and Lombok, rather inconveniently located midway between Denpasar and Sanur (see p.159). It's on the IYHA Booking Network, and staff will usually come to pick you up from the airport.

The availability of inexpensive losmen near almost every decent beach on Bali and Lombok means that it's hardly worth lugging a tent and sleeping bag all the way around the islands. To **camp** in Bali Barat National Park you need a permit and must be accompanied by a park ranger; you will also have to supply your own bag and tent. It's considered inappropriate to camp on the slopes of Bali's most sacred mountains, although camping on Lombok's Gunung Rinjani is normal practice. The villages around Rinjani are well used to trekkers, and have plenty of reasonably priced tents, sleeping bags and cooking equipment available for rent.

Long-term accommodation

Many losmen are happy to rent out rooms **long-term**, and several establishments in Legian and Ubud provide kitchen facilities and reasonable monthly rates as an incentive. Seminyak, Sanur and the Ubud area are the most popular for larger, more salubrious long-term rentals, and a number of local real-estate agents advertise their properties in English with the foreign visitor in mind; see p.136 for leads on places in Kuta–Legian–Seminyak, and p.227 for the Ubud area. For the lease and sale of both villas and land all over the island, try House of Bali (ⓦwww.houseofbali.com), Bali Real Estate Agents (☎0361/289515, ⓦwww.balirealestateagents.com), In Touch (☎0361/731047, ⓦwww.intouchbali), or Private Villas (☎0361/703060). See also the online accommodation finders, listed on p.44. The fortnightly *Bali Advertiser* always carries a page or two of property ads, and is also a good place to look; it's available from some hotels, restaurants and tourist offices. If you're thinking about **buying** or building a house in Bali, check out the Owning Property in Bali website (ⓦwww.baliproperties.com), which offers general advice on legal issues, location and architects, and has links to estate agents and developers. Be very wary of any **time-share deal**: many tourists fail to read the small print and have found themselves making unwise investments and unable to claim back their money. See p.69 for related cons.

Eating and drinking

If you come to Bali or Lombok expecting the range and exuberance of the cooking elsewhere in Southeast Asia, you'll be disappointed. Somehow the ingenuity and panache don't seem to have reached this far, or maybe they've been elbowed out of the way by pizzas, hamburgers and French fries. However, there's a considerable variety of food available, cooked in a range of styles. Ironically, the most elusive cuisines on the islands are the native Balinese and Sasak.

At the inexpensive end of the scale, you can get a bowl of *bakso ayam* (chicken soup with noodles), for Rp5000 or less from a wayside cart. These carts line the sidewalks and bus stations during the day and congregate at night markets after dark, while others ply their wares around the streets. Slightly upmarket are **warung** or *rumah makan* (eating houses), which range from a few tables and chairs in a kitchen to fully fledged **restaurants**. There's usually a menu, but in the simplest places you'll probably just find rice and noodle dishes on offer. Most places that call themselves restaurants cater for a broad range of tastes, offering Western, Indonesian, and Chinese food, while others specialize in a particular cuisine such as Mexican, Japanese or Italian. The multinational fast-food chains have also made inroads into the tourist and city areas.

Vegetarians get a good deal, with plenty of tofu (*tahu*) around as well as the equally popular *tempeh*, a fermented soybean cake, thought to have originated in Java.

Restaurant **etiquette** is pretty much the same as in the West, with waiter service the norm everywhere. Most places will have a washbasin in a corner so you can wash your hands before eating. If you're eating with friends, don't count on everyone's meal arriving together; there may be just one gas burner in the kitchen.

Prices vary dramatically depending on the location rather than the quality of the meals. In the humblest *rumah makan*, a simple rice dish such as nasi campur will set you back about Rp5000, while tourist restaurants will charge from Rp8000 upwards for the same dish. If you choose non-Indonesian food such as pizza, pasta and steak, prices start at around Rp20,000 in tourist restaurants. We've classified all restaurants that we've reviewed as inexpensive, moderate or expensive. **Inexpensive** means you will get a satisfying main dish for less than Rp15,000, **moderate** means it'll be Rp15,000–40,000, and **expensive** implies Rp40,000 and over. Bear in mind that restaurants with more expensive food also have pricier drinks and, in addition, most places add anything up to 21 percent to the bill for tax and service.

See pp.566–568 for a **menu reader** of dishes and common terms.

Styles of cooking

The most abundant style of cooking available on both Bali and Lombok is **Indonesian** rice and noodle-based meals, followed closely by Chinese (essentially Cantonese) food, as well as a vast array of Western food in the resorts. Native **Balinese** food on Bali, and **Sasak** food on Lombok, is something you'll need to search out. Should you wish to learn more about the ingredients and preparation of local food, several places offer cookery schools for visitors; see p.81for more.

Indonesian food

Based on rice (*nasi*) or noodles (*mie* or *bakmi*), with small side dishes of vegetables, fish or meat, **Indonesian food** is flavoured with chillies, soy sauce (*kecup*), garlic, ginger, cinnamon, turmeric and lemongrass. You'll also find chilli sauce (*sambal*) on offer just about everywhere.

Two dishes available in even the simplest warung are **nasi campur**, boiled rice with small amounts of vegetables, meat and fish, often served with a fried egg and krupuk (huge prawn crackers), and **nasi goreng**, fried rice with vegetables, meat or fish, also often with egg and krupuk. The noodle equivalent – mie or **bakmi goreng** – is also commonly available. The other mainstays of the Indonesian menu are **gado-gado**, steamed vegetables served with a spicy peanut sauce, and **sate**, small kebabs of beef, pork, chicken, goat or fish, barbecued over a fire and served on a bamboo stick with spicy peanut sauce.

Inexpensive and authentic Sumatran or Padang fare is sold in *rumah makan Padang*, which you'll find pretty much in every sizeable town. **Padang food** is always cold and displayed on platters piled up in a pyramid shape inside a glass-fronted cabinet. There are no menus; when you enter you either select your composite meal by pointing to the dishes on display, or just sit down, the staff bring you a selection, and you pay by the number of plates you have eaten from at the end. The range of options is variable, vegetarians are sometimes well catered for and sometimes not at all, and the food is traditionally fiery. Dishes you may encounter include boiled *kangkung* (water spinach), *tempeh*, fried eggplant with chilli, boiled eggs in curry sauce, fried whole fish or fish steaks, meat curry, squid or fish curry, potato cakes, beef brain curry and fried cow's lung.

Balinese food

The everyday **Balinese** diet is a couple of meals based on rice, essentially nasi campur, eaten whenever people feel hungry, supplemented with snacks such as krupuk. The full magnificence of Balinese cooking is reserved for festivals and ceremonies when all the stops are pulled out. One of the best dishes is **babi guling**, spit-roasted pig, served with **lawar**, a spicy raw meat mash. Another speciality is **betutu bebek**, smoked duck, cooked very slowly in an earth oven – this has to be ordered in advance from restaurants.

Although the Balinese tend not to eat desserts, they have created **bubuh injin**, black rice pudding, named after the colour of the rice husk. The rice itself is pink and served with a sweet coconut milk sauce, fruit and grated coconut. **Rice cakes** (*jaja*) play a major part in ceremonial offerings but are also a daily food. Rice flour dough is baked, steamed or fried and then eaten sugared, with coconut syrup or with fruit.

Sasak food

According to some sources, the name "Lombok" translates as "chilli pepper" – highly appropriate considering the savage heat of traditional **Sasak food**. It's not easy to track down, however, and you'll find Chinese and Indonesian food far more widely available on Lombok. Traditional Sasak food uses rice as the staple, together with a wide variety of vegetables, a little meat (although no pork), and some fish, served in various sauces, often with a dish of **chilli sauce** on the side in case it isn't hot enough already. Anything with *pelecing* in the name is served with chilli sauce. Taliwang dishes, originally from Sumbawa, are also available

Betel

One habit that you're bound to notice while in Bali and Lombok, and generally throughout Southeast Asia, is the chewing of **betel**. You'll mainly see older folk indulging in this pastime. Small parcels, made up of three essential ingredients – areca nut wrapped in betel leaf which has been smeared with lime – are lodged inside the cheek. When mixed with saliva, these work as a mild stimulant as well as producing an abundance of bright red saliva which is regularly spat out on the ground and eventually stains the lips and teeth red. Other ingredients can be added according to taste, including tobacco, cloves, cinnamon, cardamom, turmeric and nutmeg. You may also come across decorated boxes used to store the ingredients on display in museums.

on Lombok, consisting of grilled or fried food with a chilli sauce. All parts of the animals are used, and you'll find plenty of offal on the menu. There's also a wide range of sticky desserts, many of them served wrapped in leaves.

Fine dining

Just as it's possible to get by spending a dollar or less for a decent meal in Bali or Lombok, you can also enjoy some superb **fine dining** experiences on the islands. Plenty of innovative chefs, some Western, some Asian, have imported and adapted the essentials of classic French gourmet cooking and modern Pacific Rim fusion food and seasoned the resulting melange extremely well with local tastes and produce. They offer menus that are creative and imaginative and, best of all, taste great. Restaurants serving this food are invariably stylish, with excellent service, charging US$30–50 per head. This can seem a lot in the context of Indonesian prices, but when compared with restaurants of a similar standard in London or New York, it's decidedly good value. Top choices include the restaurants at *Damai Lovina Villas* in the north of the island (see p.361), *Kafé Warisan* and *The Living Room*, both in Seminyak (see p.129), *Mozaic* in Ubud (see p.220) and *Serai* in Candi Dasa (see p.288).

Fresh fruit

The range of **fresh fruit** available on Bali and Lombok is startling. You'll see **banana**, **coconut** and **papaya** growing all year round, and **pineapple** and **watermelon** are always in evidence in the markets. Of the cit-

rus fruits, the giant **pomelo** is the most unusual to visitors – larger than a grapefruit and sweeter. **Guava**, **avocado** (served as a sweet fruit juice with condensed milk), **passion fruit**, **mango**, **soursop** and its close relative, the **custard apple**, are all common. Less familiar are the seasonal **mangosteen** with a purple skin and sweet white flesh; the hairy **rambutan**, closely related to the lychee, with a large stone in the middle of distinctive, almost perfumed, white flesh; the sour **salak** or snakefruit, named after its brown scaly skin; and the **starfruit** which is crunchy but rather flavourless. **Jackfruit**, which usually weighs 10–20kg, has firm yellow segments around a large stone inside its green bobbly skin. This is not to be confused with the **durian**, also large but with a spiky skin and a distinctively pungent, sometimes almost rotten, odour. Some airlines and hotels ban it because of the smell but devoted fans travel large distances and pay high prices for good-quality durian fruit.

Drinks

Bottled water is widely available throughout the islands (Rp1800–4000 for 1.5 litres in supermarkets), as are familiar international brands of **soft drinks** (around Rp2000 per bottle in supermarkets); you'll pay higher prices in restaurants. There are also delicious **fruit drinks** on offer, but be cautious, as in many places you can't be sure of the quality of the water used or the purity of the ice (for more, see p.30). Many restaurants automatically add sugar to their juices so you'll need to specify if you don't want that. Moderately priced restaurants charge Rp6000–8000 for juice drinks, excluding tax and service.

Indonesians are great **coffee** (*kopi*) and **tea** (*teh*) drinkers. Locally grown coffee (*kopi Bali* or *kopi Lombok*) is drunk black, sweet and strong. The coffee isn't filtered, so the grounds settle in the bottom of the glass. If you want milk added or you don't want sugar, you'll have to ask (see p.568). Nescafé instant coffee is available in tourist restaurants. The tea is best when it's weak and black. You'll also find hot lemon or orange juice.

Alcohol

Locally produced **beer** includes Bali Hai, the most common, fizziest and least pleasant, as well as the two pilsners, Anker and Bintang. Expect to pay from Rp8000 for a 620ml bottle from a supermarket or in an inexpensive losmen or warung, but in a restaurant you'd be lucky to pay Rp10,000, and may be looking at Rp15,000 or more. Draught beer, usually served in a glass of about half a pint, comes in at around Rp8500 at most moderate restaurants.

Many tourist restaurants and bars offer an extensive list of **cocktails** (Rp15,000 upwards). There are reports of some places putting decidedly second-rate liquor into their cocktails, or even no liquor at all – probably difficult to detect unless you're a connoisseur. "Happy Hours" in tourist spots very often last all evening.

There are some locally produced **wines** available on Bali, made in the north and east of the island. Hatten Wines (www.hatten-wines.com) produce several different vintages available in restaurants in the main tourist areas (Rp75,000 upwards per bottle); they're perfectly drinkable, if unexciting. Imported **spirits** are only available in major tourist areas and at expensive hotels, where wines from Australia and New Zealand, California, Europe and South America are also available, mostly Rp25,000 upwards for a glass and Rp160,000 upwards for a bottle. **Local brews** include *brem*, a type of rice wine, *tuak*, palm beer brewed from palm tree sap, and powerful *arak*, a palm or rice spirit which is often incorporated into highly potent local cocktails.

Communications

Mail services in Bali and Lombok are reasonably efficient, with at least one post office in every town. The phone network however is patchy – oversubscribed in some areas, non-existent in others – though most major tourist resorts now have plenty of internet centres.

Mail

Every town and tourist centre on Bali and Lombok has a **General Post Office** (*kantor pos*) where you can buy stamps (*perangko*) and aerogrammes (*surat udara*), and can post letters (*surat*) and parcels (*paket*) and, in some cases, collect poste restante, send faxes and use the internet. All *kantor pos* keep official government office hours (Mon–Thurs 8am–2pm, Fri 8–11am, Sat 8am–12.30pm; closed on festival days and public holidays), except where otherwise stated in the guide. In larger towns and resorts you can also buy stamps and send letters and parcels from **postal agents**, who charge official rates but often open longer hours than the *kantor pos*. Post boxes (*kotak surat*) are square and orangey-red in colour, but they aren't that numerous, so you're usually better off posting letters at GPOs or postal agents. Postage is expensive, with the current rates for **airmail postcards and letters** under 200g as follows: Australia Rp4000, New Zealand Rp5000, Europe Rp6000, Canada Rp6500 and USA Rp7500. Airmail post takes about a week, while a local letter to anywhere in Bali or Lombok takes three to five days.

Kantor pos generally don't offer a **parcel-packing service**, but there's normally a stall next door where you pay to have your stuff parcelled up – don't bother packing it yourself as the contents need to be inspected before they're allowed to travel. Postal rates for parcels are also high: a parcel weighing up to 500g costs Rp90,000 to be airmailed to Europe and takes about three weeks; a 6–10kg parcel sent by sea costs Rp530,000 and could take up to three months. A parcel of 1 to 1.5kg to Australia costs Rp170,000 by airmail or Rp120,000 by sea. *Kantor pos* won't handle any parcels over 10kg, so if you want to send a large load abroad, or anything that's particularly valuable or fragile, you're best off using the services offered by the major galleries and craft shops, who will pack everything carefully and insure it as well.

Poste restante

Most *kantor pos* in major towns and resort areas offer a **poste restante** service, and in certain cases the poste restante counter is open for longer hours than the rest of the post office – details are given throughout the guide. On the whole, the poste restante system is pretty informal: letters are held for a maximum of one month and are kept in an alphabetically segregated box through which you can rifle without showing ID. Letters should be filed by family name, but mistakes do happen, so check under first-name initials as well. Some *kantor pos* ask you to sign a book when you remove mail (all of them do so for parcels and registered mail), but you're unlikely to have to pay anything for the service. Denpasar's poste restante is inconveniently located at the GPO in the southern suburb of Renon, but Kuta, Ubud, Sanur, Candi Dasa, Lovina, Singaraja, Mataram and Senggigi all have central ones – addresses are given in the guide. **American Express** also offers a limited poste restante service to its customers (Amex credit card holders and anyone in possession of Amex travellers' cheques), but this is only available at their Sanur office (see p.169), and they will only hold mail for up to one month.

Phones

Phone services in Bali and Lombok are still in their infancy. Some places, like Amed, have no phone lines at all, while others, like Pemuteran and even Ubud, have far too few to cope with demand. Although you'll find public phones in a few major centres (Kuta, Denpasar, Ubud), most phoning is done through the government-run **phone offices** – the main *kantor telkom* and the branch *wartel telkom* – or through the private "telephone shops" known simply as **wartel**. *Kantor telkom* (often open 24hr) and *wartel telkom* (usually 7am–midnight) generally have several coin-operated phones (*telepon umum*) and card phones (*telepon umum kartu*) as well as a few booths for making **IDD** (International Direct Dial) and collect (reverse-charge) calls. Wartel keep similarly long hours, but don't have coin-operated or card phones.

The **rates** at the official *telkom* outlets are standardized throughout Indonesia, but privately run wartel sometimes charge inflated prices. A ten percent tax is added to all calls made through *kantor telkom* and wartel. It's also possible to make calls from hotels, but you should confirm the price with them beforehand as it's usually extremely expensive.

Phone cards (*kartu telepon*) are sold in units of between 20 and 680 and are available at *kantor telkom* and in some wartel, postal agents and money-exchange booths. There are now several types of phone card – and two types of card phone – which can make using them very frustrating; if possible check out the phone before you buy the card, but if you get stuck with mismatching card and phone, head for the nearest large hotel, which will usually have both types of card phone in the lobby. Phonebooks are scarce, so to find a local number you might be better off calling directory enquiries or the operator.

You can send domestic and international **faxes** (*fax*) from most *kantor telkom*, *wartel telkom* and wartel, for approximately Rp15,000 per page (to Europe or the US). Many wartel will also receive faxes for you, for which they charge a small fee.

Useful numbers and codes

International operator ☏101
International directory enquiries
☏102
Domestic operator ☏100
Local directory enquiries ☏108
Long-distance directory enquiries
☏106
Police ☏110
Ambulance ☏118
Fire service ☏113

Phoning home

Dial ☏001 or ☏008 + IDD country
code + area code (minus its initial zero
if applicable) + local number. IDD rates
shown are for the standard period;
there's a 20-percent surcharge if calling during the weekday peak period,
and a 25-percent discount during
weekday off-peak periods, at weekends and on national holidays.
Australia Country code ☏61. IDD rate:
Rp8300/min (peak 9am–noon, off-peak
10pm–6am).
Ireland Country code ☏353. IDD rate:

Rp7150/min (peak 2–5pm, off-peak
3–11am).
New Zealand Country code ☏64. IDD
rate: Rp8300/min (peak 9am–noon, off-
peak 11pm–7am).
UK Country code ☏44. IDD rate:
Rp9400/min (peak 2–5pm, off-peak
3–11am).
US and Canada Country code ☏1.
IDD rate: Rp8300/min (peak
9am–noon, off-peak 11pm–7am).

Calling Bali and Lombok from abroad

Dial your international access code
(☏00 from the UK, Ireland and New
Zealand, ☏011 from the US and
Canada, ☏0011 from Australia) + **62**
for Indonesia + area code minus its initial zero + local number.

Time difference

Bali and Lombok are on Central
Indonesian Time (GMT+8, North
American EST+13, Australian EST-2).

Local, long-distance and mobile calls

A **local call** (*panggilan lokal*) is a call to any
destination that shares the same area code,
and for these you can use a coin-operated
phone, a card phone or a wartel phone.
Local calls should cost Rp180 per minute,
though hotels often charge up to Rp1000 a
minute. Some coin-operated phones still
take only the old-style Rp50 and Rp100
coins, and in most cases you put the coins in
only after the person you're calling has
picked up the phone and started to speak.
Card phones work in the same way as they
do elsewhere in the world.

Long-distance calls (*panggilan inter-lokal*),
to any destination within Indonesia that has a
different area code, can be made either at a
card phone or at any *kantor telkom* or *wartel* –
coin-operated phones don't work for long-
distance calls. Bali is divided into several code
zones while Lombok has two codes.

Calls to **mobile phones** are more expensive. Any phone number prefaced by the following code is a mobile: ☏0811; ☏0812;
☏0816; ☏0818; ☏082; ☏0828. Some

hotels and other businesses have to rely on
satellite phones (code ☏086812), which
are even costlier to call.

International calls

You can make **international calls** (*panggilan internasional*) from certain card phones,
located in major hotel lobbies and at the airport, and on special **IDD** (International Direct
Dial) phones at the *kantor telkom* and
wartel, as well as through hotel switch-
boards. Some *kantor telkom* and wartel will
also let you make **reverse-charge calls**
(collect calls) for a nominal fee.

Two phone companies provide **IDD service**: Indosat, for which you dial ☏001, and
Satelindo, accessed by ☏008. Both charge
identical rates, fixed by the government, and
use identical time bands for identical discounts, so it doesn't matter which you
choose. See box for rates. The cheapest
place to make an international call is the
kantor telkom or on a card phone, where
you're guaranteed to be charged at the
basic rate; privately run wartel always add

ten percent tax, and may add quite a bit extra too, so check first.

Home Country Direct (HCD) allows you to reach the operator in your home country, although calls end up being more expensive than dialling direct. It's available on all IDD phones as well as on certain others that have the HCD logo, such as those at Ngurah Rai Airport. You can't use cash for HCD calls, only credit cards, or make reverse-charge (collect) calls. On HCD phones you just press the designated button to reach your home-country operator; on IDD phones you need to dial ☏001-801 or ☏008-801, and then the special HCD code to reach your home-country operator: Australia ☏61, Canada ☏16, Ireland ☏353, New Zealand ☏64, UK ☏44, US ☏10.

You can in theory use BT, AT&T, MCI and other **phone chargecards** (purchased at home) to make international calls through the IDD card phones in hotel lobbies and at the airport. In practice, you may experience some difficulty getting through to the right number.

Mobile phones

If you want to use your own **mobile phone**, you'll need to check with your phone provider in advance whether it will work in Bali and Lombok. Most **UK**, **Australian** and **New Zealand** mobiles use GSM technology, which works fine in parts of Indonesia, but you'll have to inform your phone provider before leaving home in order to get international access, or "roaming", switched on. This may incur a charge. Call charges will also be different: you're likely to be charged extra for incoming calls, and there may be different price brackets for calling to an Indonesian landline, back home, and globally, as well as varying peak and off-peak times. If you want to retrieve messages while you're away, you'll have to ask your provider for a new international access code, but texting usually works as normal. Unless a **US** or **Canadian** phone is a special triband handset it probably won't work in Indonesia; check with your provider. ⊛www.gsmworld.com has full details.

The alternative is to **rent an Indonesian mobile** (*handphone*) in Bali through Bali Discovery Tours, from $5 per day (☏0361/ 286283, ⊛www.balidiscovery.com/phones).

Email and internet access

Internet access is becoming increasingly widespread on **Bali**, and there are now hundreds of tourist-friendly internet offices and cybercafés in Kuta–Legian–Seminyak, Sanur, Ubud, Lovina and Candi Dasa plus at least one in Denpasar, Tanjung Benoa and Singaraja, one at Ngurah Rai Airport, one in Toya Bungkah and one likely to appear in Nusa Lembongan; see the relevant accounts for exact locations. Due to poor-quality phone lines, Pemuteran is still an internet black hole, and Amed has no phone lines at all. On **Lombok**, there are internet facilities in Mataram, Senggigi and Kuta, as well as on all three Gili islands. All the above offer internet access as well as email services, and most charge Rp300–500 per minute online, though some charge per fifteen-minute period. Big hotels usually charge very inflated rates.

Before leaving home, check whether your existing **email account** offers a web-mail service that enables you to pick up your email from any internet terminal. Otherwise, you can set yourself up with a **free email account**, either before you leave home or in a cybercafé in Bali or Lombok. Thousands of companies offer this service, the most popular being Hotmail (⊛www.hotmail.com) and Yahoo (⊛www.yahoo.com). Every cybercafé in Bali and Lombok will have them bookmarked for speedy access.

If you plan to email from your **laptop** in Bali and Lombok, be advised that very few losmen have phone sockets in the room. The usual phone plug in Indonesia is the US standard RJ11; see ⊛www.kropla.com for detailed advice on how to set up your modem before you go, and how to hardwire phone plugs where necessary. To become a temporary subscriber to a **local ISP**, visit ⊛www.baliguide.com/net.html for reviews, prices and links. This site also links to the public ISP Telkom at ⊛plasa.com/instan/ein-dex.html, which requires no registation or fee: you simply dial ☏0809/89999 from your laptop, key the username "telkomnet@instan" and the password "telkom", and you're online. This service should cost Rp150/min, but check with the hotel first as some add surcharges or bar ☏0809 numbers.

The media

Since the ousting of Suharto in 1998 and subsequent democratic elections, the Indonesian mass media has found a confident and opinionated voice, publishing and broadcasting critical coverage of political issues.

Newspapers and magazines

Most Balinese **newspaper** readers buy the *Bali Post*, a daily Indonesian-language publication focusing on Bali and Nusa Tenggara, but also summarizing news from Jakarta and around the world. For non-Indonesian speakers, it's chiefly of interest for the cinema schedules. Indonesia's major **English-language daily**, *The Jakarta Post* (ⓦwww .thejakartapost.com), is hardly a riveting read, but it does cover Indonesian news and runs major international news agency pieces, as well as British football results. It's not that widely available on Bali and Lombok, but can be bought from hawkers and from some bookstores and minimarkets in all the major tourist centres; the published price is Rp4000 but hawkers and some shops charge as much as they can get away with. The local, tabloid-sized English-language newspaper *Bali Sun* is a much smaller venture but can be a more interesting read, if you can find it. It's published in Sanur (Mon–Fri), costs Rp2500 and is sold in a few minimarkets and supermarkets in Sanur and Kuta–Legian–Seminyak. It covers Bali news, national and international headline stories, and contains some tourist information as well. You'll find the best domestic and international news coverage in the weekly **magazine** *Tempo* (ⓦwww.tempointeractive.com), published in both Indonesian and English versions, but not widely distributed on Bali or Lombok. The best cultural read is the locally produced *Latitudes* (Rp20,000), a glossy and well-written English-language monthly magazine which looks at contemporay Indonesian society.

Bali and Lombok have numerous **free publications** aimed at tourists, including several large-format glossy magazines, published monthly and mostly available in the bigger hotels. Two recommended examples are *Hello Bali* and *Bali Tribune*, both of which carry well-written pieces on the culture of the islands and include travel articles, restaurant reviews, inspirational photographs plus tourist-oriented ads. Less glamorous-looking, but packed with similarly thought-provoking pieces, is the free, full-colour, tabloid monthly newspaper *Bali and Beyond* (ⓦwww.baliandbeyond.co.id).

There are several free **what's on** magazines too, notably the fortnightly *the beat*, which focuses on Bali's nightlife and carries listings for gigs, parties and clubs; the free monthly pamphlet *Bali Plus*, which always includes a good list of the month's festivals and dance performances; and the fortnightly glossy newspaper *Bali Travel News* (ⓦwww.bali-travelnews.com) which lists upcoming temple festivals and films showing at Denpasar's cinema, as well as running features on tourist attractions.

It's pretty easy, if costly, to get hold of **international English-language publications** in Kuta, Sanur and Ubud, but you won't find them on sale in any of the more remote areas, including Lombok (though you can read them at some of Lombok's top-notch hotels). The most popular newspapers hawked around Kuta every evening are that day's *Sydney Morning Herald*, along with the previous day's *International Herald Tribune* and *USA Today*. You'll also see *Time* and *Newsweek* fairly regularly.

TV and radio

The government-operated **TV** station, Televisi Republik Indonesia (TVRI) shows a mixture of soaps and melodramas, light entertainment shows from the US, news and international sport (Italian and British football get the most air time). Headline news and weather reports are given in English at 7.30pm every day. Most hotels also have satellite TV, which includes CNN, TV Australia and sometimes BBC World.

The main **radio** station is also government-run: Radio Republik Indonesia (RRI) broadcasts music, chat and news programmes 24 hours a day on 88.5 FM and 95 FM, with occasional English-language news bulletins. More youthful Balinese stations include the commercial Indonesian pop music station, Hot FM (93.5 FM), and the Kuta-based Top FM (89.7 FM), which plays mainly easy-listening music, interspersed with some English-language programmes, including a Sunday morning feature on Balinese culture and the US Top Forty on Sunday afternoons. Paradise FM (100.9 FM) is a Bali-based English-language station aimed at tourists, broadcasting music and tourist-oriented features daily from 8am to 7pm, with international news bulletins at 8am and 9am.

You should be able to pick up international stations such as the BBC World Service (ⓦ www.bbc.co.uk), the Voice of America (ⓦ www.voa.gov) and Radio Australia (ⓦ www.abc.net.au/ra) on a variety of **short-wave** frequencies. Broadcast times and wavelengths can change, so get hold of a schedule just before you travel. All these and more also broadcast **online** – individual programmes and/or live audio streaming. The *Rough Guide to Internet Radio* has full details.

Opening hours, holidays and festivals

Opening hours are not straightforward in Bali and Lombok, with government offices, post offices, businesses and shops setting their own timetables.

Generally speaking, **businesses** such as airline offices open at least Mon–Fri 8am–4pm, Sat 8am–noon, but have variable arrangements at lunchtime. **Banking hours** are generally Mon–Fri 8am–noon, Sat 8–11am, but foreign exchange counters may have shorter hours than this. Moneychangers in tourist areas usually keep shop rather than bank hours. Most **airline offices** open Mon–Fri 8.30am–5pm, Sat 8.30am–noon, although some close for lunch around noon or 12.30pm. **Post offices** operate roughly Mon–Thurs 8am–2pm, Fri 8–11am, Sat 8am–12.30pm, with considerable variations from office to office; main offices keep considerably longer hours although post restante counters may have different opening times. Postal agents in tourist areas tend to keep later hours. In tourist areas, **shops** open from around 10am until 8pm or later, but local shops in towns and villages tend to open and shut much earlier. **Markets** start soon after dawn and most of the business is usually completed by 10am.

Government offices are open Mon–Thurs 7am–3pm, Fri 7.30am–noon; you'll be most successful if you turn up between 8am and 11.30am. Official government hours shorten during Ramadan, usually opening an hour later in the morning; the best advice is to ring offices at that time to check before you make a long journey.

National public holidays

Most of the **national public holidays** fall on different dates of the Western calendar each year, as they're calculated according to the alternative Muslim and Balinese calendars. For fuller details, see the accounts following.

In addition to national public holidays celebrated throughout Indonesia, there are frequent **religious festivals** occurring throughout the Muslim, Hindu and Chinese communities. Each of Bali's 20,000 temples also has an anniversary celebration once every wuku year, or 210 days (see box on p.57), local communities host elaborate **marriage** and **cremation** celebrations, and both islands have their own particular **secular** holidays. Your visit is bound to coincide with a festival of one kind or another, and probably several.

National public holidays

Jan 1 – New Year's Day (Tahun Baru).
Feb – Idul Adha (Hajh), the Muslim celebration of the end of the Mecca pilgrimage.
Feb/March – 1st of Muharram, the Muslim New Year.
March/April – Good Friday and Easter Sunday.
May – Maulud Nabi Muhammad, anniversary of the birth of the Prophet.
May/June – Ascension Day.

May/June – Waisak Day, anniversary of the birth, death and enlightenment of Buddha.
Aug 17 – Independence Day (Hari Proklamasi Kemerdekaan).
Sept – Al Miraj, commemorating Muhammad's visit to heaven.
Nov/Dec – Idul Fitri, celebration of the end of Ramadan.
Dec 25 – Christmas Day.

Muslim festivals

All **Muslim festivals**, based on a lunar calendar, move backwards through the seasons, falling earlier according to the Western calendar by eleven days each year. However, dates for festivals are very approximate (and could vary from those we've published by a day or two), since each holiday is announced only when the moon has been seen clearly by an authorized cleric.

The ninth Muslim month is **Ramadan**, a month of fasting during daylight hours. It is much more apparent on Muslim Lombok than on Hindu Bali. Followers of the Wetu Telu branch of Islam on Lombok (see p.514) observe their own three-day festival of **Puasa** rather than the full month. Many Muslim restaurants, although not tourist establishments, shut down during the day so it can be hard to get a meal and, especially in central and eastern parts of Lombok, you should not eat, drink or smoke in public at this time. **Idul Fitri**, also called Hari Raya or Lebaran, the first day of the tenth month of the Muslim calendar, marks the end of Ramadan and is a two-day national holiday of noisy celebrations.

Idul Adha (Feb 12, 2003; Feb 2, 2004) commemorates Ibrahim's willingness to sacrifice his son Ishmael at God's command (given as Abraham and Isaac in the Old Testament), and is marked by the cleaning and tidying of cemeteries and by animal sacrifice. The **Muslim New Year**, the first day of

the month of Muharram (March 5, 2003; Feb 23, 2004), is followed by **Maulud Nabi Muhammad**, the celebration of the birthday of the Prophet (May 14, 2003; May 3, 2004), with festivities lasting throughout the following month. **Al Miraj** (Sept 20, 2003; Sept 9, 2004) celebrates Muhammad's visit to Allah and his return to earth with instructions for the faithful. This is the origin of the Muslim injunction to pray five times a day.

Balinese festivals

As well as the national public holidays, Bali has its own extra holidays. **Galungan** is an annual event in the wuku calendar, which means it takes place every 210 days. This ten-day festival celebrates the victory of good over evil and all the ancestral gods are thought to come down to earth to take part. Elaborate preparations take place: penjor – bamboo poles hung with offerings – arch over the road, offerings are prepared and animals slaughtered for the feasts. Galungan day itself is spent with the family, praying and making offerings. The following day, Manis Galungan, is the day for visiting friends. The final and most important day is **Kuningan**, when families once again get together, pray and make offerings as the souls of the ancestors return to heaven.

The major festival of the saka year is New Year, **Nyepi**, in March or April (April 2, 2003; later years to be announced), the major purification ritual of the year. The days before Nyepi are full of activity: religious objects are

Ramadan begins Nov 6, 2002; Oct 27, 2003; Oct 15, 2004.
Idul Fitri Dec 7, 2002; Nov 26, 2003; Nov 15, 2004.

Traditional calendars

There are two **traditional calendars** in Bali in addition to the Western (or Gregorian) calendar.

The Hindu **saka** calendar operates with years comprising 354–356 days, is divided into twelve months, and runs eighty years behind the Gregorian year: 2003 is 1923 in the saka calendar.

Also in use is the **wuku**, pawukon or uku calendar, based on a 210-day lunar cycle; these cycles are unnumbered. The wuku calendar is magnificently complex, as the 210 days are divided into weeks that are ten days long, nine days long, eight days long and so on down to weeks that are one day long. All of these weeks run concurrently and have specific names – for example, the three-day week is called Triwara, the five-day week Pancawara – and each day of each week has a specific name. This means that every day has a total of ten names, one from each of the weeks. To add to the complexity, each of the 30 seven-day weeks has its own name. You may come across the names of the days of the three-day week, Paseh, Beteng and Kajeng, as they are often used for markets which operate on a three-day cycle. You can buy tika calendars to keep track of all of this, but the different systems won't affect most visitors: they're used chiefly to determine festival dates and other auspicious days.

taken in procession from temples to sacred springs or to the sea for purification. Sacrifices are made and displayed at crossroads where evil spirits are thought to linger, to lure them into the open. The night before Nyepi is hugely exciting as the spirits are frightened away with drums, gongs, cymbals, firecrackers and huge papier-mâché monsters. On the day itself, everyone sits quietly at home to persuade any remaining evil spirits that Bali is completely deserted. No flights, except emergency medical ones, land or take off from Ngurah Rai Airport on that day and all visitors are expected to stay quietly in their hotels.

Local temple festivals may be celebrated according to wuku or saka calendars. The Bali government tourism office puts out a free comprehensive **calendar of events** booklet with colour photographs which gives you full details for the whole year. Also keep an eye on the tourist newspapers, which publish up-to-date lists.

Every temple has its annual **odalan**, an anniversary and purification ceremony which lasts about three days. The majority of these are small, local affairs, but the celebrations at the large directional temples draw large crowds (see p.510). There are also local temple festivals related to the moon, some associated with full moon and some with the night of complete darkness.

Another annual event, **Saraswati**, in honour of the goddess (see p.505), takes place on the last day of the wuku year. Books are particularly venerated and the faithful are not supposed to read, while students attend special ceremonies to pray for academic success.

Non-religious anniversaries that are celebrated in Bali include April 21, **Kartini Day**, commemorating the birthday in 1879 of Raden Ajeng Kartini, an early Indonesian nationalist and the first female emancipationist. Parades, lectures and social events are attended by women, while the men and children take over their duties for the day. September 20, the anniversary of the **Badung puputan** in Denpasar in 1906 (see p.95), is commemorated each year by a fair in Puputan Square. November 20 is **Heroes Day** in Bali, in remembrance of the defeat of the Nationalist forces led by Ngurah Rai at Marga in 1946 (see p.498). The annual **Arts Festival** is a huge celebration of all Balinese arts held at the Taman Budaya Arts Centre in Denpasar (see p.100); it usually takes place in June and July. Also watch out for **surfing championships** in

Galungan Nov 20, 2002; June 18, 2003; Jan 14 & Aug 11, 2004.
Kuningan Nov 30, 2002; June 28, 2003; Jan 24 & Aug 21, 2004.

Kuta: some are annual Balinese events, while others draw competitors from a wider area.

Lombok festivals

For **Lombok festivals**, consult the useful tourist office *Calendar of Events, West Nusa Tenggara*. **Ciwaratri** (in Jan) is celebrated by Hindus in West Lombok, where followers meditate without sleeping or eating for 24 hours to redeem their sins. **Nyale** (see p.473) takes place annually in February or March and is celebrated in certain villages along the south coast when thousands of people flock to witness the first appearance of the sea worms. **Lebaran Topat** occurs seven days after Ramadan, when Sasak people visit family graves and the grave of Loang Baloq at Batu Layar, 10km north of Mataram. **Harvest festival** is celebrated by Balinese Hindus in March/April at Gunung Pengsong, when they give thanks for the harvest by the ritual slaughter of a buffalo.

The **Anniversary of West Lombok**, a formal government event, takes place on April 17.

At the end of the year comes **Perang Topat**, celebrated at Pura Lingsar. Offerings are made here from October through to December, at the beginning of the rainy season, by Hindus and adherents of Wetu Telu to bring rain or give thanks for it. Also at this time, offerings are made at the crater lake of Segara Anak to ask for blessings, known as **Pekelem**, and the **Pujawali** celebration is held at Pura Kalasa temple at Narmada, at Pura Lingsar and at Pura Meru in Cakranegara. December 17 marks the anniversary of the political **founding of West Nusa Tenggara**. Finally, **Chinese New Year** (Imlek) is not an official holiday, but sees many Chinese-run businesses closing for two days in January or February.

The Balinese population in the west of the island celebrate the Balinese festivals described above; their temples all have their own *odalan* celebration.

Entertainment and sport

For the Balinese, leisure-time entertainment has traditionally been associated with religious festivals and ceremonies and, despite the new hi-tech distractions of discos, cinemas and TV, temple events still take up an enormous amount of time and energy. Such occasions are seen as enjoyable rather than a chore, and tourists are welcome to attend. A major feature of temple ceremonies has always been the performance of sacred dances to the accompaniment of the village gamelan orchestras – entertainments which have in the last few decades transcended the sacred/secular divide and are now also staged for tourists all over the island.

Traditional secular entertainment formerly revolved around gambling, a practice which consumed so many people's fortunes that the Indonesian government banned it in 1981. **Cockfighting** is the one sport to have survived this clampdown, and betting still continues on other sports, notably **cricket fighting** (for far smaller stakes), which now takes place only in very clandestine arenas. As a tourist you'd be lucky indeed to see a cricket fight, but the Bali

Museum in Denpasar does house an interesting collection of paraphernalia used in the sport. Wagers are also an integral part of the island's **buffalo races**, but this is considered acceptable as they're held only twice a year: in Negara, west Bali every dry season (usually once in August and then again between September and November), described on p.390; and more tourist-oriented buffalo races are held at least once a week all year round in Lovina (see box on p.360). Indonesia's national sports are badminton and football.

Dance and music

If you have any more than a passing interest in the traditional **dance and music** of Bali, you should head for Ubud, where up to five different performances are staged every night of the week for the benefit of tourists (see p.221). This is also the place to take lessons in the performing arts. Ubud and its neighbouring villages have long had a reputation for their superb dance troupes and **gamelan orchestras**, and villagers now supplement their incomes by doing regular shows in the traditional settings of temple courtyards and village compounds. None is exactly authentic, as most comprise a medley of extracts and highlights from the more dramatic temple dances, but the quality is generally high and spectators are given English-language synopses to help them fathom out what everything means. For an introduction to the major themes and styles of Balinese dance and music, see p.515.

Less taxing performances are put on for diners at numerous Sanur, Lovina and Candi Dasa restaurants and in Nusa Dua. If you go to an Ubud show, expect to **pay** Rp25,000, though be warned that tours to the same events booked through agents in Kuta and Sanur will cost at least three times as much, including return transport. If you're keen to see wholly authentic performances, then you'll need to find out about imminent temple festivals and, if you can't get to the festival itself, at least hang around at the rehearsals, most of which take place in the local *banjar* after sundown; you'll probably be welcome to watch so long as you don't distract the players.

Cockfights

Despite being banned by the Indonesian government in 1981, **cockfights** are still an extremely popular pastime in Bali, where a legal loophole allows the staging of cockfights for religious, but not entertainment, purposes. Because certain Hindu rituals require the shedding of fresh sacrificial blood to placate the most volatile of the evil *bhuta* and *kala* spirits, every temple's purification ceremony is prefaced by a cockfight, but these are far from solemn occasions, attracting massive crowds and even larger bets. Whatever your feelings about the ethics of cockfighting, these events are important occasions in Balinese life. If you're interested, ask at your losmen to find out where and when to go. Providing you wear suitable temple dress (see p.73) and can stand the gore, tourists are quite welcome to attend.

The cult of the fighting cock is so pervasive in Bali that you'll see men of all ages and incomes caressing and preening their birds in public, often gathering in groups to show them off and weigh up their rivals. When not being pampered, the birds spend their days in individual bell-shaped bamboo baskets, which are usually placed in quite noisy public places – by the side of the main drag for example – so that the bird won't be scared or distracted when it finally makes it to the ring. Prize cocks can earn their owners sizeable sums of money, and a certain status too, but despite all this the men seem remarkably unsentimental about their animals – a dead bird is a financial rather than an emotional loss.

Fights generally take place in the special cock-fighting pavilion, or *wantilan,* of the appropriate temple – an open-sided structure with a dirt floor and room for a hundred or so spectators to squeeze around the central clearing. Complicated **rules** written on ancient manuscripts govern this and every other aspect of cockfighting: there are regulations about days on which fights may take place, and a detailed classification system under which the birds are categorized according to their colour and markings, as well as height and weight. The rules and the subsequent selection of a fighting partner are the subject of a great deal of pre-fight discussion.

When a suitable opponent is finally found, the **betting** begins. The owners of each bird agree on a sum and both contribute the same amount to a central fund – this is rarely less than Rp150,000, and sometimes rises to as much as Rp1,000,000, a sum that comes mainly from the owner's pocket, but is supplemented by friends and other backers. Spectators then set their own bets among themselves.

Before the **fight**, a lethal 11–15cm long blade, or *taji*, is attached to the left ankle of each bird. Both are then released in the centre of the ring, and the competition starts. The *taji* is considered a sacred weapon and cockfights are meant to be won and lost by skilful use of the *taji*, not just by brutish pecking. Fights last for a maximum of five rounds, and the winning bird is the cock who remains standing the longest – even if he drops dead soon after. The owner of the winning cock gets the body of the losing bird plus his opponent's share of the central fund.

Outdoor activities

The sea and the mountains are the two great focuses of outdoor activities in Bali and Lombok. Bali, in particular, is renowned for its world-class surf breaks, and both islands offer some excellent diving off their shores, as well as some spectacular hikes up volcanoes.

Surfing

Bali's volcanic reef-fringed coastline has made this island one of the great **surfing** meccas of the world, and its reputation for producing an unusually high number of perfect and consistent tubes makes it particularly appealing. The tropical climate means that the water is nearly always warm enough to endure without a wetsuit and, although there are two distinct seasons, you can still surf all year round by switching to the other coast. The **best breaks** are concentrated in the south of the island, where the swell from the mighty Indian Ocean gets a chance to build up into massive waves, some of them regularly topping five metres. With this kind of challenge, Bali's breaks are a great draw for advanced surfers, but there are also plenty of gentler beach breaks, which are ideal for beginners.

From April through to October, the southeast trade winds blow offshore, fanning the waves off Bali's southwest coast (Uluwatu, Kuta, Legian) and off Nusa Lembongan, and making this both the best time of year for surf, and the pleasantest, as it's also the dry season. Breaks get very crowded during this time, particularly from June to August. From November to March, the winds blow from the northwest, bringing rain to Bali's main beach breaks, though the lesser breaks off eastern Bali (Sanur, Nusa Dua)

are still surfable at this time of year. The Balinese have been surfing since the 1930s, and from the 1970s on have become quite serious about the sport: there are now regular **competitions** on the island, and a distinctively fluid Balinese style of surfing has evolved.

As for **Lombok**, readers of Australia's *Tracks* magazine voted Desert Point as their top surfspot in the world. Other breaks in Lombok pale in comparison, and are generally not as interesting as Bali's waves either, but there are a few worth attempting around Kuta on the south coast: see p.122 for a rundown.

Information and contacts

For the best low-down on the **surfing scene** in Bali, head for Kuta (see p.121), where you'll find the biggest choice of surf shops, as well the surfers' bars *Tubes* and *All Stars Surf Café*, monthly tide charts and plenty of other surfers to compare notes with.

Details of all the best surf spots in Bali and Lombok are given in the relevant sections of the guide, but serious surfers would do well to consult the **book** *Indo Surf and Lingo*, available from Ⓦwww.indosurf.com.au in a full version for A\$29.95 or US\$19.95, or an emailed facts-only version for A\$19.95 or US\$9.95. You can also buy it from surf shops

△ Washing the salt off after swimming, Kuta, Bali

Top surf breaks

Bali

Bingin p.138. Reliable, short left-hand tubes.

Canggu p.122. Three decent breaks and fine landward views.

Kuta–Legian p.122. Good for the less confident.

Medewi p.389. Light current that's nice for beginners.

Nusa Dua p.153. Large peaks, long walls and juicy tubes.

Nusa Lembongan p.276. Six great breaks, not as crowded as some others.

Padang Padang p.138. Very challenging, and very famous.

Uluwatu p.138. Famous set of five left-hand breaks.

Lombok

Desert Point p.432. Fabulous, world-famous fast left-hander.

and bookshops in Bali. It includes detailed descriptions of all surf spots in Bali, Lombok and the rest of Indonesia, and the website has reports, news and info. Other good surf **websites** include ⑩ www.baliwaves.com, which carries a report on the current state of Bali's waves (updated several times a week) and also features stories, links, and details on surfing tours; and ⑩ www .surftravelonline.com, which has a gallery of sensational photos. The monthly **magazine** *Surf Time* is all about the Indonesian surfing scene, available free from most Kuta surf shops.

Lessons and tours

A couple of places in Kuta give **surfing lessons** for about $35 per half-day; see p.121 for details.

Several travel agents in Bali organize **surfing tours** to the awesome breaks off Sumbawa, Java, Lombok and West Timor, as well as to the fabulous G-Land off East Java, said to be the world's longest left-hand reef break and one of the top spots on the international surfing circuit. Most of these "surfaris" last about a week, and prices, which include boat transport, accommodation and food, cost around US$200–350 for four days and US$275–425 for a week, depending on the destination. See p.122 for details and websites of the Kuta agents, and p.276 for the Nusa Lembongan agent. The website ⑩ www.baliwaves.com also has some useful links to surf-tour operators.

Equipment

You'll find dozens of surf shops in Kuta (Bali) selling **equipment** – boards, spare fins and leashes and surfwear from all the top brands, including Quicksilver, Billabong, Rip Curl, Stussy, Spyderbilt, Volcom and Rusty. Brand-new surfboards in Bali cost about US$700 – twice as much as in Australia – but you can also rent boards for about Rp35,000 per day on Kuta beach, and from the Balinese surfers who hang out at the other major breaks. A two-metre board is the best for beach breaks and most reefs, though for the biggest waves you'll need one that's at least 2.1m as well. Bring reef shoes for the coral, a helmet for the reef breaks and an emergency ding-repair kit, though you'll be able to get repairs done in Kuta and at some of the other big surf beaches as well.

Most **airlines** will take boards in the hold for free so long as your total luggage weight doesn't exceed 20kg – just make sure you label them clearly and put them in well-padded **board bags** (board bags with straps are a good idea as a number of the best breaks are accessible by motorbike only). Some airlines demand compulsory insurance for your board when you check in, so it's worth calling the airline in advance. Some **tourist shuttle buses** on Bali and Lombok refuse to carry boards, though Perama buses will take them for an extra Rp6000 per board. Bemo drivers are similarly unaccommodating – so you're probably best off **renting a car** or a motorbike to get to the breaks. In Kuta, it's fairly easy to rent **motorbikes** with special surfboard clips already attached.

Surfer speak for beginners

Surfing is such a major pastime in Bali that even non-surfers might find themselves engaged in a conversation that's peppered with surfing jargon. For the uninitiated and the curious, here's a guide to some of the most common terms.

Barrel Same as a tube.

Beach break Waves that break on a sandbar right on the shore; the easiest ones to surf.

Closed out A wave that's not worth surfing because it's too dangerous or too broken, probably because the wind's blowing onshore.

Ding Hole in the board.

Dropping in Taking off on someone else's wave – considered very out of order.

Glass Perfect waves which are neither broken nor have too much white water.

Green room Same as a tube.

Kook Hopeless surfer (named after the noise the Australian bird the kookaburra makes).

Left-handers/lefts Waves which break to the surfer's left (to your right if you're watching from the shore); many surfers have a strong preference for either lefts or rights.

Offshore winds Winds that blow across the land and out to sea pitch the waves up and make them good for surfing.

Onshore winds Winds that blow in from the sea and on to the land tend to cause broken waves and white water which are frustrating and sometimes dangerous to surf.

Pipe Same as a tube.

Radical Classy waves or surfing style and action.

Reef break Waves that break over a coral reef are more difficult and more dangerous to surf.

Right-handers/rights Waves which break to the surfer's right (to your left if you're watching from the shore).

Rip tides Dangerous meeting of two tides which pull surfers and swimmers way out to sea; experienced surfers use them to get behind distant waves.

Shut down Same as closed out.

Sneaker sets Surfable waves that appear from nowhere without warning.

Stoked To have had a brilliant session in the water.

Three-sixty Doing a complete 360° turn on the wave.

Tube The hollow barrel-like shape within a breaking wave which you can fit right inside – the type of wave that every surfer dreams about.

Walling Surfing the face of the wave.

Health and safety

Bali's shoreline is notorious for its extreme currents and **rip tides** – both of which can make surfing quite hazardous – and for its reefs. Ask the lifeguards to point out where the rip tides are if you can't tell from the shore, and if you do get caught in one, stay calm and paddle sideways across the rip to get out of it; never try to paddle straight in or out of it. The beaches at both Kuta and Sanur have several **surfers' lifeguard posts**, but at the other breaks you'll have to rely on help from other surfers if you get into trouble.

Be sure to wash your **coral cuts** every night with a good disinfectant, and to remove sea urchin spines without breaking them: uri-nating on the wound is supposed to help alleviate swelling. **Sunburn** and **heatstroke** are very real problems when you're out on the waves in the heat of the tropical sun: sunblock is essential, and most surfers wear a rash-vest as well. It's also advisable to bone up on your first-aid knowledge, especially mouth-to-mouth resuscitation techniques, which can be life-saving if someone's been knocked out on a remote break. For general health considerations and details on health care in Bali and Lombok, see p.27.

Diving and snorkelling

Bali and Lombok are encircled by reefs, which not only make for excellent year-round **diving and snorkelling**, but also mean that

Top dives

Bali

Amed p.307. Huge variety and extent of coral, some of the best in Bali. Plenty of reef fish too. Wall dives down to about 43m; visibility up to 20m.

Candi Dasa p.286. Highlights include an underwater canyon (32m) and steep wall dives. Oceanic sunfish also spotted here sometimes. Currents can be strong.

Menjangan Island (Deer Island) p.401. Opinions vary on the state of the reefs, but it seems to depend on which parts you explore. Some areas, in particular the shallower flats, have been either killed by crown-of-thorns starfish or bleached as a result of the El Nino effect. However, the wall dives are still spectacular and there are plenty of gorgonians and a deep wreck. Visibility up to 50m.

Nusa Penida and Nusa Lembongan p.276. Considered the best dive spots in Bali, but also the most difficult because of strong currents and drifts. It's also very cold and only suitable for experienced divers. Good chance of spotting oceanic sunfish (*mola mola*) here from July to September.

Tulamben p.311. Popular wreck dive (3–29m deep), with visibility from 12–15m. Other rewarding dives can be found nearby, with a great diversity of coral and marine life. Good for less experienced divers but it can get very crowded. Night dives on the wreck are a highlight.

Lombok

Gili Islands p.444. A variety of dives for every level, with plenty of reef fish, but some damage to coral. Whitetip reef sharks and turtles quite frequently spotted.

---

you can get a huge variety of dive experiences within even a fortnight's holiday. There are six main areas for quality diving: around **Menjangan Island** (part of Bali Barat national park) off Bali's northwest coast, whose closest accommodation and dive centres are at Pemuteran and Lovina; off Bali's north coast at **Tulamben**, where there are also hotels and dive centres; off **Jemeluk/Amed** in the far east of Bali, close to Tulamben's amenities; off **Candi Dasa** on Bali's east coast, a resort in its own right; around the island of **Nusa Penida** (off Bali's southeast coast), whose closest dive operators and hotels are at Sanur and Nusa Lembongan, Padang Bai and Candi Dasa; and off the **Gili Islands**, near Lombok, which have their own hotels and dive bases. Whether you're an experienced diver or a complete novice, it makes most sense to stay as close as you can to one of these top dive spots; not only will your dive trips/course be a little cheaper, but you won't have to suffer long journeys to the reefs, and you may have the advantage of getting to the dive sites before the day-trippers turn up. In reality, though, relatively few divers stay at the dive sites, most tourists preferring to make day or overnight excursions from one of the big resorts in the south: Sanur and Tanjung Benoa both have dozens of dive operators and many more hotels, and nearly all tour agents in Kuta can fix you up with a dive operator.

Anyone who's thinking about diving in Bali should get hold of the very readable and highly recommended book *Diving Bali*, published by Periplus, which contains everything you need to know about sites, reefs and dive operators. For details on diving in Lombok and the rest of Indonesia, *Diving Indonesia*, also published by Periplus, is equally useful. The online version of the divers' magazine *AsianDiver*, at ⓦwww .asiandiver.com, is another good source of information and includes travellers' reports, a forum and a job shop.

Whether you're diving or snorkelling, you should be aware of your effect on the fragile **reef** structures. In reality, any human contact with the microscopic colonies that make up a reef will do some damage, but you can significantly minimize your impact by not stepping on, or supporting yourself on, any part of the reef, and by asking your boatman not to anchor in the middle of one. Don't buy coral souvenirs, as tourist demand only encourages local entrepreneurs to dynamite reefs.

Bali's only **decompression chamber** is located inside the efficient Sanglah Public Hospital, Jl Kesehatan Selatan 1, Sanglah in Denpasar (five lines ☎0361/227911–227915). Reputable dive operators should have insurance to cover their customers' emergency use of the decompression chamber, but it's essential for all divers to have travel insurance as well, in case you need medical evacuation by plane.

Diving trips and courses

There are dozens of **dive operators** on Bali and Lombok, so it's always worth checking out several before committing yourself to a trip or a course. Always check the dive centre's PADI or equivalent accreditation and, if possible, get first-hand recommendations from other divers as well. You can view a list of PADI-approved centres in Bali and Lombok at ⓦwww.padi.com, though as PADI centres have to pay to appear on this list it is not comprehensive; you can check specific credentials by emailing PADI Asia Pacific at ⓔpadi-adm@padi.com.au. Some dive operators in Bali and Lombok do fake their PADI credentials, which is why it's good to get a second opinion. Avoid booking ahead over the internet without knowing anything else about the dive centre, and be wary of any operation offering extremely cheap courses: maintaining diving equipment is an expensive business in Bali so any place offering unusually good rates will probably be cutting corners and compromising your safety. Ask to meet your instructor or dive leader, find out how many people there'll be in your group, and look over the equipment, checking the quality of the air in the tanks yourself and also ensuring there's an oxygen cylinder on board.

Many of the dive operators in Bali have a main office in Sanur, Tanjung Benoa, Lovina or Candi Dasa and one or two branch offices, for example in Tulamben or Pemuteran. For a list of some of the main dive operators in south Bali, see p.165; for those in Candi Dasa (east and northeast Bali) see p.287; and for Lovina (north and west Bali) see p.359. Most dive centres on Lombok are based in either Senggigi (see p.437) or on the Gili Islands (see p.444).

Most charge similar **rates** for dives and courses. One-day **dive trips** usually cost US$55–105 including equipment, and two- to five-day safaris cost about US$85 per day all inclusive. Yos Marine Adventures, based in Tanjung Benoa, and with branches in Pemuteran and Candi Dasa (see p.152), offers dive expeditions for **children** over twelve years old, and for **divers with disabilities**; they have specially adapted equipment available for rent. Bali International Diving Professionals in Sanur (see p.165) also offers dive trips for disabled divers and is a member of the International Association for Handicapped Divers; they do introductory courses for 8–11-year-olds, and also offer **nitrox dives** and **underwater weddings**.

All dive centres offer a range of internationally certified **diving courses**, generally with the first couple of days split between a classroom and a hotel swimming pool, and the next couple of days out on the reef (another good reason for staying close to the best sites). You can take dive courses in Kuta (Bali), Sanur, Nusa Dua, Candi Dasa, Tulamben, Amed, Lovina, Pemuteran, Senggigi and on the Gili Islands, and can book them through tour agents in most other resorts as well. Sample prices for courses include four-day open-water PADI courses for US$300–400, and two-day advanced open-water courses for around US$245–350. Many dive centres do not include the dive manual and exam papers in the price of the four-day open-water course.

Snorkelling

Snorkellers are generally welcome on dive excursions, and are usually charged fifty to sixty percent of the diver's fee, which should include the rental of mask, fins and snorkel. Specialist snorkelling trips are also arranged by the dive centres to Nusa Lembongan (p.276) for about US$45 per person, and snorkellers can charter their own boat fairly cheaply for trips to the reefs of Menjangan (see p.401). When signing up for a snorkelling trip to one of the islands, be sure to ask exactly how many hours the schedule includes for snorkelling, as a number of the bigger outfits sandwich a mere half-hour's "free time" between sightseeing.

Bird-watching and hiking

There's just one **national park** in Bali and Lombok, **Taman Nasional Bali Barat**, which covers about 760 square kilometres of mountain and coast in far western Bali (see p.394). Visitors are prohibited from exploring the park alone, but guides are available for hire at the park headquarters and will accompany you on designated hikes that can last anything from two to twelve hours (overnight camps are permitted under sufferance). The park's landscape is hardly spectacular, but its chief draw are the **birds** that inhabit it – well worth packing your binoculars for. This is also the site of a special breeding centre for Bali's only endemic bird, the endangered Bali starling (see p.398).

Other worthwhile bird-watching areas include the forested hills around **lakes Buyan** and **Tamblingan** (p.338) and Bali's second highest mountain, **Gunung Batukau** (p.385). Regular half-day bird-watching excursions are also organized from **Ubud** (p.194). The **Bali Bird Park** (Taman Burung) in nearby Batubulan (p.180) houses dozens of interesting and spectacular birds from all over the world, most of them kept in large aviaries.

For reviews of the most useful guides to the birds of Bali and Lombok, see p.559.

Volcano hikes and rice-field walks

Most **hikers** eschew the highlands of Bali Barat and head instead for the islands' grandest mountains. A trek up the active volcano of Lombok's **Gunung Rinjani** (see p.461) usually involves a night spent up on the crater rim or down inside the mountain by the crater lake. But the trip to the summit of what is Indonesia's second-highest peak, is usually a three- or four-day expedition, with some really hard work to get to the top. Guides are necessary on the routes to the summit. You can rent camping equipment and hire porters at the starting point. Bali's holiest peak, **Gunung Agung** (see p.269), also involves a strenuous climb – and guides for this walk are essential – but the ascent and descent can be managed in one day. **Gunung Batur** (see p.328), also on Bali, is a much easier proposition and by far the most popular of the volcano walks; don't be put off by this, though, as the sunrise from the top is glorious.

There are several tour companies in Bali running regular **guided hikes** to some of the island's best spots, including Gunung Batur, Gunung Batukau (see p.386), the Bedugul rainforests (see p.333) and Bali Barat (see p.396). It's also possible to join group hikes from Toya Bungkah (see p.329) and Ubud (see p.194). A number of Lombok-centred companies organize expeditions up Rinjani (see p.463), and Lotus Asia Tours (p.421) offers various treks and **bicycle tours** across the island. Sobek and Bali Adventure Tours runs guided **mountain-bike** trips down Gunung Batur, Gunung Batukau, and in the area around Sangeh Monkey Forest and neighbouring villages.

Walks through Bali's **rice-fields** are usually much less tiring than volcano climbs, need no preparation (though it's always advisable to take a sun hat and a water bottle), and always offer spectacular views. The most popular place to head for is Ubud (see p.205), as dozens of possible rice-field walks fan out from the village centre in all directions. Though we've described a few recommended walks in the Ubud area, it can be just as rewarding to strike out on your own – if you get lost there's nearly always a farmer or villager within hailing distance. Tirtagangga is another extremely pretty and worthwhile area for walking and it's straightforward to arrange guides while you're there (see p.300). Other lovely quiet spots to base yourself if you're keen on gentle but varied walks are Munduk (see p.340), up in the northern hills, and Wongayagede (see p.385), on the slopes of Gunung Batukau.

Adventure sports

Adventure sports have become a big thing in Bali. **Whitewater rafting** is popular, and as Bali's rivers range from Class 2 to Class 4, there are routes to appeal to first-timers as well as the more experienced; you can book trips in all the major coastal resorts as well as in Ubud. It's also possible to go **kayaking** on the gentler rivers, as well as on Lake Tamblingan; and a little place in Toya Bungkah offers **canoeing** on Lake Batur (see p.329). In addition you'll find several **bungee-jumping** places in Kuta–Legian–Seminyak, and one in Kemenuh, and a go-kart track in Kuta. Details on these activities are given on pp.124–25.

Golf

There are four **golf courses** on Bali: 18-hole courses at the Handara Kosaido Country Club in Bedugul (see p.335), the Bali Golf and Country Club in Nusa Dua (see p.153), and at *Le Meridien Nirwana* in Tanah Lot (see p.378); and a nine-hole course at the *Grand Bali Beach* in Sanur (see p.163). For golf packages, including transfers, green fees and club rental, contact Bali Discount Golf (☎0361/285935, ⓦwww.golf-bali.com). Lombok has two 18-hole courses: near Sira Beach on the northwest coast (see p.456), and in the centre of the island (see p.465).

Spas and traditional beauty treatments

Herbal medicines (*jamu*) and massages using oils and pastes made from locally grown plants have long played an important role in traditional Indonesian health-care. In the last few years this resource has been tapped into and adapted for the tourist market, with dozens of spas and salons now offering traditional beauty treatments to visitors.

The term **"spa"** is used very loosely in Indonesia and generally refers to an upmarket massage and beauty parlour rather than a mineral spring, though a Balinese spa complex may well have pools, jacuzzis and steam baths fed by the waters of a sacred river. You'll find spas and traditional beauty salons in all the main resorts on Bali and Lombok, both inside upper-bracket hotels and at dedicated beauty centres. Most offer a core of fairly similar massages and body rubs, plus a few in-house specialities, but the big attraction is that many use indigenous ingredients and recipes to make their own oils and body pastes, so there's plenty of scope for experiment. Settings are often gorgeous, with spas designed to capitalize on the local penchant for tropical gardens, luxury fabrics and indulgent bathrooms.

Treatments

The most famous traditional treatment is the Javanese exfoliation rub, **mandi lulur**, in which you're painted and then gently massaged with a paste made chiefly of turmeric but which may also contain ginger, jasmine, rice, ground nuts and aromatic spices. Such is its apparent power to beautify that Javanese brides are said to have a *lulur* treatment every day for the forty days before their wedding ceremonies. Another popular body wrap is the **Balinese boreh**, a warming blend of cloves, pepper, cardamom and other spices that improves circulation and invigorates muscles. There are dozens of other **body mask treatments**, using ingredients such as seaweed, aloe vera, coconut, salt and even coffee. Most scrub treatments are preceded by a gentle Balinese-style massage and followed by a moisturizing "milk bath" – actually a soothing mask treatment in which you're slathered in yogurt or condensed milk; the whole package generally takes between an hour and a half and two hours. Prices vary enormously for these scrub packages, from Rp150,000 to $100, depending on the poshness of the venue.

Most beauty centres can do several different types of **massage**, including Balinese (gentle), Thai (more vigorous), Hawaiian lomi-lomi (therapeutic), Japanese shiatsu (pressure points) and Swedish (very vigorous). Some places offer an assortment of **aromatherapy** massages to treat a range of ailments from coughs to headaches to insomnia. Massage prices range from Rp50,000 (or even less on the beach) to $42 per hour. Every spa and beauty salon does manicures, pedicures, facials and cream-bath deep-moisturizing hair treatments.

Practicalities

Spas and beauty salons in Bali and Lombok are very professional and should do their best to minimize awkwardness and embarrassment by giving you precise instructions about how much to undress and which way to lie. All treatment rooms are private but some people prefer to take swimwear with them anyway. Many places are quite happy for couples to have massages and body wraps in the same room. Most masseuses and beauty therapists are women, but some salons use male masseurs for their male customers.

We've listed some of the most famous and most popular spas and beauty salons, but there are hundreds more. Advance **reserva-** tions are recommended but not always essential, and most hotels welcome nonguests at their spas. The best include the traditional and inexpensive Nur Salon in Ubud (see p.224), which has been going for 25 years; the funky, good-value, Moroccanstyle Bodyworks in Seminyak (see p.126); the beachside massages at Indiana Massage in Lovina (see p.362); the superdeluxe and enormously expensive Ibah in Ubud (see p.224); the luxuriously classical spa at *Matahari Beach Resort* in Pemuteran (see p.405); the minimalist-chic spa at *Jepun Bali Hotel* on Bali's north coast (see p.350) and the seafront spa at Senggigi's *Sheraton* (see p.436).

Crime and personal safety

While incidents of crime of all kinds are relatively rare on Bali and Lombok, the importance of tourism to the economy, and the damage that adverse publicity could do, means that the true situation may be kept conveniently obscured. Certainly the majority of tourists have trouble-free visits, but there have been instances of theft and assault on tourists.

It makes sense to take a few **precautions**. Carry vital documents and money in a concealed moneybelt: the bum-bags that have become fashionable with travellers are far too easy to cut off in a crowd. Make sure your luggage is lockable (it's possible to get gadgets to lock backpacks) and never keep important items in the back pockets of your pack while you are wearing it – things can quickly be taken without you knowing it. Beware of **pickpockets** on crowded buses or bemos and in markets; they usually operate in pairs: one will distract you while another gets what they can either from your pockets or your backpack.

Check the **security** of a room before accepting it, make sure doors and windows can be secured and don't forget access via the bathroom. Some guesthouses and hotels have **safe-deposit boxes**, which neatly solves the problem of what to do with your valuables while you go swimming. A surprising number of tourists do leave their valuables unattended on the beach and are amazed to find them gone when they return.

Keep a separate **photocopy of your passport** so you can prove who you are if you need to get a replacement, and a separate list of travellers' cheque numbers along with the emergency phone number.

It's never sensible to carry large amounts of **cash**, and on Bali it's not necessary as there are moneychangers everywhere. However, on Lombok you may need to carry more than you would like because of the scarcity of moneychangers away from the west coast resorts. It is wise to keep a few dollars hidden somewhere away from your main stash of cash so that if you get your money stolen you can still get to the police, contact a consulate and pay for phone calls while you sort everything out. There does appear to be an increase in the number of potential rip-offs when you are **changing money**; see box on p.36 for more.

Something else to watch out for is being cornered on the street by a student or market researcher wanting to ask you a few innocent questions about your holiday in Bali. Apparently, these seemingly innocuous questionnaires are used to provide information for **time-share companies,** who have a reputation for hassling you incessantly on your hotel phone once you've divulged your details. Another common ruse is for the "researchers" to offer you a prize as a reward for participating – usually a free dinner or tour – which invariably involves a trip to the time-share company's office. Advice on this is to **never sign anything** unless you've thought about it extremely carefully, examined all the small print – and then thought about it some more. The Australian government website ⓦwww.dfat.gov.au/consular/bali.htm has some useful pages on "Common Complaints and Scams" that anyone visiting Bali or Lombok would do well to read. They warn about **spiked drinks** and emphasize that gambling is illegal in Indonesia and problems can arise from foreigners getting involved in this.

It is very foolish to have anything to do with **drugs** in Indonesia. The penalties are very tough, and you won't get any sympathy from consular officials. If you're **arrested**, or end up on the wrong side of the law for whatever reason, you should ring the consular officer at your embassy immediately (see p.23 for a list).

If you're **driving**, the chance of entanglement with the police increases; spot checks are common and by law you must make certain that you carry your own driving licence and the vehicle registration papers at all times or you're liable to a fine on the spot. See p.40 for more.

Reporting a crime or emergency

If you have anything **lost** or **stolen** you must get a **police report** for insurance purposes, so head for the nearest police station (these are marked on the maps in the guide). In areas without local police, such as the Gili Islands off the coast of Lombok, ask for the local village headman, *kepala desa* or *kepala kampung* in smaller villages, whose job it is to sort out the problem and take you to the nearest police. The police will usually find somebody who can speak some English, but it's a good idea to take along someone who can speak both Indonesian and English, if you can. Allow plenty of time for any bureaucratic involvement with the police. If you're unfortunate enough to be the victim of **violent crime**, contact your consulate at once. Government websites are listed on p.25.

In an emergency, dial the following numbers on Bali or Lombok:
Police ☏110
Ambulance ☏118
Fire service ☏113

Shopping

Shopping could easily become an all-consuming pastime in Bali: the range and quality of artefacts is phenomenal, and although the export trade has dulled the initial impact a little, the sheer volume – and reasonable price – of the wood-carvings, paintings and fabrics sold on Bali still make it a delight.

In addition, Bali acts as something of a clearing house for the arts and crafts of other Indonesian islands and has an increasing number of outlets selling works by expat designers, artists and craftspeople. Lombok's shops are fewer but no less enticing: Senggigi is a great centre for the crafts of Lombok as well as the islands further east. The real pleasure on Lombok is visiting the craft villages in the centre of the island where pottery, basketware, woodcarving and textiles are local specialities.

Locations

On Bali, you'll get the biggest overall choice in **Kuta–Legian–Seminyak** and in **Ubud**, where the streets are crammed with all manner of outlets, from makeshift stalls to sophisticated glass-fronted boutiques. Traditional covered **markets**, or *pasar*, are also rewarding places to hone your bargaining skills. Every main town has a fresh produce market, which usually opens up before dawn (some Denpasar markets stay open 24 hours) and draws traders from all the outlying villages.

Most fruit and veg markets also have a floor devoted to non-foodstuffs, a section which is known as the *pasar seni*, or **art market**, and which sells everything from sarongs and lengths of ceremonial *perada* fabric to woodcarvings, paintings, T-shirts and blankets. The term "art market" has now grown to mean any collection of tourist-oriented stalls or little shops selling inexpensive sarongs and souvenirs. Bali's best traditional *pasar seni*, at **Sukawati** near Ubud (see p.182), is so large that it's housed in a separate building from the foodstuffs; the less tourist-oriented Pasar Badung and Pasar Kumbasari in **Denpasar** (p.99) are also well worth exploring. The only *pasar*

seni on Lombok is in **Senggigi**, where there is also a variety of shops selling all sorts of desirable items. For a less touristy experience, the markets in **Cakranegara** and next to **Mandalika** bus terminal on Lombok are a jumble of stalls and alleyways where crafts of all sorts are squashed next to the fruit, vegetables and groceries.

Remember that touts, guides and drivers often get as much as fifty percent **commission** on any item sold to one of their customers – not only at the customer's expense, but also the vendor's. For information on how to ship purchases home, see p.51.

Arts and crafts

The best area for buying **paintings, woodcarvings** and **sculpture** is Ubud and its neighbouring villages, where every other family seems to be engaged in some kind of craft, and where stalls and marketplaces groan under piles of canvases and stacks of chiselled images. Here you can buy tiny unframed Keliki-style temple scenes for as little as Rp75,000, delicate abstract figurines for Rp100,000, and huge hairy Rangda masks for around Rp200,000. You can also commission your own masks, choose picture frames from highly skilled frame-carvers, and get the whole lot shipped home without having to carry it anywhere. If you have a special interest in the classical *wayang* style of painting, make a trip to Kamasan (see p.261), just south of Klungkung, which is both the historical and modern-day centre for this traditional style of art and is packed with little workshops.

Once you've perused a few painting, woodcarving or sculpture outlets, you'll soon realize that original ideas are not all that common, and that certain subjects (like carved weeping Buddhas and portraits of *baris* dancers, for example) recur in most commercial galleries. This copying is as much a traditional practice as it is a commercial one, as Balinese culture has always defined a fine artist as one who replicates the work of his or her forebears to perfection, but if you look carefully you'll be able to distinguish between a crude piece of work and one that's more delicately finished. If you're planning on investing big money, you'd be advised to stick to the bigger and better-known galleries such as those in Ubud (see p.224) and Batuan (see p.184), where assistants are well informed and quality consistently high. For smaller purchases, however, the less formal galleries and workshops can be very rewarding, and you may well get the chance to meet the artist as well.

The best way to learn about styles and artistic quality is to visit one of Bali's major arts and crafts **museums**. In Ubud, the Neka Art Museum, the Seniwati Gallery and ARMA will all give you an excellent grounding in painting genres and techniques, while the galleries of Ubud's Puri Lukisan and Denpasar's Taman Budaya Cultural Centre make reasonable introductions to fine woodcarvings. For an overview of the development of styles and techniques in Balinese painting, carving and sculpture, see p.530.

Be particularly careful when choosing **woodcarvings**, which are sometimes sold under false pretences as a more valuable wood, and which don't always travel that well. The easiest wood to fake is **sandalwood**, or *cenana*, an extremely expensive material, mainly imported from East Timor. Sandalwood's most obvious characteristic is its pungent aroma, and this is sometimes faked by packing the carvings in real sandalwood sawdust for several days, or by scenting them with sandalwood oil. In either case, the smell doesn't last that long, so either buy from an established outlet or assume that it's faked and reduce your price accordingly. Both real and fake sandalwood pieces are usually wrapped in plastic bags and kept in locked display cabinets to conserve their perfume. **Ebony**, which comes mainly from Kalimantan and Sulawesi, is another commonly faked wood. The best way to check the authenticity of an ebony image is to compare its weight with any other wood: ebony is very dense and will sink in water. Most tropical woods crack when taken to a climate that's less humid because of the uneven shrinkage that results from escaping moisture. Some carvers circumvent this problem by drying the wood in kilns, while others soak the carvings in a substance called polyethylene glycol (PEG), which fills the cracks before they have a chance to widen out. It's always worth trying to ascertain whether your purchase has undergone either of these processes, and you should definitely check for cracks before buying.

Ubud is home to several families of traditional basket weavers, who have long made a gorgeous range of **basketware** pots, urns and bowls from palm leaves. Recently, there's also been a new trend in very distinctive finely woven basketware bags, baskets, trays and mats, made from a grass known as *ato*, which apparently only grows in the rivers of central Bali. *Ato* basketware is quite pricey (Rp150,000 for a small tray) and available from many art market stalls.

Pottery is now big business in Lombok (see p.429), and most of the items you'll see in Bali tourist centres have been shipped across the water. For the best range of pots, check out the shops and production centres on Lombok itself, in particular the showrooms in Mataram and Senggigi, and the pottery villages of Banyumulek, Penunjak and Pejangik.

Fabric and soft furnishings

The main cloth-producing area on Bali is Gianyar, noted for its distinctive **ikat** or **endek** cloth – a special technique (explained on p.538) that involves dyeing the weft threads into the finished design before weaving begins. This produces a fuzzy edge to the fairly bold designs, and the fabric is popular for cushion covers and bedspreads, as well as for sarongs and other clothes. You can see *ikat* weavers at work in Gianyar, but their produce is sold at outlets all over the island. There's also a highly regarded workshop in Singaraja. The tiny Bali Aga village of Tenganan (p.291) near Candi Dasa is the only place on Bali to produce double *ikat*, or *geringsing*, a painstakingly intricate technique which produces stunning designs – at prices to match. On Lombok, the village of Sukarara (p.474) is the place to look if you're interested in weaving; here you can see both large and small workshops producing *ikat* and *songket* cloth.

Although Balinese *ikat* is occasionally used for sarongs, Javanese-style **batik** is currently much more fashionable, and is used for everything from sarongs and shirts, to tablecloths and surfers' board-bags. Some batik is now screenprinted rather than waxed, and the results are generally less good, especially as the dyes on screenprinted fabrics don't penetrate to the reverse side. Many women now favour sarongs made from rayon, which is softer, hangs better and doesn't crease so much, but is not a natural fabric and so doesn't breathe so easily. The larger fixed-price tourist shops in Kuta, Nusa Dua, Lovina and Candi Dasa tend to stock the most exhaustive range of batik goods – including exquisite hand-printed and even hand-painted silk sarongs, priced from Rp400,000 – but you'll find cheaper sarongs (Rp40,000–70,000) in the *pasar seni* frequented by the Balinese.

The ceremonial dress worn at temple festivals and other important occasions is usually fashioned from heavier, more luxurious materials such as gold-and-silver brocaded **songket** and gold-stamped **perada** (see p.538 for more on all these materials). The best places to buy *songket* and *perada* are the bigger *pasar seni*, for example at those in Denpasar or Sukawati, and at the shops along Jalan Sulawesi, the heart of Denpasar's rag trade.

In Kuta, Ubud and Candi Dasa, you'll also find a number of shops specializing in cloth woven to the traditional designs of other Indonesian islands, particularly Sumba and Flores. Prices vary enormously, depending not only on the size of the fabric, and whether or not it was hand-woven, but also on how old it is. Shawls and 100x30cm wall-hangings cost from around Rp80,000, but larger and more complicated items such as Sumbanese *ikat* bedspreads rarely start at under US$250.

A good way to display lengths of cloth at home is on the special carved **wooden hangers** sold in furniture and "antique" shops, and in some *ikat* and souvenir shops. These come in a variety of sizes (it's worth noting the width of your cloth before buying a hanger), and often have decorated finials. Most hangers are made in Lombok and Kalimantan.

In recent years local and expat designers have really gone to town with **soft furnishings**, making full use of the sumptuous fabrics available and coming up with a stunning array of cushions, bedspreads, curtains, drapes and tablecloths. Oriental-chic predominates, with the whole gamut represented from lustrous magenta silk cushions through to cream linen tableware. Legian and Seminyak have dozens of shops specializing in soft furnishings and homewares and are probably the best places to begin, but Ubud is a fruitful place to browse too.

Clothing and jewellery

With such lovely fabrics to work with, it's hardly surprising that Bali also produces some great **clothes**. The island's clothing industry is centred around Kuta–Legian–Seminyak, and this is where you'll find the classiest and most original boutiques, as well as the greatest concentration of stalls selling baggy *ikat* trousers and skimpy batik dresses. Local designers keep an astute eye on Western fashions and seem to come up with stylish but unusual collections, many of which are geared as much to Western winters (or at least to a fully air-conditioned lifestyle) as they are to Asian climes. Brand-name surfwear and urban sportswear is also good value in Kuta, as is custom-made leatherware, especially shoes, boots and jackets.

There's also a small but thriving **silver** and **gold** industry on Bali, based in the village of Celuk (p.182), where silversmiths create filigree pieces and larger items to order and sell to the public from their workshops. For more unusual jewellery you're better off scouring the jewellery shops in Kuta, Ubud, Lovina and Candi Dasa, where designs tend to be more innovative and prices similar, if not lower.

Antiques and reproduction furniture

Several shops in Bali and Lombok advertise, quite ingenuously, "**Antiques** made to order". At least they're honest. The antiques in question generally either come from Java or are reproductions of Javanese items, chiefly **furniture** such as chairs, cupboards, tables, chests, beds, screens, carved panels, window shutters and doors. Weather-worn or fashionably distressed, most of the furniture is heavy, made from teak to a Dutch-inspired design, but carved with typical Indonesian grace and whimsy. The main centres for antique and repro furniture in Bali are Batubulan, Legian and Seminyak, while in Lombok, Senggigi is the place to head for – both the resort itself, plus the road south, which is virtually lined with shops and workshops offering a huge variety of good-quality items. Bargaining is essential; reasonable sample prices are US$60 for a small table, or US$250 for a cupboard with carved doors. You should check your intended purchase, for rot and termite damage (genuine teak is resistant to termites), as well as for shoddy restoration work. In addition, be warned about the possibility of the wood cracking when transported to a less humid climate – see the advice on buying woodcarvings, above, for possible ways of preventing this.

Cultural hints

The people of Bali and Lombok are extremely generous about opening up their homes, temples and festivals to the ever-growing crowd of interested tourists but, though they're long-suffering and rarely show obvious displeasure, they do take great offence at certain aspects of Western behaviour. The most sensitive issues on the islands are Westerners' clothing – or lack of it – and the code of practice that's required when visiting holy places.

Religious etiquette

Anyone entering a **Balinese temple** (*pura*) is required to show **respect** to the gods by treating their shrines with due deference (not climbing on them or placing themselves in a higher position than them) and by **dressing modestly**: skimpy clothing, bare shoulders and shorts are all unacceptable and in some very sacred temples you'll be required to wear a sarong. In addition, you should wear a **ceremonial sash** around your waist whenever you visit a temple: these can be bought for a few thousand rupiah at most shops selling sarongs or fabric, and can be of any style and pattern (the Balinese sometimes make do with a rolled-up sarong wrapped around their waist or even a towel). At the major temples and those most visited by tourists, it's nearly always possible to rent yourself a sash and, if you're under-dressed, a sarong as well.

When attending special **temple ceremonies**, cremations and other village festivals, you should make every effort to dress up as formally as possible: sarongs and sashes are obligatory, and shirts with buttons or blouses are preferable to T-shirts. During ceremonies, you shouldn't walk in front of anyone who's praying, or take their photo, and should try not to sit higher than the priest or the table of offerings. Never use a flash.

Whether or not you rent a sarong and sash at a *pura*, you'll be expected to give a **donation** towards temple upkeep (Rp5000– 10,000 is an acceptable amount) and to sign the donation book. There's no need to be prompted into larger sums when you read how much the previous visitor donated – extra noughts are quite easy to add.

Because the shedding of blood is considered to make someone **ritually unclean** (*sebel*) in Balinese Hinduism, women are not allowed to enter a temple, or to attend any religious ceremonies, during menstruation, and the same applies to anyone bearing a fresh wound. Under the same precepts, new

Balinese caste and names

Balinese society is structured around a hereditary **caste system** which, while far more relaxed than its Indian counterpart, does nonetheless carry certain restrictions and rules of etiquette, as ordained in the Balinese Hindu scriptures. Of these, the one that travellers are most likely to encounter is the practice of **naming** a person according to their caste.

At the top of the tree is the **Brahman** caste, whose men are honoured with the title **Ida Bagus** and whose women are generally named **Ida Ayu**, sometimes shortened to **Dayu**. Traditionally revered as the most scholarly members of society, only Brahmans are allowed to become high priests (*pedanda*).

Satriya (sometimes spelt Ksatriya) form the second strata of Balinese society, and these families are descendants of warriors and rulers. The Balinese rajas were all Satriya and their offspring continue to bear tell-tale names: **Cokorda**, **Anak Agung**, **Ratu** and **Prebagus** for men, and **Anak Agung Isti** or **Dewa Ayu** for women. The merchants or **Wesia** occupy the third most important rank, the men distinguished by the title **I Gusti** or **Pregusti**, the women by the name **I Gusti Ayu**.

At the bottom of the heap comes the **Sudra** caste, the caste of the common people, which accounts for over ninety percent of the population. Sudra children are named according to their position in the family order, with no distinction made between male and female offspring. Thus, a first-born Sudra is always known as **Wayan** (or, less commonly, **Putu** or **Gede**), the second-born is **Made** (or **Kadek**), the third **Nyoman** (or **Komang**) and the fourth **Ketut**. Should a fifth child be born, then the naming system begins all over again with Wayan, and so it goes on. In order to distinguish between the sexes, Sudra caste names are often prefaced by "**I**" for males and "**Ni**" for females, eg I Wayan. Some Wayans and Madés prefer to be known by their second names, and many have distinctive nicknames, but you will come across many more Wayans than any other name in Bali.

Unlike their counterparts in the far more rigid Indian caste system, the Sudra are not looked down upon or denied access to specific professions (except that of *pedanda*). It's not at all abnormal for a university professor to hail from the Sudra caste, for example, or for a waiter or a bemo driver to be a Brahman or a Satriya, and a high-caste background guarantees neither a high income nor a direct line to political power. There are caste-related **marriage** restrictions, however. Although it's acceptable for a high-caste man to marry a woman from a lower caste, the reverse situation causes the woman to "lose caste", and is not considered desirable.

---

mothers and their babies are also considered to be *sebel* for the first 42 days after the birth (new fathers are unclean for three days), and anyone who has been recently bereaved is *sebel* until three days after burial or cremation. These restrictions apply to non-Balinese as well, and are sometimes detailed on English-language notices outside the temple.

Mosques

On the whole, the **mosques** of Lombok and Bali don't hold much interest for tourists, but should you have occasion to visit one, it's as well to be aware of certain Islamic practices. Everyone is required to take their shoes off

before entering, and to wear long sleeves and long trousers; women should definitely cover their shoulders and may also be asked to cover their heads as well (bring a scarf or shawl as there probably won't be any provided). Men and women always pray in separate parts of the mosque, though there are unlikely to be signs telling you where to go. Women are forbidden to engage in certain religious activities during menstruation, and this includes entering a mosque. Finally, you should be aware that during the month of **Ramadan** (see p.56 for more), devout Muslims neither eat, drink nor smoke during daylight hours. If visiting south or east Lombok during this time, you should be sensitive to this.

The body

Despite tolerating skimpy **dress** in Kuta and Sanur, most Indonesians are extremely offended by topless and nude bathing, and by immodest attire in their towns and villages. You'll command a great deal more respect if you recognize this and keep your shortest shorts, vests and bare shoulders for the biggest beach resorts. This is especially true in central and eastern Lombok, where Sasaks do not subscribe to the relatively relaxed attitudes of their west-coast compatriots in Senggigi and the Gili Islands.

The Balinese and Sasak people themselves regularly expose their own bodies in public when **bathing** in rivers and public bathing pools, but they are always treated as invisible by other bathers and passers-by. As a tourist you should do the same: to photograph a bathing Balinese would be very rude indeed. If you bathe alongside them, do as they do – nearly all Balinese women wash with their sarongs wrapped around them – and take note of the segregated areas: in public pools the men's and women's sections are usually clearly defined, but in rivers the borders are less tangible. For other bathing practices, see p.42.

According to Hindu beliefs, a person's body is a microcosm of the universe: the **head** is the most sacred part of the body and the feet the most unclean. This means that you should on no account touch a Balinese person's head – not even to pat a small child's head or to ruffle someone's hair in affection; nor should you lean over someone's head or place your body in a higher position than their head without some sort of apology. You should never sit with your **feet** pointed at a sacred image (best to sit with them tucked underneath you) or use them to indicate someone or something. Balinese people will never walk under a **clothes line** (for fear of their head coming into contact with underclothes), so you should try not to hang your washing in public areas, and definitely don't sling wet clothes over a temple wall or other holy building. The **left hand** is used for washing after defecating, so the Balinese will never eat with it or use it to pass or receive things or to shake hands.

Social conventions

As elsewhere in Asia, the Balinese dislike **confrontational behaviour**, and will rarely show anger or irritation of any kind. Tourists who lose their cool and get visibly rattled tend to be looked down on rather than feared.

A major source of irritation for foreigners is the rather vague notion of **time-keeping** that pervades almost every aspect of Indonesian life, but lack of punctuality is such a national institution that there is even a word for it – *jam karet*, or rubber time – and you'll save yourself a lot of stress if you remember this every time you board a bemo or visit a bank. Public **displays of affection** are also subdued – you're more likely to see affectionate hand-holding and hugging between friends of the same sex than between heterosexual lovers.

Since the downfall of Suharto in 1998, and the subsequent democratic elections, Indonesian people seem to have become much more confident about discussing **political issues** and voicing critical opinions of the state. This is mirrored by a more open press. Religious beliefs, however, are a much more sensitive issue, and it would be bad form to instigate a debate that questions a Balinese person's faith.

You will probably find Balinese people only too eager to find out about your **personal life** and habits. It's considered quite normal to ask "Are you married?" and to then express sorrow if you say that you aren't, and the same applies to questions about children: marriage and parenthood are essential stages in the life of most Balinese (see p.545).

Women travellers

Bali and Lombok do not present great difficulties for women travellers, either travelling alone or with friends of either sex; basic issues of personal security and safety are essentially the same as they would be at home. One exception to note is the parties on Gili Trawangan (see p.450) where there have been reports of attacks on women. However, an image of Western women as promiscuous and on holiday in search of sex is well established on both islands, although attitudes on Bali are a little more open-minded than on Lombok.

Observe how local women dress both on the streets and on the beach. While **topless sunbathing** has become very popular in major tourist areas – and it's unlikely that local people will say anything directly to you about it – it's worth being aware how far outside the local dress code such behaviour is. Whatever you do on the beach, you should cover up when you head inshore, and visits to temples or festivals carry their own obligations regarding dress (see p.73).

There's a large population of young men on both Bali and Lombok known variously as Kuta Cowboys, guides, mosquitoes (they flit from person to person) or **gigolos**, whose aim is to secure a Western girlfriend for the night, week, month or however long it lasts. They vary considerably in subtlety and while the transaction is not overtly financial, the woman will be expected to pay for everything. You'll see these couples all over the islands, and if a Western woman and a local man are seen together, this is the first assumption made about their relationship. Local reaction is variable, from hostility in the more traditional villages through acceptance to amusement. **Sex outside marriage** is taboo in both the Hindu and Muslim religions, and young girls on both islands – especially in the more traditional villages – are expected to conform to a strict code of morality.

Women involved in relationships abroad, either with local men or other travellers should be aware of **sexual health** issues; see p.30.

On Bali, a high proportion of women **work** in the tourist industry in shops, restaurants, hotels and, informally, as masseuses. Some have a relatively good level of English, enabling you to make contact with at least one group of the women on the island. In the villages you'll need a basic level of Indonesian or Balinese to converse with local women. In Lombok, however, it's very obvious that while there are some women (often Balinese) working in the tourist industry in the more developed resorts, once you head east into the predominantly Muslim areas, the prevalence of women in the industry drops considerably; without at least some Indonesian or Sasak, the level of your contact with local women drops radically.

Travellers with disabilities

Indonesia makes few provisions for its disabled citizens, a situation which clearly affects travellers with disabilities.

At the physical level, kerbs are usually high (rarely sloping) and pavements/sidewalks often uneven with all sorts of obstacles; access to most public places involves steps (very few have ramps); public transport is inaccessible to wheelchair users (although Perama tourist buses will take them); and the few pedestrian crossings on major roads have no audible signal. On the positive side, many hotels comprise bungalows in extensive grounds, have spacious bathrooms, and the more upmarket hotels are increasingly aware of requirements.

For all of these reasons, it may be worth considering an **organized tour** or holiday – the contacts listed below will help you start researching trips to Bali and Lombok. Read your **travel insurance** small print carefully to make sure that people with a pre-existing medical condition are not excluded. And use your travel agent to make your journey simpler: airlines can cope better if they are expecting you, with a wheelchair provided at airports and staff primed to help. A **medical certificate** of your fitness to travel, provided by your doctor, is also extremely useful; some airlines or insurance companies may insist on it. Carry spares of any clothing or equipment that might be hard to find.

Make sure that you take sufficient supplies of any **medications**, and – if they're essential – carry the complete supply with you whenever you travel (including on buses and planes), in case of loss or theft. It's also a good idea to carry a doctor's letter about your drugs prescriptions with you at all times, particularly when passing through customs at Ngurah Rai or Selaparang airport, as this will ensure you don't get hauled up for narcotics transgressions.

Yos Marine Adventures in Tanjung Benoa (see box on p.165) runs **dives** for disabled swimmers, so long as you can move your legs and equalize and don't have a heart or asthmatic condition. Bali International Diving Professionals, Jl Sekarwaru 9, south Sanur (☎0361/270759, ⊛www.bidp-balidiving .com) is UK/Balinese-run and also offers dives for disabled divers.

Contacts for travellers with disabilities

For general information on travelling abroad contact the organizations listed below. In addition there are a vast number of **websites** listed in the Travel and Leisure links at ⊛www.independentliving.org. Also consider posting a query on the Travellers with Disabilities forum on ⊛thorntree.lonelyplanet.com. For detailed information on Balinese hotels and sights and local tips for wheelchair travellers in Bali log on to ⊛www .bali-paradise.com/special-needs-traveler.

UK and Ireland

Disability Action Group 2 Annadale Ave, Belfast BT7 3JH ☎028/9049 1011. Provides information about access for disabled travellers abroad.
Holiday Care 2nd floor, Imperial Building, Victoria Rd, Horley RH6 7PZ ☎01293/774535, Minicom ☎01293/776943, ⊛www.holidaycare.org.uk. Provides free lists of accessible accommodation abroad, and information on financial help for holidays.
Irish Wheelchair Association Blackheath Drive, Clontarf, Dublin 3 ☎01/833 8241, ⓔiwa@iol.ie. Useful information provided about travelling abroad with a wheelchair.
RADAR (Royal Association for Disability and Rehabilitation) 12 City Forum, 250 City Rd, London EC1V 8AF ☎020/7250 3222, Minicom ☎020/7250 4119, ⊛www.radar.org.uk. Information on all issues related to travel, including insurance and air travel, plus a useful information phone line.
Tripscope Alexandra House, Albany Rd, Brentford TW8 0NE ☎0845/758 5641, ⊛www.justmobility .co.uk/tripscope. This registered charity offers free advice on UK and international transport for those with a mobility problem.

US and Canada

Access-Able Ⓦ www.access-able.com. Online resource for travellers with disabilities.

Directions Unlimited 123 Green Lane, Bedford Hills, NY 10507 ℡ 1-800/533-5343 or 914/241-1700. Tour operator specializing in custom tours for people with disabilities.

Mobility International USA 451 Broadway, Eugene, OR 97401, voice and TDD ℡ 541/343-1284, Ⓦ www.miusa.org. Information and referral services, access guides, tours and exchange programmes. Annual membership $35 (includes quarterly newsletter).

Society for the Advancement of Travelers with Handicaps (SATH) 347 Fifth Ave, New York, NY 10016 ℡ 212/447-7284, Ⓦ www.sath.org. Non-profit educational organization actively representing travellers with disabilities.

Travel Information Service ℡ 215/456-9600. Phone-only information and referral service.

Twin Peaks Press Box 129, Vancouver, WA 98661 ℡ 1-800/637-2256 or 360/694-2462, Ⓦ disabilitybookshop.virtualave.net. Publisher of

the *Directory of Travel Agencies for the Disabled* ($19.95), listing more than 370 agencies worldwide; *Travel for the Disabled* ($19.95); the *Directory of Accessible Van Rentals* ($12.95) and *Wheelchair Vagabond* ($19.95), loaded with personal tips.

Wheels Up! ℡ 1-888/389-4335, Ⓦ www.wheelsup.com. Provides discounted airfare, tour and cruise prices for disabled travellers, also publishes a free monthly newsletter and has a comprehensive website.

Australia and New Zealand

ACROD (Australian Council for Rehabilitation of the Disabled) PO Box 60, Curtin ACT 2605 ℡ 02/6282 4333; 24 Cabarita Rd, Cabarita NSW 2137 ℡ 02/9743 2699. Provides lists of travel agencies and tour operators for people with disabilities.

Disabled Persons Assembly 4/173–175 Victoria St, Wellington ℡ 04/801 9100. Resource centre with lists of travel agencies and tour operators for people with disabilities.

Travelling with children

The Balinese make a great fuss of their own and other people's children, and permit them to go pretty much anywhere.

One peculiar cultural convention you might encounter, though, is that the Balinese abhor young children crawling on the ground – a practice that's considered far too animal-like for young humans – and so kids are **carried** everywhere, either on the hip or in slings made from sarongs, until they're six months old. Don't be surprised if your child gets scooped off the ground for the same reason.

Activities for kids

There's plenty on Bali and Lombok to appeal to children – especially the beach, the swimming pools and the water-based activities in the more developed resorts. Active children also enjoy many of the walks on the islands as well as **mountain-biking** and **whitewater**

rafting (see box on p.125). The colour and dynamism of the **dance and music shows** could almost be tailor-made for children – from the beauty and grace of *legong* to the drama of the *barong*. Special **theme attractions** like Waterbom Park in Kuta (see p.124), the Elephant Park at Taro (see p.236), and the Taman Burung Bird Park and Reptile Park in Batubulan (see p.180) are also ideal for children. The enormous Hard Rock swimming pool in Kuta has a "beach", volleyball and a water chute: non-resident guests can pay for admission by the day. Nearly all the upmarket hotels in the main Bali resorts have a kids' club for guests with a wide variety of activities to keep younger ones occupied whilst the adults go their own way for a few hours, and many also offer babysitting services. A couple of dive operators in south Bali offer introductory **dive courses** for kids as young as eight: see box p.165 for contact details. Older, more fashion-conscious children will relish the varieties of brand-name **clothing** on offer and the endless offers to "braid your hair", while parents will appreciate the bargains to be had in the children's sections of department stores in Kuta and Denpasar and the specialist children's clothing stores. **Ubud** is especially child-friendly, with a huge amount on offer that they will love (see box p.226) including batik, gamelan and dancing.

Practicalities

A number of upmarket **hotels** make significant concessions to couples with children, many of them offering extra beds for one or two under-12s sharing a room with their parents. The Tuban area of south Kuta is particularly strong on upmarket family-oriented hotels, many of which have grounds that run right down to the sea (see p.117), while many parents rate Nusa Dua's *Sheraton Nusa Indah* hotel as having the best kids' facilities on the whole island (see p.151). In Sanur, the mid-range *Swastika* is one of several family-friendly options, complete with childrens' swimming pool (see p.161). Up near Ubud, in the village of Mas, the characterful and mid-priced *Taman Harum Cottages* also gets rave reviews from families, not least because of all the activities it organizes (see p.185). In **losmen** you may need to rent three- or four-bed rooms if your child's too big to share a bed with you, or perhaps think about renting a **villa** (see p.46). On the whole, children who occupy their own seat on **buses** and **bemos** are expected to pay full fare. Most **domestic flight** operators charge two-thirds of the adult fare for children under 14, and ten percent for infants.

Although you can buy **disposable nappies** (diapers) in the supermarkets of Kuta, Sanur, Denpasar and Ubud, the Balinese don't use them, so prices are inflated; you might want to bring your own. Bring a **changing mat**, as there are precious few public toilets in Bali and Lombok, let alone ones with special baby facilities. Also consider investing in a **child-carrier backpack** for lugging around your smallest offspring (prices start at around £30/US$45 for ones that weigh less than 2kg), as pavements and road surfaces are invariably too bumpy for a comfortable pushchair ride. **Buggies,** however, can come in handy for feeding and even bedding small children, as highchairs and cots are only provided in the most upmarket hotels. Car-rental companies never provide baby seats. A child-sized **mosquito net** might be useful as well. **Powdered milk** is available in every major tourist centre, but sterilizing bottles is a far more laborious process in Indonesian hotels and restaurants than it is back home.

Food on Bali and Lombok is generally quite palatable to children – not much spice and hardly any unfamiliar textures – but, as with adults, you should be careful about unwashed fruit and salads and about dishes that have been left uncovered for a long time (see p.30). The other main hazards are rabid dogs (keep your distance), thundering traffic, huge waves and strong currents, and the **sun** – not least because the islands' main beaches offer almost no shade at all. Sun hats, sunblock and waterproof suntan lotions are essential, and can be bought in the major resorts.

Information and advice

The **Bali for Families** website Ⓦwww.baliforfamilies.com is extremely useful, created by parents who have lots of first-hand experience of travelling in Bali with their children. As well as child-friendly hotel recommendations, lists of essential equipment to take, and ideas on how to entertain the family, there's also a travellers' forum. You might also want to canvas other travellers' opinions on the Kids To Go bulletin board at Ⓦthorntree.lonelyplanet.com. For specific advice about kids' **health issues**, either contact your doctor or consult one of the travellers' medical services listed on pp.31–33; in the UK, call the Nomad Medical Centre (☎020/8889 7014), which publishes a special information sheet on keeping kids healthy when abroad.

Gay Bali and Lombok

As members of a society that places so much emphasis on marriage and parenthood, the Balinese are generally intolerant of homosexuality within their own culture, to the point where gay Balinese men will often introduce themselves to lovers as hailing from Java, so as not to cause embarrassment to their own people. It's by no means uncommon for men to lead a gay lifestyle for ten or fifteen years before succumbing to extreme social pressure around the age of thirty, getting married and becoming fathers. Lesbians are even less visible, but subject to similar expectations.

On the positive side, it's much more common in Bali and Lombok to show a modest amount of physical affection to friends of the same sex than to friends or lovers of the opposite sex, which means that Indonesian and foreign **gay couples** generally encounter less hassle about being seen together in public than they might in the West. Indonesian law is relatively liberal: the legal **age of consent** for both gay and heterosexual sex is 16.

Despite the indigenous aversion to gay culture, Bali's tourist industry has helped establish the island as one of the two main gay centres of Indonesia (the other being Jakarta). Young gay men from islands as far afield as Borneo gravitate to Bali in search of a foreign partner, and most end up in Kuta, the focus of the island's small but enduring **scene**. Here you'll find the exuberant and long-running gay bar, the *Hulu Café* (Ⓦ www.hulucafe.com), as well as a little enclave of other gay and gay-friendly bars in Seminyak. In addition, a mixed gay crowd of Indonesians and foreigners congregates in certain Kuta venues, where they're welcomed without a problem; see p.131 for details of all these places. There are also established **cruising** areas at the far northern end of Kuta beach, in Seminyak and on Puputan Square in Denpasar. Everything is a lot quieter on Lombok, and you won't find anything resembling a gay scene in any of the resorts.

A lot of gay visitors and expatriates do have **affairs** with Indonesian men, and these liaisons tend to fall somewhere between holiday romances and paid sex. Few Indonesians would classify themselves as rent boys – they wouldn't sleep with someone they didn't like and most don't have sex for money – but they usually expect to be financially cared for by the richer man (food, drinks and entertainment expenses for example), and some do make their living this way. As a result there's no visible gay prostitution on Bali, except for the bevy of transvestites known as the "sucky-sucky girls" who hang out in central Kuta.

The Utopia website Ⓦ www.utopia-asia .com is an excellent **resource** for gay travellers in Bali and the rest of Indonesia. As well as travellers' reports on the local scene it offers tours of Bali tailor-made for the gay traveller, and provides up-to-date lists of all major Indonesian gay and lesbian **organizations**. The umbrella organization for gays and lesbians in Bali and Lombok is Gaya Dewata, at Jalan Belimbing, Gang Y 4, Denpasar 80231 (daily 9.30am–3.30pm; ℡0361/ 222620, Ⓔ ycui@denpasar.wasantara.net.id).

Directory

Addresses Many hotels and tourist businesses on Bali and Lombok have recently been obliged to change their names because the government has outlawed the use of English-language names, demanding that Indonesian names be used instead. The same law has also affected many street names in resort areas such as Kuta in Bali. Where relevant, we have included both the new name and the old one for hotels and streets; many people still refer to them by the old name, though the sign will show the new version.

Airline offices See p.21 and p.111.

Airport departure taxes International: Rp100,000 from Bali, Rp70,000 from Lombok. Domestic: Rp20,000 from Bali, Rp8000 from Lombok.

Contraceptives Condoms (*kondom*) are available from pharmacists on both islands, but don't rely on local suppliers for other contraceptives.

Cookery and cultural classes Short courses in Balinese cookery are held regularly at several venues in Ubud (see p.226), Tanjung Benoa (see p.155) and Lovina (see p.363), at Kemenuh (see p.251), Munduk (see p.340) and at the *Serai* and *Puri Bagus* hotels near Candi Dasa (see p.286). Ubud is the most popular place to take workshops in art, dance, music, carving and other Balinese arts and crafts (see pp.225–27 for details). You can learn batik painting in Kuta (see p.136).

Electricity Usually 220–240 volts AC, but outlying areas may still use 110 volts. Most outlets take plugs with two rounded pins. See wwww.kropla.com for more.

Language lessons Indonesian language lessons are available in Ubud (see p.226), Kemenuh (see p.251), Munduk (see p.340) and Denpasar (see p.103).

Laundry services There's just one public laundromat in Kuta, but most hotels and losmen have a laundry service and tourist centres have plenty of services outside the hotels as well.

Left luggage Informal services are offered by most losmen and all hotels. Bali's Ngurah Rai Airport also has a left luggage facility (see box on p.110) and many Perama offices have a left luggage/locker service for their customers.

Time Bali and Lombok are on Central Indonesian Time, which is eight hours ahead of GMT, thirteen hours ahead of US Eastern Standard Time, and two hours behind Australian Eastern Standard Time. There's no daylight saving.

Tipping It's becoming increasingly usual to tip on Bali or Lombok, generally about ten percent to waiters (if no service charge is added to the bill), drivers and tour guides; a few thousand rupiah to bell boys and chamber maids in mid-range and upmarket hotels; and a round-up to the nearest Rp1000 for metered taxi drivers.

Work Job opportunities are few and far between. A few tourists manage to set themselves up as English- or Japanese-language teachers – the best places to look for students are Kuta–Legian and Ubud. Otherwise the most common money-making ploy is the exporting of Indonesian goods (fabric, clothes, jewellery and other artefacts). The fortnightly *Bali Advertiser* always carries a "situations vacant" column and is a good place to look for office and hotel jobs. It's available free from some hotels and tourist offices.

Yoga and meditation You'll find sessions and courses for all levels in Ubud (see p.224), Lovina (see p.363), Lalang Linggah (p.388), Wongayagede (see p.385), Sidemen (see p.304) and Bondalem (see p.349).

guide

guide

South Bali

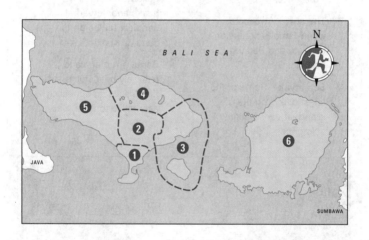

CHAPTER 1 # Highlights

* **Bali Museum, Denpasar** – A tantalizing introduction to the island's cultural and religious heritage. See p.96

* **Denpasar markets** – South Bali's most authentic, and chaotic, shopping experience. See p.99

* **The surf** – Awesome, world-famous breaks at Uluwatu and Padang Padang. See p.138

* **Seminyak** – Some of the finest dining on the island, at very reasonable prices. See p.129

* **Kuta nightlife** – Scores of easy-going bars, trendy clubs and packed dance floors make Kuta a great place to party. See p.130

* **Jimbaran beach barbecues** – Fresh fish grilled over coconut husks and served at candlelit tables on the sand. See p.141

* **Sanur** – A green and relatively peaceful resort that makes an appealing alternative to Kuta. See p.156

South Bali

The triangle of mainly flat land that makes up the south is some of the most fertile in Bali, and also the most densely populated, with more than a thousand people resident on every square kilometre. Bali's administrative capital, Denpasar, is here, and so too are the island's major tourist resorts, which have sprung up along the spectacular white-sand beaches: at Kuta in the west, and Sanur and Nusa Dua in the east. Furthermore, the combination of large offshore reefs and a peculiarly shaped coastline have made this region a genuine surfers' paradise, with some of the most sought-after breaks in the world.

Most tourists regard **Denpasar** as little more than a transit point for cross-island journeys, but it holds the island's best museum and makes an interesting contrast to the more westernized beach enclaves. Travellers tend to treat the sprawling **Kuta–Legian–Seminyak** resort on the southwest coast as the focal point for booking onward journeys, storing luggage, collecting and sending mail, and stocking up on essentials and souvenirs. It's brash and commercial – despised and adored in equal parts but not easily ignored, not least because of its proximity to Bali's airport, just 3km south of Kuta's southern fringes.

Directly east from Kuta, on the southeast coast, **Sanur** is a quieter, less youthful but more appealing alternative, with abundant greenery and decent watersports facilities. Further south, the finely manicured five-star resort of **Nusa Dua** creams off the wealthiest tourists, protecting them from all that is unnerving about Bali – as well as a lot of what is most attractive. Neighbouring **Tanjung Benoa** is known for its watersports, and its less exclusive accommodation, though not for its beaches. Beyond Nusa Dua, the barren **Bukit** limestone plateau is beginning to attract more and more overnight visitors to its peaceful, upmarket hotels at **Jimbaran**, a few kilometres south of the airport, while day-trippers continue to flock to its dramatically sited clifftop temple at **Uluwatu**, perched above the very best surf in Bali.

Aside from Denpasar which, together with Sanur, is a municipality in its own right, all the towns and villages covered in this chapter come under the administrative region known as **Badung**, a regency that was forged towards the end of the eighteenth century by the raja of Pemecutan. By 1891, Badung had expanded to include much of the land controlled by the neighbouring kingdom of Mengwi as well, but supremacy was soon wrested from the newly powerful raja of Badung by the insatiably expansionist Dutch, whose invasion of Badung in 1906 resulted in the ritual suicide of hundreds of Badung citizens, and the subsequent end to raja autocracy on the island. These days, Badung – which covers under eight percent of Bali's total land mass – is by far the richest of Bali's eight regencies, incorporating as it does nearly all the

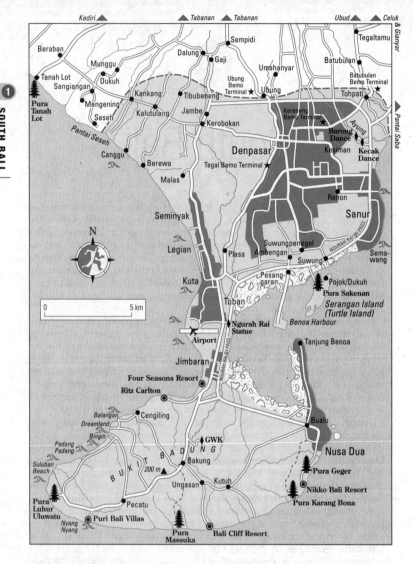

island's most lucrative tourist resorts. The regency collects over 600 million rupiah a day in hotel and restaurant taxes alone, totalling US$30 million in 2001 – approximately fifty times the daily income of West Bali's Jembrana regency, the island's poorest.

Getting around the region on **public transport** is pretty trouble-free: distances between the main centres are short, and bemo services regular and frequent. All south Bali resorts offer plenty of **cars** and **motorbikes** for rent, though traffic is tiresomely heavy throughout the day and late into the night. **Tourist shuttle buses** operate out of Kuta and Sanur to major destinations in Bali (Ubud, Candi Dasa, Lovina, Padang Bai, Kintamani, Tulamben and so on) and further afield (Nusa Lembongan, the Gili Islands, Lombok and Sumbawa). Alternatively, you can use the cheaper but slower **bemo** system: nearly all bemo journeys between places in the south and destinations on any other part of the island go via Denpasar.

Denpasar

Despite roaring motorbikes and round-the-clock traffic congestion, Bali's capital **DENPASAR** (meaning "next to the market") remains a pleasant city at heart, centred on a grassy square and dominated by family compounds grouped into traditional *banjar* districts, with just a few major shopping streets crisscrossing the centre. Bountiful flower gardens are visible over the low walls surrounding the larger houses, and in the residential quarters even the paving stones are carved with floral motifs. Streetlife is nowhere near as hectic as in Kuta, and tourists get little hassle here, not least because Denpasar makes few attempts to woo them. It's not a hedonistic city, with no nightlife, no real bars and no single outstanding restaurant or streetside café; few tourists spend much time here.

Contemporary Denpasar is a genuinely modern, urban, Balinese experience, home to a population of 500,000. **Muslims** from Java have left a strong mark on the place, **Sasaks** from Lombok make up most of the street-vending population, and **Chinese** immigrants dominate the commercial face of the city. Yet the *banjar* still exert a strong influence, and traditional community events, such as gamelan and dance rehearsals, crop up as frequently as in the island's rural villages. The city is also home to some quintessentially Indonesian markets and to the wide-ranging **Bali Museum**. For tourists, it's a convenient base from which to make trips to Batubulan (see p.179), Tanah Lot (see p.374), Sangeh (see p.373) and Mengwi (see p.372), as well as to Kuta and Sanur – all accessible by bemo in under an hour.

Before the Dutch arrived in 1906, control of the city – then known as Badung – had been divided among several rajas, most notably those at the courts of Pemecutan (southwest Denpasar) and Kesiman (east Denpasar). These districts survive to this day, but the royal families have lost their political power and have either dispersed or turned their ancestral palaces into tourist facilities. After Bali won independence from the Dutch in 1949, the island's administrative capital was moved to Badung from the north-coast town of Singaraja and the city was renamed Denpasar. Almost fifty years later Denpasar's status was upgraded again when, in 1992, it became a self-governing municipality, no longer under the auspices of Badung regency.

Arrival, information and city transport

If you're arriving in Bali by air, you'll land at **Ngurah Rai Airport**, which is not in Denpasar as sometimes implied, but just beyond the southern outskirts

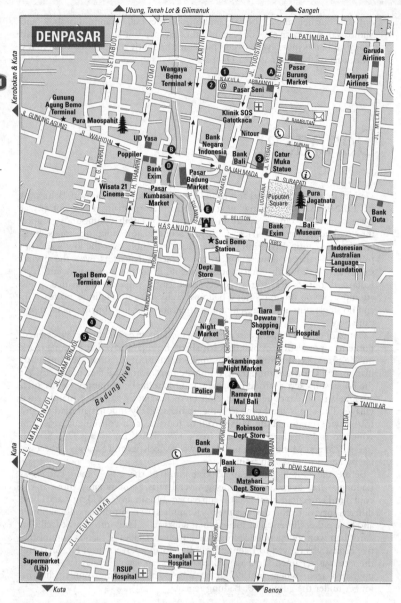

▲ *Ubung, Tanah Lot & Gilimanuk*　　　▲ *Sangeh*

DENPASAR

◄ *Kerobokan & Kuta*

◄ *Kuta*

▼ *Kuta*　　　▼ *Benoa*

of Kuta. For full airport arrival and departure information, see the box on p.110.
　Arriving by bemo or public bus from another part of the island, you'll almost
certainly be dropped at one of the four main **bemo stations**, which lie on the
edges of town: **Tegal**, on Jalan Imam Bonjol, in the southwest corner;
Kereneng, off Jalan Hayam Wuruk, in east central Denpasar; **Ubung**, way off to

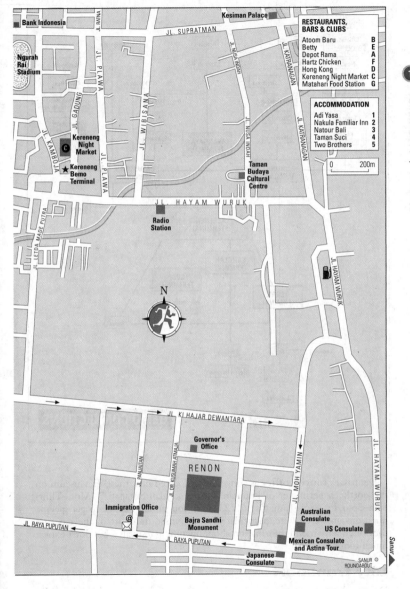

the northwest on the main road to Tabanan and effectively in its own suburb; and, even further out, **Batubulan** in the northeast. The plan on p.92 shows which terminal covers which routes. Getting from one bemo station to another is fairly easy, but connections can be quite time-consuming, as you have to wait for your bemo to fill up at each transit point.

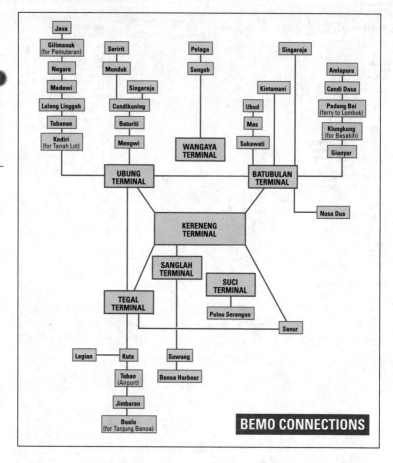

Java

Gilimanuk (for Pemuteran)

Negara

Medewi

Lalang Linggah

Tabanan

Kediri (for Tanah Lot)

Seririt

Munduk

Singaraja

Candikuning

Baturiti

Mengwi

Pelaga

Sangeh

WANGAYA TERMINAL

Singaraja

Kintamani

Ubud

Mas

Sukawati

Amlapura

Candi Dasa

Padang Bai (ferry to Lombok)

Klungkung (for Besakih)

Gianyar

UBUNG TERMINAL

BATUBULAN TERMINAL

Nusa Dua

KERENENG TERMINAL

SANGLAH TERMINAL

SUCI TERMINAL

Pulau Serangan

TEGAL TERMINAL

Sanur

Legian

Kuta

Tuban (Airport)

Jimbaran

Bualu (for Tanjung Benoa)

Suwung

Benoa Harbour

BEMO CONNECTIONS

Denpasar's **tourist office** is conveniently located near the Bali Museum on the northern perimeter of Puputan Square, at Jalan Surapati 7 (Mon–Thurs 8am–3pm, Fri 8am–1pm; ☏0361/234569). You should be able to get specific questions answered here, particularly about public transport in the city, and they often have useful information about upcoming festivals – but don't expect much more than that.

City transport

Denpasar's transport system relies on the fleet of different-coloured **public bemos** that shuttle between the city's bemo terminals. However, it isn't a particularly user-friendly network as only certain routes are covered, and the complex one-way system often means that the bemos take slightly different routes on each leg of their journey. Worse still, there are no published city transport maps. The list of city bemo routes opposite should help, and we've

Below is an outline of the major cross-city routes between Denpasar's main bemo terminals.

Some routes alter slightly in reverse because of the extensive one-way system.

Yellow

Kereneng–Jalan Plawa–Jalan Supratman–Jalan Gianyar–cnr Jalan Waribang (for *barong* dance)–Kesiman–Tohpati–**Batubulan**.

The return Batubulan–Kereneng route is identical except that bemos go down Jalan Kamboja instead of Jalan Plawa just before reaching Kereneng.

Grey-blue

Ubung–Jalan Cokroaminoto–Jalan Gatot Subroto–Jalan Gianyar–cnr Jalan Waribang (for *barong* dance)–Tohpati–**Batubulan**.

The return Batubulan–Ubung route is identical.

Dark green

Kereneng–Jalan Hayam Wuruk–cnr Nusa Indah (for Taman Budaya Cultural Centre)–Sanur roundabout (for Renon consulates)–Jalan Raya Sanur–**Sanur**.

The return Ubung–Kereneng route is identical.

Turquoise

Kereneng–Jalan Surapati (for tourist office, Bali Museum and Pura Agung Jagatnata)–Jalan Veteran (alight at the cnr of Jalan Abimanyu for short walk to Jalan Nakula losmen)–Jalan Cokroaminoto–**Ubung**.

Yellow or turquoise

Tegal–Jalan Gn Merapi–Jalan Setiabudi–**Ubung**–Jalan Cokroaminoto–Jalan Subroto–Jalan Yani–Jalan Nakula (for budget hotels)–Jalan Veteran–Jalan Patimura–Jalan Melati–**Kereneng**–Jalan Hayam Wuruk–Jalan Surapati–Jalan Kapten Agung–Jalan Sudirman–Tiara Dewata shopping centre–Jalan Yos Sudarso–Jalan Diponegoro (for Ramayana Mal Bali shopping centre)–Jalan Hasanudin–Jalan Bukit Tunggal–**Tegal**.

Beige

Kereneng–Jalan Raya Puputan (for GPO)–Jalan Dewi Sartika (for Matahari and Robinson department stores)–Jalan Teuku Umar–Hero Supermarket–junction with Jalan Imam Bonjol (alight to change onto Kuta bemos)–**Tegal**.

Because of the one-way system, the return Tegal–Kereneng route runs along Jalan Letda Tantular instead of Jalan Raya Puputan.

Dark blue

Tegal–Jalan Imam Bonjol–Jalan Teuku Umar–Hero Supermarket–junction with Jalan Diponegoro (for the Matahari and Robinson department stores)–Jalan Yos Sudarso (for Ramayana Mal Bali shopping centre)–Jalan Sudirman–Jalan Letda Tantular–junction with Jalan Panjaitan (alight for the 500m walk to the Immigration and GPO)–Jalan Hajar Dewantara–Jalan Moh Yamin–Sanur roundabout–**Sanur**.

The return Sanur–Tegal route goes all the way along Jalan Raya Puputan after the roundabout, passing the entrance gates of Immigration and the GPO, then straight along Jalan Teuku Umar, past Hero Supermarket to the junction with Jalan Imam Bonjol (where you should alight to pick up Kuta-bound bemos) before heading north up Jalan Imam Bonjol to Tegal.

Denpasar's four main bemo terminals serve towns, villages and beach resorts right across the island; see the plan on p.92 for an overview. **Tegal** bemo station serves destinations south of Denpasar, including Kuta, Jimbaran, Bualu (for Tanjung Benoa) and Uluwatu. **Kereneng** station serves Sanur. **Batubulan** station in the nearby village of Batubulan (see p.181) serves Ubud and the east coast, including Candi Dasa and Padang Bai, and is also the departure point for the Damri bus service to Nusa Dua via Sanur (dropping passengers outside the *Radisson* hotel) and the eastern outskirts of Kuta (see p.112). **Ubung** station (see p.372) runs bemos to north and west Bali, including Tanah Lot, Medewi, Gilimanuk (for Java), Candikuning (Bedugul), Munduk, and Singaraja (for Lovina), as well as **buses** to and from Java and Padang Bai (for Lombok).

There are smaller bemo terminals on Jalan **Gunung Agung**, for transport to Canggu and Kerobokan; near the **Sanglah** hospital, for Benoa Harbour and Suwung; at **Wangaya** for Sangeh and Pelaga; and at **Suci** for Pulau Serangan. For airport departure details, see box on p.111.

---

detailed the most convenient routes in the text. Nearly all Denpasar bemos have at least their first and last stop printed in large letters on the back or side of the vehicle (for example, Tegal–Ubung–Kereneng–Tegal), and most are colour coded. Wave to hail one, but be sure to state your exact destination before getting in. **Prices** are fixed, and a list of rates is displayed in the controller's office at each terminal, but tourists are often obliged to pay more – generally between Rp1000 and Rp2000 for a cross-city ride. For impartial advice on bemo routes and prices, ask at the controller's office rather than in the bemos themselves: bemo drivers often massage the facts to suit their own pockets. If you can't face the bemo system, metered **taxis** also circulate around the city, as do **dokar**, the horse-drawn carts used by locals for short journeys within town.

Accommodation

Accommodation in Denpasar is disappointingly shabby, catering more for the quick-stop Indonesian business traveller than the fussier tourist trade. The losmen and hotels listed below are the best of the bunch, though none is outstanding.

Adi Yasa Jl Nakula 23 ☎0361/222679. This long-running losmen, less than ten minutes' walk north of the museum and tourist office, is most backpackers' first choice. Rooms are exceptionally cheap and all come with fan and bathroom, though they're slightly run-down and not all that secure. From Kereneng, take an Ubung-bound bemo and walk 300m west from the Pasar Seni art market at the Jl Abimanyu junction with Jl Veteran. The weirdly routed Tegal–Kereneng bemos also pass the front door. ❶

Nakula Familiar Inn Jl Nakula 4 ☎0361/226446. Very spruce, modern and clean,

and run by a friendly family. All rooms have their own balcony, fan and bathroom. Not as popular as *Adi Yasa* across the road (see above for bemo access), or as cheap, but more comfortable. ❷

Natour Bali Jl Veteran 3 ☎0361/225681, ℱ235347, ℰntrbali@denpasar.wasantara.net.id. Central Denpasar's oldest hotel used to be the establishment of choice for the cruise passengers of the 1930s and still has a certain quaint appeal in its colonial architecture and ambience. These days it offers reasonably well-equipped if rather characterless rooms, a swimming pool and restaurant. ❺

Taman Suci Jl Imam Bonjol 45 ☎0361/485254, ℱ484724, ☯www.tamansuci.com. Modern, decently furnished mid-range hotel, just a couple of minutes' walk south of Tegal bemo station. Good value and well equipped with air-con, hot water and TVs in every room, but not terribly convenient for Denpasar's big sights. ❺

Two Brothers (Dua Saudara) Jl Imam Bonjol Gang VII 5 ☎0361/484704. Peacefully located losmen in a family compound down a *gang* off the main street, about five minutes' walk south of Tegal bemo station. Rooms are spotless if a bit scruffy, but none has its own bathroom. Good-value singles. ❶

The City

Denpasar's central landmark is **Puputan Square**, the verdant rectangle that marks the heart of the downtown area, the core of the major sights and the crossover point of the city's major north–south and east–west arteries. On the traffic island here stands a huge stone **statue of Catur Muka**, the four-faced, eight-armed Hindu guardian of the cardinal points, indicating the exact location of the city centre. The main road that runs west from the statue is **Jalan Gajah Mada** (named after the fourteenth-century Javanese prime minister), lined with shophouses and restaurants and, just beside the Badung River, the huge **Pasar Badung market**. A couple of blocks further west stands the historic **Pura Maospahit** temple, but the more visited attractions dominate the eastern fringes of Puputan Square itself – the rewarding **Bali Museum** and the state temple, **Pura Agung Jagatnata**.

Denpasar's eastern districts are less enticing, but the art gallery at the **Taman Budaya** cultural centre is worth a look, while the suburb of **Renon** is chiefly of interest for its consulates and cheap internet access.

Puputan Square

Right in the heart of Denpasar, the grassy park known as **Puputan Square** (Alun-alun Puputan or Taman Puputan) makes a pleasant retreat from the busy roads that encircle it. Kids come here to play, old men socialize on the benches under the trees, and office workers while away their lunch breaks in the shade. In September and October, at the end of the dry season, the Rose of India trees (*tangi* in Balinese) planted around the perimeter blossom into a spectacular lilac frill.

The square commemorates the events of September 20, 1906, when the raja of Badung marched out of his palace gates, followed by hundreds of his subjects, and faced the invading Dutch head on (see p.495 for the full story). Dressed all in holy white, each man, woman and child clasping a golden kris, the people of Badung had psyched themselves up for a **puputan**, or ritual fight to the death, rather than submit to the Dutch colonialists' demands. Historical accounts vary a little, but it's thought that the mass suicide took place on this square and was incited by Badung's chief priest who, on a signal from the raja, stabbed his king with the royal kris. Hundreds of citizens followed suit, and those that didn't were shot down by Dutch bullets; the final death toll was reported to be somewhere between six hundred and two thousand. The palace itself, just across Jalan Surapati on the north edge of the modern square, was razed to the ground and has now been rebuilt as the imposing official residence of the governor of Bali. The huge **bronze statue** on the northern edge of the park is a memorial to the Badung citizens who fought and died in the 1906 *puputan*, the figures bearing sharpened bamboo staves and kris – an image that you'll see repeated on town and village roadside statues across the island.

The square hosts a commemorative **fair**, with food stalls and *wayang kulit* shows, every year on September 20.

The Bali Museum

Overlooking the eastern edge of Puputan Square on pedestrianized Jalan Mayor Wisnu, the **Bali Museum** (Sun–Thurs 7.30am–3pm, Fri 7.30am–1pm; Rp750, children Rp250; on the turquoise Kereneng–Ubung bemo route) is Denpasar's most significant attraction and, with some perseverance, makes a worthwhile introduction to the island's culture past and present. Even if the exhibits hold little interest for you, the museum compound itself is charming, divided into traditional courtyards complete with *candi bentar*, *kulkul* tower, shrines and flower gardens. Work on the museum began in 1910 under the direction of the Dutch Resident, whose idea it was to construct the museum in the traditional *puri-pura* style, mixing elements from traditional palace (*puri*) architecture with temple (*pura*) features. But the project was beset with problems, and it wasn't until the 1930s and the involvement of the expatriate German artist Walter Spies (see box on p.211), among others, that the collection of ethnographic materials was really taken seriously.

Housed in four separate buildings, each designed in a specific regional and historical style, the collection is somewhat under-labelled, so you might want to hire one of the volunteer guides who hang around the entrance gate. None of the exhibition halls is named, so we've described them in the order you'll come across them: although the modern "main" building facing the entrance gate is meant to be visited first, the most rewarding place to start your museum tour is in fact the "Second Pavilion", the second building to the left of the entrance courtyard.

Main Building

The two-storey **Main Building**, which stands at the back of the entrance courtyard, houses items from Bali's prehistory as well as a selection of **traditional artefacts** from the secular daily life of the Balinese. In the downstairs hall, the cases of stone axes and bronze jewellery make less interesting viewing than the massive **stone sarcophagus**, hewn from soft volcanic rock and dating back to around the second century BC. The four black and white **photographs of the 1906 puputan** here are also well worth lingering over: one shows the landing of the Dutch troops at Sanur, the others gruesome scenes of massacred bodies heaped up in what is now known as Puputan Square.

Upstairs you'll find some fine archaic-looking implements, many of which are still in common use today. You're almost certain to see the **bamboo fans**, for example, being used by streetside barbecued-corn vendors, and the **coconut grater** features in nearly every restaurant and household kitchen – the one shown here has been carved into an animal shape, complete with genitalia, with the crucial gouging and shredding blade protruding from its head. Look out too for the bizarre containers for **fighting crickets** – tiny tubular bamboo cages designed to hold the male insects used in the popular local sport of cricket fighting (*menjangkrikan*). On the day of the contest, each competitor assembles his crickets in a special wooden box which holds up to twenty miniature cricket cages. Bets are placed, and then pairs of crickets are released from their cages to do battle in a central arena. Apparently they rarely hurt each other, and the loser is usually the insect that simply scurries away.

First (Bululeng) Pavilion

Passing through the traditional gateway that leads left off the entrance court-yard, you'll come to the compact **First Pavilion**, designed in Bululeng (or Singaraja) style, and holding some fine examples of Balinese **textiles**. The plainest and most common of the styles displayed here is **endek**, sometimes referred to as *ikat*, in which the weft threads are dyed to the finished pattern before being woven – hence the distinctive fuzzy-edged look (see p.538). **Geringsing**, or double-*ikat*, is a far rarer material which involves a complex dyeing and weaving technique practised only by the villages of Tenganan (see p.291). You'll also see gorgeously coloured heavy silk **songket** brocades, inter-woven with gleaming gold and silver threads. Finally, the less ostentatious **per-ada** (or *prada*) cloth relies less on weaving skills than on screenprint designers who stamp plain-coloured fabric with gold-painted symbols and patterns. *Perada* cloth is used for ceremonial wear and is most usually seen on tradition-al temple umbrellas.

Second (Karangasem) Pavilion

Built to resemble the long, low structure of an eighteenth-century Karangasem-style palace, the **Second Pavilion** houses the museum's most fas-cinating exhibits. It shows all manner of religious paraphernalia in an attempt to introduce the **spiritual and ceremonial life** of the Balinese – the cor-nerstone of the average islander's day-to-day existence. In the case on the far left-hand wall, the bronze image of **Sanghyang Widi Wasa** (the supreme god or being, who is also known as Acintya) is immediately recognizable because of his peculiar stance – the right leg drawn up so that his flame-shaped right foot rests against his left knee (see p.505 for more). In the same case, look out for the image constructed out of a thousand ancient **Chinese coins** strung together, meant to invoke the god of wealth. Although these coins, or *kepeng*, are no longer legal tender, they have a special religious significance and are hoarded by Balinese to use as offerings.

Along the back wall, the birthrites exhibit contains a curious bell-shaped **bamboo cage** still used by some villagers to mark the first cycle of a baby's life (210 days). Babies are never allowed to crawl on the ground, as the Balinese eschew any behaviour that appears animal-like, and until their 210th day they are continually carried around. On completion of its first cycle, the baby is placed in the cage and ceremonially lowered to the ground, after which it is expected to totter on two legs.

The Balinese **calendars** on the right-hand wall are immensely complex compositions arrived at through mathematical, astrological and religious per-mutations. The painted one here is in traditional Kamasan style (see p.531), using muted natural colours on a white cotton background, while the carved wooden calendar is much rarer. Though these particular examples are quite old, the calendar system which they depict is still widely used to determine all sorts of events from temple festivals to the starting day for the construction of a new house. For an explanation of the workings of the Balinese calendar, see box on p.57.

Third (Tabanan) Pavilion

The theme of the **Third Pavilion**, designed to replicate a palace from the Tabanan regency, is **music and dance**; exhibits include masks, costumes and puppets. Most impressive are the *barong* costumes, representing legendary crea-tures which feature in nearly every Balinese dance performance. The shaggy-haired **Barong Ket**, representing the forces of good, is probably the most popular character, and is something like a cross between a lion, a pantomime horse and a Chinese dragon. One dancer takes the part of the beast's head and front legs, the other is his hindquarters. The witch-like figure of **Rangda** who stands next to him is the embodiment of all that is evil, with her pointed fangs, unkempt hair, snarling mouth and huge lolling tongue (the box on p.249 tells Rangda's story). Less commonly seen on tourist stages, as they play a more vital role in village life, are the two towering **Barong Landung**, huge humanoid male and female puppets. At certain times of the ceremonial year, holy men will don these enormous bamboo skeletons and use them to chase away evil spirits. See p.523 for more on these ritual performances.

Pura Agung Jagatnata

Just over the north wall of the Bali Museum, and clearly visible from the museum's *kulkul* tower, stands the modern state temple of **Pura Agung Jagatnata**, set in a fragrant garden of pomegranate, hibiscus and frangipani trees. The temple, built in 1953, is dedicated to the supreme god, Sanghyang Widi Wasa, who is here worshipped in his role as "Lord of the World", or Jagatnata.

As with nearly every temple in Bali, Pura Agung Jagatnata is designed as three courtyards, though in this case the middle courtyard is so compressed as to be little more than a gallery encircled by a moat. **Carvings** of lotus flowers and frogs adorn the tiny stone bridge that spans the moat (access at festival times only) and there are reliefs illustrating scenes from the *Ramayana* and *Mahabharata* carved into the gallery's outer wall. If you walk round to the gallery's east wall, you'll see probably the most famous episode in the whole *Ramayana* story – the shooting of the golden deer by Rama, which resulted in Sita's kidnap and the subsequent bookful of battles between Rama and Rawana (see box on p.522).

The temple's focal point is the looming five-tiered **padmasana**, beneath the customary empty throne and balanced on top of a huge cosmic turtle. Built entirely from blocks of white coral, the tower is carved with demons' heads and, on the bottom level, with the face and hands of Bhoma, the son of the earth, whose job it is to repel evil spirits from the temple. The lotus throne at its summit is left empty for Sanghyang Widi Wasa to fill when descending to earth at festival times – the god is represented in a gold relief embossed on the back. Worshippers lay their offerings at the foot of this shrine, heaped up around the heads of the turtle and the two attendant *naga*, which are all swathed in lengths of holy saffron and black-and-white cloth. In the southeast corner of the outer compound stands the **kulkul** (bell) tower, with its split wooden bell hung high up from the rafters. The *kulkul* is still used to summon villagers to festivals, meetings and temple-cleaning duties.

As a state temple, Pura Agung Jagatnata is effectively open to all devotees (village temples are not). Twice a month, on the occasion of the full moon and of the new or "dark" moon, **festivals** are held here and citizens file into the temple compound to lay down their offerings and pray. On the festival evenings, *wayang kulit* shows are sometimes performed at the temple, held from around 9pm to 11pm in the outer courtyard; ask at the nearby tourist office (see p.92) for details.

Pasar Badung and Pasar Kumbasari

The Chinese shophouses and glossy department stores of modern Denpasar are nowhere near as interesting as the city's old-fashioned Balinese **markets**. The biggest and best of these is the chaotic **Pasar Badung**, which stands at the heart of the downtown area, set slightly back off Jalan Gajah Mada. It used to be housed in a traditional three-storey covered stone and brick *pasar* beside the Badung River, but this burnt down in 2000, so the stallholders now conduct their trade in the open air, in an impossibly packed warren of overflowing alleyways. Trading takes place here 24 hours a day, with buyers and sellers pouring in from all over the island. With its pungent aromas and bizarre sights assailing you from every angle, Pasar Badung epitomizes the Asian marketplace, and for tourists it's likely to be more of a cultural than a shopping experience. Easiest access into the heart of the market is from the far northern end of Jalan Sulawesi, though many of the tourist-oriented wares, including sarongs, batik clothes, ceremonial parasols and offertory baskets, are set out on the stalls that abut the western edge of Jalan Sulawesi and can be perused from the street. (Jalan Sulawesi itself is the centre of Denpasar's rag trade and well worth a browse in its own right – see p.102 for details.) Be prepared to find yourself landed with a **guide**, as well: local women hang out around the Jalan Sulawesi entrance – some even wait for their prey way up on Gajah Mada – offering to accompany you around the market. You'll be steered very persuasively towards certain stalls, and anything you buy will include a hefty commission for your guide.

Just west across the narrow Badung River from Pasar Badung, a few metres south of Jalan Gajah Mada, the four-storey **Pasar Kumbasari** is exclusively dedicated to art-market goods such as handicrafts, souvenirs and clothes. This is a good, inexpensive place to shop, particularly if you're looking for bulk buys – and if you nose around carefully you should find some more unusual artefacts alongside the carvings, wind chimes, batik sarongs and basketware items.

The much smaller, open-air **Pasar Burung**, north of Puputan Square on Jalan Veteran, specializes in a quite different sort of produce: live birds and animals sold as pets. As with similar places the world over, a visit here can be extremely depressing, both for the appalling conditions in which the creatures are kept, and for the knowledge that, behind the shuttered doors and temporary walls, there's almost certain to be a caged menagerie of more valuable, endangered birds and animals, captured and sold in secret.

Pura Maospahit

In contrast with the other major Denpasar sights, **Pura Maospahit** on Jalan Sutomo, just north of Pasar Badung, has a long and significant history that begins with the ancient fourteenth-century Javanese kingdom of Majapahit. It's thought that the oldest part of the temple may actually have been brought over to Bali from East Java, either in the fourteenth century, following the 1343 conquest of the island by the Majapahit empire, or in the sixteenth century by the Hindu aristocracy forced to flee the Islamic invasion of East Java. Certainly the architectural style is very typically Majapahit: the temple is constructed entirely from brick, and is remarkable for its total absence of superfluous ornamentation. Much of what you see today, however, is reconstruction, as the temple suffered badly in the 1917 earthquake, and has been reassembled from original and replacement brickwork.

Pura Maospahit is rarely visited by tourists, and can feel a bit forgotten – though a temple attendant is almost sure to emerge to greet you with visitors' book, donation bowl and sash. The temple rooftops are visible from Jalan Sutomo, but **access** to the outer courtyard is via a doorway down the narrow *gang* that runs along the compound's southern wall. Once inside the compound, look up at the tree to your immediate right, in whose branches you'll see a most unusual *kulkul* tower, built into its own little treehouse. Beyond this, the massive red-brick *candi bentar* connects the outer and middle courtyards, protected by two huge figures representing a giant and a *garuda*.

Through the towering, impressively chunky and unadorned *padu raksa* gateway, the **inner courtyard** is packed with a dozen or more thatched brick shrines. The central, and most important, structure here is the squat red-brick *candi raras* Maospahit, guarded by two ancient terracotta figurines. It's thought that both this shrine and the almost identical one that stands a short distance to the north were constructed in honour of the Majapahit ancestors of the Balinese people.

Taman Budaya Cultural Centre

In the eastern part of town, on Jalan Nusa Indah, fifteen minutes' walk from the Kereneng bemo station, or direct on a Sanur-bound bemo, the **Taman Budaya Cultural Centre** (daily 8am–3pm; Rp250), designed by one of Indonesia's most renowned architects, Ida Bagus Tugur, does its best to fill in the gaps left by the Bali Museum – namely the history of Balinese painting and a celebration of the island's contemporary artistic life. It's a tall order, which the purpose-built cultural centre doesn't meet, but if you don't have time to visit the far superior Neka Art Museum in Ubud (see p.206), this will at least give you a taste. And, if you're in Denpasar during the annual **Arts Festival** (usually staged between mid-June and mid-July), it's worth dropping by the centre for the huge programme of special exhibitions and dance shows.

The main **exhibition hall** is housed in the long, two-storey building towards the back of the compound, and begins with an overview of Balinese **painting**, with a few examples in the classical *wayang* style, followed by works from several different schools, taking in the so-called Ubud, Batuan and Young Artists styles (see pp.532–534 for an explanation of these). Unfortunately, there are few outstanding examples here, and the presentation and labelling is less than helpful. A selection of religious and secular **woodcarvings** fills the next room, together with an assortment of *Ramayana* and *topeng* **masks**. There are more ambitious carvings downstairs and a collection of **modern non-traditional paintings**, spanning a range of styles from batik through to works influenced by Cubism and Post-Impressionism.

Renon

Denpasar's administrative district, **Renon**, is down on the southeastern edge of the city, very close to the resort of Sanur and served by Sanur-bound bemos. Several square kilometres have been landscaped into a leafy green suburb, with wide tree-lined boulevards, shaded pavements and imposing buildings housing government offices, including the governor of Bali's headquarters and the Immigration Department.

This is also the location of the huge new **Bajra Sandhi monument** ("Balinese People's Struggle"), an ambitious project that's been under way since

1989 and will, when completed, chart the history of Bali from 300,000 BC to 1950 in a series of dioramas. Visitors are currently only permitted to admire the structure from the outside. It has been designed by the architect Ida Bagus Tugur to resemble a priest's bell, with dimensions – comprising 8 entrances, 17 corners and 45m in height – that represent the date of Indonesia's Declaration of Independence: August 17, 1945.

Eating and drinking

Eating and **drinking** hardly rates as one of Denpasar's great pleasures, but the city does harbour a fair range of authentic and very reasonably priced Indonesian and Chinese **restaurants**. Few of these make any concessions to the minimal tourist trade, which is good news for the taste buds, but does mean that you'll have to eat well before 9pm, when most places start clearing up. After hours, though, **hawkers** continue to ply the streets with their soup and noodle carts, and the **Kereneng night market** serves food till sunrise. Denpasar has a dearth of **bars**, so most people order beer with their meal or simply buy a few bottles to take away.

Atoom Baru Jl Gajah Mada 106. Popular city-centre Chinese restaurant: lots of meal-in-a-soup dishes, plus some seafood. Worth visiting in a group to share the family-sized dishes. Inexpensive to Moderate.

Betty Jl Sumatra 56. Unpretentious café with an extensive English-language menu that includes *rujak petis* (vegetable and fruit in spicy peanut and shrimp sauce), *botok daging sapi* (spicy minced beef with tofu and coconut milk), *pepes ikan laut* (steamed fish), and an imaginative and tasty vegetarian selection as well. Closes at 9pm. Inexpensive.

Depot Rama Jl Veteran 55. Neighbourhood warung serving nasi campur, nasi goreng, *nasi soto ayam* and lots of noodle dishes. Very convenient for the Jl Nakula losmen. Inexpensive.

Hartz Chicken Third floor, Ramayana Mal Bali shopping centre, Jl Diponegoro. Well-priced all-you-can-eat chicken buffet, with thirty percent discounts for the under 9s and over 65s. Last entry at 9pm. Moderate.

Hong Kong Jl Gajah Mada 99. Classy, air-conditioned Chinese restaurant offering a huge variety of set meals and à la carte choices, includ-

ing seafood and some Western dishes. Popular with middle-class Indonesian families. Karaoke at night. Moderate.

Kereneng Night Market Just off Jl Hayam Wuruk, adjacent to Kereneng bemo station. Over fifty vendors convene here from dusk to dawn every night, serving up piping hot soups, noodle and rice dishes, *babi guling*, fresh fruit juices and cold beers. Long trestle tables are set up around the marketplace. Inexpensive.

Matahari Food Station Basement of Matahari department store, cnr of Jl Teuku Umar and Jl Sudirman. Tempting range of food stalls which each specialize in a particular regional or international cuisine. Select your food, choose a table, pay at the cash desk and then wait for it to be served to you. Closes at 9pm. Inexpensive.

Puri Agung Inside the *Natour Bali Hotel*, Jl Veteran 3. The 1920s decor is of more interest than the food, with a dining room cooled by heavy-bladed fans and staffed by waiters in full formal gear. The highlight is their renowned *rijsttafel*, which includes half a dozen separate dishes plus soup and fruit salad. Moderate.

Entertainment

Most young citizens of Denpasar head out to the bars and discos of Kuta or Sanur for their **entertainment** – in fact many of the resorts' DJs, bar staff and gigolos commute from homes in Denpasar, as rents on the coast are prohibitively expensive. As a result, Denpasar lacks any kind of **nightlife**, save for a single karaoke club, *Akasaka*, on Jalan Teuku Umar and the night markets. The biggest **cinema** complex is the five-screen Wisata 21 at Jalan Thamrin 29 (T0361/424023), with a smaller one on nearby Jalan Kartini; programmes are listed in the free tourist newspaper *Bali Travel News* (Wwww .bali-travelnews.com), or consult the *Bali Post* for schedules. Films are usually shown in the original language with Indonesian subtitles.

Dance

You'll be able to see a **Balinese dance** performance on any day of the week. The shows detailed below are all performed daily, and are mostly patronized by tour groups who have booked through agents in Kuta or Sanur; tickets bought through tour agents generally cost $10–15 per person including return transport, while tickets bought at the door are Rp50,000 and are available right up until the show starts. (If coming from Sanur it's much cheaper to take a taxi and pay on the door; see p.168.) For background information on all the dances, see pp.519–527.

The **barong**, featuring the battle between the shaggy-haired lion-like Barong Ket and the evil witch Rangda, takes place at the Catur Eka Budhi on Jalan Waribang, in the eastern Kesiman district (daily 9.30–10.30am). Bemos for Batubulan from Ubung and Kereneng pass the corner of Jalan Waribang, from where the stage is a short signposted walk down the quiet side road. If you miss the stop and end up in Batubulan instead, you can also catch the *barong* there, at the Pura Puseh (daily 9.30–10.30am; see p.180 for details).

The spectacular "monkey dance", or **kecak**, is performed nightly at the Stage Uma Dewi, which is also on Jalan Waribang in Kesiman, about 300m south of the *barong* dance stage (daily 6.30–7.30pm). *Kecak* is the most accessible and popular of Bali's traditional dances and is well worth catching. Bemos heading from Ubung and Kereneng to Batubulan pass the corner of Jalan Waribang, from where the stage is a 500-metre signposted walk.

Shopping

For **crafts and souvenirs**, the best place to browse, and bargain, is Pasar Kumbasari, the four-storey art market on Jalan Gajah Mada, described on p.99. It brims over with stalls selling sarongs, textiles, woodcarvings, paintings and handicrafts. For more unusual local souvenirs, the tiny UD Yasa, Gajah Mada 148, is a specialist supplier of religious and ceremonial paraphernalia. The best place for lengths of **fabric**, including rolls of batik, is Jalan Sulawesi, whose entire course from Jalan Hasanudin in the south to Gajah Mada in the north is devoted to cloth of all descriptions, including *songket* brocades, saree silks, and of course the local women's favourite – rayon. Fabric shops also spill out east along Jalan Gajah Mada as far as Jalan Sumatra. About 100m west along Gajah Mada from the Sulawesi intersection, Poppiler, at no. 117, specializes in traditional batik prints, selling ready-made shirts and sarongs as well as some designs by the metre. You'll find a dozen outlets for **gold** on the stretch of Jalan Hasanudin that runs west from Jalan Diponegoro to the river.

The Ramayana Mal Bali shopping centre, Jalan Diponegoro 103 (daily 9.30am–9.30pm; Kereneng–Tegal and Tegal–Sanur bemos), the Matahari department store at Jalan Dewi Sartika 4 (daily 9.30am–9pm; Tegal–Sanur bemo), and the Tara Dewata shopping centre on Jalan Sutoyo (daily 9am–9pm;

Kereneng–Tegal bemo) all carry high-street **fashions** and a few handicrafts. Matahari stocks a pretty good range of English-language novels and **books** about Bali in its basement bookstore and also has a good **children's department** upstairs, with everything from baby clothes to bottles and mosquito nets (nappies and baby food are sold in the supermarket on the ground floor).

Hero Supermarket in the Libi Plaza shopping complex on Jalan Teuku Umar (daily 9.30am–9pm; Tegal–Sanur and Kereneng–Tegal bemos) is the best place in the south of Bali to buy your own **food and drink** – the Bali *kopi*, gado-gado sauces, clove cigarettes, *arak* and *brem* spirits are all much cheaper here than in the minimarts of Kuta and Sanur. An alternative is the smaller but more centrally located supermarket inside Ramayana Mal Bali.

Listings

Airline offices Most international airline offices (see box on p.111) are in Sanur or at the airport, though the domestic airlines (see p.21) have their main offices in Denpasar. Garuda has a city check-in at Jl Melati 61 ☏0361/254747, where you can get your boarding pass a day in advance.

American Express The closest office is in Sanur (see p.169).

Banks and exchange Most central Denpasar banks have exchange counters. There are ATMs for Visa, MasterCard and Cirrus Maestro every few hundred metres on the main shopping streets. Visa cash advances are available at Bank Bali, diagonally opposite the Matahari department store at Jl Dewi Sartika 88 ☏0361/261678, and at Bank Duta, Jl Hayam Wuruk 165 ☏0361/226578. The GPO in Renon (see below) is a Western Union agent; for details on receiving money wired from home, see p.37.

Dentist Bali 911 Dental Clinic, Jl Patimura 9 ☏0361/249749.

Embassies and consulates Only a few countries maintain consulates in Denpasar; p.23 has the full list.

Hospitals and clinics Sanglah Public Hospital at Jl Kesehatan Selatan 1, Sanglah (five lines ☏0361/227911–227915; public bemo from Kereneng) is the main provincial public hospital, with the island's most modern emergency ward and some English-speaking staff. It also has Bali's only divers' decompression chamber. Kasih Ibu, Jl Teuku Umar 120 ☏0361/223036, is a 24-hour private hospital that is fine for minor ailments, but not equipped for emergencies. Klinik SOS Gatotkaca, Jl Gatotkaca 21 ☏0361/223555, is open 24hr and staffed by English-speaking medics.

Immigration office At cnr Jl Panjaitan and Jl Raya Puputan, Renon (Mon–Thurs 8am–3pm, Fri 8–11am, Sat 8am–2pm; ☏0361/227828). The

Sanur–Tegal and Kereneng–Tegal bemos pass the front door; otherwise, take the Tegal–Sanur bemo, alight where the road splits into the one-way system on Jl Raya Puputan, and walk 750m.

Internet access Bali's internet HQ is Wasantara Net at the Warposnet (Mon–Sat 8am–8pm; ☏0361/228290), located at the back of the GPO compound in Renon. It's on the Sanur–Tegal bemo route. This is by far the cheapest and fastest place in Bali (Rp6000/hr) and has lots of terminals. Other useful email centres are Hello Internet on the top floor of the Ramayana Mal Bali on Jl Diponegoro, and the small internet centre handily placed across from the *Adi Yasa* losmen on Jl Veteran.

Language lessons Courses in Indonesian language at Indonesia Australia Language Foundation (IALF), Jl Kapten Agung 17 ☏0361/225243, ⓦwww.ialf.edu, and in Indonesian and Balinese language at LCC Language and Culture Centre, Jl Nusa Indah 77 ☏0361/226745, ⓔlcc.bali@eudoramail.com.

Pharmacies Inside Tiara Dewata department store on Jl Sutoyo; Matahari department store on Jl Dewi Sartika; Ramayana Mal Bali on Jl Diponegoro; and Hero Supermarket on Jl Teuku Umar. Also, Apotik Kimia Farma, Jl Diponegoro 125.

Phone offices There are Telkom offices at Jl Teuku Umar 6, and on Jl Durian. IDD phones are also available in the Tiara Dewata department store on Jl Sutoyo and there are dozens of wartels all over the city. There's a Home Country Direct phone at the Bali Museum.

Police There are police stations on Jl Pattimura and Jl Diponegoro.

Post offices Denpasar's poste restante (Mon–Sat 8am–8pm) is at the GPO, located on Jl Raya Puputan in Renon. The Sanur–Tegal and Kereneng–Tegal bemos pass the front door;

otherwise, take the Tegal–Sanur bemo, get out at the Jl Letda Tantular/Jl Panjaitan junction and walk 500m south. There's a more central post office on Jl Rambutan, north of Puputan Square.

Swimming pools Tiara Dewata shopping centre has a public pool, or you can use the one at *Natour Bali* hotel for a small fee.

Travel agents Domestic Garuda and Merpati airline tickets can be bought from Nitour next to the *Natour Bali* hotel, Jl Veteran 5 ☏ 0361/234742, ✉ nitourbali@denpasar.wasantara.net.id, and international and domestic airline tickets from Puri Astina Putra, opposite the Australian consulate in Renon, Jl Moh Yamin 1a ☏ 0361/223552, ✉ astina@denpasar.wasantara.net.id. Get Pelni boat tickets from Jl Diponegoro 165 ☏ 0361/234680, and train tickets (for Java) from Jl Diponegoro 150 Blok B4 ☏ 0361/227131.

Kuta–Legian–Seminyak

The biggest, brashest, most untraditional resort in Bali, the **KUTA–LEGIAN–SEMINYAK** conurbation continues to expand from its epicentre on the southwest coast, 10km southwest of Denpasar. Packed with hundreds of losmen, hotels, restaurants, bars, clubs, souvenir shops, fashion boutiques and tour agencies, the eight-kilometre strip plays host to several hundred thousand visitors a year, many of them regulars – all here to party, shop or surf. It's a hectic place: noisy, full of hassling hawkers, traffic jams and constant building work. The main drag, **Jalan Legian**, is often so packed that traffic just crawls along it, every inch of road jammed with taxis and tourist buses, minibuses, bemos, *dokar* and motorbikes. And yet, for all the hustle, it's a good-humoured resort, almost completely unsleazy, with no strip bars, no high-rises (nothing over the height of a tall coconut tree, in fact), and remarkably little crime.

For many travellers, it's not only the crowds and the assault on the senses that are off-putting, it's that the place seems so un-Balinese: *McDonald's*, *Billabong*, *Holiday Inn* and *Hard Rock* are all here; *Time*, *Newsweek* and *The Sydney Morning Herald* are sold on every street corner; Hollywood blockbusters show regularly at the dozens of video-bars; and almost every bartender, waiter and losmen employee engages effortlessly in slang-ridden English or Japanese banter. But the resort is, in truth, distinctly Balinese: villagers still live and work here, making religious offerings, attending *banjar* meetings and holding temple festivals. Every morning and afternoon the women of Kuta–Legian–Seminyak don their temple sashes and place **offerings** in nooks and crannies, in doorways and under tables; you're more than likely to find a tiny palm-leaf basket filled with flowers and rice on the steps of your verandah first thing in the morning. All three former villages have their own **temples**, but none is outstanding and nearly all lock their gates to tourists except at festival times, when you're usually welcome to attend so long as you're suitably attired (see p.73).

Some history

For centuries, Kuta was considered by the Balinese to be little more than a wasteland, an infertile stretch of coast haunted by malevolent spirits, and a dumping ground for the lepers and criminals cast out from their own villages. Compounding this unpleasant image was Kuta's history as a **slave port** in the seventeenth and eighteenth centuries, during which hundreds of thousands of men and women were sold by the Balinese rajas to their counterparts in Java

Mads Lange

With the arrival of the Danish adventurer and entrepreneur **Mads Lange** in 1839, Kuta's local and international reputation took a significant upward turn. In less than two decades, this astute but impetuous Dane managed not only to mark south Bali indelibly on the Asian trade map, but also to postpone the region's acquiescence to Dutch sovereignty, earning himself the title "White Raja of Bali".

The young Mads first went to sea at the age of 18, on a Danish trading ship bound for Asia. By 1833, he had built a profitable **trading post** in Ampenan, on the west coast of Lombok, shipping out regular cargoes of **rice** to China and Singapore in exchange for holds full of **kepeng** (Chinese coins), textiles and opium. But his business flourished for only a few years, and in 1839 his main competitor on Lombok, the Englishman George King, gained the protection of an influential Lombok raja, and so forced Lange out. Lange immediately decamped to Bali, determined to use **Kuta** as a base from which to rebuild his empire.

Success came quickly, with Lange once again dealing mainly in rice, though this time supplementing his income by acting as a broker for produce from all over Bali. Islanders flocked to Kuta, bringing him their coconuts, cattle, coffee and tobacco, for which he paid them in *kepeng*; he'd cleverly established a **monopoly** over these Chinese coins, which became Bali's only coinage, and set the exchange rate himself. Lange ran this burgeoning dominion from a huge fortified compound near Kuta's river (50m east of the night market on Jl Tuan Langa, named in his honour), and he lived here with a huge retinue of wives, concubines, assistants, children and servants.

Lange fraternized freely with the upper echelons of Balinese society, forging useful friendships with the powerful rajas of south Bali kingdoms. He was also singled out by **the Dutch** (who were already established in the region and unashamedly eager to extend their power base) as official agent for the Dutch Indies government in 1844. His brief was to smooth relations between the Dutch and the Balinese – an extremely tricky job considering the volatility of existing alliances between the fiery rajas and the persistent military incursions by the Dutch into northern Bali. Tensions boiled to a climax in 1849, but were skilfully diffused by Lange, who managed to negotiate a last-minute **treaty** between all the parties concerned. Although this marked the official beginning of Dutch rule in north Bali, for the rajas of the south it was a settlement to be welcomed: there had been no battle, and Balinese control of the south was, at least temporarily, assured. For Lange too it was a huge personal relief as trade between Kuta and Singapore had been paralysed for months by the Dutch blockade of the Balinese coastline. The signing of the treaty was celebrated with a huge feast at Lange's Kuta home, attended by 30,000 people.

Lange's fortunes declined after this impressive feat of diplomacy, trade slackened for a variety of political reasons, and foreign merchants focused their attentions elsewhere. By 1856 he was ready to return to Denmark, but he never made it: just before embarking he fell sick, vomited blood, and died – poisoned, so speculation ran, by a local raja. He was buried in the grounds of his Kuta home and, though the house has long since vanished, his **tomb** remains, spruced up occasionally by donations from Danish well-wishers.

and beyond. By the mid-nineteenth century, however, life had become a little less inhumane and a little more prosperous – thanks in no small part to the energetic business acumen of the Danish trader **Mads Lange** (see box above), who set up home here in 1839. A century later, Kuta's image received a drastic revision, when, in 1936, an American couple spotted Kuta's potential as soon as they saw the beach. Within months, **Bob and Louise Koke** built a small hotel on Kuta's beachfront: they named it the *Kuta Beach Hotel* (now succeeded by the

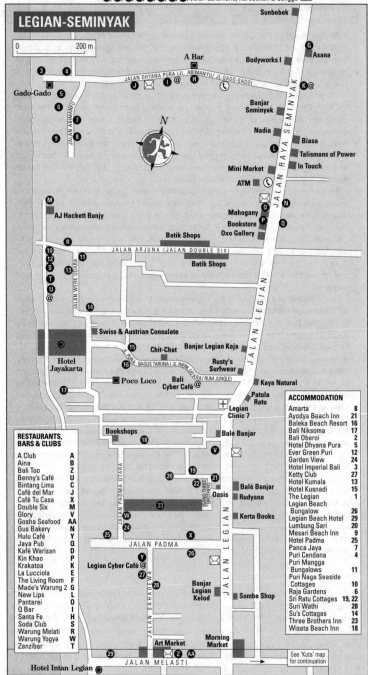

LEGIAN-SEMINYAK

❶ ❷ Ⓐ Ⓑ Ⓒ Ⓓ Ⓔ Ⓕ *Jalan Laksmana, Kerobokan & Canggu* ▲

Sunbebek

Bodyworks I

Ⓖ Asana

A Bar

JALAN DHYANA PURA (JL. ABIMANYU/ JL GADO-GADO)

Ⓙ ✉ Ⓘ @ Ⓗ

Ⓚ @

Gado-Gado

Banjar Seminyak

Nadia

Biasa

Talismans of Power

In Touch

Mini Market

ATM

Ⓝ

Ⓞ

Mahogany Bookstore

Ⓟ

Oxo Gallery

Ⓠ

AJ Hackett Bunjy

Ⓜ

Ⓡ

Batik Shops

JALAN ARJUNA (JALAN DOUBLE SIX)

Batik Shops

Ⓢ Ⓣ Ⓤ @

Swiss & Austrian Consulate

Banjar Legian Kaja

Chit-Chat

JL. PURA BAGUS TARUNA (JL. WERK UDARA / RUM JUNGLE)

Rusty's Surfwear

Hotel Jayakarta

Poco Loco

Bali Cyber Café @

Kaya Natural

Patola Ratu

Legian Clinic 7

Balé Banjar

Bookshops

Balé Banjar

Rudyana

Oasis

Kerta Books

JALAN PADMA UTARA

JALAN PADMA

Legian Cyber Café @

Banjar Legian Kelod

Sumba Shop

JALAN SAHADEWA

Art Market

Morning Market

JALAN MELASTI

Hotel Intan Legian

Jalan Benesari ▼

▼ *Kuta*

See 'Kuta' map for continuation →

0 ————— 200 m

RESTAURANTS, BARS & CLUBS

A Club — A
Aina — B
Bali Too — Z
Benny's Café — U
Bintang Lima — C
Café del Mar — J
Café Tu Casa — X
Double Six — M
Glory — V
Gosha Seafood — AA
Gus Bakery — N
Hulu Café — Y
Jaya Pub — Q
Kafé Warisan — D
Kin Khao — P
Krakatoa — K
La Lucciola — E
The Living Room — F
Made's Warung 2 — G
New Lips — L
Pantarei — O
Q Bar — I
Santa Fe — H
Soda Club — S
Warung Melati — R
Warung Yogya — W
Zanzibar — T

ACCOMMODATION

Amarta — 8
Ayodya Beach Inn — 21
Baleka Beach Resort — 16
Bali Niksoma — 17
Bali Oberoi — 2
Hotel Dhyana Pura — 5
Ever Green Puri — 12
Garden View — 24
Hotel Imperial Bali — 3
Ketty Club — 27
Hotel Kumala — 13
Hotel Kusnadi — 15
The Legian — 1
Legian Beach Bungalow — 26
Legian Beach Hotel — 29
Lumbung Sari — 20
Mesari Beach Inn — 9
Hotel Padma — 25
Panca Jaya — 7
Puri Cendana — 4
Puri Mangga Bungalows — 11
Puri Naga Seaside Cottages — 10
Raja Gardens — 6
Sri Ratu Cottages — 19, 22
Suri Wathi — 28
Su's Cottages — 14
Three Brothers Inn — 23
Wisata Beach Inn — 18

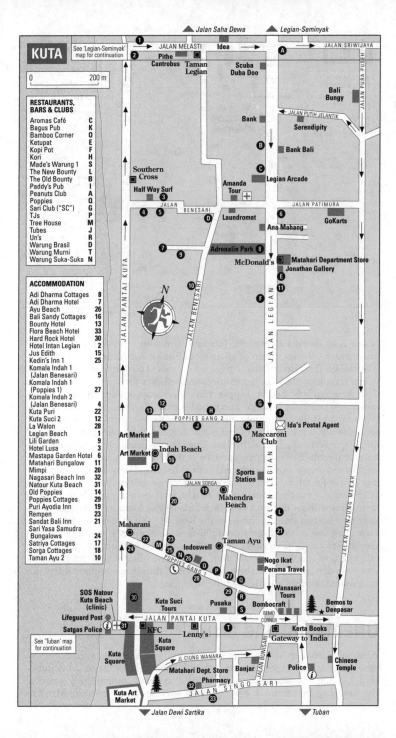

KUTA

See 'Legian-Seminyak' map for continuation

0 _____ 200 m

RESTAURANTS, BARS & CLUBS

Aromas Café	C
Bagus Pub	K
Bamboo Corner	O
Ketupat	E
Kopi Pot	F
Kori	H
Made's Warung 1	S
The New Bounty	L
The Old Bounty	B
Paddy's Pub	I
Peanuts Club	A
Poppies	Q
Sari Club ("SC")	G
TJs	P
Tree House	M
Tubes	J
Un's	R
Warung Brasil	D
Warung Murni	T
Warung Suka-Suka	N

ACCOMMODATION

Adi Dharma Cottages	8
Adi Dharma Hotel	7
Ayu Beach	26
Bali Sandy Cottages	16
Bounty Hotel	13
Flora Beach Hotel	33
Hard Rock Hotel	30
Hotel Intan Legian	2
Jus Edith	15
Kedin's Inn 1	25
Komala Indah 1 (Jalan Benesari)	5
Komala Indah 1 (Poppies 1)	27
Komala Indah 2 (Jalan Benesari)	4
Kuta Puri	22
Kuta Suci 2	12
La Walon	28
Legian Beach	1
Lili Garden	9
Hotel Lusa	3
Mastapa Garden Hotel	6
Matahari Bungalow	11
Mimpi	20
Nagasari Beach Inn	32
Natour Kuta Beach	31
Old Poppies	14
Poppies Cottages	29
Puri Ayodia Inn	19
Rempen	23
Sandat Bali Inn	21
Sari Yasa Samudra Bungalows	24
Satriya Cottages	17
Sorga Cottages	18
Taman Ayu 2	10

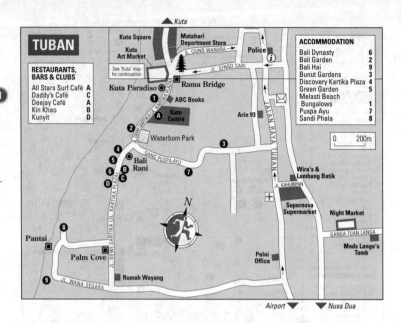

Natour Kuta Beach) and, until the **Japanese invasion** of 1942, the place flourished with a constant stream of guests from Europe and America.

World War II and its aftermath stemmed the tourist flow until the 1960s, when young travellers asked the accommodating villagers for beds, and established Kuta as a highlight on the **hippie trail**. Homestays mushroomed and were eventually joined by smarter international establishments, and Kuta quickly evolved into Bali's most sought-after real estate. Kuta–Legian–Seminyak is now the most prosperous region of the island; wages here are relatively good, and career prospects improve with every English and Japanese phrase learnt, but housing is prohibitively expensive. Many of the shopkeepers, transport touts and waiters rent grotty rooms on the edge of the resort and only return to their village homes for festivals and temple ceremonies – a development that is starting to eat away at the traditional **social fabric**, leaving young people to establish themselves without the support of their families and *banjar* members. Some villages now have so many members in the Kuta area that they've established their own expat *banjar*, so villagers can fulfil their community duties even though they're living away from home. Meanwhile, the flood of fortune-seekers from other parts of Indonesia has raised the ugly spectre of racism and religious tension – though to date there have been none of the serious confrontations that have soured relations elsewhere in the archipelago.

Orientation and arrival

Although Kuta, Legian and Seminyak all started out as separate villages, they've now merged together so completely that it's impossible for the casual visitor to recognize the demarcation lines. We've used the most common perception of the Kuta–Legian–Seminyak borders: **Kuta** stretches north from the Matahari

Alternative road names

In recent years many roads in the resort have been renamed; this can make life very confusing, not least because local residents, taxi drivers and some maps often stick to the originals, and streetsigns are rarely consistent. **Alternative road names** are given in brackets on our maps. The following list covers the most confusing examples.

Seminyak
Jl Laksmana – often referred to as Jl Oberoi (after the hotel).
Jl Petitenget (after the temple) – also known as Jl Kayu Ayu.
Jl Dhyana Pura – also known as Jl Abimanyu (which strictly speaking should only apply to the southern offshooot), and as Jl Gado Gado after the restaurant at its western end.
Jl Arjuna – also known as Jl Double Six after the famous nightclub located on the nearby beach.

Legian
Jl Bagus Taruna – also referred to as Jl Werk Udara (though this is actually the road running north off it). Nicknamed Jl Rum Jungle after a restaurant and hotel on that road.

Tuban
Jl Dewi Sartika – used to be called Jl Kartika Plaza (after one of the big hotels).

department store in Kuta Square to Jalan Melasti. **Legian** runs from Jalan Melasti as far north as Jalan Arjuna; and **Seminyak** extends from Jalan Arjuna to *The Legian* hotel and Pura Petitenget in the north. A few kilometres further up the coast from *The Legian*, and accessible via the back road to Tabanan, is the surfing beach of **Canggu**, an isolated spot which has just a handful of places to stay. Kuta's increasingly built-up southern fringes, extending south from Matahari to the airport, are defined as **Tuban**.

The resort's main road, **Jalan Legian**, runs north–south through all three districts, a total distance of 6km. A lot of businesses give their address as nothing more than "Jalan Legian", though places located on the road north of Jalan Arjuna are more accurately referred to as being on Jalan Raya Seminyak. Jalan Legian pretty much defines the eastern limit of the resort, and the coast provides the western perimeter, with the bulk of the resort facilities packed into the kilometre-wide strip between the two, an area crisscrossed by tiny *gang* (alleyways) and larger one-way roads.

The other main landmark is **Bemo Corner**, a minuscule roundabout at the southern end of Kuta that stands at the Jalan Legian–Jalan Pantai Kuta intersection. The name's a bit misleading as the Denpasar bemos don't actually depart from this very spot, but it's a useful point of reference in any case.

For information on **airport arrivals** see the box on p.110.

Arrival by bemo
Public bemos have a number of routes through the Kuta area. Coming from Denpasar's Tegal terminal, the most convenient option is the dark blue **Tegal–Kuta–Legian bemo** that goes via Bemo Corner, west and then north along Jalan Pantai Kuta, east along Jalan Melasti before heading north on Jalan Legian as far as Jalan Padma; it then turns round and runs south on Jalan Legian as far as Bemo Corner. It's up to you to decide which point on this clockwise loop is the most convenient for your chosen losmen, though for any destination a long way north of Jalan Padma you're probably better off getting a taxi.

All Bali's international and domestic flights come into the busy **Ngurah Rai Airport**, in the district of Tuban, 3km south of Kuta. For all arrival and departure **enquiries**, call ☎0361/751011, extn 1454.

Arrival

Once through immigration and customs, you'll find several 24-hour **currency exchange** booths (with different rates, so check them all out before choosing one), and a **hotel reservations desk** (open for all incoming flights), which deals in mid-range and expensive hotels only. There are several Visa, Cirrus and MasterCard **ATMs** inside the baggage claims hall and outside the Arrivals building. The **left-luggage** office (Rp5500/day per item) is located outside, midway between International Arrivals and Departures. The **domestic terminal** is in the adjacent building, where you'll find offices of the domestic airlines Garuda and Merpati.

For **onward transport**, most mid-priced and upmarket hotels will pick you up at the airport if asked in advance. Otherwise, the easiest but most expensive mode of transport to anywhere on the island is **pre-paid taxi**, for which you'll find a counter in the Arrivals area beyond the customs exit doors; you pay at the booth before being shown to the taxi. **Fares** are fixed: currently Rp15,000 to Tuban or south Kuta; Rp20,000 to central Kuta (Poppies 1 and 2); Rp22,500 to Legian (as far as Jl Arjuna); Rp25,000 to Seminyak; Rp30,000 to the *Bali Oberoi*. Further afield, you'll pay Rp20,000 to Jimbaran; Rp27,000–37,000 to Denpasar; Rp35,000 to Sanur or Nusa Dua; Rp40,000 to Tanjung Benoa; Rp55,000 to Canggu; Rp90,000 to Ubud; or Rp150,000 to Candi Dasa.

Bear these prices in mind before you start bargaining with one of the transport **touts** who gather round both the International and Domestic Arrivals areas. If you opt to go with one, make sure that the agreed price has been clearly decided on and be very firm about which hotel you're heading for, or you could easily end up at the driver's friend's losmen, miles from anywhere. **Metered taxis** ply the road immediately in front of the airport gates (turn right outside Arrivals and walk about 500m – they're not licensed to pick up inside the compound); their rates for rides into Kuta–Legian–Seminyak are at least half the pre-paid taxi equivalents.

Cheaper still are the dark blue **public bemos** whose route takes in the big main road, Jl Raya Tuban, about 700m beyond the airport gates. Note, though, that it's difficult to stash large backpacks in bemos, especially crowded ones. The northbound bemos (heading left up Jl Raya Tuban) go via Kuta's Bemo Corner and Jl Pantai Kuta as far as Jl Melasti, then travel back down Jl Legian, before continuing to Denpasar's Tegal terminal. You should pay around Rp1000–1500 to Kuta or Legian, Rp2000–3000 to Denpasar.

If you want to go straight from the airport to **Ubud**, **Candi Dasa** or **Lovina**, the cheapest way (only feasible during daylight hours) is to take a bemo to Tegal station in Denpasar and continue your journey by bemo from there; see the plan on p.92 for route outlines. A trip by bemo to Ubud will involve three different bemos and cost around Rp11,000 in total. More convenient, but a little more expensive, is to take a bemo or pre-paid taxi from the airport to Kuta's Bemo Corner, then walk 100m north up Jl Legian to Perama shuttle bus office, where you can book yourself onto the next

The dark blue **Tegal–Kuta–Tuban (airport)–Bualu** route is fine if you're staying in the southern part of Kuta as drivers on this service generally drop passengers on the eastern edge of Jalan Singo Sari – a five-minute walk away from Bemo Corner – before they turn south along Jalan Raya Tuban. Coming by bemo **from Bualu** (transfer point from Tanjung Benoa and Nusa Dua) or **from Jimbaran**, you'll probably be dropped off at the same place.

tourist shuttle bus, most of which run every two or three hours (see p.173). The priciest way is by pre-paid taxi direct from the airport (see above).

Departure

For a small fee, any tour agent in Bali will **reconfirm** your air ticket for you, and most can also change the dates of your ticket. Calling the airline yourself can be a frustrating business as lines often seem to be permanently engaged: sometimes it's easier just to visit the airline office in person. Domestic airline information is given in Basics on p.21.

If you're flying Garuda, you might want to make use of the **city check-in** offices in Kuta (see p.135), Denpasar (see p.103) and Sanur (see p.169), where you can offload your luggage the day before. This means not only that you'll get your boarding card (and therefore a much better chance of the seat you want – very worthwhile if you've got a long flight), but that you could walk along the beach to the airport from Kuta unencumbered.

Most hotels in Kuta, Sanur, Nusa Dua and Jimbaran will provide **transport to the airport** for about Rp20,000 (or occasionally for free if you've stayed a week or longer). **Metered taxis** are cheaper: around Rp16,000 from Kuta, Rp19,000 from Seminyak. All tour agents offer **shuttle buses** to the airport from major tourist destinations all over Bali: shop around for the most convenient schedule (journey times also vary), and reckon on paying about Rp10,000 from Sanur, Rp15,000 from Ubud, Rp25,000 from Candi Dasa or Rp40,000 from Lovina. During daylight hours, you can also take the dark blue Tegal (Denpasar)–Kuta–Tuban **bemo** from Denpasar, Kuta or Jimbaran, which will drop you just beyond the airport gates for Rp2000–3000.

Airport **departure tax** is Rp100,000 for international departures and Rp20,000 for domestic flights. Airside in the departures area, there's an **internet centre**, international card **phones**, a couple of snack bars, and dozens of souvenir **shops**, but be warned that prices here are hugely inflated.

International airline offices in Bali

Most airline offices open Mon–Fri 8.30am–5pm, Sat 8.30am–noon; some close for an hour's lunch at noon or 12.30pm.

Garuda has offices and city check-ins inside the *Sanur Beach Hotel* in southern Sanur (24hr ☏0361/270535), and at the *Natour Kuta Beach Hotel* in Kuta (☏0361/751179).

Offices of the following carriers are inside the compound of the *Grand Bali Beach Hotel* in Sanur: **Air France** ☏0361/288511 extn 1105; **Cathay Pacific** ☏0361/286001; **Continental Micronesia** ☏0361/287774; **JAL** ☏0361/287576; **Northwest** ☏0361/287841; **Qantas** ☏0361/288331; and **Thai International** ☏0361/288141.

Offices of the following are in Ngurah Rai Airport itself: **Air New Zealand** ☏0361/756170; **ANA** ☏0361/761101; **EVA Air** ☏0361/759773; **Malaysia Air** ☏0361/764995; **Royal Brunei** ☏0361/757292; and **Singapore Airlines/Silk Air** ☏0361/768388.

Lauda Air is at Jl Bypass Ngurah Rai 12 (☏0361/758686) and the nearest **British Airways** office is in the Indonesian capital Jakarta (☏021/230 0277).

If you're making the journey **from Sanur** to Kuta by bemo, take the dark blue Sanur–Tegal bemo as far as the Jalan Teuku Umar/Jalan Imam Bonjol junction, beside the bridge, then walk left (south) down Jalan Imam Bonjol for about 30m and you'll find Kuta-bound bemos waiting for passengers. If you miss this junction, stay on the bemo until Tegal and pick up the next Kuta-bound bemo at the start of its journey (this adds an extra 10–20min to the trip).

Arrival by shuttle bus

If arriving in Kuta by **shuttle bus**, you could be dropped almost anywhere, depending on your operator. Drivers for the biggest shuttle bus operator, Perama, drop passengers at their office on Jalan Legian, about 100m north of Bemo Corner, but will sometimes stop at spots en route if asked.

Arrival by car or motorbike

You can **park** pretty much anywhere on Kuta's streets – if you can find a space. Parking attendants charge around Rp1000 to wave you in and out and keep an eye on your vehicle; if there's an attendant there, it's almost obligatory to pay them. Otherwise, you can use the public underground car parks at the Matahari department stores on Jalan Legian and in Kuta Square.

Information and transport

All sorts of people in Kuta will be only too willing to offer you information, but the official, and pretty unhelpful, **Badung tourist office** is at Jalan Raya Kuta 2 (Mon–Thurs 7am–2pm, Fri 7–11am; ☎0361/756176), with a branch office beside the beach on Jalan Pantai Kuta (Mon–Sat 10am–5pm; ☎0361/755660).

You'll get a lot more tourist information and details about forthcoming events from the bevy of **tourist newspapers and magazines** available at hotels and some shops and restaurants. The free monthly pamphlet *Bali Plus* always includes a good list of the month's festivals and dance performances; the free fortnightly glossy newspaper *Bali Travel News* (Ⓦ www.bali-travelnews.com) introduces tourist attractions, lists upcoming temple festivals and films showing at Denpasar's main cinema, and runs interesting features on Balinese culture as well as plenty of ads for shops and entertainments. The fortnightly magazine *the beat* focuses on Bali's nightlife and carries listings for gigs, parties and clubs. Other Bali-wide cultural magazines are described in Basics on p.54.

Bemos

The dark blue public **bemos** cover only a very limited route – basically a clockwise loop around Kuta, leaving out most of Legian and all of Seminyak. Originating in Denpasar, they run up Jalan Raya Tuban, turn left at Bemo Corner along Jalan Pantai Kuta, proceed north up the beachfront Jalan Pantai, turn right along Jalan Melasti and then continue north up Jalan Legian for one block, as far as Jalan Padma, where they do a U-turn and come all the way back down Jalan Legian as far as Bemo Corner, stopping to fill up with Denpasar-bound passengers at the Jalan Pantai/Jalan Raya intersection. You can flag them down at any point along this route; the standard fare for any distance within this area is Rp1000, but tourists are sometimes obliged to pay up to Rp2000. During the day, bemos usually circulate at five- or ten-minute intervals, but very few bemos run after nightfall and none at all after about 8.30pm.

Taxis, touts and dokar

Dozens of **metered taxis** circulate throughout the resort, all with a "Taxi" sign on the roof. There are several companies, the most common being the light blue Blue Bird Taxis (☎0361/701111) and the white Ngurah Rai Airport Taxis (☎0361/724724). All charge Rp4000 flagfall and then Rp2000 per kilometre day or night; always double-check that the meter is turned on when you

Bemos

To get from Kuta to most other destinations in Bali by **bemo** will almost always entail going via Denpasar, where you'll probably have to make at least one cross-city connection.

Dark blue bemos to **Denpasar**'s Tegal terminal (Rp2000–3000; 25min) run regularly throughout the day; the easiest place to catch them is at the Jl Pantai Kuta/Jl Raya Tuban intersection, about 150m east of Bemo Corner, where they wait to collect passengers, although you can also get on anywhere on their loop around Kuta (see p.110 for details).

From Tegal, other bemos run to **Sanur** and to Denpasar's other bemo terminals for onward connections; full details are on p.94 and on the map on p.92. Note that, to get to Batubulan station (departure point for **Ubud**), the white Damri bus service from Nusa Dua is quicker than taking a bemo to Tegal and another to Batubulan; you can pick it up at the fuel station on the intersection of Jl Imam Bonjol and Jl Setia Budi, about ten minutes' walk northeast of Bemo Corner. Dark blue bemos from Tegal to Bualu (for **Nusa Dua** and **Tanjung Benoa**) also pass this intersection, and will pick you up on Jl Setia Budi if you signal. Some Tegal–Bualu bemos serve **Jimbaran** on the way, and there's also a dark blue Tegal–Jimbaran bemo, which occasionally continues on through the Bukit – possibly as far as **Uluwatu**.

Shuttle buses

If you're going anywhere beyond Denpasar, the quickest – and priciest – public transport option from Kuta is always to take a tourist **shuttle bus**. Every one of the hundred or more tour agencies in Kuta–Legian–Seminyak offers "shuttle bus services": some are little more than one man and his minivan, others are big buses run by professional operators. Prices are always competitive; most travellers choose according to convenience of timetable and pick-up points. Drop-offs are unknown on the smaller operations, most of which will drop you only at their offices in your destination.

Bali's biggest and best-known shuttle bus operator is **Perama Travel**, whose unobtrusive head office is located 100m north of Bemo Corner at Jl Legian 39 (daily 7am–10pm; ☎0361/751551, ✉perama_tour@hotmail.com). This is the departure point for all Perama buses, although you can pay an extra Rp3000 to be picked up from your hotel and can buy tickets on the phone and through other agents. Perama buses are non air-con and run between Kuta and all the obvious tourist destinations on Bali as well as to some major spots on Lombok and Sumbawa (prices include the boat transfer); see Travel details on p.173 for a full list. Perama also sells through-tickets for public buses to Java. Prices are reasonable: examples are Rp15,000 to Ubud, Rp40,000 to Lovina and Rp50,000 to Senggigi on Lombok. Some Perama routes are quite convoluted: for example, their buses from Kuta to Padang Bai/Candi Dasa go via both Sanur and Ubud, which adds an extra hour to a journey that should only take 2hr. In this case, it can make more sense, and be less time-consuming, to split a transport tout's fare between a group of you.

Transport to other islands

Many Kuta travel agents (see p.137 for a list) sell express **boat tickets** to Lombok and other Indonesian islands on a variety of operators. All these boats leave from Benoa Harbour (Pelabuhan Benoa), which is described on p.171, where you'll also find details of prices and destinations. Details of the local Pelni office (for long-distance boats to other parts of Indonesia) are on p.137. Perama **shuttle-bus** tickets to destinations on Lombok, Sumbawa and Java all include the ferry (see above).

All Kuta travel agents sell **domestic air tickets**. Sample one-way fares are Rp235,000 to Mataram on Lombok, Rp430,000 to Yogyakarta and Rp810,000 to Jakarta. Full airport information is in the box on pp.110–11.

get in the car. A longish ride, say from Jalan Bagus Taruna in northern Legian to Waterbom Park in Tuban, should cost around Rp16,000. You can often save yourself both time and money by walking a short distance to pick up a taxi on its way out of Kuta's longwinded one-way system; some drivers refuse to go along the narrow lanes of Poppies 1 and Poppies 2 anyway, forcing you to walk out to the main street.

Another option is the informal taxi service offered by the "transport, transport" **touts** who hang around on every corner. For brief journeys it's usually more hassle than it's worth even to start bargaining with a transport tout, and many won't do short rides anyway, but they can be worthwhile for longer journeys or trips with several stops.

A few **dokar** (horse-carts) also ply the streets of Kuta and Tuban, useful for short hops; again, always bargain before the journey begins.

Cars, bikes and motorbikes

Every major road in the resort is packed with tour agents offering **car rental**, and most offer air-con and non-air-con 800cc Suzuki Jimneys (Rp100,000 24hr) as well as larger, more comfortable 1600cc Toyota Kijangs (Rp150,000); try Kuta Suci, Jalan Pantai Kuta 37c (℡0361/765357, ✉kutasuci@mail.com). At the most reputable outlets, **insurance** is included, though usually with a $150 excess. Bear in mind that signposting is not always as helpful as it might be, and that traffic congestion is a fact of life in southern Bali and on the main westbound highway.

Most places will also provide a **driver** for the day, for an extra Rp50,000–100,000, including fuel. A recommended freelance English-speaking guide and driver is Wayan Artana (mobile ℡0812/396 1296, ✉iartana@hotmail.com); for other personal recommendations, you could browse the archives of the online travellers' forums listed on p.24.

You can also rent **motorbikes** from many of the same outlets, as well as from Chitchat on Jalan Bagus Taruna; average cost is Rp35,000–60,000 per day. See p.39 for general information on transport rental, costs and insurance.

The heavy main-road traffic and the irritating one-way systems can make **cycling** around Kuta rather trying, though if you stick to the back lanes it's not a bad way of getting about. Notices on the central stretch of Kuta beach forbid all vehicles, including bikes, though once you get north of Jalan Melasti, cycling along the sand seems to be perfectly acceptable. Ask about rental at your losmen or at the motorbike rental places; expect to pay Rp15,000 per 24 hours.

Accommodation

Of south Bali's main beach resorts, Kuta–Legian–Seminyak has by far the greatest amount of **accommodation**, and also the biggest range of cheap and moderately priced rooms. Many mid-range and expensive hotels are pictured on the Bali accommodation websites listed on p.44 and these always offer booking **discounts**; most hotels offer discounts on their own websites too.

The inexpensive losmen are mainly concentrated in **Kuta**, with plenty of options along Poppies 1, the *gang* (lanes) running off it, and along Poppies 2 and Jalan Benesari. **Legian** has plenty of good-value mid-range places within a few minutes' walk of the sea, most of which offer air-conditioning, hot water and a pool. Many of these quote their rates in dollars; some include the ten percent government tax as well as breakfast, others will use the tax as a bargaining tool. The expensive hotels that dominate **Tuban** and the northern reaches of **Seminyak** all offer international standard rooms and resort facilities and, almost without exception, have grounds that lead directly to the beach. The scene is much quieter in **Berewa** and **Canggu**, 10km north of Seminyak, where just a handful of mid-range and upmarket hotels occupy the shorefront.

Parts of the resort can look very unappealing during the **rainy season** (late October until March), when roads and alleyways can remain flooded for days and you literally have to walk the plank to get into some of the smaller losmen. In particular, you might want to avoid staying in the middle stretches of Jalan Sorga and Poppies 2, where the potholes make wading a necessity (although, in recompense, many places offer good discounts during this period).

Kuta

Kuta is the most congested and frantic part of the resort, where you'll find bars, restaurants, clubs and shops squashed into every available square metre of land. The beach gets crowded, but it's a good stretch of clean, fine sand and deservedly popular. It's also the surfing centre of the resort, with most of the board-rental and -repair shops, surfwear outlets and surfer-oriented bars clustered on and around Poppies 2.

Inexpensive

Ayu Beach Inn Poppies 1 ☎0361/752091, ⓕ752948. Very popular, good-value and ideally located budget option with two pools, several internet terminals and a restaurant. Rooms are not exactly spotless but are decent enough. Rooms with fan ❷ With air-con ❹

Jus Edith South off Poppies 2 ☎0361/750558. Extremely popular losmen with just eleven basic rooms, handily placed close to the action and exceptionally inexpensive for the area. ❶

Kedin's Inn 1 Poppies 1 ☎0361/756771. Twenty-seven large, adequate, fan-cooled rooms, including some very good-value three-person ones, set around a garden. ❷

Komala Indah 1 (Jl Benesari) Jl Benesari ☎0361/753185. A range of terraced bungalows set in a pretty garden less than 200m from the beach. Small basic rooms with fan and cold-water shower ❶ Better ones, with hot water ❸ With air-con ❹

Komala Indah 1 (Poppies 1) Poppies 1 ☎0361/751422. This compact square of terraced bungalows is set around a central courtyard garden and can feel slightly claustrophobic, but it's conveniently located and one of the cheapest places in Kuta. ❶

Komala Indah 2 (Jl Benesari) Jl Benesari ☎0361/754258. Simply furnished, inexpensive losmen rooms located on a quiet part of Jl Benesari, thirty seconds' walk from the beach. Prices vary a little according to size. ❶–❷

Kuta Suci 2 Bungalows Gang Mangga, off Poppies 2 ☎0361/752617. Eleven very cheap rooms in terraced bungalows in a garden; good for the price. Located close to the action but away from the noise. ❶

Lili Garden Jl Benesari ☎0361/750557, ⓕ754132, ✉duarsa@dps.centrin.net.id. Clean, simple rooms in this small, friendly, family-run losmen, set around a peaceful garden and conveniently located between Jl Legian and the beach. ❷

Hotel Lusa Jl Benesari ☎0361/753714, ⓕ765691. A quiet, better-than-average place with sprucely kept rooms, an attractive garden and a pool. Just a hop, skip and jump from the beach. Rooms with fan ❸ With air-con and hot water ❺

Mimpi Off Poppies 1 ☎ & ⓕ0361/751848. Attractive, traditional-style fan-cooled Balinese cottages in a small garden with a reasonably sized pool. It's popular and there are just nine rooms, so call ahead to reserve. ❸

Puri Ayodia Inn Jl Sorga ☎0361/754245. Exceptionally good-value losmen, with clean well-furnished rooms. One of the cheapest places to stay in this convenient but quiet location between Poppies 1 and Poppies 2. Fills up fast. ❶

Rempen Off Poppies 1 ☎0361/753150, ✉godho82@yahoo.com. Fifteen well-kept rooms, some in a three-storey tower affording rooftop views of Kuta from the verandah, others in terraced garden bungalows. ❷

Sandat Bali Inn Jl Legian 120 ☎0361/753491. Exceptionally clean and well-maintained rooms right in the heart of the action, just a few metres from *Paddy's Bar*, the *New Bounty* and the half-dozen other main nightspots. Rooms with fan and

cold-water shower ❷ With air-con ❸
Sorga Cottages Jl Sorga, running parallel
between Poppies 1 and Poppies 2
Ⓣ0361/751897, Ⓕ752417,
Ⓦwww.angelfire.com/id/sorga. Exceptionally
good-value rooms in a three-storey block set
round a small pool and a restaurant. Lacks local
character but is comfortably furnished and efficiently run. Rooms with fan and cold water ❸
With air-con and hot water ❹–❺
Taman Ayu 2 Jl Benesari Ⓣ0361/754376,
Ⓕ754640. A small block of very reasonably priced
and unusually well-maintained bamboo-walled fan
rooms plus a handful of bungalows. ❷

Moderate

Bali Sandy Cottages Off Poppies 2
Ⓣ0361/753344, Ⓕ750791. Thirty-seven sizeable,
good-value fan and air-con rooms in three two-
storey wings set around a large pool and lawn.
Attractive bamboo and *ikat* furnishings and a quiet
location, three minutes from the beach and about
100m from the shops and restaurants on Poppies
2. Rooms with fan ❹ With air-con ❺
Bounty Hotel Poppies 2 Ⓣ0361/753030,
Ⓕ752121, Ⓦwww.balibountygroup.com. Large,
very good-value operation – mainly patronized by
young Australians – with 165 exceptionally well-
maintained terraced bungalows set in a garden,
plus two pools and a games room. Each room is
equipped with air-con, TV and fridge. Guests can
choose whether to stay in the "lively" area of the
complex, near the 24-hour pool. ❻
Flora Beach Hotel Jl Singo Sari Ⓣ0361/751870,
Ⓕ754227, Ⓔflr-bh@indo.net.id. Friendly hotel
with forty air-conditioned rooms built in a terraced
ring around a central courtyard swimming pool.
Rooms are slightly faded, but good value nonetheless. Popular with package tourists. ❺
Kuta Puri Poppies 1 Ⓣ0361/751903, Ⓕ752585.
Ideal location less than a minute from the beach
and just a few minutes' walk from Kuta Square.
The cheapest rooms aren't particularly good value,
but the better bungalows have air-con and hot
water and are comfortably furnished. There's a
pretty garden, decent restaurant and a swimming
pool. Rooms with fan ❹–❺ With air-con ❻
La Walon Poppies 1 Ⓣ0361/757234, Ⓕ752463,
Ⓦbaliwww.com/bali/roomfinder/la_walon.htm,
Ⓔlawalon@hotmail.com. Small place in a convenient central location with a few fan-cooled cottages and 24 hotel rooms. Swimming pool but no
garden. Rooms with fan ❺ With air-con ❻
Mastapa Garden Hotel Jl Legian 139
Ⓣ0361/751660, Ⓕ755098,
Ⓦwww.indo.com/hotels/mastapa,

Ⓔmastapa@denpasar.wasantara.net.id. Secluded
garden haven with a pool that enjoys an ideal central location on the main drag, but is quiet
nonetheless and popular with families. All rooms
are air-con; rates depend on whether you opt for
streetside or pool-view, and are heavily discounted
online. Internet access in the lobby. Call for free
airport pick-up. ❻–❼
Matahari Bungalow Jl Legian Ⓣ0361/751616,
Ⓕ751761,
Ⓦwww.indo.com/hotels/matahari_bungalow,
Ⓔmthrbgl@indosat.net. Set in a long leafy compound that runs east off the heart of Kuta's main
shopping road, this place offers a secluded swimming pool plus a range of smartly furnished, good-
value terraced bungalows with air-con and hot
water. ❻ Suites ❼
Old Poppies Poppies 2 Ⓣ0361/751059,
Ⓕ752364, Ⓦwww.poppies.net. Pleasantly old-
fashioned if slightly faded set of Bali-style cottages
with carved wooden doors, fridges and fans. Pretty
garden, and use of the pool at the sister operation,
Poppies Cottages. Lots more character than most
other places in this price bracket. Fifty percent discounts are standard outside peak times. ❻
Sari Yasa Samudra Bungalows Jl Pantai Kuta
Ⓣ0361/751562, Ⓕ752948. Ideal location, across
the road from the beach, and just a few minutes'
walk to Kuta Square, with a big range of reasonable accommodation and a swimming pool in the
garden. Rooms with fan ❺ With air-con ❻
Satriya Cottages Poppies 2 Ⓣ0361/758331,
Ⓕ752741, Ⓦwww.balilife.com/satriya,
Ⓔsatriya@spot.net.id. Set in an appealing garden
compound 100m from the beach, with a pool and
sauna plus smartly furnished, if pricey, fan rooms
in a block. Also better value air-con bungalows. ❻

Expensive

Adi Dharma Access from both Jl Legian and Jl
Benesari: hotel Ⓣ0361/754280, cottages
Ⓣ751527, both Ⓕ753803,
Ⓦwww.indo.com/hotels/adhi_dharma,
Ⓔadhidharma@denpasar.wasantara.net.id. Nicely
furnished comfortable "cottage" rooms in a terraced block just off the main drag, with air-con,
fridge and TV. Also some more upmarket hotel
rooms in a separate building. Good value, central
location. Pool, restaurant and games room – plus
bungee jumping in the back garden. ❼–❽
Hard Rock Hotel Jl Pantai Kuta Ⓣ0361/761869,
Ⓕ762162, Ⓦwww.hardrockhotelbali.com.
Unashamedly un-Balinese hotel in a prime location, with comfortable rooms that are designed to
make you feel cool in all senses. TV and internet in
every room, and a rock-music theme throughout.

Fantastic series of swimming pools, a gym, spa and kids' club. ❾

Hotel Intan Legian Cnr of Jl Pantai Kuta and Jl Melasti ☎ 0361/751770, Ⓕ 751891, ⓦ www .balihotels.com/legian/intan.htm, Ⓔhilegb@indosat.net.id. Huge, comfortable cottages set in a series of terraced gardens, a hop across the road from the beach. Swimming pool, tennis courts, pizzeria and 24-hour coffee shop. ❽

Nagasari Beach Inn Jl Singo Sari 60 ☎ 0361/751960, Ⓕ 765058, Ⓔnsc@denpasa r.wasantara.net.id. Twenty-seven smart terraced bungalows built in two storeys around a central pool and small garden. Rooms are comfortably furnished with air-con, hot water and TV, and are set behind a popular restaurant and bar. ❼

Natour Kuta Beach Jl Pantai Kuta ☎ 0361/751361, Ⓕ 751362, Ⓔnkbh@denpasar.wasantara.net.id. Built on the site of Kuta's first-ever hotel, this place occupies an unbeatable central location and is one of only a handful of Kuta hotels that actually gives out onto the beach. Facilities include two pools, a dance stage and several restaurants, but the hotel rooms and garden cottages (all with fridge, TV, air-con) are a little disappointing for the price. ❽

Poppies Cottages Poppies 1 ☎ 0361/751059, Ⓕ752364, ⓦwww.poppies.net. Elegantly designed and extremely popular traditional-style cottages equipped with air-con, a swimming pool, laptop ports and a babysitting service. Reservations essential. Call for free airport pick-up. ❽

Tuban

A few hundred metres south of Jalan Pantai Kuta, beyond Kuta Square's Matahari department store, Kuta beach officially becomes **Tuban** beach and things quieten down a great deal. The most appealing aspect of staying in Tuban is that nearly all the hotels enjoy direct access to the beach; they charge accordingly, but facilities and standards are generally high, and the area is deservedly popular with families. No bemos run down the main drag, Jalan Dewi Sartika, so you're likely to end up forking out for taxis to Kuta's shops and entertainments as the local offerings are not especially exciting.

Bali Dynasty Resort Jl Dewi Sartika ☎ 0361/752403, Ⓕ752402, ⓦwww.balidynasty .com. International-standard hotel that's lacking in local character but nicely set in landscaped gardens that run down to the beach. Two swimming pools, a playground, tennis courts and a games room make this a good choice for families. ❾

Bali Garden Hotel Jl Dewi Sartika ☎ 0361/752725, Ⓕ752728, ⓦwww.baligarden hotel.com. Large, attractively designed low-rise hotel complex, with high-standard rooms, a pool, spa, fitness centre and garden-view restaurant. The pretty garden stretches right down to the beach; the rooms overlooking it are nicer and quieter than those on the street side. Big discounts in low season; two children free if sharing with adults; and free airport pick-up. ❽

Bali Hai Resort Jl Wana Segara 33 ☎ 0361/ 753035, Ⓕ754702, ⓦwww.balihai.holiday-inn .com. Top-grade rooms in a low-rise central block, plus some cottages in pleasantly landscaped grounds. Facilities include a spa, sports centre, tennis courts and pool. Beachfront location. ❽

Bunut Gardens Gang Puspa Ayu ☎ 0361/752971. Small operation offering 14 decent rooms in a little garden down a quiet lane. All rooms have fan and cold water. About 800m from the beach and the shops. ❸

Discovery Kartika Plaza Beach Jl Dewi Sartika ☎ 0361/751067, Ⓕ752475, ⓦwww.indo.com/hotels/kartika_plaza, Ⓔkartikaplz@denpasar.wasantara.net.id. Large, upmarket beachfront outfit where rooms are set in a lush tropical garden and most have an ocean view as well. Open-air theatre, fitness club, kids' activities, and five restaurants. ❾

Green Garden Hotel Jl Dewi Sartika 9 ☎ 0361/ 754571, Ⓕ754570, ⓦwww.greenbali.com. Well priced for its location, this is a decent enough option with 24 air-con rooms crammed around a courtyard swimming pool. There's no garden, despite the name, but the beach is a few minutes' walk away through one of the neighbouring hotels, and there's a deservedly popular restaurant on the premises. Significant discounts often available. ❻

Melasti Beach Bungalows Jl Dewi Sartika ☎ 0361/751860, Ⓕ751563, Ⓔmelasti@indo.net.id. Terraced bungalows, some with air-con and TV, set in a garden with a pool. Some rooms are a little dark, but they're fine for the location, as the garden runs right down to the shore and the hotel's just a few minutes from Kuta Square. Fifty percent discount in low season. Free airport pick-up. Rooms with fan ❻ With air-con ❼

Puspa Ayu Bungalows Gang Puspa Ayu ☎ 0361/756721. The cheapest and most popular accommodation on this residential street wreathed in bougainvillea and tropical greenery. Nice enough bungalows in a garden 200m off the main road, staffed by surfers. Rooms with fan and cold water ❸ With air-con and hot water ❹

Sandi Phala Off Jl Dewi Sartika ☎0361/753780, ℻236021. Terraced fan rooms and some much nicer, smart new wooden chalets, all with direct access to the beach – which makes them exceptional value. Some air-con, plus a pool and seafront café. ❺–❻

Legian

Significantly calmer than Kuta, **Legian** to the north has a reputation for attracting the resort's more laid-back travellers as well as long-stay surfers. There are far fewer crowds on the beach here, and many of the smaller hotels are better value than ones in Kuta, with easy access to the shore and facilities that generally include air-conditioning, hot water and a pool. Since 2000, when a new beachfront road was opened between Jalan Melasti and Jalan Arjuna, all Legian's hotels have lost their direct access to the sea, though the road itself is currently open only to local toll-paying residents and so noise and fumes are not yet a problem.

Inexpensive

Ayodya Beach Inn Gang Three Brothers ☎0361/752169, ℮ayodyabeachinn@yahoo.com. Scruffy losmen with fifteen terraced rooms with fan and cold water, set in a garden that's just 75m walk from Jalan Legian. ❶–❷

Ever Green Puri Jl Arjuna ☎0361/730386. Amazingly good value, with a prime location on the beachfront road within a few seconds' walk of a fine stretch of shore. Standard, simply furnished, fan-cooled rooms in a block and larger two-storey bungalows set around a rather dry garden. The Cheyne Horan surf school (see p.121) has its headquarters here, so this is also a great spot for aspiring and experienced surfers. ❷

Legian Beach Bungalow Jl Padma ☎0361/751087. A small, friendly operation with simple but pleasant rooms and bungalows set in a garden close to the shops but not far from the beach. Well priced considering its location and its swimming pool. All rooms have fans; rates depend on the size. ❷–❸

Su's Cottages Jl Bagus Taruna/Jl Werk Udara 532 ☎0361/730324, ℻762202. Spotless, nicely furnished rooms in a small, friendly, family-run losmen, with a tiny plunge-pool. Rooms with fan ❸ With air-con ❹

Suri Wathi Jl Sahadewa 12 ☎0361/753162, ℻758393, ℮suriwati@yahoo.com. Friendly, family-run losmen with good-value split-level bungalows and some smaller rooms. Quiet but convenient, with a decent pool and a garden. Rooms with fan ❸ With air-con ❹

Wisata Beach Inn Off Jl Padma Utara ☎0361/755987. Quiet little place at the back of a beauty parlour, with a handful of bungalows in a small garden, each offering split-level accommodation with beds and balconies on both floors. ❸

Moderate

Baleka Beach Resort Jl Bagus Taruna ☎0361/751931, ℻753976, ⊛www.balihotelsnet.com/baleka_beach_resort, ℮baleka@bali.net. Two-storey blocks scattered over a large garden area housing 45 bungalows, with a relaxed ambience despite a shopping-street location. There's a pool and restaurant. Fifty percent discounts are often available, and kids under 12 go free if they share the adults' room. Rooms with fan ❻ With air-con ❼

Bali Niksoma Beach Cottages Jl Padma Utara ☎0361/751946, ℻753587. A perfect spot across the road from the beach, with very acceptable "deluxe" air-con bungalows in a large compound that also features two restaurants and a swimming pool. Kids under 12 are free if sharing adults' room. Unexceptional rooms with fan ❻ With air-con ❼

Garden View Jl Padma Utara 4 ☎0361/751559, ℻753265, ℮gardenvc@indo.net.id. Unimaginatively designed but comfortably furnished air-conditioned cottages in a pleasant garden setting with a pool and restaurant. Also has rooms sleeping four to six people. ❻

Ketty Club aka **Ketty Beach Hotel** Jl Sahadewa 19 ☎0361/751134, ℻753265, ℮indahbkc@indo.net.id. Popular with surfers because of its proximity to the beach, this place comprises a block of reasonable, air-con rooms – some overlooking the street – built around a small swimming pool. ❺

Hotel Kumala Jl Werk Udara ☎0361/732186, ℻730407, ⊛www.kumalahotel.com. Lots of appealingly furnished rooms and more comfortable cottages, all with air-con, and some with fridge. With two pools and a good location just 250m from the beach and 100m from Jalan Arjuna, this is excellent value. ❹

Hotel Kusnadi aka **Rum Jungle Road** Jl Bagus
Taruna T0361/764948, F761330, Wwww.indo
.com/hotels/kusnadi, Eholacom@bigfoot.com. A
compact but deservedly popular hotel, with smart,
well-maintained rooms, all with hot water, set around
a courtyard swimming pool and fronted by a decent
restaurant. Rooms with fan ❹ With air-con ❺
Lumbung Sari Gang Three Brothers T &
F0361/752009, Elumbung_sari@yahoo.com.
Huge two-storey air-con bungalows with fridge
and kitchen area downstairs, ideal for long stays.
Also with a pool and some cheaper fan and air-con
rooms in a central block, all with hot water. ❹−❻
Puri Mangga Bungalows Jl Arjuna
T0361/730447, F730307. Rice-barn-style bun-
galows for two to four people, with kitchen and
bathroom included. Discounts for weekly and
monthly rental. One minute from the beach. ❻
Puri Naga Seaside Cottages Jl Arjuna
T0361/730761, F730524,
Epurinaga@indo.net.id. Standard, unimaginatively
designed air-con rooms with a pool, whose saving
grace is an ideal location across the road from a
nice stretch of beach. ❻
Sri Ratu Cottages Jl Three Brothers
T0361/751722, F754468, Wsriratu.tripod.com,
Esriratuhotel@yahoo.com. Two compounds on
either side of a quiet but conveniently located
gang, comprising seven attractive bungalows in a
garden and 19 very clean air-con rooms set
around a pool across the way. The cheapest rooms
are a bit dark, but well priced for the area, while

the better upstairs ones overlook the garden terrace. Rooms ❹−❺ Bungalows ❺−❻
Three Brothers Inn Jl Three Brothers
T0361/751566, F756082, Ethreebrothersbun-
galows@yahoo.com. One of the most characterful
places in the resort, this lush, rambling garden
complex stretches all the way from Jl Padma Utara
to Jl Three Brothers and holds dozens of large,
attractive bungalows and a pool. There are numerous different types of room, but the best are the
upstairs fan-cooled ones with open (barred) windows, mosquito nets and four-poster beds. The air-
con rooms are the least interesting options. ❺−❻

Expensive

Legian Beach Hotel Jl Melasti T0361/751711,
F752651, Wwww.legianbeachbali.com. Huge
collection of large, comfortable four-star bungalows, conveniently located on Legian's southern
boundary and set in an attractive garden that runs
down to the shorefront road. Has two decent-sized
pools and several restaurants. All bungalows have
air-con and TV, but the slightly cheaper rooms in
the hotel wing overlook a car park. ❽−❾
Hotel Padma Jl Padma 1 T0361/752111,
F752140, Wwww.hotelpadma.com. Smart, top-
notch place with classy service and thoughtful
touches. Offers rooms in a hotel wing as well as
more attractive deluxe bungalow accommodation
set around a spacious tropical garden that extends
down to the beachfront road. Two pools and a
complimentary kids' club and nursery. ❽

Seminyak

Upmarket **Seminyak**, north of Legian, is quiet and pleasant, attracting return
visitors seeking more peace and seclusion second time around. Many expats
with businesses in Bali choose to live here, so the shops and restaurants tend to
cater for these more discerning tastes. The further north you go the classier the
hotels get, with a particularly exclusive enclave now occupying the fine stretch
of shore near Pura Petitenget, off Jalan Laksmana. The beach is almost deserted
all the way along Seminyak's coast (there are no lifeguards), but away from Jalan
Raya Seminyak, the main drag, shops and restaurants are spread quite far apart,
so you may end up using a lot of taxis. There are plenty of car and motorbike
rental places on Jalan Dhyana Pura, plus the usual omnipresent transport touts.

Amarta Jl Abimanyu 2000x T0361/734793,
F736111, Wwww.amartabali.com. Boutique hotel
comprising a series of beautifully outfitted two-
storey villas, each set in its own walled compound
and with a fully equipped kitchen, two bedrooms, a
living room (with TV and CD player) and a small
patio. The high walls can make you feel rather
enclosed, but there's an attractive hotel pool area. ❽
Bali Oberoi Jl Laksmana T0361/730361,
F730791, Wwww.oberoihotels.com. One of the

resort's most exclusive and stylish hotels, set
beside the beach in the still peaceful area north of
Seminyak. Traditional-style coral-rock bungalows
complete with delightful garden bathrooms, and
some of them boasting private pools, make this
the favourite haunt of the rich and the famous.
Published rates from US$255. ❾
Hotel Dhyana Pura Jl Abimanyu T0361/730442,
F730463, Wwww.indo.com/hotels/dhyana_pura,
Edhyana-p@indosat.net.id. Good-value hotel, with

119

pleasantly furnished air-con rooms, all with TV and hot water, some in a hotel block, others in garden cottages. There's a pool and a decent restaurant, and the garden runs down to the sea. Run by the Protestant Christian Church of Bali and located next door to Seminyak's impressive church. **❼**

Hotel Imperial Bali Jl Dhyana Pura ☎0361/730730, ℻730545, ⓦwww.bali-imperial .com. Plush, classy hotel rooms and cottages (some with private pools) set in a tropical beach-front garden that affords fine views at sunset. Two swimming pools, tennis courts, open-air stage, and a recommended Japanese restaurant. **❾**

The Legian Jl Laksmana ☎0361/730622, ℻730623, ⓦwww.ghmhotels.com. Super-deluxe apartment-style rooms designed in sophisticated minimalist style with private verandahs that make the most of unparalleled ocean views. The grounds of this three-storey hotel run down to the beach and there's a shorefront pool, a spa and a restaurant. Close to the *Oberoi* and a couple of very good

restaurants but a long drive from the heart of Seminyak. Published rates from US$295. **❾**

Mesari Beach Inn Jl Abimanyu ☎0361/730401. Just three exceptionally cheap no-frills rooms in a plot that gives direct access to the beach. **❷**

Panca Jaya Jl Abimanyu ☎ & ℻0361/730458. Surprisingly inexpensive place offering simple but comfortable accommodation a couple of minutes' walk from the beach. Rooms **❷** Bungalows **❸**

Puri Cendana Jl Dhyana Pura ☎0361/730869, ℻730868, ⓦwww.puri-cendana.com. Good-value, air-conditioned Balinese-style two-storey cottages in a gorgeous garden just 30m from the beach but a longish hike from bars and restaurants. All rooms have hot water, and there's a swimming pool in the garden. Up to fifty percent discounts outside peak periods. **❽**

Raja Gardens Jl Abimanyu ☎0361/730494, ℻732805. Six unusual, nicely furnished bungalows in a garden one minute's walk from the beach. Peaceful, family-run and good value, with a pool. **❺**

Canggu and Berewa

Beyond the Jalan Laksmana turn-off to the *Bali Oberoi* in the far northern part of Seminyak, the road continues to the crossroads at Kerobokan where the left-hand fork leads to the **Canggu** stretch of coast – a road distance of 10km in all. The **Berewa** (or Brawa) beach area of Canggu is renowned for its surfing (see p.122) and long stretch of good sand, and is fronted by a handful of fairly upmarket hotels. The current is notoriously strong up here, and all the hotels advise their guests – confident surfers excepted – against swimming in the sea (they all have pools). In the rainy season the whole beachfront looks dramatically wild. There are a few warung and restaurants on the road down to Berewa beach, as well some transport rental outlets, but most people who stay in Canggu rent their own transport and use the Kuta area for entertainment and other necessities.

Bolare Beach Hotel Berewa beach ☎0361/ 730258, ℻731663, ℮bolare@indosat.net.id. Comfortably equipped cottages, if a little dark, all with air-con, TV and mini-bar; the standard ones are rather cramped so it's worth upgrading – especially as there are usually significant discounts. The garden runs down to the beach, and there's a pool and a restaurant. **❼**

Dewata Beach Berewa beach ☎0361/730263, ℻730290, ℮dewatabh@indo.net.id. The least interesting of Canggu's hotels, but comfortable enough, with well-furnished standard rooms in the main block and more attractive options in a series of smaller cottage blocks. There's a big pool, tennis courts and a kids' playground, plus bicycle rental and free transport to Kuta. **❽**

Legong Keraton Beach Cottages Berewa beach ☎0361/730280, ℻730285. By far the best option

on this beach, with 24 attractive, traditional style thatched cottages, all with air-con and sunken bath, set in a very peaceful, award-winning garden that runs right down to the beach. The more expensive ones have the best view, and there's a pool and decent mid-priced restaurant. **❻–❼**

Tugu Batu Bolong beach ☎0361/731701, ℻731704, ⓦwww.tuguhotels.com. One of the loveliest hotels in the whole of Bali, set a little further up the coast on Batu Bolong beach (just as unswimmable as Berewa). Comprising a series of traditional polished-teak houses furnished with stylish antiques, the hotel is full of character: each of the 25 elegant suites (published rates US$250–450) has a living room, bedroom and garden bathroom, and some have private plunge pools. There's a hotel pool, restaurant, spa and library, and free transport to Kuta. **❾**

The resort

There's nothing much to see in Kuta–Legian–Seminyak, but there's plenty to do, both in the resort and on day-trips out.

The **beach** is one of the most beautiful in Bali, with its gentle curve of golden sand stretching for 8km, its huge breakers, which lure amateur and experienced surfers alike, and the much lauded Kuta sunsets – at their blood-red best in April, but streaky-pink at any time of year. Though crowded with tourists from dawn to dusk every day of the year, the beach remains amazingly clean, and also refreshingly clear of hawkers, thanks to a couple of local bylaws. The most congested swath is Kuta beach itself, along Jalan Pantai Kuta; the most peaceful is at Seminyak, between Jalan Dhyana Pura and *La Lucciola* restaurant at Petitenget. The sands around Jalan Arjuna in north Legian make a pleasant alternative, fronted by a barely used road and graced with sunloungers and several restaurants where you can laze away the sweltering midday hours while admiring the local surfing talent.

The waves that make Kuta such a great beach for surfers make it less pleasant for **swimming**, with a strong undertow as well as the breakers to contend with. You should always swim between the red and yellow striped flags, and take notice of the warning signs that dot the beach. **Lifeguards** are stationed in special towers all along the Kuta–Legian stretch; the central lifeguard post is on the beach at the corner of Jalan Pantai Kuta.

Massage and **manicure** women parade the beach in their sarongs and conical hats, carrying baskets stuffed with bottles of fresh coconut oil, manicure tools, hair-beading accessories and pots of ghastly red nail polish. Balinese massage is traditionally quite rigorous, with a fair amount of pummelling and a great deal of oil; you should bargain for a session, as for anything else in Kuta.

Surfing

Kuta is the perfect **surfers' base**, with dozens of surfwear and board-repair shops, plenty of off-water entertainment facilities and some pretty good surf breaking daily on the doorstep. Because the beach is sandy and there's no coral or rocks to wipe out on, it's the best place in Bali to learn to surf, and is also within easy reach of Bali's best breaks, at Padang Padang and Uluwatu (see box on p.138). It was off this stretch of shore in 1936 that surfing was supposedly introduced to Bali by American hotel owner Bob Koke. The first pro-am competition was organized here in 1980, and local and international surf championships have since become annual events, usually held between March and July. For general surfing tips, see p.60.

Equipment, information and lessons

Poppies 2, Poppies 1 and Jalan Benesari form the heart of Kuta's surf scene, and these are the best areas to **buy boards** or get them repaired, but you can easily **rent boards** on the beach: Rp35,000 will get you a decent two-metre board for the day (beginners should take the largest they can find so as to catch the waves more easily). Boogie boards go for around Rp25,000.

Monthly **tide charts** are compiled by the helpful folk at *Tubes* bar on Poppies 2 and are available there as well as at most surfwear shops in the resort; many surf shops also keep copies of the five-day **swell forecast**. The monthly **magazine** *Surf Time* concentrates exclusively on the Indonesian scene and is available free from most Kuta surf shops.

Surfing **lessons** are offered by the Cheyne Horan School of Surf, based at the

Ever Green Puri hotel at Jl Arjuna 7a in north Legian (☎0361/735858, ⓦwww.schoolofsurf.com). They have a range of courses, from $35 for a half-day (including equipment), to $365 for a five-day session including an overnight trip to breaks elsewhere on Bali. Bali Adventure Tours (☎0361/721480, ⓦwww.baliadventuretours.com) runs two-hour lessons for $39, and many of the small board shops in Kuta will also give lessons if asked. Should you want to practise your moves in the dry, there's a mechanical surfboard at the *All Stars Surf Café* on Jalan Dewi Sartika (see p.131), where you can also watch surfing videos screened round the clock.

Surf breaks

The best time of year for surfing off Kuta is during the dry season (April–Oct), when the southeast trade winds blow offshore – at their strongest in July and August. From November to March, the wind arrives from the northwest, bringing rain and blowing onshore, sending most surfers across to Sanur and Nusa Dua on the east coast.

The surf breaks offer consistent, almost uniform waves, with lots of tubes. They are particularly appealing for beginners, especially the one known as **Kuta Beach** (beyond the Jalan Pantai lifeguard station), where high-tide beach breaks are fun but not too daunting. Further north, off the end of Jalan Padma, **Legian Beach** is slightly more exposed, with bigger waves, but still very manageable; best on a small swell at high tide. Directly in front of the *Patra Jasa* hotel at the far southern end of Kuta Beach, **Airport Lefts** provides another good beginners' wave, a left-hander best surfed on a medium swell at mid- to high tide. The trickiest of the Kuta waves is also one of the most popular, breaking over **Kuta Reef** (a 20min paddle out from the southern end of Kuta beach, or a short boat ride), where the ideal left-hand reef breaks are best ridden on mid- to high tides.

About 10km north of Seminyak by road, or about 5km along the beach, **Canggu** (see p.120) provides waves for fairly experienced surfers, with the bonus of beautiful views of paddies and coconut groves. The main break here is a right-hander, flanked by one left-hander 150m to the south, and another one 50m to the north: best on a small to medium swell at mid- to high tide.

Surfaris

An increasing number of outfits in Kuta organize "**surfari**" surfing tours to the mega-waves off Sumbawa, East Java (including the awesome G-Land), West Java, Lombok and West Timor. Prices usually include boat transport, shared accommodation and food.

Kuta's longest-established surfari operator is **Wanasari Wisata**, inside the G-Land surf shop at Jl Pantai 8b (☎0361/755588, ⓕ755690, ⓦwww.grajagan.com); they run trips to G-Land, departing every three days (March–Oct), with accommodation at Bobby's Camp, for US$350 for four days, $500 for a week. **Indoswell.com** on Poppies 1 (☎0361/763892, ⓕ763893, ⓦwww.indoswell.com) has cheaper G-Land trips, with accommodation in tents at Tiger Camp, for $250 for seven days, plus surfaris to Sumbawa (three/six days for $110/185). **Tubes** bar on Poppies 2 (☎0361/772870, ⓦwww.g-land.com) sells all-inclusive G-Land surfaris based at G-Land Jungle Surf Camp for $240 for three nights, $310 for six nights. Seminyak-based **Bali Surfing** (☎0361/730184, ⓕ730698, ⓦwww.bali-surfing.com) offers a variety of packages, from week-long south Bali surf holidays ($325 without accommodation) to a nine-day Lombok, Sumbawa and Nusa Lembongan boat-tour surf package ($750 inclusive).

△ Rujak seller, Sanur

Diving and other watersports

Surfing aside, Kuta is not a great centre for watersports. However, all tour agencies in the resort can organize **diving** trips and courses with one of south Bali's major dive centres (see pp.164–165), most of which are based in Sanur or Tanjung Benoa, and all of which charge competitive rates for near-identical packages, including local dives, trips to the best reefs on the east and north coast, and internationally certified diving courses (for more on which, see p.65). Organizing your diving through a Kuta tour agency means you don't get the chance to discuss courses and trips in advance with the dive leaders and instructors; two dive outfits who are based in the Kuta area are the American-run Scuba Duba Doo, Jl Legian 367, just south of Jalan Melasti (T & F0361/761798, W www .divecenterbali.com), and the UK-run AquaMarine Diving, Jl Raya Seminyak 56 (T0361/730107, F735368, Wwww.aquamarinediving.com).

Many of the Sanur and Tanjung Benoa dive centres also offer other **watersports**, including snorkelling, sea-kayaking and fishing trips, as well as parasailing, jet-skiing, windsurfing and waterskiing. All these can also be booked through Kuta tour agencies, but it's cheaper (though still fairly pricey) to make a day-trip and organize it yourself: ask to be dropped at places which rent out equipment – Yos Marine Adventures or Baruna in Tanjung Benoa (see p.152), or the small offices on the beaches in front of the *Grand Bali Beach* or *Sanur Beach* hotels in Sanur (see p.162).

Water parks

Kuta's **Waterbom Park** on Jalan Dewi Sartika, Tuban (daily 8.30am–6pm; adults $16.50, 5- to 12-year-olds $9), is a kind of aquatic adventure park, with water slides, chutes and helter-skelters, a lazy river to paddle inner-tubes down and facilities for water volleyball. It's quite possible to while away a whole day here, as there are lockers for your gear, and a restaurant and sunken bar on the premises. The place is very popular with families (children under 12 must be accompanied by an adult), not least because of the omnipresent corps of lifeguards. Another good watery option is to spend the day at the **Hard Rock swimming pool** (daylight hours; adults Rp50,000, kids Rp25,000, two adults plus two kids Rp125,000), inside the *Hard Rock* hotel complex on Jalan Pantai Kuta. It's a huge, fantastic construction, hundreds of metres long, with several sections plus water chutes, a sandy beach area, volleyball net and poolside food and drink waiters. For an extra Rp100,000 (or Rp60,000 after 3pm) you can even rent a little waterside "cabana" for the day, complete with day-bed and room service. Non-guests can use the swimming pool at *Poppies Cottages* on Poppies 1 for Rp18,000.

Adventure sports

The craze for **bungee jumping** has subsided, but there are still three jumps in the resort – all of them from towers that dangle you over a swimming pool. Each place sells you videos of your jump and, at around $30 a go, prices are a lot cheaper than in the West. Bali Bungy Co (daily 9am–7pm) is on Jalan Pura Puseh in north Kuta; Adrenalin Park (daily 10am–9pm), is based in the compound of *Adi Dharma* hotel at Jalan Benesari 69, also accessible from the hotel entrance on Jalan Legian; and A.J. Hackett Bungy (daily 11am–6pm & Sat night 2–4am) is further north, in the grounds of the *Double Six* nightclub on Jalan Arjuna; their **2am jumps** on Saturday nights are popular with tripped-out clubbers from next-door.

Active days out

All the following activities can be booked through travel agents or hotels in the resort, but you may want to phone the activity operator direct to find out more specific details. (Bali Adventure Tours offers discounted rates to customers who book at their office in Kuta Square.) All operators do free picks-up from hotels in the major tourist centres of Kuta, Sanur, Nusa Dua and Ubud, and some will pick up from Candi Dasa.

Whitewater rafting is a big thing in Bali, and dozens of companies now offer two-hour trips for around US$70 (kids $45), including lunch and showering facilities. Safety standards vary, so it's worth grilling your chosen operator before you sign up. Two of the most reputable long-established outfits are **Bali Adventure Tours** (T0361/721480, Wwww.baliadventuretours.com) and **Sobek** (T0361/287059, Wwww.sobekbali.com), which both offer rafting on the Class 2 and 3 rapids of the Ayung River, just west of Ubud. Unda River Rafting (T0361/227444) takes people to the Class 2–4 rapids of east Bali's Unda River. Bali Rafting (T0361/270744) races the Class 4 rapids of Telaga Waja River in central Bali.

You can go **kayaking** on Lake Tamblingan for $68 with Sobek, and on the Ayung River for $66 with Bali Adventure Tours. Sobek also takes guided **mountain-bike** trips down the side of Gunung Batur and down Gunung Batukau for $55, and Bali Adventure Tours does bike rides in Sangeh Monkey Forest and neighbouring villages ($54; kids $37). Both outfits lead **jungle treks** in the rainforest and **rice-paddy walks** ($50/$37). Rice-paddy activities are the speciality of **Paddy Venture** (T0361/289748, Wwww.baliadventures.com), which does guided walks ($45), cycling trips ($45) and jaunts on all-terrain vehicles (ATVs) and Land Rovers ($69) through the spectacular scenery around Jatiluwih. The Trekker (T0361/725944) does an Indiana Jones Adventure ($34; 2hr 30min) with canoeing, biking and trekking in the Lake Tamblingan area.

Perama (T0361/751551, Eperama_tour@hotmail.com) has guided sunrise **mountain climbs** up Gunung Agung ($40). Waka Tangga (T0361/484085, Wwww.wakaexperience.com) offers more cultural **guided hikes** to the temples dotted along the slopes of the sacred mountain Puncak Tedung in central Bali ($57).

Umalas Stable (T0361/731402) and Pony Day Tours (T0361/751672) offer **horse riding** through rice terraces or along the beach; or you could go **camel riding** (T0361/286356) along the east coast sands, or **elephant trekking** (T0361/721480) through the forests around the village of Taro near Ubud. Kids will almost certainly enjoy the package **"A Day with the Animals"** offered by Bali Adventure Tours, which takes you to the Elephant Park as well as the Bird and Reptile Parks in Batubulan for $62 (kids $43; family $189).

Late-night drinkers are also the main customers of the **Bali Slingshot** (daily 11am until late; $25), based in front of the *New Bounty* on Jalan Legian, in the heart of Kuta's nightlife area. Here, before hordes of drunken revellers, you can get catapulted 52m into the air in just over one second – and have it all captured on video. There's a **go-kart** track (daily 10am–10pm) on Gang Menuh in north central Kuta.

Spas and beauty treatments

Massages and **beauty treatments** are becoming more popular in Bali: many of Kuta's upper-bracket hotels have built their own **spa** centres to cater for this appetite, and there are plenty of smaller spas offering good-value massages, facials and manicures, as well as the ever-popular Javanese *mandi lulur* body

Organized sightseeing tours from South Bali

Every tour agent in south Bali sells about ten standard **sightseeing tours**, designed to take in the maximum number of attractions in the shortest possible time. The tours (around 8.30am–4.30pm) generally travel in an air-con eight- to ten-person minibus, cost Rp60,000–100,000 per person, and should be booked the night before. Most of these operators are also happy to take private tours (usual minimum two people) to the same places, but for as much as US$35 per person; a potentially more rewarding way to go is to hire a car with driver (see p.114) and customize your own itinerary. Typical tours include:

Bedugul Tour – including the Monkey Forest at Sangeh, the temple at Mengwi, the lake and mountain resort at Bedugul and sunset at the coastal Tanah Lot temple.

Besakih Tour – via the Kerta Gosa at Klungkung and the rice-field panorama at Bukit Jambul, ending up at Bali's holiest mountainside temple, Pura Besakih.

Denpasar Tour – a half-day round-up of the city's museums and temples.

Karangasem Tour – via the Kerta Gosa at Klungkung, the ancient Bali Aga village at Tenganan, the old court centre of Karangasem (modern day Amlapura) and the water palace at Ujung.

Kintamani Tour – the morning *barong* dance show at Kesiman or Batubulan, the holy springs at Goa Gajah or Tampaksiring, the volcano at Kintamani and a shopping break in Ubud.

North Bali Tour – via Bedugul and Lake Bratan to Gitgit waterfall and on to Lovina beach, the Banjar hot springs and the coffee plantations and rice terraces round Pupuan.

Singaraja Tour – via the temple at Mengwi and the lake at Bedugul to the former Balinese capital of Singaraja and the black-sand beach resort of Lovina.

Ubud Tour – a half-day trip via the silver village of Celuk and the woodcarving centre at Mas to Ubud and the Neka Museum of Balinese art.

Uluwatu Tour – a half-day outing to the rock-perched temple on the far southwestern corner of the island in time for sunset, *kecak* dance show and dinner.

Further afield

Most tour agents in south Bali also organize one- and two-day tours to major sights on **neighbouring islands**; many agents will also work out additional, longer, tailor-made tours on request. The three standard tours out of Bali are to:

Lombok – one day, with transport on the express ferry boat. Sights include the weaving village of Sukarara, a visit to one of Lombok's three main pottery villages, the traditional Sasak village of Rembitan and Kuta beach. $75 per person.

Mount Bromo – two days; transport by ferry from Gilimanuk to Java, then minibus. Early-morning hike to see the sunrise. $225 per person.

Yogyakarta – one day, including return flight. Spectacular ancient Buddhist temple complex at Borobudur. $230 per person.

---

scrub (there's a description of this on p.67). Many places make their own products so there's plenty of scope for experimenting.

One long-running outfit that gets good reviews is Bodyworks, which has two centres – the more convenient Bodyworks 1, Jl Raya Seminyak 63 (☎0361/730454), and Bodyworks 2, in a quieter location at Jl Kayu Jati 2 (☎0361/733317), near the *Bali Oberoi* in Petitenget. Both have private treatment rooms designed in earthy, Moroccan-influenced style around a courtyard, and both offer a long menu of massages (Rp129,000–219,000) including Balinese, Javanese (*mandi lulur*) Thai, shiatsu and aromatherapy, plus hair, facial and manicure treatments. Advance reservations are recommended but not essential. Putri Bali beauty salon, next to *Wisata Beach Inn* on Jalan Padma (☎0361/755987) offers exceptionally inexpensive treatments, including hour-long *mandi lulur* (exfoliation) rubs, Balinese *boreh* (blood-circulation), and coconut (after-sun) scrubs for Rp50,000 each.

Eating

There are hundreds of **places to eat** in Kuta–Legian–Seminyak, and the range is phenomenal, from tiny neighbourhood warung to plush international restaurants in the smartest hotels. Unless otherwise stated, all places listed below are open daily from breakfast-time through to at least 10pm. In general the most sophisticated and interesting restaurants are located in the northern reaches of Legian and in Seminyak – though relatively expensive at around Rp50,000–70,000 for a main course. At the other end of the scale, you'll come across familiar **fast-food** places, including *KFC* and *McDonalds*, as well as a lot of places specializing in **tourist food** – spaghetti, pizza, ham sandwiches, jaffles (toasted sandwiches) and fried eggs. While the latter are certainly worth visiting for their fresh fruit juices, their menus are almost indistinguishable; only the best are listed below.

Alternatively, try any of the numerous cheap and cheerful Sumatran **Masakan Padang** restaurants dotted along Jalan Legian between Jalan Melasti and Jalan Bagus Taruna; they're easily spotted by their pyramid window display of available dishes, from which you create your own combination meal (see p.48 for more details). Kuta's main **night market** (*pasar senggol*) is another enjoyable culinary event, which gets going after sundown on Gang Tuan Langa at the southern edge of Kuta: hawkers gather here to brew up noodle soup, barbecued corn and ayam goreng, while the warung barbecue fresh fish, which you can sometimes select yourself from the pails outside. Elsewhere in the resort, you can be sure to find **itinerant vendors** serving up steaming hot dishes right through the night; try the lay-bys all the way down the beachfront Jalan Pantai Kuta, or anywhere along Jalan Legian.

Kuta

Aromas Café Jl Legian. Delicious vegetarian food served in large portions in a garden dining room out of sight of the street. The menu includes Lebanese, Italian, Indian and Indonesian dishes, mostly made with organically grown ingredients, plus cheesecakes, chocolate mousse and lots of vegetable juices. Moderate to Expensive.

Bamboo Corner Poppies 1. Small travellers' restaurant that serves especially delicious *fu yung hai* (fluffy Chinese omelettes stuffed with seafood or vegetables). Inexpensive.

Ketupat Behind the Jonathan Gallery jewellery shop at Jl Legian 109. Superb menu of exquisite Indonesian dishes based around fish, goat and chicken, plus vegetarian options using interesting combinations of banana flowers, jackfruit and eggplant. Deep-fried squid with pickles and rainbow sauce (*chumi chin chin*) is recommended, also the curried vegetables (*sayur tiga warna*). Upmarket in both style and quality, but not overpriced. Tables are set around a swimming pool away from the road. Moderate to Expensive.

Kopi Pot Jl Legian. Café-restaurant serving several different coffee blends, plus *mie goreng* and some quality seafood, including lobster thermidor. Pleasant outdoor setting, with tables on a palm-shaded stepped terrace. Moderate to Expensive.

Kori Poppies 2. Refined dining in a cool, sophisticated setting, where the menu features delicious swordfish plus unusual grill-your-own "stone cuisine" dishes such as pork medallions, lobster mornay, red fish curry and roasted-vegetable lasagne. Also home-made ice creams and sticky-toffee pudding. Not great for vegetarians, but otherwise worth the money. Moderate to Expensive.

Buffet breakfasts

Though many of the cheaper losmen and hotels include breakfast in their room rates, these are not always very appetizing; lots of tourists head instead for the **buffet breakfasts** (daily 7.30–11.30am) at nearby restaurants. At around Rp13,000, these are a good deal, with most places giving you rice or noodles, toast, eggs, fruit salad, coffee and juice – plus bacon, beans and cereal at the more expensive ones. There are lots in Legian, particularly along Jalan Melasti and Jalan Sahadewa. Alternatively, you could try the set breakfasts at *Glory Restaurant* on Jalan Legian, which does Indonesian breakfasts (with fried rice) and Outback ones (with steak).

Made's Warung 1 Jl Pantai Kuta. Long-standing Kuta favourite whose table-sharing policy encourages sociability. Serves standard Indonesian fare (gado-gado, nasi campur, rice and noodle dishes) as well as seafood, multi-dish *rijsttafels* at Rp60,000 per person, plus cappuccino and cakes. Moderate.

Matahari Food Court Top floor of the Matahari department store, Kuta Square. A dozen canteen-style food stalls serving very cheap dishes from all over Asia, including Jakarta sate, west Javanese and Sulawesi specialities, plus Balinese and Thai food. Closes at 9pm. Inexpensive.

Poppies Poppies 1 (✆0361/751059). Another Kuta landmark that doesn't really deserve to be so popular – or so expensive. Disappointingly small menu that accents Western meat dishes and lacks unusual choices, but it all tastes fine. Covered garden setting, though the tables are squashed together. It's advisable to reserve a table a few hours in advance. Moderate to Expensive.

TJs Poppies 1. Popular, long-running Californian/Mexican restaurant with tables set around a watergarden. The menu covers the full gamut of tortillas, fajitas, buffalo wings and potato skins, and includes chicken wraps, Mexican coffees (spiced up with Kahlua) and those all-important margaritas and strawberry daiquiris. Moderate.

Tree House Poppies 1. Tasty travellers' fare served in large, well-prepared portions, including good fruit salads with yogurt and filling *tahu* burgers. Inexpensive.

Un's Poppies 1. Small but perfectly executed menu dominated by pastas, steaks and seafood. The "three-in-one combo" of mushroom ravioli, gnocchi and spinach ravioli is delicious but pricey. Pleasant ambience, with in-house serenading musicians in the evenings. Expensive.

Warung Brasil Jl Benesari. Cheap and cheerful guacamole, enchiladas and the like, plus standard tourist dishes. Inexpensive to Moderate.

Warung Murni Jl Pantai. Exceptionally cheap, old-style travellers' warung with just half a dozen formica tables, where the nasi goreng costs a bargain Rp5000. Inexpensive.

Warung Suka-Suka Poppies 1. Popular, extremely cheap warung with just a few tables and a menu that includes select-your-own Padang food, nasi campur, *bakso* (soup) and omelettes. Cheap beer too. Inexpensive.

Legian

Bali Too Jl Melasti. Popular place serving spicy Thai soup and some less interesting Indonesian and Western standards. Especially popular for its good-value breakfast buffets. Inexpensive.

Benny's Café Beachfront spot off Jl Arjuna. Run-of-the-mill tourist fare – juices, noodles and the like – but tasty enough, and a perfect wave-gazing location. Inexpensive.

Café Tu Casa Jl Padma. Smart streetside restaurant fronting the *Casa Padma Hotel*, with a wide-ranging menu that includes pastas, DIY pizzas, Mexican burritos, seafood curries, a mini one-person *rijsttafel*, heaps of cocktails and draught Bintang. Moderate to Expensive.

Glory Jl Legian 445, 200m north of Jl Padma. Hearty breakfast buffets and weekly Saturday-night Balinese home-cooking buffets featuring suckling pigs, chilli-fried fish, sate and plenty of veggie dishes for Rp30,000 per person (half-price for kids). Call ✆0361/751091 for free local transport to the Saturday-night buffets. Moderate.

Gosha Seafood Jl Melasti. Deservedly the most popular seafood restaurant in Legian; lobster is a speciality. Inexpensive to Moderate.

Warung Melati Jl Arjuna. A favourite of economy-minded expats, this Masakan Padang-style place is a bargain, with a good range of ready-cooked foods from which to assemble your Rp5000 meal, including deep-fried *tahu*, curried eggs, *tempeh* chips, corn fritters and chilli-spiked water spinach. Inexpensive.

Warung Yogya Jl Padma Utara 79. Another

deservedly popular, unpretentious and very cheap Indonesian eatery, charging such genuine Indonesian prices that it attracts local customers as well as tourists. The menu covers the range of tasty home-cooked classics, including the perenni-

al favourite nasi campur (veg or non-veg), *nasi pecel* and fried chicken. Inexpensive.

Zanzibar Beachfront spot off Jl Arjuna. Good sandwiches, cakes and pizzas with uninterrupted sea views. Inexpensive.

Seminyak and beyond

Bintang Lima Jl Laksmana 5a, at the head of the road down to the *Oberoi* ☎ 0361/733038. Closed Sat. Unpretentious, unusual Indonesian restaurant which serves food from all over the archipelago, including grilled tuna with lemongrass and fish in spicy green curry, and brews a huge range of herbal teas and *arak* cocktails. Has only eight tables so it's worth phoning ahead to reserve. Inexpensive to Moderate.

Gus Bakery Jl Raya Seminyak 16b. Tempting French bakery and coffee shop, with croissants, Danish pastries, chocolatines, gooey cakes, fruit tarts and selection of breads. Moderate.

Kafé Warisan Jl Raya Kerobokan, about 1km north of the *Oberoi* turn-off ☎ 0361/731175. Mon–Sat lunch and dinner, Sun closed for lunch. Reservations strongly advised. Delicious, beautifully cooked, gourmet French food is the trademark of this long-running expats' favourite overlooking the rice-fields. The menu includes artichoke-stuffed ravioli with scallops in a citrus sauce, duo of lamb with mashed potato and rosemary juice, duck confit and red berry millefeuille. The imported wine list is as long as it is pricey. Expensive.

Kin Khao Jl Legian, between Jl Arjuna and Jl Dhyana Pura. Upmarket Thai food served in stylish surroundings. Specialities include fried chicken in pandanus leaves, and mixed vegetables in green curry. Portions are small but reasonably priced so you can create your own gastronomic experience. Moderate.

Krakatoa Jl Raya Seminyak 56, opposite Jl Dhyana Pura. Fabulous home-made cakes (banana, walnut and chocolate), breads (baguettes, wholemeal, rolls) and yogurts; also available as take-outs. Moderate.

La Lucciola Jl Petitenget, accessed only by a footpath from the Pura Petitenget car park, or from the beach ☎ 0361/730838; reservations advisable, especially for a sea-view table. Fanned by the sea breezes and built right on the edge of the shore, this two-storey open-sided pavilion is a favourite spot for sunset cocktails – which you can also enjoy on sun-loungers beside the sea – and for romantic dinners under the glow of flaming torches. The Mediterranean-inspired menu doesn't always live up to the setting, but includes Moroccan duck pie, swordfish steak with eggplant

salsa, Tasmanian salmon, king prawns with sweet-potato chips and an array of tropical fruit sorbets. Expensive.

The Living Room Jl Petitenget 2000xx, about 350m beyond Pura Petitenget ☎ 0361/735735. Nightly from 7pm; reservations advisable. Elaborate presentation is the hallmark of this delightful, colonial-style eating experience, where the dining pavilion is draped in white linen, the waitresses are clad in designer summer dresses, and the courtyard tables hide amongst the candlelit shrubbery. Every dish on the outstanding pan-Asian menu is a similarly detailed work of art, and includes red-on-red swordfish with red capsicum coulis, baby squid marinated in lemongrass, honey-glazed roasted Balinese duckling and duo-chocolate mousse laced with five different fruit coulis. The wine list is interesting, and diners are offered a taster "wine rainbow" menu as well. Moderate to Expensive.

Made's Warung 2 Jl Raya Seminyak, about 100m north of Jl Dhyana Pura. More stylish offshoot of the long-running Kuta eatery, with a lively plaza setting and an Indo-European menu that looks unadventurous but tastes extremely good. Both the meat and veggie versions of the nasi campur are exceptionally tasty and served in copious portions. Moderate to Expensive.

Pantarei Jl Raya Seminyak 17. Stylish place with a contemporary Mediterranean ambience where the outdoor tables are illuminated by garden candles. The menu is predominantly Greek and includes perfect mixed meat kebabs, unusually good multi-coloured salads, grilled swordfish, some mezze dishes and the famous (and famously expensive) spaghetti lobster. Moderate to Expensive.

Soda Club Beachfront, off the west end of Jl Arjuna. Trendy seafront bar and restaurant built on several levels and fanned by the sea breezes, with plenty of stylish furnishings, lots of sofas with a sea view and some low tables with cushions. Perfect place to watch the sunset, or for pre-club drinks. The imaginative menu covers everything from seafood to beef stroganoff, plus pizzas, salads, foreign breads and plenty of veggie options. Moderate.

Tuban

Daddy's Café Opposite *Bali Dynasty Resort* on Jl Dewi Sartika. Reasonably priced Greek restaurant with an unrivalled selection of mezze, including aubergine imam, cheese saganaki, and delicious potatoes stuffed with spinach, feta and aromatic herbs. Good-value mixed seafood platters, plus genuine kebabs, souvlaki and moussaka. Moderate.

Golden Lotus Inside the *Bali Dynasty Resort* on Jl Dewi Sartika. Upmarket dim sum and à la carte Chinese restaurant that's pricey but tasty. Very popular with local Chinese and Indonesian families, especially for the all-you-can eat buffets on Sundays (10am–2.30pm). On other days, dim sum

is served from noon to 2.30pm. Moderate to Expensive.

Kin Khao Jl Dewi Sartika 170. This Tuban branch of the reliable chain of Thai restaurants does great deep-fried chicken breasts with chilli sauce, aromatic *tom yam kung* soup, and offers a range of red and yellow curries. Portions are small but not too expensive, so it's worth ordering a good selection. Moderate.

Kunyit Jl Dewi Sartika. Breezy, fairly elegant pavilion restaurant whose specialities are its sevencourse Indonesian and Balinese *rijsttafels* priced at Rp118,000 for two people. Expensive.

Nightlife and entertainment

Kuta–Legian–Seminyak boasts the liveliest and most diverse **nightlife** on the island, with at least six major clubbing venues and lots more bars, many featuring live bands. Most places stay open until at least 1am, with several clubs continuing to churn out the sounds until 6am. As much of the action is concentrated in Kuta, it's quite possible to walk from bar to bar and then home again: the main streets are well-lit and usually pretty lively until at least 3am (although be aware that muggings do occur). There are always plenty of metered taxis running down the main drag.

As a rule, the clubs and bars are safe and unthreatening places to be, and friendly enough towards lone drinkers – male or female. Women are unlikely to get serious hassle, although you will get seriously chatted up by the resident gaggle of **gigolos** who haunt the dance floors and bars. Female prostitution is on the increase in Kuta, but is mainly confined to the beach, certain stretches of Jalan Legian and a few well-known pick-up joints. There's also quite a public **transvestite** scene, which includes a group known as the "sucky sucky girls" who tout for custom on Jalan Legian after the nightclubs close.

Bars and clubs

There's a marked difference between the **bars** and **clubs** of Kuta and those of Legian–Seminyak.

Kuta's nightlife is very much a younger travellers' scene, with the most popular bars and clubs (*Paddy's, Sari Club, The New Bounty*) packed out by 11pm and still raging at 2am. The dance floors in these places are lively and friendly and in *Paddy's* at least are enlivened by a lot of young Indonesian gigolos. Some of the smaller bars also have dance floors, others offer live music, have pool tables or show all-night videos. To avoid the prospect of drinking alone, you could join the twice-weekly **Peanuts Pub Crawl**, which transports punters to the main drinking spots along Jalan Legian, including the *Peanuts* disco-bar (every Tues & Sat from 6.30pm; Rp15,000; call ☎0361/754149 for details). With an upper limit of two hundred participants, this has become a Kuta institution – so much so that there are organized *Peanuts* reunions held regularly in several Australian cities. A number of the venues listed below feature **live music** from local and Javanese bands, as do the restaurants at the *Barong* and

Indah Beach hotels on Poppies 2. For listings of special gigs, club events and parties, check the free fortnightly **magazine** *the beat*, available at some restaurants and nightlife venues.

The scene in **Legian–Seminyak** is more self-consciously cool and fashionable, and attracts a much bigger crowd of expats and well-heeled Indonesians, though younger tourists still end up here too. It's correspondingly more expensive, with some of the larger clubs charging admission and asking ridiculous prices for drinks. For a more intimate experience, the best place to make for is Jalan Dhyana Pura (aka Jalan Abimanyu), where there's a cluster of trendy little dance-bars. The Seminyak clubs keep well abreast of current mainstream dance sounds from around the world and employ plenty of Western as well as local DJs; the Ecstasy-fuelled rave scene is well established at most of the major venues.

The **gay scene** is becoming more developed, with a dedicated gay bar in Legian at *Hulu Café*, another one at *Q Bar* on Jalan Dhyana Pura in Seminyak, and a strong gay presence at other venues on the same road. Most of the other Seminyak clubs attract a good mixed crowd of gays and straights, Indonesians, expats and tourists. The most popular **cruising** area for male homosexuals has always been the beach, in particular the stretch between the *Maharani* and the *Natour Kuta Beach*, and the beachfront area north of the *Oberoi* in Seminyak. As with the heterosexual gigolo scene, the local gay community thrives not on payment for sex but on the assumption that the richer man will pay for food, drink and accommodation.

Kuta and Tuban

All Stars Surf Café Kuta Centre, Jl Dewi Sartika 8x. Popular, long-running Tuban surf bar with different bands playing nightly (9pm–2.30am), surfing videos screened back-to-back on 15 screens, autographed boards and other surfing hall-of-fame memorabilia on the walls and ceiling, a mechanical surfboard, plus pool tables and dartboards.

Bagus Pub Poppies 2. Large and loud tourist restaurant and video bar, popular with Australians and surfers.

Deejay Café Behind the *All Stars Surf Café* in Kuta Centre, Jl Dewi Sartika 8x. Sophisticated club that's part open-air and part air-con, where the resident and guest DJs spin mainly trance and tribal underground. Nightly 11pm–6am.

Hard Rock Café Jl Pantai. Despite being part of the international chain, this place has a good reputation with local youth and attracts a huge crowd from around 11pm when the nightly band comes on stage. Expect slick performances of cover songs, with some audience participation, plus the occasional big-name appearance. Drinks are expensive. Closes 2am (weekends 3am).

The Old Bounty Jl Legian, just north of Jl Benesari; and **The New Bounty** Jl Legian, between Poppies 1 and Poppies 2. These two identical novelty buildings, both built to resemble Captain Bligh's eighteenth-century galleon, dress their bar staff in sailor suits, show daredevil-sports footage on the outsize video screens, and play mainly contemporary hits on the turntables. Both places are especially popular with young Australians, and the dance floors are generally heaving by 10pm. The *New Bounty* runs happy hours nightly from 7pm to 2am, when the crowd really starts to get going, and doesn't shut down until dawn. Both venues stage regular special events, and you can ride the Slingshot (see p.125) in the courtyard in front of the *New Bounty* any night you want. Moderately priced drinks, with food served day and night.

Paddy's Pub Jl Legian, between Poppies 1 and Poppies 2. Loud music and reasonably priced beer make this Kuta's liveliest and most popular venue, with young tourists and local gigolos packing the bar and dance floor night after night. It's right in the heart of Kuta's unofficial nightlife district and stays open from 8pm until the last drunk slumps to the ground.

Peanuts Club Jl Legian, just south of the Jl Melasti intersection. Large disco and bar with low-grade live music in the streetside section, and a classic rock sound system plus glitterball to dance to inside. Popular throughout the week, but the crowds get swollen by the Peanuts Pub Crawlers on Tues and Sat. Pool table and karaoke bar and reasonably priced drinks; closes around 2am.

Sari Club ("SC") Jl Legian. Hugely popular bar and club which attracts a hip young crowd of drinkers and clubbers. Mostly plays current international dance hits, though nothing very hardcore. Friendly, party atmosphere and no cover charge. Closes 3am.

Tubes Poppies 2. The top surfers' hangout in Kuta, fully kitted out with noticeboards, surfing videos and signed champion boards (you can get tide tables from here too), plus a bar and pool tables. Spacious, airy and friendly to non-surfers. Live music every Mon, Wed and Fri. Closes around 2am.

Legian and Seminyak

A Club Jl Basangkasa 10a (just before the *Oberoi* turn-off), Seminyak. Trendy spot where the resident DJs play mainly house music and host regular one-off parties and special events (check flyers and *the beat*). Tues–Sat from 10pm.

Aina Jl Lasmana 41, at the head of the road down to the *Oberoi*, Seminyak. A low-key, arty kind of place, very much part of the Seminyak scene. It serves a good selection of wines, beers and cocktails and plays decent music. Nightly 6pm–2am.

Café del Mar Jl Dhyana Pura 1000x, Seminyak. Fairly cool place, with nightly DJs spinning up-to-date sounds, a fashion-conscious crowd and a bar full of cocktails. Nightly from 9pm.

Double Six ("66") Off the beachfront end of Jl Arjuna, Seminyak. Upmarket, but not untrendy, club which attracts a fashion-conscious local and expat crowd plus some stray backpackers. Huge dance floor, encircled by tables, and two bars. Current club sounds from around the world, often spun by European DJs (check flyers for one-off nights from visiting UK clubs). On Saturday nights you can do a bungee jump in the club grounds (see p.124). Pricey drinks, and a hefty admission charge of Rp30,000 (weekdays) or Rp50,000 (Sat), which includes one small beer. Nightly midnight–6am.

Hulu Café Jl Sahadewa, Legian. Kuta's most outré gay venue stages glamorously over-the-top drag shows nightly from 10.30pm (except Mon) and is a

friendly, lively place with reasonably priced drinks and a nice mix of Indonesians, expats and tourists. Tues–Sun 4pm till late.

Jaya Pub Jl Raya Seminyak 2. Fairly sedate live music venue and watering-hole for older tourists and expats. Twenty or so tables and no real dance floor.

New Lips Jl Raya Seminyak. Slightly seedy country-and-western pub, with nightly music from a poor-quality live band. Small and dark, with pool tables, but not without character. Also a popular pick-up joint for older Western men. Closes about 4am.

Q Bar Jl Arjuna, Seminyak. Seminyak's main gay venue stages different nights every day of the week, including drag shows, cabarets and retro theme nights. Most of the action is downstairs around the bar and diminutive dance floor, while upstairs is the chill-out zone, cybercafé and restaurant. Nightly 6pm till 1.30am.

Santa Fe Jl Abimanyu, Seminyak. Very popular bar and restaurant, larger than many on this road, that gets lively quite soon after dark and has live music from cover bands several nights a week. Shuts about 1.30am.

Soda Club Beachfront, off the west end of Jl Arjuna, Seminyak. This trendy split-level seafront bar and restaurant is ideal for pre-club drinks, including cocktails and a good selection of imported wines – *Double Six* is just 150m away.

Entertainment

Kuta's not exactly renowned for its wealth of cultural entertainment, but most tour agencies organize regular trips to see **Balinese dancing** at venues outside the resort – only worth considering if you're not planning to visit Ubud (where there are dance performances every night). *Kecak* and *barong* dances are performed every day in Denpasar (see p.102) and Batubulan (see p.180), both well worth seeing and within easy reach of Kuta. Tour agencies charge a lot more than you'd expect to pay on the door at these places – $10–15 per person, including return transport, for a show that costs Rp50,000. A few of Kuta's top hotels put on regular dance performances on their purpose-built stages, open to non-guests but pricey: the *Natour Kuta* hotel on Jalan Pantai has a medley show of several Balinese dances with a buffet dinner (Fri 7.30pm; $12, kids $6).

The nearest **cinema** is the Wisata 21 complex in Denpasar, not far from Tegal bemo terminal (see p.102). Kuta's numerous tourist restaurants – most of them on Poppies 2, with a couple on Poppies 1 – show free, back-to-back **videos** from early afternoon until midnight; screens tend to be large and the volume is turned up full blast. The day's programmes are always posted outside and usually comprise three or four very recent releases, with an emphasis on action blockbusters.

Shopping

Kuta–Legian–Seminyak is a great place to **shop**, especially for clothes, surfing gear and souvenirs. For basic necessities, cosmetics and mass-produced clothes, go for a browse at **Matahari department store** in Kuta Square, Kuta (the smaller branch on Jalan Legian is not so interesting). The ground-floor supermarket is a good place to buy packets of gado-gado sauce and Bali *kopi* to take home with you, the kids' department stocks child-sized mosquito nets, baby bottles and dummies, and the fashion department sells traditional Balinese formal wear such as women's lacy tops and men's batik shirts. Both Matahari stores have a floor dedicated to **arcade games** that's usually packed out with kids. Most stores stay open until at least 9pm and, while you're expected to bargain hard in the smaller shops and stalls, the more sophisticated stores deal in fixed-price goods only.

Books and music

There are plenty of second-hand **bookstores** on Jalan Legian and the east–west stretch of Jalan Pantai Kuta, as well as along Poppies 1, Poppies 2, Jalan Benesari and Jalan Padma Utara. Prices are not as competitive as in Ubud or Candi Dasa, though the selection compares favourably.

ABC Bookshop Opposite *Melasti Hotel* just off Jl Dewi Sartika, Tuban. Decent enough stock of second-hand books.

Asana In the same complex as *Made's Warung 2*, Jl Raya Seminyak. Small selection of new English-language books about Bali, plus some magazines, regional Indonesian maps and unusual Balinese greetings cards.

Bombocraft Jl Pantai Kuta 8c, Kuta. Hand-made musical instruments, mainly African-inspired *jimbeh* drums carved from teak and mahogany and bamboo didgeridoos.

Bookshop Jl Raya Seminyak. Keeps a range of new books in English, particularly hardbacks on Bali and the other islands of Indonesia. It also stocks some recent paperback fiction, and a few American and Australian newspapers.

Fuji Jaya Poppies 2, Kuta. A reasonable stock of good condition second-hand books.

Kerta Books Four branches: two on Jl Legian, plus one each on Jalan Pantai and Jl Padma Utara. Good stocks of second-hand books in English, German, Swedish, Italian and Japanese.

Mahogany Next to *Pantarei* on Jl Raya Seminyak. Good collection of CDs (from Rp70,000) arranged in a shopper-friendly layout and spanning most current music genres. Also some DVDs and Playstation games.

Matahari department store Kuta Square, Kuta. Keeps a few new English-language books on Bali and Indonesia.

Men at Work Jl Singo Sari, Kuta. A fair selection of CDs, from country to club hits, methodically categorized.

Clothes and jewellery

Bali's **clothing** industry is based in the resort and the shops here stock some superb one-off designs in highly original prints and fabrics – unquestionably Kuta's best bargain, a lot of them designed with cooler climes in mind. On the whole, you'll find the most stylish and exclusive boutiques quite far north up Jalan Legian and along its continuation, Jalan Raya Seminyak; Kuta Square has several international designer outlets, including Versace, Polo and Armani, though these clothes (mostly jeans and T-shirts) are locally produced and not "export quality".

Animale Kuta Square, and several outlets along Jl Legian. One of Bali's most popular womenswear chains, with a good line in stylish, loose-fitting, unstructured trousers, dresses and tops in both plain-coloured cottons and bold prints.

Athletes Foot Jl Melasti, Legian. Big stock of brand-name sports shoes.

Biasa Jl Raya Seminyak. Specializes in elegant chiffon, cotton and silk creations for women and men.

Jonathan Gallery Jl Legian 109, Kuta. Stunning, idiosyncratic silver and semi-precious jewellery, plus a fair collection of antique trinkets brought in from other parts of Indonesia. Expensive.

Komodo Jl Pantai Kuta. Up-to-date Western street fashions plus T-shirts, combats, skate- and surf-wear.

Kuta "Art Market" Beach end of Jl Singo Sari. Collection of small shops and stalls selling racks of inexpensive clothing such as baggy cotton trousers, strappy tie-dyed beach dresses, shorts and T-shirts.

Kuta Kids Jl Pantai (Bemo Corner) and Jl Legian. Bright fabrics and cute designs for under-12s.

Rascals Kuta Square, and two branches on Jl Legian. Sophisticated and tasteful good-quality batik-print swimwear and beachwear.

Sports Station Jl Legian, Kuta, 200m north of Perama Travel. Brand-name sports shoes including Tevas and Converse, plus sportswear, snorkel sets and badminton racquets, all at slightly lower prices than in the UK.

Suarti Jl Legian, near *Mastapa Garden* hotel. Eye-catching window displays which use huge lumps of rock to set off their distinctive silver necklaces, bracelets and earrings.

Surfwear shops Dozens of outlets including Bali Barrel, Billabong, Mambo, Quicksilver, Stussy and Surfer Girl – along Jalan Legian and every other shopping street in the resort. All stock brand-name surf- and skate-wear, plus some surfing equipment.

Talismans of Power Jl Raya Seminyak. Dramatic silver jewellery in highly individual designs, generally set with semi-precious stones. Especially interesting necklaces, pendants and rings. Also sells sumptuous silk cushions and scarves in vibrant shades.

Uluwatu Jl Pantai and several branches on Jl Legian. The original Balinese chain specializing in hand-made Balinese lace (it's spawned several imitators). Clothes are feminine though not too over the top, and mostly in white lace and good-quality white and cream cotton.

Handicrafts, souvenirs and homewares

The shops and stalls that line the Kuta end of Jalan Legian are the place to start looking for **artefacts**, **antiques** and other **souvenirs** from all over Indonesia – although you'll have to run the gamut of artificially aged sculptures and carvings, factory-produced paintings and mechanically woven lengths of cloth, all of which tend to be very convincing to a non-expert eye. As with fashions, the most interesting and well-made **handicrafts** and **homewares** are found in the shops of Legian and Seminyak.

Arin 93 Gang Kresek 5a, off Jl Singo Sari, Tuban. Batik paintings in traditional, surrealist and modern styles by master batik artist Heru, plus cheaper pictures by his students. You can also study batik painting with Heru (see Listings on p.136) and buy batik dyes and waxes from him. Paintings cost from Rp50,000.

Bali Onyx Jl Legian 440, Legian, opposite *Glory* restaurant. If you like onyx stone, this is the place to come. The shop is stacked high with mugs, plates, ashtrays, figurines, even artificial fruit, all made from East Javanese creamy orange onyx.

Idea Jl Melasti, Legian. Stylish handicrafts and gifts, including table mats and photo frames made of finely polished coconut shell, plus batik cosmetic bags and graceful wooden figurines.

Kaya Natural Jl Legian 466, Legian, opposite the Jl Bagus Taruna junction. Inexpensive but tasteful cushion covers, soapdishes and other homewares.

Kuta Metelu Jl Singo Sari 14, cnr of Jl Bunisari. In among the usual woodcarvings and other rather derivative Balinese souvenirs, you'll some very interesting traditional temple artefacts, still used regularly in religious ceremonies. These include gaily painted square offering baskets, gold-printed *perada* temple parasols, and painted wooden pedestals for fruit offerings.

Lombok Pottery Blok C11, Kuta Centre, Jl Dewi Sartika, Tuban. An outlet for the attractive earthen-ware plates, bowls, vases and water jars under the auspices of the Lombok Crafts Project (see p.429).

Nadia Jl Raya Seminyak 39. Attractive handicrafts including bowls, trays, lampshades and even washbasins made from coconut wood laminate.

Oxo Jl Raya Seminyak, just north of Jl Arjuna. An amazing collection of hand-crafted wooden puppets from all over Asia.

Pithe Canthrobus Jl Melasti 88, Legian. Traditional sarongs, attractive batik-print clothing, and unusual, classy handicrafts.

Pusaka Jl Pantai Kuta 20d. A branch of Pithe Canthrobus (see above), selling the same upmarket batik sarongs, shirts and skirts, and quality handicrafts.

Rumah Wayang Southern end of Jl Dewi Sartika, Tuban. Big selection of hand-made wooden traditional wayang golek puppets for sale and to order.

Serendipity Antiques Jl Putih Jelantik, Kuta. One of several shops along this road specializing in reproduction antique wooden furniture, including heavy Dutch-style chests and traditional Balinese carved doors and window frames.

Sunbebek Jl Raya Seminyak 6, north of *Made's Warung 2*. Arresting geometric silk and cotton designs made into cushion covers, drapes, bedspreads, handbags and wallets.

Sarongs and traditional textiles

The cheapest places to buy everyday **sarongs** are the street stalls and art markets of Kuta, where you'll find piles of rayon and cotton wraps in traditional Javanese designs as well as *ikats* and modern patterns, plus the occasional much more expensive silk version. Several shops in Kuta and southern Legian also specialize in **traditional textiles** from other parts of the archipelago, chiefly the distinctive, mass-produced *ikat* wall-hangings, scarves, bags and jackets from Sumba and Flores.

Ana Mahang Jl Legian 159, Kuta. A large selection of *ikat* textiles and weavings from Sumba and Flores, including scarves, bedspreads and hangings.

Batik textiles Jl Arjuna, Seminyak. This road has more than a dozen batik textile shops (sarongs, bedspreads and throws) and is the best place to browse and compare styles and prices. Most designs are bright, bold and modern, and textiles come in sarong lengths or by the metre.

Lumbung Batik East of Supernova Supermarket on Jl Kahuripan, Tuban. Useful fixed-price one-stop shop for traditional batik sarongs, Sumbanese hangings and *ikat* bedspreads. Also some basketware and Lombok pottery.

Nogo Ikat Jl Legian 47, Kuta. This branch of this chain of upmarket *ikat* textile shops is smaller than its Sanur flagship but the quality is high and the service professional, with clothes and home furnishings sold ready-made or designed to suit. Fabric is also available by the metre.

Patola Ratu Jl Legian 456, Legian. Recommended outlet for traditional woven *ikat* hangings from the island of Sumba. Run by an effervescent Sumbanese woman who will happily fill you in on the meanings of the motifs. Also stocks all sizes of carved wooden textile hangers.

Sumba Shop Jl Legian, Legian. Tiny shop crammed full of bedspreads, jackets, purses, scarves and hangings all made from Sumbanese-style woven *ikat*. Also some textiles from Flores, Timor and Toraja.

Wira's Above Lumbung Batik near Supernova Supermarket on Jl Kahuripan, Tuban. Has a whole floor stuffed full of fabrics by the metre, with everything from plain linen to thick cotton weaves and brightly printed rayons, and offers a very reasonably priced and professional dressmaking service. The downstairs showroom carries traditional batik fabrics.

Listings

Airline offices Most international airline offices are in Sanur (see box p.111), though the domestic airlines (see p.21) have their main offices in Denpasar. Garuda city check-in (for reconfirmation, and boarding passes, which can be obtained here 4–24hr before departure) is at *Natour Kuta Beach* on Jl Pantai Kuta (℡0361/751179).

American Express Lost cheques refunded at the Amex office in Sanur (see p.169).

Banks and exchange There are Visa, MasterCard

and Cirrus ATMs every few hundred metres throughout the resort. The Bank Bali opposite *The Bounty* at Jl Legian 118 offers Visa cash advances, as do several banks in Kuta Square, Kuta. There's a Moneygram agent in Blok E of the Kuta Centre complex on Jl Dewi Sartika in Tuban. Be very careful about being ripped off at exchange counters in Kuta: many places short-change tourists by using several well-known rip-offs (see p.36 for details). One chain of recommended moneychangers is PT Central Kuta, which has several branches on Jalan Legian plus one on Jalan Melasti, many of them inside Kodak film shops. There's another reputable money-changer just a few metres north up Jalan Legian from Bemo Corner, on the east side of the road. If you do get caught in a money-changing scam, contact the community police (see below).

Batik- and silk-painting classes Batik artist Heru gives workshops for beginners and experienced artists at his studio on Gang Kresek 5a, off Jl Singo Sari, Tuban ☎0361/765087, ℮arin93batik@hotmail.com. Three-day workshops cost Rp350,000 including materials and artwork, five-day courses cost Rp500,000. He also sells batik-painting materials and comprehensive starter kits. At Sacred River Silks on Gang Keraton, opposite In Touch in Seminyak (mobile ☎0812/381 6936, ℮sacredriversilks@yahoo.com), you can paint your own silk sarong or wall-hanging for $59 (kids $29.50); the price includes instruction and materials, and you can get an idea of the type of designs from the Sacred River scarves they sell at nearby Talismans of Power.

Email and internet access You're rarely more than 500m away from an internet centre in the resort. Prices are competitive, with most places charging Rp300–500/minute. Most of the smaller places offer internet access only, but a few of the longest established cybercafés are much more hi-tech and will scan graphics for you and print out emails. These include the fast and helpful *Bali @ Cyber Café and Restaurant*, Jl Pura Bagus Taruna 4 in Legian (daily 8.30am–11pm; ☎0361/761326, ℉757401; Rp500/min); *Legian Cyber C@fe*, Jl Sahadewa 21, Legian (daily 8am–10.30pm; ☎0361/7621804, ℉752455; Rp300/min); and *Krakatoa*, Jl Raya Seminyak 56, opposite Jl Dhyana Pura (Mon–Fri 8am–10pm, Sat & Sun 8am–8pm; ☎0361/730849, ℉730824; Rp500/min). The Lazale chain of internet cafés charges a ridiculous Rp1000/min. For more, see p.53.

Embassies and consulates Only a few consulates have offices in Kuta; the full list is on p.23.

Hospitals and clinics Bali's efficient chain of tourist-oriented 24hr clinics, known as Legian Clinics numbers 1–7, has two branches in Kuta–Legian–Seminyak. Legian Clinic 1 is on Jl Benesari, north Kuta ☎0361/758503; Legian Clinic 7 is on Jl Legian, 100m north of *Glory* restaurant, in Legian ☎0361/752376. Both offer 24hr consultation with an English-speaking doctor (Rp100,000), emergency call-out (Rp400,000), ambulances, minor surgery and dental services. A

similar service is offered by the SOS Natour Kuta Beach, next to the *Natour Kuta* hotel on Jl Pantai Kuta ☎0361/751361, and the Kuta Clinic on Jl Raya Tuban ☎0361/753268. Nearly all the large, upmarket hotels have an in-house doctor. A couple of places on the outskirts of Kuta also have good reputations for dealing with expat emergencies: Bali International Medical Centre (BIMC) at Jl Bypass Ngurah Rai 100x ☎0361/761263, and International SOS at Jl Bypass Ngurah Rai 24x ☎0361/755768. The nearest hospitals are in Denpasar; see p.103.

House rental Both Krakatoa business centre at Jl Raya Seminyak 56 (opposite Jl Dhyana Pura) and *Bali@Cyber Café* on Jl Bagus Taruna have large noticeboards full of adverts offering long- and short-term house rentals in Legian and Seminyak. Alternatively, contact the nearby property agent In Touch, Jl Raya Seminyak 22 ☎0361/731047, ℣www.intouchbali.com. Also check the classified ads in the fortnightly *Bali Advertiser* newspaper, available at many restaurants. See p.47 for useful websites.

Laundry Many losmen and all hotels offer laundry services. There's a coin-operated laundromat at Jl Benesari 19.

Left luggage All hotels and losmen will store your luggage if you reserve a room for your return; some charge a nominal fee. There's also left luggage at the airport (see p.110).

Newspapers *The Jakarta Post*, Indonesia's national English-language paper, is available every morning and sold by street hawkers for as much as they can get (published price is Rp4000). The same day's Australian and American newspapers usually appear on the streets at around sundown.

Pharmacies You'll find a pharmacy on every major shopping street, as well as Legian Clinic 1, on Jl Benesari, north Kuta; next to Bemo Corner on Jl Legian, south Kuta; inside the Matahari department store in Kuta Square; and on Jl Singo Sari.

Phones The government wartel is inconveniently sited down at the airport, but there are dozens of private wartels in the resort, most of them open from 8am–midnight.

Police The helpful and energetic local community police, Satgas Pantai Desa Adat Kuta, are English-speaking and in 24hr attendance at their office on the beach in front of *Natour Kuta Beach Hotel* (☎0361/762871). The government police station is at the intersection of Jl Raya Tuban and Jl Singo Sari.

Post offices Kuta's GPO is on a small *gang* between Jl Raya Tuban and Jl Tanjung Mekar (Mon–Thurs 8am–2pm, Fri 8am–noon, Sat 8am–1pm), and services include parcel-packing and poste restante. Ida's Postal Agent opposite the Poppies 2 intersection at Jl Legian 61, Kuta, is more central and keeps much longer hours (Mon–Sat 8am–8pm); services here include poste restante and a fax-receiving service (℗0361/751574). In Legian, Asthini Yasa Postal Agent is conveniently located opposite *Glory* restaurant on Jl Legian (Mon–Sat 8am–8pm; ℗0361/752883). Many other shops throughout the resort double as postal agents (selling stamps and weighing mail) and keep normal shop hours. All the email centres listed above also offer efficient fax-sending and -receiving services, as do some of the private wartels.

Travel agents Domestic and international airline tickets are available from the following agents, some of which also sell express boat tickets: Kuta Suci, Jl Pantai Kuta 37c ℡0361/765357, ℮kutasuci@mail.com; Lila Tours, inside *Natour Kuta Beach* hotel, Jl Pantai Kuta ℡0361/761827, ℮lilatur@indosat.net.id; Perama Travel, Jl Legian 39 ℡0361/751551, ℮perama_tour@hotmail .com; and Ananda Tour, Century Plaza complex, Jl Benesari 7, ℡0361/755660, ℮amantour@indosat .net.id. Pelni boat tickets from the Pelni office, about 250m south of Supernova at Jl Raya Tuban 299 ℡0361/763963 or 723689.

The Bukit and Nusa Dua

Some 4km south of Kuta, Bali narrows into a sliver of land before bulging out again into the **Bukit**, a harsh, scrubby limestone plateau that dangles like a football from a thread off the far southern end of the island. Officially called Bukit Badung (*bukit* means "hill" in Bahasa Indonesia), this part of the south has more in common with the infertile scrub of Nusa Penida across the water than with the generously lush paddies of the rest of Bali. While its inhospitable terrain leaves most Bukit residents in despair, it's a source of great delight for **surfers**, with some of Bali's best surf breaks off the craggy shoreline. Real-estate developers are starting to get interested too as they toe the government line on targeting only infertile land for tourist projects. This has meant a gradual mushrooming of upmarket hotel complexes on the Bukit, particularly in Jimbaran, and a blossoming of tiny losmen and warung on or near the best surfing beaches.

This account follows an anti-clockwise route around the plateau, beginning at the fishing village of **Jimbaran**, which lies just a couple of kilometres south of the airport on the isthmus, and has a fine beach and several luxury hotels. Continuing southwest, the road passes a number of good surf spots before reaching **Uluwatu**, location not only of some internationally renowned surf, but also of one of Bali's major clifftop temples, perched right on the island's far southwestern tip. The road then sweeps round southeast to **Nusa Dua**, a purpose-built deluxe resort offering superb facilities but distinctly lacking in character, and its adjacent alter-ego **Tanjung Benoa**, a centre for watersports and location of some cheaper accommodation.

Public **transport** in the Bukit is sporadic at best, and there are several parts where bemos just don't penetrate; more details are given in the relevant sections below. It's easy enough to join a tour to Uluwatu from any of the resorts, but the best option is to **rent your own transport** and explore by yourself. Motorbikes are often more practical than jeeps for negotiating the pitted and potholed tracks down to the surfing beaches. South of Ngurah Rai Airport,

Bukit surf breaks

The Bukit **surf breaks** are the most thrilling and the most popular in Bali, especially the Padang Padang and Uluwatu breaks which, though consistent, are tantalizingly difficult even for competent surfers. They're at their best from April to October when the southeast winds blow offshore.

Travelling along the coast from north to south, the first break is **Airport Rights**, located halfway down the Jimbaran side of the airport runway, and accessible by boat from Kuta Reef or from Jimbaran fishing village. This high-speed series of right-handers is best on a strong swell at mid- to high tides, and dangerous at low tide. At **Balangan** (see p.144), a speedy walling left-hander over a shallow reef sometimes provides long rides; best at high tide, and unsurfable at low tide. The beach break at nearby **Dreamland** (see p.144) has a fast left and right peak, sometimes gives very long rides, and can get pretty big. More consistent, and clearly signed off the main Jimbaran–Uluwatu road, **Bingin** and **Impossibles** are always busy. Bingin offers short left-hand tubes, while, breaking over the reefs beyond, Impossibles provides long and speedy walling left-handers, surfable at all tides.

Signed off the main Jimbaran–Uluwatu road, and also accessible by coast path from Uluwatu, **Padang Padang** (see p.144) is considered to be one of the classiest and most exciting surf spots in Indonesia (and was voted the tenth best wave in the world by Australia's *Tracks* magazine), but it's also one of the trickiest because of a twist in the final section. It offers great left-hander tubes, best on a big swell at mid-through high tide. Accessed via Suluban beach, close to Pura Luhur Uluwatu, **Uluwatu** (see p.144) gets the most swell of all the breaks along the west coast. There are actually five separate left-hand surf breaks here, offering rides from high through to low tide. The main break is the **Peak**, best at mid- through to high tides, and the most consistent of the Bukit breaks.

The Bukit also offers a couple of good, though tricky, waves off the **south-facing coast**, which can be surfed at any time of year, so long as there's a north wind or no wind at all. **Nyang Nyang** (see p.146), accessed via a steep track down the cliffside (follow signs for *Puri Bali Villas* off the Uluwatu–Nusa Dua road) is an unpredictable right-hander best surfed between mid- and high tides on a small swell. **Green Ball**, another right-hander, best at mid-tide, lies just offshore from the *Bali Cliff Resort* near Ungasan (see p.147).

See the box on p.153 for an rundown of Nusa Dua's surf breaks.

most of the through traffic zips down the bypass, turning right at the Ngurah Rai statue and continuing along this major road all the way to Nusa Dua, 11km southeast. To get to the southwest coast of the Bukit, to Jimbaran and Uluwatu, you need to turn right off the bypass down one of two slip roads (one is signed Jalan Ulun Siwi) that will take you straight into Jimbaran.

Jimbaran

The tiny fishing village of **JIMBARAN** has flowered into a quieter, more interesting alternative to purpose-built Nusa Dua. There are now a dozen developments spaced out along the beach, most of them upmarket chain hotels, but the pace here is still unhurried, the atmosphere unhassled and the sand soft and golden. The crescent-shaped bay is safe for swimming, and is used almost exclusively by guests of the Jimbaran hotels.

Jimbaran is famous throughout Bali for its **fish**, and every morning at dawn the fishermen return with hundreds of kilos of sardines, tuna, mackerel, snap-

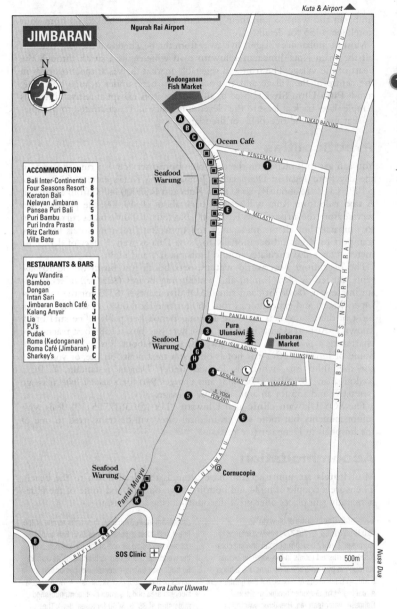

JIMBARAN

ACCOMMODATION

Bali Inter-Continental	7
Four Seasons Resort	8
Keraton Bali	4
Nelayan Jimbaran	2
Pansea Puri Bali	5
Puri Bambu	1
Puri Indra Prasta	6
Ritz Carlton	9
Villa Batu	3

RESTAURANTS & BARS

Ayu Wandira	A
Bamboo	I
Dongan	E
Intan Sari	K
Jimbaran Beach Café	G
Kalang Anyar	J
Lia	H
PJ's	L
Pudak	B
Roma (Kedonganan)	D
Roma Café (Jimbaran)	F
Sharkey's	C

per and baby sharks. Most of the trading goes on between about 5am and 7am, at the fish market at the far northern end of the beach in the *banjar* of Kedonganan, close by the airport runway. In the evening, the day's catch is served up on the seafront at the dozens of beach warung that specialize in barbecued fish and seafood. The Balinese **cooking schools** in Nusa Dua begin their lessons with a tour of Jimbaran fish market, so if you're staying in

Jimbaran and want to join them, you can arrange to be picked up from your hotel: see p.155 for details.

Most of Jimbaran's villagers live away from the beach, down the *gang* that run off the main Kuta–Jimbaran–Uluwatu road which cuts a swath through the heart of the village. The fruit and vegetable market thrives at the crossroads in the centre of the village and, just across from here, under a huge holy tree, stands **Pura Ulun Siwi**. Closed to all casual visitors except at festival time, this temple dates back at least to the eleventh century and is dedicated to the spirits that inhabit the rice-fields of the island.

Practicalities

You can get to Jimbaran on the dark blue **bemo** service that runs throughout the day from Tegal in Denpasar to Jimbaran, via Kuta's eastern fringes (see p.109). Fares are about Rp2000 from Kuta and Rp3000–4000 from Denpasar. A **taxi** ride from Kuta will set you back about Rp19,000; the pre-paid taxi service from the airport costs Rp20,000. No tourist shuttle buses currently run to Jimbaran, but all the mid-range and upmarket Jimbaran hotels have free transport to Kuta and occasionally to Nusa Dua as well. A fleet of dark blue metered taxis also circulates around Jimbaran day and night.

The beachfront Waterworld **watersports** booth just north of the *Keraton* rents out jetskis ($25/15min) and windsurfing boards ($25/hr), offers windsurfing lessons ($60/3hr), and runs PADI dive courses ($375 for the four-day Open Water) and expeditions (from $60 for one local dive); however, they bus most of their customers across to Tanjung Benoa (see p.147). The **surf** break known as Airport Rights is off the coast here (see box p.138), best reached by chartering a *prahu* from an off-duty fisherman (about Rp15,000 one-way). Some of Jimbaran's five-star hotels offer **spa** treatments on site, or you could try the Tulip Spa, which is located under *Dongan* restaurant, Jl Raya Kedonganan 18 (☎0361/704688) and charges $40 for a *mandi lulur* massage (see p.67) and $35 for an aromatherapy massage.

The SOS Uluwatu **clinic** at Jl Uluwatu 111x (☎0361/705110) deals with minor ailments, but more serious medical cases will be transferred to one of the hospitals in Denpasar (see p.103).

Accommodation

Most **hotels** are upmarket and have grounds that lead down to the beach. There are a couple of mid- and bottom-range options, and some of the independently run places offer great discounts during low season.

Bali Inter-Continental Jl Uluwatu 45 ☎0361/701888, ℱ701777, ℠www.interconti .com/bali. Luxury beachfront hotel offering comfortably furnished rooms in big, low-rise blocks surrounded by lush tropical gardens. It's a huge outfit, with hundreds of rooms, but the gardens are a real highlight, designed around traditional Balinese water features. Has three swimming pools, tennis and squash courts, and several bars and restaurants. ⑨

Four Seasons Resort South Jimbaran ☎0361/701010, ℱ701020, ℠www.fourseasons.com. A cut above every other establishment in Jimbaran, this ranks as one of the finest, and most expensive, hotels in Bali, and is consistently voted as one of the top ten hotels in the world. Each villa here is built inside its own little traditional Balinese compound, comprising a series of three thatched pavilions – a living area, a sleeping area and a garden bathroom; published rates start at $575 ($650 for a sea view). The resort is situated high up on a hillside overlooking the far southern end of Jimbaran Bay and facilities include infinity-edge swimming pools, a spa and tennis courts. ⑨

Keraton Bali Jl Merajapati ☎0361/701961,

ⓕ701991, ⓦwww.keratonjimbaranresort.com. Smart rooms in a series of tasteful, attractively designed cottage-style buildings dotted around a peaceful tropical garden that stretches right down to the beach. All rooms have air-con, TV and fridge. Swimming pool, tennis court, table tennis and watersports. One child under 12 goes free if sharing with parents. ⑨

Nelayan Jimbaran Jl Pemelisan Agung ⓣ & ⓕ0361/702253. Jimbaran's cheapest beachfront place offers a good range of spacious rooms, friendly service and a restaurant (but no garden). Its cheapest rooms offer losmen-style accommodation, with fan and cold-water showers, but there are more appealing bamboo-walled rooms with air-con, as well as a four-person suite with two connecting rooms plus a kitchen. Rooms with fan ❸ With air-con ❺

Pansea Puri Bali Jl Uluwatu ⓣ0361/701605, ⓕ701320, ⓦwww.pansea.com. Forty-one gorgeously designed individual cottage compounds, each with elegantly minimalist furnishings in the bedrooms, plus a walled garden, a terrace and a garden bathroom. One child under 12 goes free if sharing adults' cottage. Adult and kids' swimming pools, a children's play area and babysitting service. Thirty percent discounts offered outside peak periods. ⑨

Puri Bambu Jl Pengeracikan, Kedonganan, north Jimbaran ⓣ0361/701377, ⓕ701440, ⓦwww.puribambu.com. This comfortable place keeps its prices reasonable because there's no beachfront access. However, the beach is about three minutes' walk away and the 48 rooms are well equipped with air-con and TVs; there's a pool and internet access on the premises. Thirty percent discounts are nearly always available and there's a free shuttle bus service into Kuta. Call for free airport pick-up. ❼–❽

Puri Indra Prasta Jl Uluwatu 28a ⓣ0361/701552. Clean, simple, but fairly attractive losmen rooms set around a swimming pool, in this small hotel located on the main road, about five minutes' walk from the beach. Rooms with fan ❸ With air-con ❺

Ritz Carlton Jl Karang Mas Sejahtera, south of Jimbaran ⓣ0361/702222, ⓕ701555, ⓦwww.ritzcarlton.com. Renowned for its excellent service and a frequent contender for one of Asia's top ten hotels, this deluxe outfit enjoys a very impressive location on a cliffside several kilometres south of the Jimbaran beachfront. The luxuriously furnished rooms are all in a central block and most offer a sea view. There's a spa, several swimming pools and tennis courts, plus six restaurants and an 18-hole putting green, but the nearest swimmable beach is a couple of kilometres away and you'll need to rent transport if you want to go exploring. Forty percent discounts available out of season and online. Published rates from $240. ⑨

Villa Batu Jl Pemelisan Agung 21a ⓣ & ⓕ0361/703186. Attractive and unusual collection of six rooms and villas across the road from the beach, all idiosyncratically decorated and stylishly furnished with artefacts from Sulawesi, Kalimantan and Irian Jaya. The most appealing options are the two villas, sleeping two to four, both with kitchen/living area and sharing a small pool. Cheaper accommodation comprises double and connecting rooms, some with a living-room area, and use of the pool if the villas are unoccupied. Huge discounts in low season. Rooms with fan ❹ With air-con ❺ Villas ❼–❽

Eating

Jimbaran has an island-wide reputation for its fresh seafood served at the countless tiny warung strung along the beachfront. But there are other **places to eat** too, most notably the restaurants inside the more exclusive Jimbaran hotels, where you can expect a classy meal, and an equally classy bill.

The seafood warung

The **fresh fish barbecues** served up by Jimbaran's beachfront warung are so good that people travel here from Kuta, Nusa Dua and Sanur just to sample them, and restaurants across the island try to recreate the taste in their "Jimbaran-style fish barbecues". There are over fifty of these beach-shack warung, grouped in three distinct areas along the shorefront between Kedonganan in the north and Jalan Bukit Permai in the south. Some warung look a little more polished than others, but the setup is similar in every one, with chairs and tables set out on the sand, and a menu that sells the day's catch (priced per 100g), grilled in front of you over smoky fires of coconut husks. You can almost guarantee having the choice of lobster, prawns, red snapper, squid, mussels and clams at the very least. Though food is served during the day, the warung are at their liveliest from around 7pm. It's always a good idea to eat at the busier places, to be sure that the fish really is that morning's catch; some of the warung chefs stage quite a show with the coconut embers, so you may get a performance thrown in with your dinner. They all serve beer and soft drinks, and fish prices usually include various marinades and sauces plus a generous spread of rice and vegetable dishes, so accompanying vegetarians will not starve.

Broadly speaking, the knot of warung up near the fish market in **Kedonganan** offer the cheapest food and the least refined ambience (plastic chairs and no-frills table settings). Competition is extremely fierce up here and several of the most crowded places attract customers by offering commission, and even lottery tickets, to taxi drivers. As margins have tightened some places have started to **rig their scales** so that diners unwittingly get less than what they paid for: if doubtful, the easiest way to check this is to place a full one-litre bottle of water on the scales first and see if they read "1kg" (which they should). The most popular warung here include *Sharkey's*, *Pudak* and *Ayu Wandira*; do not confuse the copycat *Roma* warung next to *Sharkey's* with the more reputable original, *Roma Café*, further south in central Jimbaran.

The warung that occupy the shorefront between Jalan Pemelisan Agung and the *Keraton Bali* hotel in **central Jimbaran** are not quite as basic as those up at Kedonganan and are popular with domestic tourists; prices are reasonable and the atmosphere is good. Reputable options include *Bamboo*, *Lia*, *Jimbaran Beach Café* and the recommended *Roma Café*.

Some distance further south, at the foot of the road up to the *Four Seasons* on the very attractive stretch of beach sometimes referred to as **Pantai Muayu**, you'll find the most upmarket of the Jimbaran warung, with more salubrious setups (comfortable chairs, tiled kitchens and customer toilets) and slightly more expensive price lists. Here, *Kalang Anyar* gets good reviews, and *Intan Sari* is usually pretty busy.

Restaurants

Dongan Jl Raya Kedonganan, Kedonganan, north Jimbaran. Less formal and much less expensive than the restaurants attached to the five-star hotels, this independent eatery serves a tasty and good-value menu of Western and Indonesian dishes as well as competitively priced fish and seafood, barbecued in the same style as at the beach warung. Moderate.

Nelayan At the *Pansea Puri Bali*, Jl Uluwatu. Occupies a perfect spot right on the sand and serves drinks, snacks and light meals, including delicious European breads and good prawn sate. Expensive.

PJ's Jl Bukit Permai, south Jimbaran. This *Four Seasons* restaurant has an island-wide reputation for exquisite Mediterranean and Southeast Asian food, as well as for wood-fired pizzas with innovative toppings; it also occupies a fantastic position in a couple of gazebos perched right over the sand. Expensive.

Sami Sami Inside the *Ritz Carlton*, Jl Karang Mas Sejahtera, south of Jimbaran. This restaurant occupies a particularly awesome spot on a cliff ledge right over the waves, and the menu includes Middle Eastern dishes, seafood barbecues and Mediterranean favourites. Expensive.

Singaraja At the *Bali Inter-Continental*, Jl Uluwatu. Elegant eatery specializing in seafood dishes inspired by cuisines from Morocco, the Middle East and Asia. Expensive.

Around the Bukit

Just a couple of kilometres south of Jimbaran, the road climbs up on to the limestone plateau, and it's well worth pausing for a look back across the stunning **panorama** of southern Bali. Once up on the plateau, past a massive limestone quarry, typical **Bukit** landscape begins in earnest, a mostly dismal and depressing combination of cracked earth and leafless trees, with the occasional roadside hamlet along the way. Bukit people do grow a few crops here, mainly cassava, a root tuber vegetable used to make tapioca flour, and grass-like sorghum whose seeds are also pounded into flour. You'll see plenty of **kapok trees** too, instantly recognizable from the fluffy white fibre that bursts out of the long brown pods. This fibre is water resistant and extremely soft, and is the stuff that fills cushions, cuddly toys and even life-jackets the world over. Every mature tree produces about 20kg of fibre a year, and the kapok seeds are pulped for oil.

Garuda Wisnu Kencana (GWK)

About 2km south of the *Four Seasons* junction, a huge sign points you east off the main Uluwatu road to **Garuda Wisnu Kencana**, or **GWK** (daily 8am–10pm; cars Rp5000, motorbikes Rp1000). This controversial project, which is still being carved out of the hillside, is set to be a cultural park and events centre, centred around a towering 146-metre gold-plated **statue** of the Hindu god Vishnu astride his sacred vehicle, the half-man, half-bird Garuda. When completed, the statue (said to be the world's largest) will stand on top of an eleven-storey **entertainments complex**, the intention being to make the whole monument so high (230m above sea level) that it will serve as a Welcome-to-Bali landmark for passengers arriving at Ngurah Rai Airport, 9km to the north. The complex is to feature shops and galleries as well as an open-air stage and a museum about Balinese culture.

The whole project is due to be completed by 2003, and at the moment all that's open is a **restaurant** offering a commanding view of southern Bali's coastlines, a couple of souvenir shops, an **art gallery** (free) which hosts temporary exhibitions by contemporary Balinese artists and the partially constructed statue, currently comprising Vishnu's 23-metre head and shoulders plus the head of the gigantic Garuda; if you want to climb the statue, you have to pay an extra Rp15,000. The **kecak dance** is performed in the complex (Tues & Thurs 7pm; $5, or $25 including dinner).

GWK is privately funded and is intended to attract more tourists to the area. The respected artist and sculptor who conceived the idea, Nyoman Nuarta, sees it as a celebration of Bali's past as well as its future. Opposition has been fierce, however, with critics deploring the commercial rather than religious motivation of the project and accusing GWK's supporters of trying to turn Bali into a Hindu theme park (see p.551 for more on this). It is also seen by some as threatening Bali's cosmological balance, which centres on the holy mountain Gunung Agung. Many local people also think the $200 million earmarked for the project could be better spent on improving the region's basic infrastructure.

Surfing beaches

About 1km south of the GWK turn-off, the road forks at the village of Bakung, veering right for Uluwatu via several **surfing beaches**, and left for Nusa Dua. The box on p.138 has a description of the surf breaks in this area.

Follow the Uluwatu road for a kilometre and you'll pass a couple of **places to stay**, patronized mainly by surfers. On the west side of the road, *Bukit Inn* (formerly *Villa Koyo*; ℡0361/702927, ℻703362, ⓦwww.indo.com/hotels/villakoyo; ◑) has thirty attractive and well-maintained rooms with air-con, hot water and TV, all set round the swimming pool, and there's internet access in the lobby. Across the road, *Mr Ugly's* (℡0361/702874; ●) has three basic but perfectly decent rooms.

Dreamland and Balangan

Just a few kilometres south of *Bukit Inn*, a large sign announces the turn-off to **DREAMLAND** and **BALANGAN** surf beaches. The access road runs through an abandoned condo project, one of several unpopular development schemes on Bali that were associated with Tommy Suharto, the notorious son of the former president. Having bought a huge swath of prime land between the road and the coast, the condo company built a network of roads and just a few houses before being forced to a standstill following the downfall of the Suharto family. Since then, local villagers have reclaimed ownership of some of the land and have established clusters of small warung and rooms for rent down at the beaches. The village association also charges a Rp5000 **toll** per person to get to the beaches, payable about halfway down the access road.

About 4km after leaving the main road, a couple of short dirt tracks veer off to Dreamland beach, a stunning stretch of coast with great surf, gloriously white sands and breathtakingly aquamarine waters. About ten **warung** have been rigged up under the cliff here, serving standard travellers' fare in huge surfer-sized portions, and selling water and cigarettes; a couple of them also offer overnight crash pads (●) and some have a few sun-loungers for rent. The setup at Balangan, accessed via a nearby dirt track, is similar, and you might be lucky enough to spot the white-collared kingfisher here too.

Bingin, Impossibles and Padang Padang

Back on the main Bukit road, a couple of kilometres south of the Dreamland turn-off, there's a right fork signed to **BINGIN**, **IMPOSSIBLES** and **PADANG PADANG**: take this road for the surf spots and the longer, more scenic route to Pura Luhur Uluwatu, or the left fork for the more direct road to the temple.

Bingin and Impossibles are accessible only via a potholed dirt track which takes you a couple of kilometres off the road, and Padang Padang is visible from the main road. All three breaks attract a hardy group of surfers every day and a knot of **warung** have sprung up along the cliffside at Bingin to cater for them. The usual system is that surfers are free to crash at the warung so long as they eat all their meals there. Even if you don't surf, both these spots are worth visiting for their magnificent rocky views, but the beaches are unsuitable for swimming because of the tricky currents and huge expanses of shallow reef that lie just offshore. At Padang Padang, the warung have been moved off the beach and are now gathered in a cluster on the east side of the road, a couple of minutes' walk from the shore. Some of these warung also offer **beds** (●–◐), or you could try the more comfortable *lumbung*-style bungalows at *Ayu Guna Inn* (mobile ℡082/361 1517; ◐), 300m further north beside the main road, where you get a mattress, fan, balcony and outside bathroom.

Suluban

It's also not recommended to swim at **SULUBAN**, location of the famous **Uluwatu surf breaks**, which is signed off the Uluwatu road about 2km south of Padang Padang. The views here are gorgeous – the golden curves of Kuta and Legian in the distance, and the turquoise water, crashing white surf and olive-green seaweed of Suluban in the foreground. But for surfers the Uluwatu breaks (named after the nearby temple) are something of a mecca, with five separate left-handers, all of them consistent and surfable at anything from two to fifteen feet. There's a tiny off-beat surfers'"resort" at Suluban, with the informal deal of **free accommodation** at the warung where you eat your meals. There's also more upmarket accommodation in the vicinity, notably at *Uluwatu Resort* (☏0361/709648, ℻775319, ⓦwww.uluwaturesort.com; ❼) which is set on the cliff beside the steps down to the beach and offers, as well as a pool, the most attractive rooms on this entire stretch of coast – sixteen of them, stylishly furnished with four-poster beds and linen drapes, each enjoying an uninterrupted sea view from enormous windows and balcony. Cheaper but also very comfortable rooms are available at *Rocky Bungalows* (mobile ☏0818/351643; ❸), a short bike-ride from the surf, down a side road off the main Uluwatu road; the ten rooms here also afford great (long-range) views of the sea from their picture windows and verandahs.

Uluwatu

One of Bali's holiest and most important temples, **Pura Luhur Uluwatu** commands a superb position on the tip of a sheer rocky promontory jutting out over the Indian Ocean, 70m above the foaming surf, at the far southwestern tip of Bali – 18km south of Kuta and 16km west of Nusa Dua. Views over the serrated coastline to left and right are stunning, and, not surprisingly, this is a favourite spot at sunset, when tour buses pour in to admire the added drama of a pink and orange horizon. The temple structure itself, though, lacks magnificence, being relatively small and for the most part unadorned.

Accounts of Uluwatu's early **history** are vague and shrouded in myth, but it's fairly certain that two of Bali's most influential holy men played significant roles in its evolution. The first was a Hindu priest from Java called Empu Kuturan (sometimes known as Empu Rajakerta) who arrived in the tenth century and constructed *meru* (multi-tiered thatched shrines) all across southern Bali – including one at Uluwatu. Six hundred years later, another Hindu priest from Java, Nirartha, landed in west Bali and set about founding some of the island's most awesome sea temples: one at Rambut Siwi (p.389) and another at Tanah Lot (p.376), as well as adding to the cliffside shrine at Uluwatu.

Pura Luhur Uluwatu is now sanctified as one of Bali's sacred **directional temples**, or *kayangan jagat* – state temples having influence over all the people of Bali, not just the local villagers or ancestors. It is the guardian of the southwest and is dedicated to the spirits of the sea. Its festivals are open to all and during the holy week-long period at Galungan, for example, Balinese from all over the island come here to pay their respects.

The temple complex

The access roads lead right into the **car park** in front of Pura Luhur Uluwatu, usually overflowing with tour buses and souvenir stalls (parking fee Rp1000). At the booth at the base of the temple steps, you'll need to borrow a sarong and sash if you haven't brought your own, and pay the Rp3000 admission fee.

Climbing the frangipani-lined stairway to the temple's **outer courtyard**, you'll get your first brush with Uluwatu's resident troupe of monkeys, who have a reputation for stealing earrings, sunglasses and cameras. The outer courtyard is dominated by the elegant **candi bentar** that connects this area with the middle courtyard, built of greyish-white coral blocks to a very unusual winged design. Images of the elephant god Ganesh flank the entrance.

If you peer through the gate into the middle courtyard (casual visitors are no longer allowed in here), you'll see the **paduraksa**, the archway which divides the middle from the inner courtyard, which is made of coral blocks and crowned by an unusual three-pronged tower. Both sides of the structure are studded with mythological images fashioned from the coral bricks. The **inner sanctum** extends right to the cliff edge and over its low walls you can see the three thatched *meru* and the stone *padmasana*, set off to their best advantage by the deep blue sea beyond. A tiny courtyard leading from the temple's outer courtyard contains a locked shrine housing a very old statue, thought by some to depict the sixteenth-century priest Nirartha. The statue is kept here in his honour as it is thought that the priest achieved his own spiritual liberation, or *moksa*, on this very spot.

You'll get some of the best **views** of Pura Luhur Uluwatu's astonishingly dramatic position if you follow the pathway that heads off to the right as you stand with your back to the temple stairway. This track winds its way along the cliff-edge for a few hundred metres, affording fine silhouetted vistas of the three-tiered *meru* perched daintily atop the massive sheer wall of limestone.

Practicalities

If you don't have your own **transport**, the easiest way to visit the temple is by joining the daily "Sunset Uluwatu" trip arranged by Perama in Kuta (see p.137); the round trip costs Rp50,000 per person, departs Kuta at 4pm, and includes the option of watching the *kecak* performance (see below). You'd be lucky to find a **bemo** from Denpasar or Kuta going all the way to Uluwatu, so your cheapest option is to get a dark blue Tegal (Denpasar)–Kuta–Jimbaran bemo to its Jimbaran terminus and then flag down a metered taxi for the last leg. Coming back from Uluwatu is more of a problem as you're very unlikely to find a taxi here: either ask your taxi to wait for you, try and hitch a ride from the temple car park, or take an unofficial motorcycle taxi ride with one of the lads who hang around the temple complex. The **kecak and fire dance** (*sanghyang jaran*) are performed at Uluwatu every evening (6–7pm; Rp35,000).

The Bukit's south coast

Returning from Uluwatu along the main Jimbaran road you'll soon pass *Puri Bali Villas* (mobile ℡0816/471 0741, ℻0361/701363, ⓦwww.puribalivillas.com; ➑), whose dramatically located restaurant enjoys a fine outlook over the **Nyang Nyang** surf breaks (see box on p.138), and where you can rent spacious villas set around English-style parkland. Access to the sea is via a long, steep path.

Continuing almost as far as the Bakung T-junction, a sign for **Pura Massuka** diverts a tiny trickle of traffic off to the right, down to the southern coast of the Bukit. No bemos cover this area, so you'll need **private transport** to visit anything east of the Jimbaran–Uluwatu road, except Nusa Dua. The road to Pura Massuka winds its way for 12km right down to the coast, through an almost uninhabited landscape of parched red earth, dotted with the occasional kapok tree. At the end of the road, the minuscule Pura Massuka hardly seems to merit the title of temple, but the **views** most definitely make up for it. This is the southernmost point of Bali that is accessible, offering an uninterrupted panorama out over the clear blue ocean. The backdrop adds to the drama of the setting, with coarse thorny bushes interspersed with the bright orange flower clusters of lantana shrubs.

Back on the main Uluwatu–Nusa Dua road, another side road to the coast (about 2km east of the Bakung T-junction) takes you through the village of Ungasan and on to the exclusive **Bali Cliff Resort** (℡0361/771992, Ⓕ771993; Ⓦwww.balicliff.co.id; ❾) right on the edge of the south-facing coast, about 1km east of Pura Massuka. It's well worth stopping by for a drink or a meal (both expensive) at one of the hotel's cliffside **restaurants** and a swim off the pristine shores of the beach below. To get down to the beach you have to use a series of **cable-cars** that plunge 75m down the cliff face, one level at a time. There are restaurants at levels one and two, with high-class seafood a speciality at *The Ocean*; level three is the beach, with an open-air theatre space where *kecak* is sometimes performed. If you're considering booking a room here, be aware that the *Bali Cliff* is miles from anywhere and that you'll have to rely on tours or rented cars to get to shops or sights. Facilities are very good though, with a spectacular clifftop, infinity-edge swimming pool and several tennis courts.

Nusa Dua and Tanjung Benoa

Some 11km southeast of Kuta, Bali's most artfully designed high-class beach resort luxuriates along a coastal stretch of reclaimed mangrove swamp. This is **NUSA DUA**, a sparklingly pristine enclave that was purpose-built to indulge the whims and smooth away the grievances of upmarket tourists, while simultaneously protecting the Balinese from too many negative touristic influences (see p.549 for the full story). The dozen or so five-star hotels all boast expansive grounds running down to one of Bali's prettiest white-sand beaches, and each one offers huge swimming pools, tennis courts, and several bars and restaurants. Aside from a central shopping and entertainments complex, there's absolutely nothing else in Nusa Dua: no losmen or mid-range hotels and no markets, *banjar* or noodle stalls.

There are, however, a few more signs of real life along the narrow sandbar that extends north from Nusa Dua. **TANJUNG BENOA**, as this finger-like projection is known, still functions as a fishing village, but has developed a rash of realistically priced tourist accommodation and a whole heap of watersports facilities as well. The main drawback is the northern stretch of Tanjung Benoa's beach, which is scruffy and unappealing, but if you have your own transport, you can easily make day-trips to Jimbaran, Kuta, Sanur and the Bukit surfing beaches. In addition, Tanjung Benoa has the dubious distinction of being the centre of Bali's turtle trade (see box p.149).

Sandwiched between Nusa Dua and Tanjung Benoa, the village of **BUALU** is where you'll find the *banjar*, temples, warung, family homes and non-tourist-oriented business common to any small Balinese town. The cluster of tourist restaurants on the Bualu side of Nusa Dua's South Gate, and to a lesser extent the stalls around the Main Gate, are a useful enticement to explore beyond the too-perfect confines of Nusa Dua itself.

Don't confuse Tanjung Benoa with **Benoa Harbour** (Pelabuhan Benoa; described on p.171) which lies about a kilometre north across the water from Tanjung Benoa's northern tip, but is only accessible to the public by a circuitous land route. Fast boats to Lombok, Pelni boats to other parts of the Indonesian archipelago, sea planes and most excursion boats depart from Benoa Harbour, not Tanjung Benoa.

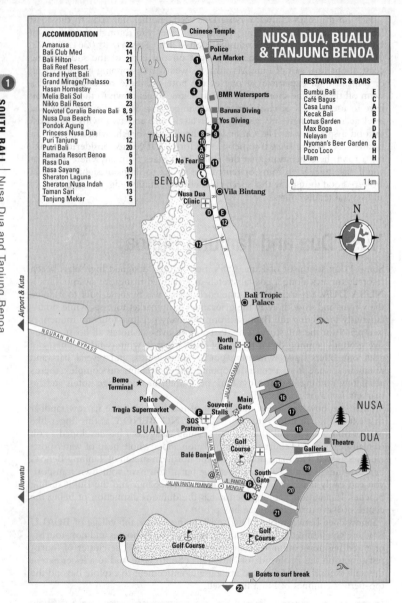

ACCOMMODATION

Amanusa	22
Bali Club Med	14
Bali Hilton	21
Bali Reef Resort	7
Grand Hyatt Bali	19
Grand Mirage/Thalasso	11
Hasan Homestay	4
Melia Bali Sol	18
Nikko Bali Resort	23
Novotel Coralia Benoa Bali	8, 9
Nusa Dua Beach	15
Pondok Agung	2
Princess Nusa Dua	1
Puri Tanjung	12
Putri Bali	20
Ramada Resort Benoa	6
Rasa Dua	3
Rasa Sayang	10
Sheraton Laguna	17
Sheraton Nusa Indah	16
Taman Sari	13
Tanjung Mekar	5

NUSA DUA, BUALU & TANJUNG BENOA

RESTAURANTS & BARS

Bumbu Bali	E
Café Bagus	C
Casa Luna	A
Kecak Bali	B
Lotus Garden	F
Max Boga	D
Nelayan	A
Nyoman's Beer Garden	G
Poco Loco	H
Ulam	H

0   1 km

Arrival

If you're arriving straight from the **airport** (see p.110) and staying in one of the more expensive hotels, you'll almost certainly be picked up by a hotel limousine. The official taxi rate from the airport is Rp35,000 to Nusa Dua and Rp40,000 to Tanjung Benoa, a journey of around twenty minutes. A **metered taxi** from Kuta–Legian–Seminyak costs about Rp33,000.

The turtles of Bali

Turtle meat is a popular luxury in Bali, and also plays a part in certain religious rituals: the flippers are made into sate, and the flesh ground down into the ceremonial *lawar* served at weddings, tooth-filing ceremonies and cremations. Weighing up to 180kg as adults, **green turtles** are the most sought-after source of meat (they are, in fact, mottled brown in colour, but get their name from the colour of the soup made from their flesh) but over-hunting has resulted in the near-extinction of turtles in Balinese waters. Bali also used to have a number of turtle **hatching grounds** on its shores – female turtles will only lay their eggs on the beach on which they themselves were born, each pregnant female swimming thousands of miles to return to her original birthplace – including at Sanur, Nusa Dua, Tanjung Benoa, Pulau Serangan, Jimbaran and Pemuteran. But nearly all have become unsafe or unusable, either as a result of tourist development or because they are well known to **hunters** and poachers eager to get their hands on turtle eggs and flesh. Over the last four decades, this plunder has been so extensive that turtle sightings off the coast have become quite rare and many hatching grounds have been abandoned. As only one in a thousand eggs produces a turtle which survives thirty years to adulthood, Bali's turtle population is in crisis. Local fishermen now trawl the seas much further afield, bringing back thousands of live green turtles to Bali every year for sale and slaughter.

The situation has become so dire, and attracted so much adverse international publicity, that in 1999 a local law was passed banning the sale, possession and consumption of all green turtles except those destined for ceremonial feasts – and fishermen are supposed to apply for special licences for these. However, with a single turtle fetching up to a million rupiah, poaching can seem a risk worth running: according to a 2001 study by the Indonesian animal conservation organization KSBK, Bali's **turtle trade** is still thriving in Tanjung Benoa. KSBK documented an average of 199 turtles a month passing through the half-dozen clandestine holding pens and slaughter-houses in Tanjung Benoa, despite the trial and conviction in 2000 of two key players in the local turtle trade. **Hawksbill turtles** are also much prized, captured for their beautiful shells rather than their meat, but since 1992 international trade in tortoiseshell has been banned under the Convention on International Trade in Endangered Species (CITES), which effectively means that tourists now have tortoiseshell souvenirs impounded.

Campaign organizations and hatcheries

Greenpeace **campaigns** against the unnecessary slaughter of all turtles, and travellers can support this by avoiding all products made from turtle flesh or tortoiseshell, and by boycotting restaurants that serve turtle meat, informing the managers exactly why. Many organizations in Indonesia are dedicated to **conserving** local turtle populations, including KSBK Bali in Denpasar (℡0361/424731, @www.ksbk.or.id); PPLH in Sanur (℡0361/281648, @www.pplhbali.or.id); and the Denpasar branch of the World Wide Fund for Nature (℡0361/247125, @www.wwf.or.id). Several people have established small turtle **hatcheries** on Bali and Lombok, including at *Bumbu Bali* restaurant in Tanjung Benoa (see p.154), at Reef Seen Aquatics in Pemuteran (see p.407), and at Reefseekers on Gili Air (see p.453).

The only means of **public transport** to Nusa Dua and Tanjung Benoa are the dark blue Tegal–Kuta–Bualu bemos that depart Denpasar's Tegal bemo station (see p.110). They operate throughout the day (about every 30min; takes 45min), and go via the eastern edge of Kuta (picking up passengers from the Jalan Imam Bonjol/Jalan Setia Budi intersection) and then via Jimbaran before racing back down the highway to terminate at **Bualu**, where the main road forks right for Nusa Dua and left for Tanjung Benoa. If you're returning by bemo to Kuta, tell the driver before you get in and he'll drop you close to Kuta's Badung tourist office on Jalan Raya (see p.112); however, getting bemos back from Bualu to Kuta or Denpasar is a very unreliable business after about 3pm, and you may be forced to charter one.

A **free shuttle bus** runs approximately hourly from Kuta Square's Matahari department store (the Jalan Ciung Wanara entrance) to the Galleria shopping complex in the heart of Nusa Dua, a five-minute walk from the beach – useful for making a day-trip.

Transport and tours

As the resorts, restaurants and shops are strung over a distance of some 6km from the northern tip of Tanjung Benoa to southern Nusa Dua, getting around can be a hot and time-consuming business.

Bemos are not allowed inside the Nusa Dua gateway, so to get from Bualu to Nusa Dua's beaches and hotels you'll either have to walk (1–2km) or hail a taxi. Infrequent **green bemos** (about every 30min) do serve Tanjung Benoa however, running between the Bualu terminal and the Chinese temple at the northern end of Tanjung Benoa.

A fleet of multi-coloured **free shuttle buses** (hourly 8am–11pm) operates between the Galleria shopping complex at the heart of Nusa Dua and the big Nusa Dua and Tanjung Benoa hotels; all the big hotels in both resorts offer free transport to the Galleria, and some will also take you to restaurants in Bualu or even to Jimbaran. If staying in one of the cheaper Tanjung Benoa hotels, you're limited to the green public bemos that ply the main beachfront road, or to the pale brown Kowinu Bali **metered taxis** (☎0361/771661; Rp4000 flagfall, then Rp2000/km) which circulate fairly regularly around both resorts.

You could capitalize on the flat terrain and virtually traffic-free roads by **renting a bicycle** from your hotel or from one of the shops in Tanjung Benoa, on the stretch of Jalan Pratama between *Vila Bintang* and *Rasa Sayang* (Rp30,000/day). **Car rental**, with or without driver, can also be arranged through Nusa Dua hotels (around $30/day) or from Tanjung Benoa rental outlets, most of which have offices on the same stretch of Jalan Pratama (from about Rp100,000).

All hotels in Nusa Dua, and most in Tanjung Benoa, offer **organized tours** to major sights on and around Bali, following standard itineraries as outlined on p.126. You'll probably have to pay above average if booking through a Nusa Dua hotel, but this is likely to include an English-speaking guide.

Accommodation

In Nusa Dua, you can expect deluxe **accommodation** in rooms that are fully equipped to international standards, though often a little characterless as a result, set on grounds that run down to the beach. Published prices start at around US$160 per double room, excluding tax and a possible high-season supplement, but most travel agents should be able to get you a decent discount on a package deal; you could also try some of the internet hotel-booking services (see box on p.44) which offer up to 55 percent off certain hotels.

Tanjung Benoa caters for a wider span of budgets, with some inexpensive losmen and lower- and mid-range hotels at the north end of the peninsula and a decent showing of upmarket four-star operations further south; nearly all the expensive hotels have a well-maintained stretch of beach immediately in front of their property.

Nusa Dua

Amanusa ☎0361/772333, ℻772335,
ⓦwww.amanresorts.com. Beautiful property on
the edge of the eighteen-hole Bali Golf and
Country Club, but some distance from the sea.
Thirty-five stunningly designed thatched cottage
compounds all with private terraces and ultra-
luxurious facilities. Published rates from $575. ❾

Bali Hilton ☎0361/771102, ℻771616,
ⓦwww.hiltonindonesia.com. Grandly designed
complex with spacious, comfortable rooms in the
central block. Lush gardens with impressive water
features, a free-form swimming pool, tennis and
squash courts and five restaurants. Plenty of activities for kids. ❾

Grand Hyatt Bali ☎0361/771234, ℻772038,
ⓦwww.hyatt.com. Terraced rooms and cottages
grouped into "villages" surrounded by sumptuous
grounds with all sorts of ponds, fountains and
tropical flowers. Tennis and squash courts, a gym,
a kids' club, and an amazing series of free-form
swimming pools complete with water chutes,
bridges and sunken bars. Free shuttle bus to the
sister operation, the *Bali Hyatt*, in Sanur. ❾

Nikko Bali Resort and Spa ☎0361/773377,
℻773388, ⓦwww.nikkobali.com. Occupies a
spectacular cliffside position about 3km south of
the *Bali Hilton*, with one block of rooms built right

on the shorefront in what is effectively a private
golden-sand bay. Other rooms have back doors
that open right on to small swimming pools.
Facilities include a spa, a lagoon swimming pool, a
children's pool and kids' club. ❾

Sheraton Laguna ☎0361/771327, ℻772163,
ⓦwww.sheraton.com. A super-deluxe hotel, with
fabulous rooms, six restaurants, and a spa, set on
a secluded stretch of beach. All rooms feature
huge marble bathrooms and balconies, and the
most expensive have direct access onto the star
attraction – a huge lagoon-like swimming pool
with its own little sandy beaches, islands and
waterfalls. ❾

Sheraton Nusa Indah ☎0361/771906,
℻771908, ⓦwww.sheraton.com. Adjacent to
the *Sheraton Laguna* complex and slightly
cheaper. Rooms are in a central hotel block,
although there are lovely beachfront pavilions
decked out with cushions for guests to relax on
beside the sea, as well as a tennis court, gym
and swimming pool with water volleyball.
Especially good for families as the children's
facilities are outstanding and include family
suites, toys, computer games, an extensive programme of kids' activities and a creche, plus
good family deals. ❾

Tanjung Benoa

Bali Reef Resort Jl Pratama ☎0361/776291,
℻776294, ⓦwww.balireef-resort.com. Small
beachfront hotel with 28 smart bungalows, all furnished with air-con and TV, lining a long, narrow
garden that runs down to the sea. Rooms are quite
compact but comfortable and there's a pool and
spa, internet access in the lobby, and a shorefront
restaurant and bar. ❽

Hasan Homestay North end of Jl Pratama
☎0361/772456. A handful of terraced rooms,
clean and modern if a bit dark; the cheapest place
in the area. Rooms with fan ❷ With air-con ❸

Novotel Coralia Benoa Bali Jl Pratama
☎0361/772239, ℻772237,
ⓦwww.novotelbali.com. Elegant but comfortable
low-rise hotel where every spaciously designed
room has its own balcony or small garden and is
furnished in Balinese style. The grounds run down
to a nice stretch of beach and are spread over
both sides of the road. Facilities include three
swimming pools (one for kids), a children's club,
plus a games room and tennis courts. Has a good
babysitting service and is child-friendly. Discounts
of up to fifty percent for internet bookings. ❾

Pondok Agung Jl Pratama 99 ☎ & ℻0361/
771143, ℮roland@eksadata.com. Small, stylish
place with attractive garden and comfortably furnished rooms. The best value, though not the cheapest, accommodation at this end of Tanjung Benoa.
Rooms with fan and hot water ❸ With air-con ❺

Princess Nusa Dua Jl Pratama ☎0361/771604,
℻771394, ⓦwww.nusadua.freeservers.com.
Well-equipped though rather unstylish terraced air-
con rooms (all with fridge, phone and mini-bar),
plus swimming pool, a sunken bar and tennis
courts. Good low-season discounts. ❼

Puri Tanjung Jl Pratama 62 ☎0361/772121,
℻772424, ℮ptanjung@bali.net. Good value
because of its location right on the beach. All
rooms come with air-con and TV; the cheaper ones
are unexceptional but the larger bungalows are
comfortable and spacious, if not particularly elegant, and some have sea views. Swimming pool
and table tennis. One child under 12 goes free if
sharing with parents. ❼–❽

Ramada Resort Benoa Jl Pratama 97a
☎0361/773730, ℻773840, ⓦwww.ramadahotels
.com. Attractive, low-key hotel complex occupying

plots on both sides of the road, with rooms and a pool on the non-beach side, and a restaurant, watersports centre and bar on the shorefront. Facilities also include tennis courts and table tennis. Rooms in the hotel wings are luxurious but still manage to feel cosy, with attractive furnishings, TV, air-con and balconies; some rooms are wheelchair-friendly. Good value. **❽**

Rasa Dua Jl Pratama 98 ☎0361/771922, ℗773515, ✉baliyacht-service@yahoo.com. Four simple but pleasant rooms in a small garden area, with bamboo furniture and partially open-air mandi. Friendly, homestay-style atmosphere. **❷**

Rasa Sayang Jl Pratama 88x ☎0361/771643,

℗777268, ✉rsbind@yahoo.com. Popular, good-value small hotel in central Tanjung Benoa offering twenty simple rooms in a terraced block. Rooms with fan **❷** With air-con **❸** With air-con and TV **❹**

Taman Sari Jl Pratama 61b ☎0361/773953, ℗773954, ⓦwww.tamansarisuite-bali.com. One of the most stylish places in Tanjung Benoa, comprising ten nicely designed bungalows, each one with air-con, TV, fridge and a garden bathroom. Large pool, spa and restaurant on the premises, but no beach access. **❼**

Tanjung Mekar Jl Pratama ☎0361/772063. Small house with four fairly basic rooms (better ones upstairs) and a garden. **❷**

The resorts

The **beach** here is long, white and sandy, reasonably wide even at high tide and, down in **Nusa Dua** at least, kept scrupulously clean. The areas in front of each Nusa Dua hotel often feel like private bays, but it's quite easy to walk from one to another and there's no law against outsiders on the sand (although non-guests have to pay to use the sun-loungers). It's a safe enough stretch for swimming, and from September to March, the offshore breakers are big enough to attract a fair number of surfers. Halfway down the shoreline, the land blossoms out into two little clumps, or "islands" (Nusa Dua means "Two Islands"), on which stand two of the area's original temples. The quiet and pretty stretch of shore near the *Nikko* hotel, 3km south of Nusa Dua and accessible down a small track, is known as **Pantai Samudra Indah** and makes a pleasant change from the busier Nusa Dua beach; there's a warung here too for refreshments.

Few people swim or sunbathe on the beach at **Tanjung Benoa** (except in front of the smarter beachfront hotels) because much of the shorefront is strewn with debris and dominated by watersports facilities. There are around half a dozen watersports operators along the shore towards the peninsula's northernmost tip, most of them offering a very similar range of activities for competitive prices (see below). The sand along here is uninviting and the road is often within view, so it's definitely worth walking down to the more pristine parts of the beach, which begin at *Bali Reef Resort*.

Sports and activities

Nearly every Nusa Dua hotel rents out some **watersports** equipment, often from a booth erected on the beach; prices are similar, but facilities are more extensive at the Tanjung Benoa end of the beach. Two of the best-known and longest-running operators in Tanjung Benoa are Yos Marine Adventures, Jl Pratama 106x (☎0361/773774, ⓦwww.yosdive.com), and the adjacent Baruna (ⓦwww.baruna.com), both of which do **parasailing** ($15 per round), **water-skiing** ($20 for 10mins), **jetskiing** ($20 for 15min), and **wakeboarding** ($25 for 15min), and offer morning boat rides to see **dolphins** off the south Bukit coast, apparently with a ninety percent chance of actually seeing some ($60), plus a range of **fishing** expeditions ($70-180 per person).

Most Nusa Dua hotels and Tanjung Benoa operators organize **snorkelling trips** ($15-50 depending on destination) and **diving** expeditions and courses. Many are run by the dive centres who advertise in Kuta and Sanur and, while the courses tend to take place in and around Nusa Dua, most diving tours

Nusa Dua surf breaks

Best surfed from September to March, when the prevailing northwest winds are offshore, Nusa Dua's **surf breaks** catch the most swell of all the breaks in Bali, and are good through all tides. Big boards are recommended, though, as currents can get pretty vicious on this stretch. The main break, known simply as **Nusa Dua** (accessible by boat from a signposted point south of the *Bali Hilton* and the golf course), is a right-hander about 1km offshore, providing large peaks that turn into fine long walls and some juicy tubes as well; best on a smallish swell at low to mid-tide. Further north, a brief paddle beyond the *Bali Club Med*, **Sri Lanka** is a short speedy right-hander, providing the best waves at mid-tide and with medium to large swells. The No Fear **surf shop** on Jl Pratama in Tanjung Benoa sells boards and surf gear and can organize board rental and repair.

head off to the reefs and wrecks elsewhere; see the box on pp.164–165 for full information. Prices in Nusa Dua tend to be noticeably higher than the same deals offered in Kuta.

There are also a fair number of ground sports to keep you occupied at the Nusa Dua hotels. At most places you can rent equipment as well as facilities: **tennis** courts (around $65/hr), **squash** courts (around $5/hr), and use of the **gym** ($5/hr). Nusa Dua has a world-class, eighteen-hole championship **golf** course within the resort boundaries: the Bali Golf and Country Club (☏0361/771791), spread across three areas of the resort, the main part dominating the southern end of Nusa Dua. Green fees are $142 including cart and caddy, and you can rent clubs for $25. The Bali Club Med resort (daily 10am–6.30pm; ☏0361/771521), just inside Nusa Dua's North Gate, issues a good-value **day pass** to non-guests (Rp165,000; kids Rp82,500), which buys use of all sports facilities, including windsurfing equipment, tennis courts and swimming pools, as well as a buffet lunch.

For **bird-watchers**, the mangrove swamp and sewage works to the west of Nusa Dua's North Gate, at the far southern end of Tanjung Benoa, is a rewarding place to spend an hour or two in the early morning; you're likely to see several species of kingfisher here, as well as lots of wading birds. *Nikko Bali Resort* (☏0361/773377, extn 210) does one-hour **camel safaris** along the beach (four times daily; $33, or $17 for under-12s).

Spa treatments

Many of the top-notch hotels have **spas** on their premises, offering a full menu of traditional Balinese, Thai, Swedish and aromatherapy massages as well as the popular Javanese *mandi lulur* (see p.67). Non-guests are usually welcome to use the facilities, though it's always advisable to phone ahead for a reservation. One of the best-known and longest-established spas in Bali is the award-winning spa at *Nusa Dua Beach* (☏0361/771210) which enjoys a beautiful tropical watergarden setting and where the treatments include a jet-lag massage. At the *Grand Mirage* (☏0361/771888) in Tanjung Benoa, the speciality is therapies using seawater, while the well-respected chain of Mandara spas has spa centres at *Nikko Bali Resort* (☏0361/773337) and *Club Med* (☏0361/771521).

Eating and drinking

You'll find the cheapest and most authentic Balinese **food** at the warung along Jalan Srikandi in **Bualu** village; some have English-language menus. Some pricier tourist restaurants have emerged on the Bualu side of Nusa Dua's South

Gate, where the atmosphere is livelier and less stilted than in Nusa Dua and the Galleria, though prices are still pretty high. **Tanjung Benoa** has a decent range of eateries, though they're quite spread out along the main beachfront road, Jalan Pratama. **Nusa Dua** has the most upmarket selection, most within the compounds of the big hotels. Food here is expensive, but quality is of a high standard and there's a big choice of options. **Hotel restaurants** worth seeking out include the Japanese *Hanabe* at the *Sheraton Nusa Indah*; the night-market-style food stalls at *Pasar Senggol* in the *Grand Hyatt*; and the French *Semeru Rotisserie* in the *Putri Bali*.

The shopping and entertainments plaza at the centre of the resort, the **Galleria**, also has dozens of restaurants which are worth browsing, though the ambience is rather contrived. You'll find everything from sushi to pizza and lobster to Peking duck, but the prices are ridiculous compared to elsewhere in Bali: a simple nasi goreng can cost up to ten times as much as it does in Kuta.

Many restaurants in Tanjung Benoa and Bualu offer **free transport** from local hotels to their establishment; where this service is available, we have included the phone number in the review.

Bumbu Bali Next to *Matahari Terbit Bungalows*, Jl Pratama, Tanjung Benoa ☎0361/774502. Founded and managed by renowned chef and food-writer Heinz von Holzen, this is one of the best restaurants in the area. It serves exquisite Balinese cuisine, including such delights as duck roasted in banana leaves and roast suckling pig, as well as seven-course *rijsttafels* and seafood set meals. Diners have an open-plan view of the chefs at work in the traditional Balinese kitchen, and you can also take Balinese cooking lessons here (see opposite). Expensive.

Café Bagus Jl Pratama, Tanjung Benoa ☎0361/772716. The place to come for breakfast with a good range of different set options. Also serves reasonably priced pizzas, pastas, sandwiches and some fish dishes, and cheap beer during early evening happy hour. Moderate.

Kecak Bali Jl Pratama, Tanjung Benoa ☎0361/775533. Formerly a sister restaurant to the *Bumbu Bali*, and still offering a similar if slightly cheaper menu, specializing in fine Balinese food. The menu includes duck sate, a multi-course seafood dinner, and a meat- or fish-based *rijsttafel*. Food is pricey but worth it, and the setting, in a series of pavilions, is pleasant. Expensive.

Lotus Garden Just outside the Main Gate on Jl Bypass Ngurah Rai in Bualu ☎0361/773378. The Bualu branch of this prolific Bali-wide chain serves a lot of Italian dishes including its trademark wood-fired pizzas, plus Indonesian specialities and Chinese-style seafood. Moderate to Expensive.

Max Boga Jl Pratama 67, Tanjung Benoa. Relatively reasonably priced snacks and light meals, including seafood and meat sate, burgers, salads and Indonesian standards. Moderate.

Nelayan Jl Pratama, Tanjung Benoa. Deservedly popular place which serves great Balinese curries and a good range of fresh fish and seafood dishes. Delicious rum-and-raisin ice cream too. Moderate.

Nyoman's Beer Garden Just outside the South Gate on Jl Pantai Mengiat in Bualu. Cheap draught beer, pool tables, bar food and a lively atmosphere. Moderate.

Poco Loco Just outside the South Gate at Jl Pantai Mengiat 12 in Bualu ☎0361/773923. Mexican restaurant (sister to the long-running Legian eatery), serving the usual array of enchiladas and tortilla dishes plus grills, steaks, tequila shots and frozen margaritas. Moderate.

Taman Sari Beside *Taman Sari* bungalows, Jl Pratama 61b, Tanjung Benoa ☎0361/773953. Known for its Thai cuisine, including a recommended dish of fried chicken with cashew nuts, and spicy squid salad. Also serves quality fish meals, such as bouillabaisse fish soup, and lobster and asparagus salad. Expensive.

Ulam Just outside the South Gate at Jl Pantai Mengiat 14 in Bualu ☎0361/773776. Fairly pricey seafood restaurant with fresh fish and seafood cooked to order to any number of Balinese and international recipes. Moderate to Expensive.

Shopping and entertainment

Every hotel in Nusa Dua has some kind of souvenir shop on the premises, but for a proper **shopping** experience you'll need to visit the **Galleria** shopping plaza (daily 9am–10pm) in the middle of the resort; all major hotels offer free transport to the place, and there's a complimentary return shuttle bus to the hotels, as well as to and from Kuta's Matahari department store. Spread over a huge landscaped area and contained in a series of pavilions connected by walkways and encircled by streams, the Galleria sells everything from coconut carvings to Nike trainers, framed paintings to glossy coffee-table books, and even includes a golf supplies shop and a toy department. Prices are high and there's no bargaining. For **books**, **handicrafts** and **food**, the best place to look is Tragia supermarket, in Block B of the Galleria; the department store Galeri Kris in Block C has a huge section dedicated to good-quality **batik wear**, especially men's shirts, and has handicrafts, some books and some foreign design outlets. Most of Bali's brand-name **clothes stores** are represented at the Galleria, including Mama et Leon (stylishly simple, tailored womenswear), Animale (bold, floaty, cotton prints) and Uluwatu (lacy fabrics and good-quality white cotton and linen outfits). There are also locally produced "ateliers" of Versace, Armani and Polo and a duty-free shop. To have your own outfit custom-made, head for Tanjung Benoa's Jalan Pratama, which has about fifteen **tailors'** shops along its course. Stalls in Bualu village, just beyond Nusa Dua's Main Gate, sell inexpensive Balinese **souvenirs** such as bamboo windchimes, sarongs, batik paintings and woodcarvings.

The Galleria is also one of Nusa Dua's main venues for **Balinese dance** shows (☎0361/771662), with a different show staged in front of a different restaurant every night of the week (7.30pm; free). All the hotels also stage regular **cultural events**; the *Nikko Bali* (☎0361/773377) does a particularly interesting "Desa Bali Night" which includes fire-blowing, cock-fighting, Balinese dance and village food stalls (Wed 7–9.30pm; $35, kids $17.50), as well as a cultural dinner that includes a *kecak* dance performance (Mon same hours and prices). At *Club Med* (☎0361/771521), non-guests can buy an **evening pass** for Rp275,000 which gives access to all their evening entertainments – chiefly a buffet dinner (including unlimited wine), cultural show (from 7pm) and hotel disco.

Listings

Airline offices Most international airline offices (see p.111) are in Sanur, though the domestic airlines (see p.21) have their main offices in Denpasar.
American Express The nearest office is in Sanur (see p.169).
Banks and exchange There are ATMs for Visa, MasterCard and Cirrus at Bank Central Asia (BCA) in the Galleria. You can change money in Tanjung Benoa at any number of little shops on the stretch of Jl Pratama between *Vila Bintang* and *Rasa Sayang*, at the Galleria, and at all Nusa Dua hotels. See p.36 for advice on money-changers' scams.
Cookery lessons You can learn how to prepare the finest Balinese cuisine from chef and food writer Heinz von Holzen: lessons are held at his *Bumbu Bali* restaurant in Tanjung Benoa (Mon–Fri; ☎0361/774502, ⓦwww.balifoods.com; $85/65 per day/half-day, book two days ahead, individuals accepted). Lessons are also available from the chefs at *Kecak* restaurant in Tanjung Benoa ($55 for a full day including two meals, or $40 for a

morning programme with lunch; ☎0361/775533, ⓦwww.kecakbali.com); and at *Casa Luna* restaurant on Jl Pratama in Tanjung Benoa (Mon, Wed & Fri 8.30am–2pm; Rp350,000; minimum two people; ☎0361/773845, ⓦwww.palomabalitours .com). Lessons at all three schools begin with a trip to Jimbaran fish market (see p.139) and the local fruit and veg market.
Email and internet At all major hotels and some minor ones; also at email centres opposite the *Grand Mirage* hotel in Tanjung Benoa and on Jl Srikandi in Bualu.
Hospitals and clinics Nusa Dua Clinic, Jl Pratama 81a, Tanjung Benoa (daily 24hr; ☎0361/771324), staffed by English-speaking medics; or SOS Pratama, beside the main junction in Bualu, Jl Pratama 1a (☎0361/773409). All Nusa Dua hotels provide 24hr medical service.
Postal services There's a postal agent in the Galleria complex, and another one in Bualu, and all Nusa Dua hotels sell stamps.

Sanur and around

Stretching down the southeast coast 18km from Ngurah Rai Airport, **SANUR** is an appealing, more peaceful alternative to Kuta, with a long, fairly decent white-sand beach, plenty of attractive accommodation in all price brackets and a distinct village atmosphere. Because it lacks the clubs and all-night party venues of Kuta, Sanur can seem a bit tame to younger travellers, but there are plenty of restaurants and enough bars to keep most visitors entertained, and nearly everyone appreciates the calmer ambience. It's also a good place to bring the kids, is one of Bali's main centres for watersports, and works well as a base for exploring other parts of Bali, particularly Ubud, which is about forty minutes' drive north, and the craft villages in between.

The written history of Sanur dates back to 913 AD, as inscribed on the ancient stone pillar **Prasasti Blanjong**, which is enshrined in a glass case at the back of Pura Blanjong on Jalan Danau Poso in southern Sanur. You can't actually see the inscriptions, as the two-metre-high pillar is wrapped in cloth, but they tell of a Javanese king who arrived in Sanur to set up a Mahayana Buddhist government.

Ten centuries later, Sanur began to attract significant numbers of foreigners to its shores, many of whom chose to build homes here. Of these, the house of the Belgian artist, **Le Mayeur** (now a museum), is the only one that still stands, but his more influential contemporaries included the American dancer Katharane Mershon and her husband Jack, Vicki Baum (author of *A Tale from Bali*), and art collectors Hans and Rolf Neuhaus. After World War II, Australian artist Donald Friend also made his home here. In the 1960s, during the Sukarno era, Sanur was chosen as the site of Bali's first major beach hotel, the *Grand Bali Beach*, an ugly high-rise. It has been rebuilt after suffering severe fire damage in 1992 and remains a blot – but, amazingly, is the only such disfigurement in the resort.

Sanur is famous across the island as the source of some of Bali's most powerful **black magic** and home of the most feared sorcerers and most respected healers, or *balian*. It's not uncommon, for example, to hear stories of police enquiries that use the black magic practitioners of Sanur to help them track down and capture wanted criminals.

Arrival and information

Sanur is Rp35,000 by pre-paid-taxi from the **airport** (see box p.110), or about Rp33,000 by metered taxi from central Kuta. The fastest and most direct way of getting to Sanur from most other places on Bali is by tourist **shuttle bus**. The biggest operator, Perama, has several ticket agents in Sanur; the main one, which is also the official drop-off point, is Warung Pojok minimarket, Jl Hang Tuah 31 in north Sanur (℡0361/287594); if you ask the bus driver in advance he may agree to drop you off elsewhere along Jalan Danau Tamblingan, otherwise you'll need to take a bemo or taxi to your hotel from opposite Warung Pojok.

The slightly cheaper but more long-winded way of getting to Sanur is by **bemo**, though this will entail travelling via Denpasar and changing at least once. Dark green bemos from Denpasar's **Kereneng** terminal run to north

SANUR

RESTAURANTS, BARS & CLUBS

Bali Janger	F
Banjar	S
Bonsai Café	G
Café Batu Jimbar	N
Cat and the Fiddle	X
Jazz Bar & Grille	A
Kafé Wayang	A
Le Pirate	C
Made's Pub	J
Mango Bar	E
Matahari Beach Bar	D
Mezzanine	U
Penjor	L
Resto Ming	Q
Ryoshi	N
Sari Bundo	R
Segara Agung	B
Spago	M
Swastika 1	H
Swastika Garden 2	K
Telaga Naga	O
The Trophy	W
The Village	I
Warung Agung	P
Warung Blanjong	T
Warung Muslim	V

ACCOMMODATION

Agung & Sue 1 (Watering Hole)	1
Bali Hyatt	22
Bali International Youth Hostel	24
Bali Wirasana	16
Baruna Beach	5
Coco Homestay	7
Desa Segara (Segara Village)	4
Diwangkara	2
Enny's Homestay	21
Gazebo	10
Grand Bali Beach	3
Griya Santrian	13
Keke Homestay	11
Hotel Kesumasari	25
La Taverna	8
Laghawa Beach Inn	15
Luisa Homestay	7
Natour Sindhu Beach	6
Pondok Prima	14
Respati Bali	9
Hotel Santai	19
Hotel Sanur Beach	26
Hotel Segara Agung	23
Simon Homestay	20
Swastika	17
Taman Agung	18
Tandjung Sari	12
Waka Maya	27
Yulia Homestay	7

Denpasar

Kuta & Airport

Public boats to Nusa Lembongan

Warung Pojok

Ananda

KFC

Radisson

Bemo stop

Museum Le Mayeur

Police

Bali Beach Golf Course

JALAN HANG TUAH

JL. DANAU BATUR

JL. PEMAMORAN

Gelael Supermarket

JALAN DANAU BUYAN

McDonalds

JALAN SEGARA AYU

Art Market

Pura Segara

JALAN TEGEH AGUNG

Kite Shop

In Touch

JALAN SINDHU

Sinar Bagus Kite

Bali Moon

Sumanindo Tour

Sanur Clinic

Art Market

Market

Art Market

Gazebo Piazza

Nogo Ikat

Bali Club Diver

German Consulate

JALAN P. KARANG

Alas Arum

Banjar Batu Jimbar

Legian Clinic 2

Pacto Tours

Supermarket

Crystal Divers

Tunas Tour

Surf Info

Bali Dive

Bemo terminal

British Consulate

Satriavi Tour

Raddin

Toba

TORA

JALAN DANAU

JALAN SEGARA AYU

NGURAH RAI BY-PASS

JALAN PUNGUTAN

GANG BUMI AYU

JALAN TAMBLINGAN

JALAN DUHUR

JALAN DIVING

JALAN DANAU POSO

JALAN SUDAMALA

JL. KESUMASARI

JALAN MERTASARI

JALAN SEKAR WARU

JALAN PANTEMBAK

NGURAH RAI BY-PASS

JALAN TANJUNG

N

0   1 km

157

Moving on from Sanur

Most hotels and losmen will arrange transport to the **airport** from around Rp35,000, or you can hail a metered taxi for slightly less. It costs about the same for private transport to **Benoa Harbour**, departure point for express boats to Lombok, Pelni shipping services, cruise liners and excursion boats.

The most painless way of moving on to most other tourist destinations is by **tourist shuttle bus**. Dozens of tour agents and small shops advertise shuttle bus services; the largest operator is Perama. Perama's main ticket agent and pick-up point is Warung Pojok minimarket, Jl Hang Tuah 31 in north Sanur (☎0361/287594); other Perama ticket outlets, where you may also be able to be picked up, include Nagasari Tours (☎0361/288096) opposite *Gazebo* hotel on the central part of Jalan Danau Tamblingan, and Tunas Tour, Jl Danau Tamblingan 102 (☎0361/288581), next to *Resto Ming*. Perama buses are not air-con; sample fares include Rp10,000 to Kuta/Ngurah Rai airport or Ubud, Rp25,000 to Candi Dasa, and Rp75,000 to Kuta in Lombok. See Travel Details, p.173, for more.

Moving on by **bemo** to anywhere on Bali entails going via Denpasar – either the green bemo to Kereneng, or the blue bemo to Tegal. For **Kuta** and **Jimbaran**, it's easiest to go via Tegal (see below for a handy short-cut); for most other destinations the Kereneng service is more efficient, though you'll have to make another cross-city bemo connection from Kereneng in order to get to the Batubulan terminal (for **Ubud and the east**) or the Ubung terminal (for **the west and the north**).

Sanur is the main departure point for **boats** to **Nusa Lembongan**, which leave from a jetty at the eastern end of Jalan Hang Tuah in north Sanur. There are currently two public services a day, for which tickets are sold from the beachfront office near the *Ananda Hotel* (daily 8am & 10am; 1hr 30min; Rp30,000); and one Perama shuttle boat, which should be booked the day before at the Perama office (daily 10.30am; 1hr 30min; Rp40,000). See p.272 for more details.

Sanur (15min; Rp2000–3000), where they drop off outside the *Grand Bali Beach* compound at the Ngurah Rai By-Pass/Jalan Hang Tuah junction only if asked; otherwise they usually head down Jalan Danau Beratan and Jalan Danau Buyan, before continuing down Jalan Danau Tamblingan to the *Trophy Pub Centre* in south Sanur. Dark blue bemos from Denpasar's **Tegal** terminal run direct via Jalan Teuku Umar and Renon (30min; Rp2000–3000) and then follow the same route as the green Kereneng ones, depending on passenger requests.

From Kuta, you'll need to change at Tegal in Denpasar, though you can save time if you get off the Kuta bemo at the bridge where Jalan Imam Bonjol intersects with Jalan Teuku Umar and hop onto a blue Sanur-bound bemo instead. Coming **from Nusa Dua** you can take the white, Batubulan-bound Damri bus, which drops passengers on the Ngurah Rai By-Pass, near the *Radisson* hotel in north Sanur; you can also use this service if coming **from Ubud**, changing onto the Damri bus at Denpasar's **Batubulan** terminus.

There are no official tourist offices in Sanur, but plenty of tour agents are only to happy to provide **information** about potential day-trips.

Transport and tours

Sanur stretches 5km from its northernmost tip to the far southern end. The green and blue public **bemos** to and from Denpasar's two terminals (see "Arrival", above) are quite useful if you're sticking to the main streets; the standard tourist price is Rp1000–2000 for any journey within Sanur. Otherwise, flag down one of the numerous **metered taxis**. The two main companies are the light blue Blue Bird Taxis (☎0361/701111) and the white Ngurah Rai Airport Taxis (☎0361/724724); all metered taxis charge Rp4000 flagfall, then Rp2000 per km, day and night, but you should always check that the meter is turned on before starting your journey. If you're planning a long trip, it may be worth negotiating a fee with one of the roadside **transport touts**, but they rarely offer competitive prices for short transfers.

The transport touts also **rent cars** ($25–35/day, excluding insurance) and **motorbikes** (from Rp60,000) by the day and the week, as will most of Sanur's tour agencies. Most tour agencies will also supply a **car with driver**; try JBA, inside the compound of the *Diwangkara Hotel*, Jl Hang Tuah 54 in north Sanur (☎0361/286501, ✉jbadwkbl@denpasar.wasantara.net.id). Although you can't assume that your driver will also act as a guide (and some drivers hassle you into visiting tourist shops), many of the transport touts are multilingual and knowledgeable about their culture; they usually charge about Rp350,000 for a full day's tour. For first-hand recommendations of Sanur drivers, check the archives of the online travellers' forums listed on p.24.

Sanur is an ideal place for **bicycles** as it's almost completely flat and traffic is pretty light, so long as you keep off the thundering Ngurah Rai By-Pass on the western perimeter. Most hotels will be able to get hold of a bike for you to rent, or try the *Bali Wirasana* hotel minimarket on Jalan Danau Tamblingan: expect to pay Rp12,000–20,000 a day.

Tours

Most tourist businesses in Sanur, including tour agents and hotels, offer a range of **sightseeing tours** to popular attractions in Bali as well as further afield to neighbouring islands. Itineraries tend usually follow identical routes to those arranged by the agents of Kuta and Nusa Dua, but numbers are generally limited to a minibus of eight or ten people and prices kept fairly low. For full details, see the box on p.126.

Accommodation

Sanur's budget **accommodation** is nothing like as prolific as Kuta's, but there are a number of reasonable possibilities, none of which is more than ten minutes' walk from the beach. Mid-priced hotels are particularly good in Sanur, the majority of them small, cosy setups with beautiful gardens, a pool and rooms with air-conditioning and hot water; some even occupy beachfront spots. The best of the beachfront is taken up by upmarket hotels, most of which have grounds that lead down to the sea: a couple of Sanur's top hotels rank amongst Bali's most appealing. Many of the mid-priced and expensive hotels listed below are featured on the Bali accommodation **websites** detailed in the box on p.44, which are also worth checking out for discounts.

Inexpensive

Agung & Sue 1 (Watering Hole) Jl Hang Tuah 37, north Sanur ☎ & ℗0361/288289. The cheapest rooms in this part of Sanur, only 250m from the beach. The better rooms have air-con, you can access the internet from here, and there's a good

restaurant. Very handy for boats to Nusa Lembongan, and staff will store your luggage here for as long as you want. Rooms with fan ❷ With air-con ❸

Bali International Youth Hostel Jl Mertasari 19,

Banjar Suwung Kangin, Sidakarya ⏀ & ⏁ 0361/ 720812. Inconveniently situated 1km south of the far southern end of Sanur, but providing free trans-fers to and from Sanur, Kuta, Denpasar and the airport. Clean, modern rooms for two and four people (some air-con), shared bathrooms and a small swimming pool. Very good rates for single travellers. ②

Coco Homestay Jl Danau Tamblingan 42, central Sanur ⏀ 0361/287391. Archetypal homestay offer-ing a few budget rooms behind the family art shop. Some of the cheapest accommodation in Sanur. ②

Enny's Homestay Jl Danau Tamblingan 172, south-central Sanur ⏀ 0361/287363, ⏁ 287306. The seven rooms behind the family shoeshop are immaculately tiled and attractively furnished in mod-ern losmen style. There's a tiny upstairs garden balcony and you're just across the road from a path down to the beach. Discounts offered in low season. Rooms with fan and cold water ② With fan and hot water ③ With air-con and private balcony ④

Keke Homestay Gang Keke 3, off Jl Danau Tamblingan 96, central Sanur ⏀ 0361/287282. Tiny losmen that's basic but friendly and offers simple fan rooms with cold-water mandi. ②

Luisa Homestay Jl Danau Tamblingan 40, central Sanur ⏀ 0361/289673. One of three very similar losmen clustered together in family compounds behind streetside businesses. Basic accommoda-tion that's among the cheapest in Sanur, but cheerful. ②

Simon Homestay Down a tiny *gang* at Jl Danau Tamblingan 164d, south-central Sanur ⏀ 0361/ 289158. Small, sparklingly clean family losmen with nicely furnished, well-maintained rooms. Rooms with fan ③ With air-con ④

Yulia Homestay Jl Danau Tamblingan 38, central Sanur ⏀ 0361/288089. This friendly, family-run losmen is the longest-running and best of the three similar outfits in this cluster; accommodation is in nice bungalows rather than rooms in a block. ②

Moderate

Bali Wirasana Jl Danau Tamblingan 138, Batu Jimbar, central Sanur ⏀ 0361/288632, ⏁ 288561, ⏂ wirasana@indosat.net.id. Though the cheapest rooms here aren't that great, they're large, clean and centrally located, plus there's internet access and guests can use the pool at *Swastika* next door. Choice of fan or air-con. ④

Baruna Beach Jl Sindhu, north-central Sanur ⏀ 0361/288546, ⏁ 289629, ⏃ www.geocities.com/baruna_hotel. Tiny beach-front complex of six pleasant bungalows, all with air-con and fridge. Popular with travellers and surfers. Friendly, and good value for the location. ⑤

Hotel Kesumasari Jl Cemara 22, Semawang, south Sanur ⏀ 0361/287492, ⏁ 288876. Attractive, spacious bungalows, including some built to traditional designs, with hot water and a fridge, plus a two-storey family bungalow that sleeps four. Swimming pool and restaurant. Rooms with fan ⑤ With air-con ⑥

Laghawa Beach Inn Jl Danau Tamblingan 51, central Sanur ⏀ 0361/288494, ⏁ 282533, ⏃ www.laghawahotel.com. Smartly furnished ter-raced rooms set in a garden, with pool, that leads right down to the beach. Internet access in the lobby. Good value for the location. Rooms with fan ⑥ With air-con ⑦

Pondok Prima Gang Bumi Ayu 23, central Sanur ⏀ 0361/286369, ⏁ 289153, ⏂ primacottage@telkom.net. Very quiet, good-value place that's well off the main road and offers a range of rooms including some very spacious and well-furnished bungalows in secluded spots around a tropical garden. The rooms in the main two-storey block are less interesting. There's a pool and a restaurant, and in most rooms you can choose to pay extra for use of the air-con. Rooms with fan ④ With air-con ⑤

Respati Bali Jl Danau Tamblingan 33, central Sanur ⏀ 0361/288427, ⏁ 288046, ⏂ brespati@ indo.net.id. A pristine collection of well-kept, good-value bungalows in a compact compound that runs down to the sea.. Also has a pool and a restaurant. Rooms with fan ⑥ With air-con ⑦

Hotel Santai Jl Danau Tamblingan 148, Batu Jimbar, central Sanur ⏀ 0361/281648, ⏁ 287314, ⏃ www.pplhbali.or.id. Small, centrally located hotel run by the environmental group PPLH. Rooms are spartan but well equipped (all with air-con, TV and hot water) and there's a pool, a recommended restaurant and an internet café in the lobby, as well as an environmental resource centre and a library of fiction and reference books. ⑤

Hotel Segara Agung Jl Duyung 43, Semawang, south Sanur ⏀ 0361/288446, ⏁ 286113, ⏃ bali-www.com/bali/roomfinder/segaraagung.htm. Occupying a very quiet spot down a residential *gang* just a couple of minutes' walk from the beach, this is an attractive place of twenty bunga-lows set in a pretty garden compound with a swimming pool. Rooms are clean and well fur-nished; the cheapest ones have a fan and cold water, the most expensive air-con and water.

Rooms with fan ⑤ With air-con ⑥

Swastika Jl Danau Tamblingan 128, Batu Jimbar, central Sanur ☎ 0361/288693, ⑤ 287526, ⓦ www.homestead.com/colb/swastika.html, ⓔ swastika@indosat.net.id. Deservedly popular mid-range place, with 78 comfortable rooms in variously styled bungalows set around a delightful garden with two sizeable swimming pools and a kids' pool. Most of the fan-cooled rooms have pretty garden bathrooms, and many of the air-con ones have private garden-view gazebos. Named after the ancient Buddhist symbol, not the Nazi emblem. Discounts of up to twenty percent, or more if booked online. ⑥

Taman Agung Jl Danau Tamblingan 146, Batu Jimbar, central Sanur ☎ 0361/288549, ⑤ 289161, ⓔ tamanagung@yahoo.com. Large, immaculate rooms, some with air-con, set around a swimming pool and small garden. The fan rooms are in a two-storey block and have outdoor seating on a shared balcony, while the slightly more expensive air-con terraced bungalows have private verandahs. Family bungalows are also available. Rooms with fan ⑤ With air-con ⑥

Expensive

Bali Hyatt Jl Danau Tamblingan, south-central Sanur ☎ 0361/281234, ⑤ 287693, ⓦ www.bali.hyatt.com. Enormous, appealingly plush establishment, offering a range of top-notch rooms and 36 acres of award-winning tropical gardens stretching down to the beach. Watersports facilities, tennis courts, several swimming pools and a spa. One child under 12 can stay free if sharing parents' room, and there are regular organized kids' activities. Free shuttle bus to sister hotel in Nusa Dua. ⑧

Desa Segara (Segara Village) Jl Segara Ayu, north-central Sanur ☎ 0361/288407, ⑤ 287242, ⓔ segara1@denpasar.wasantara.net.id. Understated elegance pervades the "village", which is made up of six compounds of very attractive traditional-style accommodation (in hotel rooms and bungalows) set amongst ponds, fountains, a swimming pool and tennis courts. The grounds run down to the sea. ⑦–⑧

Diwangkara Jl Hang Tuah, north Sanur ☎ 0361/288577, ⑤ 288894, ⓔ jbadwkbl@denpasar.wasantara.net.id. Modern concrete terraced bungalows with good facilities (air-con, TV, bathtub and hot water) in a garden compound with a small swimming pool. Fairly good value for its beachfront location, but quite a hike from central Sanur. ⑦

Gazebo Jl Danau Tamblingan 35, central Sanur ☎ 0361/288212, ⑤ 288300, ⓦ www.baligazebo.com. This set of bungalows occupies one of the prettiest tropical gardens in Sanur, complete with its own little river and two swimming pools. It's good value for its beachfront location, though some of the bungalows have rather faded furnishings and decor. The more expensive split-level and mezzanine bungalows (with TV) are the most appealing. Comfortable seafront lounge and library and two restaurants. ⑦

Grand Bali Beach Off Jl Hang Tuah, north Sanur ☎ 0361/288511, ⑤ 287917, ⓔ gbb@indosat.net.id. Huge establishment covering a long stretch of the northern end of the Sanur coast. Most rooms are in the central tower block, but there are also a fair number of cottages in the extensive grounds. The hotel fronts a good beach and offers lots of watersports, as well as four swimming pools, tennis courts and table tennis, but is some way from the central restaurant and shopping area. Two kids under 12 go free if sharing with parents. Internet centre in the lobby. ⑨

Griya Santrian Jl Danau Tamblingan 47, central Sanur ☎ 0361/288181, ⑤ 288185; ⓦ www.santrian.com. A series of smart, roomy, detached and semi-detached bungalows scattered around an attractive garden compound that runs down to the beach. All have air-con and hot water. There are two swimming pools and four restaurants. ⑧

La Taverna Jl Danau Tamblingan 29, central Sanur ☎ 0361/288497, ⑤ 287126, ⓦ www.indo.com/hotels/la_taverna, ⓔ latavern@dps.mega.net.id. Small hotel offering comfortable, cosy bungalows, including some stylish split-level ones beautifully furnished with antiques and Balinese fabrics; most have verandahs overlooking the garden, and the grounds run down to the beach. Discounts often available. ⑧

Natour Sindhu Beach Jl Pantai Sindhu 14, Sindhu, north-central Sanur ☎ 0361/288351, ⑤ 289268, ⓦ www.natoursindhubeach.com. Fairly small but upmarket chain hotel that's especially popular with domestic tourists. The garden leads down to the seafront, there's a swimming pool and games room, and you can choose between a room in the hotel wing or bungalow accommodation. ⑧

Hotel Sanur Beach Semawang, south Sanur ☎ 0361/288011, ⑤ 287566, ⓦ www.aerowisata.co.id/sanur. Sprawling complex with a disappointing lack of local architectural features, but pretty enough landscaped gardens giving direct access to a fine stretch of sandy, tree-shaded beach. Luxury-grade rooms in the central block plus swimming pools, tennis courts, a delightful Mandara spa complex and a well-equipped Blue Oasis watersports centre. ⑧–⑨

1

Tandjung Sari Jl Danau Tamblingan 41, central Sanur (☎0361/288441, ⓕ287930, ⓦwww .tandjungsari.com. Elegant if slightly dated collection of 28 personal cottage compounds each with its own courtyard garden, shaded gazebo and garden shower; some also have an upstairs living room. There's a swimming pool and the garden runs down to the shore. Reservations strongly advised. ⑨

Waka Maya Jl Tanjung Pinggir, south Sanur ☎ & ⓕ0361/289912, ⓦwww.wakaexperience.com. Far removed from all other tourist developments in Sanur at the end of a winding village lane, with fourteen air-con bungalows designed in luxurious minimalist-chic style, using rough-cut rock, dressed slate and polished woods. Each one has a garden bathroom and its own private garden (the villas have a private pool too), and there's a hotel pool, spa and restaurant. The beach in front of the hotel is unappealing, but there's frequent transport to the *Grand Bali Beach* sands. ⑧–⑨

The resort

Sanur's five-kilometre **shoreline** changes character several times along its length, with some stretches kept cleaner than others and certain parts remaining the province of boatmen and fishing activities. A huge expanse of shore gets exposed at low tide and the reef lies only about 1km offshore at high tide; the currents beyond it are dangerously strong. This makes it almost impossible to swim here at low tide (though it's okay for paddling kids), but at other times of day swimming is fine and **watersports** are popular.

The coastline has been severely eroded in the last few years as a direct result of the ill-advised land-reclamation project on nearby Serangan Island (see p.170). The sudden eating away of the beach in the Sanur area – in places by up to fifty metres – has angered fishermen in particular as they now find it difficult to lodge their *jukung* safely at high tide. Following complaints by them and other Sanur *banjar* representatives, there are now plans to restore the beaches to their original state with sand that has been dredged from elsewhere.

For the time being there are still some very attractive stretches of beach left in Sanur. The resort's best **sand** is made up of tiny coral granules and fringes the northern reaches of the shore in front of the *Grand Bali Beach*. Non-guests can rent sun-loungers and thick hotel towels on this stretch for a few dollars a day (which also includes use of the hotel pool), but there's nothing to stop you from just laying out your sarong on the sand. Most of Sanur's natural shade has been uprooted to make way for the beachfront hotel complexes, but a few coconut palms do remain at the southern end of the resort, in front of the *Sanur Beach*, itself another very pleasant stretch of sandy shore. And you can walk almost the whole length of the beachfront in partial shade, on the paved esplanade that runs from Jalan Hang Tuah, north of the *Grand Bali Beach* down to Gang Kesumasari.

Sports and activities

Sanur's two biggest **watersports** operators are associated with hotels but are open to all: the *Grand Bali Beach* watersports centre (☎0361/288511) is in the northern part of the resort, and the Blue Oasis Beach Club (☎0361/288011) is at *Sanur Beach* in the south. Many of the dive centres listed on p.165 also rent out watersports equipment; sample rates include **kayaks** for $6 an hour, **wind-**

surfers $10–15 an hour, and **jet-skis** $20 for a quarter-hour. **Parasailing** usually costs about $10 a round, and **waterskiing** $16 for fifteen minutes. Blue Oasis offers a range of different watersports **courses**, including half-day windsurfing and sailing courses ($80), kite-surfing instruction at $22 per hour, and PADI **dive** courses and dive excursions.

Sanur is a popular base for **divers**: see the box on pp.164–165 for details of local reefs, dive operators and courses. **Snorkellers** can usually join organized dive excursions, as well as specialist snorkelling trips; or you can charter glass-bottomed boats or *prahu* to take you out to the Sanur reef ($10–15/hr).

The main departure point for **fishing** expeditions off southern Bali is Tanjung Benoa (see p.152, though some boats do leave from Sanur: ask at any Sanur tour agent or watersports outlet. A four-hour trip will generally cost $50–75 per person for coral fishing, including tackle and bait, and $75–100 per person for trolling; for a full day's game fishing expect to pay $485 for a four-person boat.

A number of the biggest hotels offer extensive indoor and outdoor sporting facilities, usually open to non-guests as well. All the major hotels have **gyms** ($5) and **tennis courts** ($10–12/hr), and they generally rent out all sorts of equipment from rackets to shoes to partners and ball boys if necessary. Sanur also has its own nine-hole **golf course** in the grounds of the *Grand Bali Beach*, whose guests get a fifty percent reduction on the $50 green fees. Clubs and shoes can be rented at the club house (T0361/288511, extn 1388).

Many of the more expensive hotels have built luxury **spa** treatment centres where you can receive a range of massages, including aromatherapy, traditional Balinese and the Javanese *mandi lulur* exfoliation scrub (see p.67) as well as facials and hair treatments. Two of the best known are the beautifully designed Mandara spa complex in the grounds of *Sanur Beach* (T0361/288011), and the spa at the *Bali Hyatt* (T0361/281234). There are several other smaller and much cheaper centres too, including Atma, Jl Danau Tamblingan 94 in central Sanur (T0361/283850), which charges Rp190,000 for a two-hour *mandi lulur*, and the In Touch reflexology centre on Jalan Sindhu. Plus massage-and-manicure ladies hang out on the beach, charging around Rp20,000 for a half-hour massage.

Sanur surf breaks

Surf conditions in Sanur are best during the wet season from September to March, when the northwest winds blow offshore along this stretch of the east coast. The northernmost break, **Sanur** (directly in front of the *Grand Bali Beach*), is a respectable right-hand reef break with the possibility of some great barrels, but needs a large swell to break and is best on a mid- to high tide. Further south, in front of *Tandjung Sari Hotel*, the **Tandjung Sari Reef** is a more unpredictable right-hander, but can sometimes come up with long high-speed walls if surfed at high tide. The **Hyatt Reef**, 1.5km offshore from the front of the *Bali Hyatt*, provides very good right-handers on an incoming mid-tide.

There's a Hyatt Reef surfers' **information** hut on the beach south off Jalan Duyung, beyond *Banjar* and Bali Dive, where you should be able to get info on the local waves and rent a board. You can also **rent boards** at the Blue Oasis Beach Club, in front of *Sanur Beach* for $10 per day, or $6 for a boogie board; Blue Oasis can also organize a fishing *prahu* to take you out to nearby breaks, but you'll probably get a cheaper deal if you negotiate direct with the boat owners. The Sombak Surf shop, next to *Resto Ming* on the nearby stretch of Jalan Danau Tamblingan, sells boards and surfwear.

Diving in south Bali

Sanur is one of south Bali's two main **diving** centres (the other is Tanjung Benoa, see p.152), and many of the outfits that sell dive excursions from shops in Kuta and Nusa Dua have their headquarters in this area. It's a good place to learn to dive, or to refresh your memory after a long break, as the local dive sites are close by. More experienced divers usually prefer the dives off the east and north coast of Bali, either arranging them as day or overnight trips from Sanur, or basing themselves in accommodation nearer those places. For **general advice** on diving in Bali and Lombok, see p.63.

There is one **divers' decompression chamber** on Bali, located at Sanglah Public Hospital, Jl Kesehatan Selatan 1 in Denpasar (℡0361/227911).

Dive courses and excursions

All the centres listed below run internationally **certificated diving courses**, including four-day open-water PADI **courses** ($300–400) and two-day advanced open-water courses ($245–350); most also offer half-day introductory dives ($50–75). Prices are competitive, but be sure to check whether equipment rental, insurance and course materials are included. Be wary of any operation offering extremely cheap courses: maintaining diving equipment is an expensive business in Bali so any place offering unusually good rates will probably be cutting corners and compromising your safety.

Despite the proliferation of dive shops, **Sanur's own dive sites**, which lie just a short distance off the coast along the east-facing edge of the reef, are a bit of a disappointment. The coral is not that spectacular here, and visibility is only around 6 to 10m, with dives ranging from 2 to 12m, but the area does teem with polychromatic fish, especially parrotfish, angelfish, butterflyfish, groupers and fusiliers. Even though the reef is only about five to ten minutes' boat ride from the beach, most boats can't get to and from the reef at low tide, so check with operators how long you're likely to have for diving. The average cost of a single dive off Sanur is about $40, including guide, tank and weights. Accompanying snorkellers pay $15 each, including equipment.

Rates for **one-day dive excursions** to the more interesting reefs elsewhere in Bali (including two tanks but not necessarily all equipment) include: the northeast-coast reefs and wrecks of Tulamben (see p.311) or Amed (see p.307) for $55–85; the island of Pulau Menjangan (Deer Island, p.401) for $70–105; and the east-coast islands of Nusa Lembongan (p.271) and Nusa Penida (p.278) for $75–105. **Diving safaris** to Tulamben, Amed, Nusa Penida or Menjangan cost around $85 per person per day including equipment, accommodation and food.

Museum Le Mayeur

One of Sanur's earliest expatriate residents was the Belgian artist Adrien Jean Le Mayeur de Merpres (1880–1958), whose home has remained standing for more than sixty years and is now open to the public as **Museum Le Mayeur** (Sun–Fri 8am–4pm; donation); access is via the beachfront path that turns right off Jalan Hang Tuah in north Sanur. Le Mayeur arrived in Bali at the age of 52, and after travelling down from the north of the island chose to settle for a while in the village of Klandis on the outskirts of Denpasar. The teenage Ni Pollok was at this time the chief *legong* dancer of Klandis and considered by many to be the best dancer in the whole of Bali. An outstandingly beautiful young woman, she began to pose regularly for the middle-aged Le Mayeur. Romance blossomed, and by 1935 the two were married. The couple subsequently moved to this house on Sanur beach where he painted and she posed, and every so often they would make the journey to Singapore to hold an exhibition and sell some work.

Dive centres

All tour agents in south Bali sell diving trips organized by Bali's major **diving operators**, which is handy because many operators have offices that are quite far out of central Sanur. But for specific queries, especially about the difficulty of the dives, you should try to speak directly to one of the dive leaders, or at least call them up. Some of the most established operators include:

AquaMarine Diving Jl Raya Seminyak 56, Kuta ⊤0361/730107, ⑤735368, ⓦwww.aquamarinediving.com. UK-run.

Bali Club Diver Jl Danau Tamblingan 110, opposite *Laghawa* hotel in central Sanur ⊤ & ⑤0361/287263, ⓦwww .baliclubdiver.com. Also Jl Legian 64, Kuta ⊤ & ⑤0361/752147.

Bali Dive Jl Danau Poso 38, south Sanur. Also next to *Banjar* restaurant at the beach end of Jl Duyung, Semawang, south Sanur ⊤0361/286520, ⑤287692, ⓦwww.bali-dive.com.

Bali International Diving Professionals Jl Sekarwaru 9, south Sanur ⊤0361/270759, ⑤270760, ⓦwww .bidp-balidiving.com. Also offers nitrox dives, underwater weddings, dive courses for 8–11-year-olds, and special dives for disabled divers. UK/Balinese-run.

Bali Pesona Bahari (formerly Bali Marine Sports), Jl Bypass Ngurah Rai, Blanjong, south Sanur ⊤0361/289308, ⑤287872, ⓦwww.bmsdivebali.com. One of the first PADI dive shops in Bali and now a PADI Gold Palm Resort.

Baruna Jl Bypass Ngurah Rai 300b, Kuta ⊤0361/753820, ⑤753809, ⓦwww.baruna.com. Also in the *Grand Bali Beach* hotel, off Jl Hang Tuah, north Sanur ⊤0361/288511 extn 1381; and on Jl Pratama in Tanjung Benoa. Long-established operator.

Blue Oasis Beach Club *Sanur Beach* hotel, south Sanur ⊤0361/288011, ⓦwww.blueoasisbc.com.

Crystal Divers Jl Duyung 25, south-central Sanur ⊤ & ⑤0361/286737, ⓦwww.crystal-divers.com. One of only a few PADI five-star dive centres in Bali. Run by English and Danish divers.

ENA Dive Center Jl Tirta Ening 1, Sanur ⊤0361/288829, ⑤287945, ⓦwww.enadive.co.id. Long-running PADI five-star Gold Palm Resort, with a good reputation.

Scuba Duba Doo Jl Legian 367, Kuta ⊤ & ⑤0361/761798, ⓦwww.dive centerbali.com. US-run.

Yos Marine Adventures Jl Pratama 106x, Tanjung Benoa ⊤0361/773774, ⑤752985, ⓦwww.yosdive.com. Large, efficient and reliable outfit that's been going for years. Also offers diving excursions for children and for disabled divers if arranged in advance.

When World War II hit Bali, many foreign residents were interned, but Le Mayeur somehow avoided this indignity and stayed put in Sanur, though the couple's house was looted by the Balinese, apparently acting under Japanese orders. Most of the paintings survived the looting, but wartime shortages meant that Le Mayeur had to switch from canvas to sackcloth, and several of these raw-looking works are now on show in the museum. When Le Mayeur died, he left his house and his work to his wife, with the proviso that his paintings and his home would eventually be donated to the Indonesian government. On Ni Pollok's death in 1985, the marital home became the Museum Le Mayeur.

Le Mayeur's house dates back to around 1935 and is stunningly located right on the shore, with a compound gate that still opens directly onto the sand. Much of the original structure remains: a typical low-roofed wooden building, sumptuously carved with red and gold painted doors, lintels and pediments, and partitioned into rooms by walls that reach only two-thirds of the way up to the ceiling. He did most of his painting in the courtyard garden – a

165

compact tropical wilderness ornamented with stonecarvings, shrines, and tiny *bale*, which features in many of his paintings and photographs.

Inside the house, dozens of the artist's **paintings** – mostly oils – are displayed, though there's a disappointing absence of his Balinese work and a huge number of rather unexciting European scenes. The few Balinese paintings here show a distinct preference for a lurid interpretation of tropical light. But there are some evocative charcoal and crayon sketches on show as well – the charming 1937 drawing of Ni Pollok entitled *Panorama in the House* is the highlight of the first room. And there is another gorgeous portrait of her, this time a photographic one, in room four. It's easy to become irritated, however, with Le Mayeur's many depictions of recumbent beauties with dreamy expressions in their eyes and overtly sensuous pouts on their lips.

Eating

Sanur has plenty of **restaurants**, most of them located either along the main road through the resort, Jalan Danau Tamblingan, or along the **beachfront** walkway between *La Taverna* and Jalan Sindhu (north-central Sanur) and between Jalan Kesumasari and Jalan Duyung (south Sanur). All the beachfront hotels have seafront restaurants, and though the food can be indifferent in these places, the views – which encompass both the mountain Gunung Agung and the island of Nusa Lembongan – and sea breezes are always good, and they're ideal for kids who can play safely on the sand in front. All the beachfront places offer fresh-fish barbecues at night.

Sanur has dozens of inexpensive, almost indistinguishable little warung offering the standard range of pizzas, pastas, sandwiches, fried rice and fresh juices. You'll find the most authentic Indonesian food at restaurants beyond the main drag, particularly along Jalan Danau Poso, where homes outnumber hotels and tourist businesses. The **night market** which sets up at the Jalan Danau Tamblingan/Jalan Sindhu intersection is another good place for cheap Indonesian dishes, or you can always buy takeaway noodles, rice and soups from the handcarts that set up along Jalan Danau Tamblingan after sundown.

Bonsai Café Beachfront walkway just north of *La Taverna* hotel, access off Jl Danau Tamblingan, central Sanur. Breezy seafront café, restaurant and bar (open until 2am) whose expansive views make it a relaxing place to eat and drink at any time of day. Opens for breakfast around 7am and serves the usual range of nasi goreng, pizza, pasta and seafood, plus good-value cocktails. The restaurant is dotted with bonsai and there's a huge nursery of these artfully pruned little trees round the back. Inexpensive to Moderate.

Café Batu Jimbar Jl Danau Tamblingan 152, central Sanur. Slightly arty terrace café serving a sophisticated range of hearty Mexican and Italian favourites, plus salads, home-baked cakes, breads and herbal teas. Moderate.

Kafé Tali Jiwa In front of the *Santai Hotel*, Jl Danau Tamblingan 148, central Sanur. Serves one of the best vegetarian menus in Sanur, including spicy *nasi pecel* and energy salads, plus traditional Balinese fish and chicken dishes and delicious steamed bananas with cinnamon cream sauce. Inexpensive to Moderate.

Le Pirate Seafront restaurant belonging to the *Desa Segara* hotel, north-central Sanur. The extensive menu lists lots of wholesome dishes, including plenty of pizzas plus seafood, pastas, and some Indian and Thai specialities. Occupies a very pleasant seaside location. Moderate.

Mezzanine Beside *Puri Santrian* hotel on Jl Danau Tamblingan, south Sanur. The impressively chic barn-like dining hall, complete with comfy chairs for aperitifs and coffees, adds a touch of class to an unexceptional but decent enough menu of Asian classics that runs to Sumatran beef *rendang* curry, Thai seafood platter with lemongrass, and Manado pan-fried snapper. Live music from around 9.30pm. Expensive.

Resto Ming Jl Danau Tamblingan 105. Seafood is a speciality here, particularly lobster thermidor and king prawns, and the genial chef-owner has filled his restaurant with an outstanding collection of Balinese artefacts, paintings, and statues. Moderate.

Ryoshi Jl Danau Tamblingan, central Sanur. As well as a decent selection of sushi, the Sanur branch of Bali's ever-reliable chain of Japanese restaurants has an admirable menu of appetizers – spinach and sesame salad, deep-fried tofu, barbecued chicken, baked aubergine – which, when ordered tapas-style make a satisfying meal. Moderate.

Sari Bundo Jl Danau Poso. Typical *Masakan Padang* place (see p.48) serving spicy Sumatran dishes 24 hours a day. Inexpensive.

Segara Agung Beachfront next to *Desa Segara*, north-central Sanur ☎ 0361/288574. Superbly located capacious restaurant with a huge choice of dishes from lobster and *babi guling* to less flashy seafood and Chinese standards. It's run as a co-operative with all profits going to local schools and clinics; call for free transport. Moderate.

Spago Jl Danau Tamblingan 79, central Sanur. Sleek, elegantly styled restaurant where the outstanding menu of Mediterranean-fusion cuisine includes chilled gazpacho, Moroccan-style kebabs with tzatziki, red snapper with olives and roast vegetable salad with crumbled feta. You can choose to dine on the (noisy) streetside terrace or in the cavernous thatched *wantilan* behind. Expensive.

Swastika Garden 2 Jl Danau Tamblingan, central Sanur. Pleasant garden setting, with dances staged two evenings a week, and a reasonable enough menu of Indonesian and seafood dishes, plus pas-tas and Chinese specialities. Cheap beer. Moderate.

Telaga Naga Opposite the *Bali Hyatt* on Jl Danau Tamblingan, south-central Sanur. Very upmarket *Hyatt* restaurant comprising a series of traditional pavilions set in extensive gardens across the road from the hotel compound. Specializes in pricey Cantonese and Szechwan dishes and is famous for its smoked duck, and scallops in blackbean sauce. Nightly 6–11pm.

The Village Opposite *La Taverna* hotel, Jl Danau Tamblingan, central Sanur. Classy menu of unusual dishes including spicy chicken, cinnamon and pumpkin bisque, delicious European breads, plenty of seafood and mouthwatering macadamia nut ice cream. Moderate.

Warung Agung Jl Danau Tamblingan 97, south-central Sanur. Friendly little place serving well-priced tourist fare including Balinese grilled chicken and seafood. Inexpensive to Moderate.

Warung Blanjong Jl Danau Poso 78. Serves only Balinese dishes, including exceptionally good veggie delights such as *tipat* (fried vegetables with sticky rice cakes and peanut sauce), veggie nasi campur, and non-veg specialities like *pepes pe pasih* (grilled fish in banana leaves). Inexpensive.

Warung Muslim Jl Sudamala, south Sanur. For really cheap, authentic, mainly Javanese food, head for the bemo terminus on Jl Sudamala where you'll find a string of small Muslim warung serving bargain-priced standards including grilled chicken, sate, *bakso* and nasi goreng. Inexpensive.

Nightlife and entertainment

There are plenty of **bar-restaurants** along Sanur's beachfront, particularly between *La Taverna* and Jalan Sindhu (north–central Sanur) and between Jalan Kesumasari and Jalan Duyung (south Sanur). Pleasant, genial places to while away the evening, most stay reasonably lively till around 1am; some stage live music and all offer imported beers and spirits as well as local brew. There are only a few **clubs** in the resort, and these are rather formal places compared to Kuta's nightspots, attracting a mostly Indonesian clientele.

If you're carousing in south Sanur you might find it difficult to find a taxi after 10pm: if you get fed up with waiting for one to pass, either ask bar staff to phone one for you (see p.159), or look for one at the nearest large hotel.

Bars, clubs and live music

Bali Janger Jl Danau Tamblingan 21, central Sanur. Flashy, cavernous disco with glitter balls but not much character. A bit of a pick-up joint. Midnight–5am.

Banjar Beachfront end of Jl Duyung, south-central Sanur. Shoreside bar and restaurant, with occasional club-nights fronted by local and international DJs. Check flyers for details.

The Cat and the Fiddle Near the *Raddin* hotel on Jl Mertasari, south Sanur. Mid-priced expat-oriented restaurant with live Irish music every Tuesday from 7pm.

Jazz Bar & Grille Beside *KFC* at the Jl Bypass Ngurah Rai/Jl Hang Tuah crossroads, north Sanur. In the downstairs bar, some of Bali's best jazz and blues bands play live sets every night from about

9.30pm; the atmosphere is mellow but lively and the place attracts a friendly mix of locals, expats and the occasional tourist. The upstairs restaurant serves quality food including a whole range of fish and seafood barbecued over coconut husks – the grilled tuna is delicious – and a bizarre but tasty banana pizza concoction. There's a pool table too. Daily 8am–1am.

Kafé Wayang Next-door-but-one to *KFC* at the Jl Bypass Ngurah Rai/Jl Hang Tuah crossroads, north Sanur (T0361/287591). Bar-restaurant that stages live music from local bands every Saturday night and a local famous jam session every Friday from 9pm. Call for free transport.

Made's Pub Opposite *Gazebo* hotel on Jl Danau Tamblingan, central Sanur. A young, trendy staff keeps the punters plied with beers and cocktails at this lively streetside drinking spot that sometimes hosts live music. Closes about 1am.

Mango Bar and Restaurant Beachfront end of Jl

Sindhu, north-central Sanur. Beachfront bar and restaurant which features live reggae (Mon & Fri 9pm), a local band (Wed 8pm) and children's traditional *legong* dance (Mon & Fri 8pm).

Matahari Beach Bar Beachfront end of Jl Sindhu, north-central Sanur. Breezy beachfront bar and restaurant attached to the *Natour Sindhu* hotel, with a pool table and a well-stocked bar. Stages live music and dance performances from 7pm five nights a week. Closes around 1am.

Tandjung Sari Beach Bar Inside the *Tandjung Sari Hotel* compound, Jl Danau Tamblingan 41, central Sanur. Elegant shorefront bar, known for its fiery local brew, the *arak bumbu*, in which rice liquor is spiced up with honey, lime, ginger, garlic and pepper.

The Trophy In the Trophy Pub Centre, Jl Danau Tamblingan 49, south Sanur. Very popular, typical expat pub with a dart board, pool table and satellite TV. Live music (Wed & Sat) and Western bar food.

Entertainment

You can see **Balinese dancing** in or around Sanur on any day of the week, either at one of the hotels or restaurants, or by making a trip to dance stages in nearby Denpasar.

To see two of Bali's most spectacular dances, you'll need to venture out. The exuberant shaggy-haired lion dance, the **barong**, is performed every morning (9.30–10.30am) at the Catur Eka Budhi on Jalan Waribang in the Kesiman district on Denpasar's eastern fringes (see p.102), 3km by taxi from Sanur's Jalan Hang Tuah. The spectacular "monkey dance", or **kecak**, is performed nightly (6.30–7.30pm) at the Stage Uma Dewi, also on Jalan Waribang, about 300m south of the *barong* dance stage. All Sanur tour agencies offer trips to these for about $10–15 including return transport, but it's usually cheaper to make your own way there and buy the fixed-price Rp50,000 tickets at the door.

Balinese dance performances are staged free for diners at some restaurants on Jalan Danau Tamblingan, with times and details advertised on boards outside: *Penjor* stages nightly shows from 7.30pm, with different dances on three successive nights; or try either *Swastika Garden 2*, next to *Bali Wirasana* hotel, or *Lotus Pond*, opposite *Bali Moon* in north-central Sanur. The *Grand Bali Beach* (T0361/288511) hosts a **cultural evening** which includes traditional dances and a buffet dinner (Mon, Wed & Fri from 7pm; $15). Most other top hotels stage similar events.

Shopping

Most **shopping** in Sanur is done in the shuttered stalls and glass-fronted boutiques along Jalan Danau Tamblingan and its arterial *gang*. These places offer the same range of designer clothes and "antique" handicrafts, books, jewellery, fabric and leatherware as Kuta, and though prices are higher, quality tends to be better.

For cheap cotton clothes, beachwear, sarongs, bamboo wind-chimes and woodcarvings, the best-value places to shop are the clusters of stalls known as "**art markets**". There are a couple of these alongside the beachfront walkway in north-central Sanur, one behind the *Desa Segara* hotel and the other a little further south, just before the *Bonsai Café*. The stall-holders near the *Bonsai Café* have a reputation for hassling tourists, so you may want to avoid even venturing in, but if you do, *Tootsies* at no. 39 has been recommended for its reasonable, fixed-price policy, and *Sarina* at no. 19 is said to be a good dressmaker.

There are small **bookstores**, selling mainly new books about Bali plus a few English-language novels, in the piazza next to *Gazebo* hotel, and inside the *Grand Bali Beach* and the *Sanur Beach* hotels; the supermarket on the corner of Jalan Duyung also stocks a reasonable selection.

Alas Alarum Jl Danau Tamblingan, central Sanur. The entire first floor of Sanur's main supermarket is devoted to local handicrafts, with a good choice of reasonably priced souvenirs ranging from baskets and sarongs to jewellery and woodcarvings. Everything is fixed-price and the quality is reasonably high. Among other things, the ground floor supermarket sells groceries, pharmacy items, sandals and motorbike helmets. Daily 9am–11pm.

Animale Next to *Bali Wirasana* hotel on Jl Danau Tamblingan, central Sanur. One of Bali's most popular womenswear chains, with a good line in well-made, loose-fitting trousers, dresses and tops in both plain cottons and bold prints.

Bé Opposite *Tandjung Sari* hotel, Jl Danau Tamblingan 80, central Sanur. Beautifully made, quality handicrafts, including palm-leaf photo albums and notebooks of hand-made paper, coconut-shell spoons, bowls and tablemats, and batik wallets.

Karina Across from *Bali Janger* at Jl Danau Tamblingan 34, north-central Sanur. All manner of basketwear handbags (made in Gianyar) in attractive and fashionable designs, ranging from traditional natural-coloured weaves to exuberant pink, yellow and green versions.

Kite Shop Jl Sindhu, north-central Sanur. Sanur is famous for its fantastic, creative, and often enormous kites, and for its annual inter-village kite festival which is held on the beach every July. This is one of several places where you can buy charismatic ready-made papier-mâché kite-creatures, and you can get them custom-made here too.

Mama & Leon Opposite *Griya Santrian* at Jl Danau Tamblingan 99a, central Sanur. Elegantly understated women's fashions in plain coloured natural fabrics. Reasonably priced.

Nogo Ikat Jl Danau Tamblingan 100, central Sanur. This is the flagship store of the chain of pricey but high-quality fabric shops that specializes in *ikat* cloth (also known as *endek*, see p.71). *Ikat* is sold by the metre, as well as being made up into bedspreads, tablecloths, cushion covers and clothes. They will also tailor-make almost anything on request.

Pisces Two branches on Jl Danau Tamblingan. Womenswear shop whose trademark clothes are all black and white, in innovative modern batik-style prints.

Sinar Bagus Kites Jl Danau Tamblingan, north-central Sanur. Great selection of kites, ready-made and designed to order, many of them built around papier-mâché bodies, including bats complete with viciously pointed teeth.

Uluwatu Several branches on Jl Danau Tamblingan in central and south Sanur. Balinese chain specializing in hand-made Balinese lace and good-quality womenswear made in white and cream cotton and linen.

Listings

Airline offices Most international airline offices (see p.111) are in Sanur, though the domestic airlines (see p.21) have their main offices in Denpasar. You can use the Garuda city check-in service (Mon–Fri 9am–3pm, Sat, Sun & hols 9am–noon; 24hr phoneline ℡0361/270535) at the Garuda offices inside the *Sanur Beach Hotel* in southern Sanur (℡0361/287915) or at the *Bali Hyatt* (℡0361/288011), but check-in must be completed the day before flying. Both offices also sell domestic and international Garuda tickets.

American Express Room 1111 inside the *Grand Bali Beach* in north Sanur (Mon–Fri 8.30am–4.30pm, Sat 8.30am–1pm; ℡0361/288449; toll-free number for lost cards and cheques ℡001-803-61005). Travellers' cheque refunds and help with lost cards, plus a poste restante service for Amex card and cheque holders (Poste Restante, c/o American Express, Room 1111, *Grand Bali Beach Hotel*, Sanur, Bali). Post is kept for one month. For poste restante faxes use the hotel fax number (℻0361/287917) and state clearly that it's for the Amex office. Amex also acts as a Moneygram agent; the money must be sent from an Amex agent and will be received as an Amex cheque in dollars, which can then be cashed into rupiah.

Banks and currency exchange There are ATMs for Cirrus, MasterCard and Visa dotted all over the resort. The best rates are from the exchange counters and booths across the resort; see p.36 for advice on how to avoid scams.

Cultural classes At *Segara Village* on Jl Segara Ayu (☎0361/288407): woodcarving, flower arranging, batik and Balinese dance courses by arrangement.

Email and internet There are email centres every few hundred metres in central Sanur, most of which charge Rp300–500/min and open daily from 8am–11pm. The most efficient places include: Ocha, opposite *Besakih* hotel at Jl Danau Tamblingan 84; the Environmental Information Centre (PIL) in the lobby of the *Hotel Santai*, Jl Danau Tamblingan 148; and the nearby UFO, near Legian Clinic 2. The *Grand Bali Beach* has three terminals in its lobby and charges a whopping $5 for the first ten minutes.

Embassies and consulates Only a few consulates have offices in Sanur. See p.23 for the full list.

Hospitals and clinics The efficient, tourist-oriented Legian Clinic 2, near the *Hotel Santai* on central Jl Danau Tamblingan ☎0361/287446 is open 24hr, has a full English-speaking staff, will respond to emergency call-outs, can perform minor surgery and charges Rp100,000 per consultation. A similar service is operated by Sanur Clinic at Jl Danau Tamblingan 27, central Sanur ☎0361/282678. SOS Sanur, c/o *Hotel Santai*, Jl Danau Tamblingan 148 ☎0361/287314, operates a 24hr emergency call-out service. All the major hotels provide 24hr medical service; if yours doesn't, try the doctor at the *Grand Bali Beach* (☎0361/288511) or the *Bali Hyatt* (☎0361/288271). The nearest hospitals are all in Denpasar; see p.103.

Library You can find information on the environment from the resource library at PPLH in the lobby of *Hotel Santai* at Jl Danau Tamblingan 148, central Sanur ☎0361/281648, ⓦwww.pplhbali.or.id.

Pharmacies Several on Jl Danau Tamblingan, as well as one inside the Alas Alarum Supermarket on central Jl Danau Tamblingan.

Phones There are plenty of private wartels in central Sanur, and direct dial public phones in the basement shopping arcade of the *Grand Bali Beach* in north Sanur.

Police The police station is on the Ngurah Rai Bypass in north Sanur, just south of the *Radisson* hotel.

Post office Sanur's main post office is on Jl Danau Buyan, north-central Sanur. There are numerous small postal agents throughout the resort, including at the wartel next to *Diwangkara* hotel on Jl Hang Tuah in north Sanur; opposite *Respati* hotel at Jl Danau Tamblingan 66 in central Sanur; and inside the Trophy Centre at the southern end of the same road. Most major hotels also offer general postal facilities. You can receive poste restante c/o Agen Pos, Jl Danau Tamblingan 66, Sanur 80228 (Mon–Fri 8.30am–5.30pm, Sat 8.30am–1pm).

Travel agents International and domestic flights, plus day-trips and organized tours, from Satriavi Tours (also the local Garuda agent), Jl Danau Tamblingan 27, south Sanur ☎0361/287074; Sumanindo Tour, Jl Danau Tamblingan 22, north-central Sanur ☎0361/288570, ⓔsumandps@ indosat.net.id; JBA, inside the compound of the *Diwangkara Hotel*, Jl Hang Tuah 54 in north Sanur ☎0361/286501, ⓔjbadwkbl@denpasar.wasantara.net.id; and Nagasari Tours, Jl Danau Tamblingan 102, central Sanur ☎0361/288096, ⓔnagasari@mega.net.id. Domestic flights and day-trips from Tunas Tour, next to *Resto Ming*, Jl Danau Tamblingan 102, south-central Sanur ☎0361/288581, ⓔtunas@denpasar.wasantara.net.id.

Serangan (Turtle) Island

A few hundred metres off southern Sanur's coastline, almost blocking the entrance to Benoa Harbour, lies the sandbar settlement of Pulau Serangan, more commonly referred to as **Serangan Island** or **Turtle Island**. The reefs around Serangan Island used to be popular with local snorkelling tours – and tourists used to visit the turtle breeding pens on the island too – but all this changed in the mid-1990s when big chunks of Serangan Island were bought up for a huge real-estate development project, **Bali Turtle Island Development** (BIDT). Phase One of this project, which originally centred around a huge hotel resort complex, involved connecting the island to the mainland by a kilometre-long causeway and tripling the size of the island by encircling it with "reclaimed" land made up of dredged sand and limestone. By the summer of 1997, this phase had been successfully completed and Pulau Serangan was no longer an island.

As with several other tourist-oriented mega-projects on Bali (including *Hotel Nirwana* at Tanah Lot, see p.376), the Serangan development caused a lot of local resentment, partly because it was associated with Tommy Suharto, the unpopular son of the former president, and partly because the land reclamation and destruction of mangrove forest around the island has caused a significant change in local tidal patterns – resulting in much faster **erosion** of Sanur's beaches (see p.162). Worse still, however, is the fact that Serangan is the site of an important temple, Pura Sakenan, whose outlook is now dominated by the new causeway. With the downfall of the whole Suharto family, the hotel project came to a standstill halfway through construction and the latest twist in the saga is the plan to build a golf course and **casino** on the island. Casinos are illegal in Muslim Indonesia, and gambling is an illegal (though still popular) activity on Bali, but this "island" off the archipelago's only Hindu enclave could be considered a special case – much to the continuing irritation of local groups. At the time of writing, the pro- and anti-development lobbies were at stalemate, though in response to the erosion problems in Sanur there is now talk of trying to restore some normality to the tidal flows by blowing up the causeway and replacing it with a bridge. In the meantime the World Bank has agreed to finance the restoration of Sanur's beaches.

As for Serangan's former tourist attractions, the surrounding **reefs** have all been pulverized into sand or buried beneath landfill, and the **turtles** – which were always a sorry sight anyway – have been moved to a plot on the northwest tip of Tanjung Benoa (see p.154 for more). Although lots of south Bali tour operators still advertise trips to see the reefs and turtles of Turtle Island, they actually cheat and take you to Tanjung Benoa instead – by boat of course so that you aren't disappointed. These tours are well worth missing.

Pura Sakenan

On the northwest coast of this small, beleaguered island stands **Pura Sakenan**, which is thought to have been founded in the sixteenth century by the Javanese priest Nirartha (the same man associated with the coastal temples at Tanah Lot, Uluwatu and Rambut Siwi). It figures very importantly in the spiritual life of the people of south Bali, for whom it's a public temple – as opposed to an ancestral or village temple. The **annual festival** held here at Kuningan (see p.56) is a huge event that lasts for several days and attracts throngs of worshippers in full ceremonial gear. At low tide when boats are unable to make the crossing, devotees have traditionally waded across the exposed mudflats from Tanjung Benoa, sarongs hoisted up around their knees and piles of offerings balanced on their heads. It is a scene that recurs in numerous traditional Balinese paintings but is fast being consigned to the history books now that cars, bemos and bikes can drive onto the island.

Benoa Harbour (Pelabuhan Benoa)

BENOA HARBOUR (Pelabuhan Benoa) is located off the end of a long causeway that juts out into the sea 5km southwest of southern Sanur, and is the arrival point for most of Bali's public and tourist **boat services,** including the

Bounty Cruise boat from Gili Meno and Lombok, the Mabua Express and *Osiana 3* from Lombok, all Pelni and Barito ships from elsewhere in Indonesia, plus cruise liners and sea planes.

Despite the shared name, there's just over a kilometre of sea between the harbour and the northern tip of the Tanjung Benoa peninsula (see p.147), and the journey between the two has to be done the long way round, by land. The easiest way to reach Benoa Harbour is by **metered taxi**; it's a short ride of about Rp20,000 from Sanur, or about Rp26,000 from Kuta, plus the Rp1000 toll. Occasional public **bemos** also run here from near Denpasar's Sanglah hospital, and there is also a sporadic return service.

Boats and sea planes

Tickets for **Pelni** boats to other islands must be bought in advance (booking opens three days before departure), either through travel agents or at the Pelni offices in Benoa Harbour (Mon–Fri 8am–4pm, Sat 8am–12.30pm; ☏0361/723689) or Kuta (see p.137). For more on Pelni, see p.20.

Bounty Cruise, **Mabua Express** and **Osiana 3** boats can be booked through almost any tour agent in the main tourist resorts, as can long-distance trips to other islands on the **Barito** express boats. Only Mabua includes transport from Kuta to Benoa Harbour in its prices. The main boat services include: with Bounty Cruise, express to Gili Meno and Lombok ($35); with Mabua, express to Lombok ($30); on *Osiana 3* to Lombok, via Padang Bai (Rp129,000); and with Barito, express to Surabaya on Java (Rp170,000), Bima on Sumbawa (Rp200,000), Maumere on Flores (Rp200,000), Waingapu on Sumba (Rp300,000), and Kupang on Timor (Rp425,000). See opposite for journey times and frequencies. Day cruises to Nusa Lembongan also depart from Benoa Harbour, but these are all-inclusive.

Benoa Harbour is also the main departure point for the **sea planes** run by Island Sea Planes (☏0361/728967, ⊛www.islandseaplanes.org). These can be chartered for fixed-route sightseeing flights (from $55 for a half-hour round-trip), or you can take a day-trip to and from Nusa Lembongan, with the option of returning by sailing boat ($125 day return). They can also be hired as private taxis, for example to get to Pemuteran on the northwest coast ($225; 30min). All prices are per person for a minimum of two people.

Travel details

Bemos and public buses

It's almost impossible to give the **frequency with** which bemos and public buses run, as they only depart when they have enough passengers to make the journey worthwhile. However, on the most popular routes, you should be able to count on getting a ride within half-an-hour if you travel before noon; things quieten down in the afternoon and come to a standstill by around 5pm. **Journey times** also vary a great deal: the times given below are the minimum you can expect.

Only the direct bemo and bus routes are listed below. As most of south Bali's bemos run through Denpasar, you'll probably need to change at one of

Denpasar's four main bemo stations to get further afield (full details on p.94).

Bualu to: Denpasar (Batubulan terminal; 1hr); Denpasar (Tegal terminal; 35min); Kuta (20min); Ngurah Rai Airport (20min).

Denpasar (Batubulan terminal) to: Amlapura (2hr 30min); Bualu (1hr); Candi Dasa (1hr); Gianyar (1hr); Klungkung (1hr 20min); Mas (35min); Padang Bai (for Lombok; 1hr 40min); Sukawati (20min); Ubud (50min).

Denpasar (Kereneng terminal) to: Sanur (15–25min).

Denpasar (Tegal terminal) to: Jimbaran (40min); Kuta (25min); Ngurah Rai Airport (35min); Nusa Dua (35min); Sanur (25min).

Denpasar (Ubung terminal) to: Bedugul (1hr 30min); Gilimanuk (3hr 15min); Jakarta (Java; 24hr); Kediri (for Tanah Lot; 30min); Lalang Linggah (for Balian Beach; 1hr 15min); Medewi (1hr 30min); Mengwi (30min); Singaraja (Sukasada terminal; 3hr); Solo (Java; 15hr); Surabaya (Java; 10hr); Tabanan (35min); Yogyakarta (Java; 15hr).

Denpasar (Wangaya terminal) to: Sangeh Monkey Forest (45min).

Jimbaran to: Denpasar (Tegal terminal; 40min); Kuta (15min); Ngurah Rai Airport (10min).

Kuta to: Bualu (20min); Denpasar (Tegal terminal; 25min); Jimbaran (15min); Ngurah Rai Airport (10min).

Ngurah Rai Airport to: Bualu (20min); Denpasar (Tegal terminal; 35min); Jimbaran (10min); Kuta (10min).

Sanur to: Denpasar (Kereneng terminal; 15–25min); Denpasar (Tegal terminal; 25min).

Perama shuttle buses

STO = overnight stopover is sometimes needed
Kuta to: Air Sanih (1 daily; 5hr 30min); Bangsal (1 daily; 9hr 30min); Bedugul (1 daily; 2hr 30min–3hr); Bima (2 daily; STO); Candi Dasa (3 daily; 3hr); Jakarta (1 daily; 25–26hr); Kintamani (1 daily; 2hr 45min); Mataram (2 daily; 8hr 30min); Ngurah Rai Airport (6 daily; 30min): Kuta, Lombok (1 daily; STO); Lovina (2 daily; 3hr); Malang (1 daily; 16–17hr); Nusa Lembongan (1 daily; 2hr 30min); Padang Bai (3 daily; 2hr 30min); Sanur (7 daily; 30min); Sape (2 daily; STO); Senggigi (2 daily; 9hr); Surabaya (1 daily; 12–13hr); Tetebatu (1 daily; STO); Tirtagangga (1 daily; 4hr); Tulamben (1 daily; 5hr); Ubud (7 daily; 1hr–1hr 30min); Yogyakarta (1 daily; 16–17hr).
Sanur to: Air Sanih (1 daily; 4hr 30min–5hr); Bangsal (1 daily; 9hr); Bedugul (1 daily; 2hr–2hr 30min); Bima (2 daily; STO); Candi Dasa (3 daily; 2hr–2hr 30min); Jakarta (1 daily; 25–26hr); Kintamani (1 daily; 2hr 15min); Kuta/Ngurah Rai airport (6 daily; 30min–1hr); Kuta, Lombok (2 daily; STO); Lovina (2 daily; 2hr 30min–3hr); Malang (1 daily; 16–17hr); Mataram (2 daily; 8hr); Padang Bai (3 daily; 1hr 30min–2hr); Sape (2 daily; STO); Senggigi (2 daily; 8hr 30min); Surabaya (1 daily;

12–13hr); Tetebatu (2 daily; STO); Tirtagangga (1 daily; 3hr 30min); Tulamben (1 daily; 4hr–4hr 30min); Ubud (7 daily; 30min–1hr); Yogyakarta (1 daily; 16–17hr).

Boats

Pelni

For more on Pelni, see p.20.

Denpasar (Benoa Harbour) Except where indicated, fortnightly services to: Badas (16hr); Balikpapan (3 days); Bima (twice a fortnight; 31hr); Bitung (twice a fortnight; 4 days); Ende (2 days); Gorontalo (4–5 days); Jayapura (5 days); Kupang (3 times a fortnight; 26hr); Labuhanbajo (twice a fortnight; 2 days); Larantuka (36hr); Makassar (3 times a fortnight; 2 days); Maumere (3 days); Pantoloan (3 days); Surabaya (twice a fortnight; 15hr); Tanjung Priok (39hr); Waingapu (26hr).

Others

Benoa Harbour to: Bima (Sumbawa; 1–2 weekly by Barito express; 7hr); Gili Meno (daily by Bounty Cruise; 2hr 30min); Kupang (Timor; 1 weekly by Barito express; 20hr); Lembar (Lombok; 1 direct boat daily by Mabua Express; 2hr; also 1 daily via Padang Bai on *Osiania 3*; 3hr 15min); Maumere (Flores; 1 weekly by Barito express; 12hr); Surabaya (Java; 1 weekly by Barito express; 7hr); Teluk Nara/Senggigi (Lombok; daily by Bounty Cruise; 3hr) and Waingapu (Sumba; 1 weekly by Barito express; 13hr).

Sanur to: Jungutbatu (Nusa Lembongan; 3 daily; 1hr 30min).

Domestic flights

Denpasar (Ngurah Rai Airport) to: Bima (6 weekly; 1hr 15min); Dili (2 daily; 1hr 50min); Jakarta (6 daily; 1hr 40min); Kupang (2–3 daily; 1hr 35min); Labuhanbajo (5 weekly; 1hr 45min–2hr 20min); Makassar (2–3 daily; 1hr 15min); Mataram (6 daily; 30min); Maumere (daily; 2hr 20min); Sumbawa (2 weekly; 1hr 40min); Surabaya (4–5 daily; 50min); Waingapu (3 weekly; 1hr 50min); Yogyakarta (3 daily; 1hr 10min).

Ubud and around

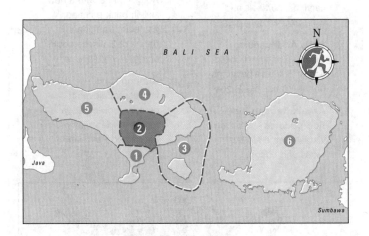

CHAPTER 2 # Highlights

* **Bali Bird Park** – A vast and beautifully landscaped aviary, with elusive Bali starlings in residence. See p.180

* **Sukawati Art Market** – A great place for bargain-price baskets, sarongs, paintings, fabrics, wood-carvings, parasols and wind-chimes. See p.182

* **Neka Art Museum, Ubud** – The finest collection of Balinese paintings on the island. See p.206

* **A walk through the rice-paddies** – Classic vistas of emerald terraces and coconut groves, framed by distant volcanoes. See p.205

* **Traditional dance performances** – Gods and demons flirt and fight by torchlight. See p.221

* **Cultural classes** – Return home with a new skill in batik painting, gamelan, traditional dance or Balinese cookery. See p.225

* **Gunung Kawi** – Impressive eleventh-century rock-cut royal tombs in the valley of the sacred Pakrisan River. See p.237

Ubud and around

The inland village of **Ubud** and its surrounding area form Bali's cultural heartland, home to a huge proliferation of temples, museums and art galleries, where Balinese dance shows are staged nightly and a wealth of arts and crafts studios provide the most absorbing shopping on the island. It's also surrounded by a stunning physical environment – a lush landscape watered by hundreds of streams (including Bali's longest waterway, the Ayung River), with archetypal terraced paddy vistas at every turn – all of which gives plenty of scope for leisurely hikes and bicycle rides. In addition, Ubud's elevated position in the hills means that the air feels noticeably cooler than at the steaming coastal resorts. The route to Ubud **north of Denpasar** takes you through a string of craft villages dubbed the "tourist corridor", a great shopping experience where you can also watch craftspeople at work. You'll need to venture out to the villages around Ubud, however, for a sense of old-fashioned Bali – to the classic adobe-walled settlements of **Penestanan** and **Peliatan**, for example, or to **Pejeng**, which still boasts relics from its Bronze Age inhabitants.

Tour agents from every major resort organize day-trips into this region, but a longer stay is far more rewarding and, together with the smaller villages on its perimeters, Ubud has hundreds of losmen and hotels to choose from, spanning all price ranges. Ubud and all the other villages described in this chapter lie within the boundaries of **Gianyar district**, formerly an ancient kingdom. (Gianyar itself, 10km east of Ubud, lies on the main route into east Bali and is described in Chapter 3, as are all the villages east of the T-junction at Sakah.) Roads within the Ubud region tend to run north–south down river valleys, making it very difficult in places to travel east–west; this chapter reflects that restriction, and follows the main bemo routes.

Ubud has always played second fiddle to the royal and political centre of Gianyar, and it has only been with the advent of mass tourism in the last few decades that it has assumed such a dominant role. Ubud's development is closely bound to the fortunes of the **Sukawati family**, who for centuries ruled over much of Gianyar regency from their court, 10km south of Ubud. The Sukawati royal household was established in the early eighteenth century by **Dewa Agung Anom**, who called in musicians, dancers, puppeteers, artists and sculptors from all over the island to live and work at his court. This was the foundation of the strong **artistic** heritage of the area, and over the next two hundred years, Dewa Agung Anom's like-thinking descendants established satellite courts in Peliatan, Ubud and Singapadu, among others.

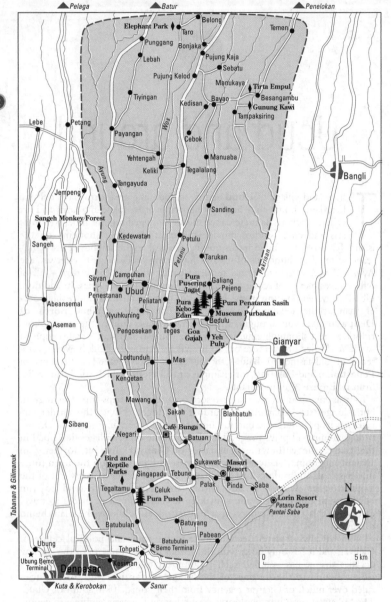

Gianyar was one of only two kingdoms to remain intact after the **Dutch** takeover in 1908, and it became the island's centre for royal patronage of the arts, with Ubud, in particular, flourishing under the rule of Cokorda Gede Agung Sukawati. The 1930s saw the arrival of a bevy of expat artists in Ubud, injecting a new vigour into the region's **arts and crafts**, which have thrived ever since.

North of Denpasar

The stretch of road running 13km **north of Denpasar** to Ubud has become something of a sightseeing attraction in itself due to the almost unbroken string of **arts- and crafts-producing villages** that line its course. Over the last decade, these villages have mushroomed so dramatically that they now merge into each other, coalescing into one extended shopping experience. Despite the obvious commercialization, these villages all have genuine histories as centres of refined artistic activity. Most villages were renowned as specialists of a certain craft, and this trend continues today; **Mas**, for example, is the place for woodcarvings, and **Batubulan** for stone sculptures.

Nearly all the craft villages described below lie on the main **bemo** route between Denpasar's **Batubulan terminal** and Ubud, which makes transport very easy – although since most villages extend quite a way from end to end, it's worth trying to give bemo drivers as precise directions as possible. There's nowhere much **to stay** along this route: the majority of visitors pass through the area on a day-trip from Kuta, Sanur or Nusa Dua, or base themselves in Ubud and make their excursions out from there. Access from Sanur is particularly easy, with Batubulan less than 10km north of Sanur's northern outskirts.

Batubulan

Barely distinguishable from the northeastern suburbs of Denpasar, **BATUBULAN** acts as the capital's public transport interchange for all bemos heading east and northeast, but it's also an important village in its own right, home of the most famous *barong* **dance troupes**, and respected across the island for its superb stonecarvers. There's also a **bird park** and a **reptile park** here.

The village is strung out over 2.5km along the main road, defined by the bemo station in the south and the huge Barong statue at the Singapadu/Celuk junction in the north. Beyond the Barong statue, along the minor road to Singapadu, the northern stretch of the village – known as **Tegaltamu** – is the most interesting bit, and it's here that you'll find the shops selling Batubulan's finest **stonecarvings**, displayed to their best advantage in disorderly ranks along the roadside. Local sculptors specialize in free-standing images, using the distinctive rough grey lava stone known as *paras*, whose texture gains great character after a few months' exposure to the elements, and smooth, almost crumbly sandstones which come in grey, yellow and pink hues. As with all other artistic disciplines in Bali, you'll find that the stonecarvers here tend to copy each others' ideas a lot, and the same pieces recur in pretty much every workshop and storefront. These include all sorts of demons and deities, mythological and religious figures, as well as pigs, monkeys, fish and people. The elephant god Ganesh is a hugely popular subject, as are *garuda*, the *raksasa* giants that guard every temple gateway, and Buddha heads.

There are plenty of outlets in which to browse, but particularly good are Rote Adhi (opposite the entrance to the Bird Park) and Yuliani, further south on the east side of the main road, between Pura Puseh and the Bird Park. In among the stonecarving outlets, you'll come across a number of eye-catching **woodcarving** places, which specialize in elegant antique-style furniture, doors and window frames; avoid the large, multipurpose emporia at the southern end of the village, which cater for tour groups and overcharge for unexciting goods.

Pura Puseh

As you'd expect in a village so renowned for its fine carvings, the main temple, **Pura Puseh**, 200m east off the main road in the north of the village (follow the signs for the *barong* dance held next door), is exuberantly decorated. It's built to an unusual design which includes a five-tiered gateway tower inspired by Indian religious architecture, and a number of Buddha images not normally associated with Bali's Hindu temples. The rest of the icons and decorations, however, are characteristically and flamboyantly Balinese: a grimacing Bhoma head overlooks the main gateway and, to his right, the god Wisnu poses proudly astride a bull; to the right of him, Siwa stands ankle-deep in skulls and wears a string of them around his neck, while majestic elephant torsos protrude from the central stairway balustrade.

Traditional dance shows

The plot adjacent to Pura Puseh has been given over to a purpose-built **barong dance** stage, where, every morning of the year (daily 9.30–10.30am; Rp50,000), the local dance troupes perform the spectacular drama of the fight between good and evil, as represented by the shaggy-haired lion-like creature, the Barong Ket, and the macabre widow-witch Rangda. It's quite feasible to get here by public bemo (see below), but most spectators come on tours arranged through agents in Kuta, Sanur or Ubud.

If you come under your own steam, consider attending the well-regarded show at the Denjulan Barong and Kris stage instead (daily 9.30–10.30am; Rp50,000), whose dancers are said to be the best in the region. The Denjulan stage is 300m south down the main Denpasar road from the Pura Puseh junction.

Batubulan dancers also put on nightly performances of the **kecak dance** in a double bill with the **fire dance** (daily 6.30–7.30pm; Rp50,000) at the Barong Sahadewa stage, signed off the main Denpasar road about 500m south of the Pura Puseh junction.

Bali Bird Park and Bali Reptile Park

Both the Bali Bird Park and the Bali Reptile Park (not to be confused with the vastly inferior reptile park in Mengwi) are fun places for children and fairly interesting for adults, too. The parks are right next door to each other, about 500m beyond the Barong statue at the Singapadu/Celuk intersection, or about 3km northwest of Batubulan bemo terminal. All bemos between Batubulan and Ubud or Gianyar can drop you at the intersection. Both parks have the same **opening hours** and ticket prices (daily 8am–6pm; $7.50, kids $3.80, joint ticket for both parks $14/$7). Bali Adventure Tours (☎0361/721480) runs a **tour** to them and the Elephant Safari Park (see p.236), with transport, admission prices and lunch included ($62, kids $43; family discounts available). There's a good but expensive **restaurant** inside the Bird Park, or you can get cheap food at a tiny warung about 30m outside the car park.

The **Bali Bird Park (Taman Burung)** is beautifully laid out with ponds, pavilions, flowers and an impressive array of birds, all identified with English-language labels. Highlights include various birds of paradise (most of them from Irian Jaya), bright scarlet egrets, the weird-looking rhino hornbill, a massive pair of cassowaries and iridescent blue Javanese kingfishers, which you should be able to catch sight of in the rice-fields around Ubud. You shouldn't miss this rare chance to see the fluffy white Bali starling, Bali's only endemic bird and a severely endangered species (it's thought there may be as few as six left in the wild); see the box on p.398 for more.

All the creatures at the **Bali Reptile Park (Rimba Reptil)** are informatively labelled: look out for the green tree pit viper which is very common in Bali, and very dangerous, as well as for the astonishing eight-metre-long reticulated python, thought to be the largest python in captivity in the world. The Komodo dragons here are only about a metre long and not that interesting but you're welcome to pick up and cuddle one of the park's scaly green iguanas.

Practicalities

Batubulan's **bemo station** is at the far southern end of the village, well organized with clearly signed bays for each destination. Chocolate-brown bemos from Batubulan to **Ubud** (50min; Rp5000; last departure 5.30pm) travel via Celuk, Sukawati and Mas. Destinations east of Batubulan are served by both dark blue and fawn-coloured bemos, which run through Gianyar, Klungkung, **Padang Bai** and **Candi Dasa** on their way to **Amlapura** (Rp10,000; last departure 5.30pm). Bemos across **Denpasar** to the Kereneng or Ubung terminals (see plan on p.92) cost Rp2000. **Buses** also depart from Batubulan bemo station on the same route to Amlapura, as well as to **Kintamani** via Tegalalang (Rp5000; last departure 2pm), and to **Singaraja** (Rp7000; last departure 2pm). White Damri buses also run to **Nusa Dua**, via the western edge of Sanur and the eastern outskirts of Kuta (Rp3000).

There's nowhere to stay in Batubulan, and the only recommended **restaurant** is the exceptionally good Sumatran-style *Masakan Padang* place on the southern approach to the village, before you reach the bemo station. There's no nameboard, but the window display is always piled high with bowls full of the distinctive daily fare: everything from fish curry and spinach stir-fried with chillies to fried tuna steaks. The bemo terminal is transformed into a **night market** every evening, with a good selection of street food and food carts.

Singapadu and the back road to Ubud

The main road from Denpasar divides at Batubulan's Barong statue roundabout, the principal artery and bemo routes veering right (east) to Celuk (see below), and the left-hand (north) prong narrowing into an exceptionally scenic **back road**. This runs past the Bali Bird Park and on through very traditional villages as far as Sayan, a few kilometres west of Ubud, before continuing to Payangan and eventually to Kintamani.

Just over 1km north of the T-junction, you'll pass through the charming village of **SINGAPADU**, a classic central Bali settlement that hides behind its low roadside walls. The bright reds, purples, yellows and oranges of frangipani, bougainvillea, hibiscus and champak flowers bloom dramatically against the muted walls, while the thatched roof towers of household shrines rise up behind, backed by vibrant green rice terraces. Some of Bali's most expert mask-carvers come from this village, but as most of them work only on commissions from temples and dance troupes there's no obvious commercial face to the local industry.

Some 13km north of Singapadu the road runs through the village of **SAYAN**, located in the spectacular Ayung River valley, site of several superb hotels (see p.200) and a couple of **whitewater rafting** centres (see p.125). The American composer and ethnomusicologist Colin McPhee lived here for several years in the 1930s with his anthropologist wife Jane Belo, and Sayan village life is described in great detail in his book, *A House in Bali*. To reach Ubud from Sayan, follow the narrow right-hand turning off the main road, which will take you 3km down a winding route via Penestanan to Campuhan, where you turn right for Ubud.

For a more direct, quieter and even more scenic route to Ubud, turn east off the Sayan road a couple of kilometres north of Singapadu, in the heart of the village of **NEGARI**. This route soon takes you over a wide river, just beyond which there's a junction: the northern arm leads you through delightful countryside via the art galleries and mask-making workshops of **LODTUNDUH** before arriving in Pengosekan near the ARMA museum on the southern edge of Ubud (see p.216), about 4km in total from the bridge. But it's worth detouring along the eastbound arm towards Batuan for 400m to enjoy coffee and cake at the *Café Bunga* restaurant and **East Bali Poverty Project charity centre**, whose menu includes delicious lemongrass tea and other herbal infusions, plus cappuccinos, home-made cakes and wholesome sandwiches. All profits go to the East Bali Poverty Project (see p.34; Ⓦwww.eastbalipovertyproject.org) whose inspiring work with malnourished and uneducated children is described in displays around the café's walls. You can also buy products made by the villagers and learn about their anti-erosion and organic farming techniques.

Celuk

Strung out along the main road just east of Batubulan, in between large swathes of paddy-field, is **CELUK**, known as the "silver village" because of its reputation as a major centre for **jewellery**. The local silversmiths have extended their homes to include workshops and salerooms, though they are now having to compete with far wealthier outside entrepreneurs whose goods are factory-produced. Nevertheless, if you head down any of the tiny *gang* leading north off the main eastbound road, you can watch individual artisans at work. You'll find all sorts of earrings, bracelets, chains, necklaces and rings on sale, but the range of designs is unimaginative compared with outlets in Kuta or Ubud and not inexpensive either.

Batubulan–Ubud **bemos** pass through Celuk, but as the shops and workshops are spread out over a three-kilometre stretch, you'd be advised to wait for a kilometre or so before you get out, until you see the small lanes off to the left.

Sukawati and around

The lively market town of **SUKAWATI**, 4km east of Celuk, is a major commercial centre for local villagers and a chief stop on the tourist arts and crafts shopping circuit, especially convenient for anyone reliant on public transport: Batubulan–Ubud **bemos** stop right in front of the central marketplace.

Sukawati's chief draw is its **art market** (*pasar seni*), at the heart of the village, which trades every day from dawn till dusk inside a traditional covered two-storey building. Here you'll find a tantalizing array of artefacts, paintings, fabrics, clothing and basketware, piled high on stalls that are crammed together so tightly you can barely walk between them. There doesn't seem to be a huge amount of method in the chaos, so if you're looking for something specific it's worth asking to be pointed in the right direction. Sarongs, light blankets, and lengths of *ikat* cloth are all excellent buys, as are ceremonial temple parasols and huge decorative fans made from gold-stamped *perada* cloth, palm baskets, bamboo wind-chimes and woodcarvings. Prices are very reasonable if you bargain – so much so that coachloads of domestic tourists flock here to do their shopping. If you can't face the scrum in the market, head for the several good basket shops on the main road, just to the north.

Sukawati is also famous for its *wayang kulit* **shadow puppet makers and performers**. *Wayang kulit* shows are still very popular across the island, and puppet masters (*dalang*) are often commissioned to entertain villagers at temple festivals with performances of traditional Hindu legends such as the *Mahabharata* that run right through the night. The puppets (*wayang*) they use are made out of very thin animal hide, perforated to let the light shine through in intricate patterns, and designed to traditional profiles that are instantly recognizable to a Balinese audience (for more, see p.527). Several of Sukawati's *dalang* make, and perform with, both *wayang kulit* puppets and the wooden *wayang golek* puppets, selling their creations from workshops inside their homes (prices start at Rp200,000): **I Wayan Nartha** (℡0361/299080) has a shop on Jalan Padma (the road that runs east off the main Ubud road, one block south of the Pasar Seni); and **I Wayan Mardika** (℡0361/299646) sells from inside his home, which is on the road that runs parallel to the east of the main road, reached by walking east down Jalan Ciung Wanara (opposite the *pasar seni*) and then turning left about 100m. Both workshops are in the *banjar* of Babakan and are signed off the main road.

Just outside the *pasar seni*, a small warung-cum-grocery store serves **food** throughout the day, mainly nasi goreng and variations on the same theme but good enough. The *Masakan Padang* place, across the main road from the *pasar seni*, next to the covered *pasar umum* fruit and vegetable market, lets you make your selection from a tasty choice of cold Sumatran curries, stews and fry-ups. *Depot Mulya*, a couple of blocks north of the markets on the east side of the road, serves up perfectly decent noodles, *bakso* and nasi campur at very cheap prices.

To Pantai Saba and the coast

If you're in Sukawati with your own transport, you might consider making a side trip down to the black-sand beach of **Pantai Saba** (shown on some maps as **Petanu Cape**), not least because it's an excuse to absorb some typical inland scenery en route as you snake your way through broad flat expanses of paddyfield, punctuated by the occasional settlement and the odd coconut, papaya, and banana grove. Even on a bicycle it makes quite a feasible day-trip from Ubud or even Sanur.

The easiest route **from Sukawati** is to follow the signs for the *Lorin Resort Saba Bai*, which lead you east off Sukawati's main road and all the way down to the posh *Lorin* hotel on the coast. On the way, you pass through the village of **PALAK**, with signs for the new *Bali Masari Resort* in the *banjar* of Gelumpang (℡0361/290029, ℉290050, ⓦwww.masari-resorts.com; published rates from $300; ⑨), a luxurious retreat comprising twelve self-catering villas with private plunge pools overlooking the Petanu River valley and enjoying fine panoramas of the surrounding hills, paddies and palm groves.

The road continues through **Pinda**, home of one of the best gamelan orchestras in Bali, and then through the village of **Saba**, famous for its *legong* dancers, before finally hitting the new coastal road, about 6km in total from Sukawati market. This new road is Stage One in a plan that aims to develop the tourist potential of this whole stretch of coast, and will run all the way from Ketewel, near Pabean, to Kusamba, 10km short of Padang Bai; using it to drive **from Sanur** is fairly straightforward as it's perfectly driveable as far as the *Lorin*, though still unsurfaced in parts.

PANTAI SABA has suffered a fair amount of erosion recently, not least from the Petanu River, which flows into the sea here. However, at low tide the band of coal-black sand is still a magnificent sight, glittering in the sunlight and adding a glacial blue sheen to the waves crashing against the offshore reef. The undertow is way too strong for swimming here, but you can paddle in the rockpools. Beyond the reef, the hilly profiles of Nusa Lembongan (to the left) and Nusa Penida (to the right) are clearly visible and if you look back to the mainland you'll see Gunung Agung, rising up as if out of nowhere. If you want to linger, you can **stay** on the seafront at the *Lorin Villa Resort Saba Bai* (℡0361/297070, ℱ297171, ⓦwww.lorinresortsababai.com; ➒), though only the most expensive of the villas here enjoys a sea view. The villas are ranged around a tropical garden with a swimming pool, spa centre, library and restaurant, and there's free transport to Ubud and Denpasar.

Batuan

Northern Sukawati merges into southern **BATUAN**, another ribbon-like roadside development, which was the original home of the **Batuan style of painting** and is now a commercial centre for all the main Balinese styles. The Batuan style first evolved in the 1930s when a group of young villagers, notably Ida Bagus Made Togog and Ida Bagus Made Wija, started experimenting with ink-washed paintings on black backgrounds, peopling their visions with dozens of figures cowering beneath ominously dense forests. Later the artists changed to gouache, and then acrylics, but the atmosphere remained just as forbidding and the canvases just as congested and full of minute detail, creating a sense of frenetic activity.

The public face of modern Batuan is now dominated by **galleries**, a disappointing number of which pander to the least discriminating tour groups, churning out endless pastel reproductions of uninspiring bird and flower compositions. There are some notable exceptions, however, many of them hidden in houses in the traditional core of the village, west of the main road, with "painter" signboards hanging above their gateways. One of the larger galleries is the **I Wayan Bendi Gallery**, on the west side of the main road, named after a contemporary artist whose Batuan-style pictures have been exhibited all over the world. A few examples of his work hang in the gallery (not for sale) along with a sizeable collection by other artists. Prices are fairly high, with nothing much under $200, but the quality is excellent. Another worthwhile if undeniably commercial gallery is **Dewa Putu Toris**, 250m west off the southern end of the main Batuan–Ubud road in the *banjar* of Tengah: just follow the signs. It's a huge emporium with a fair share of tat, but plenty of well-executed works as well, including interesting modern pieces plus some unusually fine Pengosekan-style paintings; staff are well informed and prices range from Rp200,000 to Rp10,000,000.

At the northern limit of Batuan, a plump stone **statue** of a prosperous-looking Buddha (sometimes referred to as the Fat Baby Statue) marks the Sakah turn-off to Blahbatuh and points east (see p.250), while the main road continues north.

Mas and Teges

Long established as a major **woodcarving** centre, **MAS** is a rewarding place both to browse and to buy, but as it stretches 5km from end to end, you'll need plenty of time or your own transport to do it justice.

The woodcarvers of Mas gained great inspiration from the Pita Maha arts movement during the 1930s (see box on p.202), which encouraged the carving of secular subjects as well as the more traditional masks and religious images. Today the range of carvings on display in the Mas shops is enormous; you'll find superbly imaginative portraits of legendary creatures and erotic human figures, alongside tacky cats, dogs and fish. Some of the woodcarving outlets in Mas are managed by the carvers and their families, while others buy their pieces in from less commercially minded villagers.

A good place to start is the studio of one of Bali's most famous woodcarving families, the **Nyana Tilem Gallery**, located approximately half-way along the Mas–Ubud road. Born in 1912, Ida Bagus Nyana (also spelt Njana) was one of the most prolific and innovative craftsmen in the 1930s and 1940s, closely associated with the Pita Maha arts movement, and credited with introducing the sleek, simple and slightly surreal style of elongated figures that's now so popular across the island (for more, see p.536). The Mas gallery was founded by his son Ida Bagus Tilem who has continued the quest for new forms and is especially renowned for highly expressive pieces using gnarled and twisted wood. It has plenty of works by father and son on show, alongside a huge range of other carvings, including valuable collectors' items from the 1930s and 1940s, plus plenty of more affordable pieces created by contemporary woodcarvers working for the gallery.

The large and impressive **Tantra Gallery**, housed in two buildings on either side of the main road, about 500m south of Nyana Tilem, is run by Ida Bagus Tilem's younger brother, Tantra. All the works sold here are contemporary, mostly high-quality interpretations of fairly standard subjects, such as elegantly tapered hands, masks, chess sets and weeping Buddhas; prices are on the high side, but everything is finely crafted. The Tantra compound on the east side of the road also contains a delightful small hotel (see below).

About 300m north of the Nyana Tilem Gallery, in among a knot of workshops on the west side of the main road, it's worth seeking out the tiny shop **Wayan Mendra**, belonging to a superb craftsman whose highlights are exquisite carvings of the elephant god Ganesh, each of which take a month to complete. North another 300m, on the west side of the road, the showroom of the **Nyoman Togog** gallery is a huge supermarket of a place specializing in lifelike carvings of fruit. Even if the idea of replica rambutans, mandarins, bananas and mangosteens doesn't appeal, it's hard not to be impressed by the sheer class of the imitations displayed here.

Practicalities

All Batubulan–Ubud **bemos** zip through Mas, but be prepared for a long walk if you get off in the wrong part of the village. At its northern end, Mas runs into the village of Teges, and can also just about be reached on foot from Peliatan on the outskirts of Ubud. There are **warung** at intervals along the Mas road, but nothing outstanding. The charming *Taman Harum Cottages* (℡0361/975567, ℻975149, ⓦwww.tamanharumcottages.com; ❼–❽) is currently the only **place to stay** in Mas, located in the compound of Tantra Gallery, at the southern end of the village. The standard rooms in its small two-storey block are pleasant if not exceptional, but the two-storey villas and suites are delightful and excellent value, affording fine rice-field views from upstairs; they're especially recommended for families with children, and should be reserved well ahead. All rooms are air-conditioned, there's a pool and a restaurant, free transport to Ubud, and a popular programme of **cultural classes** such as cooking, woodcarving, batik painting and making temple offerings.

Museum Rudana, Teges

Sandwiched between Mas to the south and Peliatan to the north, the main attraction in the woodcarving village of **TEGES** is the **Museum Rudana** (daily 9am–6pm; Rp10,000), 200m north of the Nyoman Togog gallery in Mas (see above) and about 1500m south of the southern end of Jalan Peliatan, a ten-minute bemo ride from central Ubud (Rp1000) or an hour's walk. The museum focuses on an overview of **Balinese painting**, from Kamasan-style traditional calendars through Batuan-style and Ubud-style pictures to contemporary works. Many of the artists represented here also feature in the Neka Art Museum (see p.206) and the Agung Rai Museum of Art (see p.216); there's more information on the history of Balinese art on pp.530–534. The best thing about this collection – apart from the inspiring rice-paddy views out of the picture windows – is the informative labelling. Each picture has a caption that discusses the subject of the painting rather than the artistic style, so you can learn a fair bit about temple festivities for example, about certain Balinese dances and Hindu legends, and about the Balinese attitude to the sea. The collection of contemporary work in the **basement gallery** is especially good, unrivalled by any art museum in Ubud. Artists to look out for here include Made Budhiana and Nyoman Erawan, both of whom are associated with the influential Sanggar Dewata Indonesia style, best described as Balinese Hindu abstract expressionism, which has been the dominant form of modern Balinese painting since the 1970s.

Ubud

Ever since the German artist Walter Spies arrived here in 1928, **UBUD** has been a magnet for any tourist with the slightest curiosity about Balinese arts. Though its evolution into a fully fledged resort is fairly recent, Ubud is now firmly established on the tourist trail, visited by nearly every holidaymaker on the island – if only as part of a day-trip to the much-publicized Monkey Forest.

Although it's fashionable to characterize Ubud as the "real" Bali, especially in contrast with Kuta, it bears little resemblance to a typical Balinese village. Cappuccino cafés and chic boutiques crowd its central marketplace and, during peak season, foreigners seem to far outnumber local residents. There is major development along the central **Monkey Forest Road** (now officially named **Jalan Wanara Wana**), a kilometre-long, almost continuous strip of hotels, restaurants, tour agencies and souvenir shops and the village has expanded to take in the neighbouring hamlets of **Campuhan**, **Penestanan**, **Sanggingan**, **Nyuhkuning**, **Padang Tegal**, **Pengosekan** and **Peliatan**. Yet the traditional village of dancers and craftspeople is still apparent, and the atmosphere remains undeniably seductive – an appealing blend of ethnic integrity and tourist-friendly comforts. The people of Ubud and adjacent villages really do still paint, carve, dance and make music, and religious practices here are so rigorously observed that hardly a day goes by without there being some kind of festival celebrated in the area.

The surrounding countryside and traditional hamlets give ample opportunity for exploration on foot or by bike, and **shopping** tends to become a major pastime too, with Balinese carvers and painters selling their wares at every corner and a proliferation of outlets run by expat fashion designers and artists. But, above all, it's the **restaurants** and **accommodation** that set Ubud apart from Bali's other tourist centres: mouthwatering menus of imaginative wholesome fare are the norm here, and most hotels and homestays make full use of their charming locations. An increasing number of travellers are now choosing to stay in Ubud for the duration of their holiday, using it as a convenient base

△ Rock carvings, Yeh Pulu

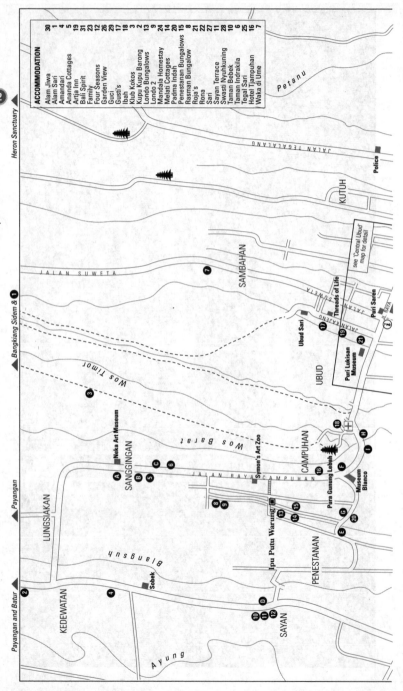

ACCOMMODATION

Alam Jiwa	30
Alam Sari	1
Amandari	4
Ananda Cottages	5
Artja Inn	19
Bali Spirit	31
Family	23
Four Seasons	12
Garden View	26
Guci	29
Gusti's	17
Ibah	18
Klub Kokos	3
Kupu Kupu Barong	2
Londo Bungalows	13
Londo 2	9
Mandala Homestay	24
Melati Cottages	14
Padma Indah	15
Penestanan Bungalows	8
Rasman Bungalow	20
Roja's	21
Rona	22
Sari	27
Sayan Terrace	11
Swasti Nyuhkuning	28
Taman Bebek	10
Taman Indrakila	6
Tegal Sari	25
Hotel Tjampuhan	16
Waka di Ume	7

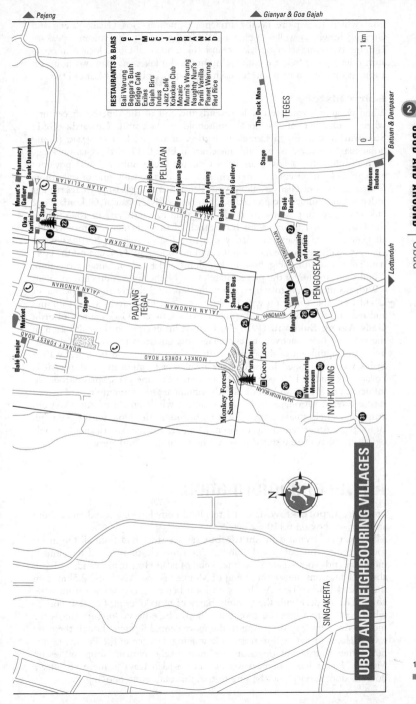

UBUD AND NEIGHBOURING VILLAGES

▲ Pejeng   ▲ Gianyar & Goa Gajah

RESTAURANTS & BARS

Bali Warung	G
Beggar's Bush	F
Bridge Café	I
Exiles	M
Gajah Biru	E
Indus	C
Jazz Café	J
Kokokan Club	L
Mozaic	B
Murni's Warung	H
Naughty Nuri's	A
Panili Vanilla	N
Planet Warung	K
Red Rice	D

TEGES

The Duck Man

▶ Batuan & Denpasar

Museum Rudana

0   1 km

UBUD AND AROUND | Ubud

2

PELIATAN

Balé Banjar

Puri Agung Stage

JALAN PELIATAN

Pura Agung

Balé Banjar

Agung Rai Gallery

Stage

JALAN PELIATAN

Munut's Gallery   Pharmacy

Bank Danamon

Oka Kartini's   Stage   Pura Dalem

22

23

JALAN SUKMA

24

Balé Banjar   Stage   JALAN HANOMAN

PADANG TEGAL

Market

Monkey Forest Sanctuary

MONKEY FOREST ROAD

Perama Shuttle Bus

K

25

JL HANOMAN

Pura Dalem   Coco Loco

27

Community of Artists

Balé Banjar

JALAN PENGOSEKAN

PENGOSEKAN

ARMA   L

M

Mangku   29   N

Woodcarving Museum   30

28   26

JALAN NYUH BULAN

NYUHKUNING

31

▶ Lodtunduh

N

SINGAKERTA

189

from which to explore nearby attractions (such as Goa Gajah, Pejeng and Gunung Kawi), as well as sights a little further afield: the volcanic peak of Gunung Batur and its crater lake are just 40km north of Ubud; local tour operators offer sunrise treks up Gunung Agung; and it takes less than two hours on a tourist shuttle bus or bemo to reach the east-coast beach of Candi Dasa.

Some history

Ubud became a royal seat only towards the end of the nineteenth century, when a member of the royal household in Sukawati, **Cokorda Gede Sukawati**, distinguished himself in battle and was made a *punggawa* (ruling nobleman), choosing to establish his court at Ubud. When the Gianyar kingdom disintegrated a few years later, Cokorda Gede Sukawati was powerful enough to fight off encroaching armies and Ubud became one of only three former districts of Gianyar (along with Peliatan and Tegalalang) to assert their independence, under the protection of the raja of Karangasem. Cokorda Gede Sukawati grew in power, continuing to extend his lands, and in 1893 helped the Gianyar royal family wrest back much of their former territory. Ubud's allegiances were once again firmly tied to those of Gianyar. In 1900, when Gianyar finally acknowledged that it could no longer hold out against the constant incursions from neighbouring kingdoms, and asked for Dutch protection, Ubud too came under the protectorate of the Netherlands Indies government.

With no more wars to worry about, the Sukawati family and the people of Ubud were able to get on with the business of making carvings and paintings and refining their dancing and gamelan skills. Cokorda Gede's son, **Cokorda Gede Agung Sukawati** (1910–78) focused his energy on the cultivation of the arts, and began actively to encourage foreign artists to live in his district. The most significant of these early visitors was a German artist called **Walter Spies** who established himself in the hamlet of Campuhan on the western border of Ubud in 1928 (see p.211). Over the next nine years, Spies introduced influential new ideas to Ubud's already vibrant artistic community and helped secure foreign patronage. In his wake came a whole crowd of other Western artists and intellectuals, some of whom, including the Dutch artist Rudolph Bonnet, the American musician Colin McPhee, and the American anthropologist Jane Belo, were inspired to set up home in the Ubud area.

Arrival and information

From the **airport**, a fixed-fare taxi to Ubud costs Rp90,000 and takes about an hour; see box on p.110 for details.

Perama runs several daily **shuttle bus** services to Ubud from all the major tourist centres on Bali and Lombok. Unfortunately, their Ubud terminus is inconveniently located at the southern end of Jalan Hanoman in Padang Tegal, about 750m from the southern end of Monkey Forest Road, and 2.5km from the central marketplace. As there's no local bemo or taxi service from here, you'll have to deal with the feeding frenzy of touts offering free transport to whichever losmen they are promoting. If you have heavy luggage, this is the most convenient way of getting to the more central losmen, though there are several places to stay within reasonable walking distance of the Perama terminus. Other shuttle bus operators are more likely to make drops either on Monkey Forest Road or near the market on Jalan Raya (some even offer a door-to-door service), but be sure to find this out before booking.

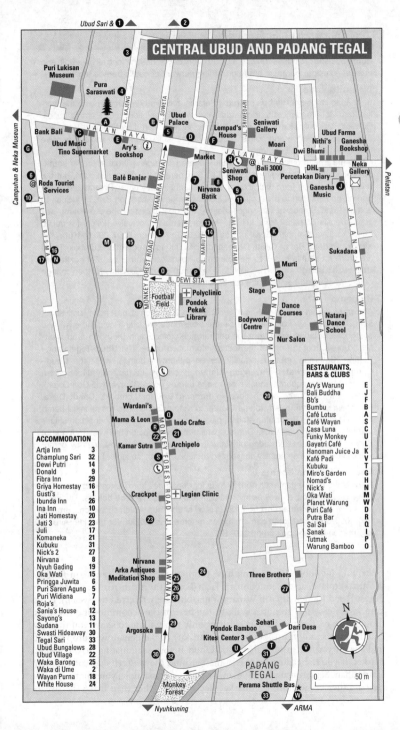

CENTRAL UBUD AND PADANG TEGAL

Ubud Sari &

Puri Lukisan Museum

Pura Saraswati

Ubud Palace

Lempad's House

Seniwati Gallery

Moari

Ubud Farma
Nithi's   Ganesha Bookshop
Dwi Bhumi

Bank Bali
Ubud Music
Tino Supermarket
Ary's Bookshop

Market

DHL

Neka Gallery

Roda Tourist Services

Seniwati Shop

Bali 3000

Percetakan Diary

Ganesha Music

Balé Banjar

Nirvana Batik

Sukadana

Murti

JL DEWI SITA

Football Field

Polyclinic
Pondok Pekak Library

Stage

Dance Courses

Nataraj Dance School

Bodywork Centre

Nur Salon

Kerta

RESTAURANTS, BARS & CLUBS

Ary's Warung	E
Bali Buddha	J
Bb's	F
Bumbu	B
Café Lotus	A
Café Wayan	S
Casa Luna	C
Funky Monkey	U
Gayatri Café	L
Hanoman Juice Ja	K
Kafé Padi	V
Kubuku	T
Miro's Garden	G
Nomad's	H
Nick's	N
Oka Wati	M
Planet Warung	W
Puri Café	D
Putra Bar	R
Sai Sai	Q
Sanak	I
Tutmak	P
Warung Bamboo	O

Wardani's
Mama & Leon
Indo Crafts

Kamar Sutra
Archipelo

Tegun

Crackpot
Legian Clinic

ACCOMMODATION

Artja Inn	3
Champlung Sari	32
Dewi Putri	14
Donald	9
Fibra Inn	29
Griya Homestay	16
Gusti's	1
Ibunda Inn	26
Ina Inn	10
Jati Homestay	20
Jati 3	23
Juli	17
Komaneka	21
Kubuku	31
Nick's 2	27
Nirvana	8
Nyuh Gading	19
Oka Wati	15
Pringga Juwita	6
Puri Saren Agung	5
Puri Widiana	7
Roja's	4
Sania's House	12
Sayong's	13
Sudana	11
Swasti Hideaway	30
Tegal Sari	33
Ubud Bungalows	28
Ubud Village	22
Waka Barong	25
Waka di Ume	2
Wayan Purna	18
White House	24

Nirvana
Arka Antiques
Meditation Shop

Three Brothers

Argosoka

Sehati
Pondok Bamboo
Kites Center 3
Dari Desa

PADANG TEGAL

Perama Shuttle Bus

Monkey Forest

Nyuhkuning   ARMA

0   50 m

Moving on from Ubud

Numerous **shuttle buses** run out of Ubud every day to destinations all over Bali, and there's a cheaper but more time-consuming network of public **bemos** too.

By shuttle bus

Bali's ubiquitous **shuttle bus** operator, Perama, has pretty much cornered the market from Ubud and most tour operators in town only sell tickets for Perama buses. Currently the only alternative is the transfer service offered by transport touts and certain larger losmen and hotels, though this generally works out more expensive unless you have a full car-load.

Perama's head office is inconveniently located in Padang Tegal at the far southern end of Jalan Hanoman (T0361/973316, ©perama_tour@hotmail.com), but the buses do pick-ups from their tour operator agents in the centre. Perama buses are non-air-con and run to most of the major tourist destinations on Bali, as well as to Lombok and Sumbawa (all prices include the boat transfer where relevant); see Travel details on p.239 for a full list. Perama also sells inclusive tickets for public buses to Java. Sample prices include Rp10,000 to **Sanur**; Rp15,000 to **Kuta**, the **airport**, **Padang Bai** or **Candi Dasa**; and Rp45,000 to **Senggigi** on Lombok. There are no direct shuttle buses to Pemuteran, Gilimanuk and other parts of **northwest Bali**, but it's straightforward enough to take a shuttle bus to **Lovina** and then change onto a westbound bemo for the last coastal stretch.

By bemo

All **bemos** depart at least half-hourly until around 2pm, then at least hourly until about 5pm. They all leave from near the central crossroads on Jalan Raya; the east- and southbound bemos leave from the central marketplace, and the north- and westbound ones from in front of the tourist information office. The **Ubud–Tegalalang–Pujung–Kintamani** route is usually served by brown bemos, while the **Ubud–Campuhan–Kedewatan–Payangan–Kintamani** bemos are generally either brown or bright blue. Frequent turquoise or orange bemos go to **Gianyar** (via Goa Gajah), where you can make connections to **Padang Bai** (for Lombok), **Candi Dasa**, **Singaraja** and **Lovina**. Any journey south, to Kuta or Sanur, involves an initial bemo ride to Denpasar's **Batubulan** station, plus at least one cross-city connection unless you take the Batubulan–Nusa Dua bus which makes drops on the western fringe of Sanur and at the eastern edge of Kuta. To reach western Bali and Java by bemo, you'll need to take an equally convoluted route via Batubulan as well.

Boat and airline tickets

Many Ubud travel agents sell **boat tickets** for departures from Benoa Harbour to Gili Meno and Lombok, as well as international and domestic **airline tickets**. The easiest way to get **to the airport** from Ubud is by shuttle bus, which should cost around Rp15,000; transport touts can charge as much as Rp100,000 for the ride. Airport information is in the box on pp.110–11.

Arriving by public **bemo**, you'll be dropped right in the centre, in front of the marketplace, at the junction of Jalan Raya (the main road) and Monkey Forest Road (signed as Jalan Wanara Wana, but rarely referred to as such). From here it's an easy few minutes' walk to the best of the accommodation centres, though you're likely to be met by touts only too willing to show you the way. Any bemo coming from Batubulan (Denpasar) or Kintamani will drop you off in Peliatan on the eastern fringe of Ubud before terminating at the central market. If you're heading for the losmen around the western edge of Ubud, in Campuhan, Sanggingan, Penestanan, or Sayan, for example, you might want to take another bemo from the market (see below) rather than make the sweaty thirty-minute walk. For Nyuhkuning, you'll either have to walk or negotiate a ride with a transport tout.

Information

Ubud's **tourist office** (daily 10am–7.30pm; ☎0361/973285) is located just west of the Jalan Raya/Monkey Forest Road intersection, right at the heart of central Ubud. It has useful outdoor noticeboards giving weekly dance performance schedules, news on special events and a directory of emergency numbers. The staff sell tickets for nearly all the dance shows in the area, organize free transport to the less accessible venues and run their own inexpensive day-trips to local sights (see p.194).

The tourist office doesn't stock **maps**, so if you're planning to do any serious walking around the Ubud area, you should buy one with the paths and tracks detailed on it. The best of these is the Travel Treasure Maps' *Indonesia VI – Ubud Surroundings*, available in all the Ubud bookstores.

Another good investment is the slim volume of **guided walks**, *Bali Bird Walks*, written by the local expatriate ornithologist Victor Mason, who lives in Campuhan, west Ubud; it's a delightful, offbeat guidebook which describes over a dozen walks of varying lengths, highlighting notable flora and fauna. The best place to buy it is at the author's bar and restaurant, the *Beggar's Bush*, in Campuhan (see p.221).

Transport, tours and activities

The most enjoyable way of seeing Ubud and its immediate environs is **on foot**, making your way via the tracks through the rice-paddies and the narrow *gang* that weave through the more traditional *banjar*. **Bicycles** make a pleasant alternative, and can be rented from nearly every losmen and some of the tour agencies (about Rp20,000 a day).

There are no metered taxis in Ubud, so you have to go through the time-consuming process of bargaining for rides with the **transport touts** who hang around outside the tourist office, the central market, and along Monkey Forest Road; if you're staying outside central Ubud this can make getting around a real headache, so it's well worth renting your own transport. (Typically, you can expect to pay around Rp10,000 for a ride from the Neka Art Museum north of the centre in Campuhan to *Café Wayan* halfway down Monkey Forest Road.) Some of the outlying losmen and most of the larger mid-range and expensive hotels provide free transport in and out of central Ubud.

It's also possible to use the public **bemos** for certain short hops: to get to the Neka Art Museum, for example, flag down any bemo heading west (such as the turquoise ones going to Payangan) or ask at the terminal in front of the central market; tourists are generally charged Rp2000 for the ten-minute ride from the market. You can get to Pengosekan or Peliatan on bemos heading for Batubulan, or to Petulu on the orange bemos to Pujung or the brown bemos to Tegalalang and Kintamani. These local rides should cost about Rp1500–2000, and they all go via Ubud's central market and/or tourist office.

Cars and motorbike rental

The transport touts and rental agencies along Monkey Forest Road all rent out **motorbikes** (from Rp35,000/day) and **cars** (Rp70,000–130,000); if you're driving up to the Kintamani volcanoes or to the north coast, it's well worth getting a more powerful Kijang rather than opting for the cheaper Jimny. Two recommended car-rental places are the very efficient Ary's Business and Travel Service (☎0361/973130), next to Ary's Bookshop on Jalan Raya, and Three Brothers (☎0361/973240), which has two outlets on Monkey Forest Road and another on Jalan Hanoman (☎0361/975525). Many car-rental outlets can also provide you with a driver, which makes longer day-trips from your base in Ubud easier; two local freelance **drivers** who have been recommended by readers are Nyoman Swastika (☎0361/980027, evenings only) and Nyoman Dan (☎0361/978320); for other personal recommendations, browse the archives of the online travellers' forums listed on p.24.

Organized tours

Ubud is well stocked with **tour agencies** – most located along Monkey Forest Road – offering a range of their own organized and tailor-made tours as well as acting as agents for specialist operators.

The itineraries and prices of organized **day-trips** vary little from agency to agency: most run daily, use air-conditioned minibuses seating eight to ten people and cost Rp65,000–110,000 per person. The most popular routes include trips to the temple complex at **Besakih**, the volcano and lake at **Kintamani** via Goa Gajah and Tampaksiring, and the monkey forest at **Sangeh**. Ubud's tourist office (see p.193) organizes eight different day-trips covering standard itineraries, according to demand, while the reputable Ary's Business and Travel Service, a few doors further west along Jalan Raya (☎0361/973130, ⓔ ary_s2000@yahoo.com) has twelve similarly priced itineraries. However, you might be better off working out your own sightseeing route and renting a car for a day, with or without driver (see above).

Most tour agencies also advertise inclusive trips to local **festivals** and **cremations**, though prices for these tend to be a bit high, especially when the celebrations are happening within walking distance of Ubud; forthcoming events are posted weekly on the board outside the tourist office. If possible, ask for advice and directions from losmen managers instead and make your own way there. Note that whether you go to a temple ceremony with a group or on your own, formal dress (sashes and sarongs) is required.

Walks, treks and other activities

One of Ubud's more unusual attractions is its regular **Bali bird walks**, organized by Victor Mason, landlord of the *Beggar's Bush* pub in Campuhan (☎0361/975009 from 8am–5pm; mobile ☎0812/391 3801 after 5pm). The walks (Tues, Fri, Sat & Sun 9am) cost $33, or more if you book through an agent, including lunch and the use of shared binoculars. Routes vary according to the season, but are all based around the Campuhan hinterland; guides guarantee sightings of several dozen species of indigenous and visiting birds.

Keep Walking Tours, alongside Tegun Galeri, Jl Hanoman 44 (☎0361/973361), has an interesting programme of guided **cultural and ecological walks** (minimum two people), where the emphasis is on learning about rural traditions and meeting village craftspeople; per-person prices range from Rp45,000 for a one-hour walk to Rp150,000 for a seven-hour excursion. They also offer **sunrise treks** up Gunung Batur ($55). The reputable and long-running Bali Sunrise 2001, Jl Raya Sanggingan 88, Campuhan/Sanggingan (mobile ☎0818/552669, ⓦ www.balisunrise2001.com), with another office in

Toya Bungkah (see box on p.329) also have sunrise treks up Gunung Batur (pick-up from Ubud hotels at 3am; $55 per person, minimum two participants; see p.319) and Gunung Agung (pick-up 10pm; $100; see p.270).

The stretch of the Ayung River just west of Ubud is the island's centre for **whitewater rafting** and **kayaking**; several companies based on the south coast run whitewater excursions along its course – you can either contact Bali Adventure Tours (℡0361/721480, ⓦwww.baliadventuretours.com) or Sobek (℡0361/287059, ⓦwww.sobekbali.com) direct, or book the trips through any Ubud tour agent. The two-hour courses stretch about 8km along the Ayung River, cross Class 2 and 3 rapids and pass through gorges and alongside cliffs and waterfalls en route. Prices are around $70 per person ($45 for under-12s where appropriate), and include all equipment, hotel transfers and food.

Sobek and Bali Adventure Tours also do guided **hikes** in the area. Bali's only **elephant treks** are organized out of the Elephant Safari Park in the village of Taro, 13km north of Ubud (see p.236). Most Ubud tour agents also sell **diving packages** run by the dive operators of south Bali, picking up from Ubud and always covering transport to major dive sites (see box on p.64).

Bike rides

There are all sorts of possibilities for good **bike rides** in the Ubud area. The two walks described on p.205 and p.213 are good routes for mountain bikes, or you might consider cycling down to the art market at Sukawati (see p.182) and then on to the coast at Pantai Saba (see p.183), a round-trip of about four hours. The box below outlines a ride to Tegalalang, with an optional extension to Lake Batur.

You can also join a **guided mountain-bike ride** (Rp360,000 including lunch): Bali Budaya Tours on Jalan Raya Pengosekan (℡0361/975557) and Ary's Business and Travel Service on Jalan Raya, central Ubud (℡0361/973130, ⓔary_s2000@yahoo.com) both run full-day cycling trips that drive you up to Kintamani and Gunung Batur and then let you cycle back down on minor village roads. Sobek and Bali Adventure Tours (see above) do guided cycle trips around Gunung Batukau, Gunung Batur and Sangeh Monkey Forest.

A bike ride to Tegalalang and Lake Batur

A two-and-a-half-hour round trip takes you to the rice terraces of **Tegalalang** (see p.235), about 13km north of Ubud. The most peaceful route is via Jalan Suweta in central Ubud, a back road that's both calm and fairly traffic-free, if a little hilly. When you get to Tegalalang (about 1hr) the road feeds into the busy main road; ten minutes on, past all the woodcarving workshops, is a spectacular **viewpoint** overlooking some classic stepped rice terraces. You can carry on from here for another 16km to the Kintamani–Penelokan road and the unbeatable views over **Lake Batur** (see p.319; 6–7hr round-trip); this is a hard and very steep road, and needs decent gears, strong muscles and good nerves to cope with the volume of lorries and other constantly tooting traffic. If you decide to head homewards instead, you're best off going back the way you came as the alternative route veers eastwards at Penusuan to follow the busy main road via Gentong and Petulu (see p.217) to the T-junction at the eastern edge of Ubud's Jalan Raya.

Accommodation

Anywhere in Ubud, you're almost certain to find that your **accommodation** is set in gorgeously lush surroundings, and that there are plenty of terraces or balconies from which to appreciate them. Many losmen and hotel managers also supply free **breakfasts**, as often as not served on your balcony. Rooms in all price brackets in Ubud are, however, subject to a local **tax** of 10–21 percent; some places include this in their published rates, but most do not, so it's always worth asking in advance. Many mid-range and expensive hotels are featured on the accommodation **websites** detailed on p.44, which will definitely get you a discount.

New losmen are opening all the time, so it's often worth listening to the **touts** who meet the bemos in the marketplace; some even ride the bemo all the way from Batubulan. If you do take up a tout's suggestion, make sure they pinpoint the exact **location** of the losmen on a map, as it's often the more outlying homestays that rely on such custom. The further away from Monkey Forest Road you look, the more traditional the losmen, and the better the views, though restaurant and entertainment options will be limited.

Ubud's accommodation explosion has played havoc with its **address system**, particularly along Monkey Forest Road, where hardly a single losmen has an official road number. To make it easier to find the Monkey Forest Road losmen listed below, we've described their approximate location. Every place we've listed is marked on a **map** – either the Central Ubud and Padang Tegal map (p.191) or the Neighbouring Villages map (pp.188–189). For accommodation in Mas, the woodcarving village to the south of Ubud, see p.185.

Central Ubud

The kilometre-long **Monkey Forest Road** is the most central, but also the most congested and commercial, part of town. It has few genuine homestays, with the emphasis instead on small mid-range or upmarket hotels comprising a dozen bungalows set in fairly spacious gardens, often with a swimming pool and restaurant. The tiny roads that run off Monkey Forest Road or parallel to it have a very different feel and, amazingly, still retain a peaceful village atmosphere. Much of the accommodation on these conveniently central lanes – Jalan Karna, Jalan Maruti, Jalan Gautama, Jalan Kajeng and Jalan Bisma, for example – is in small, archetypal homestays, where just a handful of rooms have been built in the family compound; they're usually very friendly places, though some people find the compounds too enclosed.

Inexpensive

Artja Inn Jl Kajeng ☎0361/974425. Six simple but pleasant bamboo-walled cottages with open-roofed, cold-water mandi. Set in a nice garden away from the road. ❷

Dewi Putri Jl Maruti 8 ☎0361/973304. Good-value place down a quiet little *gang*, offering two bungalows in a typical homestay compound. Run by a family of painters. ❷

Donald Jl Gautama 9 ☎0361/977156. Tiny but well-run and friendly homestay offering four exceptionally cheap, sparsely furnished bungalows in a secluded garden compound. ❶

Griya Homestay Jl Bisma ☎0361/975428. Some of the cheapest accommodation on this idyllically quiet hillside *gang* looking down over the terraced paddies. Just three large, spruce rooms. ❷

Jati 3 Down a *gang* off south-central Monkey Forest Rd ☎ & ℱ0361/973249. Place at the end of a quiet *gang* with five pleasant standard losmen bungalows in a losmen courtyard, all with hot water. But the real attraction are the four gorgeous split-level bungalows in an adjacent plot of land that slopes down to the river. Each of these has huge glass windows to make the most of the view and can accommodate up to four people. Losmen bungalows ❷ Riverside bungalows ❹

Juli Jl Bisma 102 ☎0361/97714. Good-value

place on a quiet road, offering six well-maintained rooms overlooking the paddies, all with hot showers. ❷

Nyuh Gading Central Monkey Forest Rd ☎0361/973410. A handful of very simple bungalows set in a pretty garden behind a restaurant; one of the cheapest places on Monkey Forest Road itself. ❷

Puri Widiana Jl Karna 5 ☎0361/973406. Very inexpensive, good-value basic rooms in a small family compound that's centrally located but peaceful. All rooms have fans, cold-water showers, and mosquito nets. ❶–❷

Roja's Bungalows Jl Kajeng 1 ☎0361/975107. Small, friendly, centrally located homestay offering five large rooms with character at a range of prices. Rooms with cold water ❷ With hot water ❸

Sania's House Jl Karna ☎0361/975535, ✉inengah_merta@hotmail.com. Everything about this place is well done: whitewashed bungalow rooms are clean and well furnished; service is exceptionally attentive; breakfasts are enormous; the location central but quiet; and there's hot water and a small swimming pool. The drawback is that with over twenty bungalows crammed into the smallish compound it can feel lacking in privacy. Rooms with cold water ❷ With hot water ❸–❹

Sayong's Bungalows Jl Maruti ☎0361/973305. Seven simply furnished bungalow rooms in a variety of sizes but all with hot water, set around a typical losmen garden at the end of a very quiet residential *gang*. Swimming pool across the lane. ❶–❸

Sudana Jl Gautama 11 ☎0361/976435. A typical homestay: small, friendly and family-run, offering clean if slightly spartan rooms in a small garden. ❷–❸

The White House (Three Brothers' Bungalows) Access from the southern end of Monkey Forest Rd ☎0361/974855. One of the few places in central Ubud still to be surrounded by rice-fields. Ten sizeable but plain, whitewashed rooms, each with a hot-water bathroom, fan and balcony. Nice views from the upstairs rooms. ❸

Moderate

Gusti's Garden Bungalows Jl Kajeng 27 ☎0361/973311, ℻972159. Fifteen pleasant, better-than-average losmen rooms, all with hot water, set around a swimming pool, and enjoying a convenient yet peaceful location. ❹

Ibunda Inn Central Monkey Forest Rd ☎ & ℻0361/973252. A dozen two-storey brick bungalows (all with hot water), with the more expensive rooms upstairs. The compound's a little cramped, but there's a good-sized pool in the garden. ❹

Ina Inn Jl Bisma ☎0361/973317, ℻973282, ✉inainn@eudoramail.com. Located in a quiet and panoramic spot on a small *gang* surrounded by rice-fields, these twelve well-maintained and nicely furnished cottages all have bathtubs and hot water (but no air-con). The most expensive rooms have huge glass windows affording pleasant views, and there's a rooftop swimming pool. Good value. ❹–❺

Nirvana Pension and Gallery Jl Gautama 10, Padang Tegal ☎ & ℻ 0361/975415, ✉rodanet@denpasar.wasantara.net.id. Spotless and comfortably furnished rooms in the traditional house compound of painter and batik teacher I Nyoman Suradnya (see p.225). ❺

Oka Wati's Sunset Bungalows Down a *gang* off north-central Monkey Forest Rd ☎0361/973386, ℻975063, ⊛www.okawatihotel.com. Set back from the road but still centrally located, the nineteen terraced bungalows at this long-running hotel all have hot water, and most enjoy decent views. There's a good pool, a restaurant and internet access in the reception area. ❻–❼

Swasti (Monkey Forest) Hideaway Far southern end of Monkey Forest Rd ☎ & ℻0361/975354, ✉swasti@dps.centrin.net.id. Eight attractively designed and smartly maintained bungalows. All have hot water and a couple have air-con, and the more expensive upstairs rooms look down over the lush riverbank below. ❺

Ubud Bungalows Central Monkey Forest Rd ☎0361/971298, ℻975537, ✉w_widnyana@hotmail.com. Good value, comfortable, detached fan-cooled bungalows set in a pretty garden with an attractive pool at the bottom. Also some expensive rooms with air-con and bathtubs. Rooms with fan ❹–❺ With air-con ❼

Expensive

Champlung Sari Southern end of Monkey Forest Rd ☎0361/975418, ℻975473, ⊛www.indo.com/hotels/champlungsari. Classy accommodation right at the bottom of Monkey Forest Road. The 58 rooms are all comfortably outfitted with air-con and TV, and the deluxe ones have a private garden, but there's nothing especially stylish about the place. Has a pool and two restaurants. Twenty percent discounts outside peak periods. ❽

Fibra Inn Southern end of Monkey Forest Rd ☎ & ℻0361/975451, ⊛www.thefibra.com. This mid- to upper-range little fifteen-room hotel is set in an elegant tropical sculpture garden and has some very appealing "superior" and "deluxe" rooms, which are smartly furnished and stylish. The standard fan-cooled rooms are fine but not particularly good value. There's also a pool, a delightfully designed spa and a restaurant. ⑦

Komaneka Resort Central Monkey Forest Rd ☏0361/976090, ⑤977140, ⑩www.komaneka .com. Comprising twenty large, light, air-con bungalows elegantly designed with sleek furnishings, huge beds and verandahs overlooking the paddy-fields, this is a good choice for anyone wanting upmarket accommodation in central Ubud. There's a beautiful pool, a spa, and an expensive art shop on the premises. Run by the son of the man who founded the Neka Art Museum. ⑨

Pringga Juwita Water Garden Cottages Jl Bisma ☏ & ⑤0361/975734, ⑩www.thefibra.com/pringga.htm. Beautifully designed, characterful bungalows, including some exceptionally attractive two-storey deluxe ones, all featuring traditional rooms in dark wood with antique furniture and garden bathrooms. Surrounded by a series of lotus ponds, this is a peaceful, scenic hideaway and there's a swimming pool too. Most rooms are fan-cooled, though a few have air-con. ⑦–⑧

Puri Saren Agung Jl Raya ☏0361/975057, ⑤975137. This superb collection of eight pavilions, some new and some renovated, occupies part of the palace belonging to Ubud's influential Sukawati family (see p.190). Accommodation is stylish and fairly traditional, complete with four-poster beds, carved doors, sculpted wall panels and elegant outdoor sitting rooms. Some rooms have air-con. Good value and right in the heart of Ubud. ⑦

Ubud Village Hotel Central Monkey Forest Rd ☏0361/975571, ⑤975069, ⑩www.indo.com/hotels/ubud_village. Stylish, good-value hotel where each room occupies its own small compound, complete with elegant furnishings, air-con, a courtyard garden and a sunken marble bath. The most expensive rooms have spacious terraces overlooking the river and are the best of their class in central Ubud. There's a large pool, a restaurant and an attractive lounge-pavilion too. Very central. ⑦–⑨

Waka di Ume About 1.8km north along Jl Suweta from Ubud market, in the hamlet of Sambahan ☏0361/973178, ⑤973179, ⑩www.wakaexperience.com. Delightful set of sixteen thatched bungalows designed in the Waka group's distinctive natural-chic style, with an antique flavour to the soft furnishings. Each bungalow has a picture-perfect rice-paddy view from its generous windows (the upstairs rooms are the nicest), and the hotel has two stunningly sited pools (one for kids), a spa and a restaurant. Regular shuttle buses ferry guests into central Ubud. Good value. ⑧–⑨

Padang Tegal and Peliatan

The village of **Padang Tegal** merges with the eastern borders of central Ubud, so staying here means you're rarely more than a fifteen-minute walk from Monkey Forest Road, though you may be quite a hike from the marketplace. It's quieter than Monkey Forest Road but has plenty of shops and restaurants. To the east of Padang Tegal, **Peliatan** has more of a village feel and its losmen tend to be more traditional.

Family Guest House Jl Sukma 39, Peliatan ☏0361/974054, ⑤978292. Exceptionally friendly place offering a dozen well-designed bungalows with comfortable furniture and garden verandahs (the deluxe ones are enormous and undeniably luxurious). Famous for its excellent breakfasts. Fifteen minutes' walk from central Ubud. ②–⑤

Jati Homestay Jl Hanoman, Padang Tegal ☏0361/977701. Ten comfortably furnished bungalows built in a two-storey block facing the rice paddies (upstairs rooms cost a little extra). All have hot water and peaceful views. Run by a family of painters. ②

Kubuku Off the southeastern end of Monkey Forest Rd, Padang Tegal ☏0361/974742, ⑤971552. Seven bungalow rooms marooned in the rice-fields near one of Ubud's most prettily set cafés. Upstairs rooms have the best views and cost more. ④–⑤

Mandala Homestay Jl Sukma 63, Peliatan ☏0361/973230. One of the very first homestays in Peliatan and still very much a typical family-run losmen, if a little run-down. There are just three rooms, and they're among the cheapest in Ubud. The owner makes and plays the *genggong*. ①

Nick's Pension 2 Jl Hanoman 57, Padang Tegal ☏0361/975526, ⑤975636. Seven good-value, clean, whitewashed rooms with bamboo beds and hot showers in a typical losmen-style garden compound. Guests can use the pool at *Nick's 1* (some way away on Monkey Forest Rd). ②

Rona Jl Sukma 23, Peliatan ☏ & ⑤0361/973229. Good-value terraced bungalows, furnished with comfortable bamboo beds and armchairs. There's a second-hand bookstore, library, kids' playroom and big bar-restaurant on the premises, and a babysitting service is available. Well managed and deservedly popular. Free pick-up from Ubud area. Rooms with cold water ② With bathtub and hot water ③–④

Sari Bungalows Off the southern end of Jl Peliatan, Peliatan ☎0361/975541. Some of the cheapest rooms in Ubud. Thirteen basic bungalows fronted by verandahs which afford superb views out over the paddies beyond. Excellent value. ①

Tegal Sari Jl Hanoman, Padang Tegal ☎ & ⑤0361/973318, ⑥www.travelideas.net/bali .hotels/hanoman-ubud.html. Exceptionally good-

value set of fourteen comfortable fan and air-con rooms in two-storey blocks strung alongside the paddyfields (the upstairs rooms are nicest). With fine sunset views, thoughtful service, free tea and coffee, a massage service and a pool, this is a deservedly popular spot. Located just across the road from the Perama shuttle bus depot, but quite a hike from central Ubud (free local transport is provided). Rooms with fan ③ With air-con ④–⑤

Wayan Purna Jl Hanoman, Padang Tegal ☎0361/978387. Tiny archetypal homestay in the family home of a picture framer. Good clean rooms, if a bit box-like. ①

Nyuhkuning

Stretching south from the Monkey Forest, **Nyuhkuning** is peaceful and still fairly rural, offering lots of uninterrupted paddy-field views while still being just a pleasant ten-minute walk from the shops and restaurants at the southern end of Monkey Forest Road. The one drawback is that you need to walk or cycle through the Monkey Forest after dark if you're going into central Ubud in the evening.

Alam Jiwa 100m east off the Nyuhkuning road ☎ & ⑤0361/977463, ⑥alambali@indosat.net.id. Ten large, stunningly sited bungalows, secluded alongside a small river, each one enjoying uninterrupted views of rice-fields and Gunung Agung from the bathtub as well as the balcony. There's a pool, room service is provided by *Café Wayan* (see p.219) and there's free transport into Ubud. Good value. ⑦–⑧

Bali Spirit (Bali Taksu) Southern end of Nyuhkuning ☎0361/974013, ⑤974012, ⑥www.balispirithotel.com. Prettily located upmarket spa resort, overlooking a bend in the river, with a swimming pool that's filled from a holy spring, a spa and massage programme. The nineteen air-

con rooms are large and stylish and all have either balconies or private terraces. Free shuttle service into Ubud. Forty percent discounts often available. ⑧

Garden View Cottages Nyuhkuning ☎ & ⑤0361/974055, ⑥gardenviewubud@yahoo.com. Plush, nicely furnished downstairs rooms and two-storey, two-room bungalows, all with uninterrupted rice-paddy views. Fan and hot water; swimming pool in the garden. Rooms ⑥ Bungalows ⑦

Swasti Hideaway Nyuhkuning Nyuhkuning ☎0361/974079. Seven large, spacious and comfortably furnished rooms, all with hot water and unsurpassed rice-field views from the balcony. There's a pool in the garden. Good value. ⑤

Campuhan, Sanggingan, Bangkiang Sidem and Keliki

West of central Ubud, **Campuhan** and **Sanggingan** hotels can only be reached via the busy main road, which is not a particularly pleasant walk, but public bemos run this way, and some hotels offer free transfers into central Ubud. Rural **Bangkiang Sidem**, on the other hand, is accessible via a delightful path. If you're staying in the remote but charming village of **Keliki**, you'll need your own transport.

Alam Sari Keliki ☎ & ⑤0361/240308, ⑥www.alamsari.com. Prettily located set of ten attractively furnished bungalows on a slope overlooking the terraced rice-fields and coconut groves of Keliki village, about 10km north of Ubud. Air-con, swimming pool and babysitting service, plus free pick-up from Ubud or the airport. The design is environmentally aware and the hotel tries hard

to be a positive addition to the village. Good place to base yourself if you have your own transport: Ubud is about two hours' walk away, though the hotel has bikes for rent. Good discounts if you reserve online. ⑧

Ananda Cottages Jl Raya, Sanggingan/ Campuhan ☎0361/975376, ⑤975375, ⑥anandaubud@denpasar.wasantara.net.id. Atmospheric collection of one- and two-storey bungalows set in attractive gardens that include miniature rice paddies, ornamental ponds (with resident frog chorus), a pretty swimming pool and paths lit by flaming torches at night. Rooms are characterfully furnished with carved doors, antique furniture and garden bathrooms: the upper-level fan ones are the nicest and enjoy paddy views. Smart modern air-con rooms also available. A half-hour walk, or five-minute bemo ride, from central Ubud; bicycles, motorbikes and cars are available for rent. Rooms with fan ❻ With air-con ❼

Klub Kokos Bangkiang Sidem ⓣ & ⓕ 0361/978270, ⓦ www.klubkokos.com. Located on the edge of the remote ridgetop village of Bangkiang Sidem, midway along the Campuhan ridge walk (see p.213) this is an ideal spot from which to soak up traditional village life. The seven one- and two storey bungalows are comfortably furnished and set in a garden; there's also a swimming pool, restaurant, library, internet access and kids' games room. A delightful 25-minute walk from the Campuhan bridge, following signs from

the *Ibah* hotel (or 45min from Ubud market); also accessible by car via Payogan. ❻–❼

Taman Indrakila Jl Raya, Sanggingan/Campuhan ⓣ & ⓕ 0361/975017. Offering a five-star view at two-star prices, this is a low-key operation with sixteen rooms ranged along the hillside, all affording fine uninterrupted views over the Campuhan ridge. Rooms are simply but comfortably furnished with fans and mosquito nets, and there's a pool. ❺

Hotel Tjampuhan Jl Raya, Campuhan ⓣ 0361/975368, ⓕ 975137, ⓦ www.tjampuhan.com. Cottages stunningly positioned on terraces that drop right down to the Wos Barat river, built on the site of the artist Walter Spies's former home (see p.210). The large and elegantly designed fan and air-con rooms (the old-style air-con ones have more character) are secluded amid the stepped tropical gardens, which also contains tennis courts, two swimming pools and an unusual grotto-like spa complex (see p.225). Not ideal for guests with mobility problems. Fifteen minutes' walk from Ubud market. Reservations essential. Rooms with fan ❼ With air-con ❽ Walter Spies's house ❾

Penestanan

Occupying a ridgetop and a river valley between Campuhan and Sayan, **Penestanan** offers some fabulous and very affordable hilltop bungalows and an increasing number of mid-range options, all within walking distance of Campuhan.

Londo Bungalows ⓣ & ⓕ 0361/976548, ⓔ londobungalows@hotmail.com. Friendly little place offering four large two-storey cottages, fairly basic but furnished with two double beds and an attached kitchen. Guests can use the swimming pool at *Melati Cottages* next door (see below). Run by the son of I Nyoman Londo, one of the original Young Artists. ❸

Londo 2 ⓣ 0361/976764. Located towards the end of the track that runs east from the top of the Penestanan steps, the three two-storey bungalows here offer spectacular Young Artist-style views of the surrounding ricefields and palm groves. The bungalows are simply furnished but sleep four, have spacious balconies and kitchen facilities and are exceptionally good value. Run by one of the original Young

Artists, I Nyoman Londo, whose studio is here too. ❷

Melati Cottages ⓣ 0361/974650, ⓕ 975088, ⓔ melaticottages@hotmail.com. Large, traditional-style rooms with huge picture windows, fans and hot water in a lovely rice-paddy setting. There's a pool too. ❻

Penestanan Bungalows ⓣ 0361/975604, ⓕ 288341. Comfortable mid-range bungalow rooms, pleasingly furnished and with hot water. A quiet spot high above Ubud, with a pool and rice-terrace views from some of the upstairs rooms. ❺

Rasman Bungalow ⓣ 0361/975497. Simple, fairly spartan two-storey bungalows, suitable for four people and very similar to the nearby *Londo 2*. Great views over the paddies; friendly and quiet, and run by the charming Rasman himself. ❸

Sayan and Kedewatan

Overlooking the spectacular Ayung River valley to the west of central Ubud, **Sayan** and **Kedewatan** are famous for their luxurious five-star resorts, all of which capitalize on the stunning panoramas. A couple of cheaper places share the same vistas.

Amandari Kedewatan ⓣ 0361/975333, ⓕ 975335, ⓦ www.amanresorts.com. Exclusive thirty-room hotel (part of the Aman chain), which

is repeatedly voted one of the best in the world. All guests live in their own traditional walled compounds, enclosing a garden bathroom complete with sunken marble bath and minimalist-chic accommodation; some have private plunge pools as well. Glorious views out over the Ayung River; published rates from $575. ⑨

Four Seasons Resort Bali at Sayan Sayan/Kedewatan ☎0361/977577, ⑤977588, ⓦwww.fourseasons.com. Innovatively designed, ultra-modern five-star deluxe hotel built on a series of levels in the spectacular Ayung River valley. The style is unadorned chic, and the suites and villas are beautifully appointed. All have a huge living area with TV and video, as well as a bedroom and private garden. Villas have plunge pools as well. There's a large pool, a spa and a restaurant. Because of the location it's not ideal for children, but is popular with honeymooners. Considered to be one of the best hotels in the world. Published rates from $475. ⑨

Kupu Kupu Barong Kedewatan ☎0361/975478, ⑤975079, ⓦwww.kupukupubarong.com. Small, long-running deluxe hotel with lots of character, comprising nineteen traditional rice-barn bunga-lows in a tropical terraced garden, all with a fine view over the Ayung River. It's worth upgrading to the luxury bungalows, which have a separate living room (no TV) as well as a bedroom, plus a private river-view balcony. The hotel has two pools, a spa and a restaurant. Published rates from $335. ⑨

Sayan Terrace Sayan ☎0361/974384, ⑤975384, ⓦwww.geocities.com/sayanterrace. Shares land with the adjacent *Taman Bebek* (see below), and while both enjoy an awesome location overlooking the classically Balinese Ayung River vista, the panoramas from the rooms at *Sayan Terrace* have a slight edge. All enjoy these fine views and make the most of it with enormous windows and scenic balconies. Fan rooms are particularly good value, though there are air-con options too. There's also a pool. A ten-minute drive from central Ubud. Rooms with fan ⑥ With air-con ⑦–⑨

Taman Bebek Sayan ☎0361/975385, ⑤976532, ⓦwww.baliwww.com/tamanbebek. Top choice here are the three delightful self-contained valley-view villas, built in breezy colonial style with verandahs, sliding screens, kitchen facilities and fabulous views over the breathtakingly beautiful Ayung River valley terraces. Also has a swimming pool and restaurant. A ten-minute drive from central Ubud. ⑧–⑨

Central Ubud

Covering the area between Jalan Raya in the north and the Monkey Forest in the south, and between Campuhan bridge in the west and the GPO in the east, **Central Ubud**'s chief attractions are its restaurants and shops. However, it does hold a few notable sights, including the atmospheric lotus-garden temple, **Pura Saraswati**, Ubud's oldest art museum, **Puri Lukisan**, and the much more modern **Seniwati Gallery of Art by Women**.

Puri Lukisan

Although billed as central Ubud's major art museum, the **Puri Lukisan** on Jalan Raya (daily 8am–4pm; Rp10,000) comes as a disappointment and should be visited only as an adjunct to the far superior Neka Art Museum, 2km west in neighbouring Sanggingan (see p.206).

Set in attractive gardens, complete with lotus-filled ponds and shady arbours, Puri Lukisan ("Palace of Paintings") was founded in 1956 by the Ubud *punggawa* Cokorda Gede Agung Sukawati (whose descendants are still involved with the museum) and the Dutch artist Rudolf Bonnet. Both men had amassed a signif-icant collection of work by local artists through their involvement with the Pita Maha group (see box on p.202) and almost the whole of the **First Pavilion**, located at the top of the garden, is still given over to these works (identifiable by the words "donated by Rudolf Bonnet" on the label). Some of these are **wayang-style** canvases, but most are early **Ubud-style**, depicting local scenes, with great attention paid to the detail of the foliage, the temple carvings and the villagers' attire (see p.532 for more). There are also plenty of works that don't fit into the recognized Balinese "schools", including a good selection of distinctive ink drawings by the multi-talented I Gusti Nyoman Lempad (see p.204).

The Pita Maha arts movement

By the early 1930s, Bali was firmly established on the cruise-liner circuit and the island was playing host to a stream of well-heeled visitors from Europe and America. Bowled over by the extraordinary local artefacts, these tourists began to buy significant numbers of paintings and woodcarvings and, in response, the artists churned them out in ever-increasing numbers. The result was a dramatic drop in standards, with contemporary artists and collectors bemoaning the lowering in quality and the mushrooming of shoddy imitations. To combat this decline, Ubud's patrician prince, **Cokorda Gede Agung Sukawati**, joined forces with his architect and chief carver **I Gusti Nyoman Lempad**, and enrolled the help of his expatriate painter friends **Walter Spies** and **Rudolf Bonnet**. Together, the four men founded the **Pita Maha arts movement** in Ubud in 1936.

The main aim of the movement was to preserve high artistic standards and to steer artists away from the temptation to mass-produce their works. Weekly meetings were held at Walter Spies's Campuhan home, at which the four founding members led discussions on work brought in by any of the other Pita Maha members. Over its six-year existence, the group's membership grew to include about 150 painters, carvers and sculptors, some of whom came from villages as distant as Sanur on the southeast coast, but most of whom were from the neighbouring villages of Nyuhkuning, Padang Tegal and Pengosekan. Members were encouraged to explore new themes and subjects in their work, particularly secular ones, and to give full expression to their individual interpretations. The best of the submitted pieces were registered and then exhibited in shows organized by the Pita Maha founders, who also made determined efforts to sell the works both to tourists in Bali as well as to collectors in Java, Europe and America.

The movement ground to a halt with Spies's death in 1942 and has defied all subsequent attempts to revive it; the only legacy of works from that era are the paintings and carvings bought from Pita Maha members by Bonnet and Sukawati and then donated to the **Puri Lukisan museum** in central Ubud. With hindsight, some anthropologists and art historians have criticized Pita Maha as being overly colonialist in its imposition of Western artistic ideals and techniques on an already sophisticated artistic heritage. Others see the movement as a crucial breathing of new life into a native art that was in danger of stagnating or even dying out. What seems indisputable, though, is that without the commercial stimulation of the Pita Maha movement in the 1930s, the majority of modern Ubud's artists and craftspeople would be struggling much harder to make a living from their work.

The Pita Maha group also promoted the art of **woodcarving**, and a handful of these finely crafted pieces from the 1930s, 1940s and 1950s are scattered about the First Pavilion gallery. Especially notable are the elegantly surreal figure of the earth goddess, *Dewi Pertiwi* by Ida Bagus Nyana, the charming hibiscus-wood *Buffalo Bathing in a River* by I Mangku Tama, and the sinuous portrait of the rice goddess *Dewi Sri* by I Ketut Djedeng. I Nyoman Cokot's energetic figures of weird animals and terrifying human forms were so innovative that he spawned a now much-emulated Cokot style; his *Garuda Eating Snake* is a typical example.

The **Second Pavilion**, to the left of the First Pavilion, contains a pretty extensive showcase of works in the **Young Artists** style, though the place is unfortunately not very well lit. Many of these pictures were donated to the museum by the painter Arie Smit, who was closely associated with the early years of this naive expressionist school of local art in the 1960s. Most were produced by the young people of nearby Penestanan (see p.214), who drew their inspiration from daily village life. I Nyoman Mundik is an especially prolific painter in this style, and several of his canvases displayed here were painted in his teenage years. Also in this pavilion you'll find works in the so-called **modern traditional** style such as Ida Bagus Nadera's *Story of Rajapala*.

The **Third Pavilion**, to the right of the First Pavilion, houses temporary exhibitions.

Pura Saraswati

At the end of the nineteenth century, I Gusti Nyoman Lempad arrived in Ubud from service at the court of Blahbatuh and was employed as chief stonecarver and architect to the Sukawati royal family; **Pura Saraswati** was one of his many commissions. He set the whole temple complex in a delightful watergarden, landscaped around a huge lotus pond, and dedicated it to Saraswati, a sacred Hindu river and the goddess of water and learning. A **restaurant**, *Café Lotus*, now capitalizes on the garden view.

To get to the temple, you can either take the gateway that opens onto Jalan Raya, or go through the restaurant. A forest of metre-high lotus plants leads you right up to the red-brick *paduraksa* whose main entrance is blocked by a very unusual **aling-aling** (the wall device built into nearly every temple to disorient evil spirits), which is in fact the back of a rotund statue of a *raksasa* demon guardian. Inside the **courtyard** on the right, you'll find a *bale* housing the two huge *barong* costumes used by local villagers for exorcizing rituals: the lion-like Barong Ket and the wild boar Barong Bangkal. Nearby, the main lotus-throne **shrine** is covered with a riot of *paras* carvings, with the requisite cosmic turtle and *naga* forming the base, while the tower is a swirling mass of curlicues and floral motifs. The walk-in shrine occupying the northeast corner of the complex displays some more distinguished Lempad carvings, the central wall-panel describing a farewell scene.

Puri Saren Agung (Ubud Palace)

A few hundred metres east of Pura Saraswati, **Puri Saren Agung** – generally known as **Ubud Palace** – stands at the heart of Ubud, opposite the main market and junction of Jalan Raya and Monkey Forest Road. From the late nineteenth century until the 1940s, Ubud and its catchment area was ruled from this palace complex by the resident Sukawati clan and, despite its modern incarnation as a hotel and dance stage, Puri Saren Agung has retained much of its original style and elegance. Casual visitors are welcome to walk around the compact central courtyards, and every night the outer courtyard is transformed into a spectacular backdrop for traditional dance performances (see p.222).

Built to a classic design that is really just a grander version of the traditional family compound, the palace was divided into a series of **pavilions**, each serving a particular purpose. The centrepiece was the open-sided reception *bale*, its imposing wooden pillars, sculpted stone panels and huge guardian statues of elephants, lions and *raksasa* still much as they were in the Sukawatis' heyday. The verandah is still furnished with Dutch-style carved wooden armchairs, and piles of old photograph albums lie heaped on the floor, full of early pictures of the Ubud gentry. The small thatched *bale* nearby is decorated with stonecarvings and painted wooden reliefs ascribed to the artist I Gusti Nyoman Lempad. Most of the **hotel rooms** have been adapted or purpose-built, but retain authentic features (see p.198).

Lempad's house

Ubud's most versatile and accomplished artist, **I Gusti Nyoman Lempad**, lived on Ubud's main street for most of his life in a **house** that still belongs to his family but is now also open to the public (daily 8am–6pm; free). Lempad was said to be quite a traditionalist in certain matters and would only work on propitious days; significantly, he is said to have chosen the day of his death – the auspicious *Kajeng Kliwon* day of the Balinese calendar, April 25, 1978. He was approximately 116 years old. His friends Rudolf Bonnet and Cokorda Gede Agung Sukawati both died within a few months of Lempad, and the three men were cremated together at a spectacular ceremony held in Ubud in January 1979.

Disappointingly, there's little evidence of the great man on show in his former residence, as the place now functions chiefly as a gallery and showroom for a group of artists working under the "Puri Lempad" by-line. Some of them are descendants of I Gusti Nyoman and much of their work takes inspiration from his impressive canon of paintings and drawings. Only a couple of Lempad's original ink drawings are exhibited here: for the best collection of his work you'll need to visit the Neka Art Museum (see p.208), though the Puri Lukisan museum also owns a few examples. The *bale* at the back of the Lempad compound does, however, house a small exhibition of Lempad **memorabilia**, including the Piagam Anugerah Seni certificate, government recognition of his lifetime's contribution to the island's cultural heritage, and a magazine article on the biographical film, *Lempad of Bali*, made by local expats John Darling and Lorne Blair in 1980.

Seniwati Gallery of Art by Women

Balinese women feature prominently in the paintings displayed in both the Neka Art Museum and the Puri Lukisan, but there is barely a handful of works by women artists in either collection. To redress this imbalance, British-born artist Mary Northmore set up the Association of Women Artists in Bali, out of which was born the **Seniwati Gallery of Art by Women** on Jalan Sriwedari, off Jalan Raya (daily 9am–5pm; free). Committed to the promotion, display and sale of work by women artists, the Seniwati organization currently represents about forty local and expatriate women, many of whom have pictures on show in the gallery's permanent collection. Another element of the project is the regular art classes held for young girls in the studio across the road from the gallery.

The Seniwati Gallery's small but charming permanent collection covers the complete range of mainstream Balinese art styles, and the works are admirably supported by excellent information sheets on each of the artists and by a staff of highly informed gallery attendants. A few of the most notable exhibits include a classical Kamasan style depiction of the *Vindication of Sita* by **Ni Made Suciarmi**, whose childhood was spent helping with the 1930s renovations on the Kerta Gosa painted ceilings in Klungkung. Batuan-born **Ni Wayan Warti** continues the traditional style of her village, producing dark and highly detailed scenes, while the already well-known young painter **I Gusti Agung Galuh** works chiefly in the popular Ubud style, her landscapes of watery paddies showing distinct Walter Spies's influences. Pengosekan resident **Gusti Ayu Suartini** also reflects her roots, concentrating on the pastel bird and flower compositions characteristic of the Pengosekan Community of Artists. **Tjok Istri Mas Astiti**, on the other hand, strikes out on her own to record the daily lives and activities of local women, tackling less aesthetic aspects, such as fading *legong* dancers and obvious poverty. Working in a more abstract vein, Sumatran-born **Januar Ernawati** favours an expressionist style to reflect her experiences within contemporary Indonesian culture, while **Gusti Ayu Kade Murni** channels dreams and supernatural images into her pictures.

Threads of Life Textile Arts Center

The **Threads of Life Textile Arts Center and Gallery** (Mon–Sat 10am–6pm), next to *Rumah Roda* restaurant at Jl Kajeng 24, aims to introduce visitors to the complex and highly skilled art of traditional weaving in Bali, Sumba, Flores, Lembata and Sulawesi, on all of which certain weaving designs and techniques are in danger of being lost forever. The Threads of Life foundation was established to try and halt the decline by commissioning modern-day weavers to recreate the ritual textiles of their grandmothers, using natural dyes and traditional methods. Many of these commissioned pieces, which can

A rice-paddy walk through Ubud Kaja

Running east of, and almost parallel to, the Campuhan ridge walk (see p.213) is a track defining an almost circular **rice-paddy walk** that begins and ends in the northern part of Ubud known as Ubud Kaja (*kaja* literally means "upstream, towards the mountains"); the walk is a two-and-a-half hours round trip, is flat and not at all strenuous. There's no shade for the first hour, though, so you'll need a hat, sunblock and some water. Most of the route (with one deviation) is suitable for mountain bikes too.

The walk begins from the western end of Ubud's **Jalan Raya**, between the Casa Lina shop and the overhead aqueduct, where a track leads up to the *Abangan Hotel* on the north side of the road. Head up the slope and, at the top, follow the track which bends to the left before straightening out and heading north. From here the route is straightforward, following the dirt track for about 3km as it slices through gently **terraced rice-fields** fringed with coconut palms on either edge. Whatever the time of day, you'll see people working in the fields, and you'll probably get offers of fresh coconut milk too (even if you're not that thirsty it's worth taking up the offer just for the chance of seeing someone shin effortlessly up a palm tree). You'll also see scores of beautifully coloured dragonflies zooming around, and plenty of birdlife – including, possibly, iridescent blue Javanese kingfishers.

After about 1hr 10min, the track comes to an end at a sealed road. Turn right here to cross the river, then look for the **southbound track** that starts almost immediately after the bridge and runs east of the river. (If you're on a bike, you're better off carrying on along the road east of the bridge as the track peters out quite soon, and then heading back to Ubud via Sakti on the road that merges into central Ubud's Jalan Suweta.) The southbound track becomes indistinct in places and for the next ten minutes you should try to follow the narrow paths along the top of the rice-field dykes and stick to a southerly direction by keeping the river in view on your right. Get back on the proper track as soon as you see it emerging from the woods alongside the river; don't forget to look back at the amazing **views of Gunung Agung** (cloud cover permitting): with the mountain in the background and the conical-hatted farmers working in the glittering rice-fields, these views are perfect real-life versions of the Walter Spies-style paintings you see in the museums and galleries of Ubud. This track will take you back down to Ubud Kaja again, finishing at the far northern end of Ubud's **Jalan Kajeng**, the little road paved with graffitied stones that runs all the way down to Jalan Raya. The stones are inscribed with the names, messages and doodlings of the Ubud residents and businesses who helped finance the paving of the lane.

take two years to complete, are on display in the Arts Center, alongside information on the origin and meaning of the most important motifs, plus exhibitions on the ritual use of the textiles, their cultural context and the specialized weaving and dyeing implements and techniques. The centre also **sells textiles** and runs regular **classes** on traditional textile appreciation (see p.225).

Campuhan, Sanggingan and Penestanan

Sited at the confluence of the rivers Wos Barat and Wos Timor, the hamlet of **CAMPUHAN** officially extends west from Ubud only as far as the *Hotel Tjampuhan*, and is famous as the home of several of Bali's most charismatic expatriate painters, including the late **Antonio Blanco**, whose house/gallery has been turned into a museum; the late **Walter Spies**, whose delightful early twentieth-century villa has become the centrepiece of the *Hotel Tjampuhan*; and **Symon**, who still paints and presides at his enticing studio-gallery across the road from the hotel.

North up the Campuhan hill from this knot of artistic abodes, Campuhan turns into **SANGGINGAN** (though few people bother to distinguish it from its neighbour), and it's here that you'll find Bali's best art gallery, the **Neka Art Museum**.

Otherwise, Campuhan and Sanggingan comprise little more than a sprinkling of residences sandwiched between the road and the rivers, a couple of notable restaurants and hotels, plus a few commercial galleries. Campuhan/Sanggingan also makes a good starting point for **walks** around Ubud, including the picturesque route to the neighbouring and still rather traditional hamlet of Penestanan. If you don't fancy walking or cycling along the busy main road that tears through its heart, you can take any west-bound **bemo** from in front of the tourist information office on Jalan Raya.

Campuhan's westerly neighbour **PENESTENAN** is famous for its home-grown artists, in particular the band of so-called **Young Artists** who in the 1960s forged a naive style of painting that's since been named after them. Some are still painting, and many of their fellow villagers produce similar-styled pictures.

The Neka Art Museum

Boasting the most comprehensive collection of traditional and modern Balinese paintings on the island, the **Neka Art Museum** (daily 9am–5pm; Rp10,000) is the perfect preface to any stay in the Ubud area, not least if you're intending to buy paintings from the many art shops in the region. Housed in a series of purpose-built pavilions set high on a hill overlooking the Wos Barat river valley, the museum stands alongside the main Campuhan/Sanggingan road.

The museum was founded in 1982 by the Ubud collector and art patron, **Wayan Suteja Neka**, a former teacher and son of the award-winning woodcarver I Wayan Neka, who was a member of the influential 1930s art movement, Pita Maha (see p.202). In establishing this private collection, Suteja Neka's stated intention was "to document the history of paintings inspired by the Balinese environment", a brief which neatly encompasses traditional works as well as those by expatriate and visiting artists. Highly informative English-language labels are posted alongside every one of the museum's several hundred paintings, which makes the confusing official gallery guidebook redundant. Nevertheless, you might consider splashing out on one of the more recent and better written **books** on the Neka collection: both *Perceptions of Paradise: Images of Bali in the Arts* by Garrett Kam, and *The Development of Painting in Bali: Selections from the Neka Art Museum* by Suteja Neka and Garrett Kam, are on sale at the museum as well as in several Ubud bookstores. For more on styles of art on display, see pp.530–534.

First Pavilion: Balinese Painting Hall

Divided into fairly distinct sections, the first pavilion attempts to give an overview of the three major schools of **Balinese painting** from the seventeenth century to the present day. The collection opens with an introduction to the earliest-known "school", the two-dimensional narratives inspired by *wayang kulit* shadow puppets (also displayed here), which earned the label **Kamasan style** after the east Bali town where most of them were produced. The Kamasan style dates back to the seventeenth century, but the nineteenth-century pictures displayed here show all the hallmarks, notably the use of distinctive, naturally produced ochre, brown and red pigments, and the stylized figures drawn in three-quarter profile. Kamasan paintings traditionally depict episodes from popular *wayang* stories, in particular the *Ramayana* and *Mahabharata* epics, and these tales continue to be the inspiration for contemporary artists, such as the late **Ketut Kobot**. A former puppet-maker himself, Kobot adapted the stark outlines of the *wayang* style, introducing softer pastel shades and filling out the canvases with more modern decorative motifs, as you can see from *Rajapala Steals Sulasih's Clothes*. Similarly, the *Pendawa Brothers Disguised as Common Beings*, painted in black and white by **Ida Bagus Rai**, fuses classical elements with a more modern sensuality.

The rest of the galleries in the first pavilion are given over to the other major schools of painting which evolved from the *wayang* style and took some inspiration from foreign artists as well. In the 1930s, Ubud artists began to paint scenes from everyday life, such as festivals, marketplaces and temple dances, while at the same time experimenting with perspective and the use of light and shadow. These works have retrospectively been given the umbrella label **Ubud style**, and many contemporary artists still work with the same techniques and subject matters today. One of the finest Ubud-style paintings in the museum is *The Bumblebee Dance* by **Anak Agung Gede Sobrat**, a prolific member of the Pita Maha group who was said to have been much influenced by his sometime teacher, the German artist Walter Spies; the scene shows a traditional flirtation dance (*oleg tambulilingan*) which is still regularly performed on local Ubud stages.

Of all the four major Balinese art styles, the dark and densely packed canvases that characterize the **Batuan style** lend themselves most to humour, political observation and social commentary. Originally attributed to a group of young 1930s painters from the nearby village of Batuan, these works are often very small and peopled by a jumble of mythical demons and legendary figures as well as by scores of contemporary villagers. The most dramatic Batuan-style pictures in this pavilion, however, are huge and tackle major themes: **I Wayan Bendi**'s depiction of the 1949–1950 *Indonesian War of Independence* and his wry portrait of the effect of tourism on the island, *Busy Bali*, both use the traditional juxtaposition of disparate characters and objects to fine effect. **I Made Budi**'s 1987 work, *President Suharto and his wife visit Bali*, is a similarly humorous take that rewards detailed examination.

Second Pavilion: Arie Smit Pavilion

The second pavilion is devoted to the hugely influential Dutch expatriate artist **Arie Smit**, a Campuhan resident who has been based in Bali since 1956, and to works by the group of painters with which he was associated, who came to be known as the Young Artists. You enter the pavilion via the upstairs gallery, which is filled with pictures by Smit. His pictures are instantly recognizable from their bold, expressionist tone; many feature imaginative landscapes inspired by Ubud scenes, generally depicted in vibrant oils, often pierced by fractured light. The collection includes some breathtakingly beautiful recent works, including *A Tropical Garden by the Sea*, which has a Cézanne-like quality.

The ground-floor hall exhibits works in the **Young Artists style**, a term coined by Arie Smit to describe the pictures created by a group of teenagers living in Ubud's neighbouring village of Penestanan in the 1960s. Smit encouraged this particular group of youngsters to express themselves freely without sticking to the conventional styles, giving them Western paints and materials to experiment with. The resulting works were naive, childlike and expressionistic, distinguished by their bold use of unrealistic colour, an absence of perspective and their largely expressionless, even featureless, figures. **I Wayan Pugur**'s *In the Village* is a typical example. The downstairs gallery also exhibits works by other Balinese artists who don't fit so neatly into the more traditional schools of Balinese art, including the energetic abstracts by **I Made Sumadiyasa**.

Third Pavilion: Photography Archive Center

The third pavilion houses a very interesting archive of black-and-white **photographs** from Bali in the 1930s and 1940s, all of them taken by the remarkable American expatriate **Robert Koke**. He and his wife Louise founded the first hotel in Kuta in 1936 (see p.105) and spent the next six years entertaining guests there as well as getting involved with artists, dancers and musicians from all corners of Bali. His photographic record includes some stunning shots of village scenes, temple festivals and cremations, but its highlights are the pictures of the *legong* and *kecak* performances and the portraits of the charismatic dancer Mario (see p.525) who invented the *oleg tambulilingan* (bumblebee dance) and of the *kecak* choreographer I Wayan Limbak. The photos are labelled with extracts from Louise Koke's enjoyable book *Our Hotel in Bali* (reviewed on p.554).

Fourth Pavilion: Lempad Pavilion

The small fourth pavilion is dedicated to the works of local renaissance man **I Gusti Nyoman Lempad** (see p.204), and holds the largest collection of his pictures in Bali. Lempad took up painting fairly late in his long and varied artistic career, quickly developing a very idiosyncratic style. Using deft and deceptively simplistic brushstrokes, he produced scores of line drawings mainly in black Chinese ink, with occasional highlights in vermilion and gold leaf. These sparse but delicate sketches generally describe scenes from religious mythology and secular folklore, and many of them seem almost cartoon-like. Some of his best-known works are from a series on **Men and Pan Brayut** (see box), a humorous reworking of the well-known folk story about a poor couple who have a family of eighteen children to bring up. Lempad shows the family in various states of harmony and discord, either engaged in typical domestic activities, as in *Making Pork Saté*, or in wryly observed comical situations as in *Mother Brayut Eats the Offerings* (she is reduced to doing this, apparently, because looking after her huge brood means she's too tired to cook).

The tale of Men and Pan Brayut

Men and Pan Brayut ("Mother and Father Brayut"), are the protagonists of a popular Balinese folk tale about a poverty-stricken couple who have an unruly brood of eighteen children to care for. Men Brayut has become the archetypal symbol of any poor woman with lots of kids and, together with her huge family, is the subject of numerous paintings showing episodes from their lives. The most famous illustrator of the Brayut story is the Ubud artist **I Gusti Nyoman Lempad** who did a series of ink drawings featuring the family, which serve as close-up illustrations of typical Balinese activities. Scenes from the Brayut story are also depicted in the classical *wayang*-style murals that cover the walls and ceilings of Klungkung's Bale Kambang hall (see p.257), and in the earthy stonecarved reliefs at Pura Dalem Jagaraga, near Singaraja (see p.347). The fullest account is to be found in an epic poem called *Gaguritan Brayut*, housed in Singaraja's Gedong Kirtya library.

According to one version of the **story**, the reason that Men Brayut has so many children is her enormous and uncontrollable appetite. When hungry, she gets irritable and rows with her husband, Pan Brayut. After fighting, the couple always make up in the time-honoured fashion – hence the constantly expanding brood. Another version puts the size of the family down to Pan Brayut's insatiable desire for his wife, which he acts upon regardless of place or circumstance. The family name, Brayut, is thought to have come from an old Javanese word which translates as "burdened with many children".

Men Brayut is both full-time mother and part-time weaver, and so her husband does the bulk of the domestic chores. Lempad shows him cleaning the yard and cooking ceremonial dishes, and in his spare time he studies religious practice. One of the highlights of their story is the **wedding ceremony** of their amorous son I Ketut Sabaya (an episode pictured in the Bale Kambang murals). Eventually, after all their hard parenting, Men and Pan Brayut renounce the material world and enter a retreat (still common practice, especially among elderly Balinese men), leaving their home and its contents to be divided among the children.

Although the Brayut story is always illustrated to accent its strong **Hindu** overtones with lots of scenes showing temple offerings, ceremonies and blessings, Men Brayut is also associated with **Buddhist** lore. In this mythology she is said to have evolved from an evil ogress named Hariti who spent her time devouring children until she converted to Buddhism and became not only a protector of children, but also a fertility goddess. Statues of Men Brayut in her Hariti manifestation can be found at Goa Gajah, near Ubud (p.230), and at the temple in Candi Dasa (p.286).

Fifth Pavilion: Contemporary Indonesian Art Hall

The fifth pavilion focuses on works by artists from other parts of Indonesia, whose style is sometimes labelled "**Academic**", partly because the painters were academically trained and partly because the style doesn't fit easily into any of the four major Balinese schools and so has come to be regarded as Western-inspired. Outstanding works displayed here include a couple of large oils by Javanese-born **Anton H**, who moved to Ubud in 1969. His *Three Masked Dancers* is a dynamic composition of ancient symbols and modern portraiture on the theme of traditional *topeng* dancers, while *Divine Union* shows the symbolic fusion of the male and female aspects of the Hindu deity Siwa, which resulted in the creation of the world. Also displayed in this pavilion is **Abdul Aziz**'s cute and much reproduced diptych entitled *Mutual Attraction*.

Sixth Pavilion: East–West Art Annex

The sixth pavilion opens with a roomful of portraits of members of the Neka family by various contemporary Indonesian and expatriate artists, including

Suteja Neka Waking Up on a Cold Morning and *Portrait of Mrs Suteja Neka*, both painted by the Javanese artist **Jeihan**. On this floor you'll also find pictures by the internationally admired Javanese artist **Affandi**. Although Affandi never lived in Bali, he visited the island frequently and his portrait of fighting cocks, *Fight to the Finish*, was done here. With its thick applications of oils, bold colours and dramatic movement, this expressionist painting is typical of his later work, and his depiction of a *Barong and Rangda* dance is another fine example.

The upstairs galleries feature the paintings of **foreign artists in Bali**, many of whom lived and worked here in Ubud, such as the Dutch painter **Rudolf Bonnet** whose *Temptation of Arjuna* is a sensual portrait of the *Mahabharata* hero. Bonnet's style, as encapsulated by the *Temptation*, is said to have been very influential in creating what became known as the Ubud style. Although his friend Walter Spies also influenced a great number of artists with his distinctive use of light and dark in landscapes peopled by elongated silhouettes of farmers, he is currently not represented in the Neka collection.

The bright Gauguinesque oils of Swiss-born **Theo Meier** draw on the lurid light and tropical emotions of Bali, in strong contrast to the Dutchman **Willem Gerard Hofker**'s minutely observed crayon studies of temples such as *Temple at Campuhan, Ubud* and his romanticized soft-focus portraits of local women. More recent expatriate artists are also represented here, including some erotically charged portraits by the Catalan-born **Antonio Blanco**, whose nearby studio-gallery is open to the public (see p.212); the Australian **Donald Friend**, whose *Carrying Deer Effigies* refers to Bali's fourteenth-century Majapahit ancestors from East Java; and the Dutchman **Han Snel**, whose striking *Girls Carrying Offerings* is characteristic of this versatile painter's work.

There are also a couple of interesting works by foreigners better known for their books on Bali: American **Louise Koke** has a study of a Balinese girl displayed here, and Mexican **Miguel Covarrubias**, who wrote the seminal *Island of Bali* in 1937, is represented by a black and white watercolour, *A Balinese Girl Carrying Rice on her Head*.

Walter Spies's house

Descending the Campuhan hill, in the direction of Ubud, you'll pass a few hotels and restaurants before reaching the elegant roadside **Hotel Tjampuhan** on your left, 100m west of the Campuhan bridge. "Tjampuhan" is the old Dutch spelling of Campuhan, and this stylish hotel is built on the site of the home of the expatriate German artist and musician **Walter Spies**. Even if you're not staying here, you're free to explore the grounds, which slope steeply down in terraced steps to the Wos Barat river gully below, with views across to the temple of Pura Gunung Lebah and the Campuhan ridge beyond. Non-guests can also use the swimming pool and spa here for a small fee (see p.200).

Spies's house remains intact: the simple two-storey thatched wooden building is still furnished with some of the artist's antiques, and the adjacent wall bears a stonecarved epitaph to its former resident. The house is now used as accommodation for hotel guests and gets booked up some way in advance, so you'll be lucky to get a look inside, but the breezy verandahs, heavy terrace furniture and lush tropical surroundings evoke a tangible sense of its former charm. Building began in 1928 on land donated by friends in the Sukawati royal family, and Spies tried hard to balance local style with imported sophistication. He designed the oval swimming pool (still in use today), filling it with spring water channelled from a nearby hillside via a series of bamboo pipes. He held pool-hall

Walter Spies in Campuhan

The son of a German diplomat based in Moscow, **Walter Spies** (1895–1942) left Europe for Java in 1923, and relocated to Bali four years later. He set up home in Campuhan, and began devoting himself to the study and practice of Balinese art and music. He sponsored two local gamelan orchestras and was the first Westerner to attempt to record **Balinese music**. Together with the American composer Colin McPhee, he set about transposing gamelan music for Western instruments, and with another associate, Katharane Mershon, encouraged Bedulu dancer I Wayan Limbak to come up with the enduringly popular **kecak dance** (see p.202).

Spies was an avid collector of Balinese **art**, and became one of the founding members of the Pita Maha arts group in 1936 (see p.202), holding the weekly meetings in his Campuhan house. He is said to have inspired, if not taught, a number of talented young Ubud artists, among them the painter Anak Agung Gede Sobrat and the woodcarver I Tegelan. Characteristic of Spies's own Balinese works are dense landscapes of waterlogged paddies set within double or triple horizons and peopled with elongated silhouettes of conical-hatted farmers, often accompanied by water buffaloes – a distinctive style that continues to be imitated by contemporary painters. There's currently only one Walter Spies painting on show in Ubud, at the Agung Rai Museum of Art (ARMA) in Pengosekan (see p.217).

In 1937, Spies retired from his increasingly hectic social life in Ubud to the tranquil hillside village of Iseh in the Karangasem district (see p.304). He decided to turn his Campuhan home into a **guesthouse**, the first of its kind in the Ubud area, and employed a couple of Germans to manage it. He died in 1942, and the guesthouse became *Hotel Tjampuhan*.

side parties and gave concerts on his grand piano, entertaining a constant stream of local and expatriate artists, musicians and anthropologists, not to mention visiting celebrities such as Charlie Chaplin, Noel Coward and Barbara Hutton, the Woolworth heiress.

Symon's Studio

"Danger! Art" warns the yellow roadsign across the road from the *Hotel Tjampuhan* complex, and it is hard to ignore this ebullient studio-gallery of American-born artist **Symon**, with its assortment of vivacious paintings and weird artefacts suspended around the steps leading up to the entrance. Inside, the **gallery** spaces house unconventional displays of Symon's paintings, sculptures and other creations, as well as a working atelier for the artist and his assistants. Born in 1947, Symon has lived in Bali since 1978 and is best known for his bold portraits of sensual young Balinese men, done in vivid tropical colours and often to an exaggerated scale, as in his series of Big Heads. His energetic and sometimes whimsical take on Balinese life and landscapes makes a refreshing change from the more sedate traditional views so popular with many other Ubud artists, and his pictures are well priced (from around $400). A browse around his studio is likely to be an enjoyable experience and you may get to meet Symon himself, if he's not at the Art Zoo, his rustic retreat near Alassari on the northeast coast (see p.348), where he's constructed another workshop, studio and exhibition space. An insightful **book** about Symon and his work, *Property of the Artist* by Philip Cornwel-Smith (reviewed on p.557), is available at the Ubud studio, as well as at some local bookshops.

Museum Blanco

A few hundred metres down the main road into Ubud from Symon's Studio and *Hotel Tjampuhan*, the ostentatious gateway announcing in huge curly letters "Antonio Blanco", and then in a slightly smaller script "The Blanco Dynasty", sets the tone for the Blanco experience beyond. This is the entrance to the former home of the flamboyant Catalan expatriate artist, now open to the public as the **Museum Blanco** (daily 10am–5pm; Rp10,000).

Blanco, who died in 1999 at the age of 88, specialized in **erotic paintings** and drawings, particularly portraits of Balinese women in varying states of undress and abandon. As with countless other Western male artists before and since, Blanco fell for a local girl, Ni Ronji, soon after arriving in Ubud in 1952, singling her out as his top model and later marrying her. Aside from his erotica, Blanco's collection also includes lots of his multimedia pieces, many of them surreal flights of poetic fancy, humorous and bizarre musings presented with mischievous ebullience. Blanco also created picture frames for all his works, most of them made from unorthodox materials. Whatever you think of the man's artistic achievements, it's hard not to enjoy the sheer panache of this ultimate self-publicist and his undeniably camp museum, complete with gilded pillars and sweeping Spanish balustrades.

Pura Gunung Lebah and around

Just across the road from Museum Blanco, **Pura Gunung Lebah** (sometimes known simply as Pura Campuhan) stands on the tip of a grassy spur at the confluence of the Wos Barat and Wos Timor rivers, a site occupied by holy buildings since the eighth century. These days, it makes a pleasant vantage point for views up- and downstream and across to the Campuhan ridge. The temple itself is hardly spectacular, though its shrines and *bale* all boast impressive red and gold paintwork on their woodcarved lintels and doors, and immaculate wiry thick thatch made from layers and layers of the elephant grass that carpets the hilly ridge beyond.

The healthy gurgling of the two rivers all but drowns out the thunderous roar of the road traffic and the temple compound gives access to both waterways and to several enticing **bathing spots** nearby. A hibiscus-lined path leads down from the west (Campuhan-side) temple steps and along the riverbank facing the *Hotel Tjampuhan* (though the river is fast-flowing it's fairly easy to wade across), while over to the east you just follow the signs for *Klub Kokos* that lead you off the roadside forecourt of the *Ibah* hotel and down some steps to the back of the temple complex, above the rocky pools of the Wos Timor, from where you can veer off along the track that runs along the Campuhan ridge (see box).

Penestanan

Just west of the Campuhan bridge, but invisible from the main road, the hamlet of **PENESTANAN** is more traditional than its neighbour and makes a good focus for a pleasant two-hour circular walk. It's accessible from a side road that turns off beside Museum Blanco, but the most dramatic approach is via the steep flight of steps a few hundred metres further north along the Campuhan road, just before Symon's Studio. The steps leads up the hillside, past arterial paths leading to some very panoramic and inexpensive hilltop accommodation (see p.200), before dropping down through rice-fields into the next valley, across the Blangsuh River and through a small wooded area, before coming to a crossroads with Penestanan's main street. This street connects

The Campuhan ridge walk

The track that extends north along the grassy spine behind Pura Gunung Lebah forms part of a very pleasant ninety-minute circular **walk** around the outskirts of Campuhan, bringing you back to the main road about 1.5km northwest of the Neka Art Museum. Alternatively, if you continue the complete length of the ridge, you'll eventually reach the tiny village of **Keliki** (7km), renowned for its intricate miniature paintings of *barong* dances, beyond which the track, asphalted in some sections, proceeds to **Taro** (13km), and eventually, with a few deviations, on to **Kintamani** (32km). All routes are good for **mountain bikes** too. If you have an umbrella and reasonable shoes, the shorter, circular walk also makes a pleasant outing in the rain: you don't get hot and the scenery looks even more lush when everything is glistening.

If you're starting the walk **from central Ubud**, walk (or take a bemo) west from Ubud market almost as far as the Campuhan bridge, turning north (right) off the main road about 100m before the bridge, into the entrance of the *Ibah* hotel, where an immediate left fork, signed for *Klub Kokos* hotel, takes you down some steps to the back of Pura Gunung Lebah. From here, the **track** (which is paved for the first 1500m) ascends a fairly gentle slope before quickly levelling out along the flattened ridgetop between the two river valleys. The perspective from this elevated route is breathtaking: to the left, you'll see the steep, increasingly developed westerly banks of the Wos Barat valley, and some way off, the distinctive orange rooftops of the Neka Art Museum. To the right, the eastern panorama across the Wos Timor valley remains unadulterated – nothing but savannah, coconut grove and rocky river gorge. There are few trees to speak of along this first stretch of the ridge walk, and therefore no shade, just a seemingly endless long-haired carpet of **elephant grass** (*alang-alang*) swaying in the breeze. The grass is a valuable resource for local villagers who harvest it regularly and dry the sheaves for thatch for houses and shrines across the island. Down below, the rocky riverbeds also provide a good source of income: the Wos valleys harbour a rich supply of **volcanic sandstone**, or *paras*, swept down from the mountains, which is quarried out in blocks for carving.

About 20min from Pura Gunung Lebah, the track passes through the first ridgetop settlement, shaded by an avenue of specially planted trees and comprising little more than a handful of houses, a couple of warung and the *Klub Kokos* hotel (see p.200) and restaurant. The villagers here have sculpted nearly all the grassland beyond into rice-fields (*sawah*), irrigating them by means of a complex system of water channels that draw on the Wos Barat below. About 1500m further on, the track enters **Bangkiang Sidem**, whose main street extends just a few hundred metres from end to end, skirting a row of family compounds built mainly from adobe bricks and elephant-grass thatch, a single warung, a *bale banjar* and a temple. Just beyond the temple, the route **forks**: left for the round trip back to the Campuhan road, straight on for Keliki. On a clear day you get a superb view of **Gunung Agung** from this junction.

The left-hand branch of the track has been upgraded into a sealed all-weather road, but it's only used for local access so is still a pleasant walk. It cuts through an ocean of *sawah* – the waterlogged rice-fields attract a number of **bird** species, in particular the iridescent royal blue Javanese kingfisher and the chubby brown cisticola warbler – before dropping down quite steeply towards the Wos Barat. Fifteen minutes after crossing the river, you'll reach the adjacent hamlets of **Payogan** and **Lungsiakan**, both slightly more prosperous-looking than Bangkiang Sidem because of their proximity to the main road, but still very traditional in style and not really accustomed to foreign visitors. Lungsiakan runs down to the main **Campuhan road**, from where you can either hop onto any bemo heading east (left) for a ten-minute ride into Ubud, continue walking for twenty minutes east down to the Neka Art Museum, or twenty minutes west (right) to Kedewatan and the main Kintamani road.

Campuhan to the east with Sayan to the west; go straight on if you're heading for Sayan, or left for a walk through the village and then back down to Museum Blanco in Campuhan. Alternatively, if you've got a compass or a good sense of direction, you could strike out **across the rice-fields** in a southeasterly direction and wend your way across the dykes back to central Ubud. There's no direct path, but it's an enjoyable hike through classic emerald-green vistas; en route you'll pass through cassava and soya plantations dotted with the occasional grove of peanut trees, clove trees, papaya trees and banana trees. It should take you about an hour to reach Ubud; anyone working in the fields will point you in the right direction or, for a small fee, guide you themselves.

Penestenan's main claim to fame is as the original home of the **Young Artists**. The Dutch painter Arie Smit settled in Penestanan in the 1960s, and set about encouraging village children as young as 12 to paint pictures dictated by their own instinct rather than sticking to the conventional styles and themes passed down by their fathers. He supplied the materials, and the young artists came up with pictures that were bright, bold and expressionist both in colour and form. As their subjects, they tended to choose scenes from daily life in Penestanan or Ubud – market day, bathing in the river or a temple festival, for example. These first naive paintings were warmly received by collectors, the style soon became recognized and labelled "Young Artists", and the technique was quickly adopted by artists in other Balinese villages as well. One of the first young artists to come under Smit's influence, albeit briefly, was I Nyoman Londo. Now in his sixties, Londo is still painting in the recognized Young Artists' style and has a studio attached to his *Londo 2* bungalow accommodation on the hilltop (see p.214).

You can still find scores of painters in Penestanan, though not all of them stick to their village's home-grown style; many are also proficient in the detailed Ubud-style paintings of dancers and riverside scenes, as well as bird and animal pastels. The village has about a dozen browsable **galleries**. Recently, a new craft has hit Penestanan, and villagers here are now the most skilful bead-workers on the island. They apply this **beadwork** to all sorts of jewellery and accessories, making shoes, handbags, belts, caps, earrings and bracelets from hundreds of painstakingly strung beads, which they then sell in shops in Penestanan and across Bali.

Penestanan makes a pleasantly tranquil, if slightly out-of-the-way, **place to stay** (see p.200). The *Bali Warung*, across the road from the *Padma Indah* bungalows, serves up a tasty selection of standard Indonesian and travellers' **food**, and *Sari Bungalow's Warung* prides itself on its authentic Balinese home-cooking.

The Monkey Forest and Nyuhkuning

Ubud's best-known tourist attraction is its **Monkey Forest Sanctuary** (daylight hours; Rp3000, kids Rp1500), which occupies the land between the southern end of Monkey Forest Road and the northern edge of the wood-carvers' hamlet of **Nyuhkuning**.

The focus of numerous day-tours because of its resident troupe of 125 malevolent but photogenic long-tailed macaques, the forest itself is actually small and disappointing, traversed by a concrete pathway and with little exceptional flora to look at. The only way to visit is on foot, but it's hardly a strenuous hike: the entrance to the sanctuary is a fifteen-minute walk south from Ubud's central market, and a stroll around the forest and its temple combines well with a walk around neighbouring Nyuhkuning.

Pura Dalem Agung Padang Tegal

Five minutes into the forest, you'll come to **Pura Dalem Agung Padang Tegal**, the temple of the dead for the *banjar* of Padang Tegal (you can borrow the requisite sarong and sash at the temple entrance, for which a small donation is requested). *Pura dalem* are traditionally places of extremely strong magical power and the preserve of *leyak* (evil spirits); in this temple you'll find half a dozen stonecarved images of the witch-widow **Rangda** (see box on p.249) flanking the main stairway, immediately recognizable from the hideous fanged face, unkempt hair, lolling metre-long tongue and large pendulous breasts. Two of the Rangda statues are depicted in the process of devouring children – a favourite occupation of hers.

Casual visitors are not allowed to enter the inner sanctuary, but in the outer courtyard you can see the ornate *kulkul* **drum tower**, built in red brick and lavishly decorated with *paras* carvings of Bhoma heads and *garuda*. When not being used to summon villagers to a cremation or a festival, the drums themselves sit high up on the red-and-gold-painted platform, swathed in lengths of holy black-and-white checked *kain poleng*.

You can stop for **refreshments** at the *Coco Loco* café, just south of the temple at the start of the track into Nyuhkuning, or there are several restaurants further along the track.

Nyuhkuning

Continuing south from the Pura Dalem Agung Padang Tegal, the track enters the tiny settlement of **NYUHKUNING**, whose villagers are renowned for their woodcarving skills. Both sides of the track are dotted with shops selling all manner of **woodcarvings**, from dolphins to elfin figurines and weeping Buddhas, most of them sculpted from coconut, hibiscus and "crocodile" wood. Prices are reasonable and the whole commercial process is much more low-key and workshop-oriented than in Mas, for example. Many of the carvers will give woodcarving lessons to interested tourists – just ask inside the shops.

A number of the best local carvings have been preserved in the **Widya Kusuma Woodcarving Museum**, a tiny makeshift gallery that keeps random hours and is set on its own in a sea of rice-fields about ten minutes south of the temple of the dead. The rather small collection is hardly riveting, though it does include a few lovely carvings of fish and monkeys, some of them made back in the 1960s. Scattered in amongst the woodcarving shops are several beautifully sited small **hotels**, each one offering uninterrupted rice-paddy views; see p.199 for a list.

Just beyond the museum, beside Nyuhkuning football field, the track feeds into a minuscule roundabout; whichever of the two routes you choose will take you on a circular tour of the tiny hamlet. Heading straight on, along the peaceful **main street**, you'll pass walled family compounds where many of the carvers have their workshops. At the southern end of main street, a five-minute walk, the left arm of the T-junction leads into the next village of Pengosekan (see below), while the right one completes the circular tour of Nyuhkuning, taking you west past the *Bali Spirit* hotel, overlooking the River Wos, and north again to the football field at the top of the village, from where you can head back to the Monkey Forest and central Ubud.

Pengosekan, Peliatan and Petulu

The villages of **Pengosekan**, **Peliatan** and **Petulu** lie to the east of central Ubud, and can be reached fairly easily on foot in an hour or less from the main market. It's quite possible to base yourself in these villages as there are losmen here, especially in Peliatan (see p.198), noted for their traditional family-style facilities.

Pengosekan

At the southern end of Jalan Hanoman, the road enters **PENGOSEKAN**, known locally as the centre of the Pengosekan Community of Artists, a cooperative that was founded in 1969 by I Dewa Nyoman Batuan and his brother I Dewa Putuh Mokoh, to help villagers share resources, exhibition costs and sales. The cooperative was so successful that most of the original members have now established their own galleries, but the spirit of the collective lives on in the **Pengosekan Community of Artists showroom** (daily 9am–6pm), which stands just east of the river on the main Pengosekan road. As with other local communities of artists, the Pengosekan painters developed a distinct style, specializing in large canvases of birds, flowers, insects and frogs, painted in gentle pastels and depicted in magnified detail. In recent years the artists have sought new outlets for their work, and now many villagers paint their pastel birds and flowers onto wooden knick-knacks such as picture frames and boxes, as well as carving small figurines and wooden flowers. The showroom has two separate galleries, one for the paintings and another for the carvings; most of the work is for sale but the selection is a bit disappointing.

Agung Rai Museum of Art (ARMA)

For a good selection of much meatier Balinese art you should go instead to the **Agung Rai Museum of Art**, usually referred to as **ARMA** (daily 9am–6pm; Rp10,000), which is a few hundred metres west of the river, and has entrances next to the *Kokokan Club* restaurant as well as on Jalan Hanoman. It's the brainchild of the same collector who runs the impressive commercial gallery on Jalan Peliatan (see below) and has as an excellent, public-access **library** and research centre on the premises, as well as a small bookshop and an open-air dance stage.

From the main entrance on Jalan Pengosekan, pass through the temporary exhibition hall and across the garden to the large pavilion signed as **Bale Daja**. The upstairs **Ruang Pita Maha** gallery gives a brief survey of the development of Balinese art, though the labels aren't that helpful and there's no obvious order to the exhibition. Historically speaking, you should begin with the **wayang style** (also known as Kamasan style) canvases that are hung high up on the walls overlooking the central well. Because they're way beyond eye-level you can't make out the detail but they all depict episodes from the *Mahabharata*, and are in typical seventeenth-century style, though they probably date from much later. Ida Bagus Belawa's *Cockfight* probably dates from the 1930s or 1940s and is a good example of how some early twentieth-century painters stuck with the two-dimensional Kamasan style but chose more modern subject-matter.

Most **Batuan-style** artists painted real-life scenes too and there are lots of pictures in this style – instantly recognizable by the sheer volume of detail and activity that gets packed in. The very early examples from the 1930s and 1940s were done in black and white ink, but contemporary Batuan artists such as the innovative and very popular I Wayan Bendi use plenty of colour. *Life in Bali* is typical of his work: crammed with typical Balinese scenes including a temple procession, a dance performance, a market scene and a cockfight, it's also laced with satirical comments, notably in the figures of long-nosed tourists who pop up in almost every scene, poking their camera lenses at village events. If you look closely you'll find a surfer in the picture too. Anak A Sobrat's *Baris Dance* is a typical example of **Ubud-style** art, and look out too for the pen and ink cartoons of I Gusti Nyoman Lempad, an important Ubud character whose former house is open to the public (see p.204). The **downstairs** gallery in the Bale Daja houses temporary exhibitions.

Across the garden, the **Bale Dauh** is dedicated to works by expatriate artists who lived in, worked in or were inspired by Bali. The middle gallery, **Ruang Walter Spies**, reads like a directory of Bali's most famous expats, and includes works by Adrien Jean Le Mayeur (see p.164), Rudolf Bonnet (p.201), Antonio Blanco (p.212) and Arie Smit (p.208). The highlight is *Calonarang* (1930) by the influential German artist **Walter Spies** (p.211), a very dark portrait of a demonic apparition being watched by a bunch of petrified villagers; this is the only Spies painting currently on show in Bali. The other major work is the double portrait of the *Regent of Magelan and His Wife* (1837) by the Javanese artist **Raden Saleh**, considered to be the father of Indonesian painting. In the adjacent **Ruang Affandi** gallery you'll find a classic Affandi (see p.210) picture of a cockfight, as well as portraits of ARMA founder Anak Agung Gede Rai and his wife Agung Rai Suartini, both by Srihadi Sudarsono.

Peliatan

The best way to approach **PELIATAN** from central Ubud is on foot via Jalan Sukma, which runs south from Jalan Raya. The upper part of Jalan Sukma is peppered with losmen and a few warung, but the pace of life is still gentle here, with rice-fields and narrow river gorges stretching beyond the roadside houses to east and west, accessed only by small dirt tracks that turn to sticky mud during the rainy season. Peliatan's eastern flank, however, has a completely different character, as the main Denpasar–Ubud–Kintamani roads roars right through it. This heavily trafficked route is lined with an almost continuous string of arts and crafts shops.

To the Balinese, Peliatan is best known as the home of one of the island's finest **dance troupes**, and particularly for its highly skilled pre-pubescent *legong* dancers. When a Balinese dance group was invited to perform at the Paris Colonial Exhibition in 1931, it was the Peliatan dancers that made the grade, and contributed to the first serious wave of European interest in Bali and Balinese culture. Peliatan dancers again represented Bali on a 1952 tour of Europe and the United States. There are currently over a dozen different dance and gamelan groups active in the village – including, very unusually, a women's gamelan – most of which perform in Peliatan and Ubud on several nights every week (see p.221).

Petulu

Every evening at around 6pm, hundreds of thousands of white herons fly in from miles around to roost in certain trees in the village of **PETULU**, immediately northeast of Ubud. To find the **white heron sanctuary**, follow the main Tegalalang–Pujung road north from the T-junction at the eastern edge of Ubud for about 1500m, then take the left-hand (signed) fork for a further 1500m. You may be asked to give a donation just before reaching the roosting area. Lots of public bemos ply the main Pujung road, but you'll have to walk the section from the fork.

The nightly roosting is quite an astonishing spectacle, with the elegant long-necked birds striking delightfully balletic poses as they glide into the tops of the tall trees, joining the dozens of birds already ensconced in the same branches. If you look closely from the official viewing point in the rice-fields below (binoculars are handy), you might be able to distinguish between the four different species of wading birds that frequent the heronry. The **Javan pond heron** is easiest to spot during the breeding season, when its usual plumage of grey feathers streaked with white darkening to brown on the breast and black along the back. The three types of egret are much harder to differentiate: the **plumed egret** is the largest and has pure white plumage, a long neck, black legs and either a black or a yellow beak; the shorter-necked **little egret** also has white feathers, black legs and a black beak. The smaller, yellow-billed **cattle egret** is at its most distinctive during the breeding season when its normally white feathers become flecked with reddish brown.

No one knows for certain why the herons and egrets have chosen to make their home in Petulu, though one local story claims that the birds are reincarnations of the tens of thousands of men and women who died in the civil war that raged through Bali in 1966. Many of the victims were buried near here, and the birds are said to have started coming here only after an elaborate ceremony was held in the village in memory of the dead.

When you've seen enough roosting activity, it's well worth continuing along the same tiny road for another kilometre or so to watch the sun sink down over the paddies and palm groves.

Eating

With some 250 **restaurants** to choose from, eating in Ubud is a major pleasure. The quality of the food is high, with an emphasis on wholesome ingredients and attractive presentation. You'll find European breads, cappuccinos and salads in nearly every Ubud café, and there'll usually be a good selection of vegetarian options too. Where phone numbers are given for restaurants outside central Ubud it's worth calling to ask about free transport (generally provided when business is good). A mandatory ten percent local government tax is added to all restaurant bills.

Be a good tourist...

... and **recycle** your plastic water bottle. Discarded plastic bottles pose a major problem in Bali, as they don't decompose and tend to pile up in nasty heaps at the back of losmen and restaurants; they're also relatively expensive and wasteful to manufacture. To help minimize this problem, some restaurants in Ubud sell drinking water only in recyclable glass bottles, but as most people need to carry water with them during the day that's not a solution. The obvious, if unrealistic, answer is for you to filter your own water from hotel taps, but the next best option is to **refill** your plastic water bottle with the filtered water supplied at certain clued-in outlets in Ubud. These include Pondok Pekak Resource Centre off Jalan Dewi Sita in central Ubud; Dwi Bhumi Cultural Workshops on Jalan Raya in central Ubud; *Bali Buddha* café opposite the GPO on Jalan Jembawan; *Roda Internet Café* on Jalan Bisma; *Kubuku* café, off the southeastern end of Monkey Forest Road in Padang Tegal; and Tegun arts and crafts shop on Jalan Hanoman. All will refill your bottles for less than what it would cost to buy a replacement.

Central Ubud

Ary's Warung Jl Raya. Classic Ubud indulgence at this elegant local landmark, where the menu includes wonderful crab fishcakes, slowly roasted duck in Balinese spices, pomfret fillet with jackfruit, and white cheesecake, but not much of a vegetarian selection. Stays open until about 1am. Expensive.

Bali Buddha Jl Jembawan, opposite the GPO. The perfect place to compose postcards or digest news from home: floor cushions and comfortable chairs, organic juices, filled bagels, chocolate mud pie, and brown-bread sandwiches. Plus a noticeboard with details of yoga and language classes and houses for rent. Inexpensive to Moderate.

Bb's (Boga Buan Café and Deli) Jl Raya. Streetside place offering a great selection of huge and very satisfying ciabatta and focaccia sandwiches made with a variety of imaginative filings. Also does platters of seafood, sushi, Indian foods and antipasti, and you can choose to sit on cushions or at top-floor tables overlooking the river. Moderate.

Bumbu Jl Suweta 1. Delicious Indian and Balinese fare, with plenty of veggie options, served in a pleasant water-garden setting. The menu includes banana and coconut curry, chilli-fried fish, mango and papaya salsa, vegetarian thalis and nasi campur, plus a range of unusual lassis and excellent iced coffees. Also offers cookery classes (see p.226). Moderate.

Café Lotus Jl Raya. Long-established Ubud landmark which overcharges for its rather average food, but it's worth the price of a mango juice or a chocolate brownie for the setting, which overlooks an enormous lotus pond in the grounds of Pura Saraswati. Moderate to Expensive.

Café Wayan Monkey Forest Rd. Scrumptious though not inexpensive breads and cakes (eat in and take-away) plus a fairly good menu of Indonesian, Thai and European dishes, served in thatched *bale* furnished with cushions and low tables. Traditional Balinese feasts are occasionally served here, buffet-style. Moderate to Expensive.

Casa Luna Jl Raya. Another very popular Ubud institution specializing in mouthwatering breads and cakes, but also offering great salads, Indonesian and Indian fare plus plenty of veggie dishes. Occasional musical performances in the evenings, and nightly videos in a separate room. Also runs cookery classes (see p.226). Moderate.

Gayatri Café 67 Monkey Forest Rd. Deservedly popular, not least because the prices are some of the cheapest in Ubud. The menu is varied, ranging from chilli (vegetarian or meat), red bean soup and pizza to salads and nasi campur. Inexpensive.

Miro's Garden Jl Bisma. Lovely garden terrace, candlelit at night, serving international and Balinese dishes, including very good nasi campur and *babi guling*. Moderate.

Nick's Southern end of Jl Bisma, central Ubud. Traditional Balinese food, including fish and rice cooked in a banana leaf. Inexpensive.

Puri Café Jl Raya. One of Ubud's most inexpensive options boasts a pleasantly low-key atmosphere, a well-stocked bar and a menu that includes sate, sweet and sour dishes, *soto ayam* and several vegetarian dishes. Inexpensive.

Sanak Rumah Makan Padang Jl Hanoman. Authentic Sumatran fare (see p.48), including fried chicken, baked eggs, potato cakes and fish curry. Assemble your own meal from the selection of cold platters in the window display. Inexpensive.

Tutmak Jl Dewi Sita. Highly recommended for its large, wholesome and interestingly varied menu that includes three versions of *nasi campur* (meat, fish and vegetarian), delicious sunflower and other breads, plus assorted curries, fabulously sticky cakes, espressos and cappuccinos. Board games, newspapers and lots of cushions make this another good spot to idle away an afternoon. Moderate.

Warung Bamboo Jl Dewi Sita. Tasty authentic Indonesian dishes, with recommended seafood and some interesting veggie options. Inexpensive.

Padang Tegal and Pengosekan

Hanoman Juice Ja North end of Jl Hanoman, Padang Tegal. Tiny juice bar and café serving a long list of fresh fruit and vegetable juices, all of them available with added wheatgerm, chlorophyll, ginseng or royal jelly. Also bakes its own brownies, apple-, carrot- and banana cakes, and sells bagels, sandwiches and soups. Moderate.

Kafé Padi Southern end of Jl Hanoman, Padang Tegal. Funky little place painted Mediterranean-style in blues and yellows and with a similarly eclectic menu that includes spicy Singaporean *laksa* noodle soup, Thai-inspired vegetable curry and Japanese-style *soba* noodles. Inexpensive to Moderate.

Kokokan Club Inside *Kokokan Hotel*, Jl Pengosekan, Padang Tegal ☎0361/973495. Classy fairly formal Thai restaurant serving delicious renditions of Thai favourites. Moderate.

Kubuku Off south end of Monkey Forest Rd, Padang Tegal. Ubud's most laid-back café stands on the edge of the rice-fields and serves a limited but scrumptious vegetarian menu that includes home-baked bread. It's the perfect place to chill out for an hour or two, and if you come on a windy day you'll get treated to a concert of wind-powered chimes and gongs. Great for sunset views over the paddies too. Inexpensive to Moderate.

Panili Vanilla Far southern end of Jl Hanoman, Padang Tegal/Pengosekan. Out-of-way-café that uses mainly organic fruit and veg, and bakes a good range of home-made breads and croissants. Offers a large menu of fruit and vegetable health juices, as well as tempting Breton pancakes, served with mushrooms and roquefort, or even with foie gras, plus lots of large, healthy salads as well as home-made ice creams and sorbets. Moderate.

Campuhan, Sanggingan, Penestanan and Sayan

Gajah Biru Jl Raya Penestanan ☎0361/979085. Although it opens from 11am, you need to come here after dark to appreciate the romance of the candlelit watergarden and its dining pavilions that look out onto fountains and ponds. The food is Indian and, aside from the set vegetarian and non-vegetarian thalis, the menu changes daily, though it always features half-a-dozen vegetable dishes as well as a chicken course and a lamb speciality. Moderate to Expensive.

Indus Jl Raya Sanggingan ☎0361/977684. Occupying a fine position overlooking the Campuhan ridge and the Wos Barat river valley, this is a good place to come for breakfast (muffins on the menu from 7am), lunch or at sunset, as you'll miss out on the view after dark. Run by the same team behind *Casa Luna* restaurant in central Ubud, the menu here is smaller but still good, featuring lots of dishes using local *tenggiri* river fish – cooked in Thai, Vietnamese or Indian style – plus the trade-mark cakes, home-made breads, vegetable juices and healthy salads. The multi-course Balinese *rijsttafel* is served every Sunday evening from 6pm (Rp70,000 per person). Moderate to Expensive.

Mozaic Jl Raya Sanggingan ☎0361/975768; open for dinner only. This elegant, slightly formal and fairly expensive restaurant serves a menu inspired by contemporary French and Asian cuisine

that includes duck foie gras with mango in an Armagnac sauce, Tasmanian salmon sashimi, steamed oysters, Bedugul rabbit and New Zealand rack of lamb in black olive sauce. Also offers tantalizing six-course Tasting Menus. Expensive.

Murni's Warung Jl Raya Campuhan. Good-quality curries, thick home-made soups and Indonesian specialities in this relaxed Ubud institution that's built downwards over half-a-dozen storeys into the side of the Wos River valley. Moderate.

Naughty Nuri's Jl Raya Sanggingan. Long-running warung that's a favourite expat hangout and is ideally located right opposite the entrance to the Neka Art Museum. Fresh tuna is a speciality – served as steaks, sashimi and sate – and barbecues are a regular event. All sorts of Indonesian standards too, plus great Martinis. Inexpensive to Moderate.

Red Rice Opposite *Sayan Terrace*, Jl Raya Sayan ☎0361/974433. Unpretentious but stylish restaurant that disingenuously calls itself "a warung with wine" but actually serves an eclectic and adventurous menu that fuses Asian and Western cuisines, including Donald Bebek (duck) spring rolls, quiche lorraine, *soto ayam* and banana soup; some experiments are more successful than others. The wine list is reasonable and good value. Moderate.

Nightlife and entertainment

Ubud is hardly a hotbed of hedonistic **nightlife**: most tourists spend the early part of the evening at one of the numerous Balinese **dance performances**, staged every night in and around central Ubud, before catching last orders at a restaurant at around 9pm. Less traditional entertainment is limited to the live music staged at some of Ubud's **bars**, or the nightly **video showings** at some of the restaurants, including *Casa Luna* on Jalan Raya and *Bridge Café* in Campuhan.

Bars and live music venues

Beggar's Bush Jl Raya, Campuhan. Long-running British-style pub and restaurant, owned by the expat author and ornithologist Victor Mason and his Balinese wife. Good range of beers, a menu that stretches to roast potatoes and cauliflower cheese, and a dartboard.

Exiles Across from the main ARMA entrance on Jl Pengosekan. Small restaurant where local jazz players meet for weekly jamming sessions on Saturday nights.

Funky Monkey (Kafe Kera Lucu) Off the southern end of Monkey Forest Rd, Padang Tegal. Currently Ubud's main gay venue, though it attracts a mixed crowd, this small, urban-style disco-bar has trendy decor and fairly reasonably priced drinks. It tends to get going late in the evening and is liveliest on Thursday nights. Shuts about 1am. Closed Mon.

Jazz Café Jl Sukma 2, Peliatan. Lively, popular and rather stylish bar-restaurant that stages quality live jazz every night from about 7.30pm. The atmosphere is usually good, there's just about room to dance in between the tables, and the perfectly respectable mid-priced menu of Indonesian and continental dishes is enlivened by jugs of draught beer and assorted margaritas. Check fly-

ers and the board outside for performance details. Free transport is usually available from the Archipelo shop on Monkey Forest Rd.

Nomad's Jl Raya, central Ubud. This restaurant serves unexceptional Indonesian standards – ayam goreng, sweet-and-sour pork and gado-gado – throughout the day, but stays open for beer and snacks until the last customers leave, usually well after midnight.

Planet Warung Opposite *Tegal Sari* hotel at the southern end of Jl Hanoman, Padang Tegal. This bar-restaurant is the main nightlife venue in this part of town, with live music twice a week – rock (Wed) and reggae (Sat) – and occasional video shows on other nights.

Putra Bar Central stretch of Monkey Forest Rd. Very lively bar-restaurant that runs a weekly schedule of differently themed nights, including frequent reggae evenings, complete with live band. There's a dance floor, live international sports on the TV and a faintly Kuta-ish atmosphere. Check boards outside for upcoming events.

Sai Sai Central stretch of Monkey Forest Rd. Restaurant-bar that serves beer till late and has live bands playing most nights from around 8pm.

Dance

When the first wave of expatriates settled here in the 1920s, Ubud was more renowned as a centre of **Balinese dance** and **gamelan** than for its arts and crafts; today, the region still boasts dozens of outstanding dance and music groups, many of which stage regular performances for tourists. The **kecak** (monkey dance) and the **barong** (lion dance) are the most exciting, accessible and visually interesting, with lots of drama and fairly easy plot lines. Both are performed in venues across the island, as is the more refined and understated **legong**, but Ubud also stages some highly unusual shows such as the village exorcism, **calonarang**, in which half the village seems to participate. Here, too, you'll also get a rare chance to see Javanese shadow puppet dramas, or **wayang kulit**, and to hear the unique **all-female gamelan**.

A lot of the dance groups combine up to eight different dances into a medley show. Sometimes this is not indicated in the publicity – the show at Ubud Palace by the Sadha Budaya dance group, for example, is advertised as *legong*, but also features the brilliantly eloquent flirtation dance **oleg tambulilingan** (bumblebee dance) and the touching **topeng tua** (old man's mask dance). Similarly, the Tirta Sari group's show in Peliatan includes a superbly melodramatic solo dance, the **kebyar trompong**, performed as a highly camp repartee between the dancer and the gamelan players.

Practicalities

There are up to five different dance shows every night in the Ubud area; the tourist office has details of the regular weekly schedule and also arranges **free transport** to the more outlying venues. Most **tickets** are Rp25,000 and can be bought either at the tourist office, from touts or at the door. Performances generally start between 7pm and 8pm, and it's advisable to arrive at least half-an-hour early as there are no seat reservations. For more on Balinese dance, see pp.519–527.

If you have only one evening to catch a show, then consider seeing whatever is playing at **Puri Saren Agung (Ubud Palace)**, opposite the market in the very centre of Ubud (see p.203). The setting is breathtaking, with the torchlit courtyard gateways furnishing a memorable backdrop. You can also watch Ubud children doing their dance practice here (Sun 9.30am–noon, Tues 3–5.30pm; free).

Shopping

Shopping for arts and crafts is a major pastime in Ubud; you might also want to explore the specialist "craft villages" on the Denpasar–Ubud road (see p.179) before making any significant purchases. If you're thinking of splashing out on paintings, take a tour round either the Neka Art Museum or the Seniwati Gallery first, to get some idea of the range of styles and talents.

Most Ubud shops open daily, many not closing until 8pm or 9pm. Tino Supermarket, on Jalan Raya, stocks all major essentials, from suntan lotion to beer. There's a DHL courier agent on Jalan Raya in central Ubud, across from Ganesha Bookshop, for shipping things home.

Books and cards

Adi Bookshop Corner of Jl Hanoman and Ubud's Jl Raya. Small second-hand bookstore.

ARMA Bookshop Inside Agung Rai Museum of Art, Pengosekan. Small range of books on Bali and Indonesia.

Ary's Bookshop Jl Raya, central Ubud. Fairly extensive stock of books on Bali and Indonesia, plus a number of maps. Also sells some European, American and Australian newspapers and magazines.

Cinta Bookshop Jl Dewi Sita. Great number and range of second-hand books for sale; some also available to borrow at Rp15,000 per fortnight.

Ganesha Bookshop Jl Raya, central Ubud Ⓦwww.ganeshabooksbali.com. The best bookshop in Bali, with a huge stock of new books on all things Balinese, from language to culture, gardens to recipes, as well as academic works and other specialist tomes, plus a large, intelligently

categorized collection of reasonably priced second-hand books. Also sells maps, Balinese cartoon postcards and the Baliopoly board game. Online ordering service also available.

GPO Jl Jembawan. The post office shop keeps a good range of greetings cards, including humorous Balinese ones, as well as a small range of books about Bali.

Igna Bookshop North end of Monkey Forest Rd. Reasonable number of second-hand books, plus a few new books.

Neka Art Museum Bookshop Jl Raya Sanggingan/Campuhan. Extensive range of Balinese, Indonesian and expat artists' monographs plus some more general books about Balinese art and culture.

Rona Bookshop Jl Sukma 23, Peliatan. Well-organized second-hand bookstore and library attached to *Rona Losmen*.

Clothes and jewellery

Animale Western end of Jl Raya, central Ubud. The local branch of the womenswear chain stocks trademark floaty cotton and rayon outfits in a variety of bold prints.

Baingin Jl Hanoman, Padang Tegal. Distinctive collection of women's fashions made from hand-woven Balinese cotton dyed in beautiful, arresting colours.

Kamar Sutra Monkey Forest Rd. Stunning batik

designs on gorgeous but very expensive silk, crêpe and chiffon fabrics, made into scarves, wraps and shawls.

Mama & Leon Monkey Forest Rd. Another Bali chain that fits in well with the Ubud scene with its smart range of tailored outfits in plain-coloured cotton and linen.

Pasar Seni Jl Raya, central Ubud. The two-storey

"art market" holds dozens of stalls selling cheap cotton clothes, sarongs and batik shirts. There are several good, inexpensive tailors in the art market too.

Suarti Monkey Forest Rd. Part of a chain of modern jewellery shops specializing in original designs at reasonable prices.

Crafts, textiles and homewares

Archipelo Southern end of Monkey Forest Rd. Quality handicrafts and home accessories, including napkin rings made of cloves and coconut-shell tablemats. Smart but pricey.

Argosoka Southern end of Monkey Forest Rd. Exceptional and expensive batik textiles made in traditional style to classic designs.

Dari Desa Off the far southern end of Monkey Forest Rd, Padang Tegal. Soft furnishings, including duvet covers and beanbags, made in a range of traditional textiles from Bali, Lombok, Java and India, much of it commissioned directly from village women.

Indo Crafts Central Monkey Forest Rd. Fabulous array of well-priced traditional heavy *ikat* cottons from Sumba and Flores, including hangings, bedspreads, scarves, bags and clothes.

Kites Center 3 Off the far southern end of Monkey Forest Rd, Padang Tegal. Outlet for traditional kites, most of them huge, in spectacular designs such as butterflies, vampire bats, dragons and *barong*. Also can be made to order.

Mangku Made Gina Beside ARMA at the southern end of Jl Hanoman in Padang Tegal/Pengosekan. Unrivalled collection of exquisite palm-leaf baskets made by a family of Pengosekan basket-weavers. The baskets come in all sizes, from huge flat discs the size of a car tyre to large urns and smaller pot-sized ones. The finest are woven in three different colours and take a fortnight to complete. Highly recommended. Rp125,000–700,000.

Murti Jl Hanoman 19, Padang Tegal, junction Jl Dewi Sita. Outlet for the distinctive ceramics from the kilns at Pejaten in west Bali (see p.378), mainly tiny pots, ashtrays, vases, candlesticks, mosquito-coil burners and bowls glazed in mint green and pale blues. Also sells elegant coconut-wood trays, bowls and plates.

Nithi's Collection Jl Raya, central Ubud. Huge range of inexpensive cotton and rayon wraps and sarongs, dyed in muted shades and to idiosyncratic batik designs.

Pasar Seni Jl Raya, central Ubud. The two-storey "art market" is stacked full of stalls selling sarongs, batik bags, bamboo wind-chimes, tightly woven *ato* grass baskets and the like.

Percetakan Diary Jl Raya, central Ubud. Interesting handicrafts made from bamboo paper, rice paper and banana-tree bark as well as coconut shell and recycled paper.

Sely Southern end of Monkey Forest Rd, and midway down Jl Hanoman, Padang Tegal. Cute and inexpensive little cosmetic bags, purses and shoulder bags, all made from brightly coloured Balinese silk.

Seniwati Shop Jl Raya, central Ubud. The commercial outlet for the Seniwati Gallery of Women Artists stocks reproductions of the gallery collection made into greetings cards, calendars and prints.

Tegun Jl Hanoman 44, Padang Tegal. Exceptionally fine crafts and artefacts, including exquisite wooden bowls, trays, boxes and picture frames painted with Javanese batik motifs.

Wardani's Opposite *Sai Sai* on central Monkey Forest Rd. The best fabric shop in Ubud, with scores of different cotton *ikats* sold by the metre, plus other designs in silk and cottons, as well as ready-made cushion covers and other soft furnishings.

Musical instruments and CDs

Ganesha Music Jl Jembawan, eastern Ubud ⊛ www.ganeshabooksbali.com. Long established as a venue for workshops in Balinese music (see p.227), this new branch of the Ganesha bookshop sells CDs and tapes of Indonesian and Balinese music. The selection is good and includes unusual finds. Online ordering service also available.

Genggongs At *Mandala Homestay*, Jl Sukma 63, Peliatan. Traditional vibrato wooden instruments, something like a Jew's harp (see p.517), made by the family who run this losmen. The father gives lessons on request, and also plays in local performances of the frog dance.

Moari Music Jl Raya, central Ubud. Specializes in traditional Balinese musical instruments, from bamboo flutes to full-sized gamelan.

Pondok Bamboo Off the far southern end of Monkey Forest Rd, Padang Tegal. Sells the full range of Balinese instruments made from bamboo, with everything from *genggong* and wind-chimes to the component parts of the *gamelan joged bumbung*, the bamboo gamelan.

Ubud Music Jl Raya, central Ubud. Ubud's main outlet for inexpensive CDs, offering the usual selection of current Western hits as well as classics.

Paintings and carvings

Agung Rai Fine Art Gallery Jl Peliatan, Peliatan. High-quality outlet for paintings of all types, starting at around $40 for a Keliki-style miniature, to $100 and above for Ubud scenes and into the thousands for the large abstracts and detailed Batuan-style canvases. Helpful, well-informed staff.

Arka Antiques Art Monkey Forest Rd. Massive collection of wooden masks, from frogs to Rangdas, crude Papua New Guinea pieces to modern abstract faces.

Duck Man of Bali About 1500m east along the road to Goa Gajah, southeast of central Ubud. Phenomenal gallery of wooden ducks in all sizes, stances and permutations, carved by "the duck man", Ngurah Umum, and his assistants. Also a range of more traditional carvings.

Munut's Gallery Far eastern end of Jl Raya, eastern Ubud. Recommended dealer in paintings of all styles, with a large selection on display. Prices start at around $35 for an unframed Batuan- or Keliki-style miniature; $60 for a traditional portrait of a *baris* dancer.

Neka Gallery Jl Raya, eastern Ubud. Huge warren of a showroom owned by the founder of the Neka Art Museum. Specializes in good-quality works, many by well-known artists. Prices range from $75 for small works in the Batuan and Young Artists styles to thousands of dollars for huge canvases by Han Snel and Faizal.

Wayan Purna Jl Hanoman, Padang Tegal. Picture frames carved to order on the premises.

Spas, beauty treatments and alternative therapies

Almost every upmarket hotel in Ubud now has its own in-house **spa**, where guests can pamper themselves in whirlpools and herbal baths, take traditional massages and mud wraps and have **beauty** and **alternative therapies** (for more, see p.67). Ubud also has a number of walk-in spas and beauty treatment centres, which offer the same range of treatments, sometimes without the need for an appointment. All are open daily until at least 7pm.

One of the most popular local specialities is the **mandi lulur** ($15–20), a Javanese herbal exfoliation massage in which your body gets rubbed with a slightly abrasive paste of turmeric, nuts and rice; the end result is said to be a very smooth and polished skin. There are usually half-a-dozen other **massage treatments** ($10–12) and **body scrubs** ($8) available, for relieving tension, invigorating or detoxifying your body. The popular **cream bath** ($10) is actually a deep nourishing treatment for hair, combined with a head, neck and shoulder massage. All these centres also offer manicures, pedicures, facials and haircuts, and some organize **yoga** and **meditation** sessions.

The Bodywork Centre Jl Hanoman 25 ☎0361/975720. Traditional baths and massages, beauty treatments, acupressure and reflexology. Also organizes yoga sessions and courses and sells essential oils. (Not related to Bodyworks in Legian and Seminyak.)

Ibah Spa Jl Raya Campuhan ☎0361/974466, ⓦwww.ibahbali.com. The elegantly sumptuous treatment rooms at this luxury boutique hotel are considered among the most indulgent in Ubud, and the spa treatments include the Mandara massage where each client is massaged by two therapists at the same time, using five different massage styles. Advance booking essential.

Reassuringly expensive.

Meditation Shop Monkey Forest Rd. Regular meditation sessions and talks from various spiritual teachers. Weekly highlights are posted outside the entrance.

Nirvana Monkey Forest Rd (mobile ☎0812/394 6702). Large menu of massages, body scrubs, body masks, and skin- and hair-care treatments.

Nur Salon Jl Hanoman 28, Padang Tegal ☎0361/975352, ⓔnursalon@yahoo.net. Ubud's first massage and beauty salon has been in operation since the 1970s and enjoys a very good reputation with lots of repeat customers; the *mandi lulur* treatments are especially famous, and prices are among the lowest in Ubud. The salon occupies a traditional Balinese compound and treatment rooms are designed in keeping. Uses male masseurs for male customers.

Tegun Galeri Jl Hanoman 44, Padang Tegal ☎0361/973361. Holds regular classes in Kundalini and Hatha yoga, ancient Hula dance and chanting, and Middle Eastern belly dancing. Phone for schedules.

Tjampuhan Spa At *Hotel Tjampuhan*, Jl Raya Campuhan ☎0361/975368, ⓦwww.tjampuhan.com. Unusual, fairly kitsch, grotto-like spa complex where the treatment cabins have been built into the cliffside near the river

below the *Hotel Tjampuhan*. The whole place is designed with pools, waterfalls and surreal figurines to evoke a watery fantasy land, and there are saunas, a whirlpool and a steam room as well as a large programme of massages, scrubs and facials. Non-guests can use all the facilities for \$15; or \$49 including one treatment (\$89 per couple).

Ubud Sari Health Resort Jl Kajeng 35, central Ubud ☎0361/974393, ⓦwww.ubudsari.com. The most serious, and expensive, of Ubud's health and beauty centres. Alongside the standard range of massages, wraps and scrubs are aromatherapy, reflexology, shiatsu, reiki, sports massage and sessions with a chiropractor.

Courses and workshops

Ubud's reputation as a centre for the performing and visual arts means there are plenty of opportunities to take **courses** and **workshops**, even if you're only in the area for a few days. It's also well worth asking about lessons at the more traditional homestays, whose managers are often dancers, musicians or painters.

Batik painting, textiles and arts and crafts

ARMA Jl Pengosekan, Pengosekan ☎0361/976659, ⑤975332, ⓔkokokan@dps.mega.net.id. Classes in Balinese painting, woodcarving, and batik. \$15–50 per person, depending on subject and class size.

Crackpot Batik Monkey Forest Rd, central Ubud. Design your own batik fabrics, paintings and T-shirts. Staff supply all the necessary implements, give instruction as required and encourage you to turn up as and when you want to. Rates depend on the size and complexity of your artwork, but are always reasonable.

Dwi Bhumi Art and Cultural Workshops Jl Raya, central Ubud ☎ & ⑤0361/974153, ⓦwww.dwibhumi.com. Regular classes in all sorts of arts and crafts, including woodcarving, beadwork, painting, basketry, kite-making, mask painting and shadow puppet making. Prices range from Rp65,000 for half-day classes to Rp275,000 for two-day workshops (minimum two participants; 25-percent discount for under-11s); book one day ahead.

Nirvana Batik Course Jl Gautama 10, Padang Tegal ☎ & ⑤0361/975415, ⓔrodanet@denpasar.wasantara.net.id. Renowned Ubud painter, village activist and batik artist I Nyoman Suradnya

runs one- to five-day courses in batik painting, charging \$35 per day for one-day courses and \$25 per day for four- and five-day courses, including all materials. His family also runs the *Nirvana Pension* guesthouses (see p.197).

Nyuhkuning woodcarving shops Nyuhkuning. There are plenty of opportunities to learn woodcarving in this village of woodcarvers; just ask at any of the shops.

Studio Perak North end of Jl Gautama, mobile ☎0812/361 1785. Courses in silversmithing, where in half a day you can produce your own ring (Rp100,000 inclusive). In two to five days (Rp120,000 per day excluding materials) you can learn more advanced techniques and design skills.

Threads of Life Jl Kajeng 24, central Ubud ☎0361/972187, ⑤976582, ⓦwww.threadsoflife .com. The Threads of Life Textile Art Center and Gallery (see p.205) holds scheduled weekly classes on textile appreciation: an introduction to the textiles of Bali, the *ikat* process and/or batik (Tues morning; Rp50,000); and the historical and cultural influences in Indonesian textiles (most Thurs mornings; Rp70,000). Phone ahead to check times and reserve.

Ubud for kids

Many of the **courses and workshops** listed on pp.225–27 welcome younger participants. In particular, most kids enjoy creating their own **batik** T-shirts and paintings, which they can do on an informal basis at the batik centres. Ganesha Bookshop on Jalan Raya, central Ubud (℡0361/976339, ℻973359, ⓦwww.ganeshabooksbali.com) welcomes all over-10s to its weekly **music** workshop, and Pondok Pekak Resource Centre, Jalan Dewi Sita, central Ubud (℡0361/970194, ℮pondok@denpasar.wasantara.net.id) runs multilingual children's classes in **gamelan** and Balinese **dance**, which are suitable for most over-6s. Pondok Pekak also has a well-stocked library of **children's books**. Ganesha Bookshop sells the Baliopoly **board game**, a Balinese version of Monopoly.

Traditional **dance-drama performances** can also be entertaining for kids, particularly the *kecak* (monkey) dance, which is performed somewhere in the Ubud vicinity almost every night (see p.221), and the *wayang kulit* shadow puppet shows which are staged several nights a week at *Kerta Accommodation* on Monkey Forest Road (check posters outside the venue for details).

The three animal parks within 45 minutes' drive of Ubud make fun days out for children of most ages. The **Elephant Park** in Taro (see p.236) gives everyone the chance to feed the elephants and watch them bathe, and you can also join a short elephant safari ride through the surrounding forest. In Batubulan, the **Bali Bird Park** (see p.180) is a pleasure to wander through, with plenty of pretty specimens to admire and an attractively landscaped setting. Next door, the **Reptile Park** has strange, slimy creatures, including huge pythons, chameleons and little Komodo dragons. See p.180 for details of a tour taking in all three.

Most **whitewater rafting** operators (see p.195) also accept children, but river kayaking is unsuitable for children under 14.

Cookery

Bumbu restaurant Jl Suweta 1, central Ubud ℡0361/974217, ℮wizbali@indosat.net.id. One-day workshops in Balinese cooking, which begin with a trip to the local market and culminate in lunch. Rp120,000. Reserve ahead.

Casa Luna restaurant Jl Raya, central Ubud ℡0361/973282, ℮casaluna@bali-paradise.com.

Balinese cooking workshops (Mon, Tues & Wed morning; Rp150,000; minimum five people). Advance booking essential.

Sua Bali Kemenuh. Residential cookery courses are held in the village of Kemenuh, 7km east of Ubud (see p.250).

Language

Dwi Bhumi Art and Cultural Workshops Jl Raya, central Ubud ℡ & ℻0361/974153, ⓦwww.dwibhumi.com. Tailor-made private Indonesian language lessons (evenings only); Rp45,000 per person per hour, minimum two people.

Oka Wati's restaurant Off Monkey Forest Rd, central Ubud. Lessons in Indonesian and Balinese.

Pondok Pekak Jl Dewi Sita, central Ubud ℡0361/976194, ℮pondok@indo.net.id.

Indonesian language courses (24hr; Rp540,000), usually spread over four weeks but can be changed to suit.

Sua Bali Kemenuh. Residential Indonesian and Balinese language courses are held in the village of Kemenuh, 7km east of Ubud (see p.250).

Sukadana Jl Jembawan, Padang Tegal ℡0361/974131. Classes and courses in Balinese and Indonesian with schedules and rates fixed according to the individual.

Music, dance and Balinese culture

ARMA Jl Pengosekan, Pengosekan ℡0361/976659, ℻975332, ℮kokokan@dps.mega.net.id. A wide range of interesting, if pricey, cultural workshops on

demand, including gamelan, Balinese dance and theatre, traditional Balinese architecture, traditional healing, trance and possession and making offerings. Topics generally cover both theoretical and practical aspects. $15–50 per person, depending on subject and class size.

Dewi Sekar Ayu Jl Hanoman 26, central Ubud ☎0361/976011. If you have a serious interest in Balinese dance, Ayu will be happy to arrange a tailor-made course for you.

Dwi Bhumi Art and Cultural Workshops Jl Raya, central Ubud ☎ & ℻0361/974153, ⓦwww.dwibhumi.com. Regular classes in gamelan, dance, *kecak* singing, flute playing and making offerings. Ninety-minute classes cost around Rp50,000 (minimum two participants; 25-percent discount for under-11s); book one day ahead.

Ganesha Bookshop Jl Raya, central Ubud ☎0361/ 976339, ℻973359, ⓦwww.ganeshabooksbali.com. Weekly group workshops on traditional Balinese music are held in the upstairs room (Tues 6–7.30pm; Rp45,000), for any interested person over the age of 10. They incorporate a historical and practical introduction to the gamelan as well as a chance to experiment with the instruments of your choice. Private music lessons are also available on request.

Nataraja Dance School Jl Sugriwa 20, Padang Tegal. Dancer and musician Wayan Karta gives informal individual dance and gamelan lessons in the dance of your choice (*legong* or *baris* for example). To get a good grounding, students are advised to sign up for at least fourteen hours of tuition.

Pondok Pekak Jl Dewi Sita, central Ubud ☎0361/976194, ℮pondok@indo.net.id. No formal courses in music or dance, but plenty of talented Balinese musicians at this library and resource centre who are happy to arrange classes.

Sehati Southeast off the far southern end of Monkey Forest Rd, central Ubud. Learn to play the gamelan and various other Balinese instruments, or to master the rudimentary elements of Balinese dance from a local graduate of Denpasar's prestigious school of performing arts. Rp45,000 per hour.

Sukadana Jl Jembawan, Padang Tegal ☎0361/974131. Private classes and courses in traditional Balinese dance.

Listings

Airline offices Most international (see p.111) and domestic (see p.21) airline offices are in Sanur or Denpasar.

Banks and exchange There are plenty of Visa, MasterCard and Cirrus ATMs on Ubud's Jalan Raya, a couple on Monkey Forest Rd, and one just north of Perama on Jalan Hanoman in Padang Tegal; there are no ATMs in Campuhan, Sanggingan, Penestanan or Sayan, but all these areas have currency exchange booths. Numerous tour agents (daily 8am–6pm) throughout the Ubud area, and particularly on Jl Raya and Monkey Forest Rd, offer exchange services at reasonable rates. See p.36 for details of common scams. You can get Visa and MasterCard cash advances (Mon–Fri 8am–1pm) from Bank Bali opposite Puri Lukisan Museum on Jalan Raya, and from Bank Danamon at the far eastern end of Ubud's Jalan Raya. The Ubud GPO is an agent for Western Union money transfers.

Email and internet Because of a dearth of phone lines, internet access can be slow in Ubud. Average price is Rp4000 for 15min. Some of the most efficient internet centres are: Bali 3000 on Jl Raya (daily 9am–11pm); Roda Tourist Services, Jl Bisma 3 (daily 9am–9pm); and Ary's Business and Travel Service, just west of the market on Jl Raya,

central Ubud (daily 8am–10pm). The GPO has internet terminals.

Embassies and consulates See p.23.

Hospitals and clinics For minor casualties go to the Legian Medical Clinic 5, Monkey Forest Rd ☎0361/976457, or to the Ubud Clinic near the Pura Gunung Lebah on Jl Raya Campuhan ☎0361/974911. Both are open 24hr, are staffed by English-speakers, will respond to emergency call-outs and have an ambulance service. A consultation should cost about Rp100,000. For anything more serious, the nearest hospitals are in Denpasar (p.103).

House rental There are always plenty of fabulous villas and houses available for long- and short-term rent in the Ubud area. Check the noticeboards at *Bali Buddha* café on Jl Jembawan, at *Casa Luna* restaurant on Jl Raya, and at *Bali 3000* internet café on Jl Raya, or browse the free fortnightly newspaper *Bali Advertiser* (available at many restaurants). See p.47 for online agencies.

Libraries The Pondok Pekak Library and Resource Centre on the east side of the football field, off Jl Dewi Sita (Mon–Sat 9am–9pm, Sun 10am–1pm) has a good collection of books about Bali as well as Asia travel guides and English-language novels. You can read them on the spot in the comfortable upstairs reading room or borrow them for a small fee. There is also a children's library and learning centre here, which aims to encourage Ubud children to read Indonesian- and English-language books; donated books and funds are always welcome, see p.34 for more details. The Agung Rai Museum of Art (ARMA) has the island's best library of books about Bali, with esoteric volumes such as Margaret Mead's famous anthropological studies and photos from the 1930s, monographs on artists like Hofker and Affandi, plus plenty of cookery books, language books, travelogues and novels. There's a photocopier on the premises too.

Pharmacies The two central branches of Ubud Farma on Jl Raya and Monkey Forest Rd (daily 8am–9pm) are staffed by helpful English-speaking pharmacists who stock a big range of brand-name essentials and their local equivalents.

Phone and fax services The government Kantor Telcom is inconveniently located at the eastern end of Ubud's Jl Raya, but there are IDD direct-dial phones at the GPO on Jl Jembawan (daily 8am–6pm) as well as at several more central private wartels that charge almost the same rates, including: Ary's Business and Travel Service just west of the market on Jl Raya, central Ubud (daily 8am–10pm); Nomad Wartel, above *Nomad* restaurant on Jl Raya (daily 8am–10.30pm); Roda Tourist Services, Jl Bisma 3 (daily 9am–9pm); and Wartel Pertiwi on central Monkey Forest Rd (daily 8.15am–8.45pm). There's a Home Direct public telephone at the Kantor Telcom, and outside the GPO. Phone cards are available at the Kantor Telcom, and at most minimarkets. You can also send and receive faxes at any of the email bureaus listed above.

Police The main police station is on the eastern edge of town, on Jl Tegalalang. There's a more central police booth beside the market at the Jl Raya/Monkey Forest Rd crossroads.

Post offices There are plenty of postal agents all over Ubud where you can buy stamps and send mail and parcels. The Ubud GPO on Jl Jembawan (daily 8am–6pm) keeps poste restante, and there's a parcel-packing service next door.

Safety boxes For rent (Rp5000 per day) at Ary's Business and Travel Service on Jl Raya, central Ubud (☎0361/973130), and at many mid-range and all expensive hotels.

Travel agents Any Ubud agent will be able to sell you a flight, change your existing ticket or reconfirm your flight. Try the reputable Ary's Business and Travel Service just west of the market on Jl Raya, central Ubud (☎0361/973130, ℱ975162, ℮ary_s2000@yahoo.com).

East of Ubud

Slicing through the region immediately **east of Ubud**, the sacred rivers Petanu and Pakrisan flow down from the Batur crater rim in parallel, framing a narrow strip of land imbued with great spiritual and historical importance. This fifteen-kilometre-long sliver has been settled since the Balinese Bronze Age, around 300 BC, and now boasts the biggest concentration of antiquities on Bali. Ranging from the stone sarcophagi and Bronze Age gong of **Pejeng** to the eleventh-century rock-hewn hermitage at **Goa Gajah** and fourteenth-century **Yeh Pulu** reliefs, these relics all lie within 7km of Ubud.

A few of the Pejeng area sites are popular with tour groups, but most get hardly any visitors. Access by **bemo** is very easy from Ubud – take any Gianyar-bound one – and similarly straightforward by bike or motorbike. This area also combines well with Tirta Empul and Gunung Kawi, 11km further north, and direct bemos connect the two. There are a couple of places to stay near Goa Gajah and at Yeh Pulu.

The legend of Dalem Bedaulu

Between the tenth and the fourteenth centuries, the sacred land between the Pakrisan and Petanu rivers was the seat of the **Pejeng dynasty**, which ruled the region from a court located a few kilometres south of modern Pejeng, in the village of Bedulu. The most notorious of the Pejeng rulers was also its last, **Dalem Bedaulu**, whose armies were the last on the island to capitulate to the invading forces of East Java's Majapahit empire in 1343. Legend relates how Dalem Bedaulu had enormous supernatural power, which he liked to show off to his courtiers by regularly cutting off his own head and then replacing it. The god **Siwa** became so incensed by this boastful behaviour that, on one occasion, he made Dalem Bedaulu's severed head roll away into a fast-moving river. The king's quick-thinking servant cut off the head of the nearest living creature, a pig, and placed it on the royal neck. After this, the king was so embarrassed about his pig's head that he established himself in a special high tower, passed a law forbidding anyone to look up at his face, and forced everyone to speak to him from ground level, eyes downcast. When East Javanese prime minister **Gajah Mada** heard of this, he plotted to get round the prohibition by asking, in Dalem Bedaulu's presence, to be brought drinking water from a traditional vessel with a very long spout. To drink he was obliged to tip his head backwards, and so caught a glimpse of Dalem Bedaulu's pig's head. Dalem Bedaulu was so furious at Gajah Mada's cunning that he immediately self-combusted; that was the end of the Pejeng dynasty and the start of Majapahit's complete hegemony over Bali.

Goa Gajah

Thought to have been a hermitage for eleventh-century Hindu priests, **Goa Gajah** (Elephant Cave; daylight hours; Rp3100, children Rp1600) has now become a major tourist attraction, owing more to its proximity to the main Ubud–Gianyar road than to any remarkable atmosphere or ancient features. Besides the cave itself, there's a traditional bathing pool here, as well as a number of ancient stone relics, and the usual collection of stalls selling refreshments and souvenirs. As it's a holy place, you'll need to borrow a **sarong** and **sash** if you haven't brought your own.

The pools and the cave

Descending the steep flight of steps from the back of the car park, you get a good view of the rectangular **bathing pool**, whose elegant sunken contours dominate the courtyard below. Such pools were usually built at holy sites, either at the source of a holy spring as at Tirta Empul (see p.238) or, like this one, near a sacred spot so that devotees could cleanse themselves before making offerings or prayers. Local men and women would have bathed here in the segregated male (right-hand) and female (left-hand) sections, under the jets of water from the Petanu tributary channelled through the protruding navels of the full-breasted statues lining its back wall. Although the water still flows, the pools are now maintained for ornamental purposes only.

The carvings that trumpet the entranceway to the hillside cave are certainly impressive, if a little hard to distinguish. The **doorway** is a huge gaping mouth, framed by the upper jaw of a monstrous rock-carved head that's thought to represent either the earth god Bhoma, or the widow-witch Rangda, or a hybrid of the two. The grotesque image is almost certain to have served both as a repeller of evil spirits and as a suggestion that on entering you were being swallowed up into another, holier, world. Early visitors thought it looked like an elephant's head, which is how the cave got its modern name. A series of mythical creatures is also said to be carved into the bare rock face to the left and right of the head, but from the ground it's very hard to spot them.

Passing into the monster's mouth, you enter the T-shaped **cave**, hewn by hand from the rocky hillside to serve as meditation cells, or possibly living quarters, for the priests or ascetics. As with most of Bali's rock-cut monuments, the mythical giant Kebo Iwa is also associated with Goa Gajah, and legends describe how he gouged out the cells and the carvings here with his powerful fingernails, a feat that took him just one night. The dank and dimly lit **interior** holds little of interest: a statue of the Hindu elephant-headed god Ganesh sits in a niche to the left of the far end, while to the right are three *lingga*, phallic emblems of the god Siwa.

Outside the cave, in the small pavilion to the left of the monstrous gateway, sits a weatherworn **statue** of a woman surrounded by a horde of kids. Carved from a single block of stone, this piece shows the Balinese folk heroine **Men Brayut**, a typical village woman whose resolute struggle against poverty has made her into a saint-like figure in Bali (see the box on p.209). Men Brayut is known as the goddess Hariti in Buddhist literature, and this statue – along with a number of other relics found nearby – have led archeologists to believe that the site may have a **Buddhist** as well as a Hindu history. You can see some of the other Buddhist fragments by following the concrete steps that climb down the side of the ravine just beyond the bathing pool. These include the relief of a multi-tiered stupa carved into a huge fragment of rock, and a couple of small seated stone Buddha images.

Practicalities

To get to Goa Gajah, either **walk** or **drive** the 3km east from Ubud's Jalan Peliatan, or take one of the numerous (usually orange) Ubud–Gianyar **bemos**, which go past the entrance gate. The site car park borders the main Ubud–Gianyar road and is clearly signposted from both directions. You can also walk here from the nearby Yeh Pulu rock carvings (see below), along the irrigation channels that zigzag through the rice-fields, but to do this you'll need to hire one of the guides who hang around at both Yeh Pulu and Goa Gajah.

There's a pleasant **place to stay** nearby, on the edge of the lively but untouristed village of **BEDULU**: continue along the main road about 500m east of Goa Gajah and then turn to the south (right), following signs for *Puri Yeh Pulu Bungalows* (℡0361/941566; ❹). The five bungalows here are spacious and comfortable and sit in a garden that enjoys nice views down over the Petanu valley.

Yeh Pulu

In contrast with the overcrowded and overrated carvings at Goa Gajah, the rock cut panels at **YEH PULU** (daylight hours; Rp3100 including sarong and sash rental, kids Rp1600) are delightfully engaging, and the site is often empty – partly due to its relative inaccessibility.

Chipped away from the sheer rock face, the 25-metre-long series of Yeh Pulu **carvings** are said to date back to the fourteenth or fifteenth century. They are thought by some historians to depict a five-part story and, while the meaning of this story has been lost, it's still possible to make out some recurring characters and to speculate on the connections between them; local people, how-ever, simply describe the carvings as showing daily activities from times past. The name of the site – *yeh* ("holy spring"), *pulu* ("stone vessel") – refers to the holy spring that rises from near the Ganesh statue at the far end of the carved sequence, and it's possible that the jar featured in scene three is for carrying holy water.

The series begins with an **introductory panel** separated from the others, showing a man with his arm raised skywards, thought to be the Hindu god Krishna. In the **first scene**, a man carrying two jars of river water suspended from a shoulder pole follows in the footsteps of a woman of higher caste, who is bedecked in necklaces and bracelets. **Scene two** shows a different woman, seated, with her feet tucked elegantly to one side, and her right arm stretched out towards a man carrying a hoe on his shoulder. To the left of this man sits a figure in the foreground, wearing a distinctive turban-like hat which indi-cates that he is either a priest or an ascetic (modern Balinese priests still wear very similar headdresses). A sarong-clad boy stands alone at the end of this panel, and in front of him kneels a three-dimensional statue of a Jaga Desa, the mythical village giant whose job it is to protect the village from evil spirits. **Scene three** is a hunting scene, in which one man is thrusting a weapon into a wild boar's mouth while another pulls the creature's tail; at the top of the panel, two figures kneel facing each other, with a water jar (possibly a holy water jar) standing between them. **Scene four** shows two men carrying five boars away on a pole (if you look closely you can just about make out the five piled on top of each other). In **scene five**, another hunter looks set to gallop off, and is either aided or hindered by a woman pulling on the animal's tail. Just as the story opened with a religious image, so the **concluding panel** is carved into a niche containing the elephant-headed god Ganesh.

The small **holy spring** after which the site is named rises close by the stat-ue of Ganesh and is sacred – hence the need for all visitors to wear temple dress and, for the same reason, you will probably also be asked by the temple guardian for a donation when you get to this point. The Balinese believe that all water is a gift from the spirits, so on the occasions when the spring fails to rise, this is seen as an indication of troubled or even angry spirits and special ceremonies are required to restore a harmonious flow.

Practicalities

The prettiest approach to Yeh Pulu is **on foot** along the dykes that skirt the sculpted terraces of rice-fields behind Goa Gajah, but you'll need to hire a guide to lead the way (they wait for customers at both sites and charge Rp50,000). It's also possible to walk from Yeh Pulu to the Durga Kutri temple, Pura Bukit Dharma Durga Kutri, in the village of Kutri (see p.249), which is about 2.5km to the east; guides can lead you there through the rice-fields and back (Rp100,000 per group; 3–5hr).

If you're coming by the Ubud–Gianyar **bemo**, get off at the Yeh Pulu signs just east of Goa Gajah or west of the Bedulu crossroads, and then walk the kilo-metre south through the hamlet of Batulumbang to Yeh Pulu. If driving, fol-low the same signs to where the road peters out, just a few hundred metres above the stonecarvings.

For **food**, *Made's Café* occupies a perfect position at the end of this road, with gloriously lush panoramas of forest and paddy-field and a perfectly respectable menu of cold drinks, hot snacks and rice dishes served by the convivial Made. There's a small **losmen** next door, *Pondok Wisata Lantur* (☏0361/942399; ❶), which offers simple accommodation on the edge of the family compound.

Pejeng

Inhabited since the Bronze Age, and considered a holy site ever since, the village of **PEJENG** and its immediate environs harbour a great wealth of religious antiquities, from carvings and rock-cut *candi* to bronze artefacts and massive stone statues. Some of these have been left in their original location, alongside riverbeds or buried in among the paddy-fields, while others have been housed in local temples; a number have also been carted off to museums, here and in Denpasar, Jakarta and Amsterdam. The remains have rather an esoteric appeal, and the area gets relatively few visitors and rarely features on the tour-bus circuit.

Practicalities

Pejeng's three main temples all lie within a few hundred metres of each other on the Bedulu–Tampaksiring Road and are clearly signposted.

Coming from Ubud, take an orange, Gianyar-bound **bemo** to the Bedulu crossroads and then either wait for a bluey-grey Tampaksiring-bound one, or walk the kilometre to the temples. The alternative route from Ubud – by bike or motorbike – is the quiet, fairly scenic five-kilometre **back road** that heads east from the Jalan Raya/Jalan Peliatan junction at the eastern edge of Ubud and then zigzags through paddies and small villages before finally emerging at the market on the main road, just 25m north of Pura Penataran Sasih (turn right for the temple). There are several potentially confusing junctions en route, but if you just keeping heading east, taking the right-hand fork wherever necessary (after the *Maya Ubud* hotel for example, and again in the village of Desa Pejeng Kawan) you should be fine.

Although all the major temples are clearly signed, you might want to engage the help of a local **guide** for the more out-of-the-way sites; the best place to find a guide is in the compound of Pura Penataran Sasih.

To **eat** in Pejeng, the sizeable *Warung Pejeng* is easy to spot amongst the cluster of shops on the side of the main road between Pura Pusering Jagat and Pura Kebo Edan.

Pura Penataran Sasih

Balinese people believe **Pura Penataran Sasih** (donation requested during daylight hours; obligatory sarong and sash can be borrowed at the entrance) to be a particularly sacred temple, because this is the home of the so-called Moon of Pejeng – hence the English epithet **Moon Temple**.

The moon in question is a large **bronze gong**, shaped almost like an hourglass, suspended so high up in its special tower at the back of the temple compound that you can hardly see the decorations scratched onto its surface. It probably dates from the Balinese Bronze Age, from sometime during the third century BC, and – at almost two metres long – is thought to be the largest such kettledrum ever cast. Etched into its green patina are a mass of geometric and abstract **designs** and, around the central rim, a chain of striking heart-shaped **faces**, punctured by huge round eyes and framed with distended earlobes. Legend tells how the gong fell towards earth one day from its home in heaven, where it had served as the wheel of a chariot that transported the moon through the skies. At that time, the wheel shone just as brightly as the moon itself, and when its fall was broken by a tree in Pejeng, a local thief became so incensed by the incriminating light it gave out that he tried to extinguish it by urinating over it. The wheel exploded with a thunderous echo, killed the thief outright, and then dropped to the ground in its present form. Ever since, the Balinese have treated the Moon of Pejeng as a sacred object, making offerings to it whenever they need to move it, and always keeping a respectful distance.

Though now faded and rather dilapidated, the **temple** itself was once the most important *pura* of the area, and there's little doubt that, whatever the origins of the gong, it would have been used for much the same purposes as its modern counterpart, the *kulkul* – sounded with a stick to summon the people of Pejeng to religious ceremonies and secular gatherings, to announce war and also to invite rain to fall.

Pura Pusering Jagat

Pura Pusering Jagat, literally translated as the "Temple of the Navel of the World", stands 100m south down the main road from Pura Penataran Sasih. As elsewhere in Pejeng, a donation is requested at the temple entrance, where you can also borrow the obligatory sarong and sash.

The most interesting feature of this temple is its metre-high, elaborately carved **vessel** for storing holy water, whose exterior is sculpted with a detailed relief thought to depict the Hindu myth "The Churning of the Sea of Milk". There are several versions of this legend, but they all relate the story of the gods and the demons desperately trying to get their hands on the elixir of immortal life. Under Wisnu's guidance, the celestial residents set about churning the Cosmic Soup (also known as the Sea of Milk) with the aid of a holy mountain as their pestle and serpentine *naga* as the pulleys. Finally, through a combination of trickery and good sense, the gods managed to extract, distil and drink the precious elixir. The vessel was carved in the fourteenth century from a single block of sandstone, and although the detail has become rather worn, you can still make out several figures, including the undulating *naga* ropes and a number of dancing deities supporting them.

Housed in a pavilion in front of the holy water vessel is another significant icon, the metre-high phallic *linggam* and its female receptacle, the *yoni*. Naturally enough, newly-wed and infertile couples make pilgrimages to this little shrine.

Pura Kebo Edan

Some 200m south of Pura Pusering Jagat, **Pura Kebo Edan** (donation requested) is also considered lucky for childless couples. The attraction here is a massive lifelike phallus, attached to the huge stone body of a man, nicknamed the **Pejeng Giant**. In fact, this giant, nearly four metres tall, is said to possess six penises in all; aside from the one swinging out for all to see, one is supposed to have dropped to the ground during his very vigorous dancing, and four more are said to be hidden inside him, awaiting the correct point of the dance before emerging. His principal penis is pierced from front to back with a huge bolt-like pin, probably a realistic reference to an age-old Southeast Asian practice designed to increase women's sexual pleasure. With his hands on his hips, the giant – his face hidden behind a blank mask – dances on a prone female figure thought to represent the earth. The giant's identity is debatable; some think he's Bhima, one of the chief characters from the *Mahabharata*, while others see him as a manifestation of the Hindu deity Siwa, who harnessed enormous cosmic power whenever he danced.

Gedung Koleksi Kepurbakalan

As the main treasure house of such a historically significant region, **Gedung Koleksi Kepurbakalan** – the government-run archeological **museum** – 500m south of Pura Penataran Sasih (Mon–Fri 7.30am–2.30pm; free), makes disappointing viewing. Its four tiny pavilions house a small, eclectic assortment of artefacts found in the Pejeng area, ranging from Paleolithic chopping tools to bronze bracelets and Chinese plates. Objects are poorly labelled, with very little indication of dates, and the more valuable pieces have all been snapped up by the Bali Museum in Denpasar.

The most interesting part of the collection lies through the *candi bentar* at the back of the museum compound, where you'll find a dozen **sarcophagi**, massive coffins fashioned from two fitted sections of hollowed-out stone that probably date back to around 300 BC. They range in size from one to nearly three metres, though it's thought that all these sarcophagi were designed to hold adult skeletons – those placed in the smallest vessels would have been flexed at knees, hips and shoulders – as only the more important members of a community would have merited such a relatively elaborate burial. Bronze jewellery, coins and weapons were found in some of the sarcophagi, though most of the tombs are thought to have been robbed at a much earlier date. Some of the sarcophagi are little more than simple containers, but others were obviously carved with symbols or even sculpted into figures. The one labelled "Taman Bali" looks remarkably like a turtle, with a thick protruding neck and lumpen head that may have doubled as a pulling handle, and its stubby limbs scratched out from the main body.

North of Ubud: routes to Gunung Batur

All three major roads **north of Ubud** lead eventually to the towering peak of Gunung Batur and its huge crater. Whether you go via **Payangan** to the west, **Tegalalang** directly to the north, or **Tampaksiring** to the east, the scenery along the way makes it a pleasant drive, with the invariable stretches of lush green or yellow *sawah* punctuated by remarkably pretty villages of adobe-walled compounds, flowering shrubs and thatch-roofed *meru*. Most villagers still make their living off the land, and you'll see them planting or harvesting in the fields and carrying sheaves of rice, lengths of bamboo or pots of water balanced on their heads. Distances along these three routes are comparable, about 40km to Batur, but the most significant tourist sights are located along the most easterly route, around the Tampaksiring area.

The most frequent and reliable **bemo** service running north from Ubud is the brown fleet that covers the **central route** via Tegalalang and Pujung; there are frequent turquoise and brown bemos along the first section of the **westerly route**, as far as Payangan, but only some of them continue as far as

Kintamani. For the **easterly route** via Tampaksiring, you'll need to change bemos at the Bedulu crossroads.

Although there's little of specific interest on the westerly route, which takes you via Campuhan (see p.206) and Payangan, this is the quietest, least congested and prettiest of the three routes, and the best one to take if you have **private transport**. The villages on the way are exceptionally picturesque, interspersed with lychee, durian and pineapple plantations, and in Payangan you pass the village's famously huge roadside banyan tree. The road ends up at the impressive Pura Ulun Danu Batur (see p.323) on the Batur–Kintamani road, about 5km west of Penelokan.

Tegalalang, Pujung, Sebatu and Taro

The **central route** up to Gunung Batur begins at the eastern edge of Ubud, from the point where Jalan Raya intersects with Jalan Peliatan; if heading up here on a bicycle you might prefer the more peaceful route which starts on Ubud's Jalan Suweta (see box on p.195).

Tegalalang

Turning left (north) to pass through the village of Petulu (see p.217), the road reaches the woodcarving village of **TEGALALANG** after about 7km. The central stretch of this elongated village is lined with ostentatious Bali-baroque style shops and banks, but the northern and southern fringes retain their adobe-walled compounds and thatched shrines. The speciality here is simple, brightly painted wooden birds, fish and fruit trees, vast quantities of which are snapped up for export. Other carvings worth looking out for in Tegalalang include *topeng* masks, and antique-style doors, furniture and wall panels. Of the dozen or more major showrooms, **Tambora Wood Craft Centre**, towards the northern end of the settlement, stands out for its high-quality pieces, particularly animal carvings and figurines of *Ramayana* characters, which are all made from unpainted Sumbawan "gold" wood. Also worth stopping off for is **Mitra Bali's Fair Trade Shop**, which is a Balinese-run not-for-profit organization that ensures the craftspeople get a fair percentage of the profit.

As you pass through Tegalalang, the views get increasingly spectacular, with Bali's greatest mountains looming majestically ahead: Gunung Batur (to the north) and Gunung Agung (to the east). The *sawah* are also particularly eye-catching around here, so much so, in fact, that there's a specially signposted roadside rice-terrace **viewpoint** 3km out of Tegalalang, where the panorama stretches over aesthetically sculpted terraces and across to a lushly wooded river gorge. Most tour buses pull in here, and this patch seethes with hopeful hawkers. For a more peaceful stop-with-a-view you could call in at the elegant and beautifully situated **restaurant**, *Kampung Café*, a couple of kilometres further north in the *banjar* of Ceking. It's built on two levels overlooking the valley and serves classy *nouvelle cuisine* and Southeast Asian dishes; there's quite often gamelan music in the evenings too.

Pujung and Sebatu

The northern end of Tegalalang pretty much merges into southern **PUJUNG KELOD**. Like its neighbour, Pujung also thrives on the demand for woodcarvings, and many of the workshops here employ whole teams of carvers and painters, displaying only a fraction of their produce in the handful of roadside showrooms. Pujung's hallmark is its production of *garuda*, fashioned in all sizes from ten-centimetre-high mantelpiece ornaments to massive two-metre giants. Pujung Kelod's most interesting **restaurant**, the *Blue Yogi Café* (T0361/901368; ❸) makes a very pleasant place to break your journey with its mouthwatering menu of sandwiches, salads, casseroles and rice dishes. You can also **stay** here in one of the two attractive two-storey cottages set in the garden behind the restaurant.

If you continue north along the main road for another 16km, you'll reach the Batur crater rim; alternatively, a right turn 2km beyond Pujung Kelod takes you to Tampaksiring via the village of **SEBATU**. Fed by holy water from the mountain springs beyond, Sebatu's traditional-style **bathing pools** are genuine public amenities, though rarely visited by tourists. The cool, sparkling water flows through carved stone spouts into the segregated sections of the sunken basin, which stands in the grounds of **Pura Panti Pasek Gelgel**.

Taro and the Elephant Safari Park

Turning left off the main Kintamani road a couple of kilometres beyond Pujung Kelod, a signposted little road leads you the 6km west to the village of **TARO** and the Elephant Safari Park. The route to the park is attractive, passing through a handful of traditional small villages. The area is known for its distinctive grey and black flecked tufa stone, used all over Bali to build temples, houses and hotels, and in the villages you'll see lots of outdoor **workshops** where the stone is also carved into sculptures and ornaments. Taro itself is famous as the home of a small herd of sacred white Brahmin cows. Balinese people come here to pay their respects to the cows, who play an important role in certain temple ceremonies; as you pass into the Elephant Safari Park itself, you may be asked by the local priest to give a donation for their upkeep.

Elephant Safari Park

The **Elephant Safari Park** (daily 9am–5pm; $7.50, kids $3.75, family discounts available) is a landscaped area of grassy fields, pools and village forest, and is home to seventeen Sumatran elephants. It is the brainchild of the man behind the Bali Adventure Tours company; he dreamt up the project partly as a way of "rescuing" Sumatran elephants (there are no wild elephants in Bali) who had been trained to work in the logging industry but were then abandoned when the industry declined. The elephants were shipped over to Bali, along with their Sumatran mahouts, and now look healthy and well cared for.

The admission fee allows you to **feed** and stroke the elephants, admire their **painting** skills – the trunk is apparently as adept with a paintbrush as the human hand, and some of these elephants have exhibited their work internationally – listen to them playing the harmonica and watch them having their twice-daily **baths** (a real highlight; 9.30am & 3pm). There's also an exhibition and a gift shop stuffed full of elephant memorabilia. The chief attraction, however, is the rather pricey half-hour elephant **safari ride** (an additional $39 for adults, $29 for kids, $10 for under 10s, or $117 for families); this takes you, on elephant-back, through a fairly sparse forest, with occasionally impressive views of local rice-paddies.

Most people visit the park as part of a **tour**, which includes transport from your hotel, lunch and the elephant safari ride ($68/47/17/207); book at any travel agent or contact Bali Adventure Tours (T0361/721480, Wwww.bali adventuretours.com).

Tampaksiring

The most **easterly route** from Ubud to the mountains takes you along the Bedulu–Penelokan road, passing through Pejeng (see p.232) before reaching **TAMPAKSIRING**, 11km further on. A fairly nondescript town that's really only interesting as the access point for nearby **Tirta Empul** and **Gunung Kawi**, Tampaksiring is nonetheless well stocked with craft and souvenir shops: carved wooden chess sets and knick-knacks made from bone are a speciality. The bluey-grey Gianyar–Bedulu–Tampaksiring **bemos** terminate in the centre of the long settlement, close by several warung. The bemo service between Tampaksiring and Penelokan, about 20km north, is patchy and unreliable at best, but you should at least be able to charter a bemo.

Gunung Kawi

A few hundred metres north of Tampaksiring's bemo terminus, a sign points east off the main road to **Gunung Kawi** (daylight hours; Rp3100, kids Rp1600, including sarong and sash rental), the site of a series of eleventh-century royal tombs hewn from the rock face. It's a lovely, impressive spot, completely enclosed in the lush valley of the sacred Pakrisan River and rarely visited by tour groups. To reach it, walk past the snack and souvenir stalls and down the steep flight of three hundred steps, through a massive rock-hewn archway, to the river.

Archeologists have come up with a number of theories about the **origins** and **function** of the Gunung Kawi "tombs", or *candi*, of which the least contentious is that they were erected as memorials to a king – possibly the eleventh-century Anak Wungsu – and his queens. The four Queens' Tombs are thought to be for Anak Wungsu's minor consorts, while the five Royal Tombs across the river are believed to honour the king himself and his four most favoured wives. There are no signs of bones or ashes in the *candi*, so the structures were not actual tombs, yet over the false door of each were found inscriptions (most of them unreadable) thought to be the names or at least titles of the deceased. As well as being a lasting testament to the existence of these people, the *candi* may also have represented concrete proof that the full programme of religious rites had been completed.

Before crossing the river, turn sharp left for the **Queens' Tombs**. Like the larger more important series of structures on the other side of the river, these four *candi* are huge square-tiered reliefs, chiselled from the riverside cliff face to resemble temple facades. Originally, the surface of these *candi* would have been decorated with plaster carvings, but despite being protected from the harshest effects of the elements by their individual niches, the carvings have all been worn away, leaving only the outlines of a single false door on each one. The design of the *candi* is very similar to that of structures in central and east Java (though the Balinese versions are a slightly different shape), built in three distinct sections to reflect a hell–earth–heaven cosmology, and with a stone-lidded hollow dug at the foot of each.

Crossing the Pakrisan River you enter the Gunung Kawi temple complex, which contains an unusual **cloister**, complete with courtyard, rooms and cells, entirely cut from the ravine rock wall. This was probably built for the caretakers of the *candi*, holy men who looked after the tombs, and ensured that the necessary religious rituals were attended to. The five **Royal Tombs** at the back of the temple complex are in better condition than the Queens' Tombs, and you can see the false doors and facades quite clearly. Because the *candi* at the far left end is slightly higher than the others, this is believed to be that of Anak Wungsu.

Returning across the river, follow the exit signs up the track beside the rice-paddies and then veer off along the narrow path, branching left through the fields to reach the so-called **Tenth Tomb**, an often slippery five-minute walk away. Thought to have been erected in memory of an important member of the royal household who died after the king and his wives, possibly a prime-ministerial figure, this *candi* stands on its own, framed only by rock-cut cloisters. Despite having been eroded by the water that pours off from the field above, you can still make out quite a distinct inscription above the false door.

Tirta Empul and around

Balinese from every corner of the island make pilgrimages to **Tirta Empul** (daylight hours; Rp3100, kids Rp1600 including sarong and sash rental), signposted off the main Tampaksiring–Kintamani road, about 500m north of the turn-off to Gunung Kawi. They come seeking to cleanse themselves spiritually and to cure their physical ailments by bathing in the **holy springs** here. Legend describes how the springs were first tapped by the god Indra during his battle with the evil Mayadanawa, an early ruler of the Pejeng kingdom. Mayadanawa had poisoned the nearby river and made hundreds of Indra's retainers sick, so Indra pierced the earth to release a spring of pure and sacred water – the elixir of immortality – that would revive his flagging troops. The new spring was named Tirta Empul, and has been considered the holiest in Bali ever since the tenth century, if not longer.

A **temple** was built around the springs and special bathing pools constructed for devotees, and the complex is now an extremely popular destination, both for Balinese and foreign tourists. The temple's car park is crammed with small shops selling crafts and souvenirs, as well as with an impressive assortment of inexpensive warung, many of which specialize in regional Indonesian food.

The shallow red-brick **bathing pools** are sunk into the ground of the outer courtyard of the temple, fed by water from the springs in the inner sanctuary. Men, women and priests each have their own segregated sections in which to immerse themselves, though most modern devotees just splash their faces and smile for the camera. However, for pregnant women and anyone who's just recovered from a long illness, a visit to Tirta Empul has particular significance as one of three places in which they must bathe for a special ritual called **melukat**. This ceremony requires immersion in the waters of each of the three holiest springs in Bali: the "holy waters of the mountain" at Tirta Bungkah, the "holy springs of the plain" here at Tirta Empul, and the "holy springs of the sea" at Tirta Selukat. In the inner courtyard, you can see the clear slate-blue spring water bubbling up into its own enclosed rectangular pool through a sedimentary layer of black sand. The pool was built to protect the springs in the 1960s, and a massive restoration job was carried out on the shrines and *bale* at the same time. The brightly painted and neatly thatched buildings that you see in the temple courtyards are all relatively recent.

Istana Tampaksiring

High up on the hill that overlooks the Tirta Empul complex sit two squat and unprepossessing buildings connected to each other by a bridge. They are both part of the **Istana Tampaksiring** (Mon–Fri 8am–5pm; Rp2000), a palace designed by and built for President Sukarno in the 1950s. Although there are steps up the hillside to the palace, they are closed to the general public, who are expected to enter the compound from the main Tampaksiring road, 350m north of the Tirta Empul turn-off. The effort, however, is a complete waste of time, as you're not allowed inside the unimpressive-looking palace. Sukarno's mother was Balinese, and the president spent a lot of time on his ancestral island; it's said that he built this residence so that he could spy on the local women as they bathed in the pools below (a telescope was set up on the palace terrace for that very purpose), and Sukarno is reputed to have summoned the most appealing women to climb the hillside to his lodgings. Following Sukarno's fall from power in 1967, the palace became a lodging house for visiting members of the Jakarta government. These days only the Indonesian president and vice-president are entitled to stay here.

Travel details

Bemos and public buses

It's almost impossible to give the **frequency** with which bemos and public buses run, as they only depart when they have enough passengers to make the journey worthwhile. However, on the most popular routes, you should be able to count on getting a ride within the half-hour if you travel before noon; things quieten down in the afternoon and come to a standstill by around 5pm. **Journey times** also vary a great deal: the times given below are the minimum you can expect.

Only the direct bemo and bus routes are listed here; for longer journeys you'll probably find that you have to go first either to Batubulan (and possibly cross Denpasar to make connections from a different terminal, see p.92) or to Gianyar (see p.246). **Batubulan (Denpasar)** to: Amlapura (2hr 30min); Candi Dasa (2hr); Celuk (10min); Gianyar (1hr); Kintamani (1hr 30min); Klungkung (1hr 20min); Mas (35min); Nusa Dua (1hr); Padang Bai (for Lombok; 1hr 40min); Peliatan (45min); Singaraja (Penarukan terminal; 3hr); Sukawati (20min); Tegalalang (1hr 15min); Ubud (50min).

Ubud to: Campuhan/Sanggingan (5–10min); Celuk (40min); Denpasar (Batubulan terminal; 50min); Gianyar (20min); Goa Gajah (10min); Kedewatan (10min); Kintamani (1hr); Mas (15min); Peliatan (5min); Pujung (25min); Sukawati (30min).

Perama shuttle buses

STO = overnight stopover is sometimes needed
Ubud to: Air Sanih (1 daily; 3hr 30min–4hr); Bangsal (1 daily; 8hr); Bedugul (1 daily; 1hr 30min); Bima (2 daily; STO); Candi Dasa (3 daily; 1hr 30min–2hr); Jakarta (1 daily; 25–26hr); Kintamani (1 daily; 1hr 15min); Kuta/airport (6 daily; 1hr–1hr 30min); Kuta, Lombok (3 daily; STO); Lovina (2 daily; 1hr 30min–2hr); Malang (1 daily; 16–17hr); Mataram (2 daily; 7hr); Nusa Lembongan (1 daily; 2hr 30min); Padang Bai (3 daily; 1hr–1hr 30min); Sanur (6 daily; 30min–1hr); Sape (2 daily; STO); Senggigi (2 daily; 7hr 30min); Surabaya (1 daily; 12–13hr); Tetebatu (2 daily; STO); Tirtagangga (1 daily; 2hr 30min); Tulamben (1 daily; 3hr–3hr 30min); Yogyakarta (1 daily; 16–17hr).

East Bali

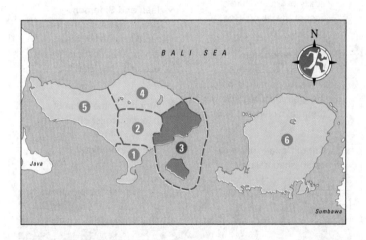

CHAPTER 3 Highlights

✳ **Besakih** – The "Mother Temple", most venerated in Bali, is stunningly positioned on the lower slopes of Gunung Agung. **See p.264**

✳ **Gunung Agung** – Volcano towering majestically over the entire east of the island. **See p.269**

✳ **Nusa Lembongan** – Islanders, surfers and sun-seekers mingle on the great beaches and in the rural hinterland. **See p.271**

✳ **Candi Dasa** – This well-established, relaxed

resort is an ideal base for exploring the east. **See p.282**

✳ **Tirtagangga** – Lovely views of the mountains, attractive rice-fields, a water palace and cool temperatures. **See p.300**

✳ **Iseh and Sidemen** – Small villages famed for fabulous rice terraces, among the most picturesque on the island. **See p.304**

✳ **Amed** – Some 14km of beautiful coast offering get-away-from-it-all peace and quiet. **See p.305**

East Bali

The east of Bali is dominated both physically and spiritually by the towering volcano Gunung Agung, and the Besakih temple complex high on its slopes. The landscape ranges from sweeping rice terraces, built on the fertile soil deposited by successive volcanic eruptions, to the dry, rocky expanses of the north coast and the far east.

Formerly divided into a multitude of ancient Balinese kingdoms, the area has witnessed vicious internal battles and power struggles, followed later by the incursions of the invading **Dutch**. During the fourteenth century, the first Majapahit capital was in **Samprangan**, now a small village just east of Gianyar and, in the following centuries, each of the towns of the area had its own royal dynasty; the now sleepy town of **Gelgel** once ruled a kingdom stretching from the island of Sumbawa in the east to Java in the west. Evidence of these ancient courts remains in the Taman Gili in **Klungkung**, the Puri Agung in **Amlapura** and the **Puri Gianyar**. Once the focus of the area which they dominated, these small relics of past glory are now surrounded by busy administrative and market towns with traffic pouring past the walls.

Most visitors come to the east for the **coast**, which extends from the wide black-sand bays south of Gianyar, through the natural deep-water harbour of **Amuk Bay**, to the peaceful but fast-developing beaches known collectively as **Amed** that range along the northeast coast, The area offers some of the best diving and snorkelling in Bali: the laid-back resorts of **Candi Dasa**, **Padang Bai**, **Tulamben** and **Amed** are the main centres. Off the south coast lie three islands: **Nusa Lembongan** with its excellent white-sand beaches, tiny **Nusa Ceningan** and little-visited **Nusa Penida**, whose south coast consists of towering limestone cliffs. Only Lembongan, with easy access from Sanur, has a developed tourist trade, catering for surfers who come for the breaks off the northwest coast, day visitors on luxury cruises from southern Bali and those in search of a few peaceful days away from the bustle of the southern resorts.

Inland, Gunung Agung and Besakih are the major tourist draws, although the hassles, rampant commercialism and frequent mist disappoint many who make the journey. However, there are other peaks and other impressive **temples**, especially Pura Kehen in Bangli, Pura Lempuyang Luhur in the far east and Pura Pasar Agung above Selat, where you can escape the crowds. **Tenganan**, within easy reach of Candi Dasa, is the most welcoming of the traditional Bali Aga villages on the island, home to descendants of the early inhabitants of Bali who resisted Javanization in the fourteenth century. This is the place to head for if you are interested in **textiles** and craftwork.

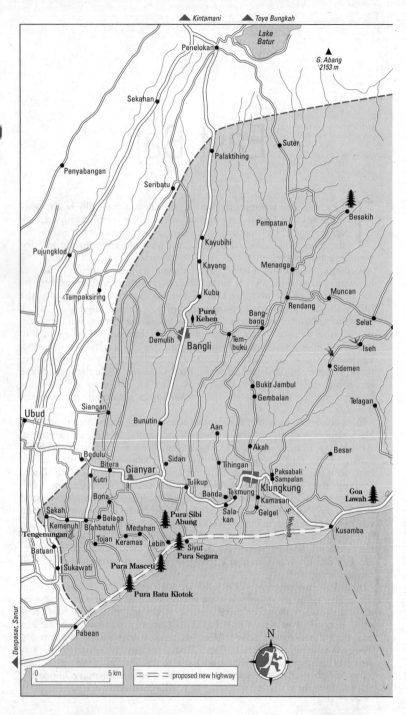

▲ Kintamani   ▲ Toya Bungkah

Lake Batur

Penelokan

▲ G. Abang 2153 m

Sekahan

Penyabangan

Suter

Palaktihing

Seribatu

Besakih

Pempatan

Pujungklod

Kayubihi

Kayang

Menanga

Muncan

Tampaksiring

Kubu

Selat

Pura Kehen

Bang-bang

Rendang

Demulih

Bangli

Tembuku

Iseh

Sidemen

Bukit Jambul

Gembalan

Telagan

Ubud

Siangan

Bunutin

Aan

Bedulu

Akah

Besar

Bitera

Gianyar

Sidan

Kutri

Tulikup

Tihingan

Paksabali
Sampalan

Bona

Banda

Klungkung

Sakah

Takmung

Kamasan

Goa Lawah

Belaga

Kemenuh

Blahbatuh

Medahan

Pura Sibi Abung

Salakan

Gelgel

Tengenungan

Tojan

Keramas

Lebih

Siyut

Kusamba

Batuan

Pura Segara

Sukawati

Pura Masceti

Pura Batu Klotok

Pabean

Denpasar, Sanur

N

0   5 km   = = = proposed new highway

Kubu & Singaraja

Tulamben

G. Agung
3142 m

Pura Pasar
Agung

Jemeluk

Culik   Amed
Bunutan
Lipah   Selang
Ibus
Banyuning
Abang   Aas
G. Lempuyang
1058 m
Sebudi   Ababi   Ngis   Kusambi
Tista
Pura
Lempuyang   G. Seraya
Tirtagangga   Luhur   1175 m

Jungutan   Budakling
Duda   Pandesari
Putung   Sibetan   Bebandem   Seraya
Bungaya
Amlapura

Ujung
Yehpoh   Bakung   Tenganan
Asak   Jasri
Manggis   Bugbug   Perasi
Ulakan   Pasir Putih
Candi
Dasa
Amuk Bay

Gili Mimpang
Gili Biaha
Gili Tepekong

Padang Bai

Ferries to Lembar (Lombok)

Nusa Lembongan
Sampalan
Jungutbatu   Ped
Toyapakeh
Lembongan   Karangsari
Nusa   Sakti
Ceningan   Sewana
Bukit Mundi
529 m
Sebuluh   Nusa Penida

Tanglad

N

0   5 km

Ferries to Nusa Penida and Nusa Lembongan

Transport practicalities

The east is easily accessible by public **transport** from Kuta and Ubud and it's possible to explore the area on day-trips (Ubud is only 13km from Gianyar). Heading to the east on the main road from Denpasar through Gianyar and Klungkung, it's easy to imagine that eastern Bali is one long exhaust-belching traffic jam of trucks, tankers, cars and swarms of motorbikes. However, once past the port turn-off for Padang Bai and the petrol depot slightly further east things do quieten down, getting calmer the further east and north you get. When the planned coastal road from Pabean to Kusamba is completed, things will hopefully improve. However this is a relaxed and relaxing part of the country, and the best way to enjoy it is to give it a bit of time. The ideal bases are Candi Dasa, Padang Bai (the port for the Lombok ferries), Tirtagangga, surrounded by attractive rice terraces, and the section of the far east coast between Culik and Aas, the fastest developing area of the east. Outside these spots, **accommodation** options are more limited. However, the lack of facilities is amply compensated for by the opportunity to experience the slow pace of village life.

Gianyar and around

GIANYAR is the administrative capital of Gianyar district, the second most densely populated district in Bali. Something of a travel hub, it's hard to avoid if you're heading east, but there's no need to stay long. The **coast** south of Gianyar consists of mile upon mile of wide curving bays with fine views across to Nusa Penida and Nusa Lembongan, that are still pretty much ignored by tourists and developers because the sand is pure black and the water too treacherous for swimming. It's likely that things will change once the new coastal road from Pabean to Kusamba is complete, but there are currently few facilities along here and no accommodation.

Some history

Gianyar was established as a separate **kingdom** in the late seventeenth century and during the next hundred years became one of the most powerful of the southern kingdoms. However, in 1883, it was annexed to Klungkung after the ruling raja, **Dewa Manggis VII**, fell victim to the political machinations of the far more wily and experienced politicos of the neighbouring kingdoms. He was interned in the village of Satria (3km east of Klungkung) with his entire family, where he eventually died, leaving two sons, the crown prince Dewa Pahang and his younger brother, Dewa Gde Raka. In 1893, they managed to escape from Klungkung and, raising a local army, re-established the Gianyar kingdom over much of its previous area. The neighbouring kingdoms, however, were out for blood, and to save Gianyar from its neighbours, the new raja made a request to the Dutch Resident in Singaraja for Gianyar to be placed under the authority and protection of the Netherlands Indies government. The Dutch agreed, and in March 1900, Gianyar became a **Dutch Protectorate**. Thus Gianyar was spared the fighting between the Dutch and the other southern Balinese kingdoms during the early years of the century – instead it thrived and became a centre for the arts. The aristocratic line and lifestyle continued; in the 1930s the raja of the time drove around in a Fiat with a solid gold *garuda* radiator cap. These days the royal family still live in some grandeur in Puri Gianyar but have ceremonial and religious rather than political duties.

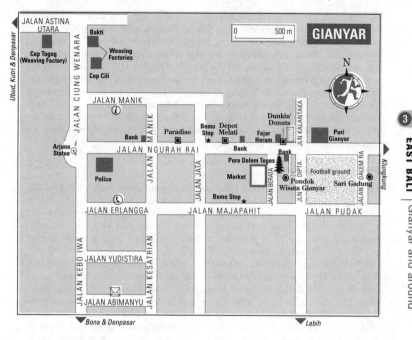

The Town

Gianyar has little to detain you other than its culinary speciality of spit-roasted suckling pig (*babi guling*) and showcase *endek* weaving factories. The most impressive feature of the town is the massive white **statue** on the main road in from the west, which shows Arjuna in his three-horsed chariot along with his godly charioteer, Krishna. Gianyar seems to go in for exuberant statuary: there's another huge Arjuna statue on the eastern side of town, this time surrounded by *naga*. The rest of Gianyar feels pretty low-key.

The town centres on the main road just west of the royal palace, **Puri Gianyar**, first built in 1771 by Dewa Manggis IV, but destroyed by the 1917 earthquake and largely rebuilt. Still the home of the descendants of the Gianyar royal family, it's not open to the public, and well-maintained walls, iron gates and no-entry signs ensure you don't wander in by mistake. All you can do is admire from afar the open *bale* with easy chairs, the statues dotted here and there and an especially fine carved and gilded gateway.

A short walk away on Jalan Berata, Gianyar's **market** is a large modern structure comprising two buildings, each three storeys high, with food in one and clothes and household goods in the other. The main market takes place every three days, but there are always some stalls here. At the north end of Jalan Berata stands **Pura Dalem Teges**, flanked by guardian monsters, along with statues of two Western gentlemen, one in a top hat and one in a uniform, both wielding swords. Stonecarvers of the past were clearly influenced by Western visitors and you'll spot many examples of such earthly figures accompanying the mythological in the island's temples.

Gianyar is well known for the **endek weaving** (see p.538 for more on this), produced in the factories on the western outskirts of town, just over 1km from the centre. Two of the most established are Cap Cili and Bakti (both daily 8am–5pm) close together on Jalan Ciung Wenara, which are good starting points. Cap Togog (daily 8am–5pm), slightly further west from the centre, on Jalan Astina Utara, is another big concern where everything has price labels. These operations cater largely for the tour-bus market and they are happy for you to wander around and watch both the preparation of the thread and the actual weaving. *Endek* cloth starts at Rp40,000 a metre for cotton, increasing to Rp60,000 for silk/cotton mixes. Sarongs cost upwards of Rp100,000, bedspreads from Rp200,000 and cushion covers from Rp35,000 depending on the thread used. You'll also find clothing and small gift items although there's a depressingly large amount of imported cloth from Java.

Practicalities

Heading east **from Denpasar** (Batubulan terminal), most public transport follows the route to Gianyar via Sakah, Kemenuh, Blahbatuh, Kutri and Bitera, although there are also local bemos from Blahbatuh which ply the alternative road through Bona and Jasri. Coming **from Ubud**, your best bet is to get a bemo down to the large junction at Sakah and then change onto another bemo for Kemenuh, Blahbatuh and Bona.

At the Gianyar government **tourist office**, Jl Manik 12b (Mon–Thurs 7am–3pm, Fri 7am–noon; ☎0361/943401), staff appear rather startled to see visitors but they do have English-language leaflets on some of the local attractions. The main **telephone office** is on Jalan Erlangga (daily 24hr) where there is also **internet access** (Rp5000/hr, minimum Rp1500). *Paradiso* snack bar, Jl Ngurah Rai 49 (daily 24hr), doubles up as a wartel and internet café (Rp2000 for 15min). The **post office** (a Western Union agent) is at Jl Abimanyu 4. **Bank** Pembangunan Daerah is on the corner of Jalan Ngurah Rai and Jalan Manik, and BNI is further south on Jalan Kesatrian; there are BNI and Bank of Central Asia ATMs for Visa, MasterCard and Cirrus opposite each other by the *Fajar Harum* shopping centre.

With Ubud so close at hand, there's no reason to stay overnight, especially as the **accommodation** options in town are nothing special. Both *Pondok Wisata Gianyar*, Jl Anom Sandat 10x (☎0361/942165; ❶), just off Jalan Ngurah Rai, and *Sari Gadung*, Jl Dalem Rai 5 (no phone; ❶), in the road along the east side of the football field, are pretty basic. About 5km northwest of Gianyar, in the small village of **SIANGAN**, are the excellent *Siangan Bungalows* (☎0361/954832, ✉siangan_bungalows@yahoo.com; ❺–❻), located in a gorgeous garden on the edge of paddy-fields. There are nine well-furnished rooms, most with hot water, and a choice of air-con or fan, plus deep verandahs and *bale* in the garden for relaxing and adult and child swimming pools. They offer a free pick-up from the airport if you stay for three days, and free transport to Ubud, 8km west. This really is a delightful spot although rather difficult to find. To get there, turn north in Bitera, just by Bitera Palace, about 500m west of Gianyar. After 1km, take the first significant turning on the left. Follow the road as it climbs and turns for almost exactly 3km. Turn right in the village of Siangan between the volleyball court/football field and the somewhat derelict Siangan Palace, then turn right again along the far side of the volleyball court. *Siangan Bungalows* are at the end of this track.

For **food**, Gianyar is rightly famous for its *babi guling* (spit-roasted suckling pig), a great Balinese speciality which is, essentially, roast pork stuffed with chillies, rice, herbs and spices, served with rice and usually *lawar* (chopped meat, vegetables and coconut mixed with pig's blood). The shops in the main street are good places to sample it; try *Depot Melati*, Jl Ngurah Rai 37, but get there before 2pm as they shut up early. *Paradiso* wartel/internet café, Jl Ngurah Rai 49 (daily 24hr), also has inexpensive nasi goreng, pizza slices, sandwiches and plenty of hot and cold drinks. Western fast food has hit Gianyar in the form of a *Dunkin Donuts* counter at the front of the *Fajar Harum* shopping centre in the middle of town.

West of Gianyar

A number of interesting **craft villages** lie to the west and southwest of Gianyar, although they don't form the same kind of commercial corridor that those on the road between Batubulan and Ubud do (see p.179).

Some 4km west of Gianyar, the small village of **KUTRI** is home to the **Pura Bukit Dharma Durga Kutri**. Well established on the tour-bus circuit, this temple has fine carvings of elephants guarding the outer gate and pigs at the inner gate, above which sits a splendid Bhoma. The most interesting feature is the statue of the goddess **Durga**; head up the staircase from the back of the inner courtyard and through a small forest of banyan trees to the top of the hill,

> ### Rangda
>
> The image of **Rangda**, Queen of the Witches, is everywhere in Bali: you'll see her in dance-dramas and on masks, temple carvings, paintings and batiks. Although there's a certain amount of variation in the way she's portrayed, several features are standard and all contribute to her grotesque and terrifying appearance. She has a long mane of hair, often in thick strands and sometimes in different colours, with flames protruding from her head. Her face is fierce and hideous with bulging eyes, a gaping mouth, huge teeth or tusks and a long tongue often reaching to her knees. Her fingernails are spectacularly long and curled, and she has enormous, pendulous breasts. She wears a striped shirt and pants, with a white cloth around her waist, an important instrument of her evil magic.
>
> Several versions of the Rangda story are enacted across the island, the most common being the **barong** and **calonarang** (see p.521 for more details of these dramas), but she always speaks in the ancient Javanese Kawi language and alternates between high whining tones, loud grunts and cackles. To the Balinese, Rangda represents the forces of evil, death and destruction, and she's often associated with the Hindu goddess Durga.
>
> It's possible that Rangda may have been based on a real woman, **Mahendratta**. Mahendratta was a princess of ancient times from Java, who married the Balinese Prince Udayana and bore him a son, Erlangga, in 1001 AD. According to legend, the king later banished Mahendratta to the forest for practising witchcraft. When Udayana died, Mahendratta, now a *rangda* (widow), continued to build up grudges against her powerful and unrelenting son. Eventually, she used her awful powers to call down a plague upon Erlangga's kingdom, nearly destroying it. Erlangga, learning the source of the pestilence, despatched a troop of soldiers who stabbed Rangda in the heart; she survived, however, and even killed the soldiers in return. In desperation, the king sent for a holy man, **Empu Bharadah**, whose assistant stole Rangda's book of magic with which he was able to restore Rangda's victims to life, and eventually destroy the witch by turning her own magic on herself.
>
> Even in performances of the story, the figure of Rangda is believed to have remarkable powers, and offerings are made and prayers said before each show to protect the actors from the evil forces they are invoking. Village performances of the drama are often a means of pacifying Rangda's anger so that she will not turn her destructive forces against them.

where you'll find the statue shrouded in holy white cloths and shaded by parasols. The figure is somewhat eroded, but you should be able to make out a many-armed Durga slaughtering a bull, with her weapons of conch, flames, bow and arrow, javelin and shield. Many people believe, however, that the carving depicts **Mahendratta**, the original of the legendary Rangda (see box on p.249), and that this is her burial place. It's also possible to walk to Kutri from the Yeh Pulu rock carvings east of Ubud, but you'll need to hire a guide to show you the way (see p.231).

At the village of **BLAHBATUH**, 5km south of Kutri, the main road, lined with bamboo furniture workshops, meets an alternative road from Gianyar through Bona and Belaga. A few hundred metres along the Bona road, the splendid entrances of **Pura Gaduh**, guarded by stone elephants outside and mounted horsemen inside, lead into a maze of linked courtyards, which were rebuilt following the 1917 earthquake. Of particular interest is a gigantic carved head with bulging eyes, supposedly the legendary **Kebo Iwa**, who is said to have created this and many other temples in the area. **BONA** village has a huge number of shops selling wooden and bamboo furniture plus plenty of smaller items made from bamboo and the fronds of the sugar palm, including baskets, bags, purses and lampshades.

Kemenuh

At **KEMENUH**, 7km southwest of Gianyar, **Tegenungan waterfall**, also known as **Srog Srogan**, drops a sheer 30m. There are two access points. One side road heads south about 500m west of the market in Blahbatuh. Follow the signs through the village back roads for 2km to reach the eastern riverbanks where a **bungee-jumping** operation (℡0361/941102, ℻752666), allows you to leap from a crane erected over the site. The views of the falls aren't great from this side unless you're on the crane or negotiate the steep descent to the river. Alternative access is via another side road, 1km east, signed to the *Waterfall Restaurant*. Another path leads to the riverside from here – it's a long climb down, the area isn't especially pristine and the strong current is a deterrent to swimming. A small warung perched on the edge of the gorge boasts tremendous views, and the moderately priced *Waterfall Restaurant* has an upper floor where you can catch the breeze; you can **stay** in their one very comfortable guest room, which features an attached garden bathroom including a huge bathtub and hot water (℡0361/299265, ℻298437; ❼).

About 400m south of the main road, on the left as you head towards the restaurant, a narrow avenue of coconut palms marks the path to the **Pura Dalem** of Kemenuh, a large and dramatic temple notable for its intricate carvings and freestanding statues; you'll spot the imposing red roofs of the *bale* from the road. On the *kulkul* tower is a carving of Pan Brayut, the legendary character with numerous children (see box on p.209), who according to local belief has the power to help infertile couples.

Back on the main road, opposite the turning to the *Waterfall Restaurant,* a side road leads past a concentration of **woodcarving** shops; a good range of subject, style and wood is on show and, as much of the carving is done in sheds outside the shops, you can watch the work as well as tour the showrooms. Some of the shops are on the tour-bus circuit, but groups don't stay long, and you can usually have the place to yourself, especially if you explore all the way through to the northern end of this twisting road at Goa Gajah (see p.229), a distance of about 5km.

One of the most innovative tourist developments in Bali is located on the northern side of Kemenuh, near the hamlet of Medahan. **Sua Bali**

(☎0361/941050, ☏941035, ⓦwww.suabali.co.id; ❼), located in gorgeous gardens on the banks of the Petang river, is committed to sustainable village tourism within the context of an involved local community. On offer are **courses** in Indonesian and Balinese cookery (US$60 per person, minimum two people); Indonesian language (group tuition $8/hr per person, minimum 40hr; individual tuition $10/hr, minimum 20hr); and batik, gamelan, woodcarving and dance (individual tuition $10/hr, minimum 20hr). Superb **accommodation** in lovely bungalows is available with or without participation in any of the courses, but the reputation of *Sua Bali* is spreading internationally and booking is essential.

Sakah

Some 3km west of Kemenuh, at the junction of the road and bemo route north to Ubud, sits the small village of **SAKAH**, with its giant Buddha statue resembling a podgy baby. There are a few woodcarving and art shops to pass the time in if you're waiting for a connection, but they're nothing out of the ordinary. Don't bother with Pura Hyang Tibha, signposted from the village – now a sorry shadow of a very ancient temple. However, temple buffs may find it worth walking a few hundred metres east along the road to Gianyar to see **Gapura Canggi**, which stands 500m off the main road, beside a gigantic banyan tree. This grand fourteenth-century red-brick temple is based around three courtyards and is guarded by splendidly solid pairs of rams and bulls, while the highlight of the inner courtyard is a fabulously carved *padmasana* complete with *garuda*.

The coast south of Gianyar

The coast **south of Gianyar** is an attractive and little-visited part of Bali, best accessed by private transport, with long beaches of pure black sand, lots of peace and quiet and some fine views. However, when the proposed road along the coast from Pabean to Kusamba is finished, the area will be wide open for development and its whole character is likely to change. Bear in mind, too, that this is an area for beach walks rather than for swimming, as the Badung Strait – the patch of ocean between the mainland and Nusa Lembongan – is one of the deepest and most treacherous stretches of water off Bali. There are plenty of temples to base your explorations around. Bear in mind that there's no coastal road yet, so travelling between these temples means returning inland, heading east and returning back to the coast.

Pura Batu Klotok, one of the four state temples of Klungkung, stands in a stunning beachside position, although the building itself is unexceptional. Klotok is particularly revered: the sacred statues from the "mother temple" Besakih, are brought here during the annual cleansing ritual of *malasti*. During the 1963 and 1979 Eka Dasa Rudra ceremonies at Besakih (see box on p.268), the procession to the sea was over a mile long, and tens of thousands gathered on the beach for the rituals, which included the sacrificial drowning of a buffalo. To reach the temple, turn left (south) a little west of Belaga, 5km from Gianyar. At Tojan, head left again; the road winds between fields of rice, chillies, corn and soya beans for several kilometres until it reaches the coast.

Pura Masceti, east of Pura Batu Klotok, is one of Bali's directional temples, or *kahyangan jagat* (see p.507). Serving the south of the island, it's an extremely important temple built from whitish-grey coral stone rather than the usual red brick, with highly ornate carvings and statues. To get here, take the road out of Gianyar towards Bona and then the first road south. This leads 4km to

Keramas (bemos come this far on the Gianyar–Keramas–Blahbatuh route), where you turn left for the final 4km to the coast.

LEBIH, 7km southeast of Gianyar, is home to two more temples. Heading south at the main crossroads in Gianyar, the road winds through fields and the hamlet of Serongga to the ocean and a broad bay with plenty of local fishing boats, a few simple warung and fine views of the islands and the hills to the east behind Candi Dasa. Close to the beach, the entrance of **Pura Segara** (Sea Temple) is imposing, but there's no real hint of the importance of this site. Magical forces are believed to be focused on the temple, and an annual ceremony is held here to placate the demon I Macaling, who is thought to bring disease and ill-fortune to the mainland from the island of Nusa Penida (see box on p.280). Inland, **Pura Sibi Agung**, 2km from the beach, has a wonderfully grand and splendidly carved entrance gate; its large *padmasana* complete with turtle and *naga* is rather curiously positioned at the front of the temple.

One of the most picturesque stretches of the south coast is at **SIYUT**, equidistant from Gianyar and Klungkung. Here the beach is pure black and the bay stretches in a wide sweep for several kilometres, with the rice terraces inland forming a fabulous foreground to the bulk of Gunung Agung. It's a good place to spend a day on the beach, but you'll need your own transport; head for Tulikup on the main Gianyar–Klungkung road and take the road that heads south just east of the football field. After a few hundred metres, turn left at the crossroads in the village centre and follow the road for 5km round to the coast.

Northeast of Gianyar

Essential viewing for anyone even vaguely interested in Balinese temples is the **Pura Dalem** at **SIDAN**, 1km north of the main Gianyar–Klungkung road, on a sharp bend about 2km east of Gianyar, with parking spaces opposite. This incredible temple of the dead, dating from the seventeenth century, drips with gruesome carvings and statues of the terrible Rangda squashing babies, while the *kulkul* tower graphically depicts the punishments that await evildoers in the afterlife – which include having your head sawn off or being boiled up in a vat. The small shrine in front of the temple is dedicated to Merajapati, the caretaker of the dead, and is a common feature of *pura dalem*. There are occasional performances of the **barong** including the **kris** dance (see p.521 for more), generally during full-moon ceremonies; ask at the Ubud tourist office for details (see p.193).

At **BUNUTIN**, 3km north of Sidan and 7km south of Bangli, **Pura Penataran Agung** (also known as Pura Langgar), is signed east off the main road. It's an attractive temple, set about 100m down the small track, overlooking a large, palm-shaded, water-lilied lake, with two small shrines built on artificial islands. The **red-brick shrine** with the two-tiered red roof is the main point of interest, having four unusual doors, one in each side. There's a local story of a seventeenth-century Hindu prince whose brother became very sick; when he went to ask advice from a traditional healer, a *dukun*, he was told about a Muslim ancestor, originally from Java, who had settled in the Bunutin area. On being told to build a temple to honour this man, the young prince designed one that partly incorporated Muslim principles, with four doorways corresponding to the directions of the four winds. The sick prince recovered, and the descendants of his family are said still to abstain from eating pork in honour of their ancestor.

Bangli and around

Situated between Gianyar and the massive volcanic formations of the Batur area, **BANGLI** is often passed by in the headlong rush from beach to volcano. Set high enough in the hills to be cool yet low enough not to be cold, the administrative capital of Bangli district is a spacious and peaceful market town, with plenty of temples to keep you busy for a day or two. It's a pretty spot; every temple in the area seems to shower forth bold and exuberant carving. It fits in well on any itinerary to or from Batur, but don't be fooled by its proximity to Besakih: there are no public bemos on the Bangli–Rendang road.

Some history

While it was never one of the major Balinese kingdoms, Bangli played a crucial role at pivotal points in Balinese history. Originally set up under the rule of the **Majapahit** dynasty based in Gelgel, Bangli, along with the other small kingdoms, gradually asserted its **independence**. By the nineteenth century, all the kingdoms were involved in a complex game of infighting, attempted

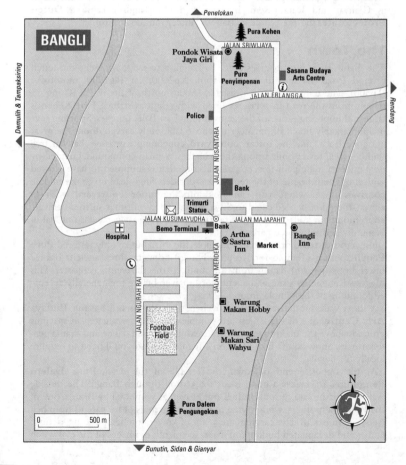

expansion and intrigue. **Gusti Ngurah Made Karangasem**, ruler of Buleleng in the north, annexed the entire Batur area from Bangli, and the Bangli raja, **Dewa Gde Tangkeban**, could only bide his time for revenge.

Between 1841 and 1843, the princes of Bali signed "friendship agreements" with the Dutch government. The disparity between the Dutch and Balinese interpretation of these eventually led to a crisis in which it became clear that the Dutch were ready to use force against Buleleng. Gaining his revenge for the loss of Batur, Dewa Gde Tangkeban announced his support for the Dutch, refusing help to Buleleng, and reoccupied the Batur area, thereby helping to cut off the Buleleng troops. Following a **Dutch victory** in 1849, Dewa Gde Tangkeban reclaimed his former lands as well as annexing Gianyar and Mengwi. Fighting between the kingdoms, including a long-running war between Bangli and Gianyar, dominated the second half of the nineteenth century, until the common threat from the Dutch diverted attention. Following the defeat of Badung regency in the south, and the *puputan* in Denpasar in 1906, the Dutch forced the raja of Bangli to sign away his powers in return for permission to remain as a figurehead. However, he became convinced that the Dutch would eventually overrun his kingdom, and requested the same status as Gianyar and Karangasem. In January 1909, Bangli became a **Dutch Protectorate**, and the whole of Bali was under outside control.

The Town

The main reason most tourists come to Bangli is to see the ancient and much revered **Pura Kehen** (daily 8am–5pm; Rp2600, car Rp1000, motorbike Rp500), state temple of Bangli district, 1500m north of the town. Rising up steeply from the road in **terraces** lined with religious statues, Pura Kehen is large and imposing – one of the gems among East Bali's temples. Sporting several remarkably fierce Bhoma leering above fabulously carved doors, the great entrance leads into the **outer courtyard** containing a massive banyan tree with a *kulkul* tower built among the branches. A small compound, guarded by *naga* under a frangipani tree, contains a stone that is supposed to have glowed with fire when the site of the temple was decided. Steps lead up to the middle courtyard, from where you can look into the **inner courtyard**, with its eleven-roofed *meru*, dedicated to Siwa, and a variety of other shrines dedicated to mountain gods. Over in the far right corner, the *padmasana* is unusual in being divided into three parts.

Just across the road from the main temple, the small but lavishly restored **Pura Penyimpenan** (Temple for Keeping Things) contains three ancient bronze inscriptions (*prasasti*) dating from the ninth to the thirteenth centuries. This suggests Kehen was a site of ancient worship even before the generally accepted founding of the temple around 1206.

A short walk southeast from Pura Kehen, the rather grand **Sasana Budaya Arts Centre**, one of the largest arts complexes in Bali, is situated in spacious grounds above the main town, and hosts exhibitions and dance and drama performances. Shows don't take place on a regular basis so you'll need to enquire locally for details.

At the opposite end of town, the temple of the dead, **Pura Dalem Pengungekan**, makes a good focus for a stroll through Bangli. The outside walls depict the fate of souls in hell and heaven as witnessed by Bhima, one of the Pandawa brothers, while trying to retrieve the souls of his parents from hell (see box on p.520). The carvings are a riot of knives, torches, pleading victims, flames and decapitated bodies. You'll also see plenty of images of the evil witch

Rangda. The central shrine is especially fine and details stories of Siwa, Ganesh, and Uma.

Practicalities

The turning to Bangli leaves the main Gianyar–Klungkung road 2km east of Gianyar. Blue public bemos lurk at the junction, but if you're coming from the west you can also pick up a bemo in Gianyar, on Jalan Berata, just outside the market entrance. Buses plying between Denpasar (Batubulan terminal) and Singaraja (Penarukan terminal) pass directly through Bangli.

The Bangli government **tourist office** is in the grounds of the Sasana Budaya Arts Centre at Jl Sriwijaya 23 (℡0366/91539), but seems to lack either personnel or opening times. There are full **exchange** facilities at Bank Rakyat Indonesia and Bank Pembangunan Daerah in the town centre. The **wartel** (daily 24hr) is on Jalan Ngurah Rai, and the **post office** is at Jl Kusumayudha 18. Bangli's **market** bursts into activity every three days.

There are several places **to stay** in town. The *Artha Sastra Inn*, Jl Merdeka 5 (℡0366/91179; ❷), is central, just opposite the bemo terminal, near the bold new *kulkul* tower and close to the market. The building was once the royal palace of Bangli and guests can enjoy the kudos of staying in an old palace with endless interlinking courtyards, though the grandeur is very faded indeed. Rooms currently have attached cold-water bathrooms although building of more luxurious accommodation is under way. The more conventional *Bangli Inn*, Jl Rambutan 1 (℡0366/91419; ❷–❹) has clean rooms in two storeys built around a small courtyard containing a restaurant, and all rooms have attached bathrooms. Bangli also offers a small **homestay** – *Pondok Wisata Jaya Giri*, Jl Sriwijaya 6 (℡0366/92255; ❶), almost opposite Pura Kehen; rooms are basic with attached mandis but this is the real thing – a family letting out a few rooms in their own compound.

For **food** during the day, the bus terminal has several stalls selling *es campur* and other snacks, while the road beside the terminal transforms into a small **night market** with the full range of sates, soups, rice and noodle dishes. *Warung Makan Hobby*, Jl Merdeka 45, offers a small menu of extremely good-value, well-cooked food; main courses are Rp3000–5000, and a large beer is less than Rp10,000. If this doesn't suit, *Warung Makan Sari Wahyu* is a few hundred metres further south on the same road, offering a similar menu.

Demulih

The quiet and pleasant village of **DEMULIH**, about 4km west of Bangli, has some well-carved temples in the main street, and a fine *kulkul* tower opposite the *bale banjar*. To get there, catch a dark red Tampaksiring-bound bemo outside the hospital in Bangli, and get out after crossing the iron bridge, before the bemo starts to climb up out of the valley. Take the first paved road to the left, by a small temple, Pura Manik Mudera; this shady road winds along a hillside for 1km to Demulih. A track to the right, 50m beyond the school, leads up to **Bukit Demulih**; anybody in the village will point you in the right direction. The track leads initially to a small, unwalled temple in the wood, where it forks; either way will take you to the top of the hill, which is actually a long wooded ridge, with temples nestling among the foliage. Trees obscure much of the view, but you should be able to spot Gunung Agung, Nusa Penida and Sanur.

Klungkung and around

It's tempting to lump **KLUNGKUNG**, also known by its older name of **Semarapura**, together with Gianyar, only 16km away. They are both district capitals, both were far grander in ancient times than they are today, and both are on the main east–west road across the island.

However, whereas Gianyar is somewhat devoid of sights, Klungkung is a bustling trading town, with plenty of things to see. Its highlights are the remains of the royal palace, collectively known as the **Taman Gili**, which include the ancient **Kerta Gosa painted ceiling**. These murals are the only surviving examples of classical wayang painting *in situ* on the island (see p.531) and they are incredibly detailed and finely worked. They underwent major restorations in the 1930s, 1960 and 1982 and although the pictures are decidedly grubby, being located on the corner of the main Klungkung crossroads, they remain required viewing. The centre of modern classical-style Balinese painting is at **Kamasan**, only a few kilometres south of town, while one of the newest museums on the island, the **Gunarsa Museum of Modern and Classical Art,** to the west of Klungkung just beyond Takmung, houses a moderately diverting collection. South of Klungkung, the sleepy village of **Gelgel** is these days a shadowy remnant of the thriving royal capital which ruled Bali for three hundred years.

Some history

Following the **Majapahit conquest** of Bali under the leadership of Gajah Mada in 1343, the conquerors set up a court in Samprangan, moving in 1400 to **Gelgel**, just south of modern Klungkung. From this base, Bali was ruled by a dynasty appointed by Gajah Mada, each ruler taking the title **Dewa Agung** (Great God). When the Majapahit empire in Java collapsed in 1515, large numbers of Javanese royalty in exile swelled the community in Bali. In 1550, when **Batu Renggong** became *dewa agung*, his area of influence increased dramatically and the Gelgel court flourished, becoming a centre for art, literature and culture. However, decline set in gradually, and under the rule of Batu Renggong's grandson, Dewa Agung Di Made, control of the empire was gradually lost. Towards the end of the seventeenth century, Di Made's son, Gusti Sideman, moved the palace and the court to **Klungkung**, believing that the decline of the kingdom was due to a curse upon the Gelgel palace. But it was downhill from then on: Gianyar was established as a separate kingdom in 1667, and the *dewa agungs* of Klungkung never again reached such influential heights.

The Dutch attacked southern Bali in 1906, and by 1908 had subdued all the kingdoms except Klungkung and Bangli. Gelgel was destroyed, and when the Dutch set up their weapons outside the Semarapura palace in Klungkung on April 28, 1908, the *dewa agung* led two hundred members of his family and court in the traditional **puputan**. When he marched into the guns and was killed, six of his wives surrounded his body and stabbed themselves with their kris. The rest of those present were either shot down or killed themselves. The monument opposite the Taman Gili in Klungkung commemorates the *puputan*. Surviving members of the Klungkung royal family were then exiled to Lombok and didn't return until the 1920s.

On several **bemo routes**, most notably from Padang Bai, the name **Semarapura** is used instead of Klungkung.

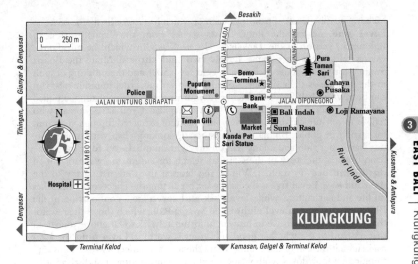

The Town

On first arrival, Klungkung can appear rather confusing – especially coming by public transport, as buses and bemos are forced to complete a wide one-way circuit of the town. Klungkung centres on a crossroads, marked by the dramatic white **Kanda Pat Sari statue** which guards the four cardinal directions. Beside it is the Taman Gili, with the Puputan Monument opposite and the market tucked away just to the east, behind the main street.

The Taman Gili

The **Taman Gili** (daily 7am–5.30pm; Rp5000), meaning "Island Gardens", has its entrance on Jalan Puputan. It's the only surviving part of the Semarapura, the palace of the Klungkung rulers. Built around 1710, and large-ly destroyed by fighting in 1908, the only remains of the palace are the Kerta Gosa (Consultation Pavilion for Peace and Prosperity), the Bale Kambung (Floating Pavilion), a *kulkul* tower, and a massive red-brick **gateway**, decorat-ed with stone carvings, which marked the entrance from the outer to the inner courtyards of the palace. Legend tells how the gateway was created by two craftsmen who, while sleeping in separate temples on the nearby coast, each dreamt about half of a massive and wonderful doorway. When they met and compared their dreams they realized that their visions fitted together perfectly, and they built the doorway. Legend also claims that at the time of the *puputan* in Klungkung in 1908, the wooden doors sealed themselves shut and nobody has been able to open them since.

Perched on one corner of the main crossroads, the **Kerta Gosa** is a square open *bale* on a raised platform. It's sometimes described as a criminal court, which adds poignancy to the pictures of gruesome punishments on the ceil-ing, but it's more likely that it was the pavilion where the king and his minis-ters met to debate law and other matters of importance. The **painted ceiling** is a unique, superlative and intricate example of the Kamasan style of classical painting, often referred to as the wayang style because the figures are essential-ly the same as the characters in the wayang puppet theatre.

There are nine levels of paintings, each of which has a specific theme or story. **Level one**, nearest the floor, shows scenes from the Tantri stories, an Indonesian version of the *Thousand and One Nights*, in which the girl, Tantri, weaves tales night after night. **Levels two and three** illustrate the Bhima Swarga story (part of the *Mahabharata* epic; see p.520), and the suffering of souls in the afterlife as their sins are atoned for by various cruel punishments: you can be sawn in half for disobedience to your parents, have your tongue pulled out for witchcraft, be suckled by a giant caterpillar if you are a woman who refuses to nurture children, or have your intestines extracted through your anus for farting in public. Bhima is the aristocratic-looking chap with moustache, tidy hair, a big club and a long nail on his right thumb. **Level four** shows the Sang Garuda, the story of the Garuda's search for *amerta*, the water of life, so that he can free his mother, Winita, and himself from eternal slavery to the thousand *naga*. **Level five** is the *palalindon*, predicting the effects of earthquakes on life and agriculture, while **levels six and seven** are a continuation of the Bhima Swarga story. **Level eight** is the Swarga Roh, which shows the rewards that the godly will receive in heaven; unfortunately, it's so far above your head that it's hard to see whether good behaviour is worth it. **Level nine**, the *loka-pala*, right at the top of the ceiling where the four sides meet, shows a lotus surrounded by four doves symbolizing good luck, enlightenment and salvation.

The **Bale Kambung**, almost beside the Kerta Gosa and surrounded by a moat, was the venue for royal tooth-filing ceremonies (see p.546). Its ceiling is less famous than its neighbour's but equally interesting; six levels of paintings cover Balinese astrology, the tales of Pan Brayut (see box on p.209) and, closest to the top, the adventures of Satusoma, who was a legendary Buddhist saint, adopted into a Hindu context. Satusoma's adventures consist of a series of battles and selfless acts through which he defeats evil and brings peace to the world.

Museum Daerah Semarapura

The **Museum Daerah Semarapura** in the Taman Gili grounds is worth a quick look. It contains a motley collection from varying periods of history including kris, textiles and stones from the ancient monuments of Gelgel. Only a few labels are in English and descriptions are rather scant. Of most interest are the photographs from the early 1900s of the Klungkung royal family and a Barong Ket dance costume.

Pura Taman Sari

Just under 1km northeast from the town centre, **Pura Taman Sari** (Flower Garden) is impressively large. With its expansive grassy compounds, it's a pleasant place to relax and there are some intriguingly original features: the grey stone eleven-roofed *meru* is highly unusual, as it stands in the middle of a moat. The structure rests upon a stone turtle, looking rather squashed and beady-eyed, while just one (rather than the traditional two) massive *naga* curves around the base, its head to the right of the turtle's head and its tail to the left. During the reign of the *dewa agung* in Bali, this temple was the site of an annual ceremony in which offerings were made to the kris and other weapons belonging to the royal family of Klungkung.

Practicalities

The main **bus and bemo terminal**, Terminal Kelod, is about 1km south of the town centre; most public transport stops or passes through. In addition, a small terminal lies just north of the main crossroads, a bit hidden away off Jalan Gunung Rinjani, where you can pick up bemos for Rendang and Besakih

△ Nusa Lembongan

(which don't stop at Kelod). Bemos for Padang Bai and minibuses for Amlapura also pass through here heading east.

The Klungkung government **tourist office** is in the same building as the Museum Daerah Semarapura, Jl Untung Surapati 3 (Mon–Thurs 7.30am–3.30pm, Fri 7am–1.15pm; ℡0366/21448), and produces a small brochure on the town's sights. Across the road from the Kerta Gosa is the **wartel** (daily 24hr), while the **post office** is just west of the museum on Jalan Untung Surapati. Several banks along Jalan Diponegoro to the east of the main crossroads **change money**, including Bank Pembangunan Daerah. BNI is just around the corner in Jalan Nakula and there's a Bank of Central Asia ATM in the main street.

Most people visit Klungkung as a day-trip from Candi Dasa. The best **accommodation** is at the *Loji Ramayana* in the eastern part of town (℡0366/21044; ❷), which has simple rooms set back from the road in a court-yard with a small restaurant. If you're counting the rupiah, consider the *Cahaya Pusaka* opposite (℡0366/22118; ❶), with rooms closer to the main road and therefore noiser. Klungkung has a few reasonable, inexpensive **places to eat** and drink. On Jalan Nakula, *Bali Indah* at no. 1, and *Sumba Rasa* at no. 5, both have small menus written in English and are used to foreign diners. Local people eat at the inexpensive warung gathered around the small bemo terminal just off Jalan Gunung Rinjani. There's a **supermarket**, Cahaya Melati, on Jalan Puputan opposite the entrance to the Taman Gili; *Dunkin Donuts* has a take-away counter here.

Around Klungkung

There are several places worth a trip **around Klungkung**, especially if you're on the trail of classical painting. With the exception of the beautiful black-sand **beach** at Siyut, all are accessible by public transport.

Gunarsa Museum of Classical and Modern Art

Some 5km west of Klungkung, just beyond the village of Takmung on the main road to Gianyar, the spacious and modern art gallery, **Gunarsa Museum of Classical and Modern Art** (daily 9am–5pm; Rp10,000), formerly known as Museum Seni Lukis Klasik Bali, is worth a visit for anyone with an interest in Balinese arts. Take any westbound bemo and get out when you see the massive Trimurti statue with mock policemen at the base.

Having started life in one large building, the museum is slowly expanding, with separate buildings for modern art, a centre for herbal medicine, a library and a cultural centre across the road. However, at the time of writing most of the collection remained in the original building.

On the far side of the white-tiled entrance area is a sunken **performance space**, used for occasional, but sadly private, events, with a set of stunning carved doors painted in red and gold. **Upstairs** is displayed a vast collection of historical objects and traditional art, including painting, embroidery, stone sculptures, masks and ancient furniture. The majority show scenes from the *Mahabharata*, the *Ramayana* and the *Karmapala*. It's a fascinating hoard to wander through; everything is labelled but there's very little explanation of each piece's significance – although the young guides will do their best to answer questions. A guidebook in English (Rp60,000) is descriptive rather than explanatory.

The museum also contains a collection of works by **Nyoman Gunarsa**, the founder of the museum. Born in nearby Banda village, he is one of the foremost modern Balinese painters. Initially his work appears quite abstract, but resolves into the forms of dancers and musicians, the artist's constant theme. His studio within the museum is also sometimes open to visitors.

In the entrance hall, a small **cafeteria** selling cold drinks is a cool and attractive spot to relax for a while.

Tihingan

From the Gunarsa Museum a side road leads 3km to **TIHINGAN**. Bemos ply this route through the small village of Banda, past fields with lovely views across to Agung, Lempuyang and Seraya, and through the village of Penasan with local brickworks lining the road. Tihingan is a small, unassuming village, home to a number of **gong-makers**. Using tin and copper from Java and beyond, the bronze gongs produced range from tiny tourist models on wooden stands, no bigger than a handspan, to giants, 1m in diameter and costing several million rupiah. Many of the gong-makers also produce metal bars for the gamelan. There are several showrooms on the main street, open from about 7am to 3pm, where you can try out both the gongs and the gamelan; if you come early, you may be able to see the craftsmen at work.

Kamasan

South of Klungkung, 500m beyond the Kelod bemo terminal, is the turning to **KAMASAN**, a tiny village packed with artists' houses, studios and small shops, and renowned on Bali as the historical and present-day centre of **classical wayang painting** (see p.531). Wayang style traditionally depicts religious subjects, astrological charts and calendars, and you'll be struck immediately by the uniform colours used: muted reds, ochres, blues, greens and blacks. Many of the artists here work in family concerns where one member of the family sketches out the work and others make and mix the colours and fill in the outlines.

After visiting a few workshops you'll find it surprisingly easy to pick out the better drawn, more carefully coloured pictures. While the artists obviously want to make sales, the atmosphere is pleasant and relaxed – although you should shop around and still bargain hard. **I Nyoman Mandra**, in particular, has a very good reputation and his work will give you a basis for comparison. His showroom has a collection of very high-quality pieces that are not available for sale; notice the fine but solid outlines, the absence of large unfilled spaces on the canvas and the careful, detailed colouring and shading. He also organizes a local school (Mon–Sat 2–5pm) where local boys and girls learn the techniques of classical painting and visitors are welcome to see their efforts; you may also be entertained by an *ad hoc* gamelan concert. Donations are appreciated and it's a heartening attempt to keep the skills of classical art alive. **Ni Made Suciarmi** is one of very few **women artists** working in Kamasan in what is very much a male preserve; many women mix colours and fill in the outlines, but she does the drawing too. She comes from a family of artists and was involved in the 1930s renovation of the Kerta Gosa ceiling in Klungkung when she was just six years old. Her work is represented in the Seniwati Women's Art Gallery in Ubud (see p.204).

There is **accommodation** at Kamasan Art Centre (T & F0361/462611, @g_legong@hotmail.com; 4), in small, neat bungalows around a courtyard. There's usually an artist working here and they can arrange programmes for individuals and groups involving local walks and visits to artists' studios.

Gelgel and beyond

The ancient court centre of **GELGEL**, 4km south of Klungkung, is a village of wide streets crammed full of temples. Today it's a quiet little place with nothing but its history to offer visitors (for more, see p.256); large numbers of its ancient stones have been removed to museums.

Why Bali has remained Hindu

Gelgel is home to a **Muslim** community, one of the three communities established on Bali at the time of the **Majapahit** rule over the island. It's believed that Muslim missionaries who came to Bali to convert the people failed, and were too ashamed to go home, so the *dewa agung* allowed them to stay. Legend tells that the *dewa agung*'s main objection to Islam was the ritual of circumcision. The missionaries explained that the bamboo knife they used was very sharp so it would be perfectly straightforward. The *dewa agung* demanded to see the knife, tried to cut his finger-nail and failed. He then tried to cut the hairs on his arm and failed. Refusing to allow the knife near any other parts of his anatomy, he gave it back and declared that he and Bali would remain Hindu.

Pura Dasar on the main street is the highlight, with massive courtyards, *bale* and nine-roofed and eleven-roofed *meru* in the inner courtyard. Each year this temple is the site of the **Pewintenan ceremony**, held on the fourth full moon of the Balinese calendar (check the *Calendar of Events* produced by the tourist office for exact dates), which attracts pilgrims from all over Bali. The purpose of the ceremony is to cleanse and purify those ready to become *pemangku* (village priests). Each potential priest brings an enormous entourage of family and friends along and donates Rp15,000 and 4kg of rice to the temple. The ritual lasts all day and at midnight culminates with the new *pemangku* walking over the skin and sometimes the head of a dead buffalo. As with most festivals on the island, visitors are welcome to watch.

Besakih and Gunung Agung

The major tourist draw in the east of Bali, with around a quarter of a million tourists a year, is undoubtedly the **Besakih** temple complex, the most venerated site in Bali, situated on the slopes of **Gunung Agung**, the holiest and highest mountain on the island. It's an irresistible combination, and inevitably attracts swarms of attendant hustlers, hassling the daily crowds of visitors. Bus tours start arriving around 10.30am, after which the sheer volume of tourists, traders and self-styled guardians of the temple make the place pretty unbearable: it's well worth **arriving early** in the morning to get the best of the atmosphere.

The two sides of Besakih's personality rarely intersect. On the one hand it's the holiest spot on the island for Balinese Hindus, who believe that the gods descend to earth and reside here occasionally – most reliably during certain ceremonies. During these times they don their finery and bring elaborate offerings for them. On the other hand Besakih is a jumble of buildings, unremarkable in many ways, around which has evolved the habit of separating foreign tourists from as much money as possible in as short a time as possible. Balinese worshippers pay little or no heed to the hundreds of camera-toting visitors milling around them as they pray, and tourists search in vain for any sacred aura around the place as they seek to evade local guides, stumble across soft-drink sellers around every corner and struggle to take photographs that don't include the *Hard Rock Café*-sponsored rubbish bins.

Even the stark grandeur of Besakih's location is often shrouded in mist, leaving Gunung Agung towering behind in all-enveloping cloud, and the splendid panorama back south to the coast an imaginary delight. However the scale of Besakih is impressive and on a clear day, with ceremonies in full swing, before

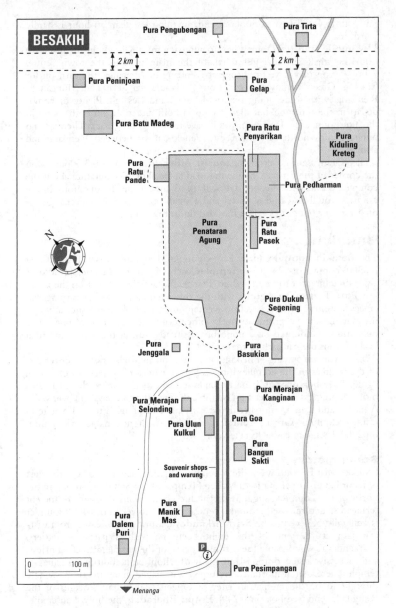

the hordes of foreign visitors arrive, it is a wonderful place. At other times you can well end up wandering around wondering why you bothered.

Arrival and information

Without your own transport, the easiest but least desirable way of getting to Besakih is to take an **organized tour**. If you decide to do this, check how much time you'll have to look around; anything less than an hour is hardly worth it.

By **public transport**, one way is to approach from Klungkung: bemos leave from the small terminal just north of the main road in the town centre, although you may have to change at Rendang or Menanga, the turn-off for Besakih. Green bemos also run from Amlapura via Selat and Muncan to Rendang, with some going on to Menanga and Besakih. Plenty of bemos depart in the morning, but they dry up in both directions on both routes in the afternoon: after 1 or 2pm, you'll have trouble getting back. There are no public bemos north of Menanga to Penelokan, or between Rendang and Bangli.

The Karangasem government **tourist office** (daily 8.30am–3.30pm) is on the corner of the car park beside the road at Besakih. No literature about the complex is available here, but staff will try to answer specific questions. In the car park you'll also find a wartel and a small post office. Moneychangers – offering very poor rates – line the road up to the temple.

Besakih

The **Besakih complex** (daily 8am–5pm; Rp3100, camera Rp1100, parking Rp500) consists of 22 separate **temples**, each with its own name, spread over a site stretching for more than 3km. The central temple – largest on the island – is **Pura Penataran Agung**, with the other temples ranged at varying distances around it. There's as yet no written guide available at the site, although the Karangasem government tourist office claims to have one planned. The only **map** is mounted on a noticeboard situated just at the top of the road leading from the car park to the temples.

Unless you are praying or making offerings, you are **forbidden to enter** any of the temples in the complex (unless you've paid for the services of a local "guide"; see box opposite); most temples remain locked unless there's a ceremony in progress. However a lot is visible through the gateways and over walls. A sarong and scarf are not strictly necessary, but you'll need them if you're in skimpy clothing; **sarong rental** is available, with negotiable prices from Rp2000. It's much easier to take your own.

Some history

It's likely that Besakih was a site of religious significance long before the start of recorded history; Pura Batu Madeg (Temple of the Standing Stone), in the north of the complex, suggests megalithic connections through its ancient terraced structure based around a central stone. However, Besakih's founder is generally believed to be **Sri Markandeya**, a priest who came from eastern Java at the end of the eighth century with a party of settlers. Markandeya's son became the first high priest of the temple, attracting priests and successive rulers of the island, many of whom built additional shrines or temples here. An important ceremony was staged here in 1007, widely thought to be the cremation rites of Queen Mahendratta, origin of the Rangda legend (see box on p.249). **Empu Bharadah**, the holy man credited with subduing Rangda, took part and there are shrines dedicated to him throughout the complex.

In 1343, the **Majapahit dynasty** conquered Bali. Two ancient *lontar* books indicate the importance of Besakih on the island at this time. It became, in turn, the state temple of the powerful Gelgel and Klungkung courts, and its pre-eminent position on the island was confirmed. The **earthquake** of 1917

Unofficial guides at Besakih

There are many **unofficial guides** hanging around Besakih, adept at attaching themselves to tourists and then demanding large sums in payment for their services. They now resist the label of guides and have styled themselves **"guardians"** or **"keepers"** of the temple. They pester, harass and harangue visitors to engage them to escort them around the main temple. There's no reason why you need to engage one of these men – although with one you'll be allowed to go through the two outer courtyards of Pura Penataran Agung, and it can be interesting to have a local perspective (even though many of them don't speak brilliant English, have limited knowledge of the temples and seem interested only in getting round as quickly as possible and receiving payment). With more than two hundred local men earning their living like this, you'll be approached whenever you arrive. Always establish the **fee** beforehand; Rp10,000–20,000 is the going rate. Whether recent complaints to the authorities about this situation will bring about an improvement remains to be seen.

severely damaged the buildings, but repairs were carried out by the Dutch, and in 1932 the road to the temple was completed. Further damage occurred in 1963 during the eruption of Gunung Agung (see box on p.268), and Besakih again underwent restoration. As a result, the temples in the complex are a vibrant mix of old and new, and fresh building and restoration work continues all the time.

The temples

To get the best out of Besakih, it's a good idea to see **Pura Penataran Agung**, the most important temple, first, and then wander at will; most of the tourist crowds tend to stick to the immediate area around the central temple. The *meru* of **Pura Batu Madeg**, rising among the trees in the north of the complex, are particularly enticing, while, if you feel like a longer walk, **Pura Pengubengan**, the most far-flung of the temples, is a good 2km through the forest.

While it's possible to consider each of the temples as a single entity, they do fall into various groups. The **Trimurti**, the "three shapes" of the supreme God, consists of three temples: Pura Kiduling Kreteg (Temple South of the Bridge), dedicated to Brahma, the creator; Pura Batu Madeg (Temple of the Standing Stone), dedicated to Wisnu, the preserver; and Pura Penataran Agung, dedicated to Siwa, the destroyer. Each of the gods has a colour associated with him, and on festival days the respective temples are decked with flags and banners: black for Wisnu, red for Brahma and a multi-coloured array for Siwa at the centre.

Five of the temples are considered to represent the **panca dewata**, the five gods of the four directions and the centre – Pura Ulun Kulkul the west, Pura Gelap the east, Pura Batu Madeg the north, Pura Kiduling Kreteg the south and Pura Penataran Agung the centre.

As in every village in Bali, there are also the three temples of **pura puseh, pura desa** and **pura dalem** (see p.507), which here symbolically serve the entire population of Bali. Pura Basukian is the Temple of Origin (*pura puseh*) where Besakih's founders completed their original ritual; Pura Penataran Agung is the Temple of the Community (*pura desa*); and Pura Dalem Puri the Temple of the Dead (*pura dalem*). This last temple is especially significant for the Balinese and, during the seventh lunar month, pilgrims come to pray for the souls of the dead.

Besakih festivals

Every temple in the Besakih complex has its timetable of **festivals**. There are more than fifty annual festivals in all, so you're likely to see one of them. Exact dates are published annually by the Bali government tourist office in their *Calendar of Events* booklet. The most important is the **Bhatar Turun Kabeh** ("the gods descend together"), which takes place in March or April and lasts a month, with the high point on the full moon of the tenth lunar month. At this time, the gods of all the shrines are believed to come and dwell in Besakih; people converge here from all over the island for the ceremonies.

Besakih's most revered festival is **Eka Dasa Rudra** (see box on p.268), supposedly held every hundred years, but which took place in 1963 and then again in 1979.

Pura Penataran Agung

The Great Temple of State, or **Pura Penataran Agung**, is the central and most dramatic building in the complex, although its drama lies in size, position and the great reverence in which it is held rather than in intricate carving.

The temple is built on **seven ascending terraces**, and altogether there are more than fifty structures including *bale*, shrines and stone thrones inside; about half are dedicated to specific gods, while the others have various ceremonial functions such as receiving offerings, providing seating for the priests or the gamelan orchestra, or as residences for the gods during temple festivals.

A giant stairway, lined by seven levels of **carved figures**, leads to the small first courtyard; the figures to the left are from the *Mahabharata* and the ones to the right from the *Ramayana*. You can look into the courtyard, although views are obstructed by the *bale* just inside the gate. This pavilion is in two parts with a small walkway between. As worshippers process through here they symbolically sever their connection with the everyday world, praying at the *bale ongkara* before proceeding into the second courtyard – the most important in the temple. The courtyards ascend consecutively in terraces, but, without employing a "guardian", visitors can go no further than the top of the main stairway.

A path skirts the entire perimeter wall of Pura Penataran Agung and you can see most of the temple's terraces from it, although you're too close to get a proper sense of the whole building. If you're hoping to see religious ceremonies, the second courtyard is the one to watch (the best views are from the west side). It's the largest courtyard in the temple and contains the **padmatiga**, the three-seated lotus throne dedicated to Brahma, Siwa and Wisnu, where all pilgrims pray.

Practicalities

The shops that line the road up from the car park, and the enormous number of stalls dotted throughout the complex, offer a huge range of **souvenirs** – all pretty standard stuff that you can buy anywhere on the island, including bedspreads, clothes, woodcarvings, baskets and paintings in all styles. The artist W. Sutama is worth seeking out; he displays original work by himself, his friends and family in a variety of styles with a wide range of subject-matter. All pictures are extremely well framed, and start at US$40.

Accommodation near Besakih is very limited. The *Lembah Arca* hotel (℡0366/23076; ❹) on the road between Menanga and Besakih, a couple of kilometres before the temple complex, has two neat, tiled bungalows in an attractive garden, but the altitude means it gets chilly at night. There are also a few unsigned and unauthorized lodgings (❷–❸) behind the shops and stalls

LEVEL I

1. Candi bentar An earlier entrance was toppled in the earthquake following the 1963 eruption.
2–3. Bale kulkul Contains the wooden kulkul (slit gongs).
4. Bale pegat Two part *bale* to symbolize pilgrims passing from the material to the spiritual world.
5–6. Bale palegongan and **bale pagambuhan** Used for dance performances during festivals.
7–8. Bale ongkara Represent the sacred syllable *om*.

LEVEL II

9. Kori agung Gateway into next courtyard.
10. Bale gong For the gamelan orchestra.
11. Bale pawedan Where high priests prepare holy water.
12. Bale kembangsirang For conducting rituals.
13. Panggungan Place for offerings.
14. Bale agung For meetings.
15. Bale kawas Dedicated to Ida Bhatara Ider Buwana.
16. Padma capah Throne dedicated to Ida Ratu Sula Majemuh, lord of the weather.
17. Bale paruman alit Containing a stone *lingge*.
18. Nine-roofed meru Dedicated to Sanghyang Kubakal, god of instruments used in ceremonies.
19. Eleven-roofed meru Dedicated to Ratu Manik Maketel.
20. Bale pepelik For offerings.
21. Bale tegeh Dedicated to Empu Bharadah.
22. Padmatiga Triple lotus throne and centrepiece of the temple, where homage is paid to the supreme god Sanghyang Widhi Wasa in his three manifestations.
23. Bale pasamuhan agung Home of the gods at festival time.
24. Bale pepelik For offerings.

LEVEL III

25–30. Meru and shrines Dedicated to spirits
31–32. Shrines to the ancestors of a clan from the Besakih area.
33. Bale pepelik For offerings.
34–35. Shrines to the ancestors of another local clan.
36. Panggungan For offerings during ceremonies at the shrines.
37. Seven-roofed meru Dedicated to Saraswati, Hindu goddess of learning.
38. Panggungan For offerings during ceremonies at the shrines.
39. Bale pepelik For offerings.
40. Eleven-roofed meru Dedicated to Ida Ratu Maspahit.
41. Three-roofed kehen Temple store for sacred objects.

LEVEL IV

42. Bale Containing ancient statues.
43. Gedong Dedicated to Ida Ratu Ulang Alu, god of wandering salesmen.
44. Gedong Dedicated to Ida Ratu Ayu Subandar, god of merchants.
45. Bale pepelik For offerings.
46. Bebaturan Dedicated to Ida Ratu Sedahan Panginte.
47. Bale pepelik For offerings.
48. Eleven-roofed meru Dedicated to Ida Ratu Sunaring Jagat, god of the light of the whole.
49–51. Bale tegeh Dedicated to the courtiers and nymphs of heaven (*widadara* and *widadari*).

PURA PENATARAN AGUNG

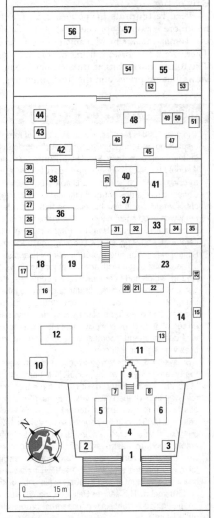

LEVEL V

52–53. Bale pepelik For offerings.
54. Three-roofed meru Dedicated to Ida Ratu Ayu Mas Magelung, goddess of performing arts.
55. Eleven-roofed meru Dedicated to a manifestation of Sanghyang Widh.

LEVEL VI

56. Gedong Dedicated to Ida Ratu Bukit Kiwa, god of the left mountain.
57. Gedong Dedicated to Ida Ratu Bukit Tengen, god of the right mountain.

lining the road from the car park up to the temple; ask at the tourist office for details. These places are very simple, with few private bathrooms, but are useful if you get stranded, are climbing Gunung Agung or want to explore the site early or late.

Several **restaurants** in the area cater for the tour-bus trade, though you'll find more reasonably priced food at the *Lembah Arca* hotel (see above) and at the *Warung Mawar* in Menanga, just on the left as you turn off to Besakih. There are a few basic warung on the walk up to Besakih from the car park. The tourist restaurants at Bukit Jambul, 6km north of Klungkung, have great views, but are pricey and the food is nothing special.

1963

The year **1963** is recalled in Bali as a time of terrible disaster, in which the gods were displeased and took their revenge in dramatic fashion. Ancient texts prescribe that an immense ceremony, **Eka Dasa Rudra** – the greatest ritual in Balinese Hinduism – should be held every hundred years for the spiritual purification of the island and to bring future good fortune. Before 1963 it had only been held a couple of times since the sixteenth century. In the early 1960s, religious leaders believed that the trials of World War II and the ensuing fight for independence were indicators that the ritual was once again needed, and these beliefs were confirmed by a **plague of rats** that overran the entire island in 1962. Preparations began on October 10, 1962, with ceremonies inviting and welcoming the gods from Gunung Semeru in Java and Rinjani in Lombok and the purification of sacrificial animals.

The climax of the festival was set for March 8, 1963, but on February 18, **Gunung Agung**, which had been dormant for centuries, started rumbling; the glow of the fire became visible within the crater and ash began to coat the area. Initially, this was interpreted as a good omen sent by the gods to purify Besakih, but soon doubts crept in. Some argued that the wrong date had been chosen for the event and wanted to call it off. However, by this time it was too late to cancel; President Sukarno was due to attend, together with an international conference of travel representatives who were meeting in Jakarta.

By March 8, black smoke, rocks and ash were billowing from the mountain, but the ceremony went ahead, albeit in a decidedly tense atmosphere. Eventually, on March 17, Agung **erupted** with such force that the top hundred metres of the mountain was ripped apart. The whole of eastern Bali was threatened by the poisonous gas and molten lava that poured from the volcano, villages were engulfed, and between 1000 and 2000 people are thought to have died, while the homes of another 100,000 were destroyed. In the district of Klungkung alone, twenty percent of the arable land was destroyed. Roads were wiped out, some towns were isolated for weeks and the ash ruined vast amounts of crops, causing serious food shortages for many months afterwards. The lava tracks are still clearly visible on the north coast around Tianyar and Kubu, and less obviously on the road between Klungkung and Kusamba. The east of Bali took many years to recover; hundreds of homeless people joined Indonesia's *transmigrasi* programme (see p.500) and moved to the outer islands.

Despite the force of the eruption and the position of the Besakih complex high on the mountain slopes, a surprisingly small amount of damage occurred within the temples themselves, and the **closing rites** of Eka Dasa Rudra took place in Pura Penataran Agung on April 20. Subsequently, many Balinese felt that the mountain's eruption at the time of such a momentous ceremony was an omen of the civil strife that engulfed Bali in 1965 (see p.499).

In 1979, the year actually specified by the ancient texts, Eka Dasa Rudra was held again and this time passed off without incident.

Gunung Agung

According to legend, **Gunung Agung** was created by the god Pasupati when he split Mount Mahmeru (the centre of the Hindu universe), forming both Gunung Agung and Gunung Batur. At 3014m, superb conical-shaped Agung is the highest Balinese peak and an awe-inspiring sight from anywhere in East Bali. The spiritual centre of the Balinese universe, it is believed that the spirits of the ancestors of the Balinese people dwell on Gunung Agung. Villages and house compounds are laid out in relation to the mountain, and many Balinese people prefer to sleep with their heads towards it. Directions on Bali are always given with reference to Agung, *kaja* meaning towards the mountain and *kelod* meaning away from it.

Climbing the mountain

Two **routes** lead up Gunung Agung, both involving a long hard climb. One path leaves from Besakih and the other from Pura Pasar Agung over on the southern slope of the mountain, near Selat (described on p.303). You'll need to set out very early in the morning if you want to be at the top to see the spectacular **sunrise** around 7am. It's essential to take a **guide** with you, as the lower slopes are densely forested and it's easy to get lost. You'll also need strong footwear, a good flashlight, water and snacks to keep you going; for the descent, a stout stick is very handy.

This is an extremely sacred peak for the Balinese, and while it's not possible to climb the mountain at certain times of the year because of the weather, it's also not permitted at many other times because of **religious festivals**: March and April are generally impossible from the Besakih side because of ceremonies. You'll also have to make **offerings** at temples at the start and on the way. **Weather**-wise, the dry season (April to mid-October) is the best time to climb Gunung Agung, but don't even contemplate it during January and February, the wettest months. At other times during the rainy season you may get a few dry days, but bear in mind that the weather up on the mountain can be very different from what it is on the beach.

From Pura Pasar Agung, it's at least a three-hour climb with an ascent of almost 2000m, so you'll need to set out at 3am or earlier, depending on how fit you are. You'll also have to either sleep at the temple or wake up even earlier to get to the start of the climb. The track initially passes through forest, ascending onto bare, steep rock. It doesn't go to the actual summit, but ends at a point on the rim which is about 100m lower. From here, the summit masks views of part of the island, but you'll be able to see Rinjani, the south of Bali and Gunung Batukau and look down into the 500-metre crater.

From Besakih, the climb is longer (5–6hr); you'll need to leave between midnight and 2am. This path starts from Pura Pengubengan, the most distant of the temples in the Besakih complex, and takes you up to the summit of Agung with views in all directions. As with the other route, you climb initially through forest but, once on the bare mountain, the path is extremely steep. The descent is particularly taxing from this side, too; allow four or five hours to get down.

Practicalities

There are established **guiding** operations to the south of the mountain, although new ones are appearing all the time and you can arrange climbs from several other areas as well. It's important to bear in mind that this is a serious trek: talk to potential guides carefully and satisfy yourself that they have the necessary experience and knowledge.

To climb **from Pura Pasar Agung**, you'll find guides at both Muncan, 4km east of Rendang, and at Selat (see p.302 for more on the road east of Rendang). I Ketut Uriada, a part-time teacher and guide, is one of the most experienced guides and has climbed Agung over 200 times in recent years; these days, he doesn't always do the climb himself but has trained several assistants to stand in. His house is marked by a blue sign advertising his services, on the left as you enter the village of Muncan from the east. He'll help you arrange a bemo charter between Muncan and Pura Pasar Agung (about $10, which includes simple accommodation in his house). To climb the mountain, expect to pay around $30 for a guide for one person, $40 for two, $50 for three. Larger groups may need more than one guide. You're expected to provide food for them. Alternative **accommodation** is at *Pondok Wisata Puri Agung* (☎0366/23037; ❸–❹) in Selat, 4km east of Muncan on the Amlapura road. They can also provide a guide for the climb, quoting Rp150,000 per person for a minimum of two people. This does not include accommodation or transport to and from Pura Pasar Agung (about Rp60,000 from Selat).

From Besakih, guides can be arranged at the tourist office; they can also help with nearby lodgings. The going rate from this side is $50 per guide, each of whom will lead up to five people.

Inevitably, prices are higher if you arrange the trek **from further afield**. Nyoman Budiarsa at **Tirtagangga** (see p.300) arranges dinner the evening before, transport and food; his small shop is on the right as you head north through the town. The *Pondok Lembah Dukuh* and *Geria Semalung* losmen in the nearby village of Ababi (see p.301) also arrange Agung climbs. The guiding operations in **Toya Bungkah** in the area of Gunung Batur (see box on p.329) charge $75–95 per person (minimum numbers apply). Bali Sunrise 2001 in **Ubud** (☎0361/980470, mobile ☎0818/552669, ⓦ www.balisunrise2001.com) will arrange pick-ups from various parts of **southern Bali** or **Lovina** for the trek, charging $100–110 per person depending on where you start from. The Perama bus company also organizes the trip (from $45 per person); enquire at any of their offices.

Nusa Lembongan, Nusa Ceningan and Nusa Penida

Southeast of Bali, across the deep and treacherous Badung Strait, the islands of Nusa Lembongan, Nusa Ceningan and Nusa Penida rise alluringly out of the ocean swell. Relatively few visitors make the crossing, and it's hard to discern one island from another at a distance.

The nearest island to the mainland is **Nusa Lembongan**, which is less than two hours by boat from Sanur and encircled by a mixture of white-sand **beaches** and mangrove. Seaweed farming is the major occupation, while the island's other main source of income is the tourist facilities in Mushroom Bay (Tanjung Sanghyang), Chelegimbai and Jungutbatu. The **surf** breaks off the northwest coast brought the first visitors to the island and the first losmen grew up in Jungutbatu to cater for them. They were followed by visitors on high-speed day-trips from the mainland to the more secluded Mushroom Bay, where luxury accommodation sprang up for those who wanted to stay longer. These days the range of places to stay caters for all tastes and budgets, drawing anyone seeking attractive beaches, a bit of gentle exploring and relaxation in an addictively somnolent atmosphere.

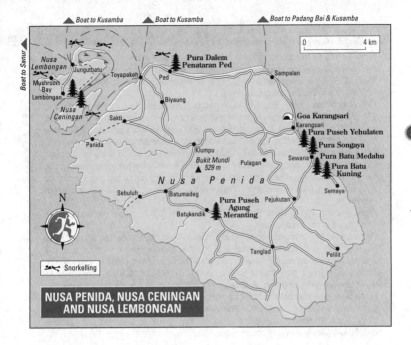

Only a few hundred metres separates Nusa Lembongan from tiny **Nusa Ceningan**, essentially a hill sticking out of the sea, where tourist facilities are just beginning to develop.

Beyond is **Nusa Penida**, roughly 20km long, dominated by a high, limestone plateau with a harsh, dry landscape reminiscent of the Bukit, the far southern tip of the mainland. The island is crisscrossed by miles of small lanes ripe for exploring, and its south coast has some of the most spectacular scenery in Bali.

Nusa Lembongan

A small island, 4km long and less than 3km at its widest part, **Nusa Lembongan** is sheltered by offshore coral reefs which provide excellent snorkelling and create the perfect conditions for seaweed farming (see box on p.281). You can **walk** around the whole island in three to four hours, and there are **bikes** (Rp10,000 per hour, discounts for longer times) and **motorbikes** (Rp25,000–30,000 per hour) for rent in Jungutbatu. A bridge, sturdy enough for motorbikes, spans the narrow strait that separates Nusa Lembongan and Nusa Ceningan.

All the accommodation is in **Jungutbatu** on the west coast and around **Chelegimbai** and **Mushroom Bay** (Tanjung Sanghyang), informally named after the mushroom coral in the offshore reef, to the southwest of this, where most of the upmarket places are situated. There's no post office, and electricity is produced by a somewhat unreliable generator from 4pm to 9am only, which some individual guesthouses supplement with their own generators for the inevitable power cuts. The recently delivered new generator may improve this situation.

Boats and trips to the islands

From Benoa to Nusa Lembongan (Jungutbatu). US$25 economy fare, $30 executive; takes 1hr. On the *Bounty* catamaran, which makes 4 trips weekly (Sun, Tues, Thurs & Sat), returning same day. Book in advance (on Bali ☏0361/733333 or 726666, ⓦwww.balibountygroup.com).

From Gili Meno (Lombok) to Nusa Lembongan (Jungutbatu). US$25 economy fare, $30 executive; takes 2hr 30min. On the *Bounty* catamaran, which makes 4 trips weekly (Sun, Tues, Thurs & Sat), returning same day. Book in advance (on Lombok ☏0370/693666, or on Gili Meno ☏0370/649090, ⓦwww.balibountygroup.com).

From Kusamba to Nusa Penida (Toyapakeh and Sampalan), and Nusa Lembongan (Jungutbatu). Rp25,000; takes 1–2hr. Boats leave when (very) full, most heading out early in the morning. These are local *prahu* used mostly for cargo, and are not for the faint-hearted. For return times enquire in the villages or, from Jungutbatu, ask at *Perama*.

From Padang Bai to Nusa Penida (Sampalan). Rp10,000; takes 1hr. Boats leave when full, starting around 7am.

From Sanur to Nusa Lembongan (Jungutbatu). Rp30,000; takes 1hr 30min. Boats leave at 8am and 10am, returning at 8am. Buy tickets from the office near the *Ananda Hotel* beachfront in Sanur, and from the beachfront office in Jungutbatu. Perama operates a daily tourist shuttle boat (Rp40,000) at 10.30am from Sanur to Nusa Lembongan (Jungutbatu), returning at 8.30am; book one day in advance.

From Senggigi (Lombok) to Nusa Lembongan (Jungutbatu). US$35 economy fare, $40 executive; takes 2hr. On the *Bounty* catamaran, which makes 4 trips weekly (Sun, Tues, Thurs & Sat), returning same day. Book in advance (on Lombok ☏0370/693666, ⓦwww.balibountygroup.com).

Luxury trips

Sold by tour operators in the southern mainland resorts, a day-trip out to the **luxury resorts** in the Mushroom Bay area or to a pontoon moored just offshore at Toyahpakeh is a pleasant, if pricey, way to visit Nusa Lembongan or Nusa Penida in some style. Most include free snorkelling, many of the resorts have pools and there are plenty of activities laid on. All trips include transfers between your hotel and the boat, and lunch; some also throw in an island tour. Prices vary quite considerably so it pays to shop around.

Jungutbatu

Spread out along the west coast for well over 1km, the attractive village of **JUNGUTBATU** is a low-key place, with plenty of losmen and restaurants, a bank, moneychanger, wartels and a few shops selling textiles and crafts. Arriving by boat, you'll be dropped off according to the tide and the skipper's favourite route through the reef; this could be anything up to 1km along the beach from the majority of the accommodation. The places to stay are not that obvious from the sea, so ask somebody to point you in the right direction.

You can **change money** at the moneychanger (daily 7am–7pm) behind *Mainski Inn*, or at Bank Pembangunan Daerah Bali (Mon–Fri 10am–1pm), but expect rates around five percent worse than on the mainland. There are **wartels** for local and international calls attached to *Bunga Lembongan* and *Mainski Inn*, open when there's electricity (when the new generator gets going they'll probably operate regular opening hours). The Perama office (daily 7am–6pm) is situated between *Pondok Baruna* and *Nusa Indah* bungalows and also serves as the **tourist information** service. You can book tickets here to all the main tourist destinations on Bali and Lombok and on to Sumbawa. Departures are at least daily, but many destinations require a stopover on the way.

Bali Hai ☎0361/720331, ℱ720334, ⓦwww.balihaicruises.com. The biggest operator offers a choice of vessels. Trips (from $69) include watersports based on the pontoon moored on the reef off Mushroom Bay or relaxing at the Lembongan Island Beach Club on the coast at Mushroom Bay where there's an excellent pool. Parasailing and diving are available for an extra charge. A high-speed ocean rafting trip is also possible ($64), taking in the incredible scenery of the south coast of Nusa Penida and snorkelling at Crystal Bay. Cruise and dive packages and overnight stays at the Hai Tide Huts are available.

Island Explorer ☎0361/728088, ℱ728089, ⓦwww.baliabc.com/explorer.html. With a choice of sailing, power boat or fast catamaran, full-day and half-day trips (from $39) are available to the Coconuts Beach Resort where staying overnight is a possible add-on. There's a pool at the resort, from where it's a short walk to the beach. Fishing and diving are optional extras.

Lembongan Island Discovery Day ☎ & ℱ0361/287431, ⓦwww.lembongan-discovery.com. Visitors use Villa Wayan and Chelegimbai beach for the day's relaxation ($45); there's no pool but the beach is attractive and peaceful. It's possible to arrange overnight stays at Villa Wayan or its other properties nearby.

Quicksilver ☎0361/729564, ℱ729503, ⓦwww.quicksilver-bali.com. Transport is by catamaran to the pontoon moored off Toyahpakeh on Nusa Penida where watersports are the speciality with trips on a semi-submersible included in the price ($89). Diving is an optional extra.

Sail Sensations ☎0361/725864, ℱ725866, ⓦwww.bali-sailsensations.com. Visitors use the facilities at the Anchorage resort on the coast at Mushroom Bay. Day cruises are available on board a luxurious sailing catamaran with a high level of comfort and service ($89). A trip to Nusa Penida, sailing around the south coast, exploring the mangrove swamps and a village tour are all included in the price, with diving and a snorkelling safari as optional extras. Overnight stays are possible at the super-luxury Nusa Lembongan Resort.

Waka Louka ☎0361/723629, ℱ722077, ⓦwww.wakaexperience.com. Day cruise to the Waka Nusa private resort on the beach at Mushroom Bay using a sailing catamaran ($80). Diving or fishing are optional extras. Longer trips are also available with accommodation at Waka Nusa.

The ticket office for **public boats** is at the southern end of the beach; boats leave at 8am. Currently the ticket-seller tours the accommodation in the morning and tells passengers where the boat will leave from (check with your guesthouse); if there's enough water they'll come and collect you at the northern end of the beach, in front of the accommodation, otherwise you'll have to go down to the village. You can also **charter** a local boat to take you back to the mainland: it'll cost about Rp300,000 to Padang Bai.

Accommodation

Most of the **accommodation** is grouped close together, just behind the beach to the north, spreading out the further south you go. There are traditional thatch, wood and bamboo two-storey buildings with upstairs verandahs, some older concrete losmen rooms, usually further away from the sea, and an increasing number of newer brick and tiled places offering slightly better quality. Rooms at the front with sea views are more expensive than those behind, and upstairs rooms are pricier than downstairs. All the places below offer en suite cold-water bathrooms.

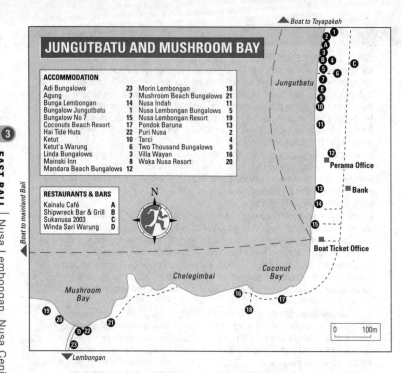

JUNGUTBATU AND MUSHROOM BAY

ACCOMMODATION

Adi Bungalows	23	Morin Lembongan	18
Agung	7	Mushroom Beach Bungalows	21
Bunga Lembongan	14	Nusa Indah	11
Bungalow Jungutbatu	1	Nusa Lembongan Bungalows	5
Bungalow No 7	15	Nusa Lembongan Resort	19
Coconuts Beach Resort	17	Pondok Baruna	13
Hai Tide Huts	22	Puri Nusa	2
Ketut	10	Tarci	4
Ketut's Warung	6	Two Thousand Bungalows	9
Linda Bungalows	3	Villa Wayan	16
Mainski Inn	8	Waka Nusa Resort	20
Mandara Beach Bungalows	12		

RESTAURANTS & BARS

Kainalu Café	A
Shipwreck Bar & Grill	B
Sukanusa 2003	C
Winda Sari Warung	D

Agung ☎0811/386986, ℮agungs_lembongan@mailcity.com. Some rooms in a concrete building, but the two-storey bamboo, wood and thatch places have most character; ones at the front have the best views and there's a good sun-bathing area just above the beach. ❶–❷

Bunga Lembongan ☎0361/415184. Next to *Bungalow no. 7* at the southern end of the beach, with various kinds of rooms in two-storey buildings. The better, pricier rooms are upstairs. ❶–❷

Bungalow Jungutbatu No phone. The most northerly accommodation, about 200m beyond *Puri Nusa*. Rooms are in two-storey bamboo and tile buildings widely spaced in the compound. It's a busy local beach up here, set a little apart from the main tourist area. ❶–❷

Bungalow No. 7 ☎0812/380 1537. Popular, extremely good-value, clean, simple rooms at the far southern end of the beach, all with balconies or verandahs. There are sitting areas overlooking the beach. ❶

Ketut ☎082/361 4895. Well-built, well-furnished attractive accommodation, some of it with excellent sea views, set in pleasant grounds. The two-storey places at the front have good sea-views; the better-built places are behind. ❹

Ketut's Warung No phone. Tucked away behind *Nusa Lembongan Bungalows*, this great little warung has a couple of simple, tiled rooms. ❶

Linda Bungalows ☎0812/394 3988. Rooms are in two-storey buildings which all face seawards but they don't all have sea views. They are well built with good-quality furnishings. ❷

Mainski Inn ☎ & ℮082/361 1153. A long-standing favourite with a wide choice of accommodation. Some upstairs rooms have hot water. There are plenty of hammocks for relaxing in the garden. ❶–❷

Mandara Beach Bungalows ☎0812/391 4908. Clean, tiled bungalows set in a garden next to and behind the *Perama* office, so a short walk to the busier area to the north. ❷

Nusa Indah ☎082/361 4071. Set back from the beach behind the *Surfer's Beach Café*. The views aren't so great but there's a choice of older and cheaper rooms or better-quality newer ones. Upstairs ones are better. ❶–❷

Nusa Lembongan Bungalows No phone. Accommodation at this popular place is in two-storey bamboo and thatch buildings with upstairs balconies set in a spacious compound. The ones at the front have especially good sea views. ❸

Pondok Baruna ☏0812/390 0686, ℱ0361/288500, ⊛www.world-diving.com. A few hundred metres south of the main accommodation area, this small, quiet place has clean tiled rooms looking straight onto the beach and a small attached restaurant. The operator World Diving Lembongan is based here. ❷—❸
Puri Nusa ☏ & ℱ0361/298613. Well-built, comfortably furnished rooms in two-storey buildings with good verandahs or balconies in an attractive garden. One of the most northerly places. ❸
Tarci ☏0812/390 6300, ℮lembongansurf@yahoo.com. Next door to *Puri Nusa*, with simple rooms just behind the beach. Best rooms are at the front, cheaper ones behind. ❶—❸
Two Thousand Bungalows ☏0812/394 1273. Simple but adequate rooms in two-storey buildings set back behind the attached café. ❷—❸

Eating

All the places to stay have **restaurants** attached, most of them right on the beachfront with pleasant views of the sea and a cooling breeze. Part of the pleasure of Nusa Lembongan is finding your own favourite; they all offer a good range of Indo-Chinese favourites and the usual travellers' fare plus local seafood, depending on the catch that day. *Agung* is a two-storey place with the shipwreck out on the reef clearly visible offshore. Further north, *Kainalu Café* is another imposing two-storey building just behind the beach, also with a pool table. This is the most upmarket dining on the beach. *Ketut's Warung* is rather hidden away behind *Nusa Lembongan Bungalows* but is well worth searching out for well-cooked, cheap local food – it's always packed. Keep an eye open for developments at the *Shipwreck Bar and Grill*, since they plan to offer the opportunity for diners to select uncooked seafood which will then be barbecued to order.

To escape the beach for a more intimate meal, head for *Sukanusa 2003* on the road through the village. Tables are set in pleasant open *bale*, furnishings are stylish and music is soothing.

Chelegimbai and Mushroom Bay

About 1km around the coast southwest of Jungutbatu, the tiny white-sand bay of **Chelegimbai** is a peaceful and relaxing spot. It's gradually developing a few accommodation choices, mostly more luxurious and expensive than those in Jungutbatu but not as plush and expensive as the Mushroom Bay options, a couple of kilometres to the southwest. **Mushroom Bay** itself, a fabulous white-sand cove, has long been a favourite snorkelling spot and destination for day-trippers from the mainland, but has now developed facilities for visitors who want to stay longer. Don't expect peace down on the beach once the day-trippers arrive – but it's a beautiful, idyllic spot before and after.

You can **charter a boat** to Mushroom Bay from Jungutbatu (expect to pay Rp50,000 per boat). **On foot**, the most straightforward route follows the first turning to the right as you enter Lembongan village coming over the hill from Jungutbatu; it's 1km from the turning to Mushroom Bay and takes about an hour in total. A more attractive alternative is to walk around the coast. Climb the steps that lead up from the extreme southern end of the beach at Jungutbatu to a path which leads along the hillside past *Coconuts Resort* to Coconut Bay, then up the far side of the bay to *Morin Lembongan* and *Villa Wayan* and on to Chelegimbai beach. Another path leads up from the far southern end of Chelegimbai and passes above a couple of tiny bays before descending to the Mushroom Bay accommodation.

A daily boat heads direct from Mushroom Bay back to Sanur on the mainland; check times locally. The Perama boat from Jungutbatu on its way back to Sanur will call at Cheligimbai so long as you book in advance.

Diving, snorkelling and surfing

The area around the islands is popular for **diving**, but most operators come out from the mainland; the sea can be extremely cold and difficult here, with currents over four knots, so care is needed. There are plenty of sites, hosting enormously varied fish life, with reef sharks especially common, as well as manta rays and the occasional oceanic sunfish.

The only **dive operator** based on the islands is the very experienced World Diving Lembongan (℡0812/390 0686, ℉0361/288500, ⓦwww.world-diving.com), based next to *Pondok Baruna* in Jungutbatu. They offer dives for certified divers (US$30 each, including equipment, for the first two; less for more dives), the PADI Open Water ($295) and Advanced ($225) courses up to Divemaster level, a Scuba Review ($30) if you have a certificate but haven't dived for some time, and Discover Scuba ($50) for those new to the sport. They dive the more frequented sites less rarely and have explored and opened up eighteen sites in the area, including three near Nusa Ceningan that are rarely dived, where the coral is in better condition and the larger ocean life more likely to appear. They have an absolute ban on dropping anchor on the reefs, using fixed moorings instead.

For **dive sites**, Toyapakeh, SD Point and Mangrove are the most reliable, predictable and frequently dived, and can get quite busy. **Toyapakeh** offers huge coral boulders and pillars which protect an inland area with gorgonians and soft coral bushes. It's an area where it is possible to see *mola mola* and other pelagics such as manta rays and hammerhead sharks. At **SD Point** there are large coral heads, an extremely diverse collection of corals and sponges and the chance to see green and hawksbill turtles, manta rays, sea snakes, octopus and white-tipped reef sharks. **Mangrove** is an easy site, used a lot for training dives. It has a 45° sloping reef with excellent coral coverage off the northeast corner of Nusa Lembongan.

You can charter boats from Nusa Lembongan to take you to **snorkelling** spots (ask at your losmen); one of the best is off **Mushroom Bay** with others at **Mangrove Corner** (also known as **Jet Point**) to the north, and **Sunfish** nearby. Boats will also take you to Nusa Penida where **Crystal Bay**, on the Penida coast looking towards Nusa Ceningan, is renowned for its crystal-clear waters; **Gamat**, off the coast near Sakti, and the reef off the coast at **Ped** are also popular. Prices depend on distance; start negotiating at around Rp100,000 per hour for a boat holding up to four people, including equipment.

Surfing off Nusa Lembongan

The best **surfing** off Nusa Lembongan – easily accessible from Sanur, and much less crowded than Kuta – is from June to September, although full moons during other months are worth a try. Bring your own board and repair and first aid kits.

The breaks are mostly offshore from Jungutbatu. Just off the beach are **Lacerations** (to the south) and **Surgery** (to the north). Lacerations is playful on a small swell, but becomes a serious barrelling right-hander. Surgery is a fast left-hander. Next to Lacerations on the other side of the deep channel, **Playgrounds** is a gentle short left-hander on a small swell, and particularly good when the swell is up to 2m. The most famous break is **Shipwreck**, a powerful right-hander that breaks off the remains of a shipwreck on the reef, a 300m paddle from the beach. There's usually some sort of wave here unless the ocean is totally flat, giving a 50–100m ride over the coral. About 1km west of Jungutbatu, **Tanjung Sanghyang** has both a left and a right. The left can be quite a ride across the reef into Mushroom Bay while the right is better for a long board or body board. **Ceningan**, in the channel between the two islands, is another popular left-hander.

Several places advertise **surf safaris** from Nusa Lembongan, the most obvious being Purnama Indah (mobile ℡0811/398553, in Sanur ℡0361/289213, ⓦwww.purnamaindah.com). They take in the main surf breaks along the southern coast of Lombok and Sumbawa; prices depend on the length of trip and the destination. Most of the boats are moored on the coast in the channel between Nusa Lembongan and Nusa Ceningan, so it's easy to go and check them out before you commit yourself.

Accommodation

The **accommodation** around this part of the coast is generally more upmarket than in Jungutbatu, although there's one notable budget option. It's worth repeating that several of the luxury places are best booked as an add-on to the day cruises that operate to the island (see pp.272–73). Doing this will get you the best rates as well as a luxurious trip to and from the mainland.

Adi Bungalows ✆081/735 3587. The cheapest option on this part of the island. Clean, tiled, well-furnished bungalows of brick and thatch set in a pretty garden a few hundred metres inland from Mushroom Beach; follow the track between *Hai Tide Huts* and *Waka Nusa*. There's a small restaurant attached. ❸

Coconuts Beach Resort ✆0361/728088, ⒻE728089, Ⓦwww.bali.activities.com. Book as an add-on to an *Island Explorer Cruise*. Accommodation is in circular, thatched bungalows (with fans or air-con) ranged up the hillside. The bungalows higher up have glorious views. There are two pools, and it's a short walk to the nearest beach. ❼

Hai Tide Huts ✆0361/720331, ⒻE720334, Ⓦwww.balihaicruises.com. A large set-up with accommodation in attractive, two-storey brick and thatch huts; the ones on the beachfront have stunning views. Bathrooms are not attached to each hut but a planned expansion will include huts with en-suite facilities. The terrific pool even has a small island in the middle. Book as part of a package with a *Bali Hai* cruise. ❼

Morin Lembongan Contact in Sanur ✆ & ⒻE0361/288993. The three lovely bungalows here have the best views on the island. They are way up on the cliffside and are light, airy and comfortable with cold-water attached bathrooms. Features a tiny restaurant. It's a short walk to Cheligimbai beach. ❻–❼

Mushroom Beach Bungalows/Tanjung Sanghyang Bungalows ✆082/361 2161. Well-built simple rooms with attached cold-water bath-

rooms, in a brilliant location on a small headland at the northern end of Mushroom Bay with a small, deserted cove down the other side. There's a small attached restaurant. Bungalows are over-priced for the facilities but you're paying for the location. ❹–❺

Nusa Lembongan Resort ✆0361/727564, ⒻE725866, Ⓦwww.nusa-lembongan.com. The most expensive resort on the island, with accommodation in twelve superbly appointed air-con villas with stunning bathrooms including a sunken bath, positioned in an excellent garden with a huge pool. Prices start at $200. Can be arranged as an add-on to a *Sail Sensations* cruise but day visitors do not disturb the peace here as they use another location. ❾

Villa Wayan ✆ & ⒻE0361/287431, Ⓦwww.lembongan.discovery.com. There are several accommodation options here, with some bungalows ranged up the hillside and other rooms in imposing houses just behind Cheligimbai beach. There's no pool but the beach is close and the restaurant has splendid views, plus binoculars to help you enjoy them. ❺–❻

Waka Nusa Resort ✆0361/723629, ⒻE722077, Ⓦwww.wakaexperience.com. Accommodation is in very comfortable fan-cooled, thatched bungalows with plenty of natural fabrics and attractive decor that are the hallmark of the Waka group – although this one does lack the wow factor enjoyed by many of the others. Located just behind the beach, there's a small pool. Book as an add-on to a *Waka Louka* cruise. ❻

Eating

All the places to stay have attached **restaurants**, with ambience, decor and price in direct relation to the luxury and cost of the accommodation. The cheapest place to eat is *Warung Adi* attached to *Adi Bungalows*, offering a small menu of inexpensive breakfasts and Indonesian main meals. A reasonable alternative is *Winda Sari Warung*, in a prime spot on the beach next to *Hai Tide Huts*, with good views and a large menu of Indonesian and Western food at moderate prices.

Around Nusa Lembongan

For a trip **around Nusa Lembongan,** it's best to walk or cycle in a clockwise direction, avoiding a lengthy, painful climb up out of Jungutbatu to the south. The road is tarmac most of the way round, although is a bit rough in places. Allow three to four hours to walk around the island, two hours to cycle, less than an hour by motorbike.

Heading north on the tarmac road that runs parallel to the coast about 200m behind the beach, and a couple of kilometres north of Jungutbatu the road splits. The left-hand fork follows the coast and a few hundred metres later passes **Pura Sakenan**, recognizable by a highly decorated central shrine. This road leads a couple of kilometres to the dead end at the northernmost tip of the island; the mangrove is very thick and high and there are few views of anything.

Taking the right fork leads to **Pura Empuaji**, with its highly carved doorway, the most venerated temple on the island (take a sarong if you want to visit). The road continues south from here for four almost uninhabited kilometres with mangroves on the left and scrub on the right where cacti seem to thrive. You may spot a few derelict salt-makers' huts here (see box on p.479) but very little production continues on the island, as this traditional way of life has been largely replaced by more lucrative **seaweed farming**. Gradually the mangrove clears and there are views of Nusa Ceningan just across the water with Nusa Penida rising up dramatically behind. At the point where the channel between Nusa Lembongan and Nusa Ceningan is narrowest, matching temples face each other across the water and a bold new **bridge** has been built to link the islands: you can walk, cycle or ride a motorbike across (see below). The waters here are crystal clear over white sand almost completely filled with frames for seaweed farming.

A steep hill climbs up into **LEMBONGAN**, the largest town on the island, 3km south of Jungutbatu. It's a crisscross of streets and alleyways and is much busier than Jungutbatu. The island's only "sight" is here, the **Underground House** (open on request; Rp10,000), dug by a traditional healer, or *dukun*, named Made Biasa. One night in 1965 he supposedly dreamt that he lost a fight with a spirit and, taking this to mean he would soon die, decided to dig an underground house as his memorial. Hale and hearty, he dug every night from 7pm to midnight with the energy of a young man and, having dug for over fifteen years, eventually died in the 1980s, never having completed his work. There's a bedroom, kitchen, dining room, bathroom and meditation room, but it's all dank and enclosed.

All roads leading uphill through the village eventually join to become the main road up past the school and over the hill to Jungutbatu, with some fine views back down to the coast on the way and good views of the surf breaks as you descend on the other side.

Nusa Ceningan

The tiny island of **NUSA CENINGAN**, 4km long by 1km wide, is essentially a hill sticking out of the water, located picturesquely between Nusa Lembongan and Nusa Penida. With around four hundred inhabitants, it's a sleepy place with only a small section of tarmac road. The only **accommodation** is at *The Bungalows* (℡0361/750550, ℻754749, ⓦwww.surftravelonline.com; ❸) on the southeast coast. Situated just above a pure white-sand beach are six fan-cooled, grass-roofed bungalows with hot and cold water and floor-to-ceiling windows which can be opened to catch the breeze. There's 24-hour electricity and nearby surfing, and local cycling trips can be arranged. Transfers from the mainland ($40 per person) use the *Quicksilver* to Toyapakeh and then a local boat.

Nusa Penida

Tell a Balinese person you're heading to **Nusa Penida** and you won't get a positive reaction. The island is renowned as the home of the legendary evil figure **I Macaling** and was also formerly a place of banishment for the kingdom of Klungkung. It's still regarded as *angker*, a place of evil spirits and ill fortune, and many Balinese make the pilgrimage to the island expressly to ward off bad luck by making offerings at Pura Dalem Penataran Ped, home of the dreaded I Macaling.

Nusa Penida is too dry to cultivate rice, and while you'll see maize, cassava, beans and tobacco in the fields during the rainy season, there's nothing at all in the dry season. The island can sustain a population of only around 45,000, and many have already left both to work on the mainland or as part of the government's *transmigrasi* programme (see p.500), although road improvements and construction are taking place. There have also been recent reports that a new casino will be built up in the mountains; time will tell whether this happens and what effect it may have on the local economy.

There are no dive operators based on Nusa Penida, but those on the mainland and the one on Nusa Lembongan offer trips to the island's north and west coasts; see p.276 for more.

Sampalan

SAMPALAN is Nusa Penida's largest town, and has a shady street of shops, a bemo terminal, a market and the only post office, hospital and phone office on the island. The town is spread out along the **beach**, and its highlight, the **Pura Dalem**, close to the cemetery near the football field, has a six-metre-tall gateway adorned with five leering Bhoma and a pendulous-breasted Rangda.

There are several **warung** in the main street, serving rice and noodles, and the town has a couple of **places to stay**. *Losmen Made* (☎0818/345204; ❷), on Jalan Segara, 100m west of the bemo terminal, is small and friendly and has four rooms with attached mandi and squat toilet set in nice gardens 200m from the beach and 100m from the main road. At the other end of town, next to the beach, the government-run *Bungalows Pemda* (☎0366/21448; ❶–❷) has standard rooms with mandi and squat toilets and more expensive, better-quality rooms with Western-style toilets, showers and bathtubs.

Toyapakeh and around

Some 9km from Sampalan, on the northwest coast of the island, the fishing town of **TOYAPAKEH** is separated from Nusa Ceningan by a channel less than 1km wide but over 100m deep in places. With its lovely white **beach** and peaceful atmosphere, it's the best place to stay on Nusa Penida. There's a small daily **market** and a tiny mosque serving the town's Muslim population. The only **accommodation** is at *Losmen Trang* (☎082/361 4868; ❶), which has five basic rooms right next to the beach with attached mandi and squat toilet, and also serves simple meals.

Pura Dalem Penataran Ped, dedicated to Jero Gede Macaling and built from volcanic sandstone and local limestone, lies 5km east of Toyapakeh on the Sampalan road. There are few statues or intricate carvings, but the size of the courtyards and the grand entrances are impressive, emphasizing the prestige of the temple, which many regard as one of the most important in Bali. There are three **courtyards**, the inner one containing an unusually large red and pink shrine, three storeys high, with intricately carved doors, used to store the sacred statues of the temple. The small red and white tiled compound to the west contains the shrine of Jero Gede Macaling, where worshippers make their offerings. The *odalan* festival here is extremely well attended by pilgrims hoping to stave off sickness and ill fortune; every three years a larger *usaba* festival draws enormous crowds.

I Macaling

I Macaling, also known as Jero Gede Macaling, is feared throughout Bali. His name derives from *caling*, Balinese for "fang", and he is believed to be responsible for disease and floods which he brings across to the mainland from Nusa Penida, landing at Lebih, south of Gianyar.

The legends of his deeds are numerous and diverse but all refer to the era following the Majapahit invasion of Bali when **King Dalem Dukut** was ruler of Nusa Penida. Batu Renggong, crowned in 1550, was the most dynamic of the *dewa agungs* of Bali, and expanded his kingdom from Java in the west to Sumbawa in the east. He then turned his eyes on Nusa Penida. I Macaling was the king's minister, and had invisible, supernatural creatures called *wong gamang* at his command. The forces of Batu Renggong came to the island twice, but were repelled by I Macaling and the *wong gamang*. On the third occasion, the invading commander brought with him a tooth of one of the sacred *naga*, with which he killed King Dalem Dukut. In his death throes, the king handed over I Macaling and the *wong gamang* to Batu Renggong, guaranteeing that if he was given a correct burial and I Macaling was treated with due respect, the *wong gamang* would protect the people of Bali and ensure good fortune. If they were treated disrespectfully, they would bring nothing but disaster to the land.

I Macaling and his wife, Jero Luh, appear regularly in the drama **barong landung** (for more details of the drama see p.523), portrayed respectively as a gigantic black creature on two legs and a white-faced woman. The drama is frequently performed to protect villages from illness and evil spirits.

Around Nusa Penida

By far the best way to see Nusa Penida is by **motorbike** – ask at your guesthouse for rental details – although you shouldn't drive unless you are confident on very steep terrain. The island is a maze of country lanes and signposts are few, so make sure you start early and have plenty of fuel. A full circuit is only about 70km but, allowing time to visit the major attractions, it takes most of a day. The road between Toyapakeh and Sampalan is the busiest on the island and roughly follows the coast; traffic elsewhere is much lighter.

About 10km south of Sampalan, you reach the limestone cave of **Goa Karangsari**. The tiny entrance is about 100m above the road and is quite tight, but opens up into a large, impressive cavern. Children lurk around the entrance as "guides"; you might like to choose the one with the best flashlight (or preferably a pressure lantern). The cave emerges after 300m onto a ledge with fine views looking out across a quiet mango grove, surrounded by hills on all sides. However, there's no path down at this end, so you have to retrace your steps. The annual festival of Galungan (see p.56) is celebrated here with a procession and ceremony inside the cave.

On the way to **SEWANA** (or Suana), a prosperous village with concrete houses strung along the coast, you'll pass **Pura Puseh Yehulaten**, with its seven-roofed *meru*, perched on a cliff edge offering great views back along the coast. Look out for the attractive **Pura Songaya** at the southern end of Sewana village, whose two *meru* are backed by a sheer cliff. Just beyond, a side road to the left leads 2km further down the coast to **SEMAYA**. This track isn't good, but a couple more impressive temples can be found along here: first is the large **Pura Batu Medahu** on the coast side of the road and, further down, with grand views back to the north, **Pura Batu Kuning**, with some fabulous carvings (especially on the *padmasana*, which sports a sexually explicit image of Sanghyang Widi). Semaya itself is a small fishing village around a long bay completely lined with frames for seaweed farming.

Returning to the main road, you climb dramatically and steeply up to the plateau that forms the centre of the island. Approaching the village of

PEJUKUTAN, 6km from Sewana, the land is dotted with giant concrete dishes for catching rainwater which is then stored in massive underground tanks. Some 2km further on, a right fork heads to **TANGLAD**, an extremely quiet and pleasantly cool upland village, with an ancient throne to the sun god, Surya, on the village green. Nestling among hills 9km from Tanglad is the village of **BATUKANDIK**, whose **Pura Puseh Agung Meranting** houses a remarkable – though much eroded – carving of a woman supporting the top of a stone altar. Supposedly prehistoric, the figure is swathed in holy clothes which are still discernible. **BATUMADEG**, 6km beyond Batukandik, is the island's second-largest village, but otherwise of no especial interest.

Turn left at Batumadeg to **SEBULUH**, where the road eventually ends a couple of hundred metres beyond the village green. From here, a path leads to the left between high stone walls and heads out to the coast, a walk of about 45 minutes. There are numerous paths through the outskirts of the village to the cliffs and you may be lucky enough to find an English-speaking guide. The coast here is similar to the coastline at the south end of the Bukit, with dramatic limestone cliffs rising sheer out of the ocean and views that are utterly spellbinding. There are also two **temples**, one out on a promontory linked to the mainland by an exposed ridge, and the other, somewhat amazingly, sited at the bottom of an extremely narrow, incredibly exposed path that winds down the face of the cliff to a freshwater spring at the bottom. If you're with a guide, you'll be expected to wear a sarong and a sash on the path. This type of scenery is typical of the whole southern coast of the island; there are waterfalls in places and several spots where hairy descents to the sea are possible – ask locally.

Returning to Batumadeg, the road turns inland and skirts close to the summit of **Bukit Mundi**, the highest point on the island, at 529m, where the goddess Dewi Rohini, a female manifestation of Siwa, is said to dwell. The road reaches the edge of the plateau, dropping down through the small, red-roofed village of **KLUMPU** and continuing to **SAKTI**, from where you can walk the 4km to the freshwater spring on the coast at **PANIDA** or continue straight back to Toyapakeh.

Seaweed farming

Areas of Nusa Penida, Nusa Lembongan and Nusa Ceningan, the Geger beach in south Bali and some areas of Lombok are big producers of **seaweed**, source of two lucrative substances: **agar**, a vegetable gel used in cooking, and **carrageenan**, used in cosmetics and foodstuffs. It grows best in areas protected by a reef so it doesn't get battered by strong currents but has a flow of water through it. The temperature must not get too high, the salinity needs to be constant, and at low tide the seaweed must remain covered by water.

To "farm" seaweed, a simple bamboo frame is made with lengths of twine tied across it. Farmers tie small pieces of seaweed – both green *cotoni* and red *spinosum* varieties (*cotoni* produces better-quality carrageenan and fetches almost twice the price) – to the twine, harvesting the long offshoots every two weeks. The seaweed is then dried and compressed into bales; 8kg of wet seaweed reduces to 1kg when dry.

In the 1980s the dried seaweed fetched around $50 a tonne, a long way from the market high of more than $600 a tonne in the 1960s, but still enough to make a reasonable living of around Rp200,000 a month (which compares very favourably with the Rp50,000 a month that traditional salt producers can expect to make). However, by the 1990s the situation had deteriorated: prices dropped on the world market, producers hadn't realized quickly enough the advantages of *cotoni* over *spinosum* and there were problems with adulteration of the product. Once again farmers are making a good living but, like anyone selling their produce on the open world market, they remain subject to forces way beyond their control.

Candi Dasa and Amuk Bay

CANDI DASA is a laid-back holiday resort at the eastern end of **Amuk Bay**, a good centre for snorkelling and diving with a wide choice of accommodation and restaurants to suit every taste and every pocket. It's also a relaxed and pleasant base from which to explore the east of Bali, with easy road access to many of the main sights.

Tourism began to develop at the end of the 1970s and Candi's transformation from fishing village into tourist centre is now complete, although many fishing boats remain to catch fish for the restaurants and ferry visitors out for sailing and snorkelling. However, development has not been without its costs, and throughout the 1980s Candi's offshore reef was systematically crushed to produce lime for cement. The beach was left so exposed that it simply washed away. Large sea walls now protect the land and jetties protrude into the sea in the hope, largely justified, that the beach will build up behind them: there are many little pockets of pretty, white sand nestling here and there. Excellent views encompass the tiny offshore islands and Nusa Lembongan and Nusa Penida in the distance.

Candi Dasa grew around its attractive lagoon, but the tourist developments have now spread west around the bay, through the villages of **Senkidu**, **Mendira**, **Buitan** and **Manggis**, where the beach is still a respectable size. Further west, just around the headland, the tiny cove of **Padang Bai** is home to the bustling access port for Lombok, and also has a small tourist infrastructure.

The entire coastal area is well served by **public transport**, both by the long-distance buses and minibuses from Denpasar (Batubulan terminal) to Amlapura, and local bemos on shorter runs. You can expect a ride every five to ten minutes for short hops early in the day, diminishing to every half-hour or so by the end of the afternoon. You'll also notice much less hassle here than in the resorts in the south: a local bylaw has made street-vending illegal, although you will be offered transport or snorkelling trips every few yards along the street.

Arrival and information

Hotel development now extends about 8km west of Candi Dasa into neighbouring villages, just to the south of the main Denpasar–Amlapura road; it's

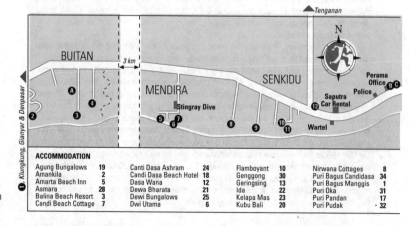

ACCOMMODATION

Agung Bungalows	19	Canti Dasa Ashram	24	Flamboyant	10	Nirwana Cottages	8
Amankila	2	Candi Dasa Beach Hotel	18	Genggong	30	Puri Bagus Candidasa	34
Amarta Beach Inn	5	Dasa Wana	12	Geringsing	13	Puri Bagus Manggis	1
Asmara	28	Dewa Bharata	21	Ida	22	Puri Oka	31
Balina Beach Resort	3	Dewi Bungalows	25	Kelapa Mas	23	Puri Pandan	17
Candi Beach Cottage	7	Dwi Utama	6	Kubu Bali	20	Puri Pudak	32

Day-trips from Candi Dasa

If your time is limited, you may want to consider a **day-trip**, available at Perama, any of the tourist booths on the main road, or through many hotels and car rental companies. Alternatively talk to the guys offering transport who linger on the main road. **Prices** range upwards from Rp200,000 per vehicle for a full-day trip, but you should shop around and be clear whether prices quoted are per person or per vehicle. The standard tours on offer are to:

Amlapura The palace, Tirtagangga and Tenganan

Besakih Putung, Muncan, Besakih, Klungkung

Kintamani Bangli, Kintamani, Penelokan, Tampaksiring, Gunung Kawi

Kuta Kuta, Nusa Dua, Sanur, Uluwatu (sometimes including the sunset at Uluwatu)

Sangeh Sangeh, Mengwi, Bedugul and Lake Bratan, Tanah Lot

Singaraja Tirtagangga, Tulamben, Air Sanih, Lovina

Ubud Goa Gajah, Monkey Forest, Mas, Celuk

easy to get **bemo** drivers to drop you off where you want. **Shuttle buses** from the main tourist destinations serve Candi Dasa, and Perama has an office with arrivals three times daily from southern Bali destinations and from Senggigi on Lombok, and daily arrivals from north and east Bali and from other resorts on Lombok (see Travel details on p.313 for more details). Fixed-price taxis serve Candi Dasa from Ngurah Rai Airport (Rp150,000; takes up to 2hr).

There's a centrally located **tourist office** in the main street close to the lagoon which has somewhat erratic opening hours.

Accommodation

Plenty of **accommodation** to suit every taste and pocket is available in Candi Dasa itself and spread in the coastal villages to the west. Most of the places listed below do not have street addresses, but all are keyed on the map.

Candi Dasa

There's a vast choice of accommodation spread about 1km along the main road running just behind the beach at **Candi Dasa**. Beware of places that are too close to the road and therefore noisy.

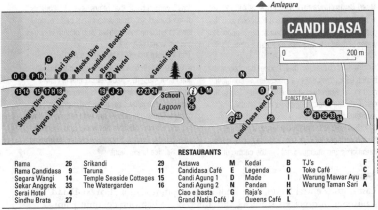

				RESTAURANTS			
Rama	26	Srikandi	29	Astawa	**M**	Kedai	**B**	TJ's	**F**
Rama Candidasa	9	Taruna	11	Candidasa Café	**E**	Legenda	**O**	Toke Café	**C**
Segara Wangi	14	Temple Seaside Cottages	15	Candi Agung 1	**D**	Made	**I**	Warung Mawar Ayu	**P**
Sekar Anggrek	33	The Watergarden	16	Candi Agung 2	**N**	Pandan	**H**	Warung Taman Sari	**A**
Serai Hotel	4			Ciao e basta	**G**	Raja's	**K**		
Sindhu Brata	27			Grand Natia Café	**J**	Queens Café	**L**		

Agung Bungalows ☎0363/41535. Well-finished seafront bungalows with good-sized verandahs, fans and hot and cold water located in a lush garden complete with ponds. ❷–❸

Asmara ☎ & ℱ0363/41929, ⊛www.asmarabali .com, ℮yosbali@indosat.net.id. New boutique dive resort and spa. There are Balinese minimalist bungalows with tiled floors, thatched roofs and open bathrooms with cold and warm water, each set beside its own fish pond. All have air-con and there is an environmentally-friendly waste-water treatment system in place. There's a beach-side restaurant, swimming pool, and Yos Marine Adventures has a dive-shop here. ❼

Canti Dasa Ashram ☎ & ℱ0363/41108, contact in Denpasar ☎0361/225145, ℮iwgunarto@ satelindo.co.id. The only Ghandian ashram in Southeast Asia gets some of its income from renting out bungalows set in one of the best sites in Candi, with the lagoon on one side and the ocean on the other. Guests are free to take as much or as little part in the daily round of puja, meditation and lectures as they wish, but are asked not to smoke, drink or sunbathe nude; only married couples may share rooms. Charges include three vegetarian meals a day. Booking is recommended in advance. Price on application.

Dasa Wana ☎0363/41444, ℱ0361/242993. Air-con rooms and villas with hot water and tea- and coffee-making facilities, in landscaped grounds across the road from the sea. A small restaurant overlooks an attractive pool. Good value in this price bracket. ❺

Dewa Bharata ☎0363/41090, ℱ41091. Attractive, good-value bungalows, all with hot water, plus a good pool and seafront restaurant set in well-maintained gardens. More expensive rooms have air-con; best of all are the ones with sea views. ❺–❻

Dewi Bungalows ☎0363/41166, ℱ41177. Set in a spacious garden close to the lagoon and the sea, the best bungalows overlook the lagoon. Hot water is available in more expensive ones. ❷–❸

Geringsing ☎0363/41084. Budget bamboo and thatch bungalows set in a small central compound next to the sea, offering excellent value. The real gems are the three bungalows right on the seafront. ❶–❷

Ida ☎ & ℱ0363/41096. Six large, wood and thatch cottages all with fan, attached cold-water bathrooms and mosquito nets in the centre of Candi with huge verandahs, set in a lovely garden stretching down to the sea. Don't confuse this with a place with a similar name on Forest Road. ❷–❸

Kelapa Mas ☎0363/41369, ℱ41947, ⊛www.welcome.to/kelapamas. Justifiably popular and centrally located, offering a range of clean bungalows set in a large well-maintained garden on the seafront. Most expensive options have hot water. ❸–❺

Kubu Bali ☎0363/41532, ℱ41531. Excellent, well-furnished bungalows with deep and shady verandahs. All have fan and air-con and hot water and are set in a glorious garden that ranges high up the hillside, dotted here and there with statues and *bale* for relaxing. There's a great swimming pool at the top of the garden and a nearby coffee shop with brilliant views. Service is friendly yet efficient. ❼

Puri Pandan ☎ & ℱ0363/41541. Attractive bungalows in central Candi Dasa, on the seafront and well shielded from the noise of the main road. All have hot water and spacious verandahs, but there's no pool. ❹

Rama ☎0363/41778. An excellent location between the sea and lagoon, with accommodation in two-storey buildings with fan and cold water in a small garden. ❷

Segara Wangi ☎0363/41159. Excellent-value clean bungalows with attached cold-water mandi set in a pretty garden. Central and with great verandahs. Seafront places are best. ❷

Sindhu Brata ☎0363/41825, ℱ41954. Tiled, clean and well-kept bungalows with cold-water bathrooms and fans, set in a neat garden which fronts onto the sea and located in a quiet spot near the lagoon. There's also a beachside restaurant. ❹

Temple Seaside Cottages ☎ & ℱ0363/41629. Small, central place that offers several standards of fan-cooled accommodation from basic bungalows to ones on the seafront with picture windows and hot water. ❶–❹

The Watergarden/Hotel Taman Air ☎0363/41540, ℱ41164, ⊛www.watergarden hotel.com. Superb, characterful hotel in central Candi Dasa. Accommodation is in excellently furnished bungalows set in an atmospheric, lush garden. Some bungalows are with fan, some have fan and air-con, all have hot water and overlook lotus ponds. There's a pretty, secluded swimming pool. Service is excellent. ❼

Forest Road

East of the central section of Candi Dasa accommodation, **Forest Road** offers a number of quiet guesthouses and hotels dotted among coconut palms.

Genggong ☏0363/41105. Bungalows plus rooms in a two-storey block with big balconies and verandahs. There's a choice of fan or air-con and there's hot water available. However, the big plus is the lovely garden and picturesque stretch of white-sand beach just over the wall. ❷—❺

Puri Bagus Candidasa ☏0363/41131, ℻41290, ⓦwww.bagus-discovery.com. In an excellent location at the far eastern end of Forest Road, this hotel offers top-quality accommodation with a poolside bar, flourishing garden and tiled well-furnished rooms. There's a long beachfront location behind a white-sand beach with fine views of the offshore islands. Two-bedroom villas are also available. For a more rural location consider the sister operation, *Puri Bagus Manggis* (see p.286). ❽

Puri Oka ☏0363/41092, ℻41093, ⓔpurioka@indo.net.id. Well-furnished, clean, tiled rooms and bungalows all with hot water, set in an attractive garden off Forest Road, with a pool and restaurant near the white-sand beach. ❹—❺

Puri Pudak ☏0363/41978. Bungalows, all with hot water and fan, overlooking the beach. There's a good sunbathing area and a nice sea breeze. ❷

Sekar Anggrek ☏0363/41086, ℻41977. The best value on Forest Road, with seven good-quality bungalows, all with fan and hot water, in a quiet seafront garden. ❷—❸

Srikandi ☏0363/41972. A neat row of simple, good-value bungalows in an attractive garden by the sea, just at the start of Forest Road so convenient for the centre of town as well. ❷

Senkidu and Mendira

To the west, the village of **Senkidu** is about 1km from the centre of Candi Dasa, slightly detached and quiet, but still convenient for the main facilities. The adjacent village of **Mendira** is located on the coast a short walk from the main road.

Amarta Beach Inn ☏0363/41230. Large, tiled bungalows, all with fan and attached cold-water bathrooms, set in a pretty garden facing the ocean at Mendira. Plenty of space for sun-bathing and a beachside restaurant. ❷

Candi Beach Cottage ☏0363/41234, ℻41111, ⓦwww.candibeachbali.com. Good-quality, top-price accommodation in rooms or bungalows in an attractive compound with excellent beachside pool, fitness centre and tennis courts. Plenty of activities are on offer including trekking and village visits, and there's a Pineapple Divers desk. A new pool is planned. ❽

Dwi Utama ☏0363/41053. A short row of clean, simple fan rooms with attached cold-water bathrooms, set in a small garden with a restaurant overlooking the pretty white-sand beach at Mendira. ❷

Flamboyant ☏ & ℻0363/41886, ⓔflamboyant_bali@hotmail.com. Spotless bungalows in a gorgeous, quiet garden beside the sea at Senkidu. There's a restaurant, a *lesehan* in the garden

above the fish ponds and you can refill mineral water bottles here. ❷—❸

Nirwana Cottages ☏0363/41136, ℻41543, ⓔnirwanacot@denpasar.wasantara.net.id. A small establishment with well-furnished rooms and bungalows in a lush garden with an excellent pool and beachside restaurant. Bottom-end rooms with fan and hot-water are not brilliant value but the bungalows, especially with a sea view are excellent. Very popular, so booking is recommended. ❻—❼

Rama Candidasa ☏0363/41974, ℻41975, ⓔramacan@denpasar.wasantara.net.id. All accommodation has air-con and hot water, but the rooms are rather distant and less appealing than the bungalows. There's a good-sized pool, attractive garden, tennis courts and a beachside restaurant. ❽

Taruna ☏0363/41823, ℻41886, ⓔtaruna _bungalows@hotmail.com. A neat row of good-value bungalows in a pretty garden with a small seaside bar, in a quiet location next to *Flamboyant*. ❷

Buitan and Manggis

If you decide to stay any further west towards **Buitan** you'll need your own transport to enjoy Candi's nightlife, as public transport stops at dusk. Also, sea views at the far west of the resort are somewhat marred by the tankers going to the oil storage terminal further east along the coast. Further west, most of **Manggis** village is spread inland, but it does offer two luxury accomodation choices.

Amankila Manggis ☏0363/41333, ℻41555, ⓦwww.amanresorts.com. The eastern Bali representative of this exclusive chain is a jetset hideaway (rumour has it that Mick Jagger and Jerry

Hall honeymooned here). The accommodation and facilities are fabulous, ranged up the hillside with a beach at the bottom and excellent coastal views at the top. There's also a helicopter landing area. For

Rp100,000 a day, at the manager's discretion, non-residents can use the Beach Club facilities (which include a 45m pool), although you won't be allowed to use the famous, much-photographed three-tiered main pool up above. Prices start from US$600. **❾**

Balina Beach Resort Buitan ☎0363/41002, ℱ41001. Offering a variety of bungalows, all with air-con and hot water plus bath tubs, in pretty gardens with an attractive pool almost on the beach; Spice Dive has a desk here. From the main road, look out for the turning signed "Royal Bali Beach Club". **❼**

Serai Hotel Buitan ☎0363/41011, ℱ41015, ⓦwww.ghmhotels.com. One of the most impressive hotels in eastern Bali is situated in a grand coconut grove beside the sea, rooms ranged around a gorgeous pool. Stylish, modern minimal-ist chic characterizes the rooms and fabulous communal areas. Service is superb. There's a Mandara Spa attached to the hotel. The hotel is developing an international reputation for its two-day (US$220) and five-day ($550) residential cooking schools. Accommodation starts at $155. **❾**

Puri Bagus Manggis ☎0363/41304, ℱ41305, ⓦwww.bagus-discovery.com. Part of the small Puri Bagus stable of hotels, with just seven beautifully furnished rooms set in a wonderfully rural setting in Manggis – the only accommodation in the village. There's a small swimming pool and orchid garden in the paddy-fields just across the road, a temple in the gardens and free transport to the sister operation in Candi Dasa where guests can use their beachside facilities. A one or two-day cooking school runs for guests who are interested (from US$35). **❽**

The resort

Candi Dasa is an ancient settlement, with its **temple**, just opposite the lagoon, believed to have been founded in the eleventh century. The statue of the fertility goddess Hariti in the lower section of the temple, surrounded by numerous children, is still a popular focus for pilgrims (the name Candi Dasa originally derives from "Cilidasa", meaning ten children).

Even the most ardent fans of Candi admit that you don't come here for the **beach**, although there are many spots along the coast where there is at least a sliver of sand and the white sand is coming back behind the concrete jetties. However, you don't have to go too far around the bay to find some sand, and one of the best deserted stretches in the area lies just to the east of the resort. Go straight on at the crossroads at the end of Forest Road; don't take the right turn down to *Puri Bagus Candidasa*, but take the road up onto the headland where it follows the top of the cliffs for a few hundred metres but eventually descends onto a glistening black-sand beach on the other side.

There's good **walking** in the hills behind Candi Dasa, which are crossed by various footpaths. The path from the upper temple compound in Candi Dasa will take you up into the hills, where you can pick up a path to Tenganan, 4km to the north (see p.291). Some of the paths aren't that easy to follow, so if you want to head to a particular destination, it's a good idea to find a guide.

Diving and snorkelling

Just off the coast of Candi Dasa, a group of small islands offers excellent **diving**, although it's not suitable for beginners as the water is frequently very cold and the currents can be strong; patience is often needed for suitable conditions to dive the sites here. **Gili Tepekong** (also known as Gili Kambing or Goat Island) is the biggest island, although only 100m by 50m; **Gili Biaha** (also known as Gili Likman) is even smaller; and **Gili Mimpang** is just three rocks sticking out of the ocean. The area offers several walls, a pinnacle just off Mimpang and the dramatic scenery of Tepekong Canyon, lined with massive boulders. The current is too strong for the growth of big coral, but the variety of fish is excellent, including barracuda, tuna, white-tipped reef sharks, sunfish and manta rays.

Not all of these spots offer great **snorkelling**: the best places are off Gili Mimpang and Blue Lagoon on the western side of Amuk Bay, closer to Padang

Bai (see p.295). Local boat owners will approach you to fix up snorkelling trips; the going rate is around Rp50,000 per hour for a boat including equipment, but you'll pay more if you arrange it through your hotel. Many dive shops take snorkellers along on dive trips; prices vary from $25 to $39 so it pays to shop around. Always be clear whether or not equipment is included in the price.

As well as the local sites, Candi Dasa is an ideal base from which to arrange **diving trips** to Padang Bai, Nusa Penida, Nusa Lembongan, Amed and Tulamben. It's also feasible to arrange dive trips from here to Gili Selang, the most easterly point in Bali; it has a reputation as a wild and exciting diving spot and has yet to be fully explored. Although Gili Selang is closer to Tulamben than Candi Dasa, the boats in Candi Dasa and Padang Bai are better equipped to cope with the trip. Candi Dasa is also a good place to take a course, as hotel swimming pools are available for initial tuition. A PADI Open Water course costs $300–360; the two-day advanced option around $250; the two- to three-day rescue diver $300; and divemaster courses can also be arranged. On trips for experienced divers prices vary, but are about $50–60 for the Candi Dasa, Padang Bai, Tulamben and Amed areas, $70–75 for Nusa Lembongan and Nusa Penida (see p.276) and $80 for Menjangan Island (see p.401). See p.65 for general advice on choosing a dive operator.

Candi Dasa dive operators

Baruna Has a counter in town ☎ 0363/41185, and one at *Puri Bagus Candidasa* hotel ☎ 0363/41217. These are the Candi Dasa offices for this large Bali-wide operator, offering the full range of trips and courses.

Calypso Bali Dive At *Hotel Candi Dasa* ☎ 0363/41126 or 41536, ☏ 41537. Courses as well as dive trips.

Divelite ☎ 0363/41660, ☏ 41661, ⓦ www.divelite.com. A full range of PADI and SSI courses plus trips for experienced divers. They offer tuition in Japanese and English.

Maoka Dive Centre ☎ 0363/41563. Offers PADI courses plus the usual destinations for experienced divers. They also offer a variety of marine sports: parasailing, fishing, jet-ski and waterskiing.

Pineapple Divers At *Candi Beach Cottage* ☎ 0363/41760. This small company offers dives

and courses and two- and three-day package tours of the dive sites around the island, including accommodation.

Spice Dive At *Balina Beach Resort* ☎ 0363/41725, ☏ 41001, ⓦ www.damai.com/spicedive. The only southern office of this extremely well-regarded north-coast operator, offering trips for certified divers and courses.

Stingray Dive Centre Senkidu ☎ 0363/41268, ☏ 41062, and an office in central Candi Dasa ☎ 0363/41063. Features the usual range of trips plus courses.

Yos Marine Adventures At *Asmara* hotel ☎ & ☏ 0363/41929, ⓔ yosbali@indosat.net.id. This well-respected southern Bali operator has now branched out into Candi Dasa, offering a range of dives and courses.

Eating, drinking and nightlife

Candi Dasa offers a great variety of **places to eat** and the quality of the food, especially seafood, is generally excellent. Several places have set meals for Rp20,000 upwards, and others feature Balinese dancing, mostly *legong*, to accompany your meal – look out for local adverts.

Unless otherwise stated, all the places listed below offer inexpensive to moderately priced food and lie on or near the main road through the resort which can, unfortunately, be rather noisy.

Astawa The most popular of a clutch of places at the eastern end of the main road, offering highly competitive prices for a large menu of well-cooked and attractively presented Western, Indo-Chinese and travellers' fare. Was undergoing renovation at the time of writing.

Candi Agung 1 & 2 The *Candi Agung 1* is at the western end of the main street, *Candi Agung 2* at the east. Both have a big food and drink menu with well-cooked main courses and set menus at Rp25,000 for three courses. There are regular *legong* dances in both places.

Candidasa Café Well-furnished place towards the western end of the main street: the waterfall at the back is probably worth a trip on its own. They offer the usual Indonesian and Western choices including lots of pizza and seafood. They also offer two Balinese and two Indonesian menus at Rp50,000–55,000 per head, with seven or eight options in each of the three courses.

Ciao e basta Slightly hidden away off the main street, this two-storey place has an extensive menu of pasta, pizza, salads, home-made ice cream and desserts plus a good selection of drinks and coffees. Pizzas are recommended.

Grand Natia Café With a huge flat-screen TV, extremely competitive prices and regular dance shows, this place is worth a look. Main courses soon after the opening were mostly less than Rp20,000 with a large choice of the usual Western and Indo-Chinese options. It's uncertain whether prices will stay this low but the food is appetizing and the service is friendly.

Kedai ☎0363/42020, ⊛www.dekco.com. This offshoot of *Ary's Warung* in Ubud is a tasteful addition to refined dining in Candi Dasa and the soaring circular *bale* is a symphony in wood, bamboo and soft, creamy stone. The menu is not huge but there are innovative, imaginative Western and Indonesian options such as sage and mustard coated chicken sate and fruit-filled sweet spring rolls for dessert. Main courses cost up to Rp43,000 but if you don't want the works, the sandwiches are top-notch. There's a tasting menu of Rp95,000 for five courses. The coffee machine ensures that coffees are excellent and there's a big choice of cocktails and wines. Expensive.

Kubu Bali The large dramatic kitchen in the restaurant at the front of the hotel in central Candi Dasa specializes in seafood, but also offers moderately priced Western, Chinese and Indonesian food in attractive, relaxed surroundings with good service. Better tables are at the back tucked away from the road near the fish ponds. There's a big list of drinks, too.

Legenda Situated close to the junction of the Forest Road with the main road, this is one of the few venues in Candi Dasa for live music. They also have a wide-ranging menu with plenty of Western dishes, including spaghetti, pizza and steak, alongside Indonesian food.

Made Located on the main road in central Candi Dasa, there's a huge menu of steaks, pork and seafood featuring Western, local and Chinese cooking. Main courses cost Rp7500 upwards and the food is well cooked.

Pandan Ignore the breakwater in the foreground and this is a pretty fair spot for a sunset drink in central Candi Dasa. There's a big menu including some good seafood, and a twice-weekly Indonesian/Western buffet.

Queen's Café There's a good buzz here. Diners get a free welcome drink and popcorn and there is often live music. Set menus are Rp20,000; although the choices aren't vast, the food is cheap and cheerful.

Raja's Lots of people come here, almost opposite the lagoon in central Candi Dasa, for the nightly videos, but there's also a vast drinks list and plenty of Indonesian and Western dishes, including sausage and mash. Pizzas are worth the 30-minute wait: they're thin and crispy with a generous topping. Visa and MasterCard accepted.

Serai Restaurant ☎0363/41011. Probably the premier dining experience in eastern Bali. The restaurant is located in an open-sided *bale* designed in modern, minimalist Asian style and full of natural materials. The huge gourmet menu changes daily but is never less than an enticing volume of Indonesian and Pacific-Asian fusion dishes including lamb, beef and kangaroo among a great deal of seafood, all constructed with interesting touches of Bali. The cooking is extremely intricate; a sample dish would be steamed fillet of snapper, mushroom soy, sweet corn cake, spring onions and long beans. The *Table d'Hôte* menu offers three courses at Rp195,000 and the Serai Tasting menu five *dégustation*-style courses at Rp225,000. Expensive.

TJ's At the *Watergarden* hotel in the middle of Candi Dasa. Has a broad menu of Indonesian, Thai, Indian and Western dishes together with an enormous drinks list including numerous cocktails and Australian and Chilean wine. Breakfast croissants are excellent as are the desserts: coconut cream pie, apple crumble and chocolate cake.

Toke Café This long-term Candi Dasa favourite with a pretty fountain is set far enough back from the main road at the western end of central Candi Dasa for the road noise to be minimal. There's a vast menu of seafood, pasta, pizza, chicken, pork and steak (Rp20,000–30,000). Set menus at Rp35,000–55,000 are real feasts.

Warung Mawar Ayu A friendly, family-run place on Forest Road. It's a quiet spot for a meal, with a menu of Indonesian food and plenty of local fish. It shuts for local ceremonies, they run out of things, the baby comes out to play and you'll hear every chop and sizzle of the cooking process but the place is still appealing and attractive.

Warung Taman Sari A small and simple, friendly place in Buitan with a small and simple menu of excellent breakfasts and a selection of Indonesian and Western favourites. Main courses are Rp8000 upwards and there's plenty of local seafood.

Nightlife

Nightlife is low-key in Candi: apart from a few late-opening restaurants, things are pretty quiet by 11pm. There's no disco scene and live music comes and goes – check out *Legenda* and *Queen's Café*. Events are advertised with flyers nailed to trees around town. Videos are the main entertainment at *Raja's* and the *Candi Bagus Pub* next door, but viewing, or rather listening, can be frustrating as heavy traffic whizzes past.

Shopping

While nobody would head to Candi Dasa just for the **shopping** alone, there's now an enticing range of Candi stores selling a variety of crafts and textiles. Although the selection isn't as great as in Ubud or Kuta, there are things here for most tastes and pockets, and shopping in Candi Dasa is a low-key and relaxed experience.

Asri Shop (daily 8am–10pm) is central, sells everything for everyday as well as souvenir needs and has fixed prices which are a good guide for your bargaining elsewhere. There's a dense stretch of **clothing** shops along the main road just east of the Perama office (although they're also popping up throughout the resort) which sell the usual range of tourist sarongs, pants, skirts, shirts and T-shirts. Gogos, near the Perama office, and Putra, just along from the Asri Shop, sell a good range of **silver** items. Nusantara Archipelago, just east of the lagoon, has an excellent selection of **paper**, **wood** and **metal** items, all well-crafted and tasteful, and, just slightly further east, Surya Gana sells lovely cotton and silk **batik** – from small bags and purses up to hand-painted pure silk sarongs at more than half a million rupiah. Also at this end of town, Balinese Ceramic, opposite *Queen's Café*, offers pretty little **ceramic** bowls, vases and incense holders as well as larger items all with an attractive glaze and with prices from Rp10,000.

Further west, the Geringsing Shop is a treasure trove of the old and not-so-old and an extensive range of **textiles** from across Indonesia. Wooden statues in all sizes, styles and prices abound and there are even a few paintings. Lenia sells great baskets, textiles and statues from throughout Indonesia, and the shop at *The Watergarden* stocks some of the most tasteful and unusual items in town including clothes, textiles, jewellery, wood and paper crafts at all prices. The shop in the wartel next to *Kubu Bali* boasts a selection of small pottery, wooden and bone items plus **jewellery** and some textiles including a few rolls of cloth sold by the metre.

At the top end of the price range, *Kedai* has a small selection of gorgeous modern, well-designed and beautifully executed items both decorative and useful. Everything is natural including wood, stone, leather and cow-hide gorgeously crafted into infinitely desirable things although there's not much under Rp50,000. If you're seriously into shopping, there's a great choice of textiles and other crafts up the hill in the village of Tenganan (see p.292).

Listings

Bike rental Enquire at your losmen or at the places in the main street, and expect to pay Rp30,000/day. *Temple Café* in the main street has a selection. Beware the busy traffic on the main road.

Books Several bookstores in Candi sell new and secondhand books; the *Candidasa Bookstore* has the largest selection.

Car and motorbike rental You'll be offered transport every few yards along the main road, or else enquire at your accommodation. There are also plenty of rental companies around the resort, with prices comparable to Kuta/Sanur (Rp70,000–75,000 for a Suzuki Jimney for one day, Rp100,000–120,000 for a Kijang). The going rate for a driver is Rp50,000 per day. A motorbike costs Rp35,000–40,000. Well-established companies are Saputra ☏ 0363/41083, close to the police post; Safari ☏ 0363/41707 and Amarta ☏ 0363/41260 in the centre of town; and Candidasa Rent Car ☏ 0363/41225, just at the start of Forest Road. The insurance included varies considerably.

Charter transport To put together your own day-trip, you'll be looking at Rp200,000–300,000/day for vehicle, driver and petrol, depending on your itinerary. Negotiate with the guys along the main street, ask at your accommodation or approach the car rental companies. One-way drops to destinations throughout Bali are a convenient and – if you're in a group – a reasonable way of moving on: Rp50,000 to Padang Bai, Rp120,000 to the Amed area, Rp130,000 to Ubud, Rp150,000 to the Kuta area (including the airport), Rp200,000 to Lovina.

Doctor Contact staff at your hotel initially if you need medical attention. Alternatively Dr I Wayan Artana ☏ 0363/41321 (or mobile ☏ 0812/390 0447) offers a 24hr service at Candidasa Clinik on the track from the main road to *Flamboyant Bungalows* and *Taruna* in Sengkidu. The nearest hospitals are at Amlapura, Klungkung or Denpasar (see p.103).

Exchange You'll find moneychangers every few metres along the main street; rates are competitive although not quite as good as in Kuta.

Internet access Available at several spots including Safari Rent Car and Kelapa Mas, both on the main street. Prices are Rp300–400/min. Be aware that phone lines can be a bit unreliable and access can be suspended for a day or so every now and again.

Massage You'll be approached throughout the resort and on the beach. The going rate is Rp30,000/hr – more if you arrange it through your hotel.

Phones The wartel (daily 8am–11pm) is next to the *Kubu Bali Restaurant.*

Postal agents Several postal agents along the main street sell stamps. Asri Shop provides a poste restante service: mail should be addressed to you, c/o Asri Shop, Candi Dasa, PO Box 135, Karangasem, Bali.

Tourist shuttle buses Plenty of places offer shuttle buses from Candi Dasa to destinations throughout Bali and Lombok and further east to Bima and Sape. Perama ☏ 0363/41114 (daily 8am–9pm) is the most established operator. See Travel details on p.313 for destinations and frequencies.

Around Candi Dasa

It's worth making the trip out to **Pura Gomang** for good views of the area around Candi Dasa. Take an Amlapura-bound bemo for a couple of kilometres east of the resort, up the hill to the pass marked by a small shrine on the road. Concrete steps followed by a steep path head seawards from here to the temple at the top of the hill. Every two years, around October, four of the local villages – Bugbug, Bebandem, Jasi and Ngis – participate in a ritual battle near the top of Gomang Hill to settle an ancient dispute.

Some 6km northeast of Candi, the cove of **Pasir Putih** has a 500-metre pure white beach sheltered by rocky headlands with good views of Gili Biaha. Take a bemo as far as Perasi, from where a small road called Jalan Segara Madu with a little shop on the corner leads past paddy-fields to the coast. Two or three kilometres along the track, you reach a small temple where the path forks. The left fork leads to two black-sand beaches; the right descends through coconut groves to Pasir Putih. There are no facilities here at present, but the beach is rumoured to be earmarked for a big resort development.

About 2km further north in the village of **JASRI**, a right turn at a huge monument of a young girl wearing a sarong (with a basket of what appear to be salak fruit) leads after 100m to a fork; head right, and it's 200m to *Jasri Villas* (☏ 0363/22943, ☏ 22941; ⑥), well-built, two-bedroom bungalows with hot and cold water and kitchens. The minimum rental period is one week and they operate a shopping service for guests. Though you can self-cater, there's a small restaurant in the attractive compound, overlooking the swimming pool. About 100m further is the rather grubby beach.

From Manggis, 6km west of Candi, a very poorly surfaced road – check the condition before setting off in a vehicle – heads up into the hills. It's a lovely eight-kilometre walk up the steep, quiet lane, with stunning views of the entire coastal area, to Pesangkan (see p.303) on the Amlapura–Rendang road, where you can have lunch at *Pondok Bukit Putung*. For the return journey, bemos connect Pesangkan with Amlapura, where you can change for Candi Dasa.

Tenganan

The village of Tenganan Pergringsingan, usually known as **TENGANAN** (admission by donation), is unique among the Bali Aga communities of the island in its strong adherence to traditional ways. Rejecting the Javanization of their land, the caste system and the religious reforms that followed the Majapahit conquest of the island in 1343, the **Bali Aga** or Bali Mula, meaning "original Balinese", withdrew to their village enclaves to live a life based around ritual and ceremony. Today, Tenganan is an extremely wealthy village, and the only place in Indonesia that produces the celebrated **geringsing** cloth.

Laid out on either side of two broad cobbled avenues that run north–south, Tenganan rises in a series of terraces up the hill. The *bale agung* is the most imposing building, and the meeting place for the *krama desa* (village council). All the house compounds are identical, with small *bale* in courtyards behind high stone walls. Despite the emphasis on tradition, however, you'll still see noisy motorbikes scurrying around the village, a public telephone just inside the entrance to the village and television aerials and satellite dishes crowding the skyline.

The road up to Tenganan is an easy **walk** from the centre of Candi Dasa but **ojek** (Rp2000) wait at the bottom to transport you the 3km up to the village. It's a major stop on the tour-bus circuit: avoid the 11am–2pm rush if you can.

Rituals, ceremonies and festivals

Tenganan's land is owned communally; the villagers do not work it, but have sharecropping agreements with other local people, leaving them free to pursue a complex round of **rituals and ceremonies**. The rituals are laid down in ancient texts and their observance is believed to prevent the wrath of the gods destroying the village. Strict regulations maintain that only the physically and mentally healthy, who were born and live in Tenganan and successfully complete all the traditional stages of initiation, can be admitted to the village council. Anyone who marries outside the community is denied the benefits of communal land ownership and banished to live in the *banjar pande*, the area to the east of the village.

The founding of Tenganan

The story of the **founding of Tenganan** is told in a famous legend. Before the Majapahit invasion of Bali, **King Bedaulu** ruled the island. One day his favourite horse went missing, and the king offered a large reward for anybody who found it. The horse was eventually found dead near Tenganan and the king decided that he would give the local people the land near where the horse was found; in fact, he would donate the area within which the stench of the rotting animal could be smelled. One of the king's ministers was sent to the village to adjudicate, and he and the village headman set out to draw the boundaries. Incredibly, the smell of the horse could be detected over a huge area. The lines were duly drawn and the minister departed. At this point, the devious village headman took out from under his clothes the piece of rotting horse meat with which he had fooled the minister. The limits of the village lands are still the ones set at that time, and cover over ten square kilometres.

Most of the daily rituals observed by the villagers are not open to the public, but there are so many **festival** days that the *Calendar of Events* printed by the Bali government tourist office has an entire section devoted to events in Tenganan. During the month-long Usaba Sambah festival, generally in May and June, a massive wooden swing, like a giant ferris wheel, is set up by the young men of the village for the young girls to swing on. You may also see the *perang padan* or *mekare-kare*, a fight between combatants armed with shields of woven bamboo and weapons made of the thorny pandanus leaves.

Tenganan crafts and skills

The most famous product of Tenganan is **geringsing**, or double *ikat* (see p.539), a highly valued brown, deep red, blue-black and tan cloth. Bhatara Indra, the god of creation, supposedly taught the women of Tenganan the art of making it and commanded them to wear it. Many textiles carry the name of the place where they are woven but *geringsing* is so important that the village, officially Tenganan Pergringsingan, takes its name from the cloth. It is prized throughout Bali, as it's thought to provide protection against evil; many ceremonies require the use of the cloth. For example, during the tooth-filing ceremony (see p.546) a piece of it is placed beneath the head; during part of the cremation ritual it is wrapped around the coffin. An item can take many years to make, owing to the scarcity of the dyestuff to create the characteristic red colour, as well as the intricacy of the process. The origins of the technique remain shrouded in mystery and it is uncertain whether it's evidence of an outside influence or whether it was created within the village.

In recent years **basketwork** from *ata* grass has become another distinctive product of the village. This is an ancient skill, with small baskets made for personal and home use from the grass which was found locally. Since the 1980s it has gradually become more commercial, and supplies of grass are now imported from Flores, Sulawesi and East Java. Depending on the complexity, it can take a month to weave a basket: the grass is first split and woven, then boiled for two to five minutes to tighten the weave, dried for up to a week and smoked over a coconut wood or husk or *cempaka* wood fire for three days, turning every three hours, to give its glossy, golden finish. You can see all the stages of production at I Nyoman Uking's Ata Shop (☎0363/41167) up towards the top of the village over in the right-hand section, the *banjar pande*. There's a small sign outside, you're welcome to take photographs, and Nyoman speaks English. Baskets are sent from here to outlets in Nusa Dua and other southern resorts, and you can buy them for Rp55,000–200,000.

Traditional calligraphy is another attractive product of the village. Calendars and pictorial representations of traditional stories are incised on narrow lengths of *lontar* palm. which are then strung together to create a small hanging. They are attractive souvenirs. Compare several before you buy: it soon becomes easy to spot the more detailed, more finely drawn examples.

Tenganan is also famous for its unusual gamelan **selonding** music using instruments which are believed to have considerable religious power. Musicians in the village make and play the *genggong*, a bamboo jew's harp, and it's possible to arrange lessons here.

Padang Bai

Deriving from two languages – *padang* is Balinese for grass and *bai* is Dutch for bay – **PADANG BAI**, the port for Lombok, nestles in a small cove with a

ACCOMMODATION

Bagus Inn	4
Darma	11
Kembar Inn	12
Kerti Beach Inn	7
Made Homestay	9
Mahayani	3
Padang Bai Beach Homestay	5
Padang Bai Beach Inn	6
Pantai Ayu	2
Parta	10
Pondok Wisata Serangan	14
Puri Rai	8
Serangan Inn	1
Tirta Yoga	13

RESTAURANTS & BARS

Café Papa John	N
Celagi	I
Depot Segara	M
Dharma	L
Kasandra	K
Kendedes	A
Kledate	D
Manalagi	J
Marina	F
Omang Omang	B
Ozone	H
Pantai Ayu	G
Purnama Café	C
Warung Made	E

white-sand beach lined with fishing boats. Fast and slow boats run regularly to Lembar on **Lombok**; the jetty, ferry offices and car park are all at the western end of the bay, from where everything is within easy walking distance.

Increasingly, visitors are choosing to stay a night or two, and Padang Bai village has developed into a small laid-back resort. The pace of life only speeds up when a cruise ship comes to town: there are several a month in the peak cruising season (Nov–Feb), when you can watch the hundreds of visitors being decanted ashore and whisked off for trips around the island.

Arrival and transport

Bemos arrive at, and depart from, the port entrance; orange bemos from Amlapura via Candi Dasa, blue or white bemos from Klungkung (also known as Semarapura). Plenty of counters along the seafront offer tourist information, but these are commercial set-ups; the nearest government tourist office is in Candi Dasa (see p.283). The ticket office for **Nusa Penida** (marked on the map) is a little way east of the port; from 7am onwards, boats leave from the beach when they're full for Sampalan (Rp10,000).

Perama **tourist shuttle buses** operate from their office (daily 7am–7pm; ☏0363/41419) near the jetty; see Travel details on p.313 for more. If you're heading to the far east of Bali it's worth noting that the bus to Tirtagangga and Tulamben can drop you at Culik. You can also book with Perama to Bima and Sape on Sumbawa. If you're heading to southern Bali and can't bear the congested roads, try the boat *Osiania 3* (daily; 1hr; Rp54,000), which calls daily at Padang Bai on its way back from Lombok and goes on to dock at Benoa; book at Wannen (☏0363/41780) on the seafront.

Moving on to Lombok

The following operate from Padang Bai to **Lembar** on Lombok. See p.416 for information on other routes to Lombok.

Slow ferry Every 90min; takes 4hr–4hr 30min. Tickets cost Rp16,500 for VIP (air-con lounge with soft seats and TV), or Rp9000 for *ekonomi* (hard seats and TV). An extra charge is made for bicycles (Rp10,000), motorbikes (Rp25,000) and cars (from Rp175,000). See p.40 for information on taking rental vehicles between the islands.

Fast boat (the *Osiania 3*). Daily; takes 1hr 30min; Rp75,000. Book in Padang Bai at Wannen ℡0363/41780.

Tourist shuttle Tickets to destinations throughout Lombok are available at Perama; other operators advertise throughout the resort.

There's a **post office** near the port entrance and a **wartel** on the seafront (daily 7am–midnight) with another in the main road near the port (daily 6am–midnight). **Internet** services are springing up in many places – *Made* and *Ozone* to name just two; access (Rp350/min) can be rather erratic because of problems with the phone lines. Many seafront restaurants **change money**, and **car rental** (Rp80,000–90,000/day for a Suzuki Jimney, Rp150,000 for a Kijang) and **motorbike rental** (Rp40,000/day) are widely available.

Accommodation

A wide choice of **accommodation** in available both in the village and strung out along the road behind the beach; Padang Bai is experiencing something of a building boom, so expect more to be added and others to be renovated any time soon. The general shift is upmarket, with some offering hot water and air conditioning, although there are still plenty of budget rooms to be had. Accommodation on the seafront tends to be more expensive than in the village. The beach places benefit from a sea breeze and are generally bigger and airier, but the ones in the village, especially up on the hill, have some excellent upstairs rooms.

Bagus Inn ℡0363/41398. An excellent budget choice with small rooms with attached bathroom in a friendly family compound. ❶

Darma ℡0363/41394. A small family set-up in the village; the downstairs rooms are dark but upstairs ones are bigger and have good sitting areas outside. ❷

Kembar Inn ℡ & ℻0363/41364. Clean, pleasant tiled place in the village. There are many options: air-con and hot water at the top end, to fan and cold water at the bottom end. There's also a pleasant sitting area upstairs. ❸–❺

Kerti Beach Inn ℡0363/41391. Near the beach; some accommodation is in bungalows, some in two-storey *lumbung*-style barns. ❷

Made Homestay ℡0363/41441. Clean, tiled rooms with fan and attached cold-water bathrooms in a two-storey block convenient for both the beach and the village. ❷

Mahayani No phone. Three rooms in a small family compound tucked away in Gang Luhur off Jalan

Silayukti at the top of town. Rooms have attached bathrooms plus large verandahs. ❶

Padang Bai Beach Homestay ℡0812/360 7946. A set of attractive well-built, clean bungalows on the seafront in a garden complete with ponds. All have verandahs and cold-water bathrooms attached. ❷–❹

Padang Bai Beach Inn With a large, attractive location near the beach, this previously single set-up seems to have divided itself into inns 1, 2, 3 and 4 – all run independently with indistinct boundaries and no communication between staff. The administrative details are tedious but worth knowing as the place covers a large area with plenty of accommodation and you may well be passed from person to person to view different rooms – all offer bungalows and two-storey *lumbung*-style barns with fan and attached cold-water bathroom. Some accommodation faces seawards and some has a less attractive outlook. ❷–❸

Pantai Ayu ⓣ0363/41396. Long-established place in the village up on the hill with good views, a pleasant breeze and a small attached restaurant. The better, pricier rooms are upstairs. All are extremely clean. ❶–❷

Parta ⓣ0363/41475. Pleasant, clean village place with rooms upstairs and down, some with hot water. There's a great sitting area on the top floor and the real gem is the room perched way up here. *Tirta Yoga* is across the alleyway here and also worth a look. ❶–❷

Pondok Wisata Serangan ⓣ0363/41425. Newly renovated rooms in a small compound in the village; upstairs rooms are lighter and better but the downstairs ones are much cheaper. ❶–❷

Puri Rai ⓣ0363/41385, ⓕ41386. Large, clean, tiled rooms and bungalows with hot water and fan or air-con; try to get a room at the back which doesn't overlook the car park. The only place in town with a swimming pool – and it's a good one. ❹–❺

Serangan Inn ⓣ0363/41425. Spotless place built high up with some great views. Catches the breeze and boasts good rooms, all with fan and attached cold-water bathroom. ❷–❹

The beaches

If you find the main beach a bit busy, head for the smaller, quieter bay of **Biastugal** (also known as Pantai Kecil), to the west. It has just a few tiny warung that organize occasional beach parties in high season. Follow the road past the post office and, just as it begins to climb, take the track to the left. There are rumours that this area is lined up for the development of a luxury resort, with uncertain implications for public access to the beach. Alternatively, head over the headland in the other direction and take the path from Pura Silayukti to another small, white cove named **Blue Lagoon** after the snorkelling and diving site located just offshore here.

Padang Bai snorkelling and diving

Several places in Padang Bai rent **snorkelling** equipment (Rp15,000 per day); the water in the bay is surprisingly clear, although the best snorkelling is at Blue Lagoon. You can snorkel off the beach at Blue Lagoon, but you'll see far more if you charter a boat (about Rp150,000 for 2hr for two people); you'll be approached on the beach about this, or ask at *Celagi* restaurant or your guesthouse.

There are now several **dive** operations in Padang Bai. The most established is Geko Dive (ⓣ0363/41516, ⓕ41790, ⓦwww.gekodive.com), a large set-up on the seafront with a lot of experience diving in the area. It offers the full range of PADI courses, dives for experienced divers and the Discover Scuba introductory day, which includes one dive. Diving Groove (ⓣ0812/398 9746, ⓦwww.divinggroove.com) offers both English and German, and pride themselves on their fish briefing prior to diving. Other operators are Bali Moon Divers, Jl Silayukti 15 (ⓣ0363/41727), Equator (ⓣ0363/41509) on the seafront and Water Worxx, in the *Padang Bai Beach Inn* compound. Expect to pay $45 for two dives in the Padang Bai area (including equipment rental), $55 for two dives in Amed, Tulamben or Candi Dasa, and $70–75 for two dives at Nusa Lembongan, Nusa Penida, Pulau Menjangan or Gili Selang. The Discover Scuba day is approximately $75, and the PADI Open Water course $280–300. See p.65 for general advice on selecting a dive operator.

The local reef is **Tanjung Sari**, around and beyond the headland to the east of the bay, where you can reliably spot hawksbill and green turtles. The animal life is remarkable and includes several varieties of sharks, rays, scorpionfish, stargazers and plenty of species that you won't spot elsewhere in Bali. As it's so close to Padang Bai this is also a feasible area for night diving. The bay itself is worth exploring; it's largely composed of seagrass but is good for spotting wrasses, eels and razorfish plus creatures such as sea cucumbers.

Temples

To the east of Padang Bai, the paved road around the bay climbs up to the headland, which is topped with three temples. The largest and most important is **Pura Silayukti**, where the priest Empu Kuturan supposedly lived and meditated in the eleventh century. The three-roofed *meru* is dedicated to him and there's a finely carved *kulkul* tower. Just behind the main temple is the smaller **Pura Telagamas**. A path from the back of Pura Silayukti leads down the cliff face to a tiny shrine in a rock crevice above the pounding waves. Although surrounded by a modern wall and *candi bentar*, the ancient stones shrouded in holy cloths and a tiny turtle sarcophagus looking out across the vast ocean conjure a feeling of absolute timelessness. About 100m along the headland you'll see **Pura Tanjunsari**, also with a three-roofed *meru*, dedicated to Empu Bharadah, the brother of Kuturan, who came to Bali about two years after Kuturan and was connected with the early history of Besakih (see p.264) and the defeat of the evil witch, Rangda (see box p.249).

Eating and drinking

Seafood is the speciality in Padang Bai **restaurants**, with marlin, barracuda, snapper and prawns on offer, depending on the catch. You'll also find regular tourist menus featuring chicken, steaks, French fries and sandwiches, as well as rice and noodle dishes. The small places on the beach side of the road are unbeatable value, offering the perfect setting for that first cool drink of the evening. All are in the inexpensive to moderate price range and have happy hours, but tend to stop serving around 10pm.

Café Kerti At *Kerti Beach Inn*. The restaurant is upstairs in a two-storey building near the beach with fine views and a good breeze. The usual menu is on offer with plenty of drinks. A good spot to cool down in the heat of the day.

Café Papa John A relaxed atmosphere, soothing music and an enormous menu of all the favourites. You can refill mineral-water bottles here.

Depot Segara Offers simple, well-cooked food on the seafront.

Kendedes A two-storey building up on the hill – an excellent spot from which to catch the breeze and watch the port. Food is good quality and good value.

Marina Last in line on the beach – a very popular place with great views. If this doesn't suit, try the nearby *Manalagi*, *Kasandra*, *Celagi* or *Dharma*.

Ozone Conveniently located near the accommodation in the village offering good food in slightly wacky surroundings. Philosophy covers every surface. The menu is a long and entertaining read, full of staff pictures and opinion and the usual travellers' fare plus some Balinese specialities. Specials are advertised on the blackboards; the spare ribs get good reports.

Pantai Ayu Two places share this name and the same menu, both in prime locations. One is at the top of the village, in the homestay of the same name, and the other in the row of tiny warung on the seafront. Both serve good, inexpensive food and a variety of drinks in relaxed surroundings.

Purnama Café Up out of the bustle of the village on the top road near the market, attached to a small art shop; there are a few tables in the garden and a limited menu of drinks and snacks.

Warung Made Small place attached to the homestay on the seafront serving simple, well-cooked food from an extensive menu of seafood and Western specialities. Shows regular movies.

Nightlife

Padang Bai is a quiet laid-back place without an established **nightlife**. An exception is *Kledate*, an open-air reggae bar towards the eastern end of the beach. They offer live music (some reggae and some not) most evenings, getting going around 10pm just as most other places are shutting down, and they keep open while there are customers. They don't operate when there are large local ceremonies. *Omang Omang*, up in the village, offered regular live music at one stage; at the time of writing, though, it had closed and it's uncertain whether it will re-open.

Goa Lawah and Kusamba

Positioned right on the coast, **Goa Lawah** (Bat Cave; daily 7am–6pm; Rp2000, sarong rental Rp1000, parking Rp500), 7km west of Padang Bai, is a major tourist draw. The hawkers here are some of the pushiest on the island and will follow you across the road to the beach, where there's a pleasantly laid-out garden and picnic area with views of Nusa Penida and even Lombok on a clear day. The **temple**, probably founded by Empu Kuturan in 1007, is quite small but much revered by the Balinese, being one of the island's nine directional temples (see p.507). This one is dedicated to the southeast and many drivers stop on their way to make offerings at the small shrine on the road. The inner courtyard is crowded with *bale, meru* and shrines with fine carving, but the focus is the **cave** at the base of the cliff, which heaves with thousands of fruit bats; you'll hear their squeaks and smell the cloying odour of their droppings long before you spot them. The cave is supposedly the start of a tunnel that stretches 30km inland to Pura Goa in Besakih and is said to contain the cosmic *naga* Basuki.

Some 3km further west, the farming, fishing and salt-producing village of **KUSAMBA** spreads about 2km along the beach (see box on p.479 for more on salt production). One of the three original Muslim communities on the island, this was the site of fierce fighting between the Balinese and Dutch during the Third Military Expedition in 1849. **Boats** run daily from here to Nusa Penida and Nusa Lembongan, but they're very small and get loaded above the gunwales – you'd be wise to take an alternative route (see box on p.272). From Kusamba it's 6km west to Klungkung along a road that was cut by lava during the 1963 eruption of Gunung Agung.

East of Candi Dasa

The far east of Bali, **east of Candi Dasa**, offers lush rice terraces carpeting picturesque valleys just a few kilometres from parched landscapes where cultivation is all but impossible. The central volcanic mass of the island, most apparent in the overpowering bulk of Gunung Agung, extends right through to the smaller, forest-covered slopes at the far eastern end of the island, with settlements and road systems clinging to the coastal areas or the more hospitable foothills of Gunung Lempuyang and Seraya, not as tall as Agung but rugged and imposing nonetheless.

The main road beyond Candi Dasa cuts inland, passing close to the sleepy market town of **Amlapura**, before crossing the hills to the north coast and continuing on the long coastal strip right round to Singaraja (see p.342). You can follow this route by public transport, but if you want to get further off the beaten track and explore the far eastern end of the island, with its remote beach hideaways and excellent snorkelling and diving, or the fabulous scenery of the **Iseh** and **Sidemen** areas, you'll ideally need your own transport.

Amlapura

Formerly known as Karangasem, **AMLAPURA**, 40km east of Klungkung, was renamed after the 1963 eruption of Gunung Agung, when much of the outskirts of the town were flattened by the lava flow. (Balinese people will sometimes change their name after a serious illness, believing that a name-change

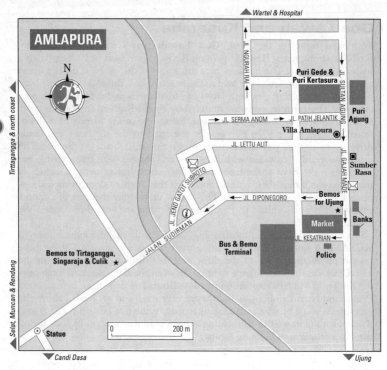

will bring about a change of fortune.) A rather remote district capital, its quiet and relaxed atmosphere makes it a pleasant place to spend a few hours, but the only sight, **Puri Agung**, one of the palaces of the rajas of Karangasem, is an unremarkable example of very faded grandeur.

Some history

Throughout its history, the far eastern **regency of Karangasem** has been involved as much with Lombok, only 35km across the Lombok Strait, as it has with Bali. Initially under the authority of the *dewa agung* of Klungkung, Karangasem began to develop its independence and, during the late seventeenth century, wrested control of Lombok from Muslim Sulawesi. Four Hindu rajas were installed to rule over the Sasak population, but ended up fighting among themselves. In 1849 the raja of Lombok, seeking to even old scores, provided four thousand troops to help the Dutch in their attack against Karangasem (see p.493). The Lombok troops ambushed and killed **Jelantik**, the hero of the Buleleng military, and the raja of Karangasem and his family committed *puputan*. The raja of Lombok was rewarded with Karangasem regency, which he ruled from 1849 to 1893.

Following a series of adventures in Bali and Lombok, the colourful **Gusti Gede Jelantik** was appointed as Dutch regent in 1894 and ruled until 1902, succeeded by his son, Anak Agung Gede Jelantik, who built the Puri Agung. Today his descendants occupy the other palaces in Amlapura.

Puri Agung

Built around a hundred years ago by Anak Agung Gede Jelantik, **Puri Agung** (daily 8am–6pm; Rp3000), also known as Puri Kaningan, is the only one of the Amlapura royal palaces open to the public. Puri Gede and Puri Kartasura across the road to the west are occupied and can only be seen from the outside.

The palace compound is fairly small with red-brick entrance gateways in a very unusual pagoda style. Within the compound, the extremely faded highlight is the **Maskerdam building**, a corruption of the name "Amsterdam", as a tribute to the Dutch. It has intricately carved doors and furniture donated by Queen Wilhelmina of the Netherlands arranged in several rooms, which you can admire only through the windows. The verandah is decorated with photographs and paintings, explained in the English-language guide to the palace, and includes a picture of the last king of Karangasem who died in 1966.

In front of the Maskerdam building, the **Bale Kambang**, formerly used for meetings, dancing and dining, rises from the middle of a murky lily pond. Royal tooth-filing ceremonies took place in the smaller **Bale Pemandesan** next door, while the **Bale Lunjuk** nearer the entrance gate was used for religious ceremonies.

Practicalities

Public transport coming into Amlapura terminal completes a massive circle around the top end of town, passing the **wartel** (open 24hr) on the way up, and Puri Agung on the way down to the terminal. The **post office** is at Jl Jend Gatot Subroto 25, with a smaller sub-office at Jl Gajah Made 45. **Exchange** facilities are at Bank Dannamon and BRI on Jalan Gajah Made, and BNI on Jalan Kesatrian near the bus/bemo terminal.

It's worth noting that in the afternoon Amlapura seems to die more quickly and completely than the other main towns, so you'd do best to travel early. **Bemos** from the terminal serve Candi Dasa and Padang Bai (orange); some of those to Selat and Muncan (green) go on to Besakih. Bemos for Ujung and Seraya (blue) leave from the southern end of Jalan Gajah Made not far from the terminal. There are also **buses** north to Singaraja, with some on to Gilimanuk (not after 3.30pm), and around the south to Batubulan (final departure 4pm). On both these routes minibuses may well make runs later than this, especially on busy days, but don't count on it. Bemos to Culik and Tianyar via Tirtagangga leave from the turn-off on the outskirts of town, as do dark-red minibuses to Singaraja. This turning is marked by a huge black and white pinnacle, a monument to the fight for independence, which is adorned with a *garuda*.

The staff in the **tourist office** on Jalan Diponegoro (Mon–Thurs 7am–3pm, Fri 7am–noon; ☎0363/21196) seem a bit startled to see visitors, but may be able to rustle up some brochures and, if you're lucky, an up-to-date calendar of ceremonies at Tenganan (see p.291).

Most people stop off in Amlapura for a couple of hours on their way elsewhere, and both Tirtagangga or Candi Dasa offer more **accommodation**. However, *Villa Amlapura* on Jalan Gajah Made (☎0363/23246; ❶–❹) has neat, pleasant rooms, the most expensive with hot water, in a small, pretty compound just south of Puri Agung. The attached *Café Lima* has a small **food** menu, with main courses up to Rp20,000, while *Sumber Rasa* further south on Jalan Gajah Made offers a similar selection of soups, sate, steak, spaghetti, noodles and rice. There are also warung near the market and bemo terminal.

Tirtagangga and around

Some 6km northwest of Amlapura, **TIRTAGANGGA**'s main draw is its lovely Water Palace, but the town is also surrounded by beautiful paddy-fields offering pleasant walks and glorious views of Gunung Agung and Gunung
Lempuyang in the distance. The refreshingly cool temperatures make this one
of the best day-trips from Candi Dasa, and if you want to spend a night or two
– or longer – you'll find it a quiet and restful spot.

Tirtagangga is served by **minibuses** and **buses** plying between Amlapura
and Singaraja, and by Perama tourist shuttle buses. There are two Perama
departures daily from Tirtagangga – one heading north for Culik, Tulamben
and Lovina and one around to the south for Candi Dasa, Padang Bai for
Lombok, Ubud and the southern resorts. See Travel details p.313 for frequency and journey durations.

There are several **moneychangers** and a postal agent on the track to the
Water Palace from the main road. **Internet** access is at *Purnama Restaurant*
(daily 7am–9pm), also on the track to the Palace from the main road.

It's worth checking out Nyoman Budiarsa's small shop (☎0363/22436), next
to *Genta Bali Warung* on the main road. He sells a printed **map** of walks to local
villages and temples (Rp2500) although it's most useful as a guide to the possibilities rather than a map to follow on the ground. He can also arrange
guides for walking trips (Rp15,000/hr per person) plus longer trips involving
transport in one or both directions and climbs up Gunung Agung (see p.270).

Accommodation

All the **accommodation** listed below is in or near Tirtagangga and accessed
by road from the village or from Temega, slightly to the south. It's also worth
considering the accommodation around the village of **Ababi** (see below): most
is around 2km from Tirtagangga by road, but there are short footpaths that lead
down to Tirtagangga in twenty minutes or less.

Tirtagangga

Cabé Bali ☎0363/22045, ⊛www.cabebali.com.
The most luxurious accommodation in the area,
offering superb, tasteful bungalows, all with hot
water, in lovely gardens surrounded by rice-fields
with excellent views of Gunung Agung and Gunung
Lempuyang. There's a relaxed atmosphere, excellent, friendly service and a swimming pool.
Accessed from Temega; about 1500m south of
Tirtagangga look out for the sign opposite the market. The site lies 500m along a rough road into the
paddy-fields. There's also a café with a small
menu of snacks and meals, open to non-residents.
❻–❼

Dhangin Taman Inn ☎0363/22059. Close to the
Water Palace with a good sitting area overlooking
the pools, this place has some reasonable rooms,
but the compound is very crowded and only more
expensive rooms have fans. **❶–❷**

Good Karma ☎0363/22445. Tiled, clean, simple
rooms set in a small garden in the paddy-fields.
Take the track on the left of the main road above
Good Karma restaurant that follows the water-

channel, then take the first path to the left. **❷**

Kusumajaya Inn ☎0363/21250. About 300m
north of the centre of Tirtagangga, on a hill; you'll
see the bungalows perched high on the hill if you
approach from the south and it's a climb of about
100 steps to reach them from the road. There's hot
water in the more expensive rooms and all have
verandahs that make the most of the splendid
views south across the fields to the coast. **❷–❸**

Pondok Wisata Pandan ☎0363/22883,
⊛www.pandanhouse.myweb.nl. Rooms with
attached hot-water bathroom are in a large,
ornately furnished house with television and sound
system set in the rice-fields north of *Cabé Bali* and
accessed via Temega. The four-poster bed with
gold fabric hangings in the room upstairs is for
real lovers of exuberance. **❺**

Puri Prima ☎0363/21316. About 500m north of
the *Kusumajaya Inn*, with quite basic rooms offering great views of Gunung Lempuyang. All rooms
have cold water but the bigger, newer ones have
huge picture windows. **❷–❸**

Puri Sawah ☎0363/21847. Just 100m beyond the Water Palace, on a track heading left from a sharp turn in the main road. There are four well-furnished rooms with verandahs in a small, peaceful garden. More expensive ones have hot water and there's a family room sleeping 4 to 6. The attached *Rice Terrace Coffee Shop* serves good food in a lovely location among the fields. ❷–❺

Rijasa ☎0363/21873. Across the main road from the track leading to the Water Palace, this is a good-value, centrally located place with a neat row of bungalows in an attractive garden. The more expensive rooms are further from the main road and have hot water. ❷

Tirta Ayu ☎0363/21697, ℱ21383. Set on the hill in the grounds of the Water Palace. All rooms have cold water but many of the bathrooms are extremely dramatic, featuring imposing statues. More expensive rooms are grander, with better furnishings. ❹–❺

Villa Tirta Mas ☎ & ℱ0363/21383. Right next door to *Tirta Ayu* overlooking the Water Palace, with two two-storey villas, both comfortably furnished with hot water and great views. ❼–❽

Ababi

Heading north from Tirtagangga, the road climbs through the small village of **ABABI**, which has no especial sights but is a lovely cool, peaceful rural spot. It's also gradually developing a number of **accommodation** options, all of which are reached along a left-hand turn signed from the main road just over 1km from Tirtagangga.

About 700m along this road, another left onto a track leads 200m to the hidden *Geria Semalung* (☎ & ℱ0363/22116; ❹), with four clean, tiled, attractive bungalows with hot- and -cold-water bathrooms in a peaceful, pretty garden and stunning views as far as Nusa Penida and Lombok on a clear day. There's a small restaurant attached. Staff here can arrange a **guide** for local treks and climbs (Rp35,000/hr per person) and for Gunung Agung climbs ($60 for one person; negotiable for more). From here, it's about thirty minutes' walk along local footpaths to Tirtagangga.

Another 500m further along the road is another track to the left, leading to two more accommodation options. Taking the left fork when the track divides brings you to *Pondok Batur Indah* (☎0363/22342, ✉pbaturindah@netscape.net; ❷), which offers simple rooms with fan and attached cold-water bathrooms in a small family compound with fine views to Gunung Lempuyang. Walking down to Tirtagangga from here takes fifteen minutes or so. Taking the right fork in the track brings you to *Pondok Lembah Dukuh* (no phone; ❶–❷), with three similarly simple rooms, cold-water bathrooms and fine views, just ten minutes' walk from Tirtagangga. Staff can arrange trekking both locally (Rp10,000/hr for two people) or further afield to Gunung Agung (Rp400,000 for two people including transport).

The Water Palace

Tirtagangga's **Water Palace** (daily 7am–6pm; Rp3100, Rp1000 for camera, Rp2500 for video camera; ⓦwww.tirtagangga.nl) was built in 1946 by Anak Agung Anglurah, the last raja of Karangasem, as one of the three testaments to his obsession with pools, moats and fountains. The others are the now ruined Ujung Water Palace (see p.310) and the rather less accessible Tirta Telaga Tista at Jungutan (see p.303). Tirtagangga's elegant palace was damaged on several occasions, including the 1963 eruption of Gunung Agung. However, it is being well restored and is an impressive terraced area featuring numerous pools, water channels and fountains set in a well-maintained garden. Check the website for historic photographs and information, plus up-to-the-minute details of the restoration efforts. You can **swim** in an upper, deeper pool (Rp4000) or a lower, shallower pool (Rp2000). **Paddle-boats** cost Rp10,000 for fifteen minutes.

Eating

Tirtagangga caters primarily for passing tourists; the **warung** on the track to the palace offer the usual rice and noodle options. The **restaurants** at the *Kusumajaya* and the *Prima Bamboo* have good views and serve similar inexpensive Indo-Chinese dishes. The *Rice Terrace Coffee Shop* attached to *Puri Sawah* is one of the quietest spots in the village and has excellent food including baguettes, apple or mango crumble, crêpes, salads, stuffed potatoes and soups, plenty of vegetarian choices and a children's menu; main courses cost Rp15,000–23,000. Above the car park, the *Good Karma* restaurant offers comfortable seating, a relaxed atmosphere and a cheap tourist menu, while across the main road *Genta Bali Warung* is also worth a try. The location of the restaurant at *Tirta Ayu*, within the Water Palace grounds and looking down across the gardens and pools, is excellent but their food is pricey and service can be offhand. After a twenty-minute walk from the main part of the village through the local paddy-fields, the restaurant at *Cabé Bali* offers a small menu of moderately priced snacks, main courses and desserts in a pretty garden in a totally rural setting. A *Ryoshi* Japanese restaurant (to match the one in Kuta) is due to open just below the road between *Kusumajaya Inn* and *Prima*.

Pura Lempuyang Luhur

From Ababi the road continues to climb gradually to the village of **ABANG**, where a large sign points the way east to the important temple of **Pura Lempuyang Luhur**, on the upper slopes of Gunung Lempuyang, 8km off the main road and impressively visible, gleaming white on the hillside against the verdant greens of the surrounding forest. One of the *kahyangan jagat*, or directional temples, of Bali (see p.507), giving protection from the east, it's among the most sacred temples on the island. Festival days are the best time to visit, when the 1700 steps up to the temple swarm with worshippers, and extra public **bemos** run almost all the way to the temple. On other days, bemos only run from Abang to **NGIS TISTA**, about 2km of the way.

However, in return for the difficulties of getting here, you'll be rewarded with one of the most staggering **views** in Bali. Pura Telaga Mas marks the bottom of the staircase, where two impressively carved *naga* greet visitors. It's a two-hour climb up the staircase through the forest to the temple, with several convenient spots for a rest on the way. Pura Lempuyang Luhur, believed to be the dwelling place of the god Genijaya (Victorious Fire), has recently been renovated – but it's the view of Gunung Agung, perfectly framed in the *candi bentar*, that makes it all worthwhile. The **courtyard** unusually contains a small stand of bamboo and on festival days the priest makes a cut in the bamboo to release holy water.

From the temple, a 90-minute climb up another staircase brings you to the **summit** of Gunung Lempuyang, where there's another small temple and even more spectacular views (the coast around Amed is clearly visible). The day after Galungan is the most popular day for local people to make a pilgrimage to the temple and on up to the summit.

The Amlapura–Rendang road

From Amlapura, a **picturesque road** heads about 32km west through Sibetan and Muncan, joining the main Klungkung–Penelokan road 14km north of Klungkung at Rendang. Public **bemos** ply the Amlapura–Rendang route, but they're not very frequent, and without **private transport** the highlights of this area – the Tirta Telaga Tista at Jungutan, Pura Pasar Agung above Selat and the rice-paddies around Iseh and Sidemen – are very difficult to get to.

Some 4km west of Amlapura (look out for a small sign by a temple), *Lila Homestay* (no phone; **❷**) is a lovely little place just above a small river in a garden overflowing with fruit trees. There are walks in the area (guests get a hand-out about these), and Bukit Kusambi, a couple of kilometres away, gives great views of Agung, Seraya and even Rinjani – especially good at sunrise.

About 5km west of *Lila Homestay*, **BEBANDEM** holds a large cattle market every three days. On the outskirts of town at **PANDESARI**, the road is lined with blacksmiths forging knives in their tiny workshops. A couple of kilometres along small lanes to the northwest of Bebandem, the village of **BUDA-KELING** is known for silverwork, and a few workshops line the road where you can watch the smiths and buy pieces.

Tirta Telaga Tista and westwards

Just west of Bebandem there's a sign off the main road to **Tirta Telaga Tista** at **JUNGUTAN**, one of the water palaces built by the last raja of Karangasem. The route isn't very clear, but after 1km you should head left at the family monument and then left again 500m further on, at the *padmasana* in the village. Tirta Telaga Tista is a square artificial lake fed by a freshwater spring, with an island temple shaded by frangipani trees. It was never as grand as Tirtagangga or Ujung, but it's an attractive and quiet spot surrounded by rice-fields, with hills rising up behind.

Continuing west, with excellent views of Gunung Agung along the way, the road heads through **SIBETAN,** about 12km from Amlapura, and climbs gradually into the salak centre of Bali. Salak, or snakeskin fruit, has a brown scaly skin hiding a crisp flesh with the crunch of an apple, but a totally unique flavour. It grows on an aggressively prickly palm about 3m high, usually planted among coconuts for shade; the main season is January to February, but fruit is available for a couple of months either side of this.

At the small village of **PESANGKAN**, 9km west of Sibetan, *Pondok Bukit Putung* (**☎** & **ℱ** 0366/23039; **❺**) is signed from the main road. Its accommodation is very poor value, but it has brilliant views from the **restaurant** terrace, where moderately priced food is available; the countryside down to the coast is spread out in an amazing panorama before you. A narrow road winds 8km down through Bakung to Manggis with gorgeous views of the entire area (see p.282); enquire locally as to the road condition – the surface is very poor and it may not be passable.

Selat and around

A further 4km west is the small village of **SELAT**, with accommodation in pleasant, tiled, well-furnished rooms set in a nice garden at *Pondok Wisata Puri Agung* (**☎**0366/23037; **❸**–**❹**), on the east side of the village just after the post office. The rooms are a bit close to the road but there's a pleasant sitting area in the garden behind. They also offer rice-field **trekking** (Rp75,000 per person for two-and-a-half hours) and **climbing** up Gunung Agung (Rp150,000 per person, minimum two people, not including transport).

Selat also marks the turn-off to **Pura Pasar Agung** (Temple of Agung Market), one of the nine directional temples of Bali, which is signposted prominently in the middle of the village. The temple was completely destroyed by the 1963 eruption of Gunung Agung and has been rebuilt. The road to the temple climbs steeply 10km through bamboo stands and a few salak and acacia forests, set in countryside scored by deep lava-carved gorges. From the car park, five hundred concrete steps lead up to the temple. Rising in three terraces to the inner courtyard, it's an impressive and dramatic place, perched at about 1200m on the slopes of Gunung Agung, and is the starting-point for one of the routes up the mountain (see p.269). Even if you're not climbing Agung, this is a lovely spot with fabulous views.

Iseh and Sidemen

From **DUDA**, just east of Selat, a beautiful route leaves the Amlapura–Rendang road, heading south through Iseh and Sidemen to Klungkung. The views of the rice-fields along this road are among the most lovely in Bali, rising into terraces on the hills behind.

Artists Walter Spies (see p.211) and Theo Meier (see p.210) both lived in **ISEH** for some time, and Anna Mathews wrote her wonderfully evocative *Night of Purnama* about her life in the village before and during the 1963 eruption of Gunung Agung. Just south of Iseh a small sign on the left points to *Pondok Wisata Patal Kikian* (T & F 0366/23005; ●), with three gorgeous bungalows sitting in mature grounds on the hillside in an utterly peaceful, blissful spot with fabulous views straight towards Gunung Agung. All bungalows have hot water and the price includes all meals. Reserve ahead to ensure things are ready for you.

A couple of kilometres south, at **SIDEMEN**, there are plenty of tracks through the fields for strolls: the village is an attractive base to experience a Bali that seems a million miles away from the bustle of the south. You can watch *endek*-weaving on foot looms at the Pelangi workshop, and, in the middle of the village, a signed turning leads to **accommodation** out in the rice-fields. After a few hundred metres the road forks. A short distance along the right-hand turn is *Pondok Wisata Lihat Sawah* (T 0366/24183; ●–●) the closest accommodation to the village. They have clean, tiled bungalows with fine ricefield views – cold-water bathrooms are at the bottom end and hot-water ones at the top. Better rooms are further away from the road, which is surprisingly noisy. Several kilometres further along this road out into the countryside is *Sacred Mountain Sanctuary* (T 0366/24330, F 23456, W www.sacredmountainbali.com; ●–●), a gorgeous, top-quality place with several standards of accommodation in well-designed wood, bamboo and thatch bungalows (some with outside bathing pavilions and dipping pools) in lush gardens with a huge swimming pool. There are several secluded sitting/meditation areas in the grounds and down near the river, and tour guides are available for local walks and treks.

Take the left fork in the road from Sidemen brings you after 1500m to the *Nirarta Centre for Living Awareness* (T 0366/24122, F 21444, W www.awareness-bali.com; ●–●) set up by psychologist and author Peter Wrycza. The accommodation is often used by groups from overseas for residential courses and seminars, but guided individual retreats are also available. Visit the website to read more about "The Way of Unfolding", the philosophical and spiritual base of the centre. The attached **restaurant** is semi-vegetarian (serving chicken and fish) and guests may join in the twice-daily Awareness Meditation sessions if they wish. A kilometre further along this road is *Tabola Inn* (T 0366/23015), now looking extremely neglected although the bungalows are set in great gardens with a small pool and a peaceful location. Check the situation and current prices before making a trip out here.

Back on the main road through the village, the *Pondok Wisata Sidemen* (T 0366/23009; ●) has little to recommend it apart from relative cheapness and accessibility. From Sidemen the road drops down through small villages before reaching the main Klungkung–Kusamba road at Paksabali and Sampalan.

Muncan and Rendang

About 4km west of Selat along the Amlapura–Rendang road, **MUNCAN** is a quiet little village and another possible base for climbing Agung (see p.270). It's also developing as a centre for making reproduction antiques; there are several workshops in the village and along nearby roads. Some 6km south, Barking Dog Rock (*Batu Ngongkong*) gives a great panorama over Iseh and Sidemen.

West of Muncan, the vistas close in and the valleys become narrower and deeper. The River Telaga Waja is used by several rafting companies: Sobek and Bali International Rafting both start their trips here amidst lovely scenery (see box on p.125 for more information). A further 4km west at **RENDANG**, an attractive village with colourful gardens lining the street, the route joins the main Klungkung–Penelokan road, and there are bemos to Besakih.

Amed

The stretch of coast in the **far east of Bali** from Culik to Aas has acquired the name of "**Amed**" in traveller-speak, although Amed is just one small village in a wonderful area offering peaceful bays, calm and clear waters, stunning coastal views and attractive inland scenery. The area is developing fast but anything further from a concrete jungle is impossible to imagine. It's an ideal spot for a quiet few days (or more), with little to do but sunbathe and indulge in some gentle snorkelling and diving. An increasing number of accommodation options cater for all tastes and budgets; all rent out snorkelling gear and are able to arrange dive trips. It's worth taking a bit of time to choose a dive operator; see p.65 for general advice on this.

The **beaches** vary from black to white sand, via a mix of the two, and you'll share them with plenty of little local boats (*jukung*). Don't expect a post office out here and, although there are several moneychangers, rates are terrible so bring plenty of cash. At the time of writing there are still very few phones, although lines are currently being erected. You'll notice that much of the accommodation has the same fax number: they all use an agency in Amlapura, so be sure to write the name of the hotel you are communicating with very prominently and don't expect a speedy response.

The coastal route from **CULIK**, on the Singaraja road 10km northeast of Tirtagangga, around to Amlapura is only 42km, but if you do decide to do it all, allow yourself the best part of a day to negotiate the road and enjoy the scenery. **Transport** is slim. From Culik, **bemos** ply via Amed to Aas in the morning. After that you'll need to charter one or use an ojek (hard bargaining should get a fare of around Rp5000 to Lipah Beach, Rp10,000–12,000 to Selong). Staff at your accommodation will help arrange transport for your return. In early 2002 this section from Culik to Aas was in superb condition: incredibly smooth without a pothole in sight. Only time will tell what the ravages of a rainy season or two manage to do to it.

For the part of the coastline from Aas south to Seraya you'll need your own vehicle. It's certainly a lovely trip, climbing over headlands and down into coves in a totally rural area. However, at the time of writing, the road was appalling and only passable by skilled motorcyclists with plenty of time and patience. This situation may change, so check before setting off from either direction.

Amed and Jemeluk

From Culik, it's 3km east to the picturesque, sleepy fishing village of **AMED**. The village features a kilometre-long black-sand beach and hills rising up behind – although the stench of drying fish can rather detract from the scenery.

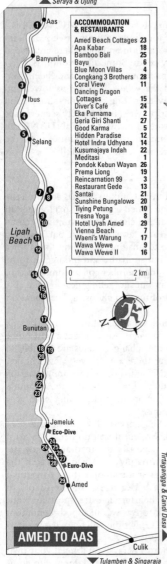

ACCOMMODATION & RESTAURANTS	
Amed Beach Cottages	23
Apa Kabar	18
Bamboo Bali	25
Bayu	6
Blue Moon Villas	4
Congkang 3 Brothers	28
Coral View	11
Dancing Dragon Cottages	15
Diver's Café	24
Eka Purnama	2
Geria Giri Shanti	27
Good Karma	5
Hidden Paradise	12
Hotel Indra Udhyana	14
Kusumajaya Indah	22
Meditasi	1
Pondok Kebun Wayan	26
Prema Liong	19
Reincarnation 99	3
Restaurant Gede	13
Santai	21
Sunshine Bungalows	20
Tiying Petung	10
Tresna Yoga	8
Hotel Uyah Amed	29
Vienna Beach	7
Waeni's Warung	17
Wawa Wewe	9
Wawa Wewe II	16

0   2 km

AMED TO AAS

Tirtagangga & Candi Dasa ▶

▼ Tulamben & Singaraja

Much of the area around here is lined with salt manufacturing (see p.479), although you'll only see it taking place in the dry season. The following **accommodation** and **eating** options are described in order, as you come across them heading east.

Just beyond Amed village, *Hotel Uyah Amed* (☎0361/285416, ℱ412592, ℯnature@naturebali.com; ❺–❻) has eight, gleaming bungalows nestling between the road and the beach. They're well furnished, with air conditioning and solar-powered hot water, clustered around the pool and have large windows to make the most of the beach views. The attached *Café Garam* is an attractive, open *bale* with displays and artefacts detailing the salt-making process. It has a large menu of moderately priced Western and Indonesian food and a wood-burning pizza oven.

About 2km beyond Amed, almost next door to Euro-Dive, *Geria Giri Shanti* (no phone; ❷) has five large, tiled, good-value bungalows just above the road all with fine verandahs to relax on. Almost opposite, *Congkang 3 Brothers* (no phone; ❹) offers clean, tiled bungalows right beside the beach facing seawards in a lush, well-kept garden with excellent views west as far as Gunung Agung for fine sunsets. Next door, *Pondok Kebun Wayan* (no phone; ❷–❺) has an inexpensive-to-moderate beachside restaurant and sun-bathing area, plus good-quality accommodation across the road and ranged up the hillside, with air-con and hot water in the priciest rooms and fan and cold-water bathrooms at the bottom. All have deep verandahs, there are plenty of sitting areas for relaxation and there's a small pool.

Some 300m further east, *Bamboo Bali* (no phone; ❷) is a good budget choice seconds from the beach, with clean, tiled, fan-cooled bungalows in a pretty garden on the hillside that catch the breeze and enjoy good views. A few hundred metres further on, just before the village of Jemeluk, *Diver's Café* (no phone; ❷–❸) has a few bungalows, some with hot water, in a garden across the road from the beach and is very convenient for divers and snorkellers.

Diving at Amed and Jemeluk

There are several **dive operators** along this stretch of coast. Transport difficulties make it tempting to go with the one that is closest to where you are staying. However, see our general notes (p.65) on choosing an operator.

About 2km beyond Amed, English and Dutch-speaking **Euro-Dive** (no phone, ℗0363/22958, ⓦwww.eurodivebali.com) is a smart Dutch-owned dive operation just above the road. They offer all PADI courses up to Divemaster level, an introductory dive for new divers and a pool for the early stages of training. Dives for experienced divers are also available. Further east, **Stingray Dive** (☎086812/163639), at the *Divers Café* just before Jemeluk, charges $40 for two dives in the area for certified divers. They also have an office in Candi Dasa (see p.287). East again, **Eco-Dive** in Jemeluk (no phone, ⓦwww.ecodivebali.com) is well established in the area and arranges local dives and snorkelling trips as well as diving at Candi Dasa and Menjangan. They teach PADI Open Water courses and offer instruction in English, French, Dutch and German. Staff here are also developing their skills in underwater videography. **Mega Dive** (☎ & ℗0361/754165, ⓦwww.megadive.com), at *Amed Beach Cottages* in Jemeluk, offers introductory dives, dives for certified divers and PADI courses.

The main **diving area** is around the rocky headland to the east of the parking area at Jemeluk: a massive sloping terrace of coral, both hard and soft, leads to a wall dropping to a depth of more than 40m. The density of fish on the wall is extremely high – gorgonians, fans, basket sponges and table coral are especially good, sharks, wrasses and parrotfish have been spotted in the outer parts, and the current is generally slow.

Jemeluk

A couple of hundred metres further brings you to **JEMELUK**, the diving focus of the area, with a big car park for visiting divers plus a few stalls and warung along the road.

Just behind Eco-Dive's restaurant are very basic bamboo and thatch rooms (no phone; ❶) with attached bathroom. Hardened backpackers will relish the bamboo doors, lack of windows and limited comfort – such places are hard to find in Bali these days. About 1km further on, over an imposing headland and into the next bay, *Amed Beach Cottages* (no phone; ❸–❺) are situated in a pretty garden between the road and the beach. They offer bungalows with fan, some with hot water and there's a small but deep swimming pool just by the beach. Just beyond is a **wartel** (7am–10pm) providing satellite communication with the outside world. Prices are steep: Rp3000/min to call within Bali, Rp18,000/min for all overseas calls. Slightly further east, *Kusumajaya Indah* (no phone; ❹–❺) has attractive, clean brick and tile bungalows in a mature, shady garden that slopes down to their restaurant right by the beach. More expensive rooms have air-con.

Next door, the delightful *Santai* (previously *Gubuk Kita*; ☎086812/103519, ℗0363/21044, ⓦwww.santaibali.com; ❼) remains the **best hotel** in the area despite increased competition. Accommodation is in lovely wooden and thatch bungalows with gorgeous decor and comfortable verandahs, the more expensive have ocean views. All have air-conditioning and hot water, and the pool is terrific. A large restaurant serves excellent, moderately priced food, including the addictive "Santai chocolate pudding cake". Tours and transport are available as are fishing and sunset sailing. Local children come here regularly to dance.

Some 700m further around the coast, *Sunshine Bungalows* (☎086812/103660; ❻–❼) are eight new bungalows clustered around a small pool beside the beach.

All have air-con and hot water and the best have ocean views. There's a small poolside restaurant. Next door *Apa Kabar* (℡086812/103753, ℱ0363/21044, Ⓦwww.apakabarvillas.com; ❽) has two villas, each with two bedrooms, a living room and cooking facilities. Both are air-conditioned and have indoor and outdoor bathrooms and are situated next to the beach and pool. The restaurant here gets good reports; they have plenty of moderately priced pizzas, barbecued seafood and meat as well as local dishes. Across the road *Prema Liong* (no phone, ℱ0363/21044, Ⓦwww.bali-amed.com; ❺) comprises two-storey bungalows topped by thatch up on the hillside away from the road, with stunning views, fans and cold-water bathrooms.

Bunutan

The next bay to the east is the location of the small, peaceful village of **BUNUTAN**, about 8km from Culik. On the climb up out of the village look out for tiny *Waeni's Warung* (no phone; ❷) on the cliff side of the road, right on the headland – a perfect spot for a sunset drink. Their simple bungalows are clean and tiled with attached cold-water bathrooms and have excellent views west to Gunung Agung, Gunung Batur and beyond.

Down the other side of the headland, about 500m further on, *Wawa Wewe II* (no phone, ℱ0363/22074, Ⓔwawawewe@hotmail.com; ❹) are straightforward bungalows set down from the road overlooking the coast with fans and attached cold-water bathrooms. In addition there are a couple of large family villas each with two bedrooms. Next door *Dancing Dragon Cottages* (℡ & ℱ0363/41177, Ⓦwww.dancingdragoncottages.com; ❽) is designed using Balinese and feng shui principles. There's stylish wooden furniture, marble floors, a vast triangular bath in each bathroom and a pretty swimming pool. All cottages have hot water and air-con, with a choice of smaller ones on the seafront or larger ones in the garden behind.

About 1km beyond, perched on a headland, is the top-quality *Hotel Indra Udhyana* (℡0361/241107, ℱ234907, Ⓦwww.indo.com/hotels/indra_udhyana; ❽–❾), which boasts superb rooms, all with air-conditioning and hot water, and a great pool set in fine grounds stretching down to the coast. Just around the bend as the road begins to descend, *Restaurant Gede* is on the hill above the road. Their ambition must be admired – they have more than 250 items on the menu – but the cheap to moderately priced food is well cooked, the place is attractively furnished and it gets a good breeze.

Lipah Beach

LIPAH BEACH is the most developed beach in the area (although still very peaceful), located around 10km from Culik. There's **accommodation** at *Hidden Paradise* (℡ & ℱ0361/431273, ℱ0363/22958, Ⓦwww.hiddenparadise-bali.com; ❻) and, slightly beyond this, *Coral View* (same contact details; ❻–❼). Both offer large, well-furnished bungalows in lush gardens with pools beside the beach. A couple of restaurants are located nearby both with attached accommodation: *Tiying Petung* (no phone; ❷) has simple tiled rooms with attached bathroom, while next door *Wawa Wewe* (no phone, ℱ0363/22074, Ⓔwawawewe@hotmail.com; ❷) has slightly better verandahs in front of the rooms. Both have similar inexpensive to moderately priced menus offering the usual Indonesian and Western travellers' choices in relaxed and relaxing surroundings. It's about 100m to the beach from these places. There's reasonable **snorkelling** just off the coast here and, for **divers**, Lipah Bay is the site of the wreck of a small freighter at 6–12m depth, which is now covered with coral, gorgonians and sponges. The reef nearby is also rich and diverse.

Into the next bay, accommodation at *Vienna Beach* (☎082/837 0342, Ⓕ0363/21883, Ⓦwww.bali-amed.com; ❺–❻) is ranged along the seafront in a small compound. All rooms have sea views; more expensive ones have air-conditioning and hot water. The room price includes an evening meal. Across the road, away from the beach, *Tresna Yoga* (no phone; ❸–❹) is perched so high on the hillside that only the fittest need apply; its bungalows are attractive and tiled with attached cold-water bathrooms. Next door *Bayu* (no phone, Ⓕ0363/21044; ❸–❹) offers similar accommodation. The beach is a short walk across the road from both these places.

Selang and Ibus

Another 1500m past the headland is the bay at **SELANG**, almost 12km from Culik, where the long-standing, ever-popular *Good Karma* (no phone; ❸–❹) is located right on the beach, which combines black and white sand and offers good snorkelling. Various standards of accommodation are on offer, all with cold water and verandahs and set in a gorgeous garden – an oasis in the midst of a parched landscape. There are plans to upgrade the accommodation with hot water and air-con.

About 500m further on are *Blue Moon Villas* (☎0812/362 2597, Ⓕ0363/21044, Ⓦwww.bluemoonvilla.com; ❼), up on the headland as you climb out of Selang bay. They have top-quality bungalows with air-conditioning and hot water, brilliantly designed to give superb views from the balcony. The attached café has an extensive menu of moderately priced food and drinks and there's a wonderfully relaxed atmosphere.

Some 700m further, in the village of **IBUS**, *Reincarnation 99* (no phone; ❹) has five good-quality bungalows just above the coast with fan and outdoor cold-water bathrooms that are themselves jungles. The restaurant is up high near the road with views down onto the coast. Just 300m further along, on the way down into Banyuning, the popular *Eka Purnama* (Ⓕ0363/21044, Ⓔgeo-cowan@yahoo.com; ❹–❺) has bamboo bungalows with tiled roofs perched on the hillside above the road. All have large verandahs looking seawards, fan and attached cold-water bathroom. There's a Japanese wreck not far off the coast here, which is visible to snorkellers. From here the road descends to the long bay of **Banyuning** where the beach is lined with colourful *jukung* and the inland hills slope steeply and impressively upwards.

Aas

The village of **AAS** is 2km beyond *Eka Purnama*, almost 15km from Culik. *Meditasi* (no phone, Ⓕ0363/22166; ❹) is situated just behind a sandy beach here, offering three bamboo bungalows with entire walls that slide open to reveal a fine seaward view for the sunrise or an inland view towards Gunung Seraya. The attached *Kick Back Café* can arrange local treks, including climbing Gunung Seraya. Diving groups do come here to explore the offshore reefs but the bungalows are well tucked away. Accommodation doesn't come much more isolated than this in modern Bali.

Kusambi, Seraya and Ujung

If you continue around the coast from Aas you'll pass through dry, barren country east of the mountains where the local farmers have a tough time scratching a living from the soil. It's far too dry to grow rice and the only crops are peanuts, soya beans and corn, grown in the wet season. The scenery is dramatic, with hills sweeping up for hundreds of metres from the coast and fields at crazy angles, their terracing supported by dry stone walls. Clinging to the

EAST BALI | East of Candi Dasa

side of the hills, the road twists and turns and the pace of travel is slow.

The road leaves the coast at **KUSAMBI**, marked by a massive beacon. This is the most easterly point on Bali – on clear days you'll be able to see Lombok, 35km across the strait. Further on, the small market town of **SERAYA** features a grand temple, dominated by the looming Gunung Seraya. From here the road heads down to the coast, where rows of colourful boats line the beach, before it turns inland at **UJUNG**, 5km south of Amlapura, where you'll spot a jumble of ruins down in a dip on the right. This is the third of the **water palaces** built by the water-loving last raja of Karangasem, Anak Agung Anglurah, in 1921 (see 301). Situated among large artificial lakes, it must once have been a wonderful place. All that remains, save the avenue of mango and frangipani trees leading through the compound, are tumbled columns, portals to nowhere and foundations, although there are some signs of renovation. From here, the road passes through attractive rice terraces with views across to Gunung Lempuyang and Seraya, before reaching the southern side of Amlapura.

Tulamben and around

Heading north from Culik, you move into an entirely different landscape: from lush and green, the land becomes parched and dry. Rice-fields give way to scrub and cactus and the landscape is comprised of boulder-strewn folds and channels, relics of the lava flow from the 1963 eruption of Gunuing Agung (see p.268).

The small, rather unattractive village of **TULAMBEN**, about 10km north-west of Culik, appears an unlikely target for visitors and, indeed, there's little to draw you here unless you are into **diving** or **snorkelling**. This is the site of the most famous and most popular dive in Bali, the **Liberty wreck**, attracting thousands of visitors every year. Built in 1915 in the US as a cargo steamship, the 120-metre-long *Liberty* was equipped with two guns at the outbreak of World War II. Carrying a cargo of rubber and rail parts, she was torpedoed on January 11, 1942, 15km southwest of Lombok. Two US destroyers tried to tow her to port at Singaraja, but the ship filled up with water and was beached at Tulamben. Everything valuable was gradually removed, including the cargo, propeller and metal parts, until in 1963 the eruption of Gunung Agung followed by earth tremors caused the hull to slip off the beach into deep water where it broke into two pieces. Up to a hundred divers a day now visit the site, so it's worth avoiding the rush hours (11.30am–4pm). Night dives here are especially exciting.

Practicalities

Tulamben is easily **accessible** from either Singaraja or Amlapura by public minibus or bus. There's a Perama office in the *Ganda Mayu* hotel (daily 8am–10pm): one service daily heads around to the north and Lovina, while another heads via Culik and Candi Dasa and on to Ubud and the southern resorts. See Travel Details (p.313) for frequency and journey times. Several **restaurants** offer the usual range of rice, noodles and pasta, and the area has seen a recent building boom, with accommodation options on the increase.

Agung (no phone). A kilometre east of the village, with bungalows in a row perpendicular to the beach. Rooms are simple and tiled, the ones closest to the beach being very peaceful. At the time of writing it looked extremely quiet and there was no restaurant. It's advisable to check at *Agung Bungalows* in Candi Dasa (see p.284) whether it's still open. **②**

Bali Coral Bungalows ☎ & ℱ 0363/22909. On the track leading to *Tauch Terminal Resort*. Set in a small garden, rooms have fan and cold-water bathrooms. More expensive ones have balconies and good views. **③–⑤**

Di Riboet (no phone). Basic but clean rooms just above the road opposite *Matahari Tulamben*

Most divers come to Tulamben on day-trips from elsewhere. However, there are **dive operations** attached to most of the accommodation places: check out *Tauch Terminal Resort*, *Mimpi Resort* and Dive Paradise Tulamben at *Paradise Palm Beach Bungalows* as well as the places along the main road, which all arrange local dives for certified divers and run courses. See p.65 for general notes about choosing a dive operator. Expect to pay around $50 for two dives at Tulamben, $55 for two dives at Amed or Jemeluk and $340–400 for a PADI open-water course. Snorkelling gear is also available for rent.

Operators arrange dives to other parts of Bali such as Menjangan (see p.401), Gili Tepekong and Gili Mimpang (see p.286) and Nusa Penida (see p.276), while *Tauch Terminal* offers all-in **dive safaris** incorporating several dive destinations in Bali and Lombok (from $300 for 3 days and 2 nights on Gili Air) and **liveaboard safaris** to further-flung locations from $1500 per person. They're considering introducing a dive package trip to Christmas Island; check their website for more. They also offer dive and accommodation packages, with unlimited diving in Tulamben including equipment rental.

Many places offer a variety of **languages** in addition to English, including several European languages and Japanese; at the time of writing, Deep Blue Studio (℡0363/22919, ⓦwww.subaqua.cz) was offering Czech, Slovak, Polish and Russian.

Dive sites

The **Liberty wreck** lies almost parallel to the beach, on a sandy slope about 30m offshore, and is encrusted with soft **coral**, gorgonians and hydrozoans plus a few hard corals, providing a wonderful habitat for around three hundred species of reef fish that live on the wreck and over a hundred species which visit from deeper water. A lot of the fish are very tame and often fed by divers, so they allow you to get close. The wreck is now pretty broken up and there are plenty of entrances letting you explore inside. Parts of the stern are only about 2m below the surface, making this a good snorkelling site too.

Although most divers come to Tulamben for the wreck, there are plenty of other excellent sites in the area; enough, in fact, to keep most divers happy for a week or more. The **Tulamben Drop-off**, sometimes called "The Wall", off the eastern end of the beach, comprises several underwater fingers of volcanic rock, which drop to 60m and are home to an enormous variety of fish, including unusual species such as comets, though it's also a good place for black coral bushes. Many divers rate this area at least as highly as the wreck itself – if not higher – although there can be more of a current to contend with. **Batu Kelebit** lies further east again and consists of two huge boulders with underwater coral-covered ridges nurturing a somewhat different but equally rewarding sea-life; it's possibly the best local site for the bigger creatures such as sharks, barracuda, jacks, mantas, molas and tuna. Back in the bay, the site known as **The River** or **The Slope** is actually a bowl lined with sand and rocks and is possibly the best place in the whole of Bali to see rare, although perhaps not large or dramatic, species.

Resort. Fine if you're not worried about frills or being near the beach. ❶
Emerald Tulamben Beach Hotel ℡0363/22925, ⓕ22928, ⓦwww.iijnet.or.jp/INC/BALI. An imposing, luxury place, 2km east of the village, popular with tour groups and offering excellent facilities, watersports and well-appointed rooms. There's a helicopter landing area, a brilliant swimming pool and a cable-car to transport guests around the

site. The operator Indonesian Cactus Divers is based here. ❽
Ganda Mayu ℡0363/22912. A clean place (with the Perama office attached) offering tiled bungalows with fans and cold-water bathrooms just above the main road: a reasonable budget choice. ❶–❷
Matahari Tulamben Resort ℡0363/22907, ⓕ22908. On a track that runs from *Café*

Tulamben to the coast at the eastern end of the village. There are two standards of rooms: clean, tiled fan rooms with cold-water bathrooms or well-furnished cottages with air-con and hot water near the beach, pool and sunbathing area. ❷–❻
Mimpi ☏0363/21642, ☏21939, @www.mimpi.com. Located about 500m east of the village, this is one of three Mimpi hotels in Bali. All rooms have air-con and hot water. Top-end cottages are gorgeous with great furnishings and comfortable sitting areas. Rooms at the bottom end are less good value: near the car park with small verandahs. Also has a dive centre offering courses and dives for experienced divers. ❽
Paradise Palm Beach Bungalows ☏0363/22910, ☏22917. Long-established bungalows with several standards of accommodation in the cosy compound – the more expensive having air-con and hot water – and a small restaurant overlooking the sea. ❷–❺

Puri Madha ☏0363/22921. The most westerly place, about 300m beyond the village and the beach, very near the *Liberty* wreck. Rooms are simple and tiled but there's a bit of a gap between the bungalows and the beach. This is a good place from which to watch the daily diving activity. There's a pleasant beachside restaurant. ❷
Tauch Terminal Resort ☏0363/22911, or contact in Kuta ☏0361/730200, ☏0361/730201, @www.tauch-terminal.com. Huge, gleaming, lively establishment that fronts a long section of the coast. Features large landscaped gardens, an attractive little pool and a very busy dive centre. The more expensive rooms are the best in the area with high ceilings, huge windows and lovely furnishings, although standard rooms with fan and cold-water bathrooms are less impressive, but also much cheaper. Accommodation and diving packages are also available; see box on p.311. ❺–❼

North of Tulamben

From Tulamben it's a long haul along the parched north coast to Singaraja (see p.342), featuring very little in the way of population centres, the lush, verdant landscape usually associated with Bali or anything spectacular in the way of coastal views. However there are fine views of the mountains inland, initially to Gunung Agung and then to the mountains of the Batur area. The land here supports relatively few people; cashew orchards are the most apparent produce. Heading on from Tulamben the villages of **Tembok**, **Sembirenteng** and **Bondalem** (see p.349) offer accommodation. From Bondalem a pretty although very steep back road leads to Kintamani (see p.323).

Travel details

Bemos and public buses

It's almost impossible to give the **frequency** with which bemos and public buses run, as they only depart when they have enough passengers to make the journey worthwhile. However, on the most popular routes, you should be able to count on getting a ride within the half-hour if you travel before noon; things quieten down in the afternoon and come to a standstill by around 5pm. **Journey times** also vary a great deal: the times given below are the minimum you can expect.

Only direct bemo and bus routes are listed; for longer journeys you'll have to go first to either Gianyar (see p.246) or to Denpasar (see p.89).
Amlapura to: Air Sanih (2hr); Batubulan (2hr); Candi Dasa (20min); Culik (45min); Gianyar (1hr 20min); Gilimanuk (4–5hr); Klungkung (1hr); Lovina (3hr 30min); Seraya (40min); Singaraja

(Penarukan terminal; 3hr); Tirtagangga (20min); Tulamben (1hr); Ujung (20min).
Bangli to: Denpasar (Batubulan terminal; 1hr 30min); Gianyar (20min); Singaraja (Penarukan terminal; 2hr 15min).
Candi Dasa to: Amlapura (20min); Denpasar (Batubulan terminal; 2hr); Gianyar (1hr); Klungkung (40min); Padang Bai (20min).
Culik to: Aas (1hr 30min); Air Sanih (1hr 30min); Amed (20min); Amlapura (45min); Bunutan (45min); Jemeluk (30min); Lipah Beach (1hr); Lovina (2hr 30min); Selang (1hr 15min); Singaraja (Penarukan terminal; 2hr 30min).
Gianyar to: Amlapura (1hr 20min); Bangli (20min); Batur (40min); Blahbatuh (30min); Candi Dasa (1hr); Denpasar (Batubulan terminal; 1hr); Klungkung (20min); Ubud (20min).
Klungkung to: Amlapura (1hr); Besakih (45min); Candi Dasa (40min); Denpasar (Batubulan terminal;

1hr 20min); Gianyar (20min); Rendang (30min).
Padang Bai to: Amlapura (40min); Candi Dasa
(20min); Gilimanuk (3–4hr); Klungkung (20min).
Tirtagangga to: Air Sanih (2hr); Culik (30min);
Amlapura (20min); Lovina (3hr); Singaraja (2hr
30min); Tulamben (1hr).
Tulamben to: Air Sanih (1hr); Culik (30min);
Amlapura (1hr); Lovina (2hr 30min); Singaraja
(2hr).

Perama shuttle buses

STO = overnight stopover is needed
Candi Dasa to: Air Sanih (daily; 2hr–2hr 30min);
Bangsal (daily; 6hr–6hr 30min); Bedugul (2 daily;
STO); Kintamani (daily; 3hr 15min); Kuta/Ngurah
Rai Airport (3 daily; 3hr); Kuta, Lombok (2 daily;
STO); Lovina (2 daily; 3hr–3hr 30min); Mataram (2
daily; 5hr–5hr 30min); Nusa Lembongan (2 daily;
STO); Padang Bai (3 daily; 30min); Sanur (3 daily;
2hr–2hr 30min); Senggigi (2 daily; 5hr
30min–6hr); Tetebatu (2 daily; STO); Tirtagangga
(daily; 30min); Tulamben (daily; 1hr 30min); Ubud
(3 daily; 1hr 30min–2hr).
Nusa Lembongan to: Air Sanih (daily; 6hr–6hr
30min); Bangsal (daily; STO); Bedugul (daily; STO);
Candi Dasa (daily; 3hr); Kintamani (daily; 4hr);
Kuta/Ngurah Rai Airport (daily; 2hr 30min–3hr);
Kuta, Lombok (daily; STO); Lovina (daily; 5hr);
Mataram (daily; 9hr); Padang Bai (daily; 3hr
30min); Senggigi (daily; 9hr); Tetebatu (daily; STO);
Tirtagangga (daily; 5hr), Tulamben (daily; 5hr
30min–6hr).
Padang Bai to: Air Sanih (daily; 2hr 30min–3hr);
Bangsal (daily; 5hr 30min–6hr); Bedugul (2 daily;
STO); Candi Dasa (3 daily; 30min); Kintamani
(daily; 2hr 45min); Kuta/Ngurah Rai Airport (3 daily;
2hr 30min); Kuta, Lombok (2 daily; STO); Lovina (2
daily; 2hr 30min–3hr); Mataram (2 daily; 4hr

30min–5hr); Nusa Lembongan (2 daily; STO);
Sanur (3 daily; 1hr 30min–2hr); Senggigi (2 daily;
5hr–5hr 30min); Tetebatu (2 daily; STO);
Tirtagangga (daily; 1hr); Tulamben (daily; 2hr);
Ubud (3 daily; 1hr–1hr 30min).
Tirtagangga to: Air Sanih (daily; 2hr); Bangsal
(daily; STO); Bedugul (daily; STO); Candi Dasa
(daily; 30min); Kintamani (daily; STO); Kuta/Ngurah
Rai Airport (daily; 4hr); Kuta, Lombok (daily; STO);
Lovina (daily; 2hr 30min); Mataram (daily; 6hr–6hr
30min); Padang Bai (daily; 2hr); Sanur (daily;
4hr–4hr 30min); Senggigi (daily; 7hr 30min–8hr
30min); Tetebatu (daily; STO); Tulamben (daily;
1hr); Ubud (daily; 2hr 30min).
Tulamben to: Air Sanih (daily; 1hr); Bangsal (daily;
STO); Bedugul (daily; STO); Candi Dasa (daily; 1hr
30min); Kintamani (daily; STO); Kuta/Ngurah Rai
airport (daily; 5hr); Kuta, Lombok (daily; STO);
Lovina (daily; 1hr 30min); Mataram (daily; 7–8hr);
Padang Bai (daily; 2hr); Sanur (daily; 4hr–4hr
30min); Senggigi (daily; 7–8hr); Tetebatu (daily;
STO); Tirtagangga (daily; 1hr); Ubud (daily; 3hr–3hr
30min).

Boats

Jungutbatu (Nusa Lembongan) to: Benoa (4
weekly; 1hr); Gili Meno (4 weekly; 2hr 30min);
Kusamba (daily; 1–2hr); Sanur (daily; 1–2hr);
Senggigi (4 weekly; 2hr); Toyapakeh (daily; 45min).
Kusamba to: Nusa Lembongan (daily; 1–2hr);
Nusa Penida (daily; 1–2hr).
Padang Bai to: Benoa (daily; 1hr); Lembar
(Lombok; slow ferry, every 1hr 30min; 4–5hr; fast
boat, daily; 1hr 30min); Nusa Penida (daily; 1hr).
Sampalan (Nusa Penida) to: Kusamba (daily;
1–2hr); Padang Bai (daily; 1hr).
Toyapakeh (Nusa Penida) to: Jungutbatu (daily;
45min); Kusamba (daily; 1–2hr).

North Bali and the central volcanoes

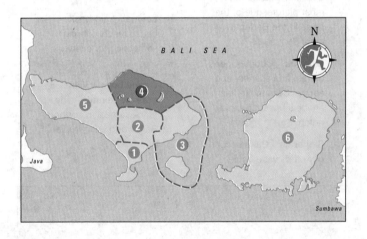

CHAPTER 4

Highlights

* **Gunung Batur** – Volcano set amidst incredibly dramatic scenery; wonderful views from the summit at sunrise or as part of the panorama from Penelokan. See p.319

* **Lake Tamblingan** – The quietest, smallest and most picturesque of the lakes in the Bedugul area. See p.339

* **Munduk** – Cool temperatures, fine scenery and easy access make this an ideal base for exploration. See p.340

* **Singaraja** – Bali's second city offers wide boulevards, a stimulating ethnic mix and down-to-earth street life. See p.342

* **Pura Meduwe Karang** – The best example of the exuberant carving, typical of northern temples. See p.348

* **Lovina** – Laid-back beach resort offering something for everyone. See p.350

* **Damai Lovina Villas gourmet dinner** – The fanciest meal in northern Bali, worth every rupiah. See p.361

North Bali and the central volcanoes

Heading into north Bali from the humid and crowded southern plains and foothills, you initially enter another world, with a slower pace, cooler climate and hugely varied countryside. The centre of the island is occupied by the awesome volcanic masses of the Batur and Bedugul areas, where dramatic mountain ranges shelter crater lakes, and small, peaceful villages line their shores. With few peaks rising above 2000m, the mountains don't rival Gunung Agung in stature, but their accessibility and beauty are unbeatable. Most people come to the Batur area either on a day-trip to gaze at the crater panorama, or to stay down by the lake and trek up Gunung Batur, the most climbed peak in Bali, which is still periodically sending up puffs of smoke and plumes of flame since it started its most recent period of activity in 1994. The Bedugul area offers more lakes, mountains and forests, but on a smaller scale, and is regularly besieged by tour groups swarming to the stunning lakeside temple of Pura Ulun Danu. (The third of Bali's central mountain areas, Batukau, is described on p.383, as access is via routes covered in Chapter 5.)

Once through the mountain ranges, the dry northern **coast** is harsh and rugged as the mountains drop steeply to the coastal plain. In the east of the region, villages and roads appear squeezed between shore and mountains while, over in the west, you'll find rolling foothills, attractive river valleys and typical Balinese rice terraces. Many visitors, seeking to avoid the excesses of Kuta, head straight for the coastal resort of **Lovina** which, despite its black sand, has rapidly grown in popularity so that it's now the largest resort outside the Kuta–Legian–Seminyak conurbation. Lovina is still developing fast, but somehow manages to retain a laid-back air: it's a great place to spend a few days by the sea or to use as a base for exploring the north and centre of the island.

For hundreds of years, the north was the part of the island most open to foreign influence, as Chinese and Muslim traders plied their wares through the port of **Singaraja**. The north was the first area to be subdued by the Dutch, almost half a century before the south, and Singaraja was their administrative capital right up until World War II. After 1924 and the start of the weekly KPM steamship service from Java, a steady stream of tourists and longer-term visitors began to arrive through Singaraja, initially using the Dutch government rest houses, but gradually switching to hotels in Denpasar and Kintamani. When

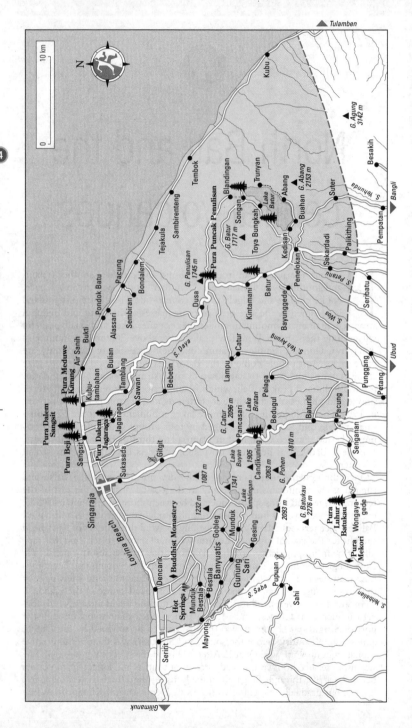

▲ *Tulamben*

▼ Gilimanuk

▲ *Bangli*

▶ *Ubud*

N

10 km

0

4

G. Agung
3142 m

Besakih

Suter

G. Abang
2153 m

Kubu

Trunyan

Abang

Blandingan

Buahan

Songan

*Lake
Batur*

G. Batur
1717 m

Kedisan

Pura Puncak Penulisan

Toya Bungkah

Penelokan

Sekardadi

Palikthing

Pempatan

Serbatu

Tembok

Sambirenteng

Tejakula

G. Penulisan
1745 m

Batur

Kintamani

Bayunggede

Pacung

Dusa

Bondalem

Pondok Batu

Alassari

Sembiran

Bukti

Air Sanih

Kubu-
tambahan

Bulian

Tamblang

Sawan

Catur

Lampu

Pelaga

Punggang

Petang

S. Petanu

S. Yehuda

S. Wos

S. Ayung

S. Yeh Ayung

S. Daya

Bebetin

Pura Meduwe
Karang

Pura Dalem Sangsit

Pura Beji

Pura Dalem
Jagaraga

Jagaraga

Sukasada

Sangsit

Gitgit

G. Catur
2096 m

Pancasari

*Lake
Bratan*

Bedugul

Baturiti

Pacung

Senganan

Singaraja

Lovina Beach

1232 m

1087 m

*Lake
Buyan*

1905

*Lake
Tamblingan*

1341

Candikuning

2063 m
G. Pohen

1810 m

2033 m

G. Batukau
2276 m

Pura Luhur
Batukau

Wongaya-
gede

Pura
Mekori

S. Kebbalan

Buddhist Monastery

Dencarik

Munduk

Bestala

Banyuatis

Gobleg

Munduk

Gunung
Sari

Gesing

Pupuan

Sahi

S. Saba

Hot
Springs

Bestala

Mayong

Seririt

the first commercial hotels opened in Kuta in the 1930s, and Ngurah Rai Airport was completed in 1969, the pendulum swung away from the north, leaving it to become a quiet tourist backwater. Today Singaraja, administrative capital of Buleleng district, is a bustling, modern city and, being a transport hub, is impossible to avoid. The busy Singaraja–Gilimanuk road passes through Lovina carrying traffic to Java, and the three main southbound roads through the mountains – from Seririt via Pupuan, Singaraja via Bedugul, and Kubutambahan via Kintamani – are all heavily used by trucks.

The exuberant and distinctive **temple carvings** and **sculptures** of the north depict bicycle-riding, car-driving Dutch invaders and ordinary Balinese folk alongside the usual legendary religious figures. The best-known temples of the area – **Kubutambahan**, **Jagaraga** and **Sangsit** – offer an accessible and light-hearted interlude, in pleasant contrast to the awesome and somewhat over-powering temple experiences further south. Close to Lovina, the sole **Buddhist** temple on the island is at Banjar and several important temples dedicated to the goddess of the lake are the focus for pilgrimages to the central volcanoes by farmers throughout the lowlands. In Singaraja, the **Gedong Kirtya** is the only *lontar* manuscript library in the world and, although pretty esoteric, is a good way to while away an hour or so in the city.

Transport practicalities

With good **bus** links from Java, Denpasar and Amlapura and **bemo** connections within the area, most of the sights in the north are fairly easy to get to on public transport, although with your own vehicle you'll be able to explore the maze of quiet inland roads and reach some of the less popular places such as Lake Tamblingan and Munduk. A good range of accommodation throughout the region makes this an ideal touring area.

Batur and Bedugul

The lakes within the ancient volcanic craters of the **Batur** and **Bedugul** areas are the source of water for a vast area of agricultural land and, as home to the goddess of the lake, are pivotal to religious belief and practice on the island. The cool mountain air, the variety of walks and the good transport services have long made this region a favourite with local and foreign day-trippers and led to the more recent growth of tourist facilities for the increasing numbers now staying here longer.

Gunung Batur and Lake Batur

The **Batur** area was formed thirty thousand years ago by the eruption of a gigantic volcano. Confusingly, the entire area is sometimes referred to as **Kintamani**, although this is the name of just one of several villages dotted along the rim of the ancient crater. Another group of villages is situated around **Lake Batur** at the bottom of the crater: **Toya Bungkah** is the start of the main route up Gunung Batur and the chief accommodation centre, although **Kedisan** offers a couple of options, and is the access point for boat trips across the lake to the Bali Aga village of **Trunyan**. Around on the southern shore of the lake, **Buahan** is the quietest spot of all. **Songan**, at the furthest end of the lake, has only one place to stay but is convenient for walks up to the crater rim.

The highest points on the rim are **Gunung Abang** (2153m) on the eastern side, the third highest mountain in Bali, and **Gunung Penulisan** (1745m) on the northwest corner, with Pura Puncak Penulisan perched on its summit. Rising from the floor of the main crater, **Gunung Batur** (1717m) is an active volcano with four craters of its own. Every morning, trekkers set off before dawn to climb the peak and watch the sunrise from the top, where tiny warung have sprung up to cater for them.

Sadly, the Batur area has developed a reputation among travellers for hassles, over-charging and unfriendliness. While it doesn't compare in either scale or grandeur with Indonesia's other famous volcanic crater, Gunung Bromo in East Java, the dramatic contrast between Batur and the rest of Bali makes it well worth taking a deep breath, keeping a hold on your patience and heading upwards for at least a glimpse of its remarkable scenery.

The crater rim

Spread out along the road that follows the rim of the crater for 11km, the villages of **Penelokan**, **Batur** and **Kintamani** almost merge with each other. The road itself is one of the main routes across the mountains between north and south coasts, so, while public transport along the rim and to towns beyond is frequent, and the views spectacular, this isn't a road for a quiet stroll. If you're planning to stay up here, be aware that the mist and sometimes rain that roll in and obscure the view in late afternoon bring a creeping dampness, and the nights are extremely chilly; at the very least, you'll need a good sweater.

There's an **admission charge** for visiting the crater area, of Rp4000 per person (Rp1000 for a car or motorbike). The ticket offices are just south of Penelokan on the road from Bangli, before the final few yards up to the crater rim, and at the junction of the road from Ubud and the rim road. In practice, collection of the money appears rather haphazard, with rental cars and tour buses the main targets.

Practicalities

Getting to the rim is straightforward from any direction, with **buses** running about every half-hour until mid-afternoon between Singaraja (Penarukan terminal) and Denpasar (Batubulan terminal), via Gianyar and Bangli. If you're coming from Tulamben or Tejakula on the northeast coast, you can pick up the bus from Singaraja at the junction at Kubutambahan, from where Kintamani is 40km away. The route from Ubud is served by brown (Kintamani) **bemos**, and the roads via Suter, Tampaksiring and Payangan are good and easy to drive on.

Perama operates daily **tourist shuttle buses** to the area from both north and south Bali, stopping at the *Gunung Sari* restaurant – inconveniently positioned midway between Kintamani and Penelokan (although the driver should be able to drop you off anywhere along the crater rim).

Penelokan is included in many of the **day-trips** on offer at the major resorts, although this usually encompasses only a quick stop to admire the view from the crater rim amid serious hassle from hawkers. Air Bali Helicopters (℡0361/766582, ℻766581, ⓦwww.airbali.com) operates a ten-minute **helicopter volcano flight** (US$50), which takes off from the helipad at *Gunawan*

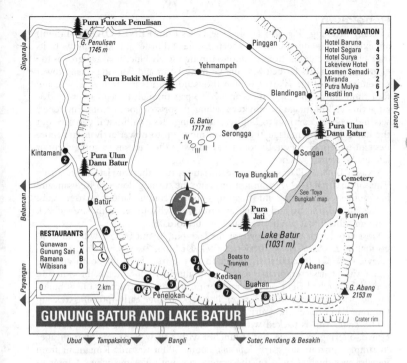

GUNUNG BATUR AND LAKE BATUR

Restaurant (☎0366/51050), where you can also book flights, and does a figure-of-eight around and between Gunung Batur's main craters, giving an amazing panorama of the whole area.

The **post office** and **phone office** are close together just off the main road 2km north of Penelokan. There are usually several places to **change money** along the road, but rates are poor and during times when tourist numbers are low they tend to cease trading. You'd be well advised to take plenty of cash.

Eruptions at Gunung Batur

Gunung Batur has **erupted** more than twenty times since 1800. In 1917, a major eruption killed over a thousand people, but the lava flow curiously stopped just outside the temple of Batur village, then situated in the crater on the western side of the lake. Considering this a good omen, the population remained in the village until August 3, 1926, when another eruption (which formed the volcano's main crater of today, Batur I) completely engulfed the village and the temple. Such was the faith of the people of Batur that the Dutch had to evacuate some of them forcibly up onto the crater rim.

The longest-lasting eruption took place in September 1963, a few months after the massive explosion of Gunung Agung (see p.268). Although the force was considerably less than that of Agung, the eruption continued until May 1964. At Yehmampeh, on the road around the base of the mountain, you'll see lava flows from the March 1974 eruption. The most recent crater, Batur IV, was formed during the eruption which started on August 7, 1994, and which continues periodically. It's certainly a bit startling to see clouds of smoke emerging skywards but local belief is that it's better if Batur lets off a little steam regularly rather than saving it all up for a major blow.

Penelokan

Literally meaning "Place to Look", the views from **PENELOKAN** (1450m) are excellent, a panorama of unexpected scale and majesty. Lake Batur, with its ever-changing colours, from turquoise through steely blue to savage grey as the clouds roll over, lies far below, while Gunung Batur and Gunung Abang tower on either side of the lake. Over two thousand tourists in the low season, and four thousand in the high, are estimated to pass through Penelokan every day, attracting an entourage of **hawkers** selling all sorts of goods, from fruit, chess sets and wooden carvings to T-shirts and sarongs. It's a pain but if you give out the correct body-language, they'll soon move on to newer arrivals and more hesitant targets. However, the only way to avoid the circus is to come early or late in the day, or stay overnight.

Yayasan Bintang Danu, a local organization, runs the **tourist office** (daily 9am–3pm; ℡0366/51730), almost opposite the turning down to Kedisan, and has noticeboards giving information about accommodation, charter rates, routes up the volcano and leaflets and maps on what to see in the area (check with an official that the noticeboards are up to date).

Most people opt **to stay** down at the lake but, if your budget will run to it, go for the *Lakeview Hotel* (℡0366/51394, ℻51464, ⓦwww.indo.com/hotels/lakeview; ❺–❻), located at the junction of the road from the south and the crater rim: it has comfortable rooms with attached hot-water bathrooms and verandahs perched right on the crater's rim (they're constructing a new building, so prices may rise in the future). They also arrange early-morning treks up Gunung Batur to see the sunrise.

The crater rim is packed with plush **restaurants** catering for the daytime crowd, offering expensive buffet lunches with a view. For something cheaper in simpler surroundings, try *Ramana*, about 300m towards Kintamani from Penelokan, which is right on the crater's rim with glorious views. Closer to Penelokan, on the opposite side of the road, *Wibisana* is also good value.

Climbing Gunung Abang

Thickly forested and lacking sweeping panoramic views, the climb up **Gunung Abang** (Red Mountain), is far less popular and rewarding than the Batur climb. Allow a couple of hours to get to the top from the start of the footpath, and be sure to take enough food and water and tell somebody responsible where you're going. To arrange a **guide**, enquire at the trekking agencies, Yayasan Bintang Danu, the losmen *Miranda* in Kintamani or the Association of Mount Batur Trekking Guides in Toya Bungkah (see box p.329).

The route starts on the Suter road that heads east around the rim from Penelokan, from just below the *Lakeview Hotel* (there are no public bemos along here). Approximately 4km from Penelokan, the road to Suter turns abruptly south away from the crater rim, but a rough track continues along the edge. Follow the track for a further 2km, passing **Pura Munggu** in the middle of the forest. The track eventually turns away from the crater rim; at this point take the footpath straight in front of you that heads up the mountain. You'll pass the small forest temple, **Pura Manu Kaya**, about halfway, reaching **Pura Puncak Tuluk Biyu**, enclosed by trees, at the summit.

A track continues down the other side of Gunung Abang, eventually bringing you to just above Songan (see p.328) on the far side of the crater. However, this path is much longer than the one from the Suter side and is used even less; you definitely need a guide to attempt it.

Pura Ulun Danu Batur

About 4km north of Penelokan, four temples stand in a row along the crater's rim. The most northerly – and most imposing – is **Pura Ulun Danu Batur**, the second most important temple on the island after the Besakih complex, and one of the highly venerated *kayangan jagat* (directional temples): this one protects Bali from the north. It's a fascinating place to visit at any time as there are usually pilgrims making offerings or praying here; the mist that frequently shrouds the area adds to the atmosphere, with grand structures looming out of the cloud. The eleven-day *odalan* festival (see p.511) is particularly spectacular and attended by people from all over the island.

The original temple was located down in the crater until the 1926 eruption of Gunung Batur destroyed the whole of Batur village. Shrines and relics that could be saved were taken up onto the crater rim and the village and temple were rebuilt. The present structures are modern (inaugurated in 1935), and construction is still under way with a total of three hundred shrines planned. The temple honours **Ida Batara Dewi Ulun Danu**, the goddess of the crater lake, who controls the water for the irrigation systems throughout the island and shares dominion of Bali with the god of Gunung Agung. The reverence in which the goddess is held is underlined by a manuscript in the temple which proclaims, "Because the Goddess makes the waters flow, those who do not follow her laws may not possess her rice terraces."

The temple is very different from any other in Bali in several respects. A virgin priestess selects 24 boys who will serve the goddess as **priests** in the temple for life. The high priest, Jero Gde or Sanglingan, is selected by the virgin priestess, and is believed to be the earthly representative of the goddess of the lake. His days are spent making offerings to her on behalf of the many visiting pilgrims, and at night he dreams under her guidance. Any farmers or *subak* with plans that may affect the flow of the water in their area, or who are in conflict with others about irrigation systems, come to confer with the Jero Gde, whose word is accepted as final.

With two extra courtyards to the right of the traditional outer, middle and inner ones, Pura Ulun Danu Batur is overwhelming for most visitors, simply because of the sheer number of shrines. Most significant is the **eleven-roofed meru** in the inner courtyard, dedicated both to Dewi Danu, the goddess of the lake, and to the god of Gunung Agung. On the left side of the middle courtyard is a rather unusual **shrine**, tended by the local Chinese community. Dedicated to Ratu Gde Subandar, the great lord harbourmaster and storekeeper for the gods, it's likely that this image dates back to precolonial times when each king had a harbourmaster or trading master who was often Chinese. Most of the other shrines are either dedicated to specific gods or honour the deified ancestors of particular ruling houses or clans. The *kulkul* tower in the outer courtyard to the left houses a drum that is beaten 45 times each morning to honour the 45 deities worshipped in the temple.

Kintamani

Consisting almost entirely of concrete buildings with rusty corrugated iron roofs, **KINTAMANI**, 2km north of Pura Ulun Danu, isn't particularly appealing, and is too far north along the rim of the crater for the best views of Lake Batur. It's famous for its breed of furry dogs, and the huge outdoor market held every three days.

Penelokan or the villages in the crater beside the lake (see below) are better choices **to stay**, although Kintamani has the only budget accommodation on the rim – *Miranda* (☏0366/52022; ❷), about 100m north of the market on the left; all bemos and pick-ups plying between Kintamani and Penelokan pass the door. The rooms are variable (you should look at several before choosing) but all have attached mandi and squat toilet. The lounge cheers up when there are a few people staying and the open fire is lit. The owner, Made Senter, also works as a **tour guide**, taking parties from the losmen down into the crater and up Gunung Batur. He charges Rp150,000 per person (in a group up to four) including transport to and from the start of the climb, leaving at 3am to get to the top for sunrise. The price is the same for treks up Gunung Abang (see p.322), and it's US$100 for a group of up to four people to climb Gunung Agung (see p.269).

Pura Puncak Penulisan

About 5km north of Kintamani on the road towards Singaraja, in the village of Sukawana, **Pura Puncak Penulisan**, also known as Pura Tegeh Koripan, built on the summit of Gunung Penulisan, is the highest temple on Bali and one of the most ancient, being referred to in ninth-century inscriptions. Its antiquity is confirmed by its layout, on a series of rising terraces. The temple grounds are peaceful and well cared for, although the views from the top are somewhat marred by television masts. There's an admission fee of Rp1000.

It's a climb of 333 concrete steps from the road to the top temple, **Pura Panarajon**, dedicated to Sanghyang Grinatha, a manifestation of Siwa, and god of the mountains. On this top terrace, *bale* shelter various shrines and an array of ancient *lingga* and worn statues from the eleventh to thirteenth centuries, which pre-date the Majapahit invasion of the island. These include a wedding portrait widely believed to portray the marriage of King Udayana and Queen Mahendratta, possible source of the Rangda myth (see box on p.249). Some of the statues appear to have Chinese features although a large number are headless; many were apparently destroyed in 1965 during the civil strife between government forces and those accused of being Communists.

Lake Batur

Home to Dewi Danu, the goddess of the crater lake, **Lake Batur** is especially sacred to the Balinese. Although it has no river outlets, the waters from the lake, generated by eleven springs, are believed to percolate through the earth and reappear as springs in other parts of the island. Situated 500m below the crater rim, this is the largest lake in Bali, 8km long and 3km wide, and one of the most glorious: the villages dotted around its shores are referred to as *bintang danu* (stars of the lake). See p.321 for a **map** of the area.

The road to the lakeside, served by **public bemos**, leaves the crater rim at Penelokan. Bemos, in theory, go as far as Songan on the western side of the lake and Abang on the eastern side, but you'll have to bargain hard to get reasonable fares beyond Toya Bungkah and Buahan. Currently, the tourist fare to Toya Bungkah or Songan is Rp5000 from Penelokan (Rp10,000 from the Perama bus drop-off at *Gunung Sari* restaurant); to Kedisan or Buahan it's Rp3000 from Penelokan (Rp8000 from the *Gunung Sari*).

It's worth noting that however gorgeous and peaceful the lake and the nearby area appears from the crater rim at Penelokan, once you're down on the western shores of the lake, peace is sadly lacking. Around on the western side of Gunung Batur there is a large quarry; huge, **noisy** convoys of trucks ferrying the volcanic stone *paras* use the road down from the crater rim and on through Kedisan, Toya Bungkah and Songan from early morning until night-

△ Pura Ulun Danu Bratan

fall. Barely a minute passes without a truck on the road. To avoid the noise consider staying in Buahan, although this is further from Gunung Batur and so less convenient if you're trekking.

In addition to noise, the hassles of the lake area can make a visit far more stressful than the stunning scenery deserves. A lot of visitors have negative experiences and, in some cases, suffer intimidation and extortion. Most people stay the minimum amount of time needed to complete their trek.

If you **arrive by car**, there's huge pressure on you to pay someone to "look after" your vehicle while you climb – sometimes followed up by threats of damage to the car if you decline. The best advice is to leave vehicles in the care of staff at a hotel you've stayed at or restaurant where you've eaten, or to take a driver with the car and ask him to stay with it while you trek.

Kedisan

At the bottom of the steep descent, 3km from Penelokan, the road splits in the southernmost lakeside village of **KEDISAN**: the right fork leads to the jetty for boats to Trunyan and continues on to the villages of Buahan and Abang; the left fork leads to Toya Bungkah and Songan.

In Kedisan there are a couple of **homestays**. A few hundred metres from the junction, towards Toya Bungkah, *Hotel Segara* (℡0366/51136, ℱ51212; ❷–❸) has a huge variety of accommodation, with hot water and TV in the most expensive rooms and cold-water bathrooms attached to the cheaper ones – all have small sitting areas outside although they overlook a car park. The hotel offers half-price pick-ups from Penelokan (Rp10,000 per car), Kuta (Rp80,000 per car), Lovina or Ubud (Rp50,000 per car); this applies even if guests stay for just one night, although it's advisable to check the details of the transport offer when you phone to arrange it. Next door, *Hotel Surya* (℡0366/51378; ❷–❸) also has clean rooms, some with cold water only, some with hot. Many of the balconies here have lovely views. They offer a free pick-up service from local areas plus Ubud, Bangli, Besakih, Gianyar and Klungkung, plus discounted pick-ups from Kuta, Sanur, Air Sanih and Lovina (all Rp100,000 per car). Again this offer applies even if guests stay for just one night, but you should check the details when you phone ahead.

Turning right at the bottom of the road from Penelokan brings you to the quietest part of the lake: quarry trucks don't come along here. Some 300m from the junction, *Putra Mulya* (℡0366/51754; ❶) has simple, comfortable tiled rooms; ask for Made Darsana, as the older folk don't speak English. About 200m further on, *Losmen Semadi* (℡0366/51819; ❷) is small with basic rooms; those at the front have a pleasant view of the lake through the foliage.

Toya Bungkah and around

TOYA BUNGKAH, 8km from Penelokan, is the accommodation centre of the lakeside area and the main starting-point for climbs up Gunung Batur.

About 4km before Toya Bungkah, **Pura Jati**, dedicated to the god Wisnu, has some finely decorated shrines and carved entrance gates. There are plans to build a wall within the lake, surrounding the temple area, to form a holy bathing place, as it's here that Magening, one of the eleven springs within the lake, rises. Every five years, the festival of Bakti Pekelem takes place, involving considerable sacrifice of animals to Dewi Danu through ritual drowning in the lake.

Toya Bungkah's stylish **hot springs**, Tirta Sanjiwani (daily 8am–5pm) were rebuilt in 1997 amidst considerable controversy as they moved stratospherically upmarket. They look extremely good, with a cold-water swimming pool and smaller hot-water pools ($5 for both) and private jacuzzis ($20), but the prices

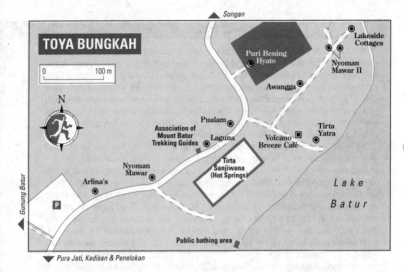

Songan

TOYA BUNGKAH

0   100 m

N

Gunung Batur

Lakeside Cottages

Puri Bening Hyato

Nyoman Mawar II

Awangga

Pualam

Association of Mount Batur Trekking Guides

Laguna

Tirta Yatra

Volcano Breeze Café

Tirta Sanjiwana (Hot Springs)

Nyoman Mawar

Arlina's

P

Lake Batur

Public bathing area

▼ Pura Jati, Kedisan & Penelokan

mean they've moved beyond the reach of many of the backpackers who are the mainstay of the local economy. Traditionally, the springs here, known as Tirta Bungkah (the Holy Waters of the Mountain), form a trinity along with Tirta Empul (the Holy Waters of the Plains) at Tampaksiring and Tirta Selukat (the Holy Waters of the Sea) at Medahan in Gianyar. Pilgrims, especially women in early pregnancy and anyone who has recovered from a long illness, bathe in each of the three waters in turn.

In normal circumstances you can **change money** and travellers' cheques at several places in the village, although rates aren't great. There's a 24-hour **wartel** at the start of Toya Bungkah, and *Joy* **internet** café is nearby.

Accommodation

There are plenty of **accommodation** options lining the road in Toya Bungkah, with a few more down by the lakeside. Given the perpetual daytime noise from the trucks, there's something to be said for getting away from the road. The most expensive hotel is the featureless multistorey *Puri Bening Hayato* but most of the accommodation is much simpler and cheaper.

Arlina's ☎0366/51165. A friendly, popular set-up at the southern end of town, with clean rooms, small verandahs and some rooms with hot water. ④–⑤

Awangga No phone. A newer, quiet place on the road down to the lake with simple accommodation, all with good verandahs. ①

Laguna ☎0366/51297. Simple, good-quality place set back from the road in the middle of the village. ②

Lakeside Cottages ☎0366/51249, ℻51250. Aptly named place, with three standards of room, from large cottages with good verandahs, lake view, hot water and TV, to cheaper, cold-water rooms further from the lake. ③–⑥

Nyoman Mawar *(Under the Volcano)*
☎0366/51166. Located in the village, with clean, good-value rooms. Cold-water bathrooms only. ①

Nyoman Mawar II *(Under the Volcano II)*
☎0366/52508. Some bungalows close to the lake with great views and some in a small garden further away; all are simple and adequate, with cold water only. ①

Pualam ☎0366/52024. Quiet losmen, close to the hot springs, with clean, good-quality rooms set around a pleasant garden. ①

Puri Bening Hyato ☎0366/51234, ℻51248, ⓦwww.indo.com/hotels/puribening. Enormous, ostentatious place offering poor value at the bottom end with cold water only; at least the more expensive rooms have hot water. ⑤–⑦

Tirta Yatra No phone. A small establishment with extremely cheap, basic rooms and unenticing bathrooms. The position right down on the lakeside is excellent. ①

Climbing Gunung Batur

With a choice of four main craters and a variety of access points, there are several ways to approach **climbing Gunung Batur**. In your own or chartered transport, the easiest way to get to the top is to drive to **Serongga**, up a signed turning off the Yehmampeh road, west of Songan. From the car park here, it's a climb of thirty minutes to an hour to the largest and highest crater, **Batur I** – not particularly deep and now grassed over, with a few alpine flowers here and there. Steam holes just below the crater rim confirm that this volcano is far from extinct (they're useful, though, for cooking eggs and bananas for a summit breakfast!).

The most common **route** up to Batur I for those without their own transport – and who are reasonably fit – is from either Toya Bungkah or Pura Jati. If you're staying at Kedisan you can either start your climb from there or go by road around to the more well-trodden paths. The path from Pura Jati is shadeless and largely across old lava fields, while about half of the ascent from Toya Bungkah is in the man-made eucalyptus forest planted to try to stabilize the slopes. From Toya Bungkah, numerous paths head up through the forest (one starts just south of the car park near *Arlina's*); after about an hour you'll come out onto the bare slope of the mountain, from where you can follow the paths that head up to the tiny warung perched way up on the crater rim on the skyline. This is the steep bit, often slippery with black volcanic sand. Allow two to three hours to get to the top from Toya Bungkah or Pura Jati, and about half that time to get back down.

A **medium-length trek** involves climbing to Batur I, walking around the rim and then descending by another route. The **long-trek** option (about 8hr in total) involves climbing up to Batur I, walking around the rim to the western side, descending to the rim of crater II and then to the rim of crater III. From here, the descent is to Toya Bungkah or Yehmampeh.

Practicalities

Climbing Batur is best done in the **dry season** (April–Oct). The path becomes extremely unpleasant in the wet, and when clouds engulf the summit there's nothing to see anyway. However, the wet season doesn't bring unrelenting rain, and you might hit a dry few days – more likely at the beginning and end of the rains than in the middle.

In **daylight**, you don't need a guide to find the way if you're just intending to climb up to Batur I from Toya Bungkah or Pura Jati. For the longer treks or the less well-trodden paths, you do need a guide: routes are trickier and harder to find – and it's important to stay away from the most active parts of the volcano. Fewer people climb during the day because of the heat, and the chance that the view from the top may be clouded over.

Most people decide to climb **in the dark** to reach the top for dawn: the view over the lake as the sun rises behind Gunung Abang and Gunung Rinjani on Lombok is definitely worth the effort, and gets progressively less dramatic during the day. You'll

Eating and drinking

Many losmen have inexpensive **restaurants** serving a good range of Western and Indo-Chinese options and freshwater fish from the lake. *Arlina's* is good-value (main courses Rp5000–15,000) and offers a wide choice and the liveliest surroundings, while the *Volcano Breeze Café* on the track down to the lake is a quiet spot with an effective sound system and mellow music.

Songan and the volcano road

At the northern end of the lake, 12km from Penelokan and 4km beyond Toya Bungkah, the village of **SONGAN** is a thriving and extensive community of need to leave early (by 4–5am), and a guide is a very good idea as it's easy to get lost in the forest in the dark.

Anyone who wants to climb Batur is under intense pressure to engage a local guide. These are now organized into the **Association of Mount Batur Trekking Guides** (⊕0366/52362, ℮volcanotrekk@hotmail.com), known locally as "the Organization", which has one office in Toya Bungkah and another on the road near-by at Pura Jati. The price for the short climb up Batur to see the sunrise is fixed at a rather steep Rp300,000 per guide for a maximum of four people, with higher prices for the longer climbs. Despite recent assurances that prices have been cut by government order, nothing seems to have changed on the ground. The situation in Batur strikes many visitors, with justification, as being confused, confusing and likely to cost them a lot of money.

Trekking and tour agencies

If you prefer not to deal directly with the Association of Mount Batur Trekking Guides, or if you just want to check out the details you've had from them, you can get **information** about the Gunung Batur area and **organized trekking services** from three companies in Toya Bungkah: Roijaya Wisata (⊕0366/51249, ℉51250, Ⓦwww.balitrekking.com), which has an office at *Lakeside Cottages* and another at the start of Toya Bungkah; Bali Sunrise 2001, at the *Volcano Breeze Café* (⊕0366/51824, Ⓦwww.balisunrise2001.com); and Arlina's (⊕0366/51165). They use guides from the Association of Mount Batur Trekking Guides, but are more used to working with tourists (which can sometimes make the whole process easier) – although you do end up paying more than if you went through the Association. All the agencies charge a fairly standard US$20 per person for the short climb to see the sunrise, or $25 for the medium trek; prices vary for the long trek ($30–38). There are minimum numbers required – sometimes two people, sometimes four. Bali Sunrise 2001 can also arrange pick-ups for Batur treks in Nusa Dua, Kuta, Sanur, Ubud, Candi Dasa or Lovina but transport costs are high: you'll pay $45–70 for the sunrise trek, depending on where you start.

In addition, all can arrange various treks in the area; prices vary, so it pays to shop around. There are climbs up **Gunung Abang** ($50 per person) and **Agung** ($75–95 per person), and it's also possible to climb to the outer caldera above Songan for the sunrise and then continue around the ridge to approach Trunyan from above ($15–25, depending on the length of the trek). Arlina's has **canoes** for rental ($15/hr or $30/day with "driver", $10 or $25/day without), and they rent out **fishing** gear at Rp20,000 per day. Roijaya Wisata and Bali Sunrise 2001 offer treks in the **Bedugul** area (May–Nov; $85 per person including one night's accommodation), and Roijaya Wisata arranges **jungle trekking** (May–Nov; one day $100 per person, two days $200).

Enquire at any of the trekking agencies about **shuttle bus** tickets and charter transport.

farmers. Not to be confused with the bigger, more important temple of the same name up on the crater rim, **Pura Ulun Danu Batur** in Songan is built on the site of a pre-Majapahit temple and is believed locally to be one of the oldest temples in Bali. While some of the shrines in the inner of the two courtyards are very ancient, much sympathetic building is under way, with a whole line of *meru* planned along the back wall. A ceremony is held in Songan every ten years to honour the goddess of the lake, involving the ritual drowning of a range of animals (buffaloes, pigs, goats, chickens and geese), all adorned with gold ornaments.

For **accommodation**, *Restiti Inn* (no phone; ❶) – undergoing renovation – provides simple bungalows in a quiet setting, several hundred metres beyond

Directly behind the temple in Songan, a small **footpath** winds up onto the rim of the outer crater. To the right, the path heads up towards Abang, passing above Trunyan and the cemetery, but this is the hard way to climb Abang and shouldn't be attempted without a guide; see p.322 for the alternative route via Suter.

As you head left, several footpaths pass through small strung-out villages of traditional bamboo huts whose inhabitants farm the steep dry hillsides on the outer edge of the crater rim. There are some fine lookout spots with views down to the north coast, and back to Abang, Agung and even – on a clear day – Rinjani on Lombok. With a good supply of food and water (it gets hotter the further down you go), a reasonable sense of direction and a bit of Indonesian, you should be able to locate and follow the footpath that leads down from the crater rim to the **north coast** where you can pick up public transport west to Air Sanih (see p.348) or east to Tulamben (see p.310).

Alternatively follow the tracks on the crater rim for about 3km until a track leads down to the village of **Blandingan**, from where there's a direct path back to Songan.

the village towards the temple. There are warung in the village for meals. Not many bemos serve Songan and you may end up walking to or from Toya Bungkah; either follow the road or take the more peaceful lakeside track.

From a junction in the middle of Songan, a **road** circles the base of Gunung Batur, passing through **Yehmampeh** on its way round to Penelokan. This is a round trip of about 26km, but it was impassable to vehicles for years due to damage from the 1974 lava flows south of Yehmampeh and isn't in the best condition. Nevertheless, if you have your own transport, it's worth getting off the tourist track at least part of the way around here to enjoy the different views of the crater rim and Gunung Batur – although you'll be accompanied by quarry trucks. The road is reasonable for the 7km from Songan to Yehmampeh; 3km further is **Pura Bukit Mentik**, surrounded by banyan and frangipani trees and usually closed, although it's easy enough to walk around the back and peek over the walls. It's known locally as Lucky Temple, because lava from the 1974 eruption surrounded it but did not damage the structure. The lava fields now supply the grey-black stone *paras*, used in building.

Buahan and Abang

The most attractive section of road in the crater follows the eastern shore of the lake beyond Kedisan (see p.326), offering great views across the lake to Toya Bungkah, with Gunung Batur rising up behind. A couple of hundred metres beyond the village of **BUAHAN**, 2.5km from the junction with the Penelokan road at Kedisan, *Hotel Baruna* (℡0366/51221; ❶–❷) is one of the quietest places to stay near the lake. It has basic rooms with cold-water bathrooms plus a perfect view; there's a *bale* to sit and admire it from.

From here the road edges between the lake and the cliffs, which rise up into the mass of Gunung Abang, and finally ends at the tiny village of **ABANG**, where a couple of shops sell soft drinks. From Abang, there's a lakeside footpath to Trunyan (4km).

Trunyan

The best-known Bali Aga village in Bali, inhabited by the original people of Bali who rejected the changes brought about by the Majapahit invasion in 1343 (see p.488), the village of **TRUNYAN** and its nearby cemetery at

Kuban are a well-established tourist attraction. Situated in a dramatic position right beside Lake Batur with Gunung Abang rising up sheer behind, there are two main routes to the village: by boat from Kedisan or by footpath from Abang village. The **boat trip** is beautiful but chilly and takes less than an hour. Boats leave from the pier at Kedisan; tourists aren't allowed on the public boats but must charter one, at a cost (advertised as including a guide and all donations) of Rp196,500 for a boat for one, Rp99,500 per person for two people, Rp67,175 per person for three people – and so on, up to a maximum of seven people, at Rp30,335 per person. They complete a circuit from the pier to Trunyan village, on to the cemetery, then Toya Bungkah and back to Kedisan.

The origin of the name "Trunyan" is open to some dispute. Some say it derives from *taru*, meaning wood, and *munyan*, meaning perfume, referring to the banyan tree in the cemetery; others claim it derives from *turun hyang*, meaning descendants from heaven. There's no doubt that Trunyan was inhabited in ancient times: ninth-century copper inscriptions refer to the foundations of a temple here and a statue of Bhatara Da Tonta that must be bathed, painted and decorated with jewellery. It's possible this refers to the four-metre-high **statue** of Dewa Ratu Gede Pancering Jagat that stands in the village temple today, referred to as Da Tonta by the people of Trunyan.

The village keeps many of the ancient **Bali Aga customs**, the most notorious being the traditional way of disposing of the dead, which involves neither burial nor cremation. Bodies are placed in open pits covered only by a cloth and a rough bamboo roof and left to decompose in the air, the banyan tree in the cemetery supposedly preventing the exposed corpses from smelling. Trunyan's tiny **cemetery** is at Kuban, just north of the village, and is accessible only by boat. For many tourists, this is the reason for their visit, but you'll be disappointed if you're expecting mountains of rotting human remains, as the bodies are totally covered by the bamboo roofs and only moved into the open when the pits are full. All you're likely to see are a few artfully arranged bones and skulls, the towering banyan tree and the covered graves.

Apart from growing cabbages and onions, the village's main source of income is from tourists, and although the boat fee is supposed to include donations you'll be asked for more. Some people have even been pressed for a donation to be allowed to leave. While it's easy to suggest you stand firm on these demands, Trunyan can feel rather isolated and forbidding; you'd do well to make sure you have plenty of small notes to give away.

Routes to the north coast

It's a long 40km from Kintamani down the main road through the foothills to the **north coast** at Kubutambahan. This is one of the main north–south routes across the island and is invariably busy with trucks, buses, cars and motorbikes. There's some pretty scenery, with more mountains to the west and verdant valleys and forested ridges gradually descending to the coast. The vegetation changes too as the hardier, high-altitude vegetables and crops give way to more tropical growth.

The village of **PEGINYAHAN**, 19km from Kintamani, makes a good stopping place. *I.Ris Warung*, owned by a Balinese–Dutch family, Ketut Widiada and his wife Paula, is just beside the road offering simple, inexpensive Indonesian **food** and drinks. There are two small losmen rooms with hot-water bathrooms in a pretty garden – with the local vegetation carefully labelled – below the road where you can **stay** (no phone; ❶). Along the river down in the bottom of the valley are three **waterfalls**, the highest and most impressive being Mesanti, about 40m high and surrounded by lush forest in an unspoiled location; the river isn't really suitable for swimming, though. You can trek from the warung to Mesanti (2hr each way), although it's possible to drive part of the way and then walk about half-an-hour each way. The warung staff can give you directions, a map or a guide (Rp50,000 for the short trek or Rp150,000 for the longer one, including some simple local food).

From Peginyahan downwards the temperature increases; another forty minutes or so brings you to the north coast at Kubutambahan (see p.348), from where Singaraja is 11km west and Air Sanih is 6km east.

The back road to Bondalem

To avoid the often extremely busy main road, you can follow a **back road** that delivers you to Bondalem, east of Air Sanih. It's a narrow, twisting and very steep 16km, but with private transport it's an attractive proposition through rural scenery with some lovely views.

The route leaves the main road at the village of Lateng, 13km from the market at Kintamani, and 500m after the split gate flanking the road that marks the end of the village of Dausa. The main road swings left on a sharp bend and there's a row of shops on the right at the start of this side road; check if you've got the correct turning (which is known as the Tejakula road).

The road initially descends through vegetable gardens and stands of cloves, cocoa, coffee and avocado in the cool highlands, with great views of nearby villages on neighbouring ridges and fine views westwards to the area around Gunung Batukau. There are few villages; **MADENAN** is a neat, cool settlement about 10km along the way down. After this the temperature rises significantly and coconut plantations stretch into the distance all the way to the north coast. The road reaches the main north-coast road at the village of **BONDALEM** (see p.349 for information on accommodation in the area). It's 15km west to Air Sanih, and a long, hot 36km east to Tulamben (see p.310) via Sembirenteng and Tembok.

The back road west to Bedugul

An enticing **back road** enables anyone with their own transport, plenty of fuel, a reasonable map (these lanes are omitted from several maps of the island) and a few phrases of Indonesian to explore the attractive, remote area – all of it well off the beaten tourist track – between the huge volcanic masses around Batur and the Bedugul region further west.

The unsigned road leaves the main Kintamani–Singaraja road 2km north of Pura Puncak Penulisan. The surface isn't brilliant but it winds pretty much due west for 12km through rural, upland scenery with the mountains impressively close before reaching the tiny village of **Catur**. From here the route turns due south, sloping steadily and slightly downhill, for around 9km before another 2km of dipping and rising, twisting and turning to the small village of **PELAGA**, where you'll find the only **place to stay** on this route – *Pondok Wana Plaga* (T & F0361/485738; ❾), on the main road in the village and comprising simple bungalows set in a pretty garden with attached cold-water bathrooms: hot water can be supplied in buckets on request. It's used by adventure-tour companies from the south but, apart from that, is essentially deserted. Regular dark red **minibuses** run between Pelaga and Denpasar (Wangaya terminal), the only public transport on this route, heading due south via **Petang**, where some rafting companies start their river descents (see box on p.125), the smaller **Getasan** and **Sangeh Monkey Forest** (see p.373) to the west of Ubud.

The back route to Bedugul follows this same road from Pelaga, heading 10km south away from the towering masses of the volcanoes into a more domestic landscape of chilli gardens, soya bean and peanut fields and citrus orchards. At the hamlet of **Angin Tiga**, an even smaller, quieter road forks off to the right, heading 9km northwest to the village of **Baturiti** on the main Mengwi–Bedugul road, which it joins 1km or so north of *Pacung Indah* and *Pacung Mountain Resort* (see p.335).

The Bedugul region

Neither as big nor as dramatic as the Batur region, the Lake Bratan area, sometimes just known as **Bedugul**, has impressive mountains, beautiful lakes, quiet walks and attractive and important temples. In many ways, the area is an Indonesian destination rather than one favoured by foreign tourists. Farmers make offerings to Dewi Danu, the goddess of the crater lake, at **Pura Ulun Danu Bratan** on the shores of **Lake Bratan**, while lowland dwellers come to the **Bali Botanical Gardens** in Candikuning on weekend picnics, and to the **Taman Rekreasi** (Leisure Park) on the shores of Lake Bratan, where a vast array of watersports is available. The entire area is frequently referred to as Bedugul or Bratan, but it's actually very spread out and it's sensible to know where you are aiming for: Bedugul is, strictly speaking, the small area on the shore of Lake Bratan occupied by the Taman Rekreasi.

Lake Bratan nestles in the lee of Gunung Catur, on the main Denpasar–Mengwi–Singaraja road 53km north of Denpasar and 30km south

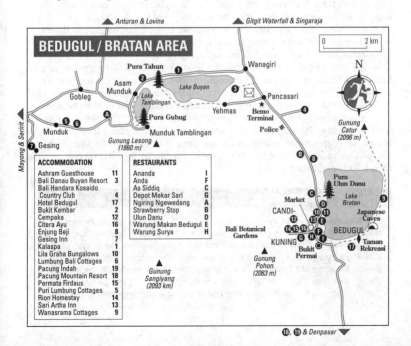

of Singaraja; no direct route links it to Batur. As you approach from the south, the road rises from the tropical heat into cooler temperatures through a series of small villages that line the road and almost merge into each other. **Pacung** offers a couple of extremely good accommodation choices; just north of it, near the market in **Baturiti**, a road is signed to Senganan which takes an extremely picturesque route through Jatiluwih to the Batukau region (see p.386). The main road completes another steep 8km north to the rim of an ancient volcanic crater at the market village of **Candikuning** from where it descends through the village of **Pancasari**, skirting the western shore of Lake Bratan. It then climbs again to the pass out of the crater at **Wanagiri** (known locally as Puncak), where it begins the steep descent to the northern plains. The smaller, quieter **Lake Buyan** and **Lake Tamblingan** lie about 6km northwest of Lake Bratan.

All the lakes have superbly situated shoreside temples and the area is dotted with attractive villages. Most tourists visit as part of a round-trip including Lake Batur and the north coast; relatively few stay overnight, although this is a pleasant area with a reasonable range of accommodation. The main road is well served by frequent north–south bemos and buses, but having your own transport means you can enjoy the glorious road that passes north of lakes Buyan and Tamblingan before heading to the coast at Seririt via Munduk and Mayong or exploring the peaceful back roads to the west of Lake Tamblingan.

Candikuning and Lake Bratan

The small village of **CANDIKUNING**, situated above the southern shores of Lake Bratan, is the centre for many of the sights in the area and home to one of the gems of central Bali, the **Bali Botanical Gardens**. However, it's very easy to miss the village completely and drive straight through; look out for the large concrete corn-on-the-cob at the roadside marking the village.

Candikuning's daily **market**, Bukit Mungsu, is small but extremely diverse and colourful; although catering largely for the tourist trade these days, it offers a vast range of fruit, spices and plants, including orchids. There's a **wartel** (daily 8am–9.30pm) in the market and another next to the *As Siddiq* restaurant near Pura Ulun Danu Bratan. You can **change money** at the moneychangers in the car park at Pura Ulun Danu Bratan or in Bukit Mungsu market but rates are poor compared with lowland areas. For **tourist shuttle bus** tickets (see p.366 for journey details), the Perama office (℡0368/21011) is at the *Sari Artha* losmen, just below the market on the main road in Candikuning. It's also possible to arrange charter transport in the area, for example at the *Ashram Guesthouse*; it's around Rp125,000 per car to Lovina, or Rp150,000 per car to Ubud, Kuta and other southern resorts.

Trekking around Bedugul

The Bedugul area offers plenty of opportunities for **trekking**, although very few places are set up to provide guides. An exception is *Lila Graha Bungalows* (see opposite). With them, a four-to-five hour trek taking in Lake Buyan or Tamblingan costs US$40 per person, while a seven-to-eight hour trek taking in both lakes costs $70 per person. It's also worth noting that the losmen *Bukit Kembar* (see p.339), on the road above Lake Tamblingan, as well as *Puri Lumbung* (see p.340) in Munduk and the trekking agencies in Toya Bungkah (see box on p.329) also arrange treks in the area.

Accommodation

Most accommodation in the area is in or near Candikuning village, although there are a few options slightly further afield.

Ashram Guesthouse ☏0368/21450, ☏21101. Situated in a good position in attractive grounds on the lakeside, this is a large establishment, offering a range of options from basic rooms boasting shared cold-water bathrooms to comfortable bungalows with wonderful views and hot water. ❶–❸

Bali Handara Kosaido Country Club ☏0362/22646, ☏23048, ⓦwww.balihandara.co.id. Accessed from the main road north of Lake Bratan, 6km from Bedugul, this luxury establishment caters mostly for the Japanese market. Facilities include tennis courts, a health and fitness centre and a karaoke bar. The view of Lake Buyan from the bar is glorious but, unless you have your own transport, it involves a 3km walk up the drive. Its world-famous golf course is a 6434-yard par 72, and claims to be the only one in the world situated in the crater of a volcano. It is fabulously picturesque – a brilliant lush green, with the crater walls rising up sheer behind. Expect to pay US$10 per hour for the tennis courts (free for guests) and US$100 for a round of golf (guests half-price) with additional charges to rent rackets, clubs and shoes. ❽

Hotel Bedugul ☏0368/21197, ☏21198. Located in the Taman Rekreasi, on a hill overlooking the lake. The position is good and most expensive rooms have stunning views; cheaper ones overlook the car park. All have hot water. ❷

Cempaka ☏0368/21402. Clean, quiet place just behind *Permata Firdaus* off the road to the Botanical Gardens. Accommodation is in a two-storey block and pricier rooms upstairs have hot water. ❷

Citera Ayu No phone. On the road to the Botanical Gardens; rooms are simple and set in a small, quiet compound. ❷

Enjung Beji ☏0368/21490, ☏21022. A pricey option, with accommodation in well-furnished cottages set in an attractive garden: less expensive ones are on the road down to the compound. All have hot water. ❺–❻

Lila Graha Bungalows ☏0368/21446, ☏21710. Located almost opposite the *Ashram Guesthouse*, 100m back towards Candikuning. Many bungalows overlook the lake, although they're across the

road and have bathrooms with hot water; larger family rooms are also available. The restaurant is in a large old wooden colonial house. You can also arrange local treks from here. ❷–❹

Pacung Indah ☏0368/21020, ☏21964, ⓦwww.pacung.com. Situated 9km south of Bedugul just before the village of Pacung. There are bungalows and suites, all with hot water and with self-catering facilities at the more expensive end of the range. Each is very private but there are fine views from the communal terrace. ❹–❼

Pacung Mountain Resort ☏0368/21038, ☏21043, ⓦwww.bali-pacung.com. Across the road from Pacung Indah, this is a luxurious resort with a lovely little swimming pool and splendid views offering the most comfortable accommodation in the area. Cheaper rooms have views of the pool but more expensive rooms have a fabulous panorama across the local fields. There are also upmarket bungalows situated down in the middle of the rice-fields; a cable-car brings guests up to the main buildings. ❽–❾

Permata Firdaus ☏0368/21531. Just off the road to the Botanical Gardens, this place has clean good-value rooms with hot water, and is in a quiet location. ❷

Rion Homestay ☏ & ☏0368/21184, ✉dheinze@indosat.net.id. A cosy homestay with an Australian–Balinese family on the road to the Botanical Gardens. Rooms have hot showers and satellite TV. There are reductions for longer stays, and lunch and dinner can be provided (breakfast is included). A popular place – it's advisable to book. ❺

Sari Artha Inn ☏0368/21011. Situated north of the market, there's a choice of rooms here with or without hot water, all with verandahs, set in a pretty garden but with no views. The most expensive rooms have TV. The Perama office is here so this place is especially convenient if you're using their bus services. ❶–❸

Wanasrama Cottages ☏0368/21197, ☏21198. Owned and adminstered by *Hotel Bedugul*, these thatched cottages are on the far side of the lake, clearly visible across the water and only accessible by boat from Bedugul. Transport is included in the price. ❻

Bali Botanical Gardens

A short walk south from the Bukit Mungsu market area in Candikuning, along a small side road by the giant corn-on-the-cob, are the **Bali Botanical Gardens** (Kebun Raya Eka Karya Bali; daily 8am–4pm; Rp2000; parking for

The birds of Bedugul

The Bali Botanical Gardens and the southern shores of Lake Bratan are fringed by montane forest and home to an amazing variety of **birds**. The most common sightings are of the forest-dwelling **grey-cheeked green pigeons** and **blue-crowned barbets**, almost entirely green in colour with a blue crown and yellow forehead. The barbet is found only on Java and Bali, and you'll often hear its monotonous call from high in the forest canopy. You're also likely to see **flycatchers**, especially the snowy-browed flycatcher, which has a distinctive white line above the eye, a slate-blue back and orange breast. It pays to stand near flowering or fruiting trees and watch, as they attract a whole range of different birds: the gregarious **Philippine glossy starling**, with its greenish purple feathers, feeds in fruiting trees, while the tiny **yellow-throated hanging parrot**, green with a red rump, heads for buds and flowers. The **collared kingfisher** is also a regular in the area, a noisy bird, frequently heard before it is seen, giving a loud "chek, chek" call. Iridescent blue-green in colour with white underparts and a white collar, it hunts for lizards, large insects and frogs in open areas near water.

cars Rp1000, for motorbikes Rp500; entry for cars Rp5000; motorbikes prohibited). The gardens, a branch of the National Botanical Gardens at Bogor on Java, were set up in 1959 and cover over a square kilometre on the slopes of Gunung Pohon (Tree Mountain). There are more than 650 different species of **tree** here – most of them unlabelled – and over four hundred species of **orchids**. The gardens are also a rich area for **bird-watching** (see box above).

At weekends, it seems as if half of Denpasar comes here for the cool air and the pleasant surroundings, but the grounds are big enough to find a peaceful corner; during the week you'll see few visitors. There are three small temples, all marked on the map near the entrance and signposted. **Pura Teratai Bang** is fairly grand, with a two-roofed *meru*, a tilting *kulkul* tower and a couple of fierce Rangdas guarding the gate. It's built on ground containing sulphur, hence the rotten-egg smell, and many visitors come here for the soil which is believed to be useful in treating skin complaints. **Pura Giri Putri**, built for the staff of the Botanical Gardens, is set in the middle of the woods and sports an intricately carved *padmasana* and carved outer walls that are a riot of flowers, humans, monsters and animals; look for the monkeys on the seesaw. The oldest of the temples, **Pura Batumeringgit**, is the least prepossessing as it's unwalled and has modern additions.

The gardens are a centre for the study of the plants of the region and there's also a herbarium and a library. The office in the grounds is open for study purposes, but serious students should contact the gardens beforehand; write to Cabang Balai Kebun Raya, Eka Karya Bali, Candikuning, Baturiti, Tabanan 82191.

Lake Bratan

Situated at 1200m above sea level and thought to be 35m deep in places, **Lake Bratan** lies in the bottom of a once gigantic, but now almost indistinguishable, volcanic crater. Surrounded by rolling forested hills, with the bulk of Gunung Catur rising sheer behind, the lake becomes the scene of rampant watersports on holidays and at weekends – although the awesome scenery more than compensates for the buzz of motorboats.

Revered by Balinese farmers as the source of freshwater springs across a wide area of the island, the lake (and its goddess) are worshipped in the immensely attractive temple of **Pura Ulun Danu Bratan** (daily 7am–5pm; Rp3300, cars Rp1000), one of the most photographed temples in Bali and the highly revered *kayangan jagat* (directional temple) for the northwest. Built in 1633 by the raja of Mengwi on a small promontory on the western shore of the lake, it's dedicated to Dewi Danu, source of water and hence fertility for the land and people of Bali. Set in well-maintained grounds, the temple consists of several shrines, some spread along the shore and others dramatically situated on small islands. On the mainland, Pura Teratai Bang is the main compound, featuring a seven-roofed *meru* dedicated to Brahma. The real highlights, though, are the island shrines, which appear to float on the surface of the lake, with the water stretching behind and the mountain looming in the distance. Closest to the bank, the eleven-roofed *meru* is dedicated to Wisnu and Dewi Danu, and the three-roofed *meru* just beyond it, housing an ancient *linggam*, to Siwa.

Taman Rekreasi Bedugul

The **Taman Rekreasi Bedugul** (Bedugul Leisure Park; daily 8am–5pm; Rp3300, cars Rp1500, motorbikes Rp600), on the southern shores of the lake, is signed "Bedugul" from the main road. You can indulge in waterskiing, parasailing and jet-skiing (expect to pay US$10 for 15min for these) or rent a speedboat (Rp65,000 for once round the lake) or rowing boat (Rp70,000 per hour). A vast number of private boat operators can be found around the lake, both near the Taman Rekreasi and the *Ashram Guesthouse*; with a bit of hard bargaining you should be able to get a boat for about Rp50,000/hour.

From the Taman Rekreasi you can walk around the shoreline for a few hundred metres to three **caves**, supposedly dug by Indonesian labourers for the Japanese during World War II. It's said that when the caves were completed, the labourers were shot. You'll need a torch to see anything (you can just wander in), but there's not much there.

Climbing Gunung Catur

The path up **Gunung Catur** (2096m), sometimes called Gunung Mangu, is easy to find and as long as you don't visit on a festival day, is unlikely to be overrun by people. To reach it, turn away from the lake just past the third of the Japanese caves and take the short track that zigzags up onto the ridge, about 20m above. It hits another, bigger path heading along the ridge; turn left onto this path and simply follow it – and the trail of plastic water bottles and other litter – to the top of Catur. The climb is through shady forest with some tantalizing glimpses of the lake far below; allow two to three hours' fairly unrelenting uphill climb (in a couple of places, you'll even need to haul yourself up by the tree trunks). Take plenty of water and some snacks for the way, and let somebody responsible know where you're going in case of accident. It should take about an hour and a half to get down again.

At the **summit**, Pura Pucak Mangu, supposedly built by the first raja of Mengwi, is a small forest temple with three-roofed and five-roofed *meru*, surrounded by yellow canna lilies and inhabited by a troop of grey monkeys. A small path from the back of the temple heads down the other side of the mountain, which eventually descends to the main road above Pancasari, but this is wild and uninhabited country and you'd need a **guide** (for which, you should ask at your accommodation or *Lila Graha Bungalows*).

Eating and drinking

Most **restaurants** in the area cater for the passing **lunchtime** trade. In the Taman Rekreasi, the moderately priced restaurant by the lake has an excellent position, but the service is nothing special. North of Bedugul, next to Pura Ulun Danu on the shore of Lake Bratan, *Restaurant Ulun Danu* has a pretty garden, a children's play area and a pricey buffet lunch. For simpler, better-value food, a lengthy row of stalls lines the road where it runs along the lakeside south of Pura Ulun Danu. In addition, several inexpensive places, including *Depot Mekar Sari*, line the road to the Botanical Gardens, and the warung in the temple car park are worth a try, as is *As Siddiq*, about 100m north of the car park on the opposite side of the road – a good-value place serving Taliwang and Sasak food. The inexpensive-to-moderate *Warung Makan Bedugul* just above the *Ashram Guesthouse* on the way to the market has views of the lake as well as decent food. *Strawberry Stop*, 2km towards Pancasari, does a good range of juice and drinks; it serves the tasty strawberries that grow in the market garden behind the restaurant – with cream or ice cream, in milkshakes or in pancakes.

In the **evenings**, the range of options isn't so good: most places tend to close around 8pm. The more expensive hotels all have restaurants, but if you want to eat more simply in Candikuning, *Ananda* and *Anda* just across the road from the turning to the Botanical Gardens are both a good bet, as is *Warung Surya* on the opposite corner; all offer a range of inexpensive Indonesian and Chinese food.

Lake Buyan

Less frequently visited than Lake Bratan, the smaller lakes of Buyan and Tamblingan are far enough off the beaten track to deter most day-trippers, and are accessible either with your own transport or by a combination of bemos and walking. It's well worth the effort of getting here to experience a little oasis of peaceful, undisturbed rural Bali. There are fine views of both lakes from the road that runs west from Wanagiri (see opposite).

The best way to explore **Lake Buyan**, 6km northwest of Bedugul, is on foot, although you can drive on the good, motorable side road that heads west just to the north of the Pancasari bemo terminal, between the terminal and a *kulkul* tower. This is lined with houses with beautifully carved household shrines, and leads directly to the village of **YEHMAS**. After about 3km, you pass the last house and the road turns rapidly into a dirt path which is no longer motorable. It follows close to the southern shores of the lake, mostly in the forest. Keep walking on the biggest and most level path for another 2km and you'll come out onto the shores of the lake; if you look carefully, you'll spot the *meru* of Pura Tahun in the trees at the western end. As the path reaches the far end of the lake, it's tempting to try and clamber over the rocks to get to the temple, but there's no way through here. Continue on the path as it heads up to the ridge and along towards the temple; within about thirty minutes the forest gives way to fields, with Pura Tahun set among them, surrounded by trees. An eleven-roofed *meru* dominates the **temple** and there's a small *bale* to sit in and another for offerings. A short track leads west from here over to Lake Tamblingan across a raised shoulder of land, but it's extremely difficult to find and it's easy to lose your sense of direction in the densely forested terrain.

Currently, the only choice of **accommodation** close to Lake Buyan is *Bali Danau Buyan Resort* (☎0362/21351 or 23739, ℱ21388; ❻), self-catering cottages in a beautiful position at the east end of the lake, accessed from the main road south of Wanagiri. There is, though, quite a bit of building going on around the lake, with a plush-looking hotel under construction on the slopes on the south side of the lake – it's likely that accommodation options will increase in the area.

Lake Tamblingan and beyond

To reach **Lake Tamblingan**, you need to take the road west from **WANA-GIRI**, 2km north of Pancasari – this is signed "scenic route" and runs along the ridge a couple of hundred metres above the northern shore of Lake Buyan.

About 4km from Wanagiri, the luxury *Kalaspa* (℡0361/419606, ℻419607, Ⓦwww.bali-kalaspa.com; ➒) has large, well-decorated wooden bungalows set in wonderful grounds, giving great views to the north coast as far as the ocean. The room price, which starts at US$175, includes a number of massages and treatments. Some 500m further west, *Bukit Kembar* (℡082/836 1386; ➒) has a small row of simple rooms with hot water; there's an attached restaurant and extremely fine views from the sitting area just across the road. This is where the road passes above the shoulder of land separating the two lakes, the site of the spring which feeds them, before arriving above the western shore of Lake Tamblingan.

About 1500m beyond the *Bukit Kembar*, the road divides. Take the left fork and it's another 3km down to the lakeside and the small village of **MUNDUK TAMBLINGAN**, where people make their living from growing vegetables, fishing for carp and rearing cattle on the *tunjung* (lotus) that grows on the lake. On the shore just in front of the village, **Pura Gubug**, sporting eleven-, nine- and five-roofed *meru*, is dedicated to Dewi Danu. Farmers come here frequently on pilgrimages to the three lakeside temples of Batur, Bratan and Tamblingan to worship the lake goddess and pray for good harvests. Across the lake, in the trees, you can just see **Pura Dalem Tamblingan**, the temple of the dead. The area is particularly renowned for bird-watching, as the forest is relatively undisturbed, and you may spot babblers, woodpeckers, ground thrushes and malkohas if you take the path around to the temple.

The scenic route to the north coast

The road from Wanagiri turns away from the lakes as it continues west and descends through coffee fields and roads lined with clove trees. If you take the right fork at the junction beyond the *Bukit Kembar*, about 1500m further you'll come to *Ngiring Ngewedang* restaurant, a great place to stop. The **views** from here are among the best in Bali with a glorious panorama across the whole of the west of the island. The restaurant has a small inexpensive-to-moderate menu of Indo-Chinese favourites. You can also see all the stages of the coffee process here in miniature, from the green beans to the production of the box of ground coffee for sale.

The road continues to Munduk and on down to the coast, but an **alternative scenic route**, even further off the beaten track, takes the road towards Gobleg from above Lake Tamblingan and descends via a narrow and winding lane, past spectacularly fertile slopes rich in bananas, durian, papaya and jackfruit trees, to Asah Gobleg and then down through Selat before reaching the coast at **Anturan** towards the east of Lovina. Take a good-quality road map to explore these by-ways.

Munduk and around

Another 4km down from *Ngiring Ngewedang* is a sign for **Munduk waterfall** at the *Sunset Bar and Restaurant*, with two more signs further on along the road, one with parking spaces next to a defunct warung and one signed opposite *Warung Sire Malih*. The falls are high, powerful and far more impressive than the falls at the more famous Gitgit (see p.346) on the road north to Singaraja; this is a quiet, peaceful and pleasantly landscaped spot, only one of several waterfalls on this river – anyone staying at *Puri Lumbung Cottages* (see below) can arrange a trek to visit the other falls as well.

A kilometre further along from the last of the three paths to the falls is the village of **MUNDUK**, an excellent base for exploration either on foot or with your own transport. The area around here and around **GOBLEG**, 2km north, is being explored by archeologists who have found evidence of a tenth- to fourteenth-century religious and administrative centre on the shores of Lake Tamblingan, ancient Chinese ceramics near Munduk, and a copper inscription in Gobleg describing a mountain kingdom in the area as early as the eighth century.

Munduk's most established **place to stay** is *Puri Lumbung Cottages* (☎0362/ 92810, ℻92514, ⓦwww.travelideas.net/bali.hotels/lumbung.html; ❻–❼), where accommodation is in replicas of traditional *lumbung* (rice storage barns) that used to stand on the site. They're well furnished and sit in lovely grounds. There's a moderately priced two-storey **restaurant** attached, *Warung Kopi Bali*, with an attractive lounge area downstairs offering a selection of books and English-language newspapers. *Puri Lumbung* also has some bungalows nearby (US$40) and administers several local **homestays** (❺) in Munduk village. These aren't luxurious places, nor are they especially cheap, but all have hot water and breakfast included. Just above, *Lumbung Bali Cottages* (☎ & ℻0362/92818, ⓔlumbungbali@hotmail.com; ❻) offers comfortable bungalows with good-quality furnishings set in attractive gardens. A restaurant is attached. There are also several warung in the village which you can head to as an alternative to eating at the hotels.

On to Mayong

Some 7km south of Munduk – via a four-kilometre branch signed off the main road – is the pretty village of **GESING**. Its friendly little homestay, the *Gesing Inn* (no phone; ❶), has just three rooms, and the owners cook simple food and can advise you on local walks, including a short one to a huge, locally famous tree and a much longer hike to Lake Tamblingan. You can get to the *Gesing Inn* by ojek (Rp2500–3000) from Tabog, which is 3km south of Munduk and served by all bemos and minibuses that run between Seririt and Munduk.

Back on the main road, you'll pass through the attractive ridge villages of Gunung Sari and Banyuatis before reaching **MAYONG** (see p.365 for details of a detour inland from here through Bestala), where there's a tiny warung, *Mayong Bali Panorama*, with a couple of tables on the side of the road. The views across the local paddy-fields are stunning and this is a great spot to stop for a drink. From Mayong, you can turn north to **Seririt** on the north coast.

Cloves

It was the search for **cloves**, among other spices, that first drove Europeans to explore the Indonesian archipelago, and for hundreds of years they were one of the region's most lucrative exports. Native to certain islands of the Moluccas (the original "Spice Islands") clove production is now centred in Maluku, Sumatra, Sulawesi and Bali. You'll spot the tall trees in the mountains around Bedugul, and if you're there during harvest time in August and September you'll see huge piles of cloves beside the road – buds that must be picked and dried before the petals open, after which the amount of clove oil declines sharply.

Today, Bali's cloves are shipped direct to factories in Java where they're used in the manufacture of Indonesia's distinctively pungent **kretek cigarettes**. These consist of up to fifty percent cloves mixed with tobacco, and demand is so great, with over 138 billion of them smoked annually, that the former clove capital of the world now imports them from Madagascar and Zanzibar to supplement local production.

The north coast

The **north coast** of Bali is a rugged and, in places, dramatic landscape, the northern flanks of the mountains dropping steeply towards long, sweeping black-sand beaches. The land is dry and parched towards the east, where villages are widely spread out and the lava flows from the last eruption of Gunung Agung are still visible. To the west, more fertile territory supports a greater population density and there are some finely sculpted rice terraces.

The major north-coast settlement is **Singaraja**, whose colonial architecture attests to the lengthy Dutch influence on the city. Its now decaying waterfront area was once the busiest port on the island. Most tourists, however, come to the north for the burgeoning beach resort of **Lovina**, west of Singaraja, a great place to relax or to use as a base for exploring the temples, hot springs and inland scenery of the region.

Some history

While the north coast of Bali has been inhabited for centuries, with local villages mentioned in tenth-century inscriptions, the ascendancy of the area only really began at the end of the sixteenth century, when **Ki Gusti Ngurah Panji Sakti** founded Buleleng, and in 1604 built a new palace called Singaraja. He was a skilful operator who gained control of Karangasem, Jembrana and parts of eastern Java, in addition to his own kingdom. These dominions expanded even further when, in 1711, the throne was taken by his son-in-law **Gusti Agung Sakti**, the raja of Mengwi, who established a joint Mengwi–Buleleng kingdom which flourished for most of the eighteenth century.

In the nineteenth century, the kingdom's fortunes declined, culminating in the expeditions of the invading **Dutch**, whose First Military Expedition in 1846 was directed against the north of the island. After the Balinese defeat in 1849, the Dutch began to administer Buleleng. This encouraged more Europeans, including journalists, merchants and scholars, to visit and settle in the area, while the south of the island was still pursuing its own battles against the Dutch. In an effort to make their colony profitable, the Dutch built roads, improved irrigation systems and encouraged coffee as a cash crop in the north. However, it was not all plain sailing: in 1864 **Ida Made Rai** rebelled in Banjar, near Seririt, and it took the Dutch until 1868 to subdue him and his followers.

As the Dutch gradually strengthened their hold, the administrative importance of the north coast grew. When Bali and Lombok were finally combined in one regency by the Dutch in 1882, their capital was established in Singaraja. During World War II, the invading **Japanese** also made their headquarters here, but when the Dutch subsequently returned to the island, they moved their capital to Denpasar due to its proximity to the new airport and the far greater density of population.

Singaraja and around

The second-largest Balinese city after Denpasar, **SINGARAJA** has an airy spaciousness created by its broad avenues, impressive monuments and colonial bungalows set in attractive gardens. With a population of over 100,000, it's home to an interesting religious mix of Hindus, Muslims and Buddhists. Behind the old harbour you can still see the shophouses and narrow streets of the original trading area; Jalan Hasanuddin is known locally as Kampong Bugis and Jalan Imam Bonjol as Kampong Arab after the Muslim Bugis settlers from Sulawesi whose descendants still live in the area.

As the transport hub for the north of the island, you're bound to pass through Singaraja on your way to or from Lovina, though most tourists head straight out again. It isn't a great place to stay and there aren't many sights, but you can spend a few interesting hours exploring this pleasant, tourist-friendly town. There is also straightforward access from Singaraja to all points eastwards. Short excursions can include the fabulous temples of **Pura Meduwe Karang** – best of the bunch – or **Sangsit**, **Jagaraga** or **Bebitin**, and it's equally easy to carry on further east to the small resort of **Air Sanih** and on round the coast to Amlapura via Tulamben.

Arrival, orientation and information

Singaraja has three bus and bemo terminals: **Sukasada** (locally called Sangket) to the south of the town, serving Gil-Git, Bedugul and Denpasar (Ubung terminal); **Banyuasri** on the western edge of town serving the west, including Lovina, Seririt and Gilimanuk; and **Penarukan** in the east, for services eastwards along the coast via Tulamben to Amlapura and inland along the road to Kintamani, Penelokan (for the Batur area) and on to Denpasar via Bangli. For information on travelling to and from Ngurah Rai **Airport**, see the box on pp.110–11.

Small bemos (flat rate Rp1000) ply main routes around town linking two of the terminals – marked on the back of the vehicle – but things can get complicated if you're trying to get to somewhere on the back streets. There are no metered taxis in Singaraja, although you'll see a few dokar; negotiate the destination and price before you get in.

Spread out along the coast and stretching inland for several kilometres, Singaraja can be quite confusing initially. It helps to remember that the main thoroughfare of **Jalan Jen Achmad Yani / Jalan Dr Sutomo** is oriented east–west and will eventually take you out onto the road to Lovina, while **Jalan**

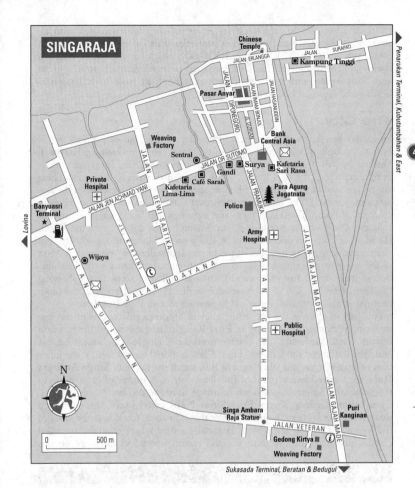

Sukasada Terminal, Beratan & Bedugul ▼

Gajah Made is oriented north–south and heads, via Sukasada, inland to the Bedugul area. The busy area around the major junction where these two main roads meet has hotels, restaurants, banks, post office, telephone office and night market all within walking distance; it's a useful focal point and feels as much like the town centre as anywhere.

The **tourist office** is south of the town centre at Jl Veteran 23 (Mon–Thurs 8.30am–2pm, Fri & Sat 8.30am–1pm; ☎0362/25141). Staff may be able to produce a brochure or map but are generally a bit startled by the arrival of tourists. Bemos heading to Sukasada terminal pass the eastern end of Jalan Veteran, 100m from the office.

Accommodation

Most of the **hotels** in Singaraja cater for Indonesian businesspeople, government officers visiting the city or extra-marital assignations. Most are centrally located – many lining Jalan Jen Achmad Yani – but are pretty soulless and not really used to tourists. One reasonable option is *Sentral*, Jl Jen Achmad Yani 48

(☎0362/21896; ❶–❷) which offers fan or air-conditioned rooms with an attached cold-water mandi. The most professional set-up in town is *Wijaya*, Jl Sudirman 74 (☎0362/21915, ℗25817; ❶–❹), which has the widest range of rooms and is conveniently close to Banyuasri terminal. At the bottom end are very basic rooms with a shared bathroom through to those with air-conditioning and attached hot-water bathrooms.

The City

Singaraja's best-known attraction is somewhat esoteric, but surprisingly interesting. A couple of kilometres south of the town centre is **Gedong Kirtya**, Jl Veteran 20 (Mon–Thurs 7am–2.30pm, Fri 7am–noon, Sat 7am–1pm; contribution expected), the only library of **lontar manuscripts** in the world. These are ancient and sacred texts inscribed on specially prepared leaves from the *lontar* palm (see box). The library contains over three thousand texts on religion, customs, philosophy, folklore, medicine, astrology and black magic, written in Balinese, Old Javanese and Indonesian. Established by L.J.J. Caron, the Dutch Resident of Bali, and opened in 1928, this is an establishment for scholars, but visitors are welcome; a member of the library staff will show you around. Most of the *lontar* manuscripts are stored in metal boxes, but there's a small exhibition of manuscripts from India and Burma as well as illustrated ones showing the Tantri tales. You can also see *prasasti*, inscribed bronze plates from the tenth century, which are amongst the oldest written records found on Bali.

This part of town is the site of the ancient Singaraja palace; one of the few surviving remnants, the gateway of **Puri Kanginan**, stands across the junction of Jalan Gajah Made and Jalan Veteran from the library, looking somewhat lost amid the traffic and modern buildings. A few hundred metres west, at the junction of Jalan Veteran and Jalan Ngurah Rai, stands the statue of **Singa Ambara Raja**, the winged lion symbol of Buleleng district. A source of great pride to the citizens of Singaraja, you'll see its image all round the city.

Just behind Gedong Kirtya, **Puri Sinar Nadi Putri** (daily 8am–4pm) is a small **weaving factory**, built on part of the old palace. You'll hear the clack of the looms before you see what is essentially a shed where exquisite weft *ikat* cloth is produced, mostly from silk and cotton (see p.538 for more on this

---

Lontar manuscripts

The leaves of the **lontar palm**, or *punyan ental*, are prepared for inscription through a long process of drying and pressing. After removal of the central rib, the leaves are soaked in water for three days to destroy the chlorophyll and brushed to remove insects, eggs and dirt from the surface, before being boiled with traditional herbal ingredients to increase flexibility and strength. At this stage, the leaves must be slow-dried to prevent wrinkling and, after being pressed for ten days, are cut to the required size (35–40cm long and 3–4cm wide), and punched with three holes for threading. The palms are then bound between thin wooden boards, pressed, and their edges coloured red with *kincu* to deter insects. Storing for about six months after binding produces the perfect texture.

The text is engraved on the prepared palm using an iron tool with a sharpened tip, and carbon black from a lamp is rubbed into the inscription to make it visible. Due to the humidity on Bali, the manuscripts only last between fifty and a hundred years, so decaying manuscripts are continuously copied onto new palm leaves, ensuring the survival of this ancient art. To see *lontar* palm being inscribed, head to the village of Tenganan (see p.291), in the hills above Candi Dasa.

craft). A small shop is attached, but you'll get a wider choice in the showrooms of Gianyar or the shops of the south. A larger concern than the factory, and a better bet if you are interested in superb textiles, is **Berdikari**, Jl Dewi Sartika 42 (daily 7am–7pm), where they produce top-quality silk and cotton *ikat*. Some of the patterns are reproduced from traditional materials and their work is highly regarded nationally. Scarves (Rp220,000 and upwards) and sarongs (Rp420,000 and upwards depending on the type of thread) are on sale; if you want to watch the weavers, come before they go home at 4pm. There's a smaller workshop at *Hotel Berdikari* (see p.347), east of Singaraja.

Almost in the middle of town, on Jalan Pramuka, you can't miss the extremely impressive **Pura Agung Jagatnata**, dedicated in 1993. Built on a grand scale, every available surface is covered in a typically northern style of effusive decoration. The *candi bentar* rises dramatically for 15m, and the main shrine, the *padmasana* to the supreme god, Sang Yang Widi, in the inner courtyard, is even higher. Although the temple is only rarely open to visitors, you can see some of the shrines from the road, and a three-metre-tall Ganesh on the pavement outside, draped in a *kain poleng* cloth, receives contributions from passers-by. The local gamelan orchestra often practises in the outer courtyard in the evenings.

North along Jalan Pramuka, and over the intersection with Jalan Jen Achmad Yani, alleys run down to **Pasar Anyar**, a two-storey maze of stalls and tiny shops selling pretty much everything needed for everyday life. Continue north and you'll reach Singaraja's **waterfront**, site of the ancient harbour of Buleleng. A quiet spot, backed by deserted warehouses, with views of traditional fishing villages further along the coast, it's hard to imagine the days when this was the most important and busiest port on Bali. In 1987, a monument, Yudha Mandala Tama, showing an independence fighter guarded by the traditional *garuda* and *naga*, was erected here. It commemorates the independence struggle of the 1940s, and in particular an incident in 1945 when the Balinese resistance attempted to lower a Dutch flag that was flying on the coast. They succeeded but were spotted by a Dutch navy vessel offshore, who fired on them, killing one; a tiny shrine to Telah Gugur, the man who died, is just around the corner, opposite the local Chinese temple, Ling Gwan Kiong.

Eating, drinking and nightlife

The largest concentration of **restaurants** is at Jl Jen Achmad Yani 25, in a small square set slightly back from the road; the Chinese restaurant here, *Gandi*, is a good bet, as is *Surya*, just at the entrance, selling Padang food. Further west along the same street there's another cluster of places which are all used to tourists, have menus in English and offer good, inexpensive rice and noodles, soft drinks and some iced desserts: *Kafetaria Lima-Lima* at no. 55a is most obvious, with *Café Sarah* a few doors east opposite *Sentral* hotel. Also worth a look during the day is *Kafetaria Sari Rasa* on Jalan Gajah Made, just south of the main post office, with a limited menu of inexpensive chicken dishes, soups, rice, noodles and drinks. For really cheap eats, *Kampung Tinggi*, just east of the bridge close to the Chinese temple, used to be a bemo terminal and is now lined with food stalls every afternoon (2–8pm), some of which have a basic written menu.

As darkness falls and the temperature drops, the **night market** in the Jalan Durian area springs into life. Lit by gloomy electric bulbs and kerosene lanterns, shoppers amble between mountains of fruit and vegetables, exchange gossip or eat an evening meal at the bustling food stalls. This is the only local nightlife and a pleasant way to spend a couple of hours.

Listings

Banks and exchange The most central place to change money is Bank Central Asia on Jl Dr Sutomo (exchange counter Mon–Fri 11am–1pm) where you can also get Visa cash advances. The ATM machine outside accepts Visa, MasterCard and Cirrus cards.

Bus tickets (long-distance) Menggala, Jl Jen Achmad Yani 76 ☎0362/24374, and Puspasari, Jl Jen Achmad Yani 90 ☎0362/23062 – both about 300m east of Banyuasri terminal – operate daily direct night buses to Surabaya (Rp55,000; takes 11hr), leaving at 6.30pm. They go via Probolinggo and Pasuruan in East Java, access points for the Bromo region, but the arrival times there are in the middle of the night. Pahala Kencana, Jl Jen Achmad Yani 95a ☎0362/29945, operates daily buses to Jakarta (Rp200,000) and Bogor (Rp205,000).

Hospitals Rumah Sakit Umum (the public hospital), Jl Ngurah Rai ☎0362/22046; Rumah Sakit Umum Angkatan Darat (staffed by army personnel, but open to the public), Jl Ngurah Rai ☎0362/22543; and Rumah Sakit Kerta Usada (a private hospital which also has a dentist), Jl Jen Achmad Yani 108 ☎0362/22396.

Internet access At the main post office, Jl Gajah Made 156 (Mon–Sat 9am–9pm, Sun & hols 8.30am–5.30pm; Rp10,000/hr).

Pharmacies Many of Singaraja's medical facilities, including doctors and pharmacies, are concentrated on Jl Diponegoro.

Phones The main phone office (daily 24hr) is at the southern end of Jalan Kartini. There are wartels on main roads in the city.

Post office The main office is at Jl Gajah Made 156 (Mon–Thurs & Sat 7.30am–4pm, Fri 7.30am–3pm). Poste restante service is to the above address, Singaraja 81113, Bali. This office acts as an agent for Western Union. A smaller post office is just south of *Wijaya* hotel at Jl Sudirman 68a, a short walk from Banyuasri terminal.

South of Singaraja

Just to the **south** of the city, the village of **BERATAN** is known locally for its silverwork – mainly large and ornate platters, vases and other household goods, but some jewellery too. The number of workshops and showrooms is small, and the variety is greater in Celuk in the south, but browsing here is a leisurely affair. Bemos to Sukasada terminal pass through the village.

Further south, 10km along the road to Bedugul, are two well-signposted waterfalls at **Gitgit** (daily 8am–5.30pm; Rp3000). All buses between Singaraja (Sukasada terminal) and Denpasar via Bedugul pass the place. A multi-tiered upper fall descends in fairly unimpressive steps and, 2km further north, is a forty-metre single drop, 500m from the road along a concrete path lined with textile and souvenir stalls. A local belief has it that if you come to Gitgit with your partner you will eventually separate. There is little reason to **stay** here rather than down at the coast, but just above the road is *Gitgit Hotel* (☎0362/26212, ☞41840; ❸) – in a noisy spot although the rooms, with hot water, are OK.

East of Singaraja

Many of the villages and the wealth of carved temples to the **east of Singaraja** can be visited on a day-trip from Singaraja or Lovina. The main sights are fairly close together and all lie on regular bemo routes.

Sangsit

Some 8km east of Singaraja, a small road north takes you 200m to the pink sandstone **Pura Beji** of **SANGSIT**, highly unusual in an area where every other temple is built of grey volcanic *paras*. Dedicated to Dewi Sri, the rice goddess, it's justly famous for the sheer exuberance of its carvings. The *candi bentar* and the inner *paduraksa* drip with animals, plants and monsters, and both courtyards are decorated with mask carvings.

About 400m to the northeast across the fields from Pura Beji, you'll be able to spot the red roofs of **Pura Dalem**. (The fields contain rice in the wet season and soya beans in the dry, so stick to the paths.) The front wall of the temple shows the rewards that await the godly in heaven and the punishments awaiting the evil in hell. There's a preponderance of soft pornography here, and it isn't certain which of this is supposed to be hell and which heaven, but the more usual punishments are vibrantly clear: stone blocks on the head, babies flung into fires, women giving birth to strange creatures, and sharp penises descending through the tops of skulls. The village of Sangsit straggles 500m north from here to a black-sand working beach with a few fishing boats, shops and warung.

Jagaraga, Sawan and Bebitin

Back on the main road, 500m east of the Sangsit turning, you come to the road heading inland to Jagaraga, Sawan and Bebitin. Bemos go direct to Bebitin from Singaraja (Penarukan terminal), passing through Jagaraga, 4km from the main road, and Sawan on the way; if you're planning to visit all these places on public transport it makes sense to go up to Bebitin first and then walk downhill to the others.

Near the small village of **BEBITIN**, Pura Bukit Bebitin is located on the top of a local hill with fine views. It has been recently and grandly renovated with some splendid new statuary and carvings, all in the exuberant style so characteristic of northern temples. Bring a sarong and scarf and be prepared to make a donation. To reach the temple take an ojek the final 2km (Rp2500) uphill from the village.

In the village of **SAWAN**, the "Pentatone" sign marks the workshop of Sawan's gamelan maker (daily 6am–4pm). You won't necessarily find the smith at work every day, but you can try out the various sizes and styles of gamelan instruments, drums and flutes. There's another shop 1km from the main road on the way to Jagaraga, though Sawan is the main centre. The four-kilometre road between Sawan and Jagaraga is lined with mango and rambutan trees overlooking fields of rice in the rainy season and tobacco in the dry. There are several energetically carved temples along the route, including Pura Paninjoan, which is guarded by outstandingly ugly monsters.

JAGARAGA was the site of an immense battle between the Balinese and the Dutch during the Second Military Expedition in 1848, which the Balinese, led by their commander Jelantik, won with huge loss of life, their 16,000 troops fighting largely with lances and kris against 3000 well-armed Dutchmen. The two forces met here again in 1849, when the Dutch finally took control of Buleleng (see p.341). The famous temple here is **Pura Dalem Jagaraga**, about 1km north of the village, dedicated to Siwa the destroyer and renowned for its front walls which are a mass of pictorial carvings. Those on the left show a variety of village activities representing community life before the Dutch invasion – kite-flying, fishing, climbing coconut trees. Next to these are the Dutch arriving in cars, boats, planes and on bicycles, destroying the community. On the right-hand side is a much-photographed carving of two Dutch men driving a Model T Ford, being held up by bandits. Nearby are statues of uniformed Dutch officers and the legendary Pan Brayut (see box on p.209), with children climbing all over him.

The only **place to stay** is back on the main road, about 200m east of the Jagaraga turning. *Hotel Berdikari* (☎0362/25195; ❷–❺) comprises attractive bungalows set in glorious gardens, far enough back from the main road to escape the noise. Cheaper rooms have cold-water bathrooms and fans and more expensive ones feature hot-water bathrooms and air-conditioning. This is also a good place to **eat** a moderately priced lunch, with a good range of Indo-Chinese options and drinks available. There's a small weaving workshop here (open for viewing 7.30am–4pm), owned by the highly regarded Berdikari company that has a larger workshop in Singaraja (see p.345).

Pura Meduwe Karang

The most spectacular of the many fine temples in the area is **Pura Meduwe Karang** at **KUBUTAMBAHAN**, 11km east of Singaraja and 300m west of the junction with the Kintamani road. Its lively and whimsical carvings have a very human quality somehow missing in the other temples; if you only make it to one temple in the north, this is the one to go for. Dedicated to Batara Meduwe Karang (the lord possessing the ground), the temple ensures divine protection for crops grown on dry land, such as coconuts, maize and ground-nuts. It's built on a spectacular scale, with well-maintained grounds and frangi-pani trees galore. The terraces at the front support 34 figures from the *Ramayana* (see p.522), and the centrepiece shows the giant Kumbakarna in violent battle with hordes of monkeys from Sugriwa's army.

Inside, the central court is decorated with **carvings** of Balinese folk, includ-ing elderly people and mothers with babies and toddlers. In the inner court-yard, and typical of northern temples, a large rectangular base links the three central shrines, called the *bebaturan*. On the base of this you'll find one of the most famous carvings on Bali: a cyclist, wearing floral shorts, with a rat about to go under the back wheel, apparently being chased by a dog. It's possible that this depicts the Dutch artist W.O.J. Nieuwenkamp, who first visited Bali in 1904 and explored the island by bicycle. Further around, there are murals of festival-going folks and some chubby-cheeked children.

Air Sanih and around

Further east, 6km from Kubutambahan, **AIR SANIH**, also known as Yeh Sanih, is a small, quiet beach resort that has grown up around the freshwater springs on the coast, although the accommodation is spread out along the coast between Air Sanih and the small village of **BUKTI** 3km to the east, where at least one luxury place is under construction. Public transport between Singaraja and Amlapura all passes through Air Sanih, as do Perama tourist shut-tle buses (see Travel Details on p.366 for details). There's no Perama office in the village but you can either make arrangements to be picked up when you get dropped off or call one of the offices in Lovina (see p.364).

The freezing cold **springs**, widely believed to originate in Lake Bratan, are set in attractive gardens with changing rooms (daily 7am–7pm; Rp2000). A couple of kilometres east of Bukti, it's impossible to miss the exuberant, aggres-sively coloured decoration on the outside of the Art Zoo, the northern gallery of the Balinese artist **Symon** (Ⓦwww.symonbali.com) who also has a gallery in Ubud (see p.211).

Accommodation

Cilik's Beach Garden Ⓣ & Ⓕ0362/26561, Ⓦwww.ciliksbeachgarden.com. About 400m east of the springs, and the real gem in the area, with four lovely choices for accommodation: the origi-nal two superbly furnished bungalows, one with air-con; and, in equally lovely grounds a short walk along the coast, two newer places, one villa and one *lumbung*-style two-storey place. All have hot water and are set in great gardens overlooking the coast – a truly magical hideaway. ❻–❽

Puri Rahayu Ⓣ0362/26565. Just over 400m east of Air Sanih's springs, and across the road from the beach, with good-value bungalows in a small compound and a restaurant attached. Cheaper rooms have fan, more expensive have air-con. ❷–❸

Puri Rena Ⓣ & Ⓕ0362/26581, Ⓔpurirena@yahoo.com. Across the road from the springs, with simple rooms with fan and cold water plus a couple of larger suite rooms with a small private pool, again with fan and cold water. All accommodation is set in a garden but there are good views from the restaurant at the front. Rooms ❷ Suites ❺

Hotel Puri Sanih ☎0362/26563. The most convenient place to stay, next to the beach and springs, with cheaper rooms and better-value, better-positioned bungalows set in fine spacious grounds. All attached bathrooms have cold water. ❷

Hotel Tara ☎0362/26575. Right on the coast 200m east of *Puri Rahayu*, 600m east of the

springs, with a row of simple tiled bungalows, all facing seawards with nice verandahs. The bathrooms are nothing special but this is an excellent budget choice with a small attached restaurant in the grounds, too. ❷

Wira Bali Arsanih ☎0361/262812. Around 2km east of Air Sanih, offering hot water in all the bungalows, fan in the cheaper rooms, air-con in the pricier ones and a small oceanside swimming pool. The most delightful rooms have a great sea view from their verandahs and there's an attached restaurant. A good-value choice. ❺–❻

Pondok Batu and around

About 12km east of Air Sanih, the road climbs over a headland at **PONDOK BATU** where there are great views along the coast. The **temple** here, on a bend in the road, was founded by the sixteenth-century Javanese priest **Nirartha** (see p.145). According to the story, while sitting on a rock here composing poetry and gazing along the coast, Nirartha saw a wrecked ship below. All the crew were lying dead on the beach but, using his spiritual powers, he brought them back to life. Following this miracle, the local people noticed that the rock where Nirartha had been sitting shone with a magical light, and a temple was founded here. Now there's a huge car park, where Balinese drivers stop to pray and receive a blessing for themselves and their vehicle.

About 100m west of the temple, *Pondok Batu Puri Bagus* is a small **restaurant** related to the *Puri Bagus* hotel in Lovina, perched on the hillside above the road in a lovely garden. There's a small menu of moderately priced Western and Indonesian main courses (Rp20,000–27,000) and plenty of drinks; you can wander a short distance up the hill to a small reservoir with even better views in all directions.

Less than 1km east of the temple, in the village of **ALASSARI**, *Pondok Sembiran Bungalows* (☎086812/103677; ❺) is clearly signed towards the coast from the main road. There are four well-built bungalows in a pretty garden with a small pool about 300m inland from the beach; in another garden, by the beach, there are five two-storey cottages. It's an attractive little set-up in a quiet location.

Continuing east, the land becomes increasingly dry and barren, and views of the outer rim of the Batur crater dominate the inland skyline. At Pacung, 2km east of Pondok Batu, a sign points off the main road to **SEMBIRAN**, reached by a narrow lane (3km). This is one of the ancient Bali Aga villages, along with Trunyan (see p.330) and Tenganan (see p.291), but today little distinguishes it from any other village in Bali. It's an area of great antiquity, however, and **JULAH**, about 1km further east, is supposedly the oldest village in Bali.

Bondalem and around

Another couple of kilometres east brings you to **BONDALEM**. On the west side of the village is *Pacific Center* (☎0362/28508, ℱ28509, ☻www.balicenter .de; ❻ all inclusive), in a great coastal location in a coconut grove with a small swimming pool. There are twenty rooms and bungalows, all different but all with attached cold-water bathrooms. The whole place is often booked out by groups who come for courses in meditation, yoga and such like, but individuals seeking some peace and quiet are also welcome. Booking is advisable. There is a **wellness centre** and **ayurvedic massage** is available. If there are no signs on the road you'll need to ask for directions in the village as access is through a maze of lanes and alleyways. On the eastern side of Bondalem village a sign indicates a quiet **back road** that leads 26km up to Kintamani (see p.382).

The small village of **TEJAKULA**, 1km east of Bondalem, is worth a stop for its **horse bath**, a white stone confection of arches and pillars 100m south of the road. The village is a sleepy backwater these days but local historians claim that the area had trading links with distant lands as far back as the first century AD, when it far outstripped the later trading ports of Padang Bai and Benoa in fame and influence; numerous local finds of foreign relics support their case. During the seventeenth century many Balinese people moved to the area for the fertile soil, and local legend tells how a brilliant light appeared in the skies over the village, visible across the island and as far afield as China. Those who saw it believed that it signified the enormous prosperity of the area.

A few kilometres beyond here at **LES**, a sign points inland to **Yeh Mempeh**, questionably dubbed the highest waterfall in Bali.

Sembirenteng and Tembok

About 8km beyond Tejakula at **SEMBIRENTENG** is *Alam Anda* (T & F 0361/752296, W www.alamanda.de; ❻–❼), an oasis in the parched land-scape. This is a great place to relax; there's a nice little swimming pool and a dedicated **massage** house with ayurvedic massage a speciality. The **restaurant** is cool and breezy, serving a good range of moderate to expensively priced Western and Indonesian food. It's a good place to stop on the long drive along the north coast but you should phone first, as they don't open to non-residents if the hotel is busy. The **accommodation** is in traditional well-furnished bungalows with hot and cold water and fan as well as losmen-style rooms with fan and cold water, set in lovely grounds just behind the beach. One bungalow has been modified for wheelchair users. **Diving** is available, at US$30 for the first local dive ($15 for additional ones); equipment rental is $16 per day. An introductory dive costs $75, while a PADI open water course is $395. It's also possible to arrange transport and dives for other north-coast sites such as Tulamben, Amed and Menjangan.

About 5km further east at **TEMBOK** is the top-class *Jepun Bali Resort* (T 0362/32000, F 32033, W www.jepun-bali.com; ❽–❾), offering accommodation in excellently appointed rooms with a few villas and suites. It's impossible to imagine a more remote spot for such a stunningly lovely resort. Natural materials are everywhere and the cream stone glows in the sunshine, emphasized by the minimalist Bali modern style. The pool is glorious, landscaping is superb and there's an on-site spa where day-visitors are welcome. From here, it's 22km east to Tulamben (see p.310).

Lovina and around

LOVINA stretches along 8km of black-sand beach, the largest resort in Bali outside the Kuta–Legian–Seminyak conurbation. Beginning 6km west of Singaraja, the resort encompasses six villages: from east to west, **Pemaron**, **Tukad Mungga**, **Anturan**, **Kalibukbuk**, **Kaliasem** and **Temukus**. Kalibukbuk is generally accepted as the centre of Lovina and has several roads, including one about 1500m east known as **Banyualit**, leading down to the coast from the main through-route. It's in Kalibukbuk that you'll find most tourist facilities, the greatest concentration of accommodation and restaurants, and the little nightlife there is in the resort. While the peak season (Dec & June–Aug) is busy, Lovina remains far less frantic and frenetic than the southern resorts and by choosing where to stay you can easily have a quiet and relaxing time. The main Singaraja–Gilimanuk road passes right through Lovina, and while some of the accommodation and tourist facilities line this road, particularly in Kalibukbuk, most of the accommodation is along side roads leading from the main road to the beach.

The potential of the area was spotted by the last raja of Buleleng, Anak Agung Panji Tisna, who built the *Tasik Madu Hotel* at Kaliasem in the 1960s and devised the name Lovina. Today, activity centres mainly on the beach, with **snorkelling**, **diving** and **dolphin-watching** as diversions. In common with the southern resorts, Lovina has its share of hawkers – but, unlike the Kuta area, they're allowed to ply their wares on the beach. There are waterfalls, hot springs and a Buddhist temple nearby, and Singaraja and points east are easily accessible by bemo. The volcanic Bedugul and Batur areas (see p.333 and p.319 respectively) are also well within reach.

At Lovina, you can witness the local **buffalo races** (*sapi gerumbungan*), the only place in the country where the colourful tradition can be seen, apart from at Negara (see p.390). The races were formerly confined to Independence Day (Aug 17), when the biggest event still takes place. However there are now regular, lower-key races staged for tourists at the track in Kaliasem that are well worth attending.

Arrival, information and transport

Getting to Lovina is easy: inter-island **buses** from Java to Singaraja pass through, as do Gilimanuk–Singaraja and Amlapura–Gilimanuk services, and all local buses and **bemos** from the west of the island. From Denpasar and the east of Bali, you'll come via Singaraja, from whose Banyuasri terminal it's a short bemo ride (Rp1000). **Tourist shuttle buses** also serve the resort from other parts of Bali and Lombok; however, Perama drop off only at their office in Anturan – inconvenient if you want to stay elsewhere in the resort. Check with other shuttle bus operators whether they will drop you off more centrally (as the resort is so spread out, it's well worth pinning down where you want to be dropped off, especially if you arrive late in the evening as many of the inter-island buses do). For information on travelling to and from Ngurah Rai **Airport**, see the box on pp.110–111.

Lovina's **tourist office** (Mon–Sat 8am–8pm) is on the main road at Kalibukbuk next to the police post. Getting around the resort on **public transport** is no problem during the day as you can pick up the frequent bemos and minibuses that zip through between Singaraja and Seririt, although the service can be erratic in the early morning and effectively dies after dark. At these times, you'll need to negotiate with the transport touts, unless your hotel or restaurant offers transport. A huge number of places offer **vehicles for rent** or charter (see Listings, p.363) and charges are competitive, on a par with the resorts in the south. There are also **bicycles** for rent, but the Singaraja–Seririt road is very busy, traffic is fast, and the heat doesn't make this a very pleasant option.

Accommodation

Despite its reputation as a backpackers' resort, Lovina has attracted big money and plenty of upmarket hotels, although there are still many inexpensive and moderately priced **accommodation** options. Generally, those closest to the

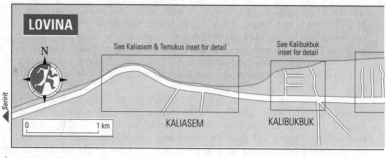

ACCOMMODATION

Adirama	39	Hotel Banyualit	53	Harris Homestay	12	Mandhara Chico	18	Padma	36
Aditya	43	Baruna Beach	26	Hepi	32	Mari	17	Parma	42
Agus Homestay	38	Bayu Kartika	1	Indra Pura	62	Mas	59	Hotel Permai	31
Aneka Lovina	54	Bayu Mantra	22	Jati Reef	28	Mas Lovina Beach	55	Hotel Permai	33
Angsoka	8	Billibo	40	Juni Arta	49	Melka	58	Pondok Elsa	11
Astina	3	Hotel Celuk Agung	60	Hotel Kalibukbuk	47	Mutiara	45	Pulestis	10
Awangga	61	Damai Lovina Villas	35	Krisna Beach	37	Nirwana Seaside	2	Puri Bagus Lovina	27
Bagus Homestay	41	Gede Homestay	16	Lila Cita	51	Nirwana Water Garden	15	Puri Bali	5
Bali Taman Beach	25	Happy Beach Inn	29	Made Janur	57	Padang Lovina	13	Puri Bedahulu	30

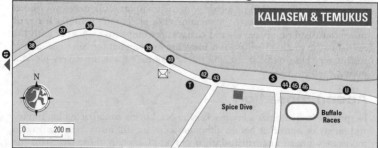

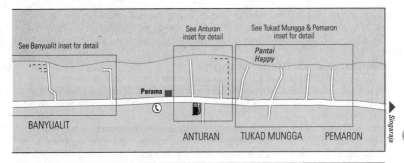

				RESTAURANTS					
Puri Mandhara	23	Rini	4	Bali Apik	F	Gula Bali	B	Warung Bambu	R
Puri Manggala	46	Sartaya	52	Bali Bintang	D	Khi Khi	L	Warung Nyoman	O
Puri Manik Sari	14	Sol Lovina	48	Barakuda	E	Kopi Bali	C	Warung Rasta	N
Puri Tasik Madu	44	Sri Homestay	21	Biyu-Nasak	U	Kubu Lalang	Q		
Puspa Rama	24	Suma	50	Bombai	H	Mailaku	G		
Putri Sari	34	Taman Lily's	6	Bu Warung	I	Malibu	J		
Rambutan	9	Villa Agung	20	Café Spice	S	Planet Lovina	K		
Ray 1	7	Yudha	19	Café 3	M	Sea Breeze	A		
Ray 2	56			Djani's	T	Warung Bamboo	P		

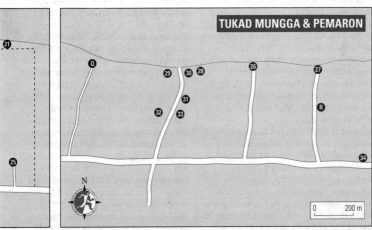

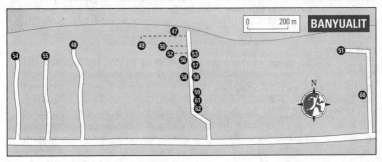

beach are more expensive, and the places lining the main road are the cheapest. The busiest season is from mid-June until late August and again in December. All accommodation is marked on the map on pp.352–53.

Pemaron and Tukad Mungga

Putri Sari, on the main road, is the marker for the eastern end of Lovina. Most of the accommodation here, in **Pemaron** and **Tukad Mungga** (also known as Pantai Happy), is along side roads leading down to the beach; upmarket places have their own drives from the main road. It's a very quiet area, with minimal hassle and a range of options including some reasonably cheap places with pools. There are no village amenities nearby and the nightlife of Kalibukbuk is several kilometres away, but you can walk 1km along the beach to the tourist facilities of Anturan (beware of the dogs that guard the fishermen's huts). The turning for Pantai Happy – the beach at Tukad Mungga – is opposite a pink split gateway and sign to Tukad Mungga. The beach here is quite scruffy but there are good views west along the coast.

Baruna Beach Cottages ☎0362/41252, ☞41745, ⓦwww.indo.com/hotels/baruna. Comfortable, quiet accommodation set in attractive gardens, with a good-sized swimming pool by the beach at the far eastern end of Lovina. Cheaper accommodation is in rooms while the top-end accommodation is in beachfront cottages with fine coastal views. ⑤—⑦

Happy Beach Inn *(Bahagia)* ☎0362/41017. Basic, cheap rooms with attached cold-water bathrooms close to Pantai Happy beach. There's a small, pleasant garden and a beachside restaurant. ②

Hepi ☎0362/41020, ☞41910, ⓦwww.balibackpacker.com. Good-quality fan and air-con rooms, all with cold water, in a quiet garden setting with a small pool, a short walk from the beach at Pantai Happy. ①—③

Jati Reef ☎0362/41052. Well located near Pantai Happy, but a bit soulless. Some accommodation is in rooms in a two-storey block but the bungalows spread out behind the beach are better. ②

Hotel Permai ☎0362/41224. There are two neighbouring places with this name near Pantai Happy. This one is closer to the sea, has no pool and no attached dive centre. Rooms are simple but adequate, with fan and cold water in the cheaper rooms and air-con and hot water in the more expensive. ②—③

Hotel Permai ☎0362/41471. The other place with this name near Pantai Happy – larger, with a good-sized pool. Permai dive centre is based here. A choice of rooms is available in two-storey buildings all with balconies or verandahs and all with hot water. There are fans in the cheaper rooms and air-con in the more expensive. A grand new restaurant and pool bar are under construction. ②—④

Puri Bagus Lovina ☎0362/21430, ☞22627, ⓦwww.bagus-discovery.com. This is one of the loveliest, most luxurious places in Lovina, offering large, airy, well-furnished villas with verandahs and indoor and open-air showers, located in superb grounds towards the far eastern end of Lovina. Rooms have TVs and tea- and coffee-making facilities. There's a lovely pool, a library and an excellent, atmospheric restaurant. Service is friendly but efficient and there's transport to central Lovina. ⑧—⑨

Puri Bedahulu ☎0362/41731. Right next to the beach at Pantai Happy with a pretty garden. The entrance resembles a temple, and there's a restaurant looking across the sand. Bungalows are elegantly carved and comfortable and the most expensive ones have air-con. All have hot water. ③—④

Anturan

The tiny fishing village of **Anturan** is developing rapidly, and many of the basic homestays have moved upmarket. While this area remains much quieter and more low-key than Kalibukbuk, there are still plenty of people around and you'll share the local beach with the villagers; they're well-used to tourists wandering around. There are plenty of beach-hawkers, but it's all fairly relaxed and amiable. To get there, take the turning almost opposite the petrol station and the imposing, two-storey Anturan health centre (*Puskesmas*); coming from the east, look out for big signs for *Bali Taman Lovina*, *Yudha* (*Simon Seaside*

Cottages) and *Villa Agung*. The Perama office is just west of the turning. All the accommodation is grouped quite close together, a five- to fifteen-minute walk from here along the side road and down to the beach.

Bali Taman Beach Hotel ☎0362/41126, ℱ41840, ⓦwww.indo.com/hotels/bali_taman. A big operation with comfortable, well-furnished rooms, a pool, tennis courts and attractive grounds accessed via its own driveway from the main road. The restaurant is near the pool which is also near the beach. Lower-end rooms only have a shower while the most upmarket are larger and have bathtubs and ocean views. ❻–❼

Bayu Mantra ☎0362/41930. Clean, tiled bungalows in a large garden set back from the beach. All rooms have fans and there is a choice of hot or cold water. ❷–❸

Gede Homestay ☎0362/41526. Good-quality accommodation is in two rows of bungalows facing each other across a small garden. There's a small sunbathing area. All rooms have fans and more expensive ones have hot water. ❶–❷

Mandhara Chico ☎0362/41271. Close to the beach, this is the upmarket version of *Puri Mandhara*. Tiled rooms, some with hot water and air-con, in a small compound with sitting areas close to the beach. The best rooms are the two bungalows at the front with verandahs facing seawards. ❷–❹

Mari ☎0362/41882. Offering some of the cheapest accommodation in Anturan: one small row of rooms near the beach with cold-water bathrooms and fan. There's an attached beachside restaurant. ❶

Puri Mandhara ☎0362/41476. Basic budget rooms in a small compound set back from the beach with an attached restaurant. ❶

Puspa Rama ☎0362/42070, ℮agungdayu@yahoo.com. A small row of six, clean rooms all with fan and hot water set in a large, attractive garden just off the lane leading to the beach with a small restaurant attached. ❷

Sri Homestay ☎0362/41135, ℮srihomstay@yahoo.com. A relaxed place in an unbeatable location – most easterly of the Anturan beachside options – with all the bungalows set in a garden and facing seawards. There are several standards of accommodation, up to the largest, newest places with hot water. There's a small restaurant with a pool table and internet access. You can reach here via a track from the main road or via the beach. ❶–❹

Villa Agung ☎0362/41527, ℱ41999, ⓦwww.balilovina.com. Rooms are set back from the sea behind the small swimming pool and are nothing special, although all have hot water, with fan in the cheaper rooms and air-con in the more costly. However, the real bonus is the seafront restaurant and the lounge on the floor above, which is ideally located for admiring the ocean views. ❹–❺

Yudha (formerly *Simon Seaside Cottage*) ☎0362/41183, ℱ41160. A long-time favourite just beside the beach, with a wide range of comfortably furnished rooms in a pretty garden and a good pool. Cheaper rooms have fan and cold-water bathroom and are situated downstairs while top-end rooms have air-con and hot water with other options in between. All rooms have a balcony or verandah and there's a restaurant overlooking the beach. ❷–❹

Banyualit

The **Banyualit** side road marks the beginning of the developed part of Lovina, about 1500m east of Kalibukbuk. It's a self-contained little enclave with plenty of accommodation, enough restaurants so you could eat somewhere different every night of the week and some shops. The places are generally simple and there aren't many swimming pools, but it isn't a long walk to the beach. There's a quieter, largely undeveloped lane a few hundred metres to the east with a couple of places to stay and, just west of the main Banyualit turning, a trio of newer, upmarket options have their own drives leading directly from the main road.

Aneka Lovina ☎0362/41121, ℱ41827, ⓦwww.anekahotels.com. West of the Banyualit turning. Accommodation is in comfortable rooms in a two-storey building or thatched bungalows, all set in attractive gardens with a beachside pool. All have air-con and hot water and some bungalows have pool views. It's a 15min walk from Kalibukbuk. A good choice in this price range. ❼

Awangga ☎0362/41561. A row of basic bungalows in a lush garden. One of the cheapest places here; don't expect anything fancy. *Made Janur* (☎0362/41056), slightly closer to the beach, is similar in price and quality. ❶

Hotel Banyualit ☎0362/41789, ℱ41563, ⓦwww.banyualit.com. This long-standing Lovina landmark has several standards of well-furnished bungalows in a lush garden wilderness with an attractive pool. The more expensive options are the best value and have air-con and hot water, with top-end villas tucked away in a private enclave near the pool. ③—⑦

Hotel Celuk Agung ⊤0362/41039, ⓕ41379, ⓔcelukabc@singaraja.wasantara.net.id. Good-quality option in this price range, often with significant discounts. All rooms have hot water and air-con and the newly refurbished rooms are especially light and airy. The grounds are extensive and attractive and there's a large pool (Rp15,000/day for non-residents), tennis courts, jogging track and a footpath to the beach. Located on a turning just to the east of the Banyualit turn-off, a few hundred metres from the main road. ⑤—⑦

Indra Pura ⊤0362/41560. Good, straightforward budget choice offering clean accommodation in bungalows with attached cold-water bathrooms, all set in a pretty garden. ②

Juni Arta ⊤0362/41885. Reached via a path behind *Hotel Kalibukbuk*, this is a small row of good-quality, good-value bungalows in a peaceful, attractive spot. All rooms have cold water and there's a choice of fan or air-con. ②—③

Hotel Kalibukbuk ⊤ & ⓕ0362/41701. The rooms here – with verandahs facing the sea – are nothing special but this place boasts an excellent location at the ocean end of Banyualit. Cheaper rooms have fan and there's air-con in the pricier ones; all have cold water. Also a small attached restaurant, beside the beach. ②

Lila Cita No phone. Right on the beach at the end of a quiet lane, a few hundred metres further on from *Hotel Celuk Agung*, with some rooms in a two-storey building and some newer bungalows – all face seawards, and the more expensive rooms have hot water. There's also a small restaurant. One of the quietest places along the coast. ①—③

Mas ⊤0362/41773. Behind an impressive gateway on the Banyualit turning to the beach, with simple rooms, some with hot water, decorated with local textiles in a pleasant garden. ②—③

Mas Lovina Beach Cottages ⊤0362/41237, ⓕ41236, ⓦwww.indo.com/hotels/maslovina. A luxurious place, just a short walk from Kalibukbuk, offering accommodation in two-storey cottages. Bedrooms either have a living room or kitchen attached or two bedrooms can be combined with living room and kitchen to provide a family villa. The gardens are attractive and there's a good pool beside the beach. ⑦

Melka ⊤0362/41552, ⓕ41543, ⓦwww.freeyellow.com/members8/melka-bali. This is a big set-up, with plenty of standards of rooms on offer. Pricier rooms with hot water and air-con are on one side of the road near the pool and restaurant. The cheaper rooms, with cold water and fan, are across the road. There's a small zoo with captive birds, deer, snakes and crocodile. It's worth looking at several rooms as the site is quite crowded in parts. ②—⑤

Ray 2 ⊤0362/41088. Clean, tiled rooms in a two-storey block with balcony or verandah. All have cold water and fan and are a good budget choice. Cheaper rooms downstairs. ①

Sartaya ⊤0362/42240. Good-quality. clean, tiled bungalows all with cold water and a choice of fan or air-con. ①—②

Sol Lovina ⊤0362/41775, ⓕ41659, ⓦwww.solmelia.com. One of the largest hotels in the region, reached via its own drive from the main road, with a huge entrance area, attractive grounds and beachside pool. All rooms have hot water and air-con; at the cheaper end rooms are in a two-storey block while more expensive options are cottages and villas. Prices start at US$90; upwards of $240 will get you a villa with private pool. There's an attached spa and many good-value packages available. ⑧—⑨

Suma ⊤0362/41566. The best budget option in this part of Lovina offers clean, well-maintained rooms in a two-storey block just a short walk from the beach, with a small restaurant attached. ①

Kalibukbuk

Centred around two side roads, Jalan Mawar, also known as Jalan Ketapang or Jalan Rambutan, and Jalan Bina Ria, **Kalibukbuk** has a huge number of places to stay and to eat, plus some nightlife and shops, money–changers, dive shops, travel agents and car rental outlets. The accommodation on the main road is the cheapest if you're on a tight budget but the road is quite noisy. The narrow entrance to Jalan Mawar is easy to miss; look out for *Khi Khi Restaurant* on the opposite side of the road and The Lovina Wellness Spa and Healing Centre on the corner. Jalan Bina Ria has the biggest concentration of buildings, and a maze of side roads leads off from it.

Angsoka ☏ 0362/41841, ⓕ 41023, ⓦ www
.baliweb.net/angsoka. A variety of good-quality
accommodation options in a large compound conveniently located off Jalan Bina Ria. Pleasant
swimming pool (Rp20,000 for non-guests). ❷–❺
Astina ☏ 0362/41187. Plenty of standards of
accommodation in this long-time budget favourite
with a large garden compound in a quiet spot a short
walk from the beach at the end of Jalan Mawar.
There are basic rooms with shared bathrooms up to
cottages with air-con and hot water. ❶–❺
Bayu Kartika ☏ 0362/41055, ⓕ 41219. Boasts
one of the best positions in Lovina, on the coast at
the end of Jalan Mawar. There is a good range of
bungalows, from cheaper ones with fan and cold
water and no view to the expensive options offering air-con and hot water; all are clean and have
mosquito nets. The rooms in the middle price
bracket have the best views of the sea. The pool is
huge with a fountain and island in the middle
(Rp20,000 for non-resident visitors) and the
restaurant superbly located to catch the sea
breezes. ❹–❻
Damai Lovina Villas ☏ 0362/41008, ⓕ 41009,
ⓦ www.damai.com. Located in the village of
Kayuputih, 4km inland from Kalibukbuk in a beautiful, cool location surrounded by paddy-fields up in
the hills. Accommodation, service and ambience
are all elegantly luxurious and among the best in
Lovina. The eight superbly appointed bungalows,
furnished with antiques and fabulous textiles (and
no TVs), are widely spaced in glorious gardens and
have all the character and facilities to be expected
at this end of the market. There's a wonderful pool,
spa treatments are available, and the restaurant is
one of the delights of northern Bali. Prices start at
US$190; diving and golf packages available. ❾
Harris Homestay ☏ 0362/41152. A popular little
gem tucked away in the back streets off Jalan
Bina Ria – worth searching out for its good-value,
good-quality rooms. ❶
Nirwana Seaside Cottages ☏ 0362/41288,
ⓕ 41090, ⓔ nirwana@singaraja.wasantara.net.id.
A large, well-organized development with a huge
choice of comfortable accommodation, all with hot
water. Has a lovely position in well-maintained
gardens near the beach at the end of Jalan Bina
Ria, with a pool (Rp20,000 for non-guests). More
expensive rooms have a beachfront location but
not uninterrupted ocean views as the foliage is
thick. New buildings near the pool will house new,
deluxe rooms. ❸–❻
Nirwana Water Garden ☏ 0362/42021,
ⓕ 41090, ⓔ nirwana@singaraja.wasantara.net.id.
Newer offshoot of Nirwana Seaside Cottages.
Attractive and unusual rooms and bungalows set

around an attractive pool in a pretty garden.
Unfortunately located close to the main road so it
does get some noise. All rooms have hot water
and there's a choice of fan or air-con. ❹–❻
Padang Lovina ☏ 0362/41302, ⓔ padanglovina@
yahoo.com. Simple accommodation in a two-
storey block just off Jalan Bina Ria. The downstairs
rooms have hot water; all rooms have good balconies or verandahs. Guests here can use the pool
at Pulestis. ❹
Pondok Elsa ☏ 0362/41186) Just off Jalan Bina
Ria, this place is newer than the others nearby.
There's good-quality accommodation in bungalows
set in a cosy compound. All have cold water and
there is a choice of fan or air-con. ❷–❹
Pulestis ☏ 0362/41035, ⓔ pulestis@hotmail.com.
Reached through a grand entrance on Jalan Bina
Ria, the small compound has comfortable rooms
with a choice of hot water or just cold, fan or air-
con, and the pleasant pool has a fun waterfall feature. Excellent value. ❷–❹
Puri Bali ☏ 0362/41485. A variety of rooms, some
with thatched roofs, in an attractive garden with a
good-sized pool; more expensive ones, closer to
the pool, have air-con and hot water. Enjoys a
quiet location on Jalan Mawar, not far from the
beach. ❷–❹
Puri Manik Sari ☏ 0362/41089. Accessible from
the main road and Jalan Bina Ria, there is a variety of bungalows in a pretty garden complete with
pools and statues. It's set far enough back from
the road to avoid the noise. There are fan-cooled
rooms with cold water at the bottom end and new
rooms with air-con at the top. ❶–❹
Rambutan ☏ 0362/41388, ⓕ 41057, ⓦ www
.rambutan.org. Halfway down Jalan Mawar with
well-furnished, clean bungalows set well apart in a
beautiful garden. Five standards of rooms to choose
from, two pools, an attractive restaurant and some
larger family villas also available. This long-standing
Lovina favourite is justifiably popular. ❹–❼
Ray 1 (No phone). Although offering good value for
the location (off Jalan Bina Ria), this is a bit
hemmed in by the larger establishments nearby;
upstairs rooms are more airy. ❶
Rini ☏ & ⓕ 0362/41386. Several choices of
accommodation in an attractive garden location on
Jalan Mawar just a short walk to the beach. More
expensive rooms have air-con and hot water and
there's a pool with a poolside restaurant. ❸–❺
Taman Lily's ☏ 0362/41307, ⓕ 26653. A small row
of attractive, spotless, tiled bungalows in a large and
well-maintained garden on Jalan Mawar, with warm-
water bathrooms. There's an attached restaurant.
More expensive rooms are larger, have a fridge and
are further from the road. Excellent value. ❷–❸

Kaliasem and Temukus

As you head west from Kalibukbuk, passing through the villages of **Kaliasem** and **Temukus**, the main road runs much closer to the coast, and is lined with restaurants and accommodation. It's generally noisier at this end though there are a few places worth considering here. The western end of the main part of Lovina is marked by *Pondok Ayu Restaurant* on the south side of the road and *Agus* on the coast side although there is one place, *Bagus Homestay*, 1km or so further west, somewhat adrift from the main resort.

Adirama ☎0362/41759, ℻41755. On the main road at Kaliasem. All rooms have hot water, bath-tubs and a choice of fan or air-con. It's looking a bit faded but there's a pool close to the beach. Worth considering if you can negotiate a consider-able (more than fifty percent) discount. **⑤**—**⑦**

Aditya ☎0362/41059, ℻41342, ⓦwww.indo.com/hotels/aditya. One of the large places that have sprung up west of Kalibukbuk, with a raised pool and plenty of accommodation options, all with hot water and air-con. **⑥**—**⑦**

Agus Homestay ☎ & ℻0362/41202. A small place, close to the sea at the far western end of the main Lovina development. Clean, tiled rooms, with verandahs that face the ocean. All have air-con and hot water. **❸**

Bagus Homestay ☎0362/93407, ℻93406. Situated about 1km west of its sister operation, *Agus Homestay*, so quite separate from the main Lovina development. Six bungalows in a lovely garden setting right beside a pleasant beach. All are spotless, with air-con and hot water. More expensive ones have a bathtub rather than shower. **④**—**⑤**

Billibo ☎ & ℻0362/41355. These tiled bunga-lows at Kaliasem are close to the beachfront in an attractive garden and there's a choice of fan or air-con and hot- or cold-water bathrooms. A large, airy restaurant is attached. All are set far enough back from the road to be sheltered from the worst of the noise. **②**—**⑤**

Krisna Beach Cottages incorporating Villa Delima ☎0362/41141. Simple budget accommo-dation in a two-storey block with plenty of places to sit and relax in the grounds, towards the far western end of Lovina and close to the beach. **①**—**②**

Mutiara ☎0362/41132. Friendly, family-run place offering simple rooms in a two-storey building. Airier rooms are upstairs. It's just a short walk to the beach. **①**—**②**

Padma ☎0362/41947, ℻41140, ⓦwww.indo.com/hotels/padma. Located towards the western end of the Lovina development. All rooms have hot water and there's a choice of fan or air-con, but the big draw here is the excellent beachside pool. Discounts often available. **⑥**

Parma ☎0362/41555. The best budget option at the western end of Lovina. Simple fan rooms in a good quiet location in a pretty garden near the sea. The best rooms overlook the sea. **①**—**②**

Puri Manggala ☎0362/41371. Clean, simple rooms in a family compound tucked between the nearby beach and the road to the west of Kalibukbuk. Rooms have cold water and fan, or hot water and air-con. **②**—**④**

Puri Tasik Madu ☎0362/41376. Situated right next to the beach at Kaliasem, this budget cheapie offers basic rooms with attached bathrooms. Some rooms overlook the sea, and it's a short walk into Kalibukbuk. **①**—**②**

The resort

Lovina's long **black-sand beach** stretches into the distance where, on clear days, the imposing peaks of East Java look surprisingly close. Fringed by palm trees, the widest stretch of beach is at Kalibukbuk, but there's at least some beach all along the resort. In many spots, most notably at Anturan, you'll share the sand with local fishing boats. There's nothing to draw surfers to Lovina – none of the huge breakers that pound the beaches on the south coast – and swimming around here is generally calm and safe, although there are no lifeguards on duty. There's not a great deal to do other than enjoy the beach and the resort life that has built up behind it, although many people consider Lovina's early-morning **dolphin trips** (see box) to be the highlight of their stay. The monument **Patung Lumba Lumba**, at the beach end of Jalan Bina Ria, depicts dolphins complete with black-and-white-checked *kain poleng* headscarves; it's pretty tacky although widely copied in hotel gardens throughout the resort.

Dolphin trips

Lovina has become famous (or infamous) for dawn trips to see the school of **dolphins** that frolics just off the coast: opinions are fairly evenly split between those who think it's grossly overrated and those who consider it one of the best things on Bali.

Boats – simple *prahu* hewn from a single tree trunk with a bamboo stabilizer on each side – leave at 6am. The vessels all have motors, but there's no shelter from the sun for passengers. As you head out to sea at dawn, in a flotilla of thirty or more boats, take a look back at the lovely views of the coast and the central mountains. The ensuing scenario is mildly comic, as one skipper spots a dolphin and chases after it, to be followed by the rest of the fleet, by which time, of course, the dolphin is long gone. Most people end up with more pictures of other boats than of dolphins, but if you can see the funny side, it's a good trip, and a lot of the skippers provide coffee and fried bananas on the way back. Very, very occasionally **whales** have been spotted.

Expect to **pay** Rp30,000 per person for the two-hour trip; you can book directly with the skippers on the beach, or hotel or losmen staff may know particularly good skippers. Captains are banned from working for a week if they're discovered to have given discounts or allowed more than four passengers per boat.

Diving and snorkelling

Situated between the main **diving** areas on the north coast of Bali – Menjangan or Deer Island to the west (see p.401) and Tulamben (see p.311) and Amed (see p.307) to the east – Lovina is a good place to base yourself for diving, although the reef here isn't particularly interesting for experienced divers. It used to stretch at least 5km along the coast, but the anchoring of boats, fish-bombing, harpoon fishing and damage from snorkellers has decimated the coral. It's now beginning to rejuvenate through local efforts which have seen tyres, an old car, and a small wrecked boat placed on the reef to encourage coral growth. There's still an excellent range of fish.

Plenty of **operators** work in the resort, all offering trips for qualified and experienced divers and some featuring introductory dives. For two-dive trips to Menjangan Island, Tulamben or Amed, the going rate is US$40–60; two dives in the Lovina area cost $35–40. Price wars break out from time to time, but maintaining dive equipment properly isn't cheap; if prices fall too low there's a risk that companies will cut costs, so don't be unduly swayed by the price. A four-day PADI Open Water course costs $250–350.

Your losmen can also arrange **snorkelling trips** for you, or you can approach the boat skippers on the beach direct; expect to pay about Rp30,000 for a trip of one-and-a-half or two hours to the local reef. Most of the dive shops will take snorkellers along on dive trips further afield if they have space; this is more expensive ($20–39) but offers more variety. It pays to shop around and see who is going where. The *Kubu Lalang* restaurant (☎0362/42207) offers **night snorkelling** trips (Rp100,000 per person).

Dive operators

Aquatropic ☎0362/42038. Has several counters on the main roads in Lovina, offering the usual dive trips for experienced divers both local and further afield, plus courses.

Baruna On the main road in Kalibukbuk ☎0362/41084, and at *Puri Bagus Hotel* ☎0362/25542, ⓦwww.comcen.com.au/~baruna. A branch of the main office near Denpasar, offering diving trips and courses.

Malibu Dive Next to *Malibu* restaurant ☎ & ⓕ0362/41225, ⓔmalibu@singaraja.wasantara.net.id. Also on Jalan Bina Ria ☎0362/41061, and with counters all over the resort. A PADI dive centre operating a full range of dives for certified divers as well as PADI courses.

Buffalo races

Lovina stages regular **buffalo races** (*sapi gerumbungan*), held in the late afternoon in a field in Kaliasem (Rp40,000) – twice weekly in the main tourist seasons and weekly at other times. Local flyers advertising the races are everywhere in the resort. Cooking, rice-pounding and martial arts displays supplement the races, turning the whole thing into a lovely, good-natured event. The buffalo are placid, dolled up in ornate yokes and headdresses to prance as quickly as possible with their high-legged gait along a set course, hampered somewhat by a huge bell around their neck, their jockeys perching on a painfully narrow seat. Spectators are encouraged to have a go themselves – and this is just as entertaining, especially the funny walks that result from bumpy contact with the aforementioned seat. A much grander, more serious event takes place annually on Independence Day (Aug 17).

Maoka On the main road in Kalibukbuk ☎0362/41968. The local office of a company which has a few branches around Bali.
Permai At *Hotel Permai*, Pantai Happy ☎0362/41471. Offers dives for certified divers, as well as PADI courses and introductory dives. The early stages of beginners' courses are in the *Permai* swimming pool.
Spice Dive Kaliasem ☎0362/41305, ℱ41171, ⓦwww.damai.com/spicedive. Also has shops on Jalan Bina Ria and Jalan Mawar. Established in Lovina for many years, and the resort's only PADI five-star dive centre, offering courses up to Assistant Instructor level, a range of trips and introductory dives. Also offer a two-day "Rainbow Tour" (US$150 per person) to Baluran National Park in Java via Menjangan Island to the west, including five dives, and more exotic trips, such as to the Kangean Islands, by special arrangement for a minimum of four people (US$560 for four days). Spice Dive instigated the AWARE Project, a local marine environmental scheme.
Sunrise Dive Jalan Bina Ria ☎0362/411820 and office ☎ & ℱ0362/42083. Offering local dives, dive trips further afield and courses.
Wisnu Resort On the main road opposite the turning to Banyualit ☎0362/42319, ⓔwisnu_diveresort@yahoo.com. The usual range of dive trips for experienced divers.

Watersports

Spice Beach (☎0362/41969), an off-shoot of the well-established operator Spice Dive, has branched out into **watersports**. They have a lovely beach location in Kaliasem, where they offer parasailing (US$10 for one run) and wake-boarding, kneeboarding and water-skiing (all $15 for 20min), plus banana boat rides (US$5 per person for 20 min, minimum four people). You can watch all the action from the highly recommended *Café Spice* (see p.361). Just next door, Indiana Massage has paddle boards for rent (Rp25,000/hr, discounts for longer periods). Lifejackets and guides are available if desired and they also rent out snorkelling and fishing gear.

Sailing (Rp75,000/hr per person), **fishing** (Rp50,000/hr per person) and **spearfishing** (Rp75,000/hr per person), are offered by the *Kubu Lalang* restaurant (☎0362/42207).

Eating, drinking and nightlife

There's a high turnover of **restaurants** in Lovina – the favourite today may well be extinct tomorrow – and a healthy level of competition ensures plenty of good "happy hour" deals, especially around Jalan Bina Ria, lasting well into the evening and in some cases including soft drinks and free nibbles. The quality of food is generally reasonable, with seafood the local speciality.

The places recommended below are all marked on the map on pp.352–53 and unless noted otherwise are in the inexpensive to moderate price range.

Bali Apik Tucked away off Jalan Bina Ria and serving an excellent choice of breakfasts as well as a large Indo-Chinese, seafood and Western menu and lots of happy hour specials. Meals are inexpensive: main courses Rp10,000–15,000 and seafood Rp25,000.

Bali Bintang Stretches back off Jalan Bina Ria and features high ceilings and more mellow music than many places. Also has internet access. The large drinks list includes liqueurs, liqueur coffees, spirits and cocktails and there's an extensive menu of the usual Indo-Chinese, Western and seafood dishes all reasonably priced: steaks Rp18,000–28,000, seafood up to Rp25,000. Also plenty of breakfast choices.

Barakuda In a quiet spot on Jalan Mawar, this place doesn't look much from the outside but they specialize in superbly cooked, extremely good-value seafood; squid, crab, fish and prawns are all under Rp15,000 and lobster is Rp140,000. Your choice is served with one of eleven Balinese or Chinese sauces and the chef will come and help you choose, based on what you like. There are plenty of vegetarian, pork and chicken options as well as pancakes for dessert.

Biyu-Nasak On the main road in Kalibukbuk. The menu is vegetarian and seafood, with lots of imaginative and appetizing choices, such as vegetable strudel, creamy mustard sauce and mash (Rp15,500) or bok choy, baby potatoes, sweet corn, *tempeh* in fresh basil and vinaigrette (Rp12,000). Also plenty of scrumptious breakfast choices and lots of drinks. Small gift shop attached.

Bombai Located on the corner of Jalan Bina Ria and the main road in Kalibukbuk, this place, despite its name, doesn't do Indian cuisine – it has the usual food but also offers some Mexican dishes. Frequent happy hours last all evening and include lassis, juices and soft drinks, and diners get free garlic bread.

Bu Warung Probably the best-value food in Kalibukbuk, this tiny place on the main road has a small menu of around a dozen main courses (Rp7500–8500) of rice, vegetables, noodles, chicken, pork and tuna dishes. There are also sandwiches, jaffles, pancakes and fried bananas and pineapple. The food is extremely well cooked and you'll not notice the noise from the nearby road.

Café Spice ☎ 0362/41969. As the base of the Spice Beach water sports set-up, this attractive café is located in a great spot beside the beach at Kaliasem. The menu includes seafood, Western and Indo-Chinese meals plus plenty of snacks, shakes and juices. Phone for a free pick-up in the

Lovina area. There are weekly parties on a Friday night, sometimes with live music, running until 3 or 4am. Open 8am–10pm.

Damai ☎ 0362/41008. The restaurant attached to the luxury *Damai Lovina Villas* offers the most exquisite gourmet dining experience in northern Bali, if not the entire island. The menu is imaginative, innovative, well-cooked, fabulously presented and exciting to eat. Meals are meticulously prepared and service is friendly yet discreet. The $38 five-course gastronomic treat is a feast beyond words – and it changes daily. There's an equally appealing à la carte menu. Expensive.

Gula Bali A quiet, attractive option on Jalan Mawar with soothing taped music, low lighting and an inexpensive menu of Indonesian and Western food, including pizzas with a range of toppings. They also offer a good-value breakfast.

Kopi Bali Popular place at the ocean end of Jalan Bina Ria. Features a big, inexpensive menu of pizza, seafood and Indo-Chinese dishes, lots of specials, plenty of breakfasts and everyone gets a free welcome drink and snack with dinner.

Kubu Lalang ☎ 0362/42207. On the coast at the eastern end of Lovina, with a free boat transfer for lunch or dinner for a minimum of two people from elsewhere in the resort (two hours' notice required). The moderately priced menu is huge, including plenty of vegetarian choices and slightly unusual, imaginative dishes. Keen anglers can go and catch their dinner beforehand. Closed Tues.

Mailaku You'll certainly notice this massive three-storey eyesore, located on Jalan Bina Ria. Still, there are good rooftop views, a bit of a breeze in the second-floor restaurant and nightly videos, although the food is standard Lovina fare.

Malibu Centre of Lovina nightlife, this large restaurant is on the main road in Kalibukbuk, screens nightly videos, stages regular live music and is open until about 2am. It has a big range of Western food, seafood and Indo-Chinese options and a huge drinks list. Even if this isn't your scene, it's worth a trip here during the day for the cakes and bread that you can eat in or take away; the croissants are especially good.

Sea Breeze Superbly located on the beach at Kalibukbuk, this is the spot for a sunset drink, with an excellent menu of soups (Rp8000–13,000), salad (Rp9000–17,000), sandwiches (Rp14,000–17,500) and main meals (Rp12,500–Rp37,500) and an equally fine selection of cakes and desserts (Rp4000–10,500). If you get that craving for crumble, brownies, lemon meringue pie, lemon cheesecake or chocolate mousse this is the place to come, although beware – they're not all available every day.

Warung Bamboo One of a trio of seafront places in Anturan, attached to *Mari Homestay*. This one has a typical Lovina menu offering inexpensive Western and Indo-Chinese travellers fare but is in a great location.

Warung Bambu ⊕0362/27080 or 31455. On the road down to *Puri Bagus Lovina* at the eastern end of Lovina; serves only Balinese and Indonesian food. An excellent range of soups and starters (Rp9000–15,000) and main courses (Rp20,000–Rp30,000), plus *rijsttafel* (Rp55,000) and "Romantic Buffet" (Rp65,000) available for as few as two diners. Balinese dancing accompanies dinner twice a week (Wed & Sun) and gets very

good reviews. There are also small gift items and original art for sale. Free transport in the Lovina area.

Warung Nyoman On the seafront just east of *Rasta* and the road to the beach at Anturan. Seafood beach barbecues are their speciality, and you can arrange an expedition with them to catch your own dinner beforehand.

Warung Rasta At the end of the road in Anturan overlooking the beach, the location is the reason for a visit to this tiny place, which has a standard menu and reggae music. Main courses are around Rp15,000 and there are plenty of vegetarian choices.

Nightlife

Anybody coming to Lovina expecting a thriving disco **nightlife** scene is in for a big disappointment: after a day relaxing on the beach, most people eat a leisurely dinner and head off to bed. *Malibu* is the liveliest spot and has the biggest video screen and most popular **live music**; *Café 3*, just off the main road in Kalibukbuk, offers something similar, and *Planet Lovina* on the main road in Kalibukbuk also has regular live music. Regular **Balinese dance shows** feature at several restaurants to accompany your dinner: look out for the flyers around town or check out the *Rambutan* bungalows. Friday-night **parties** at *Café Spice* last until the early hours, sometimes with live music.

Shopping

The number of **shops** in Lovina doesn't compare with Kuta, Sanur or Ubud but shopping is far less pressured. You'll find all the textiles, clothing and souvenirs that the island has to offer in small, family-run places lining most of the main roads that sell a range of everything. Most are along Jalan Bina Ria, Jalan Mawar and the main road in Kalibukbuk, which is also the area for secondhand **books**. The *Jakarta Post* **newspaper** arrives in the late morning or early afternoon at Kristop Shop on the main road.

One of the most impressive places is Nirwana Gallery. It has a vast array of beautifully displayed **textiles**, **paper** and **wood** items – a fair representation of most of the crafts of Bali – all labelled with fixed prices. Loviana Home Art Global has a couple of shops, one on the main road in Kalibukbuk and one further west in Kaliasem. They sell an excellent selection of natural **toiletries**, textiles and wooden items, some from other parts of Asia. The shop attached to *Biyu-Nasak* restaurant is worth a look, as is the one inside *Warung Bambu* in Pemaron (you may find more unusual items here, big and small). Take a look at Durian, next to *Rambutan* on Jalan Mawar, packed full of textiles, carvings and **jewellery**. One place that's out of the ordinary is Benny Tantra, which sells excellent hand-painted and cartoon **T-shirts** (Rp60,000 for printed ones, Rp160,000 for hand-painted ones) and cards (Rp2500).

Massage and treatments

As well as the ladies on the beach offering massages, a couple of places have opened up offering a broader range of **massages and treatments**. Indiana Massage (daily 10am–sunset, other times by appointment; ⊕0362/41570, ⊕indiana@telkom.net) has a great location on the beach next to *Café Spice*. They offer massages in a lovely open-sided pavilion which is relaxed yet private, using local techniques, Shiatsu, acupressure, Thai, or a combination (Rp65,000 for 1hr 15min), and also have open yoga classes (Tues & Thurs 8am; Rp50,000 for 1hr 30min). The Lovina Wellness Spa and Healing Centre (☎0362/27297, ✉balicenter@aol.com), on the corner of Jalan Mawar and the main road, offers several massages including ayurvedic (Rp130,000 for 2hr), spa treatments (Rp100,000 for 2hr) and, when the therapist is available, therapeutic body work. They also have Vipassana meditation classes and bodywork classes in Indonesian and English, intended for local people but open to all.

Listings

Car, bike and motorbike rental Available throughout the resort both from established firms and as charters from people who'll approach you on the street. Expect to pay around Rp85,000 a day for a Suzuki Jimney, Rp100,000 for a Kijang and Rp110,000 for a larger four-wheel drive or a people-carrier, plus Rp50,000 per day for a driver. Insurance deals vary and are only available with established companies. Motorbikes are also widely available (Rp30,000–40,000/day), as are bicycles (Rp15,0000–25,000/day). Established companies include Koperasi Marga Sakti (☎0362/41061), on Jl Bina Ria; Damar (☎0362/42154, ☏41999, ✉luhwiriadi@yahoo.com) on the main road in Kalibukbuk; or Yuli Transport, at Yuli Shop (☎0362/41184), opposite *Rambutan* on Jalan Mawar where Made Wijana (✉madewijana@hotmail.com) is a safe, reliable and recommended driver. It's also possible to charter transport for a one-way drop to destinations throughout Bali (Rp175,000–200,000 to any of the South Bali resorts, with hard bargaining): if there are several of you, this can be much more convenient, quicker and not much more expensive than a tourist shuttle bus.

Cookery courses *Djani's* restaurant (☎0362/41913), on the main road in Kaliasem, offers Indonesian cookery courses (vegetarian and non-vegetarian) for Rp110,000 – Rp125,000 per person (minimum two people; 2hr 30min), depending on the menu you choose to cook. *Barakuda* restaurant (✉restaurant_barakuda@hotmail.com) on Jalan Mawar offers classes of the same length consisting of four main courses and one dessert (Rp75,000–85,000 per person, depending on the menu; minimum two people, maximum six). A couple of hawkers on the beach also advertise cookery classes but have no means of contact; ask around at the beach in Kalibukbuk if you want to talk to them.

Doctor Lovina Clinic (☎0362/41106), on the main road in Kalibukbuk, 200m east of Jalan Mawar, has a 24-hour call-out service for doctors. The

tourist office can recommend doctors in Singaraja. The closest hospitals are in Singaraja (see p.346), although for anything serious you'll have to go to Denpasar.

Exchange and banks Moneychangers can be found every few metres along the main road, Jalan Bina Ria and Jalan Mawar. There's a BCA ATM (Visa, MasterCard and Cirrus) on the main road in Kalibukbuk, and another on Jalan Bina Ria.

Internet access Offered by many places (Rp350–400/min, often with discounts for long periods). *Outpost* and *Spice Dive* on Jalan Bina Ria are both good; *Planet Lovina* on the main road in Kalibukbuk and *Bali Bintang* on Jalan Bina Ria both have restaurants attached. In Anturan, head for Perama or *Sri Homestay*, and there's another place on the main road just west of the Banyualit turning.

Phone Wartels are dotted throughout the resort. Wartel Lovina (daily 8am–11pm) is one of the most convenient, on the main road just west of Jalan Bina Ria; Mit Surya (daily 8am–11pm) is also central, on the main road in Kalibukbuk between Jalan Bina Ria and Jalan Mawar. There's one on the main road in Anturan (daily 7.30am–10.30pm) and one on the road to Pantai Happy (daily 8am–10.30pm). Prices vary between them.

Police Located in the same building as the tourist office; they'll also try to help you with information if the tourist office is closed.

Post office The post office (Mon–Thurs 7.30am–2.30pm, Fri 8am–noon, Sat 7.30am–1pm) is about 1km west of Kalibukbuk. For poste restante, have mail addressed to you at the Post Office, Jalan Raya Singaraja, Lovina, Singaraja 81152, Bali. Several postal agents in Kalibukbuk sell stamps.

Tours Available throughout the resort, at Rp175,000–225,000 per car. The main ones on offer include Singaraja (Pura Beji, Jagaraga, Sawan, Kubutambahan, Pondok Batu and Hot Springs), Kintamani (Pura Beji, Kubutambahan,

Penulisan, Penelokan and Toyah Bungkah), Eastern Bali (Pura Beji, Kubutambahan, Penulisan, Besakih and Tenganan, Candi Dasa and Tirtaganggan), Sunset (Gigit, Lake Bratan, Taman Ayu and Tanah Lot), and Trekking (Singsing waterfall, Banjar hot springs and Buddhist temple, Pulaki and Bali Barat National Park). **Travel agents/shuttle buses** Perama has two offices in the area – at Anturan (daily 8am–9pm; ☎0362/41161) and on Jalan Mawar (daily 7am–10pm; ☎0362/41161) – offering the full range of travel services, including shuttle buses on Bali and Lombok. Perama also books buses to other parts of Indonesia, including Jakarta (leaving locally; Rp98,000) and Yogyakarta (from Ujung terminal in Denpasar; Rp65,000). Mit Surya wartel is also agent for Pahala Kencana, offering tickets to Jakarta (Rp200,000) and Bogor (Rp205,000).

Around Lovina

There are plenty of local attractions around Lovina. Several are accessible on public transport – such as the **Buddhist monastery** and **hot springs** at Banjar – while others in the area inland from Seririt are better explored with your own transport. A kilometre beyond the western limits of Lovina, Jalan Singsing leads 1km south to the **Singsing (Daybreak) waterfalls**, only really worth a look in the rainy season and not nearly as dramatic as other falls in the region.

Buddhist monastery and hot springs

Bali's only **Buddhist monastery** lies 10km southwest of Lovina and can be combined with a visit to the hot springs at Banjar, which are on a parallel road slightly further west. Catch any westbound bemo to **DENCARIK**, where a sign points inland to the monastery and ojek wait to take you the last steep 5km.

The **Brahmavihara Arama** was built in 1970 with local labour and financial help from the Indonesian and Thai governments, and consecrated in 1972. Damaged by an earthquake in 1976, the *stupa* was virtually destroyed but has been repaired and is a splendidly colourful confection. The temple complex enjoys a wonderful hillside setting: brilliant orange-tiled roofs stand over an entrance gate guarded by two fine *naga*, with a *kulkul* tower in the courtyard, a lower temple with a gold Buddha from Thailand as the centrepiece, carved stone plaques showing scenes from Buddha's life on all the main temples, and a colourful Buddhist grotto to the left of the top temple. It's a magnet for Buddhist pilgrims from across Asia and open pretty much all the time; admission is free. If you don't have a sarong, collect one from the small office near the entrance, where you make your donation.

From the temple you can walk to the **hot springs** (daily 8am–6pm; Rp3000, parking Rp1000). Head back downhill and take the first major left turn. After a few hundred metres – with fine views of the mountains of East Java in the distance – you'll reach a major crossroads and marketplace at the village of **BANJAR TEGA**. Turn left and a highly decorated *kulkul* tower will now be on your right. After about 200m you'll see a sign for the "Air Panas Holy Hot Springs" pointing you to a left turn. From here, it's a pleasant one-kilometre walk to the springs. The area has been landscaped and is well maintained, with changing rooms and toilets. There are three pools: eight *naga* spout water from their mouths into the smaller, hotter, upper pool, which then descends through another five *naga* into the lower, larger pool. Soap and shampoo are allowed only in the third pool off to the side. The water has a slight sulphur smell, and a silky, even slimy, softness. Weekends and holidays can get a bit busy but otherwise this is a lovely spot.

The pools are overlooked by a **restaurant** which offers moderately priced food and good views. *Pondok Wisata Griya Sari* (☎0362/92903, ℉92966; ❸–❹) offers comfortable, clean **rooms** ranged up the hillside, with good verandahs in a lovely garden – although the bathrooms have only cold water.

From the springs you can walk the 3km back down to the main road, or you should be able to find an ojek back in the market. This area is the main grape-growing area in Bali and you'll see the cultivated vines in the fields next to the road; the best-quality grapes are exported to Japan and Hong Kong and the rest used to produce Indonesian wine.

Inland from Seririt

If you have your own transport, you can take an interesting **inland drive** south from **Seririt**, 12km west of Lovina, along the Denpasar road. The road climbs through paddy-fields and fields of grapes, splitting after 7km at **MAYONG** (see p.340 for more on this village). The right-hand fork takes you up across the mountains to Pupuan and then the south coast, while the left fork goes through Tunjuk and Banyuatis to Munduk, and then up to the area north of Lake Tamblingan and Buyan.

Taking the left fork and following the road for just under 3km brings you to a small left turn signed "Desa Bestala". This leads to the village of **BESTALA**, where you should turn left by the statue of the independence fighter. This is a wonderful little road that winds down into the valley, across the river and then zigzags up the other side for a couple of kilometres to the tiny village of **MUNDUK BESTALA**, famous throughout Bali for its durians. January and February are the main season but you'll also find mangosteens here from December to April. There's a tiny market area just before a T-junction in the village; the road deteriorates from here on. You can either go left for about 1500m to a lookout point with good views over the north coast to the sea, or turn right and continue for about 3km to a concrete lookout spot where you'll see the entire area laid out as far as the Batukau mountains to the south. Continuing on the rough road, and taking a left fork at the next junction, brings you to **Pedawa** and **Sidetapa**, two of the Bali Aga villages of the north of the island, which still retain their narrow lanes, high-walled compounds and gates.

Travel details

Bemos and buses

It's almost impossible to give the **frequency** with which bemos and public buses run, as they only depart when they have enough passengers to make the journey worthwhile. However, on the most popular routes, you should be able to count on getting a ride within the half-hour if you travel before noon; things quieten down in the afternoon and come to a standstill by around 5pm. **Journey** times also vary a great deal: the times given below are the minimum you can expect.

Only direct bemo and bus routes are listed; for longer journeys you'll have to go first to either Singaraja (see p.342) or to Denpasar (see p.92).
Air Sanih to: Amlapura (2hr); Culik (1hr 30min); Gilimanuk (3hr); Lovina 1hr); Singaraja (Penarukan terminal; 30min); Tirtagangga (2hr); Tulamben (1hr).
Bedugul to: Denpasar (Ubung terminal; 1hr 30min); Singaraja (Sukasada terminal; 1hr 30min).
Kintamani to: Singaraja (Penarukan terminal; 1hr 30min); Ubud (40min).
Lovina to: Amlapura (3hr 30min); Gilimanuk (2hr 30min); Jakarta (24hr); Probolingo (for Bromo; 7hr); Seririt (20min); Singaraja (Banyuasri terminal; 20min); Surabaya (10–12hr).
Penelokan to: Bangli (45min); Buahan (30min); Denpasar (Batubulan terminal; 1hr 30min); Gianyar (50min); Singaraja (Penarukan terminal; 1hr 30min); Songan (45min); Toya Bungkah (30min).
Singaraja (Banyuasri terminal) to: Gilimanuk (2hr 30min); Lovina (20min); Seririt (40min); Surabaya (10–12hr); Yogyakarta (21hr).

Singaraja (Penarukan terminal) to: Amlapura (3hr); Culik (2hr 30min); Denpasar (Batubulan terminal; 3hr); Gianyar (2hr 20min); Penelokan (1hr 30min); Kubutambahan (20min); Sawan (30min); Tirtagangga (2hr 30min); Tulamben (1hr).

Singaraja (Sukasada terminal) to: Bedugul (1hr 30min); Denpasar (Ubung terminal; 3hr); Gitgit (30min).

Perama shuttle buses

STO = overnight stopover is needed

Air Sanih to: Bangsal (daily; STO); Bedugul (daily; STO); Candi Dasa (daily; 2hr–2hr 30min); Kintamani (daily; STO); Kuta/Ngurah Rai Airport (daily; 5hr 30min); Kuta, Lombok (daily; STO); Lovina (daily; 1hr); Mataram (daily; 7–8hr); Padang Bai (daily; 2hr 30min–3hr); Sanur (daily; 4hr 30min–5hr); Senggigi (daily; 7–8hr); Tetebatu (daily; STO); Tirtagangga (daily; 2hr); Ubud (daily; 3hr 30min–4hr).

Bedugul to: Air Sanih (daily; STO); Bangsal (daily; STO); Candi Dasa (daily; STO); Kintamani (daily; STO); Kuta/Ngurah Rai Airport (daily; 2hr 30min–3hr); Kuta, Lombok (daily; STO); Lovina (daily; 1hr 30min); Mataram (daily; STO); Padang Bai (daily; STO); Sanur (daily; 2hr–2hr 30min); Senggigi (daily; STO); Tetebatu (daily; STO); Tirtagangga (daily; STO); Tulamben (daily; STO); Ubud (daily; 1hr 30min).

Kintamani to: Air Sanih (daily; STO); Bangsal (daily; STO); Bedugul (daily; STO); Candi Dasa (daily; 3hr 15min); Kuta/Ngurah Rai Airport (daily; 2hr 30min–3hr); Kuta, Lombok (daily; 2hr 45min); Lovina (daily; 2hr); Mataram (daily; STO); Padang Bai (daily; 2hr 45min); Sanur (daily; 2hr 15min); Senggigi (daily; STO); Tetebatu (daily; STO); Tirtagangga (daily; STO); Tulamben (daily; STO); Ubud (daily; 1hr 15min).

Lovina to: Air Sanih (daily; 1hr); Bangsal (daily; STO); Bedugul (daily; 1hr 30min); Candi Dasa (2 daily; 3hr–3hr 30min)); Kintamani (daily; 2hr); Kuta/Ngurah Rai airport (daily; 3hr); Kuta, Lombok (daily; STO); Mataram (daily; 7–8hr); Padang Bai (daily; 2hr 45min); Sanur (daily; 2hr 30min–3hr); Senggigi (daily; 7hr 30min–8hr 30min); Tetebatu (daily; STO); Tirtagangga (daily; 2hr 30min); Tulamben (daily; 1hr 30min); Ubud (daily; 3hr 30min–4hr).

West Bali

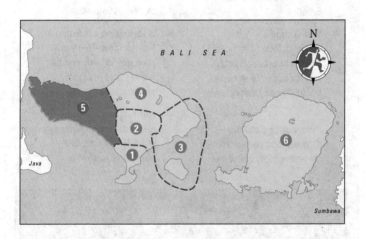

CHAPTER 5

Highlights

✳ **Tanah Lot** – Perched like a sea-bird on a wave-lashed rock, this is Bali's most famous temple. See p.374

✳ **Subak Museum, Tabanan** – Fascinating insight into Bali's rice-farming culture. See p.380

✳ **Yeh Gangga** – A dramatic stretch of remote black-sand beach with just a couple of exceptional places to stay. See p.381

✳ **Pura Luhur Batukau** – Atmospheric garden temple at the foot of a sacred mountain, full of wild birds, flowering shrubs and moss-encrusted statues. See p.385

✳ **The Jatiluwih road** – A stunning drive through classic landscapes of rice terraces sculpted from the south-facing slopes. See p.386

✳ **Snorkelling off Pulau Menjangan** – National park island with crystal waters and abundant shallow reefs. See p.400

✳ **Pemuteran** – Small, relaxed beach haven just outside the national park. See p.404

5

West Bali

S parsely populated, mountainous, and in places extremely rugged, west Bali stretches from the northwestern outskirts of Denpasar across 128km to Gilimanuk at the island's westernmost tip. Once connected to East Java by a tract of land (now submerged beneath the Bali Strait), the region has always had a distinct Javanese character. When East Java's Hindu Majapahit elite fled to Bali in the sixteenth century, the Javanese priest Nirartha started his influential preaching tour of Bali from the west – leaving the region with a stunning trinity of clifftop temples at Tanah Lot, Rambut Siwi and Pulaki. More recently, the Muslim faith has made significant inroads into western Bali too, so much so that in the region to the west of Negara, mosques now seem to outnumber temples and nearly half the male population leaves the house wearing a small black peci.

Apart from making the statutory visits to the big attractions just west of Denpasar – **Pura Tanah Lot** and **Sangeh Monkey Forest** being the main draws – few tourists linger long in west Bali, choosing instead to rush through on their way to or from Java, pausing only to board the ferry in the port town of Gilimanuk. Yet the southwest coast holds some fine black-sand **beaches**, and some good **surf** at Medewi, while the cream of Bali's **coral reefs** lies off the northwest coast around Pulau Menjangan (Deer Island). Furthermore, Bali's only national park is here: over seventy percent of the land area in the west is preserved as **Bali Barat National Park**, home to the endangered Bali starling and a lot of other unusual birds as well. The island's second highest peak, the sacred **Gunung Batukau**, dominates many west Bali vistas and, although both the extreme west and some stretches of the northwest lie in its rain shadow, which renders the land arid and infertile, the southwest boasts the most fertile paddies in Bali, not least in the area around **Jatiluwih**, focus of a famously scenic drive. Bali's rice-growing culture is celebrated by a special museum in nearby **Tabanan**.

Despite the lack of tourist centres in the west, there are a few recommended **hotels** on the west-coast beaches, most of them quiet and well off the usual tourist route.

Transport practicalities

Public transport across the region is fairly efficient, with regular bemo services from the south (out of Denpasar's Ubung bemo station) and from Singaraja on the north coast. Both these terminate at **Gilimanuk**, on Bali's westernmost tip, from where car ferries make frequent journeys across the Bali Strait to Java. Most of the bemos stick to the main round-island "ring road", though at least one service operates a direct north–south route, via Pupuan. If you're driving your own car or motorbike, be warned that **traffic** in western Bali is unpleas-

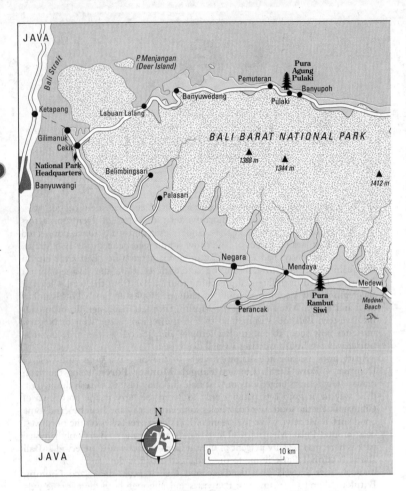

antly heavy. The roads were not intended to take anywhere near the volume that now chokes certain stretches, and truck drivers heading to and from Java seem to be little concerned about other vehicles.

The southwest

From **Ubung** bemo terminal in the northwest of Denpasar, all westbound bemos follow the busy main road through an almost continuous urban sprawl of unexciting small towns. After 15km, the conurbation becomes more distinctive as it shapes into **Kapal**, which you can't fail to notice is one of the shrine-making centres of Bali: the sidewalks here are lined with every conceivable permutation in stone, concrete and wood, some roofed with wiry black *ijuk* thatch made from sugar-palm fibres. The road branches just west of Kapal, the northbound fork being a major artery for Bedugul and Singaraja via

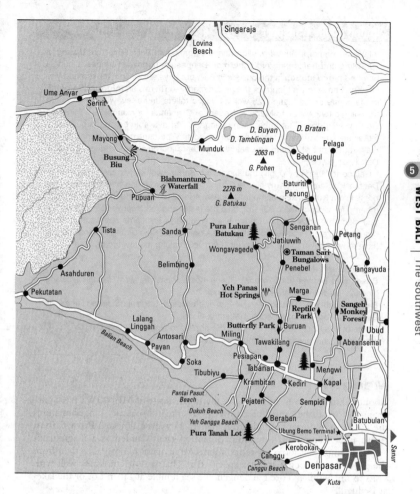

the seventeenth-century temple complex at **Mengwi**, with a side road to the **Sangeh Monkey Forest**. Continuing west towards Gilimanuk, the road reaches a crossroads at Kediri, access point for the coastal temple of **Pura Tanah Lot**. Each of these three major sights can be visited by public transport in a comfortable day-trip from Denpasar or Kuta, and they feature on the itineraries of just about every tour operator in the south of the island (see p.126). Kediri lies on the outskirts of **Tabanan**, the regency capital, from where public transport serves **Yeh Gangga beach** and the royal palace at **Krambitan**.

If you have your own transport and are heading west from Kuta or Sanur, it's worth bypassing Denpasar by taking the much more scenic and less hectic **back road** instead. From Kuta, head north up Jalan Legian, through Seminyak, until you reach the crossroads village of Kerobokan (about 9km from Kuta). The eastern arm takes you to central Denpasar, the western arm to the beach at Canggu. Continuing north, you'll soon reach Sempidi, which lies on the main Denpasar–Kediri road, 5km before the junction at Kapal.

All west- and north-bound public transport from south Bali starts from **Ubung**, a sprawling and traffic-clogged suburb on Denpasar's northwest fringes. Ubung's **bus and bemo station** is the busiest in Bali, but bays are clearly marked and you shouldn't have to wait long for the next departure. There's an **information** booth in the centre of the station, as well as public toilets and a few warung. If you're travelling a long way – to Medewi, Negara or Gilimanuk for example – it might be worth waiting for a bus rather than taking the first available bemo, as buses are faster and more comfortable (though up to fifty percent more expensive). For main routes out of Ubung see below; a guide to journey times is given in Travel Details on p.409.

Getting to Ubung by public transport **from Sanur** involves first taking a bemo to Denpasar's Kereneng terminal, then changing on to the Ubung-bound service (see p.93). **From Kuta**, take a bemo to Denpasar's Tegal terminal and then change on to a bemo for Ubung (see p.93) – or, take the faster and more convenient option of a **taxi** along the back road to Ubung (via Kerobokan). The same applies in reverse, though taxis aren't allowed to pick up passengers inside the Ubung terminal, so you have to walk down to the rank about 100m south along the main road.

Routes out of Ubung
Buses and bemos (dark green) Ubung–Kediri–Pesiapan (west Tabanan)–Lalang Linggah–Medewi–Negara–Cekik–Gilimanuk.
Bemos (bright blue) Ubung–Mengwi–Baturiti–Pancasari–Singaraja (Sukasada terminal).
Bemos Ubung–Mengwi–Bedugul–Munduk–Seririt.
Large buses Ubung–Gilimanuk–Java (Surabaya, Yogyakarta & Jakarta).
Also occasional buses to Padang Bai in east Bali.

Mengwi

About 18km northwest of Denpasar, the small village of **MENGWI** has a glittering history as the capital of a powerful seventeenth-century kingdom and is the site of an important temple from that era. However, although **Pura Taman Ayun** now features on numerous organized tours, lauded as a magnificent "garden temple", it looks far more impressive in aerial photographs than from the ground and doesn't merit a special trip. That said, it combines well with visits to the Monkey Forest at Sangeh, the sea temple at Tanah Lot or the lakes at Bedugul.

The easiest way to reach Mengwi by **bemo** is from Denpasar's Ubung terminal, from where you can take any of the numerous northbound services (30min). If you're coming from Gilimanuk or other points on the west coast, take an Ubung-bound bemo as far as Tabanan's Pesiapan terminal, then change on to a blue-and-yellow striped bemo which will take you straight to Taman Ayun.

Pura Taman Ayun
The state temple of the former kingdom of Mengwi, **Pura Taman Ayun** (daily during daylight hours; Rp3100 including sarong and sash rental, kids Rp1600) was probably built by Raja I Gusti Agung Anom in 1634 as the focus of his newly powerful dynasty. From the early seventeenth century until the close of the nineteenth, the rajas of Mengwi held sway over an extensive area, comprising parts of present-day Badung, Tabanan and Gianyar districts, by means of a series of hard-won battles and wily alliances with neighbouring

rajas. Its fortunes waned, however, and in 1885 the kingdom of Mengwi was divided between Badung and Tabanan.

Designed as a series of garden terraces with each courtyard on a different level, the whole Pura Taman Ayun complex is surrounded by a moat – now picturesquely choked with weeds and lilies – to symbolize the mythological home of the gods, Mount Meru, floating in the milky sea of eternity. For the best **view** of the temple's layout, climb to the top of the *kulkul* tower in the southwest corner of the central courtyard. Otherwise, the most interesting part is the **inner courtyard**, which is encircled by its own little moat and is inaccessible to the public except at festival time – although the surrounding wall is low enough to give a reasonable view of the two dozen separate shrines and *bale* within.

The north and east sides of the compound are lined with multi-tiered **meru**. The most important of these are the three which honour Bali's holiest mountains; they occupy positions within the temple compound that correspond to their positions on Bali in relation to Mengwi. Thus the eleven-roofed structure in the far northwest corner represents Gunung Batukau; the nine-roofed *meru* halfway down the east side stands for Gunung Batur; and Batur's eleven-roofed neighbour honours Gunung Agung. The Batur *meru* has only nine tiers because the mountain is significantly lower than the other two.

Mengwi Museum

To the west of Pura Taman Ayun's moat stands a dilapidated tourist complex housing a collection of **souvenir shops**, a small waterside **restaurant** and the **Mengwi Museum** (daily during daylight hours; donation requested). The display inside the museum shows a fairly comprehensive collection of different palm-leaf offerings made for the plethora of ceremonies, rituals and special days in the Balinese calendar. However, they're faded and badly labelled, and the whole place is lacklustre.

Reptile and Crocodile Park

Unless you have a real passion for crocodiles, there's little point making the effort to visit the **Taman Buaya dan Reptil**, known as the **Reptile and Crocodile Park** (daily 9am–6pm; $10) – not to be confused with the much better Reptile Park in Batubulan, described on p.180. The park is 8km north of Mengwi on the Bedugul road and served by all Ubung–Singaraja and Ubung–Seririt bemos. Not only is it way overpriced, but it's also badly designed, with no labels or information on the creatures – who anyway spend most of their day lying in a slothful daze. There are four species of crocodile here, fifteen types of snake, eight species of lizard and a gang of disappointingly small and unremarkable Komodo dragons. Feeding time is at 10.30am and 3pm, when there are also crocodile wrestling shows.

Sangeh Monkey Forest

Monkeys have a special status in Hindu religion, and a number of temples in Bali boast a resident monkey population, respected by devotees and duly fed and photographed by tourists. The **Monkey Forest** (Bukit Sari) in the village of **SANGEH** is probably the most visited of these on Bali, its inhabitants the self-appointed guardians of the slightly eerie Pura Bukit Sari. According to local legend, the forest itself was created when Rama's general, the monkey king Hanuman, attempted to kill off Rama's enemy Rawana, by squashing him between two halves of the sacred Mount Meru. In the process, part of the mountain fell to earth at Sangeh, with hordes of Hanuman's simian retainers still clinging to the trees, creating Bukit Sari and its monkey dynasty. The temple was built here some time during the seventeenth century, in a forest of sacred nutmeg trees which tower to heights of forty metres.

The forest borders the main road, and as soon as you pull up at the roadside car park you can see just how untamed Sangeh's monkeys are: every small warung in the vicinity is wreathed in wire netting, and the creatures race fearlessly up and down the road and over any parked vehicles. As you pass into the forest area (donation requested), huge signs warn you to beware of the monkeys, and the attendants hand out sticks in case you are attacked. This can make you feel pretty uneasy, but it's unlikely you'll have any trouble if you keep cameras and jewellery out of sight and remember to take all foodstuffs out of your bags and pockets.

Pura Bukit Sari, located in the heart of this fairy-tale forest, is best appreciated in late afternoon after the tour buses have left. During peak hours, the place can seem disappointing, but seen in waning light with only the monkeys for company, the forest and the temple take on an attractive ghostly aspect, missing from the island's other monkey forests. The square compound of the weathered and moss-encrusted grey-stone temple is out of bounds to everyone except the monkeys, but beyond the walls you can see a huge *garuda* statue, stonecarved reliefs and tiered thatched *meru*. There are no paths through the forest, but a track runs clockwise around most of its perimeter, along the edge of an expanse of cultivated land that drops down to a river a few hundred metres to the west.

Practicalities

Sangeh is on a minor road that connects Denpasar, 21km south, with the mountainside village of Pelaga. The only way of getting to the Monkey Forest by public transport is by **bemo**, direct to Sangeh from the small Wangaya bemo terminal in central Denpasar (see p.94). With your own vehicle, Sangeh is an easy drive from Mengwi, 15km southwest, or a pleasant forty-minute ride west from Ubud, via Sayan. Alternatively, you could join one of the numerous **organized tours** from any of the resorts, which usually combine Sangeh with visits to Mengwi, Tanah Lot and sometimes Bedugul (see p.126).

Pura Tanah Lot and around

Dramatically marooned on a craggy wave-lashed rock sitting just off the southwest coast, **Pura Tanah Lot** really does deserve its reputation as one of Bali's top sights. Fringed by frothing white surf and glistening black sand, its elegant multi-tiered shrines have become the unofficial symbol of Bali, appearing on a vast range of tourist souvenirs, while its links with several other coastal temples afford it an especially holy status. Unsurprisingly, the temple attracts huge crowds every day, particularly around dusk when bus-loads of local and foreign tourists come to see the magnificent temple profile silhouetted against the sunset. Even bigger crowds amass here at the time of Pura Tanah Lot's **odalan** festival. As a result, a busy tourist village has mushroomed around the approach to the temple, encompassing everything from typical art-market stalls selling sarongs, cheap clothes and souvenirs to outlets for Versace and Polo design wear.

Access is fairly easy by public bemo and there are a number of places to stay around the temple, but the vast majority of visitors come on **organized day-trips** from Bali's biggest resorts.

△ Stone statue, Pura Luhur Batukau

The construction in the mid-1990s of the *Nirwana Golf and Spa Resort* so close to Pura Tanah Lot marked a new low in the relationship between **property developers** and Balinese villagers. In Bali there are long-standing religious laws about how close to a temple one is allowed to build, and about what status the secular building should have in relation to the temple; when it became obvious that the consortium behind the *Nirwana* had managed to circumvent these rules, huge protests erupted in the press and on the streets.

This was the first time there had been such strong and widespread **opposition to tourist development** on Bali. By building a tourist resort here, it was argued, one of Bali's most important temples was being treated as nothing more than an ornament for the pleasure of foreign eyes – a serious case of disrespect. In addition, it was reported that farmers who refused to sell their ancestral land to make way for the project were forced out by underhand means (including blocking irrigation channels to make the land infertile) and that several small temples were destroyed. Nonetheless, pragmatism prevailed, and the *Nirwana* is now one of Bali's most successful luxury hotels.

With hundreds of jobs at stake and a desperate desire for the tourist dollar, the *Nirwana* controversy is typical of the tensions that have been dogging Bali ever since the first tourists arrived in the 1930s. As land gets more expensive, it is left to outside investors with little regard for Bali's religious heritage to bankroll new projects and impose their own conditions. On the other hand, cash injections like this are good for the Balinese economy, and it's unclear whether local investors would be any more ethical. For a more complete view of the effect of tourist development in Bali see p.548.

The temples

Pura Tanah Lot (daily during daylight hours, Rp3300; plus Rp1500 per car) is said to have been founded by the wandering Hindu priest **Nirartha**, who sailed across to Bali from his home in Java during the sixteenth century. Legends describe how the holy man was preaching at Rambut Siwi, about 50km northwest up the coast (see p.389), when he was distracted by a beaming light from the southeast. Setting off in search of the source, Nirartha arrived at Tanah Lot to find that the light was shining from a holy spring here. He began to preach to the local people of Beraban, but this angered the village priest who demanded that the rival holy man should leave. In response, Nirartha meditated so hard that he pushed the rock he was sitting on out into the sea; this became the Tanah Lot "island". He then dedicated his new retreat to the god of the sea and transformed his scarf into poisonous snakes to protect the place. Ever since then, Pura Tanah Lot has been one of the most holy places on Bali, closely associated with several other important temples along this coast, including Pura Rambut Siwi and Pura Luhur Uluwatu.

Because of its sacred status, only bona fide devotees are allowed to climb the temple stairway carved out of the rockface and enter the compounds; everyone else is confined to the patch of grey sand around the base of the rock (which is under water at high tide). When the waters are low enough, you can take a sip of **holy water** (*air suci*) from the spring that rises beneath the temple rock (donation requested) or stroke the docile holy coral **snakes** that are kept in nests behind the cliff face. Otherwise, your best option is to climb up to the mainland clifftop in search of the best viewing spot. Be warned however that until at least the middle part of 2003, nearly all panoramas of Tanah Lot will be ruined by the presence of a very long and unsightly temporary jetty that's been erected for anti-erosion **construction work** on the temple rock. This Japanese-financed project aims to prevent any further erosion of the rock (whose distinctive profile was of course created by erosion in the first place) by submerging six thousand giant tetrapods to make a huge breakwater around its base.

Construction work notwithstanding, if you follow the signed **clifftop path** to the southwest (right) of the temple rock you can admire the great panorama that extends as far as the raised plateau of the Bukit on Bali's southernmost tip. When Pura Tanah Lot and the other south-coast temples were built, the aim was to try and make each coastal temple visible from the next one in the "chain", thereby creating a tangible string of shrines honouring the god of the sea. The sixteenth-century builders did well here, as you can certainly make out the location, if not the actual profile, of the next in the chain, Pura Luhur Uluwatu, which stands above the Bukit cliffs.

Continuing along the coast path, you'll pass a string of small weatherbeaten **clifftop shrines** perched on the edges of narrow promontories. From the rock shelf that supports tiny **Pura Galuh** you get a fantastic view of Pura Tanah Lot's two *meru*, as well as the curved flight of rock-cut steps that leads up to them. North of Pura Galuh, the jagged coastline juts out into dozens of tiny bays, most of which are accessible from the clifftop, though the grey-sand beaches are prone to strong waves and aren't that inviting for swimming. The path itself is hardly used and you're likely to encounter more birds, lizards and butterflies along its course than people. After about 1km, the path veers inland, through a tiny hamlet comprising little more than a few mud-walled houses scattered across the rice-fields, and an imposing and well-maintained temple, **Pura Pekendungan**. Follow the path around to the right of this temple to get back to the Tanah Lot car park, or veer left to rejoin the coastal path which leads to the beach at Yeh Gangga, an hour and a half's walk away (see p.381).

Practicalities

Though there are occasional bright blue **bemos** from Denpasar's Ubung terminal direct to Tanah Lot, you'll probably end up having to go via **KEDIRI**, 12km east of the temple complex on the main Denpasar–Tabanan road. All Ubung (Denpasar)–Gilimanuk bemos pass through Kediri (Rp2000–3000; 30min). Kediri bemo station is located at the crossroads where the road branches left for Tanah Lot, right for central Tabanan and straight on for Gilimanuk. Bright blue Kediri–Tanah Lot bemos (Rp2000; 25min) run fairly regularly in daylight hours, more frequently in the morning.

If arriving under your own steam from Kuta, the prettiest **route to Tanah Lot** is via Kerobokan and Beraban, along a gorgeous road that runs through classic rice terraces and traditional small villages. Alternatively, you could arrive via the *subak* rice museum in nearby Tabanan (see p.380), or make a slight detour to the ceramic-producing village of Pejaten (see p.378).

From Tanah Lot car park, you have the choice of two **approaches to the temple complex**. Usual access is through the corridor of souvenir stalls leading straight to the temple rock; a less crowded and more dramatic route takes you through the back of the car park, via the hamlet described above.

Accommodation

Essentially a tourist village, Tanah Lot dies after the last tour bus pulls away at about 7.30pm, at which point most of the people who work here return to their homes in Kediri or Tabanan. As a result, there's little point in staying at Tanah Lot overnight unless you have to, though there are a few **hotels** to choose from.

Dewi Sinta Cottages Beside the entrance-ticket booth ☎ 0361/812933, ℻ 813956, ⓦ www.balinetwork.com/dewisinta.html, ⓔ dewisinta@dps.wasantara.net.id. Attractive place that is friendly and well managed and offers 27 fan and air-con bungalows in a soothing tropical garden with swimming pool. Rooms with fan and cold water ❹ With air-con and hot water ❻

Le Meridien Nirwana Golf and Spa Resort Signed off the access road ☎ 0361/815900, ℻ 815901, ⓦ www.lemeridien-bali.com. Huge five-star luxury hotel renowned for its quality service and much-praised Greg Norman-designed 18-hole golf course ($110). Rooms in the main hotel wing are comfortable and attractive though unremarkable, but the private villas ($450), complete with garden bathrooms, personal plunge pools and

four-poster beds, are quite special. The hotel has extensive grounds with views of Pura Tanah Lot, as well as three swimming pools (you can't swim in the sea here), tennis courts, a kids' club, a spa and several restaurants. Under-12s go free if sharing adults' room. ❾

Mutiara Tanah Lot Beside the entrance-ticket booth ☎ 0361/812939, ℻ 222672. Similar to the *Dewi Sinta* next door, if not quite so efficiently run. Nicely furnished bungalows in a garden setting; some have air-con and hot water. ❺

Pondok Wisata Atiti Graha 500m back along the access road from the temple car park ☎ 0361/812955. Surrounded by rice-fields and set well away from the commercial clutter, this is a quiet, inexpensive little losmen with spotless rooms, cold-water bathrooms and genial young staff. ❷

Eating

The coastal path overlooking the temple complex is packed with **restaurants** affording prime views, especially at sunset. As you'd expect, prices here are ridiculously high, but the location is stunning. Further back off the coast, in the cluster of hotels and souvenir stalls near the car park, you'll find a few more cafés and restaurants, including the *Mutiara Garden Restaurant* and *Dewi Sinta Restaurant*, where the prices are a little more reasonable and the menus more extensive. The most peaceful and scenic place to eat, however, is at *Bali Lestari*, located in a tranquil rice-field setting about 100m before the Tanah Lot car park; the menu is standard, but the views are nice. *Le Meridien Nirwana* stages frequent performances of traditional Balinese dance, with dinner included; phone for details.

Pejaten

About 6km northeast of Tanah Lot and signed off the Kediri–Tanah Lot road, the ceramic-producing village of **PEJATEN** is famous as the place where most Balinese roof tiles and roof-crown ornaments (*ketu*) are made. Of more interest to tourists is the distinctive Pejaten **ceramic ware**, with its idiosyncratic designs and trademark pastel grey-green, powder blue and beige glazes. Pejaten ceramicists are especially known for their tiny pots, bowls and stoppered bottles, as well as for earthenware plates and bowls, many of which are decorated with lively figurines of frogs, geckos or monkeys. Although Pejaten ceramics are now sold in most of the big resorts, you should be able to get better prices and a bigger choice in the village itself: Tanteri's Ceramic shop in the centre of the village stocks an impressive variety. There are kilns dotted all over the village, each of them fuelled by coconut husks which lie in piles along the roadside – about as industrial as rural Bali gets. To have a look inside one of the workshops, follow the signs for CV Keramic.

Tabanan and around

Despite being the former capital of the ancient kingdom of Tabanan and the administrative centre of one of Bali's most fertile districts, **TABANAN** itself is only a medium-sized town with little to encourage a protracted stop. Its one outstanding feature is the **Subak Museum**, a kind of ethnographic exhibition about rice-farming in Bali. Otherwise, Tabanan's main claim to fame is as the

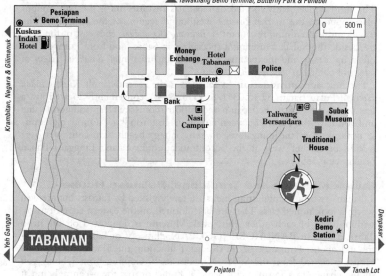

home of the outstanding dancer, I Ketut Marya, known as Mario, remembered for his astonishing performances of the *kebyar*, which he reinvented and popularized in the 1920s (see p.523).

Historically, the kingdom of Tabanan was always one of the more stable power-centres until it fell under Dutch rule in 1906. The Dutch were particularly irked with the Tabanan royal house over the issue of **self-immolation**, or *suttee*. When the old raja of Tabanan was cremated in 1903, his wives followed the traditional practice and threw themselves onto his pyre. Although the Dutch had no explicit power over Tabanan at that time, they had already outlawed *suttee* in all the areas of Bali under their control and had exerted strong pressure on the new raja of Tabanan to prohibit the practice in his kingdom. Back in Holland, the reaction to news of this *suttee* was so strong that it fuelled the Dutch decision to launch the 1906 offensive on southern Bali. After wreaking havoc in Badung, the Dutch invaders marched on Tabanan, where the new raja and his crown prince had decided to negotiate rather than commit *puputan*. The Dutch, however, refused to make a deal and, rather than face exile to Lombok or Madura, the regents committed suicide inside Denpasar prison. Little now remains of the former kingdom, as the Dutch sacked Tabanan's main *puri*, leaving only the subsidiary palace at Krambitan, 8km away (see p.382).

Practicalities

All Ubung (Denpasar)–Gilimanuk **bemos** bypass Tabanan town centre, dropping passengers at the **Pesiapan terminal**, a major transport hub on the northwest edge of town; bright yellow city bemos shuttle from Pesiapan into the centre. There are lots of regional bemo services from Pesiapan, including to Yeh Gangga, Krambitan, Kediri (for Tanah Lot) and Taman Ayun (Mengwi).

The heart of modern Tabanan is encircled by a one-way system that goes clockwise around the central market; you'll find banks with ATMs and a **money-exchange counter** plus the general stores on the eastbound section.

The most conveniently located of Tabanan's **restaurants** is the nasi campur place opposite the market on the westbound section of the ring road. The town's most interesting restaurant is *Taliwang Bersaudara*, 2km east of the centre, beside the Subak Museum; it specializes in Sasak food from Lombok and offers up a tasty and inexpensive range that includes *ayam Sasak*, a variety of sate, and chilli-hot *tahu Lombok goreng*.

The best **accommodation** in Tabanan is the recently built *Kuskus Indah Hotel*, Jl Pulau Batam 32 (℡0361/815373; ❷–❸), conveniently located just a few metres west of the Pesiapan bemo station; rooms are clean and good value and you have the choice between fan or air-con. You'll get a more panoramic outlook from the bungalows on Yeh Gangga beach 8km southwest (see p.382), or further west at the accommodation in Lalang Linggah (Balian beach; see p.388).

Subak Museum and Traditional Balinese House

Tabanan's two most interesting sights are rarely visited by tourists but are well worth a look nonetheless. They are both located on the eastern edge of town, within 100m of each other. The Subak Museum is signposted off the main Tabanan road in **BANJAR SENGGULAN**, 2km east of Tabanan town centre and about 4km west of the Kediri T-junction; the Traditional Balinese House is signed from the Subak Museum itself. Coming from Ubung, you should change to a Tabanan city bemo at Kediri or to a town-centre bemo at the Pesiapan terminal. Get out as soon as you see the prominent sign of the *Taliwang Bersaudara* restaurant on the south side of the road. The museum is 400m up the hillside road opposite, flagged by a tiny sign which says "Mandala Mathika Subak".

Subak Museum

Tabanan district has long been a major rice-producer, and the **Subak Museum** (Mon–Fri 8am–5pm; open at weekends if you ask the security guard; donation requested) celebrates the role of the rice-farmers' collectives (the *subak*) by describing traditional farming practices and displaying typical agricultural implements.

Most of the exhibits in the single-roomed museum are labelled in English, but the museum workers will probably offer to show you round. One of the most interesting sections of the display explains the highly complex and yet completely unmechanized **irrigation system** used by every *subak* on the island – a process that's known to have been in operation on Bali as early as 600 AD. Fundamental to any irrigation system is the underground tunnel that connects the river water supply to the *subak*. This artificial watercourse then feeds hundreds of small channels that are dug to crisscross the *subak* area. A system of tiny wooden dams regulates the water flow along these channels: small wooden weirs block and divert the water, while lengths of wood with angled castellations carved from them, called *tektek*, determine both the volume and the direction of the flow. Also worth looking out for are the **basket muzzles** that are placed over cows' heads to stop them eating grass while they're towing the plough, the **spiked wooden tweezers** used to catch eels from the waterlogged paddies at night and the **wooden nets** used to trap dragonflies, which are prized as delicacies by the Balinese.

Traditional Balinese House

Less than 100m from the Subak Museum, the **Traditional Balinese House** (daily during daylight hours; free) was built to give visitors an idea of the typical layout of a village home, comprising a series of thatched *bale* (pavilions) in a walled compound. Each *bale* has a specific function and must be located in a particular spot within the compound, specified by the sacred Balinese direction *kaja* (towards the sacred Gunung Agung mountain) and its counterpoint *kelod* (away from the mountain, or towards the sea). There are no labels or guides here, but for more information on sacred Balinese architecture and an annotated plan of a traditional house compound see p.543.

True to form, in this house the **family temple** occupies the *kaja* (mountainward) corner, to the far left of the entrance gate. To the right of the temple, the open-sided *bale dangin* is reserved for ceremonial functions, in particular for marriage and funeral rites. The enclosed, windowless pavilion along the left-hand (north) wall of the compound is the *bale daja* for sleeping, and next to that, immediately to the left of the entrance-gate stands the open-sided multi-functional pavilion, which can be adapted for sleeping if necessary. Straight ahead of the entrance gate in the middle of the compound, the only two-storey *bale* has an enclosed rice-storage barn upstairs and a breezy social space or guest-room below. The kitchen pavilion, or *paon*, stands to the right of the entrance in the *kelod* corner, diagonally opposite the temple, and contains a few traditional cooking implements made from bamboo and coconut wood; the nearby *bale* along the right-hand (south) wall is for rice-milling. There's no bathroom, as villagers traditionally do their ablutions outdoors.

Taman Kupu Kupu Butterfly Park

About 5km north of Tabanan, in the village of **WANASARI** on the road to Gunung Batukau, the **Taman Kupu Kupu Butterfly Park** (daily 8am–5pm; Rp30,000, kids Rp15,000) houses butterfly species from all over Indonesia in its small but prettily landscaped garden of flowering trees, pools and cascades. The best time to visit is in the morning when the butterflies flit around at their most energetic. A guide will accompany you round the park if you ask, but there are informative signs as well, giving details on each butterfly's Latin and English name and its provenance. Quite a few of them are rare enough to feature on the CITES list of protected species. One to look out for is the spectacular green and black *Ornithoptera priamus*, which comes from Irian Jaya and has a wing span of at least 10cm. The three other species of resident birdwing are also protected, though the lovely turquoise and black Balinese *Papilio perantus* is very common and is easily spotted almost anywhere on the island.

All Tabanan–Penebel **bemos** go past Taman Kupu Kupu, departing from the Tawakilang terminal, 2km north of Tabanan town centre on the Penebel road and accessed by a town-centre bemo from central Tabanan or Pesiapan terminal. Alternatively, you could charter a bemo from Pesiapan direct to Taman Kupu Kupu.

Yeh Gangga beach

Heading west out of Tabanan in the direction of Gilimanuk, nearly every minor road that branches off south leads straight to the coast, an as yet undeveloped stretch of black sand notable for its strong currents and weird offshore rock formations. One of the most appealing sections is at **YEH GANGGA**, 10km southwest of Tabanan, where there are two exceptionally attractive sets of bungalows – a good base from which to explore the area if you have your own transport. The sea gets pretty rough here, and is too dangerous for swimming, but it's a dramatic scene, punctuated by huge eroded rocks, and the beach stretches for miles in both directions. You can walk along the coast to Tanah

Lot (see p.374) in under two hours, and the Pejaten ceramics village (see p.378) is within easy cycling distance.

The access road to Yeh Gangga is signposted off the main road about 2km west of Tabanan town centre, or you can get there via back roads from Tanah Lot. Yeh Gangga **bemos** depart Tabanan's Pesiapan terminal regularly throughout the morning and early afternoon; they should take about 45 minutes.

For **accommodation**, at the end of the road you'll come to *Bali Wisata Bungalows* (℡0361/261354, ⓕ812744, ⓦwww.baliwisatabungalows.com; ❹–❻), set in a wild shorefront garden of cacti and windblown shrubs, with nothing but the sea and the rice-paddies in sight. The half-dozen fan-cooled bungalows are large and spacious, some with kitchen facilities; the most expensive have uninterrupted ocean views. There's a sea-water swimming pool and a restaurant, and the atmosphere is laid-back and friendly. Call to arrange transport from the airport.

About 1km northwest along the coast, beyond the rock with a hole, is *Waka Gangga* (℡0361/416256, ⓕ416353, ⓦwww.wakaexperience.com; ❽–❾), perhaps the nicest of the idiosyncratic Waka group of small luxury hotels. Its ten exquisite, circular bungalows are scattered across terraced rice-paddies and beautifully constructed from dark woods, rough-cut stone and natural fabrics; each one has a garden bathroom and huge glass windows affording panoramic 270° views of the ocean to the south and rice-fields to the north. There's a swimming pool, restaurant and spa here too, plus horse-riding facilities nearby.

Krambitan and around

Midway between the main road and the coast, the village of **KRAMBITAN**, 8km southwest of Tabanan, lacks obvious attractions, but makes a pleasing base for staying in a typically Balinese environment that rarely sees foreign overnight visitors. There are some pretty villages, fine rice-paddy landscapes and empty beaches within cycling distance, and you also get the chance to sleep in a royal palace. Frequent turquoise **bemos** connect Krambitan with Tabanan's Pesiapan terminal, taking about thirty minutes. If driving from Kuta or Denpasar, take the back road via Kerobokan, Beraban and Yeh Gangga for the most scenic route.

In the late seventeenth century, Krambitan became the home of one branch of the **royal family** of Tabanan, and some of their descendants still live here. Deprived of their political role, the rajas' offspring have turned to tourism, transforming part of one of their palaces into compact but elegant guest **accommodation**. The palace compound of Puri Anyar (℡0361/812668, ⓕ810885; ❻) is an impressively grand composition of elaborate carvings and tropical garden courtyards, within which are several *bale* for accommodating paying guests, each one furnished with a huge four-poster bed and garden bathroom; rooms must be reserved ahead as this is still very much a family home. If asked, *Puri Anyar* can also arrange cultural one-day programmes that incorporate demonstrations in dance, traditional games and making offerings.

Another descendant of the Tabanan royal family lives just around the corner from Puri Anyar, at **Puri Agung Wisata**, which you can visit for a small donation. Though Puri Agung (literally "big" or "main" palace) is the most important of the Tabanan palaces, it seems much less stylish than Puri Anyar, but might be worth a look for the special tooth-filing pavilion and family temple compound. Apparently it's a popular venue for tourists' wedding parties.

Both Krambitan and the neighbouring village of **PANARUKAN** have a reputation for their outstanding dancers, who sometimes give **dance per-**

formances at Puri Anyar (call for details). They are particularly renowned for their *calonarang*, a ritual-cleansing Barong and Rangda dance in which almost half the village participates (see p.523).

Tibubiyu and Pantai Pasut

A tempting alternative to royal palace **accommodation** is *Bibi's* (no phone, ⓕ0361/812744; ❷–❸), a set of five prettily designed rice-barn-style bungalows surrounded by paddy-fields in the village of **TIBUBIYU**, 4km south of Krambitan (to get there, continue for a few hundred metres south of Puri Agung Wisata and then turn right just after the sign for Tibubiyu and Pantai Pasut; turquoise Tabanan–Krambitan bemos can usually be persuaded to take passengers on to Tibubiyu). Each bungalow has sea views from its upstairs bedrooms and a garden bathroom downstairs. The place is run by an Australian artist, and there's an emphasis on peaceful and contemplative activities; the black-sand beach is ten minutes' walk away and you can borrow bicycles. It's quite isolated though, so you might be better off with your own transport if you're thinking of staying any length of time.

Southwest from Tibubiyu on the same road is **PANTAI PASUT**, a long, lonely strand of black sand and rolling surf that's invariably deserted, bar the occasional fisherman.

North to Gunung Batukau

Much of inland southwest Bali lies in the shadow of the massive **Gunung Batukau** (sometimes spelled Bautukaru; 2276m), the second-highest mountain on the island (after Gunung Agung) and one of the holiest. All west Bali temples have a shrine dedicated to the spirit of Gunung Batukau, and on the lower slopes of the holy mountain itself stands the beautiful **Pura Luhur Batukau**, Bali's directional temple (*kayangan jagat*) for the west and the focus of many pilgrimages.

Gunung Batukau and its hinterland is the **wettest** region of Bali, and the dense tropical forest that clothes the uppermost slopes has now been designated a nature reserve, a particularly rewarding area for **bird-watching**. Lower down, on the gentler slopes that effectively stretch all the way to Tabanan, 21km southeast of Pura Luhur, the superior soil provides some of the most productive agricultural land on the island: the rice-terraces around **Jatiluwih** are particularly scenic. Because of Batukau's cool, damp micro-climate, it's worth bringing warm clothes and rain gear up here with you, even if you're only making a brief visit to Pura Luhur Batukau or are planning to stay in comfort in the nearby village of **Wongayagede**.

Transport practicalities

From Tabanan, with your own transport, you have a choice of two main **routes to Batukau**. The following account describes a circular tour to Pura Luhur Batukau and back, going up via Penatahan and Wongayagede and returning via Jatiluwih, Senganan and Penebel; this route is equally viable in reverse.

It's currently impossible to get to Pura Luhur Batukau by public **bemo**, though there is a service that goes as far as Jatiluwih, via Penebel, and you may be able to charter the same bemo on to Pura Luhur. The Tabanan–Penebel–Jatiluwih bemos leave from the bemo station at Tawakilang, 2km north of Tabanan town centre – approximately hourly in the mornings, less frequently after noon.

An alternative is to join a **tour**. Most tour operators in Kuta, Sanur and Ubud do a trip to Pura Luhur Batukau, either in combination with an undemanding local walk, or featuring a few hours at the *Yeh Panas* hot springs resort, or as part of an itinerary that also takes in the Jatiluwih rice terraces and either the Pura Taman Ayun at Mengwi or Bedugul's Pura Ulun Danu. Sobek (⊤0361/287059) runs guided **mountain-bike** trips down the side of Gunung Batukau for US$55, and Paddy Ventures does bicycle and quad-bike tours through the Jatiluwih rice-fields (see the Jatiluwih account below for details). All tours can be booked direct or through tour agents in any of the major tourist centres; prices include transport from your hotel.

Tabanan to Wongayagede (via Yeh Panas)

The main **Tabanan–Wongayagede route** follows a well-maintained road all the way from Tabanan town centre: simply keep a lookout for signs to Pura Luhur Batukau. Beyond Tabanan the road passes through some lovely shrub-lined villages, past the Butterfly Park in Wanasari (see p.381) and on through archetypal Balinese scenes of rice terraces and tree-shaded roads before reaching a junction at **BURUAN**. The right-hand fork will take you up to Gunung Batukau via Penebel, Senganan and Jatiluwih, and is described in reverse on p.386.

Soon after taking the left-hand fork you pass through the village of **PENATAHAN**, site of the **Yeh Panas Hot Springs**. Tempting as they sound, these springs have been bought up by a hotel company and are now set aside for the use of guests at the *Yeh Panas Natural Hot Spring and Spa Hotel* (⊤0361/262356, Ⓕ755628; ❼). Various spa packages are available to non-guests including spa only ($15) or spa, lunch and local walk ($40).

Continuing past *Yeh Panas*, the road runs through some fine swathes of *sawah*, where you should be able to distinguish the fields planted with indigenous Balinese rice (tall and yellow) from those growing the more lucrative, faster-growing imported varieties, whose cycle is up to 30 days shorter, and which are greener and smaller. A few kilometres north of Yeh Panas, about 500m before the road enters Wongayagede, you'll see the Catholic church (*gereja*) of St Martinus de Pons, on the northern fringe of the hamlet of **TENGUDAK**. It's likely to be locked but the facade is quite an interesting example of Balinese Christian architecture: several Christian motifs have been carved onto an otherwise typical red-brick facade and the whole structure is crowned with a four-tiered Hindu-style *meru* tower.

Wongayagede

If you're planning to climb Gunung Batukau (see box on p.386 for details), you'll need to spend at least one night in **WONGAYAGEDE**, the village nearest to the trail-head, about 2km south of the temple car park. Even if you're not intending to trek up the mountain, a night or two here would be a rewarding experience – remote and extremely scenic, offering ample opportunity to explore the tranquil countryside.

The most upmarket **place to stay** in the village is the good-value *Prana Dewi* (⊤ & Ⓕ0361/732032, Ⓦwww.balipranaresort.com; ❻), signed west off the main road through the village (north of the side road to Jatiluwih) and accessed by a long, fairly rough track. *Prana Dewi* occupies an idyllic spot above a wooded riverbank, totally secluded from the road and literally surrounded by rice-fields. The seven stylish bungalows are thoughtfully designed with huge picture windows, verandahs and four-poster beds and widely spaced around the gardens; there are no fans or air-conditioning as it's relatively cool up here. The **restaurant** is worth visiting in its own right: it shares the same views and serves home-grown red rice, organic vegetables and brown bread as well as curries and pastas. You can arrange **guides** for the Batukau trek here, as well as for less taxing local walks. *Prana Dewi* also holds twice-monthly **yoga courses** ($90 for three days half-board; $190 for six days).

The other place to stay also boasts breathtaking views: *Warung Kaja* (☎0811/398052, ✉pkaler@dps.centrin.net.id; ❹) is set at the top of a steep flight of steps about 750m east along the Wongayagede–Jatiluwih road, from where you get exceptional panoramas over the sea of rice terraces. Accommodation here is in four simple wooden huts surrounded by rice-fields, and the restaurant offers a decent local menu. *Warung Kaja* also offers an extensive programme of good-value **guided walks and cycle rides**, featuring visits to local waterfalls, traditional homes, rice-fields and bird-watching ($4–12 per person). They also do guided treks up Gunung Batukau (best arranged in advance) and rent mountain bikes (Rp50,000/day).

Pura Luhur Batukau

Usually silent – except for its resident orchestra of cicadas and frogs – **Pura Luhur Batukau** (Rp5000 donation requested; sarong and sash available to rent) does full justice to its epithet, the "Garden Temple". The grassy courtyards are planted with flowering hibiscus, Javanese ixora and cempaka shrubs, and the montane forest that carpets the slopes of Gunung Batukau encroaches on the compound's perimeters to the north, east and west. Monuments are encrusted with moist green moss, and a web of paths fans out to solitary shrines set further into the forest. Batukau's **bird** population finds plenty to feed on here, so you're likely to see a fair number of forest dwellers, including bright green woodpecker-like barbets, scarlet minivets, olive-green grey-headed flycatchers and possibly even scarlet-headed flowerpeckers in the temple treetops.

Pura Luhur Batukau is thought to have become a holy site in the eleventh century, and was subsequently consecrated by the rajas of the kingdom of Tabanan who made it into their state temple and dedicated shrines here to their ancestral gods. In 1604, however, the rival rajas of Bululeng razed the shrines to the ground and, although devotees continued to worship at the ruins, the temple was not fully renovated until 1959. Many of the thatched *meru* now standing inside the **inner sanctuary** still represent a particular branch or member of the ancestral family of the rajas of Tabanan. The most important shrine, though, is the unusual seven-tiered pagoda which is dedicated to Mahadewa, the god of Gunung Batukau. To the east of the main temple compound, a large square **pond** has been dug to represent and honour the gods of nearby Lake Tamblingan (see p.339), which lies immediately to the north of Gunung Batukau. Only Batukau's priests are allowed access to the tiny island shrine in the middle of the pond, which they reach by means of a makeshift raft on a pulley.

In deference to Pura Luhur's extremely sacred status, visitors are requested to wear sarong and sash, and to obey the strict **rules of admission** that are posted at the entrance. Aside from the usual prohibitions, such as menstruating women and those who have been recently bereaved, Batukau also bars pregnant women and new mothers (who are considered ritually impure for 42 days after the birth), as well as "mad ladies/gentleman". Pura Luhur Batukau still plays a very important role in the lives of Balinese Hindus. Members of local *subak* groups come here to draw holy water from the pond for use in agricultural ceremonies, and at the annual *Galungan* festivities truckloads of devotees travel long distances to pay their respects and lay their offerings.

Climbing Gunung Batukau

Few people **climb** the sacred slopes of Gunung Batukau, and during the rainy season (Nov–March) not even the most sure-footed Balinese would attempt it. If you do decide to climb, you'll definitely need a **guide**. Although there are fairly well-defined paths nearly all the way to the summit (starting from the outer courtyard of Pura Luhur Batukau), many turn out to be false trails. In addition, the slopes are thickly wooded and offer few clearings from which to work out your bearings. When you finally reach the peak, you'll find a small temple dedicated to the god of the mountain. Constant shade and low-lying cloud also make the atmosphere damp and the paths quite slippery, so you should be prepared with warm clothes, rainwear and decent shoes. The usual guided climb takes four to six hours to reach the summit (though it has been done in two-and-a-half), and three to five hours to return to ground level. To complete the climb and descent in one day you'll need to start at sunrise, having spent the night in Wongayagede 2km down the road. Although the round trip is just about possible in one day, some people like to camp near the top.

The best place to organize a **guided hike** is *Warung Kaja* in Wongayagede (☎0811/398052, ⓔpkaler@dps.centrin.net.id; see p.385); if possible you should contact them ahead of time so they can arrange the requisite permits and guides. Prices include lunch, water and the permits, but depend on the number of trekkers and whether you require an English-speaking guide as well as a local porter and path-finder. Approximate per-person prices (depending on the exchange rate) for the trek with/without an English-speaking guide are US$55/37.50 for one person, $32.50/25 for two people or $22.50/20 for three or four people. It's also possible to arrange guides through *Prana Dewi* in Wongayagede. The guys who hang around at Pura Luhur Batukau guide tourists up the mountain for Rp500,000 per group, excluding food and water (bring your own sleeping bag and tent if planning a night on the top). It's also possible to climb Gunung Batukau via the mountain's southwestern flank, beginning near the village of Sanda on the Seririt–Pupuan–Antosari road; a guide can be arranged through *Sanda Butik Villas*, described on p.409.

Wongayagede to Tabanan (via Jatiluwih)

The road to Jatiluwih branches east from Wongayagede about 2.5km south of Pura Luhur, and then proceeds to take you through some of the most famous rice-paddy vistas on Bali, offering expansive panoramas over the broad and gently sloping terraces sculpted from the south-facing hillsides. At points you can even glimpse the sea on the distant blue horizon, but certain stretches of the road are painfully potholed, narrow and twisty, so try not to let your eyes wander too much.

A short distance along the road, you pass *Warung Kaja* (described on p.385), the first of several stunningly located **restaurants** that entice you to their tables with the prospect of a fabulous panorama. Next up is the more commercial *Paddy Venture* (☎0361/289748, ⓦwww.bali-adventures.com), which as well as serving food also runs **tours** through the rice-paddies on foot ($39), bicycle ($45), All Terrain Vehicle (ATV or quad-bike; $65 or $104 tandem), or Land Rover ($69). Prices include return transport and lunch; most tourists pre-book these tours through travel agents in one of the south-coast resorts. A couple of kilometres further east, the *Naga Puspa* restaurant makes another great vantage point as the road begins to wend through ever-more lush landscapes, dense with banana trees, *kopi bali* coffee plantations, fields of chilli peppers and tomato plants, ferns and *dadap* trees (see p.408 for more on the *dadap*), plus the occasional chicken farm – a genuine garden of the gods. This whole area is known as **JATILUWIH**, after the hamlet of the same name, where the long-running *Café Jatiluwih* is another welcoming spot for a scenic break.

About 14km in total from Wongayagede, the road arrives at the **SENGANAN** road junction. The quickest route to the north or south coasts is the northeast (left) fork, a good, fast 7.5-kilometre road that feeds into the main Denpasar–Bedugul–Singaraja artery at **PACUNG**, 6km south of Bedugul and 25km north of Mengwi. For the slower, more scenic route to Buruan and Tabanan take the southbound (right) fork which runs via the sizeable market town of **PENEBEL**. Here, on the northern outskirts of town in the *banjar* of **DUKUH**, you'll find the friendly and peaceful *Taman Sari Bungalows* (☎0361/812898; ❹), which has half-a-dozen pretty cottages set in a flower garden bordered by a rambutan orchard that drops down to the river. About 5km further south you'll arrive at back at the **BURUAN** junction, a little way north of Tabanan.

The coast road to Negara

Few tourists venture further west than Tanah Lot, but the stretch of coast beyond Tabanan holds some nice surprises at the black-sand beaches of **Balian** and **Medewi**. There are a few low-key places to stay at both, but the atmosphere may change over the next few years as this whole stretch of coast is slated for significant development. The spectacular cliffside temple of **Pura Rambut Siwi**, almost as stunningly located as Tanah Lot but far less crowded with visitors, provides a cultural focus for this area, while **Negara** really only merits a visit for its twice-yearly traditional buffalo races.

The main road divides 16km west of Tabanan at the village of **ANTOSARI**, splitting the westbound Gilimanuk and Java traffic from the vehicles heading to Seririt and the north coast. The road to the north coast, served by Ubung (Denpasar)–Seririt–Singaraja buses and dark red bemos, climbs through some pretty spectacular mountain scenery but can be a bit scary because of the truck drivers racing each other round the sharp bends (see p.408 for more on this route). After this road there's just one more route through the mountains to the north coast, 35km west of here.

Lalang Linggah and Balian beach

Heading west through Antosari and along the base of the mountain ridge, the road to Gilimanuk drops right down to the coast, affording fine sea views with shadows of southeast Java on the horizon, along with tantalizing inland panoramas of paddy-fields. You can make more of these views by stopping off at *Soka Indah* (☎0361/246004; ❸), located in **SOKA** at the point where the road hits the coast. The large, tour-group-oriented restaurant here is better than it looks and, if you follow the path down from the car park to the sea, you'll find a couple of large, surprisingly secluded, comfortable bungalows with impressive sea views.

About 10km west of Antosari, the Gilimanuk road zips through **LALANG LINGGAH**, the village closest to **Balian beach**, and a pleasant and peaceful place to base yourself for a few days. The grey-black-sand beach here is popular with surfers, but the vicious current makes it far too dangerous for casual swimmers. (There have been several fatalities in the last few years.) For non-surfers, there are a number of interesting **walks** around the locality, including north along the course of the Balian River, or east or west along the shore; Lalang Linggah hotels can advise you on the best routes.

All Ubung (Denpasar)–Gilimanuk **bemos** and buses pass through Lalang Linggah; they take about an hour and a quarter from Ubung or about half an hour from Medewi. Coming from the north coast, you can take any Seririt–Pulukan or Singaraja–Seririt–Antosari bemo and then change onto the Ubung–Gilimanuk service.

Accommodation

Lalang Linggah currently has three very different **accommodation** possibilities, but the area looks set to develop as a swath of shorefront land has recently been bought up. A number of expats have built homes along the shore in the area around Lalang Linggah so there are usually several "villa for rent" signs worth investigating.

Balian Beach Bungalows East side of the Balian River estuary ☎ & ℱ 0361/814997, ⓔ bobbali@denpasar.wasantara.net.id. Prettily set in a coconut grove beside the Balian River, about ten minutes' walk from the shore, this friendly and informally run place attracts surfers and family groups and offers a range of rooms, with good discounts for long stays and families. Rooms vary a lot in quality, but the basic losmen rooms are serviceable and a couple of the most expensive bungalows are comfortably and attractively furnished. There's a pool, a restaurant and a small soap- and candle-making workshop on the premises, which is part of the Yakeba rehabilitation programme established by the owner (see p.34 for more information). ❷–❹

Gajah Mina Signed off the Gilimanuk road, 400m west of *Sacred River* in Suraberata ☎ 0812/381 1630, ℱ 0361/731174, ⓦ www.gajahminaresort.com. Currently the most upmarket place to stay in Lalang Linggah, comprising eight air-con bungalows, designed in simple yet chic style, with a relaxed Mediterranean flavour. Each bungalow is comfortably furnished and has its own private garden verandah and pretty garden bathroom. There's a nice long swimming pool here as well as a classy restaurant specializing in fish and seafood dishes, and a bar (*Sacred River* guests can walk to the bar here in only 10min). ❽

Sacred River Retreat/Sungai Suci Signed from the Gilimanuk road on the west side of the Balian River estuary ☎ 0361/814993, ℱ 730904, ⓦ www.sacred-river.com. Designed and managed by the charismatic Australian artist and healer Shankari, this is an alternative resort with an emphasis on spiritual activities. You can join the regular meditation and yoga sessions here, take traditional *mandi lulur* herbal massages and learn Balinese painting, dancing, bamboo gamelan, cooking or singing. Horse riding is also available. The hotel tries to involve visitors in local religious ceremonies and can arrange audiences with a local *dukun* (traditional faith healer). The fifteen comfortable two-storey bungalows are simple but stylish, with upstairs bedrooms and downstairs garden bathrooms, and there's a pool and vegetarian restaurant (bring your own alcohol). ❻–❼

Medewi beach

As it skirts the coastline, the 25km stretch of road between Lalang Linggah and Medewi beach crosses more than a dozen rivers, each one streaming down from the Batukau mountain range, watering kilometre after kilometre of stunningly lush land en route. Rice-paddies dominate the landscape, some even dropping right down to the shoreline, but this area is also a major coconut-growing region as well as a big producer of vanilla pods, cloves, cocoa beans and coffee.

MEDEWI village sits on the main Tabanan–Gilimanuk road, served by frequent bemos (about 2hr from Ubung), and consists of little more than a mosque and a string of houses in among coconut groves and paddy-fields. It was first settled in 1912, when the whole area was covered in thorny *ketket* trees; the Balinese word for "thorny" is *meduwi*, hence the current name of the village, though the trees have all been cleared now. The beach is primarily a fishing beach, but there's a small enclave of shorefront bungalows which make a good short-term getaway from more crowded resorts. The black sand is fine, the current is light, and the waves are ideal for amateur **surfers**; local beach boys will be only too happy to teach you how to improve your technique. You can also rent boats here, either to go snorkelling or for a spot of fishing.

The best **accommodation** is at *Hotel Tin Jaya* (℡0365/42945; ❶–❷), which offers rooms with attached bathrooms in three comfortably furnished rice-barn-style cottages, as well as simpler losmen quarters. The cottages are set beside a long grassy lawn that slopes right down to the beach, and there's a good warung here too. The four unsignposted traditional rice-barn bungalows 100m further east along the road call themselves *Homestay Gede* (no phone; ❶), and are friendly, family-run and good value, offering fine sea views, but shared bathrooms. As there are only half a dozen rooms available here, they tend to get snapped up very quickly. Far larger, but soulless, the neighbouring *Hotel Pantai Medewi*, also known as *Medewi Beach Cottages* (℡0365/40029, ℻41555, ✉baliwest@indo.net.id; ❻–❼), overcharges for its cheapest rooms, but its more expensive cottages (with air-con and TV) do have seafront positions, and there are pleasant gardens and a swimming pool. The *Pantai Medewi* also organizes local cycling outings, day-trips and diving excursions to Menjangan Island.

All three places have **restaurants** attached: *Tin Jaya*'s tasty and wide-ranging menu covers everything from peanut-butter jaffles to fresh fish deep-fried with chillies; while the restaurant at *Pantai Medewi* serves Indonesian standards like ayam goreng, gado-gado and nasi goreng, as well as a decent repertoire of fish dishes. Every Sunday night, *Pantai Medewi* diners also get treated to a perform-ance of the locally famous *joged bumbung* dance. The *Mai Malu* café, at the head of the access road to the *Pantai Medewi*, has a big menu of pizzas, pastas and Indonesian dishes, and shows surfing movies at night.

Pura Rambut Siwi

When the sixteenth-century Hindu priest Nirartha sailed from his home in Java, he landed on Bali's southwest coast, and proceeded to explore the shore-line east of Negara. Impressed by the ruggedness of the coast, the clear views of southeast Java across the water, and the beauty of the mountainous backdrop, he claimed the spot 10km west of Medewi to be holy and set about preaching the Hindu doctrine. When he left to continue his tour of the island, Nirartha donated a lock of his hair to the villagers, who duly erected a temple and named it **Pura Rambut Siwi**, "the temple for worshipping the hair". Nirartha's choice of location was characteristically awe-inspiring and the tem-ple is now the most important in Jembrana district. After a visit, you can **swim** off the beach here, a huge swath of charcoal-black sand beneath you.

Pura Rambut Siwi is 16km west of Medewi, accessed by a 750-metre side road through the paddy-fields; if you're travelling by **bemo** from Denpasar or Gilimanuk, get out when you see the sign for the temple and the cluster of roadside warung. You'll be asked by the Brahman temple caretakers to wear a sash and give a donation, and in return they will offer to guide you around the temple, which is entered from the side.

Nirartha's sacred hair is enshrined, along with some of his clothing, in a san-dalwood box buried deep inside the central three-tiered *meru*. This shrine is the focus of the **inner courtyard**, which is inaccessible to casual visitors but can be admired from alongside its south-facing **paduraksa**. Built in tiers of solid red brick and ornamented with fierce stonecarvings of open-mouthed Bhoma, the gateway gives direct access to the cliff face and frames a stunning view of the Bali Strait. From here you pass between an assortment of guardian statues to the outer *candi bentar*, which is protected by two mythical tigers. The figure that stands in the middle of the stairway, staring out to sea with his right arm raised, is said to be looking sorrowfully at Java (you can see Mount Bromo quite distinctly from here), bemoaning the ascendance of Islam over the Hindu kingdom of Majapahit. Gently stepped garden terraces of frangipani and stubby palm trees connect the *candi bentar* with the **shrine to Dewi Sri**, goddess of rice and of water and hence of prosperity, that balances on the cliff edge.

Descending the rock-cut steps to the beach, you'll find a string of small shrines tucked into the cliff face to the left of the stairway. The first, a cave temple known as **Pura Tirta**, houses a holy freshwater spring that rises just under the cliff and is guarded by a statue of Nirartha. A series of dank, bat-infested caves links Pura Tirta to **Goa Mayan Sati** (the Cave of the Holy Tiger), 50m further east, but the underground complex is out of bounds to visitors as all new priests of Pura Rambut Siwi meditate here before becoming fully ordained. A 100-metre walk further up the beach brings you to **Pura Penataran**, dedicated to the god of the sea, Baruna, and protected by a couple of underwater snake deities, or *naga* – white for Siwa, black for Wisnu.

Negara

Formerly the home of the Jembrana royal family and still the administrative capital of Jembrana district, the prosperous but strangely empty town of **NEGARA** seems to epitomize the Islamification of western Bali. With its unnecessarily wide streets and large number of mosques, the town centre is reminiscent of many medium-sized Javanese towns. Historically, Negara was a major port of entry for the Javanese and Madurese, who would sail across the Bali Strait to the river estuary at Perancak and then head upstream to the town, 7km further north. Negara's Muslims, already well established here by the nineteenth century, came mostly from South Sulawesi, many of them people of Bugis origin, descendants of a seafaring race with a reputation as fearsome pirates. Traditional Bugis-style housing – raised, elongated wooden structures – still features in the area, notably in the hamlet of Loloan Timor, 1km south of Negara.

Negara's one significant attraction are its traditional **buffalo races**, or *Mekepung*, which are organized by the Jembrana authorities and held here every dry season, usually in August and then again between September and November (check with any Balinese tourist office for the dates and exact location; most tour agents sell all-inclusive trips to the races). The buffalo and their jockeys come from all parts of Jembrana district, divided into two teams according to whether they live east or west of Negara's Ijo Gading River.

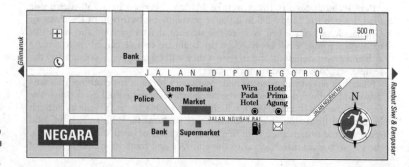

Decked out in strings of bells and decorative harness, their horns painted in bright colours, the buffalo pairs are paraded in front of the spectators before the competition begins. The races last all day and take place along a two-kilometre stretch of Negara's back roads. Buffalo pairs, both hauling along a *cikar* cart, are pitted against each other, encouraged by whip-happy jockeys. Every winning pair gains points for its team, but stylish contenders are also awarded bonuses; the victors are announced at the end of the day. It's thought that the games were introduced to Negara by the farmers who emigrated from the island of Madura, off northeast Java, where similar races are still held; the only other traditional buffalo races in Bali are held once a year near Singaraja on the north coast (see p.360).

Practicalities

All Denpasar–Gilimanuk **bemos** pass through Negara town centre, calling in at the bemo station, 100m north of the Jalan Ngurah Rai roundabout en route.

There are plenty of **places to stay**, though few are particularly welcoming. The best option is the clean and well-managed *Wira Pada Hotel*, centrally located at Jl Ngurah Rai 107 (☎0365/41161; ❷–❹), which offers a range of en-suite rooms, with either fan or air-con, set around a courtyard. It also runs a good, reasonably priced streetside **restaurant**, serving up a range of fish dishes and Indonesian standards, as well as omelettes and sandwiches for the occasional tourist. Alternatively, check out the Sumatran-style Masakan Padang food shop just east of the *Wira Pada* on Jalan Ngurah Rai, where you can either select your own combination of cold dishes from the food displayed in the glass cabinet or choose hot rice dishes and soups from the English-language menu.

The far west

Almost as soon as you leave Negara, the landscape of the **far west** changes dramatically, becoming noticeably drier and more rugged. The thickly forested, cloud-capped mountain slopes shelter very few villages and much of the land is conserved as **Bali Barat National Park**. Few tourists explore the park – the only one on the island – but it's particularly rewarding for bird-watchers and also harbours some of Bali's best coral reefs, around the fringes of **Pulau Menjangan (Deer Island)**.

If you're arriving overland from Java, the port town of **Gilimanuk** will be your first introduction to Bali. Although there's little to detain you in the town itself, the national park is just a few kilometres away, and good transport connections enable you to head either straight to Lovina and the north coast or to Denpasar and the south.

Palasari and Belimbingsari

While Muslims have long been welcomed into western Balinese society, **Christians** have generally had a much frostier reception. When the Dutch gained full control over Balinese affairs in 1908, they extended their policy of undiluted cultural preservation to include barring all Christian missionaries from practising on the island. But Dutch attentions relaxed over the next two decades, and in the 1930s a Chinese man called **Tsang To Hang** arrived to spread the Christian gospel. Tsang To Hang successfully infiltrated the local Chinese community, and by 1932 was able to boast three hundred converts, including some of "pure Balinese" ethnicity. One of his tactics was to highlight the iniquities of the entrenched Hindu caste system – which resulted in many of the new converts being ostracized by their neighbours.

The Dutch soon banned Tsang To Hang, but softened their original ruling by inviting one Protestant and one Catholic mission to establish themselves on the island. To ensure that the Christian influence was as minimal as possible, the Dutch packed these missionaries off to an inhospitable area of uninhabited land high up in the mountains of west Bali, some 30km northwest of Negara. Against massive odds and with an amazing pioneering spirit, the Protestants built themselves the village of **BELIMBINGSARI**, later adding a huge modern church to their settlement. Some 5km southeast, the Catholics did the same for their community at **PALASARI**. Interestingly, both sects have managed to separate Balinese culture from Balinese religion, a fusion that's always held to be so inextricable; Balinese music and dance, for example, are taught in Belimbingsari and Palasari, but the characters and stories are taken from the Bible rather than from the *Ramayana* and *Mahabharata*. Both settlements have populations of little more than two thousand apiece, yet the churches up here are quite astonishing, blending Balinese and Western European architecture to dramatic effect.

The two communities are accessible, and signed, via a road that runs east from Melaya on the main Tabanan–Gilimanuk road. There's no regular bemo service to either place, though gangs of **ojek** usually hang around the main road turn-offs. Just beyond Palasari, and clearly signed all the way from the main Gilimanuk road 8km away, the ultra-luxurious *Taman Wana Villas* (℡0361/728633, ℻723334, ⓦwww.bali-tamanwana-villas.com; ❽–❾) is the only **place to stay** up here. It occupies a breathtaking spot overlooking the Palasari reservoir, surrounded by rice-fields and palm groves, with the distant peaks of Gunung Klatakan and Gunung Bakingan and the waters of the Bali Strait all visible in a single panorama from the restaurant. The villas are circular to make the most of the views and there are two pools on the premises (one for kids) plus cycling, trekking and diving excursions as well as any number of watersports facilities down on the reservoir. It's also possible to arrive here by sea-plane from Benoa Harbour (see p.172) and land on the reservoir.

Gilimanuk

Situated on the westernmost tip of Bali, less than 3km from East Java, the small, ribbon-like town of **GILIMANUK** is used by visitors mainly as a transit point

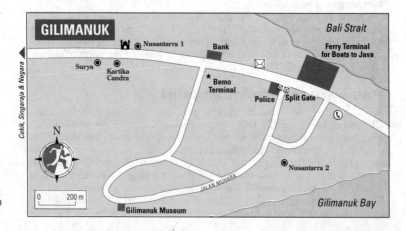

The Bali Strait

The **Bali Strait** is a notoriously difficult stretch of water to negotiate: although Bali and East Java are 3km apart here, the water is just 60m deep, and the current extremely treacherous. A regular ferry service across the Strait was only inaugurated in the 1930s, before which the crossing was made on light wooden fishing prahu all the way round to the Perancak River estuary on the southwest coast, and then north up the river to Negara (some 33km east of Gilimanuk).

According to **legend**, Bali was once connected to East Java, and its great mountain, Gunung Agung, was a holy place of pilgrimage for all sorts of spiritually minded Javanese. One such was a saintly Brahman man named Sidi Mantra who, plagued by a son who had gambled away all his parents' belongings and more, set off to ask for help from the great dragon of Gunung Agung, Naga Besukih. The *naga* agreed to pay off the Brahman's debts and, shaking his body a little, let precious stones fall from his scaly skin. But the gambling continued, and Sidi Mantra was obliged to return to the *naga* several more times. Eventually, Sidi Mantra's profligate son, Manik Angkeran, thought he'd go and bring back some of the treasure for himself. Predictably, the young gambler couldn't resist taking more than he was offered, and he sliced off the *naga*'s tail. The furious *naga* retaliated by reducing Manik to a pile of ashes. When Manik's father eventually came looking for his son, he struck a deal with the *naga*, promising to restore the tail in return for his son being brought back to life again. The deal was done, but Sidi Mantra wanted to be sure that his son wouldn't bring his parents' home into disrepute again. With his magic staff, Sidi Mantra scored a line across the land between where he and his son stood facing each other. Within seconds, the earth cracked and filled with water, and this was how the Bali Strait came into being.

Geologists corroborate some of the Bali Strait legend, as it's generally agreed that a **land bridge** did once connect Gilimanuk with East Java. Both Java and Bali rest on a continental plate known as the Sunda shelf which is sunk deep below the Java Sea. However, during the glacial age approximately one million years ago, sea levels across the world dropped, temporarily exposing the Bali Strait land bridge and enabling people from East Java to walk quite easily into Bali and back again. This may become a reality once more, if the controversial plans to construct a **Bali–Java bridge** ever come to fruition.

for journeys to and from Java. A 24-hour ferry service crosses the Bali Strait, so few travellers bother to linger in the town. Despite its dearth of attractions, though, the place does have a certain charm, with fine views west over Java's great volcanoes, and a pleasant waterside location around the edge of mangrove-fringed Gilimanuk Bay. The **Gilimanuk Museum** (Mon–Fri 8am–3pm; donation requested), about 1500m southwest of the port, houses a handful of skeletons and sarcophagi excavated nearby and is hardly worth the effort.

Getting to Gilimanuk by **bemo** from almost any major town in north, south and west Bali is fairly straightforward; all terminate at the bemo station in the town centre, ten minutes' walk from the ferry terminal or a short dokar ride. **From Denpasar** (128km southeast) and the southern beaches, take either the direct dark green bemos from Ubung terminal (Rp7500) or a Gilimanuk-bound bus (Rp11,000); see p.372. **From Singaraja** (88km northeast), dark red bemos run regularly via **Lovina**, as do a few buses (Rp5000/7500; see p.342). It's also possible to get buses here **from Padang Bai** and **Amlapura** on the east coast (Rp10,500; see p.299). For bemo and bus journeys beginning in Gilimanuk you can check fares on the noticeboard outside the controller's office.

For **eating**, there are plenty of warung and food carts clustered around the ferry terminal, as well as several restaurants along the main street. You can **change money** at the bank opposite the bemo terminal.

Crossing to Java

Crossing the Bali Strait between Bali and Java is as easy as hopping on a bemo: there are no formalities, and onward transport facilities from both ports are frequent and efficient. If you're travelling quite a way into Java, to Probolinggo (for Mount Bromo) for example, or to Surabaya, Yogyakarta or Jakarta, the easiest option is to get an all-inclusive ticket from your starting point in Bali. The cheapest **long-distance buses** run out of Denpasar's Ubung station, with pick-up points in Tabanan, Negara and sometimes Gilimanuk, but there are also more expensive **tourist shuttle buses** and **bus and train** combinations operating from major tourist centres across the island. All these services include the ferry crossing in the ticket price.

Ferries shuttle between Gilimanuk and Ketapang (East Java) and back again 24 hours a day (every 20min; takes 30min including loading and docking). **Tickets** must be bought before boarding: foot passengers buy them from the "Loket Penumpang" counter in the terminal building; seats cost Rp2000 (Rp1300 for kids). Vehicle owners pay as they drive into the compound, and the ticket price includes the driver and any passengers: bicycles cost Rp3000, motorbikes Rp5000 and cars Rp25,000. Note that most car rental agencies on Bali prohibit tourists from taking their vehicles to other islands (see p.40 for more).

Arriving in **Ketapang**, the Banyuwangi Baru train station is about 100m north of the ferry terminal, signed off to the left of the main road. Aside from frequent services to Surabaya Kota, there are three daily services from here to Probolinggo, and on to Yogyakarta. The central bus stations for cross-Java travel are in the much larger nearby town of **Banyuwangi**, 8km south of Ketapang, served by frequent bemos that depart from the ferry terminal.

Accommodation

Accommodation in Gilimanuk itself is not at all traveller-oriented: the losmen here are intended mainly for minimal overnight stops (which includes the brothel trade) or for long-stay contract workers who sometimes occupy entire losmen, making it hard to find a room here at all. Your best option near the port is *Nusantarra 2* (no phone; ❷). Peacefully located on the edge of scenic Gilimanuk Bay, it offers basic losmen-style rooms about five minutes' walk from the ferry terminal. If it's full, try *Kartika Candra* (no phone; ❷), *Nusantarra 1* (no phone; ❷) or *Surya* (no phone; ❷), all on the main road, about fifteen minutes' walk south of the ferry terminal, less than five minutes from the bemo station.

The most appealing, tourist-friendly places are on the edge of town, about 2km south of the port along the road to Cekik, or 1500m north of the Bali Barat National Park headquarters. Here you'll find the long-running *Pondok Wisata Lestari* (☎0365/61504; ❷), which has eighteen typical losmen rooms ranging from very cheap and very basic to more comfortable options with air-conditioning. There's a reasonably good restaurant here too. About 50m north, a sign leads you 250m down a side road to *Sari* (☎0365/61264, ℱ61265; ❷–❸), which has 22 rooms in two-storey bamboo bungalows set round a courtyard, a couple of hundred metres from the shore. Accommodation is fairly attractive, with the more expensive rooms running to hot water and TV but no air-conditioning. Breakfast is included, but there's no restaurant here.

Bali Barat National Park

Nearly the whole of west Bali's mountain ridge is protected as **Bali Barat National Park (Taman Nasional Bali Barat)**, a 760-square-kilometre area of wooded slopes, savannah, rainforest, monsoon forest, mangrove swamp and

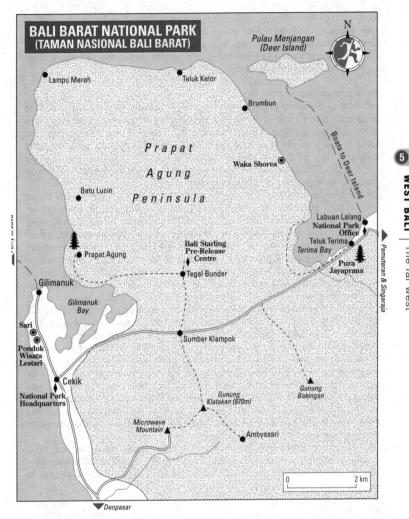

coastal flats, which is home to a range of small animals and approximately 160 species of bird – including the elusive and endangered **Bali starling**, Bali's one true endemic creature (see box on p.398). This was also once the province of the Bali tiger, but the last one was shot here in the 1930s.

Although over ninety percent of the parkland is out of bounds to visitors, there are a few trails kept open to the public. The two most rewarding are the **Tegal Bunder trail** – better for stationary bird-watching and animal-spotting – and the **Gunung Klatakan trail**, a longer hike through more interesting terrain. **Pulau Menjangan** (Deer Island), off the north coast and accessible from the park, is another worthwhile destination, particularly for divers and snorkellers. There's also a two-hour walk around **Teluk Terima**, which takes you through monsoon forest and coastal flats fairly similar to those at Tegal Bunder; this is a fruitful area for early-morning bird-spotting, with sightings likely to include sea eagles, dollar birds and even the rufous-backed kingfisher, plus monkeys and deer. The more taxing five-hour hike up the slopes of **Gunung Bakingan** and back down again follows a river course for part of the way, and traverses tropical rainforest similar to that on Gunung Klatakan, with sightings of hornbills fairly likely.

Practicalities

All dark green Ubung (Denpasar)–Gilimanuk **bemos** pass the national park headquarters at Cekik, as do all dark red Singaraja–Gilimanuk bemos; get out at the sign announcing "Taman Nasional Bali Barat". These bemo routes also make access to trailheads a bit easier: the Gilimanuk–Denpasar road skirts the southern edge of the park, while the Gilimanuk–Singaraja road zips through the middle of Bali Barat, dividing the Prapat Agung peninsula in the northwest from the mountainous ridge further east.

Anyone who enters Bali Barat National Park must be accompanied by an official park guide and must also be in possession of a permit. Both can be arranged through either the National Park Headquarters or the branch office at the Labuan Lalang jetty. The **National Park Headquarters** (daily 7am–5pm) is conveniently located at **CEKIK**, beside the Denpasar–Gilimanuk–Singaraja T-junction, 3km south of Gilimanuk. The office here is staffed by friendly and helpful park rangers, who will happily advise you on seasonal highlights in the park, and there's a scale model of Bali Barat to look at as well. For details on the branch office at the Labuan Lalang jetty, see p.400.

Most of the **guides** are English-speaking and conversant with the flora and fauna of Bali Barat; they don't necessarily need to be booked in advance. The basic fee is Rp120,000 for a two-hour hike for up to two people (plus an extra Rp30,000 for every two extra people), then Rp20,000–40,000 per extra hour, depending on the route and total duration. Specialist-interest treks can also be arranged on request. If you don't have your own transport you'll also be expected to pay for bemo or boat charters, depending on which trail you decide to follow. Having arranged a guide, you'll be granted a **permit**, which currently costs Rp2500 per person, though there are rumours of a possible price-hike to Rp20,000. Permits are good for only one day, unless you make other arrangements at the headquarters.

It's possible to join a one-day or overnight **tour** of Bali Barat National Park, arranged through tour agencies in Kuta, Sanur and Ubud from US$40 per person. All the hotels in Pemuteran, 28km northeast of Cekik (see p.404), also do day-trips to the park.

Accommodation

Although it's possible to ask the rangers' permission to **camp** in the park, they do a good job of dissuading visitors with stories of snakes and scorpions; if you're determined however, you'll need to provide your own tent, and should expect to pay Rp300,000 per person for the whole day and overnight experience. For Rp10,000, you may also pitch your own tent at the Cekik national park headquarters, though there are few facilities and you'll have to pay extra for a shower. Otherwise you'll have to stay in a **hotel** some distance from the trailheads. The best options are *Pondok Wisata Lestari* and *Sari* guesthouses, about 1500m north of the park headquarters on the road into Gilimanuk; see p.394 for details. Alternatively, make for the appealing accommodation at Pemuteran (see p.405), 28km along the road towards Singaraja.

Despite the national park status, there are now also a couple of upmarket **resorts** inside the confines of the park, both of them closer to Labuan Lalang than Cekik, and both offering guided walks and diving and snorkelling excursions. The twelve elegantly simple bungalows at *Waka Shorea* (T0828/361445, F0361/484767, Wwww.wakaexperience.com; 9) are just across the water from Pulau Menjangan on the shore of the Prapat Agung peninsula, only accessible by hotel shuttle boat from the Labuan Lalang jetty area. A couple of kilometres east of Labuan Lalang, the *Menjangan Jungle and Beach Resort* (T0361/759536, F759537, Wwww.menjangan.net; 8–9) was reportedly built under such strictly enforced restrictions that many of its buildings incorporated existing trees rather than having them cut them down. It's a huge resort, constructed entirely from Kalimantan timber, with spectacularly indulgent rooms in luxury sea-view villas (published price $300) and some disappointingly ordinary terraced "monsoon forest" rooms set around a swimming pool near the resort's riding stables.

Eating

Other than at the two resorts, there are no warung or **food** hawkers inside the national park, so you'll need to take your own supplies for the hikes. A *bakso* and noodle cart sets up outside the Cekik park headquarters every day. The nearest restaurant is at *Pondok Wisata Lestari*, 2km north up the road to Gilimanuk, where fried fish, huge locally caught prawns and various versions of nasi goreng are always on the menu. *Pondok Wisata Lestari* will also cook up food to take away if requested. The other options are all in Gilimanuk or at the Labuan Lalang jetty, 13km east of Cekik.

The Tegal Bunder trail

If your main interest is bird-spotting, then you should opt for the **Tegal Bunder trek** (1–2hr; best in the early morning), a 25-minute drive from Cekik. The focus of this trek is the monsoon forest around the Bali Starling Pre-Release Centre in the northwestern reaches of Bali Barat. The easiest way to explore is to drive to Tegal Bunder but, if you don't have your own vehicle, you can get a bemo to the access road at Sumber Klampok and then walk 2km. Or you could combine the Tegal Bunder trek with a jaunt through the mangrove forests of Gilimanuk Bay and arrive at Tegal Bunder by boat (see below).

Driving from Cekik, you'll pass through long stretches of fairly dull **dry monsoon forest**, the predominant vegetation in this area of Bali Barat, so called because its trees and plants have to be able to survive for long periods without any significant rainfall (between monsoons). To do this, many trees lose their leaves during the dry periods to help conserve water. The most interesting trees you'll see around here are **crocodile trees** (*panggal buaya*), which get their name from the thorny knobs that cover their long straight trunks. Crocodile wood is very popular with carvers who make good use of its hard white "satin" wood. **Rosewood trees** (*sonokeling*) are also eye-catching, growing up to 20m in height with distinctly gnarled trunks; they produce fine wood for furniture. Grey **macaques** and rarer **black monkeys** live in these forests, often cavorting along the side of the tracks in full view of walkers.

Once through the ranger checkpoint at **SUMBER KLAMPOK**, you'll soon come to a small side track which leads a few hundred metres to the **Bali Starling Pre-Release Centre** (see box on p.398). Here you should have a chance to see a few members of this rare and astonishingly pretty species while they're being trained for new lives in the wild. When they're ready to leave, the young birds are encouraged to settle in the area around Brumbun and Teluk Kelor, north of Batu Lucin, which is why nearly the whole of the Prapat Agung peninsula is now out of bounds to visitors.

The Bali starling

With its silky snow-white feathers, black wing and tail tips and delicate soft crest, the **Bali starling**, or Rothschild's Mynah (*Leucopsar rothschildi*), is an astonishingly beautiful bird and is the provincial symbol of Bali. It's Bali's only remaining endemic creature and survives in the dry monsoon forests and savannah grasslands that characterize the northwestern peninsula of Bali Barat National Park. Very few people get the chance to see the bird in its natural habitat: the last census in July 2001 recorded just six Bali starlings left in the wild, so all its known haunts have been made out of bounds to casual observers. It is also fairly easily confused with the much more common black-winged starling, whose wings and tail are almost completely black; the Bali starling has a blue patch of bald skin around each eye, but the black-winged starling's patches are yellow.

The Bali starling (*jalak putih Bali* in Bahasa Indonesia) was probably never a very common creature, and forest clearance in the first half of the twentieth century, followed by excessive hunting for the pet trade since the 1970s, has brought the species to the verge of extinction in the wild. In the 1930s, naturalists reported seeing "hundreds of birds", but by 1966 numbers were considered sufficiently low for the Bali starling to be put on the official list of **endangered species**. In contrast, the captive population has risen sharply. Bali starlings make docile and very pretty pets and, despite being notoriously nervous birds, they have flourished in captivity and sell for as much as US$2000.

Experts agree that the wild population needs to number at least a thousand if the species is to survive without the risk of inbreeding, and various agencies have established a breeding programme to try and ensure that this target is reached. Under this project, captive Bali starlings are mated at the **Bali Starling Pre-Release Centre** on Bali Barat's Prapat Agung peninsula. At the centre, the young birds are taught how to survive in the wild before being released at the end of the rainy season, when fruit and insects are plentiful, into known habitats further north on the peninsula, where it's hoped they'll breed with the dwindling wild population. Unfortunately, the project was dealt a severe blow in 2000 when 39 birds were stolen at gunpoint from the centre – such is the desirability of these endangered creatures. Nonetheless, visitors are usually allowed to look at the birds at the Pre-Release Centre (see p.397); the only other places you can see Bali starlings in Bali are at the Bali Bird Park in Batubulan (see p.180) and at the *Begawan Giri* hotel in Ubud, which is also sponsoring a captive breeding project, the Bali Starling Foundation Project.

The Bali starling is exceptionally sensitive to changes in its surroundings and requires a very stable habitat to survive. During the **breeding** season, the entire population is found in a small, extremely arid area (no more than three square kilometres) on the northeastern edge of the Prapat Agung peninsula. Here, the female starlings select secure tree cavities for their nests and, after hatching their young, feed the nestlings on caterpillars for the first few weeks, before mixing berries into their diet. During the dry season (April–Oct), the birds seek roosting trees a little further afield, flying 8–9km to the south and southwest of the breeding ground, and gathering there in groups of up to thirty members. Park authorities are worried that if the plans to build a Bali–Java bridge ever come to fruition, a dangerously large swath of the starlings' habit would be lost, thus reversing the good work achieved by the breeding programme. Certainly, the recent construction of an upmarket hotel on the fringes of their habitat can't have done much for the poor creatures' nerves.

The forests of Tegal Bunder harbour a large bird population, and you'll see flocks of the common **yellow-vented bulbul**, who get their name from the yellow flash on the underside of their brown body, and **black-naped orioles**, who chirp loudly and are easily distinguished by their yellow bodies, black heads and wing markings and reddish beaks. Other possible sightings include parakeets and fantails, the green jungle fowl, the pinky-brown spotted dove, which has a distinctive call, the black drongo, completely black save for its red eyes, and the tiny bright-yellow breasted olive-backed sunbird.

Gilimanuk Bay boat trip

The Tegal Bunder trail combines nicely with a boat trip round **Gilimanuk Bay**, which takes you through the mangrove forests that line most of the shore. Boats for two people for two hours cost Rp70,000 for a tiny prahu and should be arranged through the national park guides; you have to pay the statutory fee for hiring a guide on top of the boat rental.

Mangroves are best seen at low tide, when their aerial roots are fully exposed to form gnarled and knotted archways above the muddy banks. Not only are these roots essential parts of the tree's breathing apparatus, but they also reclaim land for future mangroves by trapping and accumulating water-borne debris into which the metre-long mangrove seedlings can fall. In this way, mangrove swamps also fulfil a vital ecological function: stabilizing shifting muds and protecting coastlines from erosion and the impact of tropical storms.

Boat skippers should be able to get you close enough to the mangroves for you to look for some of the most common creatures who live in the swamps. These include **fiddler crabs**, named after the male's massive reddish claw which it uses to threaten and to communicate, and is said to be so strong it can open a can of beans. You might see **mudskippers** too, specially adapted fish who can absorb atmospheric oxygen when out of the water, as long as they keep their outsides damp – which is why they spend a lot of time skipping and slithering through the mangrove mud. **Crab-eating or long-tailed macaques** hang out along the shore too, supplementing their favourite food with fruit, mussels and other small animals. They're very good swimmers and divers and have big cheek pouches for transporting and storing food.

If you get out of the boat and do a bit of beachcombing along the exposed reef, you'll see **sea cucumbers**, **sea horses**, and various species of **crab**, as well as heaps of good seashells. You might also spot some elegant dark grey **Pacific reef egrets**. The current off this shore is dangerously strong so it's not advisable to swim here, and you probably won't want to sunbathe as the beaches seem to end up with all the plastic bottles and other debris washed in from Java and the Bali Strait.

The Gunung Klatakan trail

The climb up **Gunung Klatakan** (5–6hr round trip) is the most popular and most strenuous of the Bali Barat hikes, most of it passing through moderately interesting rainforest.

The trail starts at the Sumber Klampok ranger post and for the most part follows a steep incline, via the occasional sheer descent, through **tropical rainforest**. Very little light reaches the forest floor, leaving it clear to walk through, but dark and enclosed with few clearings through which to view the surrounding peaks. However, the variety of trees and plants goes some way to compensating for the lack of panoramas. Up here the forest is thick with ferns and vines, and with vicious-looking trees like the **pandanus**, related to the palm family but with forbidding serrations along its leaf edges and knots of roots growing above ground. Climbing plants such as the spiky-stemmed **rattan** and the parasitic **strangling fig** abound too, the latter germinating on host trees way off the ground and then dropping feeder roots to the forest floor. All sorts of **orchids** grow on Gunung Klatakan and, though many of them look completely dissimilar, they all share the same flower structure of three sepals and three petals, with one of the petals quite differently shaped from the other two. Epiphytic orchids live on tree trunks and branches and absorb moisture and nutrients from the atmosphere with their specially adapted roots; one of the loveliest epiphytic orchids you'll see here is the elegant long-stemmed white-sepalled **madavellia orchid**.

You're unlikely to spot a huge amount of wildlife on this trail, but you should certainly hear the **black monkeys** swinging through the trees of the upper-most canopy, even if you can't quite see them. There's also a good chance you'll stumble across a **wild boar** or two. With a ridge of sharp spines along their backbones and fierce expressions on their faces, they can be quite scary, but they are apparently extremely poorly sighted and a bit stupid: they tend to charge in a straight line until they hit an obstacle, regardless of where their prey happens to be. (If one starts galloping towards you, the best defence is to run away in zigzags.) You could also encounter **pythons**, **green snakes** and even **flying foxes**, but don't count on it.

Two species of **hornbill** live in the national park and, even if they don't come near enough for you to see their huge beaks and bizarre bony casques, you'll certainly hear the distinctive whooshing sound they make with their powerful wings. The **southern pied hornbill** has a black head and white breast and tail feathers, with a pronounced casque on its yellow beak; the **wreathed hornbill** has a much smaller casque on its yellow beak – the female is completely black with white tail feathers, while the male has a cream-coloured head. Smaller, less dramatic birds include the multi-coloured **banded pitta**, with yellow flashes on its black head, brown wings, blue tail and yellow-and-black-striped breast, the bluey-grey **dollarbird** with its distinctive red beak, the **talking mynah** and the red and green **jungle fowl**.

Pulau Menjangan (Deer Island)

By far the most popular part of Bali Barat is **Pulau Menjangan** (**Deer Island**), a tiny uninhabited island 8km off the north coast, whose shoreline is encircled by some of the most spectacular **coral reefs** in Bali. Most visitors rate this as the best **snorkelling** spot on Bali, and divers place it high on their list too. The majority of divers and snorkellers come on organized tours, either from the north-coast resorts of Lovina and Pemuteran, or on longer excursions from Kuta, Sanur and Ubud. Unless you have your own diving equipment, tours are the only way for divers to explore the reefs. However, for snorkellers it can often work out cheaper to turn up at Labuan Lalang, the access port for Menjangan, and club together with other tourists to hire a boat. As the island comes under the jurisdiction of the national park, you have to go with a guide, but you can arrange both the guide and boat transport at the jetty in Labuan Lalang without first checking in at the Cekik headquarters.

There are no **accommodation** facilities on Pulau Menjangan, so most snorkellers and divers stay either in Pemuteran or Lovina, though you could base yourself in Gilimanuk (see p.394) or at one of the two new resorts built within the park near Labuan Lalang (see p.397).

Menjangan practicalities

The departure point for Pulau Menjangan is **LABUAN LALANG**, just east of Teluk Terima, 13km from Cekik. To get there, take any Singaraja-bound bemo or bus from Gilimanuk (30min) or Cekik (20min), or any Gilimanuk-bound bemo or bus from Lovina (2hr) or Pemuteran (30min). If you're coming from the southwest coast, take any Ubung (Denpasar)–Gilimanuk bus or bemo to Cekik, then change onto the Singaraja-bound service. There's a small

Diving and snorkelling tours to Pulau Menjangan

Pulau Menjangan is the focus of a number of day and overnight **tours** operating out of Kuta, Sanur, Candi Dasa and Lovina, with prices starting at around US$80 for two dives in one day (snorkellers $40), rising to around $180 for all-inclusive two-day, one-night dive excursions. Arranging a tour from so far away means that quite a lot of time is wasted travelling to and from the island, so you might want to consider basing yourself at Pemuteran (see p.404), 16km east along the coast from Pulau Menjangan, where dive centres arrange excursions to the island for $60–70 (two dives) or $20–25 (snorkelling). This also means you've got a better chance of getting to the reefs early in the day (8am is a good time) when the water is at its clearest and least congested – before about 10am when the tour groups from the southern resorts start pitching up.

national park office here (daily except national holidays 7.30am–3pm), as well as several restaurants.

The **hiring of boats** to Pulau Menjangan is well organized and should be arranged through the national park office in the Labuan Lalang car park. Boats can be hired at any time of day up to about 3pm; they hold up to ten people and prices are fixed at Rp200,000 for a round trip lasting a maximum of four hours, which allows two to three hours for snorkelling and/or exploring the island and thirty minutes journey-time each way. In addition you must pay Rp60,000 for one national park guide per boat, plus Rp2500 per person for the national park entry fee (the entry fee is slated to rise soon, perhaps to as much as Rp20,000). The boat can be hired for as many extra hours as you like for Rp15,000 per hour, and you can rent mask, fins and snorkel from the warung by the jetty for Rp30,000 a set. There have been recent reports of **thefts** from the boats while snorkellers are underwater, so leave your valuables back in the car or the hotel and if possible keep money with you in a waterproof neck-pouch or similar.

The Menjangan reefs

The sparkling azure-tinged water between Labuan Lalang and Pulau Menjangan is so shallow and clear that you can make out the coral reefs and their attendant fish populations even from the boat. The sea here is also incredibly calm, protected from excessive winds and strong currents by the Prapat Agung peninsula. As you near the island, the reefs form a band 100–150m around the coastline, and this is where you'll find the best **snorkelling** and **diving**, with drop-offs ranging from 40m to 60m, first-class wall dives with plenty of crevices and grottoes, and superb visibility ranging from 15m to 50m. In among the expansive sea fans, enormous barrel sponges and black tree corals so distinctive of this area, the reefs teem with all sorts of marine life (see box on pp.402–403), including turquoise and purple parrotfish, black-, yellow- and white-striped butterfly fish, yellowback fusiliers, powder-blue surgeon fish, damsel fish, puffer fish, unicorn fish, barracuda and silvery jacks. There's also an old **shipwreck** lying 45m deep off the western tip of the island, frequented by sharks and rays as well as by Moorish idols, sweetlips and snappers. It's a small prahu, known as the "Anker", but is rarely visited because it's too deep for normal PADI divers. The wreck's anchor is only about 6m deep, and features on some dive excursions, but is some way from the ship itself.

Recent reports suggest that in some areas around Menjangan the reefs are showing signs of **damage**, and for once it's not human thoughtlessness that's

Life on the reef

Coral reefs are living organisms composed of a huge variety of marine life forms, but the foundation of every reef is its ostensibly inanimate **stony coral** – hard constructions such as boulder, mushroom, bushy staghorn and brain coral. Stony coral is composed of whole colonies of polyps – minuscule invertebrates which feed on plankton, depend on algae and direct sunlight for photosynthesis, and extract calcium carbonate (limestone) from sea water in order to reproduce. The polyps use this calcium carbonate to build new skeletons outside their bodies – an asexual reproductive process known as budding – and this is how a reef is formed. It's an extraordinarily slow process, with colony growth averaging somewhere between 0.5cm and 2.8cm a year.

The fleshy plant-like **soft coral**, such as dead man's fingers and elephant's ear, generally establishes itself on and around these banks of stony coral, swaying with the currents and using tentacles to trap all sorts of micro-organisms. Soft coral is also composed of polyps, but a variety with flaccid internal skeletons built from protein rather than calcium. **Horny coral**, like sea whips and intricate sea fans, looks like a cross between the stony and the soft varieties, while **sea anemones** have much the most obvious, and poisonous, tentacles of any member of the coral family, using them to trap fish and other large prey.

The algae and plankton that accumulate around coral colonies attract a whole catalogue of fish known collectively as **reef fish**. Most are small in size, with vibrant colours which serve as camouflage against the coral, flattened bodies and broad tails for easy manoeuvring around the reef, and specially adapted features to help them poke about for food in the tiniest crannies.

Among the most typical and easily recognizable reef fish is the gorgeously coloured **emperor angelfish**, which boasts spectacular horizontal stripes in bright blue and orange, and an orange tail. The **moorish idol** is another fantastic sight, bizarrely shaped with a trailing streamer – or pennant fin – extending from its dorsal fin, a pronounced snout and dramatic black, yellow and white bands of colour. Similarly eye-catching, the ovoid **powder-blue surgeon fish** has a light blue body, a bright yellow dorsal fin and a white "chinstrap". The commonly spotted **long-nosed butterfly fish** gets its name from the butterfly-like movements of its yellow-banded silver body as it darts in and out of crevices looking for food. The bright orange **clown fish**, so called because the thick white stripes across its body

the only culprit. According to dive operators there are four different causes: a plague of coral-munching crown-of-thorns starfish arrived in 1997 and killed off a great swath of shallow reef; the warming effect of the seas caused by El Nino bleached some of the shallower corals, down to around 15m; local fishermen sometimes use dynamite to stun their catch and bring it to the surface – with obvious disastrous effects; and anchor damage is caused by boats ferrying tourists to and from the reefs. National-park patrols and the use of fixed buoys have cut down on the latter two, while the former menaces have both passed. The current consensus seems to be that if your dive operator picks their spots well (and they probably will), you won't even know there's been any damage.

The island
Boats from Labuan Lalang land at the jetty on the **southeastern shore** of Pulau Menjangan, site of a lovely white-sand beach where a shallow reef lies less than 10m offshore. The island's ranger post is here. If you want to explore the interior, follow the track which starts close to the jetty and heads east to a

resemble a clown's ruff, is more properly known as the anemone fish because of its mutually protective relationship with the sea anemone, near which it can usually be sighted. Equally predictable is the presence of **cleaner fish**, or cleaner wrasse, on the edges of every shoal of reef fish. Streamlined, with a long snout and jaws that act like tweezers, a cleaner fish spends its days picking parasites off the skins of other fish – a symbiotic relationship essential to both parties.

Some reef fish, among them the ubiquitous turquoise and purple **parrotfish**, eat coral. With the help of a bird-like beak, which is in fact several teeth fused together, the parrotfish scrapes away at the coral and then grinds the fragments down with another set of back teeth – a practice that can do quite a lot of damage to a reef. The magnificent mauve and burgundy **crown-of-thorns starfish** also feeds on coral, laying waste to as much as fifty square centimetres of stony coral in a 24-hour period. Its appearance is as formidable as its eating habits, with a body that measures up to 50cm in diameter protected by "arms" covered in highly venomous spines.

Larger, less frequent visitors to Bali and Lombok's offshore reefs include the **moray eel**, whose elongated jaws of viciously pointed teeth make it a deadly predator, and the similarly equipped **barracuda**, the world's fastest-swimming fish. **Sharks** are also common, and it's also sometimes possible to swim with a **manta ray**, whose extraordinary flatness, strange winglike fins, and massive size – up to 6m across and weighing some 1600kg – make it an astonishing presence. Weighing up to twice as much as rays, **oceanic sunfish** (sometimes known as *mola mola*) are phenomenal sights, measuring some 3m top to bottom and about 2.5m end to end. They are extremely rare, but are occasionally spotted off Nusa Lembongan (see p.276); they're very short-sighted so can often be inspected at close quarters. **Turtles** occasionally paddle around reef waters, too, but the two local species – green and hawksbill – are fast becoming endangered in Bali (see p.149).

Other commonly spotted creatures are the **sea urchin**, whose evil-looking spines grow up to 35cm in length, and the ugly but harmless **sea cucumber**, which looks like a large slug and lies half-buried on the sea bed. Deceptively slothful in appearance, sea cucumbers are constantly busy ingesting and excreting so much sand and mud that the combined force of those in a three-square-kilometre area can together redistribute one million kilograms of sea-bed material a year.

small shrine (15min) and then on round the rest of the island; the complete circuit should only take about an hour. Much of Pulau Menjangan is flat and barren: the soil is sandy and supports little **vegetation** except for a few inland patches of savannah grassland, and a ring of mangrove swamps around the coast. Although there are no rivers here, the island does have one small freshwater spring, buried in the scrub towards the east of the island, close to Menjangan's only shrine. Brahmans from the mainland make pilgrimages here in search of special medicinal herbs which grow in the area between the shrine and the spring.

Few animals live on Pulau Menjangan, save for a forty-strong herd of **barking deer**, which occasionally swim across to the mainland, but otherwise spend most of their time in the savannah. Three rarer species are also said to inhabit Pulau Menjangan: the **Java deer**, the **Bali starling** (see box on p.398) and the tiny yellow-breasted, greeny-yellow-backed **mangrove white-eye**, which in Bali is found only here and on Nusa Penida.

Pura Jayaprana

For the best aerial view of Pulau Menjangan, stop off at **Pura Jayaprana** (daylight hours; donation), 12km east of Cekik and 1km west of Labuan Lalang. The temple itself is unimpressive, but its location is superb, right at the top of a huge flight of concrete steps with panoramas that take in the island, its translucent waters, and even the shadows of the coral reefs beneath. Pura Jayaprana enshrines the grave of a local seventeenth-century folk hero who was murdered so that the king could have free access to the young man's wife. The woman in question, Layonsari, remained faithful to the memory of her dead husband and chose suicide over marriage to the king. The young couple's grave is enclosed in a glass case in the shrine's inner courtyard, watched over by kitsch doll-like statues representing Jayaprana and Layonsari.

The northwest coast

East of Cekik, the main Gilimanuk–Singaraja road emerges from the national park at the bay of Teluk Terima and runs along the narrow strip of the **northwest coast** between the sea and the mountains. Apart from Pulau Menjangan (Deer Island), described above, and a couple of minor roadside sights, the main attraction in this area is the scenery: turquoise waters to the north and increasingly sheer and dramatic mountain slopes to the south dominate the landscape as far as **Pemuteran**, beyond which the terrain softens a little and becomes noticeably more lush, and more typically Balinese, supporting crops and even rice terraces. Until recently, very few tourists paid much attention to this stretch of the north coast, but the area is starting to get a little more developed, with a scattering of attractive mid-range and upmarket hotels along the black-sand shore, and an equivalent number of dive centres too. It's still a very low-key region and one that's well worth visiting for a few days.

Banyuwedang Air Panas

About 8km east of Labuan Lalang, you'll come to a sign announcing "hot springs" at **BANYUWEDANG AIR PANAS**, 1km north off the main road. The sulphurous water here is drawn up from a well sunk into the mangrove-encrusted shore, and bathing takes place in a little wooden hut, for which you'll be charged a small fee. Constructed right alongside the hot springs, and making full use of the healthy spa waters, is the luxury **hotel**, the *Mimpi Resort* (℡0361/701070, ℻701074, ⓌWwww.mimpi.com; ❽–❾). The standard rooms here are attractive and good value, while the deluxe villas are suitably indulgent, complete with private pool, outdoor spa bath and garden verandah. The hotel has a large pool, a spa and a small PADI **dive** operation, catering mainly to Japanese clientele but with an English-speaking dive leader. The grounds run down to the mangrove-lined bay, though the hotel will transport you across the water to a more attractive beach.

Pemuteran and around

As the road heads east from Banyuwedang, the scenery gets more and more arresting, with the great craggy folds of Bali Barat's north-facing ridges rising almost perpendicular from the roadside. In the foreground of this amazing setting sits the little fishing village of **PEMUTERAN**, 28km east of Cekik, the location of some lovely, if rather pricey, accommodation and a good place to base yourself for diving and snorkelling. It's a pleasantly low-key area to stay in even if you don't want to dive, and the hotels are making a conscious effort not to upset the village ambience. You can swim and snorkel off the tree-shaded black-sand beach and each hotel has a dive centre running trips to the Menjangan reefs. There's also horse riding here and guided treks through the national park.

Just beyond the eastern edge of Pemuteran, the stark charcoal-grey stone of **Pura Agung Pulaki** peers down from a weatherworn cliff face, making a good viewpoint. The temple's history dates back to the days of the sixteenth-century Javanese priest Nirartha, but the buildings are modern and currently overrun by a band of grey macaques. All bemo drivers stop here on their first trip of the day to make an offering at the roadside shrine and get sprinkled with holy water dished out by the attendant priest. Pulaki is also locally renowned as a centre of **viticulture**, and much of the coastal land between here and Seririt 30km to the east has been set aside for vines. With its cool sea breezes, temperate climate and moderately fertile soil, this stretch of the north-west coast is ideal for vines: local growers make sweet red wine from some of the juicy black grapes, and dry the rest for export.

Practicalities

All dark red Gilimanuk–Singaraja **bemos** pass through Pemuteran and will drop you in front of your chosen hotel; they take about thirty minutes from Labuan Lalang or 1hr 20min from Lovina. If coming from Ubud or the south coast resorts, your fastest option is to take a **tourist shuttle bus** to Lovina and then hop on to a bemo. Faster still would be to charter a seaplane from Benoa Harbour (see p.172), at $225 per person for the half-hour ride.

Should you need **medical** attention while in Pemuteran, the Bhakti Yoga Clinic on the main road about 1km west of *Pondok Sari* is open 24 hours (℡082/361 1679). For anything major you'll have to go to one of the hospitals in Singaraja or Denpasar.

Accommodation

During high season, all **hotels** get booked up by diving tours, so you're strongly advised to reserve as far ahead as possible. Note however that **phone lines** in this area are extremely unreliable and none of the hotels has on-site email (nearest internet access is in Lovina), so be patient when waiting for replies to room bookings.

All accommodation occupies beachfront land. *Taman Sari*, *Pondok Sari* and *Taman Selini* are in a small cluster at the western end of Pemuteran, within a minute's walk of each other. *Matahari Beach* and *Aneka Bagus* are also near each other, about 1km east of *Taman Selini*; but *Segara Bukit* is out on its own in Banyupoh, another 2km further east. Pre-booked customers at the Reef Seen dive school (see p.407) can stay at their simple bungalows (❷).

Aneka Bagus Resort and Spa Just east of *Matahari* ℡0828/365334, ℱ365335, ℮www.anekahotels.com. Small, upmarket place comprising 14 fresh, bright, contemporary Bali-style deluxe villas facing each other across a shorefront garden. They're comfortably furnished and all have air-con and TV. Nearer the road, the standard rooms in a two-storey block are nothing special. There's a pool and a spa on the premises. ❽

Matahari Beach Resort and Spa 1km east of *Taman Selini* ℡0362/92312, ℱ92313, ℮www.matahari-beach-resort.com. Accommodation in this luxury beachfront complex comprises thirty very classy private bungalow compounds furnished with four-poster beds and pretty garden bathrooms. But the real attraction is the exceptionally elegant spa complex, reminiscent of a Roman bath-house, with its own lotus-pond tea pavilion, as well as private massage rooms and a gym. The hotel also has a swimming pool and a beachfront bar. ➒

Pondok Sari Between *Taman Sari* and *Taman Selini* ☎ & ℻0362/92337, ⓦwww.bali-hotels.co .uk/pondok.html. The cheapest, best-value hotel in Pemuteran itself, offering large, stylishly designed cottages spaced around a tropical garden that runs right down to the black-sand beach. Some cottages have air-con, and they all have attractive open-roofed garden bathrooms. Recommended. Rooms with fan ➎ With air-con ➏

Segara Bukit Seaside Cottages 3km east of *Taman Selini* in Banyupoh ☎0828/365231, ℻0362/22471. By far the cheapest place to stay in the area, with 12 decent fan and air-con rooms ranged around a small garden beside the sea, not far from a fish farm. Also has a swimming pool, a

restaurant, a small dive centre and car rental. Rooms with fan ➋–➌ With air-con ➎

Taman Sari Western end of Pemuteran ☎0362/93264, ℻0361/286879, ⓦwww .balitamansari.com. Another lovely place to stay, more upmarket than neighbouring *Pondok Sari*, with appealingly spacious and comfortable deluxe air-con bungalows and suites, though the fan rooms are better value at *Pondok Sari*. Has a swimming pool and a good Thai restaurant. Rooms with fan ➏ With air-con ➐

Taman Selini Immediately east along the shore from *Pondok Sari* ☎ & ℻0362/93449, ⓦwww.tamanselini.com. Tiny, elegant outfit with eleven rather chic rooms, all furnished with four-poster beds, pretty furnishings, air-con and hot water. Has a swimming pool and a Greek restaurant. ➑

Eating

All the hotels have **restaurants** serving freshly caught seafood, as well as a reasonable range of pastas, sandwiches, salads and Indonesian standards. *Taman Selini*'s menu stands out, as it includes a huge range of traditional Greek dishes (the owner is from Greece and also runs the quality *Pantarei* restaurant in Legian), and *Taman Sari*'s restaurant serves a famously good Thai menu. For cheap and cheerful Balinese standards, there are several small warung alongside the main road.

The *Matahari* stages frequent classical Balinese **dance** performances for diners at its very expensive restaurant, or you can watch a similar performance by local village girls at Reef Seen Aquatics dive centre, next to *Taman Selini*, on most Saturday evenings.

Snorkelling and diving

The chief activity in Pemuteran – apart from lying on the black-sand beach – is the **snorkelling and diving**. Although there are some reasonable reefs within easy reach of Pemuteran's shore, most divers agree that these are nothing compared to the underwater vistas at nearby **Pulau Menjangan** (see p.401), and snorkellers will definitely be better rewarded there.

Pemuteran reefs

As at Menjangan, some of the **Pemuteran reefs** have suffered considerable damage over the last decade, ascribed to a similar combination of bad practices by local fishermen and unavoidable environmental factors. In an attempt to try and do something about this, Yos and Arkipelago dive operators have set up a **coral-farming experiment** just off the Pemuteran shore. Using a pioneering process of "electrical mineral accretion" developed by a German professor, this involves encouraging new growth by continuously passing a low electrical current through the stony coral, causing minerals to build up at about four times the normal speed. Any snorkeller can observe the experiment in the reefs in front of *Pondok Sari* and *Taman Sari*, where two dozen large cage-like structures lie on the sea bed, bound with wires; here, in amongst the groves of deathly grey coral you can see the new growth, which is much more colourful. Arkipelago has printed information on the experiment, and staff here or at Yos will, for a fee, take you on a guided tour.

There are some healthier, more interesting **reefs** about fifteen minutes' boat ride away from the Pemuteran shore, where divers can expect to encounter a huge variety of reef fish including bright blue dancers, black- and white-striped damsel fish, and shoals of silver fusiliers, as well as snappers and the occasional white manta ray or shark; Reef Seen dive centre has mapped out the most rewarding areas.

Dive centres

Pemuteran's three main **dive centres** all run diving and snorkelling trips to local reefs as well as to Menjangan, and all are located beside the beach in front of the hotels: Reef Seen Aquatics (℡ & ℻0362/92339, ✉reefseen@den-pasar.wasantara.net.id) is beside *Taman Selini*; Yos Marine Adventures (℡ & ℻0362/92337, 🌐www.yosdive.com) is in front of *Pondok Sari*; and Arkipelago Selam (℡ & ℻0828/365296, 🌐www.archipelagodive.com) is based at *Taman Sari*.

For boat trips to the **Pemuteran reefs**, expect to pay about US$30 per diver or $6 per snorkeller. As for **Pulau Menjangan**, for divers and accompanying snorkellers it makes sense to arrange your trip through one of the Pemuteran operators, who charge an average $65 per diver and $25 per snorkeller, but unaccompanied snorkellers will probably find it cheaper, if less convenient, to go direct to Labuan Lalang, as described on p.400.

All the Pemuteran dive operators also offer **dive courses** ($310 for the four-day open-water) and diving excursions to Tulamben ($75 for two dives, or $25 for snorkellers; see p.311).

Other activities

All the Pemuteran hotels organize day-trips to local sights, including hikes through Bali Barat National Park. Pemuteran Adventure Tours (℡0362/92623) offers half-day trips ($25) through local forest and to a traditional village, which can be booked at any of the hotels. Reef Seen dive centre runs **fishing trips** and sunrise cruises for **dolphin watching** (both $6 per person for 2hr) but, although the early-morning skies are fantastic, don't count on seeing dolphins here. You can also take **horse rides** ($30 for 2hr), and horse-riding lessons ($30 for 1hr).

Reef Seen also runs a **turtle-hatching** project at its dive centre. Green and hawksbill turtles both have nesting sites in the Pemuteran area, but both species are fast becoming endangered (see box on p.149), and their eggs are particularly prized, so the idea here is to buy the eggs from fishermen and then hatch and rear them at Reef Seen. When old enough the youngsters are released off the Pemuteran coast, but at most times of the year there'll be at least a couple of turtles in the holding pens at Reef Seen, which staff will be happy to show you.

Seririt and the road south

The town of **SERIRIT** is chiefly of interest to travellers as a junction. The main north-coast road slices through the town centre, travelled by frequent dark red Gilimanuk–Singaraja bemos; this is also the departure point for the scenic back road to Munduk, Lake Bratan and Bedugul (see p.339). Most importantly, though, Seririt stands at the head of the most westerly route between the north and south coasts, described below.

About 1500m west of Seririt, in the village of **UME ANYAR**, a couple of signs point you north off the main road down a rough track to two quite different **places to stay**. About 600m from the road, the hilltop *Puri Jati Resort* (℡0362/93578, ℻93579, ✉wan2000_id@yahoo.com; ❼) offers fine views over surrounding vineyards and to the sea beyond. Its two dozen air-conditioned rooms are comfortable if plain and rather characterless, and there's a pleasant swimming pool. About 700m further down the track, the tranquil *Ratu Ayu Villas* (℡0362/93612, ℻93437, ⓦwww.travel-ideas.net/bali.hotels /sacred-sanctuary.html, ✉lumbung@indosat.net.id; ❽), are secluded in a hollow fifteen minutes' walk from the sea on a site apparently imbued with great spiritual history and power. The handful of inviting two-storey bungalows are simply but artistically designed, with balconies offering inspiring views of the rice-fields, the sea and the distant mountains. A swimming pool is likely to be built soon. Established by one of the owners of *Puri Lumbung* in Munduk (see p.340), *Ratu Ayu* also emphasizes cultural, spiritual and educational tourism and arranges workshops with local musicians.

To the south coast

The road from Seririt to the south coast commands some breathtakingly lovely views as it crosses through the mountains, rice-growing valleys and small hilltop villages that lie just beyond the eastern limits of Bali Barat National Park. But be warned that it is narrow and very twisty in parts, ill-suited to the volume of traffic that uses it daily, and dominated by truck drivers who career along at ridiculous speeds, overtaking on hairpin bends.

The first great viewpoint comes 8km south of Seririt at **BUSUNG BIU**, where you can stop in a lay-by to admire the spectacular vista of rice terraces tumbling down into the valley, framed by the peaks of Gunung Batukau to the southeast.

The road divides at the village of **PUPUAN**, 25km south of Seririt, the site of a hundred-metre-high waterfall called **Blahmantung**. Despite the height, the falls are less than spectacular, only really worth visiting in February or March when water levels are high from several months of rain. The access road is steep and rutted; look for a tiny blue sign announcing "Bend Sabah Hulu 1450m" (Sabah Hulu is the name of the river) just beyond the southernmost limit of Pupuan.

Pupuan to Pekutatan (via Tista)

From Pupuan, the more westerly route takes you via the lovely ridgetop settlement of **TISTA** (where you can veer off east, via Ceking and Bangal, down a road that ends just west of Balian beach; see p.387) and then through clove plantations and along the course of the Pulukan River to the village of **ASAHDUREN**. A few kilometres south of Asahduren, the road comes to a T-junction at **PEKUTATAN** on the main Tabanan–Gilimanuk road, 2km east of Medewi beach (see p.388).

Pupuan to Antosari (via Sanda)

The easterly branch of the road from Pupuan drops down through similarly eye-catching mountainscapes, affording especially impressive views of Gunung Batukau to the east. On the way, you'll pass dozens of **coffee plantations** (the *robusta* variety, known and drunk locally as *kopi bali*), many of them protected by liberal plantings of spindly-looking **dadap ("coral") trees**. The almost-circular leaves of the fast-growing *dadap* are commonly used in offerings, but those that are allowed to fall provide vital fertilizer for the coffee plants, while the roots simultaneously anchor the soil and prevent erosion.

In the village of **SANDA**, about 30km from Seririt, one former coffee plantation has been turned into a small upmarket **hotel** and **restaurant**, *Sanda Butik Villas* (T & F0828/369137, Wwww.sandavillas.com; ●), whose eight stylish rooms are tastefully decorated in Balinese style; all have enormous outdoor living/balcony areas that overlook the neighbouring plantations. A small patch of the original coffee plantation has also been incorporated into the hotel garden and there's a pool here too, though the 700m elevation on the slopes of Gunung Batukau means the temperature is always fairly cool. In the early mornings you get grand views of Batukau and it's possible to hire a guide here for the climb from the village to the summit and back (see box on p.386 for more on climbing Gunung Batukau).

Some 10km further south, overlooking a gorgeous valley in the village of **BELIMBING**, sits the delightful little award-winning **hotel** *Cempaka Belimbing* (T & F0361/754897, Wwww.indo.com/hotels/cempaka_belimbing, Epurwa @denpasar.wasantara.net.id; ●). The best rooms here are the valley-view villas which enjoy a breathtaking panorama of palm groves, paddy-fields and the peaks of Gunung Batukau, but all sixteen rooms have fine outlooks and are spacious and smartly outfitted; there's a swimming pool, and the place has an appealingly cosy feel to it, right in the heart of the village.

About 10km south of Belimbing, the road meets the Denpasar–Gilimanuk highway at **Antosari** (see p.387), 16km west of Tabanan on the Tabanan–Gilimanuk road.

Travel details

Bemos and public buses

It's almost impossible to give the **frequency** with which bemos and public buses run, as they only depart when they have enough passengers to make the journey worthwhile. However, on the most popular routes, you should be able to count on getting a ride within the half-hour if you travel before noon; things quieten down in the afternoon and come to a standstill by around 5pm. **Journey times** also vary a great deal: the times given below are the minimum you can expect.
For journeys in and out of west Bali, the main transport hubs are Denpasar's Ubung terminal (see p.372 for details of onward connections from there), Gilimanuk in far west Bali (see p.393) and Singaraja's Banyuasri terminal (see p.342); only the direct **bemo** and **bus** routes to and from these termini are listed below. No **shuttle buses** operate out of west Bali, but there is a shuttle bus service from Lovina on the north coast (see p.351), which is easily reached by bemo or public bus from the northwest.

Gilimanuk to: Antosari (2hr 15min); Cekik (10min); Denpasar (Ubung terminal; 3hr 15min); Kediri (for Tanah Lot; 2hr 45min); Medewi (1hr 45min); Labuan Lalang (for Menjangan; 25min); Lalang Linggah (for Balian beach; 2hr 15min); Negara (1hr); Pemuteran (1hr); Lovina (2hr 15min); Seririt (1hr 30min); Singaraja (Banyuasri terminal; 2hr 30min); Tabanan (2hr 30min).
Pemuteran to: Cekik (50min); Gilimanuk (1hr); Labuan Lalang (for Menjangan; 30min); Lovina (1hr 15min); Seririt (45min); Singaraja (1hr 30min).
Ubung (Denpasar) to: Antosari (1hr); Cekik (3hr); Gilimanuk (3hr 15min); Jakarta (Java; 24hr); Kediri (for Tanah Lot; 30min); Lalang Linggah (for Balian beach; 1hr 15min); Medewi (1hr 30min); Mengwi (30min); Negara (2hr 15min); Singaraja (Sukasada terminal; 3hr); Solo (Java; 15hr); Surabaya (Java; 10hr); Tabanan (35min); Yogyakarta (Java; 15hr).

Boats

Gilimanuk to: Ketapang (East Java; every 20min; 30min).

6

Lombok and the Gili Islands

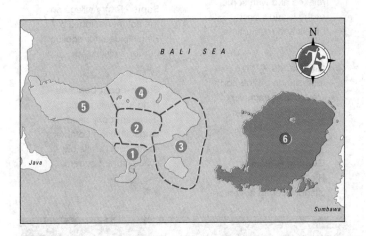

CHAPTER 6

Highlights

* **Crafts** – Pottery, textiles, woodcarving and basketware are on sale in craft villages scattered across Lombok. See p.429

* **Senggigi** – Lombok's main resort, reasonably relaxed and with some of the island's best hotels and restaurants. See p.432

* **Gili Islands** – Three perfect islands off the northwest coast, each very different in character from its neighbours. See p.441

* **Gunung Rinjani** – Highest mountain on the island, offering adventurous and rewarding trekking. See p.458

* **Sembalun valley** – Picturesque upland valley far off the tourist trail, surrounded by impressive mountain peaks. See p.461

* **Sapit** – Pretty village on the southern slopes of Rinjani, ideal for cooling out for a while. See p.470

* **South-coast beaches** – Hidden coves nestle between rocky headlands all along Lombok's south coast while big swells attract surfers. See p.473

6

Lombok and the Gili Islands

A bout 35km east of Bali at its closest point, **Lombok** is inevitably compared with its better-known western neighbour, although it differs considerably in almost every respect – physically, culturally, linguistically and historically. It also contrasts quite markedly for the visitor, with less widespread tourist facilities, sparser public transport and simpler accommodation, although things are changing pretty rapidly.

Approximately ten percent of Lombok's 2.3 million inhabitants are Balinese, and it's very easy – especially if you arrive in the west where most Balinese are settled, surrounded by their distinctive temples and household architecture – to perceive Lombok simply as an extension of Bali. However, the majority of the population are the indigenous Muslim **Sasak** people. Today the two cultures appear to coexist relatively amicably, but it doesn't take too long to discern rather less amiable emotions below the surface – perhaps not surprising given historical events and the fact that a lot of the economic advantages of increased tourism have eluded the native Sasak.

From the seventeenth century onwards, Lombok came increasingly under **Balinese influence**, after the Balinese had helped the Sasak aristocracy defeat invaders from Sumbawa. Infighting among the rajas of the four Lombok principalities – Pagasangan, Pagutan, Mataram and Cakranegara – further weakened the hold of the Sasak rulers. In 1830, **Ratu Agung** acceded to the throne of Mataram, and over the next thirteen years brought the whole of Lombok under his rule. In 1849, he also gained control of Karangasem in east Bali in return for supplying his subjects to the Dutch as troops. His brother, Ratu Agung Ngurah, succeeded him in 1872, and, seeking to serve his own ambitions in Bali, pushed the demand for troops too far. The residents of Praya **rebelled** in 1891, and unrest quickly spread. The Dutch intervened and eventually invaded Lombok in 1894, bringing the entire island under colonial rule until Indonesian independence.

Measuring 80km by 70km, Lombok is slightly smaller than Bali and divides conveniently into three geographical regions. The mountainous **north** is dominated by the awesome bulk of **Gunung Rinjani**, at 3726m one of the highest peaks in Indonesia, and until late 1994 believed to be dormant. Trekking at least part of the way up Rinjani is the reason many tourists come to Lombok, and it's an easily organized and highly satisfying trip. The **central plains**, about

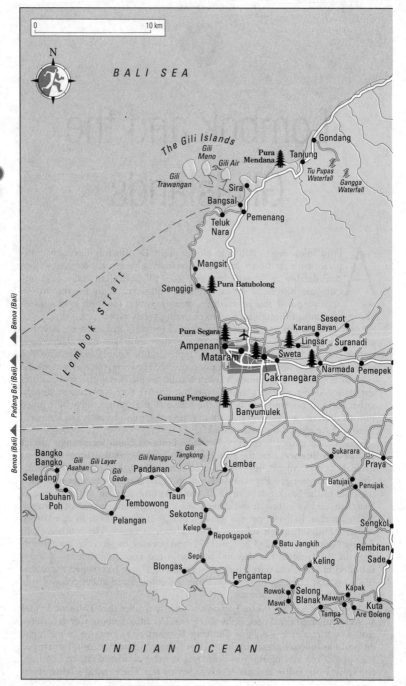

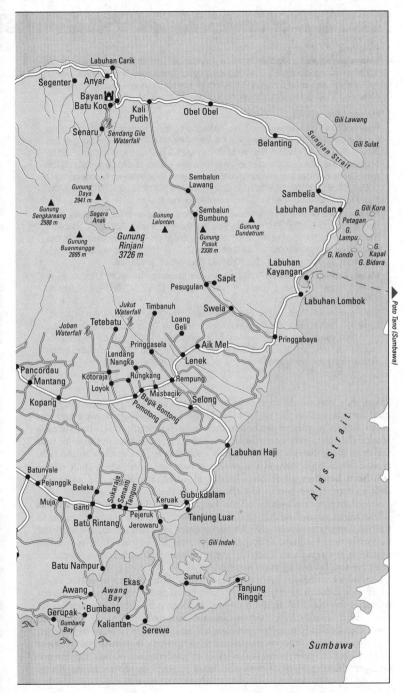

▶ Poto Tano (Sumbawa)

By plane

Selaparang Airport in Mataram is the only one on Lombok. Its only direct international flights serve Singapore (see p.11 for details) although Merpati flights from Kuala Lumpur via Surabaya also arrive here (see p.11). Regular internal flights on Garuda, Merpati and Air Mark link the airport with other points in Indonesia (see p.11–12 for more).

By boat from Bali

Bounty Cruise High-speed catamaran operating a circular route from Benoa to Nusa Lembongan, Teluk Nara (for Senggigi), Gili Meno, then back to Nusa Lembongan and Benoa (Sun, Tues, Thurs & Sat; takes 2–3hr; ⓦwww.balibountygroup.com). US$25 from Benoa or Nusa Lembongan to Teluk Nara (free shuttle bus to Senggigi); US$35 from Benoa or Nusa Lembongan to Gili Meno. Book through travel agents or direct in Bali ⓣ0361/733333, ⓕ730404; in Senggigi ⓣ0370/693666, ⓕ693678; or in Gili Meno ⓣ0370/649090, ⓕ641177, ⓔgilimeno@indo.net.id.

Fast boat (the *Osiania 3*) From Benoa to Padang Bai, and on to Lembar (daily; from Benoa 3hr 15min, Rp129,000; from Padang Bai 1hr 30min, Rp75,000). Book in Benoa on ⓣ0361/723577 or 723353; in Padang Bai at Wannen on ⓣ0363/41780; in Lembar on ⓣ0370/644051 or 641268 or 644757 or 631034; in Mataram at P.T. Indonesia, Jl Airlangga 40a1 ⓣ0370/645974 or 644051, ⓕ632849.

Mabua Express catamaran From Benoa to Lembar (daily; takes 2hr; US$25). Book through travel agents or direct in Bali ⓣ0361/721212, ⓕ723615; in Lombok ⓣ0370/681195, ⓕ681124.

Slow ferry From Padang Bai to Lembar (every 1hr 30min; takes 4hr–4hr 30min; Rp16,500 for VIP, with air-con lounge, soft seats and TV, or Rp9000 for *ekonomi*, with hard seats and TV). Bicycles cost extra (Rp10,000), as do motorbikes (Rp25,000) and cars (from Rp175,000). See p.40 for information on taking rental vehicles between the islands.

25km wide, contain the most population centres and most productive agricultural areas as well as the major road on the island linking the west and east coasts. Attractive villages perched in the southern foothills of Rinjani are easily accessible from here, and many of the island's craft centres are also in or near this cross-island corridor. Further south again is a range of dry, low inland hills, around 500m high, behind the sweeping bays and pure white sands of the **southern beaches**, all of which can be explored from **Kuta**, the accommodation centre of the south and surfing focus of the island.

Several groups of islands lie off the Lombok coast. The trio of **Gili Islands** – Trawangan, Meno and Air – off the northwest coast, are the best known to tourists, long-time favourites with backpackers in search of sea, sun and sand in simple surroundings, although Gili Trawangan, in particular, is heading upmarket at a rapid rate. Those off the southwest peninsula and the northeast coast are also becoming more accessible.

Lombok's economy is based on **agriculture**, with production of rice, cassava, cotton, tobacco (a major export), soya beans and chilli peppers. In recent centuries the island has found it impossible to support its burgeoning population, and thousands have died in **famines**, reportedly 50,000 as recently as 1966. Consequently, many people have left, and continue to leave, to settle on other Indonesian islands as part of the government's **transmigrasi scheme** (see p.500). The government is also trying to moderate the island's dependence on agriculture: pumice is now the main export, mostly to Hong Kong.

Cultivated **pearls**, farmed in co-operation with the Japanese, fetch over US$1 million a year; **seaweed** and **sea cucumber** are growing in economic importance, and income from the increasingly well-known pottery industry and tourism is rising annually.

With around 250,000 foreign visitors a year, and an equal number of visitors from other parts of Indonesia, the **tourist** presence on Lombok is nowhere near as pervasive as in Bali. Most visitors stick to a relatively well-beaten track, comprising the northwest coast around Senggigi, the Gili Islands, Senaru and Batu Koq in the Rinjani area, villages in the foothills of the mountain such as Tetebatu and Sapit and the south coast centring on Kuta, meaning that it's easy to find less popular routes, remote villages, unspoilt coastline and village people still living traditional lives. Generally, **accommodation** is more limited and slightly more expensive than on Bali, concentrated in the west-coast resorts and the capital, Mataram. Elsewhere, simple accommodation is now being supplemented by luxury five-star resorts such as the *Oberoi* on the northwest coast and *Coralia Lombok Novotel* in the south, although, as yet, the central, east-coast and Rinjani areas have not received the developers' attentions.

Lombok's tourist industry was temporarily left in tatters following the **riots** that erupted in January 2000, with zero occupancy of most hotels for several weeks afterwards, chunks of Ampenan reduced to rubble and the Lombok people deeply shocked by the speed with which their economic well-being had vanished. Initially thought to have been based on religious differences, the riots – which were extinguished within a couple of days – were later believed to have been underpinned by political motives and agitation. Tourism gradually recovered over the following months, only to be decimated again following September 11, 2001. It remains to be seen how many businesses will have been able to ride out both these storms.

West Lombok

West Lombok – stretching from the wild and remote southwest peninsula, through the port of **Lembar**, to the conurbation of the four cities **Ampenan-Mataram-Cakranegara-Sweta**, then north to **Senggigi** and the small village of Bangsal (access port for the Gili Islands) – offers by far the best facilities for tourists. With Lombok's only airport and its major port and bus station all in this area, most visitors pass through at some point during their stay, and a high proportion come to the island purely for the established beach resort of Senggigi.

Ampenan–Mataram–Cakranegara –Sweta and around

The conurbation of **AMPENAN-MATARAM-CAKRANEGARA-SWETA**, with a population of around 250,000, comprises four towns, the boundaries of which are all but indistinguishable to the casual visitor. At first sight rather overwhelming, the whole area measures over 8km from west to east, but a relatively straightforward local transport system allows you to get around easily. Most visitors pass through fairly quickly as there isn't much to see. However, this is a user-friendly Indonesian city, with markets, shops, restaurants and banks – although if you want any nightlife you'll have to head up the coast to Senggigi.

The conurbation is laid out around three parallel roads, which stretch from **Ampenan** on the coast through **Mataram** and **Cakranegara** to **Sweta** on the eastern edge. The roads change their names several times along their length, the most northerly being Jalan Langko–Jalan Pejanggik–Jalan Selaparang, which allows travel only in a west–east direction. Its counterpart running parallel to the south, Jalan Tumpang Sari–Jalan Panca Usaha–Jalan Pancawarga–Jalan Pendidikan, allows only east–west travel. The third major route, Jalan Brawijaya–Jalan Sriwijaya–Jalan Majapahit, two-way for most of its length, skirts to the south of these, and is useful as the site of the central post office and tourist office.

Arrival and information

Selaparang Airport is on Jalan Adi Sucipto at Rembiga, only a few kilometres north of Mataram and Ampenan. There's an exchange counter, open for all

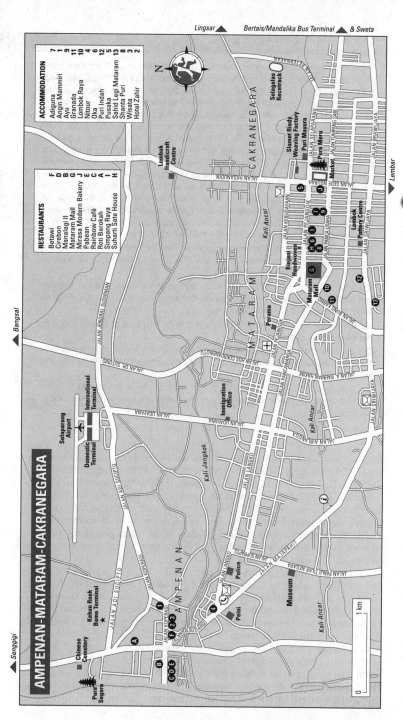

AMPENAN-MATARAM-CAKRANEGARA

RESTAURANTS

Betawi	F
Cirebon	D
Manalagi II	B
Mataram Mall	G
Mirasa Modern Bakery	J
Pabean	E
Rainbow Café	C
Roti Barokah	A
Simpang Raya	I
Suhari Sate House	H

ACCOMMODATION

Adiguna	7
Angin Mammiri	1
Ayu	9
Granada	11
Lombok Raya	10
Nitour	4
Oka	6
Puri Indah	12
Pusaka	5
Sahid Legi Mataram	13
Shanta Puri	8
Wisata	3
Hotel Zahir	2

Lingsar ▲   Bertais/Mandalika Bus Terminal ▲ & Sweta

Bangsal ▲

Senggigi ▲

N

Selagalas Racetrack

CAKRANEGARA

Lombok Handicraft Centre

JALAN HASANUDIN

Kali Ancar

JALAN JENDRAL SUDIRMAN

JALAN DR SUTOMO

Selaparang Airport

International Terminal

Domestic Terminal

JALAN ADI SUCIPTO

JALAN KOPERASI

Kebun Roek Bemo Terminal

Chinese Cemetery

Pura Segara

MATARAM

JALAN UDAYANA

JALAN UDAYANA

Immigration Office

JALAN MOS COKROAMINOTO

JALAN PEJANGGIK

Perama

JALAN PELANGGIK

Mataram Mall

Rinjani Handwoven

Slamet Riady Weaving Factory

Puri Mayura

Pura Meru

Market

JALAN SELAPARANG

JALAN GEDE NGURAH

JALAN TUMPANG SARI

JALAN BRAWIJAYA

JALAN PANCA USAHA

Lombok Pottery Centre

JALAN SRIWIJAYA

JALAN BUNG KARNO

JALAN PANCA WARGA

JALAN RA RAHIM HAKIM

Kali Ancar

JALAN AIR LANGGA

JALAN SRIWIJAYA

JALAN AIR LANGGA

Kali Jangkok

JALAN LANGKO

JALAN PANJI TILAR NEGARA

JALAN PANJI TILAR NEGARA

JALAN LANGKO

JALAN MAJAPAHIT

JALAN SUPRAPTO

Police

Pelni

Museum

Kali Ancar

AMPENAN

JALAN NIAGA SUD ARSO

JALAN KOPERASI

▼ Lembar

▼ Lembar

1 km

0

419

Lombok tours

If your time is limited you may want to join a **tour of Lombok**. You'll get the biggest range of options in Senggigi and the Ampenan-Mataram-Cakranegara-Sweta area, but it's also possible to put together your own itinerary and charter a bemo and driver to take you around (see p.41). If you're interested in arts and crafts, you'll be better off renting your own vehicle or taking public transport as tour guides demand a large commission from the craft showrooms and restaurants (thus bumping up the price you pay), and only take you to the places that they have an agreement with.

Typically the tours on offer are either **half-day** (4hr) or **full-day** (8hr). It really pays to shop around as prices vary enormously; make sure whether prices quoted are per person or for the vehicle, and whether lunch is included. Also check the itinerary carefully: the name of the each company's trip isn't always an indication of where they take you. Some trips are in a large group travelling by bus, others are in minibuses or four-seater jeeps. Aside from the tours detailed below, there are also a few trips on offer that drive you across the mountains from Sembalun Lawang to Sapit, and others that explore part of the southwest peninsula.

City tour Usually half-day. Includes some of the following: Nusa Tenggara Provincial Museum, Mayura Water Palace, Pura Meru, a shopping centre in Mataram or Cakranegara, Narmada and Lingsar.

Southern tour Usually full-day, with lunch at Kuta and stops at some of the craft and traditional villages on the way, possibly including Narmada, Sukarara, Penujak, Rembitan or Sade, Kuta and Tanjung Aan.

Northern tour Usually full-day to Senaru and back, stopping at Pusuk, Segenter, Sendang Gile waterfall and Senaru.

Central/Eastern tour Full-day. Concentrates on craft villages and the southern foothills of Rinjani including Loyok, Tetebatu, Pringgasela, Timbanuh and Masbagik/Penakak.

Gili Islands tour Full-day to Pemenang, Bangsal and various Gili Islands. If travelling from Senggigi, check whether you go by boat all the way to the islands – it's an attractive ride.

---

international arrivals, and a **taxi** counter with fixed-price fares (to Mataram Rp12,500; Senggigi Rp20,000; Mangsit Rp25,000; Bangsal Rp37,500; Tetebatu Rp74,000; Kuta Rp76,000; Sapit Rp97,000; Senaru Rp115,000; Sembalun Rp150,000; maximum four people). All the major luxury hotels have booking counters here; discounts vary from day to day, so shop around. There's also a **wartel** here (daily 7am–9pm). A few black **bemos** plying to Kebun Roek terminal in Ampenan (heading to the right) pass along the road in front of the airport. See p.442 for public transport details from the airport to Bangsal (for the Gili Islands).

If you're arriving in the city from east Lombok, from Lembar in the south (see p.430 for details of transport from Lembar), or from the airport, you'll come into the **bus station** on the eastern edge of the conurbation, known variously as **Bertais**, **Mandalika** or **Sweta**. This is the main bus terminal on the island: most public transport from the north arrives here as well. It's huge and bustling, with small local bemos jostling for space beside the long-distance buses which ply as far as Flores, Java and Sumatra. Just across the road, a maze of stalls lining tiny alleyways sell produce, household items and crafts. Arriving **from Senggigi**, and on some of the bemos from Pemenang, you'll come into the **Kebun Roek** terminal in Ampenan. The two bus terminals are linked by the frequent yellow bemos that zip around the city.

Gili Genting tour Full-day, including a boat ride to Gili Genting, Gili Gede and Gili Poh off the southwest peninsula.

Round-the-island tour Full-day. Circles the north via Senaru and then Obel Obel to Labuhan Lombok, and back across the centre of the island. You'll see most of Lombok, but the road around the north is slow going, meaning a lot of travelling time.

Tour operators

In addition to the **operators** listed below, some hotels can also put together a good deal for you: *Windy Cottages,* north of Senggigi, arranges good-value trips and *Shanta Puri,* in Cakranegara, has a range of tours. Perama also offers several tours.

Citra Lombok Indah Senggigi ℡0370/693238. All the standard tours on offer.

Coconut Cottages Gili Air ℡0370/635365, ⓦwww.coconuts-giliair.com. Tours throughout Lombok, at US$50–60 for two people (extra people are charged at $5 each), including car, driver, guide and two-way private boat charter. Alternatively they can arrange a car and driver ($35) for two people for the day (8am–3.30pm), travelling to and from Lombok on the shuttle service.

Kotasi Senggigi ℡0370/693435. Transport co-operative with two counters, one on the main street and one on the road that leads past *Maskot* cottages to the beach. Offers a huge range of tours by road and boat.

Lombok Mandiri Senggigi ℡ & ⓕ0370/693477. Has a counter on the main road.

Lotus Asia Tours Jl Raya Senggigi 1g, Ampenan ℡0370/636781, ⓕ622344, ⓦwww.lotusasiatours.com. Offers a big range of tours at $35–40 per person, including the southern beaches and trips to the southeastern peninsula looking for turtles. They also offer bicycle tours.

Nominasi Senggigi ℡0370/693690, ⓕ693832. The usual range of tours.

Vicy Senggigi ℡0370/692021, ⓕ693170, ⓦwww.vicytour.com. Most of the usual tours available.

Wannen Wisata Senggigi ℡0370/693165. Pretty much the standard tours on offer.

The most helpful **tourist office** is the Provincial Tourist Service for West Nusa Tenggara, which is rather out of the way off Jalan Majapahit in the south of the city, at Jl Singosari 2 (Mon–Thurs 7am–2pm, Fri 7–11am, Sat 7am–1pm; ℡0370/634800, ⓕ637233). There are shorter opening hours during Ramadan (see p.56). They offer leaflets, a map of Lombok and advice about travel in Lombok and Sumbawa. Yellow bemos heading via "Kekalik" pass the end of Jalan Singosari as they go along Jalan Majapahit between Bertais terminal and Kebun Roek terminal.

City transport

All **bemo** trips within the four-cities area cost Rp1000, and yellow bemos constantly ply between Kebun Roek terminal in Ampenan and Bertais/Mandalika terminal in Sweta from early morning until late evening. Most follow the Jalan Langko–Jalan Pejanggik–Jalan Selaparang route heading west to east, and Jalan Tumpang Sari–Jalan Panca Usaha–Jalan Pancawarga–Jalan Pendidikan heading east to west, although there are plenty of less frequently served variations.

The horse-drawn carts here, unlike the ones on Bali, have small pneumatic tyres and are called **cidomo**; they aren't allowed on the main streets, covering instead the back routes that bemos don't work, and are generally used for carrying heavy loads. Always negotiate a price before getting in.

There are plenty of pale blue, easily identifiable official metered **taxis**; you can flag them down anywhere. A trip across the entire city area is unlikely to be more than Rp12,000. Ordering a taxi by phone (℡0370/627000) incurs a minimum fare of Rp5000.

Accommodation

The range of **accommodation** is huge, although relatively few tourists stay here since Senggigi is only a few kilometres up the road. **Ampenan** is known for its budget backpackers' lodges, which are now looking decidedly frayed around the edges. The business hotels spread throughout the city don't offer particularly good value either, but there's a good clutch of losmen in **Cakranegara** offering cleaner and better-value accommodation. Wherever you stay, noise is a potential problem, and accommodation on the main roads is best avoided, unless it's set well back or properly soundproofed.

It's a good idea to have some notion of where you want to stay before you arrive, as accommodation is so widely spread out. The Ampenan places are twenty minutes' walk from the Kebun Roek terminal there. Those in Cakranegara are not too far from the main bemo routes, but several kilometres from both Kebun Roek and Bertais terminal in Sweta.

Ampenan

Angin Mammiri Jl Koperasi 69 ℡0370/631713. Basic but very cheap rooms with attached mandi and squat toilet, a twenty-minute walk from the bemo terminal. It's set back a bit from the road so avoids the worst of the noise. ❶

Nitour Jl Yos Sudarso 4 ℡0370/623780 or 642844, ℻625328. Noisy place close to the main road. All the rooms have air-con, hot water and TV but there's no pool. ❹

Wisata Jl Koperasi 19 ℡0370/626971, ℻621781. Tiled, reasonable-quality rooms; the expensive ones have air-con. ❶–❷

Hotel Zahir Jl Koperasi 9 ℡0370/634248. A good-value budget cheapie close to the centre of Ampenan, offering basic rooms with small verandahs around a tiny garden. ❶

Cakranegara

Adiguna Jl Nursiwan 9 ℡0370/625946. An excellent budget choice, situated in a quiet, convenient street near the bemo routes, and featuring reasonable rooms in a small garden. ❶

Ayu Jl Nursiwan 20 ℡0370/621761. This clean losmen has buildings on both sides of the road, and is popular with businesspeople, Indonesian families and foreign tourists. The most expensive rooms have air-con. ❶–❷

Granada Jl Bung Karno ℡0370/622275, ℻636015. Set in spacious grounds with a swimming pool and offering reasonable rooms although some of them are now showing their age. All have

air-con and hot water. ❸–❹

Lombok Raya Jl Panca Usaha 11 ℡0370/632305, ℻636478, ✉lora@mataram.wasantara.net.id. Yellow bemos from Bertais terminal in Sweta pass the door of this upmarket place. It has clean tiled rooms and an attractive pool. All rooms have air-con and hot water and more expensive ones have a bathtub rather than a shower. Discounts of more than 50 percent are often available. ❼

Oka Jl Repatmaja 5 ℡0370/622406. Fan rooms with attached mandi and good verandahs set in a convenient and quiet location. ❶

Puri Indah Jl Sriwijaya 132 ℡0370/637633, ℻637669. A bit out of the way, but excellent value and very popular. There's a pool and small restaurant, but no hot water; most rooms have air-con. Prices are due to rise soon. ❶–❷

Pusaka Jl Hasanudin 23 ℡0370/634189, ℻633119. Set back from the busy road with well-furnished air-con rooms, a comfortable lounge and a restaurant; more expensive rooms have hot water. ❷–❹

Sahid Legi Mataram Jl Sriwijaya 81 ℡0370/636282, ℻636281, ✉sahid@mataram.wasantara.net.id. Comfortably furnished, elegant hotel with lovely gardens, good rooms with air-con and hot water and an excellent pool. Large discounts usually available. ❻

Shanta Puri Jl Maktal 15 ℡0370/632649. The most popular travellers' place in Cakranegara, offering a wide range of rooms: the cheapest have shared bathrooms and the most expensive air-con and hot water. There's also a good-value restaurant. The compound is a bit cramped, but upstairs rooms lead off a pleasant balcony. They can arrange tours and shuttle buses and book long-distance bus tickets. **❶–❸**

The City

In the far west of the city, the old port town of **AMPENAN** is situated around the mouth of the Jangkok River. It's the liveliest part of the city, with bustling narrow streets, a flourishing **market** and an atmosphere of business and enterprise that some of the enormous tree-lined roads further east lack. The descendants of early Chinese and Arab traders settled here in a maze of shophouses, although trading has long since ceased; the *godowns* (warehouses) on the coast are decaying relics of their former glory and today Ampenan is home to a fishing community, in the shadow of the new oil depot. It's also a secondary transport hub, the jumping-off point to the tourist resort of Senggigi a few kilometres up the coast, and has a selection of **restaurants** (see p.424) and antique, pearl and art **shops** (see p.425). It's easy to spend an interesting half-day wandering around the narrows lanes and market area behind the main crossroads. When you need to feel the cooling sea breeze, wander out to the coast along Jalan Pabean: this area has now been landscaped with a big new welcome gate and is a nice spot to relax for a while.

The most interesting sight in the four towns is the peaceful and shady **West Nusa Tenggara Provincial Museum**, Jl Panji Tilar Negara 6 (Mon–Thurs 7am–2pm, Fri 7–11am, Sat 7am–1pm; Rp750), a short walk from the Pelni office. The exhibits, with only a few labelled in English, range from displays about the geological formation of Indonesia and the various cultural groups of Nusa Tenggara to household and religious items. The museum's highlight is its collection of kris, elongated daggers which are objects of reverence, treasured as family heirlooms and symbols of manhood. Blades are made from layers of different metals pounded together, always highly decorated, while the hilt often takes the form of a mythological figure – commonly Ganesh, Wisnu, Siwa or Garuda. The manufacture of kris, often taking many months, involves the harnessing of powerful magical forces and must be accompanied by suitable prayers and rituals. Stories of the magical properties of kris abound: they can bring their owners health, wealth and happiness, others can kill simply by being pointed at the victim, while some kill of their own volition or warn their owners of impending danger by rattling in their sheaths.

A few hundred metres' walk north of Ampenan is the Balinese **Pura Segara**, the temple of the sea. To get here, head 300m north on Jalan Saleh Sungkar, the road towards Senggigi, taking the first dirt track left towards the sea (Dewi Sri Murni Tours and Travel is on the corner). The temple is on the black-sand beach, and often locked, although it's possible to see the *kulkul* tower and shrines inside over the wall. Just inland from here, the **Chinese cemetery** is a sad reminder of the large Chinese population of the area who were persecuted in the purges following the attempted coup in 1965 (see p.499). More Chinese cemeteries line the main road for several hundred metres to the north; many of the graves are very ornate and colourful and well worth a look.

Mataram and Cakranegara

Merging into Ampenan to the east, **MATARAM** is the capital of West Nusa Tenggara province as well as of the district of Lombok Barat (West Lombok). It's full of offices and imposing government buildings, many set in spacious grounds on broad, tree-lined avenues, but there's little of interest.

East again, **CAKRANEGARA**, usually known as Cakra (pronounced *chakra*), was the capital of Lombok in the eighteenth century during the height of the Balinese ascendancy on the island, and was the site of savage fighting during 1894 which culminated in Dutch victory. Today, it's the commercial capital of Lombok, with shops, markets, workshops and hotels all aimed at local, or at least Indonesian, trade, but more than willing to welcome tourists as well. The main **market** centres on Jalan A.A. Gede Ngurah just south of the crossroads with Jalan Pejanggik and Jalan Selaparang; explore the alleyways here for a taste of pretty much everything that Lombok has to offer. For another vibrant and colourful market experience, take a look at the small local produce market, **Pasar Sindu**, on Jalan Hasanudin, about 500m north of the junction with Jalan Selaparang.

Built in 1744 during the rule of the Balinese in West Lombok, the **Puri Mayura** (Mayura Water Palace), on Jalan Selaparang (daily 7am–4.30pm; Rp1000), is set in well-maintained grounds which get busy at weekends. It's pleasant enough if you're looking for a bit of relaxation in the city, although the grounds at nearby Narmada (see p.464) are far more attractive. The centrepiece of the palace was the small, thatched *bale kambang* (floating pavilion), the former meeting hall and court of justice, set in the middle of a large artificial lake. The foundations of this, projecting from the surface of the lake, are all that remain of the palace, which was destroyed in November 1894 when the Dutch razed Cakra. Within the grounds is a complex of shrines, with pint-sized Rangdas guarding the entrance; you can walk around the lake to where twenty *naga* spurt or drip water.

Across the main road, **Pura Meru**, also known as Pura Mayura, is the largest Balinese temple on the island, built in 1720 by Prince Anak Agung Made Karang in an attempt to unite the various Hindu factions on Lombok. The *candi bentar* displaying scenes from the *Ramayana* is the highlight of the temple, which bustles and brims with activity on festival days but for the rest of the time is rather empty and cheerless.

Eating and drinking

There's a wide range of **places to eat**, with an excellent choice of cuisines, although the city is so spread out that you may have to travel some distance from your losmen. Great value is offered by the city's **Chinese** restaurants, and **Padang** and **Taliwang** food is also available – as is fast food should you get the urge. If you're really watching the rupiah, head for the food stalls in the Kebun Roek terminal, which sell very cheap local food.

It's worth noting that although Lombok is predominantly Muslim, visiting here **during Ramadan** does not mean long hours during the day without sustenance. Most of the places below remain open during the day at this time, although a curtain at the window discreetly hides the eating tourists, as well as the resident Balinese and local Muslims who are not fasting.

Betawi Jl Yos Sudarso 152, Ampenan. Upstairs on the corner of Jalan Koperasi. A wide range of well-prepared and well-presented Western and Indonesian dishes including seafood (Rp25,000 and upwards), soups (Rp10,000), salads (Rp10,000–15,000) and a two-person *rijsttafel* for Rp90,000. The big plus is the balcony, where you can catch the breeze and watch life in the streets below. Mon–Sat 8am–10pm. Moderate.

Mataram Mall Jl Pejanggik, Cakranegara. The gleaming shopping centre is impossible to miss as you travel into Cakranegara from the west. There's a McDonald's on the ground floor and a Swensen's ice-cream stall inside, but the top-floor food court is far more interesting, offering plenty of small stalls selling all varieties of cheap, well-cooked local food. Inexpensive.

Mirasa Modern Bakery Jl A.A. Gede Ngurah,

Cakranegara. Takeaway only. A huge selection of excellent savouries, pastries, sweet breads and cakes – although the lurid doughnuts are probably only for real sugar junkies. Moderate.

Pabean Jl Yos Sudarso 111, Ampenan. Small Chinese restaurant with large servings of basic dishes and well-cooked food. There are several other good options in this street if it's full; the closest is *Cirebon* next door, or *Manalagi II* is across the street at no. 128. Inexpensive.

Rainbow Café Jl Yos Sudarso, Ampenan. This small travellers' place has a good, welcoming atmosphere and a small menu. It also serves cold beer and plays Western music. Inexpensive.

Roti Barokah Jl Saleh Sungkar 22, Ampenan. About 100m south of the turning to Kebun Roek terminal. A little bakery and snack bar which has a

few tables where you can enjoy tasty pizzas, doughnuts and cakes – or you can take away. Inexpensive.

Shanta Puri Jl Maktal 15, Cakranegara. The restaurant attached to the popular losmen serves a range of travellers' fare and basic Indo-Chinese options in relaxed surroundings. Inexpensive to Moderate.

Simpang Raya Jl Pejangik 107, Cakranegara. Conveniently located for the Cakranegara losmen, selling a large range of well-cooked Padang food. Inexpensive.

Suharti Sate House Jl Maktal 9, Cakranegara. With a selection of sates plus seafood and chicken options, this place is just along the road from the *Shanta Puri* and is convenient for all the Cakra losmen. Very few vegetarian options. Inexpensive.

Shopping

Shopping can be a fun way to pass some time in the city – whether you're after antiques or more contemporary crafts, and whether you prefer to shop in bustling markets or small, specialized shops.

Crafts and textiles

Ampenan has a clutch of art and antique shops selling **crafts** from Lombok and the islands further east. They're good fun to browse in, although you need to take the definition of "antique" with a pinch of salt. Most places **close** for two or three hours in the middle of the day and often on Friday afternoons too, but many can arrange **shipping** (around US$250–300 per cubic metre to UK or North America; Australia is slightly cheaper and New Zealand more expensive).

Shops are concentrated in **Jalan Saleh Sungkar**, starting with Yufi Art Shop at no. 26, about 200m south of the turning to the bemo terminal, and in the area around **Jalan Yos Sudarso**, north of the bridge across the Jangkok River (check out Freti at Gang Sunda 15, towards the bridge). Amulets made from bone and buffalo horn, wooden and palm boxes and textiles are all worth looking out for. A couple of outlets have opened larger premises on the road that leads to the airport from Kebun Roek terminal. Hary is about 200m east of the terminal; Amanda is another few hundred metres away at Jl Adi Sucipto 4.

An excellent one-stop shopping spot is the **Lombok Handicraft Centre**, just beyond the Jangkok River about 2km north of Cakranegara along Jalan Hasanudin at Rungkang Jangkok, Sayang Sayang. It has numerous small shops selling every type of craftwork imaginable, although not many textiles. You can see some of them, including palm-leaf boxes, being made.

A couple of local factories producing **ikat** cloth are worth a look; both have shops attached. Rinjani Handwoven (daily 9am–9pm) is at Jl Pejanggik 44–46 in Cakranegara; and Slamet Riady is at Jl Tanun 10, just off Jalan Hasanudin in Cakranegara, with a small sign just north of *Pusaka* hotel. The process is the same as that used in Bali (see p.538), and the *ikat* is very similar.

The Cakranegara **market** (mentioned above) has some crafts scattered amongst the vegetables, fish, meat and plastic household goods, and the market near the bus terminal at Bertais is also worth a look (if you're interested in buying take a flashlight with you, as details are very hard to see in the gloom).

Pottery

Lombok **pottery** is now developing an international reputation for style and beauty, and it's possible to get a good idea of the range and quality of the products without venturing as far as the producer villages. **Lombok Pottery Centre**, Jl Sriwijaya 111a, Ampenan (℡0370/640351, ℻640350, ✉lpc_ami@ mataram.wasantara.net.id) is the shop and showroom of the Lombok Crafts Project (see box on p.429) and stocks the best-quality products of the three main pottery centres on the island; there's also a showroom in Senggigi. The work of other artisans, including handweaving and wooden items, is also on sale.

The largest pottery company on Lombok, also operating shops in several hotels, is **Sasak Pottery**, Jl Koperasi 102, Ampenan (℡0370/631687, ℻642588, ⓦwww.sasak-pottery.com), located five minutes from the airport – phone for a free pick-up in the city or Senggigi area. This is the warehouse and packing centre for overseas shipments and is the biggest earthenware showroom in Indonesia, with more than four hundred designs on display. There are prices for every pocket and sizes for every suitcase, and shipping can be arranged. Staff can advise on good workshops to visit in the villages.

Pearls and jewellery

Another increasingly popular souvenir is a string of **pearls**. There are several pearl farms dotted around the coastline and many of the pearls find their way into the shops in Ampenan. They're sold by weight and come in a variety of sizes and shapes as well as colour: aside from the many natural hues, there are a few unnatural colours created afterwards (brilliant yellow, green or purple pearls may not take your fancy). Shop around on Jalan Saleh Sungkar and you should be able to get a small string for under US$5. Check out Aneka Mutiara at no. 15, Surya Mutiara Indah at no. 51 and Central Mutiara at no. 58, just north of the turning to Kebun Roek terminal.

For **gold** and **silver jewellery**, head for Kurmasan (see map p.419), north of Mataram. Small workshops are dotted around the area to the east of Jalan Hos Cokroaminoto: quite a lot of the jewellery on sale in the tourist areas of Bali and Lombok is made here, so you'll be able to find pretty much anything that is in fashion. Bargain hard.

Listings

Airlines All the domestic airlines have ticket counters at the airport, and some have offices in the city area. Air Mark, Selaparang Airport ℡0370/643564 or 646847, and at *Hotel Selaparang*, opposite Mataram Mall, Jl Pejanggik 42–44, Mataram ℡0370/633235; Merpati, Selaparang Airport ℡0370/633691, and at Jl Pejanggik 69, Mataram ℡0370/632226; Garuda, Selaparang Airport ℡0370/622987 ext 246, and at *Hotel Lombok Raya*, Jl Panca Usaha 11, Cakranegara ℡0370/637950. Silk Air – the only international airline with offices on Lombok – is at Selaparang Airport ℡0370/636924, and at *Hotel Lombok Raya*, Jl Panca Usaha 11, Cakranegara ℡0370/628254. For details of international airline offices in Bali, see box on p.111.

Banks and exchange All the large Mataram and Cakra banks change money and travellers' cheques. The most convenient in Cakra is the Bank of Central Asia, Jl Pejanggik 67 (also with a Visa, MasterCard and Cirrus ATM). The BCA also has a convenient ATM on Jalan Sandu Jaya, about 500m west of the Mandalika bus terminal in Bertais, Sweta. The main branch of Bank Internasional Indonesia (BII), Jl Gede Ngurah 46b, Mataram ℡0370/35027, and the main post office (see below) are both Western Union agents.

Boats Pelni, Jl Majapahit 2, Ampenan (Mon–Fri 8.30am–3.30pm, Sat 8.30am–1pm; ℡0370/637212, ℻631604).

Buses If you don't want to go out to Mandalika terminal, you can buy long-distance bus tickets in Mataram from Karya Jaya, Jl Pejanggik 115d ℡0370/636065; Langsung Indah, Jl Pejanggik

△ Lombok textiles, Sukarara

56b ☎0370/634669; Perama, Jl Pejanggik 66 ☎0370/635928; Simpatik, Jl Pejanggik 115 ☎0370/634808; Vivon Sayang, Jl Langko 86. **Car rental** Biggest firm in town is Toyota Car Rental, Jl Adi Sucipto 5, Mataram ☎0370/626363, ℱ627071,℺www.trac.astra.co.id. Rinjani Rent Car is at Jl Panca Usaha 7b ☎0370/632259. You'll get a better choice if you arrange rental in Senggigi.

Dentist Dr Fjahja Hendrawan at Apotik Masyarakat III, Jl Sriwijaya, Mataram ☎0370/638363.

Departure tax Leaving Lombok by air: Rp8000 (domestic), Rp70,000 (international).

Horse racing At the Selagalas Racetrack on Jalan Gora, northeast of Cakranegara, most Sunday mornings and on some other holidays, although not at all during Ramadan; check with the tourist office. The jockeys are all young boys (they retire at 12), who ride bareback around the 1000-metre track. The night before the races, the horses are massaged and entertained with gamelan music, and in the morning they get a bucket of sweet coffee for breakfast.

Hospitals Catholic Hospital, Jl Koperasi, Ampenan ☎0370/621397; Muslim Hospital, Jalan Pancawarga, Mataram ☎0370/623498. At the public hospital (Rumah Sakit Umum, Jl Pejanggik 6, Mataram ☎0370/621354) there's a Poly Klinik (Mon–Sat 8–11am), with specialists for most problems, an English-speaking "tourist doctor", Dr Felix, and a 24hr pharmacy (☎0370/637326). Pediatrician: Dr Djelantik, Jalan A.A. Gede Ngurah, Cakranegara (phone for appointment; Mon–Sat 5–7pm; ☎0370/632169).

Immigration office *Kantor Imigrasi*, Jl Udayana 2, Mataram ☎0370/622520.

Internet access Most convenient area is Jalan Cilinaya, down the side of Mataram Mall, where Global Internet (daily 9am–11pm; Rp6000/hr) is as good as any.

Motorbike rental The main rental place is at the roadside at Jl Gelantik 21, Cakranegara, 200m west of the *Srikandi* losmen on Jl Kebudayaan; you should be confident with bikes and not worried about insurance. See p.41 for general advice.

Phones The main phone office is at Jl Langko 23, Ampenan (daily 24hr). Also plenty of wartels in town, including Jl Panca Usaha 22b, Cakranegara (daily 8am–midnight); Jl Saleh Sungkar 2g, Ampenan (daily 7.30am–midnight); Jl Langko 88, Ampenan (daily 24hr); and Jl Pejanggik 105, Mataram (daily 6.30am–11pm).

Police Jalan Langko, Ampenan ☎0370/631225.

Post office Lombok's main office is at Jl Sriwijaya 21, Mataram (Mon–Sat 8am–7pm, Sun 8am–noon). Offices at Jl Langko 21, Ampenan (Mon–Sat 8am–7pm) and on Jalan Kebudayaan in Cakranegara (same hours) are more accessible. For poste restante, the Senggigi post office is more used to dealing with tourists.

Supermarkets In the Mataram Mall, Mataram Plaza and the Cakra Plaza, all on Jl Pejanggik in Cakranegara (daily 10am–9pm).

Taxi Lombok Taxis ☎0370/627000.

Tour and travel companies See box on pp.420–421 for a run-down of some of the standard Lombok tours. Operators include Anthea Wisata Tours, at *Hotel Sahid Legi Mataram*, Jl Sriwijaya 81, Mataram ☎ & ℱ0370/641944, ℯfzz@indonet.id; Bidy Tours, Jl Ragigenap 17, Ampenan ☎0370/632127, ℱ631821, ℺www.bidytour.com; Ideal Tours, Jl Pejanggik 54b, Mataram ☎0370/622629, ℱ636982, ℯidealtour@mataram.wasantara.net.id; and Lotus Asia Tours, Jl Raya Senggigi 1g, Ampenan ☎0370/636781, ℱ622344, ℺www.lotusasiatours.com. Perama, Jl Pejanggik 66, Mataram ☎0370/635928, offers island tours and Gili Island Explorer trips in a glass-bottomed boat. The *Shanta Puri Hotel*, Jl Maktal 15, Cakranegara, arranges a variety of tours geared to travellers (Rp100,000–150,000/day per person; minimum four people).

Out of the city

The *pura* on the summit of **Gunung Pengsong**, 6km south of Mataram, is much more impressive than any temples in town, but is really only accessible with your own transport. The temple complex begins at the bottom of the hill with an extensive outer compound containing a large number of bold monkeys. From here it's a twenty-minute climb: a concrete staircase leads almost to the summit, although the final section, after the steps finish, is a bit of a scramble. The tiny temple at the top contains three small altars oriented to the south, east and north with a fifty-centimetre egg-shaped stone in the place of honour. A traditional story, that the earliest Balinese settlers on Lombok landed at the base of the hill, makes the temple the focus of regular ceremonies for the Balinese community on the island. One of the main **festivals** held here is *Bersih Dasa*, following the harvest in March or April, when Dewi Sri, the rice goddess, is honoured. There are great views across the fields and villages to the coast.

Labuapi and Banyumulek

About 7km south of the city, on the main road that leads to Lembar, the small village of **LABUAPI** is lined with several workshops and small show-rooms selling crafts. They specialize in woodcarving, including the small wooden bowls, some with painted decoration, others inlaid with shells, that you'll spot in art shops across Lombok and Bali. You can see them being painted and varnished in the workshops behind the shops, and prices are reasonable.

The village of **BANYUMULEK**, 2km south of Labuapi, is one of the three main **pottery** centres on the island, stretching west of the main road to Lembar. It's an easy one-kilometre walk from the junction, marked by traffic lights and a monument composed of a tower of large pots, to the place where the pottery workshops and showrooms begin; cidomo also serve the route. The full variety of earthenware goods is on offer: large vases are much in evidence, many engraved or covered with textiles, and there's no shortage of the bright-ly coloured, textured finishes currently in fashion. Come in the morning if you want to see the potters working. This is one of the villages involved in the **Lombok Crafts Project** (see box below); the quality is high and they can ship items directly overseas. Showrooms and shops in Ampenan and Mataram (see p.426) stock some of the items produced here.

The Lombok Crafts Project

Women in the villages of Banyumulek, Penakak (in Masbagik Timur, where there are several pottery-making hamlets east of Masbagik) and Penujak have been produc-ing hand-made **earthenware pottery** using simple tools and local materials since the early sixteenth century, passing their skills through generations from mother to daughter. The **Lombok Crafts Project** was established in the same villages in 1988, with funding from the New Zealand Development Assistance Programme with Indonesia, with the aim of raising the standard of living of the potter families, who at the start of the project had a daily income of less than US$1.

The project has supplied advisers and consultants in pottery, marketing, business and community development, targeting local hotels and restaurants and export mar-kets; to date, New Zealand has contributed some NZ$4 million. Sales are now in the region of US$350,000 annually, with about eighty percent of items being exported to Europe, Australia, New Zealand, the United States and Japan, and the remainder sold locally.

The project estimates that it has directly assisted 250–300 potters, and indirectly affected thousands more, since it has also sponsored literacy and community devel-opment programmes and helped to build better community facilities such as clean water supplies and sanitation. The average daily income of the potters now ranges from US$3 to US$4.50, an increase of 300 percent and more since the project start-ed, and there's training in place to improve skills further. One of the most positive features of the project, highly visible to anyone visiting the villages of Lombok, is that other potters and villages have realized the potential of the market, and opened many small businesses to compete.

Lembar and the southwest peninsula

With several enticing offshore islands, some wonderful beaches and bays and a totally rural atmosphere, the **southwest peninsula** is an alluring proposition for those who want to get off the beaten track – a million miles away from the bustle of the port at **Lembar** or the frenetic activity of the city area. **Bangko Bangko** at the tip of the peninsula is legendary among surfers across the world as the location of the Desert Point break, recently voted best in the world by readers of an Australian surf magazine. Even if you follow only part of the road to Bangko Bangko, you'll get a feel for this arid and harsh land, with only a few villages, whose sparse population makes its living from the sea. The road is not especially hilly and is suitable for cycling as it is pretty free of traffic; however, parts are very hot and lacking in shade – and drink and food stops are widely spaced – so you need to come prepared.

Lembar

LEMBAR, the gateway to the peninsula and the port for Bali, is 22km south of Mataram. Approaching by boat from Bali, the entrance to the rugged harbour is spectacular, but the village itself is insignificant. There's little **accommodation** here and no advantage in staying. *Tidar* (no phone; ●) is a new orange and red place where the road to the port meets the main road; and the *Sri Wahyu* losmen, Jl Pusri 1, Serumbung (℡0370/681048; ●), is signposted from the main road about 1500m north of the port, with basic bungalows set in a garden. The family provides a good chance to practise your Indonesian. There's an attached **restaurant** and you can also rent **snorkelling** gear here.

Bemos run between Sweta's Bertais/Mandalika terminal and the port at Lembar, connecting with the ferry and catamaran services to Bali (for details of which, see box on p.416). Public bemos from Lembar to the southwest peninsula leave from the large terminal 500m north of the port, at the junction of the main road and the turning to Bangko Bangko via Sekotong (this turn is clearly marked with hotel signs, including notices for *Hotel Bola Bola Paradis* and *Hotel Sekotong Indah*). Bemos operate from Lembar all the way to Selegang during the hours of daylight, although you may need to change on the way. A metered **taxi** from Lembar port to Taun is about Rp50,000.

The southwest peninsula

As the crow flies it's around 23km from Lembar to Bangko Bangko, at the far western end of the peninsula, where the road runs out. However, the journey by road is 57km, twisting around the bays and inlets of the picturesque north coast. The road is tarmacked to Selegang, 3km before Bangko Bangko, after which you're on sand tracks. The scenery is great: many of the **beaches** are glorious and there are enticing offshore **islands** with pure white sand visible across the water.

Out of Lembar, the road – often inland – traces the outline of the massive harbour. There are a few fine coastal views of fishing platforms, but much of the shore is black sand lined with mangroves. All along this stretch are piles of red building bricks, products of a local cottage industry. The small village of **SEKOTONG**, 19km from Lembar, marks the junction of the Bangko Bangko road with an equally small and equally alluring road that heads south to Sepi and Blongas on the south coast (see p.481).

The Wallace line

Bali and Lombok are separated by a narrow 35-kilometre stretch of water, the Lombok Strait, over 1300m deep in places, through which runs an imaginary boundary, the **Wallace line**, marking a division between the distribution of Asian and Australasian wildlife in Indonesia. Bali and the islands to the west have creatures mostly common to mainland Asia (rabbits, monkeys, tigers), while the wildlife on Lombok and the islands to the east is more characteristic of Australia and New Guinea (parrots, marsupials, platypus and lizards).

Between 1854 and 1862, the British naturalist **Sir Alfred Russel Wallace** travelled extensively throughout the archipelago that today forms Indonesia. Encountering obvious differences between the wildlife on Bali and that on Lombok, he suggested that during the Ice Ages, when the levels of the world's oceans dropped, animals ranged from mainland Asia down through Sumatra and Java to Bali. However, the considerable depth of the Lombok Strait meant they were unable to proceed any further. Similarly, animals from the land masses to the south roamed as far as Lombok on the other side of the strait.

Later research, showing that many animal species are in fact common to both Bali and Lombok, has now shifted opinion away from the clear-cut migration theory devised by Wallace. Today, naturalists refer not to Wallace's Line but to a **zone of transition** from the Asian type of animal life to the Australasian; in honour of Sir Alfred this is known as "Wallacea". You're likely to see **crab-eating macaques** (medium-sized grey-brown monkeys) and **silver leaf-monkeys**, with black skin and grey-tipped hairs, both in Bali Barat National Park and on the slopes of Rinjani around Tetebatu and Batu Koq, while the **yellow-crested cockatoo**, a native of Australia, and the **rainbow lorikeet** and **red-cheeked parrot** are found no further west than Lombok.

The distribution of **plant life** on the two islands has never supported Wallace's theory. The gradual transition of flora through the islands of Indonesia can be accounted for largely by climatic changes, from the rainforests of the western islands through to the drier climates in the east, and this factor is likely to have been the major influence on the differences in wildlife between Bali and Lombok.

Taun and around

Past Sekotong, the scenery improves dramatically as you pass salt pans and lobster farms, eventually reaching the village of **TAUN**, 28km from Lembar. This is an especially lovely, broad, white-sand, sweeping bay crowded with fishing platforms, with brilliant views to the islands of Gili Genting, Gili Tangkong and Gili Nanggu. **Boats** cost Rp40,000 each way for the trip to **Gili Nanggu** (takes 20min). The boat captains rent out **snorkelling** gear and are open to negotiation for trips to other islands. The only accommodation on the islands is at *Hotel Gili Nanggu* (☎0370/623783; ❶–❻), ranging from simple losmen rooms up to much more luxurious ones with air-conditioning. There's a small **restaurant** attached.

Just 2km around the coast from Taun, in the village of **LABU**, *Hotel Sekotong Indah* (☎0818/362326; ❷) has bungalows in a pleasant garden across the road from the beach and a small restaurant. Most rooms have fan and attached cold-water bathroom but there is one with air-conditioning. You can enjoy the great views from an open *bale* just above the beach.

Moving further west you'll see a certain amount of new construction, with a new hotel going up at **PANDANAN**, 4km beyond Taun, and another at **PEMALIK**, another 5km west. From here the road continues to follow tiny, pure white beaches and climb over headlands, offering great views of more islands.

At the village of **TEMBOWONG**, 11km from Taun, *Putri Duyung Homestay* (☏0812/375 2459; ❷) is a lovely little family-run place owned by Pak Gede Patra. Rooms are simple with attached mandi and squat toilet. This is an ideal base from which to explore **Gili Gede**, the largest offshore island visible from here, and the surrounding six, smaller islands; the family rents out a **boat** at Rp150,000 per day.

A further 2km west, **PELANGAN** is the largest village in this part of the peninsula, although this isn't saying much: there are only a few shops. An enticing side road heads south for about 6km to the bay of Teluk Mekaki on the south coast; ask about the condition of this road before heading off along here. *Hotel Bola Bola Paradis* (☏086812/104250, ✉batuapi99@hotmail.com; ❸) boasts a great coastal location 2km beyond Pelangan. All rooms have fan and cold water but don't live up to the grand promise provided by the towering entrance hall and restaurant. **Boat** trips are available (Rp160,000 for 3hr).

From here, the coast road is lined with more and more mangroves. It turns inland for a while before arriving at another picturesque bay at **SIUNG**, 7km from Pelangan, from where the coastline of Bali becomes visible in the far distance. The road follows the shore for another 3km to **LABUHAN POH**, where the bay appears almost circular, enclosed by hills, headlands and offshore islands, all fringed with startling and brilliantly white sand. There's a pearl-farming operation just offshore, and the views are especially lovely, a few stands of young teak trees providing a little shade.

About 3km west of Labuhan Poh the blacktopped road ends at **SELE-GANG**, a small hamlet of a few houses. A rutted, narrow dirt road, impassable in the rains, winds among the dry, scrubby coastal hills for another 3km, emerging onto a white-sand bay lined with fishermen's huts and colourful sail boats. This is **BANGKO BANGKO**, which from mid-May to September, and again in December, draws hundreds of **surfers** from as far afield as Brazil and Hawaii in search of the elusive, ultimate wave that is **Desert Point** just offshore here (see box on p.477 for surfing information).

The track continues around the bay and up the hill to look down on the next hamlet of **PANDANA**, from where the surfers also rent boats to get out to the breaks. This is a harsh landscape: the place buzzes when the surfers hit town but it's otherwise as remote and isolated spot as you'll see in Lombok, with little else to do apart from admire the scenery – there's no electricity, and fresh water is difficult to find. Bali appears incredibly close, Nusa Penida is about an hour's sail from here, and stretches of the Lombok coast way to the north are also visible.

Senggigi and the northwest coast

SENGGIGI, covering a huge stretch of coastline, with sweeping bays separated by towering headlands, has a reputation among travellers for having been spoilt by big money and big hotels. It's a pleasant surprise, then, to find that it's in fact an attractive and laid-back beach resort, offering a wide range of accommodation and restaurants and low-key nightlife. Parts of the area are packed wall-to-wall with hotels, but it's perfectly possible to have an inexpensive and relaxing stay here, and proximity to the airport makes it an ideal first- or last-night destination.

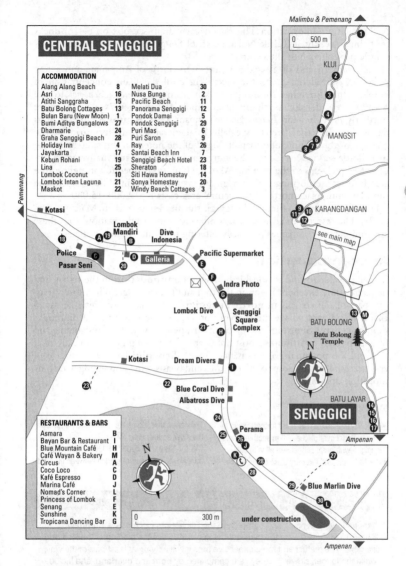

CENTRAL SENGGIGI

ACCOMMODATION

Alang Alang Beach	8	Melati Dua	30
Asri	16	Nusa Bunga	2
Atithi Sanggraha	15	Pacific Beach	11
Batu Bolong Cottages	13	Panorama Senggigi	12
Bulan Baru (New Moon)	1	Pondok Damai	5
Bumi Aditya Bungalows	27	Pondok Senggigi	29
Dharmarie	24	Puri Mas	6
Graha Senggigi Beach	28	Puri Saron	9
Holiday Inn	4	Ray	26
Jayakarta	17	Santai Beach Inn	7
Kebun Rohani	19	Senggigi Beach Hotel	23
Lina	25	Sheraton	18
Lombok Coconut	10	Siti Hawa Homestay	14
Lombok Intan Laguna	21	Sonya Homestay	20
Maskot	22	Windy Beach Cottages	3

RESTAURANTS & BARS

Asmara	B
Bayan Bar & Restaurant	I
Blue Mountain Café	H
Café Wayan & Bakery	M
Circus	A
Coco Loco	C
Kafé Espresso	D
Marina Café	J
Nomad's Corner	L
Princess of Lombok	F
Senang	E
Sunshine	K
Tropicana Dancing Bar	G

Arrival and orientation

Easily accessible by public transport, Senggigi is served by **bemos** from Ampenan throughout the day (every 15–20min). The place to pick them up is on Jalan Saleh Sungkar just north of the turn-off to the bemo terminal in Ampenan, which is where they seem to start their run. From the **airport**, fixed-price taxis charge Rp20,000 to central Senggigi, Rp25,000 to the Mangsit area to the north. Perama **tourist shuttle buses** operate to Senggigi from all the main Bali and Lombok tourist destinations; see Travel details on p.483 for more information. The *Bounty* catamaran (see box on p.416) docks four times weekly at **Teluk Nara**, north of Senggigi, from where free buses shuttle passengers into the centre.

The southern end of Senggigi is just 5km north of Ampenan, and a few places are spread out along the next 4km until the main concentration of hotels, which stretches for roughly 1km from the *Pondok Senggigi* to the *Sheraton*. Low-density development continues for another 7km to the most northerly development, *Bulan Baru* at Lendang Luar. **Bemos** ply the coast as far as here, but they aren't especially frequent and many terminate at the *Sheraton* or the Pacific Supermarket. Many of the hotels on this stretch operate free shuttle services to Central Senggigi during the day, and many restaurants offer free pick-ups in the evening. Metered blue **taxis** operate throughout the area from early morning to late at night; a ride from central Senggigi to the most far-flung place north of the central area costs Rp12,000–15,000.

There's no tourist office in Senggigi; the nearest one is in Mataram (see p.421). The resort is lined with places offering "tourist information", but these are commercial companies primarily offering tours and vehicle rental.

Accommodation

It's still possible to find reasonable budget **accommodation** in the resort, and there are some excellent hotels in the mid and luxury ranges. The most attractive part of the coast is in **north Senggigi**, which has great views across to Bali and ordinary village life carrying on behind the beachside accommodation. In **central Senggigi** there's plenty happening, with bars, restaurants and fine shopping opportunities; most hotels are set far enough back from the road to avoid the potential noise nuisance. **South Senggigi** has the advantage of easy accessibility: it's close to the city area and boasts some good budget accommodation options.

South Senggigi

Asri ☎0370/693075. This is the furthest south of the three Batu Layar places – 4km south of central Senggigi – with basic bungalows, all with cold-water bathroom and fan, very close to the beach.

The newer, tiled rooms are more appealing than the older, smaller ones. ②
Atithi Sanggraha ☎0370/693070. Well-built bungalows in a pleasant garden between the road

Trips to Sumbawa, Komodo and Flores

Various travel agencies on Lombok and the Gili Islands run trips via **Sumbawa** and **Komodo** to **Flores**, with the highlight being a visit to see the feeding of the Komodo dragons. The fastest and most expensive trips involve **flying** at least part of the way, while the longer, slower journeys are completed by **boat** and **overland**, and include several **snorkelling** stops, usually some **trekking**, a **beach party** and sometimes some **camping**. Prices vary enormously, starting at about Rp400,000 per person for a four-day/four-night boat-and-overland trip in one direction; you can pay up to several million rupiah for longer trips including some flights (air transport out of Labuhanbajo can be difficult to arrange, so allow plenty of time if you book a one-way journey). The following all organize trips: Perama (contact any office); P.T. Wannen Wisata, Senggigi ☎0370/693165; Kotasi, Senggigi ☎0370/693435; *Coconut Cottages*, Gili Air ☎0370/635365, ⊛www.coconuts-giliair.com; Lombok Mandiri, Senggigi ☎0370/693477; and Kencana Fun Sun Sea trips (available through agents in all the main resorts).

and beach, 4km south of central Senggigi. Cheaper rooms have fan and more expensive have air-con. All have cold-water bathroom and a good verandah. **①–②**

Batu Bolong Cottages ☎0370/693065, ☏693198. Just north of Batu Bolong temple, these are attractive, clean cottages with good-quality furnishings in lovely gardens, on both sides of the road; the more expensive ones have air-con and hot water and the deluxe seafront rooms have fabulous coastal views. **②–④**

Jayakarta ☎0370/693048, ☏693043, ⓦwww.jayakarta-lombok.com. This hotel marks the southern end of Senggigi. The imposing *lumbung* barn foyer with marble and rattan is the most impressive part of the hotel, although the garden is pleasant and the pool, beside the beach, is big. Most of the accommodation is in rooms, with some in cottages, and there's a lot of wood and marble around, giving a warm, appealing look, although not as grand as the entrance. It's worth enquiring about discounts. **⑦–⑨**

Siti Hawa Homestay ☎0370/693414, ⓔpondok_sitihawa@hotmail.com. Small rooms, some with attached bathroom, all with mosquito net in a simple, characterful family compound about 4km south of central Senggigi. The family has a bicycle, motorbike and kayak to rent to guests. One of the resort's cheapest options. **①**

Central Senggigi

Bumi Aditya Bungalows ☎0370/693782, ☏693862. About 500m from the main road via a track along the side of *Pondok Senggigi*. Good-quality bungalows are all set in a great garden on the hillside, with a choice of fan or air-con. There's a splendid pool – but check it's in operation. **②–⑤**

Dharmarie ☎0370/693050, ☏693099, ⓔdharmarie@mataram.wasantara.net.id. Attractive, well-furnished bungalows in a central location with grounds that go down to the beach. All rooms have air-con and hot water and the more expensive ones have ocean views. Staff are friendly and helpful. Excellent choice in this price range. **⑤**

Graha Senggigi Beach ☎0370/693101, ☏693400. Located on both sides of the road, at the southern end of the central area. Accommodation is comfortable, all rooms have air-con and hot water, there are two restaurants (including one at the beachside), a large pool (open to non-guests for Rp12,500) and a high water-slide (guests Rp10,000, non-guests Rp20,000). **⑦–⑧**

Kebun Rohani ☎0370/693018. Bamboo and thatch cottages with excellent verandahs set in a lovely garden on the hillside away from the sea, about 200m north of the Pacific Supermarket. Cheaper rooms have shared bathroom. An excellent budget choice. **①–②**

Lina ☎0370/693237. All the rooms in this tiny compound right on the seafront in the centre of Senggigi just opposite the Perama office have air-con, but only the more expensive ones facing the sea at the front have hot water. This long-standing Senggigi favourite is justifiably popular and highly recommended in this price bracket. There's a large restaurant too. **②–④**

Lombok Intan Laguna ☎0370/693090, ☏693185, ⓦwww.intanhotels.com. Part of an international chain. Accommodation, which is comfortable without being plush, is right in the heart of the central area and available in rooms, bungalows and cottages all set in extensive grounds. The highlight is undoubtedly the pool, reputedly the largest in Lombok (non-guests Rp25,000), which is just behind the beach; Dream Divers provide a free try at scuba-diving. There are several bars and restaurants. The Laguna Villa has a private swimming pool. **⑦–⑨**

Maskot ☎0370/693365, ☏693236. Good-value, central, quiet place with pleasant grounds but no pool. Located on the road that runs from the main road to the *Senggigi Beach Hotel* – there's a lengthy stretch of beach beside the gardens. The bungalows all have air-con, hot water and huge verandahs. **⑥**

Melati Dua ☎0370/693288, ☏693028. Set in attractive gardens with a choice of good-value, quality bungalows offering cold-water bathrooms and fan in the cheaper price brackets and hot water and air-con in the more expensive ones. **②–④**

Pondok Senggigi ☎0370/693277. This famous stalwart of the budget traveller has moved upmarket with a small pool, plus air-con and hot water in the pricier rooms. It's a large, relaxed place at the southern end of the central area across the road from the beach. Regular videos and live music in the restaurant at the front. **②–④**

Ray ☎0370/693439. Ranged up the hillside in central Senggigi, a short walk from the beach. Rooms are excellent value. The more expensive ones at the top of the compound have fine views and air-con. It's right next door to the *Marina Café*, which has loud, sometimes live, music until late. **①–②**

Senggigi Beach Hotel and Pool Villa Club
⊤0370/693210, ⓕ693200, ⓦwww.aerowisata
.co.id. Large establishment set in extensive
grounds that occupy an entire promontory in central Senggigi: the beach virtually surrounds the
grounds. It's reached via a turning off the main
road in the central area. The rooms in the hotel are
all very comfortable, with good-sized balconies,
and there's an attractive pool, plus several bars
and restaurants and tennis courts. Prices in the
hotel start at US$80. The *Pool Villa Club* is part of
the same establishment but is more luxurious,
with 16 superbly appointed two-storey villas each
sleeping four people in comfort, overlooking the
elegant pool and set in its own grounds. Published
prices in the Pool Villa Club start at US$300. Hotel
❽–❾ Club ❾
Sheraton ⊤0370/693333, ⓕ693140,
ⓦwww.sheraton.com The best hotel in Senggigi

North Senggigi

Alang Alang Beach Resort ⊤0370/693518,
ⓕ693194. A lovely, atmospheric choice in this
price bracket, located about 1km north of central Senggigi. All rooms and bungalows have air-
con and hot water and are attractively furnished
with local artefacts. The gardens are glorious,
there's a beachside restaurant. The pool is good
and on clear days there's a great view across to
Bali. ❽
Bulan Baru (New Moon Hotel) ⊤0370/693785,
693786, ⓔbulanbaru@hotmail.com. Situated at
Lendang Luar, 7km north of central Senggigi.
There are 12 spotless bungalows with air-con and
hot water situated in a pretty garden with a lovely
pool; the spectacular bathroom murals are almost
worth a trip on their own. It has a "no children"
policy. It's a short walk to nearby Setangi beach,
over a kilometre long and with decent snorkelling
off the coast. There's an excellent restaurant
attached. ❸–❹
Holiday Inn ⊤0370/693444, ⓕ693092,
ⓦwww.holiday-inn.com/lombok. Some 5km north
of central Senggigi, this place is upmarket with a
huge compound, comfortable rooms and good
facilities. Two-bedroom self-catering villas are
located across the road from the main hotel.
There's a giant swimming pool, a range of activities to entertain guests and a regular shuttle bus
to central Senggigi. Also several bars and restaurants. ❽–❾
Lombok Coconut ⊤0370/693195, ⓕ693593,
ⓔcoconuthotel@compuserve.com. Ranged up
the hillside about 2km north of central Senggigi,
these are good-value, attractively decorated

offers all the facilities, comfort and service that are
the hallmark of this international hotel group. In a
beachfront location at the northern end of the central area, it's convenient for all amenities while
remaining the ultimate in peace and tranquillity.
The swimming pool is brilliant (non-guests must
pay admission), the grounds are lush, and several
top-class restaurants and bars cater for Western
and Asian palates; the breakfast buffet is a real
feast. There's a seafront spa plus health centre,
shopping area and hair spa. Published prices start
at US$170, and gorgeous private villas with their
own pool are at the top of the price range.
Honeymoon packages available. ❾
Sonya Homestay ⊤0370/693447. Basic budget
rooms in a centrally located, cosy compound,
tucked away behind the main road just north of
the Galleria shopping complex. ❶

bungalows. The more expensive ones have hot
water and air-con, some have great views of
the coast, and there's also a pretty little pool.
❷–❹
Nusa Bunga Klui ⊤0370/693034, ⓕ693036,
ⓦwww.nusabunga.com. Over 5km north of the
centre, this is a fabulous place to stay, with
thatch-roofed brick cottages situated in their own
small bay and a small swimming pool in an attractive garden. An excellent choice. ❼
Pacific Beach ⊤0370/693006, ⓕ693027.
Located right beside the coast north of Senggigi
but still convenient for the centre which is only
about 1km away. Bungalows are set in a large
garden and have air-con and hot water; the ones
furthest from the road are the quietest. There's
also an attractive pool. ❼
Panorama Senggigi ⊤0370/693673, ⓕ693603.
Well-furnished and decorated bungalows, all with
hot water and air-con, set well up on the headland
north of Senggigi to make the most of the fabulous
views. There's a pleasant pool. Located about 1km
north of the central area. ❼–❽
Pondok Damai ⊤ & ⓕ0370/693019. On the
coast at Mangsit, 4km north of central Senggigi,
this is a quiet spot with good-value accommodation in bamboo and thatch bungalows built on a
tiled beach with fan and cold-water bathroom.
Beachside restaurant. ❸
Puri Mas ⊤0370/693831, ⓕ693023, ⓔlom-
bokhotels@purimasgroup.com. A variety of bungalows, all with hot water and air-con, with distinctive, quality furnishings, set in a lush and
peaceful garden next to the beach at Mangsit,

4km north of central Senggigi. There's also a pool. *Puri Mas Villas* (☎0370/693596) is an off-shoot set in the countryside behind Karandangan village. ⑤–⑦

Puri Saron ☎0370/693424, ℗693266, ℮p_saron@mataram.indo.net.id. Good-quality accommodation 2km north of central Senggigi, with air-con and hot water, close to the beachside pool and with an attached restaurant. A good choice in this price range. ⑦

Santai Beach Inn ☎ & ℗0370/693038, ⒲www.santaibeachinn.com. Right on the coast at Mangsit, these popular thatched bungalows are set in a wonderfully overgrown garden and have a very relaxed atmosphere. Meals can be provided and are eaten communally in a *bale* lit by oil lamps in the evening; the menu is ideal for fish-

eating vegetarians but they can also cater for vegans and nobody objects if carnivorous guests want to dine outside. All rooms have a fan and cold water but there are a couple of larger family rooms with hot water. Cheaper rooms are in two-storey *lumbungs* with bedrooms upstairs and bathrooms down. ②–④

Windy Beach Cottages ☎0370/693191, ℗693193, ℮lidya@mataram.wasantara.net.id. Comfortable bungalows 5km north of central Senggigi, right on the coast at Mangsit. It does get windy in the afternoons, but it's a lovely spot. The more expensive rooms have hot water. You can book shuttle bus tickets and tours of the island here, and rent snorkelling equipment; there are a couple of especially good spots off the beach here. ②–③

The resort and around

Life in Senggigi centres on the **beach** or swimming pool during the day, with some low-key shopping also a possibility, and visits to the restaurants and bars in the evening. The pace is slow; hassle from hawkers selling goods and touts offering transport, although getting worse, seems to be confined to the beach itself and the area around the supermarket. Senggigi's a good base for exploring further afield, although there are few sights very close; the only local place really worth visiting is **Batu Bolong Temple**, 1km south of the centre of Senggigi. Weighed down under an excess of lurid pink paint, the shrines are spread around a rocky promontory with fabulous views in both directions along the coast. The main part of the temple is built over an archway in the rock, the hole through which virgins were once supposedly sacrificed to appease the gods. Nowadays this is a quiet and peaceful spot, a favourite with local fishermen.

Diving and snorkelling

There are quite a few operators, many with offices in the Gili Islands, for people who want the comforts of Senggigi and don't mind the additional cost and travel to **dive** around the islands.

If you're a qualified diver expect to **pay** around US$45 for two dives, including the boat trip from Senggigi and lunch; check whether equipment rental is included in the price, and see p.65 for some general guidelines. A PADI Open Water course is around $300, an Advanced Course $200–235, and a Rescue Diver course $320. Many operators offer a "Scuba Review" (around $55) for qualified divers who haven't dived in a while, as well as "Discover Scuba" (about $75), an introductory day for those who want to get some experience without committing to a course.

Most operators run **snorkelling** trips to the Gili Islands; you go along with the divers and have to be fairly self-reliant in the water. Expect to pay $15–25, including equipment and lunch.

All dive operators are marked on the map on p.433.

Dive operators

Albatross ☎0370/693399, ℗693388, ⒲www.albatrossdive.com. Offers PADI courses up to Assistant Instructor level as well as dives for

experienced divers, Discover Scuba, Scuba Review and snorkelling trips.

Blue Coral ☎0370/693441, ℗634765, ℮bluecoral@mataram.wasantara.net.id Daily dive

and snorkelling trips and they run PADI courses. They're linked to Oceanic Diving (℡0385/41009), based in Labuhanbajo, Flores, so can help with information about diving there.
Blue Marlin ℡0370/692003, ℱ641609, ⓦwww.diveindo.com. Senggigi counter of this well-established Gili Islands operator. See p.447 for more details of all their activities. They offer the full range of trips and courses from Senggigi.
Dive Indonesia ℡0370/693367, ℱ693864, ℮deepblue@mataram.wasantara.net.id. Senggigi office, in the Galleria shopping area, of the Gili Trawangan operator offering all the usual dive trips and courses.
Divetastic ℡0370/692004, ⓦwww.divetastic.com. Liveaboard diving trips using *Felidae*, a traditional sailing yacht. Prices are much more affordable than the usual liveaboards

– recent five-day/five-night trips to Moyo National Park in Sumbawa were US$380 per person.
Dream Divers ℡0370/692047, ℱ693738, ⓦwww.dreamdivers.com. Well-established German company with offices also in Gili Air and Gili Trawangan. They offer training on the PADI Instructor Development Course and also Nitrox courses.
Lombok Dive ℡0370/693002, ℮grahampil-grim@hotmail.com. Offers diving trips, sometimes involving a beach barbecue on the way home, including wrecks and deeper dives for more experienced divers. In addition they offer trips, both liveaboards and overland, to Moyo Island off the north coast of Sumbawa where the coral is pristine and there are large fish (dog-toothed tuna and Napoleon wrasse, for example); a liveaboard costs US$900 for five days/four nights.

Adventure trips

With the enormous variety of **adventure trips** available in Bali, it was only a matter of time before operators moved across the Lombok Strait – although the selection here is not so great. Sea Kayak Adventures (℡0370/692003, ℱ641609, ⓦwww.diveindo.com), based in the Blue Marlin dive shop in Senggigi, offers guided **kayaking** trips in single-person or two-seater kayaks along the Lombok coastline (US$50) or around the Gili Islands ($45), including all equipment, snorkelling gear, lunch and as much instruction as you'd like. Their Gili Trawangan office also offers **wakeboarding** and **waterskiing** (see p.447). Lombok Inter Rafting (℡0370/693202, ℱ693867, ℮lombraft01 @yahoo.com), at Senggigi Square Complex, B-6, has half-day **rafting** trips ($54) down the Segara River on the lower slopes of Gunung Rinjani.

The road north

With your own transport, **the road north** from Senggigi to Pemenang (24km), hugging the spectacular coastline, makes a great day out. As you travel through the bays of Karang, Mangsit, Malimbu, Teluk Kodek, Nippah and Teluk Nara, there are fine views of the Gili Islands – tiny white specks atop a turquoise sea – and across to Gunung Agung on Bali when the weather is clear. However, the road is very steep, with bad bends and sheer drops, and can be especially hazardous at night. Although there are a fair smattering of hotels in the area north of Senggigi, huge expanses of the coast are totally undeveloped, with a few coastal villages dotted behind sweeping bays amidst stands of coconut palms. This remains an area where you can find peace, quiet and total relaxation.

Pemenang village (see p.442) marks the turn-off to Bangsal, from where boats depart to the Gili Islands. Only a couple of kilometres beyond Pemenang lies the stunning beach at Sira (see p.456).

Eating, drinking and nightlife

A wide range of **restaurants** in Senggigi offer international cuisines, mostly at inexpensive or moderate prices and generally of a high quality. They open daily, some in time for breakfast, closing around 10pm or 11pm.

Small street carts selling local food congregate on the main stretch not far from the Pacific Supermarket after dark, and there's a row of sate sellers along the beach at the end of the road leading to the *Senggigi Beach Hotel*. These are the only places in Senggigi that shut during the hours of daylight fasting during the month of Ramadan: all tourist places remain open.

Asmara ☎ 0370/693619. Set back from the main road in central Senggigi, this tastefully furnished and relaxed restaurant serves excellent Western, Indonesian and seafood dishes and has a massive drinks list. Salads cost Rp13,000–27,000, pasta Rp29,000–32,000, steaks up to Rp63,000. There's good home-made bread for breakfast, from 7am, and also baby and children's meals. Free pick-up throughout Senggigi. Moderate to Expensive.

Bawang Putih At *Sheraton* hotel ☎ 0370/693333. The most dramatic and romantic of the *Sheraton* restaurants, and Senggigi's most upmarket dining experience – you eat beside the fabulous, superbly lit swimming pool under vaulted white umbrellas. Food includes pizza (Rp52,000–63,000), sandwiches (Rp43,000) and nasi goreng (Rp42,000), and the huge fisherman's platter (Rp179,000). There's also a children's menu and many enormous desserts. Live music provided by a band of strolling players. Expensive.

Bayan Bar and Restaurant Imposing place on the main street in central Senggigi. There's a massive drinks list, including pricey cocktails (Rp27,000–55,000). You can eat fairly cheaply with simple Indonesian food (from Rp18,000); main courses such as steak (Rp34,000–42,000), pizza (Rp26,000–29,000), seafood (Rp23,000–48,000) and chicken (Rp23,000–42,000) feature prominently. There's good-quality live music nightly which generates a good atmosphere. Moderate to Expensive.

Blue Mountain Café One of a row of places in central Senggigi selling cheap and cheerful food with live music. There are plenty of Sasak, Indonesian and Chinese options, with many main courses Rp15,000 or less. Excellent happy hour offers on drinks, and free welcome drinks often included. *Paradise*, *Trully* and *Honey Bunny* are nearby and in the same mould. Inexpensive.

Bulan Baru (New Moon Hotel) At Lendang Luar, 7km north of central Senggigi. Well-cooked, nicely presented Indonesian and Western food, all described on the menu in mouthwatering detail, with main courses Rp18,000–45,000; for homesick travellers, "bangers and mash" is around Rp32,000. There's a big drinks list including Australian wines by the glass (Rp22,500). Staff are pleasant and welcoming. Also a good spot for lunch (toasted sandwiches and rolls Rp8500–14,000), with Setangi beach a short walk away. Moderate.

Café Wayan & Bakery An offshoot of the Ubud set-up, about 1km south of central Senggigi. Excellent Indonesian dishes (Rp14,000 upwards), seafood (Rp30,000; lobster Rp195,000), pizza and pasta (Rp25,000–30,000), and salads (Rp7000–22,000), plus plenty of vegetarian choices. Fresh bread, croissants and cakes are a highlight. Moderate to Expensive.

Circus Located in central Senggigi, and boasting mellow music and a menu of Indonesian, Sasak and Western food – with pizza and pasta as specialities. Moderate.

Coco Loco Best of several shaded seafront places in Pasar Seni in central Senggigi, with Indonesian, Sasak and Western options plus barbecued fish. All are excellent value. You'll dine within sight and sound of the lapping waves – and the local beach hawkers. Inexpensive to Moderate.

Graha Senggigi Beach Hotel A beachside restaurant that's ideal for sunset drinks, with views south to Bangko Bangko and west to Nusa Penida. There's a large menu of Indonesian meals, including pricey seafood sold by weight and a few Western options. Moderate to Expensive.

Kafé Espresso Clean, friendly place towards the north of the central area serving up an enormous range of coffees, including cappuccinos and espressos, made with a choice of local or Italian coffee – and cakes and brownies to go with them. There are plenty of excellent soups, salads, burgers, sandwiches as well as Western and Indonesian favourites. Moderate.

Lina Large, popular restaurant attached to the cottages of the same name, just opposite the Perama office in central Senggigi. There's a big menu of soups, fish, chicken and Indo-Chinese options; the tables on the terrace overlooking the beach are a fine place to watch the sunset during happy hour. Inexpensive to Moderate.

Lombok Coconut ☎ 0370/693195. Western food (pizza and pasta are specialities) as well as Indonesian and plenty of seafood, served in relaxed, attractive surroundings 2km north of Senggigi. Phone for a free pick-up in the Senggigi area. Prices are between Rp22,000 and Rp35,000 for a main course and there's a huge drinks list. Moderate.

Nomad's Corner A relaxed, sociable spot with satellite TV for sports and films, a pool table and coffee machine. The good-value menu includes breakfasts, salads (Rp11,000–14,000), soup

(Rp10,000–14,000), pasta (Rp23,000) and seafood (up to Rp33,000). Inexpensive to Moderate.

Princess of Lombok ☎0370/693011. Offering a free pick-up in the area, this restaurant right in the middle of Senggigi specializes in Mexican chilli, enchiladas, fajitas and nachos which are possibly not very authentic, but tasty nonetheless. They also serve Western steak, fish and prawn dishes. Moderate.

Senang Next to the Pacific Supermarket in central Senggigi. With formica tables and plastic chairs, and a small Indonesian menu featuring simple rice, noodle and soup options including nasi and mie goreng, *nasi soto*, *nasi pecel*, nasi ayam and *nasi rawon*. Everything is good, plentiful and cheap: main courses are from Rp7000. Inexpensive.

Sunshine A massive menu of authentic Chinese food, with seafood featured prominently, plus plenty of soup, meat and vegetarian choices. Main courses are from Rp8000 to Rp40,000; lobster is Rp250,000 per half-kilo. Located at the southern end of the central area; dine on the seafront or inside. Moderate.

Nightlife

The **nightlife** in Senggigi, and indeed everywhere on Lombok, is very low-key, in keeping with the sensibilities of the local Muslim population. Venues are limited: *Marina Café*, close to the Perama office, and *Tropicana Dancing Bar* at the front of the Senggigi Square Complex are pretty much all there is. They have nightly live music but the atmosphere and closing time depends very much on how busy they are. On Friday and Saturday evenings, local people from Mataram-Ampenan-Cakranegara-Sweta swell the crowd, and increasing numbers of domestic tourists from other parts of Indonesia also spend the weekend in Senggigi, boosting Saturday-night numbers.

Shopping

Senggigi is a souvenir **shopper**'s paradise. The main road is lined with shops selling all varieties of Lombok **crafts** including textiles, jewellery, basketware and items from across the archipelago, as well as Western clothes and bags aimed at the tourist market. **Pasar Seni** is a collection of tiny stalls selling a variety of stuff. The nearby **Galleria** has more upmarket shops, including a shop of the Lombok Pottery Centre, selling wares from the Lombok Crafts Project villages (see p.429). Asmara Art Shop sells an excellent range of extremely good-quality fixed-price items, with some lovely smaller pieces among less portable items of furniture. Pamour Art Gallery, opposite the post office, features a similarly wide choice. Oleh Oleh on the main street has a selection of good-quality Western clothes alongside attractive souvenir items, and Alxih in Senggigi Square is also worth a look.

The road south, between Senggigi and Ampenan, is gradually filling up with an eclectic variety of arts and crafts shops. Very many of them sell stonecarvings, furniture and other non-packable items but there's some smaller stuff as well. See p.425 for details of the retail opportunities on offer in Mataram-Ampenan-Cakranegara-Sweta.

Listings

Airlines See p.416 for details of airlines which serve Lombok. Information on international airline offices in Bali is on p.111.

Boats Perama (☎0370/693007, ☎693009) operate a daily boat to Gili Trawangan (1hr 30min; Rp30,000). Bounty Cruise has an office in town (daily 8am–5pm; ☎0370/693666, ☎693678), from where free shuttle buses operate to Teluk Nara, where the *Bounty* docks. Kotasi (☎0370/693435) is the local co-operative for boat skippers as well as vehicle owners, so if you're interested in chartering a boat to the Gili Islands or for local fishing it's worth contacting them; charters cost Rp170,000–190,000 one-way, Rp300,000–340,000 return per ten-person boat, depending on destination. Taun (see p.431) is the nearest place from where to explore the islands off the southwest peninsula – Gili Nanggu, Gili Genting and Gili Tangkong: boat trips are advertised from Senggigi, but it takes at least 2hr by sea just to reach the islands.

Buses Lombok Mandiri (℡0370/693477) and Perama (℡0370/693007, ℱ693009) are among the companies that offer tourist shuttles to destinations on Bali and Lombok; they advertise all along the main street. See p.483 for details of Perama services.

Car and bike rental Plenty of places rent vehicles with and without drivers. Kotasi (℡0370/693435) is the local transport co-operative and has three counters, all marked on the map on p.433. Currently, car rental includes insurance (the maximum you'll pay in case of an accident is US$100), but check the deal at the time of renting. They have Suzuki Jimneys (Rp100,000/day), Kijangs (Rp150,000), motorbikes (Rp30,000–35,000 without insurance) and bicycles (Rp15,000); remember that the road north of Senggigi is extremely steep. Expect to pay around Rp50,000/day for a driver. It's worth shopping around at other travel agents. Chartering a vehicle, driver and fuel (from Kotasi, travel agents or street touts) costs Rp200,000–300,000/day all-in, depending on where you want to go.

Doctor Some of the luxury hotels have in-house doctors, including *Holiday Inn* ℡0370/693444, *Sheraton* ℡0370/693333 and *Senggigi Beach* ℡0370/693210. There's also a clinic (℡0370/693210, ℱ693200) near *Senggigi Beach Hotel* that operates a 24hr call-out service.

Exchange BCA and BNI banks both have central ATMs for Visa, MasterCard and Cirrus. There are exchange counters (daily 8.30am–7.30pm) every few yards on the main street.

Internet access Several internet cafés can be found along the main street (daily 8am–10pm; Rp300/min).

Phones A couple of wartels are in the centre; the one above Indah Photo is as good as any (daily 8am–11.30pm).

Post office In the centre of Senggigi (Mon–Thurs 8am–7.30pm, Fri & Sat 8am–7pm). Poste restante is available here (address: Post Office, Senggigi, Lombok 83355, West Nusa Tenggara).

Supermarkets Several in the centre. Pacific (daily 8.30am–9.30pm) has the biggest selection, but tends to be pricier than the others. Most sell basic food, drink, toiletries and stationery as well as postcards, souvenirs and a selection of books about Indonesia. The English-language *Jakarta Post* usually arrives in the afternoon.

Tour companies See box on pp.420–421 for information on the range of Lombok tours on offer, and contact details for operators. The upmarket hotels usually have tour desks on the premises and operators all have offices in town; check out a few as prices vary considerably, and make sure you know the exact itinerary and whether you're being quoted for the vehicle or per person.

The Gili Islands

Prized as unspoilt paradise islands by travellers in the 1980s, the **Gili Islands** – Gili Trawangan, Gili Meno and Gili Air – just off the northwest coast of Lombok, have developed rapidly to cope with crowds of visitors. Catering until recently almost exclusively for the inexpensive end of the market, with bamboo huts a few metres from the beach, the range of accommodation has now expanded considerably and there's something for every pocket and every level of comfort.

Strikingly beautiful, with glorious white-sand beaches lapped by warm, brilliant blue waters and circled by coral reefs hosting myriad species of fish, each of the islands has developed its own character. Of the three, **Gili Trawangan** best fits the image of "party island". With its large number of places to stay, many offering hot water and air-conditioning, wide range of excellent restaurants and regular nightlife, it attracts the liveliest visitors, although it's still fairly low-key.

If you want to get away from it all, head for the smallest of the islands, **Gili Meno**, which has absolutely no nightlife and not much accommodation, although a couple of more expensive hotels are sited here. Closest to the mainland, **Gili Air** offers a choice, with plenty of facilities in the south, and more peace and quiet the further round the coast you go. All the beaches are public. The local people are probably more used to seeing scantily clad Western women than in any other part of Lombok, but you should definitely cover up when you move away from the beach. All the islands have recently established seaweed farming in the shallows (see p.281).

Prices vary dramatically depending on the season and are probably more fluid than anywhere else on Bali or Lombok, being totally dependent on what the market will bear. A traditional bungalow costing Rp50,000 in February can cost Rp100,000 or more in July and August, hovering somewhere in between if the crowds arrive early or leave late in the year. In the peak season (July, Aug & Dec), prices can double throughout the islands.

Pemenang and Bangsal

The access port for the Gili Islands is **BANGSAL**, 25km north of Senggigi. It's a short cidomo ride or a shadeless 1500m walk from **PEMENANG**, 26km beyond the Ampenan-Mataram-Cakranegara-Sweta area. Pemanang is served by **bemos** or **buses** from Bertais terminal in Sweta. (All transport between Sweta and points around the north coast passes through Pemenang.) **From the airport**, turn left on the road at the front of the terminal, head straight on across the roundabout and 500m further on, at traffic lights on a crossroads, turn left and catch a public bus marked "Tanjung", which will drop you at Pemenang. **From Senggigi**, though, there's no public bemo service along the coastal road north to Pemenang; see below for details of the boat service from Senggigi direct to the islands. A gate at Bangsal stops all vehicles 500m from the harbour itself, so prepare to **walk** the final bit or bargain very hard with the drivers of the few cidomo that do ply up and down.

Bangsal has a few **restaurants**, some moneychangers, several travel agents and, should you need a **place to stay**, the losmen *Taman Sari* (no phone; ❶–❷), just by the gate where vehicles stop on the way to the harbour. They have clean accommodation opening onto a small, quiet garden, and all rooms have fan and an attached cold-water bathroom. There's an **internet** café next door (daily 6am–11pm; Rp300/min).

Sadly, Bangsal has developed a reputation as a place full of aggravation and **hassle** for tourists; there have even been punch-ups. Keep your cool: the Gilis are worth it.

The **ticket office** for all boats to the islands is right on the seafront at the end of the road; it's all pretty organized, and there's a printed price-list covering public boats, shuttles and charters. You should go directly there and buy your ticket, since there's no advantage in even considering the numerous touts along the road who'll try to persuade you to buy from them. It's also useful to know that, despite anything you might be told, everything on sale in Bangsal is also on sale on the Gili Islands. Ideally, you should travel light enough to get your own bag onto and off the boats; if you cannot manage this, you should negotiate with the porters before you let them touch the bags – and be clear whether you're talking about rupiah, dollars, for one bag or for the whole lot.

Boats to and from the Gili Islands

From Bangsal

Public boats leave Bangsal throughout the day, when full (7.30am–4.30pm; journey time 20–45min). **Shuttle boats** depart at 10am and 4.30pm. You can also **charter** a boat, for a maximum of ten people. Day-return trips are possible, as are trips taking in more than one island; enquire at the ticket office.

	To Gili Air	To Gili Meno	To Gili Trawangan
Public boat	Rp2800	Rp2800	Rp3000
Shuttle boat	Rp7000	Rp7500	Rp8000
Charter	Rp45,000	Rp55,000	Rp58,000

From Senggigi and elsewhere

From Senggigi, you can take the twice-daily Perama shuttle boat (Rp30,000; takes 1hr 30min). It's also possible to charter a boat to the Gili Islands from the Kotasi co-operative in Senggigi (see box on p.434): it's a great trip up the coast but the boats are small – you won't be able to travel if the winds and tides make the sea too rough. At both ends of all trips you'll get your feet wet, as the boats anchor in the shallows and you have to wade to and fro.

From Benoa or **Nusa Lembongan**, you can reach Gili Meno on the *Bounty* high-speed catamaran, which follows a circular route from Benoa to Nusa Lembongan, Teluk Nara (for Senggigi), Gili Meno, then back to Nusa Lembongan and Benoa (Sun, Tues, Thurs & Sat; takes 2–3hr; US$35 from Benoa or Nusa Lembongan to Gili Meno; ⑭www.balibountygroup.com). Book through travel agents or direct in Bali on ☎0361/733333, ℉730404. Due to current agreements with the Gili Island boat owners' co-operative, you can't use the *Bounty* for the short hop between Senggigi and Gili Meno.

Perama sells **tourist shuttle bus** tickets for the Gili Islands from all main tourist destinations on Lombok and Bali.

Returning to Lombok or Bali

The times, frequencies and fares on the **public boats** are the same for the return journey as for the outward-bound trip. **Shuttle boats** leave Gili Meno and Gili Trawangan at 8.15am and Gili Air at 8.30am; note there is only one departure a day. Several operators on the islands offer shuttle tickets direct to Lombok or Bali destinations; whichever operator you use, you'll have to walk from the port at Bangsal to the *Taman Sari* losmen near the gate on the main road, where you'll be collected by the tour operator. The Perama counter on Gili Trawangan (see p.450) has full details. It's worth noting that even if you're returning to Senggigi, there is no direct boat: you must go to Bangsal and proceed overland. The **Bounty** (see above) is a speedy, if pricey, way of getting back to Nusa Lembongan or Benoa; note that you can't use it to move from Gili Meno back to Senggigi.

Several agents on Gili Trawangan can book tickets on the *Bounty*, *Mabua Express* or *Osiania* (for route details, see p.483); prices usually include transfer to the relevant departure port (Lembar or Gili Meno).

From Bangsal, you can get **shuttle bus** tickets from any of the travel agents lining the road to all main Bali and Lombok destinations. There's also a fixed-price **taxi** service (to Mataram, Senggigi or the airport Rp50,000; Lembar Rp90,000; Senaru Rp100,000; Tetebatu Rp150,000; Kuta Rp170,000; Labuhan Lombok Rp200,000) – but you'll almost certainly get a better deal if you head for Pemenang and negotiate directly with the drivers to charter a bemo from there.

Island transport and practicalities

Prices are fixed if you wish to **charter** a boat on the islands: Rp55,000 each way between Gili Air or Gili Trawangan and Gili Meno, Rp60,000 between Gili Air and Gili Trawangan. Prices for a return trip are almost double the single price, and are clearly posted at the ticket offices on each of the islands.

None of the islands has a particular **crime** problem, although there have been reports of attacks on women during and after the parties on Gili Trawangan. Do take reasonable precautions (see p.450). Many of the sturdier bungalows feature locking drawers or cupboards for your valuables while you're on the beach. There are no **police** on the islands: it's the role of the kepala desa, the head man who looks after Gili Air (where he lives) and Gili Meno, and the *kepala kampung* on Gili Trawangan, to deal with any situation – although it seems that when problems do arise they are sometimes dealt with rather poorly. You should be taken to make a report to police on the mainland (at Tanjung or Ampenan).

Snorkelling and diving

The **snorkelling** and **diving** around the Gili Islands is some of the best and most accessible in Lombok. All the islands are fringed by **coral reefs** which slope down to a sandy bottom at around 25m, although there are some coral walls. Visibility is generally around 15m. The **fish** life here is the main attraction and includes white-tip and black-tip reef sharks, sea turtles, cuttlefish, moray eels, lobster, manta rays, Napoleon wrasse and bumphead parrotfish. There are good snorkelling spots just off the beaches of all the islands; most of the best dive sites involve short boat trips, for which operators will usually also take snorkellers.

Off the west coast of Trawangan, **Andy's Reef** and **Giant Clam**, named after a clam more than 1m long that inhabits the site, are both popular dives, while the **Soft Coral Garden** on the north coast is a drift dive with plenty of soft coral. On the east side of the island, the **Trawangan Slope**, reached from the beach, is only suitable for experienced divers, as the current can get strong. Around Gili Meno, the **Meno Wall** is the most popular dive site on the west side, with the **Meno Slope** further south and the **Cabbage Coral** patch off the northeast coast. Increasingly popular among experienced divers, **Takat Malang** and **Son of Takat Malang**, off the north coast of Gili Air, with depths of 16–35m, offer a range of features including an impressive natural amphitheatre and a high density of sharks.

There are **dive operations** on all the islands, most based on Gili Trawangan.

"Hopping island" boat service

The **"hopping island"** boat service between all three Gili Islands is extremely handy. It does one circuit, Air–Meno–Trawangan–Meno–Air, in the morning, and another in the afternoon. It's fast and conveniently timetabled, and so makes taking a day-trip to another island a feasible option. The **fare** for any one leg of the route is Rp7000; for a two-leg journey (Air–Trawangan), it's Rp8000.

Gili Air to Gili Meno Departs 8.30am & 3pm.
Gili Meno to Gili Trawangan Departs 8.45am & 3.15pm.
Gili Trawangan to Gili Meno Departs 9.30am & 3.30pm.
Gili Meno to Gili Air Departs 9.45am & 4.15pm.

In theory there's a price agreement, with operators charging identical rates; however, operators vary quite a lot and you should choose one carefully. If you're a qualified diver, expect to pay US$25 for one dive, and then $20 for further dives. "Discover Scuba" (the PADI Introductory course) and "Scuba Review" are both $50. A PADI Open Water course is $300; Advanced Open Water course $225; Rescue Diver $320; and Divemaster Internships $125 a week. Some operators are qualified to take people on the Instructor Development Course, which generally costs just over $1000, including books and the exam fee. Check at the time of booking whether the price includes equipment rental.

It's sensible to be especially careful over **safety precautions** out here. The nearest hospital is in Mataram and the nearest decompression chamber in Denpasar on Bali. Note, too, that **offshore currents** around the island are strong and can be hazardous. Dive operators are aware of this and on the alert. However, if you're snorkelling or swimming off the beach you're potentially at risk: it's easy to lose an awareness of your distance from shore, get carried out further than you intend and then be unable to get back. There has been at least one fatality in recent years, when a snorkeller drowned.

Gili Trawangan

GILI TRAWANGAN, the furthest island from the mainland and the largest, with a local population of 700, attracts the greatest number of visitors and has moved upmarket at meteoric speed. The southeast of the island is virtually wall-to-wall bungalows, restaurants and dive shops, although it still manages to be pretty low-key and relaxing. For quieter, less refined and less prettified surroundings, head to the laid-back northeast, northwest or southwest coasts. The island generator provides 24-hour electricity.

Until a few decades ago, Gili Trawangan was uninhabited. In the late 1800s it had been a penal colony for 350 Sasaks exiled here for rebelling against the raja of Lombok in 1891. Hunters came irregularly from Lombok for deer (now extinct). Then, in the 1970s, ten or twelve Bugis families from Sulawesi settled here, **tourists** gradually discovered the islands, and the new settlers built cottages and began to make a profit from their visitors. The government still retains ownership of a large part of the island; rumours periodically run rife about its plans but it looks increasingly unlikely that it'll interfere.

Island **transport** is by cidomo. Ask about renting bicycles at your guesthouse or the stall near the jetty; prices vary from Rp10,000 per hour to Rp10,000 per day – but so does the quality of the bike. Only a tiny section of road in the

The Gili Eco Trust

Despite a lot of visitors, the islands' reefs remain in fair condition. Unfortunately, though, plans to make permanent moorings to prevent damage from boat anchors have so far come to nothing. Fish dynamiting in the area has decreased considerably since the local people have begun seaweed farming, but the use of harpoons and the removal of shells from the reef are all destroying the marine environment further. Dive operators on Gili Trawangan have established the **Gili Eco Trust**, funded by all divers paying a one-off fee of Rp20,000. The aim is to extend this to the other islands and use the money to safeguard the local marine environment.

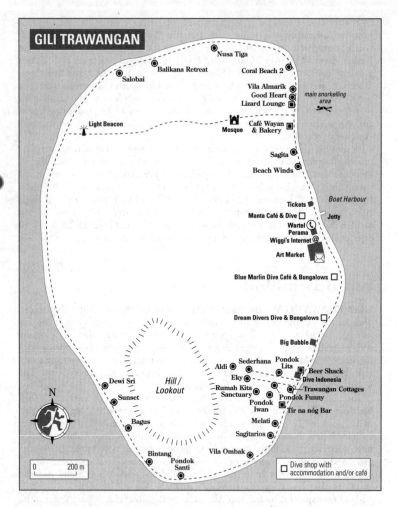

GILI TRAWANGAN

island's southeast corner is paved so be prepared for some sandy cycling: a decent bike does make the going easier.

A **walk** around the island, less than 3km long by 2km at the widest part, takes four hours or less. There's not much to see on the west side other than seaweed in the shallows, the occasional monitor lizard and the giant cacti, ixorea, eucalyptus and palms which survive throughout the dry season. Whether you're cycling or walking, take plenty of water; there's a stretch of coast (about 45min on foot) between *Salobai* in the north and *Dewi Sri* in the southwest where there's nowhere at all to get a drink. Inland, the 100-metre **hill** is the compulsory expedition at sunset – follow any of the tracks from the southern end of the island for views of Agung, Abang and Batur on Bali with the sky blazing behind.

Diving, snorkelling and watersports

The northern end of the east coast is very popular for **snorkelling**: most people hang out here during the day, ambling a few metres inland to the warung behind the beach when it gets too hot. Further around, to the south and north, you need to cross an expanse of rocks at low tide to get to the water. Enquire at the dive shops if you want to go out with one of the dive boats and snorkel further afield; it'll cost about US$10. Snorkel gear is available pretty much everywhere at around Rp10,000 per day; however, some of the more unscrupulous owners rent out extremely dodgy gear, blame you when it falls apart and demand you buy a replacement. You can buy good-quality gear on the island, for example in the Blue Marlin dive shop (mask $25, snorkel $5–10, slip-on fins $28).

Dive operators

Gili Trawangan has many resident **diving** instructors from overseas offering tuition and dive-guiding in all European languages, and dive shops with PADI materials in several languages. All the operators listed here offer dives for qualified divers and courses, and several have their own pools for the early stages of learning. They're all located close together in the southeast corner of the island, marked on the map opposite.

Big Bubble ☏0370/625020, ⓦwww.bigbubble diving.com. Small, friendly place with no groups bigger than four and often just two students per instructor on courses. They use the Dream Divers pool for the early stages of instruction. Schedules are flexible and there are evening activities in the dive shop; trips often end with a sunset drink.

Blue Marlin ☏0370/632424, ⓕ642286, ⓦwww.diveindo.com. A PADI Five Star IDC Dive Centre. There's a pool for early training on a full range of courses, including PADI IDC (Instructor Development Courses) as well as IANTD (International Association of Nitrox and Technical Divers) courses and Trimix instruction, up to the IANTD Instructor Training Course. Experienced divers on the IANTD courses get to visit the wreck of a pristine Japanese patrol boat, lying at 45m depth off the islands. They also have a Buddi Inspiration closed-circuit rebreather – quite new technology. They're currently researching and exploring wrecks off the Lombok coast as far afield as Bangko Bangko and have explored newer sites – Takat Tunang and Donyeng Wall – closer to Gili Trawangan where the coral is in very good condition. They're soon to launch a 48m traditional boat with liveaboard facitilities for Nitrox and Trimix diving as well as air.

Dive Indonesia ☏0370/642289, ⓕ642328, ⓔdeepblue@mataram.net.id. With an exceptionally enticing pool out front that is used for training, they offer the usual range of dives and courses up to Assistant Instructor level and have a busy restaurant as well, which gives this place an excellent atmosphere.

Dream Divers ☏0370/634496, ⓦwww .dreamdivers.com. A PADI Five Star IDC Centre offering German in addition to English and often other languages as well. They have a pool and offer the usual courses and dives for experienced divers. For those with more than fifty dives, they offer a two-day diving trip to southern Lombok, to experience intact coral at 30–40m depth, which attracts plenty of fish including schools of barracuda and hammerhead sharks.

Manta Diving ☏0370/643649, ⓦwww.manta -dive.com. Now under new British management but with local dive guides who are well known for their extensive local experience and knowledge. They offer dives for experienced divers and courses up to IDC level through their co-partners in Bali. The dive shop has a pleasant, laid-back atmosphere with plenty of hammocks to relax in; a new pool is planned out back.

Vila Ombak Diving Academy ☏0370/642336, ⓕ642337, ⓦwww.scubali.com. Another PADI Five Star centre. Don't be deterred by the location in one of the smartest hotels on the island – prices here are similar to those elsewhere, and they use the *Vila Ombak* pool for early training. Dives and courses offered up to IDC level through links with Bali Hai Diving Adventures in Bali. There are also very good value Dive and Stay packages on offer with *Vila Ombak*.

Watersports

There are a couple of **water sports** places to try. Manta Diving has a speedboat and offers waterskiing and wakeboarding ($40/hr); Blue Marlin do the same (Rp200,000 for 20min), as well as wakeboarding lessons (Rp400,000/hr) and courses (4 days $300; 14 days $800). Sea Kayak Adventures (☎0370/692003, ℉641609, ⓦwww.diveindo.com), attached to Blue Marlin, offers guided **kayaking** trips around the islands in single-person or two-seater kayaks ($45).

Accommodation

Traditional **accommodation**, which is now decreasing, is in bamboo and thatch bungalows on stilts, with simple furnishings, although all are fitted out with mosquito nets, a verandah and a concrete bathroom at the back with squat toilet and mandi. There are plenty of newer, bigger concrete and tile bungalows, more comfortably furnished, with fans and attached bathrooms (possibly including a Western-style toilet). The most upmarket places have hot water and air-conditioning, although only those at the very top of the scale pay much attention to ambience or luxury. *Vila Almarik, Vila Ombak* and *Salobai* provide the real hotel options; everything else is much simpler.

The north end of the island is relatively quiet, except for the mosque, while the bungalows at the southern end are livelier and closer to the restaurants and discos, though many lack views and sea breezes. There are also some pleasant, quiet developments around the southern tip and on to the west coast, but this beach is nothing special and you're a long walk from anything. A few simple, good-value places are springing up behind the warung on the northeast coast and in the village behind the main restaurant/guesthouse drag; alternatively, ask at local houses about rooms for rent.

Anyone visiting the island over a number of years will be aware that bright, gleaming new places very soon fade into dust, dirt and eventually squalor unless they are vigilantly maintained and, sadly, many of the places that were once bright and shiny now fall into that category. For that reason, it is worth keeping a keen eye out for **new places**, whether or not they're listed here: they're likely to be a good, clean bet.

Balikana Retreat ☎0370/622386, ⓦwww.balikanaretreat.com. Located in the quiet north of the island. Rooms are in two-storey buildings and have cold water and fan or air-con. A couple of rooms at the front have great sea views. ❻

Beach Winds ☎0812/376 4347. Best-quality bungalows on the northeast coast. Rooms are clean and tiled with fans, in a good location near the main snorkelling spots and five minutes' walk from the main restaurant area. ❹

Bintang No phone. A brilliant location on the quiet southern coast (a 15min walk to the restaurants) – although unless they get some maintenance soon the bungalows will be unacceptably rundown. All have a *lumbung*-style red-tiled roof, face the sea and there's a sitting area next to the beach. ❷

Blue Marlin ☎0370/632424, ℉642286, ⓔbmdc

Rat traps

When you inspect bungalows, particularly traditional ones, look under the beds. If there's a square of cardboard with food in the middle and something shiny around the edges, beware: this is a local **rat trap**. The idea is that the rat smells the food and, trying to get to it, runs into the extremely strong glue that's smeared around the food. The rat struggles pitifully and in vain, eventually collapsing into the glue. You'll be woken by the pathetic squeaking of the trapped animal which will be removed by a jubilant boy and done to death outside.

@mataram.wasantara.net.id. Bungalows behind the dive shop, with air-con and hot water. ❻

Coral Beach 2 ⓣ 0812/376 8534. A fair option in the northeast with simple, straightforward fan bungalows just behind the beach. ❷

Dewi Sri No phone, ⓔ sliehchelet@hotmail.com. Isolated place on the west coast, thirty minutes' walk from the main restaurant area. Some accommodation is in basic wood, bamboo and thatch bungalows but the newer, tiled rooms are the best ones in the area. Those at the front have excellent sea views and there's a good sitting area at the front. Nearby *Sunset* is quite basic but also worth a look. ❶–❷

Dive Indonesia ⓣ 0370/642289, ⓕ 642328, ⓔ deepblue@mataram.net.id. Located behind the dive shop and in the middle of the action in the southeast. Good-quality bungalows with hot water and air-con. ❼

Dream Divers ⓣ 0370/634496, ⓦ www .dreamdivers.com. Clean, tiled bungalows behind the dive shop in the main restaurant area. Cheaper rooms have fan and cold-water bathrooms while more expensive ones have air-con and hot water. ❹–❺

Good Heart ⓣ 0812/377 1842. Three very simple tiled rooms set back from the beach in the northeast. *Creative 2*, *Impian* and *Matahari* are nearby and of similar quality and style. ❷

Melati ⓣ 0370/642352. Decent bungalows with cold-water bathroom, fan, lockable cupboards and pleasant verandahs at the front. A fair choice, very close to the main restaurant area in the southeast. ❸

Nusa Tiga ⓣ 0370/643249. On the peaceful north coast, with traditional thatch and bamboo bungalows and more substantial concrete ones – all have seen better days. Some have sea views and there are *bale* in which to sit and admire the scenery. ❶–❷

Pondok Lita No phone. An excellent budget choice – a small family-run place, well tucked away in the village, about five minutes' walk from the beach; follow the track between Dive Indonesia and *Trawangan Cottages*. Rooms have fan and cold-water attached bathroom, set around a small garden. *Pondok Funny*, *Pondok Iwan* and *Aldi* are all close by, in the same vein. ❷

Pondok Santi No phone. Well-built traditional bungalows with a brick mandi, in a shaded location in a coconut grove near the sea in the south. A popular option as the bungalows have large verandahs, are set in a large garden and it's only a short walk (5min) to the main restaurant area. ❷

Rumah Kita Sanctuary No phone, ⓔ rumahkita99 @hotmail.com. Three bamboo and thatch bungalows in the village. They have fans and attached cold-water bathrooms, plus a pretty garden with plenty of spots to relax. ❸

Sagita ⓣ 0812/376 9580. Small family homestay with just three rooms with attached bathrooms (squat toilets), close to the snorkelling and a short walk to the main restaurant area. ❷

Sagitarios ⓣ 0370/642407. Bamboo and thatch rooms and bungalows, all with squat toilets in the attached bathrooms, in a huge garden at the southern end of the main restaurant area. The bungalows face seawards, which is rare for this part of the island. ❶–❷

Salobai ⓣ 0370/643152, ⓕ 643151. Well-built and pleasantly furnished bungalows (fan or air-con) across the track from the sea in the north, with a sunbathing area near the water. There's no pool. All rooms have cold water; the more expensive ones are better value. ❻–❼

Sederhana No phone. Another good village place; follow the track between Dive Indonesia and *Trawangan Cottages*. This is a row of four tiled cottages all with fan and attached cold-water bathroom. *Eky* (ⓣ 0370/623582) is just nearby with similar rooms. ❸

Sirwa Homestay One of several new places behind the warung on the northeast coast. This is a row of four concrete rooms, each with attached bathroom and a small verandah. ❷

Trawangan Cottages ⓣ 0370/637840. Two rows of clean, tiled good-quality cottages in the southeast corner. One set is further away from the beach along a track. All have fan and cold water and are a short walk to the beach, with plenty of restaurants nearby. ❹–❺

Vila Almarik ⓣ & ⓕ 0370/638520, ⓦ www.almarik.com. A hotel in the quiet northeast corner offering the best rooms on the island, set in an attractive garden, with air-con, hot water and stylish furnishings. The swimming pool is pretty (Rp25,000 for non-residents) and there's a sunbathing terrace near the beach. ❼

Vila Ombak ⓣ 0370/642336, ⓕ 642337, ⓦ www.hotelombak.com. Centrally located, stylishly designed place with some accommodation in two-storey *lumbung*-style places and some in bungalows. Accommodation has air-con but cold water only, although there's some fresh water for bathing. The garden is well laid out, the pool (Rp25,000 for non-residents) comes complete with waterfall and there's an attached spa. ❽

Eating, drinking and nightlife

The east coast is pretty much lined with **restaurants** and **warung**. Up in the northeastern part, simple warung provide cold drinks and simple, inexpensive Indo-Chinese food in basic surroundings, and are favourite hangouts in the middle of the day. The places in the southeast, from the jetty south, are more upmarket: furnishings are more attractive, menus larger and prices somewhat higher. Wherever you eat, the quality and variety of the food is very good and prices are reasonable, with **seafood** the best option; many places have the raw material laid out on ice at the beach. Many restaurants show videos (advertised daily); others have a strict no-video policy.

Beer Shack Attached to Dive Indonesia. Located right on the beachfront, with an excellent breakfast menu including croissants, Danish pastries, muffins and doughnuts. There are also plenty of main meals on offer later in the day, including salads, nachos and sausage and mash; main courses are Rp11,000–20,000. *The Sweet Shack* and *Seafood Shack* are nearby. Inexpensive to Moderate.

Blue Marlin Café Attached to the Blue Marlin dive shop. Either dine near the pool at the front or up in the two-storey building behind. The menu is large and food well-cooked and presented. All the usual favourites are there plus a selection of Thai food, hot-plates, baked potatoes, all-day breakfasts and weekly Indonesian buffets. Moderate.

Café Wayan and Bakery An island offshoot of the Ubud favourite – worth a visit for the bread, croissants, cinnamon rolls and other highly calorific but divine baked goods. Inexpensive to Moderate.

Lizard Lounge A large *bale* and small, attractive sitting area in the northeast. There's a mixture of Indonesian and Western main courses (Rp10,000–25,000) and a big breakfast menu, including a full English. Inexpensive to Moderate.

Salobai Huge two-storey entrance hall with the restaurant upstairs in a vast place shaped like a ship. It catches the breeze very well, has good coastal views and a menu of Indonesian and Western choices (main courses Rp21,500–27,000). A good place to stop on a walk around the island. Moderate.

Tír Na Nóg An extremely popular Irish bar with good beer, darts, daily movies and CNN news. There's an ambitious menu with plenty of barbecued seafood and Indonesian and Western food including steaks, lasagne, Irish stew and shepherd's pie (main courses Rp20,000–40,000), plus all-day breakfasts. The drinks list is equally large and includes Guinness in cans, draught Bintang and Carlsberg, and Irish whiskey. Outdoor *bale* all have individual TV screens and the sound system is good and loud.

Vila Ombak The island's most upmarket dining experience, with some tables on the outdoor terrace near the beach and some upstairs in the main two-storey building to sample the few Asian options, a large choice of pasta and pizza or some Western choices including lamb chops. There are also plenty of delightful desserts. The wine list is long, stretching to champagne (Rp750,000). Moderate to Expensive.

Nightlife

Gili Trawangan has long been renowned for its nightly **parties**, which last from roughly 11pm until 2 or 3am. Each night's venue is clearly advertised on flyers around the island; *Tír Na Nóg*, though, doesn't close until around 2am anyway, and has largely taken over as the late-night venue of choice. The Monday-night parties at *Blue Marlin* – featuring well-known European DJs – regularly attract hundreds of people from the islands and the mainland. Please note that, for reasons of **personal safety**, women should not leave these parties alone, even to go to the bathroom.

Listings

Boat and bus tickets The Perama office (daily 7am–9pm) is close to the jetty.

Exchange Moneychangers all along the main strip change cash and travellers' cheques; expect about ten percent less than on the mainland. As a last resort, the Blue Marlin dive centre can give a cash advance on a Visa card, but they charge ten percent commission plus the standard four percent Visa charge.

Internet Several places offer access (about Rp500/min; minimum 5min), including the wartel, which has the advantage of air-con, and *Wiggi's*

Internet next to the harbour. Long-stay regular users could try negotiating a discount.

Phones The wartel is open 24hr.

Post There's a postal agent in the art market.

Shopping Several shops sell and exchange secondhand books in European languages and there's a small, centrally located art market plus shops and stalls where you can buy everyday necessities.

Gili Meno

GILI MENO is a similar oval shape to Gili Trawangan, but much smaller – about 2km long and just over 1km wide. It's the most tranquil island of the three islands, with a local population of just 350 and no nightlife. There's no electricity generator; most places have their own, but operate them part-time only. Solo women travellers have reported that a few of the young men that hang around are unpleasantly persistent.

It takes a couple of hours to stroll around the island, which has a picturesque salt lake in the centre, surrounded by a few sets of salt-making paraphernalia (see p.479). The **Gili Meno Bird Park** (daily 9am–5pm; Rp30,000; Ⓦ www.balipvbgroup.com) is rather incongruously grand in the middle of the island; it has a huge aviary containing hornbills, parakeets, cockatoos, parrots, pelicans, flamingos and ibis, and there are tame deer and kangeroos to feed.

All boats arrive at the **harbour** on the east coast, apart from the *Bounty*, which sails from Bali four times weekly (see box on p.416) and docks at the jetty in the west. You can **change money** at *Gazebo* and *Casablanca*. There's a **wartel** (daily 7.30am–10pm) near the harbour, with **internet** access too (Rp750/min, minimum 5min), but phone lines aren't totally reliable. The wartel and ticket office at the harbour sell tickets for shuttle buses to destinations on Lombok and Bali.

GILI MENO

0   250 m

Karang Biru (Blue Coral)
Good Heart
Pondok Santai
Lami's
Pondok Meno
Café Sentiga
Salt lake
Casablanca
Royal Reef Resort
Bounty Resort
Gili Meno Bird Park
Blue Coral Dive
Fantastic Cottages
Boat harbour
Rawa Indah
Café Lumba-Lumba
Blue Marlin Dive
Mallia's Child
N
Tao Kombo
Biru Meno
Gazebo
Kontiki Cottages

The **snorkelling** is good all along the east coast. For **diving**, consult Blue Marlin Dive and Café – an offshoot of the Gili Trawangan setup – or Blue Coral (Ⓣ0370/632823), which also has a dive shop in Senggigi.

Accommodation

The range of **accommodation** is pretty wide, with several mid-range choices and one luxury place – most is spread along the east coast over a fairly small area. Most bungalows have their own generator for electricity, except one or two at the northern end, which is where you'll get the best budget value.

Biru Meno No phone. In a great location at the southern end of the island, ten minutes' walk from the harbour, with good-quality bamboo and thatch bungalows on a tile base, plus attached cold-water bathrooms. Electricity 7pm–midnight. ❸

Bounty Resort ☎0370/649090, ℱ641177, ℮gilimeno@indo.net.id. The plushest and most expensive place on the island, linked to the *Bounty* catamaran that serves the island. All bungalows have air-con but not hot water, and there's a big pool and other activities including a pool table. Electricity 24hr. ❽

Cafe Lumba-Lumba No phone; book through *Casablanca*. Three well-maintained, tiled bungalows on the isolated west coast, with the two at the front having excellent views to the sea. This is a great spot for the sunset. Electricity 5.30pm–midnight. ❸

Casablanca ☎0370/633847, ℱ642334, ℮lidyblanca@mataram.wasantara.net.id. Offering four standards of room set about 100m back from the beach with a pretty garden. Accommodation ranges from basic fan and cold-water rooms to large, well-furnished ones with air-con and hot water. There's a tiny pool and a pleasant restaurant. ❸–❻

Fantastic Cottages No phone. Two wood, thatch and bamboo bungalows with attached mandi with a squat toilet set back from the beach near the harbour. There are large verandahs for relaxing. *Rawa Indah* is nearby and similar. ❷

Gazebo ☎0370/635795. Ten attractive and comfortable bungalows set in a coconut grove, with air-con but no hot water. ❻

Karang Biru (Blue Coral) No phone. Quiet accommodation in an isolated location at the peaceful north end of the island. This is a row of

four traditional bungalows with attached bathrooms facing seawards. *Good Heart* is ten minutes' walk further around to the west, offering similar accommodation and equal isolation. ❷

Kontiki ☎0370/632824. Close to a good beach. Cheaper bungalows are bamboo and thatch, the more expensive ones better quality and tiled, with fans. Electricity all night. ❷–❹

Mallia's Child ☎0370/622007. Bamboo and thatch bungalows with attached bathroom in a good location near a fine beach. ❷

Pondok Meno ☎0370/643676. Traditional, very basic bungalows without electricity widely spaced in a shady garden, set slightly back from the beach towards the north of the island. ❶

Pondok Santai No phone. Traditional wood, thatch and bamboo bungalows facing seawards in a garden at the northern end of the island. The attached mandis have squat toilets. No electricity. ❶

Royal Reef Resort ☎0370/ 642340. Very close to the harbour, these wood, bamboo and thatch bungalows, set in a large garden, have fans and good verandahs to enjoy the sea views. Electricity in the evening. ❸

Tao' Kombo' ☎0812/360 6859, ℮tao_kombo@yahoo.com. Set in a shady spot about 200m behind the beach in the south, with a large bar and communal area. Three bungalows have excellent furnishings, attached bathroom, fan and a freshwater shower. Also has four *brugak* (open-sided sleeping platforms) with lockable cupboards, mattress, screen, mosquito net and shared bathrooms. In the future they hope to set up batik, art and music workshops involving local people and visitors. Electricity 6pm–midnight. *Brugak* ❶ Bungalows ❸

Eating and drinking

There are plenty of **places to eat**. Close to the harbour, *Blue Marlin Dive and Café* offers Western and Indonesian choices; the two-storey restaurant attached to *Mallia's Child* boasts an excellent pizza oven. Further south, the restaurant in front of *Kontiki* features pleasant beach views and a large menu of steak, seafood, rice and noodles. Further inland the restaurant at *Casablanca* is in an attractive open *bale* in a lovely garden, with a nearby fountain, and serves moderately priced Indonesian, seafood and Western options, plus plenty of daily specials. *Kafe Lumba-Lumba* and *Good Heart*, both on the west coast, have good food and equally fine views. A few beachside warung are springing up around the island: *Lami's*, north of *Pondok Meno* has great views across the water; and, further south, *Cafe Sentiga* also gets excellent breezes. All are inexpensive to moderately priced, but you have to eat early; they all stop serving by about 9.30pm.

Gili Air

Closest to the mainland, with a local population of one thousand – the largest of the three islands – **GILI AIR** stretches about 1500m in each direction. In terms of atmosphere, it sits somewhere between lively, social Gili Trawangan and peaceful Gili Meno. It takes a couple of hours to complete a circuit on foot, and there are great views across to Sira beach on the mainland. The conglomeration of restaurants and losmen on the southeast corner is where you'll find most of the action, and the **beach** here is the most popular, with good **snorkelling**. For snorkelling further afield, Abdi Fantastik takes boat trips (Rp160,000/day for up to four people).

Reefseekers (℡0370/641008, ℻641005, ⓦwww.reefseekers.net) is a highly regarded local **diving** company. They offer trips for experienced divers, a range of PADI courses up to IDC level and also give information for snorkellers. Reefseekers are particularly involved in conservation in the area and have established a small **turtle hatchery** for eggs they rescue from local markets, hatching them and then returning the turtles – green, hawksbill and Oliver Ridley, some of the most endangered species in the world – to the sea; they calculate they have a ninety percent survival rate and have so far released around eight hundred back into the wild. It's a great place to go and look around, and there's no admission charge (although donations to help with feeding costs are always welcome). Reefseekers also operates in Flores and can provide information on diving there (ⓦwww.angelisleflores.com). Other operators on the island include Dream Divers (℡0370/634547, ⓦwww.dreamdivers.com) and Blue Marlin (℡0370/634387, ℻643928, ⓦwww.diveindo.com), both well established on Gili Trawangan. All dive shops are marked on the map on p.454. Yan's Bookshop, also marked on the map on p.454, rents **bicycles** (Rp15,000 for 24 hours) and arranges **glass-bottomed boat trips** for Rp35,000 per person from 9.30am to 3pm for a minimum of four people.

There are plenty of **moneychangers** around the island. The **wartel** (daily 8am–10pm) is behind *Hotel Gili Indah* together with the Perama office (same hours; ℡0370/637816), where tourist shuttle tickets to destinations throughout Bali and Lombok can be booked. Postcards and stamps are available from the shops; mail gets taken to the mainland regularly by Perama. **Internet access** is at the wartel, St@rnet, and *Coconut Cottages* (Rp500–650/min).

Accommodation

You'll find a selection of good-value **accommodation**, with the quietest spots on the north and west coasts. It makes sense to engage a horse-cart to reach the more far-flung spots when you arrive with your bags. The island-wide electricity isn't very reliable so places with their own generators have a bit of an advantage when the cuts occur; keep a flashlight handy.

Abdi Fantastik No phone. In a great location looking seawards on the east coast; the wood and thatch bungalows are simple but well built, have fans and mosquito nets and offer sitting areas overlooking the water. ❷

Coconut Cottages ℡0370/635365, ⓦwww.coconuts-giliair.com. Widely-spaced bungalows in a great garden set back from the east coast, about 25min walk from the harbour. The bungalows are attractive and well maintained and

there are several standards of room, some with hot water. There's internet service, and tours can be arranged. ❷–❹

Gili Air Santay ℡0370/641022. Popular, good-quality cottages in a fine location, set slightly back from the east coast in a shady garden behind a coconut grove. The best ones face the sea. All have decent furnishings with attached tiled bathrooms with Western toilet. ❷

Gili Beach Inn No phone. Traditional bungalows

face the view and get a pleasant breeze on this part of the coast. Bungalows are simple and basic but there are *bale* for sitting and relaxing. ①–②

Gita Gili No phone. In a good location near the coast and convenient for the harbour, with thatch, wood and bamboo bungalows. More expensive ones are at the front and face the sea. The cheaper ones are smaller and further back. All have attached cold-water bathroom. ②

Gusung Indah No phone. Pleasantly located, close to the east coast, with some bungalows facing seaward and the better, larger ones behind. There are great *bale* to sit in and admire the view. Older and simpler than many on the island. ①–②

Hotel Gili Air ☎ & ℻ 0370/634435. The most upmarket option on the island, with air-con and hot water in the more expensive bungalows; cheaper ones are less good value. The swimming pool is fabulous. Negotiate large discounts when it's quiet. ⑥

Hotel Gili Indah ☎ & ℻ 0370/637328, ⓦ 202.159.75.163/gili. With a big compound near

the harbour, and several standards of bungalows (from fan and cold water to air-con and hot water). All are reasonably furnished and the ones at the front have good sea views. ⑤–⑥

Legend ☎ 0812/376 4552. Relaxed, popular spot on the northeast coast with *bale* to relax in near the beach. The bungalows are the usual, simple offering with attached cold-water bathroom. The attached warung holds weekly parties, ending at 2am. ①–②

Lombok Indah No phone. A good choice among the budget places on the mostly quiet northeast coast, set in a very pretty spot just behind the beach (be aware that the nearby *Legend* has weekly parties). There are simpler, more basic rooms at the front and better, larger places behind; all have attached cold-water bathroom. *Sandy Cottages* are just down the coast and are similar. ①–②

Lucky's ☎ 0812/376 8239. A good choice over on this side of the island (5–10min walk from the harbour). Rooms are simple but OK and there are

many *bale* to sit and relax in. ❷

Matahari No phone. Probably the best choice on the far northwest coast. The bungalows are slightly better quality than the ones nearby – but things can change. There are places to sit right beside the beach. Nearby options are *Pondok Pantai* and *Bunga*. ❶–❷

Nina No phone. Justifiably popular cottages reached by walking through *Corner Bungalows* in the southeast of the island. Bungalows are simple but good quality with attached bathroom with Western toilet. ❷

Nusa Tiga No phone. Traditionally built bungalows with Western toilets in the attached bathrooms and deep verandahs with hammocks for relaxing. A reasonable budget choice in this area. ❶

Pino No phone. Good bamboo, thatch and wood cottages in a neat garden just on the edge of the southeast corner. The best places have deep verandahs with hammocks and there are a few sitting places on the beach with brilliant views. You can also snorkel off the beach here. ❷

Pondok Gili Air Bungalows ☎0370/641014, @ sasaksavage@angelfire.com. Simple, pleasantly furnished bamboo, thatch and wood bungalows in the southeast corner of the island with attached mandi and squat toilet. *Bupatis* and *Resota*, nearby, are of similar style, quality and price. ❷

Safari No phone. Fan bungalows with attached bathrooms and deep verandahs in a lovely spot over on the west coast (5–10min walk from the harbour). Great views to Bali one way and the Lombok coast the other. ❷

Sunrise ☎0370/642370. Located behind Dream Divers on the southeast corner of the island. Accommodation is in two-storey *lumbung* barns with sitting areas upstairs and down. The ones at the front have excellent sea views. All have cold-water attached bathrooms. ❸

Eating, drinking and nightlife

There's a good range of **restaurants**, many of them attached to the accommodation. Most offer a range of Indonesian and Western food at inexpensive to moderate prices; plenty of places lay on Indonesian buffets – look for the flyers around the island.

The most popular places to hang out in the day are along the southeast coast, where all the restaurants have small *bale* on the beach: they're unbeatable for whiling away your time gazing across to Sira beach on the mainland and the foothills of Gunung Rinjani behind. *Sunrise Restaurant* is as fine as any, with a small good-value menu of Indonesian food (Rp6000–17,500), pizzas (Rp26,000–28,000) and steaks (up to Rp30,000). *Little Corner Beach Bar* is next door and just as acceptable; *Hans Café*, further north, is similar, and has a big *bale* inland. *Pondok Gili Air Café* has mostly vegetarian food (and you can refill mineral-water bottles), while *Il Pirata*, built in the shape of a pirate ship, has quality furnishings and a small Italian menu.

The most upmarket, imaginative dining experience on the island is the restaurant at *Coconut Cottages*, with seating in the main restaurant or in *bale* in the garden. It has appetizing and well-presented Western and local cuisine and seafood. **Sasak buffets** can be organized for a minimum of ten people: Sasak dishes include *gedang kelak santen* (green papaya soup with coconut milk), *pergadel kentang* (spicy potato and coconut cakes), *daging gape* (spicy beef stew with coconut) and *olah olah* (beans in coconut milk).

At the time of writing, **parties** were only permitted three times a week, alternating between *Hans Café* on Tuesday, *Legend Warung* on Wednesday and *Gogo* on Saturday (9 or 10pm until 2am). Enquire at your guesthouse about the current situation.

North Lombok

Dominated by the awesome volcanic mass of Gunung Rinjani and its neighbours, the villages in **north Lombok** nestle in the foothills of the mountains or perch along the black-sand coastline. The road from Pemenang to Bayan, Obel Obel and the east coast clings carefully to the shoreline, twisting and turning dramatically with the terrain; travel can be slow. With no major population centres, small villages are dotted throughout the area, inhabited mostly by **Sasak people**, many of whom adhere to the Wetu Telu version of Islam (see p.514).

Most tourists who come to the area either visit on a fast trip around the island or come to climb various parts of **Gunung Rinjani**, an easily arranged and extremely enjoyable adventure, although only possible in the dry season (May–Oct). However, the area offers plenty of comfortable places to stay and a clutch of attractive **waterfalls**, and its **traditional villages** are more interesting than any others on the island.

This area is easily accessible, with **buses** direct to Anyar from Bertais/Mandalika (Sweta) terminal in the west, or to Bayan from Labuhan Lombok in the east. The main advantage of having your own transport is to get to the Sembalun Lawang and Sembalun Bumbung valley more easily; there are daily buses to the valley from Aik Mel via Sapit (2–3hr) and from Kali Putih, but the services aren't frequent. You'll find very few **exchange** facilities after you leave Bangsal (see p.442).

The north coast road

From Pemenang (see p.442), the main coast road heads north. About 2km beyond the village, you'll reach a small road opposite the local school signed to Pantai Wisata Sira and Lombok Golf Kosaido Country Club. This leads a couple of kilometres to **SIRA**, the longest white-sand **beach** on Lombok. Glaringly beautiful, with palm trees swaying in the breeze and views across to Bangsal and the Gili Islands, it's still pretty much deserted, with no tourist facilities of any kind – at the moment. The entire area is slated for luxury hotel development, and just before you reach the beach a left turn brings you to Lombok Golf Kosaido Country Club (☎0370/640137, ⓕ640135, Ⓔsire-golf@mataram.wasantara.net.id), where incongruously smooth, verdant fairways and greens gleam between the coconut palms (green fees are US$80, excluding cart, shoe and club rental).

Just over 4km from Pemenang, a small asphalted road leads to **The Oberoi** (☎0370/638444, ⓕ632496, Ⓦwww.oberoihotels.com; ➒) – Lombok's most luxurious hotel and winner of several prestigious awards, which is located on the beach and benefits from lovely views. All the accommodation is tasteful and fabulously luxurious, with marble bathrooms featuring sunken baths and showers; published prices start at US$240, while villas with private swimming pool are $500. Service is superb. The hotel also offers **diving** excursions and PADI courses in its Beach Club, manicured grounds and a Banyan Tree **spa**. Several **restaurants** provide top-class, imaginative Western and Indonesian cuisine in gorgeous surroundings.

About 500m before you reach the hotel is *Medana Resort* (℡0370/628000, ℱ628100, ⓦwww.lombokmedana.com; ❼), with six well-furnished villas in an attractive garden, plus a pretty pool and sunbathing area. Accommodation is attractive and comfortable, and you can arrange sailing and glass-bottomed boat trips and rent snorkelling equipment. The beach is a few minutes' walk away along a path.

Tanjung and around

Back on the main road, 4km further east, **TANJUNG** is the largest settlement around the north coast. It's a pleasant, attractive market town with stalls overflowing with local produce, including blocks of local tobacco. The mountains of coconut husks everywhere are the remnants of coconut-oil extraction in the small processing machines that dot the area.

About 7km beyond, in the small village of **GONDANG**, *Suhadi Homestay* (℡0812/376 6668; ❶) comprises five rooms in a family house in an attractive spot. It's 300m from the main road but you'll only spot the small sign if you're coming from the west; turn seawards along the side of the huge, silver-domed mosque in the centre of the village. You pass a school on the right as the road passes fields; the homestay is in a small stand of trees on the right-hand side of the road, the beach about 400m further on. Slightly east of the centre, a sign to **Tiu Pupas waterfall** points inland, although it's slightly further than the 4km claimed. The track is very rough and narrow (only motorbikes can get through), and the area is a maze of confusing lanes. The falls are glorious, tumbling 40m down a semicircular sheer rock face into a deep pool. However, in the dry season (May–Nov), the water reduces to a trickle and the pool becomes a muddy puddle where local kids wallow and make mud castles. **Gangga waterfall** is a trek for the adventurous, about an hour's walk beyond Tiu Pupas; there are two paths – either ask the young man who looks after the visitors' book for directions, or engage him as guide. Gangga waterfall is also accessible from the turning 2km east of Gondang, which is signed to **Selelos waterfall**, 7km inland.

About 5km past Gondang in a hamlet called **MONTONG FAL**, *Montong Fal Homestay and Restaurant* (no phone; ❶) is up a steep path signed clearly from the road with fine coastal views. A few hundred metres further east the road turns inland; here, *Pondok Nusa Tiga* (no phone; ❶), comprises four rooms in a two-storey building with bathrooms just outside. The views from the verandahs are great and the upstairs rooms especially fine for catching the breeze. The owners can point you in the direction of the local waterfalls, coffee and cocoa plantations and traditional villages; fields of soya and peanuts and cashew orchards dot the landscape and the population is sparse. It's a twisty, hot 28km from here to Anyar.

Segenter, Anyar and around

Almost at the northern tip of the island, 4km west of Anyar, the traditional village of **SEGENTER** is signed 2km inland. Park just outside the gate of the fenced village and a guide will meet you; along with Senaru (see below), this is Lombok's most welcoming and interesting traditional village. Housing about sixty families, it's laid out on traditional lines with windowless houses in rows and an open *bale* between each pair of houses. The villagers grow maize, peanuts and cassava for their own consumption and cotton as a cash crop. You'll be taken inside one of the bamboo and thatch houses to see the eating platform, stone hearth and the *inan bale*, a small house-within-a-house where newly-weds spend their first night, but which is otherwise used to store rice.

At the end of the visit you'll be expected to make a **donation** to the village and sign the visitors' book.

The road from here to Anyar touches the coast here and there at pretty beaches lined with *jukung* but much of it passes inland through cashew orchards with great views across the lower slopes of Gunung Rinjani.

It's widely believed that the Majapahit prime minister, Gaja Made, landed at Labuhan Carik on the coast near **ANYAR** in the fourteenth century, although details of the Majapahit role on the island have largely been lost (see p.488). Today, it's a small, sleepy village with nothing to detain you. **Buses** from Bertais/Mandalika terminal in Sweta terminate at Anyar, from where **bemos** regularly ply to Ancak, Bayan and on to Batu Koq and Senaru. There are a few buses (morning only) that travel further east via Kali Putih to Labuhan Lombok, or you may have to travel by bemo to **ANCAK**, about 3km inland, to pick one up.

The small village of **BAYAN**, 5km south of Anyar, is generally accepted as the site of the **oldest mosque** on Lombok, said to date from before 1700. You can't enter the mosque, but even from outside it's very striking: a traditional bamboo and thatch building atop a stone and concrete circular citadel rising up in tiers. Many of Lombok's more orthodox Muslims are uncomfortable that this ancient symbol of their religion is located in an area dominated by the Wetu Telu religion (see p.514).

East of Bayan, the main road winds laboriously through the rolling foothills of Rinjani, offering many fine views of the volcano and then the hills to the east of the Sembalun valley. The extensive rice-fields of the Bayan area soon give way to a much drier, dusty terrain that continues almost 10km to the small junction at **KALI PUTIH**, with a few shops and some shady trees. From here, minibuses run to Sembalun Lawang, an alternative access-point for treks up Rinjani, and the main road continues for about 10km to Obel Obel and the east coast (see p.473).

Gunung Rinjani and around

Most of Lombok has been heavily deforested, but an extensive area of forest does remain on the slopes of the huge volcano **Gunung Rinjani** (3726m), and stretches for over 65km across the north of the island. From a distance, Rinjani – visible from Bali – appears to rise in solitary glory from the plains,

---

Gunung Rinjani National Park Project

The **Gunung Rinjani National Park Project**, started in 1999 with funding from New Zealand Official Development Assistance in conjunction with national and local government, aims to increase the involvement of the local community in managing the park and to reduce local poverty through sustainable development of human skills and resources. Early evidence of the project's impact include the Rinjani Trek Centre in Senaru, the Rinjani Information Centre and regeneration of handweaving in Sembalun Lawang, tourist maps and brochures, and organized trekking porter and guide arrangements. Clean-up campaigns of the park take place regularly, toilets and rubbish bins are planned for the trails, and radios for visitors have been introduced. Training of local people to act as guides and porters, of local women to show visitors around the villages, and courses in cookery and hygiene have already taken place. This is an ambitious project and its influence is likely to become even more apparent in future.

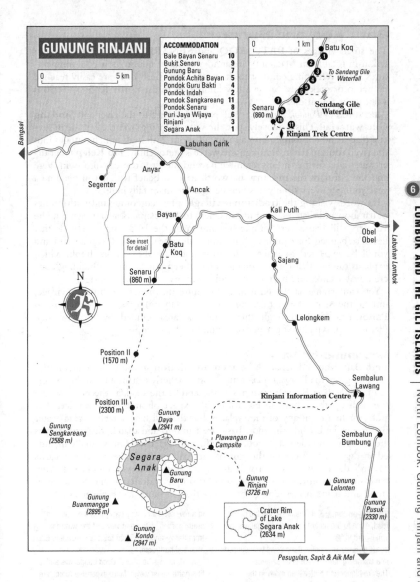

but in fact the entire area is a throng of bare and soaring summits, wreathed in dense forest. Invisible from below, the most breathtaking feature of the area is **Segara Anak**, the magnificent crater lake, measuring 8km by 6km.

The **climb** up Rinjani is the most energetic and, because of its sheer scale, the most rewarding trek on either Bali or Lombok. whether tackled independently or as part of a tour (see p.463). You can ascend from either **Senaru** or **Sembalun Lawang**.

Batu Koq and Senaru

The small villages of **BATU KOQ** and **SENARU**, south of Bayan (about 86km in total from Mataram), are at an altitude of 600m: their cool temperatures are in refreshing contrast to the north-coast heat. Both are easily reached by bemo or ojek from Anyar, a few kilometres to the north: Rp5000–6000 is a fair price for an ojek.

Just south of *Pondok Senaru*, a small path heads east to the river and **Sindang Gile waterfall**. This is a lovely spot, the water pouring over the hillside in several places and combining into a main fall about 25m high which plunges into the river. You can bathe, although the water is pretty chilly. **Tiu Kelep** is another waterfall a further hour's scramble beyond the first. You can also swim here and the effort of the trek may be worth it: local belief is that you become a year younger every time you swim behind the main falls here.

It's worth visiting the **traditional village**, a fenced compound with houses of bamboo and thatch set out in rows, next to *Bale Bayan Senaru* in Senaru. The villagers still live a very simple life and farm the land using methods that haven't changed for centuries. Someone will appear to show you around and you'll be expected to make a donation and sign the visitors' book, which explains the use that earlier donations have been put to, such as building concrete water tanks and paying for regular doctors' visits to the village.

You can arrange at the Rinjani Trek Centre (in the far south of the village, just at the start of the track up Gunung Rinjani) to go on the **Senaru Panorama Walk** through the immediate area, guided by local women (8am–noon; Rp45,000 per person; minimum two people).

Accommodation

Both Batu Koq and Senaru have **accommodation** spread for several kilometres along the road. *Segara Anak* is the most northerly (furthest from the mountain), while *Bale Bayan Senaru* lies at the end of the road, at the point where the path up the mountain begins. Don't expect phones, postal services, hot water or luxury in any of these places, but they all have attached cold-water bathrooms and, while the most basic are bamboo and thatch, the newer ones are concrete and tile with good, simple furnishings. Breakfast is usually included in the price. Places on the east of the road generally have the best views towards the mountain. Most will store your stuff while you climb, and many have small **restaurants** attached, serving simple Indonesian and Sasak meals (food and drink prices tend to be higher than in more accessible areas).

Bale Bayan Senaru No phone. At the top of the road, close to the mountain; basic bungalows in a small garden. ❶

Bukit Senaru No phone. Bungalows well spaced in a charming garden with good verandahs. They're bigger and better than many in the area, and have Western toilets. ❷

Gunung Baru No phone. Small set-up, not far from the start of the trail, with a few basic bungalows. ❶

Pondok Achita Bayan No phone. Good bungalows with verandahs both back and front for mountain and garden views. Cheaper ones have a squat toilet; newer, larger ones have a Western toilet. ❶

Pondok Guru Bakti No phone. Three bungalows

in a row set a long way back from the road in a pretty garden, with great views of the waterfall from the verandahs. Squat toilet and mandi in the attached bathroom. ❶

Pondok Indah No phone. Good bungalows and fine north-coast views. More expensive rooms are bigger, with Western toilets. ❶

Pondok Sangkareang No phone. A small row of rooms, as close to the start of the trail as it's possible to get, located in a small garden just above the Rinjani Trek Centre. ❶

Pondok Senaru ☎086812/104141. The biggest set-up, with a huge restaurant, offering good quality accommodation, all with great verandahs, set in a pretty garden with plenty of *bale* from which to admire the view. ❷–❸

Puri Jaya Wijaya No phone. Small place with verandahs overlooking the garden, rather than the great views behind. ❶

Rinjani No phone. Doesn't take advantage of the views, but the bungalows are adequate; ongoing renovation may improve things. ❶

Segara Anak No phone. The first place on the road from Bayan. There are stunning panaromas from the verandahs of the more expensive bungalows, while cheaper ones overlook the garden. There is one restaurant in the compound and a bigger one, with fine views, 100m up the road. ❶

Sembalun Lawang and Sembalun Bumbung

A steep, poorly surfaced road twists and turns 16km south from Kali Putih through several tiny villages to **SEMBALUN LAWANG**, set in countryside that is unique in Lombok – a high, flat-bottomed mountain valley virtually surrounded by hills. It's said locally that the people of this area are directly descended from the Majapahit dynasty of Java; today, though, it's Lombok's **garlic** capital – during the harvest in September and October the smell pervades the entire area. There has recently been a rennaisance of **handweaving** in the village; textiles are on show at the Rinjani Information Centre. They can point you in the direction of the weavers' homes to see work in progress (or you can look out for signs in the centre of the village). There's only one **place to stay** – *Pondok Sembalun* (no phone; ❶), which has simple rooms in a small garden just off the main road, marked by a large gate at the start of the Rinjani trail next to the Rinjani Information Centre.

South of the village is a vast, fertile plain crisscrossed by an intricate patchwork of fields and vegetable gardens. The valley closes in, the mountain walls rising steeply on all sides, apparently impenetrably. Some 4km south of Sembalun Lawang is **SEMBALUN BUMBUNG**, an attractive village with houses clustered around the local mosque in the shadows of the surrounding mountains. At the far southern end of the village, *Paer Doe* (no phone; ❶) is a tiny **homestay** with basic rooms. They can help you arrange your Rinjani trek (Rp800,000 for two people for the three-day/two-night trip to the summit) although it's probably more straightforward to do this in Senaru.

From Sembalun Bumbung, the mountain road winds for 15km across Gunung Pusuk to Pesugulan, and on to Sapit (see p.470). This road is prone to closure due to landslips; you should check on its status before heading out. There's daily **public transport** (although rather infrequent) from Kali Putih to the valley, and daily buses north from Aik Mel via Sapit, depending on road conditions.

Climbing Gunung Rinjani

The **summit of Rinjani**, the highest point of the region's volcanic mountainous mass, is reached by relatively few trekkers; the majority are satisfied with a shorter, less arduous trip to the **crater rim** – from where you can see the beautiful turquoise lake, **Segara Anak** (Child of the Sea) inside the massive crater, and the small perfect cone of **Gunung Baru** (New Mountain) rising on the far side. The lake is considered to be the abode of the gods and becomes a place of worship for the Wetu Telu people on the nights of the full moon; Balinese people come here during their Pekelem festival, which takes place during the full moon of the fifth Balinese month, to make offerings – often of gold – to the lake.

Having lain dormant since 1906, Gunung Baru **erupted** in August 1994, closing the mountain for several weeks and raising fears of a major disaster. Gunung Rinjani itself has been inactive since 1901, although it puffed a bit of smoke in 1944 and 1951. Fortunately all has gone quiet again but the mountain should be treated with respect, and the weather here is notoriously unpredictable. **Trekking** on the mountain is not for the frail or unfit and shouldn't be attempted without adequate food and water. Although not all the treks need a porter or guide, you should definitely let somebody know where you're going and when you'll be back; you can report to the Rinjani Trek Centres at Senaru and Sembalun Lawang when you set off.

Routes

The shortest trek is **from Senaru**, climbing to the **crater rim**. At the Rinjani Trek Centre, at the start of the track, you pay Rp25,000 for **admission** to the national park, and register. The route takes you from the start of the trek at the top of the village at 600m (marked on some maps as **Position I**), up through the forest to further **rest positions** (*plawangan*) with small *bale*; beware the extremely precocious monkeys at the *bale*, who will rifle through your stuff and take what they want. **Position II** is at 1550m and **Position III** at 1950m; you then leave the forest for the steep slog up to the rim at 2600m. Most people take six to seven hours (or more), not allowing for rests, to get to the rim from Senaru; unless you're extremely fit and fast, you won't be able to get to the rim and back in a day. A tent is preferable to sleeping in the *bale*, and is vital if you plan to sleep on the crater rim.

A further possibility after climbing to the rim is to descend into the crater to **the lake**, at 2050m. The path into the crater (1hr 30min) is very steep and rather frightening at the top, but gets better further down. You can bathe in the warm water of the lake or the hot springs along its shores; the best known is the Goa Susu (Cave of Milk), named for the white colour of the water. Most people get down to the lake in one day from Senaru, spend the night by the shore and return the same way the following day.

From the lake it's possible to climb out on a different path to a site called **Plawangan II** at 2900m, and from there up to the **summit** of Rinjani. This is at least a seven-hour trek in total, for which you'll need a guide. You should try to get to the summit for sunrise or by about 7am, as it clouds over and gets very windy by 9am.

A shorter route to Plawangan II and then to the summit is to climb **from Sembalun Lawang** on the east side of the mountain starting under a large archway in the village next to the Rinjani Information Centre and passing *Pondok Sembalun*. This takes around seven hours to Plawangan II (where you'll overnight) and then another three hours-plus to get to the summit the next morning.

The most complete exploration of the mountain involves a round-trip, ascending from either Senaru or Sembalun Lawang, taking in the summit and the lake, and descending to the other. The Rinjani Information Centre in Sembalun Lawang provides information, porters and guides for treks from that side of the mountain, with options and prices fixed the same as in Senaru; alternatively, you can make arrangements at the Rinjani Trek Centre in Senaru.

Rinjani practicalities

If you're climbing from Senaru to the rim or down to the lake you don't need a **guide**, although a **porter** is a great advantage. The path leaves to the left just beyond *Bale Bayan Senaru* in Senaru, and is difficult to lose. From Sembalun Lawang the route is straightforward up to Plawangan II, but you should check in the village about conditions. To climb to the **summit**, you'll need a guide and – unless you're terribly fit – a porter to carry your gear, cook your food and pitch your tent. There is spring **water** at Positions II and III from the Senaru side during and just after the rainy season, and also around the lakeshore, but you should check on this locally before setting out. It's vital to carry adequate **food and water** for the climb.

Typically, there are four options on offer: **one-night/two-day trips** to the crater rim; **two-night/three-day trips** to the rim and the lake, or to the summit (to and from Sembalun Lawang); and **three-night/four-day trips** to the summit (up from Sembalun Lawang, down to the lake and ending at Senaru).

Prices are fixed and clearly displayed throughout Senaru village and at the **Rinjani Trek Centre** (daily 7am–5pm), which should be your first port of call in arranging a trek from here. Prices depend on the trek you want to do and the number of people in the group, and include equipment, transport to and from Sembalun Lawang (if necessary), porters and food. In addition there's a new radio communication system in operation; it costs Rp10,000 to rent radio equipment for one trek.

Trip	Alone	Per person in a group of 5
Rim (two-day)	Rp600,000	Rp250,000
Lake (three-day)	Rp700,000	Rp300,000
Summit (three-day)	Rp800,000	Rp400,000
Summit (four-day)	Rp950,000	Rp500,000

All-inclusive Rinjani trips

Although it's easy to go to Senaru or Batu Koq and arrange your own climb up Rinjani from there, many companies on Lombok arrange **inclusive trips** to climb the mountain – useful if time is short but quite expensive. Prices include transport in both directions, guides, porters, accommodation, food and equipment, but costs vary according to the size of your group: the more people you have, the cheaper it becomes. Don't forget that, allowing for the guide and porters, you could end up climbing in quite a crowd. It pays to shop around between operators.

Coconut Cottages Gili Air ☎0370/635365, ⊛www.coconuts-giliair.com. Offers all four trips: Rp550,000 per person for the shortest (one night/two days), up to Rp800,000 per person for the longest trip to the peak.
Kotasi Senggigi ☎0370/693435. From US$50 per person for the short trek, up to $100 per person for the four-day/three-night trip. Minimum numbers apply.
Lombok Mandiri Opposite *Asmara Restaurant*, Senggigi ☎0370/693477. Prices for the various trips are Rp600,000, Rp700,000 or Rp800,000 per person, depending on duration. Minimum numbers apply.

Lotus Asia Tours Jl Raya Senggigi 1g, Ampenan ☎0370/636781, ⊕622344, ⊛www.lotusasiatours.com. Offers the longer trips. Contact them directly for prices.
Mahligai Senggigi Square B.09, Senggigi ☎ & ⊕0370/693139. Trips for groups of one to nine people. One person pays US$125 in a group of six for the two-day/one-night programme, or $365 alone on the longest trip to and from the summit.
Nominasi Senggigi ☎0370/693690. The short-duration trip costs US$130 alone, or $60 in a group of six or more; medium-duration $170/100; long-duration $200/125.

Central Lombok

The broad corridor of **central Lombok**, stretching from west to east coast between, to the north, the towering mass of Gunung Rinjani and its neighbours, and, to the south, the lower range of coastal hills, is the densely populated agricultural heartland of the island. It's here that you'll see typically Indonesian rice terraces in the southern foothills of the soaring volcanoes.

Stretching for 74km from Ampenan-Mataram-Cakranegara-Sweta to Labuhan Lombok, the main road across the island is the nearest thing to a highway that you'll find, and passes close to many of the most attractive destinations. Some small-scale tourist facilities have developed in the hills to cater for visitors in search of cool relaxation: the accommodation in the small village of **Tetebatu** and, to a lesser extent, in **Sapit**, is becoming increasingly popular, set high enough in the hills to be cool and situated to make the most of the local scenery. Down on the plains, **Lendang Nangka** has become something of a pilgrimage for travellers seeking the "real" village experience. The culturally minded make stops at Hindu sites at **Narmada**, **Pura Lingsar** and **Suranadi**, while the craft villages dotted throughout the area offer the chance to see potters, weavers and blacksmiths at work.

Reasonably well served by **bemos and buses**, much of the centre is accessible without your own transport. Note that there are very few moneychangers east of Sweta.

Narmada and around

Built in 1805 by the raja of Mataram, Anak Gede Karangasem, the gardens of **Taman Narmada** (daily 7am–6.30pm; Rp1000, swimming Rp1000), served by frequent bemos from Bertais/Mandalika terminal in Sweta (just 10km west), include a rather indistinct replica of Gunung Rinjani and its crater lake, made for the raja when he became too old to climb the real volcano to make his offering to the gods. More cynical commentators claim that he built the lake here to lure local women to bathe while he sat in his pavilion and watched.

The gardens lie on the south side of the main road in **NARMADA**, opposite the bemo terminal and daily market (well worth a look if you're there early in the day) and surrounded by a high wall; they're popular as a day-trip from the city for local families, while most tourists see it as a quick stop on an organized tour. However, if you have more time, this is a good place to laze around, especially if you go early before the tour groups descend. The terraces and the lake are extensive and well maintained, and there's a swimming pool as well as paddle-boats for rent. The Balinese temple here, **Pura Kalasa**, is the focus of the celebration of Pujawali (usually in Nov or Dec), when offerings of ducks are made to the lake. The aqueduct at the side of the lake is one of the few remnants of Dutch development on the island during their period of occupation (1894–1942).

Pura Lingsar

A few kilometres north of Narmada and easily reached by bemo from there, **Pura Lingsar** (daily 7am–6pm; admission by donation) was built around 1714 and then rebuilt in 1874. The complex is large, with a couple of lily ponds in the outer courtyards, and is a favourite local fishing spot in the evenings. Interestingly, this temple is a focus of worship for the Hindu religion and a place of worship for followers of Islam – including the Wetu Telu adherents on the island (see p.514). The furthest north, and highest, courtyard is the Hindu one guarded by fierce monsters at the *candi bentar*, while the Wetu Telu area has a pond overlooked by a vivid statue of Wisnu, home to some well-fed eels which emerge for hard-boiled eggs brought by devotees. The Pujawali festival is also celebrated here (Nov or Dec), and is followed by a mock battle between Hindus and Muslims throwing *ketupat* (rice wrapped in leaves) at each other.

This is a rural spot and not many tourists stay, but there is **accommodation**. About 1km west of the turning to the temple on the back road from Narmada to Cakranegara is *Puri Lingsar Homestay* (☎0370/671652; ❶), a small row of bungalows set back from the road in a pretty garden. Some 500m beyond the turning to the temple, *Losmen Ida* (☎0812/375 2083; ❶) is newer and has clean, tiled rooms set quite close to the road with attached mandi and squat toilet.

Karang Bayan

Selling itself as a "traditional village", **KARANG BAYAN**, 3km north of the main cross-island road, is easily accessible from Narmada or Lingsar with your own transport. It's a jumble of old wooden houses and newer concrete ones laid out on either side of a main path. While firmly on the tourist trail for day-trippers (one old house sports doors supposedly three hundred years old and a range of items used in local rituals), it actually has little to offer apart from the boxes woven by villagers out of fine grass. There are more picturesque villages elsewhere, where you'll see people living more obviously traditional lives.

Suranadi

Situated about 300m above sea level, **SURANADI** is 7km north of Narmada at the site of a freshwater spring. The temple here, **Pura Suranadi**, is a holy pilgrimage site for Hindus: the Hindu saint Nirartha is believed to have located the springs while in a trance. Almost next to the temple is a small forest area, the **Hutan Wisata Suranadi**, housing a pair of elephants – the male called Rinjani and the female Senggigi – given to Lombok by the government on the fiftieth anniversary of independence. They're the only elephants on the island and, having come from the famous Way Kambas elephant training school in southern Sumatra, are able to perform tricks, play football and give rides.

Suranadi Hotel (☎0370/636411, ℱ635630; ❷–❹) has **accommodation** in an old colonial bungalow with high ceilings, situated above a swimming pool (non-residents Rp2500). It's rather overpriced, however, with shared bathrooms for the cheaper rooms, although the top-end bungalows are attractive (and have hot water). Meals in the attached **restaurant** are moderately priced. Far better value is available in *Teratai Cottages* (☎081/836 0642; ❷–❸), 1km outside the village in a great rural location; take the road between Pura Suranadi and *Suranadi Hotel*. Accommodation is in cottages in a large garden with a pool and terrace, boasting fabulous views.

In a completely different league, the *GEC Rinjani Country Club* (☎0370/633488, ℱ633839, ⓦwww.lombokgolf.com; ❼), also known as *Padang Golf*, sits about 1km from the main cross-island road at Golong (there's a sign at Sedau, 5km east of Narmada), or about 3km by the back road from Suranadi. All accommodation is excellent quality (hot water and air-con), and there are tennis courts and a large swimming pool (Rp10,000 for non-residents). This is one of only two **golf courses** on the island (18-hole). Green fees are US$40 during the week, $60 at weekends, and there's a $10 caddy fee; guests get thirty percent discount. Clubs (Rp50,000) and shoes (Rp20,000) are available for rent. Prices exclude fifteen percent tax and service. Advance reservation is required.

Seseot

If you have your own transport, you can reach the attractive village of **SESEOT** from Suranadi. Head up the road that goes past the Hutan Wisata Suranadi, turn right at the T-junction and continue uphill. About 2km along here, just before the tiny hamlet of Gontoran, *Surya Homestay* (no phone; ❷) has a couple of rooms in a small replica *lumbung* barn. At the time of writing there was no sign, although it was open; ask in the village, most people know it. After another 3km you'll reach Seseot itself, where the presence of a temple as well as a mosque testifies to the mixed religion of this small but bustling village in the hills. For the casual visitor it's the situation next to the river that's the draw, with good views across the fields and plenty of places for a quiet picnic beside the river – either follow the path beside the mosque down to the river or cross the rickety road bridge at the top of the village to the other side.

Tetebatu and around

TETEBATU is situated on the southern slopes of Gunung Rinjani, 50km from Sweta (11km north of the main cross-island road), and surrounded by some of the most picturesque scenery in Lombok, with stunning views across verdant rice-paddies to the volcano. At an altitude of 400m, the area is high enough to be a cool relief from the heat of the plains, but not unpleasantly cold. Sculpted, terraced fields are lush with rice in the rainy season and tobacco in the dry. It's an excellent base from which to explore the centre of the island or simply relax for a few days – quiet, but developing rapidly as a tourist centre.

On public transport, get off the **bemo** or **bus** at Pomotong on the main road and either take an ojek straight up to Tetebatu or a bemo to Kotaraja and then a cidomo on to Tetebatu. Alternatively, you can reach Tetebatu by Perama tourist shuttle bus from many places on Bali and Lombok; see Travel details on p.483 for details but be aware that stopovers are needed on several journeys.

From Tetebatu, you can explore nearby waterfalls and craft villages: the *Green Orry* (see below) rents motorcycles (Rp35,000–40,000/day), and can arrange a guide for a trek through the fields to a local waterfall (Rp75,000 for 5hr). They can also supply **charter transport** to other Lombok destinations: sample prices are Rp100,000 to Senggigi or Labuhan Lombok, Rp150,000 to Kuta or Bangsal, Rp200,000 to Senaru.

The village has a **moneychanger**, a Perama agent (requiring one-day advance bookings), transport rental and a **wartel**, just above the *Salabuse* restaurant on the road up to *Wisma Soedjono*.

Accommodation and eating

Accommodation is mostly on the main road leading up to the *Wisma Soedjono* from Kotaraja and the road off to the east, Waterfall Street, but there are now some further-flung options. All have **restaurants** attached, although a few simple restaurants have also sprung up in the area, serving the usual inexpensive to moderately priced Indo-Chinese and travellers' fare, plus some Sasak options. *Warung Harmony* and *Salabuse*, on the main road are both worth a try.

At the time of writing phones were being installed in the area; some but not all of the accommodation places had them.

Cendrawasih ☎0376/22783. Accommodation here, in the downstairs part of four two-storey traditional *lumbung*-style barns, is some of the most attractive in the area; it's set in a great garden on Waterfall Street, and has a thatched restaurant. ❷

Green Orry ☎0376/22782, ℻23233. Traditional and modern tiled bungalows in a pleasant compound, plus a restaurant on Waterfall Street. Rooms are clean and well maintained. Plans to introduce hot water will increase prices. Guests receive a map of the local area to help exploration. This place also serves as the local Perama agent, has motorbikes for rent, can arrange a guide for local treks and charter transport. ❶–❷

Hakiki No phone. Set in the middle of paddy-fields at the eastern end of Waterfall Street, accommodation is in two-storey traditional barns with excellent verandahs upstairs and down. There's a great view of Gunung Rinjani from here; the restaurant and sitting areas make the most of it. ❶–❷

Mekarsari No phone. In a pleasant location in the fields behind *Pondok Tetebatu*, this is a small place with accommodation in brick bungalows. The turning is opposite *Pondok Tani* restaurant. ❶–❷

Nirwana Cottages and Restaurant No phone. Some 200m off Waterfall Street: two brick and thatch cottages which have verandahs facing brilliant views of Rinjani. ❷

Pondok Bulan ☎0376/22781. Located on Waterfall Street, close to the rice-fields with good views south, there are traditional bamboo and thatch *lumbung*-style bungalows as well as bigger, less traditional family rooms which are more expensive. ❶–❷

Pondok Tetebatu No phone. Tiled rooms on the main road leading up to the *Wisma Soedjono*, with good verandahs looking onto a lovely garden and a restaurant with fine views. ❶–❷

Rambutan No phone. The ultimate getaway – 400m along a rough but passable track in Kembang Kuning, with traditional bungalows of various designs in the middle of a rambutan orchard. There's a nearby spot for river-washing. It's probably best to come and check it's still open before hauling a lot of gear out here. ❶–❷

Tetebatu Homestay No phone. Around 2km from the Kotoraja–Tetebatu road in the hamlet of Penyonggok; the turning is signed a few hundred metres south of the junction with Waterfall Street. This is about as rural as it gets – just a couple of small rooms in a family compound. ❶

Wisma Soedjono ☎0818/544265, ℻0376/22522. This old house used to be the home of Dr Soedjono, the first doctor in eastern Lombok, and is still owned by his family. It offers a range of accommodation set in great grounds at the far north end of the village and is the most upmarket option in the area. Cheaper rooms are basic but have attractive verandahs; the more expensive ones provide excellent views and hot water. There's a moderately priced restaurant and a swimming pool. ❶–❸

Jukut and Joben waterfalls

With your own transport you can follow the road east from Tetebatu to **KEMBANG KUNING**, from where it's a six-kilometre steady climb to **Jukut waterfall** (Rp1500, parking Rp500). You have to complete the last couple of

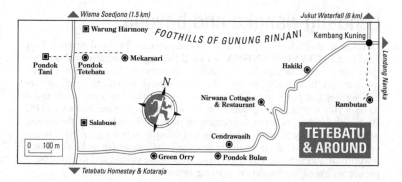

kilometres on foot, along a steep path with little shade, so you should take drinking water. The waterfall is magnificent, as the water pours over a sheer cliff about 20m high into a circular pool dammed by a jumble of large boulders and surrounded on all sides by towering walls covered in undergrowth. It's cool and shady even in the heat of the day, you can picnic near the river, and during the week it's fairly quiet. Talk to local people about the advisability of setting off alone for a trek up here, as there have been one or two recent reports of robberies. From Kembang Kunung, a seven-kilometre back road leads to Lendang Nangka.

Northwest of Tetebatu, **Joben waterfall** (Rp300), also known as Otak Kokok Gading, is not really worth the effort: the water falls only a short distance and is fed into an open-air shower block. It's believed locally, however, that this is a sacred place and that the water will turn cloudy if you're ill. The area around the waterfall is crowded with stalls selling shampoo, but it's littered with rubbish and is not the place for a peaceful swim.

Kotaraja, Loyok and Rungkang

The village of **KOTARAJA**, 5km south of Tetebatu, is something of a local transport hub. The name means "City of Kings" and relates back to ancient times when the kingdom of Langko fell to Balinese invaders and the royal family fled here. The area is known for its blacksmiths, but you'll have to ask for directions and come early to see them at work. The Kartika Art Shop, 100m beyond the crossroads on the way to Tetebatu, is the local postal agent; it has a small restaurant and a range of crafts for sale. There's a moneychanger next door. Slightly closer to the main junction, *Renjana Restaurant* offers a basic, inexpensive Indonesian menu. From time to time, Kotaraja is the setting for the traditional *peresehan*, fights in which male opponents attack each other with long rattan canes with only buffalo-skin shields to defend themselves. If you're anywhere in the area when this is due to take place, you'll hear about it.

A centre for bamboo basketware, **LOYOK** is just a few kilometres south of Kotaraja. Several handicraft shops here sell a range of local goods including bags, lamps and boxes, and even the children plait basketware as they walk along the road. Tereng Gading, in the village, has an excellent range in all styles and sizes.

Pottery is produced at **RUNGKANG**, just east of Loyok. Head for the Frisna workshop to see the pots being moulded over stones and beaten into shape with a flat stick. Made from the local grey clay, the pots turn an attractive mottled orange-black colour when fired, and are surprisingly light.

Lendang Nangka and beyond

Developed single-handedly as a tourist destination by local teacher Haji Radiah, **LENDANG NANGKA** is a small farming community of about two thousand people, 2km north of the main cross-island road, and served by cidomo and ojek from Bagik Bontong. The area around the village is rich in natural springs, but pressure on the land is huge and many villagers have moved to Irian Jaya as part of the government's *transmigrasi* policy (see box on p.500). Although the scenery is not as dramatic or picturesque as Tetebatu, the atmosphere in the village is more welcoming and friendly. This is a great place to see what Lombok life is all about and to practise your Indonesian or Sasak. There's a wealth of walks through the rice-fields around the village, and the local people are well used to strangers wandering around.

Established in 1983, *Radiah's Homestay* (no phone; ❷ ; includes three meals and tea or coffee), the original **accommodation** in the area, is a homestay in the real sense of the word. It's right in the middle of the village, but tucked away behind the school, so ask for directions. You can either stay in rooms in the family compound or in larger, newer rooms in a house in the local fields. It's a real delight to be part of a household for a while and a rare opportunity to come into contact with Sasak women, as most of the women who work in tourism in Lombok are Balinese. Many visitors enjoy an afternoon walk in the area with Radiah. Sannah, Radiah's wife, cooks traditional Sasak food and she's used to visitors in the kitchen learning recipes. There's a great *bale* in the garden where you can while away a few hours. You get a map with plenty of suggestions for local excursions and Radiah's nephew is also a Perama agent; you must book with him the day before you want to travel.

An alternative is *Pondok Bambu* (no phone; ❷ ; includes three meals), 500m north of Lendang Nangka and signed from the road that leads to Kembang Kuning. It may be a bit hard to find but the local ojek drivers know it. Its simple accommodation is in a family compound with a quiet, pleasant garden setting surrounded by fields.

Penakak and around

Further east, but not easy to find, the hamlet of **PENAKAK** lies just off the main road, 1500m east of the magical domes, spires and towering minarets of the bold new mosque, Masjid Jamal Ak'bar, on the main cross-island road in the centre of **Masbagik**. Look out for a pottery shop on the north side of the main road and you'll see the turning to Penakak almost opposite it. Penakak is one of the three villages involved in the Lombok Crafts Project (see box on p.429), and the road through the village is lined with potteries. The range of goods produced and the variety of glazes and engraving used is enormous; the potteries will ship goods overseas.

The **waterfalls** at **PANCOR KOPONG** and **PANCOR BULING** are accessible by taking a cidomo from Masbagik to Nibas (3km) and then walking the last kilometre from Nibas, or you can walk from Pringgasela (2km); either way it's best to ask for directions. The falls are not especially high, but they're impressively wide and set in the midst of attractive rice-fields with pleasant walks round about.

Pringgasela and Timbanuh

Some 5km north of **REMPUNG** on the cross-island road is the local weaving centre of **PRINGGASELA**. Local women make both *songket* and *ikat* cloth here on simple backstrap looms (see p.538 for details of production), and there are several small workshops in the village. *Akmal Homestay* (no phone; ❷ ; includes three meals), just north of the crossroads in the village centre, has a great atmosphere and small rooms in the family compound with shared bathroom. *Sasak House Homestay* (no phone; ❷ ; includes three meals) offers something very similar just across the alleyway.

For an excursion well off the beaten track, the road up to **TIMBANUH**, 8km north of Pringgasela via Pengadangan, ascends to the southern foothills of Rinjani through coffee, banana and rambutan plantations. It's a shady, picturesque trip until the road ends at *Losmen Timbanuh* (no phone; ❶), an old, very dilapidated colonial bungalow offering extremely rundown accommodation but utterly spellbinding views across to Sumbawa. You need your own transport to get here.

Loang Geli

Back on the main road at **LENEK**, another small road heads north and, after about 3km, a wide dirt track, just past the school and opposite the kepala desa's office, leads another 1km to **LOANG GELI**, the site of a cold freshwater **spring,** often listed as a local sight. From the parking spot, it's 100m down a gently sloping path to the swimming area where the spring flows into a deep concrete pool – pleasant without being exceptional. The pool is surrounded by the **Monkey Forest**, but crowds here are often so large that the monkeys keep away during the day. The accommodation here is very rundown and there is no local warung so it is best to consider this as a day-trip.

Sapit

Situated high in the hills, 1400m up on the southern slopes of Gunung Pusuk, the small mountain village of **SAPIT** is a quiet retreat with wonderful views. It's 15km from Sembalun Lawang (2–3hr by daily bus, as long as the road is open), and the same distance from the cross-island road, either via Aik Mel or Pringgabaya (there's more public transport from the latter).

Sapit is becoming increasingly popular, although it's very far from crowded. The road north is very steep and twisting and prone to being washed away – check in the Sembalun valley or Sapit on the current condition before setting off in your own transport. There's **accommodation** at *Hati Suci* (T & F 0370/636545, E hatisuci@inbox.as; ❷) and nearby *Balelangga* (same contact; ❶–❷), which are both run by the same family: *Balelangga* offers simpler accommodation with outside toilet while *Hati Suci* has bungalows with attached bathrooms. Both have great views across the paddy-fields to the coast and Sumbawa. Each has a small **restaurant** offering a basic menu, and staff here will point you in the right direction for walks to the nearby waterfalls and hot springs, the pool and Monkey Forest at Lemor, a local canyon and, for the hardy, the fifteen-kilometre trek across to Sembalun Bumbung (see p.461). They can also arrange a three-day motorcycle exploration of east Lombok with a driver (Rp70,000 per day for the bike plus all the driver's expenses).

East Lombok

With a much drier climate, smaller population and far fewer facilities than the west of the island, **east Lombok** tends to be left off most itineraries, although if you're heading to or from Sumbawa, you'll pass through the small port of **Labuhan Lombok**. While there's little to detain you for long, **Labuhan Haji**, south of Labuhan Lombok, is an attractive seaside town, with lush scenery inland. To the north of Labuhan Lombok, the land is dramatically arid, giving striking views inland to the mountains, and the accommodation at **Labuhan Pandan** gives you the chance to organize a trip to the uninhabited islands just off the coast. Accommodation options are gradually increasing, although they are still fairly limited.

Labuhan Lombok and around

LABUHAN LOMBOK, 74km east of Mataram, is probably the least interesting town in Lombok, although its near-circular bay enclosed by a small curving promontory is very attractive. Boats to Sumbawa depart from the **ferry terminal**, Labuhan Kayangan, at the far end of the promontory, a three-kilometre shadeless walk along the new road around the south side of the bay; take a local bemo if you can (Rp1000). **Kayangan Hill**, on the south side of the bay, has good views inland and across to Sumbawa; the path up the hill leaves from the road to the ferry terminal, and it's a short, dusty climb.

Buses run regularly along the cross-island road to the ferry terminal from the Bertais/Mandalika terminal at Sweta (if you're heading for Praya or Kuta from the ferry, follow this route and change at Kopang), and from Obel Obel and Bayan on the north coast via Sambelia (the best way to go, in reverse, if you're heading for Gunung Rinjani).

The best **place to stay** is *Lima Tiga*, Jl Kayangan 14 (℡0376/23316; ❷), about 150m from the town centre on the road to the ferry terminal. The rooms are adequate, although bathrooms, with mandi and squat toilet, are shared. It has places to sit, and provides local information. Several **warung**, fine for basic Indonesian food, line the same road; *Warung Kelayu* is very popular. There's a **wartel** along here, and if you head to the main road and turn left, the **post office** is 100m along on the right. If and when their Land-Sea Adventures to Sumbawa and Flores get started again, Perama will have an office (℡0376/21817) at Jalan Rajawali, a side street off Jalan Kayangan on the other side of the road from the *Lima Tiga*.

South of Labuhan Lombok

SELONG, 20km southwest of Labuhan Lombok and the capital of Lombok Timur (East Lombok), is a thriving market town, although the travel hub for the area is a couple of kilometres west at **Pancor**. Selong has broad, busy streets and was the site of the first school to be established in the east of Lombok, in 1902. It has a **tourist office**, on Jalan Lalu Muchdar (℡0376/21894), and **accommodation** at *Erina*, Jl Pahlawan 164 (℡0376/21297; ❷), on the north side of the main road – but there's little reason to linger.

About 7km southeast is **LABUHAN HAJI**, a lovely little port (served by startling green bemos from Pancor) from where Muslim pilgrims traditionally departed on the *hajj*, or pilgrimage to Mecca. The village is a maze of alleyways clustered behind the black beach but, apart from a small port office, there's little evidence of the once-thriving trading community. The Chinese merchants here suffered particularly badly during the civil conflict following the attempted coup in 1965 (see p.499); around forty were killed and the remainder fled

---

Moving on to Sumbawa

The **ferry to Sumbawa** departs Labuhan Lombok around the clock (every 45min; Rp5000; bicycle Rp6900, motorbike Rp12,500, jeeps from Rp85,000). It goes to Poto Tano on Sumbawa's northwest coast, a few kilometres from the main road across the island. Buses meet the ferries bound for Taliwang (30km south) and Alas (22km east), plus Sumbawa Besar and, occasionally, Bima. Alternatively, you can book a **long-distance bus** ticket in Mataram (see p.426) – or with Perama – through to destinations on Sumbawa.

to Sumbawa or to the west of Lombok. Even today there are no Chinese merchants living in the town. The only **accommodation** is at *Meliwis Beach Hotel* (T0376/21241; ❷–❸), which has simple bungalows made from wood, bamboo and thatch with attached bathrooms, and is conveniently close to the beach, to the north of the main harbour area. It's pretty quiet during the week, but gets busy at weekends.

North of Labuhan Lombok

Travelling north from Labuhan Lombok, you're soon out into the countryside, though the scenery quickly becomes parched and villages are few and far between. The towering mahogany trees 5km from Labuhan Lombok are welcome shade and are widely believed to be the largest such specimens in Lombok. There is basic accommodation here at *Lian Beach* (no phone; ❶) but the options further north are better. About 7km north of Labuhan Lombok, in the village of **AIK'MANIS** – served by bemos (Rp2000) and ojek (Rp5000) – is the great little *Aik Manis* (no phone, F0376/218877; ❶), owned by an Indonesian–New Zealand couple. They have a set of wood, bamboo and thatch bungalows in a neat garden just behind an excellent beach, plus a small restaurant with great views. They can help you organize snorkelling and camping trips to the offshore islands in local boats (from Rp150,000).

Labuhan Pandan and the islands

In the area of **LABUHAN PANDAN**, 13km north of Labuhan Lombok and 6km from *Aik Manis*, look out for **Pantai Pulo Lampu** beach – very popular; at weekends but otherwise peaceful. Bemos (Rp4000) and ojek (Rp10,000) run here from Labuhan Lombok. The **accommodation** here is nothing special and the two accommodation options in the excellent get-away-from-it-all spot 3km further north are far better: *Siola Cottages* (no phone; ❶–❷) has wood, thatch and bamboo bungalows with mosquito nets provided and attached concrete mandi and squat toilets set well apart in a large garden behind a black-sand beach. There are fine views on a clear day. Just next door, *Matahari* (T086812/104168; ❷) has a choice of bungalows on the seafront or larger rooms set further back in a two-storey block. All are clean and tiled, and the garden is excellent. There is an attached **restaurant**. There is **snorkelling** off the beach here but to find a reasonable variety of coral you need to swim out about 30m to where the bottom drops off steeply; both accommodation places rent snorkelling gear. *Ma Jena's* is a simple but appealing warung by the roadside a few hundred metres away.

There are two groups of **islands** off the northeast Lombok coast. The most southerly are **Gili Petangan** and its satellites, Gili Lampu and Gili Pasaran, which have beaches as well as coral walls and attract many varieties of fish; further north (and a longer boat trip away) are the larger islands **Gili Sulat** and **Gili Lawang**, surrounded by coastal mangrove, without any beaches but with a large array of offshore coral. All are uninhabited and preserved from buildings by a government ban, although some boat trips from Lombok east to Sumbawa and Flores use them for camping. Japanese scientists are involved in a mangrove study on Gili Lawang, Gili Petangan and Gili Sulat, and have built a walkway in the swamp that can be used for jungle walks without disturbing the area. You can arrange **snorkelling** and **fishing** expeditions to the islands from both *Matahari* and *Siola Cottages*. A day-trip out to Gili Lampu and the surrounding islands costs Rp150,000; to Gili Sulat and the nearby islands costs Rp200,000. Overnight **camping** trips are also possible. You can rent **snorkelling** equipment for Rp10,000 per day. Operators from Bali bring occasional dive groups here, but there's no local operator (although this may change soon; enquire at *Matahari*).

Sambelia and around

Just north of Labuhan Pandan, the small village of **SAMBELIA** is a traditional Bugis settlement with houses built on stilts – although they're gradually being replaced by concrete and brick dwellings with tile or corrugated iron roofs. The views of Gili Sulat and Gili Lawang from here around to **BELANTING** are enticing, as the islands appear very close and it's easy to see them shimmering in the heat across the Sungian Strait.

Moving on around the coast towards Obel Obel, the countryside gets even drier, traffic is rare, and the road begins to twist and turn through the hills, which slope right down to the black-sand shore. **OBEL OBEL**, about 45km from Labuhan Lombok, is a tiny oasis of green fields in among the folds of the barren hills. There are very few tourists here, but you should be able to find somewhere to buy a drink. About 10km further on is the village of Kali Putih, where a road branches south to Sembalun Lawang (see p.461); the coast road continues west to Bayan (see p.458).

South Lombok

The largely undeveloped **south coast** of Lombok is extraordinarily beautiful, with mile upon mile of picturesque curving bays of pure white sand separated by rocky headlands and backed by sparsely inhabited dry hills. Known to

---

Nyale

Celebrated on Lombok and the further-flung islands of Sumba and Savu, this annual festival centres around a seaworm, *Eunice viridis*, which is known locally as *nale*, or **nyale**. The worms live attached to rocks in the ocean, but at roughly the same time every year, February to March, they begin their sexual cycle and release male and female sexual parts which rise to the surface ready for fertilization, turning the ocean into something resembling a seething mass of spaghetti. The number of worms is believed to indicate the success of the next rice harvest, and it is estimated that around 100,000 people travel to the south coast of Lombok at this time to gather the worms (they are believed to be aphrodisiacs), to enjoy traditional songs and to watch the re-enactment of the *Putri Nyale* or *Mandalika* legend. This tells how a beautiful princess, distraught because of the number of suitors who were fighting over her hand in marriage and loath to upset any by refusing them, flung herself into the sea where her hair was changed into *nyale* seaworms.

The normally strict control over the mixing of the sexes is relaxed during the festival, and it's a good opportunity for young people to dress up in their best clothes. *Nyale* is celebrated in Kuta, Kaliantan and, to a lesser degree, some of the small villages on the shores of Awang Bay.

surfers for several years, **Kuta** is a low-key development with fewer than a dozen places to stay – pretty much the only accommodation in the area. From here you can explore out to the west, where bay after bay lines the coast, and to the east, though access is not so easy.

Awang Bay and the **southeast peninsula** are dotted with tiny villages making a living from the sea and from the desperately dry farmland around. Well off the beaten track, and accessible only with private transport, this is a part of the island largely unseen by visitors, light-years away from the towns and cities of the west and the bright lights of tourist Lombok. If you're restricted to public transport, you can still reach the inland villages specializing in pottery, weaving, basketware and carving, such as **Beleka**, **Sukarara**, **Penujak** and **Sukaraja**, and the traditional villages of **Sade** and **Rembitan**.

Several years ago the south coast was targeted for massive tourist development, with much of the land between Selong Blanak in the west and Awang Bay in the east acquired by the government and by private investors. The coastal roads were improved dramatically and the *Coralia Lombok Novotel* opened near Kuta – and, so far, that has been that. It remains to be seen what the future holds, but for the moment the area is still pristine.

Praya and the craft villages

The busy market town and transport hub of **PRAYA**, 22km southeast of Sweta, is the capital of Central Lombok (Lombok Tengah), although it lies well to the south of the island. It's a pleasant place, easily accessible by **bus** or **bemo** from Bertais/Mandalika terminal in Sweta, its administrative buildings set in broad streets; there's a market on Saturdays. You should note that Praya is in a devout Muslim area and the town is officially "dry": no strong alcohol is available, although beer is sold. The only **accommodation** is the functional *Hotel Dienda Hayu*, Jl Untung Surapati 26 (℡0370/654319; ❶–❷), which has hot water and air-conditioning in its most expensive rooms, pleasant verandahs and a small **restaurant** attached. To find it, turn right onto the main road at the bus terminal and turn left after 200m at the traffic lights; the hotel is up on the right. The **tourist office** is at Jl Gajah Made 125 (℡0370/653766), about 500m west of the bus terminal on the main road. There are BNI and BCA **bank** ATM machines for Visa, MasterCard and Cirrus on the main road between the bus terminal and the turning to *Dienda Hayu*, and several **wartels** on the main road. Most visitors change in Praya for local transport to Sengkol and Kuta (see p.476) without stopping – but there are places in the area worth exploration.

South and west of Praya

On the road to Selong Blanak, **PENUJAK**, 6km southwest of Praya, is one of the three pottery villages involved in the Lombok Crafts Project (see box on p.429). Most workshops are on or near the main road and there are plenty of designs and patterns available, including the detailed engraving that has become such a feature of Lombok pottery. Pieces come in all shapes and sizes, with vases up to 1m tall. This is a good place to watch the potters at work if you come early in the day.

Directly west of Praya, although the route is via Puyung or Batujai, the weaving village of **SUKARARA** is firmly on the tour-bus circuit and has some enormous showrooms offering the widest range of textiles that you'll find on

Lombok. Slick salesmen work the customers, while out on the verandah the weavers produce *ikat* and *songket* cloth using backstrap looms (see p.538); the latter tends to be more aggressively colourful than the former, whose subtle shades are produced by vegetable dyes from indigo, betel nut, pineapple and bay leaves. The weavers begin learning from the age of 7 and take many years to master the huge number of designs, which they weave from memory. Local girls have to be skilled at weaving in order to be considered marriageable; men do not weave as it is believed it will make them sterile. A sarong and scarf set can take anywhere from a month to more than three months to weave, depending on the thread and quality, and the weaver receives a percentage of the price when it's sold. Look out for the traditional *lumbung* barn designs as well as the "primitive" figures. There are also a few small shops in the village which have a more relaxed feel to them. Prices are generally reasonable, but you need to shop around – which you may not have time to do if you come on an organized tour.

East of Praya

East of Praya, the road to Gubukdalem is the main road across the south of the island, and most of the local **craft villages** are on or near it. With bemos plying the route, access to most is straightforward.

Noted as a weaving centre, the village of **PEJANGGIK**, 6km southeast of Praya, is tiny and easily missed. The weaving takes place in a few small workshops on the side road through the village where local women sit and work. They are perfectly welcoming if you stop and want to buy, but this is a very small-scale operation.

Turning south at **Ganti**, 7km east of Pejanggik, the road passes through Batu Rintang to the northern end of Awang Bay and the coastal village of **BATU NAMPAR**, where people make their living from fishing and seaweed cultivation; see p.481 for an alternative route to the bay. Just inland, a huge area of **salt ponds** provides another source of income (see box p.478). The views of the bay from here are excellent: you can see clearly across to Ekas on the southeast peninsula. The large rock called **Linus**, just off the shore, has a role in local weddings – the bride and groom have to sail around it together as part of the ceremony.

To reach **BELEKA**, known for the production of rattan basketware, turn north at Ganti, about 100m east of the Batu Nampar turning; it's a busy junction, with cidomo waiting to take you the 3km. There's a large number of shops and workshops here and you'll find professional operations as well as families plaiting away in their living rooms with both eyes firmly fixed on the TV. The local specialities are wares made from grass, rattan and bamboo in a huge range of shapes and sizes, up to laundry baskets large enough for you and your clothes.

Senanti and around

Back on the main road, 4km east of Ganti at Sukaraja, a turning leads for several kilometres to the village of **SENANTI** and a small woodcarving workshop, where you can see the production of many of the statues and masks you'll spot for sale around the island. One traditional carving from this area that you'll see everywhere shows three figures climbing on top of each other. Legend tells how three brothers were hunting deer in the forest one day. One of them, Doyan Medaran, was waiting for his brothers beside a deer that he had killed when a giant appeared. Doyan Medaran was so frightened that he climbed up a massive tree to hide from the giant who, after devouring the deer, disappeared into the forest. Doyan Medaran remained stuck in the tree until his brothers came along and rescued him by climbing onto each others' shoulders.

Known for its canoe-making, the village of **KERUAK**, 7km east of Sukaraja, has a few workshops east of the village in the hamlet of Batu Rimpang, to the right of the main road to Tanjung Luar. You can watch work in progress as simple hand tools are used to create dugout canoes from vast tree trunks. On completion, the boats are taken by road to **TANJUNG LUAR**, 5km east on the coast. This is a vibrant fishing village with typical Bugis houses built on high stilts with shutters instead of windows and roofs of thatch or red clay tiles. There's a small harbour packed full of boats – with a pervasive smell of drying fish – where you can watch cormorants diving for fish and look at the great views around the wide sweep of the coastline. You can charter a boat here to take you to Tanjung Ringgit on the southeast peninsula (see p.482).

Kuta and around

The only village with any degree of tourist development on the south coast is **KUTA**, 54km from Mataram and 32km from Praya, a tiny fishing village situated just behind the west end of the wide, white-sand – although fairly shadeless – Putri Nyale beach. It's rapidly becoming the favourite choice of travellers to Lombok seeking a few days by the sea, without the large tourist presence in Senggigi or the crowds on the Gili Islands, especially if you like wild coastal scenery and prefer turbulent surf rather than the calm waters needed for snorkelling. The beach is framed by rocky headlands and the coast around the village is lovely: **Seger** and **Tanjung Aan** beaches are within walking or cycling distance. Apart from Sunday when the lively **market** takes place, the area is the ultimate in peace and quiet. The big swell here makes the sea good for **surfing** (see box), but there's no diving or snorkelling; a seafront surf shop, Ocean Blue (☎0370/653911), repairs and rents boards.

Coming from the west, **buses** and **bemos** run to Praya from Bertais/Mandalika terminal in Sweta. From Praya, bemos ply either to Sengkol, where you can change, or right through to Kuta. From the east of Lombok, bemos run to Praya via Kopang on the main cross-island road. Perama also offers **tourist shuttles** to Kuta from all destinations on Bali and Lombok; see p.483 for details.

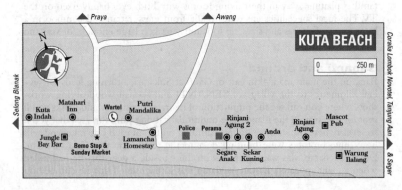

Accommodation

Kuta's **accommodation** is mostly simple losmen–style, although there are a couple of more upmarket options and the luxury end of the market is serviced by the *Coralia Lombok Novotel*. In Kuta itself the road runs about 50m inland from the beach; accommodation is spread out along the coast for about 500m on the far side, so don't expect cottages on the beach.

Anda ☎0370/654836. Several standards of very basic bungalows in a shady garden setting on the road along the beach. ❶–❷

Coralia Lombok Novotel ☎0370/653333, ℻653555, ⓦ www.novotel-lombok.com. Stunningly located 2km east of Kuta on the fabulous Seger beach, this is the only luxury development along this coast. Accommodation, all furnished in attractive, tasteful natural materials, is in low-rise buildings in lovely grounds. Prices start at US$130 (plus 21 percent tax and service) and all rooms have garden views; you'll pay more for a terrace. The villas ($250) are large, airy and lovely.

It's a fairly isolated spot but there are several bars and restaurants, a pretty pool, plenty of organized activities and watersports and a wonderful on-site spa near the beach. ❾

Kuta Indah ☎0370/653781, ℻654628, ⓔkutaindah@indo.net.id. This is one of the newest places, located at the western end of the bay. It has a good garden and clean bungalows ranged around a pool. Pricier rooms have hot water and air-con. It's a short walk to the beach and there are free transfers to Tanjung Aan and Mawun beaches. Visa and MasterCard accepted. ❷–❹

Surfing on Lombok

Generally, the quality of the **surf** breaks is not as good on Lombok as on Bali – with the exception of the world-class but elusive Desert Point. The great bonus for surfers on Lombok is fewer crowds and the wonderful south-coast scenery.

Most of the well-known breaks are off the **south coast**, with Kuta the ideal base for them. The resort's own breaks are **Kuta Left**, in front of the village, and **Kuta Right**, at the eastern end towards Aan. There's also surf off the glorious **Aan** beach (see p.481), a left-hander at the western edge and a left- and a right-hander in the centre. Climb up Batu Kotak to get a view of what's happening on the reef.

West of Kuta, most of the bays are worth a look, although they vary in accessibility and the surf is erratic. Around the headland, at **Selong Blanak** (see p.480), there's a good left-hander, best in the dry season. Further west, **Blongas** (see p.481) is less accessible, but has three good breaks, a left-hander in the east, a right in the west and another left in the centre. You'll need to charter a boat from the village to get here; it's a good spot to anchor overnight on a longer charter but you'll have to bring everything with you. Check the local situation as the area is reported to be a shark breeding-ground.

East of Kuta the best but most inaccessible breaks are off the coast of the southeast peninsula near **Serewe** (see p.482). There are two good right-handers about a mile to the west, but you'll have to come by boat. With more breaks just inside the southern headland of **Awang Bay**, as well as further into the bay, it makes sense to base yourself at *Laut Surga* (see p.482) if you can. You can charter boats from Awang (see p.481) on the west side of the bay to get out to the right-hander on the reef just south of the village. **Gumbang Bay**, which some people call Grupuk Bay, a short drive from Kuta, has the potential for big waves at its shallow mouth, plus smaller ones in the middle and to the east of the bay.

The world-famous break on Lombok is **Desert Point** off Bangko Bangko (see p.432), a fast but elusive left-hander with tubes that is at its best from June to September. The area is increasingly accessible by road, and facilities in the area are developing. An alternative option is to charter a boat, with sleeping facilities, from Bali. Elsewhere around the island, **Gili Air**'s Pertama is a renowned though erratic right-hander, **Senggigi** offers a couple of breaks, and there are several accessible from the beach at **Labuhan Haji**.

Lamancha Homestay ⊕0370/655186. Nice little place in the village, a short walk from the beach just inland from the police post, comprising a few bungalows with attached bathroom and two upstairs rooms with outside mandi. There are plenty of sitting areas and a pleasant atmosphere. ❶

Matahari Inn ⊕0370/655000, Ⓕ654909, ⓌWww.matahariinn.com. Situated in the village, just west of the main road from Praya, this is an atmospheric place set in a lush garden. More expensive rooms have air-con and hot water. There's a swimming pool and free transport to Tanjung Aan beach. ❹–❻

Putri Mandalika ⊕0370/655342. Five well-kept rooms in a small, friendly family compound in the village. There's a small, attached restaurant. ❶

Rinjani Agung ⊕0370/654849, Ⓕ654852. Stretching back a long way from the road, this

place has a huge range of accommodation on offer, the most expensive with air-con. ❶–❸

Rinjani Agung 2 ⊕0370/654849, Ⓕ654852. Further west along the beach than the original place, with a range of accommodation in two-storey buildings. ❶–❷

Segare Anak ⊕0370/654834, Ⓕ654835, Ⓔkomangsin@yahoo.com. Set in the middle of the accommodation strip along the beach road, this long-standing favourite has more expensive, newer, better bamboo rooms with red-tiled roofs and older, smaller rooms all set in a good garden behind the restaurant. ❶–❷

Sekar Kuning ⊕0370/654856. A variety of basic but adequate rooms in a garden setting on the road that runs along behind the beach. It remains in better condition than some of the competition. ❶

Eating and drinking

All Kuta's losmen have **restaurants** attached, offering inexpensive or moderately priced food; seafood is the speciality. *Segare Anak* has the biggest menu; it is currently undergoing rebuilding works following a fire, although whether they manage to complete the planned two-storey building remains to be seen. *Anda* also has good-quality food, *Warung Ilalang* at the east end of the beach has the finest spot from which to admire the ocean, and *Warung Mandalika*, attached to *Putri Mandalika* in the village, is worth a look as well. There are nightly **videos**; keep an eye out for notices.

Listings

Changing money There are several moneychangers near the losmen (*Anda*, *Kuta Indah* and *Segare Anak* bungalows also change money), but expect about ten percent less for your money than you'd get in Mataram.

Charter transport Ask at your accommodation or at Perama. It costs around Rp250,000/day for a car (including driver and fuel); Rp35,000 per half-day to rent a motorbike; Rp15,000/day for a bicycle.

Internet access is available at several places including the wartel (Rp500/min; minimum 5min).

Phones There's a wartel in the village (daily 8am–10.30pm).

Post *Segare Anak* is a postal agent and you can use it for poste restante; get mail addressed to you at *Segare Anak*, Kuta Beach, Lombok Tengah, Nusa Tenggara Barat 8357. The nearest post office is in Sengkol.

Shuttle bus tickets To book, head to the Perama office (daily 7am–10pm), attached to *Segare Anak* and opposite the wartel; they have daily departures to destinations on Bali and Lombok, although some require a stopover (see p.483).

Inland from Kuta

The traditional village of **SADE**, 6km north of Kuta, is a major stop on most day-trips to the south of the island. It lies close to the Kuta–Sengkol road and is used to visitors (donation expected). Young lads hang around offering to guide you; they speak good enough English to explain all the delights, such as the buffalo-dung foundations of the houses. It's certainly picturesque and the *lumbung* barns and traditional houses are faithfully preserved, but it does feel a bit like a theme park and you'll be constantly pestered to buy things or to take photographs of people – all at a price.

Just up the road to the north, **REMBITAN** seems less artificial and is close to a site of Muslim pilgrimage. One of the Nine Walis believed to have brought Islam to Indonesia is supposedly buried here at **MAKAM NYATO**, and on Wednesdays pilgrims come to worship at the grave, shaded by frangipani and banyan trees. Rembitan is regarded in some quarters as having the oldest mosque on the island (although Bayan in the north is more widely accepted to have that honour; see p.458). About fifteen years ago there was a big fire near the ancient mosque. It did not burn, however, and children later reported having seen figures clad in white surrounding and protecting the building. The belief in the mystical properties of the mosque grew, and when the roof was repaired many local people took part of the old one as protection for their homes.

There are several **art shops** and **batik workshops** on the road between Sade and Rembitan; at Lombok Art Painting and Rembitan Sasak Art Gallery (both daily 8am–6pm), you can watch batik painting in progress. The variety of images is huge, including classical characters from the *Ramayana*, primitive motifs, traditional scenes and a huge selection of modern designs. Prices go from about Rp80,000 for the small pieces up to Rp650,000 or more for the biggest – but you do need to bargain. There are also attractive greetings cards (Rp10,000).

West of Kuta

Along the coast **west of Kuta** you can explore half a dozen or so of the prettiest beaches on the island, backed by attractive, rolling coastal hills and widely dispersed rural communities. However bemos are few and far between so you'll need your own transport. There are few signs and not many landmarks, so be prepared for a leisurely trip and perhaps some wrong turnings. Allow two hours for the trip from Kuta around to Sekotong, southwest of Lembar.

The road out of Kuta, past *Kuta Indah*, climbs up steeply for a couple of kilometres. The view from the top of the hill back across the entire Kuta area is one of the most dramatic in southern Lombok. A restaurant is planned up here; even without a drink at the top, the scenery is worth the sweaty walk.

Making salt

On many parts of the Lombok coast, particularly around Awang Bay (and on Bali at Kusamba and on Nusa Lembongan), you'll see the salt beds and piles of white salt that indicate one of the most backbreaking occupations on the islands – **salt-making**. Vast quantities of salt water are hauled from the sea in buckets and poured into specially dug ponds, close to the shore. When the water has evaporated, the salty, sandy residue is placed in hollowed out palm-tree trunks and mixed with more sea water. The water becomes saturated with salt and a very thick brine is poured off. This is then evaporated to form salt crystals. Further stages of purification take place, and you may see large bamboo baskets suspended from frames at salt-making sites: the liquid from the wet salt crystals, which contains other more soluble impurities, drips down a string hanging from the baskets and forms long stalactites, leaving pure salt crystals behind.

The rainy season brings salt production to a halt; high tides can also flood the salt pools. A typical family of salt producers can make around 25kg of salt a day, but salt is cheap to buy and many former salt-producing areas are now turning to seaweed farming as a more lucrative way of earning a living (see box on p.281).

Some 5km out of Kuta you'll pass the "MTR 64" road marker (indicating 64km to Mataram). Just under 1km west of this, look out for a dirt track heading off to the coast; it's suitable for a motorbike with a good driver, but don't try it in a jeep. After 2km it reaches the coastal village of **ARE GOLENG**. The beach here is about 400m long and the seaweed beds in the shallows are clearly visible. A tiny island, **Gili Nungsa**, sits out in the bay, with an enticing little beach visible from the shore and villagers' huts line the area just behind the beach. Wend your way east through the coconut grove for a few hundred metres to find a more secluded part of the bay.

The next beach west is **Mawun**, 8km from Kuta and reached by a 500-metre-long sealed road a few hundred metres beyond the "MTR 66" marker. The bay is almost semicircular, enclosed on both sides by rocky headlands with the water fading from turquoise to a deep, vibrant blue, enhanced by the white of the waves crashing onto the rocks on either side. Don't expect a secluded paradise: there are usually a few other tourists here, you'll pay Rp3000 for parking, and there are cold-drink sellers plying their wares.

About 3km further west, the main road reaches the coast and runs a few hundred metres inland from the gently curving **Tampa** beach. The area is not terribly attractive – the beach is backed by flat scrub and there isn't much shade – but it's pretty deserted.

Access to the beach at **Mawi**, about 4km west of Tampa, isn't easy. Take the next sealed road branching off seaward (if you reach "MTR 75" you've gone too far). After 1500m it degenerates into a track before ending in a stand of banana, coconut and kapok trees with a couple of houses. It's a few hundred metres' walk to the lovely white-sand beach, a favourite beach with surfers and separated from nearby **Rowok** by a rocky outcrop. From here, there are great views, plus the impressive sight of Gili Lawang – three pinnacles sticking almost sheer out of the ocean.

Selong Blanak and around

Back on the road, you soon reach **SELONG BLANAK**, 18km from Kuta, also accessible via Penujak from Praya (24km). The bay here has a long curving beach with rocky headlands at each end, a few canoes pulled up on the sand, some larger boats bobbing in the waters, and the striking island of **Gili Lawang** just offshore. The only **accommodation** west of Kuta is here, at *Selong Blanak Cottages* (no phone; ❷), 2km inland from the beach; free transport to the beach is provided. The cottages are set in a lush garden and there's a moderately priced **restaurant** attached. A five-star resort is planned for the area.

From Selong Blanak there are two roads west to Pengantap. Access to the shorter, coastal road depends on the road bridge across the river at Selong Blanak. The **longer road**, curving 20km inland is a bit of an adventure. It climbs up very steeply into the coastal hills through mahogany and teak stands with fine views of the surrounding countryside. About 3km from Selong Blanak it reaches the tiny village of **KELING** where it splits. The right fork leads north to Penujak (see p.474) while the left fork continues on westwards through tiny hamlets of bamboo and thatch houses, everyone waving at you in surprise as you pass. The road is narrow and the surface deteriorates the further west you get but the views on the descent back to the coast make the whole enterprise worthwhile. Initially you see westwards into the next bay towards Sepi and Blongas and then as the road curves, you look down to the village of **PENGANGTAP**, a row of thatched houses just behind the beach. The village is served by bemos from Sekotong, 17km to the north.

Some 8km beyond Pengangtap, the road splits at the tiny fishing village of **SEPI**. You can continue 1km west to **BLONGAS**, the end of the road, where there's good snorkelling, diving and surfing. This is an isolated spot though, and there's no accommodation in the village. Alternatively, follow the road directly north from Sepi through more small villages. The road gradually improves, the density of population increases, and after 11km you reach Sekotong (see p.430) where you can turn west to Bangko Bangko or north to Lembar.

East of Kuta

The glorious beaches of **Seger** and **Tanjung Aan** are easily accessible from Kuta and, at a push, walkable if you have no transport (bicycles are a good idea). Seger is closest to Kuta (1km) and is now the location of the luxury *Coralia Lombok Novotel* development, which isn't inconspicuous, but neither is it as aesthetically horrible as it could have been. To reach Tanjung Aan (5km from Kuta), follow the road east out of the resort and take the first sealed turning to the right. There are two perfect white-sand beaches here, **Aan** to the west and **Pedau** to the east, separated by a rocky outcrop, Batu Kotak. As their popularity has grown, the beaches now see a few hawkers and there are also some drinks stalls, but no other facilities.

Past Aan, the small fishing village of **GERUPAK**, just under 8km from Kuta, perches on the western shores of Gumbang Bay. **Lobster** is one of the local specialities and buyers come here from all the big hotels on Lombok and sometimes from Bali. *Kelapa Bungalows* (no phone; ➊) are on the road in from Kuta, about 300m before the beach. They're pretty basic but have attached bathrooms and are set in a large garden; there's a small restaurant attached. Bungalows in this spot seem to come and go; you'd do well to check in Kuta in advance whether they're open. From Gerupak there are fine views across the bay to **BUMBANG** on the eastern shore, and you can rent a canoe or motorboat to take you across. From Bumbang there's a track north to the Awang road, but you can't rely on picking up transport to take you back to Kuta.

The thriving fishing village of **AWANG**, 16km east of Kuta, is well worth the trip for the views of **Awang Bay**, a massive inlet, 10km long and 8km wide in parts. As the road descends into the village, you'll be able to spot the island of Linus, just off Batu Nampar (see p.475) at the northern end of the bay, and the tiny settlement of Ekas across on the southeast peninsula (see below), and see all the way south to the open sea. You can charter boats from Awang across to Ekas, a much easier option than tackling the rough roads. Wooden Bugis-style houses on stilts line the shore and the bay is full of boats of all shapes and sizes, from large ocean-going fishing boats down to tiny dugout canoes. The **beach** here spreads magnificently both north and south from the village, and on the way down into Awang the view is stunning.

The southeast peninsula

The only road onto Lombok's wild **southeast peninsula** leaves the southern main road at **SEPAPAN**, about 500m west of Keruak, and is signposted to Kaliantan. At this point, the road is surfaced, but it deteriorates extremely fast and to venture here you'll need to be familiar with off-road driving and have a powerful motorbike or a jeep with good clearance. Make sure you fill up with fuel before leaving the main road and bear in mind that travel is slow whichever way you go.

The first village, after about 3km, is **JEROWARU**, where the road splits – turn right to continue south. About 10km from the main road the road splits again; carry straight on to Kaliantan, which is another 9km south from here, or follow the road 5km west to Ekas.

At the tiny fishing village of **EKAS**, built just behind the shoreline, about halfway along the eastern edge of Awang Bay, people make their living from fishing and seaweed farming. The views from here across and around Awang Bay are spellbinding. Just south of Ekas, a series of signs leads to *Laut Surga Cottages* (no phone), some of the hardest-to-reach **accommodation** in Lombok. They may have succumbed to their isolation and closed down by the time you read this: check at Kuta or Awang or try the surf websites on p.62 for up-to-date information as there's no way of contacting them directly. With a gorgeous situation close to the small, tightly curving beach, the cottages are set in a lovely garden. They're fairly basic, however: the water supply is unreliable and can be brackish, and electricity (not 24hr) is provided by their own generator. You can rent surfboards and there's also good snorkelling in the area.

A few **bemos** link Ekas and the main road at Sepapan, but they're very irregular. Once at Ekas, you can rent a **boat** to take you round to *Laut Surga* if it is still open. Another possibility is to get a boat from Awang on the other side of the bay. August is the busiest month here, with February and March also attracting people for the *Nyale* festival (see box on p.473), so expect prices to rise at these times. You can always sleep on the beach if the accommodation is full.

Down towards the southern tip of the peninsula the road splits again, right to **KALIANTAN** and left to **SEREWE**, both tiny fishing and seaweed-farming villages. There are good views around the coast, but they don't compare with the grand panorama you get from Ekas.

The road to **TANJUNG RINGGIT**, the southeastern tip of Lombok, is long and extremely rough, and you'll need to ask to be sure of finding the right turning – consider renting a boat from Tanjung Luar on the east coast (see p.476) rather than endure the gruesome drive. Tanjung Ringgit is reputed to be a magical place with large caves believed to be the home of a demon – but if you have to choose one side of the peninsula to explore, Ekas and the west side offers more of interest.

Travel details

Buses and bemos

It's almost impossible to give the frequency with which bemos and public buses run, as they only depart when they have enough passengers to make the journey worthwhile. However, on the most popular routes, you should be able to count on getting a ride within the half-hour if you travel before noon; things quieten down in the afternoon and come to a standstill by around 5pm. Journey times also vary a great deal: the times given below are the minimum you can expect.

Only direct bemo and bus routes are listed; for longer journeys you'll probably find that you have to go first to Bertais/Mandalika terminal in Sweta (see p.420).

Ampenan to: Senggigi (20min).
Labuhan Lombok to: Bayan (2hr); Kopang (for Praya; 1hr); Sembalun Lawang (2hr 30min); Bertais/Mandalika terminal, Sweta (2hr).
Lembar to: Sekotong (1hr); Selegang (3hr); Bertais/Mandalika terminal, Sweta (30min); Taun (2hr); Tembowong (2hr 30min).
Praya to: Gubukdalem (1hr 30min); Kuta (1hr); Bertais/Mandalika terminal, Sweta (30min).
Sapit to: Aik Mel (1hr); Pringabaya (1hr); Sembalun Lawang (2hr).
Sembalun Lawang to: Obel Obel (2hr); Sapit (2hr).

Senggigi to: Ampenan (20min).
Sweta (Bertais/Mandalika terminal) to: Bayan (for Rinjani; 2hr 30min); Bima (Sumbawa; 12hr); Dompu (Sumbawa; 10hr); Jakarta (Java; 48hr); Labuhanbajo (Flores; 24hr); Labuhan Lombok (2hr); Lembar (30min); Pemenang (50min); Pomotong (for Tetebatu; 1hr 15min); Praya (for Kuta; 30min); Ruteng (Flores; 36hr); Sape (Flores; 14hr); Sumbawa Besar (Sumbawa; 6hr); Surabaya (20hr); Yogyakarta (26hr).

Perama shuttle buses

STO = overnight stopover is needed
Bangsal to: Air Sanih (daily; STO); Bedugul (daily; STO); Candi Dasa (daily; 6hr–6hr 30min); Kintamani (daily; STO); Kuta, Bali/Ngurah Rai Airport (daily; 9hr 30min); Kuta, Lombok (daily; 3hr); Lovina (daily; STO); Mataram (daily; 1hr 30min); Padang Bai (daily; 5hr 30min–6hr); Sanur (daily; 9hr); Senggigi (daily; 45min); Tetebatu (daily; 3hr); Tirtagangga (daily; STO); Tulamben (daily; STO); Ubud (daily; 8hr).
Kuta, Lombok to: Air Sanih (daily; STO); Bangsal (daily; 3hr); Bedugul (daily; STO); Candi Dasa (daily; 8hr); Kintamani (daily; STO); Kuta, Bali/Ngurah Rai Airport (daily; 10–11hr); Lovina (daily; STO); Mataram (daily; 2hr 30min); Padang Bai (daily; 7hr 30min); Sanur (daily; 10hr); Senggigi (daily; 3hr); Tirtagangga (daily; STO); Tulamben (daily; STO); Ubud (daily; 9hr).
Mataram to: Air Sanih (daily; STO); Bangsal (daily; 1hr 30min); Bedugul (daily; STO); Candi Dasa (2 daily; 5hr–5hr 30min); Kintamani (daily; STO); Kuta, Bali/Airport (2 daily; 8hr 30min); Kuta, Lombok (daily; 2hr 30min); Lovina (daily; 7–8hr); Padang Bai (2 daily; 4hr 30min–5hr); Sanur (2 daily; 8hr); Senggigi (daily; 30min); Tetebatu (daily; 2hr 15min); Tirtangga (daily; 6hr–6hr 30min); Tulamben (daily; 7–8hr); Ubud (daily; 8hr).
Senggigi to: Air Sanih (daily; STO); Bangsal (daily; 45min); Bedugul (daily; STO); Candi Dasa (2 daily; 5hr 30min–6hr); Kintamani (daily; STO); Kuta, Bali/Ngurah Rai Airport (2 daily; 9hr); Kuta, Lombok (daily; 3hr); Lovina (daily; 7hr 30min–8hr 30min); Mataram (daily; 30min); Padang Bai (2 daily; 4hr 30min–5hr); Sanur (2 daily; 8hr); Tetebatu (daily; 2hr 45min); Tirtagangga (daily; 6hr 30min–7hr); Tulamben (daily; 7hr 30min–8hr 30min); Ubud (daily; 7hr 30min).
Tetebatu to: Air Sanih (daily; STO); Bangsal (daily; 3hr); Bedugul (daily; STO); Candi Dasa (daily; 8hr); Kintamani (daily; STO); Kuta, Bali/Ngurah Rai Airport (2 daily; 10–11hr); Lovina (daily; STO); Mataram (daily; 2hr 30min); Padang Bai (daily; 7hr 30min); Sanur (daily; 10hr); Senggigi (daily; 3hr); Tirtagangga (daily; STO); Tulamben (daily; STO); Ubud (daily; 9hr).

Boats

Bangsal to: Gili Islands (several times daily; 20–45min).
Gili Air to: Bangsal (daily; 20min); Gili Meno (daily; 20min); Gili Trawangan (daily; 40min).
Gili Meno to: Bangsal (daily; 30min); Benoa Harbour, Bali (4 weekly; 4hr 30min); Gili Air (daily; 20min); Gili Trawangan (daily; 20min); Nusa Lembongan (4 weekly; 1hr 30min).
Gili Trawangan to: Bangsal (daily; 45min); Gili Air (daily; 40min); Gili Meno (daily; 20min).
Labuhan Lombok to: Poto Tano (Sumbawa; every 45min; 2hr).
Lembar to: Benoa Harbour, Bali (daily; 2hr); Padang Bai (slow ferry: every 1hr 30min; 4hr–4hr 30min; fast boat: daily; 1hr 30min).
Senggigi to: Benoa Harbour, Bali (4 weekly; 3hr); Gili Trawangan (2 daily; 1hr 30min); Nusa Lembongan (4 weekly; 3hr).

Planes

Mataram (Selaparang Airport) to: Bima (4 weekly; 45min); Denpasar (10 daily; 30min); Jakarta (daily; 3hr); Labuhanbajo (2 weekly; 1hr 40min); Singapore (6 weekly; 2hr 30min); Sumbawa (2 weekly; 40min); Surabaya (4 daily; 45min); Yogyakarta (daily; 1hr 15min).

contexts

contexts

History

Two tiny islands, Bali and Lombok have been buffeted by powerful empires throughout their history, and their fortunes have often been tied to those of their larger neighbours, Java and Sumbawa. Relations between Bali and Lombok have been uneasy at the best of times, but more often turbulent and bloody. The origins of their present cultural, religious and economic differences are firmly rooted in past events.

Beginnings

Homo erectus, a distant ancestor of modern man, lived in Indonesia somewhere between 350,000 and 800,000 years ago during the time of the great Ice Ages. Fossilized bones of "Java Man" from this period were found in Central Java in 1890, and stone axes and adzes have been discovered on Bali, in the northern village of Sembiran.

As the earth cooled during the **Ice Ages**, glaciers advanced from the polar regions and the levels of the world's oceans fell. Many of the islands of Indonesia became joined to the land masses of Southeast Asia and Australia by exposed **land bridges**. The early humans, as well as animals, moved through these areas, across the land bridges linking the islands. It is thought there were two main routes into Indonesia from the Asian mainland; one led down through Thailand into Malaysia and then into the archipelago while the other came down via the Philippines with branches into Kalimantan and Sulawesi.

Homo sapiens first appeared around 40,000 years ago, hunter–gatherers who lived in caves and whose rock paintings have been found on some of the far eastern islands of the archipelago. The **Neolithic** era, around 3000 BC, is marked by the appearance of more sophisticated stone tools, agricultural techniques and basic pottery. Remains from this era have been found at Cekik, in the far west of Bali, where there is evidence of a settlement together with burials of around a hundred people thought to range from the Neolithic through to the Bronze Age.

From the seventh or eighth centuries BC, the **Bronze Age** began to spread south from southern China. Important centres for Bronze Age skills arose in Annam and Tonkin in what is now northern Vietnam, famed for their bronze casting, particularly of drums, decorated with animal, human and geometric patterns. The drums have been found throughout the Indonesian archipelago as have the stone moulds used in their production. The most famous example in Bali, and the largest drum found anywhere in Southeast Asia, is the **Moon of Pejeng**, nearly 2m wide, and currently housed in a temple just east of Ubud.

Discoveries of carved **stone sarcophagi** from this period have been concentrated in East Java and Bali. The most notable examples are on display in the Bali Museum in Denpasar and the Museum Purbakala in Pejeng.

Early traders and empires

From at least 200 BC, and perhaps earlier, **trade** was a feature of life in the archipelago. The earliest written records in Bali, metal inscriptions or *prasasti* dating from the ninth century AD, reveal significant Buddhist and Hindu influence from the Indian subcontinent, shown also by the statues, bronzes and rock-cut caves at Gunung Kawi and Goa Gajah.

The most famous event in early Balinese history occurred towards the end of the tenth century when a princess of East Java, Princess **Mahendratta**, married the Balinese king **Udayana**. Their marriage portrait is believed to be depicted in a stone in the Pura Korah Tegipan in the Batur area. Their son, **Erlangga**, born around 991 AD, later succeeded to the throne of the Javanese kingdom and set his regent to rule over Bali, thus bringing the two realms together until his death in 1049.

In the following centuries, the ties between the two islands fluctuated as various factions and kingdoms gained and lost power. In 1284, Kertanegara, the ruler of the Singasari empire in Java, conquered Bali for a time, but by the turn of the century the most powerful force in Bali was again a domestic one, presided over by **King Bedaulu** and based in the Pejeng district, east of Ubud.

Little is known of the ancient history of **Lombok**, which was largely the province of small, localized rulers, although it is known that the small kingdom of Selaparang controlled an area in the east of the island for a period.

The Majapahit

One of the most significant dates in Balinese history is 1343 AD, when the entire island of Bali was conquered and colonized by **Gajah Mada**, the prime minister of the powerful Hindu **Majapahit** kingdom of East Java. Establishing a court at Samprangan in eastern Bali, and granting lands to members of the aristocracy, the first Majapahit ruler of Bali was **Sri Dalem Kapikisan**. This invasion brought about massive changes in Balinese society, including the introduction of the caste system. The Balinese who did not accept these changes established their own villages in remote, mostly mountainous areas. Their descendants, known as the **Bali Aga** or *Bali Mula*, the "original Balinese", still live in separate villages, such as Tenganan near Candi Dasa and Trunyan on the shores of Lake Batur, and adhere to ancient traditions.

Kapakisan was succeeded by his son, **Dewa Ketut Ngulesir**, who set up his court in **Gelgel**, in east Bali. Throughout the fifteenth century, the power of the Majapahit empire on Java went into a decline due to the expanding influence of Islam. It finally fell in 1515, and the many small Islamic kingdoms in the island coalesced into the Islamic Mataram empire. The most dedicated Hindu believers of the Majapahit – priests, craftsmen, soldiers, nobles and artists – fled east to Bali, flooding the island with **Javanese cultural ideas** and reaffirming Hindu practices.

Given the huge influence and power of **Islam** at this time, it is something of a mystery as to why the faith did not spread to Bali, especially as it moved further east to Lombok, Sulawesi and Maluku. One reason could be that the religion spread along trade routes: with little outside trading at that time due to poor harbours and few resources, Bali was largely bypassed, and the tide of Islam swept east, although there are small Muslim communities on the island, in Kusamba, Padang Bai and Candi Kuning.

There is also evidence of Javanese influence on **Lombok** during the time of the Majapahit ascendancy. An ancient text detailing the history of the Majapahit dynasty lists Lombok as part of its empire, and the villages in the mountainous Sembalun valley on the eastern flanks of Gunung Rinjani consider themselves directly descended from the Majapahit dynasty, claiming that the brother of a Majapahit raja is buried in the valley.

Bali's Golden Age

Dewa Ketut Ngulesir was succeeded by his eldest son, **Batu Renggong**, who became king, or **dewa agung** (literally meaning "great god"), in 1550. The title of *dewa agung* continued in hereditary fashion down through the succeeding generations of the Gelgel, and later Klungkung, dynasty until the twentieth century. During Batu Renggong's reign the Gelgel kingdom achieved remarkable military successes, from Blambangan in Java in the west to Sumbawa in the east. This period coincided with a cultural renaissance in Bali and, as a result, is often referred to as the **Golden Age**. The Javanese Hindu priest **Nirartha**, who encouraged the renaissance, achieved a great following on Bali and reinforced orthodox Hindu practices.

Gradually the glory of the Golden Age faded. Batu Renggong's son, Raja Bekung, managed to maintain the court, but his grandson, **Di Made Bekung**, lost Blambangan, Lombok and Sumbawa. Eventually the chief minister, Gusti Agung Maruti, rebelled against Bekung who fled with three hundred of his court and died in exile. Gusti Agung Maruti reigned from 1650 to 1686, eventually being killed by Di Made Bekung's son, **Dewa Agung Jambe**, who moved the court to **Klungkung**, calling his new palace the Semarapura (Abode of the God of Love).

The seventeenth and eighteenth centuries were far from peaceful on Bali. The fading of the Golden Age and the move of the court to Klungkung marked the increasing prominence of other kingdoms within Bali, most notably the emergence of **Gianyar** under Dewa Manggis Kuning in 1667.

Foreigners and trade

Lacking the spices of the eastern isles, Bali appears not to have been in the mainstream of the archipelago's early trading history. It is known that the **Chinese** visited Bali, which they knew as Paoli or Rice Island, in the seventh century, but, by this time, trade had been an established part of life on nearby islands for around a thousand years. It wasn't until the end of the fifteenth century that Bali became known to **Europeans**. Following Vasco da Gama's discovery of the sea route to India via the Cape of Good Hope, numerous explorers set off from Portugal, Spain and England to search for the lucrative spice islands. They marked Bali on their maps as Balle, Ilha Bale or Java Minor, but rarely stopped, although Sir Francis Drake is reported to have visited in 1580.

During the sixteenth century, the Balinese first came into contact with Europeans. The **Portuguese**, having won the race for the spice islands, turned their eyes towards Bali, and in 1588 dispatched a ship from Malacca, complete with soldiers, builders and all the necessary materials to construct a fort and trading post on the island. Just off the island the ship hit a reef and sank with huge loss of life. The survivors were treated kindly by the *dewa agung* but not permitted to leave the island. Portuguese attempts at establishing contact do not appear to have been repeated.

Owing to the Portuguese monopoly on the spice trade in Europe, other nations continued their search for routes and sources, particularly of cloves and nutmeg. On April 2, 1595, four **Dutch** ships under the command of Commodore Cornelius Houtman left northern Holland for the long trip east. They received a hostile reception throughout the east, largely through the manipulations of the Portuguese, who were intent on protecting their trade. Having decided to give up and return home, Houtman called at Bali to stock up with supplies. His ships anchored separately off Jembrana (west Bali), Kuta (south Bali) and Labuhan Amuk (east Bali). Three sailors landed at Kuta on February 9, 1597, for reconnaissance, including Aernoudt Lintgens, whose report of his experiences is the first account by a Westerner of the island. The island so fascinated the other two crew members that they did not return to the ship. One eventually returned to Holland, but the other settled permanently in Bali.

The second visit by the Dutch came in 1601, when Cornelis Heemskerk arrived with an official letter from the prince of Holland requesting **formal trade relations**. The *dewa agung* replied on a *lontar* palm letter accepting friendly relations between the countries and agreeing to mutual trade. The Dutch trading empire continued to consolidate and expand. The VOC, or **Dutch East India Company**, was formed in 1602, and its headquarters founded in Batavia (modern-day Jakarta) in 1619. Business expanded through trading posts as far afield as Sumatra, Borneo, Makassar and the Moluccas. In 1633, the Dutch sent a mission to Bali to try to ingratiate themselves by offering the *dewa agung* assistance in his fight against the kingdom of Mataram in Java. The Dutch were themselves at war against Mataram following their establishment of Batavia on land belonging to Java's *sultan agung*. However, the *dewa agung* rejected the Dutch overtures.

From then on until the beginning of the nineteenth century, Bali was largely ignored by the European powers, as it produced little of interest to outsiders. The exception was **slaves**, who were shipped through the port of Kuta. Balinese slaves, sold by the princes of the island to Dutch merchants from Batavia and French merchants from Mauritius, had a reputation for being particularly strong and hard-working.

The situation in Lombok

During the seventeenth century, Lombok came under a combination of influences from the **Balinese** and the **Makassarese** of Sulawesi. The Balinese from Karangasem, in the far east of Bali, arrived in the early seventeenth century across the Lombok Strait, and settled in the west of Lombok, gradually achieving political control over the area. At roughly the same time, the Makassarese, who had conquered Sumbawa in 1618, invaded the east of the island. The first major conflicts between the two invaders occurred in 1677 when the Balinese, assisted by the indigenous **Sasak** aristocracy, managed to rout the Makassarese.

From the end of the seventeenth to the mid-nineteenth century, the Balinese struggled to secure their control over Lombok. Initially united and with little effective opposition from the Sasaks, this proved a simple operation. However, in 1775, **Gusti Wayan Tegah**, who had been placed on the throne by the raja of Karangasem, died, and disagreements over the succession by his two sons led to the formation of two rival principalities, with further disputes around 1800 leading to more splits. By the beginning of the nineteenth century, there were four rival Balinese principalities vying for control: Pagasangan, Pagutan, Mataram and Cakranegara. With their overlords fighting among themselves, the Sasak aristocracy in the east of the island faced little interference in their affairs from the Balinese.

In 1838, the Balinese factions were reunited when **Ratu Agung K'tut**, raja of Mataram, who had already conquered Pagasangan and Pagutan, moved against Cakranegara which was supported by the enterprising Danish trader **Mads Lange**. With Lange unable to prevent the supply of reinforcements for Mataram crossing the Lombok Strait from Karangasem, Ratu Agung K'tut eventually triumphed, and brought the east of Lombok under his control.

His greatest triumph occurred in 1849. The Dutch, at that time involved in their Third Military Expedition against Bali, wanted to move against the east Balinese kingdom of Karangasem. Providing four thousand troops to supplement the Dutch, Ratu Agung K'tut ensured the defeat of the ruling dynasty in Karangasem and, in payment for his help, won the right to put his own nominee on the throne.

European turmoil and Dutch interest

Conflicts in nineteenth-century Europe had massive repercussions in Bali. In 1795, **French** troops under Napoleon invaded the Netherlands, thus acquiring **Dutch** possessions overseas. By the turn of the century, the Dutch colonies in Southeast Asia were under the control of a governor-general appointed by Napoleon. This governor was subsequently defeated by the **British**, who had their own interests in the area to protect, and in 1811 the British also defeated the Dutch forces in Java. The British lieutenant-governor of Java, **Sir Thomas Stamford Raffles**, administered the region, but British rule in the area was shortlived.

Napoleon was defeated at Waterloo in 1815 and, as part of the peace settlement, it was agreed to return the Indies to the Dutch. A three-member commission arrived in Batavia in 1816 to take over from the reluctant Raffles, who was deeply committed to the strategic importance of the Indies for British interests. The Dutch government subsequently abolished the Dutch East India Company, which had gone bankrupt, and took over its role. In an effort to remedy the British losses, Raffles established a settlement in Singapore, in 1819. A **treaty** in 1824 gave lands north of the Straits of Malacca to the British and south of the straits to the Dutch, but Dutch fear of British motives in the region drove their colonial policy for many years to come.

Dutch incursions

By this time, the Balinese had become more hostile towards foreigners. Raffles' colonial policies had damaged the rajas' lucrative slave trade and, in 1814, there had been skirmishes between British troops and the ruler of the kingdom of Buleleng. When the **Dutch** sent an envoy, van den Broek, to Bali in 1817 to find out more about the island, he was not greeted warmly, and it was only when the conflicts in other areas of the archipelago meant that the Dutch needed allies that they ventured back to the island; in 1827, a Javanese prince, acting as Dutch intermediary, negotiated the placement of a Dutch recruiting agent in Badung.

By the mid-1830s, Dutch concerns had become more political. The Danish trader **Mads Lange** had set up a trading post in Kuta, eventually moving there permanently after the defeat of his patron, the raja of Cakranegara in Lombok. This trade, to which the Dutch were not party, was largely in rice, which both Bali and Lombok produced to excess, and it was traded directly with British-held Singapore. The Dutch evolved a plan to start trading with Bali, with the aim of gaining political control before the British. They visited Badung and Klungkung and, in 1839, established an agent in Kuta with the agreement of the raja of Badung. In 1840, the Dutch envoy, **Huskus Koopman**, began a series of visits with the aim of persuading the Balinese to agree to Dutch sovereignty over the island.

Another major aim was to resolve the issue of *tawan karang*, or reef rights, which had caused long-term grievance to the Dutch. The Balinese had always seen it as their right to do what they wished with goods salvaged from ships wrecked on the island's reefs and, with an enormous increase in the movement of shipping in the area, much of it Dutch or trading under a Dutch flag, the incidence of wrecks, and the value of these goods, had risen considerably. However, the incident of the Dutch vessel *Overijssel*, wrecked on the Kuta reef on July 19, 1841, confirmed Koopman's initial failure. Having foundered because of navigational error, the heavily armed frigate was promptly plundered by local people, which outraged the Dutch.

Koopman, however, was an extremely skilful and devious negotiator, and by 1843 he had managed to make **treaties** with the regencies of Badung, Klungkung, Buleleng, Karangasem and Tabanan, agreeing to a Dutch trade monopoly. The rajas failed to realize that they had also virtually agreed to give the Dutch sovereignty over their lands and to abolish reef rights. Following Koopman's retirement, a new commissioner arrived in 1844 to finalize the treaties, but it soon became apparent that there were huge differences in Dutch and Balinese interpretations. Most regencies did ratify the treaties, but **Buleleng** and **Karangasem** stood firm. A further Dutch mission came the following year, apparently for further discussions, but this time it included a military officer whose brief was to assess the Buleleng defences. At a meeting in Singaraja in May 1845, Gusti Ketut Jelantik, brother of the rajas of Buleleng and Karangasem, stated, "Not by a mere scrap of paper shall any man become the master of another's lands. Rather let the kris decide." The Dutch returned to Java.

Dutch military victory

On June 26, 1846, the **First Dutch Military Expedition** arrived off the Buleleng coast with 3500 men. The commissioner, Mayor, issued an ultimatum to the raja of Buleleng to comply with all the demands of the Dutch. On June 28 the military force landed, overcame resistance and marched into Singaraja to find it deserted, the Balinese troops having withdrawn to the small inland village of Jagaraga. The rajas of Buleleng and Karangasem came to Singaraja to negotiate with the Dutch and eventually signed a surrender, agreeing to Dutch sovereignty and agreeing to pay costs for the victor's military expedition.

The Dutch departed, believing they had achieved their objectives, and left behind a small garrison until the compensation was paid. However, this fitted in with Jelantik's plan, and he continued to stockpile weapons and prepare for future battle. Meanwhile, nothing was paid to the Dutch, and ships that foundered continued to be plundered by the Balinese. On March 7, 1848, the governor-general of the Dutch East Indies sent ultimatums to Buleleng, Karangasem and Klungkung, demanding compensation, payment of war debts, the destruction of defence works and, in the case of Buleleng, the delivery of Jelantik to them. The ultimatums were ignored, and the **Second Dutch Military Expedition** arrived off the northern coast at Sangsit on June 8, 1848, with almost three thousand troops. Having quickly overcome the defences on the coast, the well-armed force marched towards **Jagaraga** where Jelantik had organized his force of around 16,000, armed largely with kris and lances. What the Balinese lacked in armaments they made up for in numbers and determination and, after fierce fighting, the Dutch were put to flight, at a cost of around two hundred men dead and wounded. The Balinese suffered casualties of over two thousand, but on June 10, 1848, the Dutch forces sailed back to Batavia.

The following year, in the **Third Dutch Military Expedition**, the Dutch used almost their entire military force in the Indies to overcome the Balinese. Around seven thousand troops landed in Buleleng on April 4, 1849. The Balinese asked to negotiate and despatched twelve thousand troops in full military uniform for the meeting at Singaraja between the rajas of Buleleng and Karangasem and General Michiels, the commander-in-chief of the expedition. Both this meeting and a later one at Sangsit on April 13 failed to reach any agreement. On April 15, the Dutch attacked the fortress at Jagaraga and defeated the Balinese with the loss of only about thirty men to the Balinese thousands.

Jelantik and the rajas of Buleleng and Karangasem fled east to continue the fight from there, while the Dutch set up new headquarters at Padang Bai. With four thousand additional troops from Lombok, the Dutch decided to attack Karangasem first. On their arrival at the palace on May 20, the raja of Karangasem, Gusti Gde Ngurah Karangasem, his family, and followers, all committed **puputan** (ritual suicide). The raja of Buleleng, accompanied by Jelantik, fled to the mountains of Seraya, but they were killed in further fighting.

Dutch troops then headed west towards Klungkung, with the village of **Kusamba** their first objective. However, the Balinese still occupied the surrounding villages and, during the night of May 25, they attacked, injuring General Michiels, who later died on board ship. This episode has an important place in the local history of Klungkung and is known as the Kusamba War. The death of Michiels from what is generally regarded as a non-fatal injury is ascribed to the influence of a magical bullet, **I Seliksik**, today an heirloom of the rajas of Klungkung, and believed to have been made from parts of a martyr's body.

With demoralized, sick and massively outnumbered Dutch troops reluctant to march against the *dewa agung* in Klungkung, Mads Lange was employed as go-between, and an **agreement** was drawn up on July 13, 1849, at his house in Kuta. The Balinese recognized Dutch sovereignty and accepted that *tawan karang* was prohibited, and in return the Dutch agreed to leave the rajas to administer their own kingdoms and not to base garrisons in the areas they had conquered. A feast on July 15 put the seal on the agreement.

The strengthening of the Dutch position

Initially, the Dutch left matters pretty much alone. However, during the 1850s they began to strengthen their control and placed Dutch controllers over the rajas of Buleleng and Jembrana.

From their administrative capital in **Singaraja**, the Dutch made some improvements on the island, particularly in irrigation and by planting coffee as a cash crop. They also brought in new regulations against slavery and the tradition of *suttee*, whereby widows would throw themselves on the funeral pyres of their dead husbands. This did not mean that all the flames of Balinese rebellion were extinguished, though, and further military expeditions were needed to quell **local rebellions**, such as one in 1864 when Ida Made Rai led an uprising in the village of Banjar, close to modern-day Lovina, that was defeated only when the Dutch mobilized troops.

Meanwhile, with Dutch influence concentrated in the north, the internal politics of the kingdoms in the **south** of the island became extremely complex. The kingdoms of Klungkung, Badung, Gianyar, Mengwi, Bangli and Tabanan were all variously in conflict with each other, and politics within each kingdom were also volatile. Steadily weakening themselves, the kingdoms gradually turned more and more to the Dutch, seeking protection to save themselves from extinction by their neighbours.

Rebellion and the Dutch in Lombok

In Lombok, meanwhile, Ratu Agung K'tut continued to rule until his death in 1872, when he was succeeded by his younger brother, **Ratu Agung Ngurah**.

In the **west** of the island, where there was no Sasak aristocracy, and where the Balinese had ruled since the seventeenth century, relations were relatively harmonious, with intermarriage quite common and local involvement in Hindu festivals. In the **east**, the situation was very different: Balinese power had been re-established only in the 1840s, and the frustrated Sasak aristocracy deeply resented their Balinese masters. There were rebellions in 1855 and 1871, which the Balinese quashed, but the rebellion of 1891 proved more serious.

This **rebellion** came about when Ratu Agung Ngurah demanded several thousand Sasak troops to enable him to invade the Balinese kingdom of Klungkung. For many years he had vied with the *dewa agung* of Klungkung over claims to the title of Supreme Ruler of Bali. In 1891, when Klungkung gained land at the expense of Mengwi, he decided to take action.

In east Lombok, the request for troops was met with resistance. The atmosphere deteriorated further when peasants in **Praya** refused to obey the order to go to war and a local Sasak aristocrat was executed. On August 7, 1891, several thousand Sasaks surrounded and burned the palace of the Balinese district chief. A huge force of west Lombok troops was sent to the scene but the rebellion could not be crushed. It quickly spread and by September 22, 1891, Balinese rule had been overthrown throughout east Lombok.

At this point, the **Dutch** became involved. They blockaded the coast so that the raja of Lombok could not import weapons, and cut communications with Karangasem in Bali, so he could not send for reinforcements. The hostile situation dragged on for years, gains being made and then lost, until July 1894, when the Dutch army landed in west Lombok. Faced with this huge threat close to home, the raja recalled all his troops, and the Sasaks from the east reoccupied their land.

On the night of August 25, 1894, there were reprisals. Balinese forces attacked the Dutch camp in the **Mayura Palace** at Cakranegara, where around nine hundred soldiers were camped. The Dutch were trapped inside the massive walls and only managed to escape to Mataram and then to Ampenan with great loss of life and heavy casualties, but they soon received reinforcements and, aided by the Sasaks from the east, proved too strong for the raja. Mataram was razed to the ground and Cakranegara attacked. Some members of the royal family surrendered while others committed *puputan*. The Dutch took control of the entire island, including the district of Karangasem on Bali which had been under the raja's control.

Further confrontation in south Bali

The Dutch had wanted to extend their control to the **south of Bali** for many years, but it wasn't until the turn of the twentieth century that events conspired to give them the chance they needed. In 1901 a new Dutch resident, Eschbach, who knew little of the island and its customs, was installed. In September 1904, a new *dewa agung* was also confirmed, and in the same year a new governor-general was appointed to run the Netherlands Indies government in Batavia.

This shaky situation was further fuelled by events in Tabanan. The Dutch had decreed *suttee* to be illegal in Buleleng, and they made their displeasure at the practice known to the rajas of the south, but when Raja Ngurah Agung of Tabanan died in 1903, his two elderly wives announced they would commit *suttee* at the cremation several months later. News of the event reached Holland, and outrage at home added to Dutch colonial embarrassment when they failed to persuade the new raja to stop the ritual. The raja correctly claimed that the Dutch had no jurisdiction, and the cremation and *suttee* went ahead as planned.

In addition, on May 27, 1904, a schooner, the *Sri Kumala*, owned by a Chinese trader and under Dutch protection, hit the reef just off Sanur. The owner of the ship, receiving no satisfaction from local officials, complained to the Resident in Singaraja that copper and silver coins had been stolen from the ship, and demanded compensation. The people of Sanur swore an oath in the village temple that they had stolen nothing, but the Resident decreed a **blockade** of Badung and ordered that the raja of Badung, Gusti Gde Ngurah, should pay compensation.

Tabanan successfully defused the blockade by allowing goods to be imported through ports further north, and the situation dragged on until July 1906, when the Dutch delivered ultimatums threatening military action. Dutch forces landed at Sanur, and by September 20, 1906, had advanced to **Denpasar**. Gusti Gde Ngurah realized resistance was useless and arranged the traditional **puputan**. An eye-witness account from a Dutch observer, Dr van Weede in his book *Indies Travel Memories*, describes the full horror of the event:

The ruler and the princes with their followers, dressed in their glittering attire, with their krises girded on, of which the golden hilts were in the form of Buddha statues and studded with precious stones; all of them were dressed in red or black and their hair was carefully combed, moistened with fragrant oils. The women were wearing the best clothes and accessories that they had; most of them wore their hair loose and all had white cloaks. The prince had his palace burned down and had everything that was breakable destroyed.

When at nine o'clock it was reported to him that the enemy had penetrated Denpasar from the North, the tragic procession of 250 people started to move; each man and woman carried a kris or long lance, also the children who had the strength to do it, while the babies were carried in their arms. Thus they walked to the north along the wide road bordered by tall trees, meeting their destruction.

The prince walked in front, carried on the shoulders by his followers according to custom, and silently ... until all of a sudden, at a turning in the road, the dark line of our infantry was visible before them. Immediately a halt was commanded and Captain Schutstal ordered the interpreters to summon the arriving party to a halt with gestures and with words. However these summons were in vain, and in spite of the repeated warnings the Balinese went over to a trot.

Incessantly the Captain and the interpreters made signs, but it was in vain. Soon they had to realize that they had to do with people who wanted to die. They let them approach to a hundred paces, eighty, seventy paces, but now they went over to a double quick step with couched lances and raised krises, the prince always in front.

A longer delay would have been irresponsible in view of the safety of our men, and the first salvo was given; several killed men remained at the place. One of the first to fall was the ruler; and now one of the most horrible scenes one could imagine took place.

While those who were saved continued the attack, and the shooting on our part for self defence remained necessary, one saw lightly wounded give the death-blow to the heavily wounded. Women held out their breasts to be killed or received the death blow between their shoulders, and those who did this were mowed down by our rifle fire, other men and women got up to continue the bloody work. Also suicides took place there on a big scale, and all seemed to yearn for their death: some women threw as a reward for the violent death which they desired from them gold coins to the soldiers, and stood straight up in front of them, pointing at their heart, as if they wanted to be hit there; if no shot was fired they killed themselves. Especially an old man was busily stepping over the corpses, and used his kris left and right until he was shot down. An old woman took his task and underwent the same fate, however, nothing helped. Always others got up to continue the work of destruction.

This scene was repeated later the same day at the palace of the prince of **Pamecutan**. Estimates of the total number of people killed that day vary between four hundred (the official Dutch estimate from Commissioner Liefrinck) and two thousand (the figure reported by the *Locomotief* newspaper printed in Semarang). Having defeated Badung, on September 27, the Dutch marched on to **Tabanan**, where the raja and crown prince surrendered and were imprisoned, prior to transportation to exile in Lombok or Madura. However, they both committed suicide rather than face exile. The following month, the Dutch forced **Klungkung** and **Bangli** to sign onerous agreements in which they became colonial vassals in all but name.

The completion of Dutch control

Having subdued the regencies of Bali, the Dutch decided to assert their monopoly over **opium trading** on the island. Traditionally, opium was imported by the Chinese and Buginese traders in Bali, who paid import duties to the rajas, but were then free to sell it as they wished, in the local markets. Dutch interference would cause a massive drop in income for the rajas and the ordinary people would be forced to use designated opium houses rather than buy it direct.

On the announcement of these measures on April 1, 1908, there was **rioting** in Klungkung followed by clashes with Dutch troops who were sent to control the situation. When more troops arrived in Klungkung on April 28, 1908, they witnessed a scene that bore similarities to the Badung *puputan* two years earlier. Oral reports tell how the *dewa agung* stabbed his royal kris into the ground at his feet expecting the power of the regalia to rend the ground asunder or bring torrential rain to destroy the enemy. Nothing happened, and other portents at the time, such as the huge banyan tree in front of Pura Taman Sari bursting out into strange golden flowers, sightings of comets, beached whales and mudslides, were taken as a sign that Klungkung's time was up. Around two hundred members of the royal household committed suicide that day; the remainder were exiled and did not return for many years.

With Klungkung under direct Dutch administration, the raja of **Bangli** felt it was only a matter of time before a pretext was found to attack him, and in October 1908, requested that his kingdom should have the same status as Gianyar and Karangasem and become a Dutch Protectorate. When this was finally approved in January 1909, the whole of the island of Bali came under **Dutch control**.

Colonial rule

The *puputan* of 1906 and 1908 caused a considerable stir among the more liberal citizens, religious groups and governments in Europe and the United States and pressure was put on the Dutch to moderate their policies in Bali and throughout Indonesia. Having gained control of the island, the Dutch proceeded to rule with a philosophy and approach they called the **Ethical Policy**, which they claimed upheld Balinese values, but was entirely on their terms. Traditional rulers were left in place as regents under the authority of the Dutch administration, although not all of the old royal families were amenable to this; in Buleleng, it was not until several generations after the Dutch conquest that an obliging member of the royal family could be found, and the members of the Klungkung royal family spent nineteen years in exile after the *puputan*.

Under the Dutch, engineers, doctors and teachers were introduced to the colony. In addition, Bali was spared the less enlightened **agricultural policies** that had turned large parts of Java into plantations for rubber, tea, sugar or tobacco for export, although a few areas for coffee and copra were established in the north. Generally big businesses were discouraged from branching out into Bali, although the steamship line KPM began encouraging **tourism** on the island. The first visitors arrived in the 1920s, and by the 1930s about a hundred visitors a month were reaching the island. Many were artists, musicians, anthropologists and writers who made their homes on the island, some following in the footsteps of the artist **Walter Spies** and settling in the Ubud area, others in Iseh near Klungkung, with more maverick souls, such as K'tut Tantri and Louise and Bob Koke, preferring the then rarely visited Kuta area.

Lombok under the Dutch

The position of **Lombok** under Dutch colonial rule was different from that of Bali. The situation of the people of Lombok began to deteriorate following the Dutch victory in 1894, and continued to do so for the next fifty years, bringing the population to the point of starvation more than once. The aim of the Dutch was to rule an economically profitable colony: they taxed the population to the hilt and introduced **compulsory labour** for projects such as roadbuilding. In addition to land tax, there were **taxes** on income and on the slaughter of animals. These taxes were initially payable in local currency, but the system changed and they were demanded in Netherlands Indies currency (NIC). The Chinese rice exporters were one of the few groups on the island who traded in NIC, and increasing amounts of rice started to be sold to them to raise money for taxes. Consequently, a very high proportion of food grown on the island was exported, and local rice consumption dropped by a quarter. By 1934, the Dutch administration estimated that about a third of the population were **landless and destitute**.

World War II and independence

Following the bombing of the American Fleet in Pearl Harbour on December 7, 1941, Japan entered **World War II** and moved quickly through Asia, occupying Singapore in February 1942. The **Japanese** fleet arrived off Sanur on February 18 and landed five hundred troops, who moved unopposed to Denpasar and then through Bali, which they occupied without a fight. Many of the Dutch deserted and were later court-martialled. The larger islands to the west, Java and Sumatra, had fallen by March 9.

The Japanese **occupation** was short-lived but it was a time of hardship and fear for the islanders, who were faced with feeding the military as well as themselves. However, the occupation had very significant political effects within the islands as it showed that the Dutch colonialists were, in fact, vulnerable and could be put to flight.

Throughout the war years, the idea of liberation grew, and, on August 17, 1945, just three days after the Japanese surrender, Indonesia made its **Declaration of Independence** in an announcement by President **Sukarno**. Sukarno had established the Indonesian Nationalist Party in 1927; jailed in 1929 for advocating the overthrow of the Netherlands East Indies government, he was briefly released and then arrested again and exiled to Flores in August 1933, and then to Sumatra. Along with two other figures of the Independence movement, Dr Mohammed Hatta and Sutan Sjahrir, he was released by the Japanese invaders in 1942.

While some on Bali were strong supporters of the independence struggle, there were others who were less than happy: Java was Muslim, and the traditional enmity between the two islands made many people uncertain about joining a republic dominated by Java.

The fight for independence

Returning to retake their colony in March 1946, the **Dutch** faced ferocious fighting on Java but initially little opposition on Bali. However, the guerrilla forces, the most famous of which was led by **Gusti Ngurah Rai**, a young army officer who created the TKR (People's Military Force), set about harrying the Dutch. His tactic known as the "Long March to Gunung Agung" attempted to concentrate forces from all over the island on the slopes of the mountain and then ambush the Dutch. However, the Dutch surrounded the camp and, although the Balinese escaped across the mountains, they were again surrounded near Marga in Tabanan where all 97 of them died in a fight to the death. (Ngurah Rai is remembered as a hero: Bali's airport is named after him, as is the island's main bypass road, on which stands a commemorative statue.)

The status quo returned to Bali, with local rulers overseen by Dutch administrators. The Dutch, having lost control of the islands to the west, created the Republic of East Indonesia with a capital in Makassar in Sulawesi, and in 1948, declared Bali to be an autonomous state within that republic.

However, they were fighting a lost cause. The US questioned the sense of the Dutch expenditure of all their Marshall Plan aid (money allocated to European countries for reconstruction after the war) on fighting to keep the Indies. The Australian government was sympathetic towards Indonesia, and the other European colonial powers had their own problems, so could offer the Dutch little practical help. Finally, under pressure of world opinion in January 1949, the UN Security Council ordered the Dutch to withdraw their troops and negotiate. In December 1949, the United States of Indonesia was legally recognized and dissolved the following year to form the **Republic of Indonesia** with Sukarno as president.

The Sukarno years

The early years of independence under Sukarno were not kind to Bali; the economic situation within the new republic became perilous as inflation, corruption and mismanagement ran riot. Following a series of military coups in the islands, martial rule was instituted and parliament was abolished in 1959 with the introduction of **guided democracy**. The economic situation went from bad to worse as inflation soared and Western investment dried up. In 1960, land reforms reduced the legally allowable holdings for each individual, but land, once surrendered, was then not allocated fairly. 1963 saw a catastrophic war against Malaya to try to prevent the creation of the Federation of Malaysia.

Although Sukarno's mother was Balinese and he claimed a special understanding of the island, the Balinese felt neglected by the government in Jakarta, which, in turn, was suspicious of the Balinese lack of ferocity against the Dutch and, above all, of Bali's Hinduism. Sukarno visited the island regularly, especially his palace at Tampaksiring, with a massive entourage which demanded to be fed, entertained and then sent on its way with gifts. During the 1960s, a groundswell of resentment against the government grew in Bali. The Balinese began to believe that a state of spiritual disharmony had been reached, and preparations were made for a traditional island-wide purification ceremony, **Eka Dasa Rudra**, held in 1963 against the backdrop of a fiercely rumbling

Gunung Agung that eventually blew its top and laid waste to much of the east of the island.

Later events in Jakarta piled disaster upon disaster in Bali. During the night of September 30, 1965, a group of young left-wing army officers kidnapped and killed six high-ranking generals who, they claimed, were planning to overthrow the president. It is generally thought that the attack on the generals was an attempted Communist coup that failed when **Major-General Suharto** took control of the army and set about seizing political power amid a media blitz against the Communist Party (PKI). The entire incident, dubbed the **Gestapu** affair, has been the subject of enormous speculation, as the Communists could never have hoped to take over and were doing well politically in any case. Also, Suharto was not on the hit list although he was of higher rank than some of the generals who were killed.

A wave of killings in northern Sumatra, central and eastern Java, Bali and some of the outer islands, including Lombok, began in December 1965, continuing until March 1966, although there were sporadic outbursts right up to 1969. Estimates suggest that a hundred thousand were killed on Bali and fifty thousand on Lombok, with actual or suspected members of the PKI, or sympathizers, the main targets along with the Chinese population on both islands. Tens of thousands were also taken into military detention, and they and their families have been stigmatized ever since – an issue that is gaining some prominence as the victims begin to publicize their plight. On the whole, though, it's a period of history that nobody will discuss these days.

Following the attempted coup, Sukarno lost much of his power to Suharto, and, by March 1966, with most of Suharto's political opponents out of office, the **New Order** was in place. Sukarno signed an Instruction giving Suharto, now minister and commander of the army, power to take "all measures considered necessary to ensure peace and order and stability". Suharto officially became the second president of Indonesia in March 1968, a position which he held for over thirty years.

Indonesia under Suharto

Following the dramatic ending of the Suharto regime in May 1998, the history of his rule began to be written, and will no doubt occupy scholars for many years to come. What now seems clear is that, in some respects and at some times, his rule was beneficial to the country. The New Order policy of attracting foreign investment, curbing inflation and re-entering the global economy was largely successful. It was helped enormously by Indonesia's massive **natural resources** of copper, tin, timber and oil, and foreign investment enabled manufacturing industries to be opened up in the archipelago. The **economic situation** of the country improved, and figures looked good: the 1993 GNP per head of population was estimated at US$680, an annual increase of about five percent per year since 1985.

An unspoken but clearly understood **social contract** appeared to be in place throughout the Suharto years. Ordinary Indonesians by and large saw their material prosperity and standard of living rise, something that Suharto could and did take credit for. However, the price they paid for this was the almost total freedom they allowed the government. Until 1997 it was a price the majority of Indonesians were willing to pay, often at the expense of minority groups.

The **political** situation remained fairly stable up until 1997, mainly because of the straightforward expedient of limiting opposition. In July 1971, in the first election since 1955, the government party, Sekretariat Bersama Golongan

Karya, known as **Golkar**, won the majority of seats in the House of Representatives (Dewan Perwakilan Rakyat), and in March 1973, Suharto was re-elected as president. Despite the two main opposition parties, **Partai Demokrasi Indonesia** (PDI), the Indonesian Democratic Party, and **Partai Persatuan Pembangunan** (PPP), the Muslim-based United Development Party, this pattern was repeated in general elections until 1997, with Suharto re-elected in 1978, 1983, 1988, 1993 and 1998.

In 1996 the government engineered a special party congress of the PDI and expelled the popular and charismatic PDI leader, **Megawati Sukarnoputri**, daughter of Sukarno, behind whom opposition to the government appeared to gather. Following her removal, the PDI split and Jakarta suffered its most serious **riots** for two decades; violence and open disaffection escalated throughout the country in 1996 and 1997. Spoken opposition to the government, effectively silenced for decades, grew, as did ethnic tensions across the archipelago.

The **economic crisis** of the late 1990s that decimated the economies of Southeast Asia was never likely to leave Indonesia untouched. In August 1997, a dollar bought around Rp2400; in early 1998 it passed Rp10,000 and the rupiah kept on falling. In late 1997 and early 1998 almost a million workers lost their jobs as companies went bust or cut back in an attempt to survive. Prices of imports (including food) rose sharply, and a series of riots in the early part of the year, centred on Java, targeted Chinese shopkeepers and small businesspeople – long the scapegoats of Indonesian unrest. A rescue package from the International Monetary Fund proved to be an on-off affair, and gradually

Transmigrasi and separatism

Initially introduced as a policy during Dutch colonial times, the Indonesian government continued the practice of transmigration, **transmigrasi**, to relieve population pressure in some parts of the archipelago, most often Java, by settling other, less-populated islands. The scheme has received considerable criticism from human rights groups and environmentalists, who claim that land has been taken from indigenous peoples and massive deforestation has occurred; they also say that it is an attempt to "Javanize" the ethnically diverse Indonesians, most notoriously on **Irian Jaya**. The Organisasi Papua Merdeka (OPM, or Free Papua Movement) has been in active opposition to the government in Irian Jaya since 1977, and in January 1996 they kidnapped 26 people – including seven Westerners – to publicize their cause. Some of the most violent incidents against settlers have occurred in West Kalimantan where Dayak tribesmen have turned against Madurese settlers.

However, the Indonesian government was far more notorious overseas for its annexation of **East Timor** in 1976, and its brutal suppression of the independence movement there in the following decades, involving, some estimates suggest, the deaths of 200,000 people out of a population of 650,000. During and after the downfall of Suharto, East Timor was one of the most violent areas of the country with huge tension and strife between Muslims, Chinese, anti-Indonesian Timorese Catholics and pro-Indonesian militia. It is now acknowledged that the Indonesian army played an active and violent part in this gruesome melange. In August 1999, President Habibie held a **referendum** in which the people of East Timor were offered a choice between autonomy within Indonesia or independence. They voted, by a huge majority, for independence, which was achieved in May 2002. However, elsewhere in Indonesia this was regarded as a massive blow against the country's pride and autonomy, and added determination and anger to separatist movements across the country. At the other end of the vast archipelago, the **Free Aceh Movement** (GAM) has been active in the north of Sumatra since 1990, with more than five thousand people estimated to have been killed so far.

Indonesian anger turned against President Suharto and his family, who were seen to have been the biggest winners in the Indonesian economic success story.

Student rioting in May 1998 was the catalyst for change, at a cost of several deaths, leading to more widespread unrest and, eventually, to **Suharto's resignation** on May 21 and the appointment as president of **B.J. Habibie**, a friend of Suharto and a man many felt came from the same mould.

After Suharto

President Habibie was blamed for losing East Timor and, in the run-up to the June 1999 **elections** in which over 100 million people cast their votes, the **Bank Bali scandal** erupted to give Habibie even greater headaches. It involved Rp546 billion (US$70 million) in public funds being transferred to a company controlled by the deputy treasurer of Golkar, the party of Habibie and Suharto. It was widely believed that this money was to create a "war chest" for Habibie to buy sufficient support to win the October 1999 presidential election.

The results of the general election were unequivocal: the PDI, led by **Megawati Sukarnoputri**, won 37 percent of the vote; the old ruling party Golkar led by Habibie got twenty percent; and the PKB (National Awakening Party), led by the relatively unknown liberal Muslim cleric **Abdurrahman Wahid**, received twenty percent, with the remainder shared between smaller contenders. By October 1999, three candidates for the presidency emerged: Habibie, Megawati Sukarnoputri and Abdurrahman Wahid. Habibie withdrew just hours before the vote, and the election of Wahid brought violent protests to the streets of both Denpasar and Singaraja, where huge amounts of damage were done to government buildings in outrage that the presidency – which many felt was owed to Megawati Sukarnoputri – was denied her.

President Abdurrahman Wahid, popularly known as **Gus Dur**, will probably be remembered more for the manner he left office, rather than his achievements within it. His most notable act was to promise to curb the power of the military within the country, and immediately replaced General Wiranto as Minister of Defence with the first civilian ever to hold this post in Indonesia. By July 2001 accusations of corruption surrounded Gus Dur, and his increasingly eccentric and autocratic response alienated parliament, who forced him from office after just 21 months.

Megawati Sukarnoputri's presidency

On July 23, 2001, **Megawati Sukarnoputri** became president. Megawati – darling of the Balinese, to whom she is known simply as Mega – is regarded in Bali with something approaching fanaticism, based largely on the fact that her maternal grandmother (Sukarno's mother) was Balinese.

Her problems in ruling the country are immense. Calls for **independence** from across the archipelago are continuing, most violently in Aceh and in Irian Jaya (also known as West Papua), where violence is reported to be escalating, as Indonesian-supported militia begin to wage war against Free Papua Movement supporters in an apparent re-run of Indonesian strategy in East Timor. **Ethnic strife** across the country has continued, although the government has sponsored several peace agreements this year that look positive. In **Maluku**, Christians and Muslims have been fighting since early 1999, with three thousand reported to be dead, 200,000 homeless and the violence so extreme that aid workers and diplomats all departed. In January 2000, this religious fighting appeared to spread to normally peaceful **Lombok** (see p.417) but, fortunately, appeared to be a one-off event rather than the beginnings of a long-running conflict. More recently, fighting between Christians and Muslims in central **Sulawesi** halted.

Meanwhile the ongoing problem of prosecuting Suharto for corruption is the main topic of conversation on the average Indonesian street. The downfall of the Suharto clan has already had an effect on Bali, where several controversial construction projects associated with the discredited family have been halted or taken over by other companies. On the economic front, the rupiah has stabilized but serious problems remain: the government has vowed to remove subsidies from basic goods, and petrol prices have risen significantly, forcing up the cost of living for most people. At present, the near-reverence in which Mega is held by ordinary Indonesians has militated against outrage. It remains to be seen whether she can solve all the difficulties with which the archipelago is beset.

Religion

Over 92 percent of Balinese are Hindu. In contrast, Lombok is only three percent Hindu and the vast majority of its inhabitants are Muslim.

Religious activity permeates almost every aspect of **Balinese** life. Every morning, tiny palm-leaf offerings are laid down for the gods and spirits who need
24-hour propitiation; in the afternoons, processions of men and women parade
the streets en route to temple celebrations, towers of offertory fruit and rice
cakes balanced on their heads. Temple compounds dominate the horizons of
every village, and the desire to entice and entertain the deities inspires daily
performances of dance and gamelan music.

While Islam is as pervasive on **Lombok** as Hinduism is on Bali, it has a much
more austere presence. You'll hear the call to prayer five times a day, and streets
are often deserted on Fridays around noon, when a large proportion of the population go to the mosque. Marriage and circumcision are celebrated, but the exuberant and frequent festivals of Balinese Hinduism have no Muslim equivalents.

Balinese Hinduism

Though it's not a proselytizing faith, **Balinese Hinduism** is a demanding one,
which requires participation from every citizen. Any Balinese who gives up
their religion automatically loses their Balinese identity, and any Balinese
woman who marries a person of another faith gives up her right to worship
the Hindu gods.

Despite certain obvious similarities, Balinese Hinduism differs dramatically
from Indian and Nepalese Hinduism. Bali's is a blend of theories and practices
borrowed from Hinduism and Buddhism, grafted onto the far stronger indigenous vision of a world that is overrun by good and bad spirits. The Balinese
have practised ancestor worship and followed animist cults ever since the Stone
Age and, consequently, only the most complementary aspects of the newer
Asian theologies have been adopted.

Early influences

The **animism** of the Stone- and Bronze-Age Balinese probably differed very
little from the beliefs of their twenty-first-century descendants, who worship
certain sacred mountains and rivers and conduct elaborate rituals to ensure that
the souls of their dead ancestors are kept sweet. In among these animist practices
are elements borrowed from the **Mahayana Buddhism** that dominated much
of Southeast Asia in the eighth century – certain Buddhist saints, for example,
some of which are still visible at Goa Gajah, and a penchant for highly ornate
imagery. The strongest influences arrived with the droves of **East Javanese
Hindu priests** who fled Muslim invaders en masse in the early sixteenth century. High-caste, educated pillars of the Majapahit kingdom, these strict followers of the Hindu faith settled in all corners of Bali and quickly set about for-
malizing Bali's embryonic Hindu practices. Balinese Hinduism, or **agama
Hindu** as it's usually termed, became Bali's official religion, and the Majapahit
priests have, ever since, been worshipped as the true Balinese ancestors.

As Bali's Hinduism gained strength, so its neighbouring islands turned towards Islam, and now Bali is a tiny Hindu haven in an archipelago which contains the biggest Islamic population in the world. Hindu Bali's role within the predominantly Muslim Indonesian state has always been problematic. As part of its code of national law (Pancasila), the Jakarta administration requires that all Indonesian faiths be monotheistic – a proviso that doesn't sit easily with either Hindu or animist tenets. After concerted theological and political wranglings, however, Bali's Hindu Council came up with an acceptable compromise. By emphasizing the role of their supreme deity, **Sanghyang Widi Wasa** (who manifests himself as the Hindu Trinity of Brahma, Siwa and Wisnu), the Council convinced the Ministry of Religion that Bali was essentially monotheistic, and in 1962 Balinese Hinduism was formally recognized by Jakarta. As a result, a host of new Balinese temples were dedicated to a unifying force – Jagatnata or "Lord of the World"; two typical examples of modern *pura Jagatnata* can be seen in Denpasar and Singaraja.

The beliefs

At the root of *agama Hindu* lies the fundamental understanding that the world – both natural and supernatural – is composed of opposing forces. These can be defined as good and evil, positive and negative, pure and impure, order and disorder, gods and demons, or as a mixture of all these things – but the crucial fact is that the forces need to be balanced. The desire to achieve **equilibrium** and harmony in all things dictates every spiritual activity. **Positive forces**, or *dharma*, are represented by the gods (*dewa* and *bhatara*), and need to be cultivated, entertained and honoured with offerings of food, water and flowers, with dances, beautiful paintings and sculptures, fine earthly abodes (temples) and ministrations from ceremonially clad devotees. The **malevolent forces**, *adharma*, which manifest themselves as earth demons (*bhuta*, *kala* and *leyak*) and cause sickness, death and volcanic eruptions, need to be neutralized with elaborate rituals and special offerings.

To ensure that malevolent forces never take the upper hand, elaborate purification rituals are undertaken for the exorcism of spirits. Crucial to this is the notion of **ritual uncleanliness** (*sebel*), a state which can affect an individual (during a woman's period, for example, or after a serious illness), a family (after the death of a close relative, or if twins are born) or even a whole community (a plague of rats in the village rice-fields, or a fire in village buildings). The whole island can even become *sebel*, and **island-wide exorcisms** are held every new year (*Nyepi*) to restore the spiritual health of Bali and all its people. More elaborate island-cleansing rituals are performed every five, ten and 25 years, climaxing with the centennial *Eka Dasa Rudra* rite, which is held at the holiest temple, Besakih. In addition, there are all sorts of **purification rituals** (*yadnya*) that Balinese must go through at various significant stages in their lives (see p.545).

The focus of every purification ritual is the ministering of **holy water** – such an essential part of the religion that *agama Hindu* is sometimes known as *agama tirta*, the religion of holy water. Ordinary well or tap water can be transformed into holy water by a *pedanda* (high priest), but water from certain sources is considered to be particularly sacred – the springs at Tirta Empul in Tampaksiring and on Gunung Agung, for example, and the water taken from the lakeside Pura Danu Batur.

As the main sources of these life-giving waters, Bali's three great **mountains** are also worshipped: the highest, and the holiest, of the three is Gunung Agung, associated with the sun god Surya, and site of Bali's most sacred mother temple, Besakih; and Gunung Batur and Gunung Batukau also hold great spiritual power, as do the lakes that fill their volcanic craters. Ever since the Stone Age, the Balinese have regarded their mountains as being the realm of the deities, the sea as the abode of demons and giants, and the valleys in between as the natural province of the human world. From this concept comes the Balinese sense of direction and **spatial orientation**, whereby all things, such as temples, houses and villages, are aligned in relation to the mountains and the sea: **kaja** is the direction towards the mountains, upstream, and is the holiest direction; **kelod** is the downstream direction, the part that is closest to the sea and therefore impure.

Finally, there are the notions of karma, reincarnation, and the attaining of enlightenment. The aim of every Hindu is to attain **enlightenment** (*moksa*), which brings with it the union of the individual and the divine, and liberation from the endless painful cycle of death and rebirth. *Moksa* is only attainable by pure souls, and this can take hundreds of lifetimes to attain. Hindus believe that everybody is **reincarnated** according to their **karma**, karma being a kind of account book which registers all the good and bad deeds performed in the past lives of a soul. Karma is closely bound up with caste and the notion that an individual should accept rather than challenge their destiny.

The gods

All Balinese **gods** are manifestations of the supreme being, **Sanghyang Widi Wasa**, a deity who is only ever alluded to in abstract form by an empty throne-shrine, the *padmasana*, that stands in the holiest corner of every temple. Sanghyang Widi Wasa's three main aspects manifest themselves as the Hindu trinity: Brahma, Wisnu and Siwa. Each of these three gods has different roles and is associated with specific colours and animals.

Brahma is the Creator, represented by the colour red and often depicted riding on a bull. His consort is the goddess of learning, **Saraswati**, who rides a white goose.

As the Preserver, **Wisnu** is associated with life-giving waters; he rides the *garuda* (half-man, half-bird) and is honoured by the colour black. Wisnu also has several avatars, including **Buddha** – a neat way of incorporating Buddhist elements into the Hindu faith.

Siwa, the Destroyer or, more accurately, the Dissolver, is associated with death and rebirth, with the temples of the dead and with the colour white. He is sometimes represented as a phallic pillar, or *linggam*, and sometimes in the manifestation of **Surya**, the sun god. Siwa's consort is the terrifying goddess **Durga**, whose Balinese personality is the gruesome widow-witch **Rangda**, queen of the demons. The son of Siwa and Durga is the elephant-headed deity **Ganesh**, generally worshipped as the remover of obstacles.

Brahma, Wisnu and Siwa all have associated lesser deities, or *dewi* (*dewa* if male), many of them gods of the elements and of the physical world. **Dewi Sri** is the goddess of rice, worshipped at tiny shrines in every group of paddy-fields, and honoured at significant stages throughout the agricultural year. **Dewi Danu** is the equally important goddess of the crater lake – honoured with temples on the shores of the three volcanic lakes Bratan, Batur and Tamblingan, and so important to the rice-growers of Bali as a source of vital irrigation that annual pilgrimages are made to all three temples. **Dewa Baruna** is the unpredictable god of the sea, and **Dewi Melanting** the goddess of commerce and prosperity.

The demons

Demons also come in a variety of manifestations. The forces of evil are personified by a cast of **bhuta** and **kala**, invisible goblins and ghosts who inhabit eerie, desolate places like the temples of the dead, cemeteries, moonless seashores and dark forests. Their purpose on earth is to wreak havoc in the human world, causing horrible lingering illnesses and ruinous agricultural and economic disasters, preying on the most vulnerable babies, and entering villagers' minds and turning them insane. But their power is not invincible, and they can be appeased and placated with **offerings** just as the gods can – the difference being that the offerings for these demons consist mainly of dirty, unpleasant, unattractive and mouldy things, which are thrown down on the ground, not placed respectfully on ledges and altars. Demons are notoriously greedy too, and so the Balinese will always throw a dash of *arak* (rice liquor) on the ground before drinking, or drop a few grains of rice to the floor when eating.

Various other strategies are used to repel, confuse and banish the *bhuta* and *kala*. Most entrance gates to temples and households are guarded by fierce-looking statues and demonic images designed to be so ugly as to frighten off even the boldest demon. Many gateways are also blocked by a low brick wall, an **aling-aling**, as demons can only walk in straight lines, and so won't be able to negotiate the necessary zigzag to get around the wall. *Bhuta* and *kala* get particular pleasure from entering a person's body via their various orifices, so certain temples (especially in the north) have covered their walls with pornographic carvings, the theory being that the demons will have so much fun penetrating the carved simulation orifices on the outside walls that they won't bother to try their luck further inside the temple compound.

In addition to the unseen *bhuta* and *kala*, there are the equally fearful **leyak**, or witches, who take highly visible and creepy forms, transforming themselves into such horrors as headless chickens, bald-headed giants, monkeys with rows of shiny gold teeth, fireballs and riderless motorbikes. *Leyak* can transform themselves effortlessly from one form to another, and most assume the human form during the daytime, leading outwardly normal lives. Only at night do they release their dark spirits to wreak havoc on unsuspecting villagers, causing sickness, madness and accidents, while their human shell remains innocently asleep in bed. Even in their human form, *leyak* cannot be killed with knives or poisons, but they can be controlled and disempowered by harnessing white magic, as practised by shamanic *balian* (traditional healers; see box on p.547), or by priests.

The temples

The focus of every community's spiritual activity is the **temple**, or *pura* – a specially designed temporary abode for the gods to inhabit whenever they so desire, open and unroofed so as to invite easy access between heaven and earth. Major religious ceremonies take place inside the *pura*, and members of the community spend a great deal of their time and income beautifying the sanctuary with carvings, and consecrating offerings at its altars.

At first glance, visitors can find Balinese temples rather confusing, and even unimpressive, in appearance. Many of them seem to be rather bland affairs: open-roofed compounds scattered with a host of shrines and altars, built mainly of limestone and red brick, and with no paintings or treasures to focus on. But many of Bali's numerous temples – there are at least 20,000 on the island – do reward closer examination. Every structure within a temple complex is charged with great symbolic significance, often with entertaining legends attached, and many of the walls and gateways are carved with an ebullience of

Certain Balinese **temples** have acquired a special status because of their history, their association with a certain priest or raja, or from the sheer beauty of the carvings inside them or their stunning physical situation. The ten (in alphabetical order) that are most worth visiting are:

mythical figures, demonic spirits and even secular scenes. (Note that when **visiting a temple**, you must be appropriately dressed, even if there's no one else in the vicinity; see p.73 for details.)

The reason there are so many temples in Bali is that every *banjar* and small village is obliged to build at least three; each one serving a specific role within the community. At the top of the village, the *kaja* or holiest end, stands the **pura puseh**, the temple of origin, which is dedicated to the founders of the community. For everyday spiritual activities, villagers worship at the **pura desa**, the village temple, which always lies at the heart of the village, and often doubles as a convenient forum for community meetings and other secular activities. The essential trio is completed by the **pura dalem**, or temple of the dead, at the *kelod* (unclean) end of the village, which is usually dedicated either to Siwa, or to the widow-witch Rangda. Larger villages will often have a number of other temples as well, perhaps including a **pura melanting** for the gods of wealth and commerce, and a small agricultural temple or shrine, a **pura subak**, dedicated to the rice goddess, Dewi Sri.

Bali also has nine directional temples, or **kayangan jagat**, which are regarded as extremely sacred by all islanders as they protect the island as a whole and all its people. The *kayangan jagat* are located at strategic points across the island, especially on high mountain slopes, rugged cliff faces and lakeside shores: Pura Ulun Danu Batur is on the shores of Lake Batur (north); Pura Pasar Agung on Gunung Agung (northeast); Pura Lempuyang Luhur on Gunung Lempuyang (east); Goa Lawah near Candi Dasa (southeast); Pura Masceti near Lebih (south); Pura Luhur Uluwatu on the Bukit (southwest); Pura Luhur Batukau on Gunung Batukau (west); Pura Ulun Danu Bratan on the shores of Lake Bratan (northwest); and Besakih on Gunung Agung (centre). The most important of these is Besakih – the mother temple – as it occupies the crucial position on Bali's holiest, and highest, mountain, Gunung Agung; the others are all of equal status, and dutiful islanders are expected to attend the anniversary celebrations (*odalan*) of the one situated closest to their home.

Temple layout

Whatever the size, status or particular function of a temple, it will nearly always follow a prescribed layout (see temple plan on pp.508–509), adhering to the precepts of **religious architecture** minutely described in the ancient *lontar* texts. All Balinese temples are oriented *kaja–kelod*, and nearly all are designed around three courtyards, each section divided from the next by a low wall punctuated by a huge, and usually ornate, gateway.

The **outer courtyard**, or *jaba*, holds the secular world at bay. Cockfights take place here, as do some of the least sacred dances (tourist shows, for example),

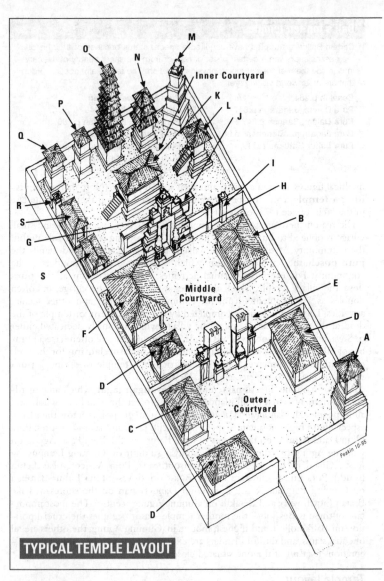

Inner Courtyard

Middle
Courtyard

Outer
Courtyard

Peakin 10-95

TYPICAL TEMPLE LAYOUT

and at festival time this is where the food stalls are set up. The **middle court-yard**, *jaba tengah*, acts as a transition zone between the human and the divine world, and generally contains pavilions for the preparing of offerings and the storing of temple paraphernalia. In some temples, particularly in north Bali, the outer and middle courtyards are merged into one. The extremely sacred **inner courtyard**, *jeroan*, houses all the shrines, and is the focus of all temple rituals. All offerings are brought here, prayers are held in front of the shrines, and the most sacred dances are performed within its confines. The *jeroan* is quite often

A – kulkul Drum tower. Tall roofed tower that contains the drum (*kulkul*) used to summon members of the *banjar* to festivals, to community meetings and, in the past, into battle. More accurately described as a wooden bell, the drum itself is made from a hollowed-out log slit down the middle and suspended by a rope from the roof.

B – wantilan Performance pavilion. Large *bale* used for cockfights and for dance performances.

C – bale gong Gamelan pavilion. Sizeable open-sided, thatched pavilion in which the gamelan instruments are stored; this is where the musicians sit and play at festivals.

D – bale All-purpose pavilion, used for village meetings and for resting devotees.

E – candi bentar The split temple gate. Looks like a tower that has literally been sliced down the middle. Its spiritual symbolism can be interpreted in several ways: the material world has been split so that the human body can enter the spiritual realm; the left side represents femaleness, the right, maleness; if an evil spirit tries to pass through, the two halves will come together to crush it.

F – paon Kitchen. Open-sided pavilion where the offerings are prepared before an *odalan* or other important festival.

G – paduraksa (or **kori agung**) Central covered gateway to the inner courtyard. Often the temple's most imposing structure, the *paduraksa* is usually approached by a flight of steps and crowned with a sculpted tower. The central wooden door is usually kept locked (except at festival times), so devotees and casual visitors generally use a side door to the inner courtyard. The archway over the central door is always crowned by a carving of a grotesque fanged head – **Bhoma**, child of the earth or son of the forest, whose role is to ward off demons.

H – raksasa Metre-high demon statues. Usually appearing in pairs on either side of gateways, *raksasa* wield clubs, have aggressive, scary faces, and act as another deterrent to malevolent spirits.

I – side gate Kept open to allow access to the inner courtyard as the central main gate is officially only for the use of the deities and their representatives.

J – aling-aling Low freestanding stone or brick wall. Located directly in front of the *kori agung*'s central doorway, this is the last line of defence against unwanted demons: evil spirits can only walk in straight lines, so the *aling-aling* will block their path.

K – gedong paruman or **pepelik** Empty pavilion nearly always located right in the middle of the inner courtyard, where the gods are invited to assemble and to watch temple festivities.

L – gedong pesimpangan The principal shrine honouring the village founder or important local deity.

M – padmasana Lotus throne. An empty stone throne built into the summit of a tall (sculpted) tower, which is reserved for the supreme deity Sanghyang Widi Wasa who is invited to sit here whenever he descends to earth. Always located in the corner that's closest to the holiest mountain, Gunung Agung (usually the northeast corner), with its back towards the peak. The tower structure is always supported by the cosmic turtle, Bedawang, and two naga or mythological sea serpents which are part of the Balinese creation myth. **Bedawang** is the creature who carries the world on his back (when he gets restless, he shakes the earth's foundations, so causing earthquakes), while **Naga Basukih** and **Naga Anantaboga** act as his steadying agents, simultaneously representing human needs, namely food, shelter, clothing and security.

N – meru Gunung Agung Three-roofed (occasionally eleven-roofed) shrine, dedicated to Bali's holiest mountain.

O – meru Sanghyang Widi Wasa Eleven-roofed shrine dedicated to the supreme deity.

P – meru Gunung Batur One-roofed (occasionally nine-roofed) shrine dedicated to the sacred Mount Batur.

Q – gedong Maospahit Shrine honouring the Javanese Majapahit (or Maospahit) people, who are considered the spiritual ancestors of the contemporary Balinese. This shrine is often only distinguishable by a sculpture of a deer's head, or a carved or real pair of antlers set over the shrine's (locked) door – the deer is the symbol of these ancestral gods.

R – taksu Stone pillar. The seat for the interpreter of the gods, who occasionally descends to inhabit the bodies of certain worshippers, sending them into a trance so that they can convey messages between the gods and the humans.

S – bale piasan Pavilions where offerings are laid.

out of bounds to the lay community and opened only during festivals.

Every *pura* contains a whole collection of small structures, each one devoted to a specific purpose. **Bale** are open-sided pavilions, usually built of wood, raised on small stilts, and thatched with black sugar-palm fibre. These are practical buildings for seating devotees or gamelan players, and for storing things. **Gedong** is the generic term for the squat, often cube-shaped shrines that are generally made of brick, with thatched roofs. Each *gedong* is dedicated to a particular deity or ancestor, and sometimes contains a symbolic image. The elegant pagoda-style shrines that tower over every temple wall are known as **meru**, after the sacred Hindu peak Mount Meru, home of the gods. Each *meru* has a small wood or brick base beneath a multi-tiered roof thatched with thick black sugar-palm fibre. There's always an odd number of roofs (three, five, seven, nine or eleven), the number indicating the status of the god to whom the temple is dedicated.

Priests

The only people who are conversant with all the rituals of *agama Hindu* are the **high priests**, or *pedanda*, men and a few women of the Brahman caste who spend years studying the complex theology. This knowledge gives them such special power that they are considered to be quite aloof from the other villagers; the *pedanda* and his or her family usually live in a special compound that stands slightly apart from the rest of the community.

Only the most important ceremonies are presided over by a *pedanda*. Wreathed in clouds of incense and dressed all in white, save for bejewelled mitres on their heads and multiple strings of beads around their necks, the *pedanda's* role is to invoke the spirit of the supreme deity with a complicated ritual performance of chanting, hand gestures and the periodic ringing of a small handbell. With legs folded into a half-lotus and eyes closed, the *pedanda* can spend hours chanting the appropriate mantras in an ancient tongue – either the old Javanese language, Kawi, or the similarly esoteric Sanskrit – which mean nothing to the lay people who generally just pause for a brief prayer before moving on. The scholarly *pedanda* are also traditionally the only people to understand the complexities of the Balinese calendar system and so they are consulted over the timing for major events – such as the most auspicious day for laying the foundation stone of a house or office, for example, or for holding a cremation ceremony.

It is the job of the **village priest**, the *pemangku*, to attend to the more mundane spiritual activities of the community. *Pemangku* are nearly always male, though their wives also help. Easily recognized by his white apparel and formal white *udeng* headdress, the *pemangku* spends a great deal of time at the temple, sweeping the grounds, repairing the buildings and, in the run-up to the *odalan* and other local celebrations, preparing the *pura* for the reception of offerings and necessary rituals. At the time of the *odalan*, it is the *pemangku* who invites the gods to partake of the offerings, and he and his wife then dispense holy water to the worshippers. Their other main duty is to advise the community on appropriate offerings and rituals for every occasion: if a household is struck down by sickness, for example, or if a family suddenly has some good fortune, they will ask the *pemangku* to help them express their sorrow or thanks. It is the *pemangku* who appears at the beginning of every dance performance (even the tourist ones) to bless the performers with sprinklings of holy water, and it is his job, too, to awaken the dancers of the *sanghyang dedari* and *sanghyang jaran* (see p.525) out of their trances.

Temple festivals

Aside from the daily propitiation of the household spirits, *agama Hindu* requires no regular act of collective worship from its devotees – no daily mass or weekly service – and so, for much of the year, Bali's 20,000 temples remain deserted, visited only by the village *pemangku* and perhaps the occasional curious tourist. But this all changes on the occasion of the temple's anniversary celebrations,

It is customary for Balinese men and women to wear **traditional dress** whenever they attend temple festivals, cremations, weddings, birth-rites and other important rituals; men also wear temple dress if playing in a gamelan orchestra and occasionally for *banjar* meetings too.

The traditional outfit for **women** is a lacy, close-fitting, long-sleeved blouse (*kebaya*) and a tightly wound sarong (*kain kamben*), set off by the all-important sash (*selempot*) around the waist, which symbolically contains the body and its physical appetites. Some women don flamboyant hair-pieces and conspicuous jewellery as well. For some big festivals, women from the same community will all wear the same-coloured *kebaya* to give their group a recognizable identity.

Men also wear a type of sarong (*kamben sarung*) and a formal, collared shirt as well (generally white but sometimes batik) or maybe even a starched jacket-like shirt. The man's sash (*selempot*) is often hidden under the shirt, but the more important item for him is the hip-cloth (*saput*), which is often yellow and usually knee-length and is worn over the sarong. Men also wear a headcloth (*udeng*) which they tie in whatever way they like, but generally leaving a triangular crest on top (shops sell ready-tied *udeng*). As with the sash, the *udeng* symbolically concentrate the mental energies and directs the thoughts heavenwards, via the perky cockscomb at the front.

or **odalan**, a three-day devotional extravaganza held at every temple either once every 210 days (every Balinese calendar year; see p.57 for an explanation of this) or once every 365 days (the *saka* year). With at least three temples gracing every sizeable community in Bali, any visitor who spends more than a week on the island will be certain to see some kind of festival. Most temples welcome tourists to the celebrations, provided they dress respectably (see p.73) and wear the temple sash, and that they don't walk in front of praying devotees.

As well as the temple anniversary celebrations, there are numerous island-wide religious festivals to mark sacred days according to both Balinese calendars; the most important of these are the *Nyepi* and *Galungan-Kuningan*, described on p.56. Although the majority of the other rituals – birth celebrations, tooth-filing, marriage and death – that punctuate every Balinese Hindu's life also have strong religious ramifications, most of these are conducted within the confines of the family's own compound, and are described on p.545.

The larger, wealthier and more important the temple, the more dramatic the *odalan* celebrations. Whatever the size, the purpose is always the same: to invite the gods down to earth so that they can be entertained and pampered by as many displays of devotion and gratitude as the community can afford. In the days before the *odalan*, the *pemangku* dresses the temple statues in **holy cloths**, either the spiritually charged black and white *kain poleng*, or a length of plain cloth in the colour symbolic of that temple's deity. Meanwhile, the women of the community begin to construct their offering towers, or *banten* (see p.512), and to cook ceremonial food.

Odalan **celebrations** start in the afternoon, with a procession of ceremonially clad women carrying their offerings to the temple. At the *pura*, the offerings are taken into the inner sanctum where the *pemangku* receives them and then blesses the devotees with holy water. Sometimes the god will temporarily inhabit the body of one of the worshippers, sending him or her into a trance and conveying its message through gestures or words. Elsewhere in the temple compound, there's generally some performance going on: the local gamelan orchestra plays, and often sacred dances are performed as well, particularly the *pendet*, or offertory dance, and perhaps a *barong* as well. After dark, a shadow play, *wayang kulit*, is often staged (see p.527 for more).

Offerings

The simplest **offerings** are the ones laid out every day by the women of each house, and placed at the household shrine, at the entrance gate, and in any nooks and crannies thought to be of interest to *bhuta* and *kala*. These offerings, called **canang**, are tiny banana-leaf trays pinned together with bamboo splinters and filled with a symbolic assortment of rice, fruit, flowers and incense. The flowers are always red or pink, to represent the Hindu god Brahma, and white for Siwa, with the green of the banana leaf symbolizing Wisnu. Sometimes the ingredients of the betel nut chew (see p.49) are added as well, the red areca nut, the white lime paste and the green betel leaf fulfilling the same symbolic function. Offerings for the gods are always placed in elevated positions, either on specially constructed altars or on functional shelves, but those meant for the demons are scattered on the ground. When she lays the offering down, the devotee sprinkles a few drops of holy water over the *canang* and wafts the incense smoke heavenwards. This sends the essence of the *canang* up to the appropriate god and ensures that he comes down immediately to enjoy it. Once the essence has been extracted, the *canang* loses its holiness and is left to rot or to be devoured by ants and dogs.

When there is a community festival or an island-wide celebration, the women of each *banjar* will band together to make great sculpted towers of fruit and rice cakes, tiny rice-dough figurines and banners woven from palm fronds. The most dramatic of these are the magnificent **banten**, pyramids of fruit, flowers, rice cakes and sometimes meat and vegetables, built up around a central skeleton made from the trunk of a young banana tree, up to three metres high. On the day of the community's *odalan*, the women dress in full ceremonial gear and then parade to the temple with the monumental *banten* balanced on their heads. At important ceremonies, the *banten* are sometimes left overnight at the temple to give the gods a decent chance to appreciate them, after which they are taken back home by the women who made them. The *banten* cannot be reused, but they can be dismantled and eaten by the families who donated them.

On the occasion of major island-wide festivals, such as *Galungan-Kuningan*, or at the Balinese new year, *Nyepi*, Bali's villages get decked out with special banners and ornamental poles, designed to attract the attention of the deities living on Gunung Agung and invite them onto the local streets. The banners, known as **lamak**, are amazing ornamental mats, often up to three metres long and woven in bold symbolic patterns from fresh green banana leaves. The most common design centres round the **cili** motif, a kind of stylized female figure with a body formed of triangles and other simple geometric shapes, wearing a spiky looking headdress; *cili* are thought by some to represent the rice goddess Dewi Sri. Seven days before the great *Galungan* festival begins, special bamboo poles, or **penyor**, are erected along the streets of every village, each one bowed down with intricately woven garlands of dried flowers and palm leaves, which arch gracefully over the roadway. Attached to the *penyor* are symbolic leafy tassels, and offerings of dried paddy sheaves and coconut shells.

Bali's other faiths

Islam is Bali's second religion – albeit one that's practised by only five percent of the population. Bali now boasts around two thousand mosques, the majority of which are in the west of the island, in the communities of people who have moved across the Bali Strait from Java.

The tiny **Christian** communities, who live in two villages on a remote mountainside in west Bali (see p.392), have adapted a number of Hindu traditions, such as dance performances, replacing the central characters with biblical ones, but retaining the tone of the originals. Roman Catholics and Protestants together make up around one percent of the Balinese population, and both communities have built huge churches in their villages.

Bali's only true **Buddhist** temple is in the village of Banjar in north Bali (see p.364), a Theravada Buddhist sanctuary based on the Thai prototype, which welcomes people of all faiths for meditation and religious instruction. Although the official statistics show that less than half a percent of the population is Buddhist, mainstream Balinese Hinduism incorporates a number of Buddhist teachings and practices.

Because **Confucianism** is not monotheistic, it's not officially recognized by the Indonesian government and so is effectively illegal. Most Chinese temples on Bali are therefore Theravada Buddhist, but suffused with enough Confucian elements to retain a distinctly Chinese character. The major Chinese temples are located near the coast and in the biggest commercial centres – close to the homes of the original Chinese traders and settlers; the most notable are in Kuta, Tanjung Benoa and Singaraja.

Lombok and Islam

Indonesia is the largest **Muslim** nation in the world, and ninety percent of its population follow the faith. On Lombok, 97 percent of the islanders are Muslim, with a tiny minority adhering to the Wetu Telu branch (see p.514). As Wetu Telu is not officially recognized, numbers of followers are uncertain, but most estimates suggest around 28,000.

Within Indonesia the practice of Islam is reasonably relaxed. Women are expected to dress modestly, but are not strictly veiled; you'll see women with and without head-coverings in Lombok, and relatively few with their entire body covered. The **mosque** is the centre of the Muslim faith, with Friday as the most religious day, when the noon service pretty much empties the villages (see p.74 for etiquette required when visiting a mosque).

It is still unclear exactly how Islam came to Indonesia, but it seems likely that it spread along trade routes, probably via traders from Gujarat in India who had converted to Islam in the mid-thirteenth century. In the fourteenth century, it spread from Sumatra, down into Java and, by the sixteenth century, had arrived in Lombok. Traditionally, the arrival of Islam in Java is thought to have more exotic roots, brought by nine Islamic saints, or *wali sangga*, one of whom is believed to be buried near Rembitan in the south of Lombok.

Wetu Telu

Followers of the **Wetu Telu** religion – the title translates as "three times", referring to the number of daily prayer-times – adhere to the central tenets of Islam, such as belief in Allah as the one God and Muhammad as his prophet, but diverge significantly from the practices of other Muslims, who, because they pray five times a day, are known as "Wetu Lima".

For the Wetu Telu, the older traditions of **ancestor worship** and **animism** are as important as the more orthodox ideas of Islam, and many follow their own three-day observation of the fast in the holy month of Ramadan, rather than the prescribed full month. The most important rituals associated with Wetu Telu are **life-cycle events** such as birth, death, marriage and circumcision, as well as rituals connected with agriculture and house-building. Their most important annual festival is **Maulid**, Muhammad's birthday.

Throughout their history, the Wetu Telu have been subjected to varying degrees of pressure. During the nineteenth century, some Muslims, many of whom had completed the *hajj*, or pilgrimage to Mecca, sought to ensure a wider orthodox adherence to the faith, and only the Dutch takeover of the island moderated the more zealous among them. Following the Indonesian declaration of independence in 1945 and the subsequent war against the Dutch, a local movement, **Nahdatul Wahtan**, was formed in Selong in East Lombok, led by Haji Zainuddin Abdul Majid, which persecuted the followers of the Wetu Telu religion. In more recent times, during the civil unrest in 1965, anyone less than scrupulously orthodox was in danger of being regarded as Communist, and there were some attacks against the Wetu Telu at that time. Today, it's almost certain that numbers are falling, for while it is possible to convert to Islam, you must be born Wetu Telu to belong to the faith.

In many ways, Wetu Telu practices have more in common with those of Balinese Hinduism: both faiths worship at Pura Lingsar in central Lombok, and some adherents believe that **Gunung Rinjani** is the dwelling place of the ancestors and the Supreme God and make pilgrimages to the mountain. Some Muslims dislike the fact that **Bayan**, in the north of Lombok, one of the first centres of Islam on Lombok and site of the oldest mosque on the island, is now a stronghold of Wetu Telu belief.

Traditional music and dance

Music and dance play an essential part in daily Balinese life, and as a visitor you can't fail to experience them, either at a special tourist show, in rehearsal or at a temple festival. You can even learn the rudimentaries at introductory classes in Ubud (see p.226). There's a vibrant tradition of music and dance on Lombok too, rarely witnessed by casual visitors to the island since it's associated almost exclusively with religious practices.

Balinese performing arts

Traditionally, **Balinese** dancers and musicians have always learnt their craft from the experts in their village and by imitating other performers. In the 1960s, however, the government felt that Bali's traditional arts were in danger of dying out and so two **schools for the performing arts** were founded – one for children of high school age, now located in Batubulan; the other for advanced degree-level students, next to the Taman Budaya Arts Centre in Denpasar. Feelings about these two establishments have been mixed, with some performers anticipating a gradual whittling away of the traditional variety of forms and styles as graduates of the schools return to teach a blander, more standardized technique to the youngsters in their home villages.

Balinese gamelan music

The national music of Bali is **gamelan**, a jangly clashing of syncopated sounds once described by the writer Miguel Covarrubias as being like "an Oriental ultra-modern Bach fugue, an astounding combination of bells, machinery and thunder". The highly structured compositions are produced by a group of 25 or more musicians seated cross-legged on the ground at a variety of bronze percussion instruments – gongs, metallophones, and cymbals – with a couple of optional wind and stringed instruments. All gamelan music is written for instruments tuned either to a five- or (less commonly) seven-tone scale, and most is performed at an incredible speed: one recent study of a gamelan performance found that each instrumentalist played an average of seven notes per second.

"Gamelan" is the Javanese word for the bronze instruments, and the music probably came over from Java around the fourteenth century; the Balinese duly adapted it to suit their own personality, and now the sounds of the Javanese and Balinese gamelan are distinctive even to the untrained ear. Where Javanese gamelan music is restrained and rather courtly, Balinese is loud and flashy, boisterous and speedy, full of dramatic stops and starts. This modern Balinese style, known as **gong kebyar** (*gong* means orchestra; *kebyar* translates, aptly, as lightning flashes), has been around since the early 1900s, emerging at a time of great political upheaval on the island, when the status of Bali's royal houses was irreparably dented by Dutch colonial aggression. Until then, Bali's music had been as palace-oriented as Javanese gamelan, but in 1915, village musicians from north Bali gave a public performance in the new *kebyar* style, and the trend spread like wildfire across the island, with whole orchestras turning their instruments in to be melted down and recast in the new, more exuberant, timbres.

Gamelan orchestras are now an essential part of village life. Every *banjar* that can afford to buy a set of instruments has its own *seka*, or **music club**, and a recent census found that there are currently 1500 active *gong kebyar* orchestras on the island. In most communities, the *seka* is open only to men (the all-female gamelan of Peliatan is a rare exception), but has no restrictions on age, welcoming keen players of any standard and experience between the ages of about eight and eighty. Players are not professional musicians: they all do other jobs during the daytime and rarely get paid for any musical performances. **Rehearsals** generally happen after nightfall, either in the *bale banjar* or in the temple's *bale gong* pavilion. Some particularly keen *seka* practise several times a week throughout the year, others just get together in the week before a performance. There's special *gong* music for every occasion – for sacred and secular dances, cremations, *odalan* festivities and *wayang kulit* shows – but players never learn from scores (in fact few *gong* compositions are ever notated), preferring instead to have it drummed into them by repetitive practice. Whatever the occasion, *gong* players always dress up in the ceremonial uniform of their music club, and make appropriate blessings and ritual offerings to the deities. Like dancers, musicians are acutely conscious of their role as entertainers of the gods.

Gamelan instruments

The type of music that a *seka* plays depends on the make-up of its particular gamelan orchestra, and every single *gong* on the island sounds slightly different. Balinese can supposedly find their way around the island in the dark by recognizing the distinctive tones of the various local gamelan.

Although the *gamelan kebyar* is currently by far the most fashionable style of music in Bali, and therefore the most common type of orchestra, there are over twenty other different ensemble variations on the island. The smallest ensemble is the four-piece **gender wayang** that traditionally accompanies the *wayang kulit* shadow-play performances; the largest is the old-fashioned classical Javanese-style orchestra comprising fifty instruments, known as the **gamelan gong**. Most gamelan instruments are huge and far too heavy to be easily transported, so nearly every *banjar* also possesses a portable orchestra known as a **gamelan angklung**, specially designed around a set of miniature four-keyed metallophones, for playing in processions and at unusual venues – at cremations for example, or at sea-shore festivals. The classic sounds of the Balinese gamelan are produced mainly by bronze instruments, but there are also a few orchestras composed entirely of bamboo instruments – split bamboo tubes, marimbas and flutes. These ensembles are a particular speciality of western Bali, where they're known as **gamelan joged bumbung** and **gamelan jegog**.

The most common orchestra, the *gong kebyar*, is composed of at least 25 individual instruments, and always features half a dozen tuned gongs, several sets of metallophones, two drums, a few sets of cymbals and one or more flutes. The leader of the orchestra is always one of the two drum players, whose job it is to link the different elements of the orchestra, as well as to take leads from the dancers during performances. This he does by fluttering or raising his hands from his seated position close to the front of the stage. Holding a double-ended cylindrical drum, the **kendang**, on his lap he controls the tempo of the piece by beating out the rhythm, usually with his hands, on both drum heads.

Cast in bronze and set in beautifully carved jackfruit-wood frames – often painted red and decorated with gold leaf – metal xylophones or **metallophones** create the distinctive clanging and shimmering gamelan sound. They come in a variety of forms, but the principle is the same for all versions. A series of bronze bars or keys are strung loosely together (the smallest metallophone has four keys, the biggest fourteen) and suspended over bamboo resonators. Players strike each key with a small wood- or metal-tipped mallet held in the right hand, while simultaneously dampening the last key with the finger and thumb of the left hand. Since the *kebyar* is often played incredibly fast, metallophone players need phenomenal co-ordination to move up and down the "keyboard", striking and dampening two different keys at the same time. The most common metallophones used for the *kebyar* are the **gangsa**, which come in three varieties. The largest and deepest toned is the **ugal**, which carries the melody, while the higher-pitched **pemade** and a corresponding number of **kantilan**, pitched higher still, add trills and melodies.

The *gangsa's* hallmark sound is produced by the gamelan technique called **kotekan**, generally translated as "the use of interlocking parts", which requires two instruments to play a single part. In many cases there are only split-second differences between the two parts. To add further depth, all pairs of Balinese instruments are tuned to slightly different pitches, a practice which produces the characteristic *vibrato* sound.

Centre-stage is nearly always dominated by the long row of ten or more bronze kettle-gongs (flattened bells with knobs on the top) strung together and set into an ornamentally carved wooden frame. This is the **trompong**, and is always played by one extremely dextrous player, who sits cross-legged before it and stretches to the left and right to embellish the melody by beating the individual gongs. There are, in fact, normally two *trompong* in an orchestra; the second is one known as a **reyong**, and played by four people sitting side by side. The large bronze **gong**, suspended from a frame at the back of the orchestra, gives structure to every musical composition, its mellow tones marking off the beginning and end of each melody.

In among these major players are several minor and occasional ones. These include sets of different-sized cymbals (**cengceng**), bamboo flutes (**suling**), and the classical two-stringed violin (**rebab**). Some orchestras also enliven their performances with guest spots from the **genggong**, a simple palm-wood Jew's harp, whose haunting vibrations sound a bit like the didgeridoo and are most popularly used for the frog dance.

Discography

Cassettes and CDs from Bali

Most of the tourist CD shops on the island have pretty good selections of Balinese music; the compilations are often the best buy. Ubud's Ganesha Bookshop (@www.ganeshabooksbali.com) offers an online ordering service for its stock of Balinese and Indonesian CDs.

Angklung Sidan (Bali Stereo). The smaller, lighter, processional gamelan orchestra from the village of Sidan plays ceremonial classics.

The Best of Gamelan Bali Parts 1 and 2 (Rick's/Maharani). Two-volume compilation of various dif-ferent gamelan styles, including the music that accompanies the Jauk demon dance, and a piece for the rarely heard wooden xylophone, the *gambang*.

The Best of Gamelan Gender (Rick's/Maharani). Sukawati village recording of the special *gender wayang* quartet, used as accompaniment to shadow-puppet plays.

Degung Instrumental: Sabilungan (SP Records). Not strictly Balinese, but played in every hotel, restaurant and tape shop, this is a classic tape of Sundanese (west Javan) *degung* music. The softer gamelan is fronted by a strong part for the bamboo flute, which lends a lovely dreamy quality to this exceptionally sensual music.

The Exotic Sounds of Bali (Rick's/Maharani). Compilation of different styles played by Ubud musicians, including pieces for the

genggong (Jew's harp) and the *gong suling* (gamelan orchestra with bamboo flute), and excerpts from the a capella *kecak* and the electrifying *kebyar duduk* dances.

Festival Gong Kebyar Se Bali 1982, Juaru 1 (Bali Stereo). Award-winning gamelan orchestra from the village of Angantaka playing a selection of its best *gong kebyar* pieces – fast, furious and quintessentially Balinese.

The Very Best of Kecak Dance (Rick's/Maharani). The haunting a capella vocals of the all-male choir that accompanies the spectacular *kecak* (monkey) dance.

CDs available outside Indonesia

Bali: Traditional Musicians – A Suite of Tropical Music and Sounds (World Network, Germany). A wonderful primer featuring every kind of Balinese music, from gamelan to flirt-dances and scat-song. Plus some great frog sounds.

Bali: Gamelan and Kecak (Elektra Nonesuch, US). Another fine cross-section of gamelan and other music, including *gong kebyar*, *gender wayang* ensemble for shadow plays, *kecak* and frog-dance *genggong*.

Bali: Musique pour le Gong Gedé (Ocora, France). A recording of the older, gentler style of Balinese gamelan, played by two ensembles from Batur and Tampaksiring.

Bali: Sebatu – les danses masquées (Ocora, France). A very lively and exciting recording of *topeng* mask dramas by the *gong kebyar* ensemble from the village of Sebatu.

Bamboo Ensemble of Sangkar Agung Village: Jegog (JVC, Japan). A wonderful recording of a *jegog* (bamboo) gamelan ensemble. If you don't manage to hear one in Bali,

then this is the next best thing. A vigorous and sonorous sound, more mellow than the bronze gamelans, enlivened further by audience reaction.

Gamelan Batel Wayang Ramayana (CMP, Germany). Village gamelan from Sading performs music from the shadow-puppet play. Excellent recording.

Gamelan Eka Cita: Gamelan Gong Kebyar (King, Japan). A terrific example in the World Music Library series of the Balinese *kebyar* style. The group is from a small village near Denpasar.

Gamelan Gong Kebyar (III) (JVC, Japan). Probably the best introduction to the *kebyar* style from the gamelan of Tejakula in northern Bali, noted for its larger than usual ensemble of instruments. Bold and glittering with strong percussion and drums.

Gamelan Semar Pegulingan: The Heavenly Orchestra of Bali (CMP, Germany). A beautifully sonorous recording of the gentle, older gamelan from the village of Kamasan in eastern Bali. Not as wild and frenetic as much Balinese music.

Gong Gedé of Batur and Tampaksiring: Musique pur le Gong Gedé (Ocora, France). Another good recording of the older pre-*kebyar* style for religious rather than courtly purposes.

Jegog of Negara (King, Japan). Another bamboo ensemble from the village of Negara in the west of Bali. Wonderful textures, both percussive and sonorous.

Music for the Gods (Rykodisc, US). Valuable not only for its unique historic recordings, but as a good all-round introduction to Balinese music. In 1941, the Fahnestock brothers, Bruce and Sheridan, American anthropologists, recorded Balinese music using disc-cutting machines and miles of cable (the cable enabled them to record performances on shore but keep the heavy equipment on board ship). The recordings were despatched

home and sat in an attic for forty years until the Library of Congress and Mickey Hart produced this disc. These are probably the oldest existing recordings of this repertoire, captured at a moment before the arrival of modern technology and tourism. Only specialists will appreciate the changes in the music, but all the same, these are fascinating examples of gamelan, *kecak*, log drum and other music rescued from another era.

Music of the Wayang Kulit: A Shadow Play from the Mahabharata (JVC, Japan). Sung narration and percussion accompaniment to the *wayang kulit*.

Peliatan Kecak, The Choral Dramas of Peliatan Village (JVC, Japan). A choral incantation of the *Ramayana* epic by a cast of 300. An amazing sound – though only devotees will last the course.

Traditional dance-dramas of Bali

Most Balinese **dance–dramas** have evolved from **sacred rituals**, and are still performed at religious events, with full attention given to the offertory and devotional aspects. Before the show begins, a *pemangku* (village priest) will always bless the players and the performance area with sprinklings of holy water, and many performances open with a *pendet*, or welcome dance, intended for the gods. The exorcist Barong–Rangda dramas continue to play a vital function in the **spiritual practices** of every village, and the *baris* dance re-enacts the traditional offering up of weapons by village warriors to the gods to invest them with supernatural power. Some of the more secular dance-dramas tell ancient and **legendary stories**, many of them adapted from the epic Hindu morality tales, the *Ramayana* and the *Mahabharata*, that came from India more than a thousand years ago. Others are based on **historical events**, embellishing the romances and battles that characterized the royal courts of Java and Bali between the tenth and the fourteenth centuries.

With the advent of mass tourism however, it's becoming less and less easy to see a traditional performance staged in its natural environment, at a temple festival or village event for example, rather than as a commercial performance. Nonetheless, some of the **tourist shows** are very good, performed by expert local troupes with traditional finesse. Practical information on where to see the best dancers is given on p.59, and a guide to some of the most inspiring and most frequently performed dances is given below.

There are few professional **dancers** in Bali; most performers spend their days working in the fields or in shops, donning costumes and make-up only at festival times or for the regular tourist shows. Almost every Balinese boy and girl is taught to dance – small boys learn the *baris* (warrior dance), girls the *legong*

Like its companion piece the *Ramayana*, the **Mahabharata** is an epic moral narrative of Hindu ethics which came originally from India in the eleventh century. Written during the fourth century AD by the Indian poet Vyasa, the original poem is phenomenally long, with over 100,000 verses in all. The **Balinese version** is translated into the ancient poetic language of Kawi and written on sacred *lontar* books kept in the Gedong Kirtya library at Singaraja.

At the heart of the story is the conflict between two rival branches of the same family, the Pandawas and the Korawas, all of them descendants of various unions between the deities and the mortals. The five **Pandawa brothers** represent the side of virtue, morality and noble purpose, though they each have idiosyncrasies that are not entirely snowy white. The eldest is **Yudhisthira**, a calm and thoughtful leader with a passion for justice, whose one vice – an insatiable love of gambling – nonetheless manages to land the brothers in a fair amount of trouble. Then comes **Bhima**, a strong, courageous and hot-headed fighter, whose fiery temper and earthy manner make him especially appealing to the Balinese. The third brother, **Arjuna**, is the real hero; not only is he a brave warrior and an expert archer, but he's also handsome, high-minded and a great lover. Arjuna's two younger brothers, the expert horseman **Nakula** and the learned **Sahadeva**, are twins. Their rivals are their cousins the **Korawas**, who number a hundred in all, and are led by the eldest male, **Durodhana**, a symbol of jealousy, deviousness and ignoble behaviour.

An early episode in the *Mahabharata* tells how the Pandawa boys are forced by the Korawas to give up their rightful claim to the kingdom's throne, and are banished unceremoniously to the mountains for a minimum of thirteen years. The Pandawa brothers grow up determined to regain their rightful heritage. Meanwhile, both families engage in all sorts of minor adventures, the best of which recur in carvings, *wayang kulit* dramas and dances. A particular favourite is the exploit known as **Bhima Swarga**, in which the second Pandawa brother, Bhima, is despatched to Hell to rescue the souls of his dead father and stepmother. While there, he witnesses all sorts of horrible tortures and punishments (many of which are graphically depicted on the ceilings of Klungkung's Kerta Gosa). When Bhima returns to earth with the souls of his relatives, he's immediately sent off again, this time to Heaven, in search of the holy water needed to smooth his dead parents' passage into Heaven. This episode is known as **Bhima Suci** and features the nine directional gods, as well as a dramatic battle between Bhima and his own godly (as opposed to earthly) father, Bayu.

Finally, a full-scale battle is declared between the two sets of cousins. On the eve of the battle, Arjuna suddenly becomes doubtful about the morality of fighting his own family, and confides as much to his friend and charioteer Krishna. Krishna, who is actually an avatar of the Hindu god Wisnu, then launches into a long theological lecture, in which he explains to Arjuna that the action is the all-important factor, not the result, and that because Arjuna is of the warrior caste, his duty is to fight, to act in a manner that's appropriate to his destiny. This episode of the *Mahabharata* is known as the **Bhagavad Gita**, and encapsulates the core Hindu philosophy of caste and the notions of karma and destiny. Duly persuaded, Arjuna joins his brothers in battle, and at the end of eighteen bloody days the Pandawa brothers are victorious.

– and the most adept are then chosen to perform at community functions, as part of the established local troupe. Dancers learn by **imitation and repetition**, the instructor often holding the pupil against his or her body and manipulating limbs until the exact angles and tensions are reproduced to perfection. Personal expression has no place in the Balinese theatre, but the skilful execution of traditional moves is always much admired, and trained dancers enjoy a high status within the village.

Female dancers keep their feet firmly planted on the ground, their legs and hips encased in restrictive sarongs that give them a distinctive forward-angled posture. They express themselves through a vocabulary of controlled **angular movements** of the arms, the wrists, the fingers, the neck and, most beguilingly, the eyes. Each pose and gesture derives from a movement observed in the natural rather than the human world. Thus a certain type of flutter of the hand may be a bird in flight, a vigorous rotation of the forearms the shaking of water from an animal's coat. Dressed in pantaloons or hitched-up sarongs, the **male dancers** are much more energetic, and whirl about a lot, emphasizing their manliness by opening shoulders and limbs outwards, keeping their knees bent and their heads high.

Most dramas are performed in superb natural settings, either within a temple compound, or in the outer courtyard of a noble family's palace. Because the stories are so familiar to the islanders, the **costumes and masks** give immediate clues to the identity of each character – and to the action which is to follow. Some dramas are performed in a combination of contemporary Bahasa Indonesia and the ancient poetic language known as **Kawi**, while others stick to modern speech – perhaps with a few humorous English phrases thrown in for the tourists.

Although most of the dances and nearly all the dance movements have long-established histories and traditions, Balinese dance is by no means a dead or stultified art form. In the last fifty years the repertoire has expanded quite considerably, not least because of the efforts of the island's most famous performer, the late I Ketut Marya. Better known as **Mario**, this superb dancer was also a highly imaginative choreographer, adapting old forms to suit the modern mood, and most famously to fit the modern gamelan style, known as *kebyar*, in the 1920s. Thirty years later, he was commissioned by a British entrepreneur to create a new "boy-meets-girl" dance – the resulting piece was the *oleg tambulilingan,* or bumblebee dance.

Baris

The **baris**, or **warrior dance**, can be performed either as a solo or in a group of five or more, and either by a young woman, or more commonly a young man. Strutting on stage with knees and feet turned out, his centre of gravity kept low, the *baris* cuts an impressive figure in a gilded brocade cloak of ribboned pennants which fly out dramatically at every turn. In his performance, he enacts a young warrior's preparation for battle, goading himself into courageous mood, trying out his martial skills, showing pride at his calling and then expressing a whole series of emotions – ferocity, passion, tenderness, rage – much of it through the arresting movements of his eyes.

Traditionally, the solo *baris* has always improvised a lot, leading the gamelan rather than following it. In its original sacred form, known as the *baris gede*, this was a devotional dance in which soldiers dedicated themselves and their weapons to the gods.

Barong–Rangda dramas

Featuring the most spectacular costumes of all the Balinese dances, the **Barong–Rangda dramas** are also among the most sacred and most important. Essentially a dramatization of the eternal conflict between the forces of good and evil, the dramas can take a variety of forms but nearly always serve as ritualized exorcisms.

The mythical widow-witch character of **Rangda** represents the forces of evil, and her costume and mask present a duly frightening spectacle (see box on p.249

The Ramayana

Written in Sanskrit around the fourth century BC, the 24,000 verses that comprise the **Ramayana** have since fired the imagination of writers, artists, dramatists, theologians and sculptors right across Southeast Asia. Like the other great Hindu epic, the *Mahabharata*, the *Ramayana* has been translated into the classical Javanese Kawi language and transcribed onto sacred *lontar* manuscripts.

It's essentially a morality tale, a dramatization of the eternal conflict between the forces of good (*dharma*) and the forces of evil (*adharma*). The forces of good are represented by Rama and his friends. **Rama** is the hero of the piece, a refined and dutiful young man, handsome, strong and courageous, who also happens to be an avatar of the god Wisnu. Rama's wife **Sita** epitomizes the Hindu ideals of womanhood – virtue, fidelity and love – while Rama's brother **Laksmana** is a symbol of fraternal loyalty and youthful courage. The other important member of the Rama camp is **Hanuman**, the general of the monkey army, a wily and athletic ape who is unfailingly loyal to his allies. On the opposing side, the forces of evil are mainly represented by the demon king **Rawana**, a lustful and devious leader whose retainers are giants and devils.

The story begins with Rama, the eldest son of the king, being banished to the forests for thirteen years, having been cheated out of his rightful claim to the throne by a scheming stepmother. Sita and Laksmana accompany him, and together the trio have various encounters with sages, giants and seductresses.

The most crucial event in the epic is the **abduction of Sita** by Rawana, a crime that inspires the generally easygoing and rather unwarlike Rama to wage battle against his avowed enemy. A favourite subject for dances and carvings, the episode starts with Sita catching sight of a beautiful golden deer and imploring her husband Rama to catch it and bring it back for her. The golden deer turns out to be a decoy planted by Rawana, and the demon king duly swoops down to abduct Sita as soon as Rama and Laksmana go off to chase the animal.

The distraught Rama determines to get Sita back and, together with Laksmana, he sets off in the direction of Rawana's kingdom. En route he meets Hanuman, the monkey general, who agrees to help him by sneaking into Sita's room at Rawana's palace and **giving her Rama's ring** (another popular theme of pictures and dramas). Eventually, Rama, Laksmana, Hanuman and his monkey army all arrive at Rawana's palace and, following a big battle, Sita is rescued and Rawana done away with.

---

for Rangda's story). The **Barong Ket** cuts a much more loveable figure, a shaggy-haired creature with a bug-eyed expression and a mischievous grin on his masked face, something like a cross between a pantomime horse and a Chinese dragon. The Barong Ket (lion) is by far the most common persona adopted by this mythical creature, but you might also see Barong Macan (tiger), Barong Bangkal (wild boar) and Barong Celeng (pig). All Rangda and Barong **masks** are invested with great sacred power and need to be treated with due respect and awe. When not in use, the masks are kept wrapped in magic cloth and stored in the temple.

Barong–Rangda dramas can be self-contained as in the *calonarang* (see opposite) or they can appear as just one symbolic episode in the middle of a well-known story like the *Mahabharata*. Whatever the occasion, the format tends to be fairly similar. Rangda is always called upon by a character who determines to cause harm to a person, a family or a village (unrequited love is a very common cause). She generally sends a minion to wage the first battles, and is then forced to appear herself when the opposition calls in the Barong, the defender of the good. In this final confrontation, the Barong enters first, occasionally joined by a monkey who teases him and plays tricks. Suddenly Rangda appears, fingernails first, from behind the central gateway. Flashing her white magic cloth, she harasses the Barong, stalking him at every turn. When the Barong looks to be on his last legs, a group of village men rush in to his rescue, but are entranced by Rangda's magic and stab themselves instead of her. A priest quickly enters before any real injury is inflicted. The series of confrontations continues, and the drama ends in stalemate: the forces of good and evil remain as strong and vital as ever, ready to clash again in the next bout.

The story of the **calonarang** is basically an embellished version of the Barong–Rangda conflict, grafted onto an ancient legend about the daughter of a witch queen whom no one will marry because they're scared of her mother. The witch queen Calonarang is a manifestation of Rangda who, furious at the lack of suitors for her daughter, demands that her followers wreak destruction in all the villages. This drama is acted out on a regular basis, whenever there are considered to be evil forces and impurities affecting the community, and sometimes the whole neighbourhood takes part, the men parading with hand-held *kulkul* drums and the women filing in to make offerings at the temple shrines.

There's also an unusual human version of the Barong, called **Barong Landung** (literally "tall barong"). These are huge puppets, one male and one female, each one operated by a single performer. The male puppet looks forbidding, his masked face is black and he has a fanged mouth and grimacing features. As a representation of the legendary Jero Gede, a giant from Nusa Penida who brought disease and misfortune to Bali, this enormous figure is also meant to scare away any similar giants. Jero Gede is always accompanied by a far sweeter-looking female puppet, known as Jero Luh, who wears a white mask with a smiling face and faintly Chinese eyes. Together they act out a bawdy comic opera which has exorcist purposes as well.

Kebyar

A great wave of artistic experimentation hit Bali in the 1920s, particularly in north Bali, where a group of young musicians started playing around with the traditional gamelan form (see p.515). They came up with a vibrant and much brasher type of music, which they named **kebyar**. The new sounds soon struck chords with musicians in the south as well, and by 1925 had also inspired the talented young dancer, Mario, to choreograph a new piece. He performed this dance while seated on the ground and so called it **kebyar duduk** (seated *kebyar*). It's a stunningly camp piece of theatre, starring just one man, who alternately flirts with the gamelan, plays the kettle gongs (*trompong*) that are placed in front of him and flutters his fan in beguiling self-dramatization. Some years later, a slightly different version of this dance was invented, the **kebyar trompong**, in which the dancer sits and plays the *trompong* for only part of the performance, in between mincing coquettishly about the stage and making eyes at the audience.

Kecak

Sometimes called the **monkey dance** after the animals represented by the chorus, the **kecak** gets its Balinese name from the hypnotic chattering sounds made by the a cappella choir. Chanting nothing more than "cak cak cak cak", the chorus of fifty or more men uses seven different rhythms to create the astonishing music that accompanies the drama. Bare-chested, and wearing lengths of black-and-white-check *kain poleng* cloth around their waists and a single red hibiscus behind the ear, the men sit cross-legged in five or six tight concentric circles, occasionally swaying or waving arms and clapping hands in unison. The **narrative** itself is taken from a core episode of the *Ramayana*, centring around the kidnap of Sita by the demon king Rawana, and is acted out in the middle of the chorus circle, with one or two narrators speaking for all the characters.

Although frequently attributed to the German artist and musician Walter Spies, the main creative force behind the *kecak* was the famous *baris* dancer **I Wayan Limbak**, who lived in Bedulu in Gianyar. In 1931 he developed the chants from the *sanghyang* trance dances (see opposite), in which the chorus chants the "cak cak cak" syncopation as part of the trance-inducing ritual, and created accompanying choreography to flesh out the episode from the *Ramayana*.

Legong

Undoubtedly the most refined of all the temple dances, the quintessentially Balinese **legong** is rather an acquired taste, which can seem tiresome to the uninitiated because of its restrained movement and lack of dramatic narrative. Its beauty is all in the intricate weavings of arms, fingers, torsos and heads. The *legong* is always performed by three pre-pubescent girls who are bound tightly in sarongs and chest cloths of opulent green or pink, with gilded crowns filled with frangipani blossoms on their heads. When village elders and former dancers are selecting aspiring *legong* dancers, they look not only for agility and vitality, but also for grace and poise, as the spirit of the *legong* is considered the acme of Balinese femininity. As a result, *legong* dancers have always enjoyed a special status in their village, a reputation that endures long after they retire at the onset of menstruation. In the past, many a *legong* dancer has ended up as a raja's wife or, latterly, as an expatriate artist's muse and subsequent partner.

The dance itself has evolved from a highly sacred *sanghyang* trance dance (see p.526) and takes several different forms. By far the most common is the **legong keraton** (dance of the court), based on a classical twelfth-century tale from Java. It tells the story of King Laksem, who is holding a princess, Rangkesari, captive against her will. Rescue is on the way in the form of Prince Daha, who plans to wage battle against King Laksem. The princess tries to dissuade the king from going to war, encouraging him to set her free instead of risking lives, but the king is adamant and sets off. As he leaves, he is attacked by a raven, an extremely bad omen, after which he duly loses the battle and is killed.

The **performance** begins with a solo dance by a court lady, known as the *condong* (dressed in pink and gold). She picks up two fans from the ground in anticipation of the arrival of the two *legong* (literally "dancer"). Dressed identically in bright green and gold, the two *legong* enact the story, adopting and swapping characters with no obvious warning. The *condong* always returns as the raven, with pink wings attached to her costume. The final fatal battle is never shown on stage.

Mahabharata dance-dramas

Many of the stories from the Hindu epic, the **Mahabharata**, are known by every Balinese and repeated endlessly in paintings, sculpted reliefs and dramatizations. The basic *Mahabharata* narrative tells of the extended rivalry between the Pandawa brothers and their usurping cousins the Korawas, and features all sorts of battles between the two sides, as well as confrontations with gods and demons, long journeys, seductions and practical jokes. The most popular

Mahabharata characters are the second Pandawa brother, **Bhima**, a passionate, tempestuous man with a good heart and a slightly coarse, earthy manner, and his younger, far more refined, brother **Arjuna**, an expert archer and all-round romantic hero. The **Ballet of Bimaniu** dramatizes the romances of Arjuna's son, Bimaniu, and features his encounter with evil, as represented by Rangda.

Oleg tambulilingan

Translated as the **bumblebee dance**, the *oleg tambulilingan* is one of the most vivacious, humorous and engaging dances of the Balinese repertoire but, unfortunately, it doesn't get performed that often. It's a flirtation dance, performed by a man and woman who act as courting bumblebees sipping honey in a flower garden, the man sexually obsessed with the female, desire burning in his eyes, the female coquettish and eventually compliant.

The *oleg tambulilingan* is one of several dances invented by the late great dancer Mario, who created it in 1952 as a commission for a world tour. The female role is complicated, needing a highly skilled performer, and so is often taken by a former *legong* dancer.

Ramayana dance-dramas

The great Hindu epic, the *Ramayana*, is a popular inspiration for all sorts of dance-dramas. By far the best-loved episode of the whole tale is the act in which Rama's queen Sita is **kidnapped** by the demon king Rawana, and whisked off to his palace. In the original poem, the kidnapping is the catalyst for all the ensuing action, prompting the hero, Rama, and his motley band of allies and retainers to struggle through all sorts of bizarre adventures in their attempt to rescue her. The kidnapping episode features prominently in two of the most frequently performed tourist dance shows, the *kecak* (see p.523) and the **Ramayana Ballet**.

Although the storyline is fairly simple, things can get confusing if you're unable to distinguish between characters, or if you fail to recognize who is siding with whom. The main **characters** have certain salient features. **Sita**, for example, always wears her hair long and is distinguishable from assorted maidservants and female friends by the two long red scarves that hang from her waist. The hero **Rama** is played by a woman, and in the opening scenes always wears a golden crown with a quiver full of arrows on his back. Confusingly, Rama's brother **Laksmana** is also played by a woman, but he generally sports a black headdress. The demon king, **Rawana**, on the other hand, has a very masculine presence, strutting around in flamboyant battle dress. It's pretty easy to recognize Rama's chief aide, the monkey general **Hanuman**, by his distinctive white monkey mask and long white tail – he always wears white, while his simian retainers dress in different colours. The monkeys are the main source of the drama's jokes and slapstick humour.

Sanghyang: trance dances

The state of **trance** lies at the very heart of traditional Balinese dance. In order to maintain the health of the village, the gods are periodically invited down into the temple arena to help in the exorcism of evil and sickness-inducing spirits. When the deities descend, they reveal themselves by possessing certain people and using them as their medium. Sometimes the deities communicate in verbal form, which may or may not have to be interpreted by the priests, and sometimes the whole physical being is taken over and the devotee is moved to dance or to perform astonishing physical feats. The chosen medium is put into a trance state through a combination of special priestly chants and protective mantras, intoned exhortations by the a cappella choir and great clouds of pungent incense wafted heavenwards to attract the gods' attention. Trance dances are traditionally only performed when the village is suffering from a particularly bad bout of sickness or bad weather – the versions that are reproduced at tourist shows have none of the spiritual dynamism of the real thing, though it is said that performers do sometimes slip into trance even then.

One of the most common trance dances is the **sanghyang dedari** (angel deity), which is widely believed to have been the inspiration for the popular courtly dance, the *legong* (see p.524). In the *sanghyang dedari*, the deities possess two young girls who perform a complicated duet with their eyes closed and, in part, while seated on the shoulders of two male villagers. Although they have never learnt the actual steps, the duo almost invariably performs its movements in tandem and sometimes continues for up to four hours. When they finally drop to the floor in exhaustion, the priest wakes them gently by sprinkling holy water over them. In the *sanghyang dedari* performed at tourist shows, however, the girls have almost certainly rehearsed the dance beforehand and probably do not enter a trance state at all. They wear the same tightly bound green and gold sarongs as the *legong* dancers, and dance to the haunting backing vocals of an a cappella chorus of men and women.

In the **sanghyang jaran** (horse deity), one or more men are put into a trance state while the temple floor is littered with burning coconut husks. As they enter the trance, the men grab hold of wooden hobbyhorse sticks and then gallop frantically back and forth across the red hot embers as if they were on real horses. The all-male *kecak* chorus fuels the drama with excited a cappella crescendos until, finally, the exhausted hobbyhorse riders are awoken by the priest.

Topeng: mask dances

In the **topeng**, or **mask dance**, the performer is possessed by the spirit of the mask. Balinese masks are extremely sacred objects, carved and painted with great reverence to the gods and spirits (see p.536). Before every entrance, the *topeng* actor sprinkles holy water on his mask and recites a mantra. Women never participate in *topeng*: female roles are played by men, and most actors play several characters in each drama.

The **storylines** of most *topeng* dramas are much more important than in most other Balinese dance-dramas. They usually centre around popular folk tales or well-known episodes from history, and every character wears a mask which makes him or her immediately recognizable. Refined and **noble characters** always wear full masks, usually painted white with almond-shaped eyes, and thick black eyebrows for the men. They communicate with elegant gestures of the hands, arms and head (speaking is impossible because of the mask), and move with rather grand, often swaggering bravado. A royal servant always acts as a narrator figure, speaking on behalf of the voiceless nobles, and he, like the coarser characters, the **clowns** and the **servants**, wears a half-mask and baggy shapeless clothing in which to roll about the floor and engage in comic antics.

One of the most popular mask dances is the **topeng tua**, a solo performance by the character of an old man, a retired first minister, who recalls his time in the king's service. The mask is always shrouded in straggly white hair and a beard, and the actor hobbles about with shaky legs and wavering fingers.

Another classic tourist *topeng* is the **frog dance** – performed to the gloriously evocative music of the Balinese Jew's harp, or *genggong* – which tells how a frog turns into a prince. The **jauk** is a masked dance of a slightly different nature, in which the solo dancer portrays a terrifying demon-king. His red or white mask has huge bulging eyes, a horribly goofy smile and a thick black moustache, and his hands are crowned with foot-long fingernails which he flashes menacingly throughout the dance. To the clashing strains of the full-blown gamelan who take their cues from the exuberant dancer, the *jauk* leaps mischievously about the stage as if darting from behind trees and pouncing on unsuspecting villagers.

Wayang kulit

On an island where cinema screens and TVs haven't yet percolated through to the smallest villages, a **wayang kulit** performance, or **shadow-puppet drama**, still draws in huge crowds and keeps them entertained well into the early hours. The stories and techniques are familiar to all, but the sheer panache, eloquence and wit of a good *dalang* (puppet master) mean the show is as likely to break news, spread gossip and pass on vital information as it is to entertain.

A typical *wayang kulit* show takes place after sundown on the occasion of a wedding, a cremation or a temple *odalan*, staged either in the outer courtyard of the village temple or in the *bale banjar* meeting area. The *dalang* (nearly always a man) sets up a white cloth screen, lights flaming rags dipped in paraffin for his illumination and assembles his collection of puppets (*wayang*). It's not unusual for a *dalang* to own 150 different **wayang**, each of them fashioned from flat lengths of buffalo hide, carved and perforated to create a lacy effect before being painted and mounted on a stick. (You can see the workshops of some well-known *dalang* in Sukawati, described on p.183.) As in many other Balinese dramas, *wayang* characters can be divided into those belonging to the refined and noble camp (royal personages, holy men and women, heroes and heroines) and those that are coarse and vulgar (clowns and servants). The refined characters speak in the ancient courtly language of Kawi, while the coarse characters use Balinese. One character may be represented by a number of different puppets, each one showing him or her in a particular mood or stance.

The **dalang** mobilizes all the puppets behind the screen, speaking for each of them and moving each one in character as well. Well-educated and humorous, with a quite astonishing memory for lines, not to mention an impressive range of different voices, the *dalang* also rehearses and conducts the special four-piece orchestra that accompanies his performances, the *gender wayang*. Not surprisingly, *dalang* are greatly revered by other villagers, who see them as being invested with great spiritual power.

From the complete *wayang* cast, the *dalang* selects between thirty and sixty puppets for any one show. The torch-lit **screen** represents the world in microcosm: the puppets are the humans that inhabit it, the torch stands in for the sun, and the *dalang* acts as god. Puppets who represent good characters always appear to the right of the *dalang*, and those who are evil appear on his left. A leaf-shaped fan-like puppet, symbolizing the tree of life, marks centre stage and is used to indicate the end of a scene as well as to represent clouds, spirits and magical forces. The most popular *wayang kulit* **stories** are taken from the *Mahabharata*.

Lombok music and dance

Lombok has a rich heritage of music and dance, linked to religious occasions on the island. The indigenous Sasak traditions have been subject to many influences, both Hindu and Islamic, direct from Bali and Java, and through Buginese and Makassarese traders. The resulting melange of puppetry, poetry, song and dance is huge and varied, but largely inaccessible to tourists. There are **no cultural shows** such as you will find in Bali, but you may happen across a wedding or other celebration on your way around the island.

There is some conflict on Lombok between the traditional forms of music and dance and the more modern Islamic ones. Some religious leaders have tried to **ban** traditional gamelan because of its association with earlier beliefs, such as animism and ancestor worship (the bronze instruments of traditional gamelan are sometimes described as "the voice of the ancestors"). The **wayang Sasak** puppets, introduced in the seventeenth century to help the spread of Islam on the island, have now also been forbidden by more conservative Muslims, on the grounds that Islam prohibits the depiction of the human form.

Lombok's gamelan music

Lombok's traditional **gamelan** music is similar to Bali's. Several common types of ensemble accompany dances and songs, comprising the familiar drums, chimes, cymbals and gongs. The **gamelan gong Sasak** resembles the Balinese *gamelan gong* in instruments and repertoire, but may be combined with the rather unusual **gamelan grantang**, consisting of bamboo xylophones. The **gamelan oncer** is also widely used, and best known for its use in the *kendang belek* dance, in which two instrumentalists carry and play large drums and dance a dramatic and confrontational duet.

Gamelan tawa–tawa and **barong tengkok** are two musical ensembles used in processions during life-cycle celebrations or other festivities such as national holidays. The usual gongs and drums are accompanied by eight sets of cymbals attached to decorated lances for marching with. The gamelan *barong tengkok* from central Lombok actually has gongs suspended within a Barong figure, and traditionally plays at wedding ceremonies, while the bride and groom are paraded on wooden horses.

Muslim ensembles were developed about a century ago in an attempt to stamp out the traditional orchestras. **Gamelan rebana** consists of up to twenty different drums which mimic the traditional sound of gamelan music, but without the use of bronze instruments. More unusual is the **gamelan klentang**, made up entirely of iron instruments. Other Muslim ensembles, **kecimol** and **cilokaq**, consist of an oboe (*preret*), flutes, lutes, violins and drums, and often accompany Sasak poetry.

Lombok's dances

Compared with the huge artistic academic interest in Balinese performance art, Lombok has been largely ignored, although several Lombok **dances** are recognizably similar to traditional Balinese ones. The **Gandrung**, for instance, which is performed mainly in central Lombok by a solo female dancer who selects a man to join her in the performance, has a counterpart on Bali.

Lombok also has examples of rare **trance dances**. The **suling dewa**, accompanied by flutes and song, is found in the north of the island, and used to induce spirits to enter the local shaman and bless the village. The **pepakon**, from east Lombok, causes the sick to become possessed so that their illness can be removed from them.

Processional dances also occur. The **batek baris** is performed in Lingsar, among other places, the dancers wearing costumes mimicking Dutch army uniforms and carrying wooden rifles while they lead a procession to the sacred springs. The **tandang mendet** takes place rarely only in the mountain village of Sembalun Bumbung, and heads a procession to the grave of a Majapahit ancestor buried in the valley.

As in Bali some dances in Lombok are based on **legends**. The **telek** is based very broadly on the tale of a princess who falls in love with a humble man; and the **kemidi rudat** on the *Thousand and One Nights* stories, complete with colourful characters and clowns.

Arts and crafts

The desire to make things look good – and to make beautiful things – is so ingrained in the Balinese way of life that there is no separate Balinese word for "art" or "artist". Villagers have traditionally considered it their unquestioned duty to honour both their gods and their rajas with attractive objects and buildings.

Lombok lacks the dynamic artistic heritage of Bali, and as a predominantly Islamic island which forbids the depiction of the human form, has virtually no indigenous fine art. However, there is a thriving crafts tradition.

For general information on **where to buy** arts and crafts in Bali and Lombok, see p.70. For details of workshops and classes in traditional Balinese arts and crafts, see Ubud p.225 and Kuta p.136.

Balinese arts and crafts

Although highly skilled, Bali's **carvers**, **sculptors**, **weavers** and **painters**, who decorated the island's temples and palaces, were never paid for their work, and would earn their living as farmers or traders, just like everybody else. They worked as **artists** only when summoned by the raja or the high priest – and they never signed their work. By the 1930s, however, Balinese society was undergoing quite significant changes. The rajas had lost a great deal of their power to the Dutch colonials (many had in fact lost their lives, or at least their homes), and foreign tourists were gradually taking their place as **patrons of the arts** – and paying for the work. Over time, this encouraged a whole variety of changes: artists began to carve and paint secular subjects, to experiment with new materials, to express themselves as individuals and to sign their own work. Making paintings and carvings became a full-time, and relatively lucrative, job, and the arts and crafts industry is now one of the most profitable on Bali.

Painting

In the last few decades, art historians have grouped **Balinese painting** into five general **schools**, most of them named after the village where a style originated or was pursued most effectively. The main schools are *wayang* (also known as classical or Kamasan), Ubud, Batuan, Young Artists and Modern or Academic. Together with the minor schools based at Pengosekan and Keliki, these are all described below. Inevitably the categories are broad and over-generalized, but Balinese painters, like artists working in other media, are not shy about copying good ideas or even reproducing successful work, and so it's not difficult to pinpoint a few representative features or techniques. One notable and extremely prolific artist, who really can't be fitted into any of the above categories, is the late **I Gusti Nyoman Lempad** (see p.204 for more on his work).

Art galleries

The best collection of Balinese painting on the island is housed in the **Neka Art Museum** in Ubud (see pp.206–210), where you'll get an excellent introduction to all the major styles and see some of the finest Balinese pictures in existence. Other worthwhile galleries include the **Seniwati Gallery of Art by Women**, the **Agung Rai Museum of Art (ARMA)**, and the **Puri Lukisan**, all in Ubud (see p.186); the **Taman Budaya Cultural Centre** in Denpasar (see p.100); and the **Gunarsa Museum of Classical and Modern Art** near Klungkung (see p.260). For unrivalled examples of classical Balinese art, visit the old **Taman Gili** palace in Klungkung (see p.257).

Online galleries

Agung Rai Museum of Art ⓦwww.nusantara.com/arma. A good chance to see some of Bali's most famous paintings, including works by Walter Spies, I Gusti Nyoman Lempad, Rudolph Bonnet and Anak Agung Gede Sobrat.

Bali Arts and Crafts ⓦbaliwww.com/bali/arts. Mini-biographies of the twenty most famous foreign artists who lived and worked in Bali between 1904 and 1967. Includes reproductions of work by Bonnet, Le Mayeur, Spies and Smit.

Don Antonio Blanco Art Foundation ⓦwww.blancobali.co.id. The online gallery of the late Antonio Blanco (see p.212), Ubud's most flamboyant expatriate resident.

Neka Art Museum ⓦwww.museumneka.com. Bali's best art museum shows off some of its wares, including a database of 73 artists from the collection with thumbnails of their major paintings.

Symon ⓦwww.symonbali.com. Exuberant and vibrant paintings from the Ubud studio of US expat artist Symon (see p.211) to browse and buy.

Wayang or Kamasan style

The earliest Balinese painters drew their inspiration from the *wayang kulit* shadow plays, re-creating puppet-like figures on their canvases and depicting episodes from the same religious and historical epics that were played out on the stage. Variously known as the **wayang style**, the **classical style** or the **Kamasan style** (after the village most noted for its *wayang*-style art), this is the most traditional genre of Balinese art, and the one that's been the least influenced by Western techniques and subjects. The oldest-known examples date back to the mid-seventeenth century, when *wayang*-style figures were painted onto banners and scrolls used to decorate shrines and temples at religious festivals, on curtains that hung in royal sleeping pavilions and on astrological charts and calendars used for determining auspicious dates. None of these has survived, however, except in descriptions from contemporary literature.

The most dramatic and famous *wayang*-style pictures – those covering the ceilings of two buildings within the old palace of Klungkung, the **Kerta Gosa** (Law Courts) and the Bale Kambung (Floating Pavilion) – are in fact less than two hundred years old and have been retouched several times. Probably painted in the early decades of the nineteenth century, the Kerta Gosa pictures are considered the yardstick of classical Balinese art (see p.257 for a full description).

All *wayang*-style pictures are packed full of people painted in characteristic **three-quarter profile** (both eyes visible), with caricature-like features and angular, puppet-like poses. There is no perspective, and stylized symbols are used to indicate the location; in lengthy narratives, the pictures are divided into scenes by borders composed of rows of mountains, flames or walls. All the major elements of a picture are first drawn onto the canvas in outlines of black ink, after which they are coloured in. Traditional *wayang* artists use only a limited palette of five different **colours** – red, blue, yellow, black and white – creating the characteristic muted effect. Paints used to be ground down from the natural pigments of bones, clay and plants, but most artists use commercial paints now. Because of all the stages involved in a *wayang*-style picture, most modern paintings are produced by a team, with the senior artist drawing the outlines in black while assistants fill in the colours.

Like the *wayang* puppets, the two-dimensional **characters** that people classical paintings are instantly recognizable by their facial features and hairstyles, by the clothes that they wear and the objects that they hold, and by their stance and their size. Convention requires, for example, that "refined" characters (heroes, heroines and other people of noble birth) have a slightly supercilious expression on all occasions (in love, in battle, in anger or in joy), and that their bodies be svelte and elegantly posed. "Coarse" characters, on the other hand, like clowns, servants and demonic creatures, have bulbous eyes, gaping mouths with prominent teeth and chunky bodies.

The *wayang* style is still popular with modern artists, some of whom keep the tradition alive by sticking faithfully to the old subjects and classical themes, while others experiment more freely. The traditional school is centred on the village of **Kamasan** near Klungkung, the home of the original Kerta Gosa artists and source of subsequent generations of restorers ever since. Probably the most famous living artist of the Kamasan school is **I Nyoman Mandra**, whose works can be bought in his Kamasan showroom. Mandra has also worked on restoration projects and has founded a school to keep the classical tradition alive. Commercially minded Kamasan artists now apply their talents to more portable artefacts, many of them producing small cloth pictures and reproductions of traditional calendars for the tourist market.

Ubud style

Although *wayang*-style pictures were occasionally peppered with incidents taken from everyday life, few artists took much interest in secular subjects until the early decades of the twentieth century. In the 1930s, however, Balinese painters started to experiment with **techniques** – including perspective, relative proportions and the use of light and shadow – which were completely at odds with the traditional *wayang* style. With these more realistic techniques came the desire to paint scenes from real life, to reproduce in acrylics the events witnessed at the market and the temple, and to illustrate festivals and dances, rice-planting and river-bathing. As tourists and expatriate artists began showing a commercial interest in the works, so the painters started to reduce their pictures to a more portable size, and to frame them as well.

The epicentre of the artistic experimentation was the village of Ubud and its neighbouring hamlets, and so this naturalistic style has been dubbed **Ubud style**. Despite its numerous innovative elements, the Ubud style still retains many typical *wayang* features. The most obvious is the overwhelming sense of **activity** that characterizes the canvases (a concept described in Balinese as *rame*), with each character engaged in some transaction or chore or conversation, and any intervening space taken up with detailed miniature reproductions of offerings or scavenging dogs. This **attention to detail** is another traditional feature: every palm leaf and blade of grass is painstakingly delineated, every sarong pattern described. People, however, are rarely given much individuality, their faces usually set in a rather stylized expression.

The two expatriate artists most commonly associated with the emergence of the

Ubud style are the German **Walter Spies** and the Dutchman **Rudolph Bonnet**. Both men lived in the Ubud area in the 1930s, and both spent a great deal of time with local painters, swapping ideas and inspirations. Most significantly, they were involved in setting up the arts group Pita Maha (see box on p.202).

Most of the best-known Ubud-style artists are represented in the Neka Museum, the Agung Rai Museum of Art (ARMA) and the Puri Lukisan in Ubud, and in the Taman Budaya Centre in Denpasar. The paintings of **Anak Agung Gede Sobrat** are particularly worth looking out for: his *Bumblebee Dance* is a perfect example of the Ubud style; the original is on show in the Neka Museum, and it's reproduced on cards and posters all over the island. The only Walter Spies painting currently on display in the whole of Bali is his *Calonarang*, which you can see at ARMA in Ubud.

Pengosekan style

During the 1960s, a group of young painters working in the Ubud style and living in the village of Pengosekan on the outskirts of Ubud came up with a new approach, subsequently known as the **Pengosekan style**. From the Ubud-style pictures, the Pengosekan school isolated just a few components, specifically the **birds**, **butterflies**, **insects** and **flowering plants** that featured, in miniature, in so many of them, and magnified these elements to fill a whole canvas. The best Pengosekan paintings look delicate and lifelike, generally depicted in soothing pastels of pinks, blues, creams, browns and greens, and slightly reminiscent of classical Japanese flower and bird pictures. To see some of the finer pictures, you can either go to the showroom run by the descendants of the original Pengosekan artists in their village, to the Seniwati Gallery in Ubud or the commercial Agung Rai Gallery in Peliatan.

Batuan style

In contrast to the slightly romanticized visions of village events being painted by the Ubud-style artists in the 1930s, a group of painters in the nearby village of Batuan were coming up with more thought-provoking interpretations of Balinese life. Like the *wayang* artists, **Batuan-style** painters filled their works with scores of people, but on a much more frantic and wide-ranging scale. A single Batuan-style picture might contain a dozen apparently unrelated scenes – a temple dance, a rice harvest, a fishing expedition, an exorcism and a couple of tourists taking snapshots – all depicted in fine detail that strikes a balance between the naturalistic and the stylized. By clever juxtaposition, the best Batuan artists (like the Neka Art Museum exhibitors **I Wayan Bendi**, **I Made Budi** and **Ni Wayan Warti**) can turn their pictures into amusing and astute comments on Balinese society. Works by their precursors, the original Batuan artists, **Ida Bagus Made Togog** and **Ida Bagus Made Wija**, focused more on the darker side of village life, on the supernatural beings that hung around the temples and forests, and on the overwhelming sense of men and women as tiny elements in a forceful natural world.

Keliki style

Easily confused with Batuan-style paintings, pictures from the village of Keliki also emphasize the supernatural elements of daily life in Bali. **Keliki-style** pictures are always tiny (rarely more than 20cm by 15cm) and set against a dark, forbidding background. The scene invariably takes place at a temple, and nearly always features a confrontation between the lion-like representative of good, the Barong, and his eternal enemy, the gruesomely fanged Rangda. Bald, snarly-mouthed witches (*leyak*) flit among the tightly packed crowd of villagers. Like Indian miniatures from Rajasthan, Keliki pictures are full of the tiniest details: each gilded ornament on the Barong's crown is outlined, each temple brick defined.

You'll rarely find a Keliki picture displayed on the walls of the big museums – and few Keliki artists sign their work – but all the commercial galleries keep large stocks of them as their size makes them easy to store and inexpensive to sell.

Young Artists style

A second flush of artistic innovation hit the Ubud area in the 1960s, when a group of teenage boys from the hamlet of **Penestanan** started producing unusually expressionist works, painting everyday scenes in vibrant, non-realistic colours. They soon became known as the **Young Artists**, a tag now used to describe work by anyone in that same style.

The inspiration for the boys' experiments is generally attributed to the interest of Dutch artist **Arie Smit**, who settled in Penestanan in the 1960s. From Smit the boys learnt to appreciate and to experiment with colour, and after a few years Smit helped them organize exhibitions and find foreign buyers for their works. The style is indisputably child-like, even naive, the detailed observations of daily life crudely drawn with minimal attention to perspective, outlined in black like a child's colouring book, and often washed over in weird shades of pinks, purples and blues. In true Balinese fashion, Young Artists' pictures tend to be mosaic-like compositions peopled by dozens of industrious men and women attending temple ceremonies, village festivals and dances, working in the ricefields or bathing in the river.

All the major museums have works by some of the original Young Artists from the 1960s, the most famous of whom include I Ketut Tagen, I Wayan Pugur, I Nyoman Londo, I Nyoman Mundik and I Nyoman Mujung. The Neka Art Museum in Ubud devotes a whole gallery to Arie Smit's outstanding body of work.

Academic (Modern) style

Many modern artists whose work doesn't fit easily into the other major schools of Balinese painting get labelled as **Academic** – meaning that they've studied and been influenced by Western techniques. The best-known Academic painters tend to be men and women from other parts of Indonesia, who have settled in Bali and painted Balinese subjects in a non-traditional style. Both the Neka Museum and ARMA devote a whole gallery to these artists, and names to look out for there include **Affandi**, **Anton H** and **Abdul Aziz**, all from Java, the Sumatran-born **Rusli** and, from Bali, **I Nyoman Tusan**, who specializes in abstract interpretations of Balinese Hindu themes, and the abstract expressionist **Nyoman Guarsa**.

Woodcarving

The oldest and most traditional forms of Balinese **woodcarvings** are those that grace the pillars, panels, doors and lintels of temples and palaces. For centuries, woodcarvers have been commissioned to decorate the most important structures of these buildings, such as the gorgeous **pillars** that support one of the *bale* at the Pura Desa in Sebatu. The Sebatu pillars represent *raksasa*, or demon guardians, and like certain other traditional wooden **figurines** are designed to repel any undesirable intruders and to protect the building from evil influence. **Door panels** and **window shutters** are often decorated with

△ Wooden garuda

carved reliefs drawn from the natural or the mythical world, the leaves, flowers, legendary figures and strange creatures set within frames of floral trellises and painted to spectacular effect. You can see some fine examples of traditional carved doors, pillars and protective figures in the reproduction palaces constructed in Denpasar's Bali Museum, and also in the former palace of Ubud's ruling family, Puri Saren, now a hotel.

Modern carvings

The idea that woodcarvings could be purely ornamental or expressive artefacts didn't really gather much credence until the early years of the twentieth century, when Balinese carvers began both to take a greater interest in **secular subjects** and to court the burgeoning, and increasingly lucrative, tourist market. Like artists working in other disciplines, woodcarvers eschewed the mythical beasts and protective guardians of their heritage to experiment with more tourist-friendly themes, such as figures of stooped rice farmers, sensually posed naked women, praying girls and lifelike animals and birds. It also became fashionable to do without the layers of bright paint that characterized traditional carvings, and instead to expose the fine grains of the timber, either polished to a sheen or varnished. The most popular styles and subjects were quickly copied, and a whole new artistic genre evolved in just a few years.

By the mid-1930s, however, certain influential artists and collectors perceived a depressing lowering of artistic standards across the island, which they attributed to the increased commercialization of the traditional arts. In response they set up the **Pita Maha Arts Movement** (see box on p.202), which encouraged and inspired some of Bali's most respected carvers. One of these was **Ida Bagus Nyana** from the village of Mas, who was always something of a trend-setter. During his most prolific years – the 1930s to the 1960s – Nyana produced works in a range of innovative styles, including abstract elongated human figures, erotic compositions of entwined limbs and smooth, rounded portraits of voluptuously fat men and women. His son, **Ida Bagus Tilem** has continued to experiment and is particularly famous for using contorted roots and twisted branches with obvious imperfections to make highly expressive pieces. Works by father and son are displayed, and sold, at the Njana Tilem Gallery in Mas (see p.185).

The Jati artist **I Nyoman Cokot** also experimented with bizarre cuts of wood, developing a "free-form" style that made wholesale use of monstrous great branches, fashioning them into weird, otherworldly creatures. Cokot's son, **Ketut Nongos**, continues to work in a similar style, letting his supernatural beings emerge from the contours of weatherworn logs and gnarled trunks. A number of Nongos' contemporaries now choose to work with haggard, seasoned forms of driftwood as well, often carving only a section of the original piece of wood.

The legacy of these innovative artists can now be seen in almost every souvenir shop in Bali, many of which sell goods that suffer from the exact same lowering of artistic standards that hit Bali in the 1930s. Aside from a few notable exceptions, few young artists have attained the same status as the stars of the Pita Maha, and carvers are now more often grouped by village rather than by individual reputation. The village of **Mas**, for example, is renowned for its fine unvarnished carvings of female figures, weeping Buddhas and *Ramayana* characters, as well as for traditional *topeng* and *wayang wong* masks (see below). **Nyuhkuning** has long been the established centre of polished wooden animals carved in uncannily natural poses, while **Tegalalang** specializes in fanciful, brightly painted birds and fish and in huge simulacra of fruit trees. **Pujung** continues the tradition of the protective figures, devoting its energies almost exclusively to the production of *garuda* figures, ranging from a few centimetres to several metres in height.

One of the most common and easily carved Balinese woods is the soft, pure white timber known as **crocodile wood** (*panggal Buaya*), which comes from trees whose trunks are covered with spiny mounds. The dark wood of the **hibiscus** tree (*waru*) and the lemony yellow to pale brown wood of the **jackfruit** tree are also relatively easy to work with, as is the lovely tan-coloured timber from the flowering **poinciana**, or *suwar*. Most of the "free-form"-style carvings are made from the gnarled trunks and branches of **frangipani** trees. Hard, dark, dense and extremely valuable **ebony** comes from Kalimantan and Sulawesi, and hard, sweet-smelling **sandalwood** (*cenana*) is imported from India and Timor.

Masks

Carved wooden **masks** play a hugely significant role in traditional Balinese dance-dramas. Many of them are treated as sacred objects, wrapped in holy cloth and stored in a high place within the temple compound when not being used, and given offerings before every public appearance. There's even an annual festival day for all masks and puppets, called Tumpek Wayang, at which actors and mask-makers honour their masks with special chants and offerings. Such is the power generated by certain masks, that some mask-makers enter a trance while working.

The undisputed centres of mask-making on Bali are the villages of **Mas** and **Singapadu**. Although the masks sold to tourists in these villages lack the spiritual power of their holy prototypes, most are still fashioned in the same way.

The best material for masks is the very pale **wood** of the *pule* (milkwood) tree. The mask-maker nearly always cuts the timber himself, making special prayers of apology and thanks to the tree before sawing away at its branches or trunk. The **carving** of any mask is a time-consuming and painstaking process, usually taking the best part of two weeks. Old-school mask-makers still make their own **paints** from natural substances, but most mask-makers now rely on commercial pigments. Facial accessories are added at the end: hair is either goat's hide or horsehair, usually glued on to the mask, and tusks are carved from the bones of wild boars or from water buffalo horns.

Traditional masks fall into three basic categories: human, animal and supernatural. Most **human** masks are made for performances of the *topeng*, literally "masked drama" (see p.526), and have both a sacred, a symbolic and a narrative role. In *topeng*, the particular features of a mask are meant to indicate personality type. **Animal** masks feature very strongly in the *wayang wong* dance-dramas, which take most of their stories and characters from the Hindu epic, the *Ramayana*. Most sacred of all are the fantastical Barong and Rangda masks, worn by the **mythical creatures** who represent the forces of good and evil and who appear in almost every drama to do battle with each other.

Stonecarving

Stonecarvings are Bali's most public art form, gracing doorways, walls, towers, shrines and gardens all over the island. Bali's best stonecarvers come from a small area around the village of **Batubulan**, still the best place to see the craftspeople at work.

Chiselled mainly from the local volcanic tuff, or *paras*, a soft grey material that yields well to pressure but disintegrates rather speedily in wind and rain, the prime function of stonecarvings has always been to entice and entertain the gods and to ward off any undesirable spirits and evil forces. The **temples** in the south are generally quite restrained in their use of carved ornamentation, being built mainly from red brick with just a few sections of carved *paras* (though Batubulan's Pura Puseh is a remarkable exception), but the northern temples, which are often built entirely from *paras*, flounder beneath a riot of reliefs and curlicues. Many of the classic northern temples are just a short bemo ride from Singaraja, and include the Pura Dalem in Jagaraga, Pura Beji and the Pura Dalem in Sangsit and, most famously, Pura Meduwe Karang at Kubutambahan.

Rajas and high-ranking nobles also commissioned fantastic carvings to embellish their **palaces** (*puri*). Unfortunately, many of these did not survive the early twentieth-century battles with the Dutch, but one notable exception is the Puri Saren Agung in Ubud. This was once the home of the culturally refined Sukawati family, and they employed Bali's most skilful stonecarver, I Gusti Nyoman Lempad (see p.204) to decorate the walls, gateways and shrines in the *puri* compound.

Interestingly, there's little to distinguish the basic **iconography** that graces religious and secular buildings. **Gateways** are normally the focus of the most elaborate carvings, as these have a symbolic as well as a practical function, dividing the outer from the inner world, whether they're leading to the inner temple courtyard, or giving access to palace compounds. Surprisingly, the Hindu trinity (Brahma, Wisnu and Siwa) are rarely depicted in stone, but a number of their spiritual relatives and manifestations do crop up fairly regularly. Temple carvings are not solely confined to deities and demons, however, and surfaces are often enlivened by playful, even risqué scenes taken from **secular** life. In the renowned temples of north Bali, you'll find beautifully observed scenes covering everything from love-making to beer-drinking parties, from car breakdowns to cartoon-style aeroplanes. Many of these were inspired by the antics of the Dutch citizens who lived in Bali in the early 1900s.

Traditional textiles

Over half-a-century after Western fashions started filtering into Bali, cloth still has a **ritual purpose** on the island – worn, given or hung at important rites of passage ceremonies such as first hair-cutting and tooth-filing. Bali's indigenous textile industry has always focused on the **ikat** technique, particular the weft *ikat* or *endek* of Gianyar and the double *ikat* or *geringsing* of Tenganan. It's possible to see weavers at work in both these places, as well as at the smaller weaving factories of Singaraja. Their fabrics are worn and sold all over the island, along with a whole range of **batik** textiles which come mainly from Java. In addition, Bali has also become something of an entrepôt for the textiles of outlying Indonesian islands, particularly Sumba and Flores. Specific details on where and how to shop for these fabrics are given on p.71, but for some of the finest examples of locally woven cloth, check out the **displays** in the Bali Museum in Denpasar and at the informative Threads of Life Textile Arts Center and Gallery in Ubud (see p.205), where you can also take workshops in traditional textile appreciation.

Ikat

Easily recognized by the fuzzy-edged motifs it produces, the **ikat** weaving technique is common throughout Indonesia, woven either on backstrap or foot-pedal looms (or, increasingly in the wealthier areas, on semi-automatic looms) from either silk, cotton or rayon. The distinctive feature of *ikat* is, however, not so much the weaving process as the dyeing technique. The word *ikat* derives from the Indonesian verb to tie or to bind, and the technique is essentially a sophisticated tie-dye process which has three variations. In **warp-ikat**, the warp yarn (the threads that run lengthwise through the material) is first threaded on to a loom frame, and then tied with dye-resistant twine into the desired pattern before being dipped into a dye vat. The binding and dyeing processes are then repeated with different colours until the final effect is achieved, after which single-coloured weft threads are woven into the patterned warp. In **weft-ikat**, the warp threads are left plain and the weft yarn (the threads running across the fabric) is dyed to the finished design. In double *ikat*, both warp and weft are dyed before weaving begins.

Nearly all the *ikat* woven in Bali is weft-*ikat*, also known as **endek**, recognizable by its predominantly geometric and abstract motifs. Weavers use mainly chemical dyes, and so colours are often bright and bold: pink, royal blue, turquoise and lime green are modern favourites. The art of embroidered *ikat*, or supplementary weft weaving, is also practised to fine effect in Bali, where it's known as **songket**. *Songket* fabric uses threads of gold and silver metallic yarn to add decorative tapestry-like motifs of birds, butterflies and flowers onto very fine silk (or, increasingly, rayon or artificial silk). *Songket* sarongs are worn by the wealthiest Balinese at major ceremonial occasions. The brocaded sashes worn by performers of traditional Balinese dance are always made from *songket*, often so heavy with gold thread that you can hardly see the silk background.

Bali is quite unusual in its favouring of weft-*ikat*; warp-*ikat* is the most widely practised technique in almost every other Indonesian island. Although it's hard for a non-expert to tell the difference, you can usually hazard a guess from the textile design, which in warp-*ikat* tends to be larger and more figurative. The warp-*ikat*s of **east Sumba** are particularly distinctive, and very popular in the shops of Bali, woven with bold humanoid motifs and images of real and mythological creatures such as horses, lizards, birds, monkeys, phoenixes and lions. They are usually dyed in combinations of indigo and deep red and often take the form of *hinggi*, or fringed shawls. Sometimes Sumbanese weavers incorporate embroidered motifs into their fabrics; this technique, known as supplementary weft, is particularly effective on wall-hangings where the raised designs – often of winged creatures – stand out in eye-catching relief. Warp-*ikat*s from **Flores** also use a distinctive blend of natural indigo and deep red dyes which generally result in lovely combinations of brown, ochre and dark red; typically these are woven into intricate non-figurative and geometric patterns. The warp-*ikat*s of Flores tend to be quite small, because of the restrictive size of the backstrap loom used to weave them. Crocodiles, fish and stylized human forms feature most frequently on the warp-*ikat*s of **Timor**, often in simple tones of indigo and white or deep red and white.

Warp- and weft-*ikat* are complicated and time-consuming processes, but are nothing in comparison to double *ikat*, or **geringsing** as it's known in Bali. The *geringsing* technique involves the dyeing of both the warp and the weft threads into their final designs before they're woven together: a double *ikat* sarong can take five years to complete. There are just three areas in the world where this highly refined weaving method is practised – India, Japan and the Bali Aga village of **Tenganan** in eastern Bali. Not surprisingly, *geringsing* is exceedingly expensive to purchase, and over the centuries it has acquired an important ritual significance. At first glance, the *geringsing* of Tenganan is quite easily confused with the warp-*ikat* of Flores, for the Flores weavers use the same combinations of natural dyes, but the Tenganan motifs have a highly charged spiritual significance, and their geometric and floral designs are instantly recognizable to the people of Bali.

Batik

Despite being far more fashionable than *ikat* for everyday wear, nearly all **batik** fabric is imported from Java, as there's very little traditional batik produced in Bali.

The essential batik **technique** involves drawing patterns in dye-resistant wax on to lengths of fabric, dyeing the fabric, then stripping off the wax to expose the undyed areas. Wax is then often reapplied in different places, and the fabric dyed with a different colour, repeating the process until the finished design is achieved. The wax used for batik design is a mixture of beeswax and paraffin wax and is sometimes softened or strengthened by additional animal and vegetable fats. All the waxing is done manually by two different methods. The most painstaking and time-consuming process involves drawing each part of the design on to the fabric with a little wooden wax-filled pen called a *canting*, which is periodically dipped into a bowl of molten wax. A far faster method uses a copper stamp or *cap*, which is fashioned from lengths of wire into one block or unit of the overall design; the *cap* is pressed into a tray of molten wax and then stamped on to the fabric.

As with *ikat*, certain batik-producing areas of Java are renowned for their characteristic dyes and designs. The refined royal cities of **Yogyakarta** and **Solo** have long been centres of high-quality batik, and the designers there continue to churn out traditional colours and patterns. Coloured mainly with rust brown and indigo dyes against a cream or white background, the patterns adorning Yogyakarta/Solo batik tend to be either abstract, or compositions of graceful birds and flowers, though mythological figures do sometimes appear, particularly *garuda*, *naga* and even lions. Birds and flowers also feature a lot in the batiks that come from Java's other main batik-producing area, **Pekalongan**, on the north coast, but these artists use a greater variety of colours, particularly blues, pinks and greens, and the designs show more Chinese and Arabic influences.

While batik is perfectly acceptable attire for most ceremonial occasions, there's a particular type of batik called **perada**, which is used only for ceremonial outfits and ornaments. This is the gold-painted cloth that you'll see fashioned into temple umbrellas, adorning some sacred statues and worn by *legong* dancers and other performers of religious dances. The background colour of *perada* fabric is nearly always bright green or yellow, sometimes purple, and onto this is painted or stamped a symbolic design (usually stylized birds or flowers) in either gold-leaf paint or, more commonly today, a bronze- or gold-coloured pigment imported from Europe.

Lombok crafts

Lombok's only native **fine art** can be found at two batik workshops near Rembitan in the south of the island. **Crafts**, however, abound, including textiles, pottery and basketware. If you want to buy crafts on Lombok with minimal effort and little travelling, head for the art shops in Ampenan, the Lombok Handicraft Centre and Senggigi, or to the markets at Cakranegara or Sweta. However, the best way to compare quality, styles and price is to go to the villages where the crafts are actually made, and buy direct from the producers.

Textiles

The *ikat* and *songket* **cloth** produced in Bali is also made in Lombok using similar colours and motifs. Footlooms are in evidence in the larger factories of **Cakranegara**, while backstrap looms predominate in the villages of **Sukarara**, **Pringgasela** and **Penjanggik**. Footlooms are faster and produce wider lengths of material.

Certain cloths are unique to Lombok, mostly with religious uses, but you won't find them for sale. The **kain usap** is a square cotton cloth either covered in geometric motifs or with alternating wide bands of floral patterns and narrow bands of geometric ones, used to cover the face of the dead. A member of the dead person's family also carries one of these cloths to the religious leader of the community to inform him of the death. The **lempot**, a rectangular stole with a simple striped pattern and fringed ends, is used to carry small children. A coarsely woven cotton striped cloth, called **kombang**, is particularly sacred; made with a continuous warp which is cut through in the course of religious ceremonies such as the naming of a child or hair-cutting, the fringes are tied with old Chinese coins for good fortune.

Pottery

Pottery is a traditional craft that has been considerably strengthened by the Lombok Crafts Project (see box on p.429) in the pottery villages of **Banyumulek**, **Penujak** and the hamlet of Penakak in **Masbagik Timur**. The potters, traditionally women who pass their techniques on to their daughters, use the local grey clay, worked by hand using a round stone and a wooden paddle to form the pots, which are often very large. As well as traditional water vessels, you'll see an enormous range of bowls, vases, lamp bases, pots and boxes.

Before firing, the pots are left for half a day to dry in the sun and are then stacked in a pile together with firewood and coconut husks. When the fire is under way the whole pile is covered with rice straw and rice husks. This covering burns too, but leaves a thick layer of ash which retains the heat for the final stages of firing, producing temperatures in the region of 800°C. A slip made from a mixture of fine clay, water and an oily plant extract is then applied to the surface of the pot and polished to a deep shine by rubbing with a smooth stone or piece of glass or shell. Patterns are often etched on to the surface of the pot at this stage.

Basketware

Lombok is also known for its **basketware** made of rattan, bamboo, palm leaves, cane and grass. The boxes, bags and baskets produced are often decorated with beads, shells or wooden carving, and many pots are also covered with a decorative cane lattice. Different villages specialize in particular materials. **Beleka**, for example, produces often enormous rattan baskets, many in a distinctive bulbous style, while **Sayang-Sayang** specializes in palm-leaf boxes, **Loyok** in bamboo and **Karang Bayan** in grass boxes with carved wooden lids.

Carving

While the **carving** of small items to decorate woven boxes is common, many of the wooden items that you'll see in the art shops on the island are actually from further east in Nusa Tenggara. The distinctive wooden boxes with interlocking lids (*tongal*) are from Sumba, and the animistic hunkered and standing carved figures from all islands further east. On Lombok, **Senanti** and **Sukaraja** are the island centres for woodcarving.

Village life

The majority of people on Bali and Lombok live in villages and earn their living from agriculture. People employed in the cities or tourist resorts may well commute from their village homes each day, and even those whose villages are far away still identify with them and return on particular festivals each year.

Balinese village layout

Orientation in the Balinese world does not correspond to the compass points of north, south, east and west. Gunung Agung, dwelling place of the gods and highest peak on Bali, is the reference point, and the main directions are **kaja** (towards the mountain) and **kelod** (away from the mountain, which in practice usually means towards the sea). Direction is therefore relative: in the south of the island, *kaja* will be roughly to the north, and in the north of Bali, *kaja* is roughly to the south. The other directions are *kangin* (from where the sun rises), and its opposite, *kauh* (where the sun sets).

All Balinese villages are oriented *kaja–kelod* and the locations of the three village temples, *pura puseh*, *pura desa* and *pura dalem* (see p.507) are determined on this axis.

House compounds

Each Balinese household consists of several structures all built within a confining wall, with variations depending on the caste and wealth of the family. When a son of the family marries, his wife will usually move into his compound, so there are frequently several generations living within the same area, each with their own sleeping quarters, but otherwise sharing the facilities. Given the climate, most domestic activities take place outside or in the partial shelter of **bale**, raised platforms supported by wooden pillars, with a roof traditionally thatched with local grass (*alang-alang*). Outside the *kelod* wall, families have their garbage tip and pig pens. The different structures of the compound are believed to reflect the human body: the family shrine is the head, the *bale* are the arms, the courtyard is the navel, the kitchen and rice barn are the legs and feet and the garbage tip is the anus.

When designing and building a compound, a set of rules laid down in ancient texts must be adhered to. The architect or master builder (*undagi*) takes a series of **measurements** from the body of the **head of the household**. For the walls of the compound he needs to measure the distance between the tips of the middle fingers with the arms stretched out sideways, the distance from the elbow to the tip of the middle finger and the width of the fist with the thumb stretched out. All these measurements are added together to give a unit length, the *depa asti musti*, and the texts specify how many of these lengths are suitable for different types of compound, location and for which caste. The *bale daja*, the sleeping quarters of the head of the household, are sited first, in relation to the *kaja* wall, and then the other structures positioned in relation to this.

Prior to calling in the *undagi*, the prospective householder also consults an

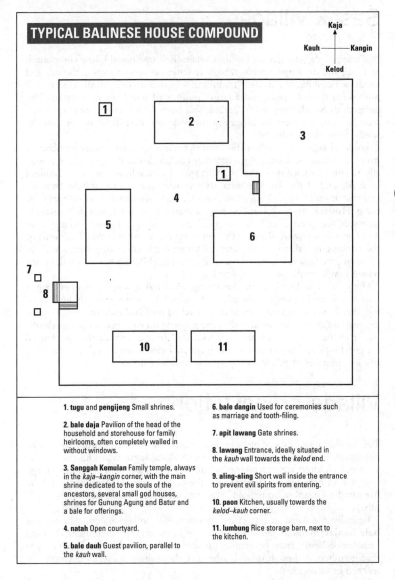

TYPICAL BALINESE HOUSE COMPOUND

Kaja

Kauh —— Kangin

Kelod

1. **tugu** and **pengijeng** Small shrines.

2. **bale daja** Pavilion of the head of the household and storehouse for family heirlooms, often completely walled in without windows.

3. **Sanggah Kemulan** Family temple, always in the *kaja–kangin* corner, with the main shrine dedicated to the souls of the ancestors, several small god houses, shrines for Gunung Agung and Batur and a bale for offerings.

4. **natah** Open courtyard.

5. **bale dauh** Guest pavilion, parallel to the *kauh* wall.

6. **bale dangin** Used for ceremonies such as marriage and tooth-filing.

7. **apit lawang** Gate shrines.

8. **lawang** Entrance, ideally situated in the *kauh* wall towards the *kelod* end.

9. **aling-aling** Short wall inside the entrance to prevent evil spirits from entering.

10. **paon** Kitchen, usually towards the *kelod–kauh* corner.

11. **lumbung** Rice storage barn, next to the kitchen.

expert in the Balinese calendar, as an auspicious day must be chosen for buying land and beginning construction. Before building starts, a **ceremony** takes place in which an offering, usually a brick wrapped in white cloth sprinkled with holy water, is placed in the foundation of each building so that work will proceed smoothly. When the building work is finished, a series of ceremonies must take place before the compound can be occupied. The final ceremony is the **melaspas**, an inauguration ritual which "brings the building to life".

Sasak villages

Balinese people who live on Lombok retain their traditional house compounds and *bale*, and the Bugis people, who have settled in coastal areas in the east and south of Lombok, live in their traditional wooden houses, constructed on tall piles with slatted floors and a large number of windows or shutters. The indigenous **Sasak** people of Lombok also have their own architectural style, seen in its purest form in villages in the Sade and Batu Rintang areas in the south, or on the north coast.

Sasak villages are traditionally walled enclosures, using either bamboo or stones and mud, and with a gateway that can be closed at night. There is usually an animal enclosure within the village so the local livestock can be brought in at the end of the day. The usual style of **mosque** is a rectangular bamboo and thatch building with a pyramid-shaped roof, though not all villages have them. **Houses**, made of bamboo with a thatch roof that slopes down steeply almost to the ground, are built on a thick base of mud and dung, and may have none or only a few windows, with a verandah on at least one side. Traditionally, the cooking hearth and eating area are inside the house, along with a walled-off room, the *inan bale*, generally used for storage, although this is also the place where newly-weds spend their first night.

The symbol of Lombok, the **lumbung rice barn**, with its bonnet-shaped roof, is a feature of only the south of the island. They are generally built close together in rows, on four piles with a thatched roof and only one small opening high up. A circular wooden disc, the *jelepreng*, on each post stops rats climbing up to the rice. Underneath each post, old Chinese coins (*kepeng*) are buried for good luck and protection. In the north, the rice barns are rectangular, their size and number of pillars indicating the wealth of the owner.

Village organizations

The smallest unit of social organization in each village is the **banjar**, or neighbourhood. Each adult male on Bali joins the local *banjar* when he marries; his wife and children are also members but only the adult men attend meetings. The size of *banjar* varies enormously: the largest ones in Denpasar may have five hundred heads of household, while the small rural ones may have as few as fifty.

Typically the *banjar* meets every month in the village meeting-house, the **bale banjar**, to discuss land issues, plans for future temple ceremonies, the local gamelan orchestra, latest government projects and any problems relating to specific members. Although there is a head of the *banjar* (*kliang*), all decisions are reached by consensus.

The *banjar* has considerable authority. If residential land in the area is left vacant for a period of time, it will revert to the *banjar* for redistribution to the members. If members neglect their duties they can be fined or even expelled from the village. This is a particularly powerful threat among people where communal life is at the heart of their existence. Expulsion also means the loss of the right to burial and cremation within the village.

The subak

Much of the daily life of a village revolves around the *sawah*, or **rice-fields**, and numerous complex rituals accompany all the stages of rice cultivation encapsulated in the worship of Dewi Sri, the goddess of rice and prosperity.

The local organization in charge of each irrigation system is the **subak**; these are known to have existed on Bali since the ninth century, and are made up of all the farmers who use the water in that system. Membership of the *subak* cuts across village and *banjar* lines. The maintenance of the irrigation system, along with detailed planning to ensure that every farmer gets the water he needs, is co-ordinated by the *kliang subak*. Any *subak* with plans that may influence the irrigation system, such as changing dry fields to wet, or causing conflict with another *subak*, has to consult the regional water temples and, ultimately, the **Jero Gede**, chief priest of Pura Ulun Danu Batur, whose decision at island level is final.

The **Subak Museum**, on the eastern outskirts of Tabanan (see p.380) is well worth a visit for more information on this unique aspect of Balinese life.

Balinese life-cycle celebrations

On **Bali**, rituals and ceremonies are carried out at important points in an individual's life to purify them, and make sure they have sufficient spiritual energy to remain healthy and calm.

The first life-cycle ritual, **pegedong-gedongan**, takes place about six months after conception, when the fetus has a definite human form; the ritual emphasizes the hope of a long healthy life for the child. Subsequent **birth rituals** focus on the placenta (*ari-ari*), which is washed and buried inside a coconut wrapped in sacred white cloth near the gateway of the parents' household. A rock is placed over the spot to protect it, and regular offerings are made there.

Following the birth of a baby, the parents and child are regarded as unclean (*sebel*), and cannot participate in religious practices. For the mother and baby this lasts 42 days, for the father it lasts until the baby's umbilical cord drops off, when the **kepus pungsed** ritual is carried out. The cord is wrapped in cloth, placed in an offering shaped like a dove and suspended over the baby's bed, along with a small shrine dedicated to Sanghyang Panca Kumara, son of Siwa. Twelve days after birth, the ceremony of **ngelepas hawon** takes place, with offerings made for the baby in the kitchen, the well and the family temple, but this is less important than the **tutug kambuhan**, 42 days after the birth, which marks the end of the *sebel* period for the mother. After 105 days, **telubulan** is a large, often elaborate ceremony at which the child is named, and may be given an amulet to guard against evil spirits.

The child's **first birthday**, *oton*, occurs after 210 days (a Balinese year according to the *wuku* calendar), and is celebrated with much feasting. This is the first occasion that the baby is allowed contact with the ground, and may be accompanied by a ritual hair-cutting ceremony. The next ceremony, **maketus**, takes place when the child's milk teeth fall out. Prayers are offered to the gods to ensure that the adult teeth will be strong. Sanghyang Kumara is sent away as the child's protector, and the child is now guarded by the family ancestors.

The next life-cycle ceremonies occur at **puberty**, with *manggah daa* rituals for a girl and *manggah teruna* for a boy, although the male ritual is often omitted.

The **tooth-filing ritual** (*mapandes*) takes place between six and eighteen years of age, preferably before marriage, but after puberty for girls, and is a huge celebration with guests, music and lavish offerings. It is considered to be an absolutely vital ritual, and the elderly, and even the dead, have been known to have their teeth filed. The aim of the ritual is to remove any hint of coarse, uncontrolled behaviour from the person by filing down the upper canine teeth or fangs – *caling*, as the Balinese call them – and the four teeth in between; six in total. Rituals are also performed to rid the person of lust, greed, anger, drunkenness, confusion and jealousy, in order that the person will lead a better life and be assured a more favourable reincarnation.

Marriage (*pawiwahan* or *nganten*) is the final life-cycle ceremony for most Balinese. There are two options when getting married. The most correct is *mamadik*, when the marriage is agreed between the two sets of parents and a huge financial outlay for ceremonies is involved. Much more common is *ngero-rod* or *malaib* – elopement. The man and woman run off and spend the night together, not so secretly that nobody knows, but with sufficient subterfuge that the girl's parents can pretend to be outraged. The following morning a simple, private ceremony (*makala-kalaan*) is carried out, and the couple are married. Frequently, rather more elaborate rituals and a reception are hosted later the same day by the boy's parents. The girl's parents will not be invited as there is supposed to be bad feeling between the two sides. However, three days later the two sets of parents meet at the *ketipat bantal* ceremony, and are reconciled.

Cremation

The ceremony that visitors to Bali are most likely to witness is **cremation** (*pengabenan* or *palebonan*). The Balinese believe that the soul of each person inhabits a temporary receptacle, the body, during each life on earth. Following death, this body must be returned to the five elements of solid, liquid, energy, radiance and ether to become ready for reincarnation. The lengthy and complex rituals, the magnificent objects and the spectacular burning itself make this the most picturesque manifestation of religious observance on the island.

Following death, the body is usually buried, sometimes for years, while the elaborate **preparations** for the cremation are made. Poorer families will often share in the cremation ceremonies of wealthier families. The entire extended family and *banjar* is involved in building temporary shelters for shrines and preparing offerings. Animals must be slaughtered, holy water acquired and gamelan, dancers and puppet shows organized. An animal-shaped sarcophagus is built from a solid tree trunk, covered with paper and cloth and decorated with mirrors, tassels and tinsel. The cremation tower, representing the Balinese universe, supported by the turtle, Bedawang, and the two *naga*, Basuki and Anantaboga, is also built, with tiers similar to the roofs on the *meru* in temples. A small *bale* at the base of the tiers houses an effigy of the dead person and the body itself, or just the bones if burial has previously taken place.

The event itself is joyful, accompanied by the soft music of the bamboo **gamelan angklung**. The sarcophagus and cremation tower are carried to the cemetery and twirled around many times to make sure the soul is completely confused and cannot find its way back home to cause mischief for the family. At the cremation ground, the body is transferred from the tower into the sarcophagus, which is anointed with holy water and set alight. The tower is burned in a separate fire. After burning, the ashes are carried to the sea or to a

Traditional healers

Known as *balian* in Bali and *dukun* in Lombok, **traditional healers** are a vital adjunct to Western medicine on the islands. Illness is believed to stem from a lack of balance between the patient and the spirit world; for example, a patient may have paid insufficient respect to a god, broken some religious custom or may be the target of black magic. There are many different kinds of *balian*, ranging from the most practical *balian tulang* (bonesetters), *balian manak* (midwives) and *balian apun* (masseurs), to the more spiritual, including *balian taksu*, mediums who communicate with the spirit world while in a trance to discover which offerings must be made and which ceremonies performed to cure the patient, and *balian kebal*, who work with charms and spells making love potions and magical amulets to protect the wearer against spiritual attack. *Balian* are also consulted to find out which ancestral souls have been reincarnated in the bodies of newborn babies, and which days are auspicious for certain events.

stream which will carry them to the ocean. A further purification ceremony takes place three days after the cremation, another at twelve days, finishing with the ritual of *nyagara-gunung* when the family take offerings to important sea and mountain temples.

Sasak life-cycle ceremonies

Some of the ceremonies performed in **Lombok** are associated with the more orthodox adherents to Islam, while others are associated only with the smaller numbers of Wetu Telu followers (see p.514). The Wetu Telu **birth ceremony** of *adi kaka* is similar to the Balinese one. A few days after birth, the **naming ceremony** of *buang au* or *malang mali* takes place. A ritual **hair-cutting ceremony** (*ngurisang*) is also obligatory for a young child, although the age it takes place is variable.

The most important ceremony for a Muslim boy is his **circumcision** (*nyunatang*), which often takes place in the Muslim month of the Prophet Muhammad's birthday, accompanied by ceremony and feasting. No anaesthetic of any kind is used, and many local people say that the boy is expected to suffer pain for Allah.

There are three **marriage** options in Sasak culture: a marriage arranged by the families concerned, one between cousins or an elopement. The man's family must pay a price for the bride, who will afterwards live in their house. This is negotiated between the families and will depend on the caste differences between the couple. Traditionally, payment is made in cows, money and rice, but also includes traditional betel nut, coconut, a white sarong and old Chinese coins. During the wedding ceremony, the couple are often carried on a type of sedan chair accompanied by a gamelan orchestra.

Under the laws of Islam, the dead are **buried**, rather than cremated. According to Wetu Telu custom the dead are ritually washed and wrapped in a white sarong, carried to the cemetery, and buried with the head towards Mecca. A death in the family sets in motion a whole cycle of possible rituals, the most important being **deena nitook**, seven days after the death, **nyatus** after a hundred days, with the final event, **nyiu**, a thousand days after death, when the grave is sprinkled with holy water and commemorative stones are placed on it.

The impact of tourism

There is no middle ground in the debate about the effects of tourism on Bali. Since the 1930s, when just a few thousand foreign tourists a year visited the island, through to the present day, when it hosts well over 1.5 million annually, one side has argued that Bali will be ruined, its culture destroyed by the tourist influx, while the other side claims that the Balinese are well able to protect their traditional culture.

Tourism within the archipelago began in 1908, the year the Dutch finally took control over the whole of Bali. Perhaps in an attempt to counter the criticism levelled both from home and elsewhere of the then-recent massacres, the Dutch began to promote the island's culture. The colonial government opened a tourist promotion bureau in Batavia (now Jakarta) to encourage tourism to the Netherlands Indies – this was initially limited to Java, but later extended to Bali, described in brochures as the "Gem of the Lesser Sunda Isles". However, it wasn't until 1924 that tourism in Bali began in earnest. KPM, the Royal Packet Navigation Company, established weekly **steamship services** connecting Bali with Batavia, Singapore, Semarang, Surabaya and Makassar (now Ujung Pandang), visitors to Bali being allowed to use the government rest houses dotted around the island. The steamships either anchored at Padang Bai for a couple of days, allowing their passengers quick sorties ashore, or landed them at Buleleng (Singaraja) on Friday morning, collecting them again on Sunday evening.

In 1928, KPM opened the first **hotel** on the island, the *Bali Hotel* in Denpasar, and by the 1930s, several thousand tourists each year were visiting lakes Tamblingan and Buyan, the Bali Museum, Goa Gajah, Tampaksiring, Gunung Kawi, Goa Lawah, Gunung Batur and the temples at Kubutambahan and Sangsit.

Following the establishment of an air link to Surabaya in 1933, a daily ferry to Java in 1934 (from the west coast town of Gilimanuk), and the opening of the airport at Tuban, near Denpasar, in 1938, Bali began to see the arrival of **independent visitors**, many of whom settled on the island. A large number of these visitors were artists, such as Walter Spies and Miguel Covarrubias, and anthropologists, including Margaret Mead and Gregory Bateson. They focused on the artistic and religious aspects of Balinese life, encouraging the Balinese to produce works of art that would appeal to tourists and, through their writing, painting, photography and film-making, enhancing the image of Bali as a paradise.

The Japanese invasion during World War II, followed by the long struggle for independence, halted the tourist influx, but under President Sukarno's rule, the **promotion of tourism** became official government policy. Until the late 1960s, though, the poor state of the Balinese economy, its limited infrastructure, political disturbance and a certain ambiguity among the authorities towards mass tourism meant that this was fairly limited. Part of the war reparation money paid to Indonesia was used to construct the **Bali Beach Hotel** in Sanur, inaugurated in 1966 when the political upheavals following the attempted coup of September 30, 1965, had closed the entire country to foreigners.

With the arrival of General Suharto and the New Order in 1967, economic development, in which tourism was to play a major part, was the primary objective for the nation, and major bodies such as the World Bank, the International Monetary Fund and the United Nations Development Project advocated tourism as a means of development. The inauguration of **Ngurah Rai International Airport** on August 1, 1969, marked the beginning of mass tourism on the island; it is now the second-busiest airport in the country, after Jakarta.

In 1972, the government-owned **Bali Tourist Development Corporation** (BTDC) was formed on the recommendations of overseas consultants; its first project was to build a major resort of a dozen hotel complexes, **Nusa Dua**, on poor agricultural land, aimed at closeting tourists away from local people and attracting high-spending tourists at the luxury end of the market. Profits were to be split between the BTDC, the foreign hotel chains who were to manage the hotels and the consortia who had built them, thus giving no guarantees about how much of the profits were to remain on Bali. Although the BTDC collapsed in 1978 with financial problems, this is the model still used within Indonesia to fund major projects. The market soon responded to Bali's entice-ments, the number of visitors climbing from 30,000 in 1969 to 700,000 in 1989. In 1991 alone, 28 new hotels with over three thousand beds were opened on the island; by 1994 there were more than 30,000 rooms and five hundred restaurants. Many resort areas have mushroomed dramatically in recent years, in particular Kuta–Legian–Seminyak and Lovina. Taking into account tourists from within Indonesia, who are as fond of Bali as a holiday spot as people from outside the country, it is estimated that over 2.5 million visitors a year arrive on the island.

There is no doubt that, in recent years, many potential visitors to Indonesia have been frightened off. The convulsions in the months leading up to Suharto's resignation in 1998 were interpreted by many as reflecting a nation on the verge of collapse, an image reinforced by the ongoing **religious strife** in Maluku. In 1999, diplomatic relations with **Australia** reached an extremely low ebb, as the suggestion was made that visiting Bali was tantamount to supporting Indonesian military actions in East Timor. Australian visitor numbers dropped dramatically as a result – very bad news, given that many Australians used Bali as a weekend getaway. Despite the fact that Lombok emptied overnight following sporadic conflict in early 2000 (and stayed empty for many weeks) – compounded by the drop in global tourism following September 11, 2001 – the figures show that tourists are now as keen to visit as ever.

Economy versus culture

The Balinese themselves have long been ambivalent about, and even openly critical of, the **effects of tourism** on Balinese society. In studies by Universi-tas Udayana, the University of Bali, some Balinese people described tourism as a tempest battering their coasts or an infectious disease spreading discord and defilement through the villages. They are particularly critical when tourism touches on **religion**, condemning the desecration of temples by tourists, the commercialization of dances and the fact that Balinese involved in the industry neglect their religious duties. However, they acknowledge the financial benefits that tourism has brought; the challenge they have given themselves is to maxi-mize these, while avoiding the wide-ranging cultural costs. As one commenta-tor noted, "Tourism is the fire that cooks your breakfast and the fire that burns down your house."

It's difficult to know to what extent either the Balinese economy or the average Balinese person has benefited from the tourist industry. The worst-case scenario sees the profits from multinational hotel chains flooding out of the island to Jakarta and abroad, with middle management jobs within these organizations beyond the reach of the average Balinese, who are often reduced to low-paid, unskilled employment. Jobs are also threatened by Indonesians from across the archipelago who are flooding to Bali, lured by the prospect of work in the tourism industry. A recent Balinese study found that seventeen percent of jobs in the prestigious Nusa Dua complex were held by non-Balinese, and it's also believed that up to ninety percent of the Balinese coast is owned by non-Balinese. Tourist businesses often prefer to employ non-Balinese rather than cope with high levels of absenteeism from Balinese staff who need to attend their own villages for traditional ceremonies.

However, as families grow and land-holdings are divided among more and more family members, many people in Bali can no longer earn a living from agriculture; the burgeoning tourist sector offers jobs for them as masseurs, touts, guides, chambermaids and gardeners, while those with some education and/or capital are opening small hotels, shops and businesses. Recent estimates suggest that eighty percent of the working population was employed in tourism-related activities. With the average annual income of the Balinese greater than that of Indonesians in other parts of the country, some benefits from tourism are clear. Indeed some commentators have noticed that the increased wealth of the Balinese is very often spent in highly traditional ways – in particular, by sponsoring extremely elaborate traditional religious ceremonies.

Environmental concerns

Tourism also generates major **environmental concerns**. It is estimated that around ten square kilometres of irrigated rice-fields are lost to tourist development every year. As an agricultural economy based on the cultivation of rice, **water** is a life or death issue on the island. One five-star hotel room alone is estimated to consume 500 litres of water each day. Not only are there fears of water shortages for farmers on the island, but also that too much water is being taken from subterranean resources that supply wells on the island. Salt water is now leaching into the water table from the ocean and spoiling the drinking water in wells.

Particular concerns have arisen about the effects of tourist developments on the island's **coral reefs** (already apparent in Candi Dasa). The coral itself is used in the production of cement, and anchors, snorkellers and divers damage it further, while sewage from hotels pollutes it. **Golf courses** are an environmental nightmare, with every eighteen holes costing at least US$25 million to create and using massive amounts of water, pesticide and herbicide. There are twenty new courses spread across the island already approved for development, including plans to build a course within the Batur crater, arousing fears for the water level in the lake and concern over pollution. Global awareness of this problem is increasing and the recent uncertainties of the tourist market have meant that few of these plans have become reality but it remains to be seen what the future holds.

The idea of a luxury hotel overlooking the highly revered temple at **Tanah Lot** was mooted as early as 1989, galvanizing local villagers into active opposition, the first time this had happened on Bali. The Parisada Hindu Dharma Indonesia (PHDI), Bali's highest Hindu body, decreed that any development needed to be at least 2km from the temple. The debate between villagers, the PHDI and the developers dragged on for several years and was eventually settled in mid-1994 with a compromise in which the hotel took the silhouette of the temple out of its logo and relocated small family shrines from the hotel's golf course area at its own expense. It was also ensured that the hotel was not visible from the temple itself.

The proposed 140-metre **Garuda Wisnu Kencana (GWK)** statue and entertainment complex (see p.143) near Jimbaran has been at least as controversial ever since it was first suggested in 1993. There is serious and ongoing concern from many people on Bali that the size of the statue, which is being hailed as the largest in the world, will very seriously upset the cosmological balance of the island, similar to the upset it suffered in the years before 1963 (see p.268) – and that disaster is bound to follow. Modernizers mock this as yet another example of backward-looking traditionalists who refuse to countenance traffic flyovers and a bridge between Bali and Java for the same reasons. Whilst the promised opening of the complex for the year 2000 was never realized, completion is now planned for 2003 and it appears that the project has developed a momentum, fuelled by a US$200 million budget, that will be impossible to stop.

Meanwhile, the future of yet another mega-development, that on **Pulau Serangan** (Turtle Island), has, like many large-scale developments on the island, ground to a halt with the demise of the Suharto family influence. The ex-president's son, Tommy, was one of the main investors in the scheme. It has already been an ecological disaster (see p.170), with some reefs obliterated, but joy at the scheme's abandonment has been short-lived: the latest idea is for a casino instead. Casinos are outlawed in Muslim Indonesia, but developers obviously hope that a small island off Hindu Bali can be exempted.

The latest touristic hot potato looks set to be the idea of a 10km cable-car in the **Bedugul** area taking in the Bali Botanical Gardens and passing over Munduk and nearby villages. Already local opposition has voiced fears about such a thing passing above temples. But, as the examples above have demonstrated, if the money and determination are there, then matters have a habit of being resolved in favour of the developers.

Social changes

Social changes are inevitably resulting from the influx of tourism, as people are displaced to make way for developments, and Western imperatives of efficiency and timekeeping are changing traditional ways of life and religious observances. Michel Picard, author of *Bali: Cultural Tourism and Touristic Culture*, presents the idea that Bali has now become a "**touristic culture**" whereby the Balinese have adopted the tourists' perceptions of themselves and their island as their own, and have "come to search for confirmation of their 'Balinese-ness' in the mirror held to them by the tourists".

There is also concern about **HIV**, **AIDS** and **drug addiction** among the young men working in the informal sex industry in the tourist areas (there are relatively few female prostitutes). This has attracted overseas aid, and the Australian International Development Assistance Bureau has been involved in HIV- and AIDS-prevention work on Bali, in Nusa Tenggara and south Sulawesi.

However, many of the problems are those of any developing country, and at least Bali has not also been subjected to the ravages of heavy industry. While many Westerners and Balinese intellectuals articulate the negative side of tourism, many of the people in the villages are keen to develop tourist facilities that will bring visitors, and their money, to them.

The situation in Lombok

On **Lombok**, part of East Indonesia, one of the poorest areas of the whole archipelago and the major focus of development efforts, there has been chronic **poverty** for generations. A few tourists started coming in the 1980s, and by 1987, local people had set up a few small losmen around Senggigi, the Gili Islands and, later, around Kuta. By 1989, over 120,000 were coming annually, and by 1993 there were many times that number. Fairly early on, government and big businesses, largely from outside the island, began to buy land for the construction of luxury hotels. Student activists highlighted the plight of fishing families losing access to the beaches because of large international hotels, households losing their land, and small food vendors going out of business. However, in practice, many of the **developers** sat on the land they had bought, and, apart from in the Senggigi area, there was little development for several years. This changed in the late 1990s as the land north of Senggigi was built on, the *Oberoi* opened in the far north, since followed by the golf course near Sira beach, and developments in the south, centred on Kuta, also started.

On the one hand, the **Lombok Tourist Development Corporation** claimed that around 25,000 jobs would be created by the developments; on the other hand, Sasak people are aware that secondary school and then tourist school **qualifications** are increasingly necessary to get anything but the most basic work in the tourist industry. As on Bali, complaints have been voiced. In February 1991, farmers demonstrated in Mataram against being forced to leave their land in Kuta where they had built up a small sea-grass industry. Plans to build a new international airport outside Praya have been indefinitely shelved following huge local protest and the reoccupation of the land by its previous owners.

Local feeling runs higher on Lombok than on Bali: the developments are new, the people are poorer, many local people feel that the gap between Muslim morals and those of their Western visitors is unacceptably wide, and they have seen the effects of mass tourism on Bali. They oppose their culture being turned into a tourist event and have had some successes: in Senggigi, a pub was closed after complaints about drunks urinating against the mosque wall next door, and provincial government regularly blocks plans for discos and bars. However, the violence of January 2000 – and the subsequent collapse in tourism – brought home to the islanders just how volatile the tourist business is; many were brought to the verge of ruin. The industry just about struggled back to its feet, only for the aftermath of September 11, 2001, to send it crashing again. Concern was expressed about the island's over-reliance on tourism, but with few resources to draw upon to change the situation, people had little alternative but to sit things out and hope.

Books

While plenty has been written on the culture, temples and arts and crafts of Bali, there has been little coverage of Lombok.

Bali's early visitors produced a clutch of fascinating first-hand accounts of a now-vanished world, many of which are available through the Oxford University Press (OUP) Asia imprint. Periplus is a specialist publisher on the region and produces a wide range of excellent, highly illustrated guides covering architecture, music, flora, fauna and food.

Many of these books are published in Indonesia – you may be able to order them from bookshops in your own country, but most are available on Bali. The best bookshop on the island is Ganesha (®www.ganeshabooksbali.com), located in Ubud; they stock a good range of specialist books and offer an online ordering service.

Where two publishers are listed, they refer to British/US publishers; "o/p" means out of print. The symbol ✦ indicates a highly recommended title.

Travel

Vicki Baum *A Tale from Bali* (Periplus). Occasionally moving, and always interesting, semi-factual historical novel based on the events leading up to the 1906 *puputan* in Denpasar. Written from the notes bequeathed to the author in 1937 by a Dutch doctor who had lived and worked in Sanur for several decades.

✦ **William Ingram** *A Little Bit One o'Clock: Living with a Balinese Family* (Ersania Books, Ubud, Bali). Warm, funny and affectionate portrait of the author's life with an Ubud family in the 1990s. The warts-and-all approach makes a nice change from more impersonal sociological studies, yet you still learn a lot about the daily rituals and concerns of a modern Balinese community. Both the author and his adoptive family still live in Ubud.

✦ **Louise G. Koke** *Our Hotel in Bali* (Pepper, Singapore). The engaging story of two young Americans who arrived in Bali in 1936 and decided almost immediately to build a hotel on Kuta beach, the first of its kind. The book describes a Bali that was just begin-

ning to attract tourists, and is an affectionate account of the locals, expats and visitors involved with the *Kuta Beach Hotel* from 1936 to 1942. It also includes some great black and white photos from the time, some of which are displayed in the Neka Art Museum.

✦ **Anna Mathews** *Night of Purnama* (o/p). Evocative and moving description of village life and characters of the early 1960s, focusing on events in Iseh and the surrounding villages from the first eruption of Gunung Agung until Mathews left in 1963. Written with affection and a keen realization of the gap between West and East.

Hickman Powell *The Last Paradise* (o/p). Highly readable reflection of an American traveller's experiences in Bali in the late 1920s. Interesting accounts of village customs and temple festivals plus a few spicy anecdotes.

Annabel Sutton *The Islands in Between* (Impact). Covers a sea voyage across Indonesia. The chapters on Bali and Lombok are informative and amusing and the whole book gives a good flavour of the variety of life within Indonesia, and a vivid insight into community life on the different islands.

★ K'tut Tantri *Revolt in Paradise* (o/p). The extraordinary story of an extraordinary woman. British-born artist and adventurer Muriel Pearson – known in Bali as K'tut Tantri and in Java as Surabaya Sue – tells the astonishing tale of her fifteen years in Bali and Java. First living in close association with the raja of Bangli, then building one of the first hotels on Kuta beach, K'tut Tantri finally became an active member of the Indonesian independence movement, operating an underground radio station and smuggling arms and other supplies between the islands, for which she suffered two years' imprisonment and torture at the hands of the Japanese invaders. A fascinating, if in places somewhat embellished, account of Bali and Java between 1932 and 1947.

Adrian Vickers (ed) *Travelling to Bali: Four Hundred Years of Journeys* (OUP Asia). Thought-provoking one-stop anthology which includes accounts by early Dutch, Thai and British adventurers, as well as excerpts from writings by the expat community in the 1930s, and the musings of late twentieth-century visitors. The editor's extensive introductions to the pieces make interesting reading, but the extracts themselves merely whet the appetite.

Travellers' health

Jude Brown *Aromatherapy for Travellers* (Thorsons). Comprehensive and inspirational pocket-sized book, explaining how aromatherapy can help prevent and then treat travel problems. Plenty of practical details on what to do and where to get supplies and further information.

Dr Jane Wilson Howarth *Bugs, Bites and Bowels* (Cadogan/Globe Pequot). Outlines nasty tropical illnesses, together with likely symptoms and what to do about them. Small enough to take with you.

Dr Nick Jones *The Rough Guide to Travel Health* (Rough Guides). Pretty much everything you need to know, in a pocket-sized, pack-friendly format.

Culture and society

Jean Couteau *Bali Today: Real Balinese Stories; Vol 1* (Spektra Communications, Bali). A very interesting little anthology of the author's newspaper columns about contemporary Bali, which he wrote for the *Bali Post*. Much of the book reads like a juicy conversation with a well-informed gossip; topics range from the role of the peeping tom and the use of sexual innuendo in the Balinese language, to true tales of cross-cultural romance and observations on the impact of tourism.

★ Miguel Covarrubias *Island of Bali* (Periplus). The Mexican artist and amateur anthropologist describes all aspects of life on Bali in the 1930s, from the daily routines of his adopted village household to the religious and philosophical meanings behind the island's arts, dramas and music. An early classic (first published in 1937) that's still as relevant and readable now.

★ Dr A.A.M. Djelantik *The Birthmark: Memoirs of a Balinese Prince* (Periplus). This very readable autobiography tells the fascinating life story of the son of the last raja of Karangasem, Made Djelantik, who was born in east Bali in 1919, became Bali's most respected and influential doctor, and still lives on the island today. Djelantik documents in a lively and enjoyable way the huge changes that have swept through Bali in his lifetime, with first-hand accounts of Dutch rule, World War II, the eruption of Gunung Agung and the Communist killings, and includes plenty of incidental detail about family life and village traditions.

★ **Fred B. Eiseman Jr** *Bali: Sekala and Niskala Vols 1 and 2* (Periplus). The fascinating and admirably wide-ranging cultural and anthropological essays of a contemporary American, thirty years resident in Bali. His pieces encompass everything from the esoteric rituals of Balinese Hinduism to musings on the popularity of the clove cigarette. Essential background reading for any interested visitor.

David J. Fox *Once a Century: Pura Besakih and the Eka Dasa Rudra Festival* (Penerbit Sinar Harapan, Citra, Indonesia). Fabulous colour pictures, and an erudite but readable text, make this the best introduction to Besakih both ancient and modern. Also includes careful and sympathetic accounts of the 1963 *Eka Dasa Rudra* festival and the eruption of Gunung Agung.

Michael Hitchcock, Victor T. King and Michael J.G. Parnwell (eds) *Tourism in South-east Asia* (Routledge). A collection of eighteen papers considering all aspects of tourism from Thailand to the Philippines, with an excellent, if somewhat overly philosophical, chapter on the development of cultural tourism in Bali.

A.J. Bernet Kempers *Monumental Bali: Introduction to Balinese Archaeology and Guide to the Monuments* (Periplus). A fairly highbrow analysis of Bali's temples and ruins, written by a Dutch ethnology and archeology professor.

Gregor Krause *Bali 1912* (January Books, New Zealand). Reprinted edition of the original black and white photographs that inspired the first generation of arty expats to visit Bali. The pictures were taken by a young German doctor and give unrivalled insight into Balinese life in the early twentieth century.

J. Stephen Lansing *Priests and Programmers: Technologies of Power in the Engineered Landscapes of Bali* (Princeton UP). Scholarly account of the *subak* system of water control and of the role of the local and regional water temples. Also includes a report on the "Green Revolution" in Bali.

Hugh Mabbett *The Balinese* (Pepper, Singapore). An accessible collection of short anecdotal essays on various aspects of contemporary Balinese life, from a look at the role of Bali's women to a discussion of the impact of tourism.

Hugh Mabbett *In Praise of Kuta* (o/p). Affectionate and very enjoyable portrait of Kuta in the 1980s, with lots of attention paid to the characters who lived and worked in and visited Bali's most exuberant resort during the decade when mass tourism took off.

★ **Michel Picard** *Bali: Cultural Tourism and Touristic Culture* (Periplus). Fascinating, readable but ultimately depressing analysis of the effects of tourism upon the people of Bali. Required reading for serious students of what's going on on the island.

Adrian Vickers *Bali: A Paradise Created* (Periplus). Detailed, intelligent and highly readable account of the outside world's perception of Bali, the development of tourism and how events inside and outside the country have shaped the Balinese view of themselves as well as outsiders' view of them.

History

Ide Anak Agung Gde Agung *Bali in the Nineteenth Century* (Yayasan Obor Indonesia, Jakarta). Meticulous account of the most eventful years in Balinese history, when conflict with the Dutch was at its most violent. Evocatively illustrated with an excellent collection of black and white photographs that you won't find elsewhere.

Alfons van der Kraan *Lombok: Conquest, Colonization and Underdevelopment 1870–1940* (Heinemann Education, Singapore). A detailed investigation into Lombok's complex relationship with Bali, its neighbour and conqueror, and subsequently with its Dutch rulers. A scathing attack on colonial-ism and its devastating effect on the local populace.

John G. Taylor *Indonesia's Forgotten War: The Hidden History of East Timor* (Zed Books/Humanities Press). Clear and incisive account of the disastrous events in East Timor, from the fifteenth century to the present day, with the final chapter looking at possible future scenarios.

Margaret J. Weiner *Visible and Invisible Realms: Power, Magic and Colonial Conquest in Bali* (Chicago UP). Academic and densely written account of Balinese history leading up to the climactic Klungkung *puputan*, as detailed in Balinese historical sources and legends.

Art, crafts and music

★ **Philip Cornwel-Smith** *Property of the Artist: Symon* (PT Sang Yang Seni, Ubud, Bali). Lively and hugely enjoyable monograph of the expat Ubud artist Symon (see p.211), which artfully interweaves the musings and *bons mots* of the painter with insights from his friends, models, collaborators and collectors. It's presented in a characteristically innovative magazine-style layout that's full of reproductions of Symon's work as well as photos of the artist and his creations.

Fred and Margaret Eiseman *Woodcarvings of Bali* (o/p). Slim but interesting volume about one of Bali's finest crafts, with particularly good sections on the history of the craft and on the types of wood used.

Edward Frey *The Kris: Mystic Weapon of the Malay World* (OUP Asia). Small but well-illustrated book outlining the history and making of the kris, along with some of the myths associated with this magical weapon. Although intended more for the collector than the visitor, this is an excellent introduction to help you appreciate what you see in the museums.

John Gillow and Barry Dawson *Traditional Indonesian Textiles* (Thames & Hudson). Beautifully photographed and accessible introduction to the *ikat* and batik fabrics of the archipelago; a handy guide if you're thinking of buying cloth in Bali or Lombok.

Brigitta Hauser-Schäublin, Marie-Louise Nabholz-Kartaschoff and Urs Ramseyer *Balinese Textiles* (Periplus). Thorough and gloriously photographed survey of Balinese textiles and their role within contemporary society. Includes sections on the more common fabrics such as *endek*, *songket* and *kain poleng*, as well as introductions to some of the much rarer weaves including the *geringsing* of Tenganan.

Garret Kam *Perceptions of Paradise: Images of Bali in the Arts* (Yayasan Dharma Seni Neka Museum, Bali). Ostensibly a guide to the paintings displayed in Ubud's Neka Art Museum, this is actually one of the best introductions to Balinese art, with helpful sections on the traditions and practices that have informed much of the work to date. Plenty of full-colour plates and wider references as well.

Jean McKinnon *Vessels of Life: Lombok Earthenware* (Saritaksu). Exhaustive and fabulously photographed book about Sasak life, pottery techniques and the significance of the items they create in the lives of the women potters.

Idanna Pucci *Bhima Swarga: The Balinese Journey of the Soul* (Bullfinch Press). Fabulously produced guide to the *Mahabharata* legends depicted on the ceiling of Klungkung's Kerta Gosa. Illustrated with large, glossy, colour photographs and a panel-by-panel description of the stories, which makes the whole creation much easier to interpret.

Hans Rhodius and John Darling *Walter Spies and Balinese Art* (Tropical Museum, Amsterdam). Biography of the German expatriate artist and musician Walter Spies, which discusses, in brief, his early life and influences and then takes up the controversial debate over the extent of Spies's influence on modern Balinese art, asking whether the received view is actually a colonialist view of art history.

Anne Richter *Arts and Crafts of Indonesia* (Chronicle Books). General guide to the fabrics, carvings, jewellery and other folk arts of the archipelago, with some background on the practices involved.

Michael Tenzer *Balinese Music* (Periplus). Well-pitched introduction to the delights and complexities of the gamelan, by an American composer who did a six-month stint at Batubulan's KOKAR high school of music and dance. Sections on theory, practice and history as well as interesting anecdotes from expert Balinese musicians.

Lifestyle

Gianni Francione and Luca Invernizzi Tetoni *Bali Modern: The Art of Tropical Living* (Periplus). A celebration of modern Balinese architecture. There's plenty of attention paid to sumptuous and tasteful reinventions of traditional themes but it's refreshing to see space given over to the modern exuberance of Waterbom Park, the *Hard Rock Hotel* and even the Kuta strip. This big, glossy hardback makes a great souvenir.

Rio Helmi and Barbara Walker *Bali Style* (Thames & Hudson). Sumptuously photographed glossy volume celebrating all things Balinese, from the humblest bamboo craftwork to some of the most fabulous buildings on the island. Both a

great souvenir and an inspiration for potential visitors.

William Warren and Luca Invernizzi Tetoni *Balinese Gardens* (Periplus). Now in its third edition, this gorgeously photographed, large-format coffee-table book concentrates mostly on modern gardens, largely in the south of the island, but with fascinating and informative sections on Balinese flora, offerings, the role of plants and gardens in Balinese culture and classical gardens across the island.

Made Wijaya and Isabella Ginanneschi *At Home in Bali* (Abbeville Press, New York). The beautiful homes of Bali's beautiful (mainly expatriate) people are here presented in enviable tropical splendour, each one introduced by the architect and landscape designer Made Wijaya, who highlights the changing trends in expat chic and points out the myriad reinterpretations of the traditional vernacular.

Food and cookery

Heinz von Holzen and Lother Arsana *The Food of Bali* (Periplus). Sumptuously illustrated paperback on all aspects of Balinese cuisine, including the religious and cultural background. The bulk of the book comprises recipes for local specialities – everything from snail soup to unripe jackfruit curry.

Jacqueline Piper *Fruits of South-East Asia: Fact and Folklore* (o/p). Although only 94 pages long, this is an exhaustive, well-illustrated book, introducing all the fruits of the region together with the influence they have had on the arts and crafts and the part they have played in religious and cultural practices.

Natural history

Guy Buckles *Dive Sites of Indonesia* (New Holland). Exhaustively researched, attractive and up-to-date guide for potential divers with good sections on Bali and Lombok. Especially good on the practical details.

Fred and Margaret Eiseman *Flowers of Bali* (Periplus). Slim, fully illustrated handbook describing fifty of the most common flowers growing in Bali, with Latin, English, Indonesian and Balinese names given where possible.

John MacKinnon *Field Guide to the Birds of Borneo, Sumatra, Java and Bali* (OUP). The most comprehensive field guide of its kind, with full colour plates, useful pointers for amateur spotters and detailed descriptions of the 820 species found on the four islands.

★ **Victor Mason** *Bali Bird Walks* (o/p). Delightful, highly personal offbeat guidebook to the Ubud area, which focuses on the neighbourhood's flora and fauna, particularly the birds. The book describes over a dozen walks of varying lengths and difficulty, highlighting notable things to look at en route.

Available from Ubud bookshops or from the author's bar and restaurant, *The Beggar's Bush* in Campuhan, west Ubud.

Victor Mason and Frank Jarvis *Birds of Bali* (Periplus). Informal, illustrated introduction to the 120 most commonly sighted birds in Bali; a slim, easy-to-digest volume by Ubud expatriate and committed birder.

Kal Muller, et al. *Diving Indonesia* (Periplus). This is the top handbook for anybody wanting to dive in Indonesia. Written by experts, it is also exquisitely photographed and supplemented with clear, useful maps. Bali and Lombok are only part of this book, but it will inspire you to venture further afield.

★ **David Pickell and Wally Siagian** *Diving Bali: The Underwater Jewel of Southeast Asia* (Periplus). Beautifully photographed and detailed account of everything you'll ever need to know about diving in Bali. Full of anecdote, humour, advice and practical knowledge, as well as plenty of detailed maps.

Fiction

Vern Cook (ed) *Bali Behind the Seen: Recent Fiction from Bali* (Darma Printing, NSW, Australia). Interesting and insightful collection of short stories by contemporary Balinese and Javanese writers. Many of the stories explore the ways in which Bali is changing, highlighting the tensions between the generations and their different outlooks on traditions, families and Westernization.

Odyle Knight *Bali Moon: A Spiritual Odyssey* (Sandstone Publishing, NSW, Australia). Riveting tale of an Australian woman's deepening involvement with the Balinese spirit world as her romance with a young Balinese priest draws her onto disturbing ground. Apparently based on true events.

Christopher J. Koch *The Year of Living Dangerously* (Penguin). Set in Jakarta, this compelling story is set in the last year of President Sukarno's rule and climaxes in the days leading up to the 1965 takeover by Suharto and the subsequent violence. Weaving a fast-moving story with classical myth and an insightful description of the people of Indonesia, it compellingly details ethnic, political and religious tensions which are still glaringly apparent in Indonesia today, and is required reading for anyone trying to understand modern Indonesia. It was made into a well-regarded film, starring Mel Gibson and directed by Peter Weir.

Victor Mason *The Butterflies of Bali* (o/p). Gentle cultural thriller about four expats who discover a Balinese village that's been hidden from the modern world for decades. The novel includes plenty of interesting detail on traditional rural Bali, but the quaint, over-elaborate writing style can grate.

Claire Messud *When The World Was Steady* (Granta). Bali is just one of several locations in this rich, elegant portrayal of two sisters, their relationship with each other and their differing approaches to life. However, the island is skilfully evoked in all its beauty and mystery, as is the cast of expatriates who came to the island to disrupt its peace, when *"dugas gumine enteg"* (the world was steady).

Putu Oka Sukanta *The Sweat of Pearls: Short Stories about Women of Bali* (Darma Printing, NSW, Australia). All the stories in this slim volume were written by a man, which somewhat detracts from their authenticity, but the vignettes of village life and traditions are enlightening, and the author is a respected writer who spent many years in jail because of his political beliefs.

Michael Wiese *On the Edge of a Dream* (Michael Wiese Productions). The story of two young Americans who settle for a while in a Balinese village in 1969. The most interesting parts of the novel show how the boys get drawn into – and freaked out by – the island's spirit world and black magic.

language

language

Bahasa Indonesia

The national language of Indonesia is Bahasa Indonesia, although there are also over 250 native languages and dialects spoken throughout the archipelago. Until the 1920s, the lingua franca of government and commerce was Dutch, but the emerging independence movement adopted a form of Bahasa Malay as a more suitable revolutionary medium; by the 1950s this had crystallized into **Bahasa Indonesia**. Now taught in every school and widely understood in Bali and Lombok, Bahasa Indonesia was a crucial means of unifying the new nation. The indigenous languages of Bali and Lombok are still spoken in the islands' villages, and brief vocabularies are given below.

Bahasa Indonesia is written in Roman script, has no tones and uses a fairly straightforward grammar – all of which makes it relatively easy for the visitor to get to grips with. The *Rough Guide to Indonesian* is a pocket-sized **phrasebook** which includes an exhaustive dictionary of useful words as well as pronunciation details, some cultural hints, and information on grammar. Otherwise, try the *Berlitz Indonesian Phrase Book and Dictionary*, which can be supplemented by a ninety-minute cassette tape. Of the numerous **teach yourself** options, Sutanto Atmosumarto's *Colloquial Indonesian: A Comprehensive Language Course* (Routledge), including two sixty-minute tapes, makes the best investment – an easy-to-follow step-by-step guide, complete with listening comprehensions, written exercises and situational dialogues. Once you're in Indonesia, you might want to get hold of the portable, though definitely not pocket-sized, **dictionary** *Kamus Lengkap Inggeris-Indonesia, Indonesia-Inggeris* (Hasta Penerbit).

Grammar and pronunciation

For **grammar**, Bahasa Indonesia uses the same subject-verb-object word-order as in English. The easiest way to make a question is simply to add a question mark and use a rising intonation. **Nouns** have no gender and don't require an article. To make a noun **plural** you usually just say the noun twice, eg *anak* (child), *anak-anak* (children). **Adjectives** always follow the noun. **Verbs** have no tenses: to indicate the past, prefix the verb with *sudah* (already) or *belum* (not yet); for the future, prefix the verb with *akan* (will).

Vowels and dipthongs

a is a cross between father and cup
e as in along; or as in pay; or as in get; or sometimes omitted (*selamat* pronounced "slamat")
i as in boutique; or as in pit

o as in hot; or as in cold
u as in boot
ai as in fine
au as in how

Consonants

Most are pronounced as in English, with the following exceptions:
c as in cheap
g is always hard, as in girl

k is hard, as in English, except at the end of the word, when you should stop just short of pronouncing it. In written form, this is often indicated by an apostrophe, for example, *beso'* for *besok*.

Useful words and phrases

Greetings and basic phrases

The all-purpose greeting is **Selamat** (derived from Arabic), which communicates general goodwill. If addressing a married woman, it's polite to use the respectful term *Ibu* or *Nyonya*; if addressing a married man use *Bapak*.

Good morning (5–11am) – **Selamat pagi**
Good day (11am–3pm) – **Selamat siang**
Good afternoon (3–7pm) – **Selamat sore**
Good evening (after 7pm) – **Selamat malam**
Good night – **Selamat tidur**
Goodbye – **Selamat tinggal**
See you later – **Sampai jumpa lagi**
Have a good trip – **Selamat jalan**
Welcome – **Selamat datang**
Enjoy your meal – **Selamat makan**
Cheers (toast) – **Selamat minum**
How are you? – **Apa kabar?**
I'm fine – **Bagus/Kabar baik**
please (requesting) – **tolong**
please (offering) – **silakan**
Thank you (very much) – **Terima kasih (banyak)**
You're welcome – **Sama sama**
Sorry/excuse me – **Ma'af**
No worries/Never mind – **Tidak apa apa**
What is your name? – **Siapa nama anda?**
My name is... – **Nama saya...**
Where are you from? – **Dari mana?**
I come from... – **Saya dari...**
Do you speak English? – **Bisa bicara bahasa Inggris?**
I don't understand – **Saya tidak mengerti**
Do you have...? – **Ada...?**
I want/would like... – **Saya mau...**
I don't want it/No thanks – **Tidak mau**
What is this/that? – **Apa ini/itu?**

another – **satu lagi**
beautiful – **cantik**
big/small – **besar/kecil**
boyfriend or girlfriend – **pacar**
clean/dirty – **bersih/kotor**
cold – **dingin**
expensive/inexpensive – **mahal/murah**
fast/slow – **sepat/lambat**
foreigner – **turis**
friend – **teman**
good/bad – **bagus/buruk**
hot (water/weather) – **panas**
hot (spicy) – **pedas**
how? – **berapa?**
hungry/thirsty – **lapar/haus**
ill/sick – **sakit**
married/single – **kawin/bujang**
men – **laki-laki**
no (with noun) – **bukan**
not (with verb) – **tidak (or tak)**
open/closed – **buka/tutup**
tired – **lelah**
very much/a lot – **banyak**
what? – **apa?**
when? – **kapan?**
where? – **dimana?**
who? – **siapa?**
why? – **mengapa?**
women – **perempuan or wanita**
yes – **ya**

Getting around

Where is the...? – **Dimana...?**
I'd like to go to the... – **Saya mau pergi ke...**
How far? – **Berapa kilometre?**
How long? – **Berapa jam?**
How much is the fare to...? – **Berapa harga karcis ke...?**
Where is this bemo going? – **Kemana bemo pergi?**
When will the bemo/bus leave? – **Bila bemo/bis berangkut?**
Where is this? – **Dimana ini?**
Stop! – **estop!**
here – **disini**

right – **kanan**
left – **kiri**
straight on – **terus**
near/far – **dekat/jauh**
airport – **lapangan terbang**
bank – **bank**
beach – **pantai**
bemo/bus station – **terminal**
bicycle – **sepeda**
bus – **bis**
car – **mobil**
city/downtown – **kota**
to come/go – **datang/pergi**

to drive – **mengendarai**
entrance/exit – **masuk/keluar**
ferry – **ferry**
fuel (petrol) – **bensin**
horse cart – **dokar/cidomo**
hospital – **rumah sakit**
hotel – **losmen**
market – **pasar**
motorbike – **sepeda motor**
motorbike taxi – **ojek**
pharmacy – **apotik**

phone office – **wartel/kantor telkom**
police station – **kantor polisi**
post office – **kantor pos**
restaurant – **restoran/rumah makan/warung**
shop – **toko**
taxi – **taksi**
ticket – **karcis**
tourist office – **kantor turis**
village – **desa**
to walk – **jalan kaki**

Accommodation and shopping

How much is...? – **Berapa harga...?**
a single room – **kamar untuk satu orang**
a double room – **kamar untuk dua orang**
Do you have a cheaper room? – **Ada kamar
yang lebih murah?**
Can I look at the room? – **Boleh saya lihat
kamar?**
to sleep – **tidur**
to buy/sell – **membeli/menjual**
money – **uang**

is there...? – **apakah ada...?**
air-conditioning – **ac**
bathroom – **kamar mandi**
breakfast – **makan pagi**
fan – **kipas**
hot water – **air panas**
mosquito net – **kelambu nyamuk**
swimming pool – **kolam renang**
toilet – **kamar kecil/wc** (pronounced "waysay")

Numbers

zero – **nol**
1 – **satu**
2 – **dua**
3 – **tiga**
4 – **empat**
5 – **lima**
6 – **enam**
7 – **tujuh**

8 – **delapan**
9 – **sembilan**
10 – **sepuluh**
11 – **sebelas**
12 – **duabelas**
20 – **duapuluh**
21 – **duapuluh satu**
30 – **tigapuluh**

100 – **seratus**
200 – **duaratus**
1000 – **seribu**
2000 – **duaribu**
10,000 – **sepuluhribu**
100,000 – **seratusribu**
1,000,000 – **sejuta**
2,000,000 – **dua juta**

Time and days of the week

What time is it? – **Jam berapa?**
When does it open/close – **Kapan dia
buka/tutup?**
3.00 – **jam tiga**
4.10 – **jam empat lewat sepuluh**
4.45 – **jam lima kurang seperempat**
6.30 – **jam setengah tujuh** ("half to seven")
... in the morning – **... pagi**
... in the afternoon – **... sore**
... in the evening – **... malam**
minute/hour – **menit/jam**
day – **hari**
week – **minggu**
month – **bulan**

year – **tahun**
today/tomorrow – **hari ini/besok**
yesterday – **kemarin**
now – **sekarang**
not yet – **belum**
never – **tidak pernah**
already – **sudah**
Monday – **Hari Senin**
Tuesday – **Hari Selasa**
Wednesday – **Hari Rabu**
Thursday – **Hari Kamis**
Friday – **Hari Jumaat**
Saturday – **Hari Sabtu**
Sunday – **Hari Minggu**

Bahasa Bali

The Balinese language, **Bahasa Bali**, has three main forms (and dozens of less widespread variations) – High (*Ida*), Middle or Polite (*Ipun*), and Low (*Ia*). The speaker decides which form to use depending on the caste of the person he or she is addressing and on the context. If speaking to family or friends, or to a low-caste (Sudra) Balinese, you use **Low Balinese**; if addressing a superior or a stranger, you use **Middle or Polite Balinese**; if talking to someone from a high caste (Brahman, Satriya or Wesya) or discussing religious affairs, you use **High Balinese**. If the caste is not immediately apparent, then the speaker will traditionally open the conversation with the euphemistic question "Where do you sit?", in order to elicit an indication of caste, but in the last couple of decades there's been a move to popularize the use of the polite Middle Balinese form, and disregard the caste factor. Bahasa Bali is essentially a **spoken language**, with few official rules of grammar and syntax and hardly any textbooks or dictionaries. Some bookshops on the island sell a useful English-language **primer**, *Bali Pocket Dictionary* by N. Shadeg (Yayasan Dharma Bhakti Pertiwi). All phrases and questions given below are shown in the Middle or Polite form.

What's your name? **Sira pesengan ragane?**
Where are you going? **Lunga kija?**
Where have you been? **Kija busan?**
How are you? **Kenken kebara?**
How are things? **Napa orti?**
(I'm/everything's) fine **Becik**
I am sick **Tiang gele**
What is that? **Napi punika?**
bad **corah**
big **ageng**
child **putra, putri**
to come **rauh, dateng**
delicious **jaen**
to eat **ngajeng, nunas**
family **panyaman, pasa metonan**
food **ajeng-ajengan, tetedan**
friend **switra**
to go **lunga**

good **becik**
house **jeroan**
husband **rabi**
no **tan, nente**
rice **pantu, beras, ajengan**
to sleep **sirep sare**
small **alit**
wife **timpal, isteri**
yes **inggih, patut**
1 **siki, diri**
2 **kalih**
3 **tiga**
4 **pat**
5 **lima**
6 **nem, enem**
7 **pitu**
8 **kutus**
9 **sia**
10 **dasa**

Menu reader

General terms

makan – to eat
makan pagi – breakfast
makan siang – lunch
makan malam – evening meal
daftar makanan – menu
Saya seorang vegetaris – I am vegetarian
Saya tidak makan daging – I don't eat meat
pisau – knife
garpu – fork
sendok – spoon

piring – plate
gelas – glass
minum – drink
dingin – cold
panas – hot (temperature)
asam manis – sweet-and-sour
goreng – fried
pedas – hot (spicy)
enak – delicious
Saya injin bayar – I want to pay

Meat, fish and basic foods

ayam – chicken

babi – pork

Sasak

The language of Lombok is **Sasak**, a purely oral language which varies quite a lot from one part of the island to another.

Realistically, Bahasa Indonesia is a more practical option for travellers, but if you can manage to come out with even a few words of Sasak, your efforts are likely to be greeted with delight.

The following words and phrases – transcribed for the English-speaker – should get you started.

There's no Sasak equivalent to the Indonesian **greetings** *Selamat pagi* and the like. If you meet someone walking along the road, the enquiry "Where are you going?" serves as a general-purpose greeting – even if the answer is blatantly obvious.

Where are you going? **Ojok um bay?**	friend **kantje**
Just walking around **Lampat-lampat**	frightened **takoot**
I'm going to Rinjani **Rinjani wah mo ojok um bay**	heavy/light **berat/ringan**
Where is...? **Um bay tao...?**	hot **beneng**
How are you? **Berem bay khabar?**	hungry **lapar**
I'm fine **Bagus/solah**	husband/wife **semame/senine**
And you? **Berem bay seeda?**	nothing **ndarak**
What are you doing? **Upa gowey de?**	thirsty **goro**
How many children do you have? **Pira kanak de?**	tired **telah**
See you (I'm going) **Yak la low**	today **djelo sine**
No problem **Nday kambay kambay**	tomorrow **djema**
Go away! **Nyeri too!**	yesterday **sirutsin**
big/small **belek/kodek**	none **ndarak**
brother/sister **semeton mama/semeton nine**	1 **skek**
child/grandchild **kanak/bai**	2 **dua**
dark/light **peteng/tenang**	3 **telu**
daughter/son **kanak nine/kanak mame**	4 **empat**
delicious **maik**	5 **lima**
fast/slow **betjat/adeng-adeng**	6 **enam**
	7 **pitook**
	8 **baluk**
	9 **siwak**
	10 **sepulu**

bakmi – noodles	kecap manis – sweet soy sauce
buah – fruit	kepiting – crab
es – ice	nasi – rice
garam – salt	petis – fish paste
gula – sugar	sambal – hot chilli sauce
ikan – fish	sapi – beef
itik – duck	soto – soup
jaja – rice cakes	telur – egg
kambing – goat	udang – prawn
kare – curry	udang karang – lobster
kecap asam – sour soy sauce	

Everyday dishes

ayam goreng – fried chicken	botok daging sapi – spicy minced beef with tofu, *tempeh* and coconut milk
bakso – soup containing meat balls	cap cai – mixed fried vegetables
bakmi goreng – fried noodles mixed with vegetables and meat	es campur – fruit salad and shredded ice

gado-gado – steamed vegetables served with a spicy peanut sauce

kangkung – water-spinach

krupuk – rice or cassava crackers, usually flavoured with prawn

lalapan – raw vegetables and sambal

lontong – steamed rice in a banana-leaf packet

lumpia – spring rolls

nasi campur – boiled rice served with small amounts of vegetable, meat, fish and sometimes egg

nasi goreng – fried rice

nasi putih – plain boiled rice

pisang goreng – fried bananas

rijsttafel – Dutch/Indonesian dish made up of six to ten different meat, fish and vegetable dishes with rice

rujak – hot spiced fruit salad

rujak petis – vegetable and fruit in spicy peanut and shrimp sauce

tahu goreng telur – tofu omelette

sate – meat or fish kebabs served with a spicy peanut sauce

sayur bening – soup with spinach and corn

sayur lodeh – vegetable and coconut milk soup

urap-urap/urap timum – vegetables with coconut and chilli

Balinese specialities

babi guling – suckling pig roasted on a spit: the Balinese national dish

betutu bebek – smoked duck

ebat – a meal of five dishes including sate, served on a tray

lawar – ceremonial dish: raw meat, blood and spices ground down to a pulpy mash, often served with *babi guling*

Sasak specialities

ayam taliwang – fried or grilled chicken served with a hot chilli sauce

beberuk – raw eggplant and chilli sauce

cerorot – rice flour, palm sugar and coconut milk sweet wrapped into a cone shape

geroan ayam – chicken liver

gule lemak – beef curry

hati – liver

kelor – vegetable soup

lapis – rice flour, coconut milk and sugar dessert wrapped in banana leaves

olah olah – beans in coconut milk

otak – brains

pangan – coconut milk and sugar dessert

paru – lungs

pelecing – chilli sauce

satay pusut – minced beef and coconut sate

sayur nangka – young jackfruit curry

sum-sum – bone marrow

tumbek – rice flour, coconut milk and palm sugar dessert wrapped in coconut leaves

usus – intestines

wajik – sticky rice and palm sugar sweet

Fruit

apel – apple

buah anggur – grapes

jeruk manis – orange

jeruk nipis – lemon

kelapa – coconut

mangga – mango

manggis – mangosteen

nanas – pineapple

nangka – jackfruit

pisang – banana

semangkha air – watermelon

Drinks

air jeruk – orange juice

air jeruk nipis – lemon juice

air minum – drinking water

arak – palm or rice spirit

bir – beer

brem – local rice beer

kopi – coffee

kopi bal – black coffee

kopi susu – white coffee

susu – milk

teh – tea

tolong tanpa es – without ice please

tolong tanpa gula – without sugar please

tuak – rice or palm wine

Glossary

adat Traditional law and custom.

aling-aling Low, freestanding wall built directly behind a house or temple gateway, in order to confuse evil spirits and deter them from entering.

Arjuna The most famous of the five heroic Pandawa brothers, stars of the epic Hindu tale, the *Mahabharata*.

bale Open-sided pavilion found in temples, family compounds and on roadsides, usually used as a resting place or shelter.

balian (or **dukun**) Traditional faith healer, herbalist or witch doctor.

banjar Village association or council to which all married men in the neighbourhood are obliged to belong; membership averages 100–500.

Barong Ket Mythical lion-like creature who represents the forces of good; frequently appears in religious rituals and dance performances.

Barong Landung Three-metre-high humanoid puppets used in temple rituals and dances.

bemo Local minibus transport.

Bhoma (or **Boma**) The son of the earth, who repels evil spirits and is most commonly represented as a huge open-mouthed face above temple gateways.

bhuta (and **kala**) Invisible demons and goblins, the personification of the forces of evil.

calonarang Exorcist dance-drama featuring the widow-witch Rangda.

candi Monument erected as a memorial to an important person; also sometimes a shrine.

candi bentar Split gateway built at the entrance to a temple compound.

cidomo Horse-drawn cart used as a taxi on Lombok.

dalang Puppet master of *wayang kulit* shadow plays.

danau Lake.

Dewi Pertiwi Earth goddess.

Dewi Sri Rice goddess.

dokar Horse-drawn cart used as a taxi in major Balinese towns.

dukun See *balian*.

endek (or **ikat**) Cloth in which the weft threads are dyed to the final pattern before being woven.

Erlangga (sometimes **Airlangga**) Eleventh-century king from East Java, son of the mythical widow-witch Rangda.

Galungan The most important Bali-wide holiday, held for ten days every 210 days in celebration of the triumph of good over evil.

gamelan Orchestra or music of bronze metallophones.

Ganesh Hindu elephant-headed deity, remover of obstacles and god of knowledge.

gang Lane or alley.

garuda Mythical Hindu creature – half-man and half-bird – and the favoured vehicle of the god Wisnu; featured in numerous sculptures and temple reliefs and as a character in several dance-dramas.

gedong Building.

genggong Crude bamboo wind instrument, played like a Jew's harp and most commonly heard in the frog dance.

geringsing Weaving technique and cloth, also known as double *ikat* because both the warp and the weft threads are dyed to the final design before being woven.

Hanuman Monkey-god and chief of the monkey army in the *Ramayana* story; an ally of Rama's.

ikat See *endek*.

jukung Traditional wooden fishing boat with outriggers.

kain poleng Black-and-white-checked cloth used for religious purposes, symbolizing the harmonious balancing of good and evil forces.

kaja Crucial Balinese direction (opposite of *kelod*) which determines house and temple orientation: towards the mountains, upstream.

kala same as *bhuta*.

kantor pos General post office.

kantor telkom Government telephone office.

Kawi Ancient courtly language of Java.

kayangan jagat Highly sacred directional temple.

Kebo Iwa Mythical giant who features in numerous legends as the builder of some of Bali's oldest monuments.

kecak Spectacular dance-drama often referred to as the monkey dance.

kelod Crucial Balinese direction (opposite of *kaja*) which determines house and temple orientation: towards the sea, downstream.

kepeng Old Chinese coins with holes bored through the middle.

ketu Terracotta crown-shaped roof ornament.

kori agung See *paduraksa*.

kris Traditional-style dagger, with scalloped blade edges, of great symbolic and spiritual significance.

kulkul Bell-like drum made from a large, hollow log slit down the middle and suspended high up in a purpose-built tower in temples and other public places. Used to summon *banjar* members to meetings and other public events, and also to raise the alarm.

Kumakarma Brother of the demon king, Rawana, in the *Ramayana* story.

Kuningan The culmination day of the important ten-day Galungan festivities.

legong Classical Balinese dance performed by two or three pre-pubescent girls.

leyak Witches who often assume disguises.

lontar Palm-leaf manuscripts on which all ancient texts were inscribed.

losmen Homestay or guesthouse.

Mahabharata Lengthy Hindu epic describing the battles between representatives of good and evil, and focusing on the exploits of the Pandawa brothers – the inspiration for a huge number of dance-dramas, paintings and sculptures.

mandi Traditional scoop-and-slosh method of showering, often in open-roofed or "garden" bathrooms.

meru Multi-tiered Hindu shrine with an odd number of thatched roofs (from one to eleven), which symbolizes the cosmic mountain Mahameru.

moksa Spiritual liberation for Hindus.

naga Mythological underwater deity, a cross between a snake and a dragon.

odalan Individual temple festival held to mark the anniversary of the founding of every temple on Bali.

ojek Motorcycle taxi.

padmasana The empty throne which tops the shrine-tower, found in every temple and dedicated to the supreme god Sanghyang Widi Wasa. The shrine is often supported by the cosmic turtle and two *naga*.

paduraksa (or **kori agung**) Temple gateway to the inner sanctuary, like the *candi bentar*, but joined together rather than split.

pancasila The five principles of the Indonesian constitution: belief in one supreme god; the unity of the Indonesian nation; guided democracy; social justice and humanitarianism; and a civilized and prosperous society. Symbolized by an eagle bearing a five-part crest.

paras Soft grey volcanic stone used for carving.

pasar Market.

pasar seni Literally art market, usually sells fabrics and non-foodstuffs, and sometimes artefacts and souvenirs.

pawukon See *wuku*.

peci Black felt or velvet hat worn by Muslim men.

pedanda High priest of the Brahman caste.

pemangku Village priest.

perada Traditional gold, screen-printed material used for ceremonial garb and temple umbrellas.

prahu Traditional wooden fishing boat.

prasasti Ancient bronze inscriptions.

pulau Island.

puputan Suicidal fight to the death.

pura Hindu temple.

puri Raja's palace, or the home of a wealthy nobleman.

raksasa Mythical Hindu demon-giant with long teeth and a large club, often used to guard temple entrances.

Ramayana Hugely influential Hindu epic, essentially a morality tale of the battles between good and evil; the source material for numerous dance-dramas, paintings and sculptures.

Rangda Legendary widow-witch who personifies evil and is most commonly depicted with huge fangs, a massive lolling tongue and pendulous breasts; features in carvings and in Balinese dance performances.

Rawana The demon king who represents the forces of evil (Rama's adversary in the *Ramayana*).

raya Main or principal ("Jalan Raya Ubud" is the main Ubud road).

saka Hindu calendar which is divided into years made up of between 354 and 356 days; runs eighty years behind the Western Gregorian calendar.

Sanghyang Widi Wasa The supreme Hindu god; all other gods are manifestations of him.

Saraswati Goddess of learning and of water.

sarong The anglicized generic term for any length of material wrapped around the lower body and worn by men and women.

sawah Rice-fields.

sebel Ritually unclean.

shophouse Shuttered building with living space upstairs and shop space on ground floor.

Siwa (Shiva) Important Hindu deity; "the Destroyer" or, more accurately, "the Dissolver".

songket Silk brocade often woven with real gold thread.

subak Irrigation committee or local farmers' council.

suttee Practice of widows choosing to burn themselves to death on their husbands' funeral pyres.

swastika Ancient Hindu and Buddhist symbol representing the wheel of the sun.

taji Sharp blade attached to the leg of fighting cocks.

teluk Bay.

topeng Masked dance-drama, performed with human masks.

tuak Rice or palm wine.

wantilan Large pavilion, usually used for cock-fights and dance performances.

wartel Phone office.

warung Food stall or tiny streetside restaurant.

wayang kulit Shadow-puppet play.

Wisnu (Vishnu) Important Hindu deity – "The Preserver". Usually shown with four arms, holding a disc, a conch, a lotus and a club, and often seated astride his vehicle, the *garuda*.

wuku (or **pawukon**) Complex Balinese calendar system based on a 210-day lunar cycle.

index

and small print

Index

Map entries are in colour

I
INDEX

Twenty years of Rough Guides

In the summer of 1981, Mark Ellingham, Rough Guides' founder, knocked out the first guide on a typewriter, with a group of friends. Mark had been travelling in Greece after university, and couldn't find a guidebook that really answered his needs.There were heavyweight cultural guides on the one hand – good on museums and classical sites but not on beaches and tavernas – and on the other hand student manuals that were so caught up with how to save money that they lost sight of the country's significance beyond its role as a place for a cool vacation. None of the guides began to address Greece as a country, with its natural and human environment, its politics and its contemporary life.

Having no urgent reason to return home, Mark decided to write his own guide. It was a guide to Greece that tried to combine some erudition and insight with a thoroughly practical approach to travellers' needs. Scrupulously researched listings of places to stay, eat and drink were matched by careful attention to detail on everything from Homer to Greek music, from classical sites to national parks and from nude beaches to monasteries. Back in London, Mark and his friends got their Rough Guide accepted by a farsighted commissioning editor at the publisher Routledge and it came out in 1982.

The Rough Guide to Greece was a student scheme that became a publishing phenomenon. The immediate success of the book – shortlisted for the Thomas Cook award – spawned a series that rapidly covered dozens of countries. The Rough Guides found a ready market among backpackers and budget travellers, but soon acquired a much broader readership that included older and less impecunious visitors. Readers relished the guides' wit and inquisitiveness as much as the enthusiastic, critical approach that acknowledges everyone wants value for money – but not at any price.

Rough Guides soon began supplementing the "rougher" information – the hostel and low-budget listings – with the kind of detail that independent-minded travellers on any budget might expect. These days, the guides – distributed worldwide by the Penguin group – include recommendations spanning the range from shoestring to luxury, and cover more than 200 destinations around the globe. Our growing team of authors, many of whom come to Rough Guides initially as outstandingly good letter-writers telling us about their travels, are spread all over the world, particularly in Europe, the USA and Australia. As well as the travel guides, Rough Guides publishes a series of dictionary phrasebooks covering two dozen major languages, an acclaimed series of music guides running the gamut from Classical to World Music, a series of music CDs in association with World Music Network, and a range of reference books on topics as diverse as the Internet, Pregnancy and Unexplained Phenomena. Visit **www.roughguides.com** to see what's cooking.

Rough Guide Credits

Text editor: Matthew Teller
Series editor: Mark Ellingham
Editorial: Martin Dunford, Jonathan Buckley, Kate Berens, Ann-Marie Shaw, Helena Smith, Judith Bamber, Orla Duane, Olivia Swift, Ruth Blackmore, Geoff Howard, Claire Saunders, Gavin Thomas, Alexander Mark Rogers, Polly Thomas, Joe Staines, Richard Lim, Duncan Clark, Peter Buckley, Lucy Ratcliffe, Clifton Wilkinson, Alison Murchie, Matthew Teller, Andrew Dickson, Fran Sandham (UK); Andrew Rosenberg, Stephen Timblin, Yuki Takagaki, Richard Koss, Hunter Slaton, Julie Feiner (US)
Production: Susanne Hillen, Andy Hilliard, Link Hall, Helen Prior, Julia Bovis, Michelle Draycott, Katie Pringle, Zoë Nobes,

Rachel Holmes, Andy Turner, Michelle Bhatia
Cartography: Melissa Baker, Maxine Repath, Ed Wright, Katie Lloyd-Jones
Cover art direction: Louise Boulton
Picture research: Sharon Martins, Mark Thomas
Online: Kelly Cross, Anja Mutic-Blessing, Jennifer Gold, Audra Epstein, Suzanne Welles, Cree Lawson (US)
Finance: John Fisher, Gary Singh, Edward Downey, Mark Hall, Tim Bill
Marketing & Publicity: Richard Trillo, Niki Smith, David Wearn, Chloë Roberts, Demelza Dallow, Claire Southern (UK); Simon Carloss, David Wechsler, Kathleen Rushforth (US)
Administration: Tania Hummel, Julie Sanderson

Publishing Information

This fourth edition published September 2002 by **Rough Guides Ltd**, 62–70 Shorts Gardens, London WC2H 9AH. Penguin Putnam, Inc. 375 Hudson Street, NY 10014, USA.
Distributed by the Penguin Group
Penguin Books Ltd,
80 Strand, London WC2R ORL
Penguin Putnam, Inc.
375 Hudson Street, NY 10014, USA
Penguin Books Australia Ltd,
487 Maroondah Highway, PO Box 257, Ringwood, Victoria 3134, Australia
Penguin Books Canada Ltd,
10 Alcorn Avenue, Toronto, Ontario, Canada M4V 1E4
Penguin Books (NZ) Ltd,
182–190 Wairau Road, Auckland 10, New Zealand
Typeset in Bembo and Helvetica to an original design by Henry Iles.

Printed in Italy by LegoPrint S.p.A

608pp includes index
A catalogue record for this book is available from the British Library

ISBN 1-85828-902-5

Help us update

We've gone to a lot of effort to ensure that the fourth edition of **The Rough Guide to Bali and Lombok** is accurate and up-to-date. However, things change – places get "discovered", opening hours are notoriously fickle, restaurants and rooms raise prices or lower standards. If you feel we've got it wrong or left something out, we'd like to know, and if you can remember the address, the price, the time, the phone number, so much the better.

We'll credit all contributions, and send a copy of the next edition (or any other Rough Guide if you prefer) for the best letters. Everyone who writes to us and isn't already a subscriber will receive a copy of our full-colour thrice-yearly newsletter. Please mark letters: **"Rough Guide Bali and Lombok Update"** and send to: Rough Guides, 62–70 Shorts Gardens, London WC2H 9AH, or Rough Guides, 4th Floor, 345 Hudson St, New York, NY 10014. Or send an email to **mail@roughguides.com**

Have your questions answered and tell others about your trip at **www.roughguides.atinfopop.com**

Acknowledgements

The authors would like to thank the the the following people:

Lesley – I Nengah Parni, Made Wijana and Man for their endless patience, good driving; Jude Armstrong for the usual Candi Welcome; Elaine and Kath on Gili Air; Mark and Shirley for invaluable details and everyone along the way who made it so pleasant. In UK, special thanks as always to Barbara Unger and Yau Sang Man.

Lucy – Wayan Artana; Wayan Patrum in Sanur; Yos in Tanjung Benoa; Suteja Neka; Bambang Supeno; Clare Dickinson; William Ingram; Bayu in Wongayagede; Phil Cornwel-Smith.

Many thanks also to all the staff at Rough Guides.

The editor would like to thank Rachel Holmes, Helen Prior and Michelle Bhatia for spot-on typesetting, Ed Wright for outstanding cartography well beyond the call, Mark Thomas for photo research, Jennifer Speake for proofreading, Zoë Nobes, Claire Saunders and Jo Mead.

Readers' letters

Thank you to all those readers who took the trouble to write in with their comments and suggestions (apologies for any misspellings or omissions): Nicholas Bull, Jess Champagne, John Cole, Bob Dixon, Emma Fairbank, Paul Farmer, Peter Finch, Yves Fleerakkers, Jim Fogden, Simon Harvey, Isabel Hopkins, Peter Kempinsky & Katarina Ulfstdotter, Jeff Lewis, Odette "Groovy Granny", Isabelle Page, Rob Pilkington, Cara Robechek, Thomas (Germany), Ceri Turnbull, Mike White & Christine Hillier, Peter Wormington, Christopher Wortley & Christobel Thomas.

SMALL PRINT

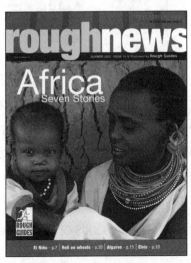

Rough Guides music, reference & CDs

Rough Guide Reference

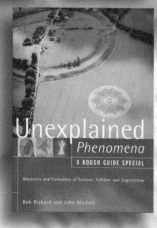

Pocket History Series

England · China · India · France

Music Reference Guides

Classical *music*

Country THE ROUGH GUIDE

Jazz THE ROUGH GUIDE

Opera

Rock THE ROUGH GUIDE

Reggae *music*

World Music
Africa, Europe and the Middle East

World Music
Latin and North America, Caribbean, India, Asia and Pacific

Music USA THE ROUGH GUIDE

World music 100 ESSENTIAL CDs THE ROUGH GUIDE

Soul 100 ESSENTIAL CDs THE ROUGH GUIDE

Country 100 ESSENTIAL CDs THE ROUGH GUIDE

Jazz 100 ESSENTIAL CDs THE ROUGH GUIDE

Blues 100 ESSENTIAL CDs THE ROUGH GUIDE

CD Guides

Classical music 100 ESSENTIAL CDs THE ROUGH GUIDE

Opera 100 ESSENTIAL CDs THE ROUGH GUIDE

Latin 100 ESSENTIAL CDs THE ROUGH GUIDE

Reggae 100 ESSENTIAL CDs THE ROUGH GUIDE

Rock 100 ESSENTIAL CDs THE ROUGH GUIDE

Mini Guides

Drum'n'bass THE ROUGH GUIDE

House THE ROUGH GUIDE

Hip-hop THE ROUGH GUIDE

Irish Music THE ROUGH GUIDE

Techno THE ROUGH GUIDE

Cuban Music THE ROUGH GUIDE

"The Rough Guides are near-perfect reference works"
Philadelphia Inquirer

www.roughguides.com

Rough Guide Music Guides

Rough Guide Instrument Guides

Essential Tipbook Series

"These Rough Guides are admirably informative. They are ideal for anyone wanting to learn or discover an instrument"
Julian Lloyd Webber

www.roughguides.com

The ideas expressed in this code were developed by and for independent travellers.

Learn About The Country You're Visiting

Start enjoying your travels before you leave by tapping into as many sources of information as you can.

The Cost Of Your Holiday

Think about where your money goes - be fair and realistic about how cheaply you travel. Try and put money into local peoples' hands; drink local beer or fruit juice rather than imported brands and stay in locally owned accommodation. Haggle with humour and not aggressively. Pay what something is worth to you and remember how wealthy you are compared to local people.

Embrace The Local Culture

Open your mind to new cultures and traditions - it will transform your experience. Think carefully about what's appropriate in terms of your clothes and the way you behave. You'll earn respect and be more readily welcomed by local people. Respect local laws and attitudes towards drugs and alcohol that vary in different countries and communities. Think about the impact you could have on them.

Exploring The World – The Travellers' Code

Being sensitive to these ideas means getting more out of your travels - and giving more back to the people you meet and the places you visit.

Minimise Your Environmental Impact

Think about what happens to your rubbish - take biodegradable products and a water filter bottle. Be sensitive to limited resources like water, fuel and electricity. Help preserve local wildlife and habitats by respecting local rules and regulations, such as sticking to footpaths and not standing on coral.

Don't Rely On Guidebooks

Use your guidebook as a starting point, not the only source of information. Talk to local people, then discover your own adventure!

Be Discreet With Photography

Don't treat people as part of the landscape, they may not want their picture taken. Ask first and respect their wishes.

We work with people the world over to promote tourism that benefits their communities, but we can only carry on our work with the support of people like you. For membership details or to find out how to make your travels work for local people and the environment, visit our website.

www.tourismconcern.org.uk

TourismConcern

Campaigning for Ethical and Fairly Traded Tourism

Don't bury your head in the sand!

Take cover!

with Rough Guide Travel Insurance